Texas Political Cultural Regions

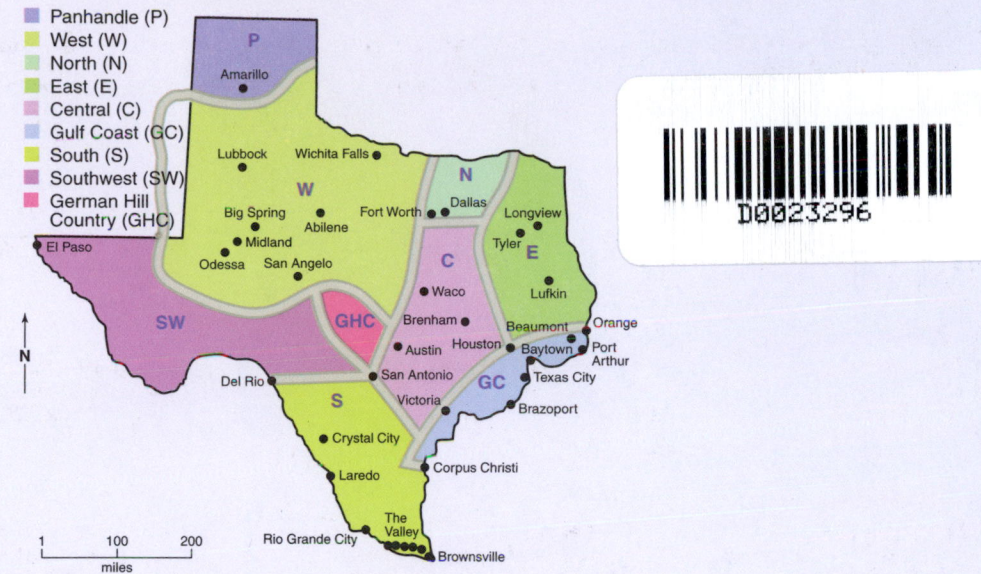

Panhandle (P)
West (W)
North (N)
East (E)
Central (C)
Gulf Coast (GC)
South (S)
Southwest (SW)
German Hill Country (GHC)

Tips on Becoming an Intelligent Consumer of Texas State Services

★ Shop for **lower utility bills** at www.powertochoose.org.

★ Apply for **property tax exemptions** and **protest property appraisals**. To locate your county appraisal authority and to find the appraised value of any property, go to **www.txcountydata.com**.

★ Get **help paying for college** at the Texas Higher Education Coordinating Board Web site **www.collegefortexans.com/**, the comptroller's Web site at **www.everychanceeverytexan.org/** and apply for federal student aid at **www.fafsa.ed.gov**.

★ Get help **collecting child support** at www.oag.state.tx.us/cs/index.shtml.

★ Financial **help for injured crime victims** is available from the crime victims compensation fund at **www.oag.state.tx.us/victims/about_comp.shtml**.

★ **Prevent child abuse** or neglect. Report them to Texas Department of Family and Protective Services at (800) 252-5400 or at **www.txabusehotline.org/**.

★ See if your family and friends are eligible to **receive state social services** by checking links at **www.yourtexasbenefits.com/** or dial 211 for human service needs.

★ Go to **www.taf.org** to learn how **whistleblowers collect bounties** for assisting in identifying false claims against the Texas Medicaid program.

★ **Don't buy a "lemon."** Before you buy a new vehicle, contact the Texas Department of Motor Vehicles, which maintains "lemon law" records and processes warranty complaints at **www.txdmv.gov/**.

★ Look for **lower auto and homeowner's insurance** rates. Check with the Texas Department of Insurance, which publishes rates and numbers of customer complaints. Go to **www.tdi.state.tx.us/consumer/index.html**.

★ If you need **emergency road assistance** or wish to report drug trafficking, call the Department of Public Safety at (800) 525-5555.

★ **Register to vote** at www.sos.state.tx.us/elections/index.shtml.

★ Find out about **drinking alcohol**, including blood alcohol laws and requirements to show ID cards at **www.tabc.state.tx.us/**.

★ For information on **educational opportunities for the blind and deaf**, visit **www.tsbvi.edu/** and **www.tsd.state.tx.us/**, respectively.

★ Texas **military veterans** get help at www.tvc.state.tx.us/.

★ **Get free legal advice, do-it-yourself and low-cost legal strategies** relating to bankruptcy, consumer complaints, divorce, identity theft, tenant rights, utility bills and a wide range of other topics at **texaslawhelp.org/**.

★ **Get tips on how to sue in small claims court, your rights as a tenant, and family law** at **www.texasbar.com**. Click on "News and Publications" and then on "Pamphlets."

★ Learn about **concealed handgun permits** at www.txdps.state.tx.us/.

★ Get **help with summer utility and telephone bills** for low income consumers at **www.puc.state.tx.us/**.

★ **Compare health insurance** plans at **http://texashealthoptions.com/**.

★ Find **lower electric and telephone rates** and stop unwanted telephone solicitations at the Public Utilities Commission Website at **www.puc.state.tx.us/**.

★ **Get a job or employment compensation** at the Texas Workforce Commission at **www.twc.state.tx.us/**.

★ The most comprehensive Web site to **use state services** is at **www.texasonline.com/**.

★ Dial 311 for nonemergency **city services** in most larger municipalities.

American
GOVERNMENT
and Politics Today

Texas Edition

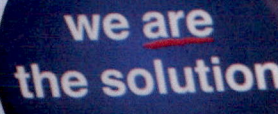
we are
the solution

voice your
opinion

ok

VOICE
YOUR
OPINION

Vote!

Schmidt

Shelley

Bardes

Ford

Maxwell

Crain

Santos

Contributing authors: Elizabeth N. Flores, Joseph Ignagni, Cynthia Opheim, and Christopher Wlezien

2011-2012

American
GOVERNMENT
and Politics Today
Texas Edition

WADSWORTH
CENGAGE Learning™

Australia • Brazil • Japan • Korea • Mexico • Singapore • Spain • United Kingdom • United States

WADSWORTH
CENGAGE Learning™

American Government & Politics Today, Texas Edition: 2011–2012 Edition
Steffen W. Schmidt, Mack C. Shelley, Barbara A. Bardes, Lynne E. Ford, William Earl Maxwell, Ernest Crain, Adolfo Santos

Publisher: Suzanne Jeans

Executive Editor: Carolyn Merrill

Managing Development Editor: Jeff Greene

Development Editor: Jennifer Jacobson, Ohlinger Publishing Services

Assistant Editor: Katherine Hayes

Editorial Assistant: Angela Hodge

Marketing Manager: Lydia LeStar

Marketing Communications Manager: Heather Baxley

Production Manager: Suzanne St. Clair

Print Buyer: Fola Orekoya

Rights Acquisition Specialist, Image: Jennifer Meyer Dare

Rights Acquisition Specialist, Text: Katie Huha

Production Service: Integra Software Services, Inc.

Photo Researcher: Bill Smith Group

Text Researcher: Christie Barros

Art Director: Linda Helcher

Cover Designer: Rokusek Design

For product information and technology assistance, contact us at **Cengage Learning Customer & Sales Support, 1-800-423-0563**

For permission to use material from this text or product, submit all requests online at **www.cengage.com/permissions**
Further permissions questions can be emailed to **permissionrequest@cengage.com**

Library of Congress Control Number: 2010943132

ISBN-13: 978-0-495-90949-1
ISBN-10: 0-495-90949-1

Wadsworth
20 Channel Center
Boston, MA 02210
USA

Cengage Learning is a leading provider of customized learning solutions with office locations around the globe, including Singapore, the United Kingdom, Australia, Mexico, Brazil, and Japan. Locate your local office at: **international.cengage.com/region**

Cengage Learning products are represented in Canada by Nelson Education, Ltd.

For your course and learning solutions, visit **www.cengage.com**

Purchase any of our products at your local college store or at our preferred online store **www.cengagebrain.com**

Printed in the United States of America
1 2 3 4 5 6 7 14 13 12 11 10

Brief CONTENTS

CONTENTS

PREFACE

The new 2011–2012 edition of *American Government and Politics Today: Texas Edition* includes significant revisions and reflects our commitment to producing the most up-to-date text possible. In 2008, the nation witnessed one of the most spirited contests for the presidential nomination in the past 40 years, culminating with a general election contest that spurred public interest in the political process, increased voter turnout, and put into office the first African American president. Voters gave control of the presidency and the Congress to the Democratic Party. Since his inauguration in 2009, President Obama, his team of advisors, and the Democratic majority have passed major legislation for stimulating the economy, reforming the entire health insurance system, and creating a new set of regulations for the banking industry to protect the nation from future crises like that of 2008. However, the continuing economic crisis and deep unemployment coupled with strong opposition to certain aspects of the president's program, have taken a toll on the popularity of the president and the Democratic majority. The 2010 elections for Congress will have long lasting effects on the Obama presidency. The foreign policy challenges facing the president include ending the American engagement in Iraq, resolving continuing conflict in Afghanistan, dealing with instability and threats from other nations in the Middle East, and building more positive relationships with allies in all parts of the globe.

The changes we have made to this edition are not limited to bringing the text up to date, however. We have also made major revisions based on the latest research. The entire textbook is more focused on showing students how participation in the system can result in changes in the political system. For instance, each chapter's *Politics with a Purpose* feature highlights political change brought about by citizens, groups, or organizations. Finally, pedagogy in the profession has evolved over time, and this edition represents our latest and best approach to introducing American government and politics to today's students.

2010 ELECTION RESULTS INCLUDED AND ANALYZED

Our experience has been that students respond to up-to-date information about political events. Consequently, we have included results of the November 2010 elections. We also analyze how these results will affect our political processes at the national, state, and local levels. While we have updated all of the text to be consistent with these results, in particular we have added throughout the text numerous special subsections dedicated to the elections.

THE INTERACTIVE FOCUS OF THIS TEXT

Whether the topic is voter participation, terrorism, or the problems that face the president, we constantly strive to involve the student reader in the analysis. We make sure that the reader comes to understand that politics is not an abstract process but a very human enterprise. We emphasize how different outcomes can affect students' civil rights and liberties, employment opportunities, and economic welfare.

Throughout the text, we encourage the reader to think critically. The features titled *Beyond Our Borders* encourage students to think globally. We further encourage interaction with the political system by ending each chapter with features titled *You Can Make a Difference*, which show students not only what they can do to become politically involved, but also why they should care enough to do so. In addition, these chapter-ending features highlight one young politically involved individual or point out actions that students can take themselves to change the system.

SPECIAL PEDAGOGY AND FEATURES

The 2011–2012 edition of *American Government and Politics Today* contains many pedagogical aids and high-interest features to assist both students and instructors. The following list summarizes the special elements that can be found in each chapter:

- **Questions to Consider**—Chapter-opening "Questions to Consider" lay out for students the most important questions explored in the chapter, allowing them to target their reading, and prompting them to think critically. These questions are now revisited directly in the chapter summary.

- **What If...?**—Now placed in the chapter-opener, these provocative questions prompt lively classroom discussion and put critical thinking skills into practice with current, real-life issues such as "What If the Constitution Had Banned Slavery Outright?" (Chapter 2); "What If One State's Same-Sex Marriages Had to be Recognized Nationwide?" (Chapter 3); "What If Roe v. Wade Were Overturned?" (new, Chapter 4); "What If Parties Were Supported Solely by Public Funding?" (new, Chapter 8); "What If Voting by Mail Became Universal?" (Chapter 9); "What If Pork Were Banned?" (new, Chapter 12); "What If There Were No Executive Privilege?" (new, Chapter 13); "What If the United States Disposed of All of Its Nuclear Weapons?" (new, Chapter 18); "What If Texas Became Five States?" (Chapter 19); "What If Texas Used Private Contractors to Administer State Government?" (Chapter 25); and "What If Texas Denied Illegal Immigrants Access to State Services?" (new, Chapter 27).

- **Politics with a Purpose**—Highlighting how a group or individual has impacted our political system, these boxes succinctly incorporate a literature review of key scholarship on the topic and offer a balance of positive and negative, modern and historical examples. Examples include "When Passions Mobilize," about the Tea Party and Coffee Party (Chapter 1); "The Innocence Project," about students fighting wrongful convictions (Chapter 4); "Let's Put It to a Vote," concerning the complexity of referenda elections across the states (Chapter 9); "Lobbying for Very Personal Interests" about one man's very personal fight to advocate for the impaired (Chapter 25); and "Fighting Tuition Hikes" about student demands for tuition relief (Chapter 27).

- **Beyond Our Borders**—Appearing in Chapters 1 through 18, this feature discusses a topic such as globalization, the war on terrorism, immigration, or comparative government that is relevant to the chapter. New *Beyond Our Borders* features in this edition are "How Short Can a Campaign Be?" (Chapter 10) and "How Green is Europe?" (Chapter 16).

- **Margin Definitions**—For all important terms. All terms and definitions are compiled in a complete glossary at the end of the book as well.

- **Did You Know?**—Margin features presenting various facts and figures that add interest to the learning process.

- **You Can Make a Difference**—These chapter-ending features show students ways to become politically involved. In the new edition, these features highlight one young adult in particular who has made or is making a difference. For example, the Chapter 4 box, "Your Civil Liberties: Searches and Seizures," features the case of Savana Redding—the Arizona eighth-grader who was strip-searched at school; the Chapter 8 box, "Electing Convention Delegates," features William Styles—a political science student at Western Carolina University who was a convention delegate in 2008; the Chapter 11 box, "Being a Critical Consumer of the News," features STAND—a student-driven organization that encourages student participation; the Chapter 12 box, "Why Should You Care About Congress?" highlights Mike Frerichs—an Illinois State Senator; Chapter 19's box highlights artist *Armando Hinojosa* of Laredo, Texas who exemplifies the value in learning about one's cultural and ethnic history; and Chapter 20's box that highlights Jesse Daniel Ames, who fought against the lynching of African Americans in Texas and battled for women's right to vote.

- **Key Terms**—A chapter-ending list with page numbers of all terms in the chapter that were boldfaced and defined in the margins.

- **Chapter Summary**—A point-by-point summary of the chapter text.

- **Selected Print, Media, and Online Resources**—An annotated list of suggested scholarly readings, as well as popular books, films, and Web sites relevant to chapter topics.

APPENDICES

Because we know that this book serves as a reference, we have included important documents for the student of American government to have close at hand. A fully annotated copy of the U.S. Constitution appears at the end of Chapter 2 as an appendix to that chapter. In addition, we have included the following appendices:

The Declaration of Independence

Federalist Papers Nos. 10 and 51

A COMPREHENSIVE SUPPLEMENTS PACKAGE

We are proud to be the authors of a text that has the most comprehensive, accessible, and fully integrated supplements package on the market. Together, the text and the supplements listed as follows constitute a total learning and teaching package for you and your students. For further information on any of these supplements, contact your Wadsworth Cengage Higher Education sales representative.

SUPPLEMENTS FOR INSTRUCTORS

PowerLecture DVD with JoinIn
(ISBN-10: 1111344698 | ISBN-13: 9781111344696)
This DVD includes two sets of **PowerPoint slides**—a book specific and a media-enhanced set, a Test Bank in both Microsoft Word and Exam View formats, an Instructor

Manual, JoinIn Clickers, and a Resource Integration Guide. The two types of Power Points are described on the next page.

Interactive book specific PowerPoint® lectures, a one-stop lecture and class preparation tool, makes it easy for you to assemble, edit, publish, and present book specific lectures for your course. You will have access to a set of PowerPoints with outlines specific to each chapter of *American Government and Politics Today,* as well as photos, figures, and tables found in the book.

The **media-enhanced PowerPoints** for each chapter can be used on their own or easily integrated with the book-specific PowerPoint outlines. Audio and video clips depicting both historic and current day events; NEW animated learning modules illustrating key concepts; tables, statistical charts, and graphs; and photos from the book, as well as outside sources are provided at the appropriate places in the chapter. You can also add your own materials—using both types of PowerPoints and your own material to culminate a powerful and personalized classroom or online presentation.

A **test bank** in Microsoft® Word and ExamView® computerized testing offers a large array of well-crafted multiple-choice and essay questions, along with their answers and page references.

An **Instructor's Manual**, written by author Lynne E. Ford and Albert Waite and Tracy Cook of Central Texas College, includes learning objectives, chapter outlines, discussion questions, suggestions for stimulating class activities and projects, tips on integrating media into your class (including step-by-step instructions on how to create your own podcasts), suggested readings and Web resources, and a section specially designed to help teaching assistants and adjunct instructors.

JoinIn™ offers book-specific "clicker" questions that test and track student comprehension of key concepts. Political Polling questions simulate voting, engage students, foster dialogue on group behaviors and values, and add personal relevance; the results can be compared to national data, leading to lively discussions. Visual Literacy questions are tied to images from the book and add useful pedagogical tools and high-interest feedback during your lecture. Save the data from students' responses all semester—track their progress and show them how political science works by incorporating this exciting new tool into your classroom. It is available for college and university adopters only.

The **Resource Integration Guide** outlines the rich collection of resources available to instructors and students within the chapter-by-chapter framework of the book, suggesting how and when each supplement can be used to optimize learning.

The Instructor Companion Web site for *American Government and Politics Today* includes the Instructor's Manual, text-specific PowerPoints containing lecture outlines, photos and figures, and NewsNow PowerPoints which are an additional set of multimedia rich PowerPoint slides posted each week. Instructors may use these slides to take a class poll or trigger a lively debate about the events that are shaping the world right now. And because this all-in-one presentation tool includes the text of the original newsfeed, along with videos, photos and discussion questions, no Internet connection is required!

Instructors also have access to the **Instructor's Guide to YouTube**, which shows American government instructors where on the Internet to find videos that can be used as learning tools in class. Organized by fifteen topics, the guide follows the sequence of an American government course and includes a preface with tips on how to use Internet videos in class.

SUPPLEMENTS FOR STUDENTS

CourseMate Instant Access Code
(ISBN-10: 1111356580 | ISBN-13: 9781111356583)
CourseMate Printed Access Code
(ISBN-10: 1111356572 | ISBN-13: 9781111356576)
The CourseMate for *American Government and Politics Today: Texas Edition* offers a variety of rich online learning resources designed to enhance the student experience. These resources include video activities, audio summaries, critical thinking activities, simulations, animated learning modules, interactive timelines, primary source quizzes, flashcards, learning objectives, glossaries, and crossword puzzles. Chapter resources are correlated with key chapter learning concepts, and users can browse or search for content in a variety of ways.

NewsNow is a new asset available on CourseMate, which is a combination of weekly news stories from the Associated Press, videos and images that bring current events to life for the student. For instructors, NewsNow includes an additional set of multimedia rich PowerPoint slides posted each week to the password-protected area of the text's instructor companion Web site. Instructors may use these slides to take a class poll or trigger a lively debate about the events that are shaping the world right now. And because this all-in-one presentation tool includes the text of the original newsfeed, along with videos, photos and discussion questions, no Internet connection is required!

How do you assess your students' engagement in your course? How do you know your students have read the material or viewed the resources you've assigned? How can you tell if your students are struggling with a concept? With CourseMate, you can use the included Engagement Tracker to assess student preparation and engagement. Use the tracking tools to see progress for the class as a whole or for individual students. Identify students at risk early in the course. Uncover which concepts are most difficult for your class. Monitor time on task. Keep your students engaged.

Coursemate also features an interactive eBook that has highlighting and search capabilities along with links to simulations, animated PowerPoints that illustrate concepts, Interactive Timelines, Videos, Primary Source Activities, Case Studies, Tutorial Quizzes and Flashcards.

> To Access CourseMate: Go to **cengagebrain.com/shop/ISBN/0495909491** to access your American Government CourseMate resources.

WebTutor™ on WebCT or Blackboard:
WebTutor on WebCT IAC
(ISBN-10: 1111303029 | ISBN-13: 9781111303020)
WebTutor on Blackboard IAC
(ISBN-10: 1111303002 | ISBN-13: 9781111303006)
Rich with content for your American government course, this Web-based teaching and learning tool includes course management, study/mastery, and communication tools.

Use WebTutor™ to provide virtual office hours, post your syllabus, and track student progress with WebTutor's quizzing material. For students, WebTutor™ offers real-time access to interactive online tutorials and simulations, practice quizzes, and Web links—all correlated to *American Government and Politics Today: Texas Edition*.

Political Theatre DVD 2.0
(ISBN-10: 0495793604 | ISBN-13: 9780495793601)
This three-DVD set, perfect for classroom use, contains video and audio clips drawn from key political events from the past 75 years: presidential speeches, campaign ads, debates, news reports, national convention coverage, demonstrations, speeches by civil rights leaders, and more.

JoinIn™ on Turning Point® for Political Theatre
ISBN-10: 0495798290 | ISBN-13: 9780495798293
For even more interaction, combine Political Theatre with the innovative teaching tool of a classroom response system through JoinIn™. Poll your students with questions created for you or create your own questions. Built within the Microsoft® PowerPoint® software, it's easy to integrate into your current lectures in conjunction with the "clicker" hardware of your choice.

The Wadsworth News Videos for American Government 2012 DVD
ISBN-10: 1111346143 | ISBN-13: 9781111346140
This collection of three- to six-minute video clips on relevant political issues serves as a great lecture or discussion launcher.

Great Speeches Collection
Throughout the ages, great orators have stepped up to the podium and used their communication skills to persuade, inform, and inspire their audiences. Studying these speeches can provide tremendous insight into historical, political, and cultural events. The Great Speeches Collection includes the full text of over sixty memorable orations for you to incorporate into your course. Speeches can be collated in a printed reader to supplement your existing course materials or bound into a core textbook.

ABC Video: Speeches by President Barack Obama
ISBN-10: 1439082472 | ISBN-13: 9781439082478
DVD of nine famous speeches by President Barack Obama, from 2004 through his inauguration, including his speech at the 2004 Democratic National Convention; his 2008 speech on race, "A More Perfect Union"; and his 2009 inaugural address. Speeches are divided into short video segments for easy, time-efficient viewing. This instructor supplement also features critical-thinking questions and answers for each speech, designed to spark classroom discussion.

Election 2010: An American Government Supplement
ISBN-10: 1111341788 | ISBN-13: 9781111341787
Written by John Clark and Brian Schaffner, this booklet addresses the 2010 congressional and gubernatorial races with both real time analysis and references.

The Obama Presidency – Year One Supplement
ISBN-10: 0495908371 | ISBN-13: 9780495908371
Much happens in the first year of a presidency, especially an historic one like that of Barack Obama. This full-color 16-page supplement by Kenneth Janda, Jeffrey Berry, and

Jerry Goldman analyzes such issues as healthcare, the economy and the stimulus package, changes in the U.S. Supreme Court, and the effect Obama policy has had on global affairs.

American Government CourseReader: Politics in Context
ISBN-10: 111147995X | ISBN-13: 9781111479954
American Government CourseReader: Politics in Context will enable instructors to create a customized reader. Using a database of hundreds of documents, readings, and videos, instructors can search by various criteria or browse the collection to preview and then select a customized collection to assign their students. The sources will be edited to an appropriate length and include pedagogical support—a headnote describing the document and critical-thinking and multiple-choice questions to verify that the student has read and understood the selection. Students will be able to take notes, highlight, and print content. The (e-Reader) allows the instructor to select exactly what students will be assigned with an easy-to-use interface and also provides an easily used assessment tool. The sources can be delivered online or in print format.

Latino American Politics Supplement
ISBN-10: 1111344817 | ISBN-13: 9781111344818
This 32-page supplement by Fernando Piñon of San Antonio College uses real examples to detail politics related to Latino Americans.

Texas Political Theatre 3.0
ISBN-10: 1111346151 | ISBN-13: 9781111346157
This 75-minute DVD contains new video and audio clips drawn from key political events in Texas, both current and historical, followed by critical thinking questions designed to engage students.

FOR USERS OF THE PREVIOUS EDITION

As usual, we thank you for your past support of our work. We have made numerous changes to this text for the 2011–2012 edition, many of which we list as follows. We have rewritten much of the text, added numerous new features, and updated the book to reflect the results of the 2010 elections.

- New and updated coverage of a multitude of topics including the 2010 midterm elections; the Obama presidency; the Tea Party movement; the political campaign advertising case *Citizens United v. FEC*; recent legislation on health care, gun control, and same-sex marriage; expanded coverage of women's rights, LGBTQ issues, illegal immigration, the impact of new media on political socialization, and the influence of changing demographics on public opinion; and expanded coverage of Latinos— America's largest majority.

- *What If…?*—Now placed in the chapter-opener, these provocative questions prompt lively classroom discussion and put critical thinking skills into practice with current, real-life issues such as "What If the Constitution Had Banned Slavery Outright?" (Chapter 2); "What If One State's Same-Sex Marriages Had to be Recognized Nationwide?" (Chapter 3); "What If *Roe v. Wade* Were Overturned?" (new, Chapter 4); "What If Parties Were Supported Solely by Public Funding?" (new, Chapter 8); "What If Voting by Mail Became Universal?" (Chapter 9); "What If Pork Were Banned?" (new, Chapter 12); "What If There Were No Executive Privilege?" (new, Chapter 13); "What

If the United States Disposed of All of Its Nuclear Weapons?" (new, Chapter 18); and "What If The United States Disposed of All of its Nuclear Weapons?" (new, Chapter 18).

- *Politics with a Purpose* features (formerly titled *Making a Difference* which opened each chapter of the last edition) how a group or individual has impacted our political system. They succinctly incorporate a literature review of key scholarship on the topic and offer a balance of positive and negative, modern and historical examples. Examples include "When Passions Mobilize," about the Tea Party and Coffee Party (revised, Chapter 1); "The Innocence Project," about students fighting wrongful convictions (new, Chapter 4); and "Let's Put It to a Vote," concerning the complexity of referenda elections across the states (Chapter 9).

- *You Can Make a Difference*—These chapter-ending features show students ways to become politically involved. In the new edition, these features highlight one young adult in particular who has made or is making a difference, resulting in greater appeal for students. For example, the Chapter 4 box, "Your Civil Liberties: Searches and Seizures," features the case of Savana Redding—the Arizona eighth-grader who was strip-searched at school; the Chapter 8 box, "Electing Convention Delegates," features William Styles—political science student at Western Carolina University who was a convention delegate in 2008; the Chapter 11 box, "Being a Critical Consumer of the News," features STAND—a student-driven organization that encourages student participation; and the Chapter 12 box, "Why Should You Care About Congress?" highlights Mike Frerichs, Illinois State Senator.

- *Questions to Consider,* which appear in the opener and help students target their reading, are now revisited directly in the chapter summary. These questions encourage students to think critically about the three most important points explored in the chapter from beginning to end.

- New coauthor Lynne E. Ford from the College of Charleston, infuses the book with stronger coverage of gender and diversity.

New political science scholarship—New citations in every chapter highlighting cutting-edge research and the latest scholarship are included. Figures and tables have been updated with the most recent data available, some added at press time.

SIGNIFICANT CHANGES WITHIN CHAPTERS

Each chapter contains updated data in figures and tables, updated citations, new photographs, updated entries for print, media and online resources, and whenever feasible, the most current information available on the problems facing the nation.

In addition, significant chapter-by-chapter changes have been made as follows:

Chapter 1 (The Democratic Republic)—Includes a new instructive section on using the Internet, "Connecting to American Government and Politics" and a new box, "What If Roe v. Wade Were Overturned?"

Chapter 2 (The Constitution)—Includes revised features: "Politics with a Purpose: How to Form a More Perfect Union?"; "What If the Constitution Had Banned Slavery Outright?"; "Beyond Our Borders: What Makes a Constitution?"; and "You Can Make a Difference: How Can You Affect the U.S. Constitution", which now includes discussion of Alondra

Jones who, as a high school student, sued her school district to provide better conditions in her school.

Chapter 3 (Federalism)—Includes expanded and updated coverage of different state approaches to income tax, same-sex marriage, and handgun laws.

Chapter 4 (Civil Liberties)—Includes expanded and updated coverage of school vouchers, political campaign advertising and the *Citizens United v. FEC* case. This chapter also features a new *Politics with a Purpose* box, "The Innocence Project."

Chapter 5 (Civil Rights)— Revised by Lynne E. Ford, the chapter includes the following: expanded coverage of women's rights, immigration and Latino rights, and LGBTQ issues; new material on race consciousness versus a post-racial society; updated information on the wage gap as it affects new college graduates; and coverage of the Lilly Ledbetter Fair Pay Act. The section on illegal immigration has been revised to include the controversy around Arizona's new law and generational differences within the Latino community in attitudes about immigration. A new section titled "Making Amends for Past Discrimination through Reparation" has been added and covers African Americans and Japanese internment. Finally, the features have been updated.

Chapter 6 (Public Opinion and Political Socialization)—Revised by Lynne E. Ford. New content has been added about the influence of new media on socialization and the development of attitudes; the ways in which expanded cell phone use and a significant decline in landlines impact public opinion polling is explored; and the material on the 2008 election has been enhanced using the latest research and election-related survey statistics. The ways in which changing demographics may influence public opinion is covered in greater depth. Some of the tables have been transformed into graphics that better display trends over time for students.

Chapter 7 (Interest Groups)—Includes a discussion of Cesar Chavez and the United Farm Workers Association, as well as updates on the pharmaceutical and health insurance lobbies.

Chapter 8 (Political Parties)—This chapter includes a recap of the 2010 elections, new discussions of perceived strengths of the different parties, and the 2008 parties' platforms on economics, as well as a revised box, "What If Parties Were Supported Solely by Public Funding?" that includes more discussion on how the flow of funds would impact power.

Chapter 9 (Voting and Elections)—Includes updated turnout numbers for the 2008 elections.

Chapter 10 (Campaigning for Office)—Includes a new discussion of the *Citizens United v. FEC* case, 2010 decision, and its possible impact on campaigns and elections, as well as updated information on 527s and their expenditures in 2008. A new *Beyond Our Orders* box, "How Short Can a Campaign Be?" compares the short national election campaign in Great Britain with that of the U.S. presidential election.

Chapter 11 (The Media and Cyberpolitics)—Updated discussion of the impact of YouTube on political campaigns and of the use of new media by the Obama White House.

Chapter 12 (The Congress)—Includes new discussion of the results of the 2010 Congressional elections; new coverage of caucuses as forums for under-represented groups in Congress; new section on partisan redistricting; new feature, "What If Pork Were Banned?" and a revised *You Can Make a Difference* feature, "Why Should You Care About Congress?"

Chapter 13 (The President)—Includes new section on Barack Obama and popular approval; new discussion of the Obama administration's use of regulatory authority and the president's new approach to foreign policy; new coverage of the executive appointment of "policy stars"; and a new box, "What If There Were No Executive Privilege?"

Chapter 14 (The Bureaucracy)—Includes update to reflect the Obama administration's changes in environmental policy.

Chapter 15 (The Courts)—Includes new discussion of the appointments of Justice Sonia Sotomayor and Justice Elena Kagan and a new *You Can Make a Difference* feature encouraging student to volunteer in the court system.

Chapter 16 (Domestic Policy)—Includes new discussion of the Gulf oil spill and the government's handling of this environmental disaster; new section, "The 2010 Health Reform Legislation," and updates on immigration reform, as well as a new *Beyond Our Borders* feature, "How Green is Europe?"

Chapter 17 (Economic Policy)—Includes new discussion of the financial crisis of 2008 and the policies passed by the president and Congress to meet the challenge of the crisis and to stimulate recovery from the recession.

Chapter 18 (Foreign Policy and National Security)—Includes updated discussions of the wars in Iraq and Afghanistan and a new box, "What If The United States Disposed of All of Its Nuclear Weapons?"

Chapter 19 (Texas History and Culture)—Expanded section on interaction between Anglos, Latinos, and Native Americans in the Republic; new section on the status of women in the Republic and their battle for equality and civil rights; expanded sections on Latinos' and African Americans' battles for civil rights; includes source material for Texas's Declaration of Independence from Mexico and Texas's Ordinance of Secession from the United States; and expanded discussion on the Texas/Mexican Border to include human, drug and weapons trafficking.

Chapter 20 (The Texas Constitution)—Includes the latest information on Texas's constitutional amendments, discussion of the recent impact of constitutionally limited legislative sessions, current data showing how Texas constitutional provisions compare among the 50 states, and Politics with a Purpose box includes new developments for those who have been wrongfully convicted.

Chapter 21 (Texas Interest Groups)—Includes updated section on noneconomic interest groups with additional discussion on motivations for joining; new mention of astro-turf lobbying; expanded section, "Which Interests are Powerful"; new data from Texans for Public Justice on 2008 campaign contributions; new update on the 2009 Supreme Court decision on the Caperton v. A.T. Massey Coal Company case and two new tables, "The Biggest Spenders on Lobbyists in Texas," and Number and Maximum Value of Contracts Signed by Selected Lobby Industry Groups: 2009."

Chapter 22 (Political Parties in Texas)—Includes a new map of Democratic and Republican strongholds in Texas based on the 2008 presidential election, impact of 2010 election results on the 2011 legislative session, and a revised discussion on whether Democrats in Texas can be competitive in the future.

Chapter 23 (Voting and Elections in Texas)—Includes the most recent data on elections and campaign spending; incorporates changes in election law; updated Beyond our Borders box that offers a comparison of voter turnout; and a new Online Resources section.

Chapter 24 (The Texas Legislature)—Includes updated info on campaign funding; updated coverage of the speaker of the house; coverage of the birth and death of a 2009 bill to require voter identification that involved use of the tactic known as chubbing; and updates throughout to reflect the 81st legislature.

Chapter 25 (The Texas Executive Branch)—Includes updated section on elected boards; updated information on governors' powers compared to other states; and new coverage of conflicts between Texas Commission on Environmental Quality and the U.S. Environmental Protection Agency on regulating plant emissions.

Chapter 26 (The Texas Judiciary, Law, and Due Process)—Covers the latest developments in death penalty issues, tort reform, and state judicial campaign finance, including discussion of U.S. Supreme Court rulings about corporate contributions to campaigns and how conflicts of interest affect due process of law.

Chapter 27 (Texas Public Policy)—Includes such cutting-edge policy issues as higher education tuition hikes, the state's use of federal stimulus funds, the state's budget shortfall, the impact of national health care reform on Texas, and the politics of the changes in public school social science curriculum; and a new feature deals with another hot-button issue—What if... Texas Denied Illegal Immigrants Access to State Services?

Chapter 28 (Local Government)—This chapter includes expanded discussions on topics such as national issues and state mandates facing local governments, municipal government structure, and local economic development; and an update on Texas municipal and county population growth.

ACKNOWLEDGMENTS

Since we started this project several years ago, a sizable cadre of individuals has helped us in various phases of the undertaking. The following academic reviewers offered numerous constructive criticisms, comments, and suggestions during the preparation of all previous editions:

Kevin Bailey, North Harris Community College, Houston, Texas

Evelyn Ballard, Houston Community College, Texas

Orlando N. Bama, McLennan Community College, Waco, Texas

Clyde W. Barrow, Texas A&M University, College Station

David C. Benford, Jr., Tarrant County Junior College, Fort Worth, Texas

Lynn R. Brink, North Lake College, Irving, Texas

Irasema Coronado, University of Texas at El Paso

Carolyn Grafton Davis, North Harris County College, Houston, Texas

Gavan Duffy, University of Texas at Austin

George C. Edwards III, Texas A&M University, College Station

Gregory Edwards, Amarillo College, Texas

Victoria A. Farrar-Myers, University of Texas at Arlington

Elizabeth N. Flores, Del Mar College, Corpus Christi, Texas

Joel L. Franke, Blinn College, Brenham, Texas

Donald Gregory, Stephen F. Austin State University, Nacogdoches, Texas

Stefan D. Haag, Austin Community College, Texas

Richard J. Herzog, Stephen F. Austin State University, Nacogdoches, Texas

Paul Holder, McLennan Community College, Waco, Texas

J. C. Horton, San Antonio College, Texas

Nancy B. Kral, Tomball College, Tomball, Texas

Harry D. Lawrence, Southwest Texas Junior College, Uvalde, Texas

Ray Leal, Southwest Texas State University, San Marcos

Sue Lee, Center for Telecommunications, Dallas County Community College District, Texas

Alan Lehmann, Blinn College, Brenham, Texas

Eileen Lynch, Brookhaven College, Dallas, Texas

J. David Martin, Midwestern State University, Wichita Falls, Texas

Helen Molanphy, Richland College, Dallas, Texas

Michael A. Preda, Midwestern State University, Wichita Falls, Texas

Mark E. Priewe, University of Texas at San Antonio

Donna Rhea, Houston Community College—Northwest, Texas

Pauline Schloesser, Texas Southern University, Houston

Robert E. Sterken, Jr., University of Texas, Tyler

John R. Todd, North Texas State University, Denton, Texas

Ron Velton, Grayson County College, Denison, Texas

Albert C. Waite, Central Texas College, Killeen, Texas

Robert D. Wrinkle, Pan American University, Edinburg, Texas

The 2011–2012 edition of this text is the result of our working closely with reviewers, who each offered us penetrating criticisms, comments, and suggestions. Although we have not been able to take account of all requests, each of the reviewers listed will see many of his or her suggestions taken to heart:

Krista Ackermann
Allan Hancock College

Teri Bengtson
Elmhurst College

Louis Battaglia
Erie Community College

Terence Lenio
McHenry County College

Jeanine Neher
Butte Glen Community College

Paul-Henri Gurian
University of Georgia

Steven Rolnick
Western Connecticut State University

In preparing this edition of *American Government and Politics Today*, we were the beneficiaries of the expert guidance of a skilled and dedicated team of publishers and editors. We would like, first of all, to thank Sean Wakely, Executive Vice President, Cengage Arts & Sciences, for the support he has shown for this project. We have benefited greatly from the supervision and encouragement given by Carolyn Merrill, executive editor; and P. J. Boardman, editor-in-chief.

Jennifer Jacobson at Ohlinger Publishing Services, our developmental editor, also deserves our thanks for her many aspects of project development. We are also indebted to editorial assistant Angela Hodge for her contributions to this project.

We are grateful to Josh Allen, our content production manager, Erica Arima, project manager at Integra Software Services, and Linda Helcher, for a remarkable design and for making it possible to get the text out on time. In addition, our gratitude goes to all of those who worked on the various supplements offered with this text, especially Katherine Hayes and Laura Hildebrand, who coordinated the Web site. We would also like to thank Amy Whitaker, marketing manager, for her tremendous efforts in marketing the text.

Any errors remain our own. We welcome comments from instructors and students alike. Suggestions that we have received in the past have helped us to improve this text and to adapt it to the changing needs of instructors and students.

STEFFEN SCHMIDT • MACK SHELLEY • BARBARA BARDES • LYNNE E. FORD • WILLIAM EARL MAXWELL • ERNEST CRAIN • ADOLFO SANTOS

ABOUT THE AUTHORS

STEFFEN W. SCHMIDT

Steffen W. Schmidt is a professor of political science at Iowa State University. He grew up in Colombia, South America, and studied in Colombia, Switzerland, and France. He obtained his Ph.D. from Columbia University, New York, in public law and government.

Schmidt has published twelve books and more than 122 journal articles. He is the recipient of numerous prestigious teaching prizes, including the Amoco Award for Lifetime Career Achievement in Teaching and the Teacher of the Year award. He is a pioneer in the use of Web-based and real-time video courses and is a member of the American Political Science Association's section on computers and multimedia. He is on the editorial board of the *Political Science Educator* and is the technology and teaching editor of the *Journal of Political Science Education*.

Schmidt has a political talk show on WOI Public Radio, where he is known as Dr. Politics, streaming live once a week at **www.woi.org**. The show has been broadcast live from various U.S. and international venues for seventeen years. Schmidt is a frequent on-air commentator for US elections on CNN en Español. He is the co-founder, Associate Editor, and Chief Political and Foreign Correspondent for a new Internet magazine InsiderIowa.com.

MACK C. SHELLEY II

Mack C. Shelley, II, is a professor of political science and statistics at Iowa State University. His B.A. is from American University, in Washington, D.C.; he received the Master's and Ph.D. at the University of Wisconsin-Madison. After two years at Mississippi State University, he arrived at Iowa State in 1979. He has served as co-editor of the *Policy Studies Journal*, and has numerous publications on public policy, including *The Permanent Majority: The Conservative Coalition in the United States Congress; Biotechnology and the Research Enterprise* (with William F. Woodman and Brian J. Reichel); *American Public Policy: The Contemporary Agenda* (with Steven G. Koven and Bert E. Swanson); and *Quality Research in Literacy and Science Education: International Perspectives and Gold Standards* (with Larry Yore and Brian Hand).

BARBARA A. BARDES

Barbara A. Bardes is professor *emerita* of political science and former dean of Raymond Walters College at the University of Cincinnati. She received her B.A. and M.A. from Kent State University and her Ph.D. from the University of Cincinnati. She held a faculty position at Loyola University in Chicago for many years before returning to Cincinnati, her hometown, as a college administrator. Bardes has written articles on public opinion and foreign policy and on women and politics. She also has authored *Thinking About Public Policy and Declarations of Independence: Women and Political Power in the Nineteenth Century American Novels* and coauthored *Public Opinion: Measuring the American Mind*.

LYNNE E. FORD

Lynne E. Ford is professor of political science and Associate Provost for Curriculum and Academic Administration at the College of Charleston in Charleston, South Carolina. She received her B.A. from The Pennsylvania State University and her M.A. and Ph.D. in government and political behavior from the University of Maryland-College Park. Ford's teaching and research interests include women and politics, elections and voting behavior, political psychology, and civic engagement. She has written articles on women in state legislatures, the under-representation of women in political office in the American South, and work-family policy in the United States. She has also authored *Women and Politics: The Pursuit of Equality* and *The Encyclopedia of Women and American Politics*. Ford served as department chair for eight years and she has led a number of campus-wide initiatives including general education reform, faculty compensation, and civic engagement.

WILLIAM EARL MAXWELL

William Earl Maxwell is a professor emeritus at San Antonio College, where he has taught courses in U.S. and Texas government since 1971. Throughout his career Maxwell has focused on innovative teaching techniques and improving the teaching and learning environments for students. As a part of that effort, in 1975 Maxwell coauthored *Understanding Texas Politics*, his first text on Texas government. He also coauthored such texts as *Politics in Texas and The Challenge of Texas Politics: Text with Readings*. He performed his undergraduate and graduate work at Sam Houston State University.

ERNEST CRAIN

A thirty-five year veteran instructor of political science, Ernest Crain specializes in political party competition, comparative state politics, and Texas public policy. Crain coauthored *Understanding Texas Politics, Politics in Texas, The Challenge of Texas Politics*, and four editions of *Introduction to Texas Politics*. Crain received his B.A. and M.A. degrees from the University of Texas in Austin.

ADOLFO SANTOS

Adolfo Santos is the chair of the Department of Social Sciences at the University of Houston-Downtown and Associate Professor of Political Science. Dr. Santos received a Ph.D. from the University of Houston in 1998. He is the author of *Do Members of Congress Reward their Future Employers? Evaluating the Revolving Door Syndrome*. He also writes about Hispanic representation in the U.S. Congress and the Texas legislature.

OTHER MEMBERS OF THE TEXAS TEAM

Elizabeth N. Flores is a professor of political science at Del Mar College in Corpus Christi. She received her M.A. degree from the University of Michigan. Flores has served as a director of the Corpus Christi Regional Transit Authority, written on politics for the Corpus Christi *Caller-Times*, and co-hosted a public affairs show on PBS.

Joseph Ignagni is a professor of political science at the University of Texas at Arlington, where he has received four teaching awards and served as an associate dean. Ignagni received a Ph.D. from Michigan State University. He has published articles in the *American Journal of Political Science, Political Research Quarterly, American Politics Quarterly, and Judicature.*

Cynthia Opheim is a professor of political science at Texas State University-San Marcos. Opheim received a Ph.D. from the University of Texas at Austin. She has published in the *Legislative Studies Quarterly, State and Local Government Review, and Public Administration Review*. She coauthored *State* and *Local Politics*: *The Individual and the Governments*. In 2003, she became president of the Southwestern Political Science Association (SWPSA).

Christopher Wlezien is a professor of political science at Temple University in Philadelphia and received a Ph.D. from the University of Iowa. Wlezien has published in the *American Journal of Political Science, British Journal of Political Science, Journal of Politics, Political Analysis, and Public Opinion Quarterly*. He is co-editor of the *Journal of Elections, Public Opinion and Parties*, and of the "Polls" section of *Public Opinion Quarterly*, and has edited the books *The Future of Election Studies and Britain Votes*. In 2004, he became president of the SWPSA.

American
GOVERNMENT
and Politics Today
Texas Edition

1

In March of 2010, 200,000 people demonstrated in favor of immigrants' rights in Washington, D.C. Image copyright Ryan Rodrick Beiler 2010. (Ryan Rodrick Beiler/Shutterstock.com)

The Democratic Republic

QUESTIONS TO CONSIDER

Why do governments exist?

Why does the United States have a representative democracy?

What are the cultural values and ideological views that support the American republic?

CHAPTER CONTENTS

what if...   Citizens Were Required To Vote?

BACKGROUND

If all eligible Americans were required to vote, elected representatives would reflect the views of a majority of the entire voting-age population. Passive consent of the nonvoters aside, today's politicians frequently ascend to their positions with the support of only a relatively small minority of citizens.

Consider the election of Barack Obama in 2008. In that election, President Obama won about 53 percent of the total popular vote and was widely hailed as a strong winner. When voter turnout is considered, however, Obama was elected by only 30 percent of the voting-age population. Given that 70 percent of age-eligible voters did *not* cast a ballot for him in 2008, any post-election claim to have earned "a mandate from the people" might seem overstated. How would the political system be changed if all citizens voted?

EFFECTS ON POLICY DECISIONS

If citizens were required to vote, elected officials would have to consider all of their constituents when making policy decisions. Today, the groups who are less likely to vote include the younger voters, the less-educated citizens, and those who are economically disadvantaged. If all citizens were required to vote, policies to assist the poor and less-skilled Americans might be implemented. On the other hand, older citizens tend to turn out in higher numbers today, keeping politicians anxious about any changes to the Social Security program.

POSSIBLE OBJECTIONS

Optimism over mandatory voting must be tempered with consideration of some of the unintended consequences that might result. First of all, requiring every citizen to vote would undoubtedly increase the number of uninformed voters. A common complaint in our existing system is that voters do not adequately follow politics or know individual candidates' stances on important issues. Uninformed voters might be more likely to be swayed by the charisma of candidates or impractical promises made by politicians. And, in the United States, voting is seen as a voluntary activity; those who are unhappy with the entire system are entitled to stay home and not vote. Imposing a fine or other punishment for not voting seems to run counter to our view of citizenship as voluntary.

FOR CRITICAL ANALYSIS

1. Do you agree with the concept that every American should be required to cast a ballot? Why or why not?
2. If citizens were required to vote, should they also be required to be well informed on the candidates and the issues? Explain your answer.
3. What are possible implications of such a change to the electoral system? Would this accomplish the reform's goals or create unintended consequences?

FRIENDS, FAMILY, JOBS, and school fill our lives. Why should it be important for anyone to register and to vote? Why should ordinary Americans take an interest in political issues or campaigns? The reason is that the citizens of the United States are more powerful than the president, Supreme Court justices, or any member of Congress. Democracies, especially this democracy, derive their powers from the citizens. Believe it or not, citizens can affect a local issue such as the level of taxes in their own town, participate in choosing the candidates for president, or influence the outcome of Supreme Court cases. The individuals who participate in the system can create change. The flip side of this truth is that if the people of a democracy fail to pay attention and fail to participate, decisions that impact their lives will be made for them, either for good or for ill. And, as with other skills we have, if we don't use the power to influence government, we may lose our inclination to do so.

What are the ways in which we can participate? Voting first comes to mind. Voting draws public attention, particularly as news coverage of campaigns fills the airwaves. Although voting is extremely important, it is only

DID YOU KNOW?

That the Greek philosopher Aristotle favored enlightened despotism over democracy, which to him meant mob rule?

one of the ways that citizens can exercise their political influence. Americans can also join a political organization or interest group, stage a protest, or donate funds to a political campaign or cause. Countless ways to become involved exist. Informed participation begins with knowledge, however, and this text aims to provide you with a strong foundation in American government and politics. We hope that this book helps introduce you to a lifetime of political awareness and activity.

POLITICS AND GOVERNMENT

What is politics? **Politics** can be understood as the process of resolving conflicts and deciding, as political scientist Harold Lasswell put it, "who gets what, when, and how."[1] More specifically, politics is the struggle over power or influence within organizations or informal groups that can grant or withhold benefits or privileges.

We can identify many such groups and organizations. In families, all members may meet together to decide on values, priorities, and actions. Wherever a community makes decisions through formal or informal rules, politics exists. For example, when a church decides to construct a new building or hire a new minister, the decision may be made politically. Politics is particularly intense when decisions are made that hit close to home, such as decisions about local schools: Where will the school be built? How will it be paid for? Will the curriculum include controversial subjects such as human sexuality? Parents, teachers, and school board members will all "politic" on these issues. Of all of the organizations that are controlled by political activity, however, the most important is the government.

What is the government? Certainly, it is an **institution**—that is, an ongoing organization with a life separate from the lives of the individuals who are part of it at any given moment in time. The **government** can be defined as an institution in which decisions are made that resolve conflicts or allocate benefits and privileges. The government is also the *preeminent* institution within society. It is unique because it has the ultimate authority for making decisions and establishing political values. Governments can, as a matter of their authority, force you to comply with laws through taxes, fines, and the power to send you to prison.

Politics
The process of resolving conflicts and deciding "who gets what, when, and how." More specifically, politics is the struggle over power or influence within organizations or informal groups that can grant or withhold benefits or privileges.

Institution
An ongoing organization that performs certain functions for society.

Government
The preeminent institution in which decisions are made that resolve conflicts or allocate benefits and privileges. It is unique because it has the ultimate authority within society.

WHY IS GOVERNMENT NECESSARY?

Perhaps the best way to assess the need for government is to examine circumstances in which government, as we normally understand it, does not exist. What happens when multiple groups compete with each other for power within a society? There are places around the world where such circumstances exist. A current example is the African nation of Somalia. Since 1991, Somalia has not had a central government. The nation has disintegrated into a collection of tribal areas, each of which has some autonomy. Neighboring nations supported the creation of the Transitional Federal Government, or TFG, in 2004, but it is primarily an alliance between rival political groups. Islamic extremist groups have taken control of some sections of the nation, even attacking the capital, Mogadishu. In general, multiple armed forces compete by fighting, and the absence of a unified government is equivalent to civil war, in which civilians suffer.

[1]Harold Lasswell, *Politics: Who Gets What, When, and How* (New York: McGraw-Hill, 1936).

SECURITY

As the example of Somalia shows, one of the original purposes of government is the maintenance of security, or **order**. By keeping the peace, the government protects the people from violence at the hands of private or foreign armies. It dispenses justice and protects the people against the violence of criminals. If order is not present, it is not possible to provide any of the other benefits that people expect from government.

Consider the situation in Iraq. In March and April 2003, U.S. and British coalition forces invaded that nation, which was governed by the dictator Saddam Hussein. The relatively small number of coalition troops had little trouble in defeating their military opponents, but they experienced serious difficulties in establishing order within Iraq when the war was over.

Once it became clear that Saddam Hussein was no longer in control of the country, widespread looting broke out. Ordinary citizens stole furniture from government buildings and thieves robbed the national museums of their treasures. In 2005, it became clear that numerous groups within Iraqi society were engaged in the struggle for power. Some groups focused on attacks on the coalition forces, while others engaged in terrorist activities against other Iraqi religious or ethnic sects.

By 2007, when the Bush administration initiated a troop surge, it was clear that the Iraq situation had deteriorated badly, and no clear agreement among Iraqis about the future of their society had emerged. The new Bush strategy created local teams of U.S. troops, aid officials, and Iraqi local leaders to rebuild towns and local institutions. It was understood that a degree of security and order would have to be restored before it would be possible to begin the reconstruction of Iraqi society. Order is a political value that we will return to later in this chapter.

BUDDHIST MONKS PROTEST the suppression of liberty by the ruling military elite in Myanmar. Does international attention to the regime help or hurt the movement for more freedom there? (AFP/Getty Images)

LIBERTY

Order cannot be the only important political value. There are many examples of countries where order exists but other threats to individuals loom large. In Myanmar, formerly called Burma, the military rulers have kept order by restricting the rights of opposition leaders, suppressing all protests including those led by Buddhist monks in 2007, and cutting off access to the Internet. Protection from the violence of domestic criminals or foreign armies is not enough. Citizens also need protection from abuses of power by the government if they are to experience any form of liberty.

Liberty—the greatest freedom of the individual consistent with the freedom of other individuals—is a second major political value, along with order. Liberty is a value that may be promoted by government, but it can also be invoked *against* government. We will further discuss this value later in this chapter.

Liberty
The greatest freedom of individuals that is consistent with the freedom of other individuals in the society.

AUTHORITY AND LEGITIMACY

Every government must have **authority**—that is, the right and power to enforce its decisions. Ultimately, the government's authority rests on its control of the armed forces and the police. Virtually no one in the United States, however, bases his or her day-to-day activities on fear of the government's enforcement powers. Most people, most of the time, obey the law because this is what they have always done, and they have been taught to believe that this is the right way to behave. Also, if they did not obey the law, they would face the disapproval of friends and family. Consider an example: Do you obey traffic laws and drive on the right side of the road because you are fearful of arrest or because you understand that these rules provide order, prevent accidents, and give you the freedom to travel where you wish to go?

Under most circumstances, the government's authority has broad popular support. People accept the government's right to establish rules and laws. When authority is broadly accepted, we say that it has **legitimacy**. Authority without legitimacy is a

Authority
The right and power of a government or other entity to enforce its decisions and compel obedience.

Legitimacy
Popular acceptance of the right and power of a government or other entity to exercise authority.

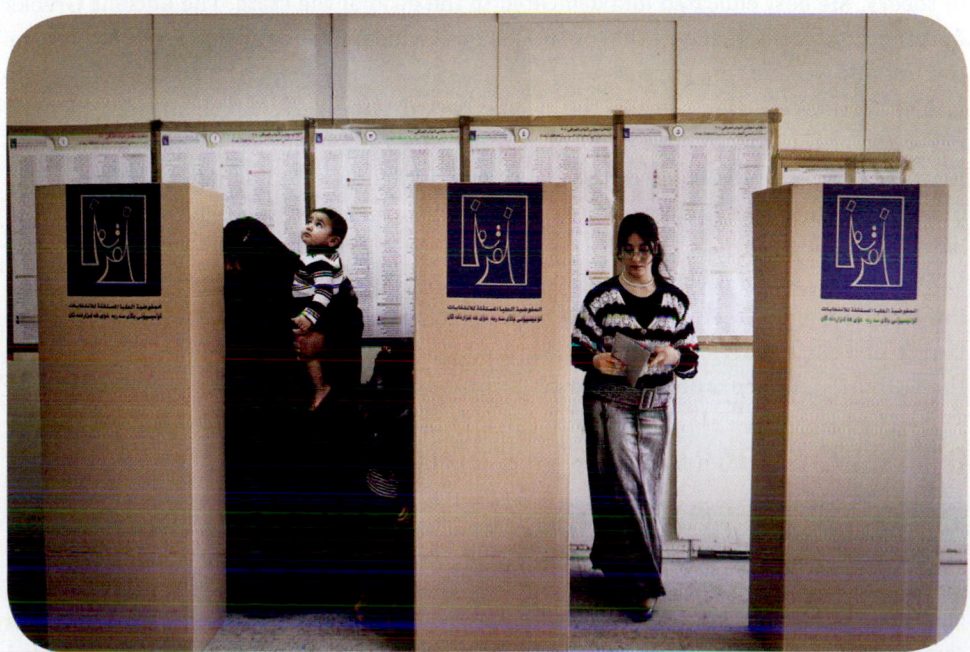

IRAQI WOMEN are seen voting in the 2010 parliamentary election. (ZHANG NING/Xinhua /Landov)

recipe for trouble. Iraq can serve as an example. Although many Iraqis were happy to see the end of Saddam Hussein's regime, they were displeased that their nation was occupied by foreign troops. Many Iraqis, especially in districts inhabited by Sunni Arabs (the former politically dominant group in Iraq), did not accept the legitimacy of the U.S.–led Coalition Provisional Authority (CPA).

Terrorists and other groups hostile to the CPA planned and carried out violent attacks on coalition forces and other groups, knowing the people would not call on government for help. After several interim steps, the Iraqi people elected the new Council of Representatives in 2005, and all ministers in the new constitutional government were in place by May 2006. In 2010, the Iraqi people participated in national elections to choose members of the parliament as called for by their constitution.

WHY CHOOSE DEMOCRACY?

Today, more than 200 nations exist in the world. All have some form of government that possesses authority and some degree of legitimacy. The crucial question for every nation is who controls the government. The answer could be a group, one person, perhaps the monarch or a dictator, or no one.

At one extreme is a society governed by a **totalitarian regime**. In such a political system, a small group of leaders or a single individual—a dictator—makes all political decisions for the society. An example of such a regime is the Soviet Union in the 1930s, 1940s, and 1950s. The leaders of the Communist Party controlled every facet of the society, including the church, schools, commerce, and government. In such a regime, the power of the ruler is total (thus the term *totalitarianism*).

A second type of system is authoritarian government. **Authoritarianism** differs from totalitarianism in that only the government is fully controlled by the ruler. Social and economic institutions exist that are not under the government's control.

Many of our terms for describing the distribution of political power are derived from the ancient Greeks, who were the first Western people to study politics systematically. One form of rule by the few was known as **aristocracy**, literally meaning "rule by the best." In practice, this meant rule by leading members of wealthy families who were, in theory, the best educated and dedicated to the good of the state. The ancient Greeks had another term for rule by the few, **oligarchy**, which means rule by a small group for corrupt and self-serving purposes.

The Greek term for rule by the people was **democracy**, which means that the authority of the government is granted to it from the people as a whole. Within the limits of their culture, some of the Greek city-states operated as democracies. Today, in much of the world, the people will not grant legitimacy to a government unless it is based on democracy.

If totalitarianism is control of all aspects of society by the government, **anarchy** is the complete opposite. It means that there is no government at all. Each individual or family in a society decides for itself how it will behave, and there is no institution with the authority to keep order in any way.

DIRECT DEMOCRACY AS A MODEL

The system of government in the ancient Greek city-state of Athens is usually considered the purest model of **direct democracy**, because the citizens of that community debated and voted directly on all laws, even those put forward by the ruling council of the city. The most important feature of Athenian democracy was that the **legislature** was composed of all of the citizens. Women, foreigners, and slaves, however, were excluded

---

Totalitarian Regime
A form of government that controls all aspects of the political and social life of a nation.

Authoritarianism
A type of regime in which only the government is fully controlled by the ruler. Social and economic institutions exist that are not under the government's control.

Aristocracy
Rule by the "best"; in reality, rule by an upper class.

Oligarchy
Rule by the few in their own interests.

Democracy
A system of government in which political authority is vested in the people. Derived from the Greek words *demos* ("the people") and *kratos* ("authority").

Anarchy
The absence of any form of government or political authority.

Direct Democracy
A system of government in which political decisions are made by the people directly, rather than by their elected representatives; probably attained most easily in small political communities.

Legislature
A governmental body primarily responsible for the making of laws.

because they were not citizens. This form of government required a high level of participation from every citizen; that participation was seen as benefiting the individual and the city-state. The Athenians believed that although a high level of participation might lead to instability in government, citizens, if informed about the issues, could be trusted to make wise decisions. Greek philosophers also believed that debating the issues and participating in making the laws was good for the individual's intellectual and personal development.

THIS TOWN MEETING in Vermont allows every citizen of the town to vote directly and in person for elected officials, for proposed policies, and, in some cases, for the town budget. To be effective, such a form of direct democracy requires that the citizens stay informed about local politics, attend town meetings, and devote time to discussion and decision making. Why might citizens be willing to spend the time necessary to attend town meetings? (AP Photo/Toby Talbot)

Direct Democracy Today. Direct democracy has also been practiced in Switzerland and in the United States, in New England town meetings. At New England town meetings, which can include all of the voters who live in the town, important decisions—such as levying taxes, hiring city officials, and deciding local ordinances—are made by majority vote. Some states provide a modern adaptation of direct democracy for their citizens; representative democracy is supplemented by the **initiative** or the **referendum**—processes by which the people may vote directly on laws or constitutional amendments. The **recall** process, which is available in many states, allows the people to vote to remove an official from state office.

Teledemocracy. Today, because of the Internet, Americans have more access to political information than ever before. Voters can now go online to examine the record of any candidate for any office. Constituents can badger their congressional representatives and state legislators by sending them e-mail. Individuals can easily and relatively inexpensively form political interest groups using the Internet. The Obama campaign in 2008 pioneered new uses of the Internet. It built a loyal following of citizens who contributed to campaign funds via the Internet and received daily messages from the candidate or his representatives. Today, many governments, like corporations, depend on the Internet to provide information to the citizens and allow them access to forms and requests for assistance. If you want to get a flag flown at the U.S. Capitol, for example, the request form is probably on your congressperson's Web site.

Although Colorado offered its citizens the opportunity of voting online in 2000, the Pentagon cancelled a plan for troops overseas to vote online in 2004 due to Internet security concerns. Several states, however, do allow for voter registration online. In 2008, the Democratic Party used online primary voting for Democrats residing overseas. On February 5, 2008, registered Democrats could go to specified cities overseas and vote online to select the candidate who would win the 11 convention delegates who would represent them. Barack Obama won the vote handily.[2]

THE DANGERS OF DIRECT DEMOCRACY

Although they were aware of the Athenian model, the framers of the U.S. Constitution had grave concerns about the stability of such a society. The Founding Fathers were well-educated men who had read the new political philosophers of the 17th and 18th centuries. The arguments for government based on the **consent of the people** were

Initiative
A procedure by which voters can propose a law or a constitutional amendment.

Referendum
An electoral device whereby legislative or constitutional measures are referred by the legislature to the voters for approval or disapproval.

Recall
A procedure allowing the people to vote to dismiss an elected official from state office before his or her term has expired.

Consent of the People
The idea that governments and laws derive their legitimacy from the consent of the governed.

[2]Since then, other jurisdictions have offered online voting.

Republic
A form of government in which sovereignty rests with the people, as opposed to a king or monarch.

Popular Sovereignty
The concept that ultimate political authority is based on the will of the people.

Democratic Republic
A republic in which representatives elected by the people make and enforce laws and policies.

Representative Democracy
A form of government in which representatives elected by the people make and enforce laws and policies; may retain the monarchy in a ceremonial role.

put forward by philosopher John Locke, who held that all individuals have certain inalienable rights and that governments are created by the people in a "social contract."[3] During America's colonial period, the idea of government based on the consent of the people gained increasing popularity. Such a government was the main aspiration of the American Revolution, the French Revolution in 1789, and many subsequent revolutions. At the time of the American Revolution, however, the masses were still considered to be too uneducated to govern themselves, too prone to the influence of demagogues (political leaders who manipulate popular prejudices), and too likely to subordinate minority rights to the tyranny of the majority.

James Madison defended the new scheme of government set forth in the U.S. Constitution, while warning of the problems inherent in a "pure democracy":

A common passion or interest will, in almost every case, be felt by a majority of the whole . . . and there is nothing to check the inducements to sacrifice the weaker party or an obnoxious individual. Hence it is that such democracies have ever been spectacles of turbulence and contention, and have ever been found incompatible with personal security or the rights of property; and have in general been as short in their lives as they have been violent in their deaths.[4]

Like other politicians of his time, Madison feared that pure, or direct, democracy would deteriorate into mob rule. What would keep the majority of the people, if given direct decision-making power, from abusing the rights of minority groups?

A DEMOCRATIC REPUBLIC

The framers of the U.S. Constitution chose to craft a **republic**, meaning a government in which sovereign power rests with the people, rather than with a king or monarch. A republic is based on **popular sovereignty**. To Americans of the 1700s, the idea of a republic also meant a government based on common beliefs and virtues that would be fostered within small communities. The rulers were to be amateurs—good citizens who would take turns representing their fellow citizens.

The U.S. Constitution created a form of republican government that we now call a **democratic republic**. The people hold the ultimate power over the government through the election process, but all policy decisions are made by elected officials. For the founders, even this distance between the people and the government was not sufficient. The Constitution made sure that the Senate and the president would be selected by political elites rather than by the people, although later changes to the Constitution allowed the voters to elect members of the Senate directly.

Despite these limits, the new American system was unique in the amount of power it granted to ordinary citizens. Over the course of the following two centuries, democratic values became increasingly popular, at first in the West and then throughout the rest of the world. The spread of democratic principles gave rise to another name for our system of government—**representative democracy**. The term *representative democracy* has almost the same meaning as *democratic republic*, with one exception. In a republic, not only are the people sovereign, but there is no king. What if a nation develops into a democracy but preserves the monarchy as a largely ceremonial institution? This is exactly what happened in Britain. Not surprisingly, the British found

---

[3]John Locke, *Two Treatises on Government*, (London: Awnshawn Churchill, 1690).
[4]James Madison, in Alexander Hamilton, James Madison, and John Jay, *The Federalist Papers*, No. 10 (New York: Mentor Books, 1964), p. 81. See Appendix B of this textbook.

the term *democratic republic* to be unacceptable, and they described their system as a representative democracy instead.

Principles of Democratic Government. All representative democracies rest on the rule of the people as expressed through the election of government officials. In the 1790s in the United States, only free white males were able to vote, and in some states they had to be property owners as well. Women did not receive the right to vote in national elections in the United States until 1920, and the right to vote was not secured in all states by African Americans until the 1960s. Today, **universal suffrage** is the rule.

Because everyone's vote counts equally, the only way to make fair decisions is by some form of **majority** will. But to ensure that **majority rule** does not become oppressive, modern democracies also provide guarantees of minority rights. If political minorities were not protected, the majority might violate the fundamental rights of members of certain groups, especially groups that are unpopular or that differ from the majority population, such as racial minorities.

To guarantee the continued existence of a representative democracy, there must be free, competitive elections. Thus, the opposition always has the opportunity to win elective office. For such elections to be totally open, freedom of the press and speech must be preserved so that opposition candidates may present their criticisms of the government.

Constitutional Democracy. Yet another key feature of Western representative democracy is that it is based on the principle of **limited government**. Not only is the government dependent on popular sovereignty, but the powers of the government are also clearly limited, either through a written document or through widely shared beliefs. The U.S. Constitution sets down the fundamental structure of the government and the limits to its activities. Such limits are intended to prevent political decisions based on the whims or ambitions of individuals in government rather than on constitutional principles.

Universal Suffrage
The right of all adults to vote for their representatives.

Majority
More than 50 percent.

Majority Rule
A basic principle of democracy asserting that the greatest number of citizens in any political unit should select officials and determine policies.

Limited Government
The principle that the powers of government should be limited, usually by institutional checks.

WHO REALLY RULES IN AMERICA?

Americans feel free to organize, to call and e-mail their representatives, to vote candidates in and out of office. We always describe our political system as a democracy or democratic republic. However, do the people of the United States actually hold power today? Political scientists have developed several theories about American democracy, including *majoritarian* theory, *elite* theory, and theories of *pluralism*. Advocates of these theories use them to describe American democracy either as it actually is or as they believe it should be.

Majoritarianism
A political theory holding that in a democracy, the government ought to do what the majority of the people want.

MAJORITARIANISM

Many people believe that in a democracy, the government ought to do what the majority of the people want. This simple proposition is the heart of majoritarian theory. As a theory of what democracy should be like, **majoritarianism** is popular among both political scientists and ordinary citizens. In the presidential election of 2000, the fact that George W. Bush became president although he did not win the majority of the popular vote led to many debates over our electoral system. He did, however, win the majority of votes in the electoral college; that is, electoral votes assigned to each state, as specified by the U.S. Constitution. The workings of the electoral college are explained in more detail in Chapter 9.

DID YOU KNOW?

That in 2010, more babies will be born to minority parents than to Caucasian parents, the first time that has happened in U.S. history?

Rooted in majoritarian theory are the contemporary debates in many states over which type of voting machine would be completely accurate and tamperproof. Many scholars, however, consider majoritarianism to be a surprisingly poor description of how U.S. democracy actually works. In particular, they point to the low level of turnout for elections. Polling data have shown that many Americans are neither particularly interested in politics nor well informed. Few are able to name the persons running for Congress in their districts, and even fewer can discuss the candidates' positions. As discussed in the opening What If . . . , a requirement that all citizens vote might bring the United States closer to a true majoritarian democracy.

ELITISM

Elite Theory
A perspective holding that society is ruled by a small number of people who exercise power to further their self-interest.

If ordinary citizens are not really making policy decisions with their votes, then who is? One answer suggests that elites really govern the United States. American government, in other words, is a sham democracy. **Elite theory** is usually used simply to describe the American system. Few people today believe it is a good idea for the country to be run by a privileged minority. In the past, however, many people believed that it was appropriate for the country to be run by an elite. Consider the words of Alexander Hamilton, one of the framers of the Constitution:

> All communities divide themselves into the few and the many. The first are the rich and the wellborn, the other the mass of the people. . . . The people are turbulent and changing; they seldom judge or determine right. Give therefore to the first class a distinct, permanent share in the government. They will check the unsteadiness of the second, and as they cannot receive any advantage by a change, they therefore will ever maintain good government.[5]

Some versions of elite theory posit a small, cohesive, elite class that makes almost all of the important decisions for the nation,[6] whereas others suggest that voters choose among competing elites. New members of the elite are recruited through the educational system so that the brightest children of the masses allegedly have the opportunity to join the elite stratum. One view suggests that the members of the elite are primarily interested in controlling the political system to protect their own wealth and the capitalist system that produces it.[7] Studies of elite opinion, however, have suggested that elites are more tolerant of diversity, more willing to defend individual liberties, and more supportive of democratic values than are members of the mass public.

PLURALISM

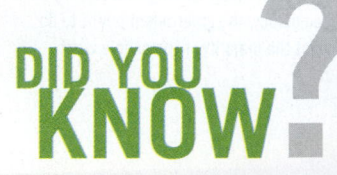

A different school of thought holds that our form of democracy is based on group interests. As early as 1831, the French traveler and commentator Alexis de Tocqueville noted the American penchant for joining groups: "As soon as the inhabitants of the United States have taken up an opinion or a feeling which they wish to promote in the world, they look out for mutual assistance; and as soon as they have found one another out, they combine. From that moment they are no longer isolated men, but a power seen from afar. . . ."[8]

That more than 500,000 officials are elected in the United States, which is more than all the bank tellers in the country?

---

[5]Alexander Hamilton, "Speech in the Constitutional Convention on a Plan of Government," in *Writings*, ed. Joanne B. Freeman (New York: Library of America, 2001).
[6]Michael Parenti, *Democracy for the Few*, 7th ed. (Belmont, CA: Wadsworth Publishing, 2002).
[7]G. William Domhoff, *Who Rules America?* 4th ed. (New York: McGraw-Hill Higher Education, 2002).
[8]Alexis de Tocqueville, *Democracy in America*, Volume II, Section 2, Chapter V, "Of the uses which the Americans make of Public Associations." (available in many editions, and as full text in several Web locations)

POLITICS WITH A purpose

When Passions Mobilize

"We the People ..." has profound meaning in the 21st century. A quick Internet search reveals literally millions of Web sites with the title "citizens against ..." and just as many more with "citizens for ..." in their title.

People organize into groups in order to influence the system and affect changes in public policy. Many groups mobilize to keep watch on government power. Some groups address specific policy problems—the environment, handgun violence, or urban gas well drilling—while others have bigger issues, such as reducing taxes or the national debt. In recent months, several interest groups have mobilized either against the Obama administration's approach to health care reform and increased government spending or in support of the president's initiatives. While it is true that such groups may have ties to a political party or to an existing political organization, many people who join do so out of real passion and may have little political experience. In 2009, the fastest-growing groups organized under the label of the Tea Party, although there was no real national organization at first. Tea Partiers rallied, marched on Washington, and went to town halls to object to the health reform legislation. Some local groups got involved in local politics, while others chose to work only on national issues.

It is generally expected that those who join such groups to express specific views are better educated, older, and more likely to be involved in community affairs. While those characteristics may describe the majority of community organizers,

soccer moms, college students, and blue-collar workers may also be found organizing groups. One of the earliest organizers of the Tea Party in Washington state was Keli Carender, a young performance artist who has a ring in her nose and a teaching degree. Carender does not fit the profile of an organizer. She began by protesting government spending by herself and then started to organize rallies.

Feeling that the Tea Party movement was too biased towards white middle-class Americans and that their form of debate was unproductive, a number of young professionals began the Coffee Party movement to provide a forum for people to have a more civil discussion of the issues. Annabel Park, a journalist and film-maker, got tired of the narrow focus of the Tea Parties and started this alternative movement by blogging, "Let's get together and drink cappuccino and have a real political dialogue with substance and compassion."*

Her call led to the organization of Coffee Parties across the nation, including one in San Antonio, where a roomful of individuals came together to organize a forum for issue discussion. The goal of the Coffee Party is to have civil discussions with no ranting or shouting. That right—and the right to have rallies and protests—is protected by the Bill of Rights.

It is interesting to consider how organizations such as the Tea Party or the Coffee Party contribute to public debates on the issues and to examine the role of the media in the growth of such organizations. Do you think that citizen organizations can become racist or extreme when passions run high? What is your passion? What are the issues about which you care most deeply? Chances are good that other similarly motivated individuals would welcome your help!

*The Texas Tribune, www. texastribune.org, March 16, 2010.

Pluralist theory proposes that even if the average citizen cannot keep up with political issues or cast a deciding vote in any election, the individual's interests will be protected by groups that represent her or him. The growth of two new groups—the Tea Party and Coffee Party movements, respectively—is discussed in the Politics with a Purpose box. Theorists who subscribe to **pluralism** see politics as a struggle among groups to gain benefits for their members. Given the structures of the American political system, group conflicts tend to be settled by compromise and accommodation. Because there is a multitude of interests, no one group can dominate the political process. Furthermore,

Pluralism
A theory that views politics as a conflict among interest groups. Political decision making is characterized by bargaining and compromise.

because most individuals have more than one interest, conflict among groups need not divide the nation into hostile camps.

Many political scientists believe that pluralism works very well as a descriptive theory. As a way to defend the practice of democracy in the United States, however, pluralism has problems. Poor citizens are rarely represented by interest groups. At the same time, rich citizens are often overrepresented, in part because they understand their own interests. As political scientist E. E. Schattschneider observed, "The flaw in the pluralist heaven is that the heavenly chorus sings with a strong upper-class accent."[9] There are also serious doubts as to whether group decision making always reflects the best interests of the nation.

Critics see a danger that groups may become so powerful that all policies become compromises crafted to satisfy the interests of the largest groups. The interests of the public as a whole, then, would not be considered. Critics of pluralism have suggested that a democratic system can be virtually paralyzed by the struggle among interest groups. We will discuss interest groups at greater length in Chapter 7.

Some scholars argue that none of these three theories—majoritarianism, elite theory, or pluralism—fully describes the workings of American democracy. These experts say that each theory captures a part of the true reality, but that we need all three theories to gain a full understanding of American politics.

FUNDAMENTAL VALUES

The writers of the American Constitution believed that the structures they had created would provide for both democracy and a stable political system. They also believed that the nation could be sustained by its **political culture**—the set of ideas, values, and ways of thinking about government and politics that are shared by all citizens.

There is considerable consensus among American citizens about certain concepts basic to the U.S. political system. Given that the vast majority of Americans are descendants of immigrants with diverse cultural and political backgrounds, how can we account for this consensus? Primarily, it is the result of **political socialization**—the process by which beliefs and values are transmitted to new immigrants and to our children. The nation depends on families, schools, houses of worship, and the media to transmit the precepts of our national culture.

The most fundamental concepts of the American political culture are those of the **dominant culture**. Those beliefs are rooted in Western European civilization and the ideas of the Enlightenment, including the ideas of popular sovereignty and the right to life, liberty, and property as expressed in the Declaration of Independence. That said, it is important to note that while Americans express broad support for these ideas and values, there are many conflicts over which values are most important to various groups within the society.

INDIVIDUAL FREEDOM

In the United States, our civil liberties include religious freedom—both the right to practice whatever religion we choose and freedom from any state-imposed religion. Our civil liberties also include freedom of speech—the right to express our opinions freely

Political Culture
The collection of beliefs and attitudes toward government and the political process held by a community or nation.

Political Socialization
The process through which individuals learn a set of political attitudes and form opinions about social issues. Families and the educational system are two of the most important forces in the political socialization process.

Dominant Culture
The values, customs, and language established by the group or groups that traditionally have controlled politics and government in a society.

---

[9]E. E. Schattschneider, *The Semi-Sovereign People* (Hinsdale, IL: The Dryden Press, 1975; originally published in 1960).

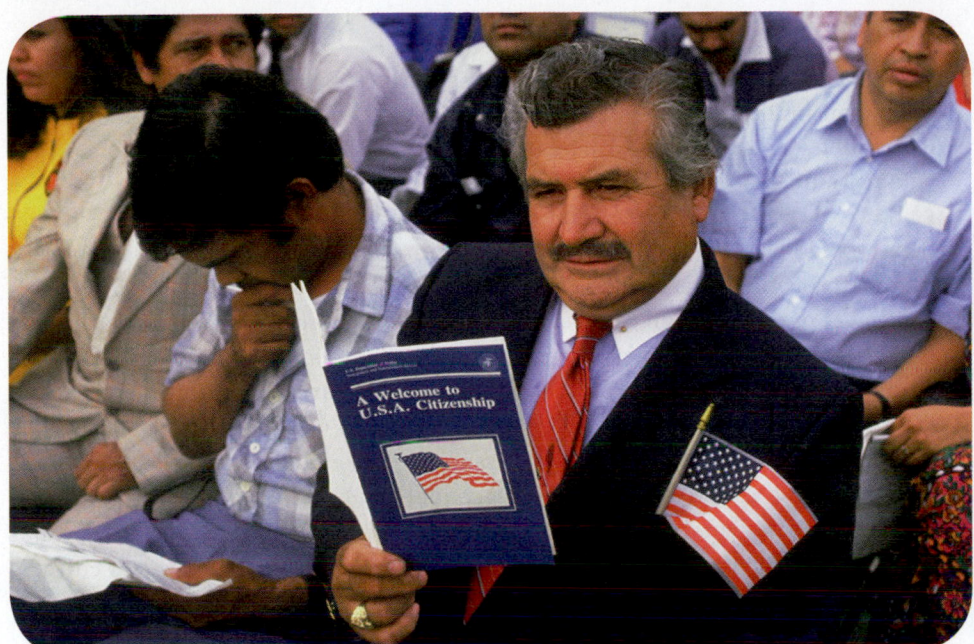

on all matters, including government actions. Freedom of speech is perhaps one of our most prized liberties, because a democracy could not endure without it. These and many other basic guarantees of liberty are found in the Bill of Rights, the first 10 amendments to the Constitution.

Liberty, however, is not the only value widely held by Americans. A substantial portion of the American electorate, those qualified to vote, believes that certain kinds of liberty threaten the traditional social order. The right to privacy is a particularly controversial liberty. The United States Supreme Court has held that the right to privacy can be derived from other rights that are explicitly stated in the Bill of Rights. The Supreme Court has also held that under the right to privacy, the government cannot ban either abortion[10] or private homosexual behavior by consenting adults.[11] Some Americans believe that such rights threaten the sanctity of the family and the general cultural commitment to moral behavior. Of course, other Americans disagree with this point of view.

Security is another issue. When Americans perceive serious external or internal threats, they have supported government actions to limit individual liberties in the name of national security. Such limits were imposed during the Civil War, World War II, and the McCarthy era of the Cold War. Following the terrorist attacks on the World Trade Center and the Pentagon on September 11, 2001, Congress passed legislation designed to provide greater security at the expense of some civil liberties. In particular, the USA PATRIOT Act (which stands for Uniting and Strengthening America by Providing Appropriate Tools Required to Intercept and Obstruct Terrorism) gave law enforcement and intelligence-gathering agencies greater latitude to search out and investigate suspected terrorists. When the news broke in December 2005 that the National Security Agency (NSA) had been engaging in warrantless secret surveillance, many wondered if civil liberties had been eroded too far in the name of national security. However, the Obama administration got approval for an extension of the act in 2010.

[10]*Roe v. Wade*, 410 U.S. 113 (1973).
[11]*Lawrence v. Texas*, 539 U.S. 558 (2003).

A HIGH POINT OF the civil rights movement of the 1950s and 1960s was the March on Washington on August 28, 1963, led by Martin Luther King, Jr. Nearly 250,000 people participated in the event. The following year, Congress passed the Civil Rights Act of 1964, one of the most important civil rights acts in the nation's history. Why does the mandate of equal treatment for all groups of Americans sometimes come into conflict with the concept of liberty? (Library of Congress, Prints & Photographs Division, U.S. News & World Report Magazine Collection [LC-U9- 10363-5])

Equality
As a political value, the idea that all people are of equal worth.

EQUALITY

The Declaration of Independence states, "All men are created equal." The proper meaning of equality, however, has been disputed by Americans since the Revolution.[12] Much of American history—and world history—is the story of how the value of **equality** has been extended and elaborated.

First, the right to vote was granted to all adult white males regardless of whether they owned property. The Civil War resulted in the end of slavery and established that, in principle at least, all citizens were equal before the law. The civil rights movement of the 1950s and 1960s sought to make that promise of equality a reality for African Americans. Other movements have sought equality for other racial and ethnic groups, for women, for persons with disabilities, and for gay men and lesbians. We discuss these movements in Chapter 5.

To promote equality, it is often necessary to place limits on the desire by some to treat people unequally. In this sense, equality and liberty are conflicting values. Today, the denial of equal treatment to members of a particular race has very few defenders. Yet as recently as 60 years ago, such denial was a cultural norm.

Economic Equality. Equal treatment regardless of race, religion, gender, and other characteristics is a popular value today. Equal opportunity for individuals to develop their talents and skills is another value with substantial support. Equality of economic status, however, is a controversial value.

For much of history, few people even contemplated the idea that the government could do something about the division of society between rich and poor. Most people assumed that such an effort was either impossible or undesirable. This assumption began to lose its force in the 1800s. As a result of the growing wealth of the Western world and a visible increase in the ability of government to take on large projects, some people began to advocate the value of universal equality, or *egalitarianism*. Some radicals dreamed of a revolutionary transformation of society that would establish an egalitarian system—that is, a system in which wealth and power would be redistributed on a more equal basis.

Many others rejected this vision but still came to endorse the values of eliminating poverty and at least reducing the degree of economic inequality in society. Antipoverty advocates believed then and believe now that such a program could alleviate much suffering. In addition, they believed that reducing economic inequality would promote fairness and enhance the moral tone of society generally.

ORDER

As noted earlier in this chapter, individuals and communities create governments to provide for stability and order in their lives. John Locke justified the creation of governments as a way to protect every individual's property rights and to organize a system of impartial justice. In the United States, laws passed by local, state, and national governments create order and stability in every aspect of life ranging from traffic laws to business laws to a national defense system. Citizens expect these laws to create a society in which individuals can pursue opportunities and live their lives in peace and prosperity.

---

[12]Gary B. Nash, *The Unknown American Revolution: The Unruly Birth of Democracy and the Struggle to Create America* (New York: Viking, 2005); and Alfred F. Young, ed., *Beyond the American Revolution: Explorations in the History of American Radicalism* (DeKalb, IL: Northern Illinois University Press, 1993).

However, the goal of maintaining order and security can run counter to the values of liberty and equality.

SECURITY

The attacks on the United States on September 11, 2001, forced Americans to consider the tension between order and liberty once again. One of the goals of any national government is to provide security for its citizens against all enemies, domestic or foreign. The terrorist attacks of September 11 convinced the president to seek dramatic changes to the federal laws regarding evidence gathering, including wiretapping and other surveillance techniques used to catch criminals, so that it would be possible to find and prosecute terrorists more easily. Congress quickly passed the PATRIOT Act.

Within months of approving the legislation, more liberal members of Congress, civil liberties watchdogs, and individuals began to question the new powers given to the federal government. Did the PATRIOT Act go too far in allowing surveillance of law-abiding Americans? Shouldn't libraries be free from such surveillance? What would happen if the government overstepped its boundaries with no real judicial scrutiny? All of these questions point to the inherent tension between individual liberty and the tools used to provide security to the nation. The PATRIOT Act has been revised to some extent, but most of the basic provisions remain in effect.

SECRETARY OF HOMELAND SECURITY Janet Napolitano testifies before a Congressional Committee. (Photo by Win McNamee/Getty Images)

PROPERTY

The value of reducing economic inequality is in conflict with the right to **property**. This is because reducing economic inequality typically involves the transfer of property (usually in the form of money) from some people to others. For many people, liberty and property are closely entwined. A capitalist system is based on private property rights. Under **capitalism**, property consists not only of personal possessions but also of wealth-creating assets, such as farms and factories. The investor-owned corporation is in many ways the preeminent capitalist institution. The funds invested by the owners of a corporation are known as *capital*—hence, the very name of the system. Capitalism is also typically characterized by considerable freedom to make binding contracts and by relatively unconstrained markets for goods, services, and investments.

Property—especially wealth-creating property—can be seen as giving its owner political power and the liberty to do whatever he or she wants. At the same time, the ownership of property immediately creates inequality in society. The desire to own property, however, is so widespread among all classes of Americans that egalitarian movements have had a difficult time securing a wide following here.

A conflict between property rights and public policy came before the United States Supreme Court in the 2005 case of *Kelo v. City of New London*.[13] The case arose when

Property
Anything that is or may be subject to ownership. As conceived by the political philosopher John Locke, the right to property is a natural right superior to human law (laws made by government).

Capitalism
An economic system characterized by the private ownership of wealth-creating assets, free markets, and freedom of contract.

[13]545 U.S. 469 (2005).

Eminent Domain
A power set forth in the Fifth Amendment to the U.S. Constitution that allows government to take private property for public use under the condition that just compensation is offered to the landowner.

Ideology
A comprehensive set of beliefs about the nature of people and about the role of an institution or government.

Socialism
A political ideology based on strong support for economic and social equality. Socialists traditionally envisioned a society in which major businesses were taken over by the government or by employee cooperatives

the city of New London, Connecticut, attempted to seize property from numerous homeowners through the power of **eminent domain**, which allows government to take private land for *public use* in return for *just compensation*. Some home owners resisted because they did not want to move, regardless of the compensation being offered by the city. They also objected because the city planned to turn the land over to private developers, who wished to build an office park and expensive condominiums. The home owners claimed that such a transfer did not constitute a public use. The Supreme Court disagreed, stating that the economic stimulation and increased tax revenues that the city would gain by the transfer of ownership fulfilled the public use requirement for eminent domain takings. The Court's decision caused an immediate uproar across the nation. The widespread disapproval compelled many state and local governments to pass laws against the kind of takings at issue in the *Kelo* case.

POLITICAL IDEOLOGIES

A political **ideology** is a closely linked set of beliefs about politics. Political ideologies offer their adherents well-organized theories that propose goals for the society and the means by which those goals can be achieved. At the core of every political ideology is a set of guiding values. The two ideologies most commonly referred to in discussions of American politics are *liberalism* and *conservatism*. In the scheme of ideologies embraced across the globe, these two, especially as practiced in the United States, are in the middle of the ideological spectrum, as noted in Table 1–1.

THE TRADITIONAL POLITICAL SPECTRUM

A traditional method of comparing political ideologies is to array them on a continuum from left to right, based primarily on how much power the government should exercise to promote economic equality as well as the ultimate goals of government activity. Table 1–1 shows how ideologies can be arrayed in a traditional political spectrum. In addition to liberalism and conservatism, the table includes the ideologies of socialism and libertarianism.

Socialism falls on the left side of the spectrum. Socialists play a minor role in the American political arena, although socialist parties and movements are very impor-

TABLE 1–1 The Traditional Political Spectrum

	SOCIALISM	LIBERALISM	CONSERVATISM	LIBERTARIANISM
How much power should the government have over the economy?	Active government control of major economic sectors	Positive government action in the economy	Positive government action to support capitalism	Almost no regulation of the economy
What should the government promote?	Economic equality, community	Economic security, equal opportunity, social liberty	Economic liberty, morality, social order	Total economic and social liberty

tant in other countries around the world. In the past, socialists typically advocated replacing investor ownership of major businesses with either government ownership or ownership by employee cooperatives. Socialists believed that such steps would break the power of the very rich and lead to an egalitarian society. In more recent times, socialists in Western Europe have advocated more limited programs that redistribute income.

On the right side of the spectrum is **libertarianism**, a philosophy of skepticism toward most government activities. Libertarians strongly support property rights and typically oppose regulation of the economy and redistribution of income. Libertarians support *laissez-faire* capitalism. (*Laissez-faire* is French for "let it be.") Libertarians also tend to oppose government attempts to regulate personal behavior and promote moral values.

Libertarianism
A political ideology based on skepticism or opposition toward almost all government activities.

IN THE MIDDLE: LIBERALISM AND CONSERVATISM

The set of beliefs called **conservatism** includes a limited role for the government in helping individuals. These values usually include a strong sense of patriotism. Conservatives believe that the private sector probably can outperform the government in almost any activity. Believing that the individual is primarily responsible for his or her own well-being, conservatives typically oppose government programs to redistribute income or change the status of individuals. Conservatism may also include support for what conservatives refer to as traditional values regarding individual behavior and the importance of the family.

The set of beliefs called **liberalism** includes advocacy of government action to improve the welfare of individuals, support for civil rights, and tolerance for social change. American liberals believe that government should take positive action to reduce poverty, to redistribute income from wealthier classes to poorer ones, and to regulate the economy. Those who espouse liberalism may also be more supportive of the rights of women and gays and diverse lifestyles. Liberals are often seen as an influential force within the Democratic Party, and conservatives are often regarded as the most influential force in the Republican Party.

YOU'LL BE HAPPY TO KNOW,
Father, he's not a Liberal, Moderate or Conservative. Jason's a nothing." (© Joseph Farris from cartoon bank.com. All rights reserved.)

THE DIFFICULTY OF DEFINING LIBERALISM AND CONSERVATISM

While political candidates and commentators are quick to label candidates and voters as "liberals" and "conservatives," the meanings of these words have evolved over time. Moreover, each term may represent a quite different set of ideas to the person or group that uses it.

Liberalism. The word *liberal* has an odd history. It comes from the same root as *liberty*, and originally it simply meant "free." In that broad sense, the United States as a whole is a liberal country, and all popular American ideologies are variants of liberalism. In a more restricted definition, a *liberal* was a person who believed in limited government and who opposed religion in politics. A hundred years ago, liberalism referred to a philosophy that in some ways resembled modern-day libertarianism. For that reason, many libertarians today refer to themselves as *classical liberals*.

Conservatism
A set of beliefs that includes a limited role for the national government in helping individuals, support for traditional values and lifestyles, and a cautious response to change.

Liberalism
A set of beliefs that includes the advocacy of positive government action to improve the welfare of individuals, support for civil rights, and tolerance for political and social change.

How did the meaning of the word *liberal* change? In the 1800s, the Democratic Party was seen as the more liberal of the two parties. The Democrats of that time stood for limited government and opposition to moralism in politics. Democrats opposed Republican projects such as building roads, freeing the slaves, and prohibiting the sale of alcoholic beverages. Beginning with Democratic president Woodrow Wilson (served 1913–1921), however, the party's economic policies began to change. President Franklin Delano Roosevelt won a landslide election in 1932 by pledging to take steps to end the Great Depression. Roosevelt and the Democratic Congress quickly passed several measures that increased federal government intervention in the economy and improved conditions for Americans. By the end of Roosevelt's presidency in 1945, the Democratic Party had established itself as standing for positive government action to help the economy. Although Roosevelt stood for new policies, he kept the old language—as Democrats had long done, he called himself a liberal. We will discuss the history of the two parties in greater detail in Chapter 8.

Outside the United States and Canada, the meaning of the word *liberal* never changed. For this reason, you might hear a left-of-center European denounce U.S. President Ronald Reagan (served 1981–1989) or British Prime Minister Margaret Thatcher (served 1979–1990) for their "liberalism." What is meant is that these two leaders were enthusiastic advocates of *laissez-faire* capitalism.

Conservatism. The term *conservatism* suffers from similar identity problems. In the United States and Western Europe, conservatives tended to believe in maintaining traditions and opposing change. Conservatives were more likely to support the continuation of the monarchy, for example. At the end of World War II, Senator Robert A. Taft of Ohio was known as "Mr. Conservative," and he steadfastly opposed the Democratic Party's platform of an active government. However, he was not a spokesperson for conservative or traditional personal values.

Today, conservatism is often considered to have two quite different dimensions. Some self-identified conservatives are "economic conservatives" who believe in less government, support for capitalism and private property, and allowing individuals to pursue their own route to achievement with little government interference. Recent presidential campaigns have seen great efforts to motivate those individuals who might be called "social conservatives" to support Republican candidates. Social conservatives are much less interested in economic issues than in supporting traditional social values, including opposition to abortion, support for the death penalty or the right to own firearms, and opposition to gay marriage. Given these two different dimensions of conservatism, it is not surprising that conservatives are not always united in their political preferences.

Libertarianism. Although libertarians make up a much smaller proportion of the population in the United States than do conservatives or liberals, this ideology shares the more extreme positions of both groups. If the only question is how much power the government should have over the economy, then libertarians can be considered conservatives. However, libertarians advocate the most complete possible freedom in social matters. They oppose government action to promote traditional moral values, although such action is often favored by other groups on the political right. Libertarians' strong support for civil liberties seems to align them more closely with modern liberals than with conservatives.

PRESIDENT GERALD FORD, served 1974–1976. President Ford is quoted as saying, "A government big enough to give you everything you want is a government big enough to take from you everything you have." (Dick Halstead/Time Life Pictures/Getty Images)

THE GLOBAL RANGE OF IDEOLOGIES

Several other ideologies have adherents today. Two of these, **communism** and **fascism**, have few followers in the United States. Their impact on Europe and Asia, however, determined the course of 20th-century history.

The first communists were a radical faction that broke away from the socialist movement. Traditionally, socialists had always considered themselves to be democrats. The communists, however, believed that they could abolish capitalism and institute socialism through a severe partisan dictatorship. The Soviet Union, founded by Russian Communists after World War I (1914–1918), succeeded in establishing government control of farms, factories, and businesses of all kinds and in replacing the market system with central planning. Under Joseph Stalin (served 1924–1953), the Soviet Union also developed into a brutal totalitarian regime.

Today, a hybrid of communism and limited capitalism is practiced by the People's Republic of China. In Cuba, Raul Castro, appointed by his brother, Fidel Castro, is the new leader of a communist nation that is repressive but has considerable support from its citizens. The leader of Venezuela, President Hugo Chavez, is a self-described socialist who has quickly moved to extend the state's reach over the economy.

The most famous example of fascism was Nazi Germany (1933–1945). As with communism, the success of fascism depended on a large body of disciplined followers and a populist appeal. Fascism, however, championed elitism rather than egalitarianism. It was strongly influenced by Charles Darwin's concept of "the survival of the fittest." It valued action over rational deliberation and explicitly rejected liberal individualism; it exalted the national collective, united behind an absolute ruler. Fascism appealed to patriotism or nationalism, but it shaped these common sentiments into virulent racism.

RADICAL ISLAM

The terrorists who attacked the World Trade Center and the Pentagon on September 11, 2001, were ideologically motivated. These terrorists were members of the al Qaeda[14] network led by Osama bin Laden. The ideology embraced by al Qaeda and several other terrorist and political movements is based on a radical and fundamentalist interpretation of Islam, an interpretation sometimes called *Islamism* or *Radical Islam*. This view rejects all Western democratic and cultural values, including equal rights for women, and calls for the establishment of a worldwide Islamic political order (the *caliphate*). The goal of this ideology is to bring all Muslim peoples back to a form of government ruled by religious leaders according to the strict interpretation of the Koran.

Given the complexity of ideological beliefs within the United States as well as the vitality of other ideologies that are directly opposed to democracy, it is clear

DID YOU KNOW?

That about 14 percent of all legal immigrants to the United States plan to live in the Los Angeles/Long Beach, California, area?

Communism
A revolutionary variant of socialism that favors a partisan (and often totalitarian) dictatorship, government control of all enterprises, and the replacement of free markets by central planning.

Fascism
A 20th-century ideology—often totalitarian—that exalts the national collective united behind an absolute ruler. Fascism rejects liberal individualism, values action over rational deliberation, and glorifies war.

MEMBERS OF AL-QAEDA train for terrorist attacks at a secret base in Afghanistan prior to September 11, 2001. (Yasser Al-ZAYYAT/AFP/Getty Images)

---

[14]*Al Qaeda*, sometimes transliterated as *al Qaida* or *al-Qa'idah*, is Arabic for "the base."

Beyond Our Borders

IMMIGRATION: CHALLENGING CULTURES IN EUROPE

One of the hottest issues on the American political scene in recent years is the debate over what to do about undocumented immigrants who have come to the United States for employment. Currently, it is estimated that approximately 12 million individuals reside in the United States without legal status. Some conservatives believe that the best solution is deporting them all to their respective native countries. Others, including President Barack Obama and moderate leaders of both parties, have argued that the United States should recognize its need for workers and implement some system by which individuals can come to this country to work and someday possibly earn a right to citizenship.

Other nations, especially in Europe, have long admitted immigrants as unskilled and semiskilled workers to fuel their economies. Today, the immigrant population of Germany is about 12 percent, while that of Austria is 15 percent. Luxembourg has a 37 percent immigrant population and Switzerland about 23 percent. For many decades, Great Britain has allowed individuals who were subjects in the British Commonwealth to enter the country, while France extended legal residency to many French citizens from the former colonies in North Africa.*

THIS SHOPPING MALL in London, England is mostly frequented by Muslim citizens and immigrants. (© Gregory Wrona/Alamy)

These European nations and many others on the European continent have faced many serious problems as their immigrant populations have reached 10 percent or more. Youths rioted in France in the last few years over the lack of employment opportunities for nonwhite French residents, while the Netherlands has seen outbreaks of violence by Muslim residents against other Dutch citizens. In Great Britain, especially after the bombings of the London subway, concern was raised over the motivations for homegrown terrorists in a nation that sees itself as offering opportunities to all its residents. Many of these states are engaged in serious internal discussion about how to socialize new residents to the culture of their new home and how to ensure that immigrants can find economic opportunities for themselves and their children. Some have even turned to examine the ways in which Americans used their school systems in the early 20th century to integrate immigrant children into the dominant culture.

FOR CRITICAL ANALYSIS

1. To what extent do you think that immigrant families should give up their customs to become part of their host country?
2. Should countries make specific efforts to socialize the children of immigrants into the language and customs of their new home?
3. How do nations ensure that immigrants accept the cultural and political values of their new home?

*United Nations statistics, 2005.

that American representative democracy will face political challenges in the future. In addition, our form of government will need to be durable enough to deal with many future challenges.

THE CHALLENGE OF CHANGE

In the next 50 years, the United States will face internal and external challenges. Not only will the face of America change as its citizens age, become more diverse, and generate new needs for laws and policies, but it will also have to contend with a lessening of its economic dominance in the world. Other nations, including China and India, have much larger populations than the United States and are assuming their respective roles in the world. The United States and its citizens will need to meet the challenges of a global economy and the impact of global environmental change. All of these challenges—demographic change, globalization, and environmental change—will impact how the American political system functions in the future.

DEMOGRAPHIC CHANGE IN A DEMOCRATIC REPUBLIC

The population of the United States is changing in fundamental ways that will impact the political and social system of the nation. Long a nation of growth, the United States has become a middle-aged nation with a low birthrate and an increasing number of older citizens who want services from the government. Both the aging of the population and its changing ethnic composition will have significant political consequences.

Like other economically advanced countries, the United States has in recent decades experienced falling birthrates and an increase in the number of older citizens (see Figure 1–1). The "aging of America" is a weaker phenomenon than in many other wealthy countries, however. Today, the median age of the population is 36.7 in the United States and 40.0 in Europe. By 2050, the median age in the United States is expected to decline slightly to 36.2. In Europe, it is expected to reach 52.7. As is already the case in many European nations, older citizens demand that their need for pensions and health care dominate the political agenda. Young people in the United States, already apathetic about politics, may become even more alienated as they witness the tilting of policies and benefits toward the aging.

ETHNIC CHANGE

As a result of differences in fertility rates and immigration, the ethnic character of the United States is also changing. Non-Hispanic white Americans have a fertility rate of just over 1.8 per two people; African Americans have a fertility rate of 2.1; and Hispanic Americans have a current fertility rate of almost 3.0. (The fertility rate in Mexico is only 2.5.) Figure 1–2 shows the projected changes in the U.S. ethnic distribution in future years.

A large share of all new immigrants is Hispanic, which also increases the Hispanic proportion of the U.S. population. A **Hispanic** or **Latino** is someone who can claim a heritage from a Spanish-speaking country (other than Spain). Today, most individuals who share this heritage prefer to refer to themselves as Latino rather than Hispanic however, government agencies such as the Census Bureau use the terms Hispanic and non-Hispanic white for their tables. In this book, Hispanic is used when referring to government statistics while Latino is used in other contexts. Table 1–2 shows the top

FIGURE 1–1
The Aging of America

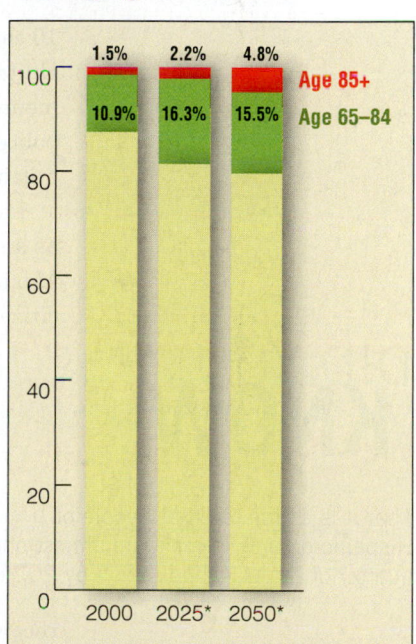

*Data for 2025 and 2050 are projections.
Source: U.S. Bureau of the Census.

Hispanic
Someone who can claim a heritage from a Spanish-speaking country other than Spain. This is the term most often used by government agencies to describe this group. Citizens of Spanish-speaking countries do not use this term to describe themselves.

Latino
Preferred term for referring to individuals who claim a heritage from a Spanish-speaking country other than Spain.

FIGURE 1–2 Distribution of U.S. Population by Race and Hispanic Origin, 1980–2075

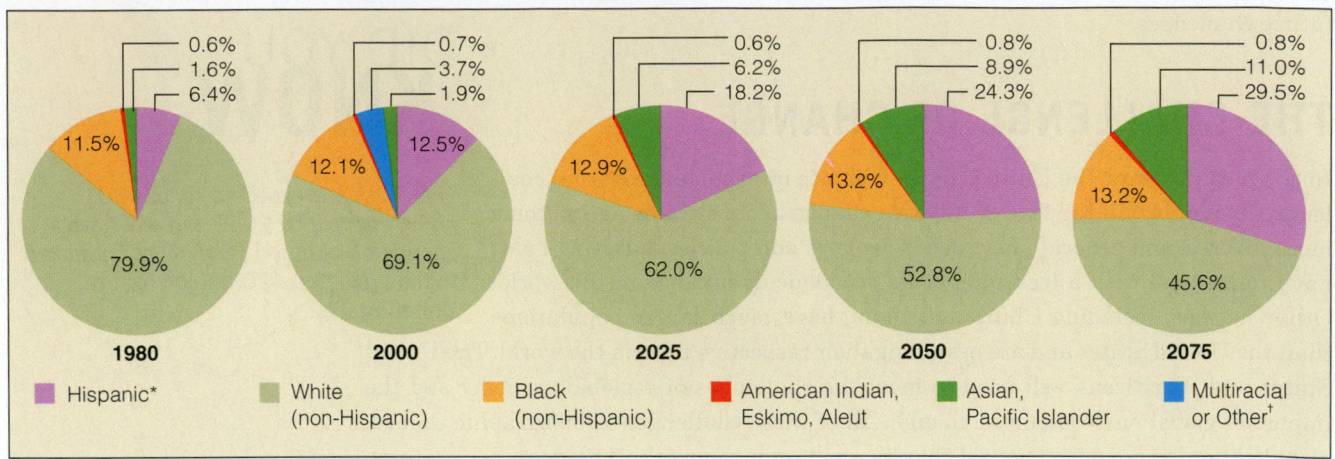

1980
- 0.6%
- 1.6%
- 6.4%
- 11.5%
- 79.9%

2000
- 0.7%
- 3.7%
- 1.9%
- 12.5%
- 12.1%
- 69.1%

2025
- 0.6%
- 6.2%
- 18.2%
- 12.9%
- 62.0%

2050
- 0.8%
- 8.9%
- 24.3%
- 13.2%
- 52.8%

2075
- 0.8%
- 11.0%
- 29.5%
- 13.2%
- 45.6%

- ■ Hispanic*
- ■ White (non-Hispanic)
- ■ Black (non-Hispanic)
- ■ American Indian, Eskimo, Aleut
- ■ Asian, Pacific Islander
- ■ Multiracial or Other†

Data for 2025, 2050, and 2075 are projections.
*Persons of Hispanic origin can be of any race.
†The "multiracial or other" category in 2000 is not an official census category but represents all non-Hispanics who chose either "some other race" or two or more races in the 2000 census.
Source: U.S. Bureau of the Census.

DID YOU KNOW?

That it is estimated that people of Hispanic origin will make up almost one-quarter of the U.S. population by 2025?

10 countries of origin for foreign-born populations (whether documented or not) in the United States in 2010. In 2010, the issue of how to deal with the 12 million or so undocumented residents was debated anew due to Arizona's adoption of a law requiring local police to check the immigration status of individuals who they stop in suspicion of committing an offense.

Latinos may come from any of about 20 primarily Spanish-speaking countries,[15] and, as a result, they are a highly diverse population. The three largest Hispanic groups are Mexican Americans at 58.5 percent of all Latinos; Puerto Ricans (all of whom are U.S. citizens) at 9.6 percent of the total; and Cuban Americans at 3.5 percent.

The diversity among Hispanic Americans results in differing political behavior. The majority of Latino Americans vote Democratic. In 2008, Barack Obama captured the majority of Latino votes across the nation. In Florida, Latino voters favored him by a margin of 57 percent to 42 percent, an increase of 14 percent over the prior presidential race. Strong voter turnout, combined with an increase in the number of Latino voters in the southwestern states, resulted in Obama victories in Colorado and New Mexico. The Latino share of the electorate increased from 8 percent to 17 percent in Colorado, and Obama received 73 percent of their votes. In New Mexico, where Latinos comprise 41 percent of the vote, Obama carried 69 percent of the Latino vote. Commentators suggested that the strong opposition of conservative talk radio to any form of immigration reform alienated many Latino voters from the Republican Party.

The United States is continuing to become a more ethnically diverse nation in every way. Nothing could be more telling than the election of Bobby Jindal, an American of Indian descent, as the governor of Louisiana in 2007. A former Republican Congressman, Jindal did not represent any major ethnic group in that state but ran on a platform of effective government and an end to corruption. The campaign of Jindal—and even more significantly of Barack Obama for president of the United States—may signal the end of white dominance in political leadership at state and national levels. A multiethnic,

---

[15]According to the census definition, "Hispanic" includes the relatively small number of Americans whose ancestors came directly from Spain. Few of these people are likely to check the "Hispanic" box on a census form, however.

TABLE 1–2 Top Ten Countries of Origin for Foreign-Born Populations in the United States

COUNTRY	2000	2004	2010*	PERCENT
Mexico	7,841,000	8,544,600	8,600,000	23.7
China	1,391,000	1,594,600	1,900,000	4.7
Philippines	1,222,000	1,413,200	1,700,000	4.2
India	1,007,000	1,244,200	2,600,000	4.0
Ireland	863,000	997,800	1,200,000	3.0
Cuba	952,000	1,011,200	1,100,000	2.7
El Salvador	765,000	899,000	1,100,000	2.7
Canada	678,000	774,800	920,000	2.3
Dominican Republic	692,000	791,600	941,000	2.3
Korea	701,000	772,600	880,000	2.2
TOTAL POPULATION—TOP TEN COUNTRIES				
	16,112,000	18,043,600	20,941,000	51.8
TOTAL FOREIGN-BORN—POPULATION				
	31,100,000	34,860,000	40,500,000	100

*Projected.
Sources: U.S. Bureau of the Census; U.S. Bureau of Citizenship and Immigration Services.

multiracial society, however, poses some real challenges in keeping the various groups from exacerbating racial differences to obtain benefits for themselves. If the United States could achieve a higher level of economic equality for all Americans, group differences could be minimized.

GLOBALIZATION

The globalization of the world economy has gone relatively unnoticed by Americans. The power of the American economy and its expansion into other parts of the world spurred similar actions by the European, South American, and Asian nations. Huge international corporations produce and market products throughout the world. American soft drinks are produced and sold in China, while Americans buy clothing manufactured in China or the former states of the Soviet Union. Jobs are outsourced from the United States to India, the Philippines, or Vietnam, while other nations outsource jobs to the United States. Companies such as General Electric employ design teams that collaborate in the design and production of jet engines, with employees working around the clock, across all time zones.

Globalization brings a multitude of challenges to the United States and all other nations, beginning with the fact that no single government can regulate global corporations. Globalization changes employment patterns, reducing jobs in one nation and increasing employment in another. Products produced in low-wage nations are cheaper to buy in the United States, but the result is little control over quality and consumer

DID YOU KNOW?

That in 2006, Washington became the first state to have both a female governor and two female U.S. senators at the same time?

safety. An economic recession triggered by one nation's economic decline may, however, affect the entire globe. Clearly, nations must come together to meet the issues of globalization, but collaborative efforts may weaken the power of the United States or any sovereign nation.

ENVIRONMENTAL CHANGE

The challenges posed by environmental change are political, technological, and global. The great majority of scientists agree that global warming is taking place. Many scientists and global organizations are focusing their efforts on measures to reduce humankind's contribution to global warming through carbon emissions and other actions. While the Bush administration balked at joining in the imposition of the measures on all nations until developing nations such as China and India were included, the Obama administration has signaled strong support for an international treaty to reduce global warming. Signing any kind of treaty on this matter is a serious issue for the United States because, as we will see in Chapter 2, according to our Constitution, treaties override U.S. law. American citizens would have their own lives determined by these treaties whether they approve of these policies or not.

While many scientists are working on the technologies to slow global warming, others believe that it is more important to concentrate on mitigating the impact of global warming, whatever the cause. The United States, like many other nations, has a concentration of population on the seacoasts: how should policies change in the face of rising seas and more hurricanes and coastal damage? Global warming is predicted to have more immediate and dire consequences on nations in Africa, where droughts will cause millions to starve. Should the United States play a much greater role in ameliorating these disasters and others caused by global warming in the near future, or should our policy priorities focus on technologies to change our lifestyles years from now?

Other challenges on a global scale include biological dangers such as bird flu and other sources of pollution. The challenge facing American democracy is to make each of these environmental issues a priority, even above domestic issues. Given the normal tendency for politics to focus on those issues most important to each of us personally, it will be very difficult to move global environmental issues to the top of the American agenda.

THE ELECTION OF BOBBY JINDAL, an Indian American, as governor of Louisiana in 2007 is an indication of how diverse the nation has become. Jindal, a Republican, was formerly a Congressman. (Tim Mueller/AP Photos)

YOU CAN MAKE A Difference

SEEING DEMOCRACY IN ACTION

One way to begin to understand the American political system is to observe a legislative body in action. There are thousands of elected legislatures in the United States at all levels of government. You might choose to visit a city council, a school board, a township board of trustees, a state legislature, or the U.S. Congress.

WHY SHOULD YOU CARE?

SCOTT, 18-year-old ncilman from Wellston, OH, orn in as City Councilman hio Secretary of State ifer Brunner. (Courtesy of Scott)

State and local legislative bodies can have a direct impact on your life. For example, local councils or commissions typically oversee the police, and the behavior of the police is a matter of interest even if you live on-campus. If you live off-campus, local authorities are responsible for an even greater number of issues that affect you directly. Are there items that the Sanitation Department refuses to pick up? Have crimes been committed in your neighborhood? You might get more action by lobbying your city councilperson. Even if no local issues concern you, benefits can still be gained from observing a local legislative session. You may discover that local government works rather differently than you expected. You might learn, for example, that the representatives of your political party do not serve your interests as well as you thought—or that the other party is much more sensible than you had presumed.

WHAT CAN YOU DO?

To find out when and where local legislative bodies meet, look up the number of the city hall or county building in the telephone directory, and call the clerk of the council or check on the Internet for the meeting times. In many communities, city council meetings and county board meetings can be seen on public-access TV channels.

Before attending a business session of the legislature, try to find out how the members are elected. Are the members chosen by the at-large method of election, so that each member represents the whole community, or are they chosen by specific geographic districts or wards? Is there a chairperson or official leader who controls the meetings? What are the responsibilities of this legislature?

When you visit the legislature, keep in mind the theory of representative democracy. The legislators or council members are elected to represent their constituents (those who live in their geographic area). Observe how often the members refer to their constituents or to the special needs of their community or electoral district. Listen for sources of conflict within a community. If there is a debate, for example, over a zoning proposal that involves the issue of land use, try to figure out why some members oppose the proposal.

If you want to follow up on your visit, try to get a brief interview with one of the members of the council or board. Ask the member how he or she sees the job of representative. How can the wishes of constituents be identified? How does the representative balance the needs of the ward or district with the good of the entire community? You might even consider running for the council yourself. In 2009, Scott Lukas, then a senior in high school, decided that his small Ohio town was in decline and that the city council needed to consider how to change this situation. He decided to run for election to the council and was elected. A freshman political science major at Ohio University, he commutes to school from Wellston, Ohio. As Scott explained his decision to run, "I believe my hometown is worth fighting for."*

*http://www.ohiodailyblog.com, August 5, 2009.

KEY TERMS

anarchy 8
aristocracy 8
authoritarianism 8
authority 7
capitalism 17
communism 21
consent of the people 9
conservatism 19
democracy 8
democratic republic 10
direct democracy 8
dominant culture 14
elite theory 12
eminent domain 18
equality 16
fascism 21

government 5
Hispanic 23
ideology 18
initiative 9
institution 5
latino 23
legislature 8
legitimacy 7
liberalism 19
libertarianism 19
liberty 7
limited government 11
majoritarianism 11
majority 11
majority rule 11
oligarchy 8

order 6
pluralism 13
political culture 14
political socialization 14
politics 5
popular sovereignty 10
property 17
recall 9
referendum 9
representative democracy 10
republic 10
socialism 19
totalitarian regime 8
universal suffrage 11

CHAPTER SUMMARY

1. **Why do governments exist?** Politics is the process by which people decide which members of society get certain benefits or privileges and which members do not. It is the struggle over power or influence within institutions and organizations that can grant benefits or privileges. Government is the institution within which decisions are made that resolve conflicts or allocate benefits and privileges. It is unique because it has the ultimate authority within society.

2. Fundamental political values are order, which includes security against violence, and liberty, the greatest freedom of the individual consistent with the freedom of other individuals. Liberty can be both promoted by government and invoked against government. To be effective, government authority must be backed by legitimacy.

3. **Why does the United States have a representative democracy?** In a direct democracy, such as ancient Athens, the citizens actually met to vote on important decisions. The American Founders believed that most citizens were not educated enough and too easily swayed by emotion to make such decisions, so they opposed a direct democracy. The United States is a representative democracy, where the people elect representatives to make the decisions.

4. Theories of American democracy include majoritarianism, in which the government does what the majority wants; elite theory, in which the real power lies with one or more elites; and pluralist theory, in which organized interest groups contest for power.

5. **What are the cultural and ideological views that support the American republic?** Fundamental American values include liberty, order, equality, and property. Not all of these values are fully compatible. The value of order often competes with civil liberties, and economic equality competes with property rights.

6. Popular political ideologies can be arrayed from left (liberal) to right (conservative). We can also analyze economic liberalism and conservatism separately from cultural liberalism and conservatism. However, other ideologies on the left (communism) and the right (fascism) also exist in the world.

7. The United States will face many challenges in the future. Among these challenges are demographic changes in the nation, the impact of globalization, and the threats of environmental change.

SELECTED PRINT, MEDIA, AND ONLINE RESOURCES

PRINT RESOURCES

Fineman, Howard. *The Thirteen American Arguments: Enduring Debates That Define and Inspire Our country.* New York: Random House Trade Paperbacks, 2009. Fineman, *the senior Washington Correspondent for Newsweek,* describes questions that have divided Americans since the Revolutionary War.

Fishkin, James S. *When People Speak: Deliberative Democracy and Public Consultation.* New York: Oxford University Press, 2009. Fishkin believes that when citizens have enough information and time to discuss an issue, they are able to make very knowledgeable decisions about political issues. In this latest work, Fishkin reports on the deliberative democracy projects in a number of countries outside the United States.

Hodgson, Godfrey. *The Myth of American Exceptionalism.* New Haven, CT: Yale University Press, 2009. A respected British commentator, Hodgson argues that America's history and political philosophy have always been influenced by European philosophy, more than most Americans will admit.

Lasswell, Harold. *Politics: Who Gets What, When and How.* New York: McGraw-Hill, 1936. This classic work defines the nature of politics.

Levy, Bernard-Henri. *American Vertigo: Traveling America in the Footsteps of Tocqueville.* New York: Random House, 2006. The author, a French journalist and philosopher, seeks to explore the question of what it means to be an American today. Just as Alexis de Tocqueville did in the 1820s, Levy provides a foreigner's description of American culture and life.

Obama, Barack. *Dreams from My Father: A Story of Race and Inheritance.* New York: Three Rivers Press, 2004. President Obama's best-selling autobiography ends before his rise to national prominence. He describes the sense of isolation he felt due to his unusual background and his attempts to come to grips with his multiethnic identity.

Tocqueville, Alexis de. *Democracy in America.* Edited by Phillips Bradley. New York: Vintage Books, 1945. Life in the United States is described by a French writer who traveled through the nation in the 1820s.

Zolberg, Aristide R. *A Nation by Design: Immigration Policy in the Fashioning of America.* New York: Russell Sage Foundation with Harvard University Press, 2006. Zolberg writes a comprehensive review of American immigration policy from before the Revolutionary War to the present, noting the common themes that undergird immigration debates.

MEDIA RESOURCES

All Things Considered—A daily broadcast of National Public Radio (NPR) that provides extensive coverage of political, economic, and social news stories.

Europe in One Room—An Emmy-Award-winning film that demonstrates Fishkin's idea of deliberative democracy with a forum including European Union citizens speaking 21 languages who come together to make decisions about their common problems.

Mr. Smith Goes to Washington—A classic movie, produced in 1939, starring Jimmy Stewart as the honest citizen who goes to Congress trying to represent his fellow citizens. The movie dramatizes the clash between representing principles and representing corrupt interests.

The Values Issue and American Politics: Values Matter Most—Ben Wattenberg travels around the country in this 1995 TV program speaking to a broad range of ordinary Americans. He examines what he calls the "values issue"—the issues of crime, welfare, race, discipline, drugs, and prayer in the schools. Wattenberg believes that candidates who can best address these issues will win elections.

ONLINE RESOURCES

American Conservative Union information about conservative positions: www.conservative.org

Americans for Democratic Action home of one of the nation's oldest liberal political organizations: www.adaction.org

Bureau of the Census—a wealth of information about the changing face of America: www.census.gov

National Security Agency/Central Security Service—the nation's cryptologic organization, which aims to protect U.S. national security systems and to produce foreign signals intelligence information: www.nsa.gov

University of Michigan—a basic "front door" to almost all U.S. government Web sites: www.lib.umich.edu/govdocs/govweb.html

U.S. Citizenship and Immigration Services—information about the rules and requirements for immigration and citizenship: www.uscis.gov/graphics/index.htm

U.S. Government—access to federal government offices and agencies: www.usa.gov

CONNECTING TO AMERICAN GOVERNMENT AND POLITICS

The Web has become our way of finding information for almost every aspect of our lives, from sports scores to election results. It can also be an exceptional aid to understanding American government and our political system. To improve your comprehension of the materials presented in this book and in lectures, the authors have created a Web site that includes many study aids, connections to news and information, and interactive pages to test your knowledge base. Please take time at the beginning of your study in American government to go to the Web site for the textbook, http://www.cengagebrain.com/shop/ISBN/0495797677, to check out all of the resources available to you. Try out the animated learning modules or audio summaries or simulations on the Web site. Find a feature on the Web site that suits your own learning style—crossword puzzles, online research projects, flash cards—and use that feature for each chapter. To check your preparation for examinations, try the interactive quizzes.

If you want a very stimulating view of today's political events, visit the home page of Dr. Politics—the Web site of Professor Steffen Schmidt, a noted news commentator and coauthor of this book.

A word of caution about Internet use: Many students surf the Web for political resources. When doing so, you need to remember to approach these sources with care. For one thing, you should be very careful when giving out information about yourself. You also need to use good judgment because the reliability or intent of any given Web site is often unknown. Some sites are more concerned with accuracy than others, and some sites are updated to include current information, whereas others are not.

Online Review: You will find a Tutorial Quiz for each chapter with questions on the chapter contents, including the features. The questions are organized to match the major sections of the chapter. You'll have access to other helpful study tools, including the book's glossary and flash cards, crossword puzzles, and Web links, as well as "Which Side Are You On?" and "Politics and . . ." features written by the authors of the book.

2

A family looks at the U.S. Constitution at the National Archives in Washington, D.C. (Alex Wong/Getty Images)

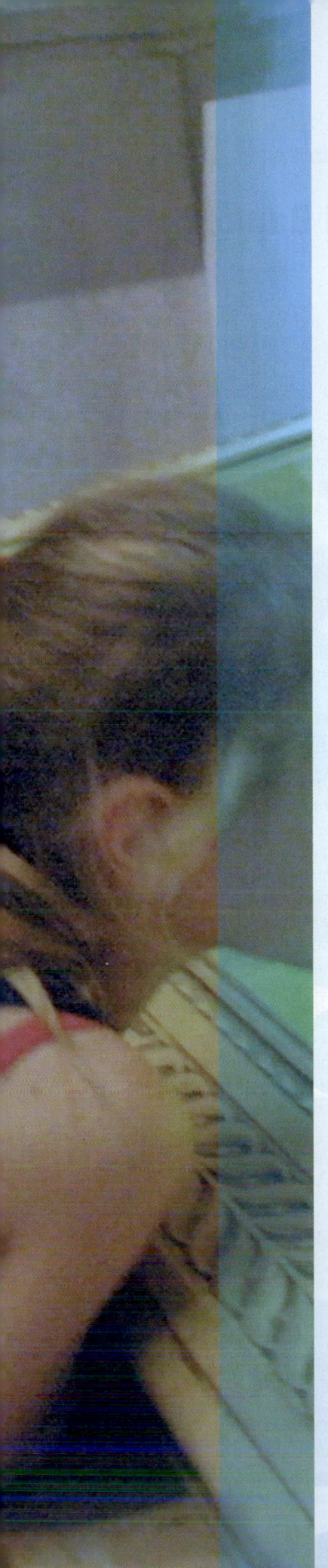

The Constitution

QUESTIONS TO CONSIDER

Why does the Constitution divide the powers of government among the three branches?

What is the purpose of the Bill of Rights?

Why is it so difficult to amend the Constitution?

CHAPTER CONTENTS

what if... The Constitution Had Banned Slavery Outright?

BACKGROUND

Slavery came to the American colonies not long after the first settlers arrived. In the earliest days of the Virginia colony about half of the immigrants were indentured servants, meaning that at some point they could earn enough or fulfill the terms of their contract to be freed. Even African Americans were often considered in this category. However, by the 1650s, great plantations had formed in the Southern states and there was a need for agricultural labor. In 1654, a Virginia court found that John Casor, an African American, was a "property," owned for life by another black colonist. Shortly after this case, law established that the children of slaves were also property. As the agricultural needs of the country grew, so did the trade in slaves, By the end of the Revolutionary War, there were almost 650,000 slaves in the new nation.

WHAT TO DO ABOUT THE SLAVE ISSUE?

One of the most hotly debated issues at the Constitutional Convention concerned slavery. Most Northern colonies had already abolished slavery and the argument over the morality of owning human property was well-known. Given the language of the Declaration of Independence, "All men are created equal, . . . that they are endowed by their Creator with certain unalienable rights, that among them are life, liberty, and the pursuit of happiness," why did the writers of the U.S. Constitution have so much difficulty with the issue of slavery? As you will learn in this chapter, the Constitutional Convention eventually agreed to two huge compromises to gain approval of the final document: slaves would count as only three-fifths of a person for purposes of representation and the slave trade could not be banned until after 1808. The debate over slavery—or, more specifically, over how the founders dealt with it—continues to this day. Some contend that those delegates who opposed slavery should have made greater efforts to ban it completely.*

DID THE FOUNDERS HAVE NO OTHER CHOICE?

Some historians argue that the founders had no choice. The South was an important part of the economy, and the Southern states depended on slave labor for their agricultural production. Virginia, perhaps the most powerful of the Southern states, counted nearly 300,000 slaves in its population in 1790; North Carolina, South Carolina, and Maryland each counted about 100,000 in that census. Although political leaders from Virginia, such as George Washington, had serious doubts about slavery, the delegates from those states may never have agreed to the Constitution if slavery had been threatened—meaning that these states would not have joined the new nation. The founders believed, as James Madison said, "Great as the evil is, a dismemberment of the Union would be worse. . . . If those states should disunite from the other states, . . . they might solicit and obtain aid from foreign powers."** Benjamin Franklin, then president of the Pennsylvania Society for the Abolition of Slavery, also feared that without a slavery compromise, delegates from the South would abandon the convention.

CRITICS ARGUE THAT ETHICS SHOULD HAVE PREVAILED

Critics of the founders' actions nonetheless believe that any compromise on slavery implicitly acknowledged the validity of the institution in 1860. According to these critics, the delegates who opposed slavery had a moral obligation to make greater efforts to ban it. At the time, many of the writers felt that slavery would eventually end. Would the Southern states actually have left the Union if slavery were banned? Would they have tried to form a separate state? If slavery had been banned in 1789 or shortly thereafter, could the Southern states have adapted to a paid labor system rather than expanding the slave population to four million in 1860? It was, of course, the importance of slaves to the economy of the Southern states as well as the moral opposition to slavery that brought the nation to civil war and led to many of the issues of race that the nation still struggles with today.

FOR CRITICAL ANALYSIS

1. Do you think that antislavery delegates to the convention should have insisted on ending slavery throughout the new nation?
2. Do you think the nation would have survived without the Southern states?
3. How would our nation be different if slavery had been abolished in 1789?

---

*See Paul Finkelman's criticism of the founders' actions on the slavery issue in *Slavery and the Founders: Race and Liberty in the Age of Jefferson*, 2nd ed. (Armonk, NY: M. E. Sharpe, 2001).

**Speech before the Virginia ratifying convention on June 17, 1788, as cited in Bruno Leone, ed., *The Creation of the Constitution* (San Diego, CA: Greenhaven Press, 1995), p. 159.

FROM TIME TO TIME A MOVEMENT ARISES in the United States that claims to be saving the Constitution. People gather at demonstrations waving their copies of the document. Why is this such a powerful tactic? The Constitution has remained largely intact for more than 200 years. To a great extent, this is because the principles set forth in the Constitution met the needs of the diverse and independent states of the confederacy and, over time, have also met the needs of a changing nation.

How and why the U.S. Constitution was created is a story that has been told and retold. It is worth repeating, because knowing the historical and political context in which this country's governmental machinery was formed is essential to understanding American government and politics today. The Constitution did not result just from creative thinking. Many of its provisions were grounded in the political philosophy of the time. The delegates to the Constitutional Convention in 1787 brought with them two important sets of influences: their political culture and their political experience. In the years between the first settlements in the New World and the writing of the Constitution, Americans had developed a political philosophy about how people should be governed and had tried out several forms of government. These experiences gave the founders the tools with which they constructed the Constitution. Milestones in the nation's early political history are shown in Table 2–1 later in this chapter.

DID YOU KNOW?

That the first English claim to territory in North America was made by John Cabot, on behalf of King Henry VII, on June 24, 1497?

TABLE 2–1 Milestones in Early U.S. Political History

YEAR	EVENT
1607	Jamestown established; Virginia Company lands settlers.
1620	Mayflower Compact signed.
1630	Massachusetts Bay Colony set up.
1639	Fundamental Orders of Connecticut adopted.
1641	Massachusetts Body of Liberties adopted.
1682	Pennsylvania Frame of Government passed.
1701	Pennsylvania Charter of Privileges written.
1732	Last of the 13 colonies (Georgia) established.
1756	French and Indian War declared.
1765	Stamp Act; Stamp Act Congress meets.
1774	First Continental Congress.
1775	Second Continental Congress; Revolutionary War begins.
1776	Declaration of Independence signed.
1777	Articles of Confederation drafted.
1781	Last state (Maryland) signs Articles of Confederation.
1783	"Critical period" in U.S. history begins; weak national government until 1789.
1786	Shays's Rebellion.
1787	Constitutional Convention.
1788	Ratification of Constitution.
1791	Ratification of Bill of Rights.

THE COLONIAL BACKGROUND

In 1607, the English government sent a group of farmers to establish a trading post, Jamestown, in what is now Virginia. The Virginia Company of London was the first to establish a permanent English colony in the Americas. The king of England gave the backers of this colony a charter granting them "full power and authority" to make laws "for the good and welfare" of the settlement. The colonists at Jamestown instituted a **representative assembly**, setting a precedent in government that was to be observed in later colonial adventures.

Jamestown was not an immediate success. Of the 105 men who landed, 67 died within the first year. But 800 new arrivals in 1609 added to their numbers. By the spring of the next year, frontier hazards had cut their numbers to 60. Of the 6,000 people who left England for Virginia between 1607 and 1623, 4,800 perished. This period is sometimes referred to as the "starving time for Virginia." Climatological researchers suggest that this "starving time" may have been brought about by a severe drought in the Jamestown area, which lasted from 1607 to 1612.

Representative Assembly
A legislature composed of individuals who represent the population.

SEPARATISTS, THE *MAYFLOWER*, AND THE COMPACT

The first New England colony was established in 1620. A group of mostly extreme separatists who wished to break with the Church of England came over on the ship *Mayflower* to the New World, landing at Plymouth (Massachusetts). Before going onshore, the adult males—women were not considered to have any political status—drew up the Mayflower Compact, which was signed by 41 of the 44 men aboard the ship on November 21, 1620. The reason for the compact was obvious. This group was outside the jurisdiction of the Virginia Company of London, which had chartered its settlement in Virginia, not Massachusetts. The separatist leaders feared that some of the *Mayflower* passengers might conclude that they were no longer under any obligations of civil obedience. Therefore, some form of public authority was imperative. As William Bradford (one of the separatist leaders) recalled in his accounts, there were

THE SIGNING OF THE compact aboard the *Mayflower*. In 1620, the Mayflower Compact was signed by almost all of the men aboard the *Mayflower* just before they disembarked at Plymouth, Massachusetts. It stated, "We . . . covenant and combine ourselves togeather into a civil body politick . . . ; and by vertue hearof to enacte, constitute, and frame such just and equal laws . . . as shall be thought [necessary] for the generall good of the Colonie." (© 2010 The Granger Collection. All rights reserved)

"discontented and mutinous speeches that some of the strangers amongst them had let fall from them in the ship; That when they came a shore they would use their owne libertie; for none had power to command them."[1]

The compact was not a constitution. It was a political statement in which the signers agreed to create and submit to the authority of a government, pending the receipt of a royal charter. The Mayflower Compact's historical and political significance is twofold: it depended on the consent of the affected individuals, and it served as a prototype for similar compacts in American history. According to Samuel Eliot Morison, the compact proved the determination of the English immigrants to live under the rule of law, based on the *consent of the people*.[2]

MORE COLONIES, MORE GOVERNMENT

Another outpost in New England was set up by the Massachusetts Bay Colony in 1630. Then followed Rhode Island, Connecticut, New Hampshire, and others. By 1732, the last of the 13 colonies, Georgia, was established. During the colonial period, Americans developed a concept of limited government, which followed from the establishment of the first colonies under Crown charters. Theoretically, London governed the colonies. In practice, owing partly to the colonies' distance from London, the colonists exercised a large measure of self-government. The colonists were able to make their own laws, as in the Fundamental Orders of Connecticut in 1639. The Massachusetts Body of Liberties in 1641 supported the protection of individual rights and was made a part of colonial law. In 1682, the Pennsylvania Frame of Government was passed. Along with the Pennsylvania Charter of Privileges of 1701, it foreshadowed our modern Constitution and Bill of Rights. All of this legislation enabled the colonists to acquire crucial political experience. After independence was declared in 1776, the states quickly set up their own new constitutions.

BRITISH RESTRICTIONS AND COLONIAL GRIEVANCES

The conflict between Britain and the American colonies, which ultimately led to the Revolutionary War, began in the 1760s when the British government decided to raise revenues by imposing taxes on the American colonies. Policy advisers to Britain's young King George III, who ascended the throne in 1760, decided that it was only logical to require the American colonists to help pay the costs of Britain's defending them during the French and Indian War (1756–1763). The colonists, who had grown accustomed to a large degree of self-government and independence from the British Crown, viewed the matter differently.

In 1764, the British Parliament passed the Sugar Act. Many colonists were unwilling to pay the tax imposed by the act. Further regulatory legislation was to come. In 1765, Parliament passed the Stamp Act, providing for internal taxation—or, as the colonists' Stamp Act Congress, assembled in 1765, called it, "taxation without representation." The colonists boycotted the purchase of English commodities in return. The success of the boycott (the Stamp Act was repealed a year later) generated a feeling of unity within the colonies.

The British, however, continued to try to raise revenues in the colonies. When Parliament passed duties on glass, lead, paint, and other items in 1767, the colonists again boycotted British goods. The colonists' fury over taxation climaxed in the Boston Tea Party: colonists dressed as Mohawk Indians dumped close to 350 chests of British tea into Boston Harbor as a gesture of tax protest. In retaliation, Parliament passed

---

[1]John Camp, *Out of the Wilderness: The Emergence of an American Identity in Colonial New England* (Middleton, CT: Wesleyan University Press, 1990).
[2]See Morison's "The Mayflower Compact," in Daniel J. Boorstin, ed., *An American Primer* (Chicago: University of Chicago Press, 1966), p. 18.

KING GEORGE III (1738–1820) was king of Great Britain and Ireland from 1760 until his death on January 29, 1820. Under George III, the British Parliament attempted to tax the American colonies. Ultimately, the colonies, exasperated at repeated attempts at taxation, proclaimed their independence on July 4, 1776. (King George III, c.1762–64 (oil on canvas), Ramsay, Allan (1713–84)/ National Portrait Gallery, London, UK/The Bridgeman Art Library International)

the Coercive Acts (the "Intolerable Acts") in 1774, which closed Boston Harbor and placed the government of Massachusetts under direct British control. The colonists were outraged—and they responded.

THE COLONIAL RESPONSE

New York, Pennsylvania, and Rhode Island proposed the convening of a colonial congress. The Massachusetts House of Representatives requested that all colonies hold conventions to select delegates to be sent to Philadelphia for such a congress.

THE FIRST CONTINENTAL CONGRESS

The First Continental Congress was held at Carpenters' Hall on September 5, 1774. It was a gathering of delegates from 12 of the 13 colonies (delegates from Georgia did not attend until 1775). At that meeting, there was little talk of independence. The Congress passed a resolution requesting that the colonies send a petition to King George III expressing their grievances. Resolutions were also passed requiring that the colonies raise their own troops and boycott British trade. The British government condemned the Congress's actions, treating them as open acts of rebellion.

The delegates to the First Continental Congress declared that in every county and city, a committee was to be formed whose mission was to spy on the conduct of friends and neighbors and to report to the press any violators of the trade ban. The formation of these committees was an act of cooperation among the colonies, which represented a step toward the creation of a national government.

THE SECOND CONTINENTAL CONGRESS

By the time the Second Continental Congress met in May 1775 (this time all of the colonies were represented), fighting had already broken out between the British and the colonists. One of the main actions of the Second Continental Congress was to establish an army. It did this by declaring the militia that had gathered around Boston an army and naming George Washington as commander in chief. The participants in that Congress still attempted to reach a peaceful settlement with the British Parliament. One declaration of the Congress stated explicitly that "we have not raised armies with ambitious designs of separating from Great Britain, and establishing independent states." But by the beginning of 1776, military encounters had become increasingly frequent.

Public debate was acrimonious. Then Thomas Paine's *Common Sense* appeared in Philadelphia bookstores. The pamphlet was a colonial best seller. (To do relatively as well today, a book would have to sell between nine and 11 million copies in its first year of publication.) Many agreed that Paine did make common sense when he argued that

a government of our own is our natural right: and when a man seriously reflects on the precariousness [instability, unpredictability] of human affairs, he will become convinced, that it is infinitely wiser and safer, to form a constitution of our own in a cool and deliberate manner, while we have it in our power, than to trust such an interesting event to time and chance.[3]

---

[3]*The Political Writings of Thomas Paine*, Vol. 1 (Boston: J. P. Mendum Investigator Office, 1870), p. 46.

Students of Paine's pamphlet point out that his arguments were not new—they were common in tavern debates throughout the land. Rather, it was the near poetry of his words—which were at the same time as plain as the alphabet—that struck his readers.

DECLARING INDEPENDENCE

On April 6, 1776, the Second Continental Congress voted for free trade at all American ports with all countries except Britain. This act could be interpreted as an implicit declaration of independence. The next month, the Congress suggested that each of the colonies establish state governments unconnected to Britain. Finally, in July, the colonists declared their independence from Britain.

THE RESOLUTION OF INDEPENDENCE

On July 2, the Resolution of Independence was adopted by the Second Continental Congress:

> RESOLVED, That these United Colonies are, and of right ought to be free and independent States, that they are absolved from allegiance to the British Crown, and that all political connection between them and the state of Great Britain is, and ought to be, totally dissolved.

The actual Resolution of Independence was not legally significant. On the one hand, it was not judicially enforceable, for it established no legal rights or duties. On the other hand, the colonies were already, in their own judgment, self-governing and independent of Britain. Rather, the Resolution of Independence and the subsequent Declaration of Independence were necessary to establish the legitimacy of the new nation in the eyes of foreign governments, as well as in the eyes of the colonists. What the new nation needed most were supplies for its armies and a commitment of foreign military aid. Unless it appeared to the world as a political entity separate and independent from Britain, no foreign government would enter into a contract with its leaders.

"You know, the idea of taxation with representation doesn't appeal to me very much either." (Cartoon by J. B. Handelsman; published in The New Yorker, June 27, 1970, © cartoonbank .com. All rights reserved.)

JULY 4, 1776—THE DECLARATION OF INDEPENDENCE

By June 1776, Thomas Jefferson already was writing drafts of the Declaration of Independence in the second-floor parlor of a bricklayer's house in Philadelphia. On adoption of the Resolution of Independence, Jefferson argued that a declaration clearly putting forth the causes that compelled the colonies to separate from Britain was necessary. The Second Congress assigned the task to him, and he completed his work on the declaration, which enumerated the colonists' major grievances against Britain. Some of his work was amended to gain unanimous acceptance (for example, his condemnation of the slave trade was eliminated to satisfy Georgia and North Carolina), but the bulk of it was passed intact on July 4, 1776. On July 19, the modified draft became "the unanimous declaration of the thirteen United States of America." On August 2, it was signed by the members of the Second Continental Congress.

Universal Truths. The Declaration of Independence has become one of the world's most famous and significant documents. The words opening the second paragraph of the Declaration are known most widely:

> We hold these Truths to be self-evident, that all Men are created equal, that they are endowed by their Creator with certain unalienable Rights, that among

these are Life, Liberty, and the Pursuit of Happiness—That to secure these Rights, Governments are instituted among Men, deriving their just Powers from the Consent of the Governed, that whenever any Form of Government becomes destructive of these Ends, it is the Right of the People to alter or abolish it, and to institute new Government.

Natural Rights and a Social Contract. The assumption that people have **natural rights** ("unalienable Rights"), including the rights to "Life, Liberty, and the Pursuit of Happiness," was a revolutionary concept at that time. Its use by Jefferson reveals the influence of the English philosopher John Locke (1632–1704), whose writings were familiar to educated American colonists, including Jefferson.[4] In his *Two Treatises on Government*, published in 1690, Locke had argued that all people possess certain natural rights, including the rights to life, liberty, and property, and that the primary purpose of government was to protect these rights. Furthermore, government was established by the people through a **social contract**—an agreement among the people to form a government and abide by its rules. As you read earlier, such contracts, or compacts, were not new to Americans. The Mayflower Compact was the first of several documents that established governments or governing rules based on the consent of the governed. In citing the "pursuit of happiness" instead of "property" as a right, Jefferson clearly meant to go beyond Locke's thinking.

After setting forth these basic principles of government, the Declaration of Independence goes on to justify the colonists' revolt against Britain. Much of the remainder of the document is a list of what "He" (King George III) had done to deprive the colonists of their rights. (See Appendix A at the end of this book for the complete text of the Declaration of Independence.)

Once it had fulfilled its purpose of legitimating the American Revolution, the Declaration of Independence was all but forgotten for many years. According to scholar Pauline Maier, the Declaration did not become enshrined as what she calls "American Scripture" until the 1800s.[5]

THE RISE OF REPUBLICANISM

Although the colonists had formally declared independence from Britain, the fight to gain actual independence continued for five more years—until the British general Charles Cornwallis surrendered at Yorktown in 1781. In 1783, after Britain formally recognized the independent status of the United States in the Treaty of Paris, Washington disbanded the army. During these years of military struggles, the states faced the additional challenge of creating a system of self-government for an independent United States.

Some colonists had demanded that independence be preceded by the formation of a strong central government. But others, who called themselves Republicans, were against a strong central government. They opposed monarchy, executive authority, and virtually any form of restraint on the power of local groups.

From 1776 to 1780, all of the states adopted written constitutions. Eleven of the constitutions were completely new. Two of them—those of Connecticut and Rhode Island—were old royal charters with minor modifications. Republican sentiment led to increased power for the legislatures. In Pennsylvania and Georgia, **unicameral** (one-body) **legislatures**

Natural Rights
Rights held to be inherent in natural law, not dependent on governments. John Locke stated that natural law, being superior to human law, specifies certain rights of "life, liberty, and property." These rights, altered to become "life, liberty, and the pursuit of happiness," are asserted in the Declaration of Independence.

Social Contract
A voluntary agreement among individuals to secure their rights and welfare by creating a government and abiding by its rules.

Unicameral Legislature
A legislature with only one legislative chamber, as opposed to a bicameral (two-chamber) legislature, such as the U.S. Congress. Today, Nebraska is the only state in the Union with a unicameral legislature.

---

[4]Not all scholars believe that Jefferson was truly influenced by Locke. For example, Jay Fliegelman states that "Jefferson's fascination with Homer, Ossian, Patrick Henry, and the violin is of greater significance than his indebtedness to Locke," in Jay Fliegelman, *Declaring Independence: Jefferson, Natural Language, and the Culture of Performance* (Palo Alto, CA: Stanford University Press, 1993).
[5]See Pauline Maier, *American Scripture: Making the Declaration of Independence* (New York: Knopf, 1997).

were unchecked by executive or judicial authority. Basically, the Republicans attempted to maintain the politics of 1776. In almost all states, the legislature was predominant.

THE ARTICLES OF CONFEDERATION: THE FIRST FORM OF GOVERNMENT

The fear of a powerful central government led to the passage of the Articles of Confederation, which created a weak central government. The term **confederation** is important; it means a voluntary association of *independent* **states**, in which the member states agree to only limited restraints on their freedom of action. As a result, confederations seldom have an effective executive authority.

In June 1776, the Second Continental Congress began the process of drafting what would become the Articles of Confederation. The final form of the Articles was achieved by November 15, 1777. It was not until March 1, 1781, however, that the last state, Maryland, agreed to ratify what was called the Articles of Confederation and Perpetual Union. Well before the final ratification of the Articles, however, many of them were implemented: the Continental Congress and the 13 states conducted American military, economic, and political affairs according to the standards and the form specified by the Articles.[6]

Under the Articles, the 13 original colonies, now states, established on March 1, 1781, a government of the states—the Congress of the Confederation. The Congress was a unicameral assembly of so-called ambassadors from each state, with each state possessing a single vote. Each year, the Congress would choose one of its members as its president (that is, presiding officer), but the Articles did not provide for a president of the United States.

The Congress was authorized in Article X to appoint an executive committee of the states "to execute in the recess of Congress, such of the powers of Congress as the United States, in Congress assembled, by the consent of nine [of the 13] states, shall from time to time think expedient to vest with them." The Congress was also allowed to appoint other committees and civil officers necessary for managing the general affairs of the United States. In addition, the Congress could regulate foreign affairs and establish coinage and weights and measures, but it lacked an independent source of revenue and the necessary executive machinery to enforce its decisions throughout the land. Article II of the Articles of Confederation guaranteed that each state would retain its sovereignty. Figure 2–1 illustrates the structure of the government under the Articles of Confederation; Table 2–2 summarizes the powers—and the lack of powers—of Congress under the Articles of Confederation.

ACCOMPLISHMENTS UNDER THE ARTICLES

The new government had some accomplishments during its eight years of existence under the Articles of Confederation. Certain states' claims to western lands were settled. Maryland had objected to the claims of the Carolinas, Connecticut, Georgia, Massachusetts, New York, and Virginia. It was only after these states consented to give up their land claims to the United States as a whole that Maryland signed the

Confederation
A political system in which states or regional governments retain ultimate authority except for those powers they expressly delegate to a central government. A voluntary association of independent states, in which the member states agree to limited restraints on their freedom of action.

State
A group of people occupying a specific area and organized under one government; may be either a nation or a subunit of a nation.

FIGURE 2–1 The Confederal Government Structure under the Articles of Confederation

Congress
Congress had one house. Each state had two to seven members, but only one vote. The exercise of most powers required approval of at least nine states. Amendments to the Articles required the consent of all the states.

Committee of the States
A committee of representatives from all the states was empowered to act in the name of Congress between sessions.

Officers
Congress appointed officers to do some of the executive work.

The States

[6]Robert W. Hoffert, *A Politics of Tensions: The Articles of Confederation and American Political Ideas* (Niwot, CO: University Press of Colorado, 1992).

TABLE 2–2 Powers of the Congress of the Confederation

CONGRESS HAD POWER TO	CONGRESS LACKED POWER TO
Declare war and make peace.	Provide for effective treaty-making power and control foreign relations; it could not compel states to respect treaties.
Enter into treaties and alliances.	Compel states to meet military quotas; it could not draft soldiers.
Establish and control armed forces.	Regulate interstate and foreign commerce; it left each state free to set up its own tariff system.
Requisition men and revenues from states.	Collect taxes directly from the people; it had to rely on states to collect and forward taxes.
Regulate coinage.	Compel states to pay their share of government costs.
Borrow funds and issue bills of credit.	Provide and maintain a sound monetary system or issue paper money; this was left up to the states, and monies in circulation differed tremendously in value.
Fix uniform standards of weight and measurement.	
Create admiralty courts.	
Create a postal system.	
Regulate Indian affairs.	
Guarantee citizens of each state the rights and privileges of citizens in the several states when in another state.	
Adjudicate disputes between states on state petition.	

DID YOU KNOW?

That the Articles of Confederation specified that Canada could be admitted to the Confederation if it ever wished to join?

Articles of Confederation. Another accomplishment under the Articles was the passage of the Northwest Ordinance of 1787, which established a basic pattern of government for new territories north of the Ohio River. All in all, the Articles represented the first real pooling of resources by the American states.

WEAKNESSES OF THE ARTICLES

Despite these accomplishments, the Articles of Confederation had many defects. Although Congress had the legal right to declare war and to conduct foreign policy, it did not have the right to demand revenues from the states. It could only ask for them. Additionally, the actions of Congress required the consent of nine states. Any amendments to the Articles required the unanimous consent of the Congress and confirmation by every state legislature. Furthermore, the Articles did not create a national system of courts.

Basically, the functioning of the government under the Articles depended on the goodwill of the states. Article III of the Articles simply established a "league of friendship" among the states—no national government was intended.

Probably the most fundamental weakness of the Articles, and the most basic cause of their eventual replacement by the Constitution, was the lack of power to raise funds for the militia. The Articles contained no language giving Congress coercive power to raise revenues (by levying taxes) to provide adequate support for the military forces controlled by Congress. When states refused to send revenues to support the government (not one state met the financial requests made by Congress under the Articles), Congress resorted to selling off western lands to speculators or issuing bonds that sold for less than their face value. Due to a lack of resources, the Continental Congress was forced to disband the army, even in the face of serious Spanish and British military threats.

SHAYS'S REBELLION AND THE NEED FOR REVISION OF THE ARTICLES

Because of the weaknesses of the Articles of Confederation, the central government could do little to maintain peace and order in the new nation. The states bickered among themselves and increasingly taxed each other's goods. At times they prevented trade altogether. By 1784, the country faced a serious economic depression. Banks were calling in old loans and refusing to give new ones. People who could not pay their debts were often thrown into prison.

By 1786, in Concord, Massachusetts, the scene of one of the first battles of the Revolution, there were three times as many people in prison for debt as there were for all other crimes combined. In Worcester County, Massachusetts, the ratio was even higher—20 to one. Most of the prisoners were small farmers who could not pay their debts because of the disorganized state of the economy.

In August 1786, mobs of musket-bearing farmers led by former Revolutionary War captain Daniel Shays seized county courthouses and disrupted the trials of debtors in Springfield, Massachusetts. Shays and his men then launched an attack on the federal arsenal at Springfield, but they were repulsed. Shays's Rebellion demonstrated that the central government could not protect the citizenry from armed rebellion or provide adequately for the public welfare. The rebellion spurred the nation's political leaders to action. As John Jay wrote to Thomas Jefferson,

> Changes are Necessary, but what they ought to be, what they will be, and how and when to be produced, are arduous Questions. I feel for the Cause of Liberty. . . . If it should not take Root in this Soil[,] Little Pains will be taken to cultivate it in any other.[7]

DRAFTING THE CONSTITUTION

Concerned about the economic turmoil in the young nation, five states, under the leadership of the Virginia legislature, called for a meeting to be held at Annapolis, Maryland, on September 11, 1786—ostensibly to discuss commercial problems only. It was evident to those in attendance (including Alexander Hamilton and James Madison) that the national government had serious weaknesses that had to be addressed if it were to survive. Among the important problems to be solved were the relationship between the states and the central government, the powers of the national legislature, the need for executive leadership, and the establishment of policies for economic stability.

Those attending the meeting prepared a petition to the Continental Congress for a general convention to meet in Philadelphia in May 1787 "to consider the exigencies of the union." Congress approved the convention in February 1787. When those who favored a weak central government realized

DID YOU KNOW?

That Daniel Shays incurred the debts that led to Shays's Rebellion because he never received pay for serving in the Revolutionary War?

DID YOU KNOW?

That the 1776 constitution of New Jersey granted the vote to "all free inhabitants," including women, but the large number of women who turned out to vote resulted in male protests and a new law limiting the right to vote to "free white male citizens"?

[7]Excerpt from a letter from John Jay to Thomas Jefferson written in October 1786, as reproduced in Winthrop D. Jordan et al., *The United States*, combined ed., 6th ed. (Englewood Cliffs, NJ: Prentice Hall, 1987), p. 135.

POLITICS WITH A purpose

How to Form a More Perfect Union?

We the People of the United States, in Order to form a more perfect Union, establish Justice, insure domestic Tranquility, provide for the common defense, promote the general Welfare, and secure the Blessings of Liberty to ourselves and our Posterity, do ordain and establish this Constitution for the United States of America.

Did you ever wonder what the framers of the Constitution meant by "a more perfect union"? Or why establishing justice and insuring domestic tranquility would be at the top of their list? The framers were reacting to the then-current problems created by the Articles of Confederation.

Adopted in 1781, the Articles of Confederation governed the emerging nation until our existing Constitution replaced it in 1787. Although the central government had very little power, the Articles held competing and disparate interests together for the first years of the nation's independence.

Any time political rules are changed, there are winners and losers. Some wish to maintain the *status quo* and others want change. Whether to amend or replace the Articles of Confederation was a dispute between those who enjoyed power under the Articles and those who found their weaknesses too dangerous and unprofitable. Under the Articles, the Congress had very little power. It could not regulate commerce or foreign trade nor levy taxes, and it had to depend on the states to begin to pay down the war debt. To deal with the difficulty of deficits without power to tax, Congress simply printed more money. This led to inflation, a lack of trust in the printed currency, and reliance on gold and silver.[a]

Members of Congress, as well as those whose economic interests were hurt by the economic instability, were frustrated. In addition to the aforementioned problems, the national government could not effectively regulate trade (all 13 states could negotiate separate trading arrangements with each other and with foreign governments). For people such as seaport merchants, large plantation owners, and commercial farmers who depended on trade, this was a trying and unstable situation.[b]

On the other hand, some people did approve of the Articles. Smaller farmers and those who lived inland depended less on trade and were more likely to believe the state governments were sufficient to solve their problems. Like Thomas Jefferson and Patrick Henry, many feared a strong national government and preferred a less active government that would keep taxes low and provide debt relief. With the success of the Articles in creating the Northwest Territory, there was a contingent in state governments that was suspicious of national encroachment on their power.

So, why would states give up the enormous power they enjoyed under the Articles of Confederation? Initially, they did not. As early as 1786, calls were made to reform the Articles, and it was through crises such as the rebellion led by Daniel Shays in Massachusetts that those favoring a stronger national government were able to organize to form a Constitutional Convention. Meeting in 1787, they deliberated for months in secret to draft a document that was acceptable to the participants. The new Constitution was ratified in July  1788 through intense efforts to persuade state leaders (including promises of positions in the new government), a promise of greater protection of civil liberties, and lobbying efforts modern politicians would recognize.[c]

[a]www.loc.gov/rr/program/bib/ourdocs/articles.html, accessed September 22, 2008.

[b]Robert A. McGuire, "Review of Keith L. Dougherty," *Collective Action under the Articles of Confederation*, EH.Net Economic History Services, April 11, 2002, http://eh.net/bookreviews/library/0469.

[c]Lee Epstein and Thomas G. Walker, *Constitutional Law for a Changing America*, 5th ed., 2 vols. (Washington, DC: CQ Press, 2004).

that the Philadelphia meeting would in fact take place, they endorsed the convention. They made sure, however, that the convention would be summoned "for the sole and express purpose of revising the Articles of Confederation." Those in favor of a stronger national government had different ideas.

The designated date for the opening of the convention at Philadelphia, now known as the Constitutional Convention, was May 14, 1787. Because few of the delegates had actually arrived in Philadelphia by that time, however, the convention was not formally opened in the East Room of the Pennsylvania State House until May 25.[8] Fifty-five of the 74 delegates chosen for the convention actually attended. (Of those 55, only about 40 played active roles at the convention.) Rhode Island was the only state that refused to send delegates.

WHO WERE THE DELEGATES?

Who were the 55 delegates to the Constitutional Convention? They certainly did not represent a cross section of American society in the 1700s. Indeed, most were members of the upper class. Consider the following facts:

1. Thirty-three were members of the legal profession.
2. Three were physicians.
3. Almost 50 percent were college graduates.
4. Seven were former chief executives of their respective states.
5. Six were owners of large plantations.
6. Eight were important businesspersons.

They were also relatively young by today's standards: James Madison was 36, Alexander Hamilton was only 32, and Jonathan Dayton of New Jersey was 26. The venerable Benjamin Franklin, however, was 81 and had to be carried in on a portable chair borne by four prisoners from a local jail. Not counting Franklin, the average age was just over 42. What almost all of them shared, however, was prior experience in political office or military service. Most of them were elected members of their own states' legislatures. George Washington, the esteemed commander of the Revolutionary War troops, was named to chair the meeting. There were, however, no women or minorities among this group. Women could not vote anywhere in the confederacy and, while free African Americans played an important part in some Northern states, they were certainly not likely to be political leaders.[9]

THE WORKING ENVIRONMENT

The conditions under which the delegates worked for 115 days were far from ideal and were made even worse by the necessity of maintaining total secrecy. The framers of the Constitution believed that if public debate took place on particular positions, delegates would have a more difficult time compromising or backing down to reach agreement. Consequently, the windows were usually shut in the East Room of the State House. Summer quickly arrived, and the air became heavy, humid, and hot by noon of each day. Also, when the windows were open, flies swarmed into the room. The delegates did, however, have a nearby tavern and inn to which they retired each evening. The Indian Queen became the informal headquarters of the delegates.

FACTIONS AMONG THE DELEGATES

We know much about the proceedings at the convention because James Madison kept a daily, detailed personal journal. A majority of the delegates were strong nationalists—

[8]The State House was later named Independence Hall. This was the same room in which the Declaration of Independence had been signed 11 years earlier.
[9]For a detailed look at the delegates and their lively debates, see Carol Berkin, *A Brilliant Solution: Inventing the American Constitution* (New York: Harcourt, 2002).

they wanted a central government with real power, unlike the central government under the Articles of Confederation. George Washington and Benjamin Franklin preferred limited national authority based on a separation of powers. They were apparently willing to accept any type of national government, however, as long as the other delegates approved it. A few advocates of a strong central government, led by Gouverneur Morris of Pennsylvania and John Rutledge of South Carolina, distrusted the ability of the common people to engage in self-government.

Among the nationalists, several went so far as to support monarchy. This group included Alexander Hamilton, who was chiefly responsible for the Annapolis Convention's call for the Constitutional Convention. In a long speech on June 18, he presented his views: "I have no scruple in declaring . . . that the British government is the best in the world and that I doubt much whether anything short of it will do in America."

Another important group of nationalists were of a more democratic stripe. Led by James Madison of Virginia and James Wilson of Pennsylvania, these democratic nationalists wanted a central government founded on popular support.

Still another faction consisted of nationalists who were less democratic in nature and who would support a central government only if it was founded on very narrowly defined republican principles. This group was made up of a relatively small number of delegates, including Edmund Randolph and George Mason of Virginia, Elbridge Gerry of Massachusetts, and Luther Martin and John Francis Mercer of Maryland.

Many of the other delegates from Connecticut, Delaware, Maryland, New Hampshire, and New Jersey were concerned about only one thing—claims to western lands. As long as those lands became the common property of all of the states, they were willing to support a central government.

Finally, there was a group of delegates who were totally against a national authority. Two of the three delegates from New York quit the convention when they saw the nationalist direction of its proceedings.

POLITICKING AND COMPROMISES

The debates at the convention started on the first day. James Madison had spent months reviewing European political theory. When his Virginia delegation arrived ahead of most of the others, it got to work immediately. By the time George Washington opened the convention, Governor Edmund Randolph of Virginia was prepared to present 15 resolutions. In retrospect, this was a masterful stroke on the part of the Virginia delegation. It set the agenda for the remainder of the convention—even though, in principle, the delegates had been sent to Philadelphia for the sole purpose of amending the Articles of Confederation. They had not been sent to write a new constitution.

The Virginia Plan. Randolph's 15 resolutions proposed an entirely new national government under a constitution. It was, however, a plan that favored the large states, including Virginia. Basically, it called for the following:

Bicameral Legislature
A legislature made up of two parts, called chambers. The U.S. Congress, composed of the House of Representatives and the Senate, is a bicameral legislature.

1. A **bicameral** (two-chamber) **legislature**, with the lower chamber chosen by the people and the smaller upper chamber chosen by the lower chamber from nominees selected by state legislatures. The number of representatives would be proportional to a state's population, thus greatly favoring the states with larger populations, including slaves, of course. The legislature could void any state laws.
2. The creation of an unspecified national executive, elected by the legislature.
3. The creation of a national judiciary, appointed by the legislature.

It did not take long for the smaller states to realize they would fare poorly under the Virginia plan, which would enable Virginia, Massachusetts, and Pennsylvania to form a majority in the national legislature. The debate on the plan dragged on for many weeks. It was time for the small states to come up with their own plan.

The New Jersey Plan. On June 15, lawyer William Paterson of New Jersey offered an alternative plan. After all, argued Paterson, under the Articles of Confederation, all states had equality; therefore, the convention had no power to change this arrangement. He proposed the following:

1. The fundamental principle of the Articles of Confederation—one state, one vote— would be retained.
2. Congress would be able to regulate trade and impose taxes.
3. All acts of Congress would be the supreme law of the land.
4. Several people would be elected by Congress to form an executive office.
5. The executive office would appoint a Supreme Court.

Basically, the New Jersey plan was simply an amendment of the Articles of Confederation. Its only notable feature was its reference to the **supremacy doctrine**, which was later included in the Constitution.

The "Great Compromise." The delegates were at an impasse. Most wanted a strong national government and were unwilling even to consider the New Jersey plan, but when the Virginia plan was brought up again, the small states threatened to leave. The issues involved in the debate included how states and their residents would be represented. Small states feared that the Virginia plan with its powerful national government would pass laws that would disadvantage smaller states. The larger states, aware that they would be the economic force in the new nation, absolutely opposed a government in which smaller states had the balance of power. Roger Sherman of Connecticut proposed a solution that gave power to both the small states and the larger states. On July 16, the **Great Compromise** was put forward for debate:

Supremacy Doctrine
A doctrine that asserts the priority of national law over state laws. This principle is rooted in Article VI of the Constitution, which provides that the Constitution, the laws passed by the national government under its constitutional powers, and all treaties constitute the supreme law of the land.

Great Compromise
The compromise between the New Jersey and Virginia plans that created one chamber of the Congress based on population and one chamber representing each state equally; also called the Connecticut Compromise.

GEORGE WASHINGTON presided over the Constitutional Convention of 1787. Although the convention was supposed to start on May 14, 1787, few of the delegates had actually arrived in Philadelphia by that date. The convention formally opened in the East Room of the Pennsylvania State House (later named Independence Hall) on May 25. Only Rhode Island did not send any delegates. (©Bettmann/CORBIS)

1. A bicameral legislature in which the lower chamber, the House of Representatives, would be apportioned according to the number of free inhabitants in each state, plus three-fifths of the slaves.
2. An upper chamber, the Senate, which would have two members from each state elected by the state legislatures.

This plan, also called the Connecticut Compromise because of the role of the Connecticut delegates in the proposal, broke the deadlock. It did exact a political price, however, because it permitted each state to have equal representation in the Senate. Having two senators represent each state in effect diluted the voting power of citizens living in more heavily populated states and gave the smaller states disproportionate political powers. But the Connecticut Compromise resolved the large-state/small-state controversy. In addition, the Senate acted as part of a checks-and-balances system against the House, which many feared would be dominated by, and responsive to, the masses. However, another important piece to the debate needed a resolution: how were slaves to be counted in determining the number of members of Congress allotted to a state?

The Three-Fifths Compromise. Part of the Connecticut Compromise dealt with this problem. Slavery was still legal in many Northern states, but it was concentrated in the South. Many delegates were opposed to slavery and wanted it banned entirely in the United States. Charles Pinckney of South Carolina led strong Southern opposition to a ban on slavery. Furthermore, the South wanted slaves to be counted along with free persons in determining representation in Congress. Delegates from the Northern states objected. Sherman's three-fifths proposal was a compromise between Northerners who did not want the slaves counted at all and Southerners who wanted them counted in the same way as free whites. Actually, Sherman's Connecticut plan spoke of three-fifths of "all other persons" (and that is the language of the Constitution itself). It is not hard to figure out, though, who those other persons were.

DID YOU KNOW?

That during the four centuries of slave trading, an estimated 10 million to 11 million Africans were transported to North and South America—and that only 6 percent of these slaves were imported into the United States?

A SLAVE AUCTION in the South, about 1850. (Peter Newark American Pictures/ The Bridgeman Art Library International)

The three-fifths compromise illustrates the power of the Southern states at the convention.[10] The three-fifths rule meant that the House of Representatives and the electoral college would be apportioned in part on the basis of *property*—specifically, property in slaves. Modern commentators have referred to the three-fifths rule as valuing African Americans only three-fifths as much as whites. Actually, the additional Southern representatives elected because of the three-fifths rule did not represent the slaves at all. Rather, these extra representatives were a gift to the slave owners—the additional representatives enhanced the power of the South in Congress.

The three-fifths compromise did not completely settle the slavery issue. There was also the question of the slave trade. Eventually, the delegates agreed that Congress could not ban the importation of slaves until after 1808. The compromise meant that the matter of slavery was never addressed directly. The South won 20 years of unrestricted slave trade and a requirement that escaped slaves in free states be returned to their owners in slave states. Could the authors of the Constitution have done more to address the issue of slavery?

Other Issues. The South also worried that the Northern majority in Congress would pass legislation that was unfavorable to its economic interests. Because the South depended on agricultural exports, it feared the imposition of export taxes. In return for acceding to the Northern demand that Congress be able to regulate commerce among the states and with other nations, the South obtained a promise that export taxes would not be imposed. As a result, the United States is among the few countries that do not tax their exports.

There were other disagreements. The delegates could not decide whether to establish only a Supreme Court or to create lower courts as well. They deferred the issue by mandating a Supreme Court and allowing Congress to establish lower courts. They also disagreed over whether the president or the Senate would choose the Supreme Court justices. A compromise was reached with the agreement that the president would nominate the justices and the Senate would confirm the nominations. These compromises, as well as others, resulted from the recognition that if one group of states refused to ratify the Constitution, it was doomed.

WORKING TOWARD FINAL AGREEMENT

The Connecticut Compromise was reached by mid-July. The makeup of the executive branch and the judiciary, however, was left unsettled. The remaining work of the convention was turned over to a five-man Committee of Detail, which presented a rough draft of the Constitution on August 6. It made the executive and judicial branches subordinate to the legislative branch.

The Madisonian Model—Separation of Powers. The major issue of **separation of powers** had not yet been resolved. The delegates were concerned with structuring the government to prevent the imposition of tyranny—either by the majority or by a minority. Madison proposed a governmental scheme—sometimes called the **Madisonian model**—to achieve this: the executive, legislative, and judicial powers of government were to be separated so that no one branch had enough power to dominate the others, nor could any one person hold office in two different branches of the government at the same time. The separation of powers was by function, as well as by personnel, with

Separation of Powers
The principle of dividing governmental powers among different branches of government.

Madisonian Model
A structure of government proposed by James Madison in which the powers of the government are separated into three branches: executive, legislative, and judicial.

---

[10]See Garry Wills, *"Negro President": Jefferson and the Slave Power* (New York: Houghton Mifflin, 2003).

Congress passing laws, the president enforcing and administering laws, and the courts interpreting laws in individual circumstances.

Each of the three branches of government would be independent of the others, but they would have to share power to govern. According to Madison, in *Federalist Paper* No. 51 (see Appendix B), "the great security against a gradual concentration of the several powers in the same department consists in giving to those who administer each department the necessary constitutional means and personal motives to resist encroachments of the others."

The Madisonian Model—Checks and Balances. The "constitutional means" Madison referred to is a system of **checks and balances** through which each branch of the government can check the actions of the others. For example, Congress can enact laws, but the president has veto power over congressional acts. The Supreme Court has the power to declare acts of Congress and of the executive unconstitutional, but the president appoints the justices of the Supreme Court, with the advice and consent of the Senate. (The Supreme Court's power to declare acts unconstitutional was not mentioned in the Constitution, although arguably the framers assumed that the Court would have this power—see the discussion of judicial review later in this chapter.) Figure 2–2 outlines these checks and balances.

Madison's ideas of separation of powers and checks and balances were not new. The influential French political thinker Baron de Montesquieu (1689–1755) had explored these concepts in his book *The Spirit of the Laws*, published in 1748. Montesquieu not only discussed the "three sorts of powers" (executive, legislative, and judicial) that were necessarily exercised by any government but also gave examples of how, in some nations, certain checks on these powers had arisen and had been effective in preventing tyranny.

In the years since the Constitution was ratified, the checks and balances built into it have evolved into a sometimes complex give-and-take among the branches of government. Generally, for nearly every check that one branch has over another, the branch that has been checked has found a way of getting around it. For example, suppose that the president checks Congress by vetoing a bill. Congress can override the presidential veto by a two-thirds vote. Additionally, Congress holds the "power of the purse." If it disagrees with a program endorsed by the executive branch, it can simply refuse to appropriate the funds necessary to operate that program. Similarly, the president can impose a countercheck on Congress if the Senate refuses to confirm a presidential appointment, such as a judicial appointment. The president can simply wait until Congress is in recess and then make what is called a "recess appointment," which does not require the Senate's approval. Recess appointments last until the end of the next session of the Congress.

The Executive. Some delegates favored a plural executive made up of representatives from the various regions. This was abandoned in favor of a single chief executive. Some argued that Congress should choose the executive. To make the presidency completely independent of the proposed Congress, however, an electoral college was adopted. To be sure, the **electoral college** created a cumbersome presidential election process (see Chapter 9). The process even made it possible for a candidate who came in second in the popular vote to become president by being the top vote-getter in the electoral college, which happened in 2000 and in three prior contests. The electoral college insulated the president, however, from direct popular control. The seven-year single term that some of the delegates had proposed was replaced by a four-year term and the possibility of re-election.

A Federal Republic. The Constitution creates a **federal system** of government that divides the sovereign powers of the nation between the states and the national

---

Checks and Balances
A major principle of the American system of government whereby each branch of the government can check the actions of the others.

DID YOU KNOW?

That Alexander Hamilton wanted the American president to hold office for life and to have absolute veto power over the legislature?

Electoral College
A group of persons called *electors* selected by the voters in each state and the District of Columbia; this group officially elects the president and vice president of the United States. The number of electors in each state is equal to the number of each state's representatives in both chambers of Congress.

Federal System
A system of government in which power is divided between a central government and regional, or subdivisional, governments. Each level must have some domain in which its policies are dominant and some genuine political or constitutional guarantee of its authority.

FIGURE 2–2 Checks and Balances

The Supreme Court can declare presidential actions unconstitutional.

The president nominates federal judges; the president can refuse to enforce the Court's decisions; the president grants pardons.

THE JUDICIARY

The Supreme Court can declare congressional laws unconstitutional.

Congress can rewrite legislation to circumvent the Court's decisions; the Senate confirms federal judges; Congress determines the number of judges.

THE PRESIDENCY

The president proposes laws and can veto congressional legislation; the president makes treaties, executive agreements, and executive orders; the president can refuse, and has refused, to enforce congressional legislation; the president can call special sessions of Congress.

Congress makes legislation and can override a presidential veto of its legislation; Congress can impeach and remove a president; the Senate must confirm presidential appointments and consent to the president's treaties based on a two-thirds concurrence; Congress has the power of the purse and provides funds for the president's programs.

THE CONGRESS

government. This structure allows for states to make their own laws about many of the issues of direct concern for their citizens while granting the national government far more power over the states and their citizens than under the Articles of Confederacy. As you will read in Chapter 3, the Constitution expressly granted certain powers to the national government.

For example, the national government was given the power to regulate commerce among the states. The Constitution also declared that the president is the nation's chief executive and the commander in chief of the armed forces. Additionally, the Constitution made it clear that laws made by the national government take priority over conflicting state laws. At the same time, the Constitution provided for extensive states' rights, including the right to control commerce within state borders and to exercise those governing powers that were not delegated to the national government.

THE FINAL DOCUMENT

On September 17, 1787, the Constitution was approved by 39 delegates. Of the 55 who had attended originally, only 42 remained. Three delegates refused to sign the Constitution. Others disapproved of at least parts of it but signed anyway to begin the ratification debate.

The Constitution that was to be ratified established the following fundamental principles:

1. Popular sovereignty, or control by the people.
2. A republican government in which the people choose representatives to make decisions for them.

3. Limited government with written laws, in contrast to the powerful British government against which the colonists had rebelled.
4. Separation of powers, with checks and balances among branches to prevent any one branch from gaining too much power.
5. A federal system that allows for states' rights, because the states feared too much centralized control.

THE DIFFICULT ROAD TO RATIFICATION

The founders knew that **ratification** of the Constitution was far from certain. Because it was almost guaranteed that many state legislatures would not ratify it, the delegates agreed that each state should hold a special convention. Elected delegates to these conventions would discuss and vote on the Constitution. Further departing from the Articles of Confederation, the delegates agreed that as soon as nine states (rather than all 13) approved the Constitution, it would take effect, and Congress could begin to organize the new government.

The federal system created by the founders was a novel form of government at that time—no other country in the world had such a system. It was invented by the founders as a compromise solution to the controversy over whether the states or the central government should have ultimate sovereignty. As you will read in Chapter 3, the debate over where the line should be drawn between states' rights and the powers of the national government has characterized American politics ever since. The founders did not go into detail about where this line should be drawn, thus leaving it up to scholars and court judges to divine the founders' intentions.

THE FEDERALISTS PUSH FOR RATIFICATION

The two opposing forces in the battle over ratification were the Federalists and the Anti-Federalists. The **Federalists**—those in favor of a strong central government and the new Constitution—had an advantage over their opponents, called the **Anti-Federalists**, who wanted to prevent the Constitution as drafted from being ratified. In the first place, the Federalists had assumed a positive name, leaving their opposition the negative label of *Anti*-Federalist.[11] More important, the Federalists had attended the Constitutional Convention and knew of all the deliberations that had taken place. Their opponents had no such knowledge, because those deliberations had not been open to the public. Thus, the Anti-Federalists were at a disadvantage in terms of information about the document. The Federalists also had time, power, and money on their side. Communications were slow. Those who had access to the best communications were Federalists—mostly wealthy bankers, lawyers, plantation owners, and merchants living in urban areas, where communications were better. The Federalist campaign was organized relatively quickly and effectively to elect Federalists as delegates to the state ratifying conventions.

The Anti-Federalists, however, had at least one strong point in their favor: they stood for the status quo. In general, the greater burden is always placed on those advocating change.

JAMES MADISON (1751–1836)
earned the title "master builder of the Constitution" because of his persuasive logic during the Constitutional Convention. His contributions to the *Federalist Papers* showed him to be a brilliant political thinker and writer. (Library of Congress Prints & Photographs Division, Washington, D.C. [LCUSZ62- 13004])

---

[11]There is some irony here. At the Constitutional Convention, those opposed to a strong central government pushed for a federal system because such a system would allow the states to retain some of their sovereign rights (see Chapter 3). The label *Anti-Federalists* thus contradicted their essential views.

The Federalist Papers. In New York, opponents of the Constitution were quick to attack it. Alexander Hamilton answered their attacks in newspaper columns over the signature "Caesar." When the Caesar letters had little effect, Hamilton switched to the pseudonym Publius and secured two collaborators—John Jay and James Madison. In a very short time, those three political figures wrote a series of 85 essays in defense of the Constitution and of a republican form of government.

These widely read essays, called the *Federalist Papers*, appeared in New York newspapers from October 1787 to August 1788 and were reprinted in the newspapers of other states. Although we do not know for certain who wrote every one, it is apparent that Hamilton was responsible for about two-thirds of the essays. These included the most important ones interpreting the Constitution, explaining the various powers of the three branches, and presenting a theory of *judicial review*—to be discussed later in this chapter. Madison's *Federalist Paper* No. 10 (see Appendix B), however, is considered a classic in political theory; it deals with the nature of groups—or factions, as he called them. Despite the rapidity with which the *Federalist Papers* were written, they are considered by many to be perhaps the best example of political theorizing ever produced in the United States.[12]

The Anti-Federalist Response. The Anti-Federalists used such pseudonyms as Montezuma and Philadelphiensis in their replies. Many of their attacks on the Constitution were also brilliant. The Anti-Federalists claimed that the Constitution was written by aristocrats and would lead to aristocratic tyranny. More important, the Anti-Federalists believed that the Constitution would create an overbearing and overburdening central government hostile to personal liberty. (The Constitution said nothing about freedom of the press, freedom of religion, or any other individual liberty.) They wanted to include a list of guaranteed liberties, or a bill of rights. Finally, the Anti-Federalists decried the weakened power of the states.

The Anti-Federalists cannot be dismissed as unpatriotic extremists. They included such patriots as Patrick Henry and Samuel Adams. They were arguing what had been the most prevalent contemporary opinion. This view derived from the French political philosopher Montesquieu, who, as mentioned earlier, was an influential political theorist at that time. Montesquieu believed that liberty was safe only in relatively small societies governed by direct democracy or by a large legislature with small districts. The Madisonian view favoring a large republic, particularly expressed in *Federalist Papers* No. 10 and No. 51 (see Appendix B), was actually the more *un*popular view at the time. Madison was probably convincing because citizens were already persuaded that a strong national government was necessary to combat foreign enemies and to prevent domestic insurrections. Still, some researchers believe it was mainly the bitter experiences with the Articles of Confederation, rather than Madison's arguments, that persuaded the state conventions to ratify the Constitution.[13]

THE MARCH TO THE FINISH

The struggle for ratification continued. Strong majorities were procured in Delaware, Pennsylvania, New Jersey, Georgia, and Connecticut. After a bitter struggle in

[12]Some scholars believe that the *Federalist Papers* played only a minor role in securing ratification of the Constitution. Even if this is true, they still have lasting value as an authoritative explanation of the Constitution.

[13]Of particular interest is the view of the Anti-Federalist position contained in Herbert J. Storing, *What the Anti-Federalists Were For* (Chicago: University of Chicago Press, 1981). Storing also edited seven volumes of the Anti-Federalist writings, *The Complete Anti-Federalist* (Chicago: University of Chicago Press, 1981). See also Josephine F. Pacheco, *Antifederalism: The Legacy of George Mason* (Fairfax, VA: George Mason University Press, 1992).

Massachusetts, that state ratified the Constitution by a narrow margin on February 6, 1788. By the spring, Maryland and South Carolina had ratified by sizable majorities. Then on June 21 of that year, New Hampshire became the ninth state to ratify the Constitution. Although the Constitution was formally in effect, this meant little without Virginia and New York—the latter did not ratify for another month (see Table 2–3).

DID THE MAJORITY OF AMERICANS SUPPORT THE CONSTITUTION?

In 1913, historian Charles Beard published *An Economic Interpretation of the Constitution of the United States*.[14] This book launched a debate that has continued ever since—the debate over whether the Constitution was supported by a majority of Americans.

Beard's Thesis. Beard's central thesis was that the Constitution had been produced primarily by wealthy property owners who desired a stronger government able to protect their property rights. Beard also claimed that the Constitution had been imposed by undemocratic methods to prevent democratic majorities from exercising real power. He pointed out that there was never any popular vote on whether to hold a constitutional convention in the first place.

Furthermore, even if such a vote had been taken, state laws generally restricted voting rights to property-owning white males, meaning that most people in the country (white males without property, women, Native Americans, and slaves) were not eligible

TABLE 2–3   Ratification of the Constitution

STATE	DATE	VOTE FOR–AGAINST
Delaware	Dec. 7, 1787	30–0
Pennsylvania	Dec. 12, 1787	43–23
New Jersey	Dec. 18, 1787	38–0
Georgia	Jan. 2, 1788	26–0
Connecticut	Jan. 9, 1788	128–40
Massachusetts	Feb. 6, 1788	187–168
Maryland	Apr. 28, 1788	63–11
South Carolina	May 23, 1788	149–73
New Hampshire	June 21, 1788	57–46
Virginia	June 25, 1788	89–79
New York	July 26, 1788	30–27
North Carolina	Nov. 21, 1789*	194–77
Rhode Island	May 29, 1790	34–32

*Ratification was originally defeated on August 4, 1788, by a vote of 84–184.

[14]Charles A. Beard, *An Economic Interpretation of the Constitution of the United States* (New York: MacMillan, 1913; New York: Free Press, 1986).

CHAPTER 2 • THE CONSTITUTION 55

to vote. Finally, Beard pointed out that even the word *democracy* was distasteful to the founders. The term was often used by conservatives to smear their opponents.

State Ratifying Conventions. As for the various state ratifying conventions, the delegates had been selected by only 150,000 of the approximately 4 million citizens. That does not seem very democratic—at least not by today's standards. Some historians have suggested that if a Gallup poll could have been taken at that time, the Anti-Federalists would probably have outnumbered the Federalists.[15]

Certainly, some of the delegates to state ratifying conventions from poor, agrarian areas feared that an elite group of Federalists would run the country just as oppressively as the British had governed the colonies. Amos Singletary, a delegate to the Massachusetts ratifying convention, contended that those who urged the adoption of the Constitution "expect to get all the power and all the money into their own hands, and then they will swallow up all us little folks . . . just as the whale swallowed Jonah."[16] Others who were similarly situated, though, felt differently. Jonathan Smith, who was also a delegate to the Massachusetts ratifying convention, regarded a strong national government as a "cure for disorder"—referring to the disorder caused by the rebellion of Daniel Shays and his followers.[17]

Support Was Probably Widespread. Much has also been made of the various machinations used by the Federalists to ensure the Constitution's ratification (and they did resort to a variety of devious tactics, including purchasing at least one printing press to prevent the publication of Anti-Federalist sentiments). Yet the perception that a strong central government was necessary to keep order and protect the public welfare appears to have been fairly pervasive among all classes—rich and poor alike.

Further, although the need for strong government was a major argument in favor of adopting the Constitution, even the Federalists sought to craft a limited government. Compared with constitutions adopted by other nations in later years, the U.S. Constitution, through its checks and balances, favors limited government over "energetic" government to a marked degree.

DID YOU KNOW?

That not all the states had ratified the Constitution by April 30, 1789, when George Washington became president of the United States of America?

THE BILL OF RIGHTS

The U.S. Constitution would not have been ratified in several important states if the Federalists had not assured the states that amendments to the Constitution would be passed to protect individual liberties against incursions by the national government. Certainly, the idea of including certain rights in the Constitution had been discussed in the convention. There were those who believed that including these rights was simply unnecessary, whereas others suggested that carefully articulating certain rights might encourage the new national government to abuse any that were not specifically defined. Some rights, including prohibiting *ex post facto lawmaking*, were included in the document. *Ex post facto lawmaking* is passing laws that make one liable for an act that has already taken place. Also prohibited were *bills of attainder*, through which a legislature could pass judgment on someone without legal process. However, many of the recommendations of the state ratifying conventions included specific rights that were considered later by James Madison as he labored to draft what became the Bill of Rights.

---

[15]Jim Powell, "James Madison—Checks and Balances to Limit Government Power," *The Freeman*, March 1996, p. 178.
[16]As quoted in Bruno Leone, ed., *The Creation of the Constitution* (San Diego, CA: Greenhaven Press, 1995), p. 215.
[17]*Ibid.*, p. 217.

Beyond Our Borders

WHAT MAKES A CONSTITUTION?

When Americans think of the Constitution, most visualize an old handwritten document that is protected in our National Archives. They may also reflect on the basic principles of the Constitution—checks and balances, separation of powers, the Bill of Rights—that structure how the national government carries out its work. However, just because a nation has a constitution does not mean that it is a short document like ours or that the constitution actually reflects the way the government operates.

WRITTEN OR UNWRITTEN

The United States Constitution is a written document that contains many lessons from the founding documents of Great Britain. However, Great Britain does not have such a written constitution. The British consider multiple historic documents, conventions, royal declarations, and other agreements to be their founding documents. And, the House of Commons can pass further legislation that would change the "constitution" of their nation. Canada's constitution is also a "set of documents" including the original Constitution Act of the 19th century creating the country and its much more recent (1982) bill of rights. Australia's constitution was approved by referendum in the Australian states between 1898 and 1900. However, in contrast to the constitution written by Americans after becoming an independent nation, the Australian constitution was submitted to the British Parliament for approval after it was approved by the Australian people.

QUEEN ELIZABETH II of England signs Canada's constitutional proclamation in 1982 as the prime minister, Pierre Trudeau looks on. (AP Photo/Canadian Press, Ron Poling)

WRITTEN OR DICTATED

In the case where one nation or group of allies defeats another nation in a war, the victorious nation may decide to take a hand in the future organization of the defeated country. After World War II, General Douglas McArthur, the commander of the Pacific forces, occupied Japan and gave strong direction to the writing of the new Japanese Constitution. That document, which is still in force and has never been amended, makes it clear that the Japanese imperial family has no political power at all. The Basic Law of Germany was also written after the Allied victory in World War II and contains provisions that are intended to prohibit the rise of a political movement like that of Adolf Hitler.

CONSTITUTION OR WINDOW DRESSING

During the Cold War between the United States and the Soviet Union, the Soviet republics held elections and called themselves democratic nations. They all had written constitutions to which they strictly adhered. However, the elections were not contested, and no opposition candidates or political parties emerged. Newspapers and other media were strictly controlled, as was any access to external information. Today, all of the former Soviet republics have new constitutions and many are democracies with the same freedoms as other nations in Western Europe or the United States. In 2008, Russia, following its popularly approved constitution of 1993, held a free election and chose a new president who was the protégé of former president Vladimir Putin. Opposition leaders claim that they are harassed and that investigative journalists have been murdered.

Similarly, the People's Republic of North Korea has a fairly new constitution (1998) and claims to be democratic. However, the military and the premier, Kim Jong Il, direct all aspects of life there, including limiting the frequencies available on radios and televisions to those approved by the government. So, it seems that just having a written document outlining the structures of government and freedoms of the people may not be enough to guarantee any form of democratic government, at least in the sense that we know it.

FOR CRITICAL ANALYSIS

1. Do you think the United States could have survived without a written constitution?
2. How important is it for the people of a nation to have approved their constitution?
3. How can you tell if a nation is following the letter and the spirit of its constitution?

If you would like to read the constitution of any country in the world, go to http://confinder.richmond.edu.

A "BILL OF LIMITS"

Although called the Bill of Rights, essentially the first 10 amendments to the Constitution were a "bill of limits," because the amendments limited the powers of the national government over the rights and liberties of individuals.

Ironically, a year earlier Madison had told Jefferson, "I have never thought the omission [of the Bill of Rights] a material defect" of the Constitution. But Jefferson's enthusiasm for a bill of rights apparently influenced Madison, as did his desire to gain popular support for his election to Congress. Madison promised in his campaign letter to voters that, once elected, he would force Congress to "prepare and recommend to the states for ratification, the most satisfactory provisions for all essential rights."

Madison had to cull through more than 200 state recommendations.[18] It was no small task, and in retrospect he chose remarkably well. One of the rights appropriate for constitutional protection that he left out was equal protection under the laws—but that was not commonly regarded as a basic right at that time. Not until 1868 did the states ratify an amendment guaranteeing that no state shall deny equal protection to any person. (The Supreme Court has since applied this guarantee to certain actions of the federal government as well.)

The final number of amendments that Madison and a specially appointed committee came up with was 17. Congress tightened the language somewhat and eliminated five of the amendments. Of the remaining 12, two—dealing with the apportionment of representatives and the compensation of the members of Congress—were not ratified immediately by the states. Eventually, Supreme Court decisions led to reform of the

DID YOU KNOW?

That 52 percent of Americans do not know what the Bill of Rights is?

---

[18]For details on these recommendations, including their sources, see Leonard W. Levy, *Origins of the Bill of Rights* (New Haven, CT: Yale University Press, 1999).

apportionment process. The amendment on the compensation of members of Congress was ratified 203 years later—in 1992!

NO EXPLICIT LIMITS ON STATE GOVERNMENT POWERS

On December 15, 1791, the national Bill of Rights was adopted when Virginia agreed to ratify the 10 amendments. On ratification, the Bill of Rights became part of the U.S. Constitution. The basic structure of American government had already been established. Now the fundamental rights and liberties of individuals were protected, at least in theory, at the national level. The proposed amendment that Madison characterized as "the most valuable amendment in the whole lot"—which would have prohibited the states from infringing on the freedoms of conscience, press, and jury trial—had been eliminated by the Senate. Thus, the Bill of Rights as adopted did not limit state power, and individual citizens had to rely on the guarantees contained in a particular state constitution or state bill of rights. The country had to wait until the violence of the Civil War before significant limitations on state power in the form of the Fourteenth Amendment became part of the national Constitution.

ALTERING THE CONSTITUTION: THE FORMAL AMENDMENT PROCESS

The U.S. Constitution consists of 7,000 words. It is shorter than any state constitution except that of Vermont, which has 6,880 words. One of the reasons the federal Constitution is short is that the founders intended it to be only a framework for the new government, to be interpreted by succeeding generations. One of the reasons it has remained short is that the formal amending procedure does not allow for changes to be made easily. Article V of the Constitution outlines the ways in which amendments may be proposed and ratified (see Figure 2–3).

FIGURE 2–3 The Formal Constitutional Amending Procedure

There are two ways of proposing amendments to the U.S. Constitution and two ways of ratifying proposed amendments. Among the four possibilities, the usual route has been proposal by Congress and ratifi cation by state legislatures.

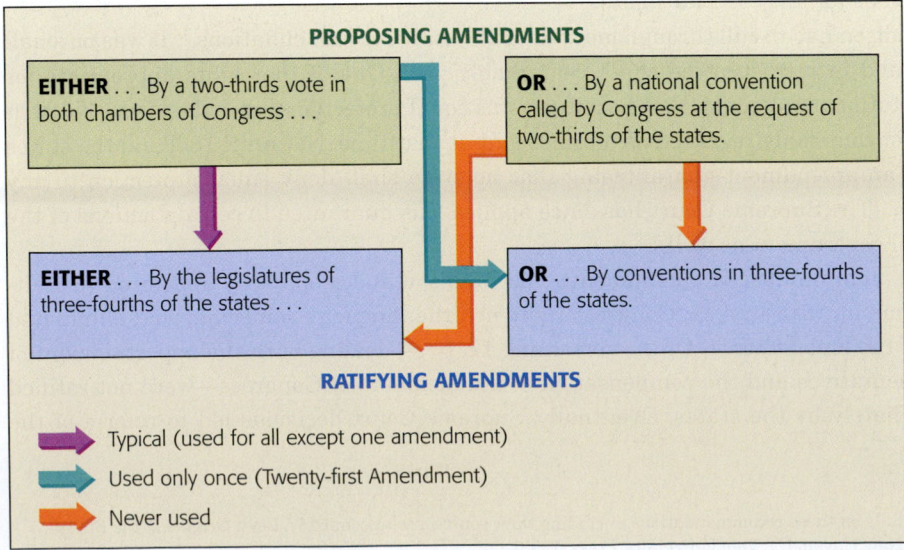

Two formal methods of proposing an amendment to the Constitution are available: (1) a two-thirds vote in each chamber of Congress or (2) a national convention that is called by Congress at the request of two-thirds of the state legislatures (the second method has never been used).

Ratification can occur by one of two methods: (1) by a positive vote in three-fourths of the legislatures of the various states or (2) by special conventions called in the states and a positive vote in three-fourths of them. The second method has been used only once, to repeal Prohibition (the ban on the production and sale of alcoholic beverages). That situation was exceptional because it involved an amendment (the Twenty-first) to repeal an amendment (the Eighteenth, which had created Prohibition). State conventions were necessary for repeal of the Eighteenth Amendment, because the "pro-dry" legislatures in the most conservative states would never have passed the repeal. (Note that Congress determines the method of ratification to be used by all states for each proposed constitutional amendment.)

MANY AMENDMENTS PROPOSED, FEW ACCEPTED

Congress has considered more than 11,000 amendments to the Constitution. Many proposed amendments have been advanced to address highly specific problems. An argument against such narrow amendments has been that amendments ought to embody broad principles, in the way that the existing Constitution does. For that reason, many people have opposed such narrow amendments as one to protect the American flag.

Only 33 amendments have been submitted to the states after having been approved by the required two-thirds vote in each chamber of Congress, and only 27 have been ratified—see Table 2–4. (The full, annotated text of the U.S. Constitution, including its amendments, is presented in a special appendix at the end of this chapter.) It should be clear that the amendment process is much more difficult than a graphic depiction such as Figure 2–3 can indicate. Because of competing social and economic interests, the requirement that two-thirds of both the House and Senate approve the amendments is difficult to achieve. Thirty-four senators, representing only 17 sparsely populated states, could block any amendment. For example, the Republican-controlled House approved the Balanced Budget Amendment within the first 100 days of the 104th Congress in 1995, but it was defeated in the Senate by one vote.

After approval by Congress, the process becomes even more arduous. Three-fourths of the state legislatures must approve the amendment. Only those amendments that have wide popular support across parties and in all regions of the country are likely to be approved.

Why was the amendment process made so difficult? The framers feared that a simple amendment process could lead to a tyranny of the majority, which could pass amendments to oppress disfavored individuals and groups. The cumbersome amendment process does not seem to stem the number of amendments that are proposed each year in Congress, however, particularly in recent years.

LIMITS ON RATIFICATION

A reading of Article V of the Constitution reveals that the framers of the Constitution specified no time limit on the ratification process. The Supreme Court has held that Congress can specify a time for ratification as long as it is "reasonable." Since 1919, most proposed amendments have included a requirement that ratification be obtained within seven years. This was the case with the proposed Equal Rights Amendment, which sought to guarantee equal rights for women. When three-fourths of the states had not ratified in the allotted seven years, however, Congress extended the limit by an additional three years and three months. That extension expired on June 30, 1982, and

TABLE 2–4 Amendments to the Constitution

AMENDMENT	SUBJECT	YEAR ADOPTED	TIME REQUIRED FOR RATIFICATION
1st to 10th	The Bill of Rights	1791	2 years, 2 months, 20 days
11th	Immunity of states from certain suits	1795	11 months, 3 days
12th	Changes in electoral college procedure	1804	6 months, 3 days
13th	Prohibition of slavery	1865	10 months, 3 days
14th	Citizenship, due process, and equal protection	1868	2 years, 26 days
15th	No denial of vote because of race, color, or previous condition of servitude	1870	11 months, 8 days
16th	Power of Congress to tax income	1913	3 years, 6 months, 22 days
17th	Direct election of U.S. senators	1913	10 months, 26 days
18th	National (liquor) prohibition	1919	1 year, 29 days
19th	Women's right to vote	1920	1 year, 2 months, 14 days
20th	Change of dates for congressional and presidential terms	1933	10 months, 21 days
21st	Repeal of the Eighteenth Amendment	1933	9 months, 15 days
22nd	Limit on presidential tenure	1951	3 years, 11 months, 3 days
23rd	District of Columbia electoral vote	1961	9 months, 13 days
24th	Prohibition of tax payment as a qualification to vote in federal elections	1964	1 year, 4 months, 9 days
25th	Procedures for determining presidential disability and presidential succession and for filling a vice presidential vacancy	1967	1 year, 7 months, 4 days
26th	Prohibition of setting minimum voting age above 18 in any election	1971	3 months, 7 days
27th	Prohibition of Congress's voting itself a raise that takes effect before the next election	1992	203 years

the amendment still had not been ratified. Another proposed amendment, which would have guaranteed congressional representation to the District of Columbia, fell far short of the 38 state ratifications needed before its August 22, 1985, deadline.

On May 7, 1992, Michigan became the 38th state to ratify the Twenty-seventh Amendment (on congressional compensation)—one of the two "lost" amendments of the 12 that originally were sent to the states in 1789. Because most of the amendments proposed in recent years have been given a time limit of only seven years by Congress, it was questionable for a time whether the amendment would take effect even if the necessary number of states ratified it. Is 203 years too long a lapse of time between the proposal and the final ratification of an amendment? It apparently was not, because the amendment was certified as legitimate by archivist Don Wilson of the National Archives on May 18, 1992.

THE NATIONAL CONVENTION PROVISION

The Constitution provides that a national convention requested by the legislatures of two-thirds of the states can propose a constitutional amendment. Congress has received approximately 400 convention applications since the Constitution was ratified; every state has applied at least once. Fewer than 20 applications were submitted during the Constitution's first hundred years, but more than 150 have been filed in the last two decades. No national convention has been held since 1787, and many national political and judicial leaders are uneasy about the prospect of convening a body that conceivably could do as the Constitutional Convention did—create a new form of government. The state legislative bodies that originate national convention applications, however, do not appear to be uncomfortable with such a constitutional modification process; more than 230 state constitutional conventions have been held.

A PROTESTOR WAVES a copy of the U.S. Constitution during a "tea party" demonstration in Lafayette Park, across the street from the White House. (KAREN BLEIER/AFP/Getty Images)

INFORMAL METHODS OF CONSTITUTIONAL CHANGE

Formal amendments are one way of changing our Constitution, and, as is obvious from their small number, they have been resorted to infrequently. If we discount the first 10 amendments (the Bill of Rights), which were adopted soon after the ratification of the Constitution, there have been only 17 formal alterations of the Constitution in the more than 200 years of its existence.

But looking at the sparse number of formal constitutional amendments gives us an incomplete view of constitutional change. The brevity and ambiguity of the original document have permitted great alterations in the Constitution by way of varying interpretations over time. As the United States grew, both in population and territory, new social and political realities emerged. Congress, presidents, and the courts found it necessary to interpret the Constitution's provisions in light of these new realities. The Constitution has proved to be a remarkably flexible document, adapting itself repeatedly to new events and concerns.

CONGRESSIONAL LEGISLATION

The Constitution gives Congress broad powers to carry out its duties as the nation's legislative body. For example, Article I, Section 8, of the Constitution gives Congress the power to regulate foreign and interstate commerce. Although there is no clear definition of foreign commerce or interstate commerce in the Constitution, Congress has cited the *commerce clause* as the basis for passing thousands of laws that have defined the meaning of foreign and interstate commerce.

Similarly, Article III, Section 1, states that the national judiciary shall consist of one supreme court and "such inferior courts, as Congress may from time to time ordain and establish." Through a series of acts, Congress has used this broad provision to establish the federal court system of today, which includes the Supreme Court, the Courts of Appeal, and District Courts. This provision allows Congress to create a court such as the Foreign Intelligence Surveillance Act (FISA) court to review requests for wiretapping suspected terrorists.

In addition, Congress has frequently delegated to federal agencies the legislative power to write regulations. These regulations become law unless challenged in the court system. Nowhere does the Constitution outline this delegation of legislative authority.

PRESIDENTIAL ACTIONS

Even though the Constitution does not expressly authorize the president to propose bills or even budgets to Congress,[19] presidents since the time of Woodrow Wilson (who served as president from 1913 to 1921) have proposed hundreds of bills to Congress each year. Presidents have also relied on their Article II authority as commander in chief of the nation's armed forces to send American troops abroad into combat, although the Constitution provides that Congress has the power to declare war.

The president's powers in wartime have waxed and waned through the course of American history. President Abraham Lincoln instituted a draft and suspended several civil liberties during the Civil War. During World War II, President Franklin Roosevelt approved the internment of thousands of Japanese American citizens. President George W. Bush significantly expanded presidential power in the wake of the terrorist attacks of 2001, especially in regard to the handling of individuals who could be defined as "enemy combatants." The creation of the detention facility at Guantánamo Bay, Cuba, made it possible for those prisoners to be held and interrogated by the military under the full control of the executive branch.

Presidents have also conducted foreign affairs by the use of executive agreements, which are legally binding documents made between the president and a foreign head of state. The Constitution does not mention such agreements.

DID YOU KNOW?

That the states have still not ratified an amendment (introduced by Congress in 1810) barring U.S. citizens from accepting titles of nobility from foreign governments?

JUDICIAL REVIEW

Another way of changing the Constitution—or of making it more flexible—is through the power of judicial review. Judicial review refers to the power of U.S. courts to examine the constitutionality of actions undertaken by the legislative and executive branches of government. A state court, for example, may rule that a statute enacted by the state legislature is unconstitutional. Federal courts (and ultimately, the United States Supreme Court) may rule unconstitutional not only acts of Congress and decisions of the national executive branch but also state statutes, state executive actions, and even provisions of state constitutions.

Not a Novel Concept. The Constitution does not specifically mention the power of judicial review. Those in attendance at the Constitutional Convention, however, probably expected that the courts would have some authority to review the legality of acts by the executive and legislative branches, because, under the common law tradition inherited from England, courts exercised this authority. Alexander Hamilton, in *Federalist Paper No. 78*, explicitly outlined the concept of judicial review. Whether the power of judicial review can be justified constitutionally is a question that has been subject to some

---

[19]Note, though, that the Constitution, in Article II, Section 3, does state that the president "shall from time to time . . . recommend to [Congress's] consideration such measures as he shall judge necessary and expedient." Some scholars interpret this phrase to mean that the president has the constitutional authority to propose bills and budgets to Congress for consideration.

debate, particularly in recent years. For now, suffice it to say that in 1803, the Supreme Court claimed this power for itself in *Marbury v. Madison*,[20] in which the Court ruled that a particular provision of an act of Congress was unconstitutional.

Allows Court to Adapt the Constitution. Through the process of judicial review, the Supreme Court adapts the Constitution to modern situations. Electronic technology, for example, did not exist when the Constitution was ratified. Nonetheless, the Supreme Court has used the Fourth Amendment guarantees against unreasonable searches and seizures to place limits on the use of wiretapping and other electronic eavesdropping methods by government officials. The Court has needed to decide whether antiterrorism laws passed by Congress or state legislatures, or executive orders declared by the president, violate the Fourth Amendment or other constitutional provisions. Additionally, the Supreme Court has changed its interpretation of the Constitution in accordance with changing values. It ruled in 1896 that "separate-but-equal" public facilities for African Americans were constitutional; but by 1954, the times had changed, and the Supreme Court reversed that decision.[21] Woodrow Wilson summarized the Supreme Court's work when he described it as "a constitutional convention in continuous session." Basically, the law is what the Supreme Court says it is at any given time. In saying what the law is, the Supreme Court sometimes consults the laws of other countries, as this chapter's *Beyond Our Borders* feature describes.

INTERPRETATION, CUSTOM, AND USAGE

The Constitution has also been changed through interpretation by both Congress and the president. Originally, the president had a staff consisting of personal secretaries and a few others. Today, because Congress delegates specific tasks to the president and the chief executive assumes political leadership, the executive office staff alone has increased to several thousand persons. The executive branch provides legislative leadership far beyond the expectations of the founders.

Changes in the ways of doing political business have also altered the Constitution. The Constitution does not mention political parties, yet these informal, "extraconstitutional" organizations make the nominations for offices, run the campaigns, organize the members of Congress, and in fact change the election system from time to time. The emergence and evolution of the party system, for example, has changed the way the president is elected. The entire nominating process with its use of primary elections and caucuses to choose delegates to the party's nominating convention is the creation of the two major political parties. The president is then selected by the electors who are, in fact, chosen by the parties and are pledged to a party's candidate.

A recent book by Bruce Ackerman argues that the rise of political parties and growth of the executive represent the failure of the Founding Fathers to understand how the government would develop over time. He proposes that the only reason that the system has maintained its checks is the development of the Supreme Court into the guarantor of our rights and liberties.[22] Perhaps most striking, the Constitution has been adapted from serving the needs of a small, rural republic to providing a framework of government for an industrial giant with vast geographic, natural, and human resources.

---

[20] 5 U.S. 137 (1803). See Chapter 15 for a further discussion of the *Marbury v. Madison* case.
[21] *Brown v. Board of Education of Topeka*, 347 U.S. 483 (1954).
[22] Bruce Ackerman, *The Failure of the Founding Fathers: Jefferson, Marshall, and the Rise of Presidential Democracy* (Cambridge: The Belknap Press, 2005).

YOU CAN MAKE A Difference

HOW CAN YOU AFFECT THE U.S. CONSTITUTION?

The U.S. Constitution is an enduring document that has survived more than 200 years of turbulent history. It is also a changing document, however. Twenty-seven amendments have been added to the original Constitution. How can you, as an individual, actively influence constitutional amendments?

WHY SHOULD YOU CARE?

The laws of the nation have a direct impact on your life, and none more so than the Constitution—the supreme law of the land. The most important issues in society are often settled by the Constitution. For example, for the first 75 years of the Republic, the Constitution implicitly protected the institution of slavery. If the Constitution had never been changed through the amendment process, slavery might still be legal today.

Since the passage of the Fourteenth Amendment in 1868, the Constitution has defined who is a citizen and who is entitled to the protections the Constitution provides. Constitutional provisions define our liberties. The First Amendment protects our freedom of speech more thoroughly than do the laws of many other nations. Few other countries have constitutional provisions governing the right to own firearms (the Second Amendment). All of these are among the most fundamental issues we face.

WHAT CAN YOU DO?

One way that you can affect the Constitution is by protecting your existing rights and liberties under it. In the wake of the September 11 attacks, several new laws have been enacted that many believe go too far in curbing our constitutional rights. If you agree and want to join with others who are concerned about this issue, a good starting point is the Web site of the American Civil Liberties Union (ACLU) at **www.aclu.org**. This organization has a special Web site, www.aclu.org/standup/, for young people as well as a Facebook page. If you follow the links for ACLU Stand Up, you will find out about Alondra Jones who, as a high school student, sued the school district to provide better conditions in her school. Her suit claimed that the substandard conditions in her school deprived students of the opportunity to access an education equal to that offered to other California students.

Do you feel that your vote makes a difference? Many voters are beginning to feel disenfranchised by the political process in presidential elections through the effects of the electoral college. A 2007 poll found that 72 percent of Americans favored replacing the electoral college with a direct election.* The Every Vote Counts Amendment proposes to abolish the electoral college and would provide for the direct popular election of the president. If you would like to further investigate Every Vote Counts, go to **www.washingtonwatch.com**, a forum for monitoring proposed legislation in Washington, D.C. Visit the Take Action box, where you can comment on the amendment, alert your friends and colleagues about the issue, and write your representative in Congress.

At the time of this writing, national coalitions of interest groups are supporting or opposing several proposed

-----

*The Washington Post–Kaiser Family Foundation–Harvard University Survey of Political Independents, Public Opinion and Media Research Program, *Kaiser Family Foundation*, July 1, 2007, p. 14; www.kff.org/kaiserpolls/7665.cfm.

ALONDRA JONES speaks to an ACLU conference about her decision to bring a lawsuit against the California school system for better funding for education. (EVIN DIETSCH/UPI/Landov)

amendments. Constitutional amendments are difficult to pass, needing supermajorities in the House and Senate, as well as three-fourths of the state legislatures. The National Popular Vote Bill seeks to reform the electoral college through individual state legislatures, which may change state laws regarding the distribution of electoral votes. With the National Popular Vote Bill, all state electoral votes would be awarded to the presidential candidate winning the popular vote in all 50 states and the District of Columbia. Check out National Popular Vote, Inc., a nonprofit group, at **www.nationalpopularvote.com**, for more information regarding this bill. Its Web site offers numerous ways to become informed and take action. You can even check the bill's progress in your own state.

KEY TERMS

Anti-Federalist 52
bicameral legislature 46
checks and balances 50
confederation 41
electoral college 50
Federalist 52

federal system 50
Great Compromise 47
Madisonian model 49
natural rights 40
ratification 51
representative assembly 36

separation of powers 49
social contract 40
state 41
supremacy doctrine 47
unicameral legislature 40

CHAPTER SUMMARY

1. The first permanent English colonies were established at Jamestown in 1607 and Plymouth in 1620. The Mayflower Compact created the first formal government for the British colonists. By the mid-1700s, other British colonies had been established along the Atlantic seaboard from Georgia to Maine.

2. In 1763, the British tried to impose a series of taxes and legislative acts on their increasingly independent-minded colonies. The colonists responded with boycotts of British products and protests. Representatives of the colonies formed the First Continental Congress in 1774. The delegates sent a petition to the British king expressing their grievances. The Second Continental Congress established an army in 1775 to defend the colonists against attacks by British soldiers.

3. On July 4, 1776, the Second Continental Congress approved the Declaration of Independence. Perhaps the most revolutionary aspects of the Declaration were its assumptions that people have natural rights to life, liberty, and the pursuit of happiness; that governments derive their power from the consent of the governed; and that people have a right to overthrow oppressive governments. During the Revolutionary War, the colonies adopted written constitutions that severely curtailed the power of executives, thus giving their legislatures predominant powers. By the end of the Revolutionary War, the states had signed the Articles of Confederation, creating a weak central government with few powers. The Articles proved to be unworkable because the national government had no way to

ensure compliance by the states with such measures as securing tax revenues.

4. **Why does the Constitution divide the powers of government among the three branches?** General dissatisfaction with the Articles of Confederation prompted the call for a convention at Philadelphia in 1787. Although the delegates ostensibly convened to amend the Articles, the discussions soon focused on creating a constitution for a new form of government. The Virginia plan and the New Jersey plan did not garner widespread support. A compromise offered by Connecticut helped to break the large-state/small-state disputes dividing the delegates. The final version of the Constitution provided for the separation of powers, checks and balances, and a federal form of government. The principles of separation of powers and the checks and balances were intended to prevent any one branch of the government from becoming too powerful.

5. **What is the purpose of the Bill of Rights?** Fears of a strong central government prompted the addition of the Bill of Rights to the Constitution. The Bill of Rights secured for Americans a wide variety of freedoms, including the freedoms of religion, speech, and assembly. It was initially applied only to the federal government, but amendments to the Constitution following the Civil War made it clear that the Bill of Rights would apply to the states as well.

6. **Why is it so difficult to amend the Constitution?** An amendment to the Constitution may be proposed either by a two-thirds vote in each house of Congress

or by a national convention called by Congress at the request of two-thirds of the state legislatures. Ratification can occur either by a positive vote in three-fourths of the legislatures of the various states or by special conventions called in the states for the specific purpose of ratifying the proposed amendment and a positive vote in three-fourths of these state conventions.

The process for amending the Constitution was made very difficult to ensure that most of the states and the majority of both houses agree to the proposed change. Informal methods of constitutional change include congressional legislation, presidential actions, judicial review, and changing interpretations of the Constitution.

SELECTED PRINT, MEDIA, AND ONLINE RESOURCES

PRINT RESOURCES

Ackerman, Bruce. *The Failure of the Founding Fathers: Jefferson, Marshall, and the Rise of Presidential Democracy.* Cambridge, MA: Belknap Press, 2005. In this book, the author sees the contested election of 1800 as exposing the failure of the new Constitution to account for the rise of presidential power and the appearance of political parties.

Armitage, David. *The Declaration of Independence: A Global History.* Cambridge, MA: Harvard University Press, 2007. The author examines the history of the Declaration of Independence and then looks at its impact on the peoples and governments of other nations.

Bailyn, Bernard. *To Begin the World Anew: The Genius and Ambiguities of the American Founders.* New York: Knopf, 2003. In a series of essays, a two-time Pulitzer Prize–winning historian discusses the themes of order and liberty in the *Federalist Papers* and the advantages of the founders' provincialism.

Breyer, Stephen G. *Active Liberty: Interpreting Our Democratic Constitution.* New York: Knopf, 2005. Supreme Court Justice Stephen Breyer offers his thoughts on the Constitution as a living document. He argues that the genius of the Constitution rests in the adaptability of its great principles to cope with current problems.

Dahl, Robert A. *How Democratic Is the American Constitution?* New Haven, CT: Yale University Press, 2002. This book compares the U.S. Constitution with the constitutions of other democratic countries in the world.

Gibson, Alan. *Understanding the Founding: The Crucial Questions.* Lawrence: The University Press of Kansas, 2007. The author looks at several oft-debated questions concerning the motivation and political views of the Founding Fathers.

Hamilton, Alexander, et al. *The Federalist: The Famous Papers on the Principles of American Government.* Benjamin F. Wright, ed. New York: Friedman/Fairfax Publishing, 2002. This is an updated version of the papers written by Alexander Hamilton, James Madison, and John Jay and published in the *New York Packet*, in support of the ratification of the Constitution.

Philbrick, Nathaniel. *Mayflower: A Story of Courage, Community and War.* New York: Penguin, 2007. The author investigates many of the myths surrounding the first colony in New England and sheds light on some little-known history.

MEDIA RESOURCES

In the Beginning—A 1987 Bill Moyers TV program that features discussions with three prominent historians about the roots of the Constitution and its impact on our society.

John Locke—A 1994 video exploring the character and principal views of John Locke.

Thomas Jefferson—A 1996 documentary by acclaimed director Ken Burns. The film covers Jefferson's entire life, including his writing of the Declaration of Independence, his presidency, and his later years in Virginia. Historians and writers interviewed include Daniel Boorstin, Garry Wills, Gore Vidal, and John Hope Franklin.

ONLINE RESOURCES

Avalon Project digital documents relevant to law, history, and diplomacy including James Madison's notes on the Constitutional Convention debates, taken from his daily journal: http://www.yale.edu/lawweb/avalon/

Emory University School of Law U.S. founding documents, including the Declaration of Independence, scanned originals of the U.S. Constitution, and the *Federalist Papers*: www.law.emory.edu/erd/docs/federalist

FindLaw.com comprehensive resource for legal information: www.findlaw.com/casecode/state.html

National Constitution Center information on the Constitution—including its history, current debates over constitutional provisions, and news articles: www.constitutioncenter.org

University of Oklahoma Law Center houses several U.S. historical documents online: www.law.ou.edu/hist

APPENDIX TO CHAPTER 2

the Constitution
OF THE UNITED STATES*

THE PREAMBLE

We the People of the United States, in Order to form a more perfect Union, establish Justice, insure domestic Tranquility, provide for the common defence, promote the general Welfare, and secure the Blessings of Liberty to ourselves and our Posterity, do ordain and establish this Constitution for the United States of America.

The Preamble declares that "We the People" are the authority for the Constitution (unlike the Articles of Confederation, which derived their authority from the states). The Preamble also sets out the purposes of the Constitution.

ARTICLE I. *(Legislative Branch)*

The first part of the Constitution, Article I, deals with the organization and powers of the lawmaking branch of the national government, the Congress.

Section 1. *Legislative Powers*

All legislative Powers herein granted shall be vested in a Congress of the United States, which shall consist of a Senate and House of Representatives.

Section 2. *House of Representatives*

Clause 1: Composition and Election of Members. The House of Representatives shall be composed of Members chosen every second Year by the People of the several States, and the Electors in each State shall have the Qualifications requisite for Electors of the most numerous Branch of the State Legislature.

Each state has the power to decide who may vote for members of Congress. Within each state, those who may vote for state legislators may also vote for members of the House of Representatives (and, under the Seventeenth Amendment, for U.S. senators). When the Constitution was written, nearly all states limited voting rights to white male property owners or taxpayers at least 21 years old. Subsequent

amendments granted voting power to African American men, all women, and everyone at least 18 years old.

Clause 2: Qualifications. No Person shall be a Representative who shall not have attained to the Age of twenty five Years, and been seven Years a Citizen of the United States, and who shall not, when elected, be an Inhabitant of that State in which he shall be chosen.

Each member of the House must be at least 25 years old, a citizen of the United States for at least seven years, and a resident of the state in which she or he is elected.

Clause 3: Apportionment of Representatives and Direct Taxes. Representatives [and direct Taxes][1] shall be apportioned among the several States which may be included within this Union, according to their respective Numbers [which shall be determined by adding to the whole Number of free Persons, including those bound to Service for a Term of Years, and excluding Indians not taxed, three fifths of all other Persons].[2] The actual Enumeration shall be made within three Years after the first Meeting of the Congress of the United States, and within every subsequent Term of ten Years, in such Manner as they shall by Law direct. The Number of Representatives shall not exceed one for every thirty Thousand, but each State shall have at Least one Representative; and until such enumeration shall be made, the State of New Hampshire shall be entitled to chuse three, Massachusetts eight, Rhode Island and Providence Plantations one, Connecticut five, New York six, New Jersey four, Pennsylvania eight, Delaware one, Maryland six, Virginia ten, North Carolina five, South Carolina five, and Georgia three.

A state's representation in the House is based on the size of its population. Population is counted in each decade's census, after which Congress reapportions House seats. Since early in the 20th century, the number of seats has been limited to 435.

---

*The spelling, capitalization, and punctuation of the original have been retained here. Brackets indicate passages that have been altered by amendments to the Constitution. We have added article titles (in parentheses), section titles, and clause designations. We have also inserted annotations in blue italic type.
[1]Modified by the Sixteenth Amendment.
[2]Modified by the Fourteenth Amendment.

Clause 4: Vacancies. When vacancies happen in the Representation from any State, the Executive Authority thereof shall issue Writs of Election to fill such Vacancies.

The "Executive Authority" is the state's governor. When a vacancy occurs in the House, the governor calls a special election to fill it.

Clause 5: Officers and Impeachment. The House of Representatives shall chuse their Speaker and other Officers; and shall have the sole Power of Impeachment.

The power to impeach is the power to accuse. In this case, it is the power to accuse members of the executive or judicial branch of wrongdoing or abuse of power. Once a bill of impeachment is issued, the Senate holds the trial.

Section 3. *The Senate*

Clause 1: Term and Number of Members. The Senate of the United States shall be composed of two Senators from each State [chosen by the Legislature thereof],[3] for six Years; and each Senator shall have one Vote.

Every state has two senators, each of whom serves for six years and has one vote in the upper chamber. Since the Seventeenth Amendment in 1913, all senators have been elected directly by voters of the state during the regular election.

Clause 2: Classification of Senators. Immediately after they shall be assembled in Consequence of the first Election, they shall be divided as equally as may be into three Classes. The Seats of the Senators of the first Class shall be vacated at the Expiration of the second Year, of the second Class at the Expiration of the fourth Year, and of the third Class at the Expiration of the sixth Year, so that one third may be chosen every second Year; [and if Vacancies happen by Resignation, or otherwise, during the Recess of the Legislature of any State, the Executive thereof may make temporary Appointments until the next Meeting of the Legislature, which shall then fill such Vacancies].[4]

One-third of the Senate's seats are open to election every two years (in contrast, all members of the House are elected simultaneously).

Clause 3: Qualifications. No Person shall be a Senator who shall not have attained to the Age of thirty Years, and been nine Years a Citizen of the United States, and who shall not, when elected, be an Inhabitant of that State for which he shall be chosen.

Every senator must be at least 30 years old, a citizen of the United States for a minimum of nine years, and a resident of the state in which he or she is elected.

Clause 4: The Role of the Vice President. The Vice President of the United States shall be President of the Senate, but shall have no Vote, unless they be equally divided.

The vice president presides over meetings of the Senate but cannot vote unless there is a tie. The Constitution gives no other official duties to the vice president.

Clause 5: Other Officers. The Senate shall chuse their other Officers, and also a President pro tempore, in the Absence of the Vice President, or when he shall exercise the Office of President of the United States.

The Senate votes for one of its members to preside when the vice president is absent. This person is usually called the president pro tempore because of the temporary nature of the position.

Clause 6: Impeachment Trials. The Senate shall have the sole Power to try all Impeachments. When sitting for that Purpose, they shall be on Oath or Affirmation. When the President of the United States is tried, the Chief Justice shall preside: And no Person shall be convicted without the Concurrence of two thirds of the Members present.

The Senate conducts trials of officials that the House impeaches. The Senate sits as a jury, with the vice president presiding if the president is not on trial.

Clause 7: Penalties for Conviction. Judgment in Cases of Impeachment shall not extend further than to removal from Office, and disqualification to hold and enjoy any Office of honor, Trust, or Profit under the United States: but the Party convicted shall nevertheless be liable and subject to Indictment, Trial, Judgment, and Punishment, according to Law.

On conviction of impeachment charges, the Senate can only force an official to leave office and prevent him or her from holding another office in the federal government. The individual, however, can still be tried in a regular court.

Section 4. *Congressional Elections: Times, Manner, and Places*

Clause 1: Elections. The Times, Places and Manner of holding Elections for Senators and Representatives, shall be prescribed in each State by the Legislature thereof; but the Congress may at any time by Law make or alter such Regulations, except as to the Places of chusing Senators.

Congress set the Tuesday after the first Monday in November in even-numbered years as the date for congressional elections. In states with more than one seat in the House, Congress requires that representatives be elected from districts within each state. Under the Seventeenth Amendment, senators are elected at the same places as other officials.

---

[3]Repealed by the Seventeenth Amendment.
[4]Modified by the Seventeenth Amendment.

Clause 2: Sessions of Congress. [The Congress shall assemble at least once in every Year, and such Meeting shall be on the first Monday in December, unless they shall by Law appoint a different Day.][5]

Congress has to meet every year at least once. The regular session now begins at noon on January 3 of each year, subsequent to the Twentieth Amendment, unless Congress passes a law to fix a different date. Congress stays in session until its members vote to adjourn. Additionally, the president may call a special session.

Section 5. *Powers and Duties of the Houses*

Clause 1: Admitting Members and Quorum. Each House shall be the Judge of the Elections, Returns, and Qualifications of its own Members, and a Majority of each shall constitute a Quorum to do Business; but a smaller Number may adjourn from day to day, and may be authorized to compel the Attendance of absent Members, in such Manner, and under such Penalties as each House may provide.

Each chamber may exclude or refuse to seat a member-elect.

The quorum rule requires that 218 members of the House and 51 members of the Senate be present to conduct business. This rule normally is not enforced in the handling of routine matters.

Clause 2: Rules and Discipline of Members. Each House may determine the Rules of its Proceedings, punish its Members for disorderly Behaviour, and, with the Concurrence of two thirds, expel a Member.

The House and the Senate may adopt their own rules to guide their proceedings. Each may also discipline its members for conduct that is deemed unacceptable. No member may be expelled without a two-thirds majority vote in favor of expulsion.

Clause 3: Keeping a Record. Each House shall keep a Journal of its Proceedings, and from time to time publish the same, excepting such Parts as may in their Judgment require Secrecy; and the Yeas and Nays of the Members of either House on any question shall, at the Desire of one fifth of those Present, be entered on the Journal.

The journals of the two chambers are published at the end of each session of Congress.

Clause 4: Adjournment. Neither House, during the Session of Congress, shall, without the Consent of the other, adjourn for more than three days, nor to any other Place than that in which the two Houses shall be sitting.

Congress has the power to determine when and where to meet, provided, however, that both chambers meet in the same city. Neither chamber may recess for more than three days without the consent of the other.

Section 6. *Rights of Members*

Clause 1: Compensation and Privileges. The Senators and Representatives shall receive a Compensation for their services, to be ascertained by Law, and paid out of the Treasury of the United States. They shall in all Cases, except Treason, Felony and Breach of the Peace, be privileged from Arrest during their Attendance at the Session of their respective Houses, and in going to and returning from the same; and for any Speech or Debate in either House, they shall not be questioned in any other Place.

Congressional salaries are to be paid by the U.S. Treasury rather than by the members' respective states. The original salaries were $6 per day; in 1857 they were $3,000 per year. Both representatives and senators were paid $165,200 in 2006.

Treason is defined in Article III, Section 3. A felony is any serious crime. A breach of the peace is any indictable offense less than treason or a felony. Members cannot be arrested for things they say during speeches and debates in Congress. This immunity applies to the Capitol Building itself and not to their private lives.

Clause 2: Restrictions. No Senator or Representative shall, during the Time for which he was elected, be appointed to any civil Office under the Authority of the United States, which shall have been created, or the Emoluments whereof shall have been encreased during such time; and no Person holding any Office under the United States, shall be a Member of either House during his Continuance in Office.

During the term for which a member was elected, he or she cannot concurrently accept another federal government position.

Section 7. *Legislative Powers: Bills and Resolutions*

Clause 1: Revenue Bills. All Bills for raising Revenue shall originate in the House of Representatives; but the Senate may propose or concur with Amendments as on other Bills.

All tax and appropriation bills for raising money have to originate in the House of Representatives. The Senate, though, often amends such bills and may even substitute an entirely different bill.

Clause 2: The Presidential Veto. Every Bill which shall have passed the House of Representatives and the Senate, shall,

---

[5]Changed by the Twentieth Amendment.

before it becomes a Law, be presented to the President of the United States; If he approve he shall sign it, but if not he shall return it, with his Objections to the House in which it shall have originated, who shall enter the Objections at large on their Journal, and proceed to reconsider it. If after such Reconsideration two thirds of that House shall agree to pass the Bill, it shall be sent together with the Objections, to the other House, by which it shall likewise be reconsidered, and if approved by two thirds of that House, it shall become a Law. But in all such Cases the Votes of both Houses shall be determined by Yeas and Nays, and the Names of the Persons voting for and against the Bill shall be entered on the Journal of each House respectively. If any Bill shall not be returned by the President within 10 Days (Sundays excepted) after it shall have been presented to him, the Same shall be a Law, in like Manner as if he had signed it, unless the Congress by their Adjournment prevent its Return in which Case it shall not be a Law.

When Congress sends the president a bill, he or she can sign it (in which case it becomes law) or send it back to the chamber in which it originated. If it is sent back, a two-thirds majority of each chamber must pass it again for it to become law. If the president neither signs it nor sends it back within 10 days, it becomes law anyway, unless Congress adjourns in the meantime.

Clause 3: Actions on Other Matters. Every Order, Resolution, or Vote to which the Concurrence of the Senate and House of Representatives may be necessary (except on a question of Adjournment) shall be presented to the President of the United States; and before the Same shall take Effect, shall be approved by him, or being disapproved by him, shall be repassed by two thirds of the Senate and House of Representatives, according to the Rules and Limitations prescribed in the Case of a Bill.

The president must have the opportunity to either sign or veto everything that Congress passes, except votes to adjourn and resolutions not having the force of law.

Section 8. *The Powers of Congress*

Clause 1: Taxing. The Congress shall have Power to lay and collect Taxes, Duties, Imposts and Excises, to pay the Debts and provide for the common Defence and general Welfare of the United States; but all Duties, Imposts and Excises shall be uniform throughout the United States;

Duties are taxes on imports and exports. Impost is a generic term for tax. Excises are taxes on the manufacture, sale, or use of goods.

Clause 2: Borrowing. To borrow Money on the credit of the United States;

Congress has the power to borrow money, which is normally carried out through the sale of U.S. treasury bonds on which interest is paid. Note that the Constitution places no limit on the amount of government borrowing.

Clause 3: Regulation of Commerce. To regulate Commerce with foreign Nations, and among the several States, and with the Indian Tribes;

This is the commerce clause, which gives to Congress the power to regulate interstate and foreign trade. Much of the activity of Congress is based on this clause.

Clause 4: Naturalization and Bankruptcy. To establish an uniform Rule of Naturalization, and uniform Laws on the subject of Bankruptcies throughout the United States;

Only Congress may determine how aliens can become citizens of the United States. Congress may make laws with respect to bankruptcy.

Clause 5: Money and Standards. To coin Money, regulate the Value thereof, and of foreign Coin, and fix the Standard of Weights and Measures;

Congress mints coins and prints and circulates paper money. Congress can establish uniform measures of time, distance, weight, and so on. In 1838, Congress adopted the English system of weights and measurements as our national standard.

Clause 6: Punishing Counterfeiters. To provide for the Punishment of counterfeiting the Securities and current Coin of the United States;

Congress has the power to punish those who copy American money and pass it off as real. Currently, the fine is up to $5,000 and/or imprisonment for up to 15 years.

Clause 7: Roads and Post Offices. To establish Post Offices and post Roads;

Post roads include all routes over which mail is carried—highways, railways, waterways, and airways.

Clause 8: Patents and Copyrights. To promote the Progress of Science and useful Arts, by securing for limited Times to Authors and Inventors the exclusive Right to their respective Writings and Discoveries;

Authors' and composers' works are protected by copyrights established by copyright law, which currently is the Copyright Act of 1976, as amended. Copyrights are valid for the life of the author or composer plus 70 years. Inventors' works are protected by patents, which vary in length of protection from 14 to 20 years. A patent gives a person the exclusive right to control the manufacture or sale of her or his invention.

Clause 9: Lower Courts. To constitute Tribunals inferior to the supreme Court;

Congress has the authority to set up all federal courts, except the Supreme Court, and to decide what cases those courts will hear.

Clause 10: Punishment for Piracy. To define and punish Piracies and Felonies committed on the high Seas, and Offences against the Law of Nations;

Congress has the authority to prohibit the commission of certain acts outside U.S. territory and to punish certain violations of international law.

Clause 11: Declaration of War. To declare War, grant Letters of Marque and Reprisal, and make Rules concerning Captures on Land and Water;

Only Congress can declare war, although the president, as commander in chief, can make war without Congress's formal declaration. Letters of marque and reprisal authorized private parties to capture and destroy enemy ships in wartime. Since the middle of the 19th century, international law has prohibited letters of marque and reprisal, and the United States has honored the ban.

Clause 12: The Army. To raise and support Armies, but no Appropriation of Money to that Use shall be for a longer Term than two Years;

Congress has the power to create an army; the money used to pay for it must be appropriated for no more than two-year intervals. This latter restriction gives ultimate control of the army to civilians.

Clause 13: Creation of a Navy. To provide and maintain a Navy;

This clause allows for the maintenance of a navy. In 1947, Congress created the U.S. Air Force.

Clause 14: Regulation of the Armed Forces. To make Rules for the Government and Regulation of the land and naval Forces;

Congress sets the rules for the military mainly by way of the Uniform Code of Military Justice, which was enacted in 1950 by Congress.

Clause 15: The Militia. To provide for calling forth the Militia to execute the Laws of the Union, suppress Insurrections and repel Invasions;

The militia is known today as the National Guard. Both Congress and the president have the authority to call the National Guard into federal service.

Clause 16: How the Militia Is Organized. To provide for organizing, arming, and disciplining the Militia, and for governing such Part of them as may be employed in the Service of the United States, reserving to the States respectively, the Appointment of the Officers, and the Authority of training the Militia according to the discipline prescribed by Congress;

This clause gives Congress the power to "federalize" state militia (National Guard). When called into such service, the National Guard is subject to the same rules that Congress has set forth for the regular armed services.

Clause 17: Creation of the District of Columbia. To exercise exclusive Legislation in all Cases whatsoever, over such District (not exceeding ten Miles square) as may, by Cession of particular States, and the Acceptance of Congress, become the Seat of the Government of the United States, and to exercise like Authority over all Places purchased by the Consent of the Legislature of the State in which the Same shall be, for the Erection of Forts, Magazines, Arsenals, dock-Yards, and other needful Buildings;—And

Congress established the District of Columbia as the national capital in 1791. Virginia and Maryland had granted land for the District, but Virginia's grant was returned because it was believed it would not be needed. Today, the District covers 69 square miles.

Clause 18: The Elastic Clause. To make all Laws which shall be necessary and proper for carrying into Execution the foregoing Powers, and all other Powers vested by this Constitution in the Government of the United States, or in any Department or Officer thereof.

This clause—the necessary and proper clause, or the elastic clause—grants no specific powers, and thus it can be stretched to fit different circumstances. It has allowed Congress to adapt the government to changing needs and times.

Section 9. The Powers Denied to Congress

Clause 1: Question of Slavery. The Migration or Importation of such Persons as any of the States now existing shall think proper to admit, shall not be prohibited by the Congress prior to the Year one thousand eight hundred and eight, but a Tax or duty may be imposed on such Importation, not exceeding ten dollars for each Person.

"Persons" referred to slaves. Congress outlawed the slave trade in 1808.

Clause 2: Habeas Corpus. The privilege of the Writ of Habeas Corpus shall not be suspended, unless when in Cases of Rebellion or Invasion the public Safety may require it.

A writ of habeas corpus is a court order directing a sheriff or other public officer who is detaining another person to "produce the body" of the detainee so the court can assess the legality of the detention.

Clause 3: Special Bills. No Bill of Attainder or ex post facto Law shall be passed.

A bill of attainder is a law that inflicts punishment without a trial. An ex post facto law is a law that inflicts punishment for an act that was not illegal when it was committed.

Clause 4: Direct Taxes. [No Capitation, or other direct, Tax shall be laid, unless in Proportion to the Census or Enumeration herein before directed to be taken.][6]

A capitation is a tax on a person. A direct tax is a tax paid directly to the government, such as a property tax. This clause was intended to prevent Congress from levying a tax on slaves per person and thereby taxing slavery out of existence.

Clause 5: Export Taxes. No Tax or Duty shall be laid on Articles exported from any State.

Congress may not tax any goods sold from one state to another or from one state to a foreign country. (Congress does have the power to tax goods that are bought from other countries, however.)

Clause 6: Interstate Commerce. No Preference shall be given by any Regulation of Commerce or Revenue to the Ports of one State over those of another: nor shall Vessels bound to, or from, one State, be obliged to enter, clear, or pay Duties in another.

Congress may not treat different ports within the United States differently in terms of taxing and commerce powers. Congress may not give one state's port a legal advantage over the ports of another state.

Clause 7: Treasury Withdrawals. No Money shall be drawn from the Treasury, but in Consequence of Appropriations made by Law; and a regular Statement and Account of the Receipts and Expenditures of all public Money shall be published from time to time.

Federal funds can be spent only as Congress authorizes. This is a significant check on the president's power.

Clause 8: Titles of Nobility. No Title of Nobility shall be granted by the United States: And no Person holding any Office of Profit or Trust under them, shall, without the Consent of the Congress, accept of any present, Emolument, Office, or Title, of any kind whatever, from any King, Prince, or foreign State.

No person in the United States may hold a title of nobility, such as duke or duchess. This clause also discourages bribery of American officials by foreign governments.

Section 10. *Those Powers Denied to the States*

Clause 1: Treaties and Coinage. No State shall enter into any Treaty, Alliance, or Confederation; grant Letters of Marque and Reprisal; coin Money; emit Bills of Credit; make any Thing but gold and silver Coin a Tender in Payment of Debts; pass any Bill of Attainder, ex post facto Law, or Law impairing the Obligation of Contracts, or grant any Title of Nobility.

Prohibiting state laws "impairing the Obligation of Contracts" was intended to protect creditors. (Shayss' Rebellion—an

attempt to prevent courts from giving effect to creditors' legal actions against debtors—occurred only one year before the Constitution was written.)

Clause 2: Duties and Imposts. No State shall, without the Consent of the Congress, lay any Imposts or Duties on Imports or Exports, except what may be absolutely necessary for executing its inspection Laws; and the net Produce of all Duties and Imposts, laid by any State on Imports or Exports, shall be for the Use of the Treasury of the United States; and all such Laws shall be subject to the Revision and Controul of the Congress.

Only Congress can tax imports. Further, the states cannot tax exports.

Clause 3: War. No State shall, without the Consent of Congress, lay any Duty of Tonnage, keep Troops, or Ships of War in time of Peace, enter into any Agreement or Compact with another State, or with a foreign Power or engage in War, unless actually invaded, or in such imminent Danger as will not admit of delay.

A duty of tonnage is a tax on ships according to their cargo capacity. No states may tax ships according to their cargo unless Congress agrees. Additionally, this clause forbids any state to keep troops or warships during peacetime or to make a compact with another state or foreign nation unless Congress so agrees. A state, in contrast, can maintain a militia, but its use has to be limited to disorders that occur within the state—unless, of course, the militia is called into federal service.

ARTICLE II. *(Executive Branch)*

Section 1. *The Nature and Scope of Presidential Power*

Clause 1: Four-Year Term. The executive Power shall be vested in a President of the United States of America. He shall hold his Office during the Term of four Years, and, together with the Vice President, chosen for the same Term, be elected, as follows.

The president has the power to carry out laws made by Congress, called the executive power. He or she serves in office for a four-year term after election. The Twenty-second Amendment limits the number of times a person may be elected president.

Clause 2: Choosing Electors from Each State. Each State shall appoint, in such Manner as the Legislature thereof may direct, a Number of Electors, equal to the whole Number of Senators and Representatives to which the State may be entitled in the Congress; but no Senator or Representative, or Person holding an Office of Trust or Profit under the United States, shall be appointed an Elector.

The "Electors" are known more commonly as the "electoral college." The president is elected by electors—that

---

is, representatives chosen by the people—rather than by the people directly.

Clause 3: The Former System of Elections. [The Electors shall meet in their respective States, and vote by Ballot for two Persons, of whom one at least shall not be an Inhabitant of the same State with themselves. And they shall make a List of all the Persons voted for, and of the Number of Votes for each; which List they shall sign and certify, and transmit sealed to the Seat of the Government of the United States, directed to the President of the Senate. The President of the Senate shall, in the Presence of the Senate and House of Representatives, open all the Certificates, and the Votes shall then be counted. The Person having the greatest Number of Votes shall be the President, if such Number be a Majority of the whole Number of Electors appointed; and if there be more than one who have such Majority, and have an equal Number of Votes, then the House of Representatives shall immediately chuse by Ballot one of them for President; and if no Person have a Majority, then from the five highest on the List the said House shall in like Manner chuse the President. But in chusing the President, the Votes shall be taken by States, the Representation from each State having one Vote; A quorum for this Purpose shall consist of a Member or Members from two thirds of the States, and a Majority of all the States shall be necessary to a Choice. In every Case, after the Choice of the President, the Person having the greater Number of Votes of the Electors shall be the Vice President. But if there should remain two or more who have equal Votes, the Senate shall chuse from them by Ballot the Vice President.][7]

The original method of selecting the president and vice president was replaced by the Twelfth Amendment. Apparently, the framers did not anticipate the rise of political parties and the development of primaries and conventions.

Clause 4: The Time of Elections. The Congress may determine the Time of chusing the Electors, and the Day on which they shall give their Votes; which Day shall be the same throughout the United States.

Congress set the Tuesday after the first Monday in November every fourth year as the date for choosing electors. The electors cast their votes on the Monday after the second Wednesday in December of that year.

Clause 5: Qualifications for President. No person except a natural born Citizen, or a Citizen of the United States, at the time of the Adoption of this Constitution, shall be eligible to the Office of President; neither shall any Person be eligible to that Office who shall not have attained to the Age of thirty five Years, and been fourteen Years a Resident within the United States.

The president must be a natural-born citizen, be at least 35 years of age when taking office, and have been a resident within the United States for at least 14 years.

Clause 6: Succession of the Vice President. [In Case of the Removal of the President from Office, or of his Death, Resignation or Inability to discharge the Powers and Duties of the said Office, the same shall devolve on the Vice President, and the Congress may by Law provide for the Case of Removal, Death, Resignation or Inability, both of the President and Vice President, declaring what Officer shall then act as President, and such Officer shall act accordingly, until the Disability be removed, or a President shall be elected.][8]

This section provided for the method by which the vice president was to succeed to the presidency, but its wording is ambiguous. It was replaced by the Twenty-fifth Amendment.

Clause 7: The President's Salary. The President shall, at stated Times, receive for his Services, a Compensation, which shall neither be encreased nor diminished during the Period for which he shall have been elected, and he shall not receive within that Period any other Emolument from the United States, or any of them.

The president maintains the same salary during each four-year term. Moreover, she or he may not receive additional cash payments from the government. Originally set at $25,000 per year, the salary is currently $400,000 a year plus a $50,000 nontaxable expense account.

Clause 8: The Oath of Office. Before he enter on the Execution of his Office, he shall take the following Oath or Affirmation: "I do solemnly swear (or affirm) that I will faithfully execute the Office of President of the United States, and will to the best of my Ability, preserve, protect and defend the Constitution of the United States."

The president is "sworn in" prior to beginning the duties of the office. The taking of the oath of office occurs on January 20, following the November election. The ceremony is called the inauguration. The oath of office is administered by the chief justice of the United States Supreme Court.

Section 2. *Powers of the President*

Clause 1: Commander in Chief. The President shall be Commander in Chief of the Army and Navy of the United States, and of the Militia of the several States, when called into the actual Service of the United States; he may require the Opinion, in writing, of the principal Officer in each of the executive Departments, upon any Subject relating to the Duties of their respective Offices,

[7]Changed by the Twelfth Amendment.
[8]Modified by the Twenty-fifth Amendment.

and he shall have Power to grant Reprieves and Pardons for Offences against the United States, except in Cases of Impeachment.

The armed forces are placed under civilian control because the president is a civilian but still commander in chief of the military. The president may ask for the help of the head of each of the executive departments (thereby creating the Cabinet). The Cabinet members are chosen by the president with the consent of the Senate, but they can be removed without Senate approval.

The president's clemency powers extend only to federal cases. In those cases, he or she may grant a full or conditional pardon, or reduce a prison term or fine.

Clause 2: Treaties and Appointment. He shall have Power, by and with the Advice and Consent of the Senate, to make Treaties, provided two thirds of the Senators present concur; and he shall nominate, and by and with the Advice and Consent of the Senate, shall appoint Ambassadors, other public Ministers and Consuls, Judges of the supreme Court, and all other Officers of the United States, whose Appointments are not herein otherwise provided for, and which shall be established by Law; but the Congress may by Law vest the Appointment of such inferior Officers, as they think proper, in the President alone, in the Courts of Law, or in the Heads of Departments.

Many of the major powers of the president are identified in this clause, including the power to make treaties with foreign governments (with the approval of the Senate by a two-thirds vote) and the power to appoint ambassadors, Supreme Court justices, and other government officials. Most such appointments require Senate approval.

Clause 3: Vacancies. The President shall have Power to fill up all Vacancies that may happen during the Recess of the Senate, by granting Commissions which shall expire at the end of their next Session.

The president has the power to appoint temporary officials to fill vacant federal offices without Senate approval if the Congress is not in session. Such appointments expire automatically at the end of Congress's next term.

Section 3. *Duties of the President*

He shall from time to time give to the Congress Information of the State of the Union, and recommend to their Consideration such Measures as he shall judge necessary and expedient; he may, on extraordinary Occasions, convene both Houses, or either of them, and in Case of Disagreement between them, with Respect to the Time of Adjournment, he may adjourn them to such Time as he shall think proper; he shall receive Ambassadors and other public Ministers; he shall take Care that the Laws be faithfully executed, and shall Commission all the Officers of the United States.

Annually, the president reports on the state of the union to Congress, recommends legislative measures, and proposes a federal budget. The State of the Union speech is a statement not only to Congress but also to the American people. After it is given, the president proposes a federal budget and presents an economic report. At any time, the president may send special messages to Congress while it is in session. The president has the power to call special sessions, to adjourn Congress when its two chambers do not agree on when to adjourn, to receive diplomatic representatives of other governments, and to ensure the proper execution of all federal laws. The president further has the ability to empower federal officers to hold their positions and to perform their duties.

Section 4. *Impeachment*

The President, Vice President and all civil Officers of the United States, shall be removed from Office on Impeachment for, and Conviction of, Treason, Bribery, or other high Crimes and Misdemeanors.

Treason denotes giving aid to the nation's enemies. The phrase "high crimes and misdemeanors" is usually considered to mean serious abuses of political power. In either case, the president or vice president may be accused by the House (called an impeachment) and then removed from office if convicted by the Senate. (Note that impeachment does not mean removal but rather refers to an accusation of treason or high crimes and misdemeanors.)

ARTICLE III. *(Judicial Branch)*

Section 1. *Judicial Powers, Courts, and Judges*

The judicial Power of the United States, shall be vested in one supreme Court, and in such inferior Courts as the Congress may from time to time ordain and establish. The Judges, both of the supreme and inferior Courts, shall hold their Offices during good Behaviour, and shall, at stated Times, receive for their Services a Compensation, which shall not be diminished during their Continuance in Office.

The Supreme Court is vested with judicial power, as are the lower federal courts that Congress creates. Federal judges serve in their offices for life unless they are impeached and convicted by Congress. The payment of federal judges may not be reduced during their time in office.

Section 2. *Jurisdiction*

Clause 1: Cases under Federal Jurisdiction. The judicial Power shall extend to all Cases, in Law and Equity, arising under this Constitution, the Laws of the United States, and Treaties made, or which shall be made, under their

---

[9]Modified by the Eleventh Amendment.
[10]Modified by the Eleventh Amendment.

Authority;—to all Cases affecting Ambassadors, other public Ministers and Consuls;—to all Cases of admiralty and maritime Jurisdiction;—to Controversies to which the United States shall be a Party;—to Controversies between two or more States; [—between a State and Citizens of another State;—][9] between Citizens of different States;—between Citizens of the same State claiming Lands under Grants of different States, [and between a State, or the Citizens thereof, and foreign States, Citizens or Subjects.][10]

The federal courts take on cases that concern the meaning of the U.S. Constitution, all federal laws, and treaties. They also can take on cases involving citizens of different states and citizens of foreign nations.

Clause 2: Cases for the Supreme Court. In all Cases affecting Ambassadors, other public Ministers and Consuls, and those in which a State shall be a Party, the supreme Court shall have original Jurisdiction. In all the other Cases before mentioned, the supreme Court shall have appellate Jurisdiction, both as to Law and Fact, with such Exceptions, and under such Regulations as the Congress shall make.

In a limited number of situations, the Supreme Court acts as a trial court and has original jurisdiction. These cases involve a representative from another country or involve a state. In all other situations, the cases must first be tried in the lower courts and then can be appealed to the Supreme Court. Congress may, however, make exceptions. Today, the Supreme Court acts as a trial court of first instance on rare occasions.

Clause 3: The Conduct of Trials. The Trial of all Crimes, except in Cases of Impeachment, shall be by Jury; and such Trial shall be held in the State where the said Crimes shall have been committed; but when not committed within any State, the Trial shall be at such Place or Places as the Congress may by Law have directed.

Any person accused of a federal crime is granted the right to a trial by jury in a federal court in that state in which the crime was committed. Trials of impeachment are an exception.

Section 3. *Treason*

Clause 1: The Definition of Treason. Treason against the United States, shall consist only in levying War against them, or, in adhering to their Enemies, giving them Aid and Comfort. No Person shall be convicted of Treason unless on the Testimony of two Witnesses to the same overt Act, or on Confession in open Court.

Treason is the making of war against the United States or giving aid to its enemies.

Clause 2: Punishment. The Congress shall have Power to declare the Punishment of Treason, but no Attainder of Treason shall work Corruption of Blood, or Forfeiture except during the Life of the Person attainted.

Congress has provided that the punishment for treason ranges from a minimum of five years in prison and/or a $10,000 fine to a maximum of death. "No Attainder of Treason shall work Corruption of Blood" prohibits punishment of the traitor's heirs.

ARTICLE IV. *(Relations among the States)*

Section 1. *Full Faith and Credit*

Full Faith and Credit shall be given in each State to the public Acts, Records, and judicial Proceedings of every other State. And the Congress may by general Laws prescribe the Manner in which such Acts, Records and Proceedings shall be proved, and the Effect thereof.

All states are required to respect one another's laws, records, and lawful decisions. There are exceptions, however. A state does not have to enforce another state's criminal code. Nor does it have to recognize another state's grant of a divorce if the person obtaining the divorce did not establish legal residence in the state in which it was given.

Section 2. *Treatment of Citizens*

Clause 1: Privileges and Immunities. The Citizens of each State shall be entitled to all Privileges and Immunities of Citizens in the several States.

A citizen of a state has the same rights and privileges as the citizens of another state in which he or she happens to be.

Clause 2: Extradition. A Person charged in any State with Treason, Felony, or other Crime, who shall flee from Justice, and be found in another State, shall on Demand of the executive Authority of the State from which he fled, be delivered up, to be removed to the State having Jurisdiction of the Crime.

Any person accused of a crime who flees to another state must be returned to the state in which the crime occurred.

Clause 3: Fugitive Slaves. [No Person held to Service or Labour in one State, under the Laws thereof, escaping into another, shall, in Consequence of any Law or Regulation therein, be discharged from such Service or Labour, but shall be delivered up on Claim of the Party to whom such Service or Labour may be due.][11]

This clause was struck down by the Thirteenth Amendment, which abolished slavery in 1865.

Section 3. *Admission of States*

Clause 1: The Process. New States may be admitted by the Congress into this Union; but no new State shall be

---

[11]Repealed by the Thirteenth Amendment.

formed or erected within the Jurisdiction of any other State; nor any State be formed by the Junction of two or more States, or Parts of States, without the Consent of the Legislatures of the States concerned as well as of the Congress.

Only Congress has the power to admit new states to the union. No state may be created by taking territory from an existing state unless the state's legislature so consents.

Clause 2: Public Land. The Congress shall have Power to dispose of and make all needful Rules and Regulations respecting the Territory or other Property belonging to the United States; and nothing in this Constitution shall be so construed as to Prejudice any Claims of the United States, or of any particular State.

The federal government has the exclusive right to administer federal government public lands.

Section 4. *Republican Form of Government*

The United States shall guarantee to every State in this Union a Republican Form of Government, and shall protect each of them against Invasion; and on Application of the Legislature, or of the Executive (when the Legislature cannot be convened) against domestic Violence.

Each state is promised a republican form of government— that is, one in which the people elect their representatives. The federal government is bound to protect states against any attack by foreigners or during times of trouble within a state.

ARTICLE V. *(Methods of Amendment)*

The Congress, whenever two thirds of both Houses shall deem it necessary, shall propose Amendments to this Constitution, or on the Application of the Legislatures of two thirds of the several States, shall call a Convention for proposing Amendments, which, in either Case, shall be valid to all Intents and Purposes, as Part of this Constitution, when ratified by the Legislatures of three fourths of the several States, or by Conventions in three fourths thereof, as the one or the other Mode of Ratification may be proposed by the Congress; Provided that no Amendment which may be made prior to the Year One thousand eight hundred and eight shall in any Manner affect the first and fourth Clauses in the Ninth Section of the First Article; and that no State, without its Consent, shall be deprived of its equal Suffrage in the Senate.

Amendments may be proposed in either of two ways: a two-thirds vote of each chamber (Congress) or at the request of two-thirds of the states. Ratification of amendments may be carried out in two ways: by the legislatures of three-fourths of the states or by the voters in three-fourths of the states. No state may be denied equal representation in the Senate.

ARTICLE VI. *(National Supremacy)*

Clause 1: Existing Obligations. All Debts contracted and Engagements entered into, before the Adoption of this Constitution shall be as valid against the United States under this Constitution, as under the Confederation.

During the Revolutionary War and the years of the Confederation, Congress borrowed large sums. This clause pledged that the new federal government would assume those financial obligations.

Clause 2: Supreme Law of the Land. This Constitution, and the Laws of the United States which shall be made in Pursuance thereof; and all Treaties made, or which shall be made, under the Authority of the United States, shall be the supreme Law of the Land; and the Judges in every State shall be bound thereby, any Thing in the Constitution or Laws of any State to the Contrary notwithstanding.

This is typically called the supremacy clause; it declares that federal law takes precedence over all forms of state law. No government at the local or state level may make or enforce any law that conflicts with any provision of the Constitution, acts of Congress, treaties, or other rules and regulations issued by the president and his or her subordinates in the executive branch of the federal government.

Clause 3: Oath of Office. The Senators and Representatives before mentioned, and the Members of the several State Legislatures, and all executive and judicial Officers, both of the United States and of the several States, shall be bound by Oath or Affirmation, to support this Constitution; but no religious Test shall ever be required as a Qualification to any Office or public Trust under the United States.

Every federal and state official must take an oath of office promising to support the U.S. Constitution. Religion may not be used as a qualification to serve in any federal office.

ARTICLE VII. *(Ratification)*

The Ratification of the Conventions of nine States shall be sufficient for the Establishment of this Constitution between the States so ratifying the Same.

Nine states were required to ratify the Constitution. Delaware was the first and New Hampshire the ninth.

Done in Convention by the Unanimous Consent of the States present the Seventeenth Day of September in the Year of our Lord one thousand seven hundred and Eighty seven and of the Independence of the United States of America the Twelfth. In witness whereof we have hereunto subscribed our Names,

Go. WASHINGTON
Presid't.
and deputy from Virginia

Attest William Jackson Secretary

Delaware	{	Geo. Read Gunning Bedford jun John Dickinson Richard Bassett Jaco. Broom	New Hampshire {	John Langdon Nicholas Gilman
Maryland	{	James McHenry Dan of St. Thos. Jenifer Danl. Carroll	Massachusetts {	Nathaniel Gorham Rufus King
Virginia	{	John Blair James Madison Jr.	Connecticut {	Wm. Saml. Johnson Roger Sherman
North Carolina	{	Wm. Blount Richd. Dobbs Spaight Hu. Williamson	New York {	Alexander Hamilton
South Carolina	{	J. Rutledge Charles Cotesworth Pinckney Charles Pinckney Pierce Butler	New Jersey {	Wh. Livingston David Brearley Wm. Paterson Jona. Dayton
Georgia	{	William Few Abr. Baldwin	Pennsylvania {	B. Franklin Thomas Mifflin Robt. Morris Geo. Clymer Thos. FitzSimons Jared Ingersoll James Wilson Gouv. Morris

AMENDMENTS TO THE CONSTITUTION OF THE UNITED STATES (The Bill of Rights)[12]

Articles in addition to, and amendment of, the Constitution of the United States of America, proposed by Congress and ratified by the Legislatures of the several states, pursuant to the Fifth Article of the original Constitution.

AMENDMENT I. *(Religion, Speech, Assembly, and Petition)*

Congress shall make no law respecting an establishment of religion, or prohibiting the free exercise thereof; or abridging the freedom of speech, or of the press; or the right of the people peaceably to assemble, and to petition the Government for a redress of grievances.

Congress may not create an official church or enact laws limiting the freedom of religion, speech, the press, assembly, and petition. These guarantees, like the others in the Bill of Rights (the first 10 amendments), are not absolute—each may be exercised only with regard to the rights of other persons.

AMENDMENT II. *(Militia and the Right to Bear Arms)*

A well regulated Militia, being necessary to the security of a free State, the right of the people to keep and bear Arms, shall not be infringed.

To protect itself, each state has the right to maintain a volunteer armed force. States and the federal government regulate the possession and use of firearms by individuals.

AMENDMENT III. *(The Quartering of Soldiers)*

No Soldier shall, in time of peace be quartered in any house, without the consent of the Owner, nor in time of war, but in a manner to be prescribed by law.

Before the Revolutionary War, it had been common British practice to quarter soldiers in colonists' homes. Military troops do not have the power to take over private houses during peacetime.

AMENDMENT IV. *(Searches and Seizures)*

The right of the people to be secure in their persons, houses, papers, and effects, against unreasonable searches and seizures, shall not be violated, and no Warrants shall issue, but upon probable cause, supported by Oath or affirmation, and particularly describing the place to be searched, and the persons or things to be seized.

Here the word warrant means "justification" and refers to a document issued by a magistrate or judge indicating the name, address, and possible offense committed. Anyone asking for the warrant, such as a police officer, must be able to convince the magistrate or judge that an offense probably has been committed.

AMENDMENT V. *(Grand Juries, Self-Incrimination, Double Jeopardy, Due Process, and Eminent Domain)*

No person shall be held to answer for a capital, or otherwise infamous crime, unless on a presentment or indictment of a Grand Jury, except in cases arising in the land or naval forces, or in the Militia, when in actual service in time of War or public danger; nor shall any person be subject for the same offence to be twice put in jeopardy of life or limb; nor shall be compelled in any criminal case to be a witness against himself, nor be deprived of life, liberty, or property, without due process of law; nor shall private property be taken for public use, without just compensation.

There are two types of juries. A grand jury considers physical evidence and the testimony of witnesses and decides whether there is sufficient reason to bring a case to trial. A petit jury hears the case at trial and decides it. "For the same offence to be twice put in jeopardy of life or limb" means to be tried twice for the same crime. A person may not be tried for the same crime twice or forced to give evidence against herself or himself. No person's right to life, liberty, or property may be taken away except by lawful means, called the due process of law. Private property taken for use in public purposes must be paid for by the government.

AMENDMENT VI. *(Criminal Court Procedures)*

In all criminal prosecutions, the accused shall enjoy the right to a speedy and public trial, by an impartial jury of the State and district wherein the crime shall have been committed, which district shall have been previously ascertained by law, and to be informed of the nature and cause of the accusation; to be confronted with the witnesses against him; to have compulsory process for obtaining witnesses in his favor, and to have the Assistance of Counsel for his defence.

Any person accused of a crime has the right to a fair and public trial by a jury in the state in which the crime took place. The charges against that person must be indicated. Any accused person has the right to a lawyer to defend him or her and to question those who testify against him or her, as well as the right to call people to speak in his or her favor at trial.

---

[12]On September 25, 1789, Congress transmitted to the state legislatures 12 proposed amendments, two of which, having to do with congressional representation and congressional pay, were not adopted. The remaining 10 amendments became the Bill of Rights. In 1992, the amendment concerning congressional pay was adopted as the Twenty-seventh Amendment.

AMENDMENT VII. *(Trial by Jury in Civil Cases)*

In Suits at common law, where the value in controversy shall exceed twenty dollars, the right of trial by jury shall be preserved, and no fact tried by jury, shall be otherwise re-examined in any Court of the United States, than according to the rules of the common law.

A jury trial may be requested by either party in a dispute in any case involving more than $20. If both parties agree to a trial by a judge without a jury, the right to a jury trial may be put aside.

AMENDMENT VIII. *(Bail, Cruel and Unusual Punishment)*

Excessive bail shall not be required, nor excessive fines imposed, nor cruel and unusual punishments inflicted.

Bail is that amount of money that a person accused of a crime may be required to deposit with the court as a guaranty that she or he will appear in court when requested. The amount of bail required or the fine imposed as punishment for a crime must be reasonable compared with the seriousness of the crime involved. Any punishment judged to be too harsh or too severe for a crime shall be prohibited.

AMENDMENT IX. *(The Rights Retained by the People)*

The enumeration in the Constitution, of certain rights, shall not be construed to deny or disparage others retained by the people.

Many civil rights that are not explicitly enumerated in the Constitution are still held by the people.

AMENDMENT X. *(Reserved Powers of the States)*

The powers not delegated to the United States by the Constitution, nor prohibited by it to the States, are reserved to the States respectively, or to the people.

Those powers not delegated by the Constitution to the federal government or expressly denied to the states belong to the states and to the people. This amendment in essence allows the states to pass laws under their "police powers."

AMENDMENT XI. *(Ratified on February 7, 1795— Suits against States)*

The Judicial power of the United States shall not be construed to extend to any suit in law or equity, commenced or prosecuted against one of the United States by Citizens of another State, or by Citizens or Subjects of any Foreign State.

This amendment has been interpreted to mean that a state cannot be sued in federal court by one of its own citizens, by a citizen of another state, or by a foreign country.

AMENDMENT XII. *(Ratified on June 15, 1804— Election of the President)*

The Electors shall meet in their respective states, and vote by ballot for President and Vice-President, one of whom, at least, shall not be an inhabitant of the same State with themselves; they shall name in their ballots the person voted for as President, and in distinct ballots the person voted for as Vice-President, and they shall make distinct lists of all persons voted for as President, and of all persons voted for as Vice-President, and of the number of votes for each, which lists they shall sign and certify, and transmit sealed to the seat of the government of the United States, directed to the President of the Senate;—The President of the Senate shall, in the presence of the Senate and House of Representatives, open all the certificates and the votes shall then be counted;— The person having the greatest number of votes for President, shall be the President, if such number be a majority of the whole number of Electors appointed; and if no person have such majority, then from the persons having the highest numbers not exceeding three on the list of those voted for as President, the House of Representatives shall choose immediately, by ballot, the President. But in choosing the President, the votes shall be taken by States, the representation from each State having one vote; a quorum for this purpose shall consist of a member or members from two-thirds of the States, and a majority of all States shall be necessary to a choice. [And if the House of Representatives shall not choose a President whenever the right of choice shall devolve upon them, before the fourth day of March next following, then the Vice-President shall act as President, as in the case of the death or other constitutional disability of the President.][13]—The person having the greatest number of votes as Vice-President, shall be the Vice-President, if such number be a majority of the whole number of Electors appointed, and if no person have a majority, then from the two highest numbers on the list, the Senate shall choose the Vice-President; a quorum for the purpose shall consist of two-thirds of the whole number of Senators, and a majority of the whole number shall be necessary to a choice. But no person constitutionally ineligible to the office of President shall be eligible to that of Vice-President of the United States.

The original procedure set out for the election of president and vice president in Article II, Section 1, resulted in a tie in 1800 between Thomas Jefferson and Aaron Burr. It was not until the next year that the House of Representatives chose Jefferson to be president. This amendment changed the procedure by providing for separate ballots for president and vice president.

---

[13]Changed by the Twentieth Amendment.

AMENDMENT XIII. *(Ratified on December 6, 1865—Prohibition of Slavery)*

Section 1.

Neither slavery nor involuntary servitude, except as a punishment for crime whereof the party shall have been duly convicted, shall exist within the United States, or any place subject to their jurisdiction.

Some slaves had been freed during the Civil War. This amendment freed the others and abolished slavery.

Section 2.

Congress shall have power to enforce this article by appropriate legislation.

AMENDMENT XIV. *(Ratified on July 9, 1868—Citizenship, Due Process, and Equal Protection of the Laws)*

Section 1.

All persons born or naturalized in the United States, and subject to the jurisdiction thereof, are citizens of the United States and of the State wherein they reside. No State shall make or enforce any law which shall abridge the privileges or immunities of citizens of the United States; nor shall any State deprive any person of life, liberty, or property, without due process of law; nor deny to any person within its jurisdiction the equal protection of the laws.

Under this provision, states cannot make or enforce laws that take away rights given to all citizens by the federal government. States cannot act unfairly or arbitrarily toward, or discriminate against, any person.

Section 2.

Representatives shall be apportioned among the several States according to their respective numbers, counting the whole number of persons in each State, excluding Indians not taxed. But when the right to vote at any election for the choice of electors for President and Vice President of the United States, Representatives in Congress, the Executive and Judicial officers of a State, or the members of the Legislature thereof, is denied to any of the male inhabitants of such State, being [twenty-one][14] years of age, and citizens of the United States, or in any way abridged, except for participation in rebellion, or other crime, the basis of representation therein shall be reduced in the proportion which the number of such male citizens shall bear to the whole number of male citizens twenty-one years of age in such State.

Section 3.

No person shall be a Senator or Representative in Congress, or elector of President and Vice President, or hold any office, civil or military, under the United States, or under any State, who having previously taken an oath, as a member of Congress, or as an officer of the United States, or as a member of any State legislature, or as an executive or judicial officer of any State, to support the Constitution of the United States, shall have engaged in insurrection or rebellion against the same, or given aid or comfort to the enemies thereof. But Congress may by a vote of two-thirds of each House, remove such disability.

This provision forbade former state or federal government officials who had acted in support of the Confederacy during the Civil War to hold office again. It limited the president's power to pardon those persons. Congress removed this "disability" in 1898.

Section 4.

The validity of the public debt of the United States, authorized by law, including debts incurred for payment of pensions and bounties for services in suppressing insurrection or rebellion, shall not be questioned. But neither the United States nor any State shall assume or pay any debt or obligation incurred in aid of insurrection or rebellion against the United States, or any claim for the loss or emancipation of any slave, but all such debts, obligations and claims shall be held illegal and void.

Section 5.

The Congress shall have power to enforce, by appropriate legislation, the provisions of this article.

AMENDMENT XV. *(Ratified on February 3, 1870—The Right to Vote)*

Section 1.

The right of citizens of the United States to vote shall not be denied or abridged by the United States or by any State on account of race, color, or previous condition of servitude.

No citizen can be refused the right to vote simply because of race or color or because that person was once a slave.

Section 2.

The Congress shall have power to enforce this article by appropriate legislation.

AMENDMENT XVI. *(Ratified on February 3, 1913—Income Taxes)*

The Congress shall have power to lay and collect taxes on incomes, from whatever source derived, without apportionment among the several States, and without regard to any census or enumeration.

This amendment allows Congress to tax income without sharing the revenue so obtained with the states according to their population.

AMENDMENT XVII. *(Ratified on April 8, 1913—The Popular Election of Senators)*

Section 1.

The Senate of the United States shall be composed of two Senators from each State, elected by the people thereof,

---

[14]Changed by the Twenty-sixth Amendment.

for six years; and each Senator shall have one vote. The electors in each State shall have the qualifications requisite for electors of the most numerous branch of the State legislatures.

Section 2.

When vacancies happen in the representation of any State in the Senate, the executive authority of such State shall issue writs of election to fill such vacancies: *Provided,* That the legislature of any State may empower the executive thereof to make temporary appointments until the people fill the vacancies by election as the legislature may direct.

Section 3.

This amendment shall not be so construed as to affect the election or term of any Senator chosen before it becomes valid as part of the Constitution.

This amendment modified portions of Article I, Section 3, that related to election of senators. Senators are now elected by the voters in each state directly. When a vacancy occurs, either the state may fill the vacancy by a special election, or the governor of the state involved may appoint someone to fill the seat until the next election.

AMENDMENT XVIII. *(Ratified on January 16, 1919—Prohibition)*

Section 1.

After one year from the ratification of this article the manufacture, sale, or transportation of intoxicating liquors within, the importation thereof into, or the exportation thereof from the United States and all territory subject to the jurisdiction thereof for beverage purposes is hereby prohibited.

Section 2.

The Congress and the several States shall have concurrent power to enforce this article by appropriate legislation.

Section 3.

This article shall be inoperative unless it shall have been ratified as an amendment to the Constitution by the legislatures of the several States, as provided in the Constitution, within seven years from the date of the submission hereof to the States by the Congress.[15]

This amendment made it illegal to manufacture, sell, and transport alcoholic beverages in the United States. It was repealed by the Twenty-first Amendment.

AMENDMENT XIX. *(Ratified on August 18, 1920—Women's Right to Vote)*

Section 1.

The right of citizens of the United States to vote shall not be denied or abridged by the United States or by any State on account of sex.

Section 2.

Congress shall have power to enforce this article by appropriate legislation.

Women were given the right to vote by this amendment, and Congress was given the power to enforce this right.

AMENDMENT XX. *(Ratified on January 23, 1933—The Lame Duck Amendment)*

Section 1.

The terms of the President and Vice President shall end at noon on the 20th day of January, and the terms of Senators and Representatives at noon on the 3d day of January, of the years in which such terms would have ended if this article had not been ratified; and the terms of their successors shall then begin.

This amendment modified Article I, Section 4, Clause 2, and other provisions relating to the president in the Twelfth Amendment. The taking of the oath of office was moved from March 4 to January 20.

Section 2.

The Congress shall assemble at least once in every year, and such meeting shall begin at noon on the 3rd day of January, unless they shall by law appoint a different day.

Congress changed the beginning of its term to January 3. The reason the Twentieth Amendment is called the Lame Duck Amendment is that it shortens the time between when a member of Congress is defeated for re-election and when he or she leaves office.

Section 3.

If, at the time fixed for the beginning of the term of the President, the President elect shall have died, the Vice President elect shall become President. If a President shall not have been chosen before the time fixed for the beginning of his term, or if the President elect shall have failed to qualify, then the Vice President elect shall act as President until a President shall have qualified; and the Congress may by law provide for the case wherein neither a President elect nor a Vice President elect shall have qualified, declaring who shall then act as President, or the manner in which one who is to act shall be selected, and such person shall act accordingly until a President or Vice President shall have qualified.

This part of the amendment deals with problem areas left ambiguous by Article II and the Twelfth Amendment. If the president dies before January 20 or fails to qualify for office, the presidency is to be filled as described in this section.

---

[15]The Eighteenth Amendment was repealed by the Twenty-first Amendment.

Section 4.

The Congress may by law provide for the case of the death of any of the persons from whom the House of Representatives may choose a President whenever the rights of choice shall have devolved upon them, and for the case of the death of any of the persons from whom the Senate may choose a Vice President whenever the right of choice shall have devolved upon them.

Congress has never created legislation pursuant to this section.

Section 5.

Sections 1 and 2 shall take effect on the 15th day of October following the ratification of this article.

Section 6.

This article shall be inoperative unless it shall have been ratified as an amendment to the Constitution by the legislatures of three-fourths of the several States within seven years from the date of its submission.

AMENDMENT XXI. *(Ratified on December 5, 1933—The Repeal of Prohibition)*

Section 1.

The eighteenth article of amendment to the Constitution of the United States is hereby repealed.

Section 2.

The transportation or importation into any State, Territory, or possession of the United States for delivery or use therein of intoxicating liquors, in violation of the laws thereof, is hereby prohibited.

Section 3.

This article shall be inoperative unless it shall have been ratified as an amendment to the Constitution by conventions in the several States, as provided in the Constitution, within seven years from the date of the submission hereof to the States by the Congress.

The amendment repealed the Eighteenth Amendment but did not make alcoholic beverages legal everywhere. Rather, they remained illegal in any state that so designated them. Many such "dry" states existed for a number of years after 1933. Today, there are still "dry" counties within the United States, in which the sale of alcoholic beverages is illegal.

AMENDMENT XXII. *(Ratified on February 27, 1951—Limitation of Presidential Terms)*

Section 1.

No person shall be elected to the office of the President more than twice, and no person who has held the office of President, or acted as President, for more than two years of a term to which some other person was elected President shall be elected to the office of President more than once. But this Article shall not apply to any person holding the office of President when this Article was proposed by the Congress, and shall not prevent any person who may be holding the office of President, or acting as President, during the term within which this Article becomes operative from holding the office of President or acting as President during the remainder of such term.

Section 2.

This article shall be inoperative unless it shall have been ratified as an amendment to the Constitution by the legislatures of three-fourths of the several States within seven years from the date of its submission to the States by the Congress.

No president may serve more than two elected terms. If, however, a president has succeeded to the office after the halfway point of a term in which another president was originally elected, then that president may serve for more than eight years, but not to exceed 10 years.

AMENDMENT XXIII. *(Ratified on March 29, 1961—Presidential Electors for the District of Columbia)*

Section 1.

The District constituting the seat of Government of the United States shall appoint in such manner as the Congress may direct:

A number of electors of President and Vice President equal to the whole number of Senators and Representatives in Congress to which the District would be entitled if it were a State, but in no event more than the least populous State; they shall be in addition to those appointed by the States, but they shall be considered, for the purposes of the election of President and Vice President, to be electors appointed by a State; and they shall meet in the District and perform such duties as provided by the twelfth article of amendment.

Section 2.

The Congress shall have power to enforce this article by appropriate legislation.

Citizens living in the District of Columbia have the right to vote in elections for president and vice president. The District of Columbia has three presidential electors, whereas before this amendment it had none.

AMENDMENT XXIV. *(Ratified on January 23, 1964—The Anti–Poll Tax Amendment)*

Section 1.

The right of citizens of the United States to vote in any primary or other election for President or Vice President, for electors for President or Vice President, or for Senator or Representative in Congress, shall not be denied or abridged by the United States, or any State by reason of failure to pay any poll tax or other tax.

Section 2.

The Congress shall have power to enforce this article by appropriate legislation.

No government shall require a person to pay a poll tax to vote in any federal election.

AMENDMENT XXV. *(Ratified on February 10, 1967—Presidential Disability and Vice Presidential Vacancies)*

Section 1.

In case of the removal of the President from office or of his death or resignation, the Vice President shall become President.

Whenever a president dies or resigns from office, the vice president becomes president.

Section 2.

Whenever there is a vacancy in the office of the Vice President, the President shall nominate a Vice President who shall take office upon confirmation by a majority vote of both Houses of Congress.

Whenever the office of the vice presidency becomes vacant, the president may appoint someone to fill this office, provided Congress consents.

Section 3.

Whenever the President transmits to the President pro tempore of the Senate and the Speaker of the House of Representatives his written declaration that he is unable to discharge the powers and duties of his office, and until he transmits to them a written declaration to the contrary, such powers and duties shall be discharged by the Vice President as Acting President.

Whenever the president believes she or he is unable to carry out the duties of the office, she or he shall so indicate to Congress in writing. The vice president then acts as president until the president declares that she or he is again able to carry out the duties of the office.

Section 4.

Whenever the Vice President and a majority of either the principal officers of the executive departments or of such other body as Congress may by law provide, transmit to the President pro tempore of the Senate and the Speaker of the House of Representatives their written declaration that the President is unable to discharge the powers and duties of his office, the Vice President shall immediately assume the powers and duties of the office as Acting President.

Thereafter, when the President transmits to the President pro tempore of the Senate and the Speaker of the House

of Representatives his written declaration that no inability exists, he shall resume the powers and duties of his office unless the Vice President and a majority of either the principal officers of the executive department or of such other body as Congress may by law provide, transmit within four days to the President pro tempore of the Senate and the Speaker of the House of Representatives their written declaration that the President is unable to discharge the powers and duties of his office. Thereupon Congress shall decide the issue, assembling within forty-eight hours for that purpose if not in session. If the Congress, within twenty-one days after receipt of the latter written declaration, or, if Congress is not in session, within twenty-one days after Congress is required to assemble, determines by two-thirds vote of both Houses that the President is unable to discharge the powers and duties of his office, the Vice President shall continue to discharge the same as Acting President; otherwise, the President shall resume the powers and duties of his office.

Whenever the vice president and a majority of the members of the Cabinet believe that the president cannot carry out her or his duties, they shall so indicate in writing to Congress. The vice president shall then act as president. When the president believes that she or he is able to carry out her or his duties again, she or he shall so indicate to the Congress. However, if the vice president and a majority of the Cabinet do not agree, Congress must decide by a two-thirds vote within three weeks who shall act as president.

AMENDMENT XXVI. *(Ratified on July 1, 1971—The 18-Year-Old Vote)*

Section 1.

The right of citizens of the United States, who are eighteen years of age or older, to vote shall not be denied or abridged by the United States or by any State on account of age.

No one 18 years of age or older can be denied the right to vote in federal or state elections by virtue of age.

Section 2.

The Congress shall have power to enforce this article by appropriate legislation.

AMENDMENT XXVII. *(Ratified on May 7, 1992—Congressional Pay)*

No law, varying the compensation for the services of the Senators and Representatives, shall take effect, until an election of representatives shall have intervened.

This amendment allows the voters to have some control over increases in salaries for congressional members. Originally submitted to the states for ratification in 1789, it was not ratified until 203 years later, in 1992.

3

President Barack Obama and Vice
President Joe Biden meet with a
bipartisan group of governors to
discuss energy policy. From left are
Alabama governor Bob Riley, West
Virginia governor Joe Manchin, the
vice president and president, Vermont
Governor Jim Douglas, Washington
governor Christine Gregoire, and South
Dakota governor Mike Rounds.
(AP Photo/Charles Dharapak)

Federalism

QUESTIONS TO CONSIDER

Why did the founders think it important to divide power between the national government and the states?

Is a federal system effective in addressing the problems of the 21st century?

How does the federal government achieve national goals in a federal system?

what if...

One State's Same-Sex Marriages Had To Be Recognized Nationwide?

BACKGROUND

The full faith and credit clause of the Constitution certainly requires states to recognize that a couple married in California is also married when they move to Nebraska. But what if one state recognizes same-sex marriages? Does that mean that all other states must recognize such marriages and give each partner the benefits accorded to partners in opposite-sex marriages?

Traditionally, all matters involving marriage, divorce, and the custody of children have been handled through state laws. However, the Supreme Court has overturned laws that forbid marriages between persons of separate races (*Loving v. Virginia,* 1967) and laws that regulate sexual conduct between consenting adults in the privacy of their own dwelling (*Lawrence v. Texas,* 2003). So, all matters of marriage have not been sacrosanct in modern times.

The issue of gay marriage is one that has arisen in the last few decades: gay and lesbian couples are faced with many legal hurdles when it comes to health benefits, care for an ill partner, fostering or adoption of children, and disposition of an estate. The right to adopt children was granted to married couples or single individuals in many states but not to gay couples. The right to visit a seriously ill person is reserved to relatives by blood or marriage.

A few jurisdictions in the United States began to respond to the needs of gay and lesbian couples by passing legislation that allows gay marriage or legally recognized civil unions. Under the Constitution, must those marriage contracts be recognized in all other states?

FEDERAL LAW INTERVENES

In 1996, Congress attempted to prevent such a result through the Defense of Marriage Act, which allows state governments to ignore same-sex marriages performed in other states. But what would happen if the United States Supreme Court ruled that the Defense of Marriage Act is unconstitutional? If this happened, then all of the state laws that refuse to recognize same-sex marriages performed in another state would be unconstitutional as well, because the U.S. Constitution is the supreme law of the land. State inheritance laws, insurance laws, and adoption laws would need to be changed to accommodate same-sex couples.

What about federal benefits? The national government has traditionally left marriage to the states. In the past, the Internal Revenue Service, the Social Security Administration, and other federal agencies recognized marriages when, and only when, the states recognized them. With the Defense of Marriage Act, the national government established its own definition of marriage for the first time. Under the act, no matter what the states do, federal agencies cannot recognize same-sex marriages. If the Defense of Marriage Act were declared unconstitutional, however, the federal government might again have to accept all state-defined marriages, and a same-sex marriage in a state that allowed such unions would entitle the couple to federal benefits, including spousal benefits under Social Security.

WHAT MUST HAPPEN TO CHANGE THE LAW

Two things must happen for nationwide recognition of same-sex marriages. One is that the Defense of Marriage Act be ruled unconstitutional. It is open to question whether the Supreme Court would actually issue such a ruling. The other requirement, however—legalization of same-sex marriage by one or more states—is in place already. In November 2003, the Massachusetts Supreme Judicial Court ruled that same-sex couples have a right to civil marriage under the Massachusetts state constitution. In 2008, the California Supreme Court overturned a law banning same-sex marriages, and ceremonies to wed couples began in June of that year. However, a referendum to amend California's constitution to outlaw same-sex marriages was on the ballot in November 2008. Voters approved the proposition to ban same-sex marriage by a vote of 52 percent to 48 percent.

By 2010, six states and the District of Columbia had approved the issuing of marriage licenses to same-sex couples, and two additional states will recognize same-sex marriages from other states as legal.

FOR CRITICAL ANALYSIS

1. If marriage is a contract between two individuals, should it be recognized in the same way as other contracts under the full faith and credit clause?
2. Why do you think that a state might adopt different marriage laws from those in other states? Can you think of an example?
3. Would a national recognition of civil unions reduce the controversies over same-sex marriages?

THE UNITED STATES IS, as the name implies, a union of states. Unlike in many other nations, the national government does not have all of the authority in the system; rights and powers are reserved to the states by the Tenth Amendment. But the situation is even more complicated than having just state governments and the national government: there are almost 89,000 separate governmental units in this nation, as you can see in Table 3–1.

Visitors from France or Spain are often awestruck by the complexity of our system of government. Consider that a criminal action can be defined by state law, national law, or both. Thus, a criminal suspect can be prosecuted in the state court system or in the federal court system (or both). Think about such a simple matter as getting a driver's license. Each state has separate requirements for the driving test, the written test, the number of years between renewals, and the cost for the license. In 2005, Congress passed the REAL ID Act requiring states to include a specified set of information on the license so that it can be used as an identity card for travel, but the act was opposed by several states that insisted on maintaining their own requirements. If the licenses issued by those states do not meet the new requirements by 2011, the IDs will not be accepted at airports for travel.

Relations between central governments and local units are structured in various ways. *Federalism* is one of these ways. Understanding **federalism** and how it differs from other forms of government is important in understanding the American political system. The impact of policies on the individual would be substantially different if we did not have a federal form of government in which governmental authority is divided between the central government and various subunits.

Federalism
A system of government in which power is divided by a written constitution between a central government and regional or subdivisional governments. Each level must have some domain in which its policies are dominant and some genuine constitutional guarantee of its authority.

THREE SYSTEMS OF GOVERNMENT

There are more than 200 independent nations in the world today. Each of these nations has its own system of government. Generally, though, we can describe how nations structure relations between central governments and local units in terms of three

TABLE 3–1 Governmental Units in the United States

With almost 89,000 separate governmental units in the United States today, it is no wonder that intergovernmental relations in this country are so complicated. Actually, the number of school districts has decreased over time, but the number of special districts created for single purposes, such as flood control, has increased from only about 8,000 during World War II to more than 36,000 today.

Federal government	1
State governments	50
Local governments	88,525
Counties	3,034
Municipalities (mainly cities or towns)	19,429
Townships (less extensive powers)	16,504
Special districts (water, sewer, and so on)	36,052
School districts	13,506
TOTAL	88,576

Source: U.S. Census Bureau.

models: (1) the unitary system, (2) the confederal system, and (3) the federal system. The most popular, both historically and today, is the unitary system.

A UNITARY SYSTEM

Unitary System
A centralized governmental system in which local or subdivisional governments exercise only those powers given to them by the central government.

A **unitary system** of government is the easiest to define. Unitary systems allow ultimate governmental authority to rest in the hands of the national, or central, government. Consider a typical unitary system—France. There are regions, departments, and municipalities (communes) in France. The regions, departments, and communes have elected and appointed officials. So far, the French system appears to be very similar to the U.S. system, but the similarity is only superficial. Under the unitary French system, the decisions of the lower levels of government can be overruled by the national government. The national government can also cut off the funding of many local government activities. Moreover, in a unitary system such as that in France, all questions of education, police, the use of land, and welfare are handled by the national government. Britain, Egypt, Ghana, Israel, Japan, the Philippines, and Sweden—in fact, the majority of countries today—have unitary systems of government.[1]

A CONFEDERAL SYSTEM

Confederal System
A system consisting of a league of independent states, each having essentially sovereign powers. The central government created by such a league has only limited powers over the states.

You were introduced to the elements of a **confederal system** of government in Chapter 2, when we examined the Articles of Confederation. A *confederation* is the opposite of a unitary governing system. It is a league of independent states in which a central government or administration handles only those matters of common concern expressly delegated to it by the member states. The central government has no ability to make laws directly applicable to member states unless the members explicitly support such laws. The United States under the Articles of Confederation was a confederal system.

Few, if any, confederations of this kind exist. One possible exception is the European Union, a league of countries that is developing unifying institutions, such as a common currency. Nations have also formed organizations with one another for limited purposes, such as military or peacekeeping cooperation. Examples are the North Atlantic Treaty Organization (NATO) and the United Nations. These organizations, however, are not true confederations.

DID YOU KNOW?

That in Florida, Michigan, Mississippi, North Carolina, North Dakota, Virginia, and West Virginia, male-female unmarried cohabitation is against the law and punishable by a short jail term, a fine of up to $500, or both?

A FEDERAL SYSTEM

The federal system lies between the unitary and confederal forms of government. As mentioned in Chapter 2, in a *federal system*, authority is divided, usually by a written constitution, between a central government and regional, or subdivisional, governments (often called *constituent governments*). The central government and the constituent governments both act directly on the people through laws and through the actions of elected and appointed governmental officials. Within each government's sphere of authority, each is supreme, in theory. Thus, a federal system differs sharply from a unitary one, in which the central government is supreme and the constituent governments derive their authority from it. Australia, Brazil, Canada, Germany, India, and Mexico are other examples of nations with federal systems. (See Figure 3–1 for a comparison of the three systems.)

---

[1]Recent legislation has altered somewhat the unitary character of the French political system. In Britain, the unitary nature of the government has been modified by the creation of the Scottish Parliament.

WHY FEDERALISM?

Why did the United States develop in a federal direction? We look here at that question, as well as at some of the arguments for and against a federal form of government. Remember that the delegates at the Constitutional Convention were often divided over how much power the national government would have over their respective states.

A PRACTICAL CONSTITUTIONAL SOLUTION

As you saw in Chapter 2, the historical basis of our federal system was laid down in Philadelphia at the Constitutional Convention, where advocates of a strong national government opposed states' rights advocates. This dichotomy continued through to the ratifying conventions in the several states. The resulting federal system was a compromise.[2] The supporters of the new Constitution were political pragmatists—they realized that without a federal arrangement, the new Constitution would not be ratified. The appeal of federalism was that it retained state traditions and local power while establishing a strong national government capable of handling common problems.

Even if the colonial leaders had agreed on the desirability of a unitary system, size and regional isolation would have made such a system difficult operationally. At the time of the Constitutional Convention, the 13 colonies taken together were much larger geographically than England or France. Slow travel and communication, combined with geographic spread, contributed to the isolation of many regions within the colonies. It could take several weeks for all of the colonies to be informed about a particular political decision.

Given the size of the United States, even in the 18th century, a federal form of government that allows many functions to be delegated by the central government to the states or provinces makes sense. The lower levels of government that accept these responsibilities thereby can become the focus of political dissatisfaction rather than the national authorities. Second, even with modern transportation and communications systems, the large area or population of some nations makes it impractical to locate all political authority in one place. Finally, federalism brings government closer to the people. It allows more direct access to, and influence on, government agencies and policies, rather than leaving the population restive and dissatisfied with a remote, faceless, all-powerful central authority.

Benefits for the United States. In the United States, federalism historically has yielded many benefits. State governments long have been a training ground for future national leaders. Many presidents made their political mark as state governors. The states have been testing grounds for new government initiatives. As United States Supreme Court Justice Louis Brandeis once observed: "It is one of the happy incidents of the federal system that a single courageous state may, if its citizens choose, serve as a laboratory and try novel social and economic experiments without risk to the rest of the country."[3]

Examples of programs pioneered at the state level include unemployment compensation, which began in Wisconsin, and air pollution control, which was initiated in California. Statewide health care plans have been pioneered in Hawaii and Massachusetts. Today, states are experimenting with policies ranging from education reforms to environmental policies to homeland security defense strategies. Indeed,

DID YOU KNOW?

That under Article I, Section 10, of the Constitution, no state is allowed to enter into any treaty, alliance, or confederation?

---

[2] For a contemporary interpretation of this compromise and how the division of power between the national government and the states has changed, see Edward A. Purcell, *Originalism, Federalism and the American Constitutional Enterprise: A Historical Inquiry* (New Haven, CT: Yale University Press, 2007).
[3] *New State Ice Co. v. Liebmann*, 285 U.S. 262 (1932).

FIGURE 3–1 The Flow of Power in Three Systems of Government

In a unitary system, power flows from the central government to the local and state governments. In a confederal system, power flows in the opposite direction—from the state governments to the central government. In a federal system, the flow of power, in principle, goes both ways.

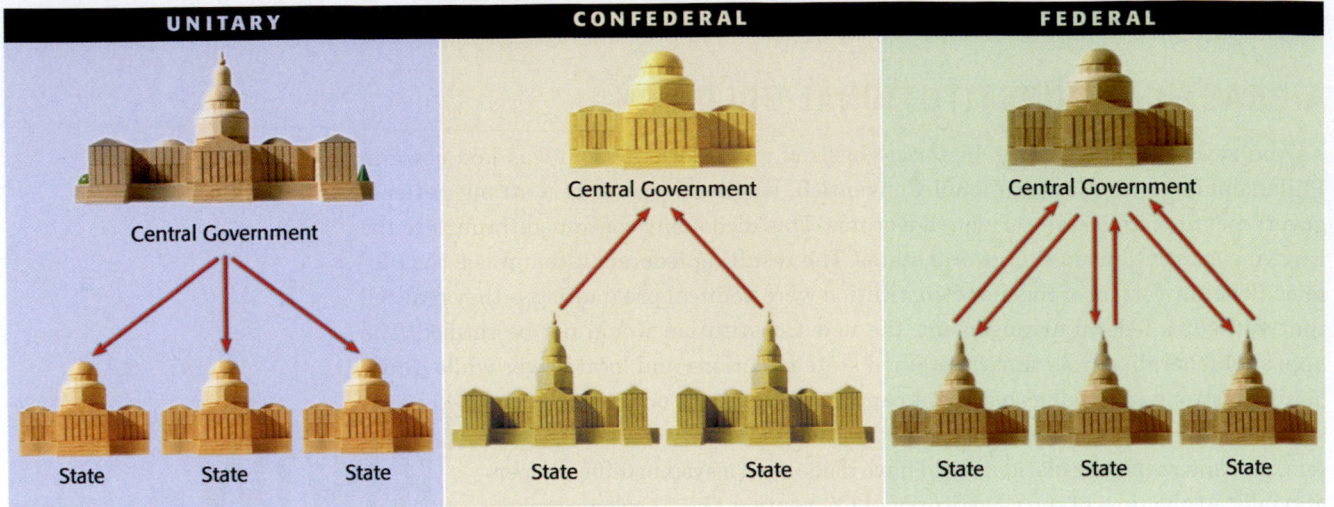

states have widely different schemes for financing government. As shown in Figure 3–2, seven states do not have an income tax, which makes them a magnet for retirees.

Allowance for Many Political Subcultures. The American way of life always has been characterized by many political subcultures, which divide along the lines of race and ethnic origin, region, wealth, education, and, more recently, degree of religious fundamentalism and sexual orientation. At the time of the writing of the Constitution, the diversity of the 13 "states" was seen as an obstacle to the survival of the nation. How could the large, rural, slaveholding states ever coexist with states where slavery was illegal? What would prevent a coalition of the larger states from imposing unfair laws on smaller states and minority groups? In *Federalist Paper* No. 51 (see Appendix B), Madison argued that adopting a federal system would protect the people from the absolute power of the national government and the will of an unjust majority. He put it this way:

> In the compound republic of America, the power surrendered by the people is first divided between two distinct governments, and then the portion allotted to each subdivide among distinct and separate departments. Hence a double security arises to the rights of the people. The different governments will control each other, at the same time that each will be controlled by itself.

Had the United States developed into a unitary system, various political subcultures certainly would have been less able to influence government behavior than they have been, and continue to, in our federal system.

Political scientist Daniel Elazar has claimed that one of federalism's greatest virtues is that it encourages the development of distinct political subcultures. These political subcultures reflect differing needs and desires for government, which vary from region to region. Federalism, he argues, allows for "a unique combination of governmental strength, political flexibility, and individual liberty."[4] The existence of political

[4]Daniel Elazar, *American Federalism: A View from the States,* 2nd ed. (New York: Crowell, 1972).

FIGURE 3–2 States with No State Income Tax

States with no income tax are shown in green, and states that tax only dividends and interest but not income are shown in yellow.

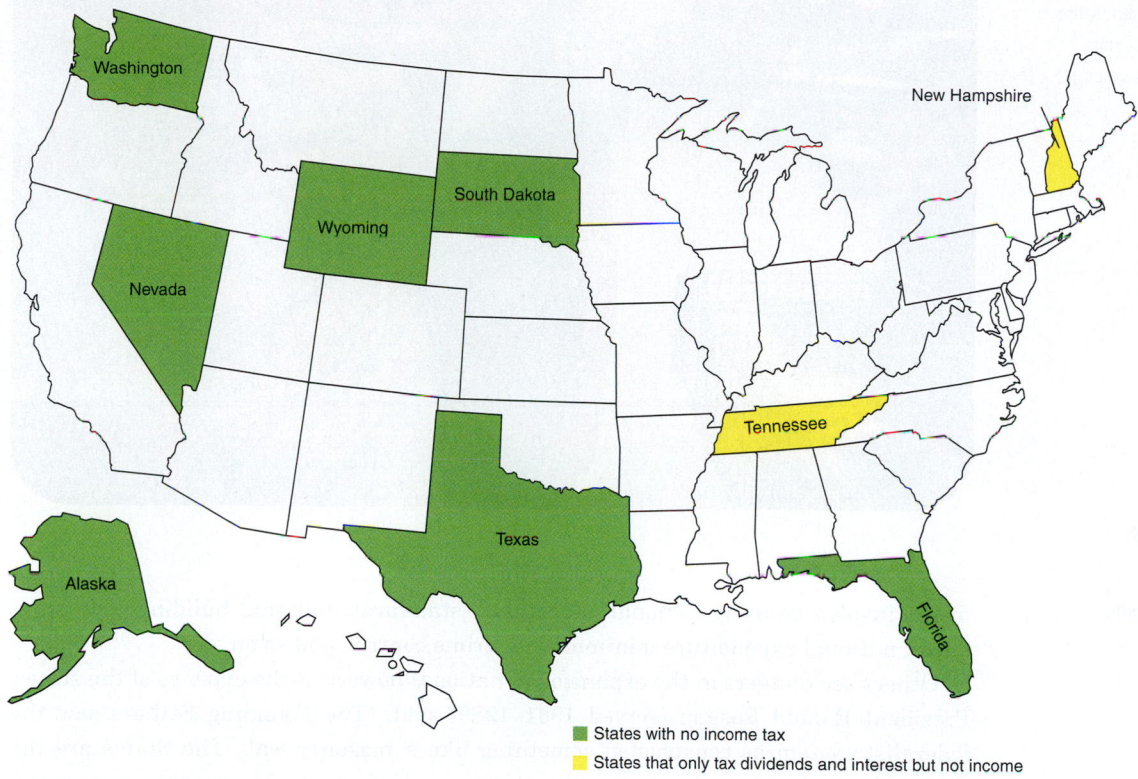

■ States with no income tax
■ States that only tax dividends and interest but not income

subcultures allows a wider variety of factions to influence government. As a result, political subcultures have proved instrumental in driving reform even at the national level, as shown by the differing state approaches to such issues as gay marriage and handgun laws. Handgun regulation runs the gamut from forbidding the ownership of such guns in the city of Chicago to allowing the open carrying of weapons in the state of Virginia.

ARGUMENTS AGAINST FEDERALISM

Not everyone thinks federalism is such a good idea. Some see it as a way for powerful state and local interests to block progress and impede national plans. Smaller political units are more likely to be dominated by a single political group, and the dominant groups in some cities and states have resisted implementing equal rights for minority groups. (This was essentially the argument that James Madison put forth in *Federalist Paper* No. 10, which you can read in Appendix B of this text.) Some argue, however, that the dominant factions in other states have been more progressive than the national government in many areas, such as the environment.

Critics of federalism also argue that too many Americans suffer as a result of the inequalities across the states. Individual states differ markedly in educational spending and achievement, crime and crime prevention, and even the safety of their buildings. Not surprisingly, these critics argue for increased federal legislation and oversight. This

A CALIFORNIA WOMAN carries her handgun into Riley's grocery in the city of Brentwood. Her right to do so is granted by the open carry law in that state. (I58/ZUMA Press/Newscom)

NEW JERSEY GOVERNOR Chris Christie signs the state's 2010 budget into law. Christie won on a platform to cut government spending, and the budget was a part of his strategy. (AP Photo/Mel Evans)

might involve creating national educational standards, national building code standards, national expenditure minimums for crime control, and so on.

Others see dangers in the expansion of national powers at the expense of the states. President Ronald Reagan (served 1981–1989) said, "The Founding Fathers saw the federalist system as constructed something like a masonry wall. The States are the bricks, the national government is the mortar. . . . Unfortunately, over the years, many people have increasingly come to believe that Washington is the whole wall."[5]

THE CONSTITUTIONAL BASIS FOR AMERICAN FEDERALISM

The term *federal system* cannot be found in the U.S. Constitution. Nor is it possible to find a systematic division of governmental authority between the national and state governments in that document. Rather, the Constitution sets out different types of powers. These powers can be classified as (1) the powers of the national government, (2) the powers of the states, and (3) prohibited powers. The Constitution also makes it clear that if a state or local law conflicts with a national law, the national law will prevail.

[5]Text of the address by the president to the National Conference of State Legislatures, Atlanta, Georgia (Washington, DC: The White House, Office of the Press Secretary, July 30, 1981), as quoted in Edward Millican, *One United People: The Federalist Papers and the National Idea* (Lexington: The University Press of Kentucky, 1990).

POLITICS WITH A purpose

LEARNING FROM EACH OTHER

Have you ever moved to a new city or town? It's a challenge to locate the goods and services you need. How do you activate your utilities or enroll yourself or your children in school? If you attend school out of state, you may wonder if you are eligible to vote and, if you are, how do you register? Or, if you wish to vote by absentee ballot in your hometown, how do you get one? Federalism is responsible for many of the differences in the answers to these questions and countless others that exist across cities and states.

The nature of power held by national, state, and local governments has changed over time. State governments, rather than the federal government, increasingly have been asked to solve the problems of their citizens' education, health care, clean air, and safe streets, to name a few. How do states accomplish these tasks? Do they decide independently, or can they work cooperatively to learn from each other how best to solve policy problems?

One way states can cope with these challenges is through associations and organizations designed to share policy ideas and provide members with support. For example, the State Legislative Leaders Foundation hosts educational programs for key state legislators so that leaders can learn from experts and each other. Other examples are mayors' groups (the United States Conference of Mayors; the National Conference of Democratic Mayors; the

Republican Mayors and Local Officials organization), governors' associations (National Governors Association), and groups for state government officials (Council of State Governments).[a] These organizations provide networking opportunities for state and local officials to learn from each other.[b] In addition, these groups provide information on how students can get involved with state government and become part of the policy innovation process. Legislative internships are available in all states[c] and many states also sponsor intercollegiate minilegislatures that recommend policy initiatives to the legislature itself.

This sharing of experiences has led to *policy innovation and diffusion.*[d] *Policy entrepreneurs* find new solutions to problems. States and localities adopt these policies, adapt them to their needs, and share information and ideas.[e] This diffusion of public policy occurs in areas as diverse as health care, accessibility issues for the disabled, education, and resource management, just to name a few.

[a] http://usmayors.org, www.ncdm.org, www.nga.org, www.csg.org
[b] For example, see Jill Clark and Thomas H. Little, "National Organizations as Sources of Information for State Legislative Leaders," *State and Local Government Review*, Volume 34 (1), Winter 2002, pp. 38–45; and T. Heikkila and A. Gerlak, "The Formation of Large-scale Collaborative Resource Management Institutions: Clarifying the Roles of Stakeholders, Science, and Institutions," *Policy Studies Journal*, Volume 33 (4), pp. 583–612.
[c] For information on state internships, go to National Council of State Legislatures and search for internships at http://www.ncsl.org.
[d] For example, see John W. Kingdon, *Agenda, Alternative, and Public Policies* (Boston: Little, Brown, and Co., 1984); M. Mintrom, "Policy Entrepreneurs and the Diffusion of Innovation," *American Journal of Political Science*, Volume 41 (3), p. 738; and M. Mintrom and S. Vergari, "Policy Networks and Innovation Diffusion: The Case of State Education Reforms," *Journal of Politics*, Volume 60 (1), February 1998, p. 126.
[e] F. Meyer and R. Baker, "An Overview of State Policy Problems," *Policy Studies Review*, Volume 11 (1), Spring 1992, pp. 75–90.

POWERS OF THE NATIONAL GOVERNMENT

The powers delegated to the national government include both expressed and implied powers, as well as the special category of inherent powers. Most of the powers expressly delegated to the national government are found in Article I, Section 8, of the Constitution. These enumerated powers include coining money, setting standards for weights and measures, making uniform naturalization laws, admitting new states, establishing post offices, and declaring war. Another important enumerated power is the power to regulate commerce among the states—a topic we deal with later in this chapter.

The Necessary and Proper Clause. The implied powers of the national government are also based on Article I, Section 8, which states that Congress shall have the power

[t]o make all Laws which shall be necessary and proper for carrying into Execution the foregoing Powers, and all other Powers vested by this Constitution in the Government of the United States, or in any Department or Officer thereof.

This clause is sometimes called the **elastic clause, or the necessary and proper clause**, because it provides flexibility to the U.S. constitutional system. It gives Congress all of those powers that can be reasonably inferred but that are not expressly stated in the brief wording of the Constitution. The clause was first used in the Supreme Court decision of *McCulloch v. Maryland*[6] (discussed later in this chapter) to develop the concept of implied powers. Through this concept, the national government has succeeded in strengthening the scope of its authority to meet the numerous problems that the framers of the Constitution did not, and could not, anticipate.

Inherent Powers. A special category of national powers that is not implied by the necessary and proper clause consists of what have been labeled as the inherent powers of the national government. These powers derive from the fact that the United States is a sovereign power among nations, and so its national government must be the only government that deals with other nations. Under international law, it is assumed that all nation-states, regardless of their size or power, have an *inherent* right to ensure their own survival. To do this, each nation must have the ability to act in its own interest among and with the community of nations—by, for instance, making treaties, waging war, seeking trade, and acquiring territory.

Note that no specific clause in the Constitution says anything about the acquisition of additional land. Nonetheless, through the federal government's inherent powers, we made the Louisiana Purchase in 1803 and then went on to acquire Florida, Texas, Oregon, Alaska, Hawaii, and other lands. The United States grew from a mere 13 states to 50 states, plus several "territories."

The national government has these inherent powers whether or not they have been enumerated in the Constitution. Some constitutional scholars categorize inherent powers as a third type of power, completely distinct from the delegated powers (both expressed and implied) of the national government.

POWERS OF THE STATE GOVERNMENTS

The Tenth Amendment states that the powers not delegated to the United States by the Constitution, nor prohibited by it to the states, are reserved to the states, or to the people. These are the reserved powers that the national government cannot deny to the states. Because these powers are not expressly listed—and because they are not limited to powers that are expressly listed—there is sometimes a question as to whether a certain power is delegated to the national government or reserved to the states. State powers have been held to include each state's right to regulate commerce within its borders and to provide for a state militia. States also have the reserved power to make laws on all matters not prohibited to the states by the U.S. Constitution or state constitutions and not expressly, or by implication, delegated to the national government. Furthermore, the states have **police power**—the authority to legislate for the protection of the health, morals, safety, and welfare of the people. Their police power enables states to pass laws governing such activities as crimes, marriage, contracts, education, intrastate transportation, and land use.

Elastic Clause, or Necessary and Proper Clause
The clause in Article I, Section 8, that grants Congress the power to do whatever is necessary to execute its specifically delegated powers.

DID YOU KNOW?

That state governments in the United States typically are unitary governments—that is, most local governments are mere creatures of the states?

Police Power
The authority to legislate for the protection of the health, morals, safety, and welfare of the people. In the United States, most police power is reserved to the states.

[6]4 Wheaton 316 (1819).

The ambiguity of the Tenth Amendment has allowed the reserved powers of the states to be defined differently at different times in our history. When there is widespread support for increased regulation by the national government, the Tenth Amendment tends to recede into the background. When the tide turns the other way (in favor of states' rights), the Tenth Amendment is resurrected to justify arguments supporting increased states' rights.

CONCURRENT POWERS

In certain areas, the states share **concurrent powers** with the national government. Most concurrent powers are not specifically listed in the Constitution; they are only implied. An example of a concurrent power is the power to tax. The types of taxation are divided between the levels of government. For example, states may not levy a tariff (a set of taxes on imported goods); only the national government may do this. Neither government may tax the facilities of the other. If the state governments did not have the power to tax, they would not be able to function other than on a ceremonial basis.

Other concurrent powers include the power to borrow funds, to establish courts, and to charter banks and corporations. To a limited extent, the national government exercises police power, and to the extent that it does, police power is also a concurrent power. Concurrent powers exercised by the states are normally limited to the geographic area of each state and to those functions *not* granted by the Constitution exclusively to the national government (such as the coinage of money and the negotiation of treaties).

Concurrent Powers
Powers held jointly by the national and state governments.

PROHIBITED POWERS

The Constitution prohibits or denies several powers to the national government. For example, the national government expressly has been denied the power to impose taxes on goods sold to other countries (exports). Moreover, any power not granted expressly or implicitly to the federal government by the Constitution is prohibited to it. For example, the national government cannot create a national divorce law system. The states are also denied certain powers. For example, no state is allowed to enter into a treaty on its own with another country.

THE SUPREMACY CLAUSE

The supremacy of the national constitution over subnational laws and actions is established in the **supremacy clause** of the Constitution. The supremacy clause (Article VI, Clause 2) states the following:

> This Constitution, and the Laws of the United States which shall be made in Pursuance thereof; and all Treaties made . . . under the Authority of the United States, shall be the supreme Law of the Land; and the Judges in every State shall be bound thereby, any Thing in the Constitution or Laws of any State to the Contrary notwithstanding.

Supremacy Clause
The constitutional provision that makes the Constitution and federal laws superior to all conflicting state and local laws.

In other words, states cannot use their reserved or concurrent powers to thwart national policies. All national and state officers, including judges, must be bound by oath to support the Constitution. Hence, any legitimate exercise of national governmental power supersedes any conflicting state action.[7] Of course, deciding whether a conflict actually exists is a judicial matter, as you will see when we discuss the case of *McCulloch v. Maryland*.

---

[7]An example of this is President Dwight Eisenhower's disciplining of Arkansas Governor Orval Faubus in 1957 by federalizing the National Guard to enforce the court-ordered desegregation of Little Rock High School.

Beyond Our Borders

FLEXIBLE FEDERALISM

The United States Constitution pretty clearly lays out the division of powers and authority between the states and the national government, as well as creating a complex election scheme to further guarantee representation for the states. As we will see, the decisions of the Supreme Court over the centuries have reinterpreted this division numerous times.

COAL-FIRED POWER PLANTS
such as this one provide most of the electricity for the midwestern United States. Limiting carbon emissions from these plants is a major goal of the environmental movement. (DAVID BOILY/AFP/ Getty Images)

Several other large, diverse countries have also adopted the federal system of government. Have they been able to construct a clear division of powers between the national government and states that has lasted? Or is federalism as a system flexible enough for nations to change their internal arrangements in response to need?

The government of Canada is a federal system with a national government and multiple provinces and territories. At its founding in 1867, the Canadian federal system differed from that of the United States in at least two major ways: (1) it was created by the United Kingdom, and the new nation owed allegiance to the British monarch; and (2) from the very beginning, provinces were divided by culture and language, with one of the largest provinces being French-speaking Quebec.

The division of powers in the Canadian system is also different from that of the United States. In general, the government has operated on the principle that all Canadians, regardless of where they live, should be taxed about equally and receive equal government benefits. The national government had power over defense, trade, transportation, and so on, whereas the provinces had control over education, civil rights, hospitals, and all natural resources within their boundaries. In the 20th century, the Canadian national government has acquired much more power over social services, the national health system, and other direct services to the people. In contrast to the American states, provinces have won increased economic independence from the central government through their control over natural resources and the money they earn from taxing their use. Today, with the price of oil skyrocketing, the province of Alberta has become the world capital of oil sand production, and the province has earned a windfall in revenue from its natural resources.[*]

Another large federal system is that of India, formed after the end of British rule in 1948. India adopted federalism to deal with its huge number of ethnic minorities

*Canadian Embassy, "A Strong Partnership," accessed at www.canadianembassy.org/government/federalism-en.asp.

and local cultures and languages. At the beginning, while powers were constitutionally divided between the capital of New Delhi and the states, the drive for economic development led to national control of some industries directly and considerable control over state decisions and economic initiatives. In the 1990s, India began to reform its economic system to encourage more development. One of the principles of that reform was to end much of the national control of the economy and allow states to develop their own laws and incentives for development. Today, the balance of power has shifted toward the states.[**]

FOR CRITICAL ANALYSIS

1. Do you think there will be a time when power will shift from the national government to the states in the United States?
2. What conditions might make that possible?

[**] Aseema Sinha, "The Changing Political Economy of Federalism in India: A Historical Institutional Approach," *India Review* 3, January 2004, pp. 25–63.

National government legislation in a concurrent area is said to *preempt* (take precedence over) conflicting state or local laws or regulations in that area. One of the ways in which the national government has extended its powers, particularly during the 20th century, is through the preemption of state and local laws by national legislation. In the first decade of the 20th century, fewer than 20 national laws preempted laws and regulations issued by state and local governments. By the beginning of the 21st century, the number had risen to nearly 120.

Some political scientists believe that national supremacy is critical for the longevity and smooth functioning of a federal system. Nonetheless, the application of this

ALTHOUGH NATIONAL legislation overturns state laws, several states sued the EPA during the Bush Administration to seek enforcement of pollution regulations on coal-fired power plants. The Obama Administration took a much stronger line on such enforcement. (Lester Lefkowitz/ PhotoLibrary)

principle has been a continuous source of conflict. As you will see, the most extreme example of this conflict was the Civil War.

VERTICAL CHECKS AND BALANCES

Recall from Chapter 2 that one of the concerns of the founders was to prevent the national government from becoming too powerful. For that reason, they divided the government into three branches—legislative, executive, and judicial. They also created a system of checks and balances that allowed each branch to check the actions of the others. The federal form of government created by the founders also involves checks and balances. These are sometimes called *vertical checks and balances* because they involve relationships between the states and the national government. They can be contrasted with *horizontal checks and balances*, in which the branches of government that are on the same level—either state or national—may check one other.

For example, the reserved powers of the states act as a check on the national government. Additionally, the states' interests are represented in the national legislature (Congress), and the citizens of the various states determine who will head the executive branch (the presidency). The founders also made it impossible for the central government to change the Constitution without the states' consent, as you read in Chapter 2. Finally, national programs and policies are administered by the states. This gives the states considerable control over the ultimate shape of those programs and policies.

The national government, in turn, can check state policies by exercising its constitutional powers under the clauses just discussed, as well as under the commerce clause (to be examined later). Furthermore, the national government can influence state policies indirectly through federal grants, as you will learn later in this chapter.

INTERSTATE RELATIONS

So far we have examined only the relationship between central and state governmental units. The states, however, have constant commercial, social, and other dealings among themselves. The national Constitution imposes certain "rules of the road" on interstate relations. These rules have prevented any one state from setting itself apart from the other states. The three most important clauses governing interstate relations in the Constitution, all derived from the Articles of Confederation, require each state to do the following:

1. Give full faith and credit to every other state's public acts, records, and judicial proceedings (Article IV, Section 1).
2. Extend to every other state's citizens the privileges and immunities of its own citizens (Article IV, Section 2).
3. Agree to return persons who are fleeing from justice in another state back to their home state when requested to do so (Article IV, Section 2).

The Full Faith and Credit Clause. This provision of the Constitution protects the rights of citizens as they move from state to state. It provides that "full faith *and credit* shall be given in each State to the public Acts, Records and judicial Proceedings of every other State." This clause applies only to civil matters. It ensures that rights established under deeds, wills, contracts, and the like will be honored by any other states. It also ensures that any judicial decision with respect to such property rights will be honored as well as enforced, in all states. The **full faith and credit clause** has contributed to the unity of American citizens, particularly as we have become a more mobile society.

Full Faith and Credit Clause
This section of the Constitution requires states to recognize one another's laws and court decisions. It ensures that rights established under deeds, wills, contracts, and other civil matters in one state will be honored by other states.

Privileges and Immunities. Privileges and immunities are defined as special rights and exemptions provided by law. Under Article IV, "The Citizens of each State shall be entitled to all Privileges and Immunities of Citizens in the several States." This clause indicates that states are obligated to extend to citizens of other states protection of the laws, the right to work, access to courts, and other privileges they grant their own citizens. It means that if you are a student from Iowa attending college in Ohio, you have the same rights as Ohioans to protest a traffic ticket, to buy a car, to hold a job, and to travel freely throughout the state.

Interstate Extradition. The Constitution clearly addressed the issue of how states should cooperate in catching criminals. Article IV, Section 2, states that "[a] person charged in any State with Treason, Felony, or another Crime who shall flee from Justice and be found in another State, shall on Demand of the executive Authority of the State from which he fled, be delivered up, to be removed to the State having jurisdiction of the Crime." While the language is clear, a federal judge will not order such an action. It is the moral duty of the governor to **extradite** the accused. From time to time, the governor of a state may refuse to do so, either because he or she does not believe in capital punishment, which might be ordered upon conviction, or because the accused has lived a law-abiding life for many years outside the state in which the crime was committed.

Following these constitutional mandates is not always easy for the states. For example, one question that has arisen in recent years is whether states will be constitutionally obligated to recognize same-sex marriages performed in other states, as you read in the What If . . . feature.

Additionally, states may enter into agreements called **interstate compacts**, if consented to by Congress. In reality, congressional consent is necessary only if such a compact increases the power of the contracting states relative to other states (or to the national government). Typical examples of interstate compacts are the establishment of the Port Authority of New York and New Jersey by an interstate compact between those two states in 1921 and the regulation of the production of crude oil and natural gas by the Interstate Oil and Gas Compact of 1935. Recently, the federal government has attempted to mediate the dispute between Georgia and Tennessee over a prior agreement about how much water can be sent from a Tennessee lake to meet Georgia's needs.

Privileges and Immunities
Special rights and exceptions provided by law. States may not discriminate against one another's citizens.

Extradite
To surrender an accused or convicted criminal to the authorities of the state from which he or she has fled; to return a fugitive criminal to the jurisdiction of the accusing state.

Interstate Compact
An agreement between two or more states. Agreements on minor matters are made without congressional consent, but any compact that tends to increase the power of the contracting states relative to other states or relative to the national government generally requires the consent of Congress. Such compacts serve as a means by which states can solve regional problems.

DEFINING CONSTITUTIONAL POWERS— THE EARLY YEARS

Recall from Chapter 2 that constitutional language, to be effective and to endure, must have some degree of ambiguity. Certainly, the powers delegated to the national government and the powers reserved to the states contain elements of ambiguity, thus leaving the door open for different interpretations of federalism. Disputes over the boundaries of national versus state powers have characterized this nation from the beginning. In the early 1800s, the most significant disputes arose over differing interpretations of the implied powers of the national government under the necessary and proper clause and over the respective powers of the national government and the states to regulate commerce.

Although political bodies at all levels of government play important roles in the process of settling such disputes, ultimately the Supreme Court casts the final vote. As might be expected, the character of the referee will have an impact on the ultimate outcome of any dispute. From 1801 to 1835, the Supreme Court was headed by Chief Justice John Marshall, a Federalist who advocated a strong central government. We look here at two cases decided by the Marshall Court: *McCulloch v. Maryland*[8] and *Gibbons v. Ogden*.[9] Both cases are considered milestones in defining the boundaries between federal and state power.

McCULLOCH v. MARYLAND (1819)

Nowhere in the U.S. Constitution does it state that Congress has the power to create a national bank, although it does have the express power to regulate currency. Twice in the history of the nation has the Congress chartered banks—the First and Second Banks of the United States—and provided part of their initial capital; thus, they were national banks. The government of Maryland, which intended to regulate its own banks and did not want a national bank competing with its own institutions, imposed a tax on the Second Bank's Baltimore branch in an attempt to put that branch out of business. The branch's cashier, James William McCulloch, refused to pay the Maryland tax. When Maryland took McCulloch to its state court, the state of Maryland won. The national government appealed the case to the Supreme Court.

The Constitutional Questions. The questions before the Supreme Court were of monumental proportions. The very heart of national power under the Constitution, as well as the relationship between the national government and the states, was at issue. Congress has the authority to make all laws that are "necessary and proper" for the execution of Congress's expressed powers. Strict Constitution constructionists looked at the word *necessary* and contended that the national government had only those powers *indispensable* to the exercise of its designated powers. To them, chartering a bank and contributing capital to it were not necessary, for example, to coin money and regulate its value.

Loose constructionists disagreed. They believed that the word *necessary* could not be looked at in its strictest sense. As Alexander Hamilton once said, "It is essential to the being of the national government that so erroneous a conception of the meaning of the word *necessary* be exploded." The important issue was, if the national bank was constitutional, could the state tax it?

Marshall's Decision. Three days after hearing the case, Chief Justice John Marshall announced the Court's decision. (Given his Federalist allegiance, it is likely he made his decision before he heard the case.) It is true, Marshall said, that Congress's power to establish a national bank was not expressed in the Constitution. He went on to say, however, that if establishing such a national bank aided the government in the exercise of its designated powers, then the authority to set up such a bank could be implied. To Marshall, the necessary and proper clause embraced "all means which are appropriate: to carry out the 'legitimate ends' of the Constitution." Only when such actions are forbidden by the letter and spirit of the Constitution are they thereby unconstitutional. There was nothing in the Constitution, according to Marshall, "which excludes incidental or implied powers; and which requires that everything granted shall be expressly and minutely described." It would be impossible to spell out every action that Congress might legitimately take—the Constitution "would be enormously long and could scarcely be embraced by the human mind."

In perhaps the single most famous sentence every uttered by a Supreme Court justice, Marshall said, "[W]e must never forget it is a constitution we are expounding." In other words, the Constitution is a living instrument that has to be interpreted to meet the practical needs of government. Having established this doctrine of implied powers, Marshall

[8]4 Wheaton 316 (1819).
[9]9 Wheaton 1 (1824).

then answered the other important question before the Court and established the doctrine of national supremacy. Marshall stated that no state could use its taxing power to tax an arm of the national government. If it could, "the declaration that the Constitution . . . shall be the supreme law of the land, is an empty and unmeaning declamation."

Marshall's decision enabled the national government to grow and to meet problems that the Constitution's framers were unable to foresee. Today, practically every expressed power of the national government has been expanded in one way or another by use of the necessary and proper clause.

GIBBONS v. OGDEN (1824)

One of the most important parts of the Constitution included in Article I, Section 8, is the so-called **commerce clause**, in which Congress is given the power "[t]o regulate Commerce with foreign Nations, and among the several States, and with the Indian Tribes." What exactly does "to regulate commerce" mean? What does "commerce" entail? The issue here is essentially the same as that raised by *McCulloch v. Maryland*: How strict an interpretation should be given to a constitutional phrase? As might be expected given his Federalist loyalties, Marshall used a liberal approach in interpreting the commerce clause in *Gibbons v. Ogden*.

The Background of the Case. Robert Fulton and Robert Livingston secured a monopoly on steam navigation on New York waters from the New York legislature in 1803. They licensed Aaron Ogden to operate steam-powered ferryboats between New York and New Jersey. Thomas Gibbons, who had obtained a license from the U.S. government to operate boats in interstate waters, decided to compete with Ogden, but he did so without New York's permission. Ogden sued Gibbons. The New York state courts prohibited Gibbons from operating in New York waters. Gibbons appealed to the Supreme Court.

There were actually several issues before the Court in this case. The first issue was how the term *commerce* should be defined. New York's highest court had defined the term narrowly to mean only the shipment of goods, or the interchange of commodities, *not* navigation or the transport of people. The second issue was whether the national government's power to regulate interstate commerce extended to commerce within a state (*intra*state commerce) or was limited strictly to commerce among the states (*inter*state commerce). The third issue was whether the power to regulate interstate commerce was a concurrent power (as the New York court had concluded), meaning a power that could be exercised by both the state or national governments, or an exclusive national power. Clearly, if such powers were concurrent, there would be many instances of laws that conflicted with each other.

Marshall's Ruling. Marshall defined *commerce* as all commercial intercourse—all business dealings—including navigation and the transport of people. Marshall used this opportunity not only to expand the definition of commerce but also to validate and increase the power of the national legislature to regulate commerce. Declared Marshall, "What is this power? It is the power . . . to prescribe the rule by which commerce is to be governed. This power, like all others vested in Congress, is complete in itself." Marshall also held that the commerce power of the national government could be exercised in state jurisdictions, even though it cannot reach *solely* intrastate commerce. Finally, Marshall emphasized that the power to regulate interstate commerce was an *exclusive* national power. Marshall held that because Gibbons was duly authorized by the national government to navigate in interstate waters, he could not be prohibited from doing so by a state court.

Commerce Clause
The section of the Constitution in which Congress is given the power to regulate trade among the states and with foreign countries.

DID YOU KNOW?

That the Liberty Bell cracked when it was rung at the funeral of John Marshall in 1835?

Marshall's expansive interpretation of the commerce clause in *Gibbons v. Ogden* allowed the national government to exercise increasing authority over all areas of economic affairs throughout the land. Congress did not immediately exploit this broad grant of power. In the 1930s and subsequent decades, however, the commerce clause became the primary constitutional basis for national government regulation—as you will read later in this chapter.

STATES' RIGHTS AND THE RESORT TO CIVIL WAR

The controversy over slavery that led to the Civil War took the form of a dispute over national government supremacy versus the rights of the separate states. Essentially, the Civil War brought to an ultimate and violent climax the ideological debate that had been outlined by the Federalist and Anti-Federalist parties even before the Constitution was ratified.

THE SHIFT BACK TO STATES' RIGHTS

As we have seen, while John Marshall was chief justice of the Supreme Court, he did much to increase the power of the national government and to reduce that of the states. During the Jacksonian era (1829–1837), however, a shift back to states' rights began. The question of the regulation of commerce became one of the major issues in federal-state relations. When Congress passed a tariff in 1828, the state of South Carolina unsuccessfully attempted to nullify the tariff (render it void), claiming that in cases of conflict between a state and the national government, the state should have the ultimate authority over its citizens.

Over the next three decades, the North and South became even more sharply divided—over tariffs that mostly benefited Northern industries and over the slavery

PRESIDENT LINCOLN meets with some of his generals and other troops on October 3, 1862. While many believe that the Civil War was fought over the issue of slavery, others point out that it was really a battle over the supremacy of the national government. In any event, once the North won the war, what happened to the size and power of our national government? (Bettmann/Corbis)

issue. On December 20, 1860, South Carolina formally repealed its ratification of the Constitution and withdrew from the Union. On February 4, 1861, representatives from six Southern states met at Montgomery, Alabama, to form a new government called the Confederate States of America.

WAR AND THE GROWTH OF THE NATIONAL GOVERNMENT

The ultimate defeat of the South in 1865 permanently ended any idea that a state could successfully claim the right to secede, or withdraw, from the Union. Ironically, the Civil War—brought about in large part because of the South's desire for increased states' rights—resulted in the opposite: an increase in the political power of the national government.

The War Effort. Thousands of new employees were hired to run the Union war effort and to deal with the social and economic problems that had to be handled in the aftermath of war. A billion-dollar ($1.3 billion, which is more than $11.9 billion in today's dollars) national government budget was passed for the first time in 1865 to cover the increased government expenditures. The first (temporary) income tax was imposed on citizens to help pay for the war. This tax and the increased national government spending were precursors to the expanded future role of the national government in the American federal system. Civil liberties were curtailed in the Union and in the Confederacy in the name of the wartime emergency. The distribution of pensions and widows' benefits also boosted the national government's social role. Many scholars contend that the North's victory set the nation on the path to a modern industrial economy and society.

The Civil War Amendments. The expansion of the national government's authority during the Civil War was reflected in the passage of the Civil War Amendments

DID YOU KNOW?

That only after the Civil War did people commonly refer to the United States as "it" instead of "they"?

FORMER SLAVES, now freedmen, prepare to cast ballots in the southern states. (© North Wind Picture Archives/Alamy)

to the Constitution. Before the war, legislation with regard to slavery was some of the most controversial ever to come before the Congress. In fact, in the 1830s, Congress prohibited the submission of antislavery petitions before it. When new states were admitted into the Union, the primary decision was whether slavery would be allowed. Immediately after the Civil War, at a time when former officers of the Confederacy were barred from voting, the three Civil War Amendments were passed. The Thirteenth Amendment, ratified in 1865, did more than interfere with slavery—it abolished the institution altogether. By abolishing slavery, the amendment also in effect abolished the rule by which three-fifths of the slaves were counted when apportioning seats in the House of Representatives (see Chapter 2). African Americans were now counted in full.

The Fourteenth Amendment (1868) defined who was a citizen of each state. It sought to guarantee equal rights under state law, stating that

> [no] State [shall] deprive any person of life, liberty, or property, without due process of law; nor deny to any person within its jurisdiction the equal protection of the laws.

For a brief time after the ratification of these amendments, the rights of African Americans in the South were protected by the local officials appointed by the Union forces. Within two decades, the Fourteenth Amendment lost much of its power as states reinstituted separate conditions for the former slaves. Decades later, the courts interpreted these words to mean that the national Bill of Rights applied to state governments, a development that we will examine in Chapter 4. The Fourteenth Amendment also confirmed the abolition of the three-fifths rule. Finally, the Fifteenth Amendment (1870) gave African Americans the right to vote in all elections, including state elections, although a century would pass before that right was enforced.

THE CONTINUING DISPUTE OVER THE DIVISION OF POWER

Although the outcome of the Civil War firmly established the supremacy of the national government and put to rest the idea that a state could secede from the Union, the war by no means ended the debate over the division of powers between the national government and the states. The debate over the division of powers in our federal system can be viewed as progressing through at least two general stages since the Civil War: dual federalism and cooperative federalism.

DUAL FEDERALISM AND THE RETREAT OF NATIONAL AUTHORITY

Dual Federalism
A system in which the states and the national government each remains supreme within its own sphere. The doctrine looks on nation and state as coequal sovereign powers. Neither the state government nor the national government should interfere in the other's sphere.

During the decades following the Civil War, the prevailing model was what political scientists have called **dual federalism**—a doctrine that emphasizes a distinction between federal and state spheres of government authority. Various images have been used to describe different configurations of federalism over time. Dual federalism is commonly depicted as a layer cake, because the state governments and the national government are viewed as separate entities, like separate layers in a cake. The national government is the top layer of the cake; the state government is the bottom layer. Nevertheless, the two layers are physically separate. They do not mix. For the most part, advocates of dual federalism believed that the state and national governments should not exercise authority in the same areas.

A Return to Normal Conditions. The doctrine of dual federalism represented a revival of states' rights following the expansion of national authority during the Civil War. Dual federalism, after all, was a fairly accurate model of the prewar consensus on state-national relations. For many people, it therefore represented a return to normal. The national income tax, used to fund the war effort and the reconstruction of the South, was ended in 1872. The most significant step to reverse the wartime expansion of national power took place in 1877, when President Rutherford B. Hayes withdrew the last federal troops from the South. This meant that the national government was no longer in a position to regulate state actions that affected African Americans. While the black population was now free, it was again subject to the authority of Southern whites.

The Role of the Supreme Court. The Civil War crisis drastically reduced the influence of the United States Supreme Court. In the prewar *Dred Scott* decision,[10] the Court had attempted to abolish the power of the national government to restrict slavery in the territories. In so doing, the Court placed itself on the losing side of the impending conflict. After the war, Congress took the unprecedented step of exempting the entire process of Southern reconstruction from judicial review. The Court had little choice but to acquiesce.

In time, the Supreme Court reestablished itself as the legitimate constitutional umpire. Its decisions tended to support dual federalism, defend states' rights, and limit the powers of the national government. In 1895, for example, the Court ruled that a national income tax was unconstitutional.[11] In subsequent years, the Court gradually backed away from this decision and eventually might have overturned it. In 1913, however, the Sixteenth Amendment explicitly authorized a national income tax.

THIS PHOTOGRAPH shows teenagers and young boys leaving a coal mine near Fairmont, West Virginia. In the 1800s, even very young children worked in coal mines. Today, national child-labor laws prohibit employers from hiring young workers for dangerous occupations. Why do you think the parents of these youths and children allowed them to work at such dangerous jobs? If no childlabor laws existed today, would a large percentage of children still be working in dangerous occupations? Why or why not? (Lewis Wickes Hine, Library of Congress Prints & Photographs Division, Washington, D.C. [LC-DIG-nclc-01082])

---

[10]*Dred Scott v. Sanford*, 19 Howard 393 (1857).
[11]*Pollock v. Farmers' Loan & Trust Co.*, 157 U.S. 429 (1895); *Pollock v. Farmers' Loan & Trust Co.*, 158 U.S. 601 (1895).

For the Court, dual federalism meant that the national government could intervene in state activities through grants and subsidies, but for the most part, it was barred from regulating matters that the Court considered to be purely local. The Court generally limited the exercise of police power to the states. For example, in 1918, the Court ruled that a 1916 national law banning child labor was unconstitutional because it attempted to regulate a local problem.[12] In effect, the Court placed severe limits on the ability of Congress to legislate under the commerce clause of the Constitution.

THE NEW DEAL AND COOPERATIVE FEDERALISM

The doctrine of dual federalism receded into the background in the 1930s as the nation attempted to deal with the Great Depression. Franklin D. Roosevelt was inaugurated on March 4, 1933, as the 32nd president of the United States. In the previous year, nearly 1,500 banks had failed (and 4,000 more would fail in 1933). Thirty-two thousand businesses had closed down, and almost one-fourth of the labor force was unemployed. The public expected the national government to do something about the disastrous state of the economy. But for the first three years of the Great Depression (1930–1932), the national government did very little.

The "New Deal." President Herbert Hoover (served 1929–1933) clung to the doctrine of dual federalism and insisted that unemployment and poverty were local issues. The states, not the national government, had the sole responsibility for combating the effects of unemployment and providing relief to the poor. Roosevelt, however, did not feel bound by this doctrine, and his new Democratic administration energetically intervened in the economy. Roosevelt's "New Deal" included large-scale emergency antipoverty programs. In addition, the New Deal introduced major new laws regulating economic activity, such as the National Industrial Recovery Act of 1933, which established the National Recovery Administration (NRA). The NRA, initially the centerpiece of the New Deal, provided codes for every industry to restrict competition and regulate labor relations.

The End of Dual Federalism. Roosevelt's expansion of national authority was challenged by the Supreme Court, which continued to adhere to the doctrine of dual federalism. In 1935, the Court ruled that the NRA program was unconstitutional.[13] The NRA had turned out to be largely unworkable and was unpopular. The Court, however, rejected the program on the ground that it regulated intrastate, not interstate, commerce. This position appeared to rule out any alternative recovery plans that might be better

PRESIDENT FRANKLIN DELANO ROOSEVELT (served 1933–1945). Roosevelt's national approach to addressing the effects of the Great Depression was overwhelmingly popular, although many of his specific initiatives were controversial. How did the Great Depression change the political beliefs of many ordinary Americans? (Bettmann/Corbis)

[12]*Hammer v. Dagenhart*, 247 U.S. 251 (1918). This decision was overruled in *United States v. Darby*, 312 U.S. 100 (1940).
[13]*Schechter Poultry Corp. v. United States*, 295 U.S. 495 (1935).

designed. Subsequently, the Court struck down the Agricultural Adjustment Act, the Bituminous Coal Act, a railroad retirement plan, legislation to protect farm mortgages, and a municipal bankruptcy act.

In 1937, Roosevelt proposed legislation that would allow him to add up to six new justices to the Supreme Court. Presumably, the new justices would be more friendly to the exercise of national power than were the existing members. Roosevelt's move was widely seen as an assault on the Constitution. Congressional Democrats refused to support the measure, and it failed. Nevertheless, the "court-packing scheme" had its intended effect. Although the membership of the Court did not change, after 1937 the Court ceased its attempts to limit the national government's powers under the commerce clause. For the next half-century, the commerce clause would provide Congress with an unlimited justification for regulating the economic life of the country.

Cooperative Federalism. Some political scientists have described the era since 1937 as characterized by **cooperative federalism**, in which the states and the national government cooperate in solving complex common problems. Roosevelt's New Deal programs, for example, often involved joint action between the national government and the states. The pattern of national-state relationships during these years created a new metaphor for federalism—that of a marble cake. Unlike a layer cake, in a marble cake the two types of cake are intermingled, and any bite contains cake of both flavors.

Cooperative Federalism
The theory that the states and the national government should cooperate in solving problems.

As an example of how national and state governments work together under the cooperative federalism model, consider Aid to Families with Dependent Children (AFDC), a welfare program that was established during the New Deal. (In 1996, AFDC was replaced by Temporary Assistance to Needy Families—TANF.) Under the AFDC program, the national government provided most of the funding, but state governments established benefit levels and eligibility requirements for recipients. Local welfare offices were staffed by state, not national, employees. In return for national funding, the states had to conform to a series of regulations on how the program was to be carried out. These regulations tended to become more elaborate over time.

The 1960s and 1970s were a time of even greater expansion of the national government's role in domestic policy. The evolving pattern of national-state-local government relationships during the 1960s and 1970s yielded yet another metaphor—**picket-fence federalism**, a concept devised by political scientist Terry Sanford. The horizontal boards in the fence represent the different levels of government (national, state, and local), while the vertical pickets represent the various programs and policies in which each level of government is involved. Officials at each level of government work together to promote and develop the policy represented by each picket.

Picket-Fence Federalism
A model of federalism in which specific programs and policies (depicted as vertical pickets in a picket fence) involve all levels of government—national, state, and local (depicted by the horizontal boards in a picket fence).

METHODS OF IMPLEMENTING COOPERATIVE FEDERALISM

Even before the Constitution was adopted, the national government gave grants to the states in the form of land to finance education. The national government also provided land grants for canals, railroads, and roads. In the 20th century, federal grants increased significantly, especially during Roosevelt's administration during the Great Depression and again during the 1960s, when the dollar amount of grants quadrupled. These funds were used for improvements in education, pollution control, recreation, and highways. With this increase in grants, however, came a bewildering number of restrictions and regulations.

Categorical Grants. By 1985, **categorical grants** amounted to more than $100 billion per year. They were spread out across 400 separate programs, but the largest five accounted for more than 50 percent of the revenues spent. These five programs involved Medicaid (health care for the poor), highway construction, unemployment benefits, housing assistance, and welfare programs to assist mothers with dependent children and people with disabilities. For fiscal year 2009 the national government gave an estimated $253 billion to the states and local governments through federal grants. Figure 3–3 shows the increase in federal transfers of funds to state and local governments from 1920 to 2010 (estimated).

Before the 1960s, most categorical grants by the national government were *formula grants*. These grants take their name from the method used to allocate funds. They fund state programs using a formula based on such variables as the state's needs, population, or willingness to come up with matching funds. Beginning in the 1960s, the national government began increasingly to offer *program grants*. This funding requires states to apply for grants for specific programs. The applications are evaluated by the national government, and the applications may compete with one another. Program grants give the national government a much greater degree of control over state activities than formula grants.

Why have federal grants to the states increased so much? One reason is that Congress has decided to offload some programs to the states and provide a major part of the funding for them. Also, Congress continues to use grants to persuade states and cities to operate programs devised by the federal government. Finally, states often are happy to apply for grants because they are relatively "free," requiring only that the state match a small portion of each grant. States can still face criticism for accepting the grants, because their matching funds may be diverted from other state projects.

DID YOU KNOW?

That the Morrill Act of 1862, providing for land grants to states to create public institutions of higher education, was the first example of the federal government providing grants to the states.

Feeling the Pressure—The Strings Attached to Federal Grants. No dollars sent to the states are completely free of strings, however; all funds come with requirements that must be met by the states. Often, through the use of grants, the national government has been able to exercise substantial control over matters that traditionally have been under the purview of state governments. When the federal government gives federal funds for highway improvements, for example, it may condition the funds on the state's cooperation with a federal policy. This is exactly what the federal government did in the 1980s and 1990s to force the states to raise their minimum drinking age to 21.

Such carrot-and-stick tactics have been used as a form of coercion in recent years as well. In 2002, for example, President George W. Bush signed the No Child Left Behind (NCLB) Act into law. Under NCLB, Bush promised billions of dollars to the states to bolster their education budgets. The funds would only be delivered, however, if states agreed to hold schools accountable to new federal achievement benchmarks on standardized tests designed by the federal government. Education traditionally had been under state control, and the conditions for receiving NCLB funds effectively stripped the states of some autonomy in creating standards for public schools. President Barack Obama proposed revising NCLB but also supports federal standards for the achievement of individual schools and students.

Block Grants. **Block grants** lessen the restrictions on federal grants given to state and local governments by grouping several categorical grants under one broad heading. Governors and mayors generally prefer block grants because such grants give the states more flexibility in how the money is spent.

One major set of block grants provides aid to state welfare programs. The Personal Responsibility and Work Opportunity Reconciliation Act of 1996 ended the AFDC program. The TANF program that replaced AFDC provided a welfare block grant to each state. Each grant has an annual cap. According to some, this is one of the most successful block grant programs. Although state governments prefer block grants, Congress generally favors categorical grants, because the expenditures can be targeted according to congressional priorities.

Federal Mandates. For years, the federal government has passed legislation requiring that states improve environmental conditions and the civil rights of certain groups. Since the 1970s, the national government has enacted literally hundreds of **federal mandates** requiring the states to take some action in areas ranging from the way voters are registered, to ocean-dumping restrictions, to the education of persons with disabilities. The Unfunded Mandates Reform Act of 1995 requires the Congressional Budget Office to identify mandates that cost state and local governments more than $50 million to implement. Nonetheless, the federal government routinely continues to pass mandates for state and local governments that cost more than that to implement.

For example, the estimated total cost of complying with federal mandates concerning water purity, over just a four-year period, is in the vicinity of $29 billion. In all, the estimated cost of federal mandates to the states in the early 2000s was more than $70 billion annually. One way in which the national government has moderated the burden of federal mandates is by granting *waivers*, which allow individual states to try out innovative approaches to carrying out the mandates. For example, Oregon received a waiver to experiment with a new method of rationing health care services under the federally mandated Medicaid program.

DID YOU KNOW?

That part of the $4.2 million federal block grants received by four Native American tribes since 1997 has gone toward the building of "smoke shops"— stores that sell discounted cigarettes and pipe tobacco?

Federal Mandate
A requirement in federal legislation that forces states and municipalities to comply with certain rules.

FIGURE 3–3 The Rise in Federal Transfers to State and Local Governments

The chart shows the percentage of state and local revenues transferred from the federal government. As noted in the text, the federal government often uses grants and other transfers of revenue to convince states to abide by federal regulations.

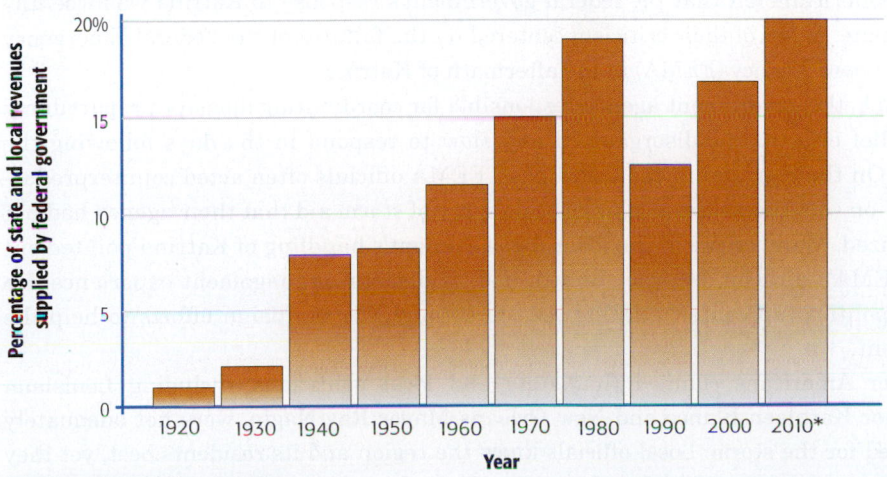

*The figure for 2010 is a projection.

Sources: *Historical Statistics of the United States; Statistical Abstract of the United States, 2008;* and *Budget of the United States Government, FY 2009.*

THE POLITICS OF FEDERALISM

As we have observed, the allocation of powers between the national and state governments continues to be a major issue. In 2005, the devastation caused by Hurricane Katrina in Louisiana unleashed a heated debate about federalism, as Americans disagreed on which level of government should be held accountable for inadequate preparations and the failures in providing aid afterward. As you know, some 1,300 people died as a result of the storm, while property damage totaled tens of billions of dollars. Many Americans felt that the federal government's response to Katrina was woefully inadequate. Much of their criticism centered on the failures of the Federal Emergency Management Agency (FEMA) in the aftermath of Katrina.

FEMA, the government agency responsible for coordinating disaster preparedness and relief efforts, was disorganized and slow to respond in the days following the storm. On their arrival in the Gulf Coast, FEMA officials often acted counterproductively—on some occasions denying the delivery of storm aid that their agency had not authorized. Many critics of the federal government's handling of Katrina pointed out that FEMA's director, Michael Brown, had no disaster management experience: He was a political appointee, earning the job through his campaign efforts to help the president.

Other Americans claimed that state and local politicians, including Louisiana Governor Kathleen Blanco and New Orleans Mayor Ray Nagin, were not adequately prepared for the storm. Local officials knew the region and its residents best, yet they failed to make proper provisions for evacuating vulnerable residents.

The real reason for the disaster was the failure of the levees that protect New Orleans from Mississippi River floods. The levees were constructed by the Army

Corps of Engineers (a federal agency) and maintained by the Corps; however, those employees took orders from both federal officials and state and local politicians, including the multiple local levee boards that could and did divert funds to other purposes.[14] It was widely known that the levees needed replacement, but Congress had declined to fund the design for many years. The aftermath of Hurricane Katrina was a classic case of failure due, perhaps, to the design of our federal system of government.

WHAT HAS NATIONAL AUTHORITY ACCOMPLISHED?

Why have conservatives favored the states and liberals favored the national government? One answer is that throughout American history, the expansion of national authority typically has been an engine of social change. Far more than the states, the national government has been willing to alter the status quo. The expansion of national authority during the Civil War freed the slaves—a major social revolution. During the New Deal, the expansion of national authority meant unprecedented levels of government intervention in the economy. In both the Civil War and New Deal eras, support for states' rights was a method of opposing these changes and supporting the status quo.

PRESIDENT LYNDON B. JOHNSON'S Great Society and War on Poverty were among programs that asserted the most national authority since the New Deal. The photo shows Johnson shaking the hand of one of the residents of Appalachia during his Poverty Tour on May 7, 1964. (Cecil Stoughton/LBJ Library Collection, National Archives)

Some scholars believe that this equation was also a subtext in the Supreme Court's defense of states' rights between the Civil War and 1937. These scholars argue that the Supreme Court, in those years, came increasingly under the influence of *laissez-faire* economics—a belief that any government intervention in the economy was improper. When the Court struck down national legislation against child labor, for example, it was not acting only in defense of the states; an underlying motivation was the Court's belief that laws banning child labor were wrong no matter which level of government implemented them.

Civil Rights and the War on Poverty. A final example of the use of national power to change society was the presidency of Lyndon B. Johnson (1963–1969). Johnson oversaw the greatest expansion of national authority since the New Deal. Under Johnson, a series of civil rights acts forced the states to grant African Americans equal treatment under the law. Crucially, these acts included the abolition of all measures designed to prevent African Americans from voting. Johnson's Great Society and War on Poverty programs resulted in major increases in spending by the national government. As before, states' rights were invoked to support the status quo—states' rights meant no action on civil rights and no increase in antipoverty spending.

Why Should the States Favor the Status Quo? When state governments have authority in a particular field, there may be great variations from state to state in how the issues are handled. Inevitably, some states will be more conservative than others. Therefore, bringing national authority to bear on a particular issue may impose national standards on states that, for whatever reason, have not adopted such standards. One example is the voting rights legislation passed under President Johnson. By the 1960s, there was a national consensus that all citizens, regardless of race, should have the right to vote. A majority of the white electorate in former Confederate states, however, did not share this view. National legislation was necessary to impose the national consensus on the recalcitrant states.

[14]Douglas Brinkley, *The Great Deluge: Hurricane Katrina, New Orleans and the Mississippi Gulf Coast* (New York: HarperCollins, 2006).

Another factor that may make the states more receptive to limited government, especially on economic issues, is competition among the states. It is widely believed that major corporations are more likely to establish new operations in states with a "favorable business climate." Such a climate may mean low taxes and therefore relatively more limited social services. If states compete with one another to offer the best business climate, the competition may force down taxes all around. Competition of this type also may dissuade states from implementing environmental regulations that restrict certain business activities. Those who deplore the effect of such competition often refer to it as a "race to the bottom." National legislation, in contrast, is not constrained by interstate competition.

A final factor that may encourage the states to favor the status quo is the relative power of local economic interests. A large corporation in a small state, for example, may have a substantial amount of political influence. Such a corporation, which has experienced success within the existing economic framework, may be opposed to any changes to that framework. These local economic interests may have less influence at the national level. This observation echoes James Madison's point in *Federalist Paper No. 10* (see Appendix B of this text). Madison argued that a large federal republic would be less subject to the danger of factions than a small state.

FEDERALISM BECOMES A PARTISAN ISSUE

Devolution

The transfer of powers from a national or central government to a state or local government.

In the years after 1968, the **devolution** of power from the national government to the states became a major ideological theme for the Republican Party. Republicans believed that the increased size and scope of the federal government—which began with the New Deal programs of Franklin Roosevelt and continued unabated through Lyndon Johnson's Great Society programs—was a threat to individual liberty and to the power of the states. As the Republicans became more conservative in their views of the extent of national government power, Democrats have become more liberal and supportive of that power.

The "New Federalism." The architects of Lyndon Johnson's War on Poverty were reluctant to let state governments have a role in the new programs. This reluctance was a response to the resistance of many southern states to African American civil rights. The Johnson administration did not trust the states to administer antipoverty programs in an impartial and efficient manner.

Republican president Richard Nixon (served 1969–1974), who succeeded Johnson in office, saw political opportunity in the Democrats' suspicion of state governments. Nixon advocated what he called a "New Federalism" that would devolve authority from the national government to the states. In part, the New Federalism involved the conversion of categorical grants into block grants, thereby giving state governments greater flexibility in spending. A second part of Nixon's New Federalism was revenue sharing. Under the revenue-sharing plan, the national government provided direct, unconditional financial support to state and local governments.

Nixon was able to obtain only a limited number of block grants from Congress. The block grants he did obtain, plus revenue sharing, substantially increased financial support to state governments. Republican President Ronald Reagan was also a strong advocate of federalism, but some of his policies withdrew certain financial support from the states. Reagan was more successful than Nixon in obtaining block grants, but Reagan's block grants, unlike Nixon's, were less generous to the states than the categorical grants they replaced. Under Reagan, revenue sharing was eliminated.

Federalism in the 21st Century. Today, federalism (in the sense of limited national authority) continues to be an important element in conservative ideology. At this point, however, it is not clear whether competing theories of federalism truly divide the Republicans from the Democrats in practice. Consider that under Democratic president Bill Clinton (served 1993–2001), Congress replaced AFDC, a categorical welfare program, with the TANF block grants. This change was part of the Welfare Reform Act of 1996, which was perhaps the most significant domestic policy initiative of Clinton's administration. In contrast, a major domestic initiative of Republican president George W. Bush was increased federal funding and control of education—long a preserve of state and local governments.

Also, in some circumstances, liberals today may benefit from states' rights. One example is the issue of same-sex marriages, which we examined in the What If . . . feature. A minority of the states is much more receptive than the rest of the nation to same-sex marriages or to civil unions for gay or lesbian partners. Liberals who favor such marriages or civil unions therefore have an incentive to oppose national legislation or an amendment to the national Constitution on this topic.

FEDERALISM AND THE SUPREME COURT TODAY

The United States Supreme Court, which normally has the final say on constitutional issues, necessarily plays a significant role in determining the line between federal and state powers. Consider the decisions rendered by Chief Justice John Marshall in the cases discussed earlier in this chapter. Since the 1930s, Marshall's broad interpretation of the commerce clause has made it possible for the national government to justify its regulation of virtually any activity, even when an activity would appear to be purely local in character.

Since the 1990s, however, the Supreme Court has been reining in somewhat the national government's powers under the commerce clause. The Court also has given increased emphasis to state powers under the Tenth and Eleventh Amendments to the Constitution. At the same time, other recent rulings have sent contradictory messages with regard to states' rights and the federal government's power.

REINING IN THE COMMERCE POWER

In a widely publicized 1995 case, *United States v. Lopez*,[15] the Supreme Court held that Congress had exceeded its constitutional authority under the commerce clause when it passed the Gun-Free School Zones Act in 1990. The Court stated that the act, which banned the possession of guns within 1,000 feet of any school, was unconstitutional because it attempted to regulate an area that had "nothing to do with commerce, or any sort of economic enterprise." This marked the first time in 60 years that the Supreme Court had placed a limit on the national government's authority under the commerce clause.

In 2000, in *United States v. Morrison*,[16] the Court held that Congress had overreached its authority under the commerce clause when it passed the Violence against Women Act in 1994. The Court invalidated a key section of the act that provided a federal remedy for gender-motivated violence, such as rape. The Court noted that in enacting this law, Congress had extensively documented that violence against women had an adverse "aggregate" effect on interstate commerce: it deterred potential victims from traveling, from engaging in employment, and from transacting business in

---

[15]514 U.S. 549 (1995).
[16]529 U.S. 598 (2000).

interstate commerce. It also diminished national productivity and increased medical and other costs. Nonetheless, the Court held that evidence of an aggregate effect on commerce was not enough to justify national regulation of noneconomic, violent criminal conduct.

STATE SOVEREIGNTY AND THE ELEVENTH AMENDMENT

In recent years, the Supreme Court has issued a series of decisions that bolstered the authority of state governments under the Eleventh Amendment to the Constitution. As interpreted by the Court, that amendment in most circumstances precludes lawsuits against state governments for violations of rights established by federal laws unless the states consent to be sued. For example, in a 1999 case, *Alden v. Maine*,[17] the Court held that Maine state employees could not sue the state for violating the overtime pay requirements of a federal act. According to the Court, state immunity from such lawsuits "is a fundamental aspect of the sovereignty which [the states] enjoyed before the ratification of the Constitution, and which they retain today."

In 2000, in *Kimel v. Florida Board of Regents*,[18] the Court held that the Eleventh Amendment precluded employees of a state university from suing the state to enforce a federal statute prohibiting age-based discrimination. In 2003, however, in *Nevada v. Hibbs*,[19] the Court ruled that state employers must abide by the federal Family and Medical Leave Act (FMLA). The reasoning was that the FMLA seeks to outlaw gender bias, and government actions that may discriminate on the basis of gender must receive a "heightened review status" compared with actions that may discriminate on the basis of age or disability. Also, in 2004, the Court ruled that the Eleventh Amendment could not shield states from suits by individuals with disabilities who had been denied access to courtrooms located on the upper floors of buildings.[20]

TENTH AMENDMENT ISSUES

The Tenth Amendment states: "The powers not delegated to the United States by the Constitution, nor prohibited by it to the States, are reserved to the States respectively, or to the people." In 1992, the Court held that requirements imposed on the state of New York under a federal act regulating low-level radioactive waste were inconsistent with the Tenth Amendment and thus unconstitutional. According to the Court, the act's "take title" provision, which required states to accept ownership of waste or regulate waste following Congress's instructions, exceeded the enumerated powers of Congress. Although Congress can regulate the handling of such waste, "it may not conscript state governments as its agents" in an attempt to enforce a program of federal regulation.[21]

In 1997, the Court revisited this Tenth Amendment issue. In *Printz v. United States*,[22] the Court struck down the provisions of the federal Brady Handgun Violence Prevention Act of 1993 that required state employees to check the backgrounds of prospective handgun purchasers. Said the Court:

> [T]he federal government may neither issue directives requiring the States to address particular problems, nor command the States' officers, or those of their political subdivisions, to administer or enforce a federal regulatory program.

[17]527 U.S. 706 (1999).
[18]528 U.S. 62 (2000).
[19]538 U.S. 721 (2003).
[20]*Tennessee v. Lane*, 541 U.S. 509 (2004).
[21]*New York v. United States*, 505 U.S. 144 (1992).
[22]521 U.S. 898 (1997).

OTHER FEDERALISM CASES

In recent years, the Supreme Court has sent mixed messages in federalism cases. At times the Court has favored states' rights, whereas on other occasions it has backed the federal government's position.

There has been a general drift toward favoring the states in cases involving federalism issues. Despite this trend, the Supreme Court argued in 2005 that the federal government's power to seize and destroy illegal drugs trumped California's law legalizing the use of marijuana for medical treatment.[23] Yet, less than a year later, the Court favored states' rights in another case rife with federalism issues, *Gonzales v. Oregon*.[24] After a lengthy legal battle, the Court upheld Oregon's controversial "Death with Dignity" law, which allows patients with terminal illnesses to choose to end their lives early and thus alleviate suffering.

As you read in Chapter 1, the decision handed down in *Kelo v. City of New London*[25] created an uproar among property rights advocates. Many state and local governments proposed legislation that would bar the taking of private land unaffected by blight if it would be transferred to a private developer. Steps taken by the states to combat *Kelo* gained so much political traction that the U.S. Congress is considering legislation that would forbid such takings nationwide. If such a law is passed, it will eventually be tested in the courts.

IN 2005, THESE PEOPLE waited at the steps of the United States Supreme Court building because they wished to be the first to find out about the Court's decision in the government's appeal against Oregon's "Death with Dignity" law. The Court decided against the federal government and in favor of Oregon. Why would the federal government go to court in an attempt to prevent legally assisted suicide in one state? (AP Photo/Charles Dharapak)

---

[23]*Gonzales v. Raich*, 545 U.S. 1 (2005).
[24]126 S.Ct. 904 (2006).
[25]545 U.S. 469 (2005).

YOU CAN MAKE A Difference

THE DEPARTMENT OF HOMELAND SECURITY AND YOU

The National Strategy for Homeland Security and the Homeland Security Act of 2002 attempted to mobilize our nation against terrorist attacks through the creation of the Department of Homeland Security (DHS). The new agency unified 22 governmental agencies in 2003 and now employs 180,000 people. Most DHS staff are focused on preventing terrorist attacks and stopping illegal immigrants at the border, but the agency has far-reaching programs that impact the states and individuals.

between the national and state governments. Since 9/11, however, it may appear that the federal government dominates the national conversation with regard to homeland security. The federal government determines risk factors for terrorism and decides how much money each state and, in some cases, city receives. State and local officials then administer the grants awarded.

But how is that money being spent? Critics say that questionable projects are being funded and argue that homeland security money should be off limits for "pork-barrel" spending. In 2005, Kentucky secured a $36,000 grant to protect bingo halls from terrorist infiltration. Five days before Christmas in 2004, the government announced a $153 million homeland security grant to provide food and shelter for the homeless. In 2006, $15.7 million in homeland security funds went for enforcement of child labor laws. Often, Congress earmarks spending; in other cases, the DHS decides how to allocate state and local grants.

FEMA ADMINISTRATOR W. Craig Fugate speaks at a 2009 conference about "The Power of Citizen Corps" in the war on terror. (FEMA/Bill Koplitz)

WHY SHOULD YOU CARE?

The Constitution and the Tenth Amendment, in particular, are supposed to define and limit the power of the national government and define the relationship between the national government and individual state governments. Federalism establishes that power be shared

WHAT CAN YOU DO?

You can find out how much money your state and local governments have received from DHS, but you may have little chance of knowing how that money was spent. Some states have laws or policies that preclude public disclosure of certain details on homeland security purchases; officials say that the information could be useful to terrorists. Some states, such as New York, will disclose general categories of purchases, such as personal protection gear, but will not give specifics. Other states are still developing disclosure policies on homeland security purchases, with requests for spending details decided on a case-by-case basis. Alabama forbids disclosure of homeland security spending specifics. To research your state's 2009 DHS grant awards and total funding history, go to **www.dhs.gov/xgovt/grants**. This page displays state grant award information for all 50 states and territories. You can click on your state for your homeland security contact and fiscal year 2009 allocation totals.

1. The state grant document gives details about grant program breakdowns. The Urban Areas Security Initiative (UASI) gives specific grants to the 45 highest-risk urban areas. Is your city designated a high-risk urban area?
2. The State Homeland Security Program (SHSP) is the core assistance program for all 50 states to implement their antiterror readiness programs. How do your fund levels compare with those of other states?
3. The Law Enforcement Terrorism Prevention Program (LETPP) provides resources to your state's public safety communities. How does your state rank?
4. The Metropolitan Medical Response System (MMRS) supports local efforts to respond to mass casualty incidents such as epidemic disease outbreaks, natural disasters, and contamination from hazardous materials. About 124 cities were eligible for funding. Is your city included?
5. The Citizen Corps Program (CCP) brings community and government leaders together to coordinate community involvement in emergency preparedness. How much did your state receive?

CAN I GET INVOLVED IN HOMELAND SECURITY?

Through the Citizen Corps Program, which probably operates in your county, individuals—including students—can get involved in a number of efforts, including emergency preparedness, flood preparedness, and citizen watch groups. In Michigan, for example, there are Citizen Emergency Response Teams at most major universities as well as at the county level. You can find information about local opportunities at **www.citizencorps.gov.**

REFERENCES

http://bensguide.gpo.gov/9-12/government/federalism.html
www.dhs.gov/xabout/strategicplan/index.shtm
www.dhs.gov/xgovt/grants
Fred Lucas, "Homeland Security Funding 'Pork' Under Fire," CNSNews.com, accessed February 23, 2007.
Eileen Sullivan, "Billions in States' Homeland Purchases Kept in the Dark," *Congressional Quarterly*, accessed June 22, 2005, at www.cq.com.

KEY TERMS

block grants 108
categorical grants 108
commerce clause 101
concurrent powers 95
confederal system 88
cooperative federalism 107
devolution 112
dual federalism 104

elastic clause, or necessary and proper clause 94
extradite 99
federalism 87
federal mandate 109
full faith and credit clause 98
interstate compact 99

picket-fence federalism 107
police power 94
privileges and immunities 99
supremacy clause 95
unitary system 88

CHAPTER SUMMARY

1. **Why did the founders think it important to divide powers between the nation and the states?** There are three basic models for ordering relations between central governments and local units: (1) a unitary system (in which ultimate power is held by the national government), (2) a confederal system (in which ultimate power is retained by the states), and (3) a federal system (in which governmental powers are divided between the national government and the states). A major reason for the creation of a federal system in the United States is that it reflected a compromise between the views of the Federalists (who wanted a strong national government) and those of the Anti-Federalists (who wanted the states to retain their sovereignty).

2. The Constitution expressly delegated certain powers to the national government in Article I, Section 8. In addition to these expressed powers, the national

government has implied and inherent powers. Implied powers are those that are reasonably necessary to carry out the powers expressly delegated to the national government. Inherent powers are those held by the national government by virtue of its being a sovereign state with the right to preserve itself.

3. The Tenth Amendment to the Constitution states that powers not delegated to the United States by the Constitution, nor prohibited by it to the states, are reserved to the states, or to the people. In certain areas, the Constitution provides for concurrent powers, such as the power to tax, which are powers that are held jointly by the national and state governments. The Constitution also denies certain powers to both the national government and the states.

4. The supremacy clause of the Constitution states that the Constitution, congressional laws, and national treaties are the supreme law of the land. States cannot use their reserved or concurrent powers to override national policies. Vertical checks and balances allow the states to influence the national government and vice versa.

5. The three most important clauses in the Constitution on interstate relations require that each state (1) give full faith and credit to every other state's public acts, records, and judicial proceedings; (2) extend to every other state's citizens the privileges and immunities of its own citizens; and (3) agree to return persons who are fleeing from justice back to their home state when requested to do so.

6. Two landmark Supreme Court cases expanded the constitutional powers of the national government. Chief Justice John Marshall's expansive interpretation of the necessary and proper clause of the Constitution in *McCulloch v. Maryland* (1819) permitted the "necessary and proper" clause to be used to enhance the power of the national government. Additionally, his decision made it clear that no state could tax a national institution. Marshall's broad interpretation of the commerce clause in *Gibbons v. Ogden* (1824) further extended the constitutional regulatory powers of the national government.

7. The controversy over slavery that led to the Civil War took the form of a fight over national government supremacy versus the rights of the separate states. Ultimately, the South's desire for increased states' rights and the subsequent Civil War resulted in an increase in the political power of the national government.

8. Since the Civil War, federalism has evolved through at least two general phases: dual federalism and cooperative federalism. In dual federalism, each of the states and the federal government remain supreme within their own spheres. The era since the Great Depression has sometimes been labeled one of cooperative federalism, in which states and the national government cooperate in solving complex common problems.

9. **How does the federal government achieve national goals in a federal system?** Categorical grants from the federal government to state governments help finance many projects, such as Medicaid, highway construction, unemployment benefits, and welfare programs. By attaching special conditions to the receipt of federal grants, the national government can effect policy changes in areas typically governed by the states. Block grants, which group several categorical grants together, usually have fewer strings attached, thus giving state and local governments more flexibility in using funds. Federal mandates—laws requiring states to implement certain policies, such as policies to protect the environment—have generated controversy because of their cost.

10. **Is a federal system effective in addressing the problems of the 21st century?** Traditionally, conservatives have favored states' rights, and liberals have favored national authority. In part, this is because the national government has historically been an engine of change, while state governments have been more content with the status quo. States have also been reluctant to increase social spending because of a fear that the resulting taxes could interfere with a "favorable business climate" and discourage new business enterprises. Some problems, such as environmental issues, seem to require either multistate cooperation or an overarching federal policy. States might argue that other problems, such as education, can best be addressed close to home.

11. Resistance to African American civil rights by the Southern states prejudiced many people against states' rights in the 1960s. Renamed "federalism," the states' rights cause received Republican support in the 1970s and 1980s. Republican presidents Richard Nixon and Ronald Reagan sought to return power to the states through block grants and other programs. Under Republican President George W. Bush, however, the national government has gained power relative to that of the states.

12. The United States Supreme Court plays a significant role in determining the line between state and federal powers. Since the 1990s, the Court has been reining in somewhat the national government's powers under the commerce clause and has given increased emphasis to state powers under the Tenth and Eleventh Amendments to the Constitution.

SELECTED PRINT, MEDIA, AND ONLINE RESOURCES

PRINT RESOURCES

Gerston, Larry A. *American Federalism: A Concise Introduction.* New York: M. E. Sharpe, 2007. The author introduces the reader to the philosophical and historical foundations of the federal system. He examines cases of conflict throughout our history.

Hamilton, Alexander, et al. *The Federalist: The Famous Papers on the Principles of American Government.* Benjamin F. Wright, ed. New York: Friedman/Fairfax Publishing, 2002. These essays remain an authoritative exposition of the founders' views on federalism.

Karmis, Dimitrios, and Wayne Norman, eds. *Theories of Federalism: A Reader.* New York: Palgrave MacMillan, 2005. This reader brings together the most significant writings on Federalism from the late 18th century to the present.

Manna, Paul. *School's In: Federalism and the National Education Agenda.* Washington, DC: Georgetown University Press, 2006. The author examines the changing relationship between the federal government and the states with regard to our public education system.

Nagel, Robert F. *The Implosion of American Federalism.* New York: Oxford University Press, 2002. The author contends that despite the states' rights trend of recent years, which has been given force by the Supreme Court in several of its decisions, the nation faces the danger of increasingly centralized power.

Nugent, John D. *Safeguarding Federalism: How States Protect Their Interests in National Policymaking.* Norman, OK: University of Oklahoma Press, 2009. Tracing the history of federalism, the author proposes that federalism is a vital force in American politics. He shows how the states protect their interest in policy innovation through a number of tactics including influencing federal legislation.

MEDIA RESOURCES

Can the States Do It Better?—A 1996 film in which various experts discuss how much power the national government should have. The film uses documentary footage and other resources to illustrate this debate.

City of Hope—A 1991 movie by John Sayles. The film is a story of life, work, race, and politics in a modern New Jersey city. An African American alderman is one of the several major characters.

The Civil War—The PBS documentary series that made director Ken Burns famous. *The Civil War*, first shown in 1990, marked a revolution in documentary technique. Photographs, letters, eyewitness memoirs, and music are used to bring the war to life. The DVD version was released in 2002.

McCulloch v. Maryland **and** ***Gibbons v. Ogden***—These programs are part of the series *Equal Justice under Law: Landmark Cases in Supreme Court History.* They provide more details on cases that defined our federal system.

ONLINE RESOURCES

Brookings—policy analyses and recommendations on a variety of issues, including federalism: www.brookings.edu

Catalog of Federal Domestic Assistance—complete listing of the federal grants that may be distributed to states and local governments: www.cfda.gov

Cato Institute—a libertarian approach to issues relating to federalism: www.cato.org

The Constitution Society—links to U.S. state constitutions, the *Federalist Papers*, and international federations, such as the European Union: www.constitution.org

Council of State Governments—information on state responses to federalism issues: www.csg.org

Emory University Law School—access to the *Federalist Papers*—the founders' views on federalism—and other historical documents: http://els449.law.emory.edu/index.php?id=3130

National Governors Association—information on issues facing state governments and federal-state relations: www.nga.org

4

A college student holds a peace sign as he speaks to a group about race relations and racist symbols at Denison College in Ohio. (Columbus Dispatch/David Foster/AP Photos)

Civil Liberties

QUESTIONS TO CONSIDER

Why is freedom of expression so fundamental to democracy?

What should be the relationship between religion and the political system?

What should be the balance between the rights of the accused and the rights of society to be protected from criminals?

CHAPTER CONTENTS

what if... *Roe v. Wade* Were Overturned?

BACKGROUND

The Bill of Rights and other provisions of the U.S. Constitution are the ultimate protections of our civil rights and liberties. But how do these rights work out in practice? How do we determine what our rights are in any given situation? One way is through judicial review, the power of the United States Supreme Court or other courts to declare laws and other acts of government unconstitutional. Supreme Court cases are often hotly contested, and the decision in the 1973 case *Roe v. Wade* is one of the most contentious ever handed down. In the *Roe v. Wade* case, the Court declared that a woman's constitutionally protected right to privacy includes the right to have an abortion. The Court concluded that the states cannot restrict a woman's right to an abortion during the first three months of pregnancy. More than 30 years later, however, the debate over the legality of abortion still rages in the United States.

WHAT IF *ROE v. WADE* WERE OVERTURNED?

If the Supreme Court overturned *Roe v. Wade*, the authority to regulate abortion would fall again to the states. Before the *Roe v. Wade* case, each state decided whether abortion would be legal within its borders. State legislatures made the laws that covered abortion. Some critics of *Roe v. Wade*'s constitutional merits have argued that allowing the Supreme Court to decide the legality of abortion nationwide is undemocratic because the justices are not elected officials. In contrast, if state legislatures regained the power to create abortion policy, the resulting laws would reflect the majority opinion of each state's voters. Legislators would have to respect popular sentiment on the issue or risk losing their next reelection bids.

THE POSSIBILITY OF STATE BANS ON ABORTION

Simply overturning *Roe v. Wade* would not make abortion in the United States illegal overnight. In many states, abortion rights are very popular, and the legislatures in those states would not consider measures to ban abortion or to further restrict access to abortion. Some states have laws that would protect abortion rights even if *Roe v. Wade* were overturned. Access to abortions would likely continue in the West Coast states and in much of the Northeast. In much of the South and the Midwest, however, abortion could be seriously restricted or even banned. Some states have "trigger laws" that would immediately outlaw abortion if *Roe v. Wade* were overturned.

Women living in conservative states such as the Dakotas, Kentucky, and Mississippi already face serious difficulties in obtaining an abortion. In each of these states, 98 percent of the counties do not have an abortion clinic. Many women desiring the procedure already have to travel long distances. If abortion were banned, these women could still cross state lines to obtain an abortion. If 21 of the most conservative states banned abortion, only 170 clinics would be affected—less than 10 percent of the national total.

STATE CHALLENGES TO *ROE v. WADE*

Undoubtedly feeling optimistic because of President George W. Bush's conservative Supreme Court appointments (John Roberts and Samuel Alito), South Dakota's legislature passed a law in February 2006 banning abortion however the law was overtuned in a statewide referendum. Another ballot effort to ban abortions was also defeated by South Dakota voters, in 2008. In 2008, "right-to-life" activists in a number of other states placed antiabortion measures on the ballot. In Colorado, for example, citizens voted on whether the state constitution should declare a fertilized egg a "person" who enjoys "inalienable rights, equality of justice, and due process of law." The measure was voted down by a three-to-one margin.

With the election of Barack Obama as president, the future of *Roe v. Wade* brightened. His first Supreme Court appointment, Sonya Sotomayor, was likely to become a supporter of the decision, and in 2010, the president nominated Elena Kagan to replace Justice Stevens, likely shoring up the coalition in support of *Roe v. Wade*.

FOR CRITICAL ANALYSIS

1. Why do you think that abortion remains a contentious topic more than 30 years after the *Roe v. Wade* decision? Should that decision be revisited? Why or why not?
2. How significant a role should the courts play in deciding constitutional questions about abortion? Do you feel that individual states should have a say in the legality of abortion within their own borders? Why or why not?

"THE LAND OF THE FREE." When asked what makes the United States distinctive, Americans commonly say that it is a free country. Americans have long believed that limits on the power of government are an essential part of what makes this country free. The first ten amendments to the U.S. Constitution—the Bill of Rights—place such limits on the national government. Of these amendments, none is more famous than the First Amendment, which guarantees freedom of religion, speech, the press, and other rights.

Most other democratic nations have laws to protect these and other **civil liberties**, but none of the laws is quite like the First Amendment, which states, "Congress shall make no law . . . abridging the freedom of speech, or of the press." Think about the issue of "hate speech." What if someone makes statements that stir up hatred toward a particular race or other group of people? In Germany, where memories of Nazi anti-Semitism remain alive, such speech is unquestionably illegal. In the United States, such speech may well be constitutionally protected, depending on the circumstances under which it occurred. In this chapter, we describe the civil liberties provided by the Bill of Rights and some of the controversies that surround them. We look at the First Amendment liberties, including religion, speech, press, and assembly, and then discuss the right to privacy and the rights of the accused.

Civil Liberties
Those personal freedoms that are protected for all individuals. Civil liberties typically involve restraining the government's actions against individuals.

THE BILL OF RIGHTS

As you read through this chapter, bear in mind that the Bill of Rights, like the rest of the Constitution, is relatively brief. The framers set forth broad guidelines, leaving it up to the courts to interpret these constitutional mandates and apply them to specific situations. Thus, judicial interpretations shape the true nature of the civil liberties and rights that we possess. Because judicial interpretations change over time, so do our rights. As you will read in the following pages, there have been many conflicts over the meaning of such simple phrases as *freedom of religion* and *freedom of the press*. To understand what freedoms we actually have, we need to examine how the courts—and particularly the United States Supreme Court—have resolved some of those conflicts. One important conflict was over the issue of whether the Bill of Rights in the federal Constitution limited the powers of state governments as well as those of the national government.

DID YOU KNOW?

That one of the proposed initial constitutional amendments—"No State shall infringe the equal rights of conscience, nor the freedom of speech, nor of the press, nor of the right of trial by jury in criminal cases"—was never sent to the states for approval because the states' rights advocates in the First Congress defeated this proposal?

EXTENDING THE BILL OF RIGHTS TO STATE GOVERNMENTS

Many citizens do not realize that, as originally intended, the Bill of Rights limited only the powers of the national government. At the time the Bill of Rights was ratified, there was little concern over the potential of state governments to curb civil liberties. For one thing, state governments were closer to home and easier to control. For another, most state constitutions already had bills of rights. Rather, the fear was of the potential tyranny of the national government. The Bill of Rights begins with the words, "Congress shall make no law . . ." It says nothing about *states* making laws that might abridge citizens' civil liberties.

In 1833, in *Barron v. Baltimore*,[1] the United States Supreme Court held that the Bill of Rights did not apply to state laws. The issue in the case was whether a property owner

---

[1] 7 Peters 243 (1833).

THESE EMPLOYEES of the National Security Agency (NSA) are working at the Threat Operations Center in Fort Meade, Maryland. This "super-secret" intelligence operation is heavily guarded. The NSA has admitted that it has engaged in domestic surveillance. Why were the actions of this agency seen as a threat to our First Amendment freedoms? (AP Photo/Evan Vucci)

could sue the city of Baltimore for recovery of his losses under the Fifth Amendment to the Constitution. Chief Justice Marshall spoke for a united court, declaring that the Supreme Court could not hear the case because the amendments were meant only to limit the national government.

We mentioned that most states had bills of rights. These bills of rights were similar to the national one, but there were some differences. Furthermore, each state's judicial system interpreted the rights differently. Citizens in different states, therefore, effectively had different sets of civil rights. Remember that the Thirteenth, Fourteenth, and Fifteenth Amendments were passed after the Civil War to guarantee equal rights to the former slaves and free black Americans, regardless of the states in which they lived. It was not until after the Fourteenth Amendment was ratified in 1868 that civil liberties guaranteed by the national Constitution began to be applied to the states. Section 1 of that amendment provides, in part, as follows:

DID YOU KNOW?

That in a recent survey, nearly one-fourth of the respondents could not name any First Amendment rights?

No State shall . . . deprive any person of life, liberty, or property, without due process of law.

INCORPORATION OF THE FOURTEENTH AMENDMENT

There was no question that the Fourteenth Amendment applied to state governments. For decades, however, the courts were reluctant to define the liberties spelled out in the national Bill of Rights as constituting "due process of law," which was protected under the Fourteenth Amendment. Not until 1925, in *Gitlow v. New York*,[2] did the United States Supreme Court hold that the Fourteenth Amendment protected the freedom of speech guaranteed by the First Amendment to the Constitution.

Only gradually, and never completely, did the Supreme Court accept the **incorporation theory**—the view that most of the protections of the Bill of Rights are

Incorporation Theory
The view that most of the protections of the Bill of Rights apply to state governments through the Fourteenth Amendment's due process clause.

[2]268 U.S. 652 (1925).

incorporated into the Fourteenth Amendment's protection against state government actions. Table 4–1 shows the rights that the Court has incorporated into the Fourteenth Amendment and the case in which it first applied each protection. As you can see in that table, in the 15 years following the *Gitlow* decision, the Supreme Court incorporated into the Fourteenth Amendment the other basic freedoms (of the press, assembly, the right to petition, and religion) guaranteed by the First Amendment. These and the later Supreme Court decisions listed in Table 4–1 have bound the 50 states to accept for their citizens most of the rights and freedoms that are set forth in the U.S. Bill of Rights. We now look at some of those rights and freedoms, beginning with the freedom of religion.

TABLE 4–1 Incorporating the Bill of Rights into the Fourteenth Amendment

YEAR	ISSUE	AMENDMENT INVOLVED	COURT CASE
1925	Freedom of speech	I	*Gitlow v. New York*, 268 U.S. 652
1931	Freedom of the press	I	*Near v. Minnesota*, 283 U.S. 697
1932	Right to a lawyer in capital punishment cases	VI	*Powell v. Alabama*, 287 U.S. 45
1937	Freedom of assembly and right to petition	I	*De Jonge v. Oregon*, 299 U.S. 353
1940	Freedom of religion	I	*Cantwell v. Connecticut*, 310 U.S. 296
1947	Separation of church and state	I	*Everson v. Board of Education*, 330 U.S. 1
1948	Right to a public trial	VI	*In re Oliver*, 333 U.S. 257
1949	No unreasonable searches and seizures	IV	*Wolf v. Colorado*, 338 U.S. 25
1961	Exclusionary rule	IV	*Mapp v. Ohio*, 367 U.S. 643
1962	No cruel and unusual punishment	VIII	*Robinson v. California*, 370 U.S. 660
1963	Right to a lawyer in all criminal felony cases	VI	*Gideon v. Wainwright*, 372 U.S. 335
1964	No compulsory self-incrimination	V	*Malloy v. Hogan*, 378 U.S. 1
1965	Right to privacy	I, III, IV, V, IX	*Griswold v. Connecticut*, 381 U.S. 479
1966	Right to an impartial jury	VI	*Parker v. Gladden*, 385 U.S. 363
1967	Right to a speedy trial	VI	*Klopfer v. North Carolina*, 386 U.S. 213
1969	No double jeopardy	V	*Benton v. Maryland*, 395 U.S. 784

FREEDOM OF RELIGION

Establishment Clause
The part of the First Amendment prohibiting the establishment of a church officially supported by the national government. It is applied to questions of state and local government aid to religious organizations and schools, the legality of allowing or requiring school prayers, and the teaching of evolution versus intelligent design.

In the United States, freedom of religion consists of two main principles as they are presented in the First Amendment. The **establishment clause** prohibits the establishment of a church that is officially supported by the national government, thus guaranteeing a division between church and state. The *free exercise clause* constrains the national government from prohibiting individuals from practicing the religion of their choice. These two precepts can inherently be in tension with one another, however. For example, would prohibiting a group of students from holding prayer meetings in a public school classroom infringe on the students' right to free exercise of religion? Or would allowing the meetings amount to unconstitutional government support for religion? You will read about several difficult freedom of religion issues in the following discussion.

THE SEPARATION OF CHURCH AND STATE— THE ESTABLISHMENT CLAUSE

The First Amendment to the Constitution states, in part, that "Congress shall make no law respecting an establishment of religion." In the words of Thomas Jefferson, the establishment clause was designed to create a "wall of separation of Church and State."[3]

Perhaps Jefferson was thinking about the religious intolerance that characterized the first colonies. Many of the American colonies were founded by groups that were pursuing religious freedom for their own particular denomination. Nonetheless, the early colonists were quite intolerant of religious beliefs that did not conform to those held by the majority of citizens within their own communities. Jefferson undoubtedly was also aware that established churches (denominations) existed within nine of the original 13 colonies.

As interpreted by the United States Supreme Court, the establishment clause in the First Amendment means at least the following:

> Neither a state nor the federal government can set up a church. Neither can pass laws which aid one religion, aid all religions, or prefer one religion over another. Neither can force nor influence a person to go to or to remain away from church against his will or force him to profess a belief or disbelief in any religion. No person can be punished for entertaining or professing religious beliefs or disbeliefs, for church attendance or nonattendance. No tax in any amount, large or small, can be levied to support any religious activities or institutions, whatever they may be called, or whatever form they may adopt to teach or practice religion. Neither a state nor the federal government can, openly or secretly, participate in the affairs of any religious organizations or groups and vice versa.[4]

The establishment clause is applied to all conflicts about such matters as the legality of state and local government aid to religious organizations and schools, the allowing or requiring of school prayers, the teaching of evolution versus intelligent design, the posting of the Ten Commandments in schools or public places, and discrimination against religious groups in publicly operated institutions. The establishment clause's mandate that government can neither promote nor discriminate against religious beliefs raises particularly complex questions at times.

---

[3]"Jefferson's Letter to the Danbury Baptists, The Final Letter, as Sent," January 1, 1802, The Library of Congress, Washington, D.C.
4 [4]*Everson v. Board of Education*, 330 U.S. 1 (1947).

Aid to Church-Related Schools. Throughout the United States, all property owners except religious, educational, fraternal, literary, scientific, and similar nonprofit institutions must pay property taxes. A large part of the proceeds of such taxes goes to support public schools. But not all children attend public schools. Fully 12 percent of school-aged children attend private schools, of which 85 percent have religious affiliations. Many cases have reached the United States Supreme Court; the Court has tried to draw a fine line between permissible public aid to students in church-related schools and impermissible public aid to religion. These issues have arisen most often at the elementary and secondary levels.

In 1971, in *Lemon v. Kurtzman*,[5] the Court ruled that direct state aid could not be used to subsidize religious instruction. The Court in the *Lemon* case gave its most general statement on the constitutionality of government aid to religious schools, stating that the aid had to be secular (nonreligious) in aim, that it could not have the primary effect of advancing or inhibiting religion, and that the government must avoid "an excessive government entanglement with religion." The three phrases above became known as the "three-part *Lemon* test" which has been applied in most of the cases under the establishment clause since 1971. The interpretation of the test, however, has varied over the years.

In several cases, the Supreme Court has held that state programs helping church-related schools are unconstitutional. The Court also has denied state reimbursements to religious schools for field trips and for developing achievement tests. In a series of other cases, however, the Supreme Court has allowed states to use tax funds for lunches, textbooks, diagnostic services for speech and hearing problems, standardized tests, computers, and transportation for students attending church-operated elementary and secondary schools. In some cases, the Court argued that state aid was intended to directly

DID YOU KNOW?

That on the eve of the American Revolution, fewer than 20 percent of American adults adhered to a church in any significant way, compared with the 60 percent who do so today?

[5]403 U.S. 602 (1971).

assist the individual child, and in other cases, such as bus transportation, the Court acknowledged the state's goals for public safety.

A Change in the Court's Position. Generally, today's Supreme Court has shown a greater willingness to allow the use of public funds for programs in religious schools than was true at times in the past. Consider that in 1985, in *Aguilar v. Felton*,[6] the Supreme Court ruled that state programs providing special educational services for disadvantaged students attending religious schools violated the establishment clause. In 1997, however, when the Supreme Court revisited this decision, the Court reversed its position. In *Agostini v. Felton*,[7] the Court held that *Aguilar* was "no longer good law." What had happened between 1985 and 1997 to cause the Court to change its mind? Justice Sandra Day O'Connor answered this question in the *Agostini* opinion: What had changed since *Aguilar*, she stated, was "our understanding" of the establishment clause. Between 1985 and 1997, the Court's makeup had changed significantly. In fact, six of the nine justices who participated in the 1997 decision were appointed after the 1985 *Aguilar* decision.

School Vouchers. Questions about the use of public funds for church-related schools are likely to continue as state legislators search for new ways to improve the educational system in this country. An issue that has come to the forefront in recent years is school vouchers. In a voucher system, educational vouchers (state-issued credits) can be used to "purchase" education at any school, public or private.

School districts in Florida, Ohio, and Wisconsin have all been experimenting with voucher systems. In 2000, the courts reviewed a case involving Ohio's voucher program. Under that program, some $10 million in public funds is spent annually to send 4,300 Cleveland students to 51 private schools, all but five of which are Catholic schools. The case presented a straightforward constitutional question: Is it a violation of the principle of separation of church and state for public tax money to be used to pay for religious education?

In 2002, the Supreme Court held that the Cleveland voucher program was constitutional.[8] The Court concluded, by a five-to-four vote, that Cleveland's use of taxpayer-paid school vouchers to send children to private schools was constitutional, even though more than 95 percent of the students use the vouchers to attend Catholic or other religious schools. The Court's majority reasoned that the program did not unconstitutionally entangle church and state, because families theoretically could use the vouchers for their children to attend religious schools, secular private academies, suburban public schools, or charter schools, even though few public schools had agreed to accept vouchers. The Court's decision raised a further question that will need to be decided—whether religious and private schools that accept government vouchers must comply with disability and civil rights laws, as public schools are required to do.

Despite the United States Supreme Court's decision upholding the Cleveland voucher program, in 2006 the Florida Supreme Court declared Florida's voucher program unconstitutional. The Florida court held that the Florida state constitution bars public funding from being diverted to private schools that are not subject to the uniformity requirements of the state's public school system. The decision could have national implications if other states mount similar challenges to voucher programs. It remains to be seen whether the United States Supreme Court will review the Florida ruling. To further complicate the issue, the Obama administration sought to cancel a school voucher program for the Washington, D.C., schools that has been funded by federal law.

---

[6]473 U.S. 402 (1985).
[7]521 U.S. 203 (1997).
[8]*Zelman v. Simmons-Harris*, 536 U.S. 639 (2002).

After protests by parents, the administration decided to continue funding only for students already enrolled in the program and continued to cut funding in 2010.

The Issue of School Prayer—*Engel v. Vitale*. Do the states have the right to promote religion in general, without making any attempt to establish a particular religion? That is the question raised by school prayer and was the precise issue in 1962 in *Engel v. Vitale*,[9] the so-called Regents' Prayer case in New York. The State Board of Regents of New York had suggested that a prayer be spoken aloud in the public schools at the beginning of each day. The recommended prayer was as follows:

> Almighty God, we acknowledge our dependence upon Thee, And we beg Thy blessings upon us, our parents, our teachers, and our Country.

Such a prayer was implemented in many New York public schools. The parents of several students challenged the action of the regents, maintaining that it violated the establishment clause of the First Amendment. At trial, the parents lost. The Supreme Court, however, ruled that the regents' action was unconstitutional because "the constitutional prohibition against laws respecting an establishment of a religion must mean at least that in this country it is no part of the business of government to compose official prayers for any group of the American people to recite as part of a religious program carried on by any government." The Court's conclusion was based in part on the "historical fact that governmentally established religions and religious persecutions go hand in hand." In *Abington School District v. Schempp*,[10] the Supreme Court outlawed officially sponsored daily readings of the Bible and recitation of the Lord's Prayer in public schools.

The Debate over School Prayer Continues. Although the Supreme Court has ruled repeatedly against officially sponsored prayer and Bible-reading sessions in public schools, other means for bringing some form of religious expression into public education have been attempted. In 1983, the Tennessee legislature passed a bill requiring public school classes to begin each day with a minute of silence. Alabama had a similar law. In 1985, in *Wallace v. Jaffree*,[11] the Supreme Court struck down as unconstitutional the Alabama law authorizing one minute of silence for prayer or meditation in all public schools. Applying the three-part *Lemon* test, the Court concluded that the law violated the establishment clause because it was "an endorsement of religion lacking any clearly secular purpose."

Since then, the lower courts have interpreted the Supreme Court's decision to mean that states can require a moment of silence in the schools as long as they make it clear that the purpose of the law is secular, not religious.

Prayer outside the Classroom. The courts have also dealt with cases involving prayer in public schools outside the classroom, particularly prayer during graduation ceremonies. In 1992, in *Lee v. Weisman*,[12] the United States Supreme Court held that it was unconstitutional for a school to invite a rabbi to deliver a nonsectarian prayer at graduation. The Court said nothing about *students* organizing and leading prayers at graduation ceremonies and other school events, however, and these issues continue to come before the courts. A particularly contentious question in the last few years has been the constitutionality of student-initiated prayers before sporting

DID YOU KNOW?

That about two-thirds of 18- to 25-year-old Americans believe that humans and other living things evolved over time, whereas about one-third believe that all living things have existed in their present form since creation?

[9]370 U.S. 421 (1962).
[10]374 U.S. 203 (1963).
[11]472 U.S. 38 (1985).
[12]505 U.S. 577 (1992).

events, such as football games. In 2000, the Supreme Court held that while school prayer at graduation did not violate the establishment clause, students could not use a school's public-address system to lead prayers at sporting events.[13]

Despite the Court's ruling, students at several schools in Texas continue to pray over public-address systems at sporting events. In other areas, the Court's ruling is skirted by avoiding the use of the public-address system. For example, in a school in North Carolina, a pregame prayer was broadcast over a local radio station and heard by fans who took radios to the game for that purpose.

The Ten Commandments. A related church–state issue is whether the Ten Commandments may be displayed in public schools—or on any public property. In recent years, several states have considered legislation that would allow or even require schools to post the Ten Commandments in school buildings. Supporters of the "Hang Ten" movement claim that schoolchildren are not being taught the fundamental religious and family values that frame the American way of life. They argue further that the Ten Commandments are more than just religious documents. The Commandments are also secular in nature because they constitute a part of the official and permanent history of American government.

Opponents of such laws claim that they are an unconstitutional government entanglement with the religious life of citizens. Still, various Ten Commandments installations have been found to be constitutional. For example, the Supreme Court ruled in 2005 that a granite monument on the grounds of the Texas state capitol that contained the commandments was constitutional because the monument as a whole was secular in nature.[14] In another 2005 ruling, however, the Court ordered that displays of the Ten Commandments in front of two Kentucky county courthouses had to be removed because they were overtly religious.[15]

The Ten Commandments controversy took an odd twist in 2003 when, in the middle of the night, former Alabama chief justice Roy Moore installed a two-and-a-half-ton granite monument featuring the Commandments in the rotunda of the state courthouse. When Moore refused to obey a federal judge's order to remove the monument, the Alabama Court of the Judiciary was forced to expel him from the judicial bench. The monument was wheeled away to a storage room.

Forbidding the Teaching of Evolution. For many decades, certain religious groups, particularly in Southern states, have opposed the teaching of evolution in the schools. To these groups, evolutionary theory directly counters their religious belief that human beings did not evolve

WORKERS REMOVE a monument of the Ten Commandments from the rotunda area of the Alabama Judicial Building where Superior Court Justice Roy Moore had refused to take it down on August 27, 2003, in Montgomery, Alabama. Judge Moore was suspended by the state judicial review board for refusing to comply with the federal court order to remove the monument. (TAMI CHAPPELL/ Reuters/Landov)

[13]*Santa Fe Independent School District v. Doe*, 530 U.S. 290 (2000).
[14]*Van Orden v. Perry*, 125 S.Ct. 2854 (2005).
[15]*McCreary County v. American Civil Liberties Union*, 125 S.Ct. 2722 (2005).

but were created fully formed, as described in the biblical story of creation. State and local attempts to forbid the teaching of evolution, however, have not passed constitutional muster in the eyes of the United States Supreme Court. For example, in 1968, the Supreme Court held in *Epperson v. Arkansas*[16] that an Arkansas law prohibiting the teaching of evolution violated the establishment clause because it imposed religious beliefs on students. The Louisiana legislature passed a law requiring the teaching of the biblical story of the creation alongside the teaching of evolution. In 1987, in *Edwards v. Aguillard*,[17] the Supreme Court declared that this law was unconstitutional, in part because it had as its primary purpose the promotion of a particular religious belief.

Nonetheless, state and local groups around the country, particularly in the so-called Bible Belt, continue their efforts against the teaching of evolution. The Cobb County school system in Georgia attempted to include a disclaimer in its biology textbooks that proclaims, "Evolution is a theory, not a fact, regarding the origin of living things." A federal judge later ruled that the disclaimer stickers must be removed. Other school districts have considered teaching "intelligent design" as an alternative explanation of the origin of life. Proponents of intelligent design contend that evolutionary theory has gaps that can be explained only by the existence of an intelligent creative force (God). They believe that teaching intelligent design in the schools is simply teaching another kind of scientific theory, so it would not breach the separation of church and state.

Critics of intelligent design have pointed out that many of its proponents have a religious agenda. Conservative evangelical Christians have often been the driving force behind efforts to teach intelligent design alongside evolution. The same religious groups also once backed creationism, a discredited theory that attempted to provide scientific evidence for the Bible's creation narrative. Furthermore, say the critics, intelligent design is not even a theory in the scientific sense of the word, as its claims cannot be disproved by examining real-world data. Therefore, intelligent design is a belief system. They insist that such religious agendas have no place in the public school system, where a firm separation between church and state must be respected.

Religious Speech. Another controversy in the area of church-state relations concerns religious speech in public schools or universities. For example, in *Rosenberger v. University of Virginia*,[18] the issue was whether the University of Virginia violated the establishment clause when it refused to fund a Christian group's newsletter but granted funds to more than 100 other student organizations. The Supreme Court ruled that the university's policy unconstitutionally discriminated against religious speech. The Court pointed out that the funds came from student fees, not general taxes, and were used for the "neutral" payment of bills for student groups.

Later, the Supreme Court reviewed a case involving a similar claim of discrimination against a religious group, the Good News Club. The club offers religious instruction to young schoolchildren. The club sued the school board of a public school in Milford, New York, when the board refused to allow the club to meet on school property after the school day ended. The club argued that the school board's refusal to allow the club to meet on school property, when other groups—such as the Girl Scouts and the 4-H Club—were permitted to do so, amounted to discrimination on the basis of religion. Ultimately, the Supreme Court agreed, ruling in *Good News Club v. Milford Central School*[19] that the Milford school board's decision violated the establishment clause.

[16]393 U.S. 97 (1968).
[17]482 U.S. 578 (1987).
[18]515 U.S. 819 (1995).
[19]533 U.S. 98 (2001).

THE FREE EXERCISE CLAUSE

The First Amendment constrains Congress from prohibiting the free exercise of religion. Does this **free exercise clause** mean that no type of religious practice can be prohibited or restricted by government? Certainly, a person can hold any religious belief that he or she wants, or a person can have no religious beliefs. When, however, religious *practices* work against public policy and the public welfare, the government can act. For example, regardless of a child's or parent's religious beliefs, the government can require certain types of vaccinations. The sale and use of marijuana for religious purposes has been held illegal, because a religion cannot make legal what would otherwise be illegal. Additionally, public school students can be required to study from textbooks chosen by school authorities.

The extent to which government can regulate religious practices has always been a subject of controversy. For example, in 1990 in *Oregon v. Smith*,[20] the United States Supreme Court ruled that the state of Oregon could deny unemployment benefits to two drug counselors who had been fired for using peyote, an illegal drug, in their religious services. The counselors had argued that using peyote was part of the practice of a Native American religion. Many criticized the decision as going too far in the direction of regulating religious practices.

The Religious Freedom Restoration Act. In 1993, Congress responded to the public's criticism by passing the Religious Freedom Restoration Act (RFRA). One of the specific purposes of the act was to overturn the Supreme Court's decision in *Oregon v. Smith*. The act required national, state, and local governments to "accommodate religious conduct" unless the government could show that there was a *compelling* reason not to do so. Moreover, if the government did regulate a religious practice, it had to use the least restrictive means possible.

Some people believed that the RFRA went too far in the other direction—it accommodated practices that were contrary to the public policies of state governments. Proponents of states' rights complained that the act intruded into an area traditionally governed by state laws, not by the national government. In 1997, in *City of Boerne v. Flores*,[21] the Supreme Court agreed and held that Congress had exceeded its constitutional authority when it passed the RFRA. According to the Court, the act's "sweeping coverage ensures its intrusion at every level of government, displacing laws and prohibiting official actions of almost every description and regardless of subject matter."

Free Exercise in the Public Schools. The courts have repeatedly held that U.S. governments at all levels must remain neutral on issues of religion. In the *Good News Club* decision discussed previously, the Supreme Court ruled that "state power is no more to be used to handicap religions than it is to favor them." Nevertheless, by overturning the RFRA, the Court cleared the way for public schools to set regulations that, while ostensibly neutral, effectively limited religious expression by students. An example is a rule banning hats, which has been instituted by many schools as a way of discouraging the display of gang insignia. This rule has also been interpreted as barring yarmulkes, the small caps worn by strictly observant Jewish boys and men.

The national government found a new way to ensure that public schools do not excessively restrict religion. To receive funds under the No Child Left Behind Act of 2002,

---

[20]494 U.S. 872 (1990).
[21]521 U.S. 507 (1997).

A MUSLIM GIRL in France arrives at school with her head covered in a traditional scarf. The French government has prohibited the wearing of such religious symbols in the schools. Could a state in the U.S. prohibit wearing a cross or another religious symbol in public schools? (Olivier Morin/ AFP/Getty Images)

schools must certify in writing that they do not ban prayer or other expressions of religion as long as they are made in a constitutionally appropriate manner.

FREEDOM OF EXPRESSION

Perhaps the most frequently invoked freedom that Americans have is the right to free speech and a free press without government interference. Each of us has the right to have our say, and all of us have the right to hear what others say. For the most part, Americans can criticize public officials and their actions without fear of reprisal by any branch of government.

NO PRIOR RESTRAINT

Restraining an activity before that activity has actually occurred is called **prior restraint**. When expression is involved, prior restraint means censorship, as opposed to subsequent punishment. Prior restraint of expression would require, for example, that a permit be obtained before a speech could be made, a newspaper published, or a movie or TV show exhibited. Most, if not all, Supreme Court justices have been very critical of any governmental action that imposes prior restraint on expression. The Court clearly displayed this attitude in *Nebraska Press Association v. Stuart*,[22] a case decided in 1976:

> A prior restraint on expression comes to this Court with a "heavy presumption" against its constitutionality. ... The government thus carries a heavy burden of showing justification for the enforcement of such a restraint.

Prior Restraint
Restraining an action before the activity has actually occurred. When expression is involved, this means censorship.

[22]427 U.S. 539 (1976). See also *Near v. Minnesota*, 283 U.S. 697 (1931).

One of the most famous cases concerning prior restraint was *New York Times v. United States*[23] in 1971, the so-called Pentagon Papers case. The *Times* and the *Washington Post* were about to publish the Pentagon Papers, an elaborate secret history of the U.S. government's involvement in the Vietnam War (1964–1975). The secret documents had been obtained illegally by a disillusioned former Pentagon official. The government wanted a court order to bar publication of the documents, arguing that national security was threatened and that the documents had been stolen. The newspapers argued that the public had a right to know the information contained in the papers and that the press had the right to inform the public. The Supreme Court ruled six to three in favor of the newspapers' right to publish the information. This case affirmed the no-prior-restraint doctrine.

Symbolic Speech
Nonverbal expression of beliefs, which is given substantial protection by the courts.

THE PROTECTION OF SYMBOLIC SPEECH

Not all expression is in words or in writing. Articles of clothing, gestures, movements, and other forms of expressive conduct are considered **symbolic speech**. Such speech is given substantial protection today by our courts. For example, in a landmark decision issued in 1969, *Tinker v. Des Moines School District*,[24] the United States Supreme Court held that the wearing of black armbands by students in protest against the Vietnam War was a form of speech protected by the First Amendment. The case arose after a school administrator in Des Moines, Iowa, issued a regulation prohibiting students in the Des Moines School District from wearing the armbands. The Supreme Court reasoned that the school district was unable to show that the wearing of the armbands had disrupted normal school activities. Furthermore, the school district's policy was discriminatory, as it banned

DEMONSTRATORS burn U.S. flags in front of the World Bank headquarters in 2002, protesting the international meetings there. Why is it legal to burn the flag in protest? (Hiroko Masuike/AFP/ Getty Images)

---

[23]403 U.S. 713 (1971).
[24]393 U.S. 503 (1969).

only certain forms of symbolic speech (the black armbands) and not others (such as lapel crosses and fraternity rings).

In 1989, in *Texas v. Johnson*,[25] the Supreme Court ruled that state laws that prohibited the burning of the American flag as part of a peaceful protest also violated the freedom of expression protected by the First Amendment. Congress responded by passing the Flag Protection Act of 1989, which was ruled unconstitutional by the Supreme Court in June 1990.[26] Congress and President George H. W. Bush immediately pledged to work for a constitutional amendment to "protect our flag"—an effort that has yet to be successful.

In 2003, however, the Supreme Court held that a Virginia statute prohibiting the burning of a cross with "an intent to intimidate" did not violate the First Amendment. The Court concluded that a burning cross is an instrument of racial terror so threatening that it overshadows free speech concerns.[27]

THE PROTECTION OF COMMERCIAL SPEECH

Commercial speech usually is defined as advertising statements. Can advertisers use their First Amendment rights to prevent restrictions on the content of commercial advertising? Until the 1970s, the Supreme Court held that such speech was not protected at all by the First Amendment. By the mid-1970s, however, more commercial speech had been brought under First Amendment protection. According to Justice Harry A. Blackmun, "Advertising, however tasteless and excessive it sometimes may seem, is nonetheless dissemination of information as to who is producing and selling what product for what reason and at what price."[28] Nevertheless, the Supreme Court will consider a restriction on commercial speech valid as long as it (1) seeks to implement a substantial government interest, (2) directly advances that interest, and (3) goes no further than necessary to accomplish its objective. In particular, a business engaging in commercial speech can be subject to liability for factual inaccuracies in ways that do not apply to noncommercial speech.

> **Commercial Speech**
> Advertising statements, which increasingly have been given First Amendment protection.

The issue of political campaign advertising is one that crosses the boundaries between individual free speech and commercial speech. For many years, federal law has prohibited businesses, labor unions, and other organizations from engaging directly in political advertising. As you will learn later in this book, corporations and other groups were allowed to create political action committees to engage in regulated activities. In recent years, new organizational forms were created to campaign for issues. However, nonprofit organizations were strictly prohibited from directly campaigning for candidates. In 2009, the Supreme Court overturned decades of law on this issue, declaring in *Citizens United vs. FEC* that corporations and other associations were "persons" in terms of the law and had free speech rights. According to the majority decision, Citizens United, an incorporated nonprofit group, was unfairly denied the right to pay for broadcasting a movie about Senator Hillary Clinton, a film which was intended to harm her campaign for president. President Obama reacted by asking the Congress to rewrite the campaign finance laws to restrict such forms of political advertising.[29]

---

[25]488 U.S. 884 (1989).
[26]*United States v. Eichman*, 496 U.S. 310 (1990).
[27]*Virginia v. Black*, 538 U.S. 343 (2003).
[28]*Virginia State Board of Pharmacy v. Virginia Citizens Consumer Council, Inc.*, 425 U.S. 748 (1976).
[29]*Citizens United v. Federal Election Commission*, 558 U.S. (2010).

PERMITTED RESTRICTIONS ON EXPRESSION

At various times, restrictions on expression have been permitted. As we have seen after the terrorist attacks of September 11, 2001, periods of perceived foreign threats to the government sometimes lead to more repression of speech that is thought to be dangerous to the nation. It is interesting to note that the Supreme Court changes its view of what might be dangerous speech depending on the times.

Clear and Present Danger. When a person's remarks create a clear and present danger to the peace or public order, they can be curtailed constitutionally. Justice Oliver Wendell Holmes used this reasoning in 1919 when examining the case of a socialist who had been convicted for violating the Espionage Act by distributing a leaflet that opposed the military draft. Holmes stated:

> The question in every case is whether the words are used in such circumstances and are of such a nature as to create a *clear and present danger* that they will bring about the substantive evils that Congress has a right to prevent. It is a question of proximity and degree.[30] [Emphasis added.]

According to the **clear and present danger test**, then, expression may be restricted if evidence exists that such expression would cause a condition, actual or imminent, that Congress has the power to prevent. Commenting on this test, Justice Louis D. Brandeis in 1920 said, "Correctly applied, it will reserve the right of free speech . . . from suppression by tyrannists, well-meaning majorities, and from abuse by irresponsible, fanatical minorities."[31]

Modifications to the Clear and Present Danger Rule. Since the clear and present danger rule was first enunciated, the United States Supreme Court has modified it. In 1925, during

Clear and Present Danger Test
The test proposed by Justice Oliver Wendell Holmes for determining when government may restrict free speech. Restrictions are permissible, he argued, only when speech creates a *clear and present danger* to the public order.

IN 2002, A STUDENT who held this banner outside his school in Alaska was suspended for supporting drug use with his "speech." The Supreme Court upheld the principal's decision in the 2007 case *Morse v. Frederick*,[29] saying that public schools are able to regulate what students say about promoting illegal drug use. Do you think banning such speech is a violation of students' free speech rights? Should colleges be able to implement such a ban as well? (Clay Good/Zuma Press)

---

[30]*Schenck v. United States*, 249 U.S. 47 (1919).
[31]*Schaefer v. United States*, 251 U.S. 466 (1920).

a period when many Americans feared the increasing power of communist and other left-wing parties in Europe, the Supreme Court heard the case *Gitlow v. New York*.[32] In its opinion, the Court introduced the *bad-tendency rule*. According to this rule, speech or other First Amendment freedoms may be curtailed if there is a possibility that such expression might lead to some "evil." In the *Gitlow* case, a member of a left-wing group was convicted of violating New York State's criminal anarchy statute when he published and distributed a pamphlet urging the violent overthrow of the U.S. government. In its majority opinion, the Supreme Court held that although the First Amendment afforded protection against state incursions on freedom of expression, Gitlow could be punished legally in this particular instance because his expression would tend to bring about evils that the state had a right to prevent.

The Supreme Court again modified the clear and present danger test in a 1951 case, *Dennis v. United States*.[33] During the early years of the Cold War, Americans were anxious about the activities of communists and the Soviet Union within the United States. Congress passed several laws that essentially outlawed the Communist Party of the United States and made its activities illegal. Twelve members of the American Communist Party were convicted of violating a statute that made it a crime to conspire to teach, advocate, or organize the violent overthrow of any government in the United States. The Supreme Court affirmed the convictions, significantly modifying the clear and present danger test in the process. The Court applied a *grave and probable danger rule*. Under this rule, "the gravity of the 'evil' discounted by its improbability justifies such invasion of free speech as is necessary to avoid the danger." This rule gave much less protection to free speech than did the clear and present danger test.

Six years after the *Dennis* case, the Supreme Court heard another case in which members of the Communist Party in California were accused of teaching and advocating the overthrow of the government of the United States. The ruling of the Court in this case greatly reduced the scope of the law passed by Congress. In *Yates v. United States*,[34] the Court held that there was a difference between "advocacy and teaching of forcible overthrow as an abstract principle" and actually proposing concrete action. The Court overturned the convictions of the party leaders because they were essentially engaging in speech rather than action. This was the beginning of a series of cases that eventually found the original congressional legislation to be unconstitutional because it violated the First and Fourth Amendments.

Some claim that the United States did not achieve true freedom of political speech until 1969. In that year, in *Brandenburg v. Ohio*,[35] the Supreme Court overturned the conviction of a Ku Klux Klan leader for violating a state statute. The statute prohibited anyone from advocating "the duty, necessity, or propriety of sabotage, violence, or unlawful methods of terrorism as a means of accomplishing industrial or political reform." The Court held that the guarantee of free speech does not permit a state "to forbid or proscribe advocacy of the use of force or of law violation except where such advocacy is directed to inciting or producing imminent lawless actions and is likely to incite or produce such action." The incitement test enunciated by the Court in this case is a difficult one for prosecutors to meet. As a result, the Court's decision significantly broadened the protection given to advocacy speech.

---

[32]268 U.S. 652 (1925).
[33]341 U.S. 494 (1951).
[34]354 U.S. 298 (1957).
[35]395 U.S. 444 (1969).

UNPROTECTED SPEECH: OBSCENITY

Many state and federal statutes make it a crime to disseminate obscene materials. Generally, the courts have not been willing to extend constitutional protections of free speech to what they consider to be obscene materials. But what is obscenity? Justice Potter Stewart once stated, in *Jacobellis v. Ohio*,[36] a 1964 case, that even though he could not define *obscenity*, "I know it when I see it." The problem is that even if it were agreed on, the definition of *obscenity* changes with the times. Victorians deeply disapproved of the "loose" morals of the Elizabethan Age. The works of Mark Twain and Edgar Rice Burroughs at times have been considered obscene (after all, Tarzan and Jane were not legally wedded).

Definitional Problems. The Supreme Court has grappled from time to time with the difficulty of specifying an operationally effective definition of *obscenity*. In 1973, in *Miller v. California*,[37] Chief Justice Warren Burger created a formal list of requirements that must be met for material to be considered legally obscene. Material is obscene if (1) the average person finds that it violates contemporary community standards; (2) the work taken as a whole appeals to a prurient interest in sex; (3) the work shows patently offensive sexual conduct; and (4) the work lacks serious redeeming literary, artistic, political, or scientific merit. The problem is that one person's prurient interest is another person's medical interest or artistic pleasure. The Court went on to state that the definition of *prurient interest* would be determined by the community's standards. The Court avoided presenting a definition of *obscenity,* leaving this determination to local and state authorities. Consequently, the *Miller* case has been applied in a widely inconsistent manner.

Protecting Children. The Supreme Court has upheld state laws making it illegal to sell materials showing sexual performances by minors. In 1990, in *Osborne v. Ohio*,[38] the Court ruled that states can outlaw the possession of child pornography in the home. The Court reasoned that the ban on private possession is justified because owning the material perpetuates commercial demand for it and for the exploitation of the children involved. At the federal level, the Child Protection Act of 1984 made it a crime to receive knowingly through the mails sexually explicit depictions of children.

Pornography on the Internet. A significant problem facing Americans and lawmakers today is how to control obscenity and child pornography disseminated via the Internet. In 1996, Congress first attempted to protect minors from pornographic materials on the Internet by passing the Communications Decency Act (CDA). The act made it a crime to make available to minors online any "obscene or indecent" message that "depicts or describes, in terms patently offensive as measured by contemporary community standards, sexual or excretory activities or organs." The act was immediately challenged in court as an unconstitutional infringement on free speech. The Supreme Court held that the act imposed unconstitutional restraints on free speech and was therefore invalid.[39] In the eyes of the Court, the terms *indecent* and *patently offensive* covered large amounts of nonpornographic material with serious educational or other value.

Later attempts by Congress to curb pornography on the Internet also encountered stumbling blocks. For example, the Child Online Protection Act (COPA) of 1998 banned the distribution of material "harmful to minors" without an age-verification system

(Image copyright Sylvana Rega 2010. Used under license from Shutterstock.com)

---

[36]378 U.S. 184 (1964).
[37]413 U.S. 5 (1973).
[38]495 U.S. 103 (1990).
[39]*Reno v. American Civil Liberties Union*, 521 U.S. 844 (1997).

to separate adult and minor users. In 2002, the Supreme Court upheld a lower court injunction suspending the COPA, and in 2004, the Court again upheld the suspension of the law on the ground that it was probably unconstitutional.[40] In 2000, Congress enacted the Children's Internet Protection Act (CIPA), which requires public schools and libraries to install filtering software to prevent children from viewing Web sites with "adult" content.

Should "Virtual" Pornography Be Deemed a Crime? In 2001, the Supreme Court agreed to review a case challenging the constitutionality of another federal act attempting to protect minors in the online environment—the Child Pornography Prevention Act (CPPA) of 1996. This act made it illegal to distribute or possess computer-generated images that appear to depict minors engaging in lewd and lascivious behavior. At issue was whether digital child pornography should be considered a crime even though it uses only digitally rendered images and no actual children are involved.

The Supreme Court, noting that virtual child pornography is not the same as child pornography, held that the CPPA's ban on virtual child pornography restrained a substantial amount of lawful speech.[41] The Court stated, "The statute proscribes the visual depiction of an idea—that of teenagers engaging in sexual activity—that is a fact of modern society and has been a theme in art and literature throughout the ages." The Court concluded that the act was overbroad and thus unconstitutional.

UNPROTECTED SPEECH: SLANDER

Can you say anything you want about someone else? Not really. Individuals are protected from **defamation of character**, which is defined as wrongfully hurting a person's good reputation. The law imposes a general duty on all persons to refrain from making false, defamatory statements about others. Breaching this duty orally is the wrongdoing called *slander*. Breaching it in writing is the wrongdoing called *libel*, which we discuss later. The government does not bring charges of slander or libel. Rather, the defamed person may bring a civil suit for damages.

Legally, **slander** is the public uttering of a false statement that harms the good reputation of another. Slanderous public uttering means that the defamatory statements are made to, or within the hearing of, persons other than the defamed party. If one person calls another dishonest, manipulative, and incompetent to his or her face when no one else is around, that does not constitute slander. The message is not communicated to a third party. If, however, a third party accidentally overhears defamatory statements, the courts have generally held that this constitutes a public uttering and therefore slander, which is prohibited.

Defamation of Character
Wrongfully hurting a person's good reputation. The law imposes a general duty on all persons to refrain from making false, defamatory statements about others.

Slander
The public uttering of a false statement that harms the good reputation of another. The statement must be made to, or within the hearing of, persons other than the defamed party.

CAMPUS SPEECH

In recent years, students have been facing free-speech challenges on campuses. One issue has to do with whether a student should have to subsidize, through student activity fees, organizations that promote causes that the student finds objectionable.

Student Activity Fees. In 2000, this question came before the United States Supreme Court in a case brought by several University of Wisconsin students. The students argued that their mandatory student activity fees—which helped to fund liberal causes with which they disagreed, including gay rights—violated their First Amendment rights of free

---

[40]*Ashcroft v. American Civil Liberties Union*, 542 U.S. 656 (2004).
[41]*Ashcroft v. Free Speech Coalition*, 535 U.S. 234 (2002).

speech, free association, and free exercise of religion. They contended that they should have the right to choose whether to fund organizations that promoted political and ideological views that were offensive to their personal beliefs. To the surprise of many, the Supreme Court rejected the students' claim and ruled in favor of the university. The Court stated that "the university may determine that its mission is well served if students have the means to engage in dynamic discussions of philosophical, religious, scientific, social, and political subjects in their extracurricular life. If the university reaches this conclusion, it is entitled to impose a mandatory fee to sustain an open dialogue to these ends."[42]

Campus Speech and Behavior Codes. Another free speech issue is the legitimacy of campus speech and behavior codes. Some state universities have established codes that challenge the boundaries of the protection of free speech provided by the First Amendment. These codes are designed to prohibit so-called hate speech—abusive speech attacking persons on the basis of their ethnicity, race, or other criteria. For example, a University of Michigan code banned "any behavior, verbal or physical, that stigmatizes or victimizes an individual on the basis of race, ethnicity, religion, sex, sexual orientation, creed, national origin, ancestry, age, marital status, handicap" or Vietnam-veteran status. A federal court found that the code violated students' First Amendment rights.[43]

Although the courts generally have held, as in the University of Michigan case, that campus speech codes are unconstitutional restrictions on the right to free speech, such codes continue to exist. Whether hostile speech should be banned on high school campuses has also become an issue. In view of school shootings and other violent behavior in the schools, school officials have become concerned about speech that consists of veiled threats or that could lead to violence. Some schools have even prohibited students from wearing clothing, such as T-shirts bearing verbal messages (such as sexist or racist comments) or symbolic messages (such as the Confederate flag), that might generate "ill will or hatred."

Defenders of campus speech codes argue that they are necessary not only to prevent violence but also to promote equality among different cultural, ethnic, and racial groups on campus and greater sensitivity to the needs and feelings of others. In recent years, law schools even attempted to bar military recruiters from their campuses. The law schools argued that the military's policy toward homosexuals was discriminatory and violated their own antidiscrimination policies.

In response, Congress passed the Solomon Amendment, which required all colleges and universities receiving federal funds to open their campuses to military recruiters. Unless the recruiters were granted the same access as any other company or prospective employer, federal funding would be forfeited.

In 2003, law schools and numerous concerned faculty members formed the Forum for Academic and Institutional Rights (FAIR) and filed a suit in federal court. The law schools claimed that the Solomon Amendment violated their rights to free speech and freedom of association. The United States Supreme Court disagreed. In March 2006, the Court handed down a unanimous eight-to-zero decision

(Image copyright Samuel Acosta 2010. Used under license from Shutterstock.com)

---

[42]*Board of Regents of the University of Wisconsin System v. Southworth*, 529 U.S. 217 (2000).
[43]*Doe v. University of Michigan*, 721 F.Supp. 852 (1989).

holding the Solomon Amendment constitutional.[44] Chief Justice John Roberts noted in his opinion that the amendment does not infringe in any way on an institution's freedom of speech. Roberts also held that Congress could even directly force schools to allow recruiting through the "raise and support Armies" clause of the Constitution.

HATE SPEECH ON THE INTERNET

Extreme hate speech appears on the Internet, including racist materials and denials of the Holocaust (the murder of millions of Jews by the Nazis during World War II). Can the federal government restrict this type of speech? Should it? Content restrictions can be difficult to enforce. Even if Congress succeeded in passing a law prohibiting particular speech on the Internet, an army of "Internet watchers" would be needed to enforce it. Also, what if other countries attempt to impose their laws that restrict speech on U.S. Web sites? This is not a theoretical issue. In 2000, a French court found Yahoo! in violation of French laws banning the display of Nazi memorabilia. In 2001, however, a U.S. district court held that this ruling could not be enforced against Yahoo! in the United States.[45]

FREEDOM OF THE PRESS

Freedom of the press can be regarded as a special instance of freedom of speech. Of course, at the time of the framing of the Constitution, the press meant only newspapers, magazines, and books. As technology has modified the ways in which we disseminate information, the laws touching on freedom of the press have been modified. What can and cannot be printed still occupies an important place in constitutional law, however. (To see how freedom of the press is viewed elsewhere in the world, see this chapter's Beyond Our Borders feature.)

DEFAMATION IN WRITING

Libel is defamation in writing (or in pictures, signs, films, or any other communication that has the potentially harmful qualities of written or printed words). As with slander, libel occurs only if the defamatory statements are observed by a third party. If one person writes a private letter to another person wrongfully accusing him or her of embezzling funds, that does not constitute libel. It is interesting that the courts have generally held that dictating a letter to a secretary constitutes communication of the letter's contents to a third party, and therefore, if defamation has occurred, the wrongdoer can be sued.

A 1964 case, *New York Times Co. v. Sullivan*,[46] explored an important question regarding libelous statements made about public officials. The Supreme Court held that only when a statement against a public official was made with **actual malice**—that is, with either knowledge of its falsity or a reckless disregard of the truth—could damages be obtained.

The standard set by the Court in the *New York Times* case has since been applied to **public figures** generally. Public figures include not only public officials but also public employees who exercise substantial governmental power and any persons who are gen-

Libel
A written defamation of a person's character, reputation, business, or property rights.

Actual Malice
Either knowledge of a defamatory statement's falsity or a reckless disregard for the truth.

Public Figure
A public official, movie star, or other person known to the public because of his or her position or activities.

[44]*Rumsfeld v. Forum for Academic and Institutional Rights, Inc.*, 547 U.S. 47.
[45]*Yahoo!, Inc. v. La Ligue Contre le Racisme et l'Antisemitisme*, 169 F.Supp. 2d 1181 (N.D. Cal. 2001).
[46]376 U.S. 254 (1964).

POLICE COMMISSIONER L. B. Sullivan (second from right) celebrates his $500,000 libel suit victory in the case *New York Times Co. v. Sullivan*. From left are attorneys J. Roland Nachman, Jr., who directed the plaintiff's suit, Calvin Whitesell, Sullivan, and Sam Rice Baker.
(Bettmann/CORBIS)

erally in the limelight. Statements made about public figures, especially when they are made through a public medium, usually are related to matters of general public interest; they are made about people who substantially affect all of us. Furthermore, public figures generally have some access to a public medium for answering disparaging falsehoods about themselves, whereas private individuals do not. For these reasons, public figures have a greater burden of proof (they must prove that the statements were made with actual malice) in defamation cases than do private individuals.

A FREE PRESS VERSUS A FAIR TRIAL: GAG ORDERS

Another major issue relating to freedom of the press concerns media coverage of criminal trials. The Sixth Amendment to the Constitution guarantees the right of criminal suspects to a fair trial. In other words, the accused have rights. The First Amendment guarantees freedom of the press. What if the two rights appear to be in conflict? Which one prevails?

Jurors certainly may be influenced by reading news stories about the trial in which they are participating. In the 1970s, judges increasingly issued **gag orders**, which restricted the publication of news about a trial in progress or even a pretrial hearing. In a landmark 1976 case, *Nebraska Press Association v. Stuart*,[47] the Supreme Court unanimously ruled that a Nebraska judge's gag order had violated the First Amendment's guarantee of freedom of the press. Chief Justice Warren Burger indicated that even pervasive adverse pretrial publicity did not necessarily lead to an unfair trial, and that prior restraints on publication were not justified. Some justices even went so far as to suggest that gag orders are never justified.

Despite the *Nebraska Press Association* ruling, the Court has upheld certain types of gag orders. In *Gannett Co. v. De Pasquale*[48] in 1979, for example, the highest court held that if a judge found a reasonable probability that news publicity would harm a defendant's right to a fair trial, the court could impose a gag rule: "Members of the public have no constitutional right under the Sixth and Fourteenth Amendments to attend criminal trials."

Gag Order
An order issued by a judge restricting the publication of news about a trial or a pretrial hearing to protect the accused's right to a fair trial.

[47]427 U.S. 539 (1976).
[48]443 U.S. 368 (1979).

The *Nebraska* and *Gannett* cases, however, involved pretrial hearings. Could a judge impose a gag order on an entire trial, including pretrial hearings? In 1980, in *Richmond Newspapers, Inc. v. Virginia*,[49] the Court ruled that actual trials must be open to the public except under unusual circumstances.

FILMS, RADIO, AND TV

As we have noted, only in a few cases has the Supreme Court upheld prior restraint of published materials. The Court's reluctance to accept prior restraint is less evident with respect to motion pictures. In the first half of the 20th century, films were routinely submitted to local censorship boards. In 1968, the Supreme Court ruled that a film can be banned only under a law that provides for a prompt hearing at which the film is shown to be obscene. Today, few local censorship boards exist. Instead, the film industry regulates itself primarily through the industry's rating system.

Radio and television broadcasting has the least First Amendment protection. Broadcasting initially received less protection than the printed media because, at that time, the number of airwave frequencies was limited. In 1934, the national government established the Federal Communications Commission (FCC) to regulate electromagnetic wave frequencies. No one has a right to use the airwaves without a license granted by the FCC. The FCC grants licenses for limited periods and imposes a variety of regulations on broadcasting. Based on a case decided by the Supreme Court in 1978,[50] the FCC can impose sanctions on radio or TV stations that broadcast "filthy words," even if the words are not legally obscene. During the George W. Bush administration, the FCC acted more frequently to sanction radio and television broadcasters for the use of words, phrases, and pictures that might be considered in the category of "filthy words."

---

[49]448 U.S. 555 (1980).
[50]*FCC v. Pacifica Foundation*, 438 U.S. 726 (1978). The phrase "filthy words" refers to a monologue by comedian George Carlin, which became the subject of the court case.

Beyond Our Borders

AN UPROAR OVER CARTOONS

An international imbroglio erupted when a Danish newspaper printed cartoon images that were deemed offensive by many Muslims. The cartoons, many of which depicted the Prophet Muhammad unfavorably and linked the Islamic faith to international terrorism, enraged Muslims all over the globe. When newspapers in some other European countries reprinted the offensive cartoons, riots broke out, European embassies were attacked, and already tense relations between Muslims and Westerners deteriorated. The dispute over the cartoons opened an international debate about freedom of expression.

THE FREEDOM TO OFFEND?

Without question, the caricatures of Muhammad were offensive. In the Islamic faith, creating any kind of image of the Prophet or Allah (God) is strictly forbidden. Thus, the offensive nature of the cartoons merely added further insult to an already taboo portrayal. Moreover, many Muslims living in Europe perceived the cartoons as yet another example of racial and religious discrimination.

In contrast, many Westerners saw the publication of the cartoons as a freedom of expression issue. Nonetheless, most Westerners viewed the cartoons as offensive and unnecessarily inflammatory. The European newspaper editors argued that they had every right to publish the images, even as they apologized for offending the Muslim community. The editors felt that freedom of expression should not be restrained, regardless of the reaction it may cause. French and German newspapers insisted that democratic freedoms include the "right to blasphemy."

THROUGHOUT THE MUSLIM WORLD, protests were held to condemn the publication of a cartoon depicting the Prophet Muhammed in a Danish newspaper. This protest took place in Islamabad, Pakistan in 2006. (AP Photo/Anjum Naveed)

REVEALING DEEPER TENSIONS AND DIFFERENCES

The cartoon dispute also revealed a deeper cultural rift between many Muslims and Westerners. Significant numbers of Muslims living in Europe and North America have been revolted by what they consider to be overly "liberal" attitudes toward personal freedom, individualism, sex, family structure, and religion. For their part, many Westerners have been critical of what they perceive as Muslims' religious fundamentalism and immigrant Muslims' unwillingness to assimilate culturally and politically to their new surroundings.

Most Westerners were shocked at the reaction spurred by the cartoons. The violent attacks on European and American embassies in the Middle East and other Muslim areas were perhaps the most bewildering. In Gaza, for example, gunmen appeared at the offices of the European Union, firing automatic weapons and threatening further violence unless the offending nations apologized for the cartoons.

U.S. MEDIA AND THE CARTOONS

Most U.S. media sources decided not to reprint the offending cartoons. Some outlets, such as NBC News, chose to offer links to the images via their Web sites. Nonetheless, the cartoons were a hot topic on television news channels and in newspaper editorial sections across the country. Some defended the cartoons as free speech, whereas others focused on the need to be more respectful of sensitive religious and cultural topics. Columnist Kathleen Parker summed up the difficulty of reconciling Western notions of free expression with the fundamentalist reactions of some Muslims: "Until Muslim nations and peoples get the idea that free expression means freedom to offend as well as the necessary correlative—to be offended—we have a problem."*

FOR CRITICAL ANALYSIS

Some commentators spoke of the need to find a balance between freedom of expression and respect for religious beliefs.

1. Do you believe that such a balance can be found?
2. Is it desirable to restrict freedom of expression in some instances? Explain.

*Kathleen Parker, *Washington Post*, February 2, 2006.

THE RIGHT TO ASSEMBLE AND TO PETITION THE GOVERNMENT

The First Amendment prohibits Congress from making any law that abridges "the right of the people peaceably to assemble, and to petition the Government for a redress of grievances." Inherent in such a right is the ability of private citizens to communicate their ideas on public issues to government officials, as well as to other individuals.

Indeed, the amendment also protects the right of individuals to join interest groups and lobby the government. The Supreme Court has often put this freedom on a par with freedom of speech and freedom of the press. Nonetheless, it has allowed municipalities to require permits for parades, sound trucks, and demonstrations so that public officials can control traffic or prevent demonstrations from turning into riots.

The freedom to demonstrate became a major issue in 1977 when the American Nazi Party sought to march through Skokie, Illinois, a largely Jewish suburb where many Holocaust survivors resided. The American Civil Liberties Union defended the Nazis' right to march (despite its opposition to the Nazi philosophy). The Supreme Court let stand a lower court's ruling that the city of Skokie had violated the Nazis' First Amendment guarantees by denying them a permit to march.[51]

ONLINE ASSEMBLY

A question for Americans today is whether individuals should have the right to "assemble" online to advocate violence against certain groups (such as physicians who perform abortions) or advocate values that are opposed to our democracy (such as terrorism). While some online advocacy groups promote interests consistent with American political values, other groups aim to destroy those values. Whether First Amendment freedoms should be sacrificed (by the government's monitoring of Internet communications, for example) in the interests of national security is a question that will no doubt be debated for some time to come.

MORE LIBERTIES UNDER SCRUTINY: MATTERS OF PRIVACY

No explicit reference is made anywhere in the Constitution to a person's right to privacy. Until the second half of the 1990s, the courts did not take a very positive approach toward the right to privacy. For example, during Prohibition, suspected bootleggers' telephones were tapped routinely, and the information obtained was used as a legal basis for prosecution. In *Olmstead v. United States*[52] in 1928, the Supreme Court upheld such an invasion of privacy. Justice Louis Brandeis, a champion of personal freedoms, strongly dissented from the majority decision in this case. He argued that the framers of the Constitution gave every citizen the right to be left alone. He called such a right "the most comprehensive of rights and the right most valued by civilized men."

In the 1960s, the highest court began to modify the majority view. In 1965, in *Griswold v. Connecticut*,[53] the Supreme Court overturned a Connecticut law that effectively prohibited the use of contraceptives, holding that the law violated the right to privacy. Justice William O. Douglas formulated a unique way of reading this right into the Bill of Rights. He claimed that the First, Third, Fourth, Fifth, and Ninth Amendments created "penumbras [shadows], formed by emanations [things sent out from] those guarantees that help give them life and substance," and he went on to describe zones of privacy that are guaranteed by these rights. When we read the Ninth Amendment, we can see the foundation for his reasoning: "The enumeration in the Constitution, of certain rights, shall not be construed to deny or disparage [belittle] others retained by the people." In other words, just because the Constitution, including its amendments,

---

[51]*Smith v. Collin*, 439 U.S. 916 (1978).
[52]277 U.S. 438 (1928). This decision was overruled later in *Katz v. United States*, 389 U.S. 347 (1967).
[53]381 U.S. 479 (1965).

does not specifically talk about the right to privacy does not mean that this right is denied to the people.

Some of today's most controversial issues relate to privacy rights. One issue involves the erosion of privacy rights in an information age, as computers make it easier to compile and distribute personal information. Other issues concern abortion and the "right to die." Since the terrorist attacks of September 11, 2001, Americans have faced another crucial question regarding privacy rights: To what extent should Americans sacrifice privacy rights in the interests of national security?

PRIVACY RIGHTS IN AN INFORMATION AGE

An important privacy issue, created in part by new technology, is the amassing of information on individuals by government agencies and private businesses, such as marketing firms, grocery stores, and casinos, to name just a few. Personal information on the average American citizen also is filed away in dozens of agencies—such as the Social Security Administration and the Internal Revenue Service. Because of the threat of indiscriminate use of private information by unauthorized individuals, Congress passed the Privacy Act in 1974. This was the first law regulating the use of federal government information about private individuals. Under the Privacy Act, every citizen has the right to obtain copies of personal records collected by federal agencies and to correct inaccuracies in such records.

The ease with which personal information can be obtained by using the Internet for marketing and other purposes has led to unique privacy issues. Some fear that privacy rights in personal information may soon be a thing of the past. However, for today's young adults, the concept of privacy seems to have evolved into a concept that individuals define for themselves. Portraits on public Web sites such as MySpace or other networking sites are created by the user and can protect personal data or make certain facts *very public*. The person who submits the information gets to decide. Whether privacy rights can survive in an information age is a question that Americans and their leaders continue to confront.

AS TECHNOLOGIES CONTINUE TO DEVELOP, more and more people use electronic devices for entertainment, for information and for social networking. Here a woman checks her Facebook page on her iPad. (© CJG - Technology/Alamy)

PRIVACY RIGHTS AND ABORTION

Historically, abortion was not a criminal offense before the "quickening" of the fetus (the first movement of the fetus in the uterus, usually between the 16th and 18th weeks of pregnancy). During the last half of the 19th century, however, state laws became more severe. By 1973, performing an abortion at any time during pregnancy was a criminal offense in a majority of the states.

Roe v. Wade. In 1973, in *Roe v. Wade,*[54] the United States Supreme Court accepted the argument that the laws against abortion violated "Jane Roe's" right to privacy under the Constitution. The Court held that during the first trimester (three months) of pregnancy, abortion was an issue solely between a woman and her physician. The state could not limit abortions except to require that they be performed by licensed physicians. During the second trimester, to protect the health of the mother, the state was allowed to specify the conditions under which an abortion could be performed. During the final trimester, the state could regulate or even outlaw abortions, except when necessary to preserve the life or health of the mother.

After *Roe*, the Supreme Court issued decisions in several cases defining and redefining the boundaries of state regulation of abortion. During the 1980s, the Court twice struck down laws that required a woman who wished to have an abortion to undergo counseling designed to discourage abortions. In the late 1980s and early 1990s, however, the Court took a more conservative approach. For example, in *Webster v. Reproductive Health Services*[55] in 1989, the Court upheld a Missouri statute that, among other things, banned the use of public hospitals or other taxpayer-supported facilities for performing abortions. And, in *Planned Parenthood v. Casey*[56] in 1992, the Court upheld a

IN 2006, ON THE 33rd anniversary of *Roe v. Wade*, opposing sides on the abortion issue argued with each other in front of the United States Supreme Court building in Washington, D.C. What was the major argument against laws prohibiting abortion that the Court used in the *Roe* case? (AP Photo/Pablo Martinez Monsivais)

---

[54] 410 U.S. 113 (1973). Jane Roe was not the real name of the woman in this case. It is a common legal pseudonym used to protect a person's privacy.
[55] 492 U.S. 490 (1989).
[56] 505 U.S. 833 (1992).

Pennsylvania law that required preabortion counseling, a waiting period of 24 hours, and, for girls under the age of 18, parental or judicial permission. The *Casey* decision was remarkable for several reasons. The final decision was a five-to-four vote with Sandra Day O'Connor writing the opinion. While the opinion explicitly upheld *Roe*, it changed the grounds on which the states can regulate abortion. The Court found that states could not place an "undue burden" on a woman who sought an abortion. In this case, the Court found that spousal notification was such a burden. Because many other conditions were upheld, abortions continue to be more difficult to obtain in some states than others.

The Controversy Continues. Abortion continues to be a divisive issue. Right-to-life forces continue to push for laws banning abortion, to endorse political candidates who support their views, and to organize protests. Because of several episodes of violence attending protests at abortion clinics, in 1994 Congress passed the Freedom of Access to Clinic Entrances Act. The act prohibits protesters from blocking entrances to such clinics. The Supreme Court ruled in 1993 that such protesters can be prosecuted under laws governing racketeering, and in 1998 a federal court in Illinois convicted right-to-life protesters under these laws. In 1997, the Supreme Court upheld the constitutionality of prohibiting protesters from entering a 15-foot "buffer zone" around abortion clinics and from giving unwanted counseling to those entering the clinics.[57] In 2006, however, the Supreme Court unanimously reversed its earlier decision that antiabortion protesters could be prosecuted under laws governing racketeering.[58]

In a 2000 decision, the Court upheld a Colorado law requiring demonstrators to stay at least eight feet away from people entering and leaving clinics unless people consent to be approached. The Court concluded that the law's restrictions on speech-related conduct did not violate the free speech rights of abortion protesters.[59]

In the same year, the Supreme Court again addressed the abortion issue directly when it reviewed a Nebraska law banning "partial-birth" abortions. Similar laws had been passed by at least 27 states. A partial-birth abortion, which physicians call intact dilation and extraction, is a procedure that can be used during the second trimester of pregnancy. Abortion rights advocates claim that in limited circumstances the procedure is the safest way to perform an abortion, and that the government should never outlaw specific medical procedures. Opponents argue that the procedure has no medical merit and that it ends the life of a fetus that might be able to live outside the womb. The Supreme Court invalidated the Nebraska law on the grounds that, as written, the law could be used to ban other abortion procedures, and it contained no provisions for protecting the health of the pregnant woman.[60] In 2003, legislation similar to the Nebraska statute was passed by the U.S. Congress and signed into law by President George W. Bush. It was immediately challenged in court. In 2007, the Supreme Court heard several challenges to the partial-birth abortion law and upheld the constitutionality of that legislation, saying that the law was specific enough that it did not "impose an undue burden" on women seeking an abortion.[61]

In a move that will likely set off another long legal battle, in 2006 the South Dakota legislature passed a law that banned almost all forms of abortion in the state. The bill's supporters hope that it will eventually force the United States Supreme Court to reconsider *Roe v. Wade*. Opponents of the bill have already filed suit.

---

[57]*Schenck v. ProChoice Network*, 519 U.S. 357 (1997).
[58]*Scheidler v. National Organization for Women*, 126 S.Ct. 1264 (2006).
[59]*Hill v. Colorado*, 530 U.S. 703 (2000).
[60]*Stenberg v. Carhart*, 530 U.S. 914 (2000).
[61]*Gonzales v. Carhart*, 550 U.S. (2007) and *Gonzales v. Planned Parenthood*, 550 U.S. (2007).

PRIVACY RIGHTS AND THE "RIGHT TO DIE"

A 1976 case involving Karen Ann Quinlan was one of the first publicized right-to-die cases.[62] The parents of Quinlan, a young woman who had been in a coma for nearly a year and who had been kept alive during that time by a respirator, wanted her respirator removed. In 1976, the New Jersey Supreme Court ruled that the right to privacy includes the right of a patient to refuse treatment and that patients who are unable to speak can exercise that right through a family member or guardian. In 1990, the Supreme Court took up the issue. In *Cruzan v. Director, Missouri Department of Health*,[63] the Court stated that a patient's life-sustaining treatment can be withdrawn at the request of a family member only if there is "clear and convincing evidence" that the patient did not want such treatment.

What If There Is No Living Will? Since the 1976 *Quinlan* decision, most states have enacted laws permitting people to designate their wishes concerning life-sustaining procedures in "living wills" or durable health care powers of attorney. These laws and the Supreme Court's *Cruzan* decision have resolved the right-to-die controversy for situations in which the patient has drafted a living will. Disputes are still possible if there is no living will. An example is the case of Terri Schiavo. The husband of the Florida woman, who had been in a persistent vegetative state for more than a decade, sought to have her feeding tube removed on the basis of oral statements that she would not want her life prolonged in such circumstances. Schiavo's parents fought this move in court but lost on the ground that a spouse, not a parent, is the appropriate legal guardian for a married person. Although the Florida legislature passed a law allowing Governor Jeb Bush to overrule the courts, the state supreme court held that the law violated the state constitution.[64]

The case escalated into a national drama in March 2005 when the U.S. Congress intervened and passed a law allowing Schiavo's case to be heard in the federal court system. The federal courts, however, essentially agreed with the Florida state courts' findings and refused to order the reconnection of the feeding tube, which had been disconnected a few days earlier. After twice appealing to the United States Supreme Court without success, the parents gave up hope, and Schiavo died shortly thereafter.

Physician-Assisted Suicide. In the 1990s, another issue surfaced: Do privacy rights include the right of terminally ill people to end their lives through physician-assisted suicide? Until 1996, the courts consistently upheld state laws that prohibited this practice, either through specific statutes or under their general homicide statutes. In 1996, after two federal appellate courts ruled that state laws banning assisted suicide (in Washington and New York) were unconstitutional, the issue reached the United States Supreme Court. In 1997, in *Washington v. Glucksberg*,[65] the Court stated, clearly and categorically, that the liberty interest protected by the Constitution does not include a right to commit suicide, with or without assistance. In effect, the Supreme Court left the decision in the hands of the states. Since then, assisted suicide has been allowed in only one state—Oregon. In 2006, the

(© tatniz/shutterstock)

---

[62]*In re Quinlan*, 70 N.J. 10 (1976).
[63]497 U.S. 261 (1990).
[64]*Bush v. Schiavo*, 885 So.2d 321 (Fla. 2004).
[65]521 U.S. 702 (1997).

Supreme Court upheld Oregon's physician-assisted suicide law against a challenge from the Bush administration.[66]

PRIVACY RIGHTS VERSUS SECURITY ISSUES

As former Supreme Court Justice Thurgood Marshall once said, "Grave threats to liberty often come in times of urgency, when constitutional rights seem too extravagant to endure." Not surprisingly, antiterrorist legislation since the attacks on September 11, 2001, has eroded certain basic rights, in particular the Fourth Amendment protections against unreasonable searches and seizures. Several tools previously used against certain types of criminal suspects (e.g., "roving wiretaps" and National Security Letters) have been authorized for use against a broader array of terror suspects. Many civil liberties organizations argue that abuses of the Fourth Amendment are ongoing.

While it has been possible for a law enforcement agency to gain court permission to wiretap a telephone virtually since telephones were invented, a roving wiretap allows an agency to tap all forms of communication used by the named person, including cell phones and e-mail, and it applies across legal jurisdictions. Previously, roving wiretaps could only be requested for persons suspected of one of a small number of serious crimes. Now if persons are suspected of planning a terrorist attack, they can be monitored no matter what form of electronic communication they use. Such roving wiretaps appear to contravene the Supreme Court's interpretation of the Fourth Amendment, which requires a judicial warrant to describe the *place* to be searched, not just the person, although the Court has not banned them to date. One of the goals of the framers was to avoid *general* searches. Further, once a judge approves an application for a roving wiretap, when, how, and where the monitoring occurs will be left to the discretion of law enforcement agents. Supporters of these new procedures say that they allow agents to monitor individuals as they move about the nation. Previously, a warrant issued in one federal district might not be valid in another.

Moreover, President George W. Bush approved a plan by the National Security Agency to eavesdrop on telephone calls between individuals overseas and those in the United States if one party was a terrorist suspect. This plan was carried out without warrants because the administration claimed that speed was more important. Critics called for immediate termination of such eavesdropping. The Congress has continued to reform legislation on this issue.

The USA PATRIOT Act. Much of the government's failure to anticipate the attacks of September 11, 2001, has been attributed to a lack of cooperation among government agencies. At that time, barriers prevented information sharing between the law enforcement and intelligence arms of the government. A major objective of the USA PATRIOT Act was to lift those barriers. Lawmakers claimed that the PATRIOT Act would improve lines of communication between agencies such as the Federal Bureau of Investigation (FBI) and the Central Intelligence Agency (CIA), thereby allowing the government to better anticipate terrorist plots. With improved communication, various agencies could more effectively coordinate their efforts in combating terrorism.

In addition, the PATRIOT Act eased restrictions on the government's ability to investigate and arrest suspected terrorists. Because of the secretive nature of terrorist groups, supporters of the PATRIOT Act argue that the government must have greater latitude in pursuing leads on potential terrorist activity. After receiving approval of the Foreign Intelligence Surveillance Court (known as FISA), the act authorizes law enforcement

---

[66]*Gonzales v. Oregon*, 126 S.Ct. 904 (2006).

officials to secretly search a suspected terrorist's home. It also allows the government to monitor a suspect's Internet activities, phone conversations, financial records, and book purchases. Although a number of these search and surveillance tactics have long been a part of criminal investigations, the PATRIOT Act expanded their scope to include individuals as suspects even if they are not agents of a foreign government.

Civil Liberties Concerns. Proponents of the PATRIOT Act insist that ordinary, law-abiding citizens have nothing to fear from the government's increased search and surveillance powers. Groups such as the ACLU have objected to the PATRIOT Act, however, arguing that it poses a grave threat to constitutionally guaranteed rights and liberties. Under the PATRIOT Act, FBI agents are required to certify the need for search warrants to the FISA Court. Rarely are such requests rejected.

In the last few years, the FBI began using another tool that it has had for several years, the National Security Letter (NSL), to avoid the procedures required by the FISA Court. The NSL allows the FBI to get records of telephone calls, subscriber information, and other kinds of transactions, although it does not give the FBI access to the content of the calls. However, as Congress tightened the requirements for warrants under the PATRIOT Act, the FBI evidently began to use the NSLs as a shortcut. While the use of NSLs has been legal for more than 20 years, recent massive use of this technique has led Congress to consider further restrictions on the FBI and its investigations in order to preserve the rights of U.S. citizens.

Opponents of the PATRIOT Act fear that these expanded powers of investigation might be used to silence government critics or to threaten members of interest groups who oppose government polices today or in the future. Congress debated all of these issues in 2005 and then renewed most of the provisions of the act in 2006. One of the most controversial aspects of the PATRIOT Act permits the government to eavesdrop on telephone calls with a warrant from the FISA Court. In 2005, it became known that the Bush administration was eavesdropping on U.S. telephone calls without a warrant if the caller was from outside the United States. After almost three years of controversy, Congress passed the FISA Amendments Act in June 2008, which regulates such calls and gives immunity from prosecution to telecommunications companies.

THE GREAT BALANCING ACT: THE RIGHTS OF THE ACCUSED VERSUS THE RIGHTS OF SOCIETY

The United States has one of the highest murder rates in the industrialized world. It is not surprising, therefore, that many citizens have extremely strong opinions about the rights of those accused of violent crimes. When an accused person, especially one who has confessed to some criminal act, is set free because of an apparent legal technicality, many people believe that the rights of the accused are being given more weight than the rights of society and of potential or actual victims. Why, then, give criminal suspects rights? The answer is partly to avoid convicting innocent people, but mostly because all criminal suspects have the right to due process of law and fair treatment.

The courts and the police must constantly engage in a balancing act of competing rights. At the basis of all discussions about the appropriate balance is the U.S. Bill of Rights. The Fourth, Fifth, Sixth, and Eighth Amendments deal specifically with the rights of criminal defendants. (You will learn about some of your rights under the Fourth Amendment in the *You Can Make a Difference* feature at the end of this chapter.)

TABLE 4–2 Basic Rights of Criminal Defendants

LIMITS ON THE CONDUCT OF POLICE OFFICERS AND PROSECUTORS
No unreasonable or unwarranted searches and seizures (Amend. IV)
No arrest except on probable cause (Amend. IV)
No coerced confessions or illegal interrogation (Amend. V)
No entrapment
On questioning, a suspect must be informed of her or his rights
DEFENDANT'S PRETRIAL RIGHTS
Writ of *habeas corpus* (Article I, Section 9)
Prompt arraignment (Amend. VI)
Legal counsel (Amend. VI)
Reasonable bail (Amend. VIII)
To be informed of charges (Amend. VI)
To remain silent (Amend. V)
TRIAL RIGHTS
Speedy and public trial before a jury (Amend. VI)
Impartial jury selected from a cross section of the community (Amend. VI)
Trial atmosphere free of prejudice, fear, and outside interference
No compulsory self-incrimination (Amend. V)
Adequate counsel (Amend. VI)
No cruel and unusual punishment (Amend. VIII)
Appeal of convictions
No double jeopardy (Amend. V)

RIGHTS OF THE ACCUSED

The basic rights of criminal defendants are outlined in Table 4–2. When appropriate, the specific constitutional provision or amendment on which a right is based is also given.

EXTENDING THE RIGHTS OF THE ACCUSED

During the 1960s, the Supreme Court, under Chief Justice Earl Warren, significantly expanded the rights of accused persons. In *Gideon v. Wainwright*,[67] a case decided in 1963, the Court held that if a person is accused of a felony and cannot afford an attorney, an attorney must be made available to the accused person at the government's expense. This case was particularly interesting because Gideon, who was arrested for stealing a small amount of money from a vending machine, was not considered a dangerous

---

[67]372 U.S. 335 (1963).

man, nor was his intellect in any way impaired. As related by Anthony Lewis,[68] Gideon pursued his own appeal to the Supreme Court because he believed that every accused person who might face prison should be represented. Although the Sixth Amendment to the Constitution provides for the right to counsel, the Supreme Court had established a precedent 21 years earlier in *Betts v. Brady*,[69] when it held that only criminal defendants in capital (death penalty) cases automatically had a right to legal counsel.

Miranda v. Arizona. In 1966, the Court issued its decision in *Miranda v. Arizona*.[70] The case involved Ernesto Miranda, who was arrested and charged with the kidnapping and rape of a young woman. After two hours of questioning, Miranda confessed and was later convicted. Miranda's lawyer appealed his conviction, arguing that the police had never informed Miranda that he had a right to remain silent and a right to be represented by counsel. The Court, in ruling in Miranda's favor, enunciated the *Miranda* rights that are now familiar to virtually all Americans:

> Prior to any questioning, the person must be warned that he has a right to remain silent, that any statement he does make may be used against him, and that he has a right to the presence of an attorney, either retained or appointed.

Two years after the Supreme Court's *Miranda* decision, Congress passed the Omnibus Crime Control and Safe Streets Act of 1968. Section 3501 of the act reinstated a rule that had been in effect for 180 years before *Miranda*—that statements by defendants can be used against them if the statements were made voluntarily. The Justice Department immediately disavowed Section 3501 as unconstitutional and has continued to hold this position. As a result, Section 3501, although it was never repealed, has never been enforced. In 2000, in a surprise move, a federal appellate court held that the all-but-forgotten provision was enforceable, but the Supreme Court held that the *Miranda* warnings were constitutionally based and could not be overruled by a legislative act.[71]

Exceptions to the *Miranda* Rule. As part of a continuing attempt to balance the rights of accused persons against the rights of society, the Supreme Court has made several exceptions to the *Miranda* rule. In 1984, for example, the Court recognized a "public-safety" exception to the rule. The need to protect the public warranted the admissibility of statements made by the defendant (in this case, indicating where he had placed a gun) as evidence in a trial, even though the defendant had not been informed of his *Miranda* rights.

In 1985, the Court further held that a confession need not be excluded even though the police failed to inform a suspect in custody that his attorney had tried to reach him by telephone. In an important 1991 decision, the Court stated that a suspect's conviction will not be automatically overturned if the suspect was coerced into making a confession. If the other evidence admitted at trial is strong enough to justify the conviction without the confession, then the fact that the confession was obtained illegally in effect can be ignored. In yet another case, in 1994, the Supreme Court ruled that suspects must unequivocally and assertively state their right to counsel in order to stop police questioning. Saying "Maybe I should talk to a lawyer" during an interrogation after being taken into custody is not enough. The Court held that police officers are not required to decipher the suspect's intentions in such situations. Most

DID YOU KNOW?

That in 18th-century England, pickpocketing and similar crimes were punishable by the death penalty?

---

[68]Anthony Lewis, *Gideon's Trumpet* (New York: Vintage, 1964).
[69]316 U.S. 455 (1942).
[70]384 U.S. 436 (1966).
[71]*Dickerson v. United States*, 530 U.S. 428 (2000).

recently, the Miranda protections were further narrowed when the Court found that a suspect must expressly announce his or her desire to remain silent, not just sit silently during questioning.

Video Recording of Interrogations. In view of the numerous exceptions, there are no guarantees that the *Miranda* rule will survive indefinitely. Increasingly, though, law enforcement personnel are using digital cameras to record interrogations. According to some scholars, the recording of *all* custodial interrogations would satisfy the Fifth Amendment's prohibition against coercion and in the process render the *Miranda* warnings unnecessary. Others argue, however, that recorded interrogations can be misleading.

THE EXCLUSIONARY RULE

At least since 1914, judicial policy has prohibited the admission of illegally seized evidence at trials in federal courts. This is the so-called **exclusionary rule**. Improperly obtained evidence, no matter how telling, cannot be used by prosecutors. This includes evidence obtained by police in violation of a suspect's *Miranda* rights or of the Fourth Amendment. The Fourth Amendment protects against unreasonable searches and seizures and provides that a judge may issue a search warrant to a police officer only on *probable cause* (a demonstration of facts that permit a reasonable belief that a crime has been committed). The question that must be determined by the courts is what constitutes an unreasonable search and seizure.

> **Exclusionary Rule**
> A policy forbidding the admission at trial of illegally seized evidence.

The reasoning behind the exclusionary rule is that it forces police officers to gather evidence properly, in which case their due diligence will be rewarded by a conviction. Nevertheless, the exclusionary rule has always had critics who argue that it permits guilty persons to be freed because of innocent errors.

This rule was first extended to state court proceedings in a 1961 United States Supreme Court decision, *Mapp v. Ohio*.[72] In this case, the Court overturned the conviction of Dollree Mapp for the possession of obscene materials. Police found pornographic books in her apartment after searching it without a search warrant and despite her refusal to let them in.

Over the last several decades, the Supreme Court has diminished the scope of the exclusionary rule by creating some exceptions to its applicability. For example, in 1984, the Court held that illegally obtained evidence could be admitted at trial if law enforcement personnel could prove that they would have obtained the evidence legally anyway. In another case decided in the same year, the Court held that a police officer who used a technically incorrect search warrant form to obtain evidence had acted in good faith and therefore the evidence was admissible at trial. The Court thus created the "good faith" exception to the exclusionary rule.

THE DEATH PENALTY

Capital punishment remains one of the most debated aspects of our criminal justice system. Those in favor of the death penalty maintain that it serves as a deterrent to serious crime and satisfies society's need for justice and fair play. Those opposed to the death penalty do not believe it has any deterrent value and hold that it constitutes a barbaric act in an otherwise civilized society.

---

[72]367 U.S. 643 (1961).

POLITICS WITH A purpose

The Innocence Project

As long as the United States has imposed capital punishment on convicted felons, there have been claims of innocence by those sentenced to die. Although police officers and judges have always known that sometimes the innocent are falsely accused and convicted, they also believe that most of the individuals were correctly prosecuted and convicted of their crimes. As most Americans know from popular television series such as *CSI* and *Bones*, new scientific techniques make it possible to find biological and chemical evidence that was completely unknown to law enforcement in the past. Most important of these new tools is the use of DNA, or deoxyribonucleic acid. DNA molecules contain all of the information about a person's or an animal's genetic makeup and are almost unique to each individual. The importance of DNA to criminal investigations is that DNA molecules that are found on a strand of hair or saliva on a handkerchief can be tested many years after they were deposited on that object.

In the early 1990s, law students at the Benjamin N. Cardozo School of Law at Yeshiva University began theorizing that DNA found in old evidence records could be used to establish the innocence of individuals wrongfully convicted of crimes. Led by Barry C. Scheck and Peter J. Neufeld, the students and faculty founded the Innocence Project, which is dedicated to helping exonerate innocent people and improving the legal system to avoid wrongful convictions. To date, more than 250 people have been exonerated through DNA evidence, and 17 of those were serving time on death row.

Why do wrongful convictions occur? Don't the safeguards of the Constitution (the right to confront witnesses, the right to an attorney, and the right to a speedy trial) protect people from wrongful imprisonment? The Innocence Project identifies a number of reasons why wrongful convictions occur. Witnesses may identify the wrong person as the suspect; individuals who are arrested may feel strongly pressured to make a confession, especially if the prosecution offers a plea bargain for a lesser sentence; forensic science may be faulty in a particular location; the police may have acted out of discriminatory motives or failed to complete an investigation; informants or snitches may have given false information; or the free counsel offered to a defendant may be incompetent.[a] The Innocence Project is a nonprofit organization located at Yeshiva University; however, the work has spread throughout the United States and to some foreign countries. There are now 54 affiliated projects, mostly at law schools and centers in 45 states. The centers form when students and faculty come together to begin the work in their own state. Law students provide most of the volunteer investigations into possible cases of wrongful conviction with guidance from their faculty. Students also research the laws governing criminal procedure in their own state and then lobby for changes to reduce the chance of wrongful convictions. In 2010, Governor Strickland of Ohio signed into law a bill that was researched by a student of the Innocence Project at the University of Cincinnati law school. The student was present at the General Assembly when the bill passed. The new legislation requires  preservation of DNA evidence forever in serious crimes, strengthens the requirements for police lineups, and gives incentives for the video recording of interrogations in most serious crimes. The legislation is considered groundbreaking for preserving evidence that might prevent wrongful convictions.

If you are interested in taking part in the Innocence Project or learning if there is a center near you, log onto the national Web site, http://www.innocenceproject.org, and look for the list of state projects. You can learn a great deal about wrongful convictions from the organization's Web site and explore changes in the law that may prevent this miscarriage of justice.[b]

[a]Barry Scheck, Peter Neufeld, and Jim Dwyer, *Actual Innocence: When Justice Goes Wrong and How to Make it Right,* New York: New American Library, 2003.
[b]Saundra Westervelt and John Humphrys, *Wrongly Convicted: Perspectives on Failed Justice,* Piscataway, NJ: Rutgers University Press, 2001.

CRUEL AND UNUSUAL PUNISHMENT?

The Eighth Amendment prohibits cruel and unusual punishment. Throughout history, "cruel and unusual" referred to punishments that were more serious than the crimes— the phrase referred to torture and to executions that prolonged the agony of dying. The

GEORGE WHITE, PICTURED in the foreground, spent seven years in an Alabama prison after he was convicted of murdering his wife. The state ultimately admitted that he had been falsely accused of the crime and released him from prison. Here, he speaks out against the death penalty. What are some of the arguments for and against capital punishment? (Independent Record/George Lane/AP Photo)

Supreme Court never interpreted "cruel and unusual" to prohibit all forms of capital punishment in all circumstances. Indeed, several states had imposed the death penalty for a variety of crimes and allowed juries to decide when the condemned could be sentenced to death. However, many believed that the imposition of the death penalty was random and arbitrary, and in 1972 the Supreme Court agreed in *Furman v. Georgia*.[73]

The Supreme Court's 1972 decision stated that the death penalty, as then applied, violated the Eighth and Fourteenth Amendments. The Court ruled that capital punishment is not necessarily cruel and unusual if the criminal has killed or attempted to kill someone. In its opinion, the Court invited the states to enact more precise laws so that the death penalty would be applied more consistently. By 1976, 25 states had adopted a two-stage, or *bifurcated*, procedure for capital cases. In the first stage, a jury determines the guilt or innocence of the defendant for a crime that has been determined by statute to be punishable by death. If the defendant is found guilty, the jury reconvenes in the second stage and considers all relevant evidence to decide whether the death sentence is, in fact, warranted.

In *Gregg v. Georgia*,[74] the Supreme Court ruled in favor of Georgia's bifurcated process, holding that the state's legislative guidelines had removed the ability of a jury to "wantonly and freakishly impose the death penalty." The Court upheld similar procedures in Texas and Florida, establishing a procedure for all states to follow that would ensure them protection from lawsuits based on Eighth Amendment grounds. On January 17, 1977, Gary Mark Gilmore became the first American to be executed (by Utah) under the new laws.

THE DEATH PENALTY TODAY

Today, 38 states (see Figure 4–1) and the federal government have capital punishment laws based on the guidelines established by the *Gregg* case. State governments are responsible for almost all executions in this country. The executions of Timothy McVeigh and Juan Raul Garza in 2001 marked the first death sentences carried out by the federal government since 1963. At this time, about 3,700 prisoners are on death row across the nation.

---

[73] 408 U.S. 238 (1972).
[74] 428 U.S. 153 (1976).

FIGURE 4–1 The States and the Death Penalty: Executions since 1976 and the Death Row Population

Today, as shown in this figure, 35 states and the federal government and military have laws permitting capital punishment. Since 1976, there have been 1,200 executions in the U.S., with 42 in 2007, 37 in 2008, 52 in 2009 and 39 thus far in 2010 at the time this book went to press.

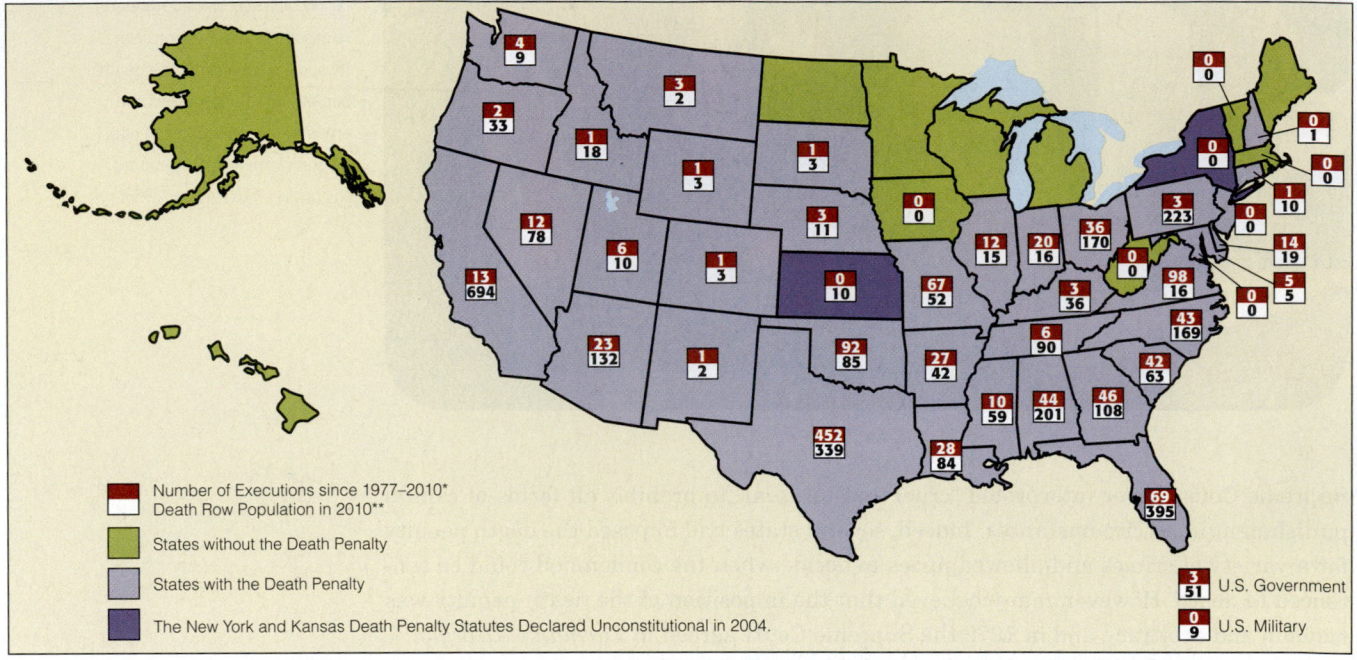

Sources: U.S. Department of Justice, Bureau of Justice Statistics, "Capital Punishment, 2006," www.ojp.usdoj.gov/bjs; Death Penalty Information Center, "Death Row Inmates of State and Size of Death Row by Year," January/February 2008; and "Facts About the Death Penalty," April 15, 2010, www.deathpenaltyinfo.org.

The most recent controversy over the death penalty concerns the method by which the punishment is carried out. Thirty-five of the 36 states that have the death penalty use a lethal injection to cause the convicted person's death. Most use a combination of three different drugs injected in an intravenous manner. Several cases have been appealed to the Supreme Court on the basis that this method can cause extreme pain and thus violates the Constitution's ban on cruel and unusual punishment. The Court has upheld the three-drug method, most recently in April 2008, although the justices wrote seven opinions in the case, indicating a lack of consensus among them.[75]

The number of executions per year reached a high in 1998 at 98, and then began to fall. Some believe that the declining number of executions reflects the waning support among Americans for the imposition of the death penalty. In 1994, polls indicated that 80 percent of Americans supported the death penalty. Recent polls, however, suggest that this number has dropped to between 50 and 60 percent, depending on the poll, possibly because of public doubt about the justice of the system. Recently, DNA testing has shown that some innocent people may have been convicted unjustly of murder. Since 1973, more than 100 prisoners have been freed from death row after new evidence suggested that they were wrongfully convicted. It is the goal of the Innocence Project, discussed in Politics with a Purpose, to continue to investigate wrongful convictions in every state.

[75]*Baze v. Rees*, 553 U.S. 35 (2008).

The number of executions may decline even further due to the Supreme Court's 2002 ruling in *Ring v. Arizona.*[76] The Court held that only juries, not judges, could impose the death penalty, thus invalidating the laws of five states that allowed judges to make this decision. The ruling meant that the death sentences of 168 death row inmates would have to be reconsidered by the relevant courts. The sentences of many of these inmates have been commuted to life in prison.

TIME LIMITS FOR DEATH ROW APPEALS

In 1996, Congress passed the Anti-Terrorism and Effective Death Penalty Act. The law limits access to the federal courts for all defendants convicted in state courts. It also imposes a severe time limit on death row appeals. The law requires federal judges to hear these appeals and issue their opinions within a specified time period. Many are concerned that the shortened appeals process increases the possibility that innocent persons may be put to death before evidence that might free them can be discovered. On average, it takes about seven years to exonerate someone on death row; however, the time between conviction and execution has been shortened from an average of 10 to 12 years to an average of six to eight years.

[76]536 U.S. 548 (2002).

YOU CAN MAKE A Difference

YOUR CIVIL LIBERTIES: SEARCHES AND SEIZURES

Our civil liberties include numerous provisions, many of them listed in the Bill of Rights, that protect persons who are suspected of criminal activity. Among these are limits on how the police—as agents of the government—can conduct searches and seizures.

WHY SHOULD YOU CARE?

You may be the most law-abiding person in the world, but that will not guarantee that you will never be stopped, arrested, or searched by the police. Sooner or later, most citizens will have some kind of interaction with the police. People who do not understand their rights or how to behave toward law enforcement officers can find themselves in serious trouble. The words of advice in this feature actually provide you with key survival skills for life in the modern world.

WHAT CAN YOU DO?

How should you behave if you are stopped by police officers? Your civil liberties protect you from having to provide information other than your name and address.

Normally, even if you have not been placed under arrest, the officers have the right to frisk you for weapons, and you must let them proceed. The officers cannot, however, check your person or your clothing further if, in their judgment, no weaponlike object is produced.

The officers may search you only if they have a search warrant or probable cause to believe that a search will likely produce incriminating evidence. What if the officers do not have probable cause or a warrant? Physically resisting their attempt to search you can lead to disastrous results. It is best simply to refuse orally to give permission for the search, preferably in the presence of a witness, and to be polite. It is usually advisable to limit what you say to the officers. If you are arrested, it is best to keep quiet until you can speak with a lawyer.

If you are in your car and are stopped by the police, the same fundamental rules apply. Always be ready to show your driver's license and car registration. You may be asked to get out of the car. The officers may use a flashlight to peer inside the car if it is too dark to see otherwise. None of this constitutes a search. A true search requires either a warrant or probable cause. No officer has the legal right to search your car simply to find out if you may have committed a crime. Police officers can conduct searches that are incidental to lawful arrests, however, such as an arrest for speeding or drunk driving.

If you are in your home and a police officer with a search warrant appears, you can ask to examine the warrant before granting entry. A warrant that is correctly made out will state the place or persons to be searched, the object sought, and the date of the warrant (which should be no more than 10 days ago), and it will bear the signature of a judge or magistrate. If the warrant is in order, you need not make any statement. If you believe the warrant to be invalid, or if no warrant is produced, you should make it clear orally that you have not consented to the search, preferably in the presence of a witness. If the search later is proved to be unlawful, normally any evidence obtained cannot be used in court.

Officers who attempt to enter your home without a search warrant can do so only if they are pursuing a suspected felon into the house. Rarely is it advisable to give permission for a warrantless search. You, as the resident, must be the one to give permission if any evidence obtained is to be considered legal. The landlord, manager, or head of a college dormitory cannot give legal permission. A roommate, however, can give permission for a search of his or her room, which may allow the police to search areas where you have belongings.

If you are a guest in a place that is being legally searched, you may be legally searched as well. But unless you have been placed under arrest, you cannot be compelled to go to the police station or get into a squad car.

If you would like to find out more about your rights and obligations under the laws of searches and seizures, you might wish to contact the following organization, which maintains a downloadable Know Your Rights Card.

SAVANA REDDING stands before the U.S. Supreme Court building on the day her case was heard. As a 13 year-old, Redding was strip-searched by school authorities looking for ibuprofen. Her parents were not asked for their consent or informed about the incident. (AP Photo/Evan Vucci, file)

American Civil Liberties Union
125 Broad St., 18th Floor
New York, NY 10004
212-549-2500
www.aclu.org

KEY TERMS

actual malice 141
civil liberties 123
clear and present danger test 136
commercial speech 135
defamation of character 139

establishment clause 126
exclusonary rule 155
free exercise clause 132
gag order 142
incorporation theory 124
libel 141

prior restraint 133
public figure 141
slander 139
symbolic speech 134

CHAPTER SUMMARY

1. Originally, the Bill of Rights limited only the power of the national government, not that of the states. Gradually and selectively, however, the Supreme Court accepted the incorporation theory, under which no state can violate most provisions of the Bill of Rights.

 2. **Why is freedom of expression so fundamental to democracy?** The First Amendment's protection of speech, press, religion, and the right to assemble and petition government is meant to protect the fundamental rights of citizens in a democracy. If a government can suppress speech, the press, religious beliefs, or the right to join a group, it can make democratic debates and elections impossible.

3. **What should be the relationship between religion and the political system?** The First Amendment protects against government interference with freedom of religion by requiring a separation of church and state (under the establishment clause) and by guaranteeing the free exercise of religion. Controversial issues that arise under the establishment clause include aid to church-related schools, school prayer, the teaching of evolution versus intelligent design, school vouchers, the posting of the Ten Commandments in public places, and discrimination against religious speech. The government can interfere with the free exercise of religion only when religious practices work against public policy or the public welfare; however, the government cannot sponsor or support religion in general or any specific religious belief.

4. The First Amendment protects against government interference with freedom of speech, which includes symbolic speech (expressive conduct). The Supreme Court has been especially critical of government actions that impose prior restraint on expression. Commercial speech (advertising) by businesses has received limited First Amendment protection. Restrictions on expression are permitted when the expression creates a clear and present danger to the peace or public order. Speech that has not received First Amendment protection includes expression that is judged to be obscene or slanderous.

5. The First Amendment protects against government interference with the freedom of the press, which can be regarded as a special instance of freedom of speech. Speech by the press that does not receive protection includes libelous statements. Publication of news about a criminal trial may be restricted by a gag order in some circumstances.

6. The First Amendment protects the right to assemble peaceably and to petition the government. Permits may be required for parades, sound trucks, and demonstrations to maintain the public order, and a permit may be denied to protect the public safety.

7. Under the Ninth Amendment, rights not specifically mentioned in the Constitution are not necessarily denied to the people. Among these unspecified rights protected by the courts is a right to privacy, which has been inferred from the First, Third, Fourth, Fifth, and Ninth Amendments. A major privacy issue today is how best to protect privacy rights in cyberspace. Whether an individual's privacy rights include a right to an abortion or a "right to die" continues to provoke controversy. Another major challenge concerns the extent to which Americans must forfeit privacy rights to control terrorism.

8. **What should be the balance between the rights of the accused and the rights of society to be protected from criminals?** The Constitution includes protections for the rights of persons accused of crimes. Under the Fourth Amendment, no one may be subject to an unreasonable search or seizure or be arrested except on probable cause. Under the Fifth Amendment, an accused person has the right to remain silent. Under the Sixth Amendment, an accused person must be informed of the reason for his or her arrest. The accused also has the right to adequate counsel, even if he or she cannot afford an attorney, and the right to a prompt arraignment and a speedy and public trial before an impartial jury selected from a cross section of the community.

9. In *Miranda v. Arizona* (1966), the Supreme Court held that criminal suspects, before interrogation by law enforcement personnel, must be informed of certain constitutional rights, including the right to remain silent and the right to be represented by counsel.

10. The exclusionary rule forbids the admission in court of illegally seized evidence. There is a "good faith exception" to the exclusionary rule: Illegally seized evidence need not be thrown out due to, for example, a technical defect in a search warrant.

11. Under the Eighth Amendment, cruel and unusual punishment is prohibited. Whether the death penalty is cruel and unusual punishment and the circumstances under which it is appropriate continue to be debated.

SELECTED PRINT, MEDIA, AND ONLINE RESOURCES

PRINT RESOURCES

Behe, Michael. *Darwin's Black Box: The Biochemical Challenge to Evolution.* New York: Simon and Schuster, 2006. Considered a seminal work in the intelligent design movement, Behe's book has been updated to include further evidence for his claims that evolution does not fully explain the origins of life.

Epps, Garrett. *To an Unknown God: Religious Freedom on Trial.* New York: St. Martin's Press, 2001. The author chronicles the journey through the courts of *Oregon v. Smith* (discussed earlier in this chapter), a case concerning religious practices decided by the Supreme Court in 1990. The author regards this case as one of the Supreme Court's most momentous decisions on religious freedom in the last 50 years.

Hamadi, Rob. *Privacy Wars: Who Holds Information on You and What They Do with It.* London: Vision Paperbacks, 2009. Hamadi sounds an alarm about the current extent of surveillance in the United States. He also provides recommendations that citizens can use to protect their own privacy.

Kitcher, Philip. *Living with Darwin: Evolution, Design, and the Future of Faith.* New York: Oxford University Press, 2007. This brief book looks at the history of the controversy over evolution as part of a larger conflict between religious faith and the discoveries of modern science.

Lewis, Anthony. *Freedom for the Thought We Hate: Tales of the First Amendment.* New York: Basic Books, 2008. Pulitzer Prize–winning journalist Anthony Lewis writes eloquently on the value of free expression and the resulting need for "activist judges." He provides a series of engaging stories of how the courts came to give real life to the First Amendment.

Lewis, Anthony. *Gideon's Trumpet.* New York: Vintage, 1964. This classic work discusses the background and facts of *Gideon v. Wainwright,* the 1963 Supreme Court case in which the Court held that the state must make an attorney available for any person accused of a felony who cannot afford a lawyer.

MEDIA RESOURCES

***The Abortion War: Thirty Years after* Roe v. Wade**—An ABC News program released in 2003 that examines the abortion issue.

The Chamber—A movie, based on John Grisham's novel by the same name, about a young lawyer who defends a man (his grandfather) who has been sentenced to death and faces imminent execution.

Execution at Midnight—A video presenting the arguments and evidence on both sides of the controversial death penalty issue.

Gideon's Trumpet—An excellent 1980 movie about the *Gideon v. Wainwright* case. Henry Fonda plays the role of the convicted petty thief Clarence Earl Gideon.

God's Christian Warriors—A controversial 2007 CNN special on how evangelical Christians seek to influence American politics and society. Reported by CNN chief international correspondent Christine Amanpour, the two-hour show is part of a broader series that includes *God's Jewish Warriors and God's Muslim Warriors.*

May It Please the Court: The First Amendment—A set of audiocassette recordings and written transcripts of the oral arguments made before the Supreme Court in 16 key First Amendment cases. Participants in the recording include nationally known attorneys and several Supreme Court justices.

The People vs. Larry Flynt—An R-rated 1996 film that clearly articulates the conflict between freedom of the press and how a community defines pornography.

Skokie: Rights or Wrong?—A documentary by Sheila Chamovitz. The film documents the legal and moral crisis created when American Nazis attempted to demonstrate in Skokie, Illinois, a predominantly Jewish suburb that was home to many concentration camp survivors.

ONLINE RESOURCES

American Civil Liberties Union (ACLU) the nation's leading civil liberties organization provides an extensive array of information and links concerning civil rights issues: www.aclu.org

The American Library Association information on free-speech issues, especially issues of free speech on the Internet: www.ala.org

Center for Democracy and Technology nonprofit institute that monitors threats to the freedom of the Internet and provides a wealth of information about issues involving the Bill of Rights. It also focuses on how developments in communications technology are affecting the constitutional liberties of Americans: www.cdt.org

Electronic Privacy Information Center information on Internet privacy issues: www.epic.org/privacy

Foundation for Individual Rights in Education (FIRE) tracks the rights to free speech, press, religion, and assembly at the nation's colleges and universities. Find a rating for your own university's speech and conduct codes: www.thefire.org

Freedom Forum nonpartisan foundation dedicated to free press, free speech, and free spirit for all people. Includes history of flag protection and the First Amendment, as well as the status of the proposed flag amendment in Congress: www.freedomforum.org

Legal Information Institute at Cornell University Law School searchable database of historic Supreme Court decisions: http://supct.law.cornell.edu/supct/search/index.html

Liberty Counsel nonprofit litigation, education, and policy organization dedicated to advancing religious freedom, the sanctity of human life, and the family: www.lc.org

The Oyez Project provides summaries and the full text of Supreme Court decisions concerning constitutional law, plus a virtual tour of the Supreme Court: www.oyez.org

5

A rainbow flag, a symbol of gay and lesbian rights, waves in front of the U.S. Capitol dome during the 2009 Equality Across America march in Washington D.C. Several of the most pressing civil rights issues today concern the interests of gays and lesbians and their families. (Richard Clement/Newscom)

Civil Rights

QUESTIONS TO CONSIDER

Why does discrimination against groups exist in the United States?

How can the government best ensure equal rights for all?

Why is the Supreme Court so important in determining civil rights?

CHAPTER CONTENTS

what if...

Undocumented Immigrants Were Granted Citizenship?

BACKGROUND

Granting citizenship to every undocumented immigrant now residing in the United States would have significant political and social implications in this country. The sheer numbers of persons involved would command attention from both political parties since the Latino vote would take on much greater significance.

A massive grant of citizenship would make employment and income tax practices (or lack thereof) associated with undocumented workers more transparent. By granting citizenship to those who had entered the country illegally, the United States might face a tide of new immigrants.

INCREASED POLITICAL CLOUT FOR THE LATINO COMMUNITY

In recent years, voter participation within the Latino community has increased as individuals have become more politically active and outspoken. Indeed, such developments are reflected in the growing number of individuals of Latino descent holding public office as mayors of major cities, governors, and members of Congress.

The fact that granting citizenship to illegal immigrants is a topic of discussion represents a significant turn of events for Hispanic Americans. Factions within both major parties have proposed different measures that would lead to citizenship for undocumented residents. Political interest groups have formed to champion immigrant rights. Some broader-based groups have advocated on behalf of both legal and illegal immigrants of Hispanic origin.

EMPLOYMENT AND TAXES

Most illegal immigrants come to the United States to work. Many of these immigrants send part of their earnings in America back to relatives in their home countries. The wages, known as remittances, sent home to family members by individuals working in the United States (both legally and illegally) are the second-largest source of foreign income in Mexico.

The Internal Revenue Service has had difficulty collecting taxes on the wages that undocumented workers earn, however. Some employers who knowingly hire illegal immigrants simply pay those workers "under the table" to avoid a paper trail. Often, the arrangement is a cash transaction, which is difficult to track. If all illegal immigrants were granted citizenship, most employers would no longer be able to engage in such tax-evasion schemes.

Employers sometimes take advantage of undocumented workers by refusing to pay them for work or changing the terms of work agreements. Other employers use illegal immigrants as employees because they often accept lower wages than American citizens would leading to the charges that undocumented workers "take Americans' jobs" and depress wages for other employees working in the same labor sector. Some employers break the law by hiring undocumented workers to get around paying state or federal minimum wages. If citizenship were granted to illegal immigrants, employers would have to reconsider their practices. Moreover, as wages were properly reported, tax revenues would increase. Alternatively, employers might eliminate some jobs if they were forced to pay higher wages.

U.S. IMMIGRATION POLICY

Obviously, illegal immigrants violate U.S. immigration laws. Anyone seeking to enter the United States legally faces an extremely lengthy application process and annual quota limitations that depend on national origin. Enforcement of immigration law has always been difficult. Granting citizenship to all illegal immigrants now residing in the United States could be considered unfair to all those who are waiting for legal entry. Record numbers of illegal immigrants continue to enter the United States despite increased efforts to control the borders. While immigration reform was central to the issues in the 2008 presidential campaign, Congress has not yet acted and the likelihood that it will do so prior to the congressional midterm elections in 2010 is quite low. This leaves border states to try to deal with the problems of border control and the issues associated with undocumented immigrants on their own and, in most cases, without sufficient resources to do so effectively.

FOR CRITICAL ANALYSIS

1. Some politicians have advocated a gradual process for granting citizenship to undocumented immigrants. Do you think that a gradual process would be more appropriate than an automatic grant of citizenship, sometimes referred to as "amnesty"? Or do you oppose any proposal—gradual or immediate—to offer citizenship to undocumented immigrants? Explain your position.

2. In January 2010, the Department of Homeland Security reported that the number of unauthorized immigrants in the United States dropped by nearly one million—the largest drop in three decades and the second consecutive annual decline. The decline is attributed to fewer jobs as a result of the recession as well as to increased border enforcement efforts. According to the same report, 63 percent of those here illegally arrived before 2000. Do you think immigration would significantly increase if the United States adopted a policy to grant citizenship to undocumented immigrants already living here? Why or why not?

DESPITE THE WORDS set forth in the Declaration of Independence that "all Men are created equal," the United States has a long history of discrimination based on race, gender, national origin, religion, and sexual orientation, among others. The majority of the population had few rights at the nation's founding. As you learned in Chapter 2, the framers of the Constitution permitted slavery to continue, thus slaves were excluded from the political process. Women also were excluded for the most part, as were Native Americans, African Americans who were not slaves, and white men who did not own property. To the nation's founders, equality required a degree of independent thinking and the capacity for rational action that they believed members of these groups did not possess. Today we believe that all people are entitled to equal political rights as well as the opportunities for personal development provided by equal access to education and employment. Thus, the story of civil rights in the United States is the struggle to reconcile our ideals as a nation with the realities of discrimination individuals and groups may still encounter in daily life.

Equality is at the heart of the concept of civil rights. Generally, the term **civil rights** refers to the rights of all Americans to equal treatment under the law, as provided for by the Fourteenth Amendment to the Constitution and by subsequent acts of Congress. Although the terms *civil rights* and *civil liberties* are sometimes used interchangeably, scholars make a distinction between the two. As you learned in Chapter 4, civil liberties are limitations on government; they specify what the government *cannot* do. Civil rights, in contrast, specify what the government *must* do—to ensure equal protection and freedom from discrimination.

The history of civil rights in America therefore is the story of the struggle of various groups to be free from discriminatory treatment. In this chapter, we first look at two movements with significant consequences for the history of civil rights in America: the civil rights movement of the 1950s and 1960s and the women's movement, which began in the mid-1800s and continues today. Each of these movements resulted in legislation that secured important basic rights for all Americans—the right to vote and the right to equal protection under the laws. Each of these movements also demonstrates how individuals working alone and with others in groups can effect significant change. Today's civil rights activists draw on insights and strategies from these earlier movements in making new claims for political and social equality. We then explore a question with serious implications for today's voters and policy makers: What should the government's responsibility be when equal protection under the law is not enough to ensure truly equal opportunities for Americans?

Civil Rights
All rights rooted in the Fourteenth Amendment's guarantee of equal protection under the law.

DID YOU KNOW?

That at the time of the American Revolution, African Americans made up nearly 25 percent of the American population of about three million?

AFRICAN AMERICANS AND THE CONSEQUENCES OF SLAVERY IN THE UNITED STATES

Before 1863, the Constitution protected slavery and made equality impossible in the sense in which we use the word today. African American leader Frederick Douglass pointed out that "Liberty and Slavery—opposite as Heaven and Hell—are both in the Constitution." As Abraham Lincoln stated sarcastically, "All men are created equal, except Negroes."

The constitutionality of slavery was confirmed just a few years before the outbreak of the Civil War in the infamous *Dred Scott v. Sanford*[1] case of 1857. The Supreme Court held that slaves were property, not citizens of the United States, and thus they were not entitled to the rights and privileges of citizenship. The Court also ruled that the Missouri Compromise, passed by Congress in 1820, which banned slavery in the territories north of 36°30' latitude (the southern border of Missouri), was unconstitutional. The *Dred Scott* decision had grave consequences. Most observers contend that the ruling contributed to making the Civil War inevitable.

ENDING SERVITUDE

With the Emancipation Proclamation in 1863 and ratification of the Thirteenth, Fourteenth, and Fifteenth Amendments during the Reconstruction period following the Civil War, constitutional inequality was ended.

The Thirteenth Amendment (1865) states that neither slavery nor involuntary servitude shall exist within the United States. The Fourteenth Amendment (1868) says that *all* persons born or naturalized in the United States are citizens of the United States. It states, furthermore, that "[n]o State shall make or enforce any law which shall abridge the privileges or immunities of citizens of the United States; nor shall any State deprive any person of life, liberty, or property, without due process of law; nor deny to any person within its jurisdiction the equal protection of the laws." Note the use of the terms *citizen* and *person* in this amendment. Citizens have political rights, such as the right to vote and run for political office. Citizens also have certain privileges or immunities (see Chapter 4). All *persons*, however, including noncitizens, have a right to due process of law and equal protection under the law.

The Fifteenth Amendment (1870) reads as follows: "The right of citizens of the United States to vote shall not be denied or abridged by the United States or by any State on account of race, color, or previous condition of servitude." Activists in the women's suffrage movements brought pressure on Congress to include in the Fourteenth and Fifteenth Amendments a prohibition against discrimination based on sex, but with no success.

THE CIVIL RIGHTS ACTS OF 1865 TO 1875

At the end of the Civil War, President Lincoln's Republican Party controlled the national government and most state governments, and the so-called radical Republicans, with their strong antislavery stance, controlled the party. From 1865 to 1875, the Republican majority in Congress succeeded in passing a series of civil rights acts that were aimed at enforcing the Thirteenth, Fourteenth, and Fifteenth Amendments even as legislatures in the Southern states moved quickly to pass laws (known as **Black Codes**) intended to limit the civil rights of African Americans and regulate their labor in ways that closely resembled slavery. For example, South Carolina's Black Code passed in

Black Codes
Laws passed by Southern states immediately after the Civil war denying most legal rights to freed slaves.

[1]19 Howard 393 (1857).

1865 stated that "all persons of color who make contracts for service or labor, shall be known as servants, and those with whom they contract, shall be known as masters."[2] Following the assassination of President Lincoln on April 15, 1865, Andrew Johnson assumed the presidency and presided over the initial period of Reconstruction. Johnson, a Southerner and former slave owner, was viewed by radical Republicans as too conciliatory toward Southern states.

Following the 1866 elections in which Southern states were not allowed to vote, an emboldened radical Republican majority in Congress moved to take control of Reconstruction. The first Civil Rights Act in the Reconstruction period was passed in 1866 over the veto of President Johnson. That act extended citizenship to anyone born in the United States and gave African Americans full equality before the law. It gave the president authority to enforce the law with military force. Johnson characterized the law as an invasion by federal authority of the rights of the states. It was considered to be unconstitutional, but the ratification of the Fourteenth Amendment two years later ended that concern.

Among the six other civil rights acts passed after the Civil War, one of the most important was the Enforcement Act of 1879, which set out specific criminal sanctions for interfering with the right to vote as protected by the Fifteenth Amendment and by the Civil Rights Act of 1866. Equally important was the Civil Rights Act of 1872, known as the Anti–Ku Klux Klan Act. This Act made it a federal crime for anyone to use law or custom to deprive an individual of his or her rights, privileges, and immunities secured by the Constitution or by any federal law.

The last of these early civil rights acts, known as the Second Civil Rights Act, was passed in 1875. It declared that everyone is entitled to full and equal enjoyment of public accommodations, theaters, and other places of amusement, and it imposed penalties for violators. What is most important about all of the civil rights acts was the belief that congressional power applied to official or government action or to private action. If a state government did not secure rights, then the federal government could do so. Thus, Congress could legislate directly against individuals who were violating the constitutional rights of others. As we will see, these acts were quickly rendered ineffective by law and by custom. However, they became important in the civil rights struggles of the 1960s, 100 years after their passage.

THE LIMITATIONS OF THE CIVIL RIGHTS LAWS

The Reconstruction statutes, or civil rights acts, ultimately did little to secure equality for African Americans. Both the *Civil Rights Cases* and *Plessy v. Ferguson* effectively nullified these acts. The election of Rutherford B. Hayes as president in 1877 marked an end to the progressive advance of rights for African Americans during Reconstruction. He withdrew federal forces from

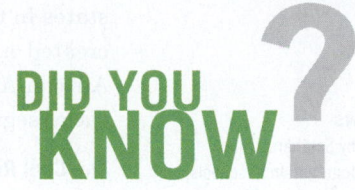

DID YOU KNOW?

That June 19th, known as Juneteenth or Freedom Day, celebrates the day in 1865 that slaves in Galveston, Texas, found out they were free three years after Lincoln signed the Emancipation Proclamation?

AN ENGRAVING of Ku Klux Klan members active in the late 1860s as Southerners rebelled against Northern influence during Reconstruction. (The Stapleton Collection/The Bridgeman Art Library International)

---

[2]"Acts of the General Assembly of the State of South Carolina Passed at the Sessions of 1864–65," pp. 291–304.

states in the former Confederacy. Without direct oversight, Southern and border states created a variety of seemingly race-neutral legal barriers that in reality prevented African Americans from exercising their right to vote while also adopting policies of racial segregation known as **Jim Crow laws**.

The Civil Rights Cases. The Supreme Court invalidated the 1875 Civil Rights Act when it held, in the *Civil Rights Cases*[3] of 1883, that the enforcement clause of the Fourteenth Amendment (which states that "[n]o State shall make or enforce any law which shall abridge the privileges or immunities of citizens") was limited to correcting actions by states in their *official* acts; thus, the discriminatory acts of private citizens were not illegal. ("Individual invasion of individual rights is not the subject matter of the Amendment.") The 1883 Supreme Court decision removed the federal government as a forceful advocate for advancing civil rights in all aspects of daily human interaction, and it was met with widespread approval throughout most of the United States.

Twenty years after the Civil War, the white majority was all too ready to forget about the three Civil War amendments and the civil rights legislation of the 1860s and 1870s. The other civil rights laws that the Court did not specifically invalidate became effectively null without any mechanisms of enforcement, although they were never repealed by Congress. At the same time, many former proslavery secessionists had regained political power in the Southern states.

***Plessy v. Ferguson*: Separate but Equal.** A key decision during this period concerned Homer Plessy, a Louisiana resident who was one-eighth African American. In 1892, he boarded a train in New Orleans. The conductor made him leave the car, which was restricted to whites, and directed him to a car for nonwhites. At that time, Louisiana had a statute providing for separate railway cars for whites and African Americans.

Plessy went to court, claiming that such a statute was contrary to the Fourteenth Amendment's equal protection clause. In 1896, the United States Supreme Court rejected Plessy's contention. The Court concluded that the Fourteenth Amendment "could not have been intended to abolish distinctions based upon color, or to enforce social...equality." The Court stated that segregation alone did not violate the Constitution: "Laws permitting, and even requiring, their separation in places where they are liable to be brought into contact do not necessarily imply the inferiority of either race to the other."[4] With this case, the Court announced the **separate-but-equal doctrine**.

Plessy v. Ferguson became the judicial cornerstone of racial discrimination throughout the United States. Even though *Plessy* upheld segregated facilities in railway cars only, it was assumed that the Supreme Court was upholding segregation everywhere as long as the separate facilities were equal, which in reality meant as long as there were separate facilities. The result was a system of racial segregation, particularly in the South—supported by laws collectively known as Jim Crow laws—that required separate drinking fountains; separate seats in theaters, restaurants, and hotels; separate public toilets; and separate waiting rooms for the two races. "Separate" was indeed the rule, but "equal" was never enforced, nor was it a reality.

Voting Barriers. The brief enfranchisement of African Americans ended after 1877, when the federal troops that occupied the South during the Reconstruction era were withdrawn. Southern politicians regained control of state governments and, using everything except race as a formal criterion, passed laws that effectively deprived African Americans of the right to vote.

Jim Crow Laws
Laws enacted by Southern states that enforced segregation in schools, on transportation, and in public accommodations.

Separate-but-Equal Doctrine
The 1896 doctrine holding that separate-but-equal facilities do not violate the equal protection clause.

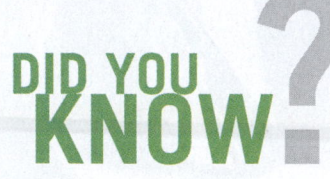

DID YOU KNOW?

That the original Constitution failed to describe the status of *citizen* or how this status could be acquired?

---

[3]109 U.S. 3 (1883).
[4]*Plessy v. Ferguson*, 163 U.S. 537 (1896).

By claiming that political parties were private organizations, the Democratic Party was allowed to restrict black voters from participating in its primaries. Since most Southern states were dominated by a single party, the Democratic Party, denying blacks the right to vote in the primary effectively disenfranchised them altogether. The **white primary** was upheld by the Supreme Court until 1944 when, in *Smith v. Allwright*,[5] the Court ruled it a violation of the Fifteenth Amendment.

Another barrier to African American voting was the **grandfather clause**, which restricted voting to those who could prove that their grandfathers had voted before 1867. **Poll taxes** required the payment of a fee to vote; thus, poor African Americans—as well as poor whites—who could not afford to pay the tax were excluded from voting. Not until the Twenty-fourth Amendment to the Constitution was ratified in 1964 was the poll tax eliminated as a precondition to voting. **Literacy tests** were also used to deny the vote to African Americans. Such tests asked potential voters to read, recite, or interpret complicated texts, such as a section of the state constitution, to the satisfaction of local registrars—who were, of course, never satisfied with the responses of African Americans. Each of these barriers to voting was, on its face, race-neutral. However, each was vigorously enforced disproportionately against African Americans by government agents and a system of racial intimidation.

Southern states, counties, and towns also passed numerous ordinances and laws to maintain a segregated society and to control the movements and activities of African American residents. In Florida, for example, no "negro, mulatto, or person of color" was permitted to own or carry a weapon, including a knife, without a license. This law did not apply to white residents. Other laws set curfews for African Americans, set limits on the businesses they could own or run and on their rights to assembly, and required the newly freed men and women to find employment quickly or be subject to penalties. The penalty sometimes meant that the men would be forced into labor at very low wages at large farms or factories against their will. Denied the right to register and vote, black citizens were also effectively barred from public office and jury service.

Extralegal Methods of Enforcing White Supremacy. The second-class status of African Americans was also a matter of social custom, especially in the South. In their interactions with Southern whites, African Americans were expected to observe an informal but detailed code of behavior that confirmed their inferiority. The most serious violation of the informal code was "familiarity" toward a white woman by an African American man or boy. The code was backed up by the common practice of *lynching*—mob action to murder an accused individual, usually by hanging and sometimes accompanied by torture. Lynching was illegal, but Southern authorities rarely prosecuted these cases, and white juries would not convict. African American women were instrumental in anti-lynching campaigns, beginning in the 1890s with the work of Ida B. Wells-Barnett. As the owner and editor of *The Free Speech*, a Memphis newspaper, she used her voice to call attention to the brutality of lynching and argued in editorials that lynching was a strategy to eliminate prosperous, politically active African Americans.

African Americans outside the South were subject to a second kind of violence—race riots. In the early 20th century, race riots were typically initiated by whites. Frequently, the riots were caused by competition for employment. For example, there were several serious riots during World War II (1939–1945), when labor shortages forced Northern employers to hire more black workers.

White Primary
A state primary election that restricts voting to whites only; outlawed by the Supreme Court in 1944.

Grandfather Clause
A device used by Southern states to disenfranchise African Americans. It restricted voting to those whose grandfathers had voted before 1867.

Poll Tax
A special tax that must be paid as a qualification for voting. The Twenty-fourth Amendment to the Constitution outlawed the poll tax in national elections, and in 1966, the Supreme Court declared it unconstitutional in all elections.

Literacy Test
A test administered as a precondition for voting, often used to prevent African Americans from exercising their right to vote.

[5]321 U.S. 649 (1944).

THESE SEGREGATED drinking fountains were common in Southern states in the late 1800s and during the first half of the 20th century. What landmark Supreme Court case made such segregated facilities legal? (Bettmann/Corbis)

THE END OF THE SEPARATE-BUT-EQUAL DOCTRINE

The successful attack on the separate-but-equal doctrine began with a series of lawsuits in the 1930s that sought to admit African Americans to state professional schools. Nearly three decades earlier, in 1909, influential African Americans and progressive whites, including W.E.B. Dubois and Oswald Garrison Villard, joined to form the National Association for the Advancement of Colored People (NAACP) with the express intention of targeting the separate-but-equal doctrine. Although all Southern states maintained a segregated system of elementary and secondary schools as well as colleges and universities, very few offered professional education for African Americans. Thus, the NAACP elected to begin its challenge with law schools believing in part that it would be too expensive for states to establish an entirely separate system of black professional schools, leaving integration as the best option. To pursue this strategy, the NAACP established the Legal Defense and Education Fund (LDF). As a result of several such challenges, law schools in Maryland, Missouri, Oklahoma, and Texas were forced to change their policies regarding admittance or matriculation of law school students, paving the way for *Brown v. Board of Education* (1954).

By 1950, the Supreme Court had ruled that African Americans who were admitted to a state university could not be assigned to separate sections of classrooms, libraries, and cafeterias. In 1951, Oliver Brown attempted to enroll his eight-year-old daughter, Linda Carol Brown, in the third grade of his all-white neighborhood school seven blocks from their home rather than travel by bus to the segregated school across town. Although Kansas law did not require schools to be segregated by race, in practice there were separate schools for white and black children. When Linda was denied admission to the all-white school, the Topeka NAACP urged Brown to join a lawsuit against the Topeka Board of Education.

Brown v. Board of Education of Topeka[6] established that segregation of races in the public schools violates the equal protection clause of the Fourteenth Amendment. First argued in 1952 by NAACP Legal Defense Fund attorney Thurgood Marshall (appointed as the first African American to the U.S. Supreme Court in 1967), the votes were almost evenly split to uphold or strike down *separate but equal*; Chief Justice Fred Vinson held the swing vote. In 1953, Vinson died, and President Dwight Eisenhower appointed Earl Warren to replace him. *Brown* was reargued, and Warren wrote a unanimous decision to strike down *separate but equal*, arguing that "separate" is inherently unequal.

"With All Deliberate Speed." The following year, in *Brown v. Board of Education*[7] (sometimes called the second *Brown* decision), the Court declared that the lower courts needed to ensure that African Americans would be admitted to schools on a nondiscriminatory basis "with all deliberate speed." The district courts were to consider devices in their desegregation orders that might include "the school transportation system, personnel, [and] revision of school districts and attendance areas into compact units to achieve a system of determining admission to the public schools on a nonracial basis."

This legal strategy was only one of many African Americans found successful in their struggle for civil rights, and there would be many difficult days ahead. The success of civil rights groups in *Brown* was a flashpoint, sparking an enormous wave of backlash among segregationists. They defied the Court, closed public schools rather than integrate them, and vowed to maintain inequality in other areas such as voting. Violence and sometimes death for civil rights activists followed.

THESE THREE LAWYERS successfully argued in favor of desegregation of the schools in the famous *Brown v. Board of Education of Topeka* case. On the left is George E. C. Hayes; on the right is James Nabrit, Jr.; and in the center is Thurgood Marshall, who later became the first African American Supreme Court justice. (Bettmann/Corbis)

REACTIONS TO SCHOOL INTEGRATION

The white South did not let the Supreme Court ruling go unchallenged. Governor Orval Faubus of Arkansas used the state's National Guard to block the integration of Central High School in Little Rock in September 1957. The federal court demanded that the troops be withdrawn. Finally, President Dwight Eisenhower had to federalize the Arkansas National Guard and send in the army's 101st Airborne Division to quell the violence. Central High became integrated.

The universities in the South, however, remained segregated. When James Meredith, an African American student, attempted to enroll at the University of Mississippi in Oxford in 1962, violence flared there, as it had in Little Rock. The white riot at Oxford was so intense that President John Kennedy was forced to send in 30,000 U.S. combat troops, a larger force than the one then stationed in Korea. There were 375 military and civilian injuries, many from gunfire, and two bystanders were killed. Ultimately, peace was restored, and Meredith began attending classes.[8]

[6]347 U.S. 483 (1954).
[7]349 U.S. 294 (1955).
[8]William Doyle, *An American Insurrection: James Meredith and the Battle of Oxford, Mississippi, 1962* (New York: Anchor, 2003).

AN INTEGRATIONIST ATTEMPT AT A CURE: BUSING

De Facto Segregation
Racial segregation that occurs because of past social and economic conditions and residential racial patterns.

De Jure Segregation
Racial segregation that occurs because of laws or administrative decisions by public agencies.

Busing
In the context of civil rights, the transportation of public school students from areas where they live to schools in other areas to eliminate school segregation based on residential racial patterns.

In most parts of the United States, residential concentrations by race have made it difficult to achieve racial balance in schools. This concentration results in *de facto* **segregation**, as distinct from *de jure* **segregation**, which results from laws or administrative decisions.

Court-Ordered Busing. One solution to both *de facto* and *de jure* segregation seemed to be transporting some African American schoolchildren to white schools and some white schoolchildren to African American schools. The courts ordered school districts to engage in such **busing** across neighborhoods. Busing led to violence in some Northern cities, such as in south Boston, where African American students were bused into blue-collar Irish Catholic neighborhoods. Indeed, busing was unpopular with many groups. In the mid-1970s, almost 50 percent of African Americans interviewed were opposed to busing, and approximately three-fourths of the whites interviewed held the same opinion.

The End of Integration? During the 1980s and the early 1990s, the Supreme Court began to back away from its earlier commitment to busing and other methods of desegregation. By the late 1990s and early 2000s, the federal courts were increasingly unwilling to uphold race-conscious policies designed to further school integration and diversity. In 2001, a federal appellate court held that the Charlotte-Mecklenburg school district in North Carolina had achieved the goal of integration,[9] meaning that race-based admission quotas could no longer be imposed constitutionally.

The Resurgence of Minority Schools. Today, schools around the country are becoming segregated again, in large part because changing population demographics result in increased *de facto* segregation. Even as African American and Latino students are becoming more isolated, the typical white child is in a school that is more diverse in large part due to the substantial decline in the number and proportion of white students in the population relative to the increase of nonwhites. In Latino and African American populations, two of every five students attend a school with more than 90 percent minority enrollment. Public school segregation is most severe in the Western states. In California, the nation's most multiracial state, half of African Americans and Asians attend segregated schools, as do one-quarter of Latino and Native American students.[10] Most nonwhite schools are segregated by poverty as well as race. A majority of the nation's dropouts occurs in nonwhite public schools, leading to large numbers of virtually unemployable young people of color. The Bureau of Labor Statistics reported that in November 2008, the month President Obama was elected, the unemployment rate for African American males (adult and teen) was nearly twice that for white males.

Generally, Americans are now taking another look at what desegregation means. In 2007, the Supreme Court handed down a decision that would dramatically change the

ANGRY WHITES shout epithets at one of eight African American students who were admitted to the previously segregated Little Rock Central High School in September 1957. Successful integration of that school required the federalization of the Arkansas National Guard with the help of the Army's 101st Airborne Division. (Bettmann/Corbis)

[9]*Belk v. Charlotte-Mecklenburg Board of Education*, 269 F.3d 305 (4th Cir. 2001).
[10]Gary Orfield, *Reviving the Goal of an Integrated Society: A 21st Century Challenge* (Los Angeles, CA: The Civil Rights Project/Proyecto Derechos Civiles at UCLA, 2009).

way school districts across the country assigned students to schools. In cases brought by white parents in Seattle and Louisville, the court, by a narrow five-to-four majority, found that using race to determine which schools students could attend was a violation of the Fourteenth Amendment. White children could not be denied admission to magnet schools or other schools designed to have racially balanced populations on account of their race. Justice Anthony Kennedy was the swing vote in this case. Although he agreed with four justices in striking down voluntary plans that assigned students to schools solely on the basis of race, he also agreed with other justices in holding that integrated education was a compelling educational goal that could be pursued through other methods.[11]

An alternative being tried in over 60 school districts across the country is to integrate schools on the basis of income. A more advantaged school environment translates into higher achievement levels. On the 2007 National Assessment of Educational Progress given to all fourth-graders in math, for example, low-income students attending more affluent schools scored almost two years ahead of low-income students attending high-poverty schools. Today more than 3.2 million students live in school districts with some form of socioeconomic integration in place.[12]

THE CIVIL RIGHTS MOVEMENT

The *Brown* decision applied only to public schools. Not much else in the structure of existing segregation was affected. In December 1955, a 43-year-old African American woman, Rosa Parks, boarded a public bus in Montgomery, Alabama. When the bus became crowded and several white people stepped aboard, Parks was asked to move to the rear of the bus (the "colored" section). She refused, was arrested, and was fined $10, but that was not the end of the matter. For an entire year, African Americans boycotted the Montgomery bus line. The protest was headed by a 27-year-old Baptist minister, Dr. Martin Luther King, Jr. During the protest period, he went to jail, and his house was bombed. In the face of overwhelming odds, the protesters won. In 1956, a federal district court issued an injunction prohibiting the segregation of buses in Montgomery. The era of civil rights protests had begun.

KING'S PHILOSOPHY OF NONVIOLENCE

The following year, in 1957, King formed the Southern Christian Leadership Conference (SCLC). King advocated nonviolent **civil disobedience** as a means to achieve racial justice. King's philosophy of civil disobedience was influenced, in part, by the life and teachings of Mahatma Gandhi (1869–1948). Gandhi had led resistance to the British colonial system in India from 1919 to 1947. He used tactics such as demonstrations and marches, as well as nonviolent, public disobedience to unjust laws. King's followers successfully used these methods to gain wider public acceptance of their cause.

Civil Disobedience
A nonviolent, public refusal to obey allegedly unjust laws.

Nonviolent Demonstrations. For the next decade, African Americans and sympathetic whites engaged in sit-ins, freedom rides, and freedom marches. Organizations including the NAACP, the Congress of Racial Equality (CORE), and the Student Nonviolent

---

[11]*Parents Involved v. Seattle School District No. 1*, 550 U.S (2007) and *Meredith v. Jefferson County Board of Education*, 550 U.S. (2007).
[12]Richard D. Kahlenberg, "Can Separate Be Equal?" *The American Prospect,* September 16, 2009.

Coordinating Committee (SNCC) organized and supported these actions. In the beginning, such demonstrations were often met with violence, and the contrasting image of nonviolent African Americans and violent, hostile whites created strong public support for the civil rights movement. In 1960, when African Americans in Greensboro, North Carolina, were refused service at a Woolworth's lunch counter, they organized a sit-in that was aided day after day by sympathetic whites and other African Americans. Enraged customers threw ketchup on the protesters. Some spat in their faces. The sit-in movement continued to grow, however. Within six months of the first sit-in at the Greensboro Woolworth's, hundreds of lunch counters throughout the South were serving African Americans.

The sit-in technique also was successfully used to integrate interstate buses and their terminals, as well as railroads engaged in interstate transportation. Although buses and railroads engaged in interstate transportation were prohibited by law from segregating African Americans from whites, they stopped doing so only after the sit-in protests.

Marches and Demonstrations. One of the most famous of the violence-plagued protests occurred in Birmingham, Alabama, in 1963, when Police Commissioner Eugene "Bull" Connor unleashed police dogs and used electric cattle prods against the protesters. People throughout the country viewed the event on television with indignation and horror. King was thrown in jail. The media coverage of the Birmingham protest and the violent response by the city government played a key role in the process of ending Jim Crow laws in the United States. The ultimate result was the most important civil rights act in the nation's history, the Civil Rights Act of 1964.

In August 1963, African American leaders A. Philip Randolph and Bayard Rustin organized a massive March on Washington for Jobs and Freedom. Before nearly a quarter-million white and African American spectators and millions watching on television, King told the world his dream: "I have a dream that my four little children will one day live in a nation where they will not be judged by the color of their skin but by the content of their character."

ANOTHER APPROACH—BLACK POWER

Not all African Americans agreed with King's philosophy of nonviolence or with the idea that King's strong Christian background should represent the core spirituality of African Americans. Black Muslims and other African American separatists advocated a more militant stance and argued that desegregation should not result in cultural assimilation. During the 1950s and 1960s, when King was spearheading nonviolent protests and demonstrations to achieve civil rights for African Americans, black power leaders insisted that African Americans should "fight back" instead of turning the other cheek. Some would argue that without the fear generated by black militants, a "moderate" such as King would not have garnered such widespread support from white America.

Malcolm Little (who became Malcolm X when he joined the Black Muslims in 1952) and other leaders in the black power movement believed that African Americans fell into two groups: the "Uncle Toms," who peaceably accommodated the white establishment, and the "New Negroes," who took pride in their color and culture and who preferred and demanded racial separation as well as power. Malcolm X was assassinated in 1965, but he became an important reference point for a new generation of African Americans and a symbol of African American identity.

MALCOLM X, right, shown here in March 1964, along with Martin Luther King, Jr., opposed the philosophy of nonviolence espoused by Dr. King, and he urged African Americans to "fight back" against white supremacy. Some people have argued that such a militant approach is almost always counterproductive. Others believe that a militant alternative may have made King's peaceful appeal more attractive. Is either of these arguments persuasive? Why or why not? (Library of Congress, Prints & Photographs Division, Washington, D.C. [LC-USZ6-1847])

THE ESCALATION OF THE CIVIL RIGHTS MOVEMENT

Police dog attacks, cattle prods, high-pressure water hoses, beatings, bombings, the March on Washington, and black militancy—all of these events and developments led to an environment in which Congress felt compelled to act on behalf of African Americans.

MODERN CIVIL RIGHTS LEGISLATION

As the civil rights movement mounted in intensity, equality before the law came to be "an idea whose time has come," in the words of then Republican Senate Minority Leader Everett Dirksen. The legislation passed during the Eisenhower administration was relatively symbolic. The Civil Rights Act of 1957 established the Civil Rights Commission and a new Civil Rights Division within the Department of Justice. The Civil Rights Act of 1960 was passed to protect voting rights. Whenever a pattern or practice of discrimination was documented, the Justice Department, on behalf of the voter, could bring suit, even against a state. However, this act, which had little enforcement power, was relatively ineffective.

The 1960 presidential election featured Vice President Richard Nixon against Senator John F. Kennedy. Kennedy sought the support of African American leaders, promising to introduce tougher civil rights legislation. When Martin Luther King was imprisoned in Georgia after participating in a sit-in in Atlanta, candidate Kennedy called Mrs. King to express his support, and his brother, Robert, made telephone calls to expedite King's release on bond. However, President Kennedy's civil rights legislation was stalled in the Senate in 1963, and his assassination ended the effort in his name. When Lyndon B. Johnson became president in 1963, he committed himself to passing civil rights bills, and the 1964 act was the result.

The Civil Rights Act of 1964. The Civil Rights Act of 1964, the most far-reaching bill on civil rights in modern times, forbade discrimination on the basis of race, color, religion, gender, and national origin. The major provisions of the act were as follows:

1. It outlawed arbitrary discrimination in voter registration.
2. It barred discrimination in public accommodations, such as hotels and restaurants, whose operations affect interstate commerce.
3. It authorized the federal government to sue to desegregate public schools and facilities.
4. It expanded the power of the Civil Rights Commission and extended its life.
5. It provided for the withholding of federal funds from programs administered in a discriminatory manner.
6. It established the right to equality of opportunity in employment.

Title VII of the Civil Rights Act of 1964 is the cornerstone of employment-discrimination law. It prohibits discrimination in employment based on race, color, religion, sex, or national origin. Under Title VII, executive orders were issued that banned employment discrimination by firms that received any federal funding. The 1964 Civil Rights Act created a five-member commission, the Equal Employment Opportunity Commission (EEOC), to administer Title VII.

The EEOC can issue interpretive guidelines and regulations, but these do not have the force of law. Rather, they give notice of the commission's enforcement policy. The EEOC also has investigatory powers. It has broad authority to require the production of documentary evidence, to hold hearings, and to **subpoena** and examine witnesses under oath.

The equal employment provisions of the 1964 act have been strengthened several times since its first passage. In 1965, President Johnson signed an Executive Order (11246) that prohibited any discrimination in employment by any employer who received federal funds, contracts, or subcontracts. It also required all such employers to establish *affirmative action plans*, which will be discussed later in this chapter. A revision of that order extended the requirement for an affirmative action plan to public institutions and medical and health facilities with more than 50 employees. In 1972, the Equal Employment Opportunity Act extended the provisions prohibiting discrimination in employment to the employees of state and local governments and most other not-for-profit institutions.

The Voting Rights Act of 1965. As late as 1960, only 29.1 percent of African Americans of voting age were registered in the Southern states, in stark contrast to 61.1 percent of whites. The Voting Rights Act of 1965 addressed this issue. The act had two major provisions. The first one outlawed discriminatory voter-registration tests. The second authorized federal registration of voters and federally administered voting procedures in any political subdivision or state that discriminated electorally against a particular group. In part, the act provided that certain political subdivisions could not change their voting procedures and election laws without federal approval. The act targeted counties, mostly in the South, in which less than 50 percent of the eligible population was registered to vote. Federal voter registrars were sent to these areas to register African Americans who had been kept from voting by local registrars. Within one week after the act was passed, 45 federal examiners were sent to the South. A massive voter-registration drive drew thousands of civil rights activists, many of whom were white college students, to the South over the summer. This effort resulted in a dramatic increase in the proportion of African Americans registered to vote.

Subpoena
A legal writ requiring a person's appearance in court to give testimony.

DID YOU KNOW?

That by September 1961, more than 3,600 students had been arrested for participating in civil rights demonstrations, and that 141 students and 58 faculty members had been expelled by colleges and universities for their part in civil rights protests?

Urban Riots. Even as the civil rights movement was experiencing its greatest victories, a series of riots swept through African American inner-city neighborhoods. These urban riots were different in character from the race riots described earlier in this chapter. The riots in the first half of the 20th century were street battles between whites and blacks. The urban riots of the late 1960s and early 1970s, however, were not directed against individual whites—in some instances, whites actually participated in small numbers. The riots were primarily civil insurrections, although these disorders were accompanied by large-scale looting of stores. Inhabitants of the affected neighborhoods attributed the riots to racial discrimination.[13] The riots dissipated much of the goodwill toward the civil rights movement that had been built up earlier in the decade among Northern whites. Together with widespread student demonstrations against the Vietnam War (1964–1975), the riots pushed many Americans toward conservatism.

The Civil Rights Act of 1968 and Other Housing Reform Legislation. Martin Luther King, Jr., was assassinated on April 4, 1968. Despite King's message of peace, his death was followed by widespread rioting. Nine days after King's death, President Johnson signed the Civil Rights Act of 1968, which forbade discrimination in most housing and provided penalties for those attempting to interfere with individual civil rights (giving protection to civil rights workers, among others). Subsequent legislation added enforcement provisions to the federal government's rules against discriminatory mortgage lending practices. Today, all lenders must report to the federal government the race, gender, and income of all mortgage loan seekers, along with the final decision on their loan applications.

PRESIDENT LYNDON B. JOHNSON is shown signing the Civil Rights Act of 1968. What are some of the provisions of that far-reaching law? (Bettmann/Corbis)

CONSEQUENCES OF CIVIL RIGHTS LEGISLATION

As a result of the Voting Rights Act of 1965 and its amendments, and the large-scale voter-registration drives in the South, the number of African Americans registered to vote climbed dramatically. Subsequent amendments to the Voting Rights Act of 1965 extended its protections to other minorities, including Latinos, Asian Americans, Native Americans, and Native Alaskans. To further protect the voting rights of minorities, the law now provides that states must make bilingual ballots available in counties where 5 percent or more of the population speaks a language other than English.

Some of the provisions in the Voting Rights Act of 1965 were due to "sunset" (expire) in 2007. In July 2006, President George W. Bush signed a 25-year extension of these provisions, following heated congressional debate in which many members, particularly those representing the states and counties still monitored by the Justice Department, argued that the Voting Rights Act was no longer needed.

Political Participation by African Americans. The movement of African American citizens into high elected office has been sure, if exceedingly slow. African American

[13]Angus Campbell and Howard Schuman, *ICPSR 3500: Racial Attitudes in Fifteen American Cities, 1968* (Ann Arbor, MI: Inter-University Consortium for Political and Social Research, 1997). Campbell and Schuman's survey documents both white participation in and the attitudes of the inhabitants of affected neighborhoods. This survey is available online at www.grinnell.edu/academic/data/sociology/minorityresearch/raceatt1968.

POLITICS WITH A purpose

Research With Impact: Slavery Reparations

Deandria Farmer-Paellmann grew up listening to stories about her ancestors, who were rice farmers in South Carolina. Her grandfather, whose own grandfather was a slave on a rice plantation on St. Helena Island, often claimed, "They still owe us 40 acres and a mule."

He was referring to a short-lived promise made by General William T. Sherman to slaves freed in 1863 by the Emancipation Proclamation that they would receive a 40-acre plot of land. The plots were drawn from "the islands from Charleston, south, the abandoned rice fields along the rivers for thirty miles back from the sea, and the country bordering the St. Johns river, Florida."[a] After Lincoln was assassinated, President Andrew Johnson revoked the order, took the land away from the freed slaves, and returned it to its original owners, who in many cases turned around and "hired" the former slaves at very low wages. Thus, the first recorded form of reparations for slavery never materialized.

Deandria Farmer-Paellmann was still interested in the issue when she enrolled in the New England School of Law. While researching a paper on slave reparations, she discovered an insurance policy from 1856 that offered slave owners in six Southern states the option of insuring the lives of their slaves so that their "property interests" could be protected in the event a slave died. A two-dollar policy on a 10-year-old, for example, would pay out $100 if the child died. Tom Baker, director of the Insurance Law center at the University of Connecticut School of Law says, "It was very common. Basically, insurance and slavery go all the way back. ..."[b] When she found a

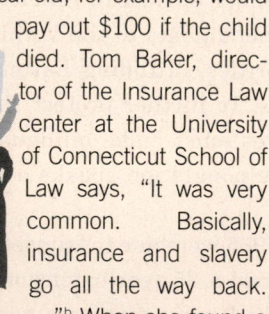

similar document from a company that is now Aetna, Inc., the nation's largest health insurer, she contacted the company and asked for archival records related to slave insurance. This discovery and request ignited a national dialogue. In 2000, Aetna issued a public apology for its role in supporting the "deplorable practice" of slavery. The state of California passed a law requiring all insurance companies that do business in the state to submit records of any slaveholder insurance policies. As a result of the law, Farmer-Paellmann learned that Aetna wrote a policy on the

life of Abel, one of her ancestors from South Carolina. This discovery provided her legal standing to pursue reparations through litigation.

In March 2002, Deandria Farmer-Paellmann and other plaintiffs filed a federal lawsuit against Aetna, a bank, and a major railroad company on the grounds that they "knowingly benefited from a system that enslaved, tortured, starved and exploited human beings" and concealed their involvement with the slave trade from consumers—an act that constitutes fraud.[c] In an interview, Farmer-Paellmann said that although she was intrigued by the idea of a national apology and federal restitution for descendants of slaves, she decided that the American public wasn't ready for a national reparations bill, and so she turned her attention to corporations.

Not all scholars and activists believe reparations are the way to settle the debts of slavery. Glenn Loury, director of Boston University's Institute on Race and Social Division, warns that a successful reparations lawsuit could end up helping white Americans feel even less responsible for slavery than they do now. Loury and others prefer progressive social policies that benefit impoverished African Americans: "What I'm advocating is politics ... reparations is not a substitute for politics."[d] Randall Robinson, author of *The Debt: What America Owes to Blacks*, links the contemporary popularity of the reparations movement to scaled-back social programs and to the backlash against affirmative action policy.

Whatever the eventual outcome of Deandria Farmer-paellmann legal actions, her curiosity about her ancestor's slave experiences led her to do research that sparked a new public dialogue on the legacy of slavery. Several universities including Harvard, Yale, and Brown have undertaken efforts to document and make public the ways in which their endowments are connected to the slave trade. The U.S. Congress passed a resolution issuing a formal apology for the institution of slavery in 2008. Law schools across the country have hosted scholarly conferences on reparations. The question of what, if any, legal and moral responsibility today's society has toward the descendants of slaves is far from settled. Yet one woman's actions helped to put the question of reparations back onto the political agenda.

[a]Major General William T. Sherman, "Special Field Orders, No. 15," Savannah, Georgia, January 16, 1865.
[b]Virginia Groark, "Slave Policies," *New York Times*, May 5, 2002.
[c]The bank is FleetBoston Financial Corporation and the railroad is CSX Corporation.
[d]Sasha Polakow-Suransky, "Sins of Our Fathers," *Brown Alumni Magazine*, July/August 2003.

representatives hold 42 of the 435 seats in the House of Representatives (9.5 percent) and only one of 100 seats in the U.S. Senate in the 111th Congress. The number of African American state legislators increased from 401 in 1986 to a record 628 (or 9 percent) in 2009. In 2008, Karen Bass was selected as the first African American woman assembly speaker in California. At the local level (city and county offices), the Joint Center for Political and Economic Studies estimated that black elected officials held over 5,700 offices in 2002. In a decisive victory, Barack Obama was elected the first African American president on November 4, 2008. In his acceptance speech on election night, the president-elect stressed the need for all Americans to come together regardless of race or ethnic background to solve the problems facing the nation.

The U.S. Census and Civil Rights. The census, which calls for a count of the country's population every 10 years and which took place in 2010, is the basis for virtually all demographic information used by policy makers, educators, and community leaders. The census is related to civil rights in a number of important ways. First, it is used for determining representation for the purposes of redistricting (covered in detail in Chapter 12). In this sense, the census data also provide an important tool for enforcing the Voting Rights Act, which forbids drawing districts with the intention of diluting the concentration and thus the political power of minority voters. Census data are also used to allocate federal dollars in support of community development, education, crime prevention, and transportation. For these reasons, civil rights leaders urged full participation from within their communities. Being counted in the census equates to political and community empowerment.

Lingering Social and Economic Disparities. According to Joyce Ladner of the Brookings Institution, one of the difficulties with the race-based civil rights agenda of the 1950s and 1960s is that it did not envision remedies for cross-racial problems. How, for example, should the nation address problems such as poverty and urban violence that affect underclasses in all racial groups? In 1967, when Martin Luther King, Jr., proposed a Poor People's Campaign, he recognized that a civil rights coalition based entirely on race would not be sufficient to address the problem of poverty among whites as well as blacks. During his 1984 and 1988 presidential campaigns, African American leader Jesse Jackson also acknowledged the inadequacy of a race-based model of civil rights when he attempted to form a "Rainbow Coalition" of minorities, women, and other underrepresented groups, including the poor.[14]

Race Conscious or Post-Racial Society? Whether we are talking about college attendance, media stereotyping, racial profiling, or academic achievement, the black experience is different from the white one. As a result, African Americans view the nation and many specific issues differently than their white counterparts do.[15] In survey after survey, when blacks are asked whether they have achieved racial equality, few believe that they have. In contrast, whites are five times more likely than blacks to believe that racial equality has been achieved.[16] As a candidate for the Democratic nomination for president, Barack Obama directly addressed race in America in his "A More Perfect Union" speech delivered in Philadelphia in

DID YOU KNOW?

That during the Mississippi Summer Project in 1964, organized by students to register African American voters, 1,000 students and voters were arrested, 80 were beaten, 35 were shot, and six were murdered; 30 buildings were bombed; and 25 churches were burned?

---

[14]Joyce A. Ladner, "A New Civil Rights Agenda," *The Brookings Review*, Vol. 18, No. 2, Spring 2000, pp. 26–28.
[15]Lawerence D. Bobo et al., "Through the Eyes of Black America," *Public Perspective*, May/June 2001, p. 13.
[16]Ibid., p. 15, Figure 2.

March 2008.[17] Since taking office, President Obama has been criticized by some within the civil rights community for not making the goal of racial equality a higher priority within his administration.

The president addressed racial profiling in ways no previous president could when one of the nation's preeminent African American scholars, Harvard Professor Henry Louis Gates, was arrested in his own home and charged with disorderly conduct for displaying "loud and tumultuous behavior" when he was asked by Cambridge police for identification to prove that he was indeed the homeowner. For their part, the police said they were responding to a call from a neighbor who reported seeing "two black men with backpacks" trying to enter the house. In reality that afternoon, Professor Gates returned home from a trip to China to find his front door stuck; he and the taxi driver were trying to get it open. The president, asked at a news conference to comment on the incident said, "What I think we know, separate and apart from this incident, is that there's a long history in this country of African Americans and Latinos being stopped by law enforcement disproportionately. That's just a fact. ..."[18]

Despite the civil rights movement and civil rights legislation, and despite the election of the first black president, many African Americans continue to feel a sense of injustice in matters of race, and this feeling is often not apparent to, or appreciated by, the majority of white America.

This cartoon highlights the issue of racial profiling, however as you know from the description of the incident in the text, Professor Gates was confronted and later arrested in his home during daylight hours. Why would the cartoonist draw this scene at night? How is neighborhood racial segregation still prevalent in the U.S. related to this incident and the way it has been portrayed by the cartoonist? (By permission of Chris Britt and Creators Syndicate, Inc.)

---

[17]Barack Obama, "A More Perfect Union," *Transcript of speech delivered*, March 18, 2008, at the Constitution Center in Philadelphia, PA. http://www.npr.org/templates/story/story.php?storyId=88478467
[18]"Obama Addresses Race and Gates Incident," *Washington Post*, July 23, 2009.

WOMEN'S CAMPAIGN FOR EQUAL RIGHTS

Like African Americans and other minorities, women also have had to make a claim for equality. Political citizenship requires personal autonomy (the ability to think and act for oneself), but at the founding, the prevailing opinion about women was that they were not endowed with reason. During the first phase of this campaign, the primary political goal of women was to obtain the right to vote.

EARLY WOMEN'S POLITICAL MOVEMENTS

The first political cause in which women became actively engaged was the movement to abolish slavery. When the World Antislavery Convention was held in London in 1840, women delegates were barred from active participation. Partly in response to this rebuff, two American delegates, Lucretia Mott and Elizabeth Cady Stanton, returned from that meeting with plans to work for women's rights in the United States.

In 1848, Mott and Stanton organized the first women's rights convention in Seneca Falls, New York. The 300 people who attended the two-day event debated a wide variety of issues important for expanding women's social, civil, and religious rights including access to education and employment, marriage and divorce reform, and most controversial of all, **suffrage**. Attendees approved a Declaration of Sentiments modeled in word and spirit on the Declaration of Independence: "We hold these truths to be self-evident: that all men and *women* are created equal." Groups that supported women's rights held similar conventions in cities in the Midwest and East.

Suffrage
The right to vote; the franchise.

With the outbreak of the Civil War, advocates of women's rights were urged to put their support behind the war effort and women in the North and South dedicated themselves to their respective causes. In 1866 the American Equal Rights Association (AERA) was formed to advance the cause of universal suffrage, but tensions arose immediately between those whose first priority was black male suffrage and those who were dedicated first to women's suffrage. The failure to include women in the Fifteenth Amendment resulted in the dissolution of the AERA and the formation of two rival women's suffrage organizations.

DID YOU KNOW?

That of all those in attendance at Seneca Falls, only one 19-year-old woman, Charlotte Woodward, lived long enough to exercise her right to vote?

WOMEN'S SUFFRAGE ASSOCIATIONS

Susan B. Anthony and Elizabeth Cady Stanton formed the National Woman Suffrage Association (NWSA) in 1869 and dedicated themselves nearly exclusively to advancing women's suffrage at the federal level by way of a constitutional amendment. In their view, women's suffrage was a means to achieve major improvements in the economic and social situation of women in the United States. Unlike Anthony and Stanton, Lucy Stone, a key founder of the American Woman Suffrage Association (AWSA), continued to support the Fifteenth Amendment restricted to males but vowed to support a Sixteenth Amendment dedicated to women's suffrage. The AWSA primarily focused its efforts on the states.

In the November election of 1872 several women attempted to vote under the revolutionary legal reasoning that the Fourteenth Amendment extended citizenship rights to all persons, and voting was among the privilege and immunities of citizenship. In

FIGURE 5–1 The Suffrage Map, Early August, 1920

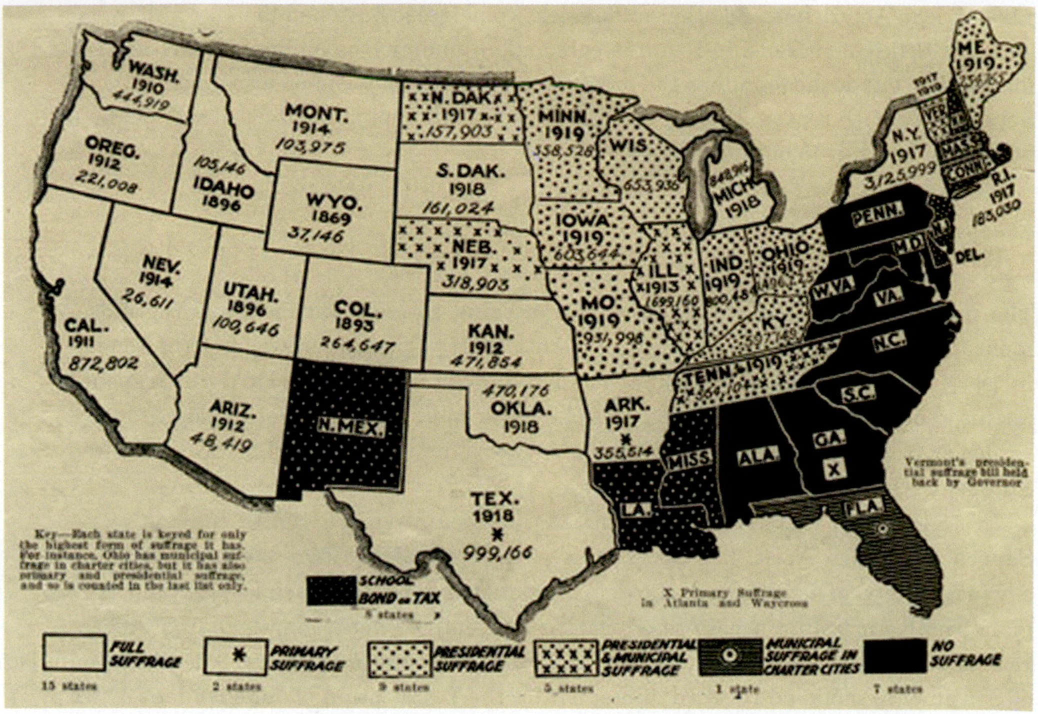

Source: From "Out of Subjection into Freedom" by Marjorie Shuler, published in *The Woman Citizen*, p. 360, September 4, 1920.

Missouri, Virginia Minor cast her vote and was arrested for illegal voting. In the case of *Minor v. Happersett*, the U.S. Supreme Court ruled that since the federal Constitution did not explicitly grant women the right to vote, the states were free to decide who had the privilege of voting. For suffragists, this left two options—an amendment to the U.S. Constitution or a state-by-state campaign.

For the next 20 years, the two organizations worked along similar paths to educate the public and legislators, testifying before legislative committees, giving public speeches, and conducting public referendum campaigns on women's suffrage. Organizations like the Women's Christian Temperance Union (WCTU) joined the campaign for suffrage, arguing that only women could be counted on to cast the votes necessary to prohibit the sale and consumption of alcohol. The combination of efforts yielded the movement's first successes. The western territory of Wyoming granted women the right to vote in 1869, and several state legislatures in other regions (outside the South) took up legislation granting women the vote. Political scientist Lee Ann Banaszak calculated that between 1870 and 1890, an average of four states a year took up the question of women's suffrage.[19] In 1890, the two organizations joined forces, creating the National American Woman Suffrage Association (NAWSA), with only one goal—the enfranchisement of women—and continued lobbying in the states and western territories.

Opposition to women's suffrage came from a number of sources including the liquor industry, big business, and the church. Brewers and distillers were interested

---

[19]Lynne E. Ford, *Women and Politics: The Pursuit of Equality*. (Boston: Cengage Learning Wadsworth, 2011).

in preventing prohibition, thus hoped to keep women from the voting booth. Industry was interested in limiting the reach of progressive policy to set wages and improve working conditions (both areas where female activists were heavily involved), and the church opposed suffrage primarily on ideological grounds. However, beginning in about 1880, the most persistent opponents to the suffrage cause emerged: other women. Suffragists at first dismissed the "antis" but later came to understand that they were a powerful, well-organized force dedicated to protecting traditional gender roles as well as women's social and economic privileges as they understood them.[20]

At the turn of the century, an impatient new generation of women introduced direct protest tactics they had observed while working alongside Emmeline Pankhurst in the British suffrage campaign. Harriet Stanton Blatch (Elizabeth Cady Stanton's daughter), Alice Paul, and Lucy Burns urged NAWSA to return to a federal amendment strategy. The new suffragists, as they were called, intended to *demand* their right to vote. They scheduled a massive parade in Washington, D.C., for March 3, 1913, timed to coincide with Woodrow Wilson's inauguration as president, scheduled for the next day. Alice Paul believed that Congress would only be persuaded to move the suffrage amendment forward if prodded to do so by the president. The parade attracted 8,000 marchers and more than half a million spectators.

Alice Paul continued to agitate for women's suffrage in ways that embarrassed NAWSA's leadership. She organized "Silent Sentinels" to stand in front of the White House with banners reading, "Mr. President, What Will You Do for Woman Suffrage?" These women were the first picketers ever to appear before the White House. When the United States joined the war against Germany in 1917, women were urged to set aside their goals in favor of the overall war effort. Paul refused and formed the National Woman's Party (NWP) to bring even greater attention to women's disenfranchisement.

Meanwhile NAWSA members, under the leadership of Carrie Chapman Catt, were pursuing the "winning plan," which entailed a two-pronged lobbying strategy focused on both federal and state legislators. In the end, scholars agree that it was the combination of patient lobbying by NAWSA members and the more militant tactics of the NWP that resulted in Congress passing the suffrage amendment in May 1919. In

SILENT SENTINELS posted in front of the White House gates. The women were often arrested and attacked by onlookers, but the protests continued. Long prison terms were imposed in an attempt to scare women away. Women who could not themselves stand on the picket line sent money to support the families of those who were jailed. Women in jail organized hunger strikes only to be force-fed through the nose. (Courtesy of the Library of Congress)

[20]Susan E. Marshall, *Splintered Sisterhood: Gender and Class in the Campaign Against Women's Suffrage* (Madison WI: University of Wisconsin Press, 1997).

TABLE 5–1 WOMEN'S VOTING RIGHTS AROUND THE WORLD
Selected Countries, Year Women's Suffrage Granted

1893	New Zealand	1920	United States	1944	France	1950	India	1971	Switzerland
1902	Austria	1928	United Kingdom	1945	Japan	1956	Egypt	1974	Jordan
1913	Norway	1930	Turkey	1947	Mexico	1961	Rwanda	1980	Iraq
1918	Canada	1934	Cuba	1948	Israel	1964	Afghanistan	1994	South Africa
1919	Germany	1939	El Salvador	1949	China	1965	Sudan	2005	Kuwait

Source: Center for the American Woman and Politics

Tennessee, the last state required to win ratification, the amendment passed by one vote on August 26, 1920. The Nineteenth Amendment reads: "The right of citizens of the United States to vote shall not be denied or abridged by the United States or by any State on account of sex."

The United States was neither the first nor the last to give women the vote. New Zealand introduced universal suffrage in 1893, while Kuwait allowed women to vote and seek public office for the first time in 2005. Saudi Arabia still does not permit women to vote (see Table 5–1).

THE SECOND WAVE WOMEN'S MOVEMENT

After gaining the right to vote in 1920, women did not flock to polls in large numbers, nor did many of the thousands of women who had lobbied for and against suffrage seek political office. There was little by way of an organized women's movement again until the second wave began in the 1960s. The civil rights movement of that decade resulted in a growing awareness of rights for all groups, including women. Women's increased participation in the workforce and the publication of Betty Friedan's *The Feminine Mystique* in 1963 focused national attention on the unequal status of women in American life.

In 1966, Betty Friedan and others who were dissatisfied with existing women's organizations, and especially with the failure of the Equal Employment Opportunity Commission to address discrimination against women, formed the National Organization for Women (NOW). NOW immediately adopted a blanket resolution designed "to bring women into full participation in the mainstream of American society *now*, exercising all the privileges and responsibilities thereof in truly equal partnership with men."

The second wave gained additional impetus from young women who entered politics to support the civil rights movement or to oppose the Vietnam War. Many of them found that despite the egalitarian principles of these movements, women remained in second-class positions. In the late 1960s, "women's liberation" organizations began to spring up on college campuses and women organized "consciousness-raising groups," in which they discussed how gender affected their lives. The new women's movement emerged as a major social force by 1970.

Historian Nancy Cott contends that the word *feminism* first began to be used around 1910.[21] At that time, **feminism** meant, as it does today, political, social, and economic equality for women. It is difficult to measure the support for feminism at

Feminism
The philosophy of political, economic, and social equality for women and the gender consciousness sufficient to mobilize women for change.

[21]Nancy F. Cott, *The Grounding of Modern Feminism* (New Haven, CT: Yale University Press, 1987).

Beyond Our Borders

THE CAMPAIGN FOR WOMEN'S RIGHTS AROUND THE WORLD

Although in the last several decades women's rights have emerged as a global issue, progress has been slow. The campaign for women's rights in countries where cultural or legal practices perpetuate the inequality of women is especially difficult. December 2009 marked the 30th anniversary of the United Nations' adoption of the Convention on the Elimination of All Forms of Discrimination against Women (CEDAW), an international treaty to promote the adoption of national laws, policies, and practices to ensure that women and girls live free from violence, have access to high-quality education, and have the right to participate fully in the economic, political, and social sectors of their society. Although it has been ratified by 186 countries, the United States is one of only seven nations that have not ratified. International agreements such as CEDAW convey a set of universal ethical standards and global norms regarding human rights.

THE PROBLEM OF VIOLENCE

Most people consider the right to be free from violence as one of the most basic human rights. Women's rights advocates point out that this right is threatened in societies that do not accept the premise that men and women are equal. Some parts of India, for example, implicitly tolerate the practice of dowry killing. (A *dowry* is a sum of money given to a husband by the bride's family.) In a number of cases, husbands, dissatisfied with the size of dowries, have killed their wives in order to remarry for a "better deal"—a crime that is rarely prosecuted.

THE SITUATION IN AFGHANISTAN

In 2001, a startling documentary, "Behind the Veil," was aired repeatedly on CNN. A courageous female reporter had secretly filmed Afghan women being beaten in the streets, killed in public for trivial offenses, and subjugated in extreme ways. Women's rights became a major issue in our foreign policy. Americans learned that Afghan girls were barred from schools, and by law women were not allowed to work. Women who had lost their husbands during Afghanistan's civil wars were forced into begging and prostitution. Women had no access to medical care. Any woman found with an unrelated man could be executed by stoning, and many were.

IRAQI GIRLS wait for the start of class at the Eastern Secondary School in Baghdad. The role of women in the new Iraq remains uncertain. What negative consequences could result if discriminatory laws forced Iraqi women—among the region's most educated— to retreat to their homes? (AP Photo/ Alexander Zemlianichenko)

NATION BUILDING AND WOMEN'S RIGHTS

After the collapse of the Taliban regime, the United States and its allies were able to influence the status of Afghan women. The draft constitution of Afghanistan, adopted in January 2004, gave women equality before the law and 20 percent of the seats in the National Assembly. Much of the country remained outside the control of the national government, however. Women continue to face abuse, including arson attacks on girls' schools, forced marriages, and reimposition of the all-covering burka garment.

Women in Iraq had enjoyed greater equality than in most Arab nations. In line with the secular ideology of the Baath Party, Saddam Hussein's government tended to treat men and women alike. A problem for the U.S.–led Coalition Provisional Authority (CPA) that governed Iraq until June 2004 was ensuring that women did not lose ground under the new regime. Some members of the Iraqi Governing Council, for example, advocated traditional Islamic laws that would have deprived women of equal rights. Women's organizations campaigned against these provisions, and they were vetoed by the CPA. The interim Iraqi constitution, adopted in March 2004, allotted 25 percent of the seats in the parliament to women.

FOR CRITICAL ANALYSIS

1. Is it fair or appropriate for one country to judge the cultural practices of another? Why or why not?
2. Are there universal norms of gender equality that should prevail? Is an international treaty such as CEDAW an effective tool to promote equality across cultures? Why has the United States failed to ratify CEDAW?

present because the word means different things to different people. When the dictionary definition of *feminist*—"someone who supports political, economic, and social equality for women"—was read to respondents in a survey, 67 percent labeled themselves as feminists.[22] In the absence of such prompting, however, the term *feminist* (like the term *liberal*) implies radicalism to many people, who therefore shy away from it. Young women have launched a third wave of feminism embracing a multitude of perspectives on what it means to be a feminist woman.[23]

DID YOU KNOW?

That 72 years passed between the time the Declaration of Independence was signed in 1776 and women first demanded the vote at the Seneca Falls Convention in 1848; it took another 72 years for women to win suffrage by the Nineteenth Amendment, ratified in 1920; and it took another 72 years before more than two women were elected to serve in the U.S. Senate *at the same time* (1992)?

The Equal Rights Amendment. Leaders of NOW and other women's rights advocates sought to eradicate gender inequality through a constitutional amendment. The proposed Equal Rights Amendment (ERA), first introduced in Congress in 1923 by leaders of the National Woman's Party, states: "Equality of rights under the law shall not be denied or abridged by the United States or by any state on account of sex." For decades the amendment was not even given a hearing in Congress, but finally it was approved by both chambers and sent to the state legislatures for ratification in 1972.

As was noted in Chapter 2, any constitutional amendment must be ratified by the legislatures (or conventions) in three-fourths of the states. Since the early 1900s, most proposed amendments have required that ratification occur within seven years of Congress's adoption of the amendment. Although states competed to be the first to ratify the ERA, by 1977 only 35 of the necessary 38 states had ratified the amendment. Congress granted a rare extension, but the remaining three states could not be added by the 1982 deadline even though the ERA was supported by numerous national party platforms, six presidents, and both chambers of Congress.

As with the antisuffrage efforts, the staunchest opponents to the ERA were other women. Many women perceived the goals pursued by feminists as a threat to their way

[22]Nancy E. McGlen and Karen O'Connor, *Women, Politics, and American Society*, 4th ed. (Upper Saddle River, NJ: Prentice Hall, 2004).
[23]See, for example, Jessica Valenti, *Full Frontal Feminism: A Young Woman's Guide to Why Feminism Matters* (Emeryville, CA: Seal Press, 2007); and Jennifer Baumgardner and Amy Richards, *Manifesta: Young Women, Feminism, and the Future* (New York: Farrar, Straus and Giroux, 2000).

of life. At the head of the countermovement was Republican Phyllis Schlafly and her conservative organization, Eagle Forum. Eagle Forum's "Stop ERA" campaign found significant support among fundamentalist religious groups and other conservative organizations. The campaign was a major force in blocking the ratification of the ERA, although 21 states have passed such amendments to their own constitutions.

Three-State Strategy. Had the ERA been ratified by 38 states, it would have become the Twenty-seventh Amendment to the Constitution. Instead, that place is occupied by the "Madison Amendment" governing congressional pay raises, first sent to the states in 1789 but not actually ratified until 1992. ERA supporters argue that acceptance of the Madison Amendment means that Congress has the power to maintain the legal viability of the ERA and the existing 35 state ratifications. The legal rationale for the three-state strategy was developed by three law students in a law review article published in 1997.[24] Support for constitutional equality remains high in the United States; however, mobilizing support for ratification of the ERA in the future may prove difficult. A 2001 poll found that although 96 percent of those polled supported constitutional equality for women and men, 72 percent mistakenly believed that the U.S. Constitution already includes the Equal Rights Amendment.[25]

Challenging Gender Discrimination in the Courts and Legislatures. With the failure of the ERA, feminists turned their attention to national and state laws that would guarantee the equality of women. In 1978, the Civil Rights Act of 1964 was amended by the Pregnancy Discrimination Act, which prohibits discrimination in employment against pregnant women. In addition, Title IX of the Education Amendments was passed in 1972; it banned sex discrimination at all levels and in all aspects of education and dealt with issues of sexual harassment, pregnancy, parental status, and marital status. Although best known for increasing women's access to sports, the legislation's most significant impact has been on equalizing admissions to professional programs, financial aid, and educational facilities. Prior to Title IX, women's entrance into professional programs in law, medicine, science, and engineering was limited by quotas. In 1996, the Supreme Court held that the state-financed Virginia Military Institute's policy of accepting only males violated the equal protection clause, leading to the admission of women at The Citadel, the state-financed military college in South Carolina, as well.[26]

Women's rights organizations challenged discriminatory statutes and policies in the federal courts, contending that **gender discrimination** violated the Fourteenth Amendment's equal protection clause. Since the 1970s, the Supreme Court has tended to scrutinize gender classifications closely and has invalidated a number of such statutes and policies. For example, in 1977, the Court held that police and firefighting units cannot establish arbitrary rules, such as height and weight requirements, that tend to keep women from joining those occupations.[27] In 1983, the Court ruled that life insurance companies cannot charge different rates for women and men.[28]

A question that the Court has not ruled on is whether women should be allowed to participate in military combat. Generally, the Supreme Court has left this decision up to Congress and the Department of Defense. In 1994 Congress repealed the "risk rule" barring women from all combat situations. As a result over 90 percent of positions in

> **Gender Discrimination**
> Any practice, policy, or procedure that denies equality of treatment to an individual or to a group because of gender.

---

[24]Allison Held, Sheryl Herndon, and Danielle Stager, "The Equal Rights Amendment: Why the ERA Remains Legally Viable and Properly Before the States." *William & Mary Journal of Women and the Law,* Spring 1997, pp. 113–136.
[25]*The ERA Campaign*, Issue #5, July 2001, accessed at http://eracampaignweb.kishosting.com/newsletter5.html.
[26]*United States v. Virginia*, 518 U.S. 515 (1996).
[27]*Dothard v. Rawlinson*, 433 U.S. 321 (1977).
[28]*Arizona v. Norris*, 463 U.S. 1073 (1983).

the military are now open to women, and most experts think it is only a matter of time until there is full gender integration. Most recently, the navy has opened service on submarines to women, beginning in 2012. While technically women cannot be "assigned" to direct combat units, the wars in Iraq and Afghanistan have stretched the limits of that law, and more women have been "attached" to front-line units in combat support positions. Generally, the public supports increasing women's combat role. A 2009 poll found that 53 percent of those polled would favor permitting women to "join combat units, where they would be directly involved in the ground fighting."

WOMEN IN POLITICS TODAY

Today women make up just 17 percent of the U.S. Congress, an all-time high. The United States is ranked 74th among 188 nations by the Inter-Parliamentary Union based on the proportion of seats held by women in the lower house. Rwanda ranks first—in that nation, women hold 56 percent of seats in the Lower House.[29] The efforts of women's rights advocates have helped increase the number of women holding political offices at all levels of government. In 2007, Nancy Pelosi of California became the first female Speaker of the House, the most powerful member of the majority party and second in the line of succession to the presidency.

Although no woman has yet been nominated for president by a major political party, in 1984 Geraldine Ferraro became the Democratic nominee for vice president. In 2008 Hillary Rodham Clinton, senator from New York, became one of two final contenders for the presidential nomination of the Democratic Party, but ultimately lost to Barack Obama. In a surprise move, Senator John McCain chose the Alaskan governor, Sarah Palin, for his running mate.

In recent presidential administrations, women are more visible in Cabinet posts. President Bill Clinton (1993–2001) appointed four women to his Cabinet, more than any

THE 111TH CONGRESS includes seventeen women in the U.S. Senate. (Courtesy of The Office of Senator Barbara Boxer)

[29]Inter-Parliamentary Union, "Women in National Parliaments," accessed at http://www.ipu.org/wmn-e/classif.htm.

previous president. Madeleine Albright was appointed to serve as secretary of state, a first for a woman. President George W. Bush also appointed several women to Cabinet positions, including Condoleezza Rice as his secretary of state in 2005.

Increasing numbers of women sit on federal judicial benches. President Ronald Reagan (1981–1989) was credited with a historic first when he appointed Sandra Day O'Connor to the Supreme Court in 1981. President Clinton appointed a second woman, Ruth Bader Ginsburg, to the Court. O'Connor retired from the Court in 2006. In 2009 President Barak Obama appointed Federal Appeals Court Judge Sonia Sotomayor to fill the vacancy created by Justice David Souter's retirement. Justice Sotomayor is the first Latina to serve on the U.S. Supreme Court. In April 2010, Justice John Paul Stevens announced his retirement, giving President Obama the chance to make a second appointment to the Court. He selected Elena Kagan, the solicitor general of the United States, to fill the vacancy thus increasing the number of women currently sitting on the Supreme Court to three.

GENDER-BASED DISCRIMINATION IN THE WORKPLACE

Traditional cultural beliefs concerning the proper role of women in society continue to be evident not only in the political arena but also in the workplace. Since the 1960s, however, women have gained substantial protection against discrimination through laws mandating equal employment opportunities and equal pay.

TITLE VII OF THE CIVIL RIGHTS ACT OF 1964

Title VII of the Civil Rights Act of 1964 prohibits gender discrimination in employment and has been used to strike down employment policies that discriminate against employees on the basis of gender. Even so-called protective policies have been held to violate Title VII if they have a discriminatory effect. In 1991, for example, the Supreme Court held that a fetal protection policy established by Johnson Controls, Inc., the country's largest producer of automobile batteries, violated Title VII. The policy required all women of childbearing age working in jobs that entailed periodic exposure to lead or other hazardous materials to prove that they were infertile or to transfer to other positions. The same requirement was not applied to men. Women who agreed to transfer often had to accept cuts in pay and reduced job responsibilities. The Court concluded that women who are "as capable of doing their jobs as their male counterparts may not be forced to choose between having a child and having a job."[30]

SEXUAL HARASSMENT

The Supreme Court has also held that Title VII's prohibition of gender-based discrimination extends to **sexual harassment** in the workplace. Sexual harassment occurs when job opportunities, promotions, salary increases, and the like are given in return for sexual favors. A special form of sexual harassment, called hostile-environment harassment, occurs when an employee is subjected to sexual conduct or comments that interfere with the employee's job performance or are so pervasive or severe as to create an intimidating, hostile, or offensive environment.

> **DID YOU KNOW?**
>
> That as of March 2010 the United States ranks 74th of 184 nations based on the percentage of women serving in the lower house (U.S. House of Representatives), while Rwanda ranks first? Women make up just 16.8 percent of the U.S. House but hold 56.3 percent of the seats in the lower chamber of Rwanda's parliament.

Sexual Harassment
Unwanted physical or verbal conduct or abuse of a sexual nature that interferes with a recipient's job performance, creates a hostile work environment, or carries with it an implicit or explicit threat of adverse employment consequences.

---

[30]*United Automobile Workers v. Johnson Controls, Inc.*, 499 U.S. 187 (1991).

In two 1998 cases, the Supreme Court clarified the responsibilities of employers in preventing sexual harassment. The Court ruled that employers must take reasonable care to prevent and promptly correct any sexually harassing behavior. Claims by the employer that it was unaware of the situation or that the victim suffered no tangible job consequences do not reduce liability.[31] In another 1998 case, *Oncale v. Sundowner Offshore Services, Inc.*,[32] the Supreme Court ruled that Title VII protection extends to same-sex harassment.

WAGE DISCRIMINATION

In 2010, largely as a result of the economic recession, women constitute a majority of U.S. workers. Although Title VII and other legislation since the 1960s have mandated equal employment opportunities for men and women, women continue to earn less, on average, than men do.

The Equal Pay Act of 1963. The issue of women's wages was first addressed during World War II (1939–1945), when the War Labor Board issued an "equal pay for women" policy largely to ensure that salaries remained high when men returned from war and reclaimed their jobs. The board's authority ended with the war. Although it was supported by the next three presidential administrations, the Equal Pay Act was not enacted until 1963 as an amendment to the Fair Labor Standards Act of 1938.

The Equal Pay Act requires employers to provide equal pay for substantially equal work. In other words, males cannot legally be paid more than females who perform essentially the same job. The Equal Pay Act did not address occupational segregation, the fact that certain types of jobs traditionally held by women pay lower wages than the jobs usually held by men. For example, more women than men are salesclerks and nurses, whereas more men than women are construction workers and truck drivers. Even if all clerks performing substantially similar jobs for a company earned the same salaries, they typically would still be earning less than the company's truck drivers.

When Congress passed the Equal Pay Act in 1963, a woman, on average, made 59 cents for every dollar earned by a man. Figures recently released by the U.S. Department of Labor suggest that women now earn 77.9 cents for every dollar that men earn. The wage gap is greater for minority women. In some areas, the wage gap is widening. According to the results of a General Accounting Office survey, female managers in 10 industries made less money relative to male managers in 2000 than they did in 1995.[33] A 2007 study on the gender pay gap for college graduates found that one year out of college, women working full time earn only 80 percent as much as their male peers, even among those men and women graduating with the same major and entering the same occupation. The same study found that women earn only 69 percent of men's wages 10 years out of college.[34] The first bill President Obama signed after taking office in 2009 was the Lilly Ledbetter Fair Pay Act. The law is an example of congressional action undertaken specifically to overturn a decision by the U.S. Supreme Court. Lilly Ledbetter, an employee of Goodyear Tire and Rubber for 19 years, discovered that she was a victim of gender pay discrimination by an anonymous tip when she retired in 1998. She filed a complaint under Title VII, but in a 5-4 ruling the U.S. Supreme Court held that race and gender discrimination claims must be made within 180 days of the employer's discriminatory act.[35] As Justice Ruth Bader Ginsburg noted in her dissenting opinion, pay disparities

---

[31]524 U.S. 725 (1998) and 524 U.S. 742 (1998).
[32]523 U.S. 75 (1998).
[33]The results of this survey are online at www.gao.gov/audit.htm. To view a copy of the results, enter "GAO-02-156" in the search box. In 2004, the name of this agency was changed to the "Government Accountability Office."
[34]Judy Goldberg Dey and Catherine Hill, "Behind the Pay Gap," *AAUW Educational Foundation*, April 2007.
[35]*Ledbetter v. Goodyear Tire & Rubber Co.*, 550 U.S. 618 (2007).

FIGURE 5–2 Women's Earnings as a Percentage of Men's Earnings in the Past 12 Months by State and Puerto Rico: 2008

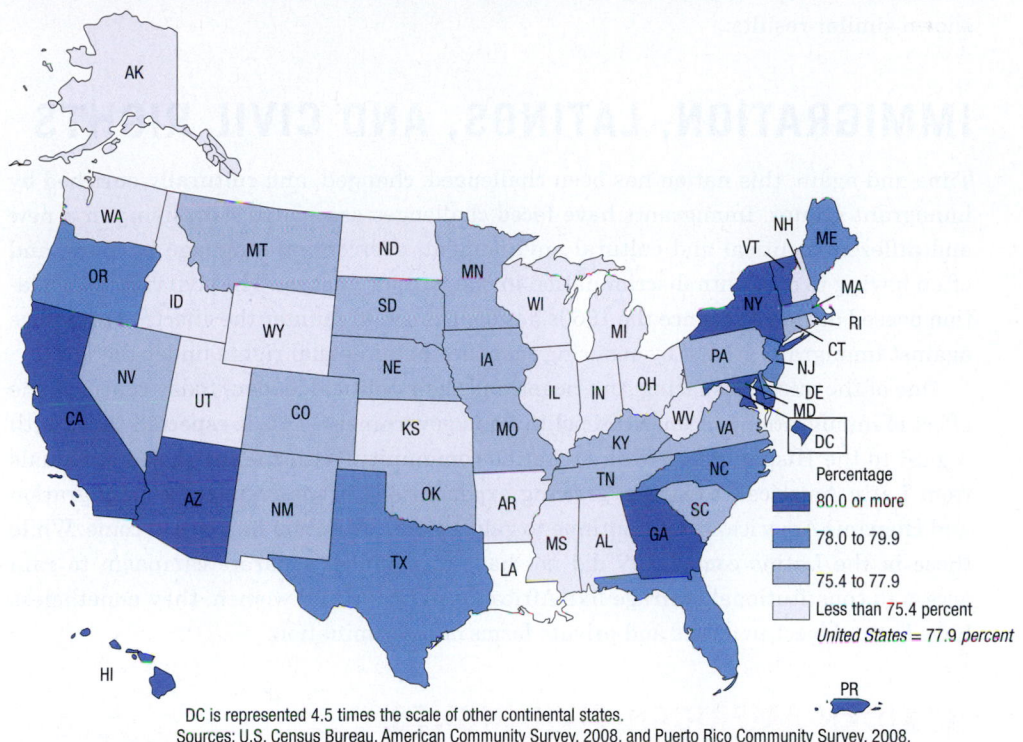

Percentage
- 80.0 or more
- 78.0 to 79.9
- 75.4 to 77.9
- Less than 75.4 percent

United States = 77.9 *percent*

DC is represented 4.5 times the scale of other continental states.
Sources: U.S. Census Bureau, American Community Survey, 2008, and Puerto Rico Community Survey, 2008.

often occur in small increments and over time, making them difficult to discover. The Ledbetter Act amends Title VII of the Civil Rights Act of 1964 by stating that the 180-day statute of limitations for filing an equal pay lawsuit regarding pay discrimination resets with each new discriminatory paycheck. It does not, however, provide any additional tools to combat wage discrimination or enforce provisions already in effect. Equal Pay Day, typically celebrated in April, marks the day each year on which women "catch up" to men in terms of wages. It is an occasion to call attention to the wage gap and to examine progress toward closing the wage gap between women and men (see Figure 5–2).

While women have made significant progress in the last decade toward equality in politics, education, and the workplace, traditional gender role expectations regarding children and family and the assignment of a disproportionate share of family responsibilities to women make achieving true equality a persistent challenge.

VOTING RIGHTS AND THE YOUNG

The Twenty-sixth Amendment to the Constitution, ratified on July 1, 1971, reads as follows:

> The right of citizens of the United States, who are eighteen years of age or older, to vote shall not be denied or abridged by the United States or by any State on account of age.

Before this amendment was ratified, the age at which citizens could vote was 21 in most states. One of the arguments used for granting the right to 18-year-olds was that, because they could be drafted to fight in the country's wars, they had a stake in public policy. At the time, the example of the Vietnam War (1964–1975) was paramount. In the first election following ratification, 58 percent of 18- to 20-year-olds were registered to vote, and 48.4 percent reported voting. But by the 2000 presidential election, of the 11.5

million U.S. residents in the 18-to-20 age bracket, 50.7 percent were registered, and 41 percent reported that they had voted. In contrast, voter turnout among Americans aged 65 or older is very high, usually between 60 and 70 percent. Subsequent elections have shown similar results.

IMMIGRATION, LATINOS, AND CIVIL RIGHTS

Time and again, this nation has been challenged, changed, and culturally enriched by immigrant groups. Immigrants have faced challenges associated with living in a new and different political and cultural environment, overcoming language barriers, and often having to deal with discrimination in one form or another. The civil rights legislation passed during and since the 1960s has done much to counter the effects of prejudice against immigrant groups by ensuring that they obtain equal rights under the law.

One of the questions facing Americans and their political leaders today concerns the effect of immigration on American politics and government. This is especially true with regard to the Hispanic American or Latino community. With the influx of individuals from Latin American countries growing exponentially, issues related to immigration and Hispanic Americans will continue to gain greater attention in years to come. While those in the Latino community did not have to mount a separate campaign to gain access to constitutional suffrage like African Americans and women, they nonetheless have been subject to public and private forms of discrimination.

MEXICAN AMERICAN CIVIL RIGHTS

The history of Mexican Americans spans more than 400 years and varies by region in the United States. Many of the most important challenges to discrimination took place in Texas and California and parallel the claims to rights made by African Americans and women. For example, Mexican American children were forced to attend segregated schools, referred to as "Mexican schools," in California. In a case that preceded *Brown v. Board of Education*, the U.S. Court of Appeals for the Ninth Circuit ruled in 1947 that segregated schools were unconstitutional. In this narrow decision, the court found that while California law provided for separate education for "children of Chinese, Japanese, or Mongolian parentage," the law did not include children of Mexican descent and therefore it was unlawful to segregate them.[36] California governor Earl Warren, who would later be appointed chief justice of the U.S. Supreme Court and preside over *Brown*, signed a law in 1947 repealing all school segregation statutes.

In 1954, an agricultural worker named Pete Hernandez was convicted of murder by an all-white jury in Texas. Hernandez maintained that juries could not be impartial unless they included members of other races. The U.S. Supreme Court ruled in *Hernandez v. Texas* that Mexican Americans and other racial groups were entitled to equal protection under the Fourteenth Amendment.[37] The Court ordered that Mr. Hernandez be retried with a jury composed without regard to race or ethnicity.

In the realm of voting rights, Mexican Americans were covered under the 1965 Voting Rights Act but they did not enjoy the singular focus of federal registration oversight as African Americans did. Poll taxes (until ended by the Twenty-fourth Amendment in 1964) limited Mexican Americans' electoral participation, particularly in Texas and California. Political organizing in the 1960s and 1970s by groups such as the La Raza Unida Party,

[36]*Mendez v. Westminster School District,* 64 F. Supp. 544 (C.D. Cal. 1946), aff'd, 161 F. 2d 744 (9th Cir. 1947) (en banc).
[37]*Hernandez v. Texas,* 347 U.S. 475 (1954).

TABLE 5–2 Latinos by Country of Origin, 2008

The ten largest Latino population groups in the United States by country of origin

	ALL HISPANICS	**48,822,000**	**100%**
1	Mexicans	30,746,000	63%
2	Puerto Ricans	4,151,000	9%
3	Cubans	1,631,000	9%
4	Salvadorians	1,560,000	3%
5	Dominicans	1,334,000	2.7%
6	Guatemalans	986,000	2%
7	Columbians	882,000	1.8%
8	Hondurans	608,000	1.2%
9	Ecuadorians	591,000	1.2%
10	Peruvians	519,000	1%

Source: Pew Hispanic Center, http://pewhispanic.org/

founded in Texas but active in other regions, increased minority representation at the local level. Although Mexican Americans potentially constitute a very large voting bloc, they tend to have low voter turnout rates, which scholars attribute to lower income and education rates as well as recent concerns over immigration status.

The Chicano movement is often characterized as an extension of the Mexican American civil rights movement but one focused on land rights, farm workers' rights, education, and voting rights, as well as the eradication of ethnic stereotypes and promotion of a positive group consciousness. At first a label with negative connotations, in the 1960s "Chicano" became associated with ethnic pride and self-determination. Movement leaders such as Cesar Chavez and Delores Huerta were instrumental in founding a number of organizations that, in addition to focusing on labor rights, offered members of the community language classes, assistance in obtaining citizenship, and advocacy for Spanish language rights (see Chapter 7). The Chicano movement has galvanized and trained successive generations of community and political activists. Recent campaigns have focused on the plight of immigrant workers in low-wage jobs such as janitors, truck drivers, and domestics.

THE CONTINUED INFLUX OF IMMIGRANTS

Every year, about one million people immigrate to this country, and those who were born on foreign soil now constitute more than 12 percent of the U.S. population—twice the percentage of 30 years ago.

Since 1977, more than 80 percent of immigrants have come from Latin America or Asia. Latinos have overtaken African Americans as the nation's largest minority. In 2008, 15 percent of the U.S. population identified itself as Hispanic or Latino, 14 percent as African American or black, and 5 percent as Asian. Non-Latino white Americans made up about 66 percent of the population. If current immigration rates continue, minority groups collectively will constitute the "majority" of Americans by the year 2042, according to estimates by the U.S. Census Bureau. If Latinos, African Americans, and perhaps Asians were to form coalitions, they could increase their political strength dramatically and would have the numerical strength to make significant changes. However, as noted in earlier discussions of civil rights campaigns and social movements, coalitions are difficult to form when common interests are not immediately obvious.

ILLEGAL IMMIGRATION

In the past few years, the issue of illegal immigration has become both a hot political issue and a serious policy concern. There may be as many as 12 million undocumented aliens residing and working in the United States. Immigrants typically come to the United States to work, and their labor continues to be in high demand, particularly in construction and farming.

One civil rights question that often surfaces is whether the government should provide services to those who enter the country illegally. Residents of southwestern states complain about the need to shore up border control and perceive that undocumented immigrants place a burden on government-provided social services and the health care industry. Some schools have become crowded with the children of undocumented immigrants. Often, these children require greater attention because of their inability to speak English, although many are themselves native-born U.S. citizens.

On April 23, 2010, Arizona governor Jan Brewer signed a highly controversial bill on immigration designed to identify, prosecute, and deport illegal immigrants. The law makes the failure to carry immigration documents a crime and gives the police broad powers to detain anyone *suspected of* being in the country illegally. Governor Brewer said the law "represents another tool for our state to use as we work to solve a crisis we did not create and the federal government has refused to fix." Leaders in the Latino community claim that the law will increase racial and ethnic profiling and create a climate of fear among residents of the state.

The Arizona law offers an opportunity to examine generational differences in attitudes about immigration. A Brookings Institution report found that Arizona has the largest "cultural generation gap" between older Americans, who are largely white (83 percent in Arizona), and children under 18, who are increasingly members of minorities (57 percent in Arizona).[38] This gap fuels conflict over policy issues such as immigration and funding allocations for education and health care. Because older people are more likely to vote and less likely to be connected to the perspectives of youth, the gap also has the potential to further alienate young people from direct political participation. A recent poll found that Americans 45 and older were more likely than young people to restrict immigration, a finding attributed to the multicultural environment young people today inhabit.

Citizenship. Members of Congress from both parties have proposed legislation that would either immediately or gradually extend citizenship to undocumented immigrants now residing in the United States. Although not all Americans agree that citizenship should be extended to illegal immigrants, the greater Latino community in the United States has taken up the cause. Numerous protests and marches calling for citizenship occurred in 2006, with more than one million individuals participating in demonstrations on May 1, 2006, alone. To be sure, the citizenship question will be an important political topic for the foreseeable future.

One expedited path to citizenship for immigrants with permanent resident status and permission to work (green card holders) is through military service. Noncitizens

---

[38]William H. Frey, *The State of Metropolitan America* (Washington, DC: Brooking Institution, 2010).

have served in the military since the Revolutionary War, and today about 29,000 noncitizens serve in uniform. Service members are eligible for expedited citizenship under a July 2002 executive order, an opportunity realized by nearly 43,000 men and women since September 11, 2001.[39]

Accommodating Diversity with Bilingual Education. The continuous influx of immigrants into this country presents another ongoing challenge—how to overcome language barriers. Bilingual education programs, first introduced in the 1960s, teach children in their native language while also teaching them English. Congress authorized bilingual education programs in 1968 when it passed the Bilingual Education Act, which was intended primarily to help Hispanic children learn English. In a 1974 case, *Lau v. Nichols*,[40] the Supreme Court bolstered the claim that children have a right to bilingual education. In that case, the Court ordered a California school district to provide special programs for Chinese students with language difficulties if a substantial number of these children attended school in the district. However, bilingual programs have more recently come under attack. In 1998, California residents passed a ballot initiative that called for the end of bilingual education programs in that state. The law allowed schools to implement English-immersion programs instead. In these programs, students are given intensive instruction in English for a limited period of time and then placed in regular classrooms. The law was immediately challenged in court on the grounds that it unconstitutionally discriminated against non-English-speaking groups. A federal district court, however, concluded that the new law did not violate the equal protection clause and allowed the law to stand, thus ending bilingual education efforts in California.

AFFIRMATIVE ACTION

As noted earlier in this chapter, the Civil Rights Act of 1964 prohibited discrimination against any person on the basis of race, color, national origin, religion, or gender. The act also established the right to equal opportunity in employment. A basic problem remained, however: Minority groups and women, because of past discrimination, often lacked the education and skills to compete effectively in the marketplace. In 1965, the federal government attempted to remedy this problem by implementing the concept of affirmative action. **Affirmative action** policies attempt to "level the playing field" by giving special preferences in educational admissions and employment decisions to groups that have been discriminated against in the past.

In 1965, President Lyndon B. Johnson ordered that affirmative action policies be undertaken to remedy the effects of past discrimination. All government agencies, including those of state and local governments, were required to implement such policies. Additionally, affirmative action requirements were applied to companies that sell goods or services to the federal government and to institutions that receive federal funds. Affirmative action policies were also required whenever an employer had been ordered to develop such a plan by a court or by the Equal Employment Opportunity Commission because of evidence of past discrimination. Finally, labor unions that had been found to discriminate against women or minorities in the past were required to establish and follow affirmative action plans.

Affirmative Action
A policy in educational admissions or job hiring that gives special attention or compensatory treatment to traditionally disadvantaged groups in an effort to overcome present effects of past discrimination.

---

[39]Department of Defense, MAVNI Fact Sheet, accessed at http://www.defense.gov/news/mavni-fact-sheet.pdf.
[40]414 U.S. 563 (1974).

THE *BAKKE* CASE

The first Supreme Court case addressing the constitutionality of affirmative action plans examined a program implemented by the University of California at Davis. Allan Bakke, a white student who had been denied admission to the medical school, discovered that his academic record was better than those of some of the minority applicants who had been admitted to the program. He sued the University of California regents, alleging **reverse discrimination**. The UC–Davis Medical School had held 16 places out of 100 for educationally "disadvantaged students" each year, and admitted to using race as a criterion for these 16 admissions. Bakke claimed that his exclusion from medical school violated his rights under the Fourteenth Amendment's provision for equal protection of the laws. The trial court agreed. On appeal, the California Supreme Court agreed also. Finally, the regents of the university appealed to the United States Supreme Court.

In 1978, the Supreme Court handed down its decision in *Regents of the University of California v. Bakke*.[41] The Court did not rule against affirmative action programs. Rather, it held that Bakke must be admitted to the UC–Davis Medical School because its admissions policy had used race as the sole criterion for the 16 "minority" positions. Justice Lewis Powell, speaking for the Court, indicated that while race can be considered "as a factor" among others in admissions (and presumably hiring) decisions, race cannot be the sole factor. So affirmative action programs, but not specific quota systems, were upheld as constitutional.

The *Bakke* decision did not end the controversy over affirmative action programs. At issue in the current debate over affirmative action programs is whether favoring one group violates the equal protection clause of the Fourteenth Amendment to the Constitution as it applies to all other groups.

FURTHER LIMITS ON AFFIRMATIVE ACTION

Several cases decided during the 1980s and 1990s placed further limits on affirmative action programs subjecting any federal, state, or local affirmative action program that uses racial or ethnic classifications as the basis for making decisions to "strict scrutiny" by the courts (to be constitutional, a discriminatory law or action must be narrowly tailored to meet a *compelling* government interest).[42] Yet in two cases involving the University of Michigan, the Supreme Court indicated that limited affirmative action programs continue to be acceptable and that diversity is a legitimate goal. The Court struck down the affirmative action plan used for undergraduate admissions at the university, which automatically awarded a substantial number of points to applicants based on minority status.[43] At the same time, it approved the admissions plan used by the law school, which took race into consideration as part of a complete examination of each applicant's background.[44]

STATE BALLOT INITIATIVES

A ballot initiative passed by California voters in 1996 amended that state's constitution to end all state-sponsored affirmative action programs. The law was challenged

Reverse Discrimination
The charge that an affirmative action program discriminates against those who do not have minority status.

---

[41]438 U.S. 265 (1978).
[42]515 U.S. 200 (1995).
[43]*Gratz v. Bollinger*, 539 U.S. 244 (2003).
[44]*Grutter v. Bollinger*, 539 U.S. 306 (2003).

immediately in court by civil rights groups and others arguing that it violated the Fourteenth Amendment by denying racial minorities and women the equal protection of the laws. In 1997, however, a federal appellate court upheld the constitutionality of the amendment. Thus, affirmative action is now illegal in California in all state-sponsored institutions, including state agencies and educational institutions. In 1998, Washington voters also approved a law banning affirmative action in that state.

MAKING AMENDS FOR PAST DISCRIMINATION THROUGH REPARATIONS

While affirmative action programs attempt to remedy past discrimination by "leveling the playing field," reparations are a way of apologizing for past discriminatory actions and providing compensation. The legal philosophy of **reparation** requires that victims of a harm be replenished by those who inflicted the harm. In criminal courts, for example, defendants are sometimes sentenced to perform community service or provide restitution to the victim in lieu of jail time. When reparation is used relative to a class of people who experienced discrimination, such as descendants of former slaves or Japanese Americans who were interned during World War II, restitution is made by the government. In 1988, Congress passed legislation that apologized and admitted that wartime government action against Japanese Americans was based on racial prejudice and war hysteria. Over $1.6 billion has been disbursed to Japanese Americans who were themselves interned or to the heirs of those who were interned.

Proposals for similar forms of restitution for the descendants of slaves in the United States have been under discussion for some time, but there is little consensus around

Reparation
Compensation, monetary or nonmonetary (e.g., formal apology), to make amends for a past transgression or harm.

ASIANS IN AMERICA have experienced a long history of discrimination. In 1922, for example, the Supreme Court ruled that Asians were not white and therefore were not entitled to full citizenship rights (*Ozawa v U.S.*, 1922). Following the Japanese attack on Pearl Harbor in 1941, Executive Order 9066 required the exclusion of all people of Japanese ancestry (including U.S. citizens) from the Pacific coast. Approximately 110,000 people were forcibly relocated to internment camps. In 1944, the Supreme Court upheld the constitutionality of the war relocation camps (*Korematsu v U.S.*) citing national security concerns during a time of war. (Prints and Photographs Division, Library of Congress. (LC-USZ62-113923))

the issue (see the Politics with a Purpose feature). On July 29, 2008, the U.S. House of Representatives passed a resolution (with 120 cosponsors from both parties) apologizing to African Americans for the institution of slavery, Jim Crow laws, and other practices that have denied people equal opportunity under the law. Democrat Steve Cohen from Tennessee introduced the resolution, saying, "... only a great country can recognize and admit its mistakes and then travel forth to create indeed a more perfect union. ..."[45] The U.S. Senate followed with a similar resolution of apology the following summer. The resolutions did not contain any mention of financial compensation for descendants of slaves.

SPECIAL PROTECTION FOR OLDER AMERICANS

Age discrimination is potentially the most widespread form of discrimination, because anyone—regardless of race, color, national origin, or gender—could be a victim at some point in life. In an attempt to protect older employees from such discriminatory practices, Congress passed the Age Discrimination in Employment Act (ADEA) in 1967. The act, which applies to employers, employment agencies, and labor organizations and covers individuals over the age of 40, prohibits discrimination against individuals on the basis of age unless age is shown to be a bona fide occupational qualification reasonably necessary to the normal operation of the particular business. To succeed in a suit for age discrimination, an employee must prove that the employer's action, such as a decision to fire the employee, was motivated, at least in part, by age bias. Even if an older worker is replaced by a younger worker who is also over the age of 40, the older worker is entitled to bring a suit under the ADEA.[46] Most states have their own prohibitions against age discrimination in employment, and some are stronger than the federal provisions.

SECURING RIGHTS FOR PERSONS WITH DISABILITIES

Persons with disabilities did not fall under the protective umbrella of the Civil Rights Act of 1964. In 1973, however, Congress passed the Rehabilitation Act, which prohibited discrimination against persons with disabilities in programs receiving federal aid. A 1978 amendment to the act established the Architectural and Transportation Barriers Compliance Board. Regulations for ramps, elevators, and the like in all federal buildings were implemented. Congress passed the Education for All Handicapped Children Act in 1975. It guarantees that all children with disabilities will receive an "appropriate" education. The most significant federal legislation to protect the rights of persons with disabilities, however, is the Americans with Disabilities Act (ADA), which Congress passed in 1990.

THE AMERICANS WITH DISABILITIES ACT OF 1990

The ADA requires that all public buildings and public services be accessible to persons with disabilities. The act also mandates that employers

---

[45]"Congress Apologizes for Slavery, Jim Crow," *National Public Radio*, July 30, 2008.
[46]*O'Connor v. Consolidated Coin Caterers Corp.*, 517 U.S. 308 (1996).

must reasonably accommodate the needs of workers or potential workers with disabilities. Physical access means ramps; handrails; wheelchair-accessible restrooms, counters, drinking fountains, telephones, and doorways; and easily accessible mass transit. In addition, other steps must be taken to comply with the act. Car rental companies must provide cars with hand controls for disabled drivers. Telephone companies are required to have operators to pass on messages from speech-impaired persons who use telephones with keyboards.

The ADA requires employers to "reasonably accommodate" the needs of persons with disabilities unless to do so would cause the employer to suffer an "undue hardship." The ADA defines persons with disabilities as persons who have physical or mental impairments that "substantially limit" their everyday activities. Health conditions that have been considered disabilities under federal law include blindness, alcoholism, heart disease, cancer, muscular dystrophy, cerebral palsy, paraplegia, diabetes, acquired immune deficiency syndrome (AIDS), and infection with the human immunodeficiency virus (HIV) that causes AIDS.

The ADA does not require that *unqualified* applicants with disabilities be hired or retained. If a job applicant or an employee with a disability, with reasonable accommodation, can perform essential job functions, however, then the employer must make the accommodation. Required accommodations may include installing ramps for a wheelchair, establishing more flexible working hours, creating or modifying job assignments, and creating or improving training materials and procedures.

LIMITING THE SCOPE AND APPLICABILITY OF THE ADA

Beginning in 1999, the Supreme Court has issued a series of decisions that effectively limit the scope of the ADA. In 1999, for example, the Court held in *Sutton v. United Airlines, Inc.*[47] that a condition (in this case, severe nearsightedness) that can be corrected with medication or a corrective device (in this case, eyeglasses) is not considered a disability under the ADA. In other words, the determination of whether a person is substantially limited in a major life activity is based on how the person functions when taking medication or using corrective devices, not on how the person functions without these measures. Since then, the courts have held that plaintiffs with bipolar disorder, epilepsy, diabetes, and other conditions do not fall under the ADA's protections if the conditions can be corrected with medication or corrective devices. The Supreme Court has also limited the applicability of the ADA by holding that lawsuits under the ADA cannot be brought against state government employers.[48]

THE RIGHTS AND STATUS OF GAYS AND LESBIANS

On June 27, 1969, patrons of the Stonewall Inn, a New York City bar popular with gays and lesbians, responded to a police raid by throwing beer cans and bottles because they were angry at what they felt was unrelenting police harassment. In the ensuing

A MAN AND A WOMAN communicating in sign language at work. Sign language is not a method of representing English, but is an entirely unique language system. Despite the fact that it is not English, should sign language be exempted from the effects of English-only laws that have been adopted in some jurisdictions? Why or why not? (Michael Newman/PhotoEdit)

---

[47]527 U.S. 471 (1999).
[48]*Board of Trustees of the University of Alabama v. Garrett,* 531 U.S. 356 (2001).

riot, which lasted two nights, hundreds of gays and lesbians fought with police. Before Stonewall, the stigma attached to homosexuality and the resulting fear of exposure had tended to keep most gays and lesbians quiescent. In the months immediately after Stonewall, however, "gay power" graffiti began to appear in New York City. The Gay Liberation Front and the Gay Activist Alliance were formed, and similar groups sprang up in other parts of the country. Thus, Stonewall has been called "the shot heard round the homosexual world."

GROWTH IN THE GAY AND LESBIAN RIGHTS MOVEMENT

The Stonewall incident marked the beginning of the movement for gay and lesbian rights. Since then, gays and lesbians have formed thousands of organizations to exert pressure on legislatures, the media, schools, churches, and other organizations to recognize their right to equal treatment.

DID YOU KNOW?

That in October 1999, Scouts Canada, the Canadian equivalent of the Boy Scouts of America, officially approved North America's first gay Scout troop?

To a great extent, lesbian and gay groups have succeeded in changing public opinion—and state and local laws—relating to their status and rights. Nevertheless, they continue to struggle against age-old biases against homosexuality, often rooted in deeply held religious beliefs, which allow discrimination to persist. For example, in a widely publicized case involving the Boy Scouts of America, a troop in New Jersey refused to allow gay activist James Dale to be a Scout leader. In 2000, the case came before the Supreme Court, which held that, as a private organization, the Boy Scouts had the right to determine the requirements for becoming a Scout leader.[49] In 1998, a student at the University of Wyoming named Matthew Shepard was brutally beaten, tortured, tied to a fence post, and left to die near Laramie, Wyoming, because he was believed to be gay. His killers could not be charged with a **hate crime** because at the time, the state law did not recognize sexual orientation as a protected class. In 2009, Congress passed the Matthew Shepard Act expanding the 1969 federal hate crime law to include crimes motivated by the victim's actual or perceived gender, sexual orientation, gender identity, or disability.[50]

Hate Crime

A criminal offense committed against a person or property that is motivated, in whole or in part, by the offender's bias against a race, color, ethnicity, national origin, sex, gender identity or expression, sexual orientation, disability, age, or religion.

STATE AND LOCAL LAWS TARGETING GAYS AND LESBIANS

Before the Stonewall incident, 49 states had sodomy laws that made various kinds of sexual acts, including homosexual acts, illegal (Illinois, which had repealed its sodomy law in 1962, was the only exception). During the 1970s and 1980s, more than half of these laws were either repealed or struck down by the courts. In 2003, the Court reversed an earlier antisodomy position[51] with its decision in *Lawrence v. Texas*.[52] The Court held that laws against sodomy violate the due process clause of the Fourteenth Amendment, stating: "The liberty protected by the Constitution allows homosexual persons the right to choose to enter upon relationships in the confines of their homes and their own private lives and still retain their dignity as free persons." The result of *Lawrence v. Texas* was to invalidate all remaining sodomy laws throughout the country.

Today, 20 states and the District of Columbia have laws protecting lesbians and gays against discrimination in employment, housing, public accommodations, and credit. Several laws at the national level have also been changed over the past two decades. Among other

[49]*Boy Scouts of America v. Dale*, 530 U.S. 640 (2000).
[50]"Obama Signs Measure to Widen Hate Crimes Law," *PBS Newshour*, October 28, 2009.
[51]478 U.S. 186 (1986).
[52]539 U.S. 558 (2003).

things, the government has lifted a ban on hiring gays and lesbians and voided a 1952 law prohibiting gays and lesbians from immigrating to the United States.

GAYS AND LESBIANS IN THE MILITARY

The U.S. Department of Defense traditionally has viewed homosexuality as incompatible with military service. In 1993 President Clinton announced a new policy, generally characterized as "don't ask, don't tell." Enlistees would not be asked about their sexual orientation, and gays and lesbians would be allowed to serve in the military so long as they did not declare that they were gay or lesbian or commit homosexual acts. Military officials endorsed the new policy, after opposing it initially, but supporters of gay rights were not enthusiastic. According to the Servicemembers Legal Defense Network, more than 13,500 soldiers have been discharged since the policy was adopted. Since 2001, discharges under the policy have declined by half.[53]

That Albert Einstein was among 6,000 persons in Germany in 1903 who signed a petition to repeal a portion of the German penal code that made homosexuality illegal?

As a presidential candidate, Barak Obama promised to help bring an end to the "don't ask, don't tell" policy (only Congress can repeal the law). In March of 2009, Secretary of Defense Robert M. Gates announced a number of interim steps designed to make it more difficult for the military to discharge openly gay men and women. The new guidelines raise the standard of evidence and prevent certain types of information (such as information provided to lawyers, doctors, or clergy) from being used as evidence in discharge proceedings. Secretary Gates also announced that the Pentagon would undertake a study to assess how lifting the ban should be carried out so that the military is prepared when the ban is repealed. This is widely viewed as an acknowledgment by the military that repeal of the policy is imminent.

SAME-SEX MARRIAGES

Perhaps one of the most sensitive political issues with respect to the rights of gay and lesbian couples is whether they should be allowed to marry, just as heterosexual couples are.

Defense of Marriage Act. The controversy over this issue was fueled in 1993, when the Hawaii Supreme Court ruled that denying marriage licenses to gay couples might violate the equal protection clause of the Hawaii constitution.[54] In the wake of this event, other states began to worry about whether they might have to treat gay men or lesbians who were legally married in another state as married couples in their state as well. Opponents of gay rights pushed for state laws banning same-sex marriages, and the majority of states enacted such laws or adopted constitutional amendments. At the federal level, Congress passed the Defense of Marriage Act of 1996, which bans federal recognition of lesbian and gay couples and allows state governments to ignore same-sex marriages performed in other states. However, in 2009 President Obama signed an order extending health care and other benefits to the partners of gay federal employees. President Obama does not support same-sex marriage.

The controversy over gay marriages was fueled again by developments in the state of Vermont. In 1999, the Vermont Supreme Court ruled that gay couples are entitled to the same benefits of marriage as opposite-sex couples.[55] Subsequently, in April 2000, the Vermont legislature passed a law permitting gay and lesbian couples to form "civil

[53]Servicemembers Legal Defense Network, http://www.sldn.org/.
[54]*Baehr v. Lewin*, 852 P.2d 44 (Hawaii 1993).
[55]*Baker v. Vermont*, 744 A.2d 864 (Vt. 1999).

DEL MARTIN (L) and Phyllis Lyon (R) are married by San Francisco mayor Gavin Newsom in a private ceremony at San Francisco City Hall June 16, 2008. Martin and Lyon, a couple since 1953, were active in the gay rights and women's rights movements. Del Martin died on August 27, 2008. (AP Photo/Marcio Jose Sanchez, Pool)

unions." The law entitled partners forming civil unions to receive some 300 state benefits available to married couples, including the rights to inherit a partner's property and to decide on medical treatment for an incapacitated partner. In 2005, Connecticut became the second state to adopt civil unions. Neither law entitled partners to receive any benefits allowed to married couples under federal law, such as spousal Social Security benefits.

State Recognition of Gay Marriages. Massachusetts was the first state to recognize gay marriage. In November 2003, the Massachusetts Supreme Judicial Court ruled that same-sex couples have a right to civil marriage under the Massachusetts state constitution and that civil unions would not suffice.[56] In 2005, the Massachusetts legislature voted down a proposed ballot initiative that would have amended the state constitution to explicitly state that marriage could only be between one man and one woman (but would have extended civil union status to same-sex couples). Although the highest courts in several states have upheld bans on gay marriage, in 2008 the Supreme Court of California held that the state was required to recognize gay marriages. Citizens immediately prepared petitions to put a constitutional amendment on the ballot in November of 2008 to outlaw such marriages. The campaign for and against Proposition 8, which would ban gay marriages in California, cost at least $74 million and was funded by contributions from almost every state. Ultimately, Proposition 8 was approved by a margin of 4 percent. The 18,000 marriages that took place between the California Supreme Court decision and the approval of Proposition 8 remain valid. On August 4, 2010, a federal judge declared California's ban on same-sex marriage unconstitutional, saying that no legitimate state interest justified treating gay and lesbian couples differently from others. The ruling was the first in the country to strike down a marriage ban on federal constitutional grounds rather than on the basis of a state constitution. Before the ban could be lifted and marriages resumed in California, the Ninth Circuit Court issued a stay and scheduled hearings for early December 2010.

Same-sex marriage is currently permitted in Massachusetts, Connecticut, Iowa, Vermont, New Hampshire, and the District of Columbia. Thirty-one states have explicitly banned gay marriage. Same-sex marriage is currently accepted nationwide in Belgium, Canada, the Netherlands, Norway, South Africa, and Spain.

[56]*Goodridge v. Department of Public Health*, 798 N.E.2d 941 (Mass. 2003).

YOU CAN MAKE A Difference

DEALING WITH DISCRIMINATION

You may think you know what "discrimination" means while applying for or working at a job. But do you really understand how it applies to your life? To "discriminate" means to treat differently or less favorably, and discrimination can happen while you are at school or at work. Discrimination can come from friends, teachers, coaches, coworkers, managers, and business owners and be based on race, color, gender, religion, age, sexual orientation, or disability. There may be tests while applying for a job that could have a discriminatory effect on being hired (tests of strength, for example, must be directly related to the requirements of the job). Genetic information, now more widely available, might some day be used by employers in making hiring decisions. Increasingly, there is evidence that employers make use of online sites such as Facebook, MySpace, blogs, and personal Web sites to learn more about applicants. While doing so may leave employers subject to "failure to hire" lawsuits if information gathered online is used to discriminate illegally, you should be very aware of how you present yourself online. Agencies at the state and federal government examine the fairness and validity of criteria used in screening job applicants and, as a result, there are ways of addressing the problem of discrimination.

WHY SHOULD YOU CARE?

Some people may think that discrimination is only a problem for members of racial or ethnic minorities. Actually, almost everyone can be affected. In some instances, white men have experienced "reverse discrimination"—and have obtained redress for it. Also, discrimination against women is common, and women constitute half the population. Therefore, knowledge of how to proceed when you suspect discrimination is another useful tool to have when living in the modern world.

WHAT CAN YOU DO?

If you believe that you have been discriminated against by a potential employer, consider the following steps:

1. Evaluate your own capabilities, and determine if you are truly qualified for the position.
2. Analyze the reasons why you were turned down. Would others agree with you that you have been the object of discrimination, or would they uphold the employer's claim?

3. If you still believe that you have been treated unfairly, you have recourse to several agencies and services. You should first speak to the personnel director of the company and explain that you believe you have not been evaluated adequately. If asked, explain your concerns clearly and provide detailed examples of behavior you believe is discriminatory.

If further action is warranted, many states and localities have antidiscrimination laws and agencies responsible for enforcing these laws. They are referred to as Fair Employment Practices Agencies (FEPAs). They can be found on your state's official government Web site and include your state attorney general; state commissions on civil rights, equal rights, equal opportunity, and antidiscrimination; and departments of labor and industry.

WHEN THE U.S. Supreme Court used a narrow interpretation of the statute to rule against Lilly Ledbetter's claim of pay discrmination, Congress passed the Lilly Ledbetter Fair Pay Act in January 2009. (Bill Clark/Roll Call/Getty Images)

You can access all local and state government agencies through www.usa.gov, the U.S. government's official Web portal to all federal, state, and local government resources and services.

Finally, the U.S. Equal Employment Opportunity Commission (EEOC) enforces federal laws concerning job discrimination and harassment, processing about 80,000 complaints a year, and partners with 90 state and local agencies that investigate an additional 50,000 complaints. You can contact the EEOC anytime you feel you are being treated unfairly on the job because of race, religion, sex (including pregnancy), national origin, disability, or age. This federal agency is an extensive resource and will answer questions about job discrimination even if you do not want to file a formal complaint.

The EEOC's main office is located in Washington, D.C., but there are 51 field offices around the country. You should contact the field office closest to you. The EEOC should be contacted promptly if you have an unresolved complaint. A charge must be filed within 180 days from the date of the alleged violation; the deadline is extended to 300 days if the charge is also covered by a state or local antidiscrimination law. To find the field office closest to you, contact:

The U.S. Equal Employment Opportunity Commission
1801 L St. NW
Washington, DC 20507

KEY TERMS

affirmative action 197
Black Codes 168
busing 174
civil disobedience 175
civil rights 167
de facto segregation 174
de jure segregation 174
feminism 186

gender discrimination 189
grandfather clause 171
hate crime 202
Jim Crow laws 170
literacy test 171
poll tax 171
reparation 199
reverse discrimination 198

separate-but-equal doctrine 170
sexual harassment 191
subpoena 178
suffrage 183
white primary 171

CHAPTER SUMMARY

1. **Why does discrimination against groups exist in the United States?** To the nation's founders, political equality required a degree of independent thinking and a capacity for rational action that at the time they believed were limited to a very few white males. Therefore, other groups and individuals were systematically excluded, not only from the exercise of political rights, but also from access to education and employment. Today we believe that all people are entitled to equal political rights as well as to the opportunities for personal development provided by equal access to education and employment. However, the roots of past discrimination live on in today's discriminatory practices, including racial profiling, the wage gap, the achievement gap in schools, and the glass ceiling. Thus, the story of civil rights in the United States is the struggle to reconcile our ideals as a nation with the realities of discrimination individuals and groups may still encounter in daily life.

2. **How can the government best ensure equal rights for all?** Although the government has the power to assert rights and the obligation to protect civil rights, it does not always do so. Individuals and groups then organize to bring pressure on government to act. The civil rights movement started with the struggle by African Americans for equality. Before the Civil War, most African Americans were slaves, and slavery was protected by the Constitution and the Supreme Court. Constitutional amendments after the Civil War legally ended slavery, and African Americans gained citizenship, the right to vote, and other rights through legislation. This legal protection was rendered meaningless in practice by the 1880s, however, and politically and socially, African American inequality continued.

3. Legal segregation was declared unconstitutional by the Supreme Court in *Brown v. Board of Education of Topeka* (1954), in which the Court stated that separation implied inferiority. In *Brown v. Board of Education* (1955), the Supreme Court ordered federal courts to ensure that public schools were desegregated "with all deliberate speed." Also in 1955, the modern civil rights movement began with a boycott of segregated public transportation in Montgomery, Alabama. Of particular impact was the Civil Rights Act of 1964 banning discrimination on the basis of race, color, religion, sex, or national origin in employment and public accommodations. The act created the Equal

Employment Opportunity Commission to administer the legislation's provisions.

4. The Voting Rights Act of 1965 outlawed discriminatory voter-registration tests and authorized federal registration of persons and federally administered procedures in any state or political subdivision evidencing electoral discrimination or low registration rates. The Voting Rights Act and other protective legislation passed during and since the 1960s apply not only to African Americans but to other ethnic groups as well. Minorities have been increasingly represented in national and state politics, although they have yet to gain representation proportionate to their numbers in the U.S. population. Lingering social and economic disparities have led to a new civil rights agenda—one focusing less on racial differences and more on economic differences.

5. In the early history of the United States, women were considered citizens, but by and large they had no political rights because they were largely viewed as dependents. After the first women's rights convention in 1848, the campaign for suffrage gained momentum, yet not until 1920, when the Nineteenth Amendment was ratified, did women finally obtain the right to vote. The second wave of the women's movement began in the 1960s alongside the civil rights and anti–Vietnam War movements. The National Organization for Women (NOW) was formed in 1966 to bring about complete equality for women in all walks of life. Efforts to secure the ratification of the Equal Rights Amendment failed, but the women's movement has been successful in obtaining new laws, changes in social customs, and increased political representation of women.

6. Although women have been slow to win positions of political leadership, their numbers in Congress and in other government bodies increased in the 1990s and early 2000s. Women continue to fight gender discrimination in employment. Federal government efforts to eliminate gender discrimination in the workplace include Title VII of the Civil Rights Act of 1964, which prohibits, among other things, gender-based discrimination, including sexual harassment on the job. Wage discrimination also continues to be a problem for women, as does the "glass ceiling" that prevents them from rising to the top of business or professional firms.

7. America has always been a land of immigrants and will continue to be so. Today, more than one million immigrants enter the United States each year, and more than 12 percent of the U.S. population consists of foreign-born persons. Demographers estimate that the foreign-born will account for 15 percent of the nation sometime between 2020 and 2025. In particular, the Latino community in the United States has experienced explosive growth. In recent years, undocumented immigration has surfaced as a significant issue for border states and the nation. Indeed, one of the pressing concerns facing today's politicians is whether U.S. immigration policy should be reformed.

8. Affirmative action programs have been controversial because of charges that they can lead to reverse discrimination against majority groups or even other minority groups. Supreme Court decisions have limited affirmative action programs, and voters in California and Washington passed initiatives banning state-sponsored affirmative action in those states. Two Supreme Court decisions in cases brought against the University of Michigan have confirmed the principle of diversity as an important educational goal and that limited affirmative action programs are constitutional.

9. The Rehabilitation Act of 1973 prohibited discrimination against persons with disabilities in programs receiving federal aid. Regulations implementing the act provide for ramps, elevators, and the like in federal buildings. The Americans with Disabilities Act of 1990 prohibits job discrimination against persons with physical and mental disabilities, requiring that positive steps be taken to comply with the act. The act also requires expanded access to public facilities, including transportation, and to services offered by such private concerns as car rental and telephone companies.

10. Gay and lesbian rights groups work to promote laws protecting gays and lesbians from discrimination and to repeal antigay laws. After 1969, sodomy laws that criminalized specific sexual practices were repealed or struck down by the courts in all but 18 states, and in 2003 a Supreme Court decision effectively invalidated all remaining sodomy laws nationwide. Gays and lesbians are no longer barred from federal employment or from immigrating to this country. The Obama administration issued an order extending benefits to partners of federal employees. Twenty states and the District of Columbia outlaw discrimination based on sexual orientation. Hate crimes based on sexual orientation or gender identity are punishable by federal law under the Matthew Shepard Act of 2009. The military's "don't ask, don't tell" policy is under review in Congress and is expected to be repealed.

11. **Why is the Supreme Court so important in determining civil rights?** The Supreme Court is in the best position within the framework of American government to interpret the values and ideals contained in the founding documents and ensure those ideas are reflected in policy and practice. As this chapter demonstrates, the Court, too, is fallible and often overly constrained in its actions by the prevailing beliefs of the time period. As will be discussed in Chapter 15, the Supreme Court may lose stature if it decides cases in a way that markedly diverges from public opinion. However, the Court is often in a good position to pull the public along as more progressive ideas are percolating throughout society by issuing rulings that speed up the timetable for social change, as it did in the *Brown* decision. In determining civil rights, the Supreme Court is called upon to reconcile our ideals as a nation with the realities of discrimination individuals and groups may still encounter in daily life.

SELECTED PRINT, MEDIA, AND ONLINE RESOURCES

PRINT RESOURCES

Anderson, Terry H. *The Pursuit of Fairness: A History of Affirmative Action.* New York: Oxford University Press, 2004. Anderson offers an evenhanded history of affirmative action. His account extends from the administrations of Franklin D. Roosevelt and Harry Truman in the 1940s to the 2003 University of Michigan cases that have established the current constitutional parameters of affirmative action policies.

Kristoff, Nicholas D., and Sheryl WuDunn. *Half the Sky: Turning Oppression into Opportunity for Women Worldwide.* New York: Alfred Knopf, 2009. Written by two Pulitzer Prize–winning journalists, this book demonstrates that the key to solving global poverty is to improve the lives of women around the globe. The book profiles women throughout Asia and Africa who have not only coped with unimaginable forms of brutal discrimination, but created opportunities for survival for themselves and other women.

Morin, Jose Luis. *Latino/a Rights and Justice in the United States: Perspectives and Approaches.* Durham, NJ: Carolina Academic Press, 2009. This book offers a thorough overview of the history and modern incarnation of Latino/a civil rights and experiences within the U.S. justice system. Case studies and a focus on taking action complement the legal analysis.

Savage, Dan. *The Commitment: Love, Sex, Marriage, and My Family.* New York: Penguin, 2005. A humorous memoir exploring the definition of "family" within the context of the gay marriage policy debate.

Valenti, Jessica. *Full Frontal Feminism: A Young Woman's Guide to Why Feminism Matters.* Emeryville, CA: Seal Press, 2007. Valenti, founder of feministing.com, a wildly popular blog, explores what it means to be a young feminist today by confronting and discounting the myths so often associated with the feminist label.

MEDIA RESOURCES

Chisholm '72: Unbought and Unbossed—A documentary about the career of Congresswoman Shirley Chisholm, the first black woman to run for president of the United States. Includes archival footage and contemporary interviews.

Eyes on the Prize: America's Civil Rights Movement 1954–1985—A 14-part *American Experience* documentary first aired on public television that features both movement leaders and the stories of average Americans through contemporary interviews and historical footage.

Fight in the Fields: Cesar Chavez and the Farmworkers' Struggle—A 1997 film documenting the first successful drive to organize farmworkers in the United States; described as a social history with Chavez as a central figure, the documentary draws from archival footage, newsreels, and present-day interviews.

Lioness—A documentary film about a group of female army support soldiers who were a part of the first program in American history to send women into direct ground combat against insurgents in Iraq.

Malcolm X—A 1992 film, directed by Spike Lee and starring Denzel Washington, that depicts the life of the controversial "black power" leader Malcolm X. Malcolm X, who was assassinated on February 21, 1965, clearly had a different vision from that of Martin Luther King, Jr., regarding how to achieve civil rights, respect, and equality for black Americans.

ONLINE RESOURCES

National Immigration Forum Established in 1982, the National Immigration Forum is the leading immigrant advocacy organization in the country, with a mission to advocate for the value of immigrants and immigration to the nation: http://www.immigrationforum.org/

Pew Hispanic Center Founded in 2001, the Pew Hispanic Center is a nonpartisan research organization that seeks to improve understanding of the U.S. Hispanic population and to chronicle Latinos' growing impact on the nation: http://pewhispanic.org/

Reporting Civil Rights an anthology of the reporters and journalism of the American civil rights movement hosted by Library of America: http://reportingcivilrights. loa.org/

Women's Rights National Historical Park Operated by the National Park Service, the Park preserves the sites associated with the first women's rights convention in 1848: http://www.nps.gov/wori/index.htm

6

Children cheer for Democratic presidential hopeful Sen. Barack Obama at a February 2008 campaign rally in Racine, Wisconsin. Although they cannot vote now, exposure to politics early in life may favorably shape their attitudes toward political participation as adults. (AP Photo/ Journal Times, Mark Hertzberg)

Public Opinion and Political Socialization

QUESTIONS TO CONSIDER

How does public opinion impact government actions?

How do individuals come to hold political opinions?

Should government officials always follow public opinion?

CHAPTER CONTENTS

what if...

Young People Were Required To Serve?

BACKGROUND

What if the United States adopted a policy that required all persons between the ages of 18 and 22 residing in the United States to engage in domestic or military service for a period of at least 18 months? Would national service create a stronger bond between young citizens and the nation? How might 18 months of service socialize new generations of young people to politics and political activity?

Young people typically know less about politics, express less interest in politics, and vote less often than their elders. But that isn't set in stone! Voter turnout by people under 30 reached 51 percent in 2008, the third highest turnout since the voting age was lowered to 18 years of age. Even more significantly, the age gap was highest for voters ages 18–29 than for any other age group; young voters supported Barack Obama over John McCain 66 percent to 32 percent. Thus, young citizens have tremendous potential to shape politics and policy *if* they get involved.

SERVICE AS POLITICAL SOCIALIZATION

The United States has a long history of citizens rendering service to their communities, including the Civilian Conservation Corps, the Peace Corps, and Volunteers in Service to America (VISTA). During the Clinton administration, AmeriCorps, a large-scale national service program designed to place young people in service positions in communities across the country, was established. The Obama administration has significantly expanded both the AmeriCorps and VISTA programs.

Would young people be willing to serve their country? This chapter reviews what we know about the process of becoming socialized into civic and political life and, as a result, how we develop and express political opinions. Forces such as the family, schools, faith communities, the media, and peers all shape how we understand public life. Likewise, direct personal experience with politics is a developmental force. From national surveys of first-year college students, we know that roughly a third of all students believe that it is important to keep up with political affairs and that roughly a third report that there is a very good chance that they will participate in community service or volunteer work while in college. These individuals are also more likely to remain engaged with their communities after they graduate from college. Those who oppose national service do so for a variety of reasons, including the disruption to education and career, as well as the belief that individual liberty would be violated.

TOWARD A NATIONAL POLICY

What would the nation gain from a service requirement? The U.S. military is an all-volunteer force today following the repeal of the draft in 1973. Representative Charles B. Rangle, a veteran of the Korean conflict, argued in a 2002 *New York Times* op-ed essay that the draft should be reinstated to promote the philosophy of shared sacrifice and enforce a greater appreciation of the consequences of war. Similarly, when President Bill Clinton proposed AmeriCorps, he said "Citizen service bridges isolated individuals, local communities, the national community, and ultimately, the community of all people." AmeriCorps members serve in communities across the United States for one or two years in return for an educational stipend.[1] The nation benefits from a diverse group of committed individuals performing public work that needs doing. Critics charge that national service amounts to forced voluntarism and that the compulsory nature undermines the benefits for individuals and communities.

FOR CRITICAL ANALYSIS

1. Do you believe a national service requirement would improve young people's connection to politics and to the country? Why or why not?
2. You have no doubt heard the phrase, "with rights come responsibilities." What responsibilities do you have as a resident of your community, of your state, and of the nation?

---

[1]William J. Clinton, "The Duties of Democracy," in E. J. Dionne et. al., eds. *United We Serve: National Service and the Future of Citizenship* (Washington, DC: Brookings Institution, 2003).

IN A DEMOCRACY, the people express their opinions in many different ways. First and foremost, they express their views in political campaigns and vote for the individuals who will represent their views in government. Between elections, individuals express their opinions in many ways, ranging from writing to the editor to calling their senator's office to responding to a blog. Public opinion is also expressed and conveyed to public officials through public opinion polls, which are reported almost daily in the media. Sometimes public opinion is expressed through mass demonstrations, rallies, or protests.

In 2003, when President George W. Bush asked the Congress to authorize the use of force against Iraq, public approval for the war was 72 percent. At that time, more than 80 percent of Americans either believed or considered it possible that Saddam Hussein was building an arsenal of biological and other extremely dangerous weapons. By 2005, support for the use of troops in Iraq had declined to 39 percent and, by mid-2007, had fallen to 36 percent. Senator Barack Obama made withdrawal of American troops from Iraq a priority of his campaign and claimed that if he had been in the Senate at that time, he would not have supported the authorization of the use of force. Senator Hillary Clinton, who had voted for the resolution, no longer supported the Iraqi campaign and claimed that she had been misled at the time of the debate. The approval rating of President Bush, inevitably connected with the unpopular war, fell to 30 percent or less. In the past, public opinion also has had a dramatic impact on presidents. In 1968, President Lyndon B. Johnson decided not to run for reelection because of the intense and negative public reaction to the war in Vietnam. In 1974, President Richard Nixon resigned in the wake of a scandal when it was obvious that public opinion no longer supported him. Although President Obama promised to make health care reform a top legislative priority, vacillating public opinion made it difficult to pressure even members of his own party in Congress to act. Thus, the extent to which public opinion affects policy making is not always clear and scholars must deal with many uncertainties when analyzing the impact of public opinion on policy making.

Public Opinion
The aggregate of individual attitudes or beliefs shared by some portion of the adult population.

Consensus
General agreement among the citizenry on an issue.

DEFINING PUBLIC OPINION

There is no single public opinion, because there are many different publics. In a nation of over 300 million people, there may be innumerable gradations of opinion on an issue. What we do is describe the distribution of opinions among the members of the public about a particular question. Thus, we define **public opinion** as the aggregate of individual attitudes or beliefs shared by some portion of the adult population.

Typically, public opinion is distributed among several different positions, and the distribution of opinion can tell us how divided the public is on an issue and whether compromise is possible. When a large proportion of the American public appears to express the same view on an issue, we say that a **consensus** exists, at least at the moment the poll was taken. Figure 6–1 shows a pattern of opinion that might be called consensual. Issues on which the public holds widely differing attitudes result

(© Mark Anderson)

"Reaction to the news was mixed, largely because we asked more than one person."

Divisive Opinion
Public opinion that is polarized between two quite different positions.

Nonopinion
The lack of an opinion on an issue or policy among the majority.

in **divisive opinion** (see Figure 6–2). Sometimes, a poll shows a distribution of opinion indicating that most Americans either have no information about the issue or are not interested enough in the issue to formulate a position. This is sometimes referred to as **nonopinion** (see Figure 6–3). Politicians may believe that the public's lack of knowledge about an issue gives them more room to maneuver, or they may be wary of taking any action for fear that opinion will crystallize after a crisis.

Sometimes public officials have a difficult time discerning the public's opinion on a specific issue from the public's expression of general anger or dissatisfaction. The Tea Party protests present just such a dilemma. The rallies began in early 2009 to express opposition to the TARP (Troubled Asset Relief Program) bailout bill passed by Congress. Drawing on themes from the Revolutionary War era in general and the Boston Tea Party in particular, the protesters often arrive dressed as Patriots and holding handmade placards with antitax slogans. Organizers have utilized social networking sites and the Internet to call for Tea Party meetings and protests in communities large and small. They have demonstrated against health care reform and increased government spending on a wide array of social programs. Several rallies were held around the country on April—15th—widely known as tax day. This coalition of disparate groups acting under a single moniker is not "for" or "against" any single policy or program, but rather an expression of negative opinion directed at incumbents of both parties. As a result, public officials and candidates for office are having a difficult time knowing how to respond.

HOW PUBLIC OPINION IS FORMED: POLITICAL SOCIALIZATION

Political Socialization
The process by which people acquire political beliefs and attitudes.

Most Americans are willing to express opinions on political issues when asked. How do people acquire these opinions and attitudes? Typically, views that are expressed as political opinions are acquired through the process of **political socialization**. By this

FIGURE 6–1
Consensus Opinion

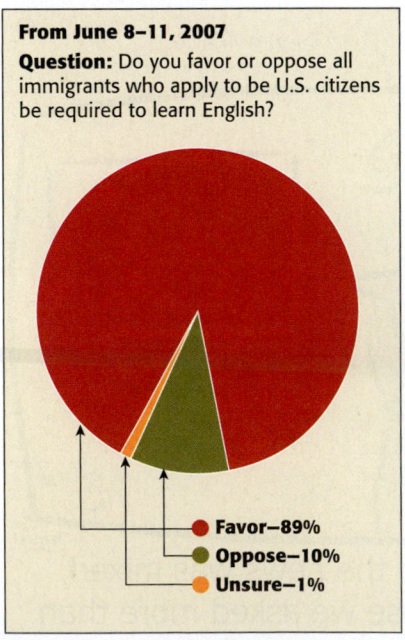

From June 8–11, 2007
Question: Do you favor or oppose all immigrants who apply to be U.S. citizens be required to learn English?

● **Favor—89%**
● **Oppose—10%**
● **Unsure—1%**

Source: NBC News/Wall Street Journal Poll

FIGURE 6–2
Divisive Opinion

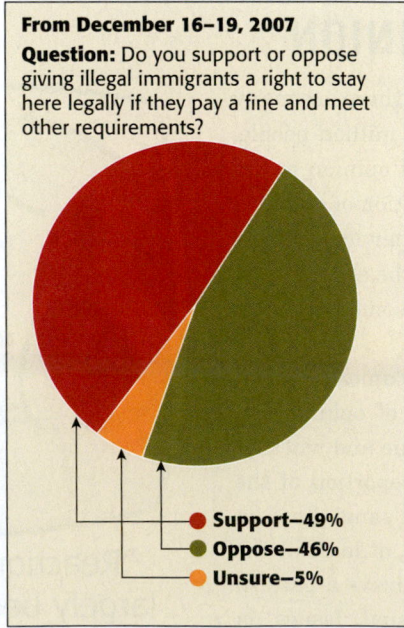

From December 16–19, 2007
Question: Do you support or oppose giving illegal immigrants a right to stay here legally if they pay a fine and meet other requirements?

● **Support—49%**
● **Oppose—46%**
● **Unsure—5%**

Source: ABCNews/Facebook Poll

FIGURE 6–3
Nonopinion

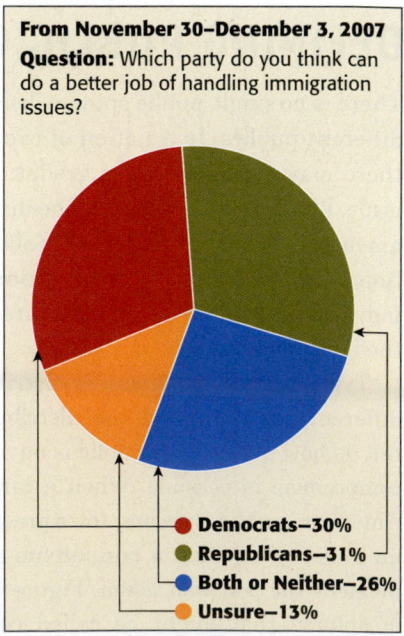

From November 30–December 3, 2007
Question: Which party do you think can do a better job of handling immigration issues?

● **Democrats—30%**
● **Republicans—31%**
● **Both or Neither—26%**
● **Unsure—13%**

Source: Los Angeles Times/Bloomberg Poll

we mean that people acquire their political attitudes, often including their party identification, through relationships with their families, friends, and coworkers.

MODELS OF POLITICAL SOCIALIZATION

The most important early sources of political socialization are found in the family and the schools. Children learn their parents' views on politics and on political leaders through observation and approval seeking. When parents are strong supporters of a political party, children are very likely to identify with that same party. If the parents are alienated from the political system or totally disinterested in politics, children will tend to hold the same attitudes. It is clear that children, who are very young, say about five or six, will express political views even when they are not mature enough to comprehend very much about the political institutions. This is the result of socialization.

In the last few decades, more sources of information about politics have become available to all Americans and especially to young people. Although their basic outlook on the political system may be formed by early family influences, young people are now exposed to many other sources of information about issues and values. It is not unusual for young adults to hold very different views on issues. The exposure of younger Americans to many sources of ideas may also underlie their more progressive views on such issues as immigration and gay rights.

THE FAMILY AND THE SOCIAL ENVIRONMENT

Not only do our parents' political attitudes and actions affect our opinions, but the family also links us to other factors that affect opinion, such as race, social class, educational environment, and religious beliefs. How do parents transmit their political attitudes to their offspring?

Studies suggest that the influence of parents is due to two factors: communication and receptivity. Parents communicate their feelings and preferences to children constantly. Because children have such a strong desire for parental approval, they are very receptive to their parents' views. Children are less likely to influence their parents, because parents expect deference from their children.[1]

Nevertheless, other studies show that if children are exposed to political ideas at school and in the media, they will share these ideas with their parents, giving the parents what some scholars call a second chance at political socialization. Children can also expose their parents to new media, such as the Internet.[2]

Education as a Source of Political Socialization. From the early days of the republic, schools were perceived to be important transmitters of political information and attitudes. Children in the primary grades learn about their country mostly in patriotic ways. They learn about the Pilgrims, the flag, and some of the nation's presidents. They also learn to celebrate national holidays. Without much explicit instruction, children easily adopt democratic decision-making tools such as "taking a vote" and democratic

THE KIDS VOTE project involves teachers, parents, and children in encouraging children to vote on an unofficial ballot in the presidential election. Do you think this project will increase the children's desire to vote when they are adults? (Charlotte Observer, John D. Simmons/AP/ Wide World Photos)

[1]Barbara A. Bardes and Robert W. Oldendick, *Public Opinion: Measuring the American Mind*, 3rd ed. (Belmont, CA: Wadsworth Publishing, 2006), p. 73.
[2]For a pioneering study in this area, see Michael McDevitt and Steven H. Chaffee, "Second Chance Political Socialization: 'Trickle-up' Effects of Children on Parents," in Thomas J. Johnson et al., eds., *Engaging the Public: How Government and the Media Can Reinvigorate American Democracy* (Lanham, MD: Rowman & Littlefield, 1998), pp. 57–66.

procedures such as "the majority wins." Later, in the middle grades, children learn more historical facts and come to understand the structure and functions of government. By high school, students have a more complex understanding of the political system, may identify with a political party, and may take positions on issues. Additionally, students in grade school and high school may gain some experience in political participation: first, through student elections and activities, and second, through their introduction to registration and voting while still in school.

Generally, education is closely linked to political participation. The more formal education a person receives, the more likely it is that he or she will be interested in politics, be confident in his or her ability to understand political issues, and be an active participant in the political process.

Peers and Peer Group Influence. Once a child enters school, the child's friends become an important influence on behavior and attitudes. For children and for adults, friendships and associations in **peer groups** affect political attitudes. We must, however, separate the effects of peer group pressure on opinions and attitudes in general from the effects of peer group pressure on political opinions. For the most part, associations among peers are nonpolitical. Political attitudes are more likely to be shaped by peer groups when the peer groups are involved directly in political activities. For example, if you join an interest group based on your passion for the environment, you are more likely to be influenced by your organizational peers than you are by classmates.

Opinion Leaders' Influence. We are all influenced by those with whom we are closely associated or whom we hold in high regard—friends at school, family members and other relatives, and teachers. In a sense, these people are **opinion leaders**, but on an *informal* level; that is, their influence on our political views is not necessarily intentional or deliberate. We are also influenced by *formal* opinion leaders, such as presidents, lobbyists, congresspersons, media figures, and religious leaders, who have as part of their jobs the task of shaping people's views. Their interest lies in defining the political agenda in such a way that discussions about policy options will take place on their terms.

THE IMPACT OF THE MEDIA

Clearly, the **media**—newspapers, television, radio, and Internet sources—strongly influence public opinion. This is because the media inform the public about the issues and events of our times and thus have an **agenda setting** effect. In other words, to borrow from Bernard Cohen's classic statement about the media and public opinion, the media may not be successful in telling people what to think, but they are "stunningly successful in telling their audience what to think about."[3]

Today, many contend that the media's influence on public opinion has grown to equal that of the family. For example, in her analysis of the role played by the media in American politics,[4] media scholar Doris A. Graber points out that high school students, when asked where they obtain the information on which they base their attitudes, mention the mass media far more than they mention their families, friends, and teachers. A national Annenberg Policy Center study found that 55 percent of those 18 to 29 used the Internet for presidential campaign information in 2008, compared to 15 percent of those 65 and older. Three in four adults now have access to the Internet either at home

Peer Group
A group consisting of members sharing common social characteristics. These groups play an important part in the socialization process, helping to shape attitudes and beliefs.

Opinion Leader
One who is able to influence the opinions of others because of position, expertise, or personality.

That CNN reaches more than 1.5 billion people in 212 countries?

Media
Channels of mass communication.

Agenda Setting
Determining which public policy questions will be debated or considered.

---

[3]*The Press and Foreign Policy* (Princeton, NJ: Princeton University Press, 1963), p. 81.
[4]See Doris A. Graber, *Mass Media and American Politics*, 7th ed. (Chicago: University of Chicago Press, 2005).

POLITICS WITH A purpose

Opinion Gaps and Advocacy

Have you ever noticed that when your friends are discussing something, the same group of people seems to be on one side of the debate more often than not? It could be that in discussing the latest movies, the fine arts majors tend to agree. Or perhaps, in conversations about politics, Democrats and Republicans find themselves on opposite sides of the fence.

Opinion split along group lines (e.g., by gender, partisanship, socioeconomic status, race, or ethnicity) is called an opinion gap. Public opinion research yields many interesting gaps. One of the most widely covered is the gender gap, which occurs when women as a group have similar opinions or behaviors as compared to those of men. For example, since the 1980 presidential election, women have tended to vote for the Democratic candidate for president at rates higher than men. Sometimes these differences can be significant; in the 2008 presidential election, 56 percent of women said they supported Senator Barack Obama, and only 43 percent said they voted for Senator John McCain. Contrast this with men, who divided their vote about evenly between the two candidates: 49 percent for Obama and 48 percent for McCain.[a] In 2009, 41 percent of women self-identified with the Democratic Party, compared to only 32 percent of men. Another example of an opinion gap is among racial or ethnic groups. African Americans historically have been more likely to identify as Democrats, and they are being joined by other minority groups. In 2009, 88 percent of Republicans were white (compared to whites' 68 percent share of the population), while only 56 percent of Democrats were white, non-Hispanic. The balance of Democratic-identifiers are African Americans (22 percent), Latinos (15 percent), and other minorities (6 percent). Since 2000, the Republican Party's racial composition has changed very little, while the Democratic Party has become more diverse.[b] With regard to attitudes about racial discrimination, a clear gap among the races emerged. While 67 percent of African Americans reported experiencing discriminatory practices in searching for a job, only 20 percent of whites and 36 percent of Latinos perceived that anti-black discrimination in employment exists.

Yet another way to understand opinion gaps is to examine differences between average people and "opinion leaders" such as elected officials, clergy, educators, and journalists. In a 2005 report on attitudes toward immigration policy, 51 percent of the public reported that reducing illegal immigration should be a top priority. Contrast this with roughly one-third of military leaders and religious leaders.[c] A 2006 report similarly found that 58 percent of the public believed that reducing illegal immigration should be among the top foreign policy goals.[d] More recently, even as the Obama administration tried to move health care reform through Congress, 83 percent of the public believed the economy should be the government's top priority versus 57 percent who listed health care and only 40 percent who put immigration first on the list.[e]  These opinion gaps can mobilize groups to form in advocacy for awareness and social change. For example, in addition to the many reports on gender equity produced by the American Association of University Women, this advocacy group also publishes a "woman-to-woman" voter turnout manual. This effort is designed to increase voter turnout among women and to aid women candidates in reaching women voters.[f]

Groups concerned with the racial gap described previously have organized to address existing inequities and to facilitate communication on these issues. For example, the Open Society Institute, funded by the Soros Foundation Network, has sponsored a project examining youth criminal offenders and the criminal justice system. As part of this initiative, it has conducted public opinion polling to determine attitudes about minority offenders and so-called get-tough initiatives. One of the project's aims is to address the differential treatment of minority youth by the criminal justice system found by its studies, and it hopes to use public opinion as a tool to accomplish its aims.[g]

[a]www.cawp.rutgers.edu/Facts/Elections/GGPresVote.pdf
[b]"Independents Take Center Stage in Obama Era," May 21, 2009, report from the Pew Research Center: Social and Demographic Trends, http://people-press.org/report/517/political-values-and-core-attitudes.
[c]http://people-press.org/reports/pdf/263.pdf.
[d]www.thechicagocouncil.org/dynamic_page.php?id=56.
[e]"Public's Priorities for 2010: Economy, Jobs, and Terrorism," January 25, 2010, report from the Pew Research Center: Social and Demographic Trends, http://people-press.org/report/584/policy-priorities-2010.
[f]www.aauw.org/advocacy/issue_advocacy/voter_ed/Woman-to-WomanVoterTurnout.cfm.
[g]www.soros.org/initiatives/usprograms/focus/justice/articles_publications/publications/public_opinion_youth_20011001?skin=printable (accessed September 16, 2008).

or at work.[5] This trend, combined with the increasing popularity of cable satires such as *The Daily Show,* talk radio, blogs, social networking sites, and the Internet as information sources, may significantly alter the nature of the media's influence on public opinion. The media's influence will be discussed in more detail in Chapter 11.

THE INFLUENCE OF POLITICAL EVENTS

Generally, older Americans tend to be somewhat more conservative than younger Americans, particularly on social issues and, to some extent, on economic issues. This effect is known as the **life cycle effect**. People change as they grow older as a result of age-specific experiences. Likewise, as new generations of citizens are socialized within a particular social, economic, and political context, this in turn affects individual members' more specific opinions and actions. In other words, political events and environmental conditions have the power to shape the political attitudes of an entire generation. You no doubt recall what you were doing and where you were when terrorists flew planes into the World Trade Center towers in New York City. Although you and your parents may have similarly witnessed the terror attacks, the ways that they have influenced your attitudes about the increased airport security measures that resulted might differ. When events produce such a long-lasting result, we refer to it as a **generational effect** (also called the *cohort effect*).[6]

Voters who grew up in the 1930s during the Great Depression were likely to form lifelong attachments to the Democratic Party, the party of Franklin D. Roosevelt. In the 1960s and 1970s, the war in Vietnam and the **Watergate break-in** and the subsequent presidential cover-up fostered widespread cynicism toward government. There is evidence that the years of economic prosperity under President Ronald Reagan during the 1980s led many young people to identify with the Republican Party. More recently the increase in non-party-affiliated Independents may mean that although young people heavily supported Democrat Barack Obama over Republican John McCain in the 2008 election, Democrats should not count on a lifelong attachment.

POLITICAL PREFERENCES AND VOTING BEHAVIOR

Various socioeconomic and demographic factors appear to influence political preferences. These factors include education, income and **socioeconomic status**, religion, race, gender, geographic region, and similar traits. People who share the same religion, occupation, or any other demographic trait are likely to influence one another and may also have common political concerns that follow from the common characteristic. Other factors, such as party identification, perception of the candidates, and issue preferences, are closely connected to the electoral process. Table 6–1 illustrates the impact of some of these variables on voting behavior.

DEMOGRAPHIC INFLUENCES

Demographic influences reflect the individual's personal background and place in society. Some factors have to do with the family into which a person was born: race and (for most people) religion. Others may be the result of choices made throughout an individual's life: place of residence, educational achievement, and occupation.

Life Cycle Effect
People change as they grow older because of age-specific experiences and thus people are likely to hold age-specific attitudes.

Generational Effect
A long-lasting effect of the events of a particular time on the political opinions of those who came of political age at that time.

Watergate Break-in
The 1972 illegal entry into the Democratic National Committee offices by participants in President Richard Nixon's reelection campaign.

Socioeconomic Status
The value assigned to a person due to occupation or income. An upper-class person, for example, has high socioeconomic status.

---

[5]Ken Winneg and Kate Kenski, National Annenberg Election Survey, March 28, 2008. accessed at www.annenbergpublicpolicycenter.org.
[6]Cliff Zukin, Scott Keeter, Molly Andolina, Krista Jenkins, and Michael X. Delli Carpini, *A New Engagement? Political Participation, Civic Life, and the Changing American Citizen* (New York: Oxford University Press, 2006).

TABLE 6–1 Votes by Groups in Presidential Elections, 1992–2008 (in Percentages)

	1992			1996		2000		2004		2008	
	CLINTON (DEM.)	BUSH (REP.)	PEROT (REF.)	CLINTON (DEM.)	DOLE (REP.)	GORE (DEM.)	BUSH (REP.)	KERRY (DEM.)	BUSH (REP.)	OBAMA (DEM.)	MCCAIN (REP.)
Total vote	43	38	19	49	41	48	48	48	51	53	46
Gender											
Men	41	38	21	43	44	42	53	44	55	49	48
Women	46	37	17	54	38	54	43	51	48	56	43
Race											
White	39	41	20	43	46	42	54	41	58	43	55
Black	82	11	7	84	12	90	8	88	11	95	3
Hispanic	62	25	14	72	21	67	31	54	44	67	31
Educational Attainment											
Not a high school graduate	55	28	17	59	28	59	39	50	50	63	35
High school graduate	43	36	20	51	35	48	49	47	52	52	46
College graduate	40	41	19	44	46	45	51	46	52	50	48
Postgraduate education	49	36	15	52	40	52	44	54	45	58	40
Religion											
White Protestant	33	46	21	36	53	34	63	32	68	45	54
Catholic	44	36	20	53	37	49	47	47	52	53	45
Jewish	78	12	10	78	16	79	19	75	24	77	22
White fundamentalist	23	61	15	NA	NA	NA	NA	21	79	24	74
Union Status											
Union household	55	24	21	59	30	59	37	59	40	58	40
Family Income											
Under $15,000	59	23	18	59	28	57	37	63	37	73	25
$15,000–29,000	45	35	20	53	36	54	41	57	41	60	37
$30,000–49,000	41	38	21	48	40	49	48	50	49	55	43
Over $50,000	40	42	18	44	48	45	52	43	56	49	49
Size of Place											
Population over 500,000	58	28	13	68	25	71	26	60	40	71	28
Population 50,000 to 500,000	50	33	16	50	39	57	40	50	50	59	40
Population 10,000 to 50,000	39	42	20	48	41	38	59	48	51	45	63
Rural	39	40	20	44	46	37	59	39	60	45	53

NA = not asked
Sources: *The New York Times*; Voter News Service; CBS News; CNN; *Wall Street Journal*

It is also clear that many of these factors are interrelated. People who have more education are likely to have higher incomes and to hold professional jobs. Similarly, children born into wealthier families are far more likely to complete college than children from poor families. Many other interrelationships are not so immediately obvious; for example, many people might not know that 88 percent of African Americans report that religion is very important in their lives, compared with only 57 percent of whites.[7]

Education. In the past, having a college education tended to be associated with voting for Republicans. In recent years, however, this correlation has become weaker. In particular, individuals with a postgraduate education (professors, doctors, lawyers, other managers) have become increasingly Democratic. Also, a higher percentage of voters with only a high school education, who were likely to be blue-collar workers, voted Republican in 2000 and 2004, compared with the pattern in many previous elections, in which that group of voters tended to favor Democrats. Demonstrating how difficult it is to speak with any certainty about these partisan trends, those with a high school education and those with less than a high school diploma supported Democrat Barack Obama in 2008 (see Table 6–1).

The Influence of Economic Status. Family income is a strong predictor of economic liberalism or conservatism. Those with low incomes tend to favor government action to benefit the poor or to promote economic equality. As indicated in Table 6–2, voters in union households have tended to vote for the Democratic candidate. Those with high incomes tend to oppose government intervention in the economy or to support it only when it benefits business. On economic issues, therefore, the traditional economic spectrum described in Chapter 1 is a useful tool. The rich tend toward the right; the poor tend toward the left.

There are no hard-and-fast rules, however. Some very poor individuals are devoted Republicans, just as some extremely wealthy people support the Democratic Party. Indeed, recent research indicates that a realignment is occurring among those of higher economic status: As just mentioned, professionals now tend to vote Democratic, while small-business owners, managers, and corporate executives tend to vote Republican.[8]

Religious Influence: Denomination. Traditionally, scholars have examined the impact of religion on political attitudes by dividing the population into such categories as Protestant, Catholic, and Jewish. In recent decades, however, such a breakdown has become less valuable as a means of predicting someone's political preferences. It is true that in the past, Jewish voters were notably more liberal than members of other groups on both economic and cultural issues, and they continue to be more liberal today. Persons reporting no religion are likely to be liberal on social issues but have mixed economic views. Northern Protestants and Catholics, however, do not differ that greatly from each other, and neither do Southern Protestants and Catholics. This represents something of a change—in the late 1800s and early 1900s, Northern Protestants were distinctly more likely to vote Republican, and Northern Catholics were more likely to vote Democratic.[9] Between 2004 and 2008 nearly all religious groups moved toward the Democratic candidate Barack Obama, with the largest shifts occurring among Catholics (+7 percentage points) and those unaffiliated with any religion (+8 percentage points).[10]

Religious Influence: Religiosity and Evangelicals. Nevertheless, two factors do turn out to be major predictors of political attitudes among members of the various Christian denominations. One is the degree of *religiosity*, or intensity in practice of beliefs, and the other is whether the person holds fundamentalist or evangelical views. A high degree

[7]The Gallup Poll, "A Look at Americans and Religion Today," March 23, 2004.
[8]Thomas B. Edsall, "Voters Thinking Less with Their Wallets," *International Herald Tribune*, March 27, 2001, p. 3.
[9]John C. Green, *The Faith Factor: How Religion Influences American Elections* (New York: Praeger, 2007).
[10]"How the Faithful Voted," The Pew Forum on Religion and Public Life, November 5, 2008.

TABLE 6–2 Percentage of Union Households Voting Republican

Although union members are more likely to identify themselves as Democrats than Republicans and labor organizations are far more likely to support Democratic candidates, the data below show that in eight of the last 14 presidential elections, Republicans have captured at least 40 percent of the votes from union households.

YEAR	UNION HOUSEHOLDS VOTING REPUBLICAN FOR PRESIDENTIAL CANDIDATES	PERCENTAGE
1952	Eisenhower vs. Stevenson	44
1956	Eisenhower vs. Stevenson	57
1960	Kennedy vs. Nixon	36
1964	Johnson vs. Goldwater	17
1968	Nixon vs. Humphrey	44
1972	Nixon vs. McGovern	57
1976	Carter vs. Ford	36
1980	Reagan vs. Carter	45
1984	Reagan vs. Mondale	43
1988	Bush vs. Dukakis	42
1992	Clinton vs. Bush	24
1996	Clinton vs. Dole	30
2000	Bush vs. Gore	37
2004	Bush vs. Kerry	40
2008	Obama vs. McCain	40

Sources: *CQ Researcher*, June 28, 1996, p. 560; *New York Times*, November 10, 1996, p. 16; and authors' updates.

of religiosity is usually manifested by very frequent attendance at church services, at least once or twice a week.

Voters who are more devout, regardless of their church affiliation, tend to vote Republican, whereas voters who are less devout are more often Democrats. In 2008, for example, people who regularly attend church regardless of denomination were more likely to support John McCain than Barack Obama (55 percent to 43 percent) compared with those who attend church less often (57 percent voted for Obama, while 42 percent voted for McCain). There is an exception to this trend: African Americans of all religious backgrounds have been and continue to be strongly supportive of Democrats.

Another distinctive group of voters who are also likely to be very religious are those Americans who can be identified as holding fundamentalist beliefs or consider themselves part of an evangelical group. They are usually members of a Protestant church, which may be part of a mainstream denomination or may be an independent congregation. In election studies, these individuals are usually identified by a pattern of beliefs: They may describe themselves as "born again" and believe in the literal word of the Bible, among other characteristics. As voters, these Christians tend to be cultural conservatives but not necessarily economic conservatives. This group made up 23 percent of the electorate in 2008 and voted overwhelmingly for John McCain (73 percent).

The Influence of Race and Ethnicity. Although African Americans are, on average, somewhat conservative on certain cultural issues such as same-sex marriage and abortion, they tend to be more liberal than whites on social welfare matters, civil liberties, and even foreign policy. African Americans voted principally for Republicans (the party of Lincoln) until Democrat Franklin Roosevelt's New Deal in the 1930s. Since then, they have nearly exclusively identified with the Democratic Party. Indeed, Democratic presidential candidates have received, on average, more than 80 percent of the African American vote since 1956. As you learned in Chapter 1, Latinos also favor the Democrats. Latinos of Cuban ancestry, however, are predominantly Republican. Most Asian American groups lean toward the Democrats, although often by narrow margins. Muslim American immigrants and their descendants are an interesting category.[11] In 2000, a majority of Muslim Americans of Middle Eastern ancestry voted for Republican George W. Bush because they shared his cultural conservatism. In the 2004 and 2008 election campaigns, however, the civil liberties issue propelled many of these voters toward the Democrats.[12]

The Gender Gap. Until the 1980s, there was little evidence that men's and women's political attitudes were very different. Following the election of Ronald Reagan in 1980, however, scholars began to detect a **gender gap**. The gender gap has reappeared in subsequent presidential elections, with women being more likely than men to support the Democratic candidate (see Figure 6–4). In the 2000 elections, 54 percent of women voted for Democrat Al Gore, compared with 42 percent of men.

Women also appear to hold different attitudes from their male counterparts on a range of issues other than presidential preferences. They are much more likely than men to oppose capital punishment and the use of force abroad. Studies also have shown that women are

Gender Gap
The difference between the percentage of women who vote for a particular candidate and the percentage of men who vote for the candidate.

ONE OF THE PREPRIMARY debates for the Democratic candidates actually took place on CNN and YouTube, with individuals using the Internet to post questions to the candidates. This debate took place on November 28, 2007. (Stan Honda/AFP/Getty Images)

---

[11]At least one-third of U.S. Muslims are actually African Americans whose ancestors have been in this country for a long time. In terms of political preferences, African American Muslims are more likely to resemble other African Americans than Muslim immigrants from the Middle East.

[12]For up-to-date information on Muslim American issues, see the Web site of the Council on American-Islamic Relations at www.cair.com.

FIGURE 6–4 Gender Gap in Presidential Elections, 1980–2008

A gender gap in voting is apparent in the percentage of women and the percentage of men voting in the last several presidential elections. Even when women and men favor the same candidate, they do so by different margins, resulting in a gender gap.

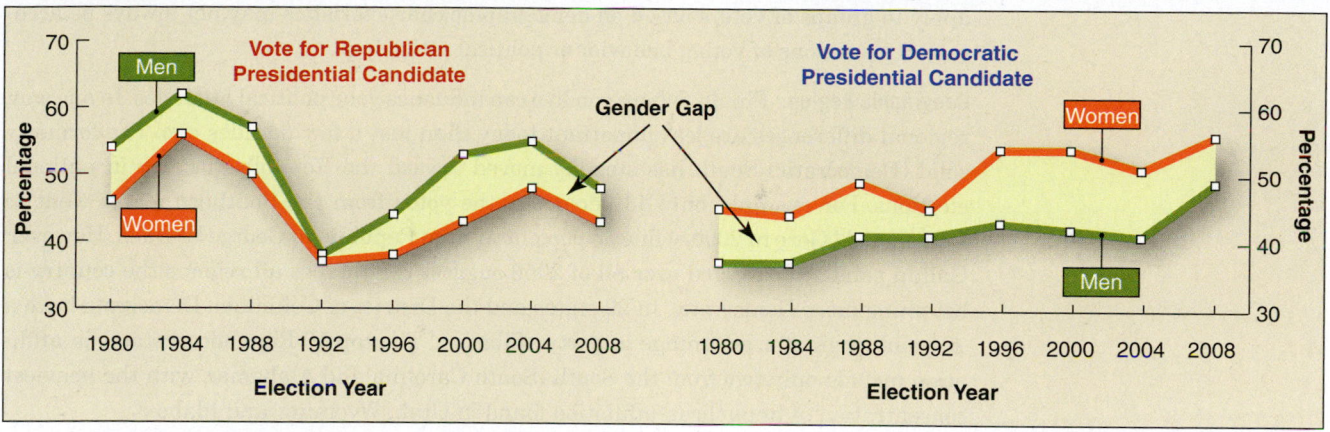

Note: Data in the chart includes votes for Republican and Democratic candidates only. The effect of third party candidates on the gender gap is nominal except in 1992, when H. Ross Perot received 17 percent of the vote among women and 21 percent among men. Perot's impact, if factored into the data, would widen the gap pictured in the chart for 1992, and to a lesser extent in 1996, when his candidacy drew fewer votes.
Sources: Center for American Women and Politics (CAWP); Eagleton Institute of Politics; and Rutgers University.

more concerned about risks to the environment, more supportive of social welfare, and more in agreement with extending civil rights to gays and lesbians than are men. The contemporary gender gap ranges from about 7 to 12 percent. In the 2004 presidential elections, the gender gap narrowed somewhat from previous elections to 7 percent. In large part this is because George W. Bush increased his share of female voters by 5 percent over 2000; 48 percent of women voted for George W. Bush, the highest percentage voting Republican since 1988. In 2008, women strongly preferred Barack Obama to John McCain (56 percent to 43 percent), while men split their votes roughly evenly between the two candidates (49 percent for Obama, 48 percent for McCain). Because more women are registered to vote and more women vote than men, as a result of the gender gap female voters can reasonably claim to have delivered victories in many electoral contests.

Reasons for the Gender Gap. What is the cause of the gender gap? A number of explanations have been offered, including the increase in the number of working women, feminism, and women's concerns over abortion rights and other social issues and the changing political attitudes of men. Researchers Lena Edlund and Rohini Pande of Columbia University, however, have identified another factor leading to the gender gap—the disparate economic impact on men and women of not being married. In the last three decades, men and women have tended to marry later in life or stay single even after having children. The divorce rate has also risen dramatically. Edlund and Pande argue that particularly for those in the middle class, this decline in marriage has tended to make men richer and women relatively poorer. Consequently, support for Democrats is higher among single or divorced women.[13]

In 2004, observers noted that women seemed more concerned about homeland security and terrorism than men, so much so that the media coined a new term: security moms. The label's origins have been traced to a poll reporting that while only 17 percent of men were personally concerned that a member of their family would be the victim of a terrorist attack, 43 percent of women and 53 percent of mothers with children under 18 expressed the same concern. However, further analysis found that although the

[13]Lena Edlund and Rohini Pande, "Why Have Women Become Left-Wing? The Political Gender Gap and the Decline in Marriage," *The Quarterly Journal of Economics*, Vol. 117, No. 3, August 2002, pp. 917–961.

Democratic candidate, John Kerry, was underperforming among female voters relative to past Democrats, "security moms" did not result in George W. Bush's victory. In fact, researchers Laurel Elder and Steven Greene found that parenthood does not move men or women in a more conservative direction.[14] These studies suggest that labels the media apply to groups of voters based on demographic characteristics may not always be accurate explanations of voting behavior or political attitudes.

Geographic Region. Finally, where you live can influence your political attitudes. In one way, regional differences are less important today than just a few decades ago. The formerly solid (Democratic) South has steadily moved toward the Republican Party in national elections. For example, only 43 percent of the votes from the Southern states went to Democrat Al Gore in 2000, while 55 percent went to Republican George W. Bush. However, Gallup poll data collected over all of 2008 suggest that across all regions the country is becoming more Democratic. In 29 states and the District of Columbia, Democrats have a 10-point or greater advantage in party affiliation. The top 10 Republican states in affiliation include only two from the South (South Carolina and Alabama), with the heaviest concentration of Republican affiliation found in Utah, Wyoming, and Idaho.[15]

There is a tendency today, at least in national elections, for the South, the Great Plains, and the Rocky Mountain states to favor the Republicans and for the West Coast and the Northeast to favor the Democrats. Perhaps more important than region is residence—urban, suburban, or rural. People in large cities tend to be liberal and Democratic. Those who live in smaller communities tend to be conservative and Republican. Because there can be so much variability in political attitudes and partisan affiliation within a single state, a map constructed at the county level looks purple rather than distinctly red (representing Republicans) or blue (representing Democrats) (See Figure 6–5).

ELECTIONS: THE MOST IMPORTANT INFLUENCES

Factors such as party identification, perception of the candidates, and issue preferences all have an effect on how people vote in particular elections. Although strong party identifiers remain loyal in most elections, independent voters change their preferences frequently, and the impact of candidate personalities and the issues changes with every election.

Party Identification. With the possible exception of race, party identification has been the most important determinant of voting behavior in national elections. Party affiliation is influenced by family and peer groups, by generational effects, by the media, and by the voter's assessment of candidates and issues.

In the middle to late 1960s, party attachment began to weaken. Whereas independent voters were only a little more than 20 percent of the eligible electorate during the 1950s, they constituted more than 30 percent of all voters by the mid-1990s, and their numbers have remained constant since that time. New voters are likely to identify themselves as independent voters, although they may be more ready to identify with one of the major parties by their mid-30s. There is considerable debate among political scientists over whether those who call themselves Independents are truly so: When asked, most say that they are "leaning" toward one party or the other. For candidates, the increase in Independents means that more campaign time and resources must be dedicated to educating and mobilizing these voters, functions political parties typically perform. (For further discussion of party affiliation, see Chapter 8).

DID YOU KNOW?

That Britain had a major gender gap for much of the 20th century—because women were much more likely than men to support the Conservative Party rather than the more left-wing Labour Party?

[14] Laurel Elder and Steven Greene, "The Myth of 'Security Moms' and 'NASCAR Dads'": Parenthood, Political Stereotypes, and the 2004 Election," *Social Science Quarterly*, Vol. 88, No. 1, March 2007, pp. 1–19.
[15] Jeffrey M. Jones, "State of the State: Party Affiliation," Gallup, January 28, 2009.

FIGURE 6–5   The "Purple" Election Map by County

We have grown used to seeing the national vote portrayed using the electoral college map (see, for example, Figure 8-2 on page 286). Because the states are colored red or blue depending on which party candidate receives the majority of votes, it appears as if all voters in the state are either Republicans (red) or Democrats (blue). Of course, we know that this is not true. Republican and Democratic voters are in every state, and states are broken down into smaller units called counties where the diversity is even more apparent. One way to reveal more accurately the nuance in the vote is to use red, blue, and shades of purple in between to indicate percentages of votes that each party candidate receives at the county level. In this way, the diversity of political affiliation within states is more visible. Areas that appear purple represent more balance between Republicans and Democrats.

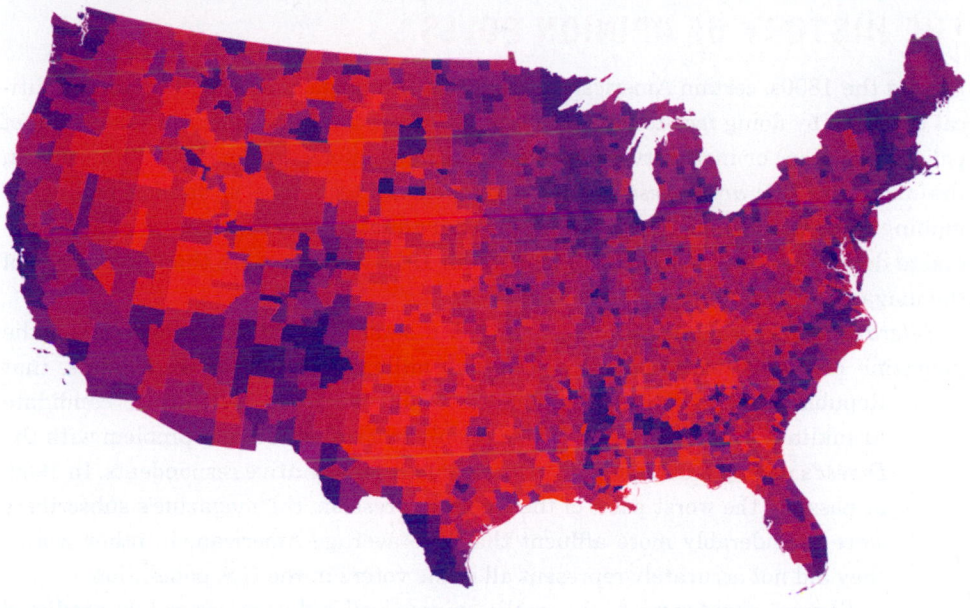

Perception of the Candidates. The image of the candidate also seems to be important in a voter's choice, especially when voting for president. To some extent, voter attitudes toward candidates are based on emotions (such as trust or attraction rather than on any judgment about experience or policy). In some years, voters have been attracted to a candidate who appeared to share their concerns and worries. (President Bill Clinton was one example.) In other years, voters have sought a candidate who appeared to have high integrity and honesty. Voters have been especially attracted to these candidates in elections that follow a major scandal, such as Richard Nixon's Watergate scandal (1972–1974) or Clinton's sex scandal (1998–1999). In 2008, Barack Obama was presented as a candidate who represented change and who would bring change to Washington. He ran an "outsider" campaign focusing on the failings of the government under President George W. Bush. His ability to deliver a charismatic speech along with his youth increased his attractiveness as a candidate. Senator John McCain tried to project the image of a reformer who could also change Washington. His age and long experience in the capital worked against that portrayal.

Issue Preferences. Issues make a difference in presidential and congressional elections. Although personality or image factors may be very persuasive, most voters have some notion of how the candidates differ on basic issues or at least know which candidates want a change in the direction of government policy.

Historically, economic concerns have been among the most powerful influences on public opinion. When the economy is doing well, it is very difficult for a challenger, especially at the presidential level, to defeat the incumbent. In contrast, inflation, unemployment, or high interest rates are likely to work to the disadvantage of the incumbent. Some studies seem to show that people vote on the basis of their personal economic well-being, while other research suggests that people vote on the basis of the nation's overall economic health.[16]

MEASURING PUBLIC OPINION

In a democracy, people express their opinions in a variety of ways, as mentioned in this chapter's introduction. One of the most common means of gathering and measuring public opinion on specific issues is, of course, through the use of **opinion polls**.

THE HISTORY OF OPINION POLLS

During the 1800s, certain American newspapers and magazines spiced up their political coverage by doing face-to-face **straw polls** (unofficial polls indicating the trend of political opinion) or mail surveys of their readers' opinions. In the early 20th century, the magazine *Literary Digest* further developed the technique of opinion polling by mailing large numbers of questionnaires to individuals, many of whom were subscribers, to determine their political opinions. From 1916 to 1936, more than 70 percent of the magazine's election predictions were accurate.

Literary Digest's polling activities suffered a setback in 1936, however, when the magazine predicted, based on more than two million returned questionnaires, that Republican candidate Alfred Landon would win over Democratic candidate Franklin D. Roosevelt. Landon won in only two states. A major problem with the *Digest*'s polling technique was its use of nonrepresentative respondents. In 1936, at possibly the worst point of the Great Depression, the magazine's subscribers were considerably more affluent than the average American. In other words, they did not accurately represent all of the voters in the U.S. population.

Several newcomers to the public opinion poll industry accurately predicted Roosevelt's landslide victory. These newcomers are still active in the poll-taking industry today: the Gallup poll founded by George Gallup and the Roper poll founded by Elmo Roper. Gallup and Roper, along with Archibald Crossley, developed the modern polling techniques of market research. Using personal interviews with small samples of selected voters (fewer than 2,000), they showed that they could predict with accuracy the behavior of the total voting population.

By the 1950s, improved methods of sampling and a whole new science of survey research had been developed. Survey research centers sprang up throughout the United States, particularly at universities. Some of these survey groups are the American Institute of Public Opinion at Princeton, in New Jersey; the National Opinion Research Center at the University of Chicago; and the Survey Research Center at the University of Michigan.

SAMPLING TECHNIQUES

How can interviewing fewer than 2,000 voters tell us what tens of millions of voters will do? Clearly, it is necessary that the sample of individuals be representative of all voters in the population. Consider an analogy: Let's say we have a large jar containing 10,000 pennies of various dates, and we want to know how many pennies were minted within certain decades (1960–1969, 1970–1979, and so on).

Opinion Poll
A method of systematically questioning a small, selected sample of respondents who are deemed representative of the total population.

Straw Polls
A nonbinding vote, often used to gauge the opinion or will of a group prior to taking a formal, binding vote.

DID YOU KNOW?

That 30 percent of people asked to participate in an opinion poll refuse?

---

[16]Warren E. Miller and J. Merrill Shanks, *The New American Voter* (Cambridge, MA: Harvard University Press, 1996). See page 270 for voting on the basis of personal income and page 196 for voting on the basis of the state of the economy.

Representative Sampling. One way to estimate the distribution of the dates on the pennies—without examining all 10,000—is to take a representative sample. This sample would be obtained by mixing the pennies up well and then removing a handful of them—perhaps 100 pennies. The distribution of dates might be as follows:

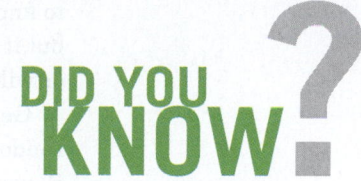

1960–1969: 5 percent
1970–1979: 5 percent
1980–1989: 20 percent
1990–1999: 30 percent
2000–present: 40 percent

If the pennies are very well mixed within the jar, and if you take a large enough sample, the resulting distribution will probably approach the actual distribution of the dates of all 10,000 coins.

The Principle of Randomness. The most important principle in sampling, or poll taking, is randomness. Every penny or every person should have a known chance, and especially an *equal chance*, of being sampled. If this happens, then a small sample should be representative of the whole group, both in demographic characteristics (age, religion, race, region, and the like) and in opinions. The ideal way to sample the voting population of the United States would be to put all voter names into a jar—or a computer—and randomly sample, say, 2,000 of them. Because this is too costly and inefficient, pollsters have developed other ways to obtain good samples. One technique is simply to choose a random selection of telephone numbers and interview the respective households. Prior to expanded cell phone use, this technique produced a relatively accurate sample at a low cost. However, in 2010 the proportion of people living in households without a landline grew to one in four (25 percent). For certain subgroups within the population the proportions are even higher; 30 percent of Latinos are cell-only, as are 30 percent of adults ages 18 to 24 and 49 percent of adults between the ages of 25 and 29. The percentage of households with only a landline continues to decrease but is estimated at about 10 percent. Only 2 percent of the U.S. population cannot be reached by a phone of any kind.

These rapid changes in use of phone technology increase the risk for what pollsters call "coverage error"; that is, the bias introduced when some portion of the population is not covered by the sample. If those missed in the sample differ substantially from those covered, the bias can lead to errors in reporting the results similar to the *Literary Digest* example described above. Whereas research in 2006 found that the likelihood of coverage bias in landline phone surveys was very small, a new study released by the Pew Research Center indicates that the size of the bias effect is increasing, as well as the likelihood of substantive consequences for social and political research reports.[17] Researchers continue to examine these issues as they develop new techniques such as address-based sampling frames to ensure that every person has a known and equal chance at being sampled.

To ensure that the random samples include respondents from relevant segments of the population—rural, urban, Northeastern, Southern, and so on—most survey organizations randomly choose, say, urban areas that they will consider as representative of all urban areas. Then they randomly select their respondents within those areas. A generally less accurate technique is known as *quota sampling*. Here, survey researchers decide how many persons of certain types they need in the survey—such as minorities, women, or farmers—and then send out interviewers

DID YOU KNOW?

That because of scientific sampling techniques, public opinion pollsters can typically measure national sentiment among the roughly 200 million adult Americans by interviewing only about 1,500 people?

AN INTERVIEWER for a public opinion polling firm speaks with a woman in Jenkintown, Pennsylvania, in a survey of households. (AP Photo/Joseph Kaczmarek)

[17]"Assessing the Cell Phone Challenge to Survey Research in 2010," Pew Research Center for the People and the Press, May 20, 2010.

to find the necessary number of these types. Not only is this method often less accurate, but it also may be biased if, say, the interviewer refuses to go into certain neighborhoods or will not interview after dark.

Generally, the national survey organizations take great care to select their samples randomly, because their reputations rest on the accuracy of their results. The Gallup and Roper polls usually interview about 1,500 individuals, and their results have a very high probability of being correct—within a margin of 3 percentage points. The accuracy with which the Gallup poll has predicted presidential election results is shown in Table 6–3.

PROBLEMS WITH POLLS

Public opinion polls are snapshots of the opinions and preferences of the people at a specific moment in time and as expressed in response to a specific question. Given that definition, it is fairly easy to imagine situations in which the polls are wrong.

Sampling Errors. Polls may also report erroneous results because the pool of respondents was not chosen in a scientific manner; that is, the form of sampling and the number of people sampled may be too small to overcome **sampling error**, which is the difference between the sample result and the true result if the entire population had been interviewed. The sample would be biased, for example, if the poll interviewed people by telephone and did not correct for the fact that more women than men answer the telephone and that some populations (college students and very poor individuals, for example) cannot be found so easily by telephone. Unscientific mail-in polls, telephone call-in polls, Internet polls, and polls completed by the workers in a campaign office are not scientific and do not give an accurate picture of the public's views.

As pollsters get close to election day, they become even more concerned about their sample of respondents. Some pollsters continue to interview eligible voters, meaning those over age 18 and registered to vote. Many others use a series of questions in the poll and

Sampling Error
The difference between a sample's results and the true result if the entire population had been interviewed.

TABLE 6–3 Gallup Poll Accuracy Record

YEAR	GALLUP FINAL SURVEY, PERCENTAGE		ELECTION RESULTS, PERCENTAGE		DEVIATION
2008	55.0	Obama	52.6	Obama	+2.4
2004	49.3	Bush	50.7	Bush	−1.7
2000	50.0	Bush	48.0	Bush	+2.0
1996	52.0	Clinton	49.0	Clinton	+3.0
1992	49.0	Clinton	43.2	Clinton	+5.8
1988	56.0	Bush	53.9	Bush	+2.1
1984	59.0	Reagan	59.1	Reagan	−0.1
1980	47.0	Reagan	50.8	Reagan	−3.8
1976	48.0	Carter	50.0	Carter	−2.0
1972	62.0	Nixon	61.8	Nixon	+0.2
1968	43.0	Nixon	43.5	Nixon	−0.5
1964	64.0	Johnson	61.3	Johnson	+2.7
1960	51.0	Kennedy	50.1	Kennedy	+0.9
1956	59.5	Eisenhower	57.8	Eisenhower	+1.7
1952	51.0	Eisenhower	55.4	Eisenhower	−4.4
1948	44.5	Truman	49.9	Truman	−5.4
1944	51.5	Roosevelt	53.3	Roosevelt	−1.8
1940	52.0	Roosevelt	55.0	Roosevelt	−3.0
1936	55.7	Roosevelt	62.5	Roosevelt	−6.8

Sources: *The Gallup Poll Monthly*, November 1992; *Time*, November 21, 1994; *Wall Street Journal*, November 6, 1996; and authors' updates.

other weighting methods to try to identify "likely voters" so that they can be more accurate in their election eve predictions. When a poll changes its method from reporting the views of eligible voters to reporting those of likely voters, the results tend to change dramatically.

Poll Questions. It makes sense to expect that the results of a poll will depend on the questions that are asked. One of the problems with many polls is the yes/no answer format. For example, suppose the poll question asks, "Do you favor or oppose the war in Iraq?" Respondents might wish to answer that they favored the war at the beginning but not as it is currently being waged or that they favor fighting terrorism but not a military occupation. They have no way of indicating their true position with a yes or no answer. Respondents also are sometimes swayed by the inclusion of certain words in a question: More respondents will answer in the affirmative if the question asks, "Do you favor or oppose the war in Iraq as a means of fighting terrorism?" Furthermore, respondents' answers are also influenced by the order in which questions are asked, by the possible answers from which they are allowed to choose, and, in some cases, by their interaction with the interviewer. To a certain extent, people try to please the interviewer. They answer questions about which they have no information and avoid some answers to try to measure up to the interviewer's expectations.

Push Polls. Some campaigns have begun using "push polls," in which the respondents are given misleading information in the questions asked to persuade them to vote against a candidate. For example, the interviewer might ask, "Do you approve or disapprove of Congressman Smith, who voted to raise your taxes 22 times?" Obviously, the answers given are likely to be influenced by such techniques. Push polls have been condemned by the polling industry and are considered to be unethical, but they are still used. In the 2000 Republican Party primary in South Carolina, for example, voters were asked "Would you be more likely or less likely to vote for John McCain for president if you knew he had fathered an illegitimate black child?" Although there was no basis for the substance of the question, and George W. Bush's campaign disavowed any connection to the calls, thousands of Republican primary voters heard a message obviously designed to *push* them away from candidate McCain. In 2008, Jewish voters in Florida and Pennsylvania were targets of a push poll linking Barack Obama to the Palestine Liberation Organization. Other than complaining to the media about such efforts, candidates are largely defenseless against this abuse of polling.

Because of these problems with polls, you need to be especially careful when evaluating poll results. For some suggestions on how to be a critical consumer of public opinion polls, see the You Can Make a Difference feature at the end of this chapter.

TECHNOLOGY AND OPINION POLLS

Public opinion polling is based on scientific principles, particularly with respect to randomness. Today, technological advances allow polls to be taken over the Internet, but serious questions have been raised about the ability of pollsters to obtain truly random samples using this medium. The same was said not long ago when another technological breakthrough changed public opinion polling—the telephone.

President Harry Truman holds up the front page of the *Chicago Daily Tribune* issue that predicted his defeat on the basis of a Gallup poll. The poll had indicated that Truman would lose the 1948 contest for his reelection by a margin of 55.5 to 44.5 percent. The Gallup poll was completed more than a week before the election, so it missed a shift by undecided voters to Truman. (AP Photo/Byron Rollins)

THE ADVENT OF TELEPHONE POLLING

During the 1970s, telephone polling began to predominate over in-person polling. By calling randomly generated telephone numbers within the targeted areas, polls could generate a random sample. Telephone polling quickly proved to be much less expensive than sending interviewers to poll respondents in their homes. Additionally, telephone interviewers do not have to worry about safety problems, particularly in high-crime areas. Finally, telephone interviews can be conducted relatively quickly. They allow politicians or the media to poll one evening and report the results the next day.

Telephone Polling Problems. Somewhat ironically, the success of telephone polling has created major problems for the technique. The telemarketing industry in general has become so pervasive that people increasingly refuse to respond to telephone polls. More than 40 percent of households now use either caller ID or some other form of call screening. This has greatly reduced the number of households that polling organizations can reach. Calls may be automatically rejected, or the respondent may not pick up the call. A potentially greater problem for telephone polling is the popularity of cell phones. Furthermore, individuals with cell phones may be located anywhere in the United States or the world, thus confounding attempts to reach people in a particular area. Federal law prohibits any sort of unsolicited calls to cell phones using "automated dialing devices" and since virtually all pollsters now conduct surveys using computerized systems, this presents a problem. As more people, and especially younger Americans and Latinos, choose to use only a cell phone and do not have a landline at all, polling accuracy is further reduced because these individuals cannot be included in any sample for a poll.[18]

Nonresponse Rates Have Skyrocketed. Nonresponses in telephone polling include unreachable numbers, refusals, answering machines, and call-screening devices. The nonresponse rate has increased to as high as 80 percent for most telephone polls. Such a high nonresponse rate undercuts confidence in the survey results. In most cases, polling only 20 percent of those on the list cannot lead to a random sample. Even more important for politicians is the fact that polling organizations are not required to report their response rates.

ENTER INTERNET POLLING

Obviously, Internet polling is not done on a one-on-one basis, because there is no voice communication. Despite the potential problems, the Harris Poll, a national polling organization, pioneered online polls during the 1998 elections. Its election predictions were accurate in many states. Nonetheless, it made a serious error in one Southern gubernatorial election. The Harris group subsequently refined its techniques and continues to conduct online polls. This organization believes that proper weighting of the results will achieve the equivalent of a random-sampled poll.

Public opinion experts argue that the Harris Poll procedure violates the mathematical basis of random sampling. Nonetheless, the Internet population is looking more like the rest of America: As many women go online as men (74 percent), 70 percent of African American adults have Internet access, and so do 64 percent of Hispanics. Important differences remain based on education (94 percent of those with a college degree use the Internet regularly as compared to 39 percent of those who fail to complete high school) and age (while 93 percent of 18- to 29-year-olds regularly go online, only 38 percent of those over age 65 use the Internet).[19]

DID YOU KNOW?

That when Americans were asked if they thought race relations were good or bad in the United States, 68 percent said that they were "bad," but when asked about race relations in their own communities, 75 percent said that they were "good"?

---

[18] J. Michael Brick et al., "Cell Phone Survey Feasibility in the U.S.: Sampling and Calling Cell Numbers versus Landline Numbers," *Public Opinion Quarterly*, Vol. 71, Spring 2007, pp. 23–39.

[19] Pew Internet and American Life Project, *May–June 2006 Tracking Survey*. The Pew Internet surveys are online at www.pewinternet.org.

"Nonpolls" on the Internet. Even if organizations such as the Harris Poll succeed in obtaining the equivalent of a random sample when polling on the Internet, another problem will remain: the proliferation of "nonpolls" on the Internet. Every media outlet that maintains a Web site allows anyone to submit her or his opinion. Numerous organizations and for-profit companies send polls to individuals via e-mail. Mister Poll (www.misterpoll.com) bills itself as the Internet's largest poll database. Mister Poll allows you to create your own polls just for fun or to include them on your home page. In general, Mister Poll, like many other polling sites, asks a number of questions on various issues and seeks answers from those who log on to its site. Although the Mister Poll Web site states "None of these polls is scientific," sites such as this one undercut the efforts of legitimate pollsters to use the Internet scientifically.

As we have noted, totally nonscientific polls sometimes get as much hype from the media as more scientifically conducted surveys. Poll results are broadcast on the Internet with no authentication at all, and the news media regularly encourage viewers to call in to their own unscientific polls. This indiscriminate use of polling may encourage Americans to see all polls as equally truthful or equally fraudulent and to refuse to respond to any poll. Public antipathy toward polling will, in the long run, make it even more difficult for the finest polling organizations to serve their clients.

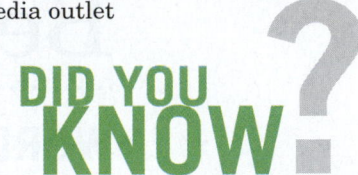

DID YOU KNOW?

That a straw poll conducted by patrons of Harry's New York Bar in Paris has an almost unbroken record of predicting the outcomes of U.S. presidential contests?

PUBLIC OPINION AND THE POLITICAL PROCESS

Public opinion affects the political process in many ways. Politicians, whether in office or in the midst of a campaign, see public opinion as important to their success. The president, members of Congress, governors, and other elected officials realize that strong support by the public as expressed in opinion polls is a source of power in dealing with other politicians. It is far more difficult for a senator to say no to the president if the president is immensely popular and if polls show approval of the president's policies. Public opinion also helps political candidates identify the most important concerns among the people and may help them shape their campaigns successfully.

During the presidential primary contests, polling becomes extremely important to candidates, contributors, and voters. Individuals who would like to make a campaign contribution to their favorite candidate may decide not to if the polls show that the candidate is unlikely to win. Voters do not want to waste their votes on the primary candidates who are doing poorly in the polls. In 2008, the two leading Democratic candidates, Senators Barack Obama and Hillary Clinton, used poll results to try to convince convention delegates of their respective strengths as the party nominee.

Nevertheless, surveys of public opinion are not equivalent to elections in the United States. Although opinion polls may influence political candidates or government officials, elections are the major vehicle through which Americans can bring about changes in their government.

POLITICAL CULTURE AND PUBLIC OPINION

Americans are divided into a multitude of ethnic, religious, regional, and political subgroups. Given the diversity of American

THE PENTAGON HONOR GUARD renders honors during a memorial ceremony commemorating the fifth anniversary of the September 11, 2001, terrorist attacks on the United States. When Americans express high levels of confidence in the military, which events or which people are they likely to be thinking about? (Mass Communication Specialist 1st Class Chad J. McNeeley/ U.S. Navy)

Beyond Our Borders

WORLD OPINION OF THE UNITED STATES

In the immediate aftermath of the September 11, 2001, terrorist attacks, most of the world expressed a great deal of sympathy toward the United States. Few nations objected to the subsequent American invasion of Afghanistan in 2001 to oust the Taliban government or to the Bush administration's vow to hunt down the terrorists responsible for the 9/11 attacks. When the United States announced plans to invade Iraq in 2003, however, world opinion was not supportive. By 2006, world opinion had become decidedly anti-American, as the United States' ongoing "war on terrorism" continued to offend other nations.

NEGATIVE VIEWS OF AMERICAN UNILATERALISM

The invasion of Iraq in 2003 marked a key turning point in world public opinion toward the United States. Most nations opposed the United States' plan to attack Iraq. They were supportive of continuing inspections by the United Nations and did not agree that Iraq was a sponsor of terrorism. The willingness of American leaders to ignore world opinion with regard to the Iraq situation led to charges of arrogance on the part of the U.S. administration.

Between 2003 and 2007, the Pew Global Attitudes Project conducted surveys of public opinion in more than 40 nations. By 2007, attitudes toward the United States had declined in many regions of the world. For example, the percentage of Canadians who had a favorable view of the United States fell from 71 percent in 2000 to 55 percent in 2007. Declines in favorable views were also found in Western Europe and in some South American countries. While the publics in many former Soviet states had been very supportive of the United States, their favorable views also declined during this period, although not as severely as in Western Europe.

ARAB AND MUSLIM OPINION TOWARD AMERICA AND ITS IDEALS

Among the majority of Middle Eastern states, approval of the United States is especially low among Muslims. This is true in such states as Egypt, Jordan, Pakistan, and Malaysia. There are, however, divisions even among Muslims based on religious views. Sunni Muslims in Lebanon are much more favorably inclined toward the United States than are their Shia countrymen and women. Many Muslim nations and their peoples are opposed to the United States' action in Iraq and continued aggressive stance toward Iran. While those nations may not support the current regimes, they are more worried that the United States has destabilized the region, and they continue to see the United States as too supportive of the state of Israel. It is worth noting, however, that most Muslim states in Africa have favorable opinions of the United States.*

Many Arabs and Muslims resent the United States' interventionism and presence in the Middle East. This does not mean that they reject all aspects of the United States or its ideals, however. The majority of Muslims do not support religious extremism or terrorism in their own nations. Nor are Arabs and Muslims dismissive of democracy. Recent polls have shown declining support for terrorist groups among Arabs and Muslims, with only 13 percent of Moroccans and 25 percent of Pakistani Muslims expressing positive views toward terrorism. There has also been broad support for democracy in the Middle East. Many individuals believe that democracy is a real possibility in their own country. Indeed, 83 percent of Lebanese and 80 percent of Jordanians believe that democracy could work in their respective nations. However, many are still suspicious of American motives in the region.

THE "OBAMA EFFECT"

A 2009–2010 poll conducted by the Program on International Policy Attitudes (PIPA) found that America's influence in the world is now seen as more positive than negative. The improved international standing coincides with Barack Obama's election as president. The survey, conducted among some 30,000 adults, found that the United States is viewed positively on balance in 20 of 28 countries, with an average of 46 percent of those surveyed now saying that the United States has a mostly positive influence in the world, while 34 percent say it has a negative influence. Germany is viewed most positively (with an average of 59 percent positive), and Iran is the least favorably viewed nation (15 percent).

Muslim women examining a mosaic of stamps depicting the image of Barack Obama during the Asian International Stamp Exhibition held in Jakarta, Indonesia in 2008. (© Dadang Tri/Reuters/Corbis)

FOR CRITICAL ANALYSIS

1. Pollsters do not know yet whether the "Obama effect" is temporary or lasting. Think back over the past year and identify events or actions taken by the government that might positively or negatively influence the world's opinion. Should the U.S. government keep world opinion in mind when making decisions? Why or why not?
2. Some polls have shown that younger Muslims and Arabs have a more positive opinion toward the United States. Why might that be the case?

*The Pew Global Attitudes Project, 2007 Survey, www.pewglobal.org.

society and the wide range of opinions contained within it, how is it that the political process continues to function without being stalemated by conflict and dissension? One explanation is rooted in the concept of the American political culture, which can be described as a set of attitudes and ideas about the nation and the government. As discussed in Chapter 1, our political culture is widely shared by Americans of many different backgrounds. To some extent, it consists of symbols, such as the American flag, the Liberty Bell, and the Statue of Liberty. The elements of our political culture also include certain shared beliefs about the most important values in the American political system, including (1) liberty, equality, and property; (2) support for religious freedom; and (3) community service and personal achievement. The structure of the government—particularly federalism, separation of powers, and popular rule—is also an important value.

Political Culture and Support for Our Political System. The political culture provides a general environment of support for the political system. If the people share certain beliefs about the system and a reservoir of good feeling exists toward the institutions of government, the nation will be better able to weather periods of crisis. Such was the case after the 2000 presidential elections when, for several weeks, it was not certain who the next president would be and how that determination would be made. At the time, some contended that the nation was facing a true constitutional crisis. In fact, however, the broad majority of Americans did not believe that the uncertain outcome of the elections had created a constitutional crisis. Polls taken during this time found that, on the contrary, most Americans were confident in our political system's ability to decide the issue peaceably and in a lawful manner.[20]

Political Trust. The political culture also helps Americans evaluate their government's performance. At times in our history, **political trust** in government has reached relatively high levels. As you can see in Figure 6–6, a poll taken two weeks after the September 11 attacks found that trust in government was higher than it had been for more than three decades. At other times, political trust in government has fallen to low levels. For example, in the 1960s and 1970s during the Vietnam War and the Watergate scandals, surveys showed that the overall level of political trust in government had declined steeply. A considerable proportion of Americans seemed to feel that they could not trust government officials and that they could not count on officials to care about the ordinary person. This index of political trust reached an all-time low in the early 1990s but then climbed steadily until 2001. Researchers disagree over exactly

Political Trust
The degree to which individuals express trust in the government and political institutions, usually measured through a specific series of survey questions.

FIGURE 6–6 Trends in Political Trust

QUESTION: How much of the time do you think you can trust the government in Washington to do what is right—just about always, most of the time, or only some of the time?

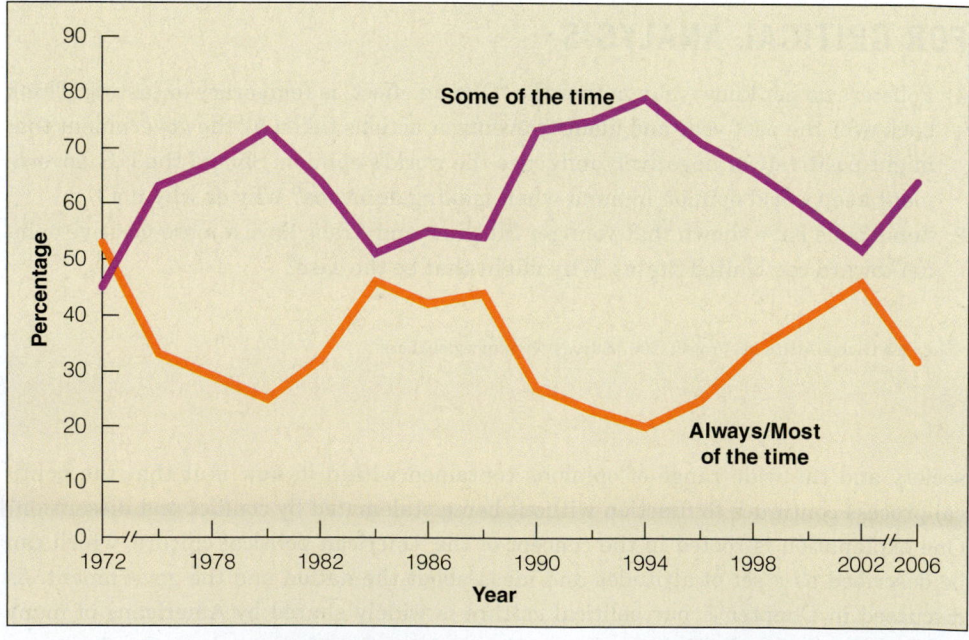

Sources: *New York Times*/CBS News Surveys; University of Michigan Survey Research Center, National Election Studies; Pew Research Center for the People and the Press; Council for Excellence in Government; *Washington Post* poll, September 25–27, 2001; and Gallup polls, Fall 2002, 2004, 2006, and 2008.

[20]As reported in *Public Perspective*, March/April 2002, p. 11, summarizing the results of Gallup/CNN/*USA Today* polls conducted between November 11 and December 10, 2000.

how much importance varying levels of trust in government should be given. There is some evidence that the traditional measures of trust bias results negatively (in other words, trust is higher than polls show), and there are scholars who argue that democracy requires healthy skepticism rather than blind trust. Scholar Marc Hetherington demonstrates that declining levels of trust have policy implications. In his book, *Why Trust Matters*, he shows that the decline in Americans' political trust explains the erosion in public support for progressive policies such as welfare, food stamps, and health care. As people have lost faith in the federal government, the delivery system for most redistributive policies, they have also lost faith in progressive ideas. The 2010 battle over health care reform offers a more recent example of this phenomenon.[21]

At times it can be instructive to look at the level of trust that the rest of the world has in the U.S. government. For many years, the United States was a trusted leader in world affairs with many allies. In recent years, however, world opinion toward the United States has soured, as discussed in this chapter's Beyond Our Borders feature.

PUBLIC OPINION ABOUT GOVERNMENT

A vital component of public opinion in the United States is the considerable ambivalence with which the public regards many major national institutions. Figure 6–7 shows trends from 1983 to 2006 in opinion polls asking respondents, at regularly spaced intervals, how much confidence they had in the institutions listed.

FIGURE 6–7 Confidence in Institutions Trend

QUESTION: I am going to read a list of institutions in American society. Would you please tell me how much confidence you, yourself, have in each one—a great deal, quite a lot, some, or very little?

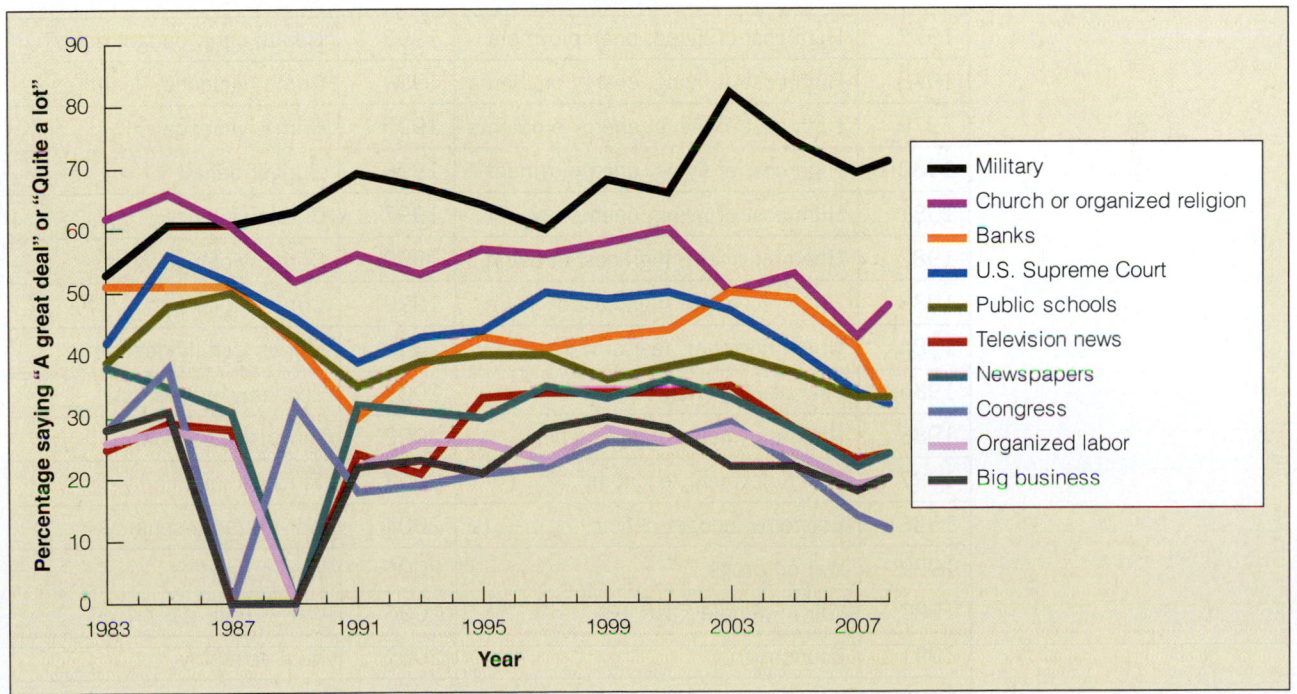

NA = Not asked.
Source: Gallup pall, May 21–23, 2004, June 11–14, 2007, June 9–12, 2008.

[21]Marc J. Hetherington, *Why Trust Matters: Declining Political Trust and the Demise of American Liberalism* (Princeton, NJ: Princeton University Press, 2006).

At times, popular confidence in all institutions may rise or fall, reflecting optimism or pessimism about the general state of the nation. For example, between 1979 and 1981, there was a collapse of confidence affecting most institutions. This reflected public dissatisfaction with the handling of the hostage crisis in Iran and with some of the highest levels of inflation in U.S. history. Some of this confidence was restored by 1985, however, when conditions had improved.

Although people may not have much confidence in government institutions, they nonetheless turn to government to solve what they perceive to be the major problems facing the country. Table 6–4, which is based on Gallup polls conducted from the years 1977 to 2008, shows that the leading problems have changed over time. The public tends to emphasize problems that are immediate and that have been the subject of many stories in the media. When coverage of a particular problem increases suddenly, the public is more likely to see that as the most important problem. Thus, the fluctuations in the "most important problem" cited in Table 6–4 may, in part, be attributed to media agenda setting. In recent years, the economy and jobs, gas and the heating oil crisis, and the war in Iraq have reached the top of the list.

When government does not respond adequately to a crisis, public reaction is swift and negative. For example, President George W. Bush's approval rating dropped precipitously following Hurricane Katrina because the majority of the public lacked confidence in the government's response to the devastating Gulf Coast hurricane. African Americans, in particular, believed the government would have responded quicker if those affected by the storm had been wealthier and primarily white.[22] Similarly, as the economy faltered in the latest recession, individuals, businesses, and even the states looked to the federal

TABLE 6–4 Most Important Problem Trend, 1977 to Present

Year	Problem	Year	Problem
1977	High cost of living, unemployment	1993	Health care, budget deficit
1978	High cost of living, energy problems	1994	Crime, violence, health care
1979	High cost of living, energy problems	1995	Crime, violence
1980	High cost of living, unemployment	1996	Budget deficit
1981	High cost of living, unemployment	1997	Crime, violence
1982	Unemployment, high cost of living	1998	Crime, violence
1983	Unemployment, high cost of living	1999	Crime, violence
1984	Unemployment, fear of war	2000	Morals, family decline
1985	Fear of war, unemployment	2001	Economy, education
1986	Unemployment, budget deficit	2002	Terrorism, economy
1987	Unemployment, economy	2003	Terrorism, economy
1988	Economy, budget deficit	2004	War in Iraq, economy
1989	War on drugs	2005	War in Iraq
1990	War in Middle East	2006	War in Iraq, gas prices
1991	Economy	2007	Iraq, economy
1992	Unemployment, budget deficit	2008	Economy, jobs

Sources: *New York Times*/CBS News poll, July 2008; and Gallup polls, 2000 through 2008.

[22]Michael A. Fletcher and Richard Morin, "Bush's Approval Rating Drops to New Low in Wake of Storm," *The Washington Post*, September 13, 2005.

government for answers and assistance. When an explosion at an offshore drilling rig operated by British Petroleum (BP) dumped unprecedented amounts of oil into the Gulf, the Obama administration took action to coordinate relief and cleanup efforts but still received criticism because it could not plug the leak. While Congress is best suited to investigate the nature of the problem, the president is best able to take action by mobilizing the resources of the federal bureaucracy.

PUBLIC OPINION AND POLICY MAKING

If public opinion is important for democracy, are policy makers really responsive to public opinion? A study by political scientists Benjamin I. Page and Robert Y. Shapiro suggests that in fact the national government is very responsive to the public's demands for action.[23] In looking at changes in public opinion poll results over time, Page and Shapiro show that when the public supports a policy change, the following occurs: Policy changes in a direction consistent with the change in public opinion 43 percent of the time; policy changes in a direction opposite to the change in opinion 22 percent of the time; and policy does not change at all 33 percent of the time. Page and Shapiro also show that when public opinion changes dramatically—say, by 20 percentage points rather than by just 6 or 7 percentage points—government policy is much more likely to follow changing public attitudes.

Setting Limits on Government Action. Although opinion polls cannot give exact guidance on what the government should do in a specific instance, the opinions measured in polls do set an informal limit on government action. For example, consider the highly controversial issue of abortion. Most Americans are moderates on this issue; they do not approve of abortion as a means of birth control, but they do feel that it should be available. Yet sizable groups of people express very intense feelings both for and against legalized abortion. Given this distribution of opinion, most elected officials would rather not try to change policy to favor either of the extreme positions. To do so would clearly violate the opinion of the majority of Americans. In this case, as in many others, *public opinion does not make public policy; rather, it restrains officials from taking truly unpopular actions.*

To what degree should public opinion influence policy making? It would appear that members of the public view this issue differently than do policy leaders. The results of a recent poll about polls showed that whereas 68 percent of the public feel that public opinion should have a great deal of influence on policy, only 43 percent of policy leaders hold this opinion.[24] Why would a majority of policy leaders *not* want to be strongly influenced by public opinion? One answer to this question is that public opinion polls can provide only a limited amount of guidance to policy makers.

The Limits of Polling. Policy makers cannot always be guided by opinion polls. In the end, politicians must make their own choices. When they do so, their choices necessarily involve trade-offs. If politicians vote for increased spending to improve education, for example, by necessity there must be fewer resources available for other worthy projects.

Individuals who are polled do not have to make such trade-offs when they respond to questions. Indeed, survey respondents usually are not even given a choice of trade-offs in their policy opinions. Pollsters typically ask respondents whether they want more or less spending in a particular area, such as education. Rarely, though, is a dollar

---

[23]See the extensive work of Page and Shapiro in Benjamin I. Page and Robert Y. Shapiro, *The Rational Public: Fifty Years of Trends in Americans' Policy Preferences* (Chicago: University of Chicago Press, 1992).
[24]Mollyann Brodie et al., "Polling and Democracy: The Will of the People," *Public Perspective*, July/August 2001, pp. 10–14.

amount assigned or the reallocation of resources that will be required made clear. Additionally, broad poll questions often provide little guidance for policy makers. What does it mean if a majority of those polled want "free" medical treatment for everyone in need? Obviously, medical care is never free. Certain individuals may receive medical care free of charge, but society as a whole has to pay for it. In short, polling questions usually do not reflect the cost of any particular policy choice. Moreover, to make an informed policy choice requires an understanding not only of the policy area but also of the consequences of any given choice.

YOU CAN MAKE A Difference

BEING A CRITICAL CONSUMER OF OPINION POLLS

Americans are inundated with the results of public opinion polls. The polls purport to tell us a variety of things: whether the president's popularity is up or down, whether gun control is more in favor now than previously, or who is leading the pack for the next presidential nomination. What must be kept in mind with this blizzard of information is that all poll results are not equally good or equally believable.

WHY SHOULD YOU CARE?

As a critical consumer, you need to be aware of what makes one set of public opinion poll results valid and other results useless or even dangerously misleading. Knowing what makes a poll accurate is especially important if you plan to participate actively in politics. Successful participation depends on accurate information, and that includes knowing what your fellow citizens are thinking.

WHAT CAN YOU DO?

Pay attention only to opinion polls that are based on scientific, or random, samples. In these so-called *probability samples,* a known probability is used to select each person interviewed. Do not give credence to the results of opinion polls that consist of shopping-mall interviews or the like. The main problem with this kind of opinion taking is that not everyone has an equal chance of being in the mall when the interview takes place. And it is almost certain that the people in the mall are not a reasonable cross section of a community's entire population.

Sometimes, even the most experienced pollsters have unreliable results. The "science" counted on for the 2008 presidential primary polling produced results that were wrong by wide margins. The evening before Super Tuesday 2008, the Reuters/C-SPAN/Zogby poll had Democrat Barack Obama with a 13-point lead over Hillary Clinton in the California primary. This same poll had Republican Mitt Romney with a 7-point lead over John McCain. The final voting results in the California primary showed Clinton ahead of Obama by 9 points; McCain held off Romney by almost 8. What happened?

Experts felt many reasons caused such faulty results. The science of political polling tries to create a microcosm of the electorate; 833 Republicans and 895 Democrats were contacted and identified as "likely to vote." Apparently, the sample included too few Latinos and too many younger voters. Also, the "refusal rate" of people unwilling to talk to pollsters is rising. Pollsters have no way of knowing if these refusing voters represent the views of the majority. The 24/7 news cycle also influences the process. Results in the New Hampshire primary demonstrated that up to 15 percent of the voters decided whom to vote for over the weekend before the actual election. Pollsters missed most of those deciders.*

Pay attention as well to how people were contacted for the poll—by mail, by telephone, in person in their homes, or in some other way (such as via the Internet). Because of its lower cost, polling firms have turned more and more to telephone interviewing. This method can produce highly accurate results. Its disadvantage is that telephone interviews typically need to be short and to deal with questions that are fairly easy to answer. Interviews in person are better for getting useful information about why a particular response was given. They take much longer to complete, however. Results from mailed questionnaires should be taken with a grain of salt. Usually, only a small percentage of people send them back.

When viewers or listeners of television or radio shows are encouraged to call in their opinions to an 800 telephone number, the polling results are meaningless. Users of the Internet also have an easy way to make their views known. Only people who own computers and are interested in the topic will take the trouble to respond, however, and that group is not representative of the general public.

Check to see if your college or university has a polling center on campus. They are often associated with one or more of the social science departments such as political science, sociology, or communication and offer a good way for you to learn firsthand about the science of polling as well as an opportunity to develop skills in interviewing. At Quinnipiac University, a small liberal arts college in Connecticut, students staff a growing Polling Institute that has become well known for its Q-poll. Student interviewers use a computer-assisted telephone interviewing system to collect data from state and national residents. The poll is regularly cited during presidential primaries and general elections by major news outlets including the *Washington Post*, *New York Times*, CNN, and Reuters.

---

*John Diaz, "Why the Polls Are So Wrong," *San Francisco Chronicle*, February 24, 2008, p. G4.

MODERN POLLING depends heavily on computerized telephone polling. The respondents are chosen by a random selection of telephone numbers. The interviewer inputs their responses directly into a computer for analysis. (Sven Martson/Image Works)

KEY TERMS

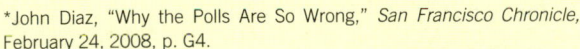

agenda setting 216	**media** 216	**political trust** 234
consensus 213	**nonopinion** 214	**public opinion** 213
divisive opinion 214	**opinion leader** 216	**sampling error** 228
gender gap 222	**opinion poll** 226	**socioeconomic status** 218
generational effect 218	**peer group** 216	**straw polls** 226
life cycle effect 218	**political socialization** 214	**Watergate break-in** 218

CHAPTER SUMMARY

1. Public opinion is the aggregate of individual attitudes or beliefs shared by some portion of the adult population. A consensus exists when a large proportion of the public appears to express the same view on an issue. Divisive opinion exists when the public holds widely different attitudes on an issue. Sometimes, a poll shows a distribution of opinion indicating that most people either have no information about an issue or are not interested enough in the issue to form a position on it.

2. **How do individuals come to hold public opinions?** People's opinions are formed through the political socialization process. Important factors in this process are the family, educational experiences, peer groups, opinion leaders, the media, and political events. The influence of the media as a socialization factor may be growing relative to the family. Voting behavior is influenced by demographic factors such as education, economic status, religion, race and ethnicity, gender, and region. It is also influenced by election-specific factors such as party identification, perception of the candidates, and issue preferences.

3. Most descriptions of public opinion are based on the results of opinion polls. The accuracy of polls depends on sampling techniques that include a representative sample of the population being polled and that ensure randomness in the selection of respondents.

4. Problems with polls include sampling errors (which may occur when the pool of respondents is not chosen in a scientific manner), the difficulty of knowing the degree to which responses are influenced by the type and order of questions asked, the use of a yes/no format for answers to the questions, and the interviewer's techniques. Many are concerned about the use of "push polls" (in which the questions "push" the respondent toward a particular candidate).

5. Advances in technology have changed polling techniques over the years. During the 1970s, telephone polling came to be widely used. Today, largely because of extensive telemarketing, people often refuse to answer calls, and nonresponse rates in telephone polling have skyrocketed. The rapid increase in the percentage of Americans who use a cell phone exclusively poses new challenges to creating representative random samples. Due to the difficulty of obtaining a random sample in the online environment, Internet polls are often "nonpolls." Whether Internet polls can overcome this problem remains to be seen.

6. **How does public opinion impact government actions?** Public opinion affects the political process in many ways. The political culture provides a general environment of support for the political system, allowing the nation to weather periods of crisis. The political culture also helps Americans to evaluate their government's performance. At times, the level of trust in government has been relatively high; at other times, the level of trust has declined steeply. Similarly, Americans' confidence in government institutions varies over time, depending on a number of circumstances. Generally, though, Americans turn to government to solve what they perceive to be the major problems facing the country. In 2008, Americans ranked the economy and jobs, the war in Iraq, and gas and the heating oil crisis as the three most significant problems facing the nation.

7. **Should government officials always follow public opinion?** Public opinion also plays an important role in policy making. Although polling data show that a majority of Americans would like policy leaders to be influenced to a great extent by public opinion, politicians cannot always be guided by opinion polls. This is because the respondents often do not understand the costs and consequences of policy decisions or the trade-offs involved in making such decisions. An important function of public opinion is to set limits on government action through public pressure.

SELECTED PRINT, MEDIA, AND ONLINE RESOURCES

PRINT RESOURCES

Asher, Herbert. *Polling and the Public: What Every Citizen Should Know.* Washington, DC: CQ Press, 2007. This clearly written and often entertaining book explains what polls are, how they are conducted and interpreted, and how the wording and ordering of survey questions, as well as the interviewer's techniques, can significantly affect the respondents' answers.

Bardes, Barbara A., and Robert W. Oldendick. *Public Opinion: Measuring the American Mind,* 3rd ed. Belmont, CA: Wadsworth, 2006. This examination of public opinion polling looks at the uses of public opinion data and recent technological issues in polling in addition to providing excellent coverage of public opinion on important issues over a period of decades.

Clawson, Rosalee A., and Zoe M. Oxley. *Public Opinion: Democratic Ideals, Democratic Practice.* Washington, DC: CQ Press, 2008. This book begins with the premise that democratic theorists disagree about the degree to which citizens should play an active role in politics. Based on the research in public opinion, the authors explore how individuals come to know and understand politics and then how they think and behave politically.

Dalton, Russell J. *The Good Citizen: How a Younger Generation is Reshaping American Politics.* Washington, DC: CQ Press, 2009. Contrary to the conventional wisdom that young people are politically disengaged, this book argues that in many ways today's youth are more engaged than those of previous generations, although the forms of engagement differ. Using public opinion surveys and other empirical research, Dalton analyzes modern citizenship norms that move away from duty-based engagement toward a more encompassing version of civic engagement.

Gimple, James G., J. Celeste Lay, and Jason E. Schuknecht. *Cultivating Democracy: Civic Environments and Political Socialization in America.* Washington, DC: Brookings Institution Press, 2003. This book examines the sources of political attitudes in adolescents by examining the characteristics of the local environments that shape their experiences as they come of age in a new century.

Youniss, James, and Peter Levine, eds. *Engaging Young People in Civic Life.* Nashville, TN: Vanderbilt University Press, 2009. The chapters in this edited volume explore the activities and attitudes that promote voting, volunteering, trust, tolerance, political talk and action, and advocacy in young people. Policies and practices that promote civic engagement are evaluated.

MEDIA RESOURCES

Blame It on Fidel—A 2007 French film in which Anna, a nine-year old girl, must figure out her own beliefs in the confusion created as her parents become increasingly radicalized. This coming of age film explores themes of stereotyping, misinformation, the power of ideologies, and idealism.

Wag the Dog—A 1997 film that provides a very cynical look at the importance of public opinion. The film, which features Dustin Hoffman and Robert De Niro, follows the efforts of a presidential political consultant, who stages a foreign policy crisis to divert public opinion from a sex scandal in the White House.

ONLINE RESOURCES

Gallup has studied human attitudes and behavior for over 75 years. Although some of the data is only available by subscription, the Gallup Daily News regularly provides information and statistics on a variety of issues and current events: www.gallup.com

Latino Decisions conducts state-level polls, primarily in states with high Latino populations, to inform candidates and policy makers about concerns in the Latino community: http://latinodecisions.wordpress.com/

Pew Forum on Religion and Public Life Part of the Pew Research Center, this forum conducts surveys, demographic analyses, and other social science research on important aspects of religion and public life in the United States and around the world. It also provides a neutral venue for discussions of timely issues through roundtables and briefings: http://pewforum.org/

Polling Report an up-to-date and easy-to-use Web site that offers polls and their results organized by topic: www.pollingreport.com

Real Clear Politics (RCP) daily digest of poll results, election analysis, and political commentary as well as an archive of past political polls: www.realclearpolitics.com

7

Lobbyists line up in the Hart Senate Office Building to observe the Senate Finance Committee deliberate on the health insurance reform bill which became law in 2010. (Douglas Graham/Roll Call/Getty Images)

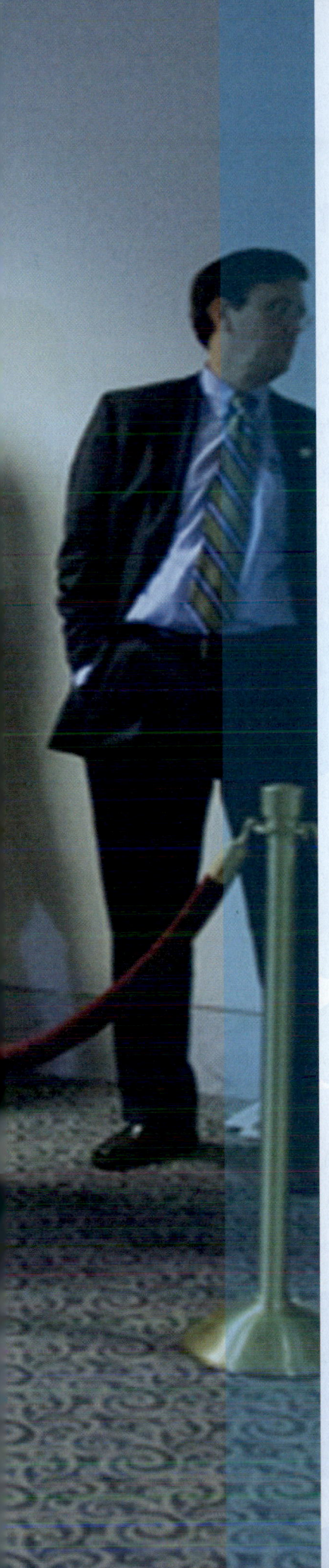

Interest Groups

QUESTIONS TO CONSIDER

Why are there so many interest groups in the United States?

Are all Americans represented by interest groups?

Do interest groups have too much influence over policies and political leaders?

CHAPTER CONTENTS

what if...

Retired Government Employees Could Not Work For Interest Groups?

BACKGROUND

Interest groups place a high value on lobbyists who "know their way around Washington." Former government employees and elected officials qualify in this regard. Often, retired government employees or congresspersons retain personal friendships with their former colleagues. There are rules in place to prevent former government employees from lobbying their former colleagues for a limited period of time after retirement. Congresspersons and their staff members also face such limits. Still, retirees can immediately engage in activities that do not technically qualify as lobbying, and they can begin full-scale lobbying as soon as the time limits expire.

WHAT IF RETIRED GOVERNMENT EMPLOYEES COULD NOT WORK FOR INTEREST GROUPS?

What if retired government employees and members of Congress were banned from lobbying for life? Would this reduce the influence of interest groups on legislation, or would it keep valuable advice out of the public sphere?

A large number of interest groups represent particular industries. Typically, such groups are concerned with legislation and administrative rules specific to their industry but of little interest to the general public. Therefore, the press pays little attention to these laws and regulations. Industry lobbying can pass unnoticed. A retired government employee with expert knowledge of the specific subject matter and of the processes and people involved in making administrative rules can be a formidable lobbyist.

Likewise, a former member of Congress can offer invaluable assistance when an interest group seeks to affect lawmaking. For example, the nation's health insurance companies, hospitals, and medical groups hired more than 350 former members of Congress and retired staff members to lobby during the health care debates of 2009–2010. Among those were individuals who used to hold staff positions on the same committees that now worked to formulate legislation. If these knowledgeable retirees were not available to interest groups, those groups would have less influence on legislation. It is possible, however, that the insights of a former senator might improve the final legislation due to his or her past experience with such laws or ability to suggest a point for compromise.

Industry-specific legislation can include tariffs on imports, tax breaks, and direct subsidies. The cost of this legislation adds up. The Cato Institute, a libertarian research group, estimates that what it calls "corporate welfare" costs nearly $100 billion per year. Barring former government employees from working for interest groups might reduce these kinds of corporate subsidies. Of course, if corporations and other interest groups could not hire former members of Congress, they would hire other lobbyists to represent their interests.

THE IMPACT ON FORMER EMPLOYEES

Some government employees—and many congresspersons—look forward to lobbying as a final stage of their careers. A government career may be more attractive if it ends with a few years of highly paid, comfortable employment. Banning such employment might make government service less appealing to some. The long-term result might be that fewer well-qualified individuals would choose to enter government and politics as a lifelong career.

FOR CRITICAL ANALYSIS

1. Why would interest groups argue that a ban on hiring retired government employees would be an unfair (or even an unconstitutional) restriction on their activities?
2. In what ways might a ban on hiring retired government employees be unfair to the former employees?

BUSINESSES, ENVIRONMENTALISTS, oil well drillers, older Americans, African American organizations, doctors, dentists, Native American tribes, colleges and universities, and foreign governments all try to influence the political leaders and policy-making processes of the United States. The structure of American government invites the participation of **interest groups** at various stages of the policy-making process. One reason why so many different types of interest groups and other organized institutions attempt to influence our government is the many opportunities for them to do so. Interest groups can hire **lobbyists** to try to influence members of the House of Representatives, the Senate or any of its committees, or the president or any of his officials. They can file briefs at the Supreme Court or challenge regulations issued by federal agencies. This ease of access to the government is sometimes known as the "multiple cracks" view of our political system. Interest groups can penetrate the political system through many, many entry points, and, as we will note, their right to do so is protected by the Constitution.

Interest Group
An organized group of individuals sharing common objectives who actively attempt to influence policy makers.

Lobbyist
An organization or individual who attempts to influence legislation and the administrative decisions of government.

INTEREST GROUPS: A NATURAL PHENOMENON

Alexis de Tocqueville observed in 1834 that "in no country of the world has the principle of association been more successfully used or applied to a greater multitude of objectives than in America."[1] The French traveler was amazed at the degree to which Americans formed groups to solve civic problems, establish social relationships, and speak for their economic or political interests. James Madison, when he wrote *Federalist Paper* No. 10 (see Appendix B), foresaw the importance of having multiple organizations in the political system. He supported the creation of a large republic with many states to encourage the formation of multiple interests. The multitude of interests, in Madison's view, would protect minority views against the formation of an oppressive majority interest. Madison's belief in the power of groups to protect a democracy was echoed centuries later by the work of Robert A. Dahl,[2] a contributor to the pluralist theory of politics, as discussed in Chapter 1. Pluralism sees the political struggle pitting different groups against each other to reach a compromise in the public interest.

Surely, neither Madison nor de Tocqueville foresaw the formation of more than 100,000 associations in the United States or the spending of millions of dollars to influence legislation. Poll data show that more than two-thirds of all Americans belong to at least one group or association. Although the majority of these affiliations could not be classified as interest groups in the political sense, Americans do understand the principles of working in groups.

Today, interest groups range from elementary school parent-teacher associations and the local "Stop the Sewer Plant Association" to statewide associations of insurance agents. They include small groups such as local environmental organizations and national groups such as the Boy Scouts of America, the American Civil Liberties Union, the National Education Association, and the American League of Lobbyists. The continuing increase in the number of groups that lobby governments and the multiple ways in which they are involved in the political process have been seen by some scholars as a detriment to an effective government. Sometimes called *hyperpluralism*, the ability of interest groups to mandate policy or to defeat policies needed by the nation may work against the public good.[3]

[1]Alexis de Tocqueville, *Democracy in America*, Vol. 1, edited by Phillips Bradley (New York: Knopf, 1980), p. 191.
[2]Robert A. Dahl, *Who Governs? Democracy and Power in an American City* (New Haven, CT: Yale University Press, 1961).
[3]Theodore Lowi, The End of Liberalism (New York: W. W. Norton, 1979).

INTEREST GROUPS AND SOCIAL MOVEMENTS

Social Movement
A movement that represents the demands of a large segment of the public for political, economic, or social change.

Interest groups are often spawned by mass **social movements**. Such movements represent demands by a large segment of the population for change in the political, economic, or social system. Social movements are often the first expression of latent discontent with the existing system. They may be the authentic voice of weaker or oppressed groups in society that do not have the means or standing to organize as interest groups. For example, most mainstream political and social leaders disapproved of the women's movement of the 1800s. Because women were unable to vote or take an active part in the political system, it was difficult for women who desired greater freedoms to organize formal groups. After the Civil War, when more women became active in professional life, the first real women's rights group, the National Woman Suffrage Association, came into being.

African Americans found themselves in an even more disadvantaged situation after the end of the Reconstruction period. They were unable to exercise their political rights in many Southern and border states, and their participation in any form of organization could lead to economic ruin, physical harassment, or even death. The civil rights movement of the 1950s and 1960s was clearly a social movement. Although the movement received support from several formal organizations—including the Southern Christian Leadership Conference, the National Association for the Advancement of Colored People, and the Urban League—only a social movement could generate the kinds of civil disobedience that took place in hundreds of towns and cities across the country.

Congressman Bennie Thompson, a Democrat from Mississippi, is the target of lobbyists Jake James (representing the AFL-CIO) and Samuel L. Maury (of the Business Roundtable). James is opposing opening trade with China while Maury is supporting it. (Scott J. Ferrell/Newscom)

In the mid-twentieth century, Hispanic or Latino? Americans became part of a social movement to improve the treatment of immigrant workers. Cesar Chavez, a farm worker, organized the Mexican farm laborers in California and other western states to demand better working conditions, better treatment, and the right to form a union. At one point, the National Farm Workers Association initiated a strike against the grape growers in California and led a successful national boycott of table grapes for six years. Chavez became a national figure and his work led to improved conditions for all farm workers. By the 1960s, other leaders within the Hispanic American community founded the National Council of La Raza to improve educational and employment opportunities for their community. Chavez's social movement became a nationally recognized union, the United Farm Workers, while "La Raz" became recognized as an advocacy group that spoke for Hispanic Americans.

Social movements are often precursors of interest groups. They may generate interest groups with specific goals that successfully recruit members through the incentives the group offers. In the case of the women's movement of the 1960s, the National Organization for Women was formed in part out of a demand to end gender-segregated job advertising in newspapers.

Caesar Estrada Chavez, leader of the farm worker rights movement. He founded the National Farm workers Association to secure the rights of migrant farm workers for better wages and living conditions. One of the tactics he used was a consumer boycott against food producers. (Peter Silva/ZUMA Press/Newscom)

WHY SO MANY?

Whether based in a social movement or created to meet an immediate crisis, interest groups continue to form and act in American society. One reason for the multitude of interest groups is that the right to join a group is protected by the First Amendment to the U.S. Constitution (see Chapter 4). Not only are all people guaranteed the right "peaceably to assemble," but they are also guaranteed the right "to petition the Government for a redress of grievances." This constitutional provision encourages Americans to form groups and to express their opinions to the government or to their elected representatives as members of a group. Group membership makes the individual's opinions appear more powerful and strongly conveys the group's ability to vote for or against a representative.

In addition, our federal system of government provides thousands of "pressure points" for interest group activity. Americans can form groups in their neighborhoods or cities and lobby the city council and their state government. They can join statewide groups or national groups and try to influence government policy through Congress or through one of the executive agencies or cabinet departments. Representatives of giant corporations may seek to influence the president personally at social events or fundraisers. When attempts to influence government through the executive and legislative branches fail, interest groups turn to the courts, filing suit in state or federal courts to achieve their political objectives. Pluralist theorists, as discussed in Chapter 1, point to the openness of the American political structure as a major factor in the power of groups in American politics.

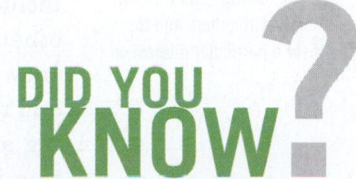

That at least half of all lobbyists in Washington, D.C., are women?

WHY DO AMERICANS JOIN INTEREST GROUPS?

One puzzle that has fascinated political scientists is why some people join interest groups, whereas many others do not. Everyone has some interest that could benefit from government action. For many individuals, however, those concerns remain unorganized interests, or **latent interests**.

According to political theorist Mancur Olson,[4] it simply may not be rational for individuals to join most groups. In his classic work on this topic, Olson introduced the idea of the "collective good." This concept refers to any public benefit that, if available to any member of the community, cannot be denied to any other member, whether or not he or she participated in the effort to gain the good.

Although collective benefits are usually thought of as coming from such public goods as clean air or national defense, benefits are also bestowed by the government on subsets of the public. Price subsidies to dairy farmers and loans to college students are examples. Olson used economic theory to propose that it is not rational for interested individuals to join groups that work for group benefits. In fact, it is often more rational for the individual to wait for others to procure the benefits and then share them. How many college students, for example, join the United States Student Association, an organization that lobbies the government for increased financial aid to students? The difficulty interest groups face in recruiting members when the benefits can be obtained without joining is referred to as the **free rider problem**.

If so little incentive exists for individuals to join together, why are there thousands of interest groups lobbying in Washington? According to the logic of collective action, if the contribution of an individual *will* make a difference to the effort, then it is worth it to the individual to join. Thus, smaller groups, which seek benefits for only a small proportion of the population, are more likely to enroll members who will give time and funds to the cause. Larger groups, which represent general public interests (the women's movement or the American Civil Liberties Union, for example), will find it relatively more difficult to get individuals to join. People need an incentive—material or otherwise—to participate.

SOLIDARY INCENTIVES

Interest groups offer **solidary incentives** for their members. Solidary incentives include companionship, a sense of belonging, and the pleasure of associating with others. Although the National Audubon Society was originally founded to save the snowy egret from extinction, today most members join to learn more about birds and to meet and share their pleasure with other individuals who enjoy bird-watching as a hobby. Even though the incentive might be solidary for many members, this organization nonetheless also pursues an active political agenda, working to preserve the environment and to protect endangered species. Most members may not play any part in working toward larger, national goals unless the organization can convince them to take political action or unless some local environmental issue arises.

Latent Interests
Public-policy interests that are not recognized or addressed by a group at a particular time.

Free Rider Problem
The difficulty interest groups face in recruiting members when the benefits they achieve can be gained without joining the group.

Solidary Incentive
A reason or motive having to do with the desire to associate with others and to share with others a particular interest or hobby.

---

[4]Mancur Olson, *The Logic of Collective Action* (Cambridge, MA: Harvard University Press, 1965).

MATERIAL INCENTIVES

For other individuals, interest groups offer direct **material incentives**. A case in point is AARP (formerly the American Association of Retired Persons), which provides discounts, automobile insurance, and organized travel opportunities for its members. After Congress created the prescription drug benefit program that was supported by AARP, it became one of the larger insurers under that program. Because of its exceptionally low dues ($16 annually) and the benefits gained through membership, AARP has become the largest—and a very powerful—interest group in the United States. AARP can claim to represent the interests of millions of senior citizens and can show that 40 million actually have joined the group. For most seniors, the material incentives outweigh the membership costs.

Many other interest groups offer indirect material incentives for their members. Such groups as the American Dairy Association and the National Association of Automobile Dealers do not give discounts or freebies to their members, but they do offer indirect benefits and rewards by, for example, protecting the material interests of their members from government policy making that is injurious to their industry or business.

> **Material Incentive**
> A reason or motive having to do with economic benefits or opportunities.

That the activities of interest groups at the state level have been growing much faster than in the nation's capital, with more than 44,000 registered state lobbyists in 2006 and with a growth rate of 50 percent in California, Florida, and Texas in the last 10 years?

PURPOSIVE INCENTIVES

Interest groups also offer the opportunity for individuals to pursue political, economic, or social goals through joint action. **Purposive incentives** offer individuals the satisfaction of taking action when the goals of a group correspond to their beliefs or principles. The individuals who belong to a group focusing on the abortion issue, gun control, or environmental causes, for example, do so because they feel strongly enough about the issues to support the group's work with money and time. They are also the most likely members to have come out of a social movement and to see that joining the group will strengthen their influence on an issue of great personal importance.

Some scholars have argued that many people join interest groups simply for the discounts, magazine subscriptions, and other tangible benefits and are not really interested in the political positions taken by the groups. According to William P. Browne, however, research shows that people really do care about the policy stance of an interest group. Members of a group seek people who share the group's views and then ask them to join. As one group leader put it, "Getting members is about scaring the hell out of people."[5] People join the group and then feel that they are doing something about a cause that is important to them.

> **Purposive Incentive**
> A reason for supporting or participating in the activities of a group that is based on agreement with the goals of the group. For example, someone with a strong interest in human rights might have a purposive incentive to join Amnesty International.

TYPES OF INTEREST GROUPS

Thousands of groups exist to influence government. Among the major types of interest groups are those that represent the main sectors of the economy. In addition, many public-interest organizations have been formed to represent the needs of the general citizenry, including some single-issue groups. The interests of foreign governments and foreign businesses are also represented in the American political arena. The names and Web addresses of some major interest groups are shown in Tables 7–1 and 7–2.

[5]William P. Browne, *Groups, Interests, and U.S. Public Policy* (Washington, DC: Georgetown University Press, 1998), p. 23.

TABLE 7–1 *Fortune*'s "Power 25"—The 25 Most Effective Interest Groups

1.	National Rifle Association of America (the NRA—opposed to gun control): www.nra.org
2.	AARP (formerly the American Association of Retired Persons): www.aarp.org
3.	National Federation of Independent Business: www.nfibonline.com
4.	American Israel Public Affairs Committee (AIPAC—a pro-Israel group): www.aipac.org
5.	American Association for Justice: www.justice.org
6.	American Federation of Labor–Congress of Industrial Organizations (the AFL–CIO—a federation of most U.S. labor unions): www.aflcio.org
7.	Chamber of Commerce of the United States of America (an association of businesses): www.uschamber.com
8.	National Beer Wholesalers Association: www.nbwa.org
9.	National Association of Realtors: www.realtor.com
10.	National Association of Manufacturers (NAM): www.nam.org
11.	National Association of Home Builders of the United States: www.nahb.org
12.	American Medical Association (the AMA—representing physicians): www.ama-assn.org
13.	American Hospital Association: www.aha.org
14.	National Education Association of the United States (the NEA—representing teachers): www.nea.org
15.	American Farm Bureau Federation (representing farmers): www.fb.org
16.	Motion Picture Association of America (representing movie studios): www.mpaa.org
17.	National Association of Broadcasters: www.nab.org
18.	National Right to Life Committee (opposed to legalized abortion): www.nrlc.org
19.	America's Health Insurance Plans: www.ahip.org
20.	National Restaurant Association: www.restaurant.org
21.	National Governors' Association: www.nga.org
22.	Recording Industry Association of America: www.riaa.com
23.	American Bankers Association: www.aba.com
24.	Pharmaceutical Research and Manufacturers of America: www.phrma.org
25.	International Brotherhood of Teamsters (a labor union): www.teamster.org

Source: *Fortune*, May 2005.

ECONOMIC INTEREST GROUPS

More interest groups are formed to represent economic interests than any other set of interests. The variety of economic interest groups mirrors the complexity of the American economy. The major sectors that seek influence in Washington, D.C., include business, agriculture, labor unions and their members, government workers, and professionals.

TABLE 7–2 Some Other Important Interest Groups (Not on *Fortune's* "Power 25" List)

American Civil Liberties Union (the ACLU): www.aclu.org
American Legion (a veterans' group): www.legion.org
American Library Association: www.ala.org
The American Society for the Prevention of Cruelty to Animals (the ASPCA): www.aspca.org
Amnesty International USA (promotes human rights): www.amnesty.org
Handgun Control, Inc. (favors gun control): www.bradycampaign.org
League of United Latin American Citizens (LULAC): www.lulac.org
Mothers Against Drunk Driving (MADD): www.madd.org
NARAL Pro-Choice America (formerly the National Abortion and Reproductive Rights Action League—favors legalized abortion): www.naral.org
National Association for the Advancement of Colored People (the NAACP—represents African Americans): www.naacp.org
National Audubon Society (an environmentalist group): www.audubon.org
National Gay and Lesbian Task Force: www.ngltf.org
National Organization for Women (NOW—a feminist group): www.now.org
National Urban League (a civil rights organization): www.nul.org
National Wildlife Federation: www.nwf.org
The Nature Conservancy: www.nature.org
Sierra Club (an environmentalist group): www.sierraclub.org
Veterans of Foreign Wars of the United States: www.vfw.org
World Wildlife Fund: www.wwf.org

Business Interest Groups. Thousands of business groups and trade associations work to influence government policies that affect their respective industries. Umbrella groups represent certain types of businesses or companies that deal in a particular type of product. The U.S. Chamber of Commerce, for example, is an umbrella group that represents businesses, and the National Association of Manufacturers is an umbrella group that represents only manufacturing concerns. The American Pet Products Manufacturers Association works for the good of manufacturers of pet food, pet toys, and other pet products, as well as for pet shops. This group strongly opposes increased regulation of stores that sell animals and restrictions on importing pets. Other major organizations that represent business interests, such as the Better Business Bureaus, take positions on policies but do not actually lobby in Washington, D.C.[6]

Some business groups are decidedly more powerful than others. The U.S. Chamber of Commerce, which has more than 200,000 member companies, can bring constituent influence to bear on every member of Congress. Another powerful lobbying organization is the National Association of Manufacturers. With a staff of more than 60 people

---

[6]Charles S. Mack, *Business, Politics, and the Practice of Government Relations* (Westport, CT: Quorum Books, 1997), p. 14.

in Washington, D.C., the organization can mobilize dozens of well-educated, articulate lobbyists to work the corridors of Congress on issues of concern to its members.

Although business interest groups are likely to agree on anything that reduces government regulation or taxation, they often do not concur on the specifics of policy, and the sector has been troubled by disagreement and fragmentation within its ranks. Large corporations have been far more concerned with federal regulation of their corporate boards and insider financial arrangements, whereas small businesses lobby for tax breaks for new equipment or new employees. One of the key issues on which businesses do not agree is immigration reform. It seems obvious that businesses that employ foreign workers should be responsible for reporting illegal immigrants, but smaller businesses, particularly in agriculture and construction, argue that checking everyone's immigration status and reporting to the government would be a heavy and expensive burden to bear. Large corporations that are normally under much greater governmental scrutiny and have very professional employment practices comply with immigration rules for their own good.

Agricultural Interest Groups. American farmers and their employees represent less than 2 percent of the U.S. population. Nevertheless, farmers' influence on legislation beneficial to their interests has been significant. Farmers have succeeded in their aims because they have very strong interest groups. They are geographically dispersed and therefore have many representatives and senators to speak for them.

The American Farm Bureau Federation, established in 1919, has several million members (many of whom are not actually farmers) and is usually seen as conservative. It was instrumental in getting government guarantees of "fair" prices during the Great Depression in the 1930s.[7] Another important agricultural interest organization is the National Farmers' Union (NFU), which is considered more liberal. As farms have become larger and agribusiness has become a way of life, single-issue farm groups have emerged. The American Dairy Association, the Peanut Growers Group, and the National Soybean Association, for example, work to support their respective farmers and associated businesses. In recent years, agricultural interest groups have become active on many new issues. Among other things, they have opposed immigration restrictions and are very involved in international trade matters as they seek new markets. One of the newest agricultural groups is the American Farmland Trust, which supports policies to conserve farmland and protect natural resources.

Labor Interest Groups. Interest groups representing the **labor movement** date back to at least 1886, when the American Federation of Labor (AFL) was formed. In 1955, the AFL joined forces with the Congress of Industrial Organizations (CIO). Today, the combined AFL-CIO is a large union with a membership of nearly nine million workers and an active political arm called the Committee on Political Education. In a sense, the AFL-CIO is a union of unions.

The AFL-CIO experienced severe discord within its ranks during 2005, however, when four key unions left the federation and formed the Change to Win Coalition. The

Labor Movement
Generally, the economic and political expression of working-class interests; politically, the organization of working-class interests.

---

[7]The Agricultural Adjustment Act of 1933 (declared unconstitutional) was replaced by the 1938 Agricultural Adjustment Act and later changed and amended several times.

FIGURE 7–1 Decline in Union Membership, 1948 to Present

As shown in this figure, the percentage of the total workforce that is represented by labor unions has declined precipitously over the last 40 years. Note, however, that in contrast to the decline in union representation in the private sector, the percentage of government workers who are unionized has increased significantly since about 1960.

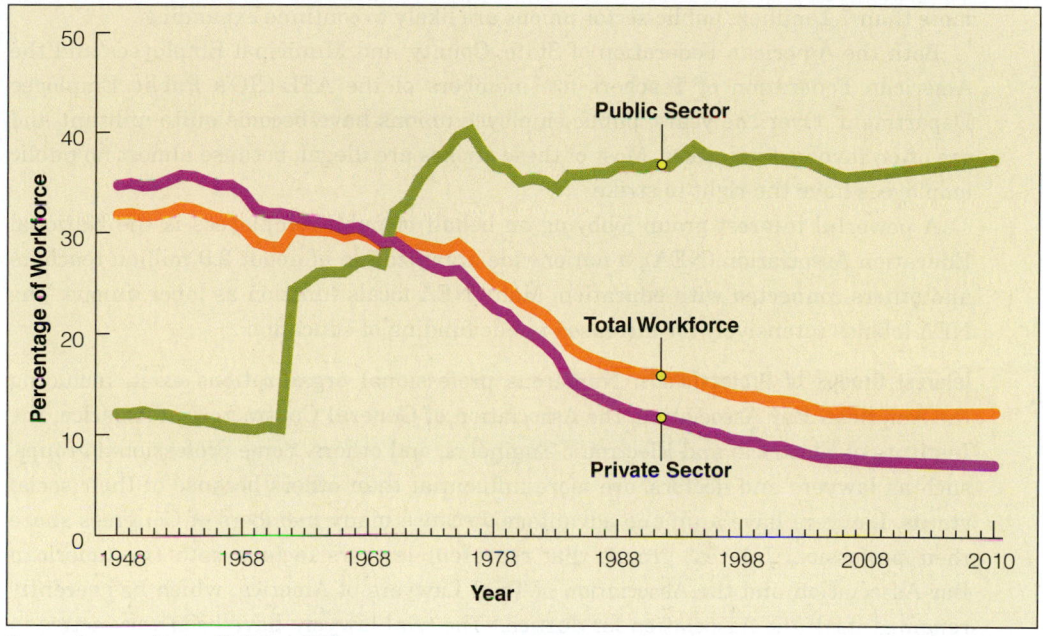

Source: Bureau of Labor Statistics, 2008.

new **Change to Win Coalition** represents about one-third of the 13 million workers who formerly belonged to the AFL-CIO. Many labor advocates fear that the split will further weaken organized labor's waning political influence. The role of unions in American society has declined in recent decades, as witnessed by the decrease in union membership (see Figure 7–1). In the age of automation and with the rise of the **service sector**, blue-collar workers in basic industries (autos, steel, and the like) represent an increasingly smaller percentage of the total working population. Although there was some growth in union membership in the early 2000s, the economic recession that began in 2008 took its toll on union workers as employees lost their jobs. At the end of 2009, total union membership in the United States stood at 15.3 million workers, or 12.3 percent of the workforce.

With the steady decline in employment in the industrial sector of the economy, national unions are looking to nontraditional areas for their membership, including migrant farm workers, service workers, and, most recently, public employees—such as police officers, firefighting personnel, and teachers, including college professors and graduate assistants. By 2009, the number of individuals who belonged to public-sector unions outnumbered those in private-sector unions.

Although the proportion of the workforce that belongs to a union has declined over the years, American labor unions have not given up their efforts to support sympathetic candidates for Congress or for state office. Currently, the AFL-CIO, under the leadership of John J. Sweeney, has a large political budget, which it uses to help Democratic candidates nationwide. Although interest groups that favor Republicans continue to assist their candidates, the efforts of labor are more sustained and more targeted. Labor offers a candidate (such as former Democratic presidential candidate Barack Obama) a corps of volunteers in

Service Sector
The sector of the economy that provides services—such as health care, banking, and education—in contrast to the sector that produces goods.

addition to campaign contributions. A massive turnout by labor union members in critical elections can significantly increase the final vote totals for Democratic candidates.

Public-Employee Unions. The degree of unionization in the private sector has declined since 1965, but this has been partially offset by growth in the unionization of public employees. Figure 7–1 displays the growth in public-sector unionization. With a total membership of more than 7.1 million, public-sector unions are likely to continue expanding.

Both the American Federation of State, County, and Municipal Employees and the American Federation of Teachers are members of the AFL-CIO's Public Employee Department. Over the years, public-employee unions have become quite militant and are often involved in strikes. Most of these strikes are illegal, because almost no public employees have the right to strike.

A powerful interest group lobbying on behalf of public employees is the National Education Association (NEA), a nationwide organization of about 2.8 million teachers and others connected with education. Many NEA locals function as labor unions. The NEA lobbies intensively for increased public funding of education.

Interest Groups of Professionals. Numerous professional organizations exist, including the American Bar Association, the Association of General Contractors of America, the Institute of Electrical and Electronic Engineers, and others. Some professional groups, such as lawyers and doctors, are more influential than others because of their social status. Lawyers have a unique advantage, because many members of Congress share their profession. Interest groups that represent lawyers include both the American Bar Association and the Association of Trial Lawyers of America, which has recently renamed itself the Association for Justice.[8] The trial lawyers have been very active in political campaigns, and are usually one of the larger donors to Democratic candidates. In terms of money spent on lobbying, however, one professional organization stands head and shoulders above the rest—the American Medical Association (AMA). Founded in 1847, it is now affiliated with more than 2,000 local and state medical societies and has a total membership of about 300,000.

THE PRESIDENT of the organization Unidad Honduruena, or Honduran Unity, counsels a young immigrant about taking the proper step to keep his temporary protected status. In this case, an interest group formed to protect nonvoters. How can such an interest group leverage its power when it does not represent voters? (AP Photo/ Wilfredo Lee)

8www.opensecrets.org

POLITICS WITH A purpose

Lobby U

When you hear the word *lobbyist*, do you think of a representative of your college or university? Though you likely do not associate lobbying with your school, almost every institution of higher education (especially public institutions) has an office on campus, and sometimes in Washington, D.C., that actively lobbies government. Usually named the "governmental affairs office" or "department of government relations," these offices are responsible for making sure that the interests of the school are best advocated to those in elective office.

These efforts can take many forms. Often, these offices serve as communication hubs between the university community and politicians. For example, through Web sites, newsletters, and e-mail updates, politicians alert faculty, staff, students, and alumni when the state legislature or Congress is working on legislation that affects the school. This legislation might be budgetary or regulatory policy or issues pertaining to financial aid or student athletes. If university officials are traveling to Washington, D.C., government relations officers help prepare them and often accompany them on their trips, introducing them to influential members of Congress.

Governmental affairs offices also help keep their schools on the minds of lawmakers. For example, the Massachusetts Institute of Technology (MIT) informs members of Congress when someone from their district has been admitted to MIT.[a] This helps publicize the school to members of Congress. Sometimes government affairs offices work in conjunction with (or are housed with) the public affairs arm of the school. This allows regular, targeted use of press releases to members of Congress to inform them of how the college or university is using tax dollars.

Some government relations offices even organize trips to the nation's capital for their alumni. The University of Missouri hosts a Legislative Day. In addition to providing a schedule of events and contact information for members of Congress, the school guides participants in the following ins and outs of meeting a member of Congress:

- When entering the congressional office, identify yourself as an alumnus of the school.
- Ask to speak with the member of Congress or the legislative aide.
- Keep the discussion focused around the talking points, which are a list of issues of concern to the alumnus. This might be funding for research, or scholarships, or increased access to financial aid.
- Be patient, courteous, and appreciative. Send a follow-up thank-you note.
- There is even a school rally in the captial Rotunda![b]

Apart from the efforts of individual colleges and universities, there are student lobbying organizations. The United States Students Association, a student-led advocacy organization, has been in existence since 1947. With its roots in union organizing, this organization has over time been associated with anti-McCarthyism, various student activism efforts in the 1960s, and now characterizes itself as a broad-based progressive advocacy group.[c] Its efforts include lobbying conferences and Lobby Days in Washington, D.C., in which its members learn about advocacy and lobbying techniques; attempts to increase voting among young people; and various diversity projects aimed at making higher education accessible to all groups.[d]

[a] http://web.mit.edu/annualreports/pres05/01.03.pdf

[b] www.umsystem.edu/ums/departments/gr/events/index.shtml
[c] www.usstudents.org/who-we-are/history
[d] www.usstudents.org/our-work

The Unorganized Poor. Some have argued that the system of interest group politics leaves out poor Americans or U.S. residents who are not citizens and cannot vote. Americans who are disadvantaged economically cannot afford to join interest groups; if they are members of the working poor, they may hold two or more jobs just to survive, leaving them no time to participate in interest groups. Other groups in the population—including non-English-speaking groups, resident aliens, single parents, disabled

Americans, and younger voters—probably do not have the time or expertise even to find out what group might represent them. Consequently, some scholars suggest that interest groups and lobbyists are the privilege of upper-middle-class Americans and those who belong to unions or other special groups.

R. Allen Hays examines the plight of poor Americans in his book *Who Speaks for the Poor?*[9] Hays studied groups and individuals who have lobbied for public housing and other issues related to the poor and concluded that the poor depend largely on indirect representation. Most efforts on behalf of the poor come from a policy network of groups—including public housing officials, welfare workers and officials, religious groups, public-interest groups, and some liberal general-interest groups—that speak loudly and persistently for the poor. Poor Americans remain outside the interest group network and have little direct voice of their own.

ENVIRONMENTAL GROUPS

Environmental interest groups are not new. We have already mentioned the National Audubon Society, which was founded in 1905 to protect the snowy egret from the commercial demand for hat decorations. The patron of the Sierra Club, John Muir, worked for the creation of national parks more than a century ago. But the blossoming of national environmental groups with mass memberships did not occur until the 1970s. Since the first Earth Day, organized in 1970, many interest groups have sprung up to protect the environment in general or unique ecological niches. The groups range from the National Wildlife Federation, with a membership of more than five million and an emphasis on education, to the more elite Environmental Defense Fund, with a membership of 300,000 and a focus on influencing federal policy. Other groups include the Nature Conservancy, which uses members' contributions to buy up threatened natural areas and either give them to state or local governments or manage them itself, and the more radical Greenpeace Society and Earth First.

PUBLIC-INTEREST GROUPS

Public Interest
The best interests of the overall community; the national good, rather than the narrow interests of a particular group.

Public interest is a difficult term to define because, as we noted in Chapter 6, there are many publics in our nation of about 300 million. It is almost impossible for one particular public policy to benefit everybody, which makes it practically impossible to define the public interest. Nonetheless, over the past few decades, a variety of lobbying organizations have been formed "in the public interest."

Nader Organizations. The best-known and perhaps the most effective public-interest groups are those organized under the leadership of consumer activist Ralph Nader. Nader's rise to the top began in 1965 with the publication of his book *Unsafe at Any Speed*, a lambasting critique of the purported attempt by General Motors (GM) to keep from the public detrimental information about its rear-engine Corvair. Partly as a result of Nader's book, Congress began to consider an automobile safety bill. GM made a clumsy attempt to discredit Nader's background. Nader sued the company, the media exploited the story, and when GM settled out of court for $425,000, Nader became a recognized champion of consumer interests. Since then, Nader has turned over much of his income to the more than 60 public-interest groups that he has formed or sponsored. Nader ran for president in 2000 on the Green Party ticket and again in 2004 and 2008 as an independent.

Other Public-Interest Groups. Partly in response to the Nader organizations, numerous conservative public-interest law firms have sprung up that are often pitted against

[9]R. Allen Hays, *Who Speaks for the Poor?* (New York: Routledge, 2001).

the consumer groups in court. Some of these are the Mountain States Legal Defense Foundation, the Pacific Legal Foundation, the National Right-to-Work Legal Defense Foundation, the Washington Legal Foundation, the Institute for Justice, and the Mid-Atlantic Legal Foundation.

One of the first groups seeking political reform was Common Cause, founded in 1970. Its goal continues to be moving national priorities toward "the public" and to make governmental institutions more responsive to the needs of the public. Anyone willing to pay dues of $20 per year can become a member. Members are polled regularly to obtain information about local and national issues requiring reassessment. Some of the activities of Common Cause have been (1) helping to ensure the passage of the Twenty-sixth Amendment (giving 18-year-olds the right to vote), (2) achieving greater voter registration in all states, (3) supporting the complete withdrawal of all U.S. forces from South Vietnam in the 1970s, and (4) succeeding in passing campaign finance reform legislation.

While Common Cause has about 300,000 members and is still working for political reforms at the national and state level, it is not as well known today as MoveOn.org. Founded in 1998 by two entrepreneurs from California, the group's original purpose was to get millions of people to demand that President Clinton be censured instead of impeached and that the country should "move on" to deal with more important problems. What was strikingly different about this organization is that it was—and continues to be—an online interest group. MoveOn (www.moveon.org) has more than three million members and is now a family of organizations that are politically active in national campaigns and in pressuring government on specific issues.

Other public-interest groups include the League of Women Voters, founded in 1920. Although nominally nonpartisan, it has lobbied for the Equal Rights Amendment and for government reform. The Consumer Federation of America is an alliance of about 200 local and national organizations interested in consumer protection. The American Civil Liberties Union dates back to World War I (1914–1918), when, under a different name, it defended draft resisters. It generally enters into legal disputes related to Bill of Rights issues.

OTHER INTEREST GROUPS

Single-interest groups, being narrowly focused, may be able to call attention to their causes because they have simple, straightforward goals and because their members tend to care intensely about the issues. Thus, such groups can easily motivate their members to contact legislators or to organize demonstrations in support of their policy goals.

A number of interest groups focus on just one issue. The abortion debate has created various groups opposed to abortion (such as the Right to Life organization) and groups in favor of abortion rights (such as NARAL Pro-Choice America). Other single-issue groups are the National Rifle Association, the Right to Work Committee (an antiunion group), and the American Israel Public Affairs Committee (a pro-Israel group). Still other groups represent Americans who share a common characteristic, such as age or ethnicity. Such interest groups may lobby for legislation that benefits their members or upholds their rights or just represent a viewpoint.

AARP, as mentioned earlier, is one of the most powerful interest groups in Washington, D.C., and, according to some, the strongest lobbying group in the United States. It is certainly the nation's largest interest group, with a membership of about 40 million. AARP has accomplished much for its members over the years. It played a significant role in the creation of Medicare and Medicaid, as well as in obtaining cost-of-living increases in Social Security payments. In 2003, AARP supported the Republican bill to add prescription drug coverage to Medicare. (The plan also made other changes to the system.) Some observers believe that AARP's support tipped the balance and allowed Congress to pass the measure on a closely divided vote. AARP also supported the health care reform legislation passed in 2010.

FOREIGN GOVERNMENTS

Homegrown interests are not the only players in the game. Washington, D.C., is also the center for lobbying by foreign governments as well as private foreign interests. The governments of the largest U.S. trading partners, such as Canada, European Union (EU) countries, Japan, and South Korea, maintain substantial research and lobbying staffs. Even smaller nations, such as those in the Caribbean, engage lobbyists when vital legislation affecting their trade interests is considered. Frequently, these foreign interests hire former representatives or former senators to promote their positions on Capitol Hill. To learn more about how foreign interests lobby the U.S. government, see this chapter's *Beyond Our Borders* feature.

WHAT MAKES AN INTEREST GROUP POWERFUL?

At any time, thousands of interest groups are attempting to influence state legislatures, governors, Congress, and members of the executive branch of the U.S. government. What characteristics make some of those groups more powerful than others and more likely to have influence over government policy? Generally, interest groups attain a reputation for being powerful through their membership size, financial resources, leadership, and cohesiveness.

SIZE AND RESOURCES

No legislator can deny the power of an interest group that includes thousands of his or her own constituents among its members. Labor unions and organizations such as AARP and the American Automobile Association (AAA) are able to claim voters in every congressional district. Having a large membership—nearly 9 million in the case of the AFL-CIO—carries a great deal of weight with government officials. AARP now has about 40 million members and a budget of approximately $1 billion for its operations. In addition, AARP claims to represent all older Americans, who constitute close to 20 percent of the population, whether they join the organization or not.

Having a large number of members, even if the individual membership dues are relatively small, provides an organization with a strong financial base. Those funds pay for lobbyists, television advertisements, mailings to members, a Web site, and many other resources that help an interest group make its point to politicians. The business organization with the largest membership is probably the U.S. Chamber of Commerce, which has more than 200,000 members. The Chamber uses its members' dues to pay for staff and lobbyists, as well as a sophisticated communications network so that it can contact members in a timely way. All of the members can receive e-mail and check the Web site to get updates on the latest legislative proposals.

Other organizations may have fewer members but nonetheless can muster significant financial resources. The pharmaceutical industry is represented in Washington, D.C., by the Pharmaceutical Research Manufacturers of America (PhRMA), sometimes called Big Pharma. In 2009, this lobby poured resources into the fight over health reform legislation, seeking and getting limits on how much the new legislation would cost the pharmaceutical industry. The industry employed more than 1,200 lobbyists, according to estimates (2.3 for every member of Congress) and spent more than $200 million on lobbying.

LEADERSHIP

Money is not the only resource that interest groups need to have. Strong leaders who can develop effective strategies are also important. For example, the American Israel Public Affairs Committee (AIPAC) has long benefited from strong leadership. AIPAC lobbies Congress and the executive branch on issues related to U.S.–Israeli relations, as well as general foreign policy in the Middle East. AIPAC has been successful in facilitating the close relationship that the two nations have enjoyed, which includes between $6 billion and $8 billion in foreign aid that the United States annually bestows on Israel. Despite its modest membership size, AIPAC has won bipartisan support for its agenda and is consistently ranked among the most influential interest groups in America.

Other interest groups, including some with few financial resources, succeed in part because they are led by individuals with charisma and access to power, such as Jesse Jackson of the Rainbow Coalition. Sometimes, choosing a leader with a particular image can be an effective strategy for an organization. The National Rifle Association (NRA) had more than organizational skills in mind when it elected the late Charlton Heston as its president. The strategy of using an actor who is identified with powerful roles as the spokesperson for the organization worked to improve its national image.

HOUSE SPEAKER NANCY PELOSI of California addresses a powerful American interest group, the American Israel Public Affairs Committee, known as AIPAC, in 2007. AIPAC often speaks for the interests of the state of Israel. (AP Photo/Evan Vucci)

Beyond Our Borders

LOBBYING AND FOREIGN INTERESTS

Domestic groups are not alone in lobbying the federal government. Many foreign entities hire lobbyists to influence policy and spending decisions in the United States. American lobbying firms are often utilized by foreign groups seeking to advance their agendas. The use of American lobbyists ensures greater access and increases the possibility of success. In 2007–2008, for example, more than 340 foreign entities were represented by lobbying firms here. With the United States holding such a dominant position in the global economy and world affairs, it is hardly surprising that foreign entities regularly attempt to influence the U.S. government.

HIS HOLINESS, THE DALAI LAMA, exiled from his native land of Tibet for the last forty years. (Image copyright ECyril Hou 2010. Used under license from Shutterstock.com)

FOREIGN CORPORATIONS AND THE GLOBAL ECONOMY

Economic globalization has had an incalculable impact on public policy worldwide. Given the United States' prominence in the global economy, international and multinational corporations have taken a keen interest in influencing the U.S. government. Foreign corporations spend millions of dollars each year on lobbying in an effort to create favorable business and trade conditions.

As an example of foreign corporations lobbying the United States, consider the pharmaceutical industry. Many of the world's largest manufacturers of prescription drugs are not American corporations. However, firms such as GlaxoSmithKline, based in England, spend extensively on lobbying in the United States to influence Medicare legislation.

INFLUENCE FROM OTHER NATIONS

Foreign nations also lobby the U.S. government. After it became clear that several Saudi Arabian citizens participated in the September 11, 2001, terrorist attacks, Saudi Arabia became very concerned about its image in the United States. The Saudi government hired Qorvis Communications, LLC, a public and government affairs consulting firm, to spread the message that Saudi Arabia backed the U.S.–led war on terrorism and was dedicated to peace in the Middle East. In 2002 alone, Saudi Arabia spent $14.6 million on lobbying and public relations services provided by Qorvis. In 2007–2008, Saudi Arabia continued to invest in lobbying, spending more than $1 million on public relations firms, according to its report to the U.S. Senate.*

Foreign governments lobby for more specific agendas as well. Numerous developing nations have lobbied Congress to cut back on domestic farm subsidies. If the subsidies were reduced or eliminated, nations with cheaper labor costs could sell their agricultural products in the United States for less than American farm products cost. In addition, smaller nations press for free-trade agreements, such as that signed with Canada and Mexico (NAFTA), so they can increase their exports to the United States. In 2008, a leading campaign executive for Hillary Rodham Clinton resigned his position in the campaign after it was disclosed that he was working as a lobbyist for Colombia on the pending free-trade bill. Senator Clinton opposed that legislation.

FOR CRITICAL ANALYSIS

1. Should foreign governments and foreign corporations be permitted to lobby the members of Congress in the same way as American interest groups?
2. Why do these governments prefer to hire former members of Congress?

*For reports on the expenditures of countries on lobbying efforts, go to the database at http://foreignlobbying.org, which is sustained by Propublica and the Sunlight Foundation, two not-for-profit organizations dedicated to making information about government more public.

COHESIVENESS

Regardless of an interest group's size or the amount of funds in its coffers, the motivation of an interest group's members is a key factor in determining how powerful it is. If the members of a group are committed to their beliefs strongly enough to send letters to their representatives, join a march on Washington, or work together to defeat a candidate, that group is considered powerful. As described earlier, the American labor movement's success in electing Democratic candidates made the labor movement a more powerful lobby.

In contrast, although groups that oppose abortion rights have had little success in influencing policy, they are considered powerful because their members are vocal and highly motivated. Other measures of cohesion include the ability of a group to get its members to contact Washington quickly or to give extra money when needed. The U.S. Chamber of Commerce excels at both of these strategies. In comparison, AARP cannot

claim that it can get its 40 million members to contact their congressional representatives, but it does seem to influence the opinions of older Americans and their views of political candidates.

INTEREST GROUP STRATEGIES

Interest groups employ a wide range of techniques and strategies to promote their policy goals. Although few groups are successful at persuading Congress and the president to completely endorse their programs, many are able to block—or at least weaken—legislation that is injurious to their members. The key to success for interest groups is access to government officials. To gain such access, interest groups and their representatives try to cultivate long-term relationships with legislators and government officials. The best of these relationships are based on mutual respect and cooperation. The interest group provides the official with excellent sources of information and assistance, and the official in turn gives the group opportunities to express its views.

Direct Technique
An interest group activity that involves interaction with government officials to further the group's goals.

Indirect Technique
A strategy employed by interest groups that uses third parties to influence government officials.

The techniques used by interest groups can be divided into direct and indirect techniques. With **direct techniques**, the interest group and its lobbyists approach the officials personally to present their case. With **indirect techniques**, in contrast, the interest group uses the general public or individual constituents to influence the government on behalf of the interest group.

DIRECT TECHNIQUES

Lobbying, publicizing ratings of legislative behavior, building coalitions, and providing campaign assistance are the four main direct techniques used by interest groups.

Lobbying Techniques. As might be guessed, the term *lobbying* comes from the activities of private citizens regularly congregating in the lobbies of legislative chambers before a session to petition legislators. In the latter part of the 1800s, railroad and industrial groups openly bribed state legislators to pass legislation beneficial to their interests, giving lobbying a well-deserved bad name. Most lobbyists today are professionals. They are either consultants to a company or interest group or members of one of the Washington, D.C., law firms that specialize in providing such services. As described in the *What If...* feature, such firms employ hundreds of former members of Congress and former government officials (e.g., former presidential candidates Bob Dole and Walter Mondale). Lobbyists are valued for their network of contacts in Washington. As Ed Rollins, a former White House aide, put it, "I've got many friends who are all through the agencies and equally important, I don't have many enemies. ... I tell my clients I can get your case moved to the top of the pile."[10] Lobbyists of all types are becoming more numerous. The number of lobbyists in Washington, D.C., has more than doubled since 2000.

Lobbyists engage in an array of activities to influence legislation and government policy. These include the following:

1. Engaging in private meetings with public officials, including the president's advisers, to make known the interests of the lobbyists' clients. Although acting on behalf of their clients, lobbyists often furnish needed information to senators and representatives (and government agency appointees) that these officials could not easily obtain on their own. It is to the lobbyists' advantage to provide accurate information so that policy makers will rely on them as a source in the future.
2. Testifying before congressional committees for or against proposed legislation.
3. Testifying before executive rule-making agencies—such as the Federal Trade Commission or the Consumer Product Safety Commission—for or against proposed rules.
4. Assisting legislators or bureaucrats in drafting legislation or prospective regulations. Often, lobbyists furnish advice on the specific details of legislation.
5. Inviting legislators to social occasions, such as cocktail parties, boating expeditions, and other events, including conferences at exotic locations. Most lobbyists believe that meeting legislators in a relaxed social setting is effective.
6. Providing political information to legislators and other government officials. Often, the lobbyists have better information than the party leadership about how other legislators are going to vote. In this case, the political information they furnish may be a key to legislative success.
7. Supplying nominations for federal appointments to the executive branch.

The Ratings Game. Many interest groups attempt to influence the overall behavior of legislators through their rating systems. Each year, the interest group selects legislation that it believes is most important to the organization's goals and then monitors how legislators vote on it. Each legislator is given a score based on the percentage of times that he or she voted in favor of the group's position. The usual scheme ranges from 0 to 100 percent. In the ratings scheme of the liberal Americans for Democratic Action, for example, a rating of 100 means that a member of Congress voted with the group on every issue and is, by that measure, very liberal.

Ratings are a shorthand way of describing members' voting records for interested citizens. They can also be used to embarrass members. For example, an environmental group identifies the 12 representatives it believes have the worst voting records on environmental issues and labels them "the Dirty Dozen," and a watchdog group describes those representatives who took home the most "pork" for their districts or states as the biggest "pigs."

---

[10]As quoted in Mahood, *Interest Groups in American National Politics*, (New York: Prentice Hall, 1999) p. 51.

Building Alliances. Another direct technique used by interest groups is to form a coalition with other groups that are concerned about the same legislation. Often, these groups will set up a paper organization with an innocuous name to represent their joint concerns. In the early 1990s, for example, environmental, labor, and consumer groups formed an alliance called the Citizens Trade Campaign to oppose the passage of NAFTA.

Members of such a coalition share expenses and multiply the influence of their individual groups by combining their efforts. Other advantages of forming a coalition are that it blurs the specific interests of the individual groups involved and makes it appear that larger public interests are at stake. These alliances also are efficient devices for keeping like-minded groups from duplicating one another's lobbying efforts.

Another example of an alliance developed when the Republicans launched the K Street Project. The project, named for the street in Washington, D.C., where the largest lobbying firms have their headquarters, was designed to alter the lobbying community's pro-Democratic tilt. Republicans sought to pressure lobbying firms to hire Republicans in top positions, offering loyal lobbyists greater access to lawmakers in return.

Campaign Assistance. Interest groups have additional strategies to use in their attempts to influence government policies. Groups recognize that the greatest concern of legislators is to be reelected, so they focus on the legislators' campaign needs. Associations with large memberships, such as labor unions, are able to provide workers for political campaigns, including precinct workers to get out the vote, volunteers to put up posters and pass out literature, and people to staff telephone banks for campaign headquarters.

In many states where certain interest groups have large memberships, candidates vie for the groups' endorsements in the campaign. Gaining those endorsements may be automatic, or it may require that the candidates participate in debates or interviews with the interest groups. Endorsements are important, because an interest group usually publicizes its choices in its membership publication and because the candidate can use the endorsement in her or his campaign literature. Traditionally, labor unions have endorsed Democratic Party candidates. Republican candidates, however,

DID YOU KNOW?

That lobbying expenditures in the United States exceed the gross national product of 57 countries?

INTEREST GROUPS from every imaginable ideological point of view issue scorecards of individual legislators' voting records as they relate to the organization's agenda. Shown here are two such scorecards. How much value can voters place on these kinds of ratings? (Left: Courtesy of Pat Carlson, Texas Eagle Forum, http://www. texaseagle.org; Right: Courtesy of Sierra Club Minnesota North Star Chapter, http:// minnesota.sierraclub.org))

often try to persuade union locals at least to refrain from any endorsement. Making no endorsement can then be perceived as disapproval of the Democratic Party candidate.

Despite the passage of the Bipartisan Campaign Finance Act in 2002, the 2008 election boasted record campaign spending. The usual array of interest groups—labor unions, professional groups, and business associations—gathered contributions to their political action committees and distributed them to the candidates. Most labor contributions went to Democratic candidates, while a majority of business contributions went to Republicans. Some groups, such as real estate agents, gave evenly to both parties. At the same time, the newer campaign groups, the so-called 527 organizations—tax-exempt associations focused on influencing political elections—raised more than $425 million in unregulated contributions and used them for campaign activities and advertising. After seeing the success of these groups in raising and spending funds, hundreds of interest groups, private and nonprofit, have founded their 527 organizations to spend funds for advertising and other political activities. The 2009 decision of the Supreme Court in *Citizens United v. FEC,* 558 U.S. (2010) makes it possible for unions, interest groups, and corporations to spend money directly on advertising for and against candidates in 2010.

INDIRECT TECHNIQUES

Interest groups can also try to influence government policy by working through others, who may be constituents or the general public. Indirect techniques mask the interest group's own activities and make the effort appear to be spontaneous. Furthermore, legislators and government officials are often more impressed by contacts from constituents than from an interest group's lobbyist.

Generating Public Pressure. In some instances, interest groups try to produce a groundswell of public pressure to influence the government. Such efforts may include advertisements in national magazines and newspapers, mass mailings, television publicity, and demonstrations. The Internet and satellite links make communication efforts even more effective. Interest groups may commission polls to find out what the public's sentiments are and then publicize the results. The intent of this activity is to convince policy makers that public opinion overwhelmingly supports the group's position.

Some corporations and interest groups also engage in a practice that might be called **climate control**. With this strategy, public relations efforts are aimed at improving the public image of the industry or group and are not necessarily related to any specific political issue. Contributions by corporations and groups in support of public television programs, sponsorship of special events, and commercials extolling the virtues of corporate research are some ways of achieving climate control. For example, to improve its image in the wake of litigation against tobacco companies, Philip Morris began advertising its assistance to community agencies, including halfway houses for teen offenders and shelters for battered women. By building a reservoir of favorable public opinion, groups believe that their legislative goals will be less likely to encounter opposition by the public.

Climate Control
The use of public relations techniques to create favorable public opinion toward an interest group, industry, or corporation.

Using Constituents as Lobbyists. Interest groups also use constituents to lobby for their goals. In the "shotgun" approach, the interest group tries to mobilize large numbers of constituents to write, phone, or send e-mails to their legislators or the president. Often, the group provides postcards or form letters for constituents to fill out and mail. These efforts are effective on Capitol Hill only with a very large number of responses, however, because legislators know that the voters did not initiate the communications on their own. Artificially manufactured grassroots activity has been aptly labeled *Astroturf lobbying*.

A more powerful variation of this technique uses only important constituents. With this approach, known as the "rifle" technique or the "Utah plant manager theory," the interest group might, for example, ask the manager of a local plant in Utah to contact

PROTESTORS for and against the health care reform plan meet outside the University of Iowa fieldhouse in 2010 where President Obama spoke on that legislation. (AP Photo/The Des Moines Register, Rodney White)

the senator from Utah.[11] Because the constituent is seen as responsible for many jobs or other resources, the legislator is more likely to listen carefully to the constituent's concerns about legislation than to a paid lobbyist.

Unconventional Forms of Pressure. Sometimes, interest groups may employ forms of pressure that are outside the ordinary political process. These can include marches, rallies, civil disobedience, or demonstrations. Such assemblies, as long as they are peaceful, are protected by the First Amendment. In Chapter 5, we described the civil disobedience techniques of the African American civil rights movement in the 1950s and 1960s. The 1963 March on Washington in support of civil rights was one of the most effective demonstrations ever organized. The women's suffrage movement of the early 1900s also employed marches and demonstrations to great effect.

Demonstrations, however, are not always peaceable. Violent demonstrations have a long history in America, dating back to the antitax Boston Tea Party described in Chapter 2. The Vietnam War (1964–1975) provoked many demonstrations, some of which were violent. In 1999, at a meeting of the World Trade Organization in Seattle, demonstrations against globalization turned violent. These demonstrations were repeated throughout the 2000s at various sites around the world. Still, violent demonstrations can be counterproductive—instead of putting pressure on the authorities, they may simply alienate the public. For example, historians continue to debate whether the demonstrations against the Vietnam War were effective or counterproductive.

Another unconventional form of pressure is the **boycott**—a refusal to buy a particular product or deal with a particular business. To be effective, boycotts must command widespread support. One example was the African American boycott of buses in Montgomery, Alabama, during 1955, described in Chapter 5. Another was the boycott of California grapes that were picked by nonunion workers, as part of a campaign to organize Mexican American farm workers. The first grape boycott lasted from 1965 to 1970; a series of later boycotts was less effective.

Boycott
A form of pressure or protest—an organized refusal to purchase a particular product or deal with a particular business.

[11]Kay Lehman Schlozman and John T. Tierney, *Organized Interests and American Democracy* (New York: Harper & Row, 1986), p. 293.

REGULATING LOBBYISTS

Congress made its first attempt to control lobbyists and lobbying activities through Title III of the Legislative Reorganization Act of 1946, otherwise known as the Federal Regulation of Lobbying Act. The act actually provided for public disclosure more than for regulation, and it neglected to specify which agency would enforce its provisions. The 1946 legislation defined a *lobbyist* as any person or organization that received money to be used principally to influence legislation before Congress. Such persons and individuals were supposed to register their clients and the purposes of their efforts and report quarterly on their activities.

The legislation was tested in a 1954 Supreme Court case, *United States v. Harriss*,[12] and was found to be constitutional. The Court agreed that the lobbying law did not violate due process, freedom of speech or of the press, or the freedom to petition. The Court narrowly construed the act, however, holding that it applied only to lobbyists who were influencing federal legislation *directly*.

DID YOU KNOW?

That lobbyists have their own lobbying organization, the American League of Lobbyists?

THE RESULTS OF THE 1946 ACT

The immediate result of the act was that a minimal number of individuals registered as lobbyists. National interest groups, such as the National Rifle Association and the American Petroleum Institute, could employ hundreds of staff members who were, of course, working on legislation, but only register one or two lobbyists who were engaged *principally* in influencing Congress. There were no reporting requirements for lobbying the executive branch, federal agencies, the courts, or congressional staff.

Approximately 7,000 individuals and organizations registered annually as lobbyists, although most experts estimated that 10 times that number were actually employed in Washington to exert influence on the government.

While lobbying firms and individuals who represent foreign corporations must register with Congress, lobbyists who represent foreign governments must register with the Department of Justice under the Foreign Agent Registration Act of 1938. The Department of Justice publishes an annual report listing the lobbyists and the nations that have reported their activities. That report is available online at the Department of Justice Web site (www.usdoj.gov/criminal/fara).

DID YOU KNOW?

That, on average, there are now 60 lobbyists for each member of Congress?

THE REFORMS OF 1995

The reform-minded Congress of 1995–1996 overhauled the lobbying legislation, fundamentally changing the ground rules for those who seek to influence the federal government. Lobbying legislation passed in 1995 included the following provisions:

1. A *lobbyist* is defined as anyone who spends at least 20 percent of his or her time lobbying members of Congress, their staffs, or executive branch officials.
2. Lobbyists must register with the clerk of the House and the secretary of the Senate within 45 days of being hired or of making their first contacts. The registration requirement applies to organizations that spend more than $20,000 in one year or to individuals who are paid more than $5,000 annually for lobbying work.

[12]347 U.S. 612 (1954).

3. Semiannual (now quarterly and electronic) reports must disclose the general nature of the lobbying effort, specific issues and bill numbers, the estimated cost of the campaign, and a list of the branches of government contacted. The names of the individuals contacted need not be reported.

4. Representatives of U.S.–owned subsidiaries of foreign-owned firms and lawyers who represent foreign entities also are required to register.

5. The requirements exempt grassroots lobbying efforts and those of tax-exempt organizations, such as religious groups.

As they debated the 1995 law, both the House and the Senate adopted new rules on gifts and travel expenses: The House adopted a flat ban on gifts, and the Senate limited gifts to $50 in value and to no more than $100 in total value from a single source in a year. There are exceptions for gifts from family members and for home-state products and souvenirs, such as T-shirts and coffee mugs. Both chambers banned all-expenses-paid trips, golf outings, and other such junkets. An exception applies for "widely attended" events, however, or if the member is a primary speaker at an event. These gift rules stopped the broad practice of taking members of Congress to lunch or dinner, but the various exemptions and exceptions have caused much controversy as the Senate and House Ethics Committees have considered individual cases.

RECENT LOBBYING SCANDALS

The regulation of lobbying activity again surfaced in 2005, when several scandals came to light. At the center of some publicized incidents was a highly influential and corrupt lobbyist, Jack Abramoff. Using his ties with numerous Republican (and a handful of Democratic) lawmakers, Abramoff brokered many deals for the special-interest clients that he represented in return for campaign donations, gifts, and various perks.

In January 2006, Abramoff pled guilty to three criminal felony counts related to the defrauding of American Indian tribes and the corruption of public officials. Investigations have not ceased, however, as lawmakers and Bush administration officials connected with Abramoff and his colleagues are under continued scrutiny. Numerous politicians have attempted to distance themselves from the embattled lobbyist by giving Abramoff's campaign donations to charity.

In 2007, both parties claimed that they wanted to reform lobbying legislation and the ethics rules in Congress. The House Democrats tightened the rules in that body early in the year, as did the Senate. The aptly named Honest Leadership and Open Government Act of 2007 was signed by President Bush in September 2007. The law made reporting requirements for lobbyists tighter, extended the time period before ex-members can accept lobbying jobs (two years for senators and one year for House members), set up rules for lobbying by the spouses of members, and changed some campaign contribution rules for interest groups. The new rules adopted by the respective houses bar all members from receiving gifts or trips paid for by lobbyists unless preapproved by the Ethics Committee. Within three months after the bill took effect, a loophole was discovered that allows lobbyists to make a campaign contribution to a senator's campaign, for example, and then go to a fancy dinner where the campaign is allowed to pay the bill.[13] As with most other pieces of lobbying legislation, additional loopholes will be discovered and utilized by members and interest groups.

[13]Robert Pear, "Ethics Law Isn't Without Its Loopholes," *New York Times*, accessed April 20, 2008, from www.nytimes.com.

INTEREST GROUPS AND REPRESENTATIVE DEMOCRACY

The role played by interest groups in shaping national policy has caused many to question whether we really have a democracy at all. Most interest groups have a middle-class or upper-class bias. Members of interest groups can afford to pay the membership fees, are generally well educated, and normally participate in the political process to a greater extent than the "average" American. Furthermore, the majority of Americans do not actually join a group outside of their religious congregation or a recreational group. They allow others who do join to represent them.

Furthermore, leaders of some interest groups may constitute an "elite within an elite," in the sense that they usually are from a different economic or social class than most of their members. Certainly, association executives are highly paid individuals who live in Washington, D.C., and associate regularly with the political elites of the country. The most powerful interest groups—those with the most resources and political influence—are primarily business, trade, or professional groups. In contrast, public-interest groups or civil rights groups make up only a small percentage of the interest groups lobbying Congress and may struggle to gain enough funds to continue to exist.

Thinking about the relatively low number of Americans who join them and their status as middle class or better leads one to conclude that interest groups are really an elitist phenomenon rather than, as discussed in Chapter 1, a manifestation of pluralism. Pluralist theory proposes that these many groups will try to influence the government and struggle to reach a compromise that will be advantageous to all sides. However, if most Americans are not represented by a group, say, on the question of farm subsidies or energy imports, is there any evidence that the final legislation improves life for ordinary Americans?

INTEREST GROUP INFLUENCE

The results of lobbying efforts—congressional legislation—do not always favor the interests of the most powerful groups, however. In part, this is because not all interest groups have an equal influence on government. Each group has a different combination of resources to use in the policy-making process. While some groups are composed of members who have high social status and significant economic resources, such as the National Association of Manufacturers, other groups derive influence from their large memberships. AARP, for example, has more members than any other interest group. Its large membership allows it to wield significant power over legislators. Still other groups, such as environmentalist groups, have causes that can claim strong public support even from people who have no direct stake in the issue. Groups such as the National Rifle Association are well organized and have highly motivated members. This enables them to channel a stream of mail or electronic messages toward Congress with a few days' effort.

Even the most powerful interest groups do not always succeed in their demands. Whereas the U.S. Chamber of Commerce may understandably have a justified interest in the question of business taxes, many legislators might feel that the group should not engage in the debate over the future of Social Security. In other words, groups are seen as having a legitimate concern about the issues closest to their interests but not necessarily about broader issues. This may explain why some of the most successful groups are those that focus on very specific issues—such as tobacco farming, funding of abortions, or handgun control—and do not get involved in larger conflicts.

DID YOU KNOW?

That, as of 2010, the average salary for a lobbyist in Washington, D.C., is $177,000?

YOU CAN MAKE A Difference

THE GUN CONTROL ISSUE

Some interest groups focus on issues that concern only a limited number of people. Others are involved in causes in which almost everyone has a stake. Gun control is an issue that concerns many people. The question of whether the possession of handguns should be regulated or even banned is at the heart of a long-running, heated battle among organized interest groups. The fight is fueled by the one million gun incidents occurring in the United States each year—murders, suicides, assaults, accidents, and robberies in which guns are involved.

WHY SHOULD YOU CARE?

Research conducted by the National School Safety Center shows that more than 300 students have died in school shootings in the past 15 years. Student gunmen at Virginia Tech and Northern Illinois University in 2007 and 2008 served as traumatic reminders that campus populations seem increasingly vulnerable to gun violence at the hands of mentally unstable young people. Given

the social outcry surrounding these terrible incidents, are interest groups being formed to deal with the crisis?

Many states are now sharing information about certain mentally unstable people with the National Instant Criminal Background Check system, prodded by a measure worked out by Congress and the National Rifle Association, one of the most powerful single-issue groups in the United States. About 32 states have started reporting mental health information to the federal database since the Virginia Tech tragedy, with other states considering laws to improve their reporting. However, people can still buy guns without anyone checking this database. According to current federal law, unlicensed gun dealers at gun shows do not need to conduct a background check before they sell a weapon. It is unclear how many weapons are sold this way; gun control groups say it could be 40 percent of guns, with gun rights groups claiming the number is less than 3 percent. Congress has repeatedly failed to pass a bill to close this gun show loophole.

Gun control advocates would also like to see a reinstatement of the Federal Assault Weapons Ban, which federal lawmakers allowed to expire in 2004. This law would ban the sale of military-style assault weapons and high-capacity ammunition magazines like those used by the Virginia Tech and Northern Illinois University killers.

Concealed Carry on Campus maintains this Web site to update students on their gun rights and to encourage college students to lobby for additional rights to carry weapons on campus. (Students for Concealed Carry on Campus, http://www.concealedcampus.org)

WHAT CAN YOU DO?

It seems that even with ample warning signs, tragedies can be very difficult to prevent. Both shooters in these university killings were apparently plagued by mental illness. Experts say that we all need to take responsibility for identifying and redirecting the energies of problematic people. We all need social ties and mentoring, especially in large colleges, where counseling staffs are boosting their numbers, offering more walk-in hours, and training faculty and residence hall advisers to become more skilled at identifying students suffering from emotional problems.

Short of installing metal detectors at every building entrance, experts think the majority of these violent events can be handled and prevented by behavioral awareness. College campuses are considering assembling "threat assessment" teams, which would consist of school resource officers and administration personnel, working with lawyers, nurses, and clinical psychologists. These teams would give students and faculty the opportunity to see a warning sign and report it to a group with enough perspective to see a possible threat and the authority to act, if necessary.

Some feel that students and educators should have the right to defend themselves, and that weapons on campus should be part of the plan. A nonprofit organization called Students for Concealed Carry on Campus has 42,000 members nationwide that include college students, faculty, and parents. This group advocates legislation that would allow licensed gun owners to carry concealed weapons on campus, believing that a well-trained citizen could stop a deranged shooter from committing mass murder. Thirteen states are currently considering a form of "concealed carry" legislation for college campuses. Proponents of the Brady Campaign to Prevent Gun Violence oppose the concealed carry legislation, believing that it would only heighten the danger on campuses, where young people drink heavily and live communally. However, a recent court decision in Colorado upheld the students' right under Colorado law to carry concealed licensed firearms on campus, striking down the Board of Regents rule against such action.

To find out more about the National Rifle Association and its positions, contact

The National Rifle Association
11250 Waples Mill Rd.
Fairfax, VA 22030
703-267-1000
www.nra.org

For more information about the rights of college students to carry weapons, contact
Students for Concealed Carry on Campus
http://www.concealedcampus.org

To learn about the positions of gun control advocates, contact

The Coalition to Stop Gun Violence
1023 15th St. N.W., Suite 301
Washington, DC 20005
202-408-0061

Brady Center to Prevent Gun Violence
Brady Campaign to Prevent Gun Violence
1225 Eye St. N.W., Suite 1100
Washington, DC 20005
Brady Center: 202-289-7319
Brady Campaign: 202-898-0792
www.bradycampaign.org

REFERENCES

Daniel McGinn and Samantha Hening, "Spotting Trouble," *Newsweek*, accessed August 21, 2007, at www.newsweek.com.

Mitch Mitchell, "School-Shooting Expert Answers Tough Questions," *Fort Worth Star Telegram*, accessed February 15, 2008, at www.star-telegram.com/.

Matthew Phillips, "Not Yet Bulletproof," *Newsweek*, accessed October 12, 2007, at www.newsweek.com.

Amanda Ripley, "Ignoring Virginia Tech," *Time*, accessed April 15, 2008, at www.time.com.

Suzanne Smalley, "More Guns on Campus?" *Newsweek*, accessed February 15, 2008, at www.newsweek.com.

KEY TERMS

boycott 266
climate control 265
direct technique 262
free rider problem 248
indirect technique 262

interest group 245
labor movement 252
latent interests 248
lobbyist 245
material incentive 249

public interest 256
purposive incentive 249
service sector 253
social movement 246
solidary incentive 248

CHAPTER SUMMARY

1. **Why are there so many interest groups in the United States?** An interest group is an organization whose members share common objectives and actively attempt to influence government policy. Interest groups proliferate in the United States, because they can influence government at many points in the political structure and because they offer solidary, material, and purposive incentives to their members. Interest groups are often created out of social movements.

2. **Are all Americans represented by interest groups?** Major types of interest groups include business, agricultural, labor, public employee, professional, and environmental groups. Other important groups may be considered public-interest groups. In addition, special-interest groups and foreign governments lobby the government. Two-thirds of Americans belong to a group or association of some kind; however, poorer Americans are less likely to have such representation.

3. Interest groups use direct and indirect techniques to influence government. Direct techniques include testifying before committees and rule-making agencies, providing information to legislators, rating legislators' voting records, aiding political campaigns, and building alliances. Indirect techniques to influence government include campaigns to rally public sentiment, letter-writing campaigns, efforts to influence the climate of opinion, and the use of constituents to lobby for the group's interests. Unconventional methods of applying pressure include demonstrations and boycotts.

4. The 1946 Legislative Reorganization Act was the first attempt to control lobbyists and their activities through registration requirements. The United States Supreme Court narrowly construed the act as applying only to lobbyists who directly seek to influence federal legislation.

5. In 1995, Congress approved new legislation requiring anyone who spends 20 percent of his or her time influencing legislation to register. Also, any organization spending $20,000 or more and any individual who is paid more than $5,000 annually for his or her work must register. Quarterly reports must include the names of clients, the bills in which they are interested, and the branches of government contacted. The 2007 lobbying reform law tightened the regulations on lobbyists and imposed other rules on members who wish to become lobbyists after leaving office.

6. **Do interest groups have too much influence over policies and political leaders?** While many interest groups are very strong and able to expend considerable resources on lobbying Congress and the president, not all are successful. Counterpressure from other organizations, public views, from the president will push legislation forward even when lobbying in opposition to it is fierce.

SELECTED PRINT, MEDIA, AND ONLINE RESOURCES

PRINT RESOURCES

Battista, Andrew. *The Revival of Labor Liberalism.* Champaign, IL: University of Illinois Press, 2008. While labor unions have lost members in recent decades, it is still true that few interest groups are as large as organized labor. Until the late 1960s, the labor movement and political liberalism were close allies. Battista, a political science professor, analyzes the political decline of labor and liberalism, especially after the breakup of the labor-liberal coalition. He also looks at recent attempts to put the coalition back together.

Berry, Jeffrey M., and Clyde Wilcox. *Interest Group Society*, 5th ed. New York: Longman, 2009. This work examines the expanding influence of interest groups as well as their relationship to the party system.

Fleshler, Dan. *Transforming America's Israel Lobby: The Limits of Its Power and the Potential for Change.* Dulles, VA: Potomac Books, 2009. Fleshler contends that America's Israel lobby, like many other lobbies, is more resistant to compromise than the people it represents. He proposes strategies to encourage moderation and promote the peace process.

Kaiser, Robert G. *So Damn Much Money: The Triumph of Lobbying and the Corrosion of American Government.* New York: Knopf, 2009. *The Washington Post* journalist, Kaiser shows how lobbyists satisfy politicians' ever-growing need for campaign funds. He argues that behavior once considered corrupt has become commonplace.

Nownes, Anthony J. *Total Lobbying: What Lobbyists Want (and How They Try to Get It).* New York: Cambridge University Press, 2006. This well-written survey of lobbying covers state and local governments, in addition to lobbying at the federal level. It concentrates on public policy, land use, and procurement.

Sifry, Micah, and Nancy Watzman. *Is That a Politician in Your Pocket? Washington on $2 Million a Day.* New York: John Wiley & Sons, 2004. The authors, staff members at Public Campaign, provide a clearly written and detailed exposé of how financial contributions by interest groups drive politics. Chapters cover pharmaceuticals, gun control, agribusiness, oil and chemical corporations, and cable TV.

Tishnet, Mark V. *Out of Range: Why the Constitution Can't End the Battle over Guns.* New York: Oxford University Press, 2007. The author, a Harvard law professor, looks at the ongoing debate between the National Rifle Association and gun control groups and offers a thoughtful analysis of both sides of the debate.

MEDIA RESOURCES

Bowling for Columbine—Michael Moore's documentary won an Academy Award in 2003. Moore seeks to understand why the United States leads the industrialized world in firearms deaths. While the film is hilarious, it takes a strong position in favor of gun control and is critical of the National Rifle Association.

Norma Rae—A 1979 Hollywood movie about an attempt by a Northern union organizer to unionize workers in the Southern textile industry; stars Sally Field, who won an Academy Award for her performance.

Organizing America: The History of Trade Unions—A 1994 documentary that incorporates interviews, personal accounts, and archival footage to tell the story of the American labor movement. The film is a Cambridge Educational Production.

The West Wing—A popular television series that was widely regarded as being an accurate portrayal of the issues and political pressures faced by a liberal president and his White House staff.

ONLINE RESOURCES

AARP (formerly the American Association of Retired Persons) a nonprofit, nonpartisan membership organization that helps people age 50 and over improve the quality of their lives: www.aarp.org

AFL-CIO (American Federation of Labor and Congress of Industrial Organizations) a voluntary federation of 56 national and international labor unions: www.aflcio.org

The Center for Public Integrity a nonprofit organization dedicated to producing original, responsible investigative journalism on issues of public concern; tracks lobbyists and their expenditures: www.publicintegrity.org/lobby

Center for Responsive Politics a nonpartisan guide to money's influence on U.S. elections and public policy with data derived from Federal Election Commission reports: www.opensecrets.org

National Rifle Association America's foremost defender of Second Amendment rights and firearms education organization in the world; provides information on the gun control issue: www.nra.org

8

The Democratic precinct chairwoman
explains the rules to the voters at the
Iowa Caucus in January of 2008 before
the debate over the candidates begins.
(AP Photo/Dave Weaver)

Political Parties

QUESTIONS TO CONSIDER

What do political parties add to the American political system?

Should candidates be chosen by political parties?

Should there be more political parties in the United States?

CHAPTER CONTENTS

what if...

Parties Were Supported Solely By Public Funding?

BACKGROUND

Today's major political parties are supported by hundreds of millions of dollars offered by unions, corporations, other groups, and individuals. Not surprisingly, some Americans lament that the winning candidates are merely the "best that money can buy." For years, members of both political parties have been linked to lobbying and campaign contribution scandals, leading some critics to call for dramatic reforms. One of those reforms would be the public financing of political parties. Such public financing would, of course, come from taxpayers.

WHAT IF PARTIES WERE SUPPORTED SOLELY BY PUBLIC FUNDING?

If parties were supported solely by public funding, one question would immediately arise: What level of funding would be required? Both major political parties now spend many millions of dollars each year to educate the public, register voters, recruit candidates, and support election campaigns. If that amount were significantly reduced, the effectiveness of the political parties would also be reduced. Also, if the public were funding the national parties, there would almost certainly be prohibitions on contributions from corporations, individuals, and interest groups. This situation would be much different from the one that exists now because corporations and interest groups currently give to candidates whom they believe will support their interests. For example, labor unions give to Democratic political action committees and chambers of commerce are more likely to give to Republican political action committees (PACs), and chambers of commerce normally give to Republican PACs. The number of paid employees of the major political parties would also fall if these parties were publicly funded, although more people might volunteer.

THE EFFECT ON LOBBYISTS

Fourteen states now provide direct public financing to candidates. An additional 10 states provide minimal public financing to candidates or political parties, usually by collecting contributions to political parties from taxpayers through their state income tax returns. California, Indiana, and Ohio give some funds to the parties. The federal government currently provides a limited amount of public funding for presidential candidates and for the political parties' conventions.

All such public financing of candidates' campaigns carries with it restrictions on acceptable sources of other funds. If both the major parties and candidates for election were publicly financed, the role of lobbies and lobbyists would be changed. No longer would they be holding fundraising social events for candidates and parties. Instead, they would have to rely on their ability to inform or persuade legislators.

THE FLOW OF FUNDS AND POWER

The public financing of the major national parties could either strengthen or weaken their influence over candidates, voters, and campaigns. Contributors might channel their contributions to candidates and parties in those states that do not offer public financing.

In recent years, the United States has seen a rapid growth in nonparty political organizations that avoid regulation by not coordinating their activities with a party or campaign. If the political parties were limited to public funding, such nonparty groups would become vastly more important.

Candidates for the U.S. House and Senate would also increase their own fundraising if they could not depend on the national parties to do it for them. Already, most politicians have their own PACs, and those would multiply. Forcing candidates to be responsible for their own funding might make them more independent of their parties, weakening party cohesion. In the long run, this might also weaken the attachment of voters to their party identification, making it possible for them to consider a third party.

MORE POLITICAL PARTIES MIGHT BE POSSIBLE

Who is to say that public funding of political parties would be limited to only the two major parties? If we adopted the French system, for example, public funds would be available for numerous political parties. The only requirement would be a minimum number of party members. As you might imagine, the result in France has been the emergence of dozens of small political parties. After all, if public funds are available, someone will figure out a way to obtain them.

Even if minor parties became more important, however, the major political parties would still be the only serious players in this country. In our winner-take-all electoral system, few independent party candidates can win public office.

FOR CRITICAL ANALYSIS

1. If political parties were publicly funded, what would be the appropriate level of funding—more than the parties are spending today, the same, or less?
2. Would the United States actually consider funding third or fourth parties, and how would that impact the political system?

DURING NATIONAL ELECTION YEARS, whether congressional years such as 2006 or presidential years like 2004 and 2008, political parties become a much more important feature in the political landscape of the United States. For the first six months of 2008, the political party primary elections focused on choosing a nominee from among their respective candidates. Commentators noted the wide variety of election processes in the Democratic primaries. John McCain, the Republican nominee, earned his party's nod fairly early in the Republican process. For the voters, it became important to know when to vote and what restrictions there might be in voting in the primary: Some states allow voters to choose either primary, whereas others restrict voting to declared or registered party "members." In some states, **independent** voters could vote in the primaries, but not in other states.

Notice that in the previous paragraph, party "member" is placed in quotation marks. This is because Americans do not join a party, nor do they really become members. We did this because hardly anyone actually belongs to a political party in the sense of being a card-carrying member. To become a member of a political party, you do not have to pay dues, pass an examination, or swear an oath of allegiance. Furthermore, individuals and groups of individuals switch their allegiance from one party to another during critical elections. Therefore, at this point, we can ask an obvious question: If nothing is required to be a member of a political party, what, then, is a political party?

Independent
A voter or candidate who does not identify with a political party.

WHAT IS A POLITICAL PARTY?

A **political party** might be formally defined as a group of political activists who organize to win elections, operate the government, and determine public policy. This definition explains the difference between an interest group and a political party. Interest groups do not want to operate the government, and they do not put forth political candidates—even though they support candidates who will promote their interests if elected or reelected. Another important distinction is that interest groups tend to sharpen issues, whereas American political parties tend to blur their issue positions to attract voters.

Political parties differ from **factions**, which are smaller groups that are trying to obtain power or benefits.[1] Factions are subgroups within parties that may try

Political Party
A group of political activists who organize to win elections, operate the government, and determine public policy.

Faction
A group or bloc in a legislature or political party acting in pursuit of some special interest or position.

[1]See James Madison's comments on factions in Chapter 2.

IN SEPTEMBER 2009, Tea Party followers rallied in front of the U.S. Capitol for lower taxes and decreased government spending. The Tea Party is an independent movement which sometimes endorses Republican Party candidates and sometimes supports candidates who are challenging incumbent Republicans. Do you think that the Tea Party will become a permanent political party? (Image copyright Rena Schild 2010. Used under license from Shutterstock.com)

to capture a nomination or get a position adopted by the party. A key difference between factions and parties is that factions do not have a permanent organization, whereas political parties do. Factions generally preceded the formation of political parties in American history, and the term is still used to refer to groups within parties that follow a particular leader or share a regional identification or an ideological viewpoint. For example, the Republican Party is sometimes seen as having a Northeastern faction that holds more moderate positions than the dominant conservative majority of the party.

Political parties in the United States engage in a wide variety of activities, many of which are discussed in this chapter. Through these activities, parties perform several functions for the political system. These functions include the following:

1. *Recruiting candidates for public office.* Because it is the goal of parties to gain control of government, they must work to recruit candidates for all elective offices. Often, this means recruiting candidates to run against powerful incumbents. If parties did not search out and encourage political hopefuls, far more offices would be uncontested, and voters would have limited choices.
2. *Organizing and running elections.* Although elections are a government activity, political parties actually organize the voter-registration drives, recruit the volunteers to work at the polls, provide most of the campaign activity to stimulate interest in the election, and work to increase voter participation.
3. *Presenting alternative policies to the electorate.* In contrast to factions, which are often centered on individual politicians, parties are focused on a set of political positions. The Democrats or Republicans in Congress who vote together do so because they represent constituencies that have similar expectations and demands.
4. *Accepting responsibility for operating the government.* When a party elects the president or governor and members of the legislature, it accepts the responsibility for running the government. This includes staffing the executive branch with loyal party supporters and developing linkages among the elected officials to gain support for policies and their implementation.
5. *Acting as the organized opposition to the party in power.* The "out" party, or the one that does not control the government, is expected to articulate its own policies and oppose the winning party when appropriate. By organizing the opposition to the "in" party, the opposition party forces debate on the policy alternatives.

The major functions of American political parties are carried out by a small, relatively loose-knit nucleus of party activists. This arrangement is quite different from the more highly structured, mass-membership party organization typical of many

European parties. American parties concentrate on winning elections rather than on signing up large numbers of deeply committed, dues-paying members who believe passionately in the party's program.

A HISTORY OF POLITICAL PARTIES IN THE UNITED STATES

Although it is difficult to imagine a political system in the United States with four, five, six, or seven major political parties, other democratic systems have three-party, four-party, or even 10-party systems. In some European nations, parties are clearly tied to ideological positions; parties that represent Marxist, socialist, liberal, conservative, and ultraconservative positions appear on the political continuum. Some nations have political parties representing regions of the nation that have separate cultural identities, such as the French-speaking and Flemish-speaking regions of Belgium. Some parties are rooted in religious differences. Parties also exist that represent specific economic interests—agricultural, maritime, or industrial—and some, such as monarchist parties, speak for alternative political systems.

The United States has a **two-party system**, and that system has been around since about 1800. The function and character of the political parties, as well as the emergence of the two-party system, have much to do with the unique historical forces operating from this country's beginning as an independent nation. James Madison (1751–1836) linked the emergence of political parties to the form of government created by the Constitution.

Generally, we can divide the evolution of the nation's political parties into seven periods:

1. The creation of parties, from 1789 to 1816.
2. The era of one-party rule, or personal politics, from 1816 to 1828.
3. The period from Andrew Jackson's presidency to just before the Civil War, from 1828 to 1860.
4. The Civil War and post–Civil War period, from 1860 to 1896.
5. The Republican ascendancy and the progressive period, from 1896 to 1932.
6. The New Deal period, from 1932 to about 1968.
7. The modern period, from approximately 1968 to the present.

THE FORMATIVE YEARS: FEDERALISTS AND ANTI-FEDERALISTS

The first partisan political division in the United States occurred before the adoption of the Constitution. As you will recall from Chapter 2, the Federalists were those who pushed for adoption of the Constitution, whereas the Anti-Federalists were against ratification.

In September 1796, George Washington, who had served as president for almost two full terms, decided not to run again. In his farewell address, he made a somber assessment of the nation's future. Washington felt that the country might be destroyed by the "baneful [harmful] effects of the spirit of party." He viewed parties as a threat to both national unity and the concept of popular government. Early in his career, Thomas

DID YOU KNOW?

That the political party with the most seats in the House of Representatives chooses the Speaker of the House, makes any new rules it wants, gets a majority of the seats on each important committee and chooses committee chairs, and hires most of the congressional staff?

Two-Party System
A political system in which only two parties have a reasonable chance of winning.

THOMAS JEFFERSON, founder of the first Republican Party. His election to the presidency in 1800 was one of the world's first transfers of power through a free election. (Library of Congress, Prints & Photographs Division, Washington, D.C. [LC-USZ62-387])

Jefferson did not like political parties either. In 1789, he stated, "If I could not go to heaven but with a party, I would not go there at all."[2]

Nevertheless, in the years after the ratification of the Constitution, Americans realized that something more permanent than a faction would be necessary to identify candidates for office and represent political differences among the people. The result was two political parties. One party was the Federalists, which included John Adams, the second president (served 1797–1801). The Federalists represented commercial interests such as merchants and large planters. They supported a strong national government.

Thomas Jefferson led the other party, which came to be called the Republicans, or Jeffersonian Republicans. (These Republicans should not be confused with the later Republican Party of Abraham Lincoln. To avoid confusion, some scholars refer to Jefferson's party as the Democratic-Republicans, but this name was never used during the time that the party existed.) Jefferson's Republicans represented artisans and farmers. They strongly supported states' rights. In 1800, when Jefferson defeated Adams in the presidential contest, one of the world's first peaceful transfers of power from one party to another was achieved.

THE ERA OF GOOD FEELINGS

From 1800 to 1820, a majority of U.S. voters regularly elected Republicans to the presidency and to Congress. By 1816, the Federalist Party had virtually collapsed, and two-party competition did not really exist. Although during elections the Republicans opposed the Federalists' call for a stronger, more active central government, they undertook such active government policies as acquiring the Louisiana Territory and Florida and establishing a national bank. Because there was no real political opposition to the Republicans and thus little political debate, the administration of James Monroe (1817–1825) came to be known as the **era of good feelings**. Because political competition now took place among individual Republican aspirants, this period can also be called the *era of personal politics*.

Era of Good Feelings
The years from 1817 to 1825, when James Monroe was president and there was, in effect, no political opposition.

Democratic Party
One of the two major American political parties evolving out of the Republican Party of Thomas Jefferson.

Whig Party
A major party in the United States during the first half of the 19th century, formally established in 1836. The Whig Party was anti-Jackson and represented a variety of regional interests.

NATIONAL TWO-PARTY RULE: DEMOCRATS AND WHIGS

Organized two-party politics returned in 1824. With the election of John Quincy Adams as president, the Republican Party split into two entities. The followers of Adams called themselves National Republicans. The followers of Andrew Jackson, who defeated Adams in 1828, formed the **Democratic Party**. Later, the National Republicans took the name **Whig Party**, which had been a traditional name for British liberals. The Whigs stood for, among other things, federal spending on "internal improvements" such as roads. The Democrats opposed this policy. The Democrats, who were the stronger of the two parties, favored personal liberty and opportunity for

[2]Letter to Francis Hopkinson written from Paris while Jefferson was minister to France. In John P. Foley, ed., *The Jeffersonian Cyclopedia* (New York: Russell & Russell, 1967), p. 677.

the "common man." It was understood implicitly that the common man was a white man—hostility toward African Americans was an important force holding the disparate Democratic groups together.[3]

The Democrats' success was linked to their superior efforts to involve common citizens in the political process. Mass participation in politics and elections was a new phenomenon in the 1820s, as the political parties began to appeal to popular enthusiasm and themes. The parties adopted the techniques of mass campaigns, including rallies and parades. Lavishing food and drink on voters at polling places also became a common practice. Perhaps of greatest importance, however, was the push to cultivate party identity and loyalty. In large part, the spirit that motivated the new mass politics was democratic pride in participation. By making citizens feel that they were part of the political process, the parties hoped to win lasting party loyalty at the ballot box.

THE CIVIL WAR CRISIS

In the 1850s, hostility between the North and South over the issue of slavery divided both parties. The Whigs were the first party to split apart. The Whigs had been the party of an active federal government, but Southerners had come to believe that a strong central government might use its power to free their slaves. The Southern Whigs therefore ceased to exist as an organized party. The Northern Whigs united with antislavery Democrats and members of the radical antislavery Free Soil Party to form the modern **Republican Party**.

THE POST–CIVIL WAR PERIOD

After the Civil War, the Democratic Party was able to heal its divisions. Southern resentment of the Republicans' role in defeating the South and fears that the federal government would intervene on behalf of African Americans ensured that the Democrats would dominate the white South for the next century.

"Rum, Romanism, and Rebellion." Northern Democrats feared a strong government for other reasons. The Republicans thought that the government should promote business and economic growth, but many Republicans also wanted to use the power of government to impose evangelical Protestant moral values on society. Democrats opposed what they saw as culturally coercive measures. Many Republicans wanted to limit or even prohibit the sale of alcohol. They favored the establishment of public schools—with a Protestant curriculum. As a result, Catholics were strongly Democratic. In 1884, Protestant minister Samuel Burchard described the Democrats as the party of "rum, Romanism, and rebellion." This remark was offensive to Catholics, and Republican presidential candidate James Blaine later claimed that it cost him the White House. Offensive as it may have been, Burchard's characterization of the Democrats contained an element of truth.

The Triumph of the Republicans. In this period, the parties were evenly matched in strength. The abolition of the three-fifths rule, described in Chapter 2, meant that African Americans would be counted fully when allocating House seats and

Republican Party
One of the two major American political parties. It emerged in the 1850s as an antislavery party and consisted of former Northern Whigs and antislavery Democrats.

ANDREW JACKSON earned the name "Old Hickory" for his exploits during the War of 1812. In 1828, Jackson was elected president as the candidate of the new Democratic Party. He is shown here, shortly before his death in 1845, in a badly scratched daguerreotype produced by the studio of Mathew B. Brady. (© Bettmann/CORBIS)

[3]Edward Pessen, *Jacksonian America: Society, Personality, and Politics* (Homewood, IL: Dorsey Press, 1969). See especially pages 246–247. The small number of free blacks who could vote were overwhelmingly Whig.

electoral votes to the South. The Republicans therefore had to carry almost every Northern state to win, and this was not always possible. In the 1890s, however, the Republicans gained a decisive edge. In that decade, the populist movement emerged in the West and South to champion the interests of small farmers, who were often heavily in debt. Populists supported inflation, which benefited debtors by reducing the real value of outstanding debts. In 1896, when William Jennings Bryan became the Democratic candidate for president, the Democrats embraced populism.

As it turned out, the few western farmers who were drawn to the Democrats by this step were greatly outnumbered by urban working-class voters who believed that inflation would reduce the purchasing power of their paychecks and who therefore became Republicans. William McKinley, the Republican candidate, was elected with a solid majority of the votes. Figure 8–1 shows the states taken by Bryan and McKinley. The pattern of regional support shown in Figure 8–1 persisted for many years. From 1896 until 1932, the Republicans were successfully able to present themselves as the party that knew how to manage the economy.

THE PROGRESSIVE INTERLUDE

In the early 1900s, a spirit of political reform arose in both major parties. Called *progressivism*, this spirit was compounded by a fear of the growing power of great corporations and a belief that honest, impartial government could regulate the economy effectively. In 1912, the Republican Party temporarily split as former Republican president Theodore Roosevelt campaigned for the presidency on a third-party Progressive, or "Bull Moose," ticket. The Republican split permitted the election of Woodrow Wilson, the Democratic candidate, along with a Democratic Congress.

Like Roosevelt, Wilson considered himself a progressive, although he and Roosevelt did not agree on how progressivism ought to be implemented. Wilson's progressivism marked the beginning of a radical change in Democratic policies. Dating back to its foundation, the Democratic Party had been the party of limited government. Under Wilson, the Democrats became for the first time at least as receptive as the Republicans to government action in the economy. (Wilson's progressivism did not extend to race relations—for African Americans, the Wilson administration was something of a disaster.)

IN 1912, Theodore Roosevelt campaigned for the presidency on a third-party Progressive, or Bull Moose, ticket. Here, you see a charter membership certificate showing Roosevelt and his vice-presidential candidate, Hiram W. Johnson. What was the main result of Roosevelt's formation of this third party? (Bettmann/Corbis)

THE NEW DEAL ERA

The Republican ascendancy resumed after Wilson left office. It ended with the election of 1932, in the depths of the Great Depression. Republican Herbert Hoover was president when the Depression began in 1929. Although Hoover took some measures to fight the Depression, they fell far short of what the public demanded. Significantly, Hoover opposed federal relief for the unemployed and the destitute. In 1932, Democrat Franklin D. Roosevelt was elected president by an overwhelming margin.

The Great Depression shattered the working-class belief in Republican economic competence. Under Roosevelt, the Democrats began to make major interventions in the economy in an attempt to combat the Depression and to relieve the suffering of the unemployed. Roosevelt's New Deal relief programs were open to all citizens, both black and white. As a result, African Americans began to support the Democratic Party in large numbers—a development that would have stunned any American politician of the 1800s.

Roosevelt's political coalition was broad enough to establish the Democrats as the new majority party, in place of the Republicans. In the 1950s, Republican Dwight D. Eisenhower, the leading U.S. general during World War II, won two terms as president. Otherwise, with minor interruptions, the Democratic ascendancy lasted until 1968.

AN ERA OF DIVIDED GOVERNMENT

The New Deal coalition managed the unlikely feat of including both African Americans and whites who were hostile to African American advancement. This balancing act came to an end in the 1960s, a decade that was marked by the civil rights movement, by several years of race riots in major cities, and by increasingly heated protests against

FIGURE 8–1 The 1896 Presidential Election

In 1896, the agrarian, populist appeal of Democrat William Jennings Bryan (blue states) won Western states for the Democrats at the cost of losing more populous Eastern states to Republican William McKinley (red states). This pattern held until the election of Franklin Roosevelt in 1932.

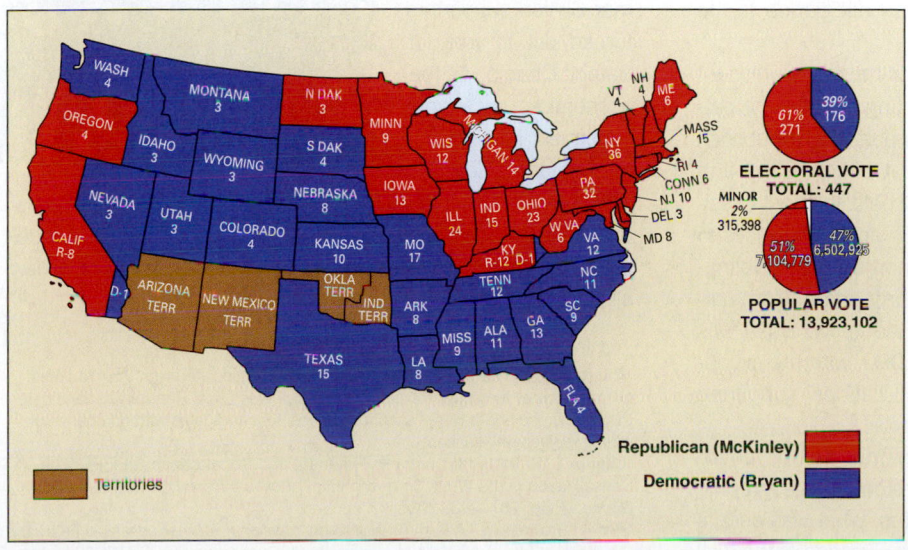

POLITICS WITH A purpose

Shifting Party Coalitions

Have you ever heard the expression "politics makes strange bedfellows"? If so, then a coalition of Protestant conservative white voters and northeastern liberal urban voters from religious and ethnic groups as diverse as Jews, Irish Catholics, and African Americans would surely fit the description. This is exactly the New Deal coalition on which Democratic Party victories were based, starting with President Franklin D. Roosevelt's win in 1932. The name, New Deal coalition, refers to those groups who were most helped by President Roosevelt's New Deal programs to address the problems created by the Great Depression. This coalition of disparate groups was a stable electoral force that elected five Democrats to the White House over the next 58 years (Presidents Roosevelt, Truman, Kennedy, Johnson, and Carter).

The electoral landscape for the political parties has changed a great deal from the early to middle 20th century. The Democratic Party, which had supported racial segregation in the South until the 1950s, advocated racial integration and other civil rights policies that drove white, Protestant conservative Southern voters who opposed these initiatives away. First Richard Nixon in 1972 and then Ronald Reagan in 1980 successfully drew these voters to the Republican Party. These voters were also drawn to the Republican Party's social conservatism and rejection of the cultural changes of the 1960s and 1970s. Often self-identifying as working class, these Reagan Democrats were attracted to President Reagan's policies. Motivated by traditional family values, anti-communism, and a strong national defense, by the 1990s they had largely switched their allegiance to the Republican Party.

The 1980 presidential election also saw the first significant gender gap; that is, men and women voting in different patterns, with women voters less likely to support the Republican candidate (see Politics with a Purpose: Opinion Gaps and Advocacy in Chapter 6). This trend has held in most presidential elections. Additionally, immigration and differences in birthrates have increased the Latino proportion of the voting-age population and decreased the white proportion. Both parties have targeted Latino voters. While George W. Bush was somewhat successful with this group in 2000, with the exception of conservative Cuban Americans, Latinos supported Democrats and Barack Obama in 2008.

In addition to racial, religious, and ethnic groups, these changing party coalitions can be understood in geographic terms. As the previous discussion indicates, what was once a solidly Democratic region of the country as a vestige of the Civil War,[a] the South, has become a bastion of Republican electoral wins since the late 1980s. The Northeast, which had been moderate and Republican, is now a Democratic stronghold, as is immigrant-rich California. Additionally, the Pacific Northwest began to trend Democratic.[b] This left the Midwest and Central/Mountain West as battleground regions, especially the more populous states such as Ohio, Missouri, and Michigan, which are crucial to a presidential victory.

What happened in the 2008 presidential election? Turnout increased across the country in the primaries as well as in the general election. This is especially true in the Democratic primaries and caucuses, where many voters who were previously turned off by the system found appeal in the historic candidacies of Senator Obama and Senator Clinton (the first viable African American and female presidential candidates, respectively). Voters participated in the Democratic primaries and caucuses in record numbers.

Who were these new Democratic voters? This is a group of younger voters (under 30 years old); some are more affluent (making over $100,000) and more liberal; and they consist of mainly women, African Americans, and Latinos.[c] While this constellation of voters was more likely to support Senator Obama in the Democratic primaries and caucuses, white men, older women, and so-called downscale voters (those in lower earning brackets) were more likely to support Senator Clinton. Indeed, Senator Hillary Clinton won the primary elections in Pennsylvania and Ohio on the strength of these voters. In the general election, almost all of the former Clinton supporters turned out to vote for Barack Obama. As the economic recession continued into 2010, the midterm elections saw some elements  of the Obama coalition including blue collar workers and independents vote Republican, thus making the creation of a new alliance less likely.

[a] The Republican Party, the party of Lincoln, was associated with the "Yankees" or Union forces long after the close of the Civil War. Local Republican candidates throughout the South were "sacrificial lambs" or candidates with no chance of wining the general election.

[b] Charles S. Bullock, III, Donna R. Hoffman, and Ronald Keith Gaddie, "The Consolidation of the White Southern Vote," *Political Research Quarterly,* Vol. 58, no. 2, pp. 231–243, 2005.

[c] Ronald Brownstein, "A Party Transformed," *National Journal,* accessed February 29, 2008, at http://nationaljournal.com/about/njweekly/stories/2008/0229nj1.htm.

the Vietnam War. For many economically liberal, socially conservative voters (especially in the South), social issues had become more important than economic ones, and these voters left the Democrats. These voters outnumbered the new voters who joined the Democrats—newly enfranchised African Americans and former liberal Republicans in New England and the upper Midwest.

The Parties in Balance. The result, since 1968, has been a nation almost evenly divided in politics. In presidential elections, the Republicans have had more success than the Democrats. Until 1994, Congress remained Democratic, but official party labels can be misleading. Some of the Democrats were Southern conservatives who normally voted with the Republicans on issues. As these conservative Democrats retired, they were largely replaced by Republicans.

In the 42 years between the elections of 1968 and 2010, there were only 12 years when one of the two major parties controlled the presidency, the House of Representatives, and the Senate. The Democrats controlled all three institutions during the presidency of Jimmy Carter (1977–1981) and during the first two years of the presidency of Bill Clinton (1993–2001). The Republicans controlled all three institutions during the third through sixth years of George W. Bush's presidency.[4] Before the 1992 elections, the electorate seemed to prefer, in most circumstances, to match a Republican president with a Democratic Congress. Under Bill Clinton, that state of affairs was reversed, with a Democratic president facing a Republican Congress. After the 2006 elections, a Republican president again faced a Democratic Congress. In 2008, Americans elected a Democrat, Barack Obama, as president, and gave the Democratic Party majorities in both houses of Congress.

Red State, Blue State. The pattern of a Republican Congress and a Democratic president would have continued after the election of 2000 if Democratic presidential candidate Al Gore had prevailed. Gore won the popular vote, but lost the electoral college by a narrow margin. Despite the closeness of the result, most states had voted in favor of either Bush or Gore by a fairly wide margin. To many observers, America had become divided between states that were solidly Republican or Democratic in their leanings, with a handful of "swing states." States that had shown strong support for a Republican candidate were deemed "red states" and so-called Democratic states were labeled "blue states."

Despite the presidential victory of Republican George W. Bush and the larger Republican margins of control in the House and Senate, the 2004 elections revealed a nation that continued to be closely divided between the two parties. Bush's 2004 victory may have been the result of cultural politics. In exit polls, more voters chose "moral values" as the most important election issue than the war in Iraq or the economy. While this result suggests the importance of cultural issues, the choice of moral issues was never offered to voters in prior elections. The fact that same-sex marriage referenda were on the ballot in many states may have increased the number of conservative voters who turned out and voted Republican.

In 2006, Democratic candidates for Congress seemed to have an edge in national politics. Several Republican members of Congress were forced to resign and face charges on corruption issues, while several others were involved in sex scandals. The Democratic Party mounted a national campaign and won back control of both houses of Congress.

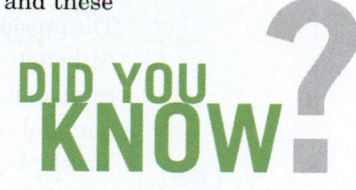

DID YOU KNOW?

That the Democrats and Republicans each had exactly one woman delegate at their conventions in 1900?

---

[4]The Republicans also were in control of all three institutions for the first four months after Bush's inauguration. This initial period of control came to an end when Senator James Jeffords of Vermont left the Republican Party, giving the Democrats control of the Senate.

PARTISAN TRENDS IN THE 2008 ELECTIONS

The presidential election year 2008 might be called a "perfect storm" for the Republicans. Although they were able to choose their nominee early, giving him plenty of time to campaign, Senator John McCain lost the 2008 election by six percentage points in the national popular vote. Not only did Senator Barack Obama win by a decisive margin, but the Democratic Party increased its majorities in both the House of Representatives and the Senate, giving the party control over both branches of government. As John McCain and the Republicans struggled to gain votes in an atmosphere dominated by an unpopular president, an unpopular war in Iraq and, by fall, a crisis in the financial markets, Barack Obama and the Democrats offered new policies and hope to the voters.

With an enormous effort to register new voters and get them to the polls, Democrats made inroads with many groups of voters who had supported Republicans in the past. African American voters increased their turnout by more than 10 percent, and 95 percent of their votes went to the Democratic ticket. Latino voters and Asian voters gave about two-thirds of their votes to the Democratic ticket. And, going against some predictions, the Democratic ticket polled strongly in white, rural areas of the Midwest.

The 2010 midterm elections for Congress saw many Obama supporters either stay home or vote Republican. Fueled by the economic recession, voters turned to Republican candidates for Congress and the state houses for new leadership. The trend was most pronounced in the Midwest where a number of Republican governors were elected, and two Democratic Senators were replaced by Republicans.

FIGURE 8–2 The Presidential Elections of 2008

In the 2008 presidential elections, Democrat Barack Obama received a majority of the electoral college votes, outdoing Republican John McCain by a large margin. Although Obama won nine more states than Democrat John Kerry had won in the 2004 presidential elections, the regional political preferences remained similar to those of previous elections.

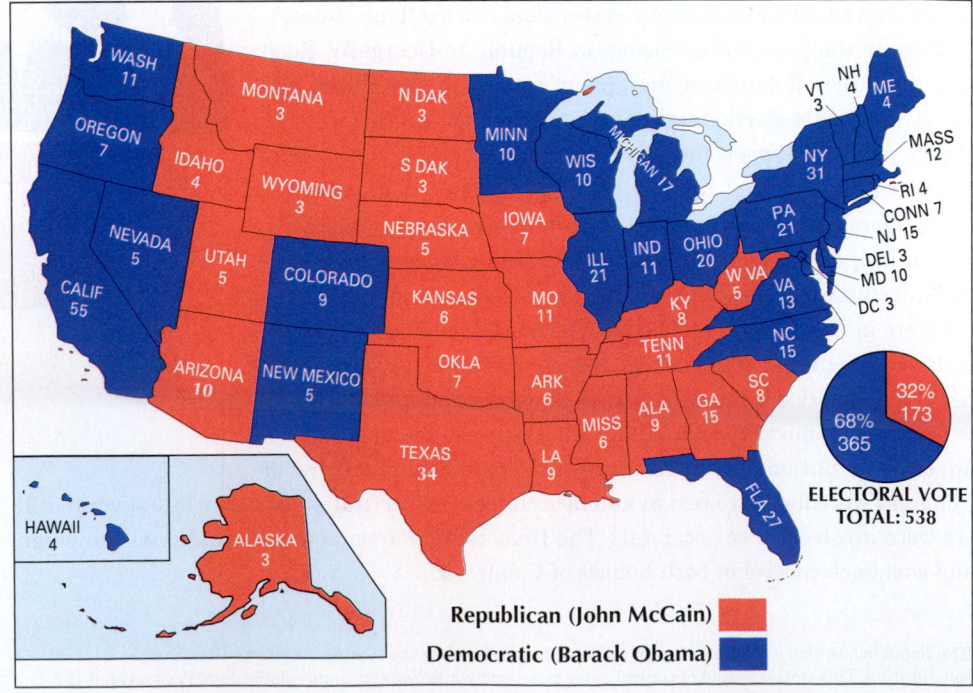

THE TWO MAJOR U.S. PARTIES TODAY

It is sometimes said that the major American political parties are like Tweedledee and Tweedledum, the twins in Lewis Carroll's *Through the Looking-Glass*. Labels such as "Repubocrats" are especially popular among supporters of third parties, such as the Green Party and the Libertarian Party. Third-party advocates, of course, have an interest in claiming that there is no difference between the two major parties—their chances of gaining support are much greater if the major parties are seen as indistinguishable. Despite such allegations, the major parties do have substantial differences, both in their policies and in their constituents.

THE PARTIES' CORE CONSTITUENTS

You learned in Chapter 6 how demographic factors affect support for the two parties. Democrats receive disproportionate support not only from the least well-educated voters but also from individuals with advanced degrees. Upper-income voters are generally more Republican than lower-income voters; businesspersons are much more likely to vote Republican than are labor union members. The Jewish electorate is heavily Democratic; white evangelical Christians who are regular churchgoers tend to be Republicans. Latinos are strongly Democratic; African Americans are overwhelmingly so. Women are somewhat more Democratic than men. City dwellers tend to be Democrats; rural people tend to be Republicans. In presidential elections, the South, the Rocky Mountain states, and the Great Plains states typically vote Republican; the West Coast and the Northeast are more likely to favor the Democrats. These tendencies represent the influences of economic interests and cultural values, which often conflict with each other.

ECONOMIC BELIEFS

A coalition of the labor movement and various racial and ethnic minorities has been the core of Democratic Party support since the presidency of Franklin D. Roosevelt. The social programs and increased government intervention in the economy that made up Roosevelt's New Deal were intended to ease the pressure of economic hard times on these groups. This goal remains important for many Democrats today. In general, Democratic identifiers are more likely to approve of social-welfare spending, to support government regulation of business, to endorse measures to improve the situation of minorities, and to support assisting older adults with their medical expenses. Republicans are more supportive of the private marketplace and believe more strongly in an ethic of self-reliance and limited government.

A poll taken in 2008 revealed that Democrats were closely associated with improving the environment, education, energy problems, and health care, while Republicans were seen as likely to do well on stopping terrorism. As Figure 8–3 demonstrates, the tide of public opinion shifted during the first two years of the Obama administration. Results from a 2010 poll on the strengths of the parties show that Republicans were seen to be strong in solving the budget deficit and defending against terrorism and were tied with Democrats in dealing with economic problems. Belief in the Democratic Party's ability to deal with education, health care, and the economy had dropped by 10 points from 2008.

Economic Directions. In his 1996 State of the Union address, Democratic president Bill Clinton announced that "the era of big government is over." One might conclude from this that both parties now favor limited government. However, up until 2010, it appeared that both parties were in favor of "big government." Deficits increased under both Ronald Reagan and George W. Bush (Republicans), and fell at the end of Bill Clinton's (a Democrat's) presidency. Clinton, despite the protectionist beliefs of many Democrats in Congress, was in practice more supportive of free trade.[5] Despite these facts, Clinton was not really a supporter of limited government. If his 1993 plan for universal health insurance had been accepted by Congress, the size and cost of the federal government would have increased considerably. In 2008 the Republican candidate, John McCain, adopted a pro-business, lower-taxes platform although most Republicans in Congress had voted for the deficits of the Bush years. Barack Obama campaigned on a platform of social change, which he then began to enact in 2009 and 2010. While the Obama campaign promised no new taxes on America's middle class, the government's efforts to limit the economic damage of the recession caused the deficit to skyrocket, once more bringing taxing and spending policies to the forefront of politics in 2010.

The 2010 midterm elections returned Republicans to control of the House of Representatives with an historic gain of more than 60 seats. Exit polling data showed that the economy was the most important factor in voter decisions along with a desire to curb deficit spending. The Tea Party clearly played a role in shaping the issues with its focus on smaller government and lower taxes although it was unclear how the new Republican majority could achieve these goals.

FIGURE 8–3 Republican Issues and Democratic Issues

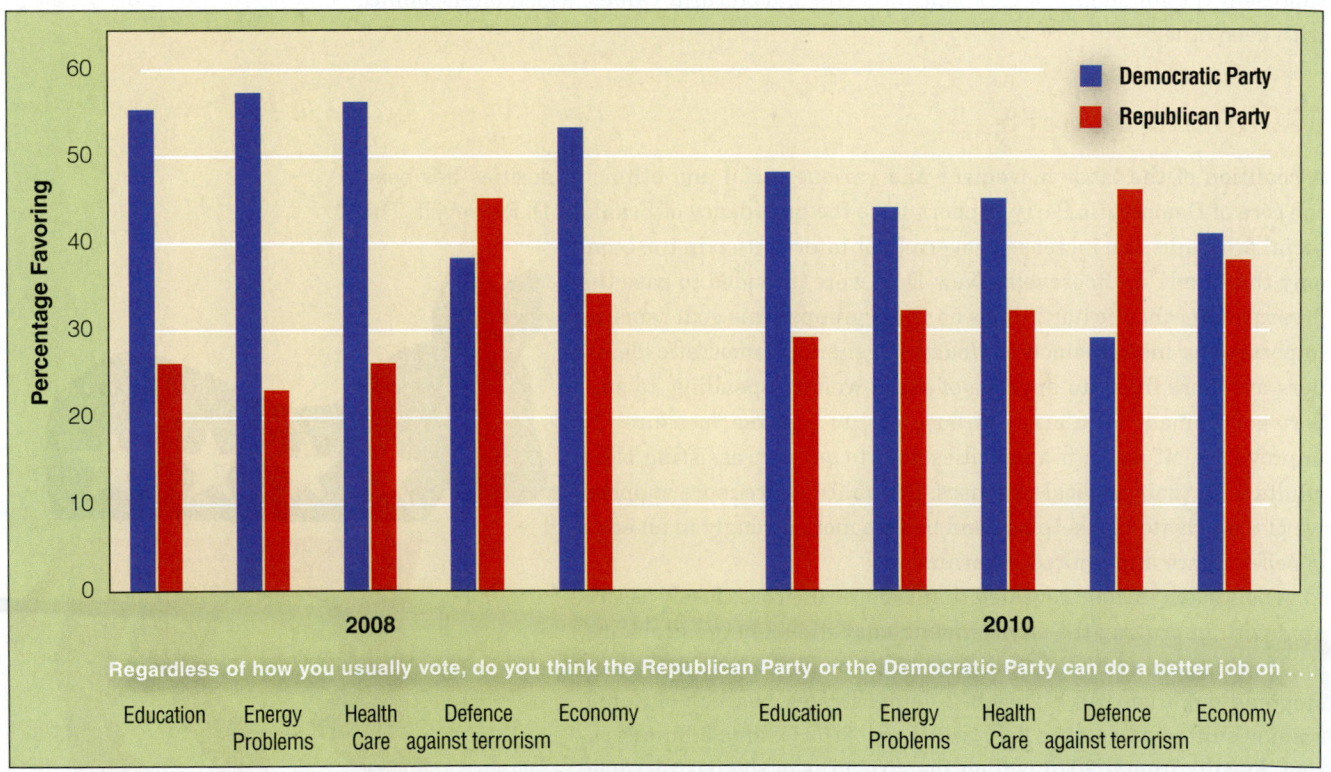

Source: "Obama's Ratings Are Flat, Wall Street's Are Abysmal: Midterm Election Challenges for Both Parties," February 12, 2010, the Pew Research Center For the People & the Press, a project of the Pew Research Center.

[5]Jeffrey Frankel, "Republican and Democratic Presidents Have Switched Economic Policies," *Milken Institute Review*, Vol. 5, No. 1, First Quarter 2003, pp. 18–25.

CULTURAL POLITICS

In recent years, cultural values may have become more important than they previously were in defining the beliefs of the two major parties. For example, in 1987, Democrats were almost as likely to favor stricter abortion laws (40 percent) as Republicans were (48 percent). Today, Republicans are twice as likely to favor stricter abortion laws (50 percent to 25 percent).

Cultural Politics and Socioeconomic Status. Thomas Frank, a writer, noticed the following bumper sticker at a gun show in Kansas City: "A working person voting for the Democrats is like a chicken voting for Colonel Sanders." (Colonel Sanders is the iconic founder of Kentucky Fried Chicken, the chain of fried chicken restaurants.) In light of the economic traditions of the two parties, this seems to be an odd statement. In fact, the sticker is an exact reversal of an earlier one directed against the Republicans.

You can make sense of such a sentiment by remembering what you learned in Chapter 6—although economic conservatism is associated with higher incomes, social conservatism is relatively more common among lower-income groups. The individual who displayed the bumper sticker, therefore, was in effect claiming that cultural concerns—in this example, presumably the right to own handguns—are far more important than economic ones. Frank argues that despite Republican control of the national government during the George W. Bush administration, cultural conservatives continued to view themselves as embattled "ordinary Americans" under threat from a liberal, cosmopolitan elite.[6]

Also, according to Republican commentator Karl Zinsmeister, many police officers, construction workers, military veterans, and rural residents began moving toward the Republican Party in the 1960s and 1970s. In contrast, many of America's rich and superrich elite, including financiers, media barons, software millionaires, and entertainers, started slowly, but surely, drifting toward the Democratic Party. Arguably, the major financial backing for Democrats is from the rich and superrich. In contrast, for the Republicans in the last two presidential elections, less than 10 percent of voters in pro-Bush counties earned more than $100,000 per year. All that can be said today is that it is difficult to stereotype what socioeconomic groups support which party.

DID YOU KNOW?

That it took 103 ballots for John W. Davis to be nominated at the Democratic National Convention in 1924?

The Regional Factor in Cultural Politics. Conventionally, some parts of the country are viewed as culturally liberal and others as culturally conservative. On a regional basis, cultural liberalism (as opposed to economic liberalism) may be associated with economic dynamism. The San Francisco Bay Area can serve as an example. The greater Bay Area contains Silicon Valley, the heart of the microcomputer industry; it has the highest per capita personal income of any metropolitan area in America. It also is one of the most liberal regions of the country. San Francisco liberalism is largely cultural—one sign of this liberalism is that the city has a claim to be the "capital" of gay America. There is not much evidence, however, that the region's wealthy citizens are in favor of higher taxes.

To further illustrate this point, we can compare the political preferences of relatively wealthy states with relatively poor ones. Of the 10 states with the highest per capita personal incomes in 2004, eight voted for Democrat John Kerry in the presidential election of that year. Of the 25 states with the lowest per capita incomes in 2004, 23 voted for Republican George W. Bush.

Given these data, it seems difficult to believe that upper-income voters really are more Republican than lower-income ones. Within any given state or region, however,

---

[6]Thomas Frank, *What's the Matter with Kansas?* (New York: Macmillan, 2004).

Reverse-Income Effect
A tendency for wealthier states or
regions to favor the Democrats and for
less wealthy states or regions to favor
the Republicans. The effect appears
paradoxical because it reverses traditional
patterns of support.

upscale voters are more likely to be Republican regardless of whether the area as a
whole leans Democratic or Republican. States that vote Democratic are often Northern
states that contain large cities. At least part of this **reverse-income effect** may simply
be that urban areas are more prosperous, culturally liberal, and Democratic than the
countryside, and that the North is more prosperous, culturally liberal, and Democratic
than the South.

THE 2008 ELECTIONS: ECONOMICS AND NATIONAL SECURITY

Senator Barack Obama and many of the other contenders for the Democratic presidential nomination expressed their opposition to the war in Iraq as well as many other
Bush administration foreign policy initiatives long before the primary season began.
Indeed, most Democrats doubted that the military surge in Iraq could be effective.
National security concerns were still very much on voters' minds in the early period of
the primaries as Obama and Senator Hillary Clinton battled for the nomination. After
the nomination was clinched in June, national security questions faded in importance.
Fewer incidents of violence occurred in Iraq, and the surge seemed to have worked. No
terrorist attacks on Americans took place.

Throughout the summer, it seemed clear that the American economy was slowing
down, and talk of recession entered the campaigns. As shown in Figure 8–3, voters
already believed that Democrats were better able to handle unemployment and the
economy than were Republicans. In the general election campaign, the presidential candidates and their respective parties staked out classic positions: Democrats espoused
tax cuts for the poor and the middle class and tax increases on the wealthiest Americans.
John McCain articulated the Republican view that tax cuts for all levels of income
would be a better way to stimulate a sagging economy. As the banking crisis deepened,
a majority of voters blamed it on the Republicans and trusted the Democratic Party to
bring the country out of recession.

THE THREE FACES OF A PARTY

Although American parties are known by a single name and, in the public mind, have a common historical identity, each party really has three major components. The first component is the **party-in-the-electorate**. This phrase refers to all those individuals who claim an attachment to the political party. They need not participate in election campaigns. Rather, the party-in-the-electorate is the large number of Americans who feel some loyalty to the party or who use partisanship as a cue to decide who will earn their vote. Party membership is not really a rational choice; rather, it is an emotional tie somewhat analogous to identifying with a region or a baseball team. Although individuals may hold a deep loyalty to or identification with a political party, there is no need for members of the party-in-the-electorate to speak out publicly, to contribute to campaigns, or to vote all Republican or all Democratic. Needless to say, the party leaders pay close attention to the affiliation of their members in the electorate.

The second component, the **party organization**, provides the structural framework for the political party by recruiting volunteers to become party leaders; identifying potential candidates; and organizing caucuses, conventions, and election campaigns for its candidates, as will be discussed in more detail shortly. The party organization and its active workers keep the party functioning between elections, as well as make sure that the party puts forth electable candidates and clear positions in the elections. If the party-in-the-electorate declines in numbers and loyalty, the party organization must try to find a strategy to rebuild the grassroots following.

The **party-in-government** is the third component of American political parties. The party-in-government consists of those elected and appointed officials who identify with a political party. Generally, elected officials do not also hold official party positions within the formal organization, although they often have the informal power to appoint party executives.

PARTY ORGANIZATION

Each of the American political parties is often seen as having a pyramid-shaped organization, with the national chairperson and committee at the top and the local precinct chairperson on the bottom. This structure, however, does not accurately reflect the relative power of the individual components of the party organization. If it did, the national chairperson of the Democratic Party or the Republican Party, along with the national committee, could simply dictate how the organization was to be run, just as if it were the ExxonMobil Corporation or Ford Motor Company. In reality, the political parties have a confederal structure, in which each unit has significant autonomy and is linked only loosely to the other units. The fact that these are not powerful national organizations can be seen in the uneven strength of local and state party organizations. In some states, parties receive significant contributions from individuals and interest groups for their operations, whereas in other states and localities political parties are very weak organizations with very little funding. This is particularly true of the minority party in a state or district where it has little chance to win a seat.

THE NATIONAL PARTY ORGANIZATION

Each party has a national organization, the most clearly institutional part of which is the **national convention**, held every four years. The convention is used to nominate the presidential and vice presidential candidates. In addition, the **party platform** is developed at the national convention. The platform sets forth the party's position on the issues and makes promises to initiate certain policies if the party wins the presidency.

Party-in-the-Electorate
Those members of the general public who identify with a political party or who express a preference for one party over another.

Party Organization
The formal structure and leadership of a political party, including election committees; local, state, and national executives; and paid professional staff.

Party-in-Government
All of the elected and appointed officials who identify with a political party.

National Convention
The meeting held every four years by each major party to select presidential and vice presidential candidates, to write a platform, to choose a national committee, and to conduct party business.

Party Platform
A document drawn up at each national convention outlining the policies, positions, and principles of the party.

After the convention, the platform frequently is neglected or ignored by party candidates who disagree with it. Because candidates are trying to win votes from a wide spectrum of voters, it is counterproductive to emphasize the fairly narrow and sometimes controversial goals set forth in the platform. Political scientist Gerald M. Pomper discovered decades ago, however, that once elected, the parties do try to carry out platform promises, and that roughly three-fourths of the promises eventually become law.[7] Of course, some general goals, such as economic prosperity, are included in the platforms of both parties.

Convention Delegates. The party convention provides the most striking illustration of the difference between the ordinary members of a party, or party identifiers, and party activists. As a series of studies by the *New York Times* shows, delegates to the national party conventions are quite different from ordinary party identifiers. Delegates to the Democratic National Convention, as shown in Figure 8–4, are far more liberal than ordinary Democratic voters. Typically, delegates to the Republican National Convention are far more conservative than ordinary Republicans. Why does this happen? In part, it is because a person, to become a delegate, must gather votes in a primary election from party members who care enough to vote in a primary or be appointed by party leaders. Also, the primaries generally pit presidential candidates against each other on intraparty issues. Competition within each party tends to pull candidates away from the center, and delegates even more so. Often, the most important activity for the convention is making peace among the delegates who support different candidates and persuading them to accept a party platform that will appeal to the general electorate.

FIREWORKS ERUPT at the end of Senator Barack Obama's acceptance speech at the 2008 Democratic National Convention. The first African American presidential nominee gave a stirring speech in Denver's football stadium. (REUTERS/Jim Young/Landov)

GOVERNOR SARAH PALIN, the vice-presidential nominee for the Republican Party, roused the delegates with her acceptance speech at the Republican National Convention. (Ethan Miller/Getty Images)

[7]Gerald M. Pomper and Susan S. Lederman, *Elections in America: Control and Influence in Democratic Politics,* 2nd ed. (New York: Longman, 1980).

The National Committee. At the national convention, each of the parties formally chooses a national standing committee, elected by the individual state parties. This **national committee** directs and coordinates party activities during the following four years. The Democrats include at least two members (a man and a woman) from each state, from the District of Columbia, and from the several territories. Governors, members

National Committee
A standing committee of a national political party established to direct and coordinate party activities between national party conventions.

FIGURE 8–4 Convention Delegates and Voters: How Did They Compare on the Issues in 2008?

At the time of the national party conventions, the *New York Times* surveys a sample of each convention's delegates, a sample of party voters, and compares their views to those of the average voter. The figure below shows that Republican convention delegates tend to be more conservative than their voters and that Democratic delegates are more liberal than their voters.

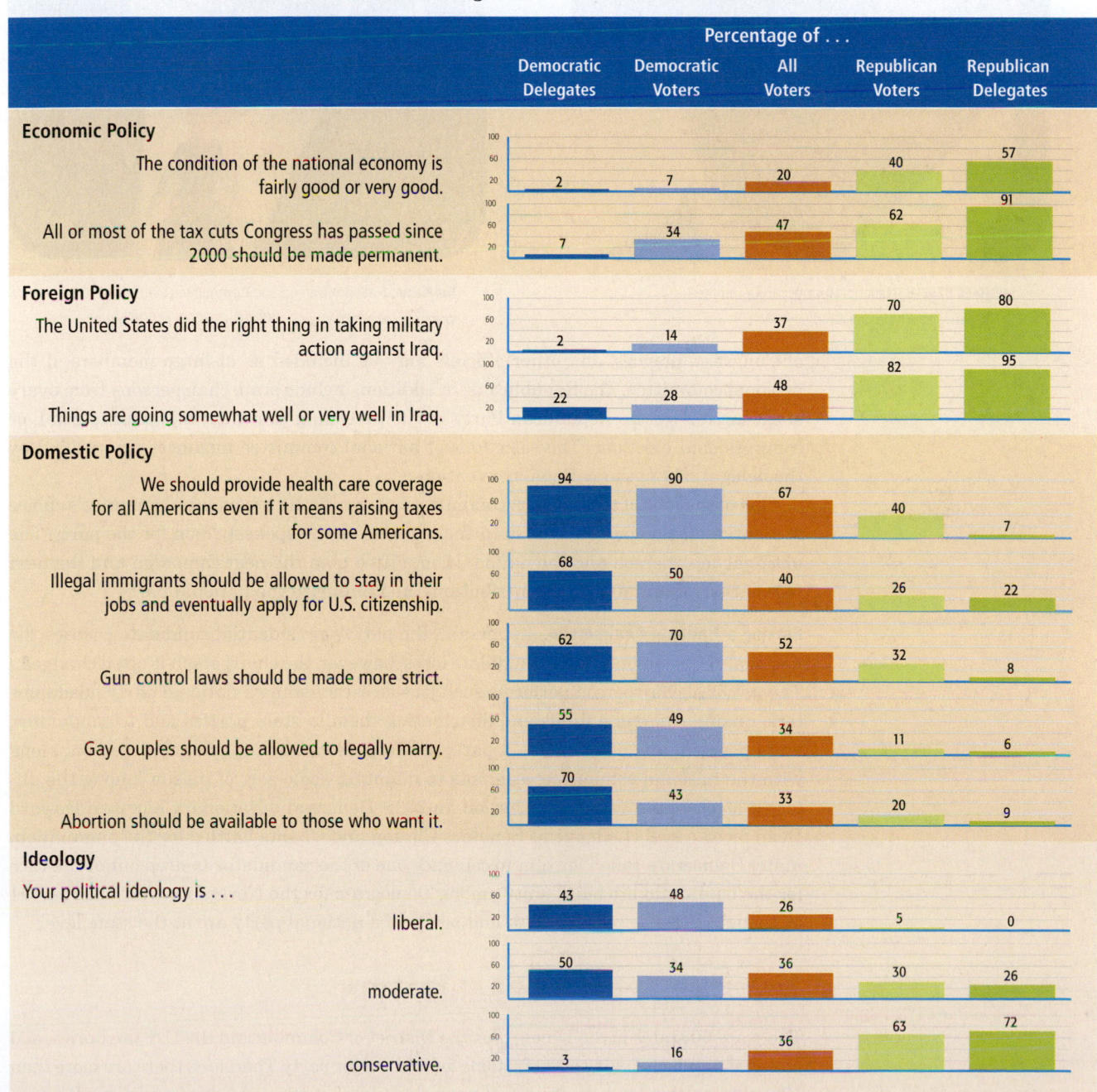

	Percentage of . . .				
	Democratic Delegates	Democratic Voters	All Voters	Republican Voters	Republican Delegates
Economic Policy					
The condition of the national economy is fairly good or very good.	2	7	20	40	57
All or most of the tax cuts Congress has passed since 2000 should be made permanent.	7	34	47	62	91
Foreign Policy					
The United States did the right thing in taking military action against Iraq.	2	14	37	70	80
Things are going somewhat well or very well in Iraq.	22	28	48	82	95
Domestic Policy					
We should provide health care coverage for all Americans even if it means raising taxes for some Americans.	94	90	67	40	7
Illegal immigrants should be allowed to stay in their jobs and eventually apply for U.S. citizenship.	68	50	40	26	22
Gun control laws should be made more strict.	62	70	52	32	8
Gay couples should be allowed to legally marry.	55	49	34	11	6
Abortion should be available to those who want it.	70	43	33	20	9
Ideology					
Your political ideology is . . . liberal.	43	48	26	5	0
moderate.	50	34	36	30	26
conservative.	3	16	36	63	72

Source: *The New York Times.*

MICHAEL STEELE, National Republican Committee Chairman. (AP Photo/Jeff Chiu)

Tim Kaine, National Democratic Committee Chairman and former governor of Virginia (KEVIN DIETSCH/UPI/Landov)

of Congress, mayors, and other officials may be included as at-large members of the national committee. The Republicans, in addition, include state chairpersons from every state carried by the Republican Party in the preceding presidential, gubernatorial, or congressional elections. The selections of national committee members are ratified by the delegations to the national convention.

One of the jobs of the national committee is to ratify the presidential nominee's choice of a national chairperson, who (in principle) acts as the spokesperson for the party. The national chairperson and the national committee plan the next campaign and the next convention, obtain financial contributions, and publicize the national party.

Picking a National Chairperson. In general, the party's presidential candidate chooses the national chairperson. (If that candidate loses, however, the chairperson is often changed.) The national chairperson performs such jobs as establishing a national party headquarters, raising campaign funds and distributing them to state parties and to candidates, and appearing in the media as a party spokesperson. The national chairperson, along with the national committee, attempts to maintain some sort of liaison among the different levels of the party organization. In 2008, Democratic National Chairman Howard Dean faced a real challenge as Senators Clinton and Obama battled for the nomination. Many Democrats called for him to convince one of the candidates to drop out of the race for the nomination to build unity among Democrats for the November election. The fact is, though, that the real strength and power of a national party are at the state level.

THE STATE PARTY ORGANIZATION

There are 50 states in the Union, plus the District of Columbia and the U.S. territories, and an equal number of party organizations for each major party. Therefore, there are more than 100 state parties (and even more, if we include local parties and minor parties). Because every state party is unique, it is impossible to describe what an "average" state political party is like. Nonetheless, state parties have several organizational features in common.

Each state party has a chairperson, a committee, and local organizations. In theory, the role of the **state central committee**—the principal organized structure of each political party within each state—is similar in the various states. The committee, usually composed of members who represent congressional districts, state legislative districts, or counties, has responsibility for carrying out the policy decisions of the party's state convention. In some states, the state committee can issue directives to the state chairperson.

Also, like the national committee, the state central committee controls the use of party campaign funds during political campaigns. Usually, the state central committee has little, if any, influence on party candidates once they are elected. In fact, state parties are fundamentally loose alliances of local interests and coalitions of often bitterly opposed factions.

State parties are also important in national politics because of the **unit rule**, which awards electoral votes in presidential elections as an indivisible bloc (except in Maine and Nebraska). Presidential candidates concentrate their efforts in states in which voter preferences seem to be evenly divided or in which large numbers of electoral votes are at stake.

> **State Central Committee**
> The principal organized structure of each political party within each state. This committee is responsible for carrying out policy decisions of the party's state convention.

> **Unit Rule**
> A rule by which all of a state's electoral votes are cast for the presidential candidate receiving a plurality of the popular vote in that state.

LOCAL PARTY MACHINERY: THE GRASSROOTS

The lowest layer of party machinery is the local organization, supported by district leaders, precinct or ward captains, and party workers. Much of the work is coordinated by county committees and their chairpersons.

Patronage and City Machines. In the 1800s, the institution of **patronage**—rewarding the party faithful with government jobs or contracts—held the local organization together. For immigrants and the poor, the political machine often furnished important services and protections. The big-city machine was the archetypal example. Tammany Hall, or the Tammany Society, which dominated New York City government for nearly two centuries, was perhaps the most notorious example of this political form.

The last big-city local political machine to exercise substantial power was run by Chicago's Mayor Richard J. Daley, who was also an important figure in national Democratic politics. Daley, as mayor, ran the Chicago Democratic machine from 1955 until his death in 1976. The current mayor of Chicago, Richard M. Daley, son of the former mayor, does not have the kind of machine that his father had.

City machines are now dead, mostly because their function of providing social services (and reaping the reward of votes) has been taken over by state and national

> **Patronage**
> Rewarding faithful party workers and followers with government employment and contracts.

VOLUNTEERS CHECK their lists as they register voters in South Dade County, Florida. Civil rights organizations trained the volunteers to register voters in hopes of avoiding the chaos of the 2000 elections. (Orjan F. Ellingvag/CORBIS)

agencies. This trend began in the 1930s, when the social legislation of the New Deal established Social Security and unemployment insurance. The local party machine has little, if anything, to do with deciding who is eligible to receive these benefits.

Local Party Organizations Today. Local political organizations—whether located in cities, in townships, or at the county level—still can contribute a great deal to local election campaigns. These organizations are able to provide the foot soldiers of politics—individuals who pass out literature and get out the vote on election day, which can be crucial in local elections. In many regions, local Democratic and Republican organizations still exercise some patronage, such as awarding courthouse jobs, contracts for street repair, and other lucrative construction contracts. The constitutionality of awarding (or not awarding) contracts on the basis of political affiliation has been subject to challenge, however. The United States Supreme Court has ruled that firing or failing to hire individuals because of their political affiliation is an infringement of the employees' First Amendment rights to free expression.[8] Local party organizations are also the most important vehicles for recruiting young adults into political work, because political involvement at the local level offers activists many opportunities to gain experience.

THE PARTY-IN-GOVERNMENT

After the election is over and the winners are announced, the focus of party activity shifts from getting out the vote to organizing and controlling the government. As you will learn in Chapter 12, party membership plays an important role in the day-to-day operations of Congress, with partisanship determining everything from office space to committee assignments and power on Capitol Hill. For the president, the political party furnishes the pool of qualified applicants for political appointments to run the government. (Although it is uncommon to do so, presidents can and occasionally do appoint executive personnel, such as Cabinet members, from the opposition party.) As we will note in Chapter 13, there are not as many of these appointed positions as presidents might like, and presidential power is limited by the permanent bureaucracy. Judicial appointments also offer a great opportunity to the winning party. For the most part, presidents are likely to appoint federal judges from their own party.

Divided Government. All of these party appointments suggest that the winning political party, whether at the national, state, or local level, has a great deal of control in the American system. Because of the checks and balances and the relative lack of cohesion in American parties, however, such control is an illusion. One reason is that for some time, many Americans have seemed to prefer a **divided government**, with the executive and legislative branches controlled by different parties. The trend toward **ticket splitting**—splitting votes between the president and members of Congress—has increased sharply since 1952. This practice may indicate a lack of trust in government (as discussed in Chapter 6) or the relative weakness of party identification among many voters. Voters have often seemed comfortable with having a president affiliated with one party and a Congress controlled by the other.

The Limits of Party Unity. There are other ways in which the power of the parties is limited. Consider how major laws are passed in Congress. Traditionally, legislation has rarely been passed by a vote strictly along party lines. Although most Democrats may oppose a bill, for example, some Democrats may vote for it. Their votes, combined with the votes of Republicans, may be enough to pass the bill. Similarly, support from some Republicans may

DID YOU KNOW?

That it takes about 700,000 signatures to qualify to be on the ballot as a presidential candidate in all 50 states?

Divided Government
A situation in which one major political party controls the presidency and the other controls the chambers of Congress, or in which one party controls a state governorship and the other controls the state legislature.

Ticket Splitting
Voting for candidates of two or more parties for different offices. For example, a voter splits her ticket if she votes for a Republican presidential candidate and a Democratic congressional candidate.

[8]*Rutan v. Republican Party of Illinois*, 497 U.S. 62 (1990).

enable a bill sponsored by the Democrats to pass. This is not to say that Congress *never* votes along strict party lines. A notable example of such partisan voting occurred in the House of Representatives in 1998. The issue at hand was whether to impeach President Bill Clinton. Almost all votes were strictly along party lines—Democrats against, and Republicans for. In 2009 and 2010, partisan voting was again in vogue in the House of Representatives. Speaker Nancy Pelosi won a number of votes on Obama initiatives including health care and an energy bill with almost all Democrats voting in favor and all Republicans opposed.

One reason that the political parties find it so hard to rally all of their members in Congress to vote along party lines is that parties have almost no control over who runs for office. In other words, the head of a political party in most instances cannot handpick candidates who share his or her views and who will be loyal to the party's views. In the United States, modern elections are "candidate centered," meaning that candidates choose to run, raise their own funds, build their own organizations, and win elections largely on their own, without significant help from a political party. This means, though, that the parties have very little control over the candidates who run under the party labels. In fact, a candidate could run as a Republican, for example, and advocate beliefs that are repugnant to the national party, such as that the United States should have a socialized health care system. No one in the Republican Party organization could stop this person from being nominated or even elected, although the likelihood that he or she would attract votes from Republican voters is very slim.

Party Polarization. Despite the forces that act against party-line voting, there have been times when the two parties in Congress have been polarized, and defections from the party line have been rare. One such period was the mid-1990s, after the Republicans gained control of both the House and the Senate. Under House Speaker Newt Gingrich, the Republicans maintained strict discipline in an attempt to use their new majority to sponsor a specific legislative agenda. In 2003, polarization peaked again. "People genuinely hate each other," lamented Louisiana Senator John Breaux, a moderate Democrat.[9]

One cause of polarization is ability of the parties to create House districts that are **safe seats**. The creation of districts will be discussed further in Chapter 12. It is also true that the two parties are each more cohesive today than in many years. That means, for example, that the Republican Party leadership, many of its contributors, and its officeholders share beliefs about government and, to some extent, cultural values. Those beliefs are more conservative than those of the grassroots voter. Democratic leaders and politicians share more liberal views than those of the grassroots voter. This makes it easier for congresspeople and senators to vote together and support a common partisan position. With both parties becoming more cohesive, the debate over policies becomes more polarized and divisive.

Safe Seat
A district that returns the legislator with 55 percent of the vote or more.

Writers and advocates in the media, who find that stridency sells, also tend to encourage an atmosphere of polarization. Some commentators, however, do not believe that this spirit of polarization extends very far into the general electorate. They contend that a majority of Americans are strongly committed to tolerance of opposing political views. Supporting this view is Morris Fiorina, who argues that the American people are no more divided over their policy preferences than they have ever been.[10]

[9]Jackie Calmes, "Set This House on Fire," *The Wall Street Journal Europe*, December 1, 2003, p. A7.
[10]Morris Fiorina, *Culture War? The Myth of a Polarized America* (New York: Longman, 2005).

WHY HAS THE TWO-PARTY SYSTEM ENDURED?

There are several reasons why two major parties have dominated the political landscape in the United States for almost two centuries. These reasons have to do with (1) the historical foundations of the system, (2) political socialization and practical considerations, (3) the winner-take-all electoral system, and (4) state and federal laws favoring the two-party system.

THE HISTORICAL FOUNDATIONS OF THE TWO-PARTY SYSTEM

As we have seen, at many times in American history, one preeminent issue or dispute has divided the nation politically. In the beginning, Americans were at odds over ratifying the Constitution. After the Constitution went into effect, the power of the federal government became the major national issue. Thereafter, the dispute over slavery divided the nation by section, North versus South. At times—for example, in the North after the Civil War—cultural differences have been important, with advocates of government-sponsored morality (such as banning alcoholic beverages) pitted against advocates of personal liberty.

During much of the 1900s, economic differences were preeminent. In the New Deal period, the Democrats became known as the party of the working class, while the Republicans became known as the party of the middle and upper classes and commercial interests. When politics is based on an argument between two opposing points of view, advocates of each viewpoint can mobilize most effectively by forming a single, unified party. Also, when a two-party system has been in existence for almost two centuries, it becomes difficult to imagine an alternative.

POLITICAL SOCIALIZATION AND PRACTICAL CONSIDERATIONS

Given that the majority of Americans identify with one of the two major political parties, it is not surprising that most children learn at a fairly young age to think of themselves as either Democrats or Republicans. This generates a built-in mechanism to perpetuate a two-party system. Also, many politically oriented people who aspire to work for social change consider that the only realistic way to capture political power in this country is to be either a Republican or a Democrat.

THE WINNER-TAKE-ALL ELECTORAL SYSTEM

Plurality
A number of votes cast for a candidate that is greater than the number of votes for any other candidate but not necessarily a majority.

At virtually every level of government in the United States, the outcome of elections is based on the **plurality**, winner-take-all principle. In a plurality system, the winner is the person who obtains the most votes, even if that person does not receive a majority (more than 50 percent) of the votes. Whoever gets the most votes gets everything. Most legislators in the United States are elected from single-member districts in which only one person represents the constituency, and the candidate who finishes second in such an election receives nothing for the effort.

Presidential Voting. The winner-take-all system also operates in the election of the U.S president. Recall that the voters in each state do not vote for a president directly but vote for **electoral college** delegates who are committed to the various presidential candidates. These delegates are called *electors*.

Electoral College
A group of persons, called electors, who are selected by the voters in each state. This group officially elects the president and the vice president of the United States.

In all but two states (Maine and Nebraska), if a presidential candidate wins a plurality in the state, then *all* of the state's votes go to that candidate. For example, let us say that the electors pledged to a particular presidential candidate receive a plurality of 40 percent of the votes in a state. That presidential candidate will receive all of the state's votes in the electoral college. Minor parties have a difficult time competing under such a system. Because voters know that minor parties cannot win any electoral votes, they often will not vote for minor-party candidates, even if the candidates are in tune with them ideologically.

Popular Election of the Governors and the President. In most European countries, the chief executive (usually called the prime minister) is elected by the legislature, or parliament. If the parliament contains three or more parties, as is usually the case, two or more of the parties can join together in a coalition to choose the prime minister and the other leaders of the government (see the Beyond Our Borders box in Chapter 10). In the United States, however, the people elect the president and the governors of all 50 states. There is no opportunity for two or more parties to negotiate a coalition. Here, too, the winner-take-all principle discriminates powerfully against any third party.

Proportional Representation. Many other nations use a system of proportional representation with multimember districts. If, during the national election, party X obtains 12 percent of the vote, party Y gets 43 percent of the vote, and party Z gets the remaining 45 percent of the vote, then party X gets 12 percent of the seats in the legislature, party Y gets 43 percent of the seats, and party Z gets 45 percent of the seats. Because even a minor party may still obtain at least a few seats in the legislature, the smaller parties have a greater incentive to organize under such electoral systems than they do in the United States. To read more about nations that utilize a proportional representation system, see this chapter's Beyond Our Borders feature.

DID YOU KNOW?

That the Reform Party, established in 1996, used a vote-by-mail process for the first step of its nominating convention and also accepted votes cast by e-mail?

The relative effects of proportional representation versus our system of single-member districts are so strong that many scholars have made them one of the few "laws" of political science. Duverger's Law, named after French political scientist Maurice Duverger, states that electoral systems based on single-member districts tend to produce two parties, while systems of proportional representation produce multiple parties.[11] Still, many countries with single-member districts have more than two political parties—Britain and Canada are examples.

STATE AND FEDERAL LAWS FAVORING THE TWO PARTIES

Many state and federal election laws offer a clear advantage to the two major parties. In some states, the established major parties need to gather fewer signatures to place their candidates on the ballot than do minor parties or independent candidates. The criterion for determining how many signatures will be required is often based on the total party vote in the last general election, thus penalizing a new political party that did not compete in that election.

At the national level, minor parties face different obstacles. All of the rules and procedures of both houses of Congress divide committee seats, staff members, and other privileges on the basis of party membership. A legislator who is elected on a minor-party ticket, such as the Conservative Party of New York, must choose to be counted with one of the major parties to obtain a committee assignment. The Federal Election Commission (FEC) rules for campaign financing also place restrictions on minor-party candidates. Such candidates are not eligible for federal matching funds in either the primary or the general election. In the 1980 election, John Anderson, running for president as an independent, sued the FEC for campaign funds. The commission finally agreed to repay part of his campaign costs after the election in proportion to the votes he received. Giving funds to a candidate when the campaign is over is, of course, much less helpful than providing funds while the campaign is still under way.

---

[11]As cited in Todd Landman, *Issues and Methods in Comparative Politics* (New York: Routledge, 2003), p. 14.

THE ROLE OF MINOR PARTIES IN U.S. POLITICS

Third Party
A political party other than the two major political parties (Republican and Democratic).

For the reasons just discussed, minor parties have a difficult (if not impossible) time competing within the American two-party political system. Nonetheless, minor parties have played an important role in our political life. Parties other than the Republicans or Democrats are usually called **third parties**. (Technically, of course, there could be fourth, fifth, or sixth parties as well, but we use the term *third party* because it has endured.) Third parties can come into existence in three ways: (1) They may be founded from scratch by individuals or groups who are committed to a particular interest, issue, or ideology; (2) they can split off from one of the major parties when a group becomes dissatisfied with the major party's policies; and (3) they can be organized around a particular charismatic leader and serve as that person's vehicle for contesting elections.

Third parties have acted as barometers of changes in the political mood. Such barometric indicators have forced the major parties to recognize new issues or trends in the thinking of Americans. Political scientists believe that third parties have acted as safety valves for dissident groups, preventing major confrontations and political unrest. In some instances, third parties have functioned as way stations for voters en route from one of the major parties to the other. Table 8–1 on page 302 lists significant third-party presidential campaigns in American history; Table 8–2 on page 303 provides a brief description of third-party beliefs.

INDEPENDENT PRESIDENTIAL candidate Ralph Nader (shown here) and former candidate Howard Dean debated the legitimacy of third-party campaigns in July 2004. After Dean's own bid for the presidency failed, the former Vermont governor became the Democratic Party's leading critic of Nader's campaign. Nader ran again in 2008. (REUTERS/Molly Riley/Landov)

IDEOLOGICAL THIRD PARTIES

The longest-lived third parties have been those with strong ideological foundations that are typically at odds with the majority mind-set. The Socialist Party is an example. The party was founded in 1901 and lasted until 1972, when it was finally dissolved. (A smaller party later took up the name.)

Ideology has at least two functions. First, the members of the minor party regard themselves as outsiders and look to one another for support; ideology provides great psychological cohesiveness. Second, because the rewards of ideological commitment are partly psychological, these minor parties do not think in terms of immediate electoral success. A poor showing at the polls therefore does not dissuade either the leadership or the grassroots participants from continuing their quest for change in American government (and, ultimately, American society).

Currently active ideological parties include the Libertarian Party and the Green Party. The Libertarian Party supports a *laissez-faire* ("let it be") capitalist economic program, together with a hands-off policy on regulating matters of moral conduct. The Green Party began as a grassroots environmentalist organization with affiliated political parties across North America and Western Europe. It was established in the United States as a national party in 1996 and nominated Ralph Nader to run for president in

Beyond Our Borders

MULTIPARTY SYSTEMS: THE RULE RATHER THAN THE EXCEPTION

The United States has a two-party system. Occasionally, a third-party candidate enters the race but really has little chance of winning. Throughout the world, though, many democracies have multiparty systems.

SOME EXAMPLES

In its first legislative elections ever, Afghanistan saw the emergence of six major parties and seven minor parties. In the 2005 Iraqi national assembly election, there were a total of 15 parliamentary alliances and parties, plus 20 other parties. In any national election in India, there are six major parties, and in the states, there are a total of 30 parties. (There are also more than 700 registered, but unrecognized, parties in India.)

In the latest elections in Germany, there were major parties and numerous minor ones. In any given presidential election in France, there are even more parties. They include the National Front that represents the extreme right, anti-immigrant part of the electorate. But there was also a party supporting hunting, fishing, nature, and traditions and one supporting the Revolutionary Communist League. All in all, there are at least 15 French parties, most of which obtain some public funding.

PROPORTIONAL REPRESENTATION AND COALITIONS

In the German elections of September 2005, the Christian Democrats received about 30 percent of the vote and obtained about 30 percent of the seats in the German Federal Congress, called the *Bundestag*. The Christian Social Union of Bavaria obtained about 8 percent of the votes and almost 8 percent of the seats. Together, these two right-of-center parties obtained 36.8 percent of the seats in Germany's equivalent of our House of Representatives. The opposition on the left, called the Social Democratic Party of Germany, obtained almost the same—36.2 percent. Not surprisingly, neither the right nor the left in Germany had a high enough percentage of seats in the *Bundestag* to move forward. Consequently, a coalition government was formed, one that had to take account of the more extreme parties represented in the *Bundestag*, including the Free Democratic Party and the so-called Greens (ecologists).

In the latest French elections, the Union for a Presidential Minority, along with assorted other right-of-center parties, obtained a clear majority and therefore did not have to form coalitions with opposition parties on the left.

Coalitions are almost a certainty in a multiparty system. Why? Because usually the leading party does not have a majority of votes in the legislature. The leading party therefore has to make compromises to obtain votes from other parties. These coalitions are subject to change due to the pressures of lawmaking.

Great Britain's first live television debate among contenders for the Prime Minister's position was held in 2010. The three candidates were, from the left, Liberal Party candidate Nick Clegg, Conservative party candidate David Cameron, and Labor candidate Gordon Brown. (© Homer W Sykes/Alamy)

Often, a minor partner in a coalition finds itself unable to support the laws or policies proposed by its larger partners. Either a compromise will be found, or the coalition will be ended and new partners may be sought to form a government coalition. If we had a multiparty system in the United States, we might have a farmers' party, a Latino party, a western party, a labor party, and others. To gain support for her or his program, a president would have to build a coalition of several parties by persuading each that its members would benefit from the coalition. The major difficulty in a multiparty system is, of course, that the parties will withdraw from the coalition when they fail to benefit from it. Holding a coalition together for more than one issue is sometimes impossible.

FOR CRITICAL ANALYSIS

Are multiparty systems necessarily more representative than the two-party system in the United States? Why or why not?

2000. Nader campaigned against what he called "corporate greed," advocated universal health insurance, and promoted environmental concerns.[12] He ran again for president as an independent in 2004 and in 2008

TABLE 8–1 The Most Successful Third-Party Presidential Campaigns Since 1864

The following list includes all third-party candidates winning more than 2 percent of the popular vote or any electoral votes since 1864. (We ignore isolated "unfaithful electors" in the electoral college who failed to vote for the candidate to which they were pledged.)

YEAR	MAJOR THIRD PARTY	THIRD-PARTY PRESIDENTIAL CANDIDATE	PERCENT OF THE POPULAR VOTE	ELECTORAL VOTES	WINNING PRESIDENTIAL CANDIDATE AND PARTY
1892	Populist	James Weaver	8.5	22	Grover Cleveland (D)
1904	Socialist	Eugene Debs	3.0	–	Theodore Roosevelt (R)
1908	Socialist	Eugene Debs	2.8	–	William Howard Taft (R)
1912	Progressive	Theodore Roosevelt	27.4	88	Woodrow Wilson (D)
1912	Socialist	Eugene Debs	6.0	–	Woodrow Wilson (D)
1920	Socialist	Eugene Debs	3.4	–	Warren G. Harding (R)
1924	Progressive	Robert LaFollette	16.6	13	Calvin Coolidge (R)
1948	States' Rights	Strom Thurmond	2.4	39	Harry Truman (D)
1960	Independent Democrat	Harry Byrd	0.4	15*	John Kennedy (D)
1968	American Independent	George Wallace	13.5	46	Richard Nixon (R)
1980	National Union	John Anderson	6.6	0	Ronald Reagan (R)
1992	Independent	Ross Perot	18.9	0	Bill Clinton (D)
1996	Reform	Ross Perot	8.4	0	Bill Clinton (D)

*Byrd received 15 electoral votes from unpledged electors in Alabama and Mississippi.
Source: *Dave Leip's Atlas of U.S. Presidential Elections,* www.uselectionatlas.org.

[12]Ralph Nader offers his own entertaining account of his run for the presidency in 2000 in *Crashing the Party: How to Tell the Truth and Still Run for President* (New York: St. Martin's Press, 2002).

TABLE 8–2 Policies of Selected American Third Parties since 1864

Populist: This pro-farmer party of the 1890s advocated progressive reforms. It also advocated replacing gold with silver as the basis of the currency in hopes of creating a mild inflation in prices. (It was believed by many that inflation would help debtors and stimulate the economy.)

Socialist: This party advocated a "cooperative commonwealth" based on government ownership of industry. It was pro-labor, often antiwar, and in later years, anti-communist. It was dissolved in 1972 and replaced by nonparty advocacy groups (Democratic Socialists of America and Social Democrats USA).

Communist: This left-wing breakaway from the socialists was the U.S. branch of the worldwide communist movement. The party was pro-labor and advocated full equality for African Americans. It was also closely aligned with the Communist Party-led Soviet Union, which provoked great hostility among most Americans.

Progressive: This name was given to several successive splinter parties built around individual political leaders. Theodore Roosevelt, who ran in 1912, advocated federal regulation of industry to protect consumers, workers, and small businesses. Robert LaFollette, who ran in 1924, held similar viewpoints.

American Independent: Built around George Wallace, this party opposed any further promotion of civil rights and advocated a militant foreign policy. Wallace's supporters were mostly former Democrats who were soon to be Republicans.

Libertarian: This party opposes most government activity.

Reform: The Reform Party was initially built around businessman Ross Perot but later was taken over by others. Under Perot, the party was a middle-of-the-road group opposed to federal budget deficits. Under Patrick Buchanan, it came to represent right-wing nationalism and opposition to free trade.

Green: The Greens are a left-of-center pro-environmental party; they are also generally hostile to globalization.

SPLINTER PARTIES

Some of the most successful minor parties have been those that split from major parties. The impetus for these **splinter parties**, or factions, has usually been a situation in which a particular personality was at odds with the major party. The most successful of these splinter parties was the Bull Moose Progressive Party, formed in 1912 to support Theodore Roosevelt for president. The Republican National Convention of that year denied Roosevelt the nomination, although he had won most of the primaries. He therefore left the Republicans and ran against Republican "regular" William Howard Taft in the general election. Although Roosevelt did not win the election, he did split the Republican vote, enabling Democrat Woodrow Wilson to become president.

Third parties have also been formed to back individual candidates who were not rebelling against a particular party. Ross Perot, for example, who challenged Republican George H. W. Bush and Democrat Bill Clinton in 1992, had not previously been active in a major party. Perot's supporters, likewise, probably would have split their votes between Bush and Clinton had Perot not been in the race. In theory, Perot ran in 1992 as a nonparty independent; in practice, he had to create a campaign organization. By 1996, Perot's organization was formalized as the Reform Party.

Splinter Party
A new party formed by a dissident faction within a major political party. Often, splinter parties have emerged when a particular personality was at odds with the major party.

H. ROSS PEROT, THIRD-PARTY candidate for president in 1992 and 1996, speaks before a California Senate committee in 2002. (Justin Sullivan/Getty Images)

THE IMPACT OF MINOR PARTIES

Third parties have rarely been able to affect American politics by actually winning elections. (One exception is that third-party and independent candidates have occasionally won races for state governorships—for example, Jesse Ventura was elected governor of Minnesota on the Reform Party ticket in 1998.) Instead, the impact of third parties has taken two forms. First, third parties can influence one of the major parties to take up one or more issues. Second, third parties can determine the outcome of a particular election by pulling votes from one of the major-party candidates in what is called the "spoiler effect."

Influencing the Major Parties. One of the most clear-cut examples of a major party adopting the issues of a minor party took place in 1896, when the Democratic Party took over the Populist demand for "free silver"—that is, a policy of coining enough new money to create inflation. As you learned earlier, however, absorbing the Populists cost the Democrats votes overall.

Affecting the Outcome of an Election. The presidential election of 2000 was one instance in which a minor party may have altered the outcome. Green candidate Ralph Nader received almost 100,000 votes in Florida, a majority of which would probably have gone to Democrat Al Gore if Nader had not been in the race. The real question, however, is not whether the Nader vote had an effect—clearly, it did—but whether the effect was important.

The problem is that in an election as close as the presidential election of 2000, *any* factor with an impact on the outcome can be said to have determined the results of the election. Discussing his landslide loss to Democrat Lyndon B. Johnson in 1964, Republican Barry Goldwater wrote, "When you've lost an election by that much, it isn't the case of whether you made the wrong speech or wore the wrong necktie. It was just the wrong time."[13] With the opposite situation, a humorist might speculate that Gore would have won the election had he worn a better tie! Nevertheless, given that Nader garnered almost 3 million votes nationwide, many people believe that the Nader campaign was an important reason for Gore's loss. Should voters ignore third parties to avoid spoiling the chances of a preferred major-party candidate?

MECHANISMS OF POLITICAL CHANGE

What does the 21st century hold for the Democrats and the Republicans? Support for the two major parties is roughly balanced today. In the future, could one of the two parties decisively overtake the other and become the "natural party of government"? The Republicans held this status from 1896 until 1932, and the Democrats enjoyed it for many years after the election of Franklin D. Roosevelt in 1932. Not surprisingly, political advisers in both parties dream of circumstances that could grant them lasting political hegemony, or dominance.

REALIGNMENT

Realignment
A process in which a substantial group of voters switches party allegiance, producing a long-term change in the political landscape.

One mechanism by which a party might gain dominance is called **realignment**. As described in the Politics with a Purpose feature, major constituencies shift their allegiance from one party to another, creating a long-term alteration in the political environment. Realignment has often been associated with particular elections, called *realigning elections*. The election of 1896, which established a Republican ascendancy,

---

[13]Barry Goldwater, *With No Apologies* (New York: William Morrow, 1979).

was clearly a realigning election. So was the election of 1932, which made the Democrats the leading party.

Realignment: The Myth of Dominance. Several myths have grown up around the concept of realignment. One is that in realignment, a newly dominant party must replace the previously dominant party. Actually, realignment could easily strengthen an already dominant party. Alternatively, realignment could result in a tie. This has happened—twice. One example was the realignment of the 1850s, which resulted in Abraham Lincoln's election as president in 1860. After the Civil War, the Republicans and the Democrats were almost evenly matched nationally.

The most recent realignment—which also resulted in two closely matched parties—has sometimes been linked to the elections of 1968. Actually, the realignment was a gradual process that took place over many years. It is sometimes referred to as a "rolling realignment." In 1968, Democrat Hubert Humphrey, Republican Richard Nixon, and third-party candidate George Wallace of Alabama all vied for the presidency. Following the Republican victory in that election, Nixon adopted a "Southern strategy" aimed at drawing dissatisfied Southern Democrats into the Republican Party.[14] At the presidential level, the strategy was an immediate success, although years would pass before the Republicans could gain dominance in the South's delegation to Congress or in state legislatures. Nixon's Southern strategy helped create the political environment in which we live today. Another milestone in the progress of the Republicans was Ronald Reagan's sweeping victory in the presidential election of 1980.

Realignment: The Myth of Predictability. A second myth concerning realignments is that they take place, like clockwork, every 36 years. Supposedly, there were realigning elections in 1860, 1896, 1932, and 1968, and therefore 2004 must have been a year for realignment. No such event took place. In fact, there is no force that could cause political realignments at precise 36-year intervals. Further, as we observed earlier in this section, realignments are not always tied to particular elections. The most recent realignment, in which conservative Southern Democrats became conservative Southern Republicans, was not closely linked to a particular election. The realignment of the 1850s, following the creation of the modern Republican Party, also took place over a period of years.

Is Realignment Still Possible? The nature of American political parties created the pattern of realignment in American history. The sheer size of the country, combined with the inexorable pressure toward a two-party system, resulted in parties made up of voters with conflicting interests or values. The pre–Civil War party system involved two parties—Whigs and Democrats—with support in both the North and the South. This system could survive only by burying, as deeply as possible, the issue of slavery. We should not be surprised that the structure eventually collapsed. The Republican ascendancy of 1896–1932 united capitalists and industrial workers under the Republican banner, despite serious economic conflicts between the two. The New Deal Democratic coalition after 1932 brought African Americans and ardent segregationists into the same party.

For realignment to occur, a substantial body of citizens must come to believe that their party can no longer represent their interests or values. The problem must be fundamental and not attributable to the behavior of an individual politician. Given the increasing cohesion of each of the parties today, it is unlikely that a realignment is in the offing. The values that unite each party are relatively coherent, and their constituents are reasonably compatible. Therefore, the current party system should be more stable than in the past, and a major realignment is not likely to take place in the foreseeable future.

---

[14]The classic work on Nixon's Southern strategy is Kirkpatrick Sales, *The Emerging Republican Majority* (New Rochelle, NY: Arlington House, 1969).

DEALIGNMENT

Dealignment
A decline in party loyalties that reduces long-term party commitment.

Party Identification
Linking oneself to a particular political party.

Straight-Ticket Voting
Voting exclusively for the candidates of one party.

Swing Voters
Voters who frequently swing their support from one party to another.

Among political scientists, one common argument has been that realignment is no longer likely because voters are not as committed to the two major parties as they were in the 1800s and early 1900s. In this view, called **dealignment** theory, large numbers of independent voters may result in political volatility, but the absence of strong partisan attachments means that it is no longer easy to "lock in" political preferences for decades.

Independent Voters. Figure 8–5 shows trends in **party identification**, as measured by standard polling techniques from 1937 to the present. The chart displays a rise in the number of independent voters throughout the period, combined with a fall in support for the Democrats from the mid-1960s on. The decline in Democratic identification may be due to the consolidation of Republican support in the South since 1968, a process that by now may be substantially complete. In any event, the traditional Democratic advantage in party identification has vanished.

Not only has the number of independents grown over the last half-century, but voters are also less willing to vote a straight ticket—that is, to vote for all the candidates of one party. In the early 1900s, **straight-ticket voting** was nearly universal. By midcentury, 12 percent of voters engaged in ticket splitting. In recent presidential elections, between 20 and 40 percent of the voters engaged in split-ticket voting. This trend, along with the increase in the number of voters who call themselves independents, suggests that parties have lost much of their hold on the loyalty of the voters.

Not-So-Independent Voters. A problem with dealignment theory is that many "independent" voters are not all that independent. Polling organizations estimate that of the 33 percent of voters who identify themselves as independents, 11 percent vote as if they were Democrats in almost all elections, and 12 percent vote as if they were Republicans. If these "leaners" are deducted from the independent category, only 10 percent of the voters remain. These true independents are **swing voters**—they can swing back and forth between the parties. These voters are important in deciding elections. Some analysts believe, however, that swing voters are far less numerous today than they were two or three decades ago.

FIGURE 8–5 Party Identification from 1937 to the Present

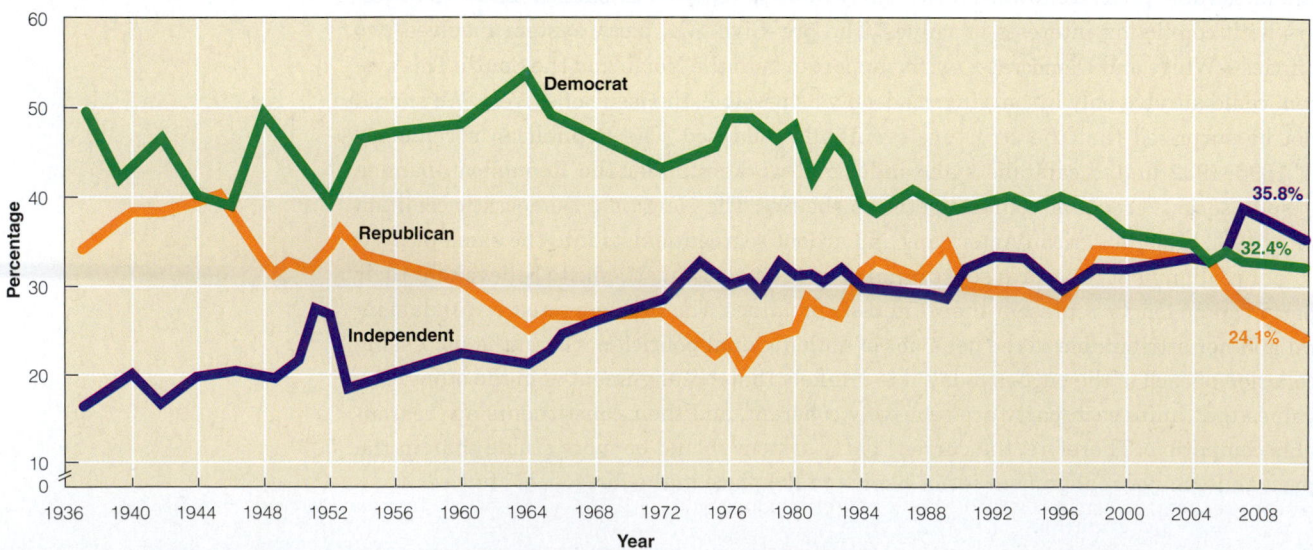

Sources: Gallup Report, August 1995; *New York Times*/CBS poll, June 1996; Gallup Report, February 1998; The Pew Research Center for the People and the Press, November 2003; and authors' updates.

TIPPING

Realignment is not the only mechanism that can alter the political landscape. Political transformation can also result from changes in the composition of the electorate. Even when groups of voters never change their party preferences, if one group becomes more numerous over time, it can become dominant for that reason alone. We call this kind of demographically based change **tipping**. Immigration is one cause of this phenomenon.

Tipping in Massachusetts. Consider Massachusetts, where for generations Irish Catholics confronted Protestant Yankees in the political arena. Most of the Yankees were Republican; most of the Irish were Democrats. The Yankees were numerically dominant from the founding of the state until 1928. In that year, for the first time, Democratic Irish voters came to outnumber the Republican Yankees. Massachusetts, which previously had been one of the most solidly Republican states, cast its presidential vote for Democrat Al Smith. Within a few years, Massachusetts became one of the most reliably Democratic states in the nation.

Tipping in California? California may have experienced a tipping effect during the 1990s. From 1952 until 1992, California consistently supported Republican presidential candidates, turning Democratic only in the landslide election of Lyndon Johnson in 1964. In 1992, however, the California electorate gave Democrat Bill Clinton a larger percentage of its votes than he received in the country as a whole. Since then, no Republican presidential candidate has managed to carry California.

The improved performance of the Democrats in California is almost certainly a function of demography. In 1999, California became the third state, after Hawaii and New Mexico, in which non-Latino whites do *not* make up a majority of the population. Latinos and African Americans both give most of their votes to the Democrats. Even before 1999, these groups were numerous enough to tip California into the Democratic column.

ON TO THE FUTURE

Some speculation about the future is reasonable, as long as we remember that unexpected events can make any prediction obsolete. We can anticipate that party advocates will continue to hope that events will propel their party into a dominant position. Either party could lose substantial support if it were identified with a major economic disaster. Noneconomic events could have an impact as well.

Republican strategists will seek to encourage substantial numbers of voters to abandon the Democrats, perhaps on the basis of cultural issues. Some of these strategists believe that the relative conservatism of Hispanic Americans on cultural matters may provide an opening for the Republicans. Others point to the increasing numbers of Americans with investments in the stock market as a possible indicator of growing economic conservatism. Finally, Republicans look at the decline in Democratic Party identification since the 1960s (see Figure 8–4) and project that trend into the future.

Tipping
A phenomenon that occurs when a group that is becoming more numerous over time grows large enough to change the political balance in a district, state, or country.

PROTESTORS GATHER in Phoenix in May 2010 to show their disapproval of Arizona's controversial immigration bill. Most of the law, which would have required Arizona law enforcement officers to check the immigration status of suspects, was held to be unconstitutional in the first court hearing. (AP Photo/Matt York)

Democratic strategists hope that the tolerant spirit of many younger voters (in attitudes toward gay rights, for example) may work to their advantage. Latino voters are of interest to the Democrats as well. Demographic changes have turned once-reliably Republican states such as Florida into swing states that can decide national elections. As noted in Chapter 1, some time after 2015, Texas—now among the most Republican states—will no longer have a non-Latinos white majority. If the Republicans do not succeed in detaching Latinos from the Democratic Party, Texas could eventually tip into the Democratic column and possibly tip the country as a whole to the Democrats as well.

YOU CAN MAKE A Difference

ELECTING CONVENTION DELEGATES

The most exciting political party event, staged every four years, is the national convention. State conventions also take place on a regular basis. Surprising as it might seem, there are opportunities for the individual voter to become involved in nominating delegates to a state or national convention or to become a delegate.

WHY SHOULD YOU CARE?

How would you like to exercise a small amount of real political power yourself—power that goes beyond simply voting in an election? You might be able to become a delegate to a county, district, or even state party convention. Many of these conventions nominate candidates for various offices. For example, in Michigan, the state party conventions nominate the candidates for the Board of Regents of the state's three top public universities. The regents set university policies, so

these are nominations in which students have an obvious interest. In Michigan, if you are elected as a party precinct delegate, you can attend your party's state convention.

In much of the country, there are more openings for district-level delegates than there are people willing to serve. In such circumstances, almost anyone can become a delegate by collecting a handful of signatures on a nominating petition or by mounting a small-scale write-in campaign. You are then eligible to take part in one of the most educational political experiences available to an ordinary citizen. You will get a firsthand look at how political persuasion takes place, how resolutions are written and passed, and how candidates seek out support among their fellow party members. In some states, party caucuses bring debate even closer to the grassroots level.

WHAT CAN YOU DO?

When the parties choose delegates for the national convention, the process begins at the local level—either the congressional district or the state legislative district. Delegates may be elected in party primary elections or chosen in neighborhood or precinct caucuses. If the delegates are elected in a primary, persons who want to run for these positions must first file petitions with the board of elections. If you are interested in committing yourself to a particular presidential candidate and running for the delegate position, check with the local county committee or with the party's national committee about the rules you must follow.

It is even easier to get involved in the grassroots politics of presidential caucuses. In some states—Iowa being the earliest and most famous example—delegates are first nominated at the local precinct caucus. According to the rules of the Iowa caucuses, anyone can participate in a caucus if he or she is 18 years old, a resident of the precinct, and registered as a party member. These caucuses,

WILLIAM STYLES, a political science major at Western Carolina University, became a convention delegate in 2008. (Courtesy of William Styles)

in addition to being the focus of national media attention in January or February, select delegates to the county conventions who are pledged to specific presidential candidates. This is the first step toward the national convention.

At both the county caucus and the convention levels, both parties try to find younger members to fill some of the seats. Contact the state or county political party to find out when the caucuses or primaries will be held or check the Web sites of the Young Democrats or Young Republicans in your state. Then gather local supporters and friends, and prepare to join in an occasion during which political debate is at its best.

For further information about these opportunities (some states hold caucuses and state conventions in every election year), contact the state party office or your local state legislator for specific dates and regulations.

You can also write to the national committee for information on how to become a delegate.

Republican National Committee
Republican National Headquarters
310 First Street, SE
Washington, DC 20003
202-863-8500
www.rnc.org

Democratic National Committee
Democratic National Headquarters
430 S. Capitol St. SE
Washington, DC 20003
202-863-8000
www.democrats.org

KEY TERMS

dealignment 306
Democratic Party 280
divided government 296
electoral college 298
era of good feelings 280
faction 277
independent 277
national committee 293
national convention 291
party identification 306
party-in-government 291

party-in-the-electorate 291
party organization 291
party platform 291
patronage 295
plurality 298
political party 277
realignment 304
Republican Party 281
reverse-income effect 290
safe seat 297

splinter party 303
state central committee 295
straight-ticket voting 306
swing voters 306
third party 300
ticket splitting 296
tipping 307
two-party system 279
unit rule 295
Whig Party 280

CHAPTER SUMMARY

1. **What do political parties add to the American political system?** A political party is a group of political activists who organize to win elections, operate the government, and determine public policy. Political parties recruit candidates for public office, organize and run elections, present alternative policies to the voters, assume responsibility for operating the government, and act as the opposition to the party in power.

2. The evolution of our nation's political parties can be divided into seven periods: (1) the creation and formation of political parties from 1789 to 1816; (2) the era of one-party rule, or personal politics, from 1816 to 1828; (3) the period from Andrew Jackson's presidency to the Civil War, from 1828 to 1860; (4) the Civil War and post-Civil War period, from 1860

to 1896; (5) the Republican ascendancy and progressive period, from 1896 to 1932; (6) the New Deal period, from 1932 to about 1968; and (7) the modern period, from approximately 1968 to the present.

3. Many of the differences between the two parties date from the time of Franklin D. Roosevelt's New Deal. The Democrats have advocated government action to help labor and minorities, and the Republicans have championed self-reliance and limited government. The constituents of the two parties continue to differ. A close look at policies actually enacted in recent years, however, suggests that despite rhetoric to the contrary, both parties are committed to a large and active government. Today, cultural differences are at least as important as economic issues in determining party allegiance.

4. A political party consists of three components: the party-in-the-electorate, the party organization, and the party-in-government. Each party component maintains linkages to the others to keep the party strong. Each level of the party—local, state, and national—has considerable autonomy. The national party organization is responsible for holding the national convention in presidential election years, writing the party platform, choosing the national committee, and conducting party business.

5. **Should candidates be chosen by political parties?** The party-in-government comprises all of the elected and appointed officeholders of a party. However, many officeholders may have won their seats with little or no help from the party, making them less susceptible to party control. If the political parties had more control over the candidates, they would be better able to carry out a cohesive program in government.

6. **Should there be more political parties in the United States?** Two major parties have dominated the political landscape in the United States for almost two centuries. The reasons for this include (1) the historical foundations of the system, (2) political socialization and practical considerations, (3) the winner-take-all electoral system, and (4) state and federal laws favoring the two-party system. For these reasons, minor parties have found it extremely difficult to win elections. If the rules for getting candidates on the ballot were changed or states adopted more proportional voting systems, other political parties might form, such as an environmental party, an ultraconservative party, or a party based on religious affiliation. Such parties might do a better job of articulating certain interests than the two major parties do at the present time.

7. Minor (or third) parties have emerged from time to time, sometimes as dissatisfied splinter groups from within major parties, and have acted as barometers of changes in the political mood. Splinter parties have emerged when a particular personality was at odds with the major party, as when Theodore Roosevelt's differences with the Republican Party resulted in the formation of the Bull Moose Progressive Party. Other minor parties, such as the Socialist Party, have formed around specific issues or ideologies. Third parties can affect the political process (even if they do not win) if major parties adopt their issues or if they determine which major party wins an election.

8. One mechanism of political change is realignment, in which major blocs of voters switch allegiance from one party to another. Realignments were manifested in the elections of 1896 and 1932. Realignment need not leave one party dominant—it can result in two parties of roughly equal strength. Some scholars speak of dealignment—that is, the loss of strong party attachments. In fact, the share of the voters who describe themselves as independents has grown since the 1930s, and the share of self-identified Democrats has shrunk since the 1960s. Many independents actually vote as if they were Democrats or Republicans, however. Demographic change can also "tip" a district or state from one party to another.

SELECTED PRINT, MEDIA, AND ONLINE RESOURCES

PRINT RESOURCES

Amato, Theresa. *Grand Illusion: The Fantasy of Voter Choice in a Two-Party Tyranny.* New York: The New Press, 2009. As Ralph Nader's campaign manager during his 2000 and 2004 presidential runs, Amato was in an excellent position to see how the political system makes it almost impossible for third-party candidates to succeed. She also examines the experiences of other challengers, including John Anderson, Ross Perot, and Pat Buchanan.

Frank, Thomas. *What's the Matter with Kansas? How Conservatives Won the Heart of America.* New York: Henry Holt & Company, 2005. This book looks at how the Republican Party gained its current dominance in the American heartland. The author examines why so many Americans vote against their own economic interests.

Gould, Lewis. *Grand Old Party: A History of the Republicans.* New York: Random House, 2003. A companion volume to the history of the Democrats by Jules Witcover, listed later. Gould provides a sweeping history of the Republican Party from its origins as an antislavery coalition to the present. A major theme of the work is the evolution of the Republicans from a party of active government to the more conservative party that it is today.

Green, John C., and Paul S. Hernson, eds. *Responsible Partisanship: The Evolution of American Political Parties since 1950.* Lawrence: University Press of Kansas, 2003. This collection of scholarly essays explores the roles and functions of political parties, both as parties-in-the-electorate and as parties-in-government.

Lublin, David. *The Republican South: Democratization and Partisan Change.* Ewing, NJ: Princeton University Press, 2007. Lublin looks at the rise of Republicanism in the Southern states, emphasizing the economic issues involved in the political realignment of the South.

McAuliffe, Terry. *What a Party! My Life among Democrats.* New York: St. Martin's Press, 2007. The former chairperson of the Democratic National Committee discusses his years of experience on the inside of a major political party.

Paul, Ron. *The Revolution: A Manifesto.* New York: Grand Central Publishing, 2008. Representative Paul (R., Tex.) ran for president on the Libertarian ticket in 2004 and as a Republican in 2008. His concise political statement is an eloquent defense of the Libertarian cause. Among Paul's more striking proposals is the abolition of the Federal Reserve System, which, in his opinion, benefits only the rich.

Paulson, Arthur. *Electoral Realignment and the Outlook for American Democracy.* Boston: University Press of New England, 2006. Paulson seeks to understand recent realignments in the light of political geography and historical divisions.

Sager, Ryan. *The Elephant in the Room: Evangelicals, Libertarians, and the Battle to Control the Republican Party.* New York: Wiley, 2006. The author describes the current coalition of subgroups within the Republican Party and predicts an eventual splintering as the individual groups struggle for greater power within the party.

Schaller, Thomas F. *Whistling Past Dixie: How Democrats Can Win without the South.* New York: Simon & Schuster, 2008. Schaller, a professor of political science at the University of Maryland, argues that the Democrats are more likely to succeed by solidifying their support in northern states than by trying to rebuild their once-predominant position in the South.

Witcover, Jules. *Party of the People: A History of the Democrats.* New York: Random House, 2003. A companion volume to the history of the Republicans by Lewis Gould, listed earlier. Witcover describes the transformation of the Democrats from a party of limited government to a party of national authority, but he also finds a common thread that connects modern Democrats to the past—a belief in social and economic justice.

MEDIA RESOURCES

The American President—A 1995 film starring Michael Douglas as a widowed president who must balance partisanship and friendship (Republicans in Congress promise to approve the president's crime bill only if he modifies an environmental plan sponsored by his liberal girlfriend).

The Best Man—A 1964 drama based on Gore Vidal's play of the same name. The film, which deals with political smear campaigns by presidential party nominees, focuses on political party power and ethics.

The Last Hurrah—A classic 1958 political film starring Spencer Tracy as a corrupt politician who seeks his fifth nomination for mayor of a city in New England.

A Third Choice—A film that examines America's experience with third parties and independent candidates throughout the nation's political history.

ONLINE RESOURCES

Democratic Party www.democrats.org

Green Party of the United States a federation of state Green Parties. Committed to environmentalism, non-violence, social justice, and grassroots organizing: www.gp.org

Libertarian Party America's third largest and fastest-growing political party; calls itself the party of principle and supports smaller government, lower taxes, and more freedom: www.lp.org

Politics1.com a pioneering political blog and news site published as a nonpartisan public service to promote fully informed decision making by the American electorate. Offers extensive information on U.S. political parties, including the major parties and 50 minor parties: www.politics1.com/parties.htm

The Pew Research Center for the People & the Press an independent, nonpartisan public opinion research organization that studies attitudes toward politics, the press, and public policy issues. Offers survey data online on how the parties fared during the most recent elections, voter typology, and numerous other issues: http://people-press.org

Republican Party www.gop.com

9

Voters stand in line to cast their ballots in the 2008 primary election in Texas. In this heavily Latino precinct, voters seemed to be divided between choosing Barack Obama and Hillary Clinton. (Karen Warren/Houston Chronicle/Rapport Press/Newscom)

Voting and Elections

QUESTIONS TO CONSIDER

What should be the qualifications to vote?

Who votes in the United States?

Does the popular vote determine all elections?

CHAPTER CONTENTS

what if... Voting By Mail Became Universal?

BACKGROUND

As pointed out in the text, so far Oregon is the only state to have eliminated precinct polling places. Washington state has also been a leader in adopting voting by mail. The majority of that state's counties now use a vote-by-mail system.

Typically, with a vote-by-mail system, ballots are mailed to the homes of registered voters, who then fill them out and return them via the postal system. Usually, ballots are sent out about three weeks before the election date. Local voting authorities determine the cut-off date for returning the ballots. In some vote-by-mail jurisdictions, volunteers pick up ballots at voters' homes and take them to drop-off booths or to drive-in quick-drop locations.

WHAT IF VOTING BY MAIL BECAME UNIVERSAL?

What if the Congress passed a law changing all federal elections—for Congress and the president—to voting by mail? Many proponents of voting by mail believe that it is the best way to increase voter participation. (Internet voting would be even easier.) Despite some initial concerns that voters would not return their ballots, Oregon has seen the highest percentage of voter participation ever, reaching 87 percent in the 2004 elections.

When questions arise about the accuracy of ballot counts, mail-in votes provide an automatic paper trail. Each vote-by-mail ballot is normally read by optical scanners, and the paper version remains available if a hand recount becomes necessary. Certainly, the elimination of polling places reduces the expense of elections for any jurisdiction. Oregon estimates that it has reduced costs by more than 30 percent since it went to a statewide vote-by-mail system.

Proponents of voting by mail argue that it is preferable to some alternative national standard that would apply new rules to an outdated system of polling places. Voting by mail is low tech, low cost, and convenient.

VOTE BY MAIL: A SUBVERSION OF THE ELECTION PROCESS

Political scientist Norman Ornstein, an early critic of mail-in voting, argues that mail balloting subverts the whole election process. He points out that voters can cast their ballots well before meaningful debates and other exchanges occur between the candidates. As a result, the voter may be casting an uninformed ballot.* The Constitution Project at Georgetown University, as well as a consortium of the Massachusetts Institute of Technology and the California Institute of Technology, came to the same conclusion after an examination of the 2004 elections.

Critics additionally argue that mail-in voting deprives voters of the secrecy guaranteed by voting at a polling place. They also believe that mail-in voting provides more opportunities for fraud. Finally, they contend that it represents the abandonment of an important civic duty of going to the polls on election day.

FOR CRITICAL ANALYSIS

1. Would citizens be more likely to vote if they could vote by mail?
2. Is there enough new information in the last weeks of a campaign to change votes?
3. Do you believe that the chances of voting fraud are greater or smaller with a mail-in voting system than with the current polling-place system?

*Norman Ornstein, "Vote-by-Mail: Is It Good for Democracy?" *Campaigns and Elections*, May 1996, p. 47.

VOTING IN FREE and fair elections is the basis of any democracy. It is true that people are allowed to vote in China, Cuba, and North Korea, but there are no opposition candidates and no opposition campaign. In other nations, individuals are coerced into staying away from the polls by guerrilla fighters or, in some cases, by the government's own forces. In yet other nations, the incumbent government or candidate may alter the results of elections by fraudulent means. All of those cases fail the test of free and fair elections.

In the United States, it is often said that we have too many elections. In addition to voting for candidates, in some states, people can vote directly on laws. In California, there are often dozens of referenda on the ballot at one time. Citizens are often asked to vote three times in one year—in a primary election to choose candidates, in elections for school taxes or other local matters, and in a general election. Americans often elect not only representatives to state and national legislatures and executive officers for the state, but also school superintendents, sheriffs, even the jailer. In addition, many states have elected judges, which can add 50 more offices in a city as large as Chicago.

TURNING OUT TO VOTE

In 2008, the voting-age population was about 231,229,500 people. Of that number, 127,500,000, or 55 percent of the voting-age population, actually went to the polls. When only half of the voting-age population participates in elections, it means, among other things, that the winner of a close presidential election may be voted in by only about one-fourth of the voting-age population (see Table 9–1).

TABLE 9–1 Elected by a Majority?

Most presidents have won a majority of the votes cast in the election. We generally judge the extent of their victory by whether they have won more than 51 percent of the votes. Some presidential elections have been proclaimed *landslides*, meaning that the candidates won by an extraordinary majority of votes cast. As indicated below, however, no modern president has been elected by more than 38 percent of the total voting-age population.

YEAR—WINNER (PARTY)	PERCENTAGE OF TOTAL POPULAR VOTE	PERCENTAGE OF VOTING-AGE POPULATION
1932—Roosevelt (D)	57.4	30.1
1936—Roosevelt (D)	60.8	34.6
1940—Roosevelt (D)	54.7	32.2
1944—Roosevelt (D)	53.4	29.9
1948—Truman (D)	49.6	25.3
1952—Eisenhower (R)	55.1	34.0
1956—Eisenhower (R)	57.4	34.1
1960—Kennedy (D)	49.7	31.2
1964—Johnson (D)	61.1	37.8
1968—Nixon (R)	43.4	26.4
1972—Nixon (R)	60.7	33.5
1976—Carter (D)	50.1	26.8
1980—Reagan (R)	50.7	26.7
1984—Reagan (R)	58.8	31.2
1988—Bush (R)	53.4	26.8
1992—Clinton (D)	43.3	23.1
1996—Clinton (D)	49.2	23.2
2000—Bush (R)	47.8	24.5
2004—Bush (R)	51.0	27.6
2008—Obama (D)	52.6	27.5

Sources: Congressional Quarterly Weekly Report, January 31, 1989, p. 137; *New York Times*, November 5, 1992; November 7, 1996; November 12, 2004; November 6, 2008; and author's update.

Voter Turnout
The percentage of citizens taking part in the election process; the number of eligible voters who actually "turn out" on election day to cast their ballots.

Figure 9–1 shows **voter turnout** for presidential and congressional elections from 1904 to 2010. According to these statistics, the last good year for voter turnout was 1960, when almost 65 percent of the voting-age population actually voted. Each of the peaks in the figure represents voter turnout in a presidential election. Thus, we can also see that turnout for congressional elections is influenced greatly by whether there is a presidential election in the same year. Whereas voter turnout during the presidential elections of 2008 was more than 50 percent, it was only 42 percent in the midterm elections of 2010.

The same is true at the state level. When there is a race for governor, more voters participate both in the general election for governor and in the election for state representatives. Voter participation rates in gubernatorial elections are also greater in presidential election years. The average turnout in state elections is about 14 percentage points higher when a presidential election is held.

Now consider local elections: In races for mayor, city council, county auditor, and the like, it is fairly common for only 25 percent or less of the electorate to vote. Is something amiss here? It would seem that people should be more likely to vote in elections that directly affect them. At the local level, each person's vote counts more (because there are fewer voters). Furthermore, the issues—crime control, school bonds, sewer bonds, and so on—touch the immediate interests of the voters. The facts, however, do not fit the theory. Potential voters are most interested in national elections, when a presidential choice is involved. Otherwise, voter participation in our representative government is very low (and, as we have seen, it is not overwhelmingly great even in presidential elections).

THE EFFECT OF LOW VOTER TURNOUT

There are two schools of thought concerning low voter turnout. Some view low voter participation as a threat to representative democratic government. Too few individuals are deciding who wields political power in society. In addition, low voter participation

FIGURE 9–1 Voter Turnout for Presidential and Congressional Elections, 1904–2010

The peaks represent turnout in presidential election years; the troughs represent turnout in off-presidential-election years.

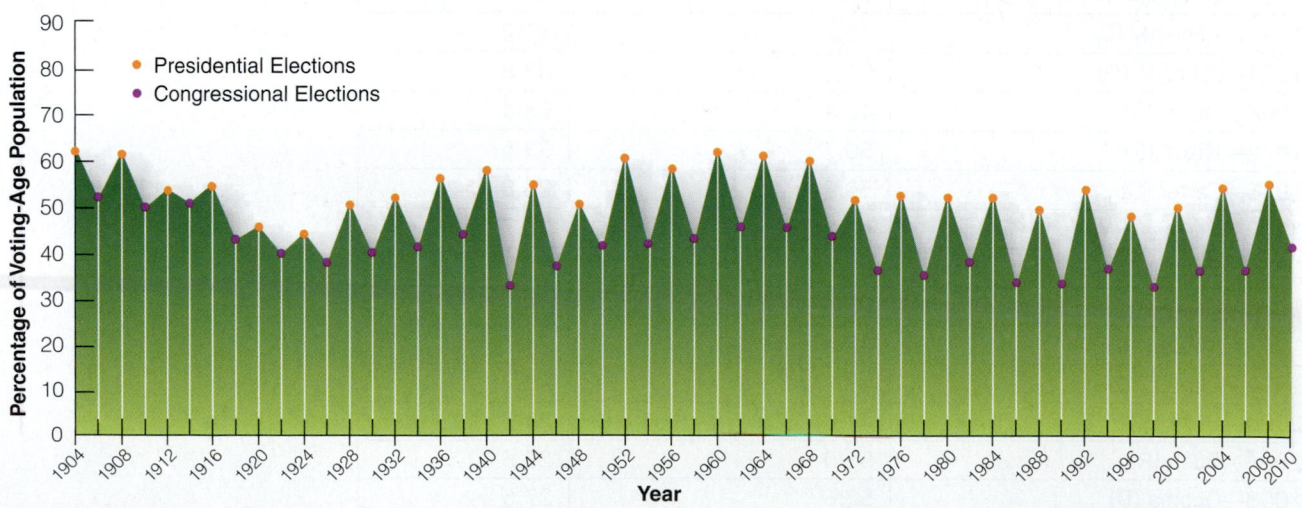

Sources: Historical Data Archive, Inter-university Consortium for Political and Social Research; U.S. Department of Commerce, *Statistical Abstract of the United States: 1980*, 101st ed. (Washington, DC: U.S. Government Printing Office, 1980), p. 515; William H. Flanigan and Nancy H. Zingale, *Political Behavior of the American Electorate*, 5th ed. (Boston: Allyn and Bacon, 1983), p. 20; *Congressional Quarterly*, various issues; and authors' updates.

presumably signals apathy or cynicism about the political system in general. It also may signal that potential voters simply do not want to take the time to learn about the issues or that the issues are too complicated. Some suggest that people do not vote because they do not believe that their vote will make any difference.

Others are less concerned about low voter participation. They believe that low voter participation simply indicates more satisfaction with the status quo. Also, they believe that representative democracy is a reality even if a very small percentage of eligible voters vote. If everyone who does not vote believes that the outcome of the election will accord with his or her own desires, then representative democracy is working. The nonvoters are obtaining the type of government—with the type of people running it—that they want to have anyway.

That in August 2000, six people offered to sell their votes for president on eBay, the online auction site? eBay quickly canceled the bidding.

IS VOTER TURNOUT DECLINING?

During many recent elections, the media have voiced concern that voter turnout is declining. Figure 9–1 appears to show somewhat lower voter turnout in recent years than during the 1960s. Pundits have blamed the low turnout on negative campaigning and broad public cynicism about the political process. But is voter turnout actually as low as it seems?

One problem with widely used measurements of voter turnout—as exemplified by Figure 9–1—is that they compare the number of people who actually vote with the voting-age population, not the population of *eligible voters*. These figures are not the same. The figure for the voting-age population includes felons and ex-felons who have lost the right to vote. Above all, it includes new immigrants who are not yet citizens. Finally, it does not include Americans living abroad, who can cast absentee ballots.

In 2008, the measured voting-age population included 3.2 million ineligible felons and ex-felons and an estimated 17.5 million noncitizens. It did not include 3.3 million Americans abroad. In 2008, the voting-age population was 225.5 million people. The number of eligible voters, however, was only 206.0 million. That means that voter turnout in 2008 was not 58 percent but about 64 percent of the truly eligible voters.

As you learned in Chapter 1, the United States has experienced high rates of immigration in recent decades. Political scientists Michael McDonald and Samuel Popkin argue that the apparent decline in voter turnout since 1972 is entirely a function of the increasing size of the ineligible population, chiefly due to immigration.[1]

FACTORS INFLUENCING WHO VOTES

A clear association exists between voter participation and the following characteristics: age, educational attainment, minority status, income level, and the existence of two-party competition.

1. *Age.* Look at Figure 9–2, which shows the breakdown of voter participation by age group for the 2008 presidential election. It is very clear that the Americans who have the highest turnout rate are those reaching retirement. The reported

---

[1]Michael P. McDonald and Samuel L. Popkin, "The Myth of the Vanishing Voter," *American Political Science Review*, Vol. 95, No. 4, December 2001, p. 963.

FIGURE 9–2 Voting in the 2008 Presidential Elections by Age Group

Turnout is given as a percentage of the voting-age citizen population. The data given in this figure is from the Census Bureau. It has been gathered by polling the American public. Generally the Census data is not available for months after the election. The data from the 2008 polls indicates that turnout among older Americans remained high.

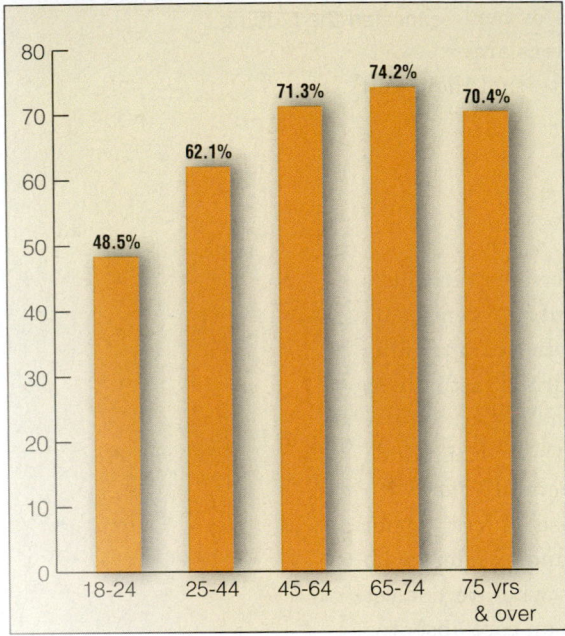

Source: U.S. Bureau of the Census, May 2010

turnout increases with each age group. Greater participation with age is very likely because older voters are more settled in their lives, are already registered, and have had more time to experience voting as an expected activity. Older voters may have more leisure time to learn about the campaign and the candidates, and communications, especially those from AARP, target this group.

What is most striking about the turnout figures is that younger voters have the lowest turnout rate. Before 1971, the age of eligibility to vote was 21. Due to the prevailing sentiment that if a man was old enough to be drafted to fight in the Vietnam War, he should be old enough to vote, the U.S. Constitution was amended (Amendment Twenty-six) to lower the voting age to 18. However, young Americans have never exhibited a high turnout rate. In contrast to older Americans, young people are likely to change residence frequently, have few ties to the community, and perhaps not see election issues as relevant to them.

Turnout among voters aged from 18 to 24 increased significantly between 2000 and 2004, from 36 percent to 47 percent in the presidential election. Evidence suggests that the candidates and political parties devoted much more attention to the younger voters. Candidates appeared on the television shows watched by younger voters, and campaigns began to utilize the Internet and other cybersources to reach younger voters. Younger voters greatly increased their turnout in the 2008 primary elections, with many supporting Barack Obama's campaign for the presidency, although the increase in turnout for the general election was only 1.5 percent.

2. *Educational attainment.* Education also influences voter turnout. In general, the more education you have, the more likely you are to vote. This pattern is clearly evident in the 2008 election results, as you can see in Figure 9–3. Reported turnout was 30 percentage points higher for those who had some college education than it was for people who had never been to high school.

3. *Minority status.* Race and ethnicity are important, too, in determining the level of voter turnout. Non-Latino whites in 2008 voted at a 66.1 percent rate, whereas the non-Latino African American turnout rate was 64.7 percent, up almost 5 percent from 2004. For Latino, the turnout rate was 49.9 percent, up 5 percent from 2008, and for Asian Americans the rate was 47.6 percent, up slightly from the previous presidential election. These low rates may occur because many Latino and Asian American immigrants are not yet citizens or due to language issues. The fact that the turnout increased 5 percent for African Americans and Latino may be due to the fact that a man of color was a candidate for president.

4. *Income level.* Differences in income also correlate with differences in voter turnout. Wealthier people tend to be overrepresented among voters who turn out on election day. In the 2008 presidential elections, voter turnout for those with the highest annual family incomes was almost twice the turnout for those with the lowest annual family incomes.

5. *Two-party competition.* Another factor in voter turnout is the extent to which elections are competitive within a state. More competitive states generally have higher turnout rates, and turnout increases considerably in states where there is an extremely

DID YOU KNOW?

That computer software now exists that can identify likely voters and likely campaign donors by town, neighborhood, and street?

competitive race in a particular year. In addition, turnout can be increased through targeted get-out-the-vote drives among minority voters.

WHY PEOPLE DO NOT VOTE

For many years, political scientists believed that one reason why voter turnout in the United States was so much lower than in other Western nations was that it was very difficult to register to vote. In most states, registration required a special trip to a public office far in advance of elections. Many experts are now proposing other explanations for low U.S. voter turnout.

Uninformative Media Coverage and Negative Campaigning. Some scholars contend that one of the reasons why some people do not vote has to do with media coverage of campaigns. Many researchers have shown that the news media tend to provide much more news about "the horse race," or which candidates are ahead in the polls, than about the actual policy positions of the candidates. Thus, voters are not given the kind of information that would provide them with an incentive to go to the polls on election day. Additionally, negative campaigning is thought to have an adverse effect on voter turnout. By the time citizens are ready to cast their ballots, most of the information they have heard about the candidates has been so negative that no candidate is appealing.

According to a yearlong study conducted in 2000 by Harvard University's Center on the Press, Politics, and Public Policy, nonvoters and voters alike shared the same criticisms of the way the media cover campaigns: Most thought the media treated campaigns like theater or entertainment. Nonvoters, however, were much more cynical about government and politicians than were voters. As the director of the study put it, "All the polls, the spin, the attack ads, the money and the negative news have soured Americans on the way we choose our president."[2]

The Rational Ignorance Effect. Another explanation of low voter turnout suggests that citizens are making a logical choice in not voting. If citizens believe that their votes will not affect the outcome of an election, then they have little incentive to seek the information they need to cast intelligent votes. The lack of incentive to obtain costly (in terms of time, attention, and so on) information about politicians and political issues has been called the **rational ignorance effect**. That term may seem contradictory, but it is not. Rational ignorance is a condition in which people purposely and rationally decide not to obtain information—to remain ignorant.[3]

Why, then, do even one-third to one-half of U.S. citizens bother to show up at the polls? One explanation is that most citizens receive personal satisfaction from the act of voting. It makes them feel that they are good citizens and that they are doing something patriotic, even though they are aware that their one vote will not change the

FIGURE 9–3 Voting in the 2008 Presidential Elections by Education Level

These statistics reinforce one another. White voters are likely to be wealthier than African American voters, who are also less likely to have obtained a college education.

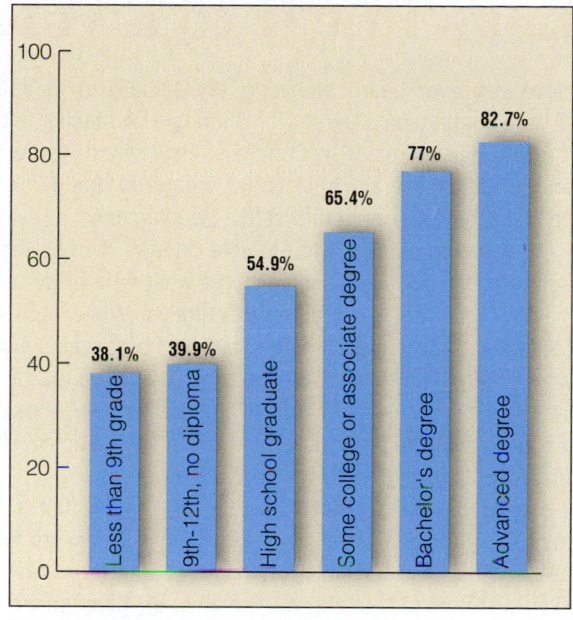

Source: U.S. Bureau of the Census, May 2010

Rational Ignorance Effect
An effect produced when people purposely and rationally decide not to become informed on an issue because they believe that their vote on the issue is not likely to be a deciding one; a lack of incentive to seek the necessary information to cast an intelligent vote.

[2]Thomas E. Patterson, *The Vanishing Voter: Public Involvement in an Age of Uncertainty* (New York: Knopf, 2002). You can continue to track the Vanishing Voter Project at the study's Web site, www.hks.harvard.edu/presspol/vanishvoter.
[3]Anthony Downs, *An Economic Theory of Democracy* (New York: Harper, 1957).

POLITICS WITH A purpose

Let's Put It to a Vote

Have you ever heard someone say, usually in indignation, "There ought to be a law . . . !"? Often this lawmaking happens in state legislatures or in Congress. However, in some states and localities, average citizens (or organized groups of "average citizens") can put an idea to a popular vote.

Why would citizens want to vote on laws themselves? The answer boils down to a debate over what type of democracy a society wants: direct or representative. While representative democracy is much more common, some states explicitly have created a means by which citizens can bypass the legislative process (through an initiative), revoke the actions of legislatures (via a referendum), or even remove elected officials from office (using recall).

While all states except Delaware require that amendments to the state constitutions go before the voters for final approval,[a] more than half of all states do not have any initiatives or referenda. In these 26 states, no mechanism exists for citizens to legislate through initiatives (enact laws by popular vote) or to overrule legislatures through referenda. The 24 states that do give citizens the ability to affect policy changes directly have seen vigorous debates over some of the most divisive and contentious issues of the day.

For example, both gay rights laws (domestic partnership laws, antidiscrimination laws) as well as laws defining marriage as a union between a man and a woman have been put to the direct democracy test. In 2006, an unsuccessful effort was made in Colorado by gay rights advocates to extend domestic partnership rights to same-sex couples through a referendum. In the same year, eight states had ballot issues to amend their constitutions to ban same-sex marriage; the amendment passed in all except one, Arizona.[b] However, in 2007, backers of a planned referendum were unable to place on the ballot referenda on two Oregon laws that extended civil rights protections, including domestic partnership, to gays and lesbians.[c] Organizers in Maine are targeting the 2009 election to attempt to add a referendum to the ballot that would repeal that state's law banning discrimination based on sexual orientation.[d]

States choose the process by which a referendum, initiative, or recall effort is allowed on the ballot and the threshold of support necessary for winning. To get on the ballot, these efforts require that signatures be collected on a petition, and the petition is allowed to circulate for a set period of time. States also choose how many signatures

are necessary for the effort to get on the ballot. Usually the minimum number is a percentage of either the total number of registered voters or the total turnout in the last general election. Sometimes states specify that the effort has to have support from across the state. Wyoming, for example, mandates that the signatures have to come from at least two-thirds of its counties.[e] Also, the signatures usually have to be from residents of that state who are registered voters. Often opponents of the effort use this stage to mount their attack. For example, in the 2007 Oregon referendum effort, supporters of gay rights were able to thwart the referendum both by challenging the validity of signatures and by effectively mobilizing in a "refuse to sign" campaign.[f]

Once it is on the ballot, the initiative, referendum, or recall must garner a certain percentage of votes. Often held in off-year elections, turnout for these votes may be very small. Some states go to great lengths, however, to ensure that the ballot issue has significant support not just from a majority of people voting in that election but also from the state's voting population. For example, Massachusetts requires that the measure receive a majority of the votes during that election and that those voting on the measure (either for or against) constitute in excess of 50 percent of those who voted in the previous general election![g] Each of these examples illustrates the importance of each vote.

[a]M. Dane Waters, "Initiative and Referendum in the United States," a presentation to the Democracy Symposium, February 16–18, 2002, Williamsburg, VA; accessed at http://ni4d.us/library/waterspaper.pdf.
[b]www.cnn.com/ELECTION/2006/pages/results/ballot.measures; accessed April 11, 2008.
[c]www.basicrights.org/?p=84; accessed April 11, 2008.
[d]www.edgeboston.com/index.php?ch=news&sc=glbt&sc2=news&sc3=&id=72878; accessed April 11, 2008.
[e]Jennifer Drage, "Initiative, Referendum, and Recall: The Process," *Journal of the American Society of Legislative Clerks and Secretaries*, Vol. 5, No. 2, 2000.
[f]www.basicrights.org/?p=84; accessed April 11, 2008.
[g]Drage, "Initiative, Referendum, and Recall: The Process."

outcome of the election.[4] Even among voters who are registered and who plan to vote, if the cost of voting goes up (in terms of time and inconvenience), the number of registered voters who actually vote will fall. In particular, bad weather on election day means that, on average, a smaller percentage of registered voters will go to the polls. It also appears that the greater the number of elections that are held, the smaller the turnout for primary and special elections. The Politics with a Purpose feature discusses the complexity of referenda elections across the states.

Plans for Improving Voter Turnout. Mail-in voting, Internet voting, registering to vote when you apply for a driver's license—these are all ideas that have been either suggested or implemented in the hope of improving voter turnout. Nonetheless, voter turnout remains relatively low.

Two other ideas seemed promising. The first was to allow voters to visit the polls up to three weeks before election day. The second was to allow voters to vote by absentee ballot without having to give any particular reason for doing so. The Committee for the Study of the American Electorate discovered, however, that in areas that had implemented these plans, neither plan increased voter turnout. Indeed, voter turnout actually fell in those jurisdictions. In other words, states that did *not* permit early voting or unrestricted absentee voting had better turnout rates than states that did. Apparently, these two innovations appeal mostly to people who already intended to vote.

What is left? One possibility is to declare election day a national holiday. In this way, more eligible voters will find it easier to go to the polls.

IN 1944, the Georgia primary was opened to African American voters as the result of a Supreme Court decision. Registrars give instructions on how to cast a ballot. (AP Photo)

---

[4]See Ilya Somin, "When Ignorance Isn't Bliss: How Political Ignorance Threatens Democracy," in *Policy Analysis*, September 22, 2004, Washington, DC: The Cato Institute, for a review of the rational ignorance theories.

LEGAL RESTRICTIONS ON VOTING

Legal restrictions on voter registration have existed since the founding of our nation. Most groups in the United States have been concerned with the suffrage issue at one time or another.

HISTORICAL RESTRICTIONS

In most of the American colonies, only white males who owned property with a certain minimum value were eligible to vote, leaving a greater number of Americans ineligible than eligible to take part in the democratic process.

Property Requirements. Many government functions concern property rights and the distribution of income and wealth, and some of the founders of our nation believed it was appropriate that only people who had an interest in property should vote on these issues. The idea of extending the vote to all citizens was, according to Charles Pinckney, a South Carolina delegate to the Constitutional Convention, merely "theoretical nonsense."

The logic behind the restriction of voting rights to property owners was questioned seriously by Thomas Paine in his pamphlet *Common Sense*:

> Here is a man who today owns a jackass, and the jackass is worth $60. Today the man is a voter and goes to the polls and deposits his vote. Tomorrow the jackass dies. The next day the man comes to vote without his jackass and cannot vote at all. Now tell me, which was the voter, the man or the jackass?[5]

The writers of the Constitution allowed the states to decide who should vote. Thus, women were allowed to vote in Wyoming in 1870 but not in the entire nation until the Nineteenth Amendment was ratified in 1920. By about 1850, most white adult males in virtually all the states could vote without any property qualification. North Carolina was the last state to eliminate its property test for voting—in 1856.

Further Extensions of the Franchise. Extension of the franchise to black males occurred with the passage of the Fifteenth Amendment in 1870. This enfranchisement was short lived, however, as the "redemption" of the South by white racists had rolled back these gains by the end of the century. As discussed in Chapter 5, African Americans, both male and female, were not able to participate in the electoral process in all states until the 1960s. The most recent extension of the franchise occurred when the voting age was reduced to 18 by the Twenty-sixth Amendment in 1971.

Is the Franchise Still Too Restrictive? There continue to be certain classes of people who do not have the right to vote. These include noncitizens and, in most states, convicted felons who have been released from prison. They also include current prison inmates, election law violators, and people who are mentally incompetent. Also, no one under the age of 18 can vote. Some political activists have argued that some of these groups should be allowed to vote. Most other democracies do not prevent persons convicted of a crime from voting after they have completed their sentences. In the 1800s, many states let noncitizen immigrants vote. In Nicaragua, the minimum voting age is 16.

One discussion concerns the voting rights of convicted felons who are no longer in prison or on parole. Some contend that voting should be a privilege, not a right, and

DID YOU KNOW?

That noncitizens were allowed to vote in some states until the early 1920s?

---

[5]Thomas Paine, *Common Sense* (London: H. D. Symonds, 1792), p. 28.

we should not want the types of people who commit felonies participating in decision making. Others believe that it is wrong to further penalize those who have paid their debt to society. These people argue that barring felons from the polls injures minority groups because minorities make up a disproportionately large share of former prison inmates.

CURRENT ELIGIBILITY AND REGISTRATION REQUIREMENTS

Voting generally requires **registration**, and to register, a person must satisfy the following voter qualifications, or legal requirements: (1) citizenship, (2) age (18 or older), and (3) residency—the duration varies widely from state to state and with types of elections. Since 1972, states cannot impose residency requirements of more than 30 days for voting in federal elections.

Each state has different qualifications for voting and registration. In 1993, Congress passed the "motor voter" bill, which requires that states provide voter-registration materials when people receive or renew driver's licenses, that all states allow voters to register by mail, and that voter-registration forms be made available at a wider variety of public places and agencies. In general, a person must register well in advance of an election, although voters in Idaho, Maine, Minnesota, Oregon, Wisconsin, and Wyoming are allowed to register up to, and on, election day. North Dakota has no voter registration at all.

Some argue that registration requirements are responsible for much of the nonparticipation in our political process. Certainly, since their introduction in the late 1800s, registration laws have reduced the voting participation of African Americans and immigrants. There also is a partisan dimension to the debate over registration and nonvoting. Republicans generally fear that an expanded electorate would help to elect more Democrats.

The question arises as to whether registration is really necessary. If it decreases participation in the political process, perhaps it should be dropped altogether. Still, as those in favor of registration requirements argue, such requirements may prevent fraudulent voting practices, such as multiple voting or voting by noncitizens. Several states have passed legislation that requires a would-be voter to show government-issued photo identification before casting a ballot.

Registration
The entry of a person's name onto the list of registered voters for elections. To register, a person must meet certain legal requirements of age, citizenship, and residency.

MANY HIGH-PROFILE ENTERTAINERS, such as actress America Ferrera, engage in charitable appearances to encourage voter registration. What might be the motivation for well-known entertainers to become part of this country's political process? (Photo by Gilbert Carrasquillo/FilmMagic/Getty Images)

EXTENSION OF THE VOTING RIGHTS ACT

In the summer of 2006, President Bush signed legislation that extended the Voting Rights Act for 25 more years. As discussed in Chapter 5, the Voting Rights Act was enacted to ensure that African Americans had equal access to the polls. Most of the provisions of the 1965 Voting Rights Act became permanent law. The 2006 act extended certain temporary sections and clarified certain amendments. For example, any new voting practices or procedures in jurisdictions with a history of discrimination in voting have to be approved by the U.S. Department of Justice or the federal district court in Washington, D.C., before being implemented. Section 203 of the 2006 act ensures that American citizens with limited proficiency in English can obtain the necessary assistance to enable them to understand and cast a ballot. Further, the act authorizes the U.S. attorney general to appoint federal election observers when there is evidence

Beyond Our Borders

WHY DO OTHER NATIONS HAVE HIGHER TURNOUT?

Most nations in the world are now democracies. Some are very new and some are still unstable, but in every democracy the question of voting turnout is important. Some scholars have speculated that voting is a matter of historic behavior: Those countries, like the democracies of Western Europe, that had the most experience with democratic practice, would naturally have greater voting turnout. Turnout data from the United States would suggest that countries in which citizens are literate and better off economically would have higher turnout. Australia and Belgium, which both have strictly enforced compulsory voting laws, do have turnout above 80 percent of the voting-age population.

However, the data in Table 9–2 show that high turnout is not restricted to nations with compulsory voting or with highly educated populations. This abbreviated table, which shows a sample of the data from the Institute for Democracy and Electoral Assistance (IDEA), finds Italy at the top of the list of democracies, followed by Iceland, New Zealand, South Africa, Austria, Belgium, Netherlands, Australia, and Denmark. While many of the nations at the head of the list are European, South Africa certainly is not. Most Central and South American countries have higher turnout than the United States, with Venezuela and Belize at 72 percent. The Philippines, Japan, Yugoslavia, and Canada have turnout just under 70 percent. Voting turnout in the United States lags behind 138 nations, at 48.3 percent average turnout for national elections. The only other advanced democracy near the United States is Switzerland at 49.3 percent.

To understand why some nations have such high turnout compared with others, IDEA looked at voting systems, compulsory voting laws, literacy and other indicators of development, and competitiveness of elections as factors impacting turnout. Its results indicate that literacy and other development factors do increase turnout, but national wealth does not in any systematic way. Proportional voting systems where the results of the election more closely mirror the proportion of votes cast for each party seem to improve turnout, but the factor that seems to be most important across all nations is competitiveness of elections. Voting turnout is considerably greater in nations where the elections are closely fought.* The competitiveness of the 2004 election in the United States following on the contested election of 2000 may well have influenced the increase in turnout here.

IN DECEMBER of 2007, Kenyans turned out to vote in the presidential election. The lines extended more than a mile through this school courtyard in Nairobi. (Roberto Schmidt/ AFP/Getty Images)

*The Institute for Democracy and Electoral Assistance (IDEA), "What Affects Turnout?" www.idea.int/vt.

FOR CRITICAL ANALYSIS

1. Why do you think the United States' turnout is so much lower than in many poorer, less-developed nations?
2. Would compulsory voting change election outcomes in the United States?
3. Would uniform voting and election laws across the United States help increase turnout?

of attempts to intimidate minority voters at the polls. Those who supported the 2006 act believe that such provisions will ensure continuing voter participation by minority groups in America. However, it is difficult to overcome the anxieties that some individuals may feel about registration and voting. Naturalized citizens may be concerned that their legal status will be questioned, and this fear may overflow to other individuals of the same ethnic background even if they were born in the United States. Indeed, individuals with limited educational backgrounds or from very rural areas may also feel as if they are not welcome at the polls.

HOW ARE ELECTIONS CONDUCTED?

The United States uses the **Australian ballot**—a secret ballot that is prepared, distributed, and counted by government officials at public expense. Since 1888, all states have used the Australian ballot. Before that, many states used the alternatives of oral

Australian Ballot
A secret ballot prepared, distributed, and tabulated by government officials at public expense. Since 1888, all U.S. states have used the Australian ballot rather than an open, public ballot.

TABLE 9–2 Turnout in Selected Countries since 1945

COUNTRIES(NO. OF ELECTIONS)	VOTE/VOTING-AGE POPULATION PERCENTAGE
Italy (14)	92.5
Iceland (16)	90.2
New Zealand (18)	86.2
South Africa (1)	85.5
Austria (16)	85.1
Belgium (17)	84.9
Netherlands (15)	84.8
Australia (21)	84.4
Denmark (22)	83.6
Bosnia and Herzegovina (1)	82.8
Germany (13)	80.6
Korea (9)	74.8
Dominican Republic (11)	68.7
Barbados (10)	63.5
India (12)	60.7
Jamaica (12)	58.5
Switzerland (13)	49.3
United States (26)	48.3

Source: IDEA, as cited in Beyond Our Borders box.

Office-Block, or Massachusetts, Ballot
A form of general-election ballot in which candidates for elective office are grouped together under the title of each office. It emphasizes voting for the office and the individual candidate, rather than for the party.

Party-Column, or Indiana, Ballot
A form of general-election ballot in which all of a party's candidates for elective office are arranged in one column under the party's label and symbol. It emphasizes voting for the party, rather than for the office or individual.

Coattail Effect
The influence of a popular candidate on the electoral success of other candidates on the same party ticket. The effect is increased by the party-column ballot, which encourages straight-ticket voting.

voting and differently colored ballots prepared by the parties. Obviously, knowing which way a person was voting made it easy to apply pressure on the person to change his or her vote, and vote buying was common.

OFFICE-BLOCK AND PARTY-COLUMN BALLOTS

Two types of Australian ballots are used in the United States in general elections. The first, called an **office-block ballot**, or sometimes a **Massachusetts ballot**, groups all the candidates for a particular elective office under the title of that office. Parties dislike the office-block ballot because it places more emphasis on the office than on the party; it discourages straight-ticket voting and encourages split-ticket voting.

A **party-column ballot** is a form of general election ballot in which all of a party's candidates are arranged in one column under the party's label and symbol. It is also called the **Indiana ballot**. In some states, it allows voters to vote for all of a party's candidates for local, state, and national offices by simply marking a single "X" or by pulling a single lever. Most states use this type of ballot. As it encourages straight-ticket voting, the two major parties favor this form. When a party has an exceptionally strong presidential or gubernatorial candidate to head the ticket, the use of the party-column ballot increases the **coattail effect** (the influence of a popular candidate on the success of other candidates on the same party ticket).

MANY STATES ALLOW paper or electronic ballots to have a "party circle" so the voter can vote for all the candidates of that party for local, state, and national offices with one mark. (Probate Court, Jefferson County, Alabama)

VOTING BY MAIL

Although voting by mail has been accepted for absentee ballots for many decades (for example, for those who are doing business away from home or for members of the armed forces), only recently have several states offered mail ballots to all of their voters. The rationale for using the mail ballot is to make voting easier for the voters. A startling result came in a special election in Oregon in spring 1996: With the mail-only ballot, turnout was 66 percent, and the state saved more than $1 million. In the 2000 presidential elections, in which Oregon voters were allowed to mail in their ballots, voter participation was more than 80 percent. Although voters in several states now have the option of voting by mail, Oregon is the only state to have abandoned precinct polling places completely. A nationwide system of voting by mail would have many pros and cons, which we explored in the *What If . . . feature.*

VOTE FRAUD

Vote fraud is something regularly suspected but seldom proved. Voting in the 1800s, when secret ballots were rare and people had a cavalier attitude toward the open buying of votes, was probably much more conducive to fraud than are modern elections. Larry J. Sabato and Glenn R. Simpson, however, claim that the potential for vote fraud

is high in many states, particularly through the use of phony voter registrations and absentee ballots.[6]

The Danger of Fraud. In California, for example, it is very difficult to remove a name from the polling list even if the person has not cast a ballot in the last two years. Thus, many persons are still on the rolls even though they no longer live in California. Enterprising political activists could use these names for absentee ballots. Other states have registration laws that are meant to encourage easy registration and voting. Such laws can be taken advantage of by those who seek to vote more than once.

After the 2000 elections, Larry Sabato again emphasized the problem of voting fraud. "It's a silent scandal," said Sabato, "and the problem is getting worse with increases in absentee voting, which is the easiest way to commit fraud." He noted that in 2000, one-third of Florida's counties found that more than 1,200 votes were cast illegally by felons, and in one county alone nearly 500 votes were cast by unregistered voters. In two precincts, the number of ballots cast was greater than the number of people who voted.[7]

Mistakes by Voting Officials. Some observers claim, however, that errors leading to fraud are trivial in number, and that a few mistakes are inevitable in a system involving millions of voters. These people argue that an excessive concern with vote fraud makes it harder for minorities and poor people to vote.

For example, in 2000, Katherine Harris, Florida's top election official, oversaw a purge of the voter rolls while simultaneously serving as co-chair of the Florida Bush campaign. According to the *New York Times*, when attempting to remove the names of convicted felons from the list of voters:

> Ms. Harris's office overruled the advice of the private firm that compiled the felon list and called for removing not just names that were an exact match, but ones that were highly inexact. Thousands of Florida voters wound up being wrongly

[6]Larry J. Sabato and Glenn R. Simpson, *Dirty Little Secrets: The Persistence of Corruption in American Politics* (New York: Random House, 1996).
[7]As cited in "Blind to Voter Fraud," *Wall Street Journal*, March 2, 2001, p. A10.

purged. . . . In Missouri, elected officials charged for years that large numbers of St. Louis residents were casting votes from vacant lots. A study conducted by *The* [St. Louis] *Post Dispatch* in 2001 found that in the vast majority of cases, the voters lived in homes that had been wrongly classified by the city.[8]

In both the Florida and Missouri examples, a majority of the affected voters were African American.

As a result of the confusion generated by the 2000 elections, many states are now in the process of improving their voting systems and procedures. Some claim that certain reforms, such as requiring voters to show a voter-registration card or photo identification, may prevent fraud but may also deter first-time voters, new citizens, and people with less educational background. By 2008, 25 states required that voters produce some sort of identification when they go to the polls. In April of that year, the Supreme Court upheld the Indiana law, which was one of the strictest in the nation, by a six-to-three vote.[9] While the court found no direct evidence of the fraud that the Indiana statute is intended to stop, there was also no evidence of any burden being placed on the voter. The ruling makes it likely that other states will pass stricter voter identification laws.

THE IMPORTANCE OF THE VOTING MACHINE

The 2000 presidential election spurred a national debate on the mechanics of how people actually cast their ballots on election day. Up until 2000, states and counties moved from hand-counted paper ballots to mechanical voting machines or electronic touch-screen devices as they could afford the move or in response to local election difficulties. The outcome of the 2000 presidential election hinged on Florida's electoral votes. The biggest problem lay in Florida's use of punch card ballots. Voters slipped their card into the voting book and then "punched" the number next to the name of the candidate they preferred. Because of the layout of the printed book in 2000, names were spread across two pages, resulting in a "butterfly" ballot. Voters could accidentally punch the wrong number and cast their vote for the wrong candidate.

NAPLES, FLORIDA election workers study punch card ballots in the state Supreme Court's ordered recount after the 2000 election. A few minutes after this photograph was taken, the U.S. Supreme Court stopped the recount and announced that it would hear the case. George W. Bush won Florida's electoral votes. (Colin Braley/Reuters/CORBIS)

[8]"How America Doesn't Vote," *New York Times: The News of the Week in Review*, February 15, 2004, p. 10.
[9]*Crawford v. Marion County Election Board*, 553 U.S.__(2008).

As the election night came to a close, it was clear that the votes in Florida between George W. Bush and Al Gore were "too close to call." Ballot problems abounded: Some voters invalidated their ballots by voting for both candidates; some punch cards were not punched all the way through, resulting in no vote being counted; some had no vote for president at all. The Democratic Party and its candidates went to court to demand a recount of the votes. The Republican political leaders in Florida tried to stop recounts in fear of losing the election. After a series of dramatic legal battles, the U.S. Supreme Court settled the election by allowing a Florida decision favoring the Republicans to stand. However, the result was a seriously flawed election process that produced tremendous cynicism about the mechanics of voting.

In 2002, Congress passed the Help America Vote Act, which established the U.S. Election Assistance Commission. The charge of the commission is to set standards for voting machines; to distribute funds to help communities acquire new, easier-to-use machines; and to act as a clearinghouse of information for the states. As expected, several companies began to create new machines for use in the voting booth. Most of these depend on digital recording of votes. Given the mistakes that occurred in Florida, many citizens wanted a record of their votes so that a mistake in tallying votes could be checked against a paper record. Election officials are deeply concerned that recording and transmitting vote counts only digitally may be subject to hacking and vote fraud. To date, no system has been devised that is totally immune to some sort of fraud, and voters continue to be concerned about the security of our election system.[10]

DID YOU KNOW?

That each new voting machine costs more than $3,000 for the equipment alone?

THE ELECTORAL COLLEGE

Many people who vote for the president and vice president think that they are voting directly for a candidate. In actuality, they are voting for **electors**, who will cast their ballots in the electoral college. Article II, Section 1, of the Constitution outlines in detail the method of choosing electors for president and vice president. The framers of the Constitution wanted to avoid the selection of president and vice president by the "excitable masses." Rather, they wished the choice to be made by a few supposedly dispassionate, reasonable men (but not women).

Elector
A member of the electoral college, which selects the president and vice president. Each state's electors are chosen in each presidential election year according to state laws.

THE CHOICE OF ELECTORS

Each state's electors are selected during each presidential election year. The selection is governed by state laws. After the national party convention, the electors normally are pledged to the candidates chosen. The total number of electors today is 538, equal to 100 senators, 435 members of the House, and three electors for the District of Columbia (the Twenty-third Amendment, ratified in 1961, added electors for the District of Columbia). Each state's number of electors equals that state's number of senators (two) plus its number of representatives. Figure 9–4 shows how the electoral votes are apportioned by state.

DID YOU KNOW?

That 42 states do not indicate on the ballot that the voter is casting a ballot for members of the electoral college rather than for the president and vice president directly?

---

[10]The AEI-Brookings Election Reform Project collects data and provides reports on progress in securing the vote at its Web site: www.electionreformproject.org.

FIGURE 9–4 Electoral Votes by State

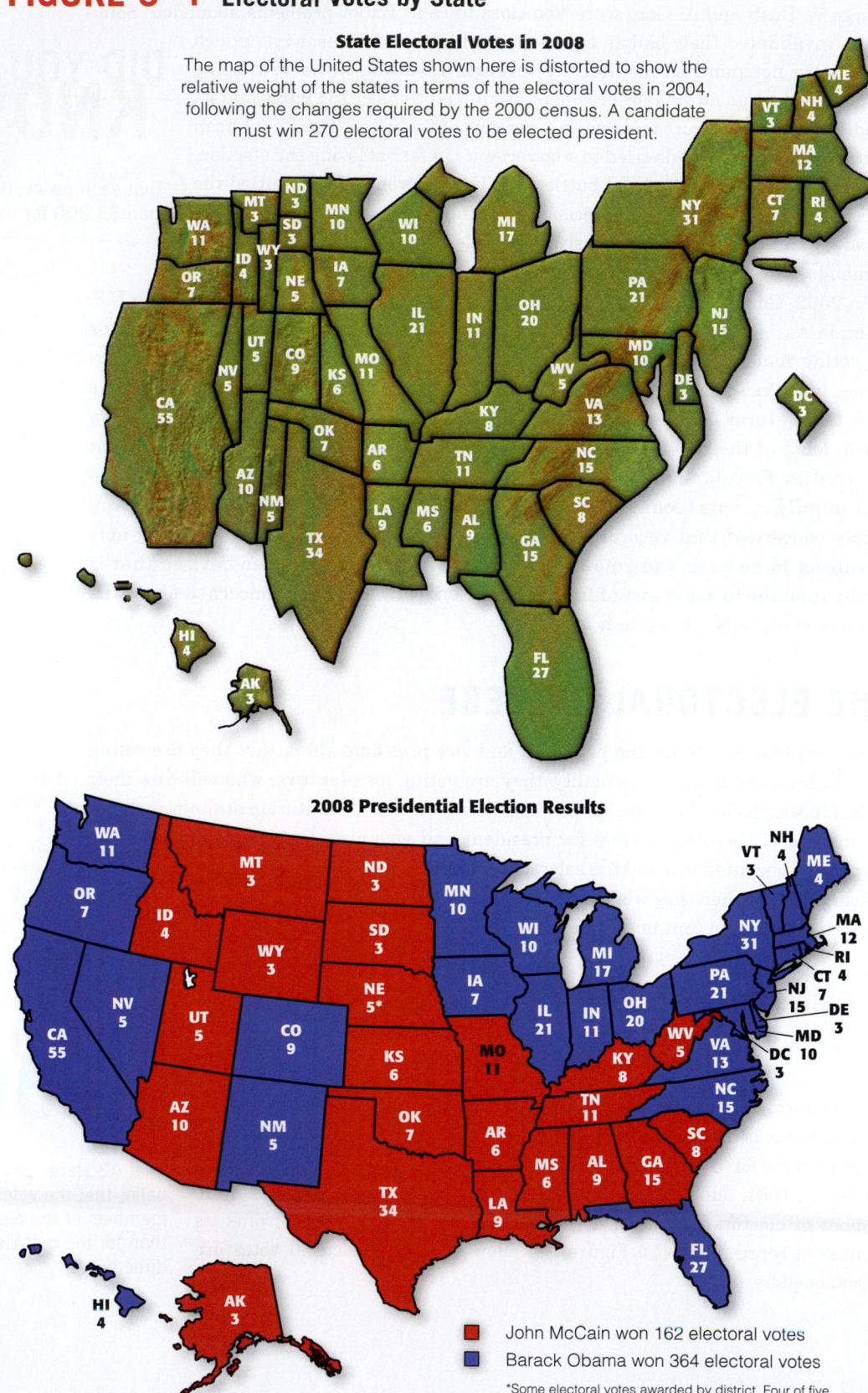

State Electoral Votes in 2008

The map of the United States shown here is distorted to show the relative weight of the states in terms of the electoral votes in 2004, following the changes required by the 2000 census. A candidate must win 270 electoral votes to be elected president.

2008 Presidential Election Results

■ John McCain won 162 electoral votes
■ Barack Obama won 364 electoral votes

*Some electoral votes awarded by district. Four of five electoral votes for NE were awarded to McCain.

(CARLSON © 2004 *The Washington Post*. Reprinted with permission of Universal Press Syndicate.)

THE ELECTORS' COMMITMENT

When a plurality of voters in a state chooses a slate of electors—except in Maine and Nebraska, where electoral votes are based on congressional districts—those electors are pledged to cast their ballots on the first Monday after the second Wednesday in December in the state capital for the presidential and vice presidential candidates of their party. The Constitution does not, however, *require* the electors to cast their ballots for the candidates of their party.

The ballots are counted and certified before a joint session of Congress early in January. The candidates who receive a majority of the electoral votes (270) are certified as president-elect and vice president–elect. According to the Constitution, if no candidate receives a majority of the electoral votes, the election of the president is decided in the House from among the candidates with the three highest numbers of votes, with each state having one vote (decided by a plurality of each state delegation). The selection of the vice president is determined by the Senate in a choice between the two candidates with the most votes, each senator having one vote. Congress was required to choose the president and vice president in 1801 (Thomas Jefferson and Aaron Burr), and the House chose the president in 1825 (John Quincy Adams).[11]

It is possible for a candidate to become president without obtaining a majority of the popular vote. There have been many minority presidents in our history, including Abraham Lincoln, Woodrow Wilson, Harry Truman, John F. Kennedy, Richard Nixon (in 1968), Bill Clinton (1992, 1996), and George W. Bush (in 2000). Such an event becomes more likely when there are important third-party candidates.

[11]For a detailed account of the process, see Michael J. Glennon, *When No Majority Rules: The Electoral College and Presidential Succession* (Washington, DC: Congressional Quarterly Press, 1993), p. 20.

Perhaps more distressing is the possibility of a candidate's being elected when an opposing candidate receives a plurality of the popular vote. This has occurred on four occasions—in the elections of John Quincy Adams in 1824, Rutherford B. Hayes in 1876, Benjamin Harrison in 1888, and George W. Bush in 2000, all of whom won elections in which an opponent received a plurality of the popular vote.

CRITICISMS OF THE ELECTORAL COLLEGE

Besides the possibility of a candidate's becoming president even though an opponent obtains more popular votes, there are other complaints about the electoral college. The idea of the Constitution's framers was to have electors use their own discretion to decide who would make the best president. But electors no longer perform the selecting function envisioned by the founders, because they are committed to the candidate who has a plurality of popular votes in their state in the general election.[12]

One can also argue that the current system, which in most states gives all of the electoral votes to the candidate who has a statewide plurality, is unfair to other candidates and their supporters. The current system of voting also means that presidential campaigning will be concentrated in those states that have the largest number of electoral votes and in those states in which the outcome is likely to be close. The other states may receive second-class treatment during the presidential campaign. It can also be argued that there is something of a bias favoring states with smaller populations, because including Senate seats in the electoral vote total partly offsets the edge of the more populous states in the House. Wyoming (with two senators and one representative) gets an electoral vote for roughly every 164,594 inhabitants (based on the 2000 census), for example, whereas Iowa gets one vote for every 418,046 inhabitants, and California has one vote for every 615,848 inhabitants. Note that many of the smallest states have Republican majorities.

Many proposals for reform of the electoral college system have been advanced, particularly after the turmoil resulting from the 2000 elections. The most obvious proposal is to eliminate the electoral college system completely and to elect candidates on a popular-vote basis; in other words, a direct election, by the people, of the president and vice president. Because abolishing the electoral college would require a constitutional amendment, however, the chances of electing the president by a direct vote are remote.

The major parties are not in favor of eliminating the electoral college, fearing that this would give minor parties a more influential role. Also, less populous states are not in favor of direct election of the president because they believe they would be overwhelmed by the large-state vote. In recent years, some states have begun to consider yet another way to make the electoral college more responsive to the popular vote. In 2007, the National Popular Vote (NPV) movement came to public attention. The movement creates a compact between the states that requires that electoral votes from NPV states will be cast for the candidate who wins the national popular vote regardless of the vote in that particular state. So far, two states have approved this law, and several more are considering it. In addition, Massachusetts, South Carolina, Virginia, and Wisconsin are among states considering adopting a district plan like that of Maine.

While the 2000 election caused considerable controversy and cynicism about the national electoral system, it also focused attention on issues that need to be resolved. Efforts to improve registration systems, to make voting easier and more secure, and to make changes to the electoral college all will work to make elections in the United States more trustworthy for the voters.

---

[12]Note, however, that there have been revolts by so-called *faithless electors*—in 1796, 1820, 1948, 1956, 1960, 1968, 1972, 1976, 1988, and 2000.

YOU CAN MAKE A Difference

REGISTERING AND VOTING

In nearly every state, before you are allowed to cast a vote in an election, you must first register. Registration laws vary considerably from state to state. Depending in part on how difficult a state's laws make it to register, some states have much lower rates of registration and voting participation than do others.

WHY SHOULD YOU CARE?

To vote, you must register. But why bother to vote? After all, the electorate is large, many elections are not close, and often your vote will not have an important effect on the election outcome. If you do vote, however, you increase the amount of attention that politicians pay to people like you. When Congress, state legislatures, or city councils consider new laws and regulations, these bodies typically give more weight to the interests of groups that are more likely to vote. So even if your single vote does not determine the outcome of an election, it does add, to a small degree, to the voter turnout for your constituency. Your vote therefore increases the chances of legislation that benefits you or that meets with your approval.

WHAT CAN YOU DO?

What do you have to do to register and cast a vote? In general, you must be a citizen of the United States, at least 18 years old on or before election day, and a resident of the state in which you intend to register. Most states require that you meet minimum-residency requirements. In other words, you must have lived in the state in which you plan to be registered for a specified period of time. If you have not lived in the state long enough to register before an upcoming election, you may retain your previous registration in another state and cast an absentee vote, if that state permits it. Minimum-residency requirements vary among the states. By a ruling of the United States Supreme Court, no state can require more than 30 days of residency. Some states require a much shorter period—for example, 10 days in Wisconsin and one day in Alabama. Thirty-one states do not have a minimum-residency requirement at all.

Can college students vote in their college town? Generally speaking, yes. Almost all students meet the 30 days of residency requirement, but states may have laws about the appropriate identification that make it more difficult to register and vote. Students should always check with the local board of elections or political party headquarters to get the right answer. And, remember, students who vote in their college town may not vote again in their parents' town.

VOTER REGISTRATION drive in Miami, Florida. (© Jeff Greenberg/Alamy)

Nearly every state also specifies a closing date by which you must be registered before an election. In other words, even if you have met a residency requirement, you still may not be able to vote if you register too close to the day of the election. The closing date is different in certain states (Connecticut and Delaware) for primary elections than for other elections. The closing date for registration varies from election day itself (Maine, Minnesota, Wisconsin, and Wyoming) to 30 days before the election in 13 states. In North Dakota, no registration is necessary.

In most states, your registration can be revoked if you do not vote within a certain number of years. This process of automatically "purging" the voter-registration lists of nonactive voters happens every two years in about a dozen states, every three years in Georgia, every four years in more than 20 other states, every five years in Maryland and Rhode Island, every eight years in North Carolina, and every 10 years in Michigan. Ten states do not require this purging at all.

Let us look at Iowa as an example. Iowa voters normally register through the local county auditor or when they obtain a driver's license (under the "motor voter" law of 1993). A voter who moves to a new address within the state must change his or her registration by contacting the auditor. Postcard registrations must be postmarked or delivered to the county auditor no later than the 15th day before an election. Voters can declare or change their party affiliation when they register or reregister, or they can change or declare a party when they go to the polls on election day. Postcard registration forms in Iowa are available at many public buildings, from labor unions, at political party headquarters, at the county auditors' offices, or from campus groups. Registrars who will accept registrations at other locations may be located by calling a party headquarters or a county auditor.

For more information on voting registration, contact your county or state officials, party headquarters, labor union, or local chapter of the League of Women Voters.*

*League of Women Voters, www.lwv.org

KEY TERMS

Australian ballot 325
coattail effect 326
elector 329

office-block, or Massachusetts, ballot 326
party-column, or Indiana, ballot 326

rational ignorance effect 319
registration 323
voter turnout 316

CHAPTER SUMMARY

1. **Who votes in the United States?** Voter participation in the United States is low compared with that of other countries. Some view low voter turnout as a threat to representative democracy, whereas others believe it simply indicates greater satisfaction with the status quo. There is an association between voting and a person's age, education, minority status, and income level. Another factor affecting voter turnout is the extent to which elections are competitive within a state. It is also true that the number of eligible voters is smaller than the number of people of voting age because of ineligible felons and immigrants who are not yet citizens.

2. **What should be the qualifications to vote?** In the United States, only citizens have been able to vote. However, in the early years of the republic, only free white male citizens who owned property were eligible to vote. Over the years, laws have excluded women, citizens under 18 years of age, felons, ex-slaves, and others. By 1973, suffrage was extended to all citizens, male and female, aged 18 or older. However, questions remain: Should felons be excluded from voting? What about resident noncitizens or people who have difficulty getting registered? Each state has somewhat different registration processes and requirements for identification at the polls. Some claim that these requirements

are responsible for much of the nonparticipation in the political process in the United States.

3. The United States uses the Australian ballot, a secret ballot that is prepared, distributed, and counted by government officials. The office-block ballot groups candidates according to office. The party-column ballot groups candidates according to their party labels and symbols.

4. Vote fraud is often charged but not often proven. After the 2000 election, states and local communities adopted new forms of voting equipment, seeking to provide secure voting systems for elections. The federal government established a commission to test new technologies and provide a clearinghouse for information.

5. **Does the popular vote determine all elections?** The voter technically does not vote directly for president but chooses between slates of presidential electors. In most states, the slate that wins the most popular votes throughout the state gets to cast all the electoral votes for the state. The candidate receiving a majority (270) of the electoral votes wins. Both the mechanics and the politics of the electoral college have been sharply criticized. There have been many proposed reforms, including a proposal that the president be elected on a popular-vote basis in a direct election.

SELECTED PRINT, MEDIA, AND ONLINE RESOURCES

PRINT RESOURCES

Alvarez, R. Michael, and Thad E. Hall. *Electronic Elections: The Perils and Promises of Digital Democracy.* Princeton, NJ: Princeton University Press, 2008. Alvarez and Hall examine all past technologies in voting and look at the new voting machines and processes that are available in the digital age. They suggest standards by which voting systems can be improved.

Fortier, John C. *Absentee and Early Voting: Trends, Promises and Perils*. Washington, DC: AEI, 2006. The author looks at all of the efforts to encourage participation by making early voting and absentee voting easier and then discusses the advantages and disadvantages of these alternatives to going to the polls.

Green, Donald P., and Alan S. Gerber. *Get Out the Vote: How to Increase Voter Turnout*. Washington, DC: Brookings Institution Press, 2004. This volume is a practical guide for activists seeking to mount Get Out The Vote (GOTV) campaigns. It differs from other guides in that it is based on research and experiments in actual electoral settings—Green and Gerber are political science professors at Yale University. The authors discover that many widely used GOTV tactics are less effective than is often believed.

Herrnson, Paul S., Richard G. Niemi, Michael J. Hanmer, Benjamin B. Bederson, Frederick C. Conrad, and Michael W. Traugott. *Voting Technology: The Not-So-Simple Act of Casting a Ballot*. Washington, DC: Brookings Institution, 2008. This book summarizes the data collected by the Brookings Institution on how voting technology impacts voters' behavior.

Martinez, Michael D. *Does Turnout Matter?* Boulder, CO: Westview Press, 2009. Scholars have expended much effort in examining why voter turnout is lower in the United States than in many other countries, but the question of whether low turnout actually matters has received less attention. Martinez is a professor of political science at the University of Florida.

Piven, Frances Fox, Lori Minnite, and Margaret Groarke. *Keeping Down the Black Vote: Race and Demobilization of American Voters*. New York: The New Press, 2009. The authors claim that under the banner of election reform, leading operatives in the Republican Party have sought to affect elections by suppressing the black vote.

Poundstone, William. *Gaming the Vote: Why Elections Aren't Fair (and What We Can Do About It)*. New York: Hill and Wang, 2009. America's first-past-the-post, winner-take-all voting system is not the only one possible, and Poundstone believes that it is actually one of the worst. In this volume, he provides a clear and witty tour of possible voting systems that may better reflect the will of the people.

Simons, Barbara, and Douglas W. Jones. *Who's Minding the Vote?* Sausalito, CA: Polipoint Press, 2008. This is a fascinating history of voting machines and technological methods that can be used to rig elections. The authors offer a scathing criticism of certain recently developed electronic voting systems.

MEDIA RESOURCES

American Blackout—A 2005 film starring former congresswoman Cynthia McKinney from Georgia as she investigates the ways in which African American voters can be challenged at the polls and kept from voting.

Election Day—This 2005 film was shot on election day in 2004 and looks at 14 different individuals who are trying to vote or who are working at the polls themselves.

Hacking Democracy—An HBO production that follows activist Bev Harris of Seattle and others as they take on Diebold, a company that makes electronic voting machines. The documentary argues that security lapses in Diebold's machines are a threat to the democratic process.

Mississippi Burning—This 1988 film, starring Gene Hackman and Willem Dafoe, is a fictional version of the investigation of the death of two civil rights workers who came to Mississippi to help register African Americans to vote in 1964.

Recount—A 2008 film nominated for an Emmy Award that chronicles the disputed 2000 presidential contest in Florida, where a mere 538 ballots separated Republican George W. Bush and Democrat Al Gore. The film makes out the victorious Republican operatives to be much more aggressive than the rather hapless Democrats.

Trouble in Paradise—Shot in Florida after the contested 2000 presidential election, the film follows Florida residents as they find out what laws have been changed and which aspects of voting are still troubling in their state. The film was released in 2004.

ONLINE RESOURCES

AEI-Brookings Election Reform Project In response to the Help America Vote Act of 2002, this project aims to synthesize voting reform research and create a bridge between the research and policy communities. Discusses election technologies and their pros and cons: www.electionreformproject.org

The Center for Voting and Democracy a source of analysis and perspective on improving how elections are held in the United States. Discusses the impact of different voting systems on election strategies and outcomes: www.fairvote.org

Institute for Democracy and Electoral Assistance (IDEA) an intergovernmental organization that supports sustainable democracy worldwide. Provides information about voting and turnout around the world: www.idea.int

National Conference of State Legislatures Find out what different states are doing to ensure the vote: www.ncsl.org/programs/legismgt/elect/elect.htm

Oregon Secretary of State Elections Division includes frequently asked questions and a brief history of voting by mail: http://www.sos.state.or.us/elections/

10

Barack Obama greets supporters as he makes his way into a rally at Bristow, Virginia, on June 5, 2008. He had already clinched the nomination for president. (Mandel Ngan/AFP/Getty Images)

Campaigning for Office

QUESTIONS TO CONSIDER

What are the hallmarks of free and fair elections?

Should all candidates have equal campaign financing?

Should party members or the general public nominate the candidates for president?

CHAPTER CONTENTS

what if...

Spending Limits Were Placed On Campaigns?

BACKGROUND

After the 2008 presidential primary campaigns ended, more than $7.5 million was distributed by the Federal Election Commission (FEC) to candidates including Joe Biden, Christopher Dodd, John Edwards, Dennis Kucinich, and Ralph Nader. However, the major primary contenders in both parties (including Barack Obama, Hillary Clinton, John McCain, Mitt Romney, and Mike Huckabee) refused the public funding, raising more than $500 million themselves. The political parties each received a little more than $16 million from the FEC for their conventions. In addition, Congress appropriated $50 million to each convention city for help with security and police issues. Both Denver and St. Paul had to raise another $50 million to $60 million from private funds to hold the conventions. For the general election, Republican nominee John McCain accepted $85 million for his campaign, but Democratic nominee Barack Obama refused public funding, preferring to raise campaign funds without the restrictions that come with public funds.

One of the most fundamental questions about campaign financing in the United States is the fairness of one candidate who raises more money to finance a strong organization and buy more media advertisements than others. Do voters have an equal chance to hear the positions and promises of all the candidates if some have greater financial resources? Should one candidate be able to buy five times more television time than another? The Supreme Court has said that individuals can spend their own funds for their campaigns as a practice of free speech. The same principle holds for interest groups that wish to express their views on the issues. So, the tension over regulating campaign finance lies between advocates of free speech and advocates of fairness.

WHAT IF SPENDING LIMITS WERE PLACED ON CAMPAIGNS?

If some sort of limit on campaign spending were found to be constitutional, one consequence would be a decline in the number of candidates with "deep pockets." In other words, fewer of the very rich would attempt to run for office, because they would not be able to use their personal wealth in the effort to win.

A limit on campaign spending would also mean a limit on campaign contributions. Consequently, special-interest groups and lobbying organizations would necessarily diminish in numbers. The lobbying industry would shrink, because one of the best ways to influence legislation is to make sure that the candidate of choice is elected or reelected. Contributions are certainly helpful in winning elections.

THE IMPACT ON TELEVISION

The television industry would also be affected. Just as the bulk of the public's entertainment time is spent on television, so too is the bulk of campaign spending. Consider that in just the month before the Iowa caucuses in 2008, $9 million was spent on television ads in Des Moines, Iowa, alone. Voters in Iowa's capital saw 22,000 ads for the candidates. In the last week of the presidential campaigns in 2004, the two candidates spent more than $40 million on TV ads. A limit on total campaign spending would, by necessity, dramatically reduce spending on television advertising. Media companies, which count on increased profits in election years, would see a decline in their revenue, and overall advertising prices would decline.

WE HAVE ALREADY ATTEMPTED TO REFORM CAMPAIGNS

Complaints about excessive campaign spending are not new. Even sitting politicians have attempted to clean up elections. The BCRA of 2002 was one such attempt. The law became effective in January 2003. This law prohibited, among other things, so-called soft money contributions and expenditures that were clearly being used to influence federal elections. It also banned supposedly nonpartisan issue ads that were funded by corporations and labor unions. Such ads cannot appear 30 days prior to a primary election or 60 days before a general election. As we saw earlier, however, campaign spending overall has increased dramatically since the act became effective.

FOR CRITICAL ANALYSIS

1. Why would it be extremely difficult to *effectively* limit campaign spending?
2. If campaign spending limits were effective, who would be hurt more—those politicians already in office or those attempting to win an election for the first time? Explain your answer.

FREE ELECTIONS ARE the cornerstone of the American political system. Voters choose one candidate from a pool of candidates to hold political office by casting ballots in local, state, and federal elections. Voters are free from intimidation or coercion and are able to get easy access to information about the election, as provided for by a free press. In 2008, the voters chose Barack Obama and Joe Biden to be president and vice president of the United States for the next four years. In addition, voters elected all of the members of the House of Representatives and one-third of the members of the Senate. The campaigns were bitter, long, and extremely expensive, with the Democratic primary contest being the closest and most expensive in history. The total cost for all federal elections in the 2007–2008 cycle was more than $5 billion.

Voters and candidates frequently criticize the American electoral process. It is said to favor wealthier candidates, to further the aims of special-interest groups, and to be dominated by older voters and those with better educations and higher incomes. Recent reforms of the campaign finance laws were tested for the first time in 2004. Although the new laws had some effect on campaign strategy, fundraising outside the system and extensive use of television advertising dominated the election season. New media, especially e-mail, text messaging, and blogging, were used to increase youth participation.

WHO WANTS TO BE A CANDIDATE?

Democratic political systems require competitive elections, meaning that opposition candidates for each office have a chance to win. If there is no competition for any office—president or local school superintendent—then the public has no ability to make a choice about its leadership or policies to be pursued. Who, then, are the people who seek to run for office?

There are thousands of elective offices in the United States. The political parties strive to provide a slate of candidates for every election. Recruiting candidates is easier for some offices than for others. Political parties may have difficulty finding candidates for the board of the local water control district, but they generally have a sufficient number of candidates for county commissioner or sheriff. The higher the office and the more prestige attached to it, the more candidates are likely to want to run. In many areas of the country, however, one political party may be considerably stronger than the other. In those situations, the minority party may have more difficulty finding nominees for elections in which victory is unlikely.

The presidential campaign provides the most colorful and exciting look at candidates and how they prepare to compete for office—in this instance, the highest office in the land. The men and women who wanted to be candidates in the 2008 presidential campaign faced a long and obstacle-filled path. First, they needed to

Mayoral candidates Mike Shallow, left, and Yvonne Scarlett-Golden answer questions during a political forum for candidates in Daytona Beach, Florida. (Daytona Beach News-Journal/Craig Litten/AP Photos)

Presidential Primary
A statewide primary election of delegates to a political party's national convention, held to determine a party's presidential nominee.

Superdelegate
A party leader or elected official who is given the right to vote at the party's national convention. Superdelegates are not elected at the state level.

raise sufficient funds to plan for the early campaigns in Iowa and New Hampshire. Then, they faced an unprecedented number of early **presidential primaries**, which determined if they could win in diverse states. The early primaries were followed by "Super Tuesday" with 22 primaries. Candidates and their campaign organizations needed to have strategies that maximized their strengths across the nation and, at the same time, raised enough donations to keep national campaigns going. They had to keep their organization alive for the primary season, plan to win caucus and primary votes, and, in the case of the Democrats in 2008, convince enough **superdelegates** to win the nomination before the convention. John McCain won his party's primaries early enough to begin raising funds for the general election, while Barack Obama and Hillary Clinton battled throughout the primary season, with Barack Obama ultimately receiving his party's nomination. These candidates raised and spent record amounts of money in their fight for the nomination.

WHY THEY RUN

People who choose to run for office can be divided into two groups—the self-starters and those who are recruited. The volunteers, or self-starters, get involved in political activities to further their careers, to carry out specific political programs, or in response to certain issues or events. Ralph Nader's campaigns for the presidency in 2000 and 2004 were rooted in his belief that the two major parties were ignoring vital issues, such as environmental protection and the influence of corporate wealth on American politics. Candidates such as Ron Paul, on the Republican side, and Dennis Kucinich, on the Democratic side, run for president to present their positions, even though they know that they have very little chance of winning.

Issues are important, but self-interest and personal goals—status, career objectives, prestige, and income—are central in motivating some candidates to enter political life. Political office is often seen as the stepping-stone to achieving certain career goals. A lawyer or an insurance agent may run for office only once or twice and then return to private life with enhanced status. Other politicians may aspire to long-term political office—for example, county offices such as commissioner or sheriff sometimes offer attractive opportunities for power, status, and income and are in themselves career goals. Finally, we think of ambition as the desire for ever-more-important offices and higher status. Politicians who run for lower offices and then set their sights on Congress or a governorship may be said to have "progressive" ambitions.[1]

THE NOMINATION PROCESS

Individuals become official candidates through the process of nomination. Generally, nominating processes for all offices are controlled by state laws and usually favor the two major political parties. For most minor offices, individuals become candidates by submitting petitions to the local election board. Political parties often help individuals obtain the petitions, pay whatever filing fee is required, and gather signatures. In most states, a candidate from one of the two major parties faces far fewer requirements to get on the ballot than a candidate who is an independent or who represents a minor or new party.

For higher-level offices, candidates may need to petition and then be nominated by a party convention at the state level. In other jurisdictions, party caucuses are empowered to nominate candidates. And, as will be discussed later, many contenders for office

[1]See the discussion of this topic in Linda Fowler, *Candidates, Congress, and the American Democracy* (Ann Arbor, MI: University of Michigan Press, 1993), pp. 56–59.

are nominated through a primary election in which two or more individuals contend for the party's nomination.

The American system of nominations and primary elections is one of the most complex in the world. In most European nations, the political party's choice of candidates is final, and no primary elections are ever held.

WHO IS ELIGIBLE?

There are few constitutional restrictions on who can become a candidate in the United States. As set out in the Constitution, the formal requirements for national office are as follows:

1. *President.* Must be a natural-born citizen, have attained the age of 35 years, and be a resident of the country for 14 years by the time of inauguration.
2. *Vice president.* Must be a natural-born citizen, have attained the age of 35 years, and not be a resident of the same state as the candidate for president.[2]
3. *Senator.* Must be a citizen for at least nine years, have attained the age of 30 by the time of taking office, and be a resident of the state from which elected.
4. *Representative.* Must be a citizen for at least seven years, have attained the age of 25 by the time of taking office, and be a resident of the state from which elected.

The qualifications for state legislators are set by the state constitutions and likewise include age, place of residence, and citizenship. (Usually, the requirements for the upper chamber of a legislature are somewhat more stringent than those for the lower chamber.) The legal qualifications for running for governor or other state office are similar.

WHO RUNS?

Despite these minimal legal qualifications for office at both the national and state levels, a quick look at the slate of candidates in any election—or at the current members of the U.S. House of Representatives—will reveal that not all segments of the population take advantage of these opportunities. Holders of political office in the United States are overwhelmingly white and male. Until the 20th century, presidential candidates were of northern European origin and of Protestant heritage.[3] Laws that effectively denied voting rights made it impossible to elect African American public officials in many areas in which African Americans constituted a significant portion of the population. As a result of the passage of major civil rights legislation in the 1960s, however, the number of African American public officials has increased throughout the United States. By 2007, the number of African American elected officials was estimated at more than 9,500,[4] and 84 percent of Americans said they would be completely comfortable voting for an African American for president.[5]

Women as Candidates. Until recently, women generally were considered to be appropriate candidates only for lower-level offices, such as state legislator or school board member. It was thought that women would be more acceptable to the voting public if they were either running for an office that allowed them to continue their family duties, or were running for an office that focused on local affairs, such as city or school issues. The last

DID YOU KNOW?

That five women received votes for vice president at the Democratic Convention in 1924, the first held after women received the right to vote in 1920?

---

[2]Technically, a presidential and vice presidential candidate can be from the same state, but if they are, one of the two must forfeit the electoral votes of his or her home state.
[3]A number of early presidents were Unitarian. The Unitarian Church is not Protestant, but it is historically rooted in the Protestant tradition.
[4]Ralph Everett, "Number of Black Elected Officials Increases, But Not by Much," *Joint Center Journal*, 2007.
[5]Gallup Poll, February/March 2007.

FIGURE 10–1 Women Running for Congress (and Winning)

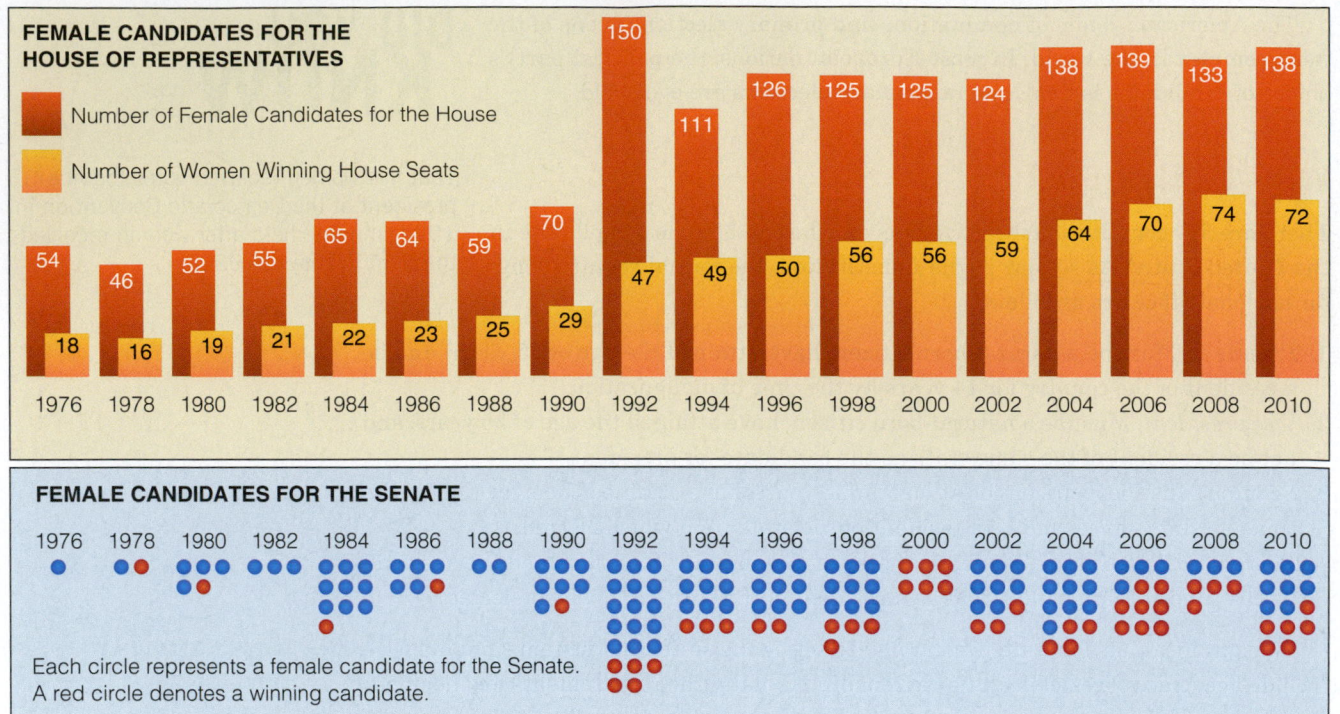

FEMALE CANDIDATES FOR THE HOUSE OF REPRESENTATIVES

■ Number of Female Candidates for the House

■ Number of Women Winning House Seats

Year	Candidates	Winners
1976	54	18
1978	46	16
1980	52	19
1982	55	21
1984	65	22
1986	64	23
1988	59	25
1990	70	29
1992	150	47
1994	111	49
1996	126	50
1998	125	56
2000	125	56
2002	124	59
2004	138	64
2006	139	70
2008	133	74
2010	138	72

FEMALE CANDIDATES FOR THE SENATE

1976 1978 1980 1982 1984 1986 1988 1990 1992 1994 1996 1998 2000 2002 2004 2006 2008 2010

Each circle represents a female candidate for the Senate. A red circle denotes a winning candidate.

20 years have seen a tremendous increase in the number of women who run for office, not only at the state level but for the U.S. Congress as well. Figure 10–1 shows the increase in female candidates. In 2010, 152 women ran for Congress, and 78 were elected. One of the most notable women of recent years has been Nancy Pelosi, the Speaker of the House until 2011.

In the past, women were not recruited because they had not worked their way up through the male-dominated party organization or because they were thought to have no chance of winning. Women also had a more difficult time raising campaign funds. Since the 1970s, there has been a focused effort to increase the number of women candidates. EMILY's List, a group that raises money to recruit and support liberal women candidates, has had a strong impact on the situation for women candidates. Other organizations with more conservative agendas also raise money for women. Today, it is clear that women can raise the necessary funds to run a campaign, run it effectively, and attract enough voters to win almost any office. According to the Gallup Poll, a vast majority of Americans (86 percent) would vote for a qualified woman for president.[6]

Lawyers as Candidates. Candidates are likely to be professionals, particularly lawyers. Political campaigning and officeholding are simply easier for some occupational groups than for others, and political involvement can make a valuable contribution to certain careers. Lawyers, for example, have more flexible schedules than do many other professionals, can take time off for campaigning, and can leave their jobs to hold public office full time. Furthermore, holding political office is good publicity for their professional practice, and they usually have partners or associates to keep the firm going while they are in office. Perhaps most important, many jobs that lawyers aspire to—federal or state judgeships, state attorney positions, or work in a federal agency—can be attained by

[6]Gallup Poll, September 8–11, 2005.

political appointment. Such appointments often go to loyal partisans who have served their party by running for and holding office. For certain groups, then, participation in the political arena may further personal ambitions, whereas it could be a sacrifice for others whose careers demand full-time attention for many years.

THE 21ST CENTURY CAMPAIGN

After the candidates have been nominated, the most exhausting and expensive part of the election process begins—the general election campaign. The contemporary political campaign is becoming more complex and more sophisticated with every election. Even with the most appealing of candidates, today's campaigns require a strong organization; expertise in political polling and marketing; professional assistance in fundraising, accounting, and financial management; and technological capabilities in every aspect of the campaign.

THE CHANGING CAMPAIGN

The goal is the same for all campaigns—to convince voters to choose a candidate or a slate of candidates for office. Part of the reason for the increased intensity of campaigns in the last decade is that they are now centered on the candidate, not on the party. The candidate-centered campaign emerged in response to several developments: changes in the electoral system, the increased importance of television and other forms of electronic media in campaigns, technological innovations such as computers, and the increased cost of campaigning.

To run a successful and persuasive campaign, the candidate's organization must be able to raise funds for the effort, obtain coverage from the media, produce and pay for political commercials and advertising, schedule the candidate's time effectively, convey the candidate's position on the issues to the voters, conduct research on the opposing candidate, and get the voters to go to the polls. When party identification was stronger among voters and before the advent of television campaigning, a strong party organization at the local, state, or national level could furnish most of the services and expertise that the candidate needed. Political parties provided the funds for campaigning until the 1970s. Parties used their precinct organizations to distribute literature, register voters, and get out the vote on election day. Less effort was spent on advertising each candidate's positions and character, because the party label presumably communicated that information to many voters.

One of the reasons that campaigns no longer depend on parties is that fewer people identify with them (see Chapter 8), as is evident from the increased number of political independents. In 1952, about one-fifth of adults identified themselves as independents, whereas in 2010, about one-third considered themselves to be independents. Political independents include not only adults who are well educated and issue oriented, but also many individuals who are not very interested in politics or well informed about candidates or issues.

THE PROFESSIONAL CAMPAIGN

Whether the candidate is running for the state legislature, for the governor's office, for the U.S. Congress, or for the presidency, every campaign has some fundamental tasks to accomplish. Today, in national elections, the lion's share of these tasks is handled by paid professionals, rather than volunteers or amateur politicians. Volunteers and amateurs are primarily used for the last-minute registration or voter turnout activities.

DID YOU KNOW?

That EMILY's List means Early Money Is Like Yeast, referring both to needing money early in a campaign and to yeast for raising bread?

Political Consultant
A paid professional hired to devise a campaign strategy and manage a campaign.

Finance Chairperson
The campaign professional who directs fundraising, campaign spending, and compliance with campaign finance laws and reporting requirements.

Pollster
The person or firm who conducts public opinion polls for the campaign.

FORMER CAMPAIGN consultant and now senior White House adviser to President Barack Obama, David Axelrod checks his wireless device for messages. (AP Photo/Alex Brandon)

The most sought-after and possibly the most criticized campaign expert is the **political consultant**, who, for a large fee, devises a campaign strategy, creates a campaign theme, oversees the advertising, and possibly chooses the campaign colors and the candidate's official portrait. Political consultants began to displace volunteer campaign managers in the 1960s, about the same time that television became a force in campaigns. The paid consultant monitors the campaign's progress, plans all media appearances, and coaches the candidate for debates. The consultants and the firms they represent are not politically neutral; most will work only for candidates from one party.

Under constant pressure to raise more campaign funds and to comply with the campaign finance laws, virtually all campaigns need a **finance chairperson** who plans the fundraising strategy and finds the legal and accounting expertise needed for the organization. Of course, campaigns will either hire an in-house **pollster** or contract with a major polling firm for the tracking polls and focus groups discussed in Chapter 6.

Candidates need to have a clear strategy to gain public attention and to respond to attacks by their opponents. The campaign's **communications director** plans appearances, the themes to be communicated by the candidate at specific points in the campaign, and the responses to any attacks. The campaign's **press secretary** is responsible for dealing directly with the press. Perhaps the most famous example of a successful communication strategy was that of Bill Clinton in his 1992 victory. The campaign organized a "War Room" to instantly respond to any attack by his opponents. Today's candidates also need a communication strategy that utilizes social networks and the Internet. At the end of the campaign is the actual election. Campaigns need to find a way to recruit and organize volunteers for the **Get Out the Vote (GOTV)** drive to persuade voters to come to the polls on election day.

THE STRATEGY OF WINNING

In the United States, unlike some European countries, there are no rewards for a candidate who comes in second; the winner takes all. A winner-take-all system is also known as a *plurality voting system*. In most situations, the winning candidate does not have to have a majority of the votes. If there are three candidates, the one who gets the most votes wins—that is, "takes it all"—and the other two candidates get nothing. Given this system, the campaign organization must plan a strategy that maximizes the candidate's chances of winning. In American politics, candidates seek to capture all of the votes of their party's supporters, to convince a majority of the independent voters to vote for them, and to gain a few votes from supporters of the other party. To accomplish these goals, candidates must consider their visibility, their message, and their campaign strategy.

CANDIDATE VISIBILITY AND APPEAL

One of the most important concerns is how well known the candidate is. If she or he is a highly visible incumbent, there may be little need for campaigning except to remind the voters of the officeholder's good deeds. If, however, the candidate is an unknown challenger or a largely unfamiliar character attacking a well-known public figure, the campaign must devise a strategy to get the candidate before the public.

In the case of the independent candidate or the candidate representing a minor party, the problem of name recognition is serious. Such candidates must present an overwhelming case for the voter to reject the major-party candidates. Both Democratic and Republican candidates use the strategic ploy of labeling third-party candidates as "not serious"—and therefore not worth the voter's time.

THE USE OF OPINION POLLS

Opinion polls are a major source of information for both the media and the candidates. Poll taking is widespread during the primaries. Presidential hopefuls have private polls taken to make sure that there is at least some chance they could be nominated and, if nominated, elected. During the presidential campaign, polling is even more frequent. Polls are taken not only by the regular pollsters—Roper, Harris, Gallup, and others—but also privately by the candidate and his or her campaign organization. As the election approaches, many candidates and commercial houses use **tracking polls**, which are polls taken almost every day, to find out how well they are competing for votes. Tracking polls enable consultants to fine-tune the advertising and the candidate's speeches in the last days of the campaign.

FOCUS GROUPS

Another tactic is to use a **focus group** to gain insights into public perceptions of the candidate. Professional consultants organize a discussion of the candidate or of certain political issues among 10 to 15 ordinary citizens. The citizens are selected from specific target groups in the population—for example, working women, blue-collar men, senior citizens, or young voters. Recent campaigns have tried to reach groups such as "soccer moms," "Wal-Mart shoppers," or "NASCAR dads."[7] The group discusses personality traits of the candidate, political advertising, and other candidate-related issues. The conversation is digitally video recorded (and often observed from behind a mirrored wall). Focus groups are expected to reveal more emotional responses to candidates or the deeper anxieties of voters—feelings that consultants believe often are not tapped into by more impersonal telephone surveys. The campaign then can shape its messages to respond to these feelings and perceptions.

FINANCING THE CAMPAIGN

In a book published in 1932 entitled *Money in Elections*, Louise Overacker had the following to say about campaign financing:

> The financing of elections in a democracy is a problem which is arousing increasing concern. Many are beginning to wonder if present-day methods of raising and

DID YOU KNOW?

That a candidate can buy lists of all the voters in a precinct, county, or state for only about two cents per name from a commercial firm?

---

[7]NASCAR stands for the National Association of Stock Car Auto Racing.

Beyond Our Borders

HOW SHORT CAN A CAMPAIGN BE?

Consider the difference between U.S. presidential campaigns and the British system of elections for Parliament and prime minister. In the United States, candidates for president begin traveling the country and building up support about two years before the general election. The primary election season starts just after January 1st of the election year, and the campaigns continue nonstop for almost 11 months.

In the United Kingdom, the prime minister makes the decision to hold elections for Parliament, or the House of Commons. In any case, parliamentary elections must be held at least every five years by law. The prime minister asks the queen to call elections either when the party's support is declining or when there might be an advantage to the majority party to hold elections. In one year, there were two general elections due to the instability of the party's majority. When the queen issues the proclamation dissolving the Parliament, the date for the general election is set, and it must be held within 17 days of the proclamation. From that moment until the election is held, the parliamentary buildings are closed to the public, and government administrators may not make any announcements of new initiatives or new decisions on policy.*

In less than three weeks, the political parties assemble their candidates for each constituency, name their leaders as contenders for the prime minister's position, and do all their campaigning, both locally and nationally. With each new election in Great Britain, more American practices have come into play. American political consultants are regularly hired to help with developing the message for the parties and planning the advertising campaign. Survey research and political polling are also well developed in Great Britain, and pre-election polls are widely read. In the 2010 election, the three major party candidates held a live debate on television, American-style, for the first time in British history. Generally, the debate seemed to highlight the performance of the third party candidate, the leader of the Liberal Democratic Party.

So, how do the parties use that time, and how much money is spent during this short campaign period? British law has focused on spending limits for the campaign rather than on donation limits. Each party is limited in its expenditures during the year before the election. The spending limits are set on a constituency basis. In 2005, each major party was limited to spending about $25,000 per seat in the House of Commons. Compare that with the United States' average expenditure of more than $1 million for each seat in the House of Representatives. Altogether, the expenditures of the three contending parties in 2005 were about $125 million, compared to the billions spent in the United States for a similar period.** Finally, after the votes were counted in 2010, no party held a majority of seats in the House of Commons, meaning that none of the three contenders for prime minister would be named leader of the government. (The leader of the government in Great Britain is an elected member of Parliament and the leader of the majority party.) The Labor Party won more seats than the Conservative Party, while the Liberal Democratic Party won enough seats to form a coalition. Several days after the election, the Liberal Democratic Party agreed to a deal with the Conservative

---

*See the excellent Web site maintained by the British parliament for more information: http://www.parliament.uk.
**Library of Congress: http://www.loc.gov/law/help/campaign-finance/uk.php.

Party, and a government was formed. It was an interesting arrangement because the Liberal Democratic Party is actually closer to the Labor Party on many issues, but its platform insisted on electoral reform, which its new partner, the Conservative Party, agreed to.

Could the United States face a similar situation in congressional elections or even the presidential election? Yes, if a third party became strong enough. Conceivably, a third party could win enough seats in Congress to deny the majority to either the Democrats or the Republicans. It is much more difficult in America for a third party to win enough electoral votes to send the presidential election into the House of Representatives, as discussed in Chapter 9, but it is possible.

The larger question is whether the United States could adopt some electoral reforms to reduce the cost of our campaigns (and the possible influence of donors) and shorten the season. While a six-week window and 17- day campaign seem very short, most Americans would like to see a shorter election season and less campaign advertising in their lives.

WITH NEITHER PARTY winning a clear majority of the seats in parliament, David Cameron of the Conservative Party and Nick Clegg of the Liberal Democratic Party formed a partnership to govern the United Kingdom. Cameron became the Prime Minister while Clegg took the title, Deputy Prime Minister. Here they walk to the opening parliamentary session together. (BEN STANSALL/AFP/Getty Images)

FOR CRITICAL ANALYSIS

1. Do you think American campaigns would generate more or less excitement and voter turnout if they were considerably shorter?
2. Is it really possible for candidates and parties to explain their platforms and present their candidates in a couple of weeks?

spending campaign funds do not clog the wheels of our elaborately constructed mechanism of popular control, and if democracies do not inevitably become [governments ruled by small groups].[8]

Although writing more than 70 years ago, Overacker touched on a sensitive issue in American political campaigns—the connection between money and elections. As mentioned earlier, more than $5 billion was spent at all levels of campaigning during the 2007–2008 election cycle. Total spending by the presidential candidates in 2008 amounted to about $1 billion. For the midterm senatorial election in 2006 in New York State alone, the two candidates together amassed $50 million in contributions for their campaigns. Arizona, Michigan, Minnesota, Missouri, Nebraska, Pennsylvania, and Washington all saw senatorial campaigns costing between $15 million and $30 million. As might be expected, candidates spend much less to retain or obtain a seat in the House of Representatives, because representatives must run for election every two

[8]Louise Overacker, *Money in Elections* (New York: Macmillan, 1932), p. vii.

years as opposed to every six years for senators. (There are other reasons, too.) Except for the presidential campaigns, all of these funds had to be provided by the candidates and their families, borrowed, or raised by contributions from individuals, political parties, or *political action committees*, described later in this chapter. For the presidential campaigns, some of the funds may come from the federal government.

REGULATING CAMPAIGN FINANCING

The way campaigns are financed has changed dramatically in the last 25 years. Today, candidates and political parties must operate within the constraints imposed by complicated laws regulating campaign financing.

A variety of federal **corrupt practices acts** have been designed to regulate campaign financing. The first, passed in 1925, limited primary and general election expenses for congressional candidates. In addition, it required disclosure of election expenses and, in principle, put controls on contributions by corporations. There were many loopholes in the restrictions, and the acts proved to be ineffective.

The **Hatch Act** (Political Activities Act) of 1939 is best known for restricting the political activities of civil servants. The act also, however, made it unlawful for a political group to spend more than $3 million in any campaign and limited individual contributions to a political group to $5,000. Of course, such restrictions were easily circumvented by creating additional political groups.

In the 1970s, Congress passed additional legislation to reshape the nature of campaign financing. In 1971, it passed the Federal Election Campaign Act to reform the process. Then in 1974, in the wake of the Watergate scandal (see Chapter 6), Congress enacted further reforms.

THE FEDERAL ELECTION CAMPAIGN ACT

The Federal Election Campaign Act (FECA) of 1971, which became effective in 1972, essentially replaced all past laws. The act placed no limit on overall spending but restricted the amount that could be spent on mass-media advertising, including television. It limited the amount that candidates could contribute to their own campaigns (a limit later ruled unconstitutional) and required disclosure of all contributions and expenditures over $100. In principle, the FECA limited the role of labor unions and corporations in political campaigns. It also provided for a voluntary $1 (now $3) check-off on federal income tax returns for general campaign funds to be used by major-party presidential candidates.

Further Reforms in 1974. For many, the 1971 act did not go far enough. Amendments to the FECA passed in 1974 did the following:

1. *Created the Federal Election Commission.* This commission consists of six nonpartisan administrators whose duties are to enforce compliance with the requirements of the act.
2. *Provided public financing for presidential primaries and general elections.* Any candidate running for president who is able to obtain sufficient contributions in at least 20 states can obtain a subsidy from the U.S. Treasury to help pay for primary campaigns. In 2004, however, neither George W. Bush nor John Kerry accepted public financing for the primaries. This allowed both of them to spend much more on advertising and other expenses than they could have if they had accepted public funding. Each of them did accept $74.62 million for the general election campaign.
3. *Limited presidential campaign spending.* Any candidate accepting federal support must agree to limit campaign expenditures to the amount prescribed by federal law.

4. *Limited contributions.* Under the 1974 amendments, citizens could contribute up to $1,000 to each candidate in each federal election or primary; the total limit on all contributions from an individual to all candidates was $25,000 per year. Groups could contribute a maximum of $5,000 to a candidate in any election. (As you will read shortly, some of these limits were changed by the 2002 campaign reform legislation.)

5. *Required disclosure.* Each candidate must file periodic reports with the FEC listing who contributed, how much was spent, and for what the funds were spent.

The 1971 and 1974 laws regulating campaign contributions and spending set in place the principles that have guided campaign finance ever since. The laws and those that have been enacted subsequently are guided by three principles: (1) set limits on what individuals and groups can give to individual candidates and within one election cycle; (2) provide some public funding for the presidential primaries, conventions, and the general election campaign; and (3) make all contributions and reports public. All contributions that are made to candidates under these laws and principles are usually called **hard money**. As will be detailed later, however, individuals and groups that wish to circumvent these principles have been successful in finding ways to do so.

Buckley v. Valeo. The 1971 act had limited the amount that each individual could spend on his or her own behalf. The Supreme Court declared the provision unconstitutional in 1976, in *Buckley v. Valeo*,[9] stating that it was unconstitutional to restrict in any way the amount congressional candidates could spend on their own behalf: "The candidate, no less than any other person, has a First Amendment right to engage in the discussion of public issues and vigorously and tirelessly to advocate his own election."

The *Buckley v. Valeo* decision, which has often been criticized, was directly countered by a 1997 Vermont law. The law, known as Act 64, imposed spending limits ranging from $2,000 to $300,000 (depending on the office sought) by candidates for state offices in Vermont. A number of groups, including the American Civil Liberties Union and the Republican Party, challenged the act, claiming that it violated the First Amendment's guarantee of free speech. In a landmark decision in August 2002, a federal appellate court disagreed and upheld the law. The court stated that Vermont had shown that, without spending limits, "the fund-raising practices in Vermont will continue to impair the accessibility which is essential to any democratic political system. The race for campaign funds has compelled public officials to give preferred access to contributors, selling their time in order to raise campaign funds."[10] In 2006, the U.S. Supreme Court declared that Vermont's campaign spending and donation limits were unconstitutional, thereby in a sense reaffirming the *Buckley v. Valeo* decision.

INTEREST GROUPS AND CAMPAIGN FINANCE: REACTION TO NEW RULES

In the last two decades, interest groups and individual companies have found new, very direct ways to support elected officials through campaign donations. Elected officials, in turn, have become dependent on these donations to run increasingly expensive campaigns. Interest groups and corporations funnel money to political candidates through several devices: **political action committees (PACs)**, **soft money** contributions, and **issue advocacy advertising**. These devices developed as a means of circumventing the campaign financing reforms of the early 1970s, which limited contributions by individuals and unions to set amounts.

Hard Money
This refers to political contributions and campaign spending that is recorded under the regulations set forth in law and by the Federal Election Commission.

Political Action Committee (PAC)
A committee set up by and representing a corporation, labor union, or special-interest group. PACs raise and give campaign donations.

Soft Money
Campaign contributions unregulated by federal or state law, usually given to parties and party committees to help fund general party activities.

Issue Advocacy Advertising
Advertising paid for by interest groups that support or oppose a candidate or a candidate's position on an issue without mentioning voting or elections.

[9]424 U.S. 1 (1976).
[10]*Randell v. Vermont Public Interest Research Group*, 300 F.3d 129 (2d Cir. 2002).

PACs AND POLITICAL CAMPAIGNS

The 1974 and 1976 amendments to the Federal Election Campaign Act of 1971 allow corporations, labor unions, and other interest groups to set up PACs to raise funds for candidates. For a federal PAC to be legitimate, the funds must be raised from at least 50 volunteer donors and must be given to at least five candidates in the federal election. PACs can contribute up to $5,000 to each candidate in each election. Each corporation or each union is limited to one PAC. As you might imagine, corporate PACs obtain funds from executives and managers in their firms, and unions obtain PAC funds from their members.

The number of PACs has grown significantly since 1976, as has the amount they spend on elections. There were about 1,000 PACs in 1976; today, there are more than 4,500. Total spending by PACs grew from $19 million in 1973 to more than $1 billion in 2005–2006. About 43 percent of all campaign funds raised by House candidates in 2006 came from PACs.[11]

Interest groups funnel PAC funds to the candidates they think can do the most good for them. Frequently, they make the maximum contribution of $5,000 per election to candidates who face little or no opposition. The summary of PAC contributions given in Figure 10–2 shows that the great bulk of campaign contributions goes to incumbent candidates rather than to challengers. Table 10–1 shows the amounts contributed by the top 20 PACs during the 2007–2008 election cycle.

As Table 10–1 also shows, many PACs give most of their contributions to candidates of one party. Other PACs, particularly corporate PACs, tend to give funds to Democrats in Congress as well as to Republicans, because, with both chambers of Congress so closely divided, predicting which party will be in control after an election is almost

FIGURE 10–2 PAC Contributions to Congressional Candidates, 1991–2008

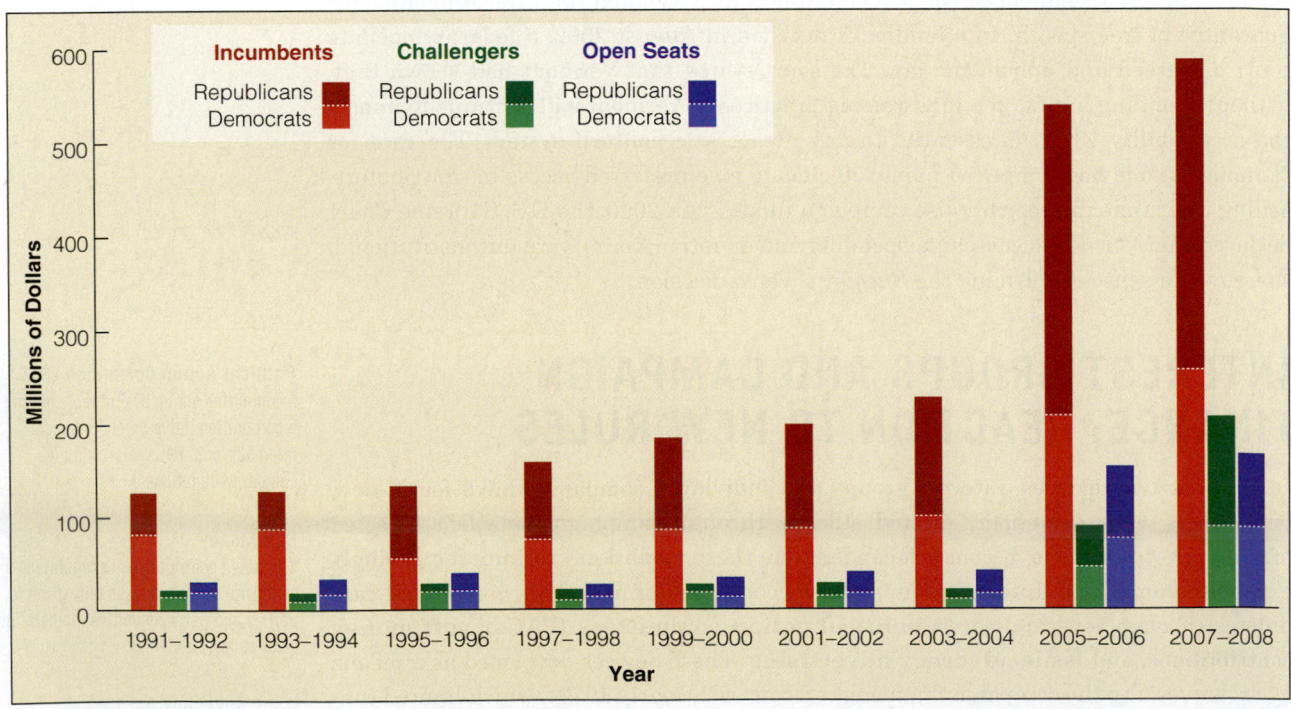

Source: Center for Responsive Politics, http://www.opensecrets.org

[11]Center for Responsive Politics, at www.opensecrets.org.

impossible. Why, you might ask, would business leaders give to Democrats who may be more liberal than themselves? Interest groups see PAC contributions as a way to ensure *access* to powerful legislators, even though the groups may disagree with the legislators some of the time. PAC contributions are, in a way, an investment in a relationship.

Campaign financing regulations clearly limit the amount that a PAC can give to any one candidate, but there is no limit on the amount that a PAC can spend on issue advocacy, either on behalf of a candidate or party or in opposition to one.

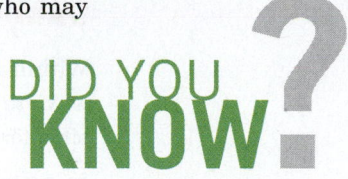

That Abraham Lincoln sold pieces of fence rail that he had split as political souvenirs to finance his campaign?

TABLE 10–1 Top 527 Committees in 2008

COMMITTEE	2008 RECEIPTS	2008 EXPENDITURES	POLITICAL PREFERENCE	AFFILIATIONS
Service Employees International Union	$27.4 million	$27.8 million	Democratic	SEIU union
American Votes	$26 million	$24.5 million	Progressive/ Democratic	
American Solutions Winning the Future	$22.7 million	$22.9 million	Conservative/ Republican	Newt Gingrich, former House Speaker
EMILYs List	$13.7 million	$12.9 million	Democratic mostly	Supports women candidates
The Fund for America	$12.1 million	$12.1 million	Democratic	Antiwar
Patriot Majority Fund	$8.2 million	$8.1 million	Democratic/ liberal	
College Republican National Comm.	$6.9 million	$7.5 million	Republican/ Conservative	
RightChange. com	$6.7 million	$5.6 million	Independent	Media Criticism/cam- paign watch
Citizens United	$6.4 million	$6.0 million	Conservative	Christian conservative
International Brotherhood of Electrical Workers	$5.8 million	$5.8 million	Democratic	IBEW union
Club for Growth	$5 million	$5.9 million	Republican/ Conservative	Business oriented
Alliance for New America	$4.8 million	$4.8 million	Democratic/ Liberal	SEIU union

Source: Center for Responsive Politics. http://www.opensecrets.org

CAMPAIGN FINANCING BEYOND THE LIMITS

Within a few years after the establishment of the tight limits on contributions, new ways to finance campaigns were developed that skirted the reforms and made it possible for huge sums to be raised, especially by the major political parties.

Contributions to Political Parties. Candidates, PACs, and political parties found ways to generate *soft money*—that is, campaign contributions to political parties that escaped the limits of federal election law. Although the FECA limited contributions that would be spent on elections, there were no limits on contributions to political parties for activities such as voter education and voter-registration drives. This loophole enabled the parties to raise millions of dollars from corporations and individuals. It was not unusual for some corporations to give more than $1 million to the Democratic National Committee or to the Republican Party.[12] Between 1993 and 2002, when soft money was banned, the amount raised for election activities quadrupled to more than $400 million. The parties spent these funds for their conventions, for registering voters, and for advertising to promote the general party position. The parties also sent a great deal to state and local party organizations, which used the soft money to support their own tickets. Although soft money contributions to the national parties were outlawed after election day 2002 (as you will read shortly), political parties saw no contradiction in raising and spending as much soft money as possible during the 2001–2002 election cycle.

(TOLES © 2004 *The Washington Post*. Reprinted with permission of Universal Press Syndicate)

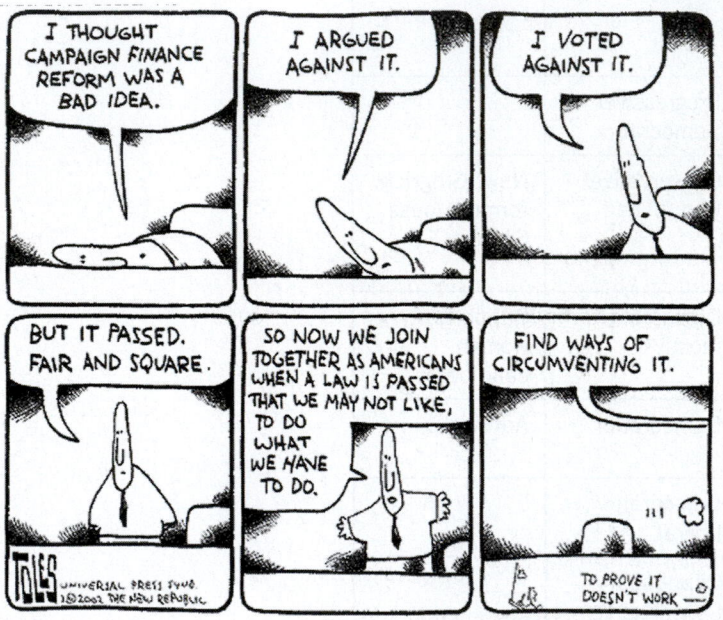

Independent Expenditures. Business corporations, labor unions, and other interest groups discovered that it was legal to make **independent expenditures** in an election campaign, so long as the expenditures were not coordinated with those of the candidate or political party. Hundreds of unique committees and organizations blossomed to take advantage of this campaign tactic. Although a 1990 United States Supreme Court decision, *Austin v. Michigan State Chamber of Commerce*,[13] upheld the right of the states and the federal government to limit independent, direct corporate expenditures (such as for advertisements) on behalf of *candidates*, the decision did not stop businesses and other types of groups from making independent expenditures on *issues*.

Issue Advocacy. Indeed, issue advocacy—spending unregulated funds on advertising that promotes positions on issues rather than candidates—has become a common tactic in recent years. Interest groups routinely wage their own issue campaigns. For example, the Christian Coalition, which is incorporated, annually raises millions of dollars to produce and distribute voter guidelines and other direct-mail literature to describe candidates' positions on various issues and to promote its agenda. In 2004, the interest group MoveOn.org began running issue ads attacking the Bush record shortly after Senator John Kerry had clinched the Democratic nomination. The Bush campaign responded by beginning its own advertising campaign.

Independent Expenditures
Nonregulated contributions from PACs, organizations, and individuals. The funds may be spent on advertising or other campaign activities, so long as those expenditures are not coordinated with those of a candidate.

---

[12]Paul Allen Beck, *Party Politics in America*, 8th ed. (New York: Longman, 1997), pp. 293–294.
[13]494 U.S. 652 (1990).

Although promoting issue positions is very close to promoting candidates who support those positions, the courts repeatedly have held, in accordance with the *Buckley v. Valeo* decision mentioned earlier, that interest groups have a First Amendment right to advocate their positions. In a 1996 decision,[14] the Supreme Court clarified this point, stating that political parties may also make independent expenditures on behalf of candidates—as long as the parties do so *independently* of the candidates. In other words, the parties must not coordinate such expenditures with the candidates' campaigns.

THE BIPARTISAN CAMPAIGN REFORM ACT OF 2002

While both Democrats and Republicans argued for campaign reform legislation during the 1990s, the bill co-sponsored by Senators John McCain, a Republican, and Russ Feingold, a Democrat, finally became the Bipartisan Campaign Reform Act (BCRA) in 2002. This act, which amended the 1971 FECA, took effect on the day after the congressional elections of November 5, 2002.

Key Elements of the New Law. The 2002 law bans the large, unlimited contributions to national political parties that are known as soft money. It places curbs on, but does not entirely eliminate, the use of campaign ads by outside special-interest groups advocating the election or defeat of specific candidates. Such ads are allowed up to 60 days before a general election and up to 30 days before a primary election.

In 1974, contributions by individuals to federal candidates were limited to $1,000 per individual. The 2002 act increased this limit to $2,000, with annual increases. In addition, the maximum amount that an individual can give to all federal candidates was raised from $25,000 per year to $95,000 over a two-year election cycle. The act did not ban soft money contributions to state and local parties. These parties can accept such contributions, as long as they are limited to $10,000 per year per individual.

Challenges to the 2002 Act. Almost immediately, the 2002 act faced a set of constitutional challenges brought by groups negatively affected. In December 2003, however, the Supreme Court upheld almost all of the clauses of the act.[15]

Soon thereafter, a coalition of conservative and liberal groups called Wisconsin Right to Life brought a lawsuit claiming that the 2002 act infringed on legitimate grassroots lobbying. Wisconsin Right to Life argued that part of the act violated its right to free speech. In 2006, the Supreme Court unanimously ruled that the Wisconsin group could go back to court to challenge a specific part of the 2002 act—the federal ban on issue-oriented ads that mention a particular candidate just before an election.[16]

Once the Supreme Court upheld the bulk of the 2002 law, it was left to the FEC to interpret the statute. Slowly but surely, the FEC opened loopholes that allowed campaign finance to return to "business as usual." In 2004, a U.S. district court struck down more than a dozen such commission regulations. When the FEC asked for these rulings to be reversed, a federal appeals court in Washington did not agree.

The Rise of the 527s. Interest groups that previously gave soft money to the parties responded to the 2002 BCRA by setting up new organizations outside the parties, called 527 organizations after the section of the tax code that provides for them. These tax-exempt organizations, which rely on soft money contributions for their funding and generally must report their contributions and expenditures to the Internal Revenue

---

[14]*Colorado Republican Federal Campaign Committee v. Federal Election Commission*, 518 U.S. 604 (1996).
[15]*McConnell v. Federal Election Commission*, 540 U.S. 93 (2003).
[16]*Wisconsin Right to Life, Inc. v. Federal Election Commission*, 126 S.Ct. 1016 (2006).

POLITICS WITH A purpose

The Emergence of 527 Groups

Money is the lifeblood of elections. Candidates for office raise and spend hundreds of millions of dollars. For example, the presidential candidates in 2004 spent about $750 million. In the 2008 presidential election, before the national conventions were held, candidates for president, including Senators McCain, Clinton, and Obama, had raised more than $1 billion.[a]

Candidates need these contributions to be successful. However, donors influence the electoral process in other significant ways. As you will learn in this chapter, before the reforms in campaign finance laws in 2002 (the Bipartisan Campaign Reform Act, or BCRA), donors could give unlimited or "soft" money to parties as long as the parties did not explicitly use that money to aid particular candidates. The BCRA outlawed that particular form of soft money, but in its place have risen so-called 527 groups, named for the section of the U.S. Tax Code that provides for these nonprofits to collect donations without having to pay taxes on the money.

The rise of these 527 groups is important for many reasons. By closing the soft money loophole, the BCRA stopped the flow of money from corporations, unions, and wealthy individuals to the political parties. One of the effects of the BCRA was that these donors avoided the provisions of BCRA by redirecting their giving to a relatively new form of organization, the 527. Since the 2002 law, corporations, unions, and wealthy individuals are among the top financial contributors to 527 groups. These groups are not limited in how much money they may accept, nor are they limited in the source of the money. This behavior is related to the way in which they spend their money. The Federal Election Commission (FEC) has ruled that if these groups wish to remain unregulated in fundraising, they may not coordinate with any candidate for a federal election (such as the president or Congress). This means they may not actively campaign for someone running for these offices, nor may they use the "magic words" "vote for" or "vote against" a particular federal candidate in advertisements they finance. If they violate these rules, they may become subject to fines. However, they can support issue ads that make clear which issues and, by the way, which candidates they are supporting or opposing.[b]

Despite these limits, these groups are very important players in campaigns. Although the tax status has existed for many years and some groups had limited exposure in 2000,[c] the presidential election of 2004 marked a turning point, making 527 groups a topic of discussion in the mainstream media. One of the more famous, although not the most financially active, groups was the Swift Boat Veterans for Truth. This group was highly critical of the Democratic nominee, Senator John Kerry, attacking his Vietnam War record. By 2008 standards, this group's financial footprint was relatively small; it raised only $158,750 in 2004. Of that sum, Bob J. Perry, a Houston, Texas-based builder, contributed $100,000. In the 2004 cycle, Mr. Perry was the fifth-highest donor to 527 groups (giving $8,085,199), and in 2006, gave the most money ($9,750,000) to 527s. All of this information is publicly accessible either through the FEC or through public-interest groups such as the Center for Responsive Politics, which runs a searchable Web site, www.opensecrets.org.

These public-interest watchdog groups, such as Democracy 21, the Campaign Legal Center, and the Center for Responsive Politics, are highly critical of the burgeoning influence of 527s. In 2004, they filed a complaint with the FEC against America Coming Together, charging that it had violated the ban on candidate advocacy. This is a Democratic-leaning group whose largest individual contributor, George Soros, donated $7.5 million in 2004.[d] In 2007, the FEC ruled against the 527, levying a fine of $775,000 against it for making more than $100 million in inappropriate contributions.[e] The public-interest groups protested that the fine was not sufficiently large to deter future 527 actions. As the 2008 primary season progressed, it became obvious that 527s were raising money and running advertisements as they did in 2004. The Supreme Court decision in *Citizens United v. FEC* may well lift all the rules on limits on the 527s as it appears to do for corporations and associations, although the tax-exempt status of 527s could keep them subject to the old rules. This will be decided in later court rulings.

[a]As of the end of September 2008, Senator McCain had raised $358 million while Senator Obama had raised more than $639 million. It has been estimated that the total raised for all candidates in this election cycle was almost $2 billion; www.opensecrets.org.org, accessed November 7, 2008.
[b]www.clcblog.org, accessed April 17, 2008.

[c]In the Republican presidential nominating contest in 2000, Senator John McCain was highly criticized by a 527 group, Republicans for Clean Air. The group was funded in part by individuals who supported then–Governor Bush's candidacy; www.dallasobserver.com/2000-04-06/news/clearing-the-air, accessed April 17, 2008.
[d]www.opensecrets.org/527s/527cmtedetail.asp?cycle=2004& format=&ein=200094706&tname=America%20Coming% 20Together, accessed April 17, 2008.
[e]www.democracy21.org/index.asp?Type=B_PR&SEC=%7B248831A-87CA-4C2D-B873-60C64918C920%7D, accessed April 17, 2008.

Service, are discussed in more detail in the Politics with a Purpose feature. What started out as a device to circumvent the campaign finance limits on donations has now grown into a complicated web of unregulated campaign financing. As noted in the box, 527 groups can be a vehicle for a particular point of view, such as the Swift Boat Veterans for Truth campaign against Senator John Kerry; however, powerful interest groups now use 527s in addition to their existing political action committees to receive monies for voter registration drives and other activities. The top names in Table 10–1 might look familiar. EMILY's List, for example, has been a long-standing PAC that supports women candidates, mostly Democrats. It still has a PAC that receives regulated contributions and makes direct limited donations to candidates. Yet EMILY's List also has a 527 organization that can accept unlimited donations and spend the funds on "uncoordinated advertising." The list of top 2008 groups includes labor unions, groups linked to business, groups headed by well-known politicians, and others that maintain both PACs and 527 organizations. This tactic gives the groups greater ability than a PAC to raise and spend money.

Overall, 527 groups spent more than $600 million in the 2003–2004 election cycle. They continued to be active during the 2007–2008 election cycle, as you can see in Table 10–2. Note the wholesome and patriotic titles of the 527 committees in the table. A few are independent, but the vast majority of these groups have a partisan preference, regardless of what they call themselves.

In contrast to the 527s, charities and true not-for-profit organizations are not allowed to participate directly in any type of political activity. If they do so, they risk fines and the loss of their charitable tax-exempt status. In 2005, the IRS reviewed more than 80 churches, charities, and other tax-exempt organizations. The IRS looked for such banned activities as the distribution of printed materials encouraging members to vote for a specific candidate, contributions of cash to candidates' campaigns, and ministers' use of their pulpits to oppose or endorse specific candidates.

RAISING CAMPAIGN FUNDS is an important task for any candidate. Barack Obama speaks to supporters at a fundraiser in Harlem's Apollo Theater in November of 2007, long before he won the nomination for president. How would presidential election campaigns change if they were publicly financed? (© Monika Graff/The Image Works)

The IRS found that churches played a particularly important role in the 2004 elections. For example, well-known fundamentalist Baptist minister Jerry Falwell used his Web site to endorse President Bush and to urge visitors to the site to donate $5,000 to the Campaign for Working Families. At the All Saints Church in Pasadena, California, a pastor gave a sermon in which he imagined a debate among Senator John Kerry, President George Bush, and Jesus Christ. Although Jesus won, the press reported that the hypothetical debate came out in favor of John Kerry.

Of the 82 churches, charities, and other tax-exempt organizations that the IRS examined, more than 75 percent engaged in prohibited political activity during the 2003–2004 election cycle. The IRS proposed to revoke the tax-exempt status of at least three of these organizations.

TABLE 10–2 The Top 20 PAC Contributors to Federal Candidates, 2007–2008 Election Cycle*

PAC NAME	TOTAL AMOUNT	DEM. (%)	REP. (%)
National Association of Realtors	$4,020,900	58	42
International Brotherhood of Electrical Workers	$3,344,650	98	2
AT&T	$3,108,200	52	47
American Bankers Association	$2,918,143	57	43
National Beer Wholesalers Association	$2,869,000	53	47
National Auto Dealers Association	$2,860,000	34	66
International Association of Fire Fighters	$2,734,900	77	22
Operating Engineers Union	$2,704,067	87	13
American Association for Justice (Trial Lawyers)	$2,700,500	94	4
Laborers Union	$2,555,350	92	8
Honeywell International	$2,515,616	52	48
National Association of Home Builders	$2,480,000	46	54
Airline Pilots Assn.	$2,422,000	110	15
Credit Union National Association	$2,3362,899	54	46
Machinists/Aerospace Workers Union	$2,321,842	97	3
Plumbers/Pipefitters Union	$2,316,559	95	5
Service Employees International Union	$2,285,850	94	6
American Federation of Teachers	$2,283,250	99	1
Teamsters Union	$2,248,950	97	3
National Air Traffic Controllers Assn.	$2,210,475	80	20

*Includes subsidiaries and affiliated PACs, if any.
Source: Center for Responsive Politics, 2010

CAMPAIGN FINANCING AND THE 2008 ELECTIONS

In 2008, the current campaign financing laws were put to the test and may have failed. Senator John McCain, who authored the most recent revision of the laws, chose not to accept private donations during the general election campaign. As a result, the total amount he raised during 2008 was about $350 million. He did, however, accept about $1 million in PAC contributions. He ran his fall campaign on the $84 million of federal campaign funds granted to him under law. In addition, the Republican National Committee was able to raise and spend funds toward his election.

Taking the completely opposite approach, Senator Barack Obama chose not to accept public funds for the general election campaign. During the 2008 campaign, he raised more than $630 million but accepted no PAC donations. The Obama campaign pioneered new ways for individuals to make contributions over the Internet, and millions of individuals chose to give in that manner. One result of the disparity in funds available was the ability of the Obama campaign to mount an exceptional Get Out the Vote campaign and to purchase four times more advertising time than did McCain. At the end of the campaign came many calls for a reexamination of campaign finance laws to fit these new realities.

CITIZENS UNITED AND THE FUTURE OF CAMPAIGN FINANCE REGULATION

The Supreme Court decision in *Citizens United v. FEC* shook the political world like no other since *Buckley v. Valeo*.[17] In many ways, the case continued the struggle of outside groups and groups not affiliated with political parties to play a bigger role in political campaigns. Although three decades of campaign finance laws and regulation had been passed to contain the influence of groups on the political process and to limit the contributions of individuals, political action committees, and corporations, the *Citizens United* decision, on its face, lifted many of those restrictions. The decision appears to allow corporations, unions, groups such as Citizens United, and others to spend money in campaign advertising without limit as long as it is not coordinated with a campaign. Indeed, the restriction against using direct campaign language such as "vote for Mr. Smith" may have been lifted as well. President Obama expressed his disagreement with the decision during his State of the Union speech, and most Democrats applauded his remarks. The Democratic leadership of the Congress pledged to write new laws to counteract this decision, but no action was taken before the 2010 election.

Campaign spending exploded in the 2010 midterm elections as Republicans tried to retake the House and the Senate. Outside groups and corporations did make large contributions to 527 organizations which then spent the money on campaign advertising. However, funds spent by the Democrats and the Republicans were roughly equal. Most of the candidates who funded their own campaigns with millions of dollars lost.

RUNNING FOR PRESIDENT: THE LONGEST CAMPAIGN

The American presidential election is the culmination of two different campaigns linked by the parties' national conventions. The presidential primary campaign lasts from

---

[17]*United v. Federal Election Commission*, 558 U.S. (2010).

January until June of the election year. Traditionally, the final campaign heats up around Labor Day, although if the nominees are known, it will begin even before the conventions.

Primary elections were first mandated in 1903 in Wisconsin. The purpose of the primary was to open the nomination process to ordinary party members and to weaken the influence of party bosses in the nomination procedure. Until 1968, however, there were fewer than 20 primary elections for the presidency. They were often **"beauty contests"** in which the candidates competed for popular votes, but the results had little or no impact on the selection of delegates to the national convention. National conventions were meetings of the party elite—legislators, mayors, county chairpersons, and loyal party workers—who were mostly appointed to their delegations. National conventions saw numerous trades and bargains among competing candidates, and the leaders of large blocs of delegates could direct their delegates to support a favorite candidate.

REFORMING THE PRIMARIES

In recent decades, the character of the primary process and the makeup of the national convention have changed dramatically. The public, rather than party elites, now generally controls the nomination process. In 1968, after President Lyndon B. Johnson declined to run for another term, the Democratic Party nomination race was dominated by candidates who opposed the war in Vietnam. After Robert F. Kennedy was assassinated in June 1968, antiwar Democrats faced a convention that would nominate LBJ's choice regardless of popular votes. After the extraordinary disruptive riots outside the doors of the 1968 Democratic Convention in Chicago, many party leaders pushed for serious reforms of the convention process. They saw the general dissatisfaction with the convention, and the riots in particular, as being caused by the inability of the average party member to influence the nomination system.

The Democratic National Committee appointed a special commission to study the problems of the primary system. Called the McGovern-Fraser Commission, the group formulated new rules for delegate selection over the next several years that had to be followed by state Democratic parties.

The reforms instituted by the Democratic Party, which were imitated in part by the Republicans, revolutionized the nomination process for the presidency. The most impor-

"Beauty Contest"
A presidential primary in which contending candidates compete for popular votes but the results do not control the selection of delegates to the national convention.

SENATOR ROBERT F. KENNEDY
tells a press conference on April 1, 1968, that he will pursue the Democratic nomination for president. He was assassinated after winning the California primary election. Then Vice President Hubert Humphrey won the nomination for president that year but lost the election to Richard Nixon. (Bettmann/CORBIS)

tant changes require that a majority of the Democratic convention delegates not be nominated by party elites; they must be elected by the voters in primary elections, in caucuses held by local parties (discussed later), or at state conventions. No delegates can be awarded on a "winner-take-all" basis; all must be proportional to the votes for the contenders. Delegates are normally pledged to a particular candidate, although the pledge is not always formally binding at the convention.

The delegation from each state must also include a proportion of women, younger party members, and representatives of the minority groups within the party. At first, virtually no special privileges were given to elected party officials, such as senators and governors. After the conventions chose candidates who were not as strong as the party hoped for, the Democratic Party invented superdelegates, who are primarily elected Democratic officeholders and state leaders. Superdelegates comprise less than 20 percent of the delegate votes.

TYPES OF PRIMARIES

Before discussing the types of primaries, we must first examine how some states use a party **caucus**. A caucus is typically a small, local meeting of party regulars who agree on a nominee. Sometimes the results of caucuses are voted on by a broader set of party members in a primary election. (If the party's chosen candidates have no opponents, however, a primary election may not be necessary.)

Alternatively, there may be a local or state party convention at which a slate of nominees of loyal party members is chosen. In any event, the resulting primary elections differ from state to state. The most common types are discussed here.

Closed Primary. In a **closed primary**, only avowed or declared members of a party can vote in that party's primary. In other words, voters must declare their party affiliation, either when they register to vote or at the primary election. A closed-primary system tries to make sure that registered voters cannot cross over into the other party's primary in order to nominate the weakest candidate of the opposing party or to affect the ideological direction of that party.

Open Primary. In an **open primary**, voters can vote in either party primary without disclosing their party affiliation. Basically, the voter makes the choice in the privacy of the voting booth. The voter must, however, choose one party's list from which to select candidates. Open primaries place no restrictions on independent voters.

Blanket Primary. In a *blanket primary*, the voter can vote for candidates of more than one party. Alaska, Louisiana, and Washington have blanket primaries. Blanket-primary campaigns may be much more costly because each candidate for every office is trying to influence all of the voters, not just those in his or her party.

In 2000, the United States Supreme Court issued a decision that altered significantly the use of the blanket primary. The case arose when political parties

DURING THE 1968 Democratic convention, thousands of protesters gathered in front of the convention headquarters, the Hilton hotel in Chicago. National Guard troops and the Chicago police used military tactics to move the protesters away from the site. (Photograph by Jo Freeman, www.jofreeman.com)

Caucus
A meeting of party members designed to select candidates and propose policies.

in California challenged the constitutionality of a 1996 ballot initiative authorizing the use of the blanket primary in that state. The parties contended that the blanket primary violated their First Amendment right of association. Because the nominees represent the party, they argued, party members—not the general electorate—should have the right to choose the party's nominee. The Supreme Court ruled in favor of the parties, holding that the blanket primary violated parties' First Amendment associational rights.[18]

The Court's ruling called into question the constitutional validity of blanket primaries in other states as well. The question before these states is how to devise a primary election system that will comply with the Supreme Court's ruling, yet offer independent voters a chance to participate in the primary elections.

Runoff Primary. Some states have a two-primary system. If no candidate receives a majority of the votes in the first primary, the top two candidates must compete in another primary, called a *runoff primary*.

FRONT-LOADING THE PRIMARIES

As soon as politicians and potential presidential candidates realized that winning as many primary elections as possible guaranteed them the party's nomination for president, their tactics changed dramatically. For example, candidates running in the 2008 primaries, such as Senator Hillary Clinton, concentrated on building organizations in states that held early, important primary elections. Candidates realized that winning early contests, such as the Iowa caucuses or the New Hampshire primary election (both in January), meant that the media instantly would label the winner as the **front-runner**, thus increasing the candidate's media exposure and escalating the pace of contributions to his or her campaign fund.

The Rush to Be First. The states and state political parties began to see that early primaries had a much greater effect on the outcome of the presidential election and, accordingly, began to hold their primaries earlier in the season to secure that advantage. While New Hampshire held on to its claim to be the first primary, other states moved theirs to the following week. A group of mostly Southern states decided to hold their primaries on the same date, known as Super Tuesday, in the hope of nominating a moderate Southerner at the Democratic convention. When California, which had held the last primary (in June), moved its primary to March, the primary season was curtailed drastically. Due to this process of **front-loading** the primaries, in 2000 the presidential nominating process was over in March, with both George W. Bush and Al Gore having enough convention delegate votes to win their nominations. This meant that the campaign was essentially without news until the conventions in August, a gap that did not appeal to the politicians or the media. Both parties discussed whether more changes in the primary process were necessary.

In 2006, the Democratic Party announced that the Nevada caucus and the South Carolina primary would be held in the same time frame traditionally dominated by New Hampshire and Iowa. The Democrats reasoned that they wanted to add diversity to an early primary calendar that has been dominated by the predominantly white, rural voices of New Hampshire and Iowa. Nevada boasts a quickly growing Hispanic population, and South Carolina has a long-standing African American community.

Closed Primary
A type of primary in which the voter is limited to choosing candidates of the party of which he or she is a member.

Open Primary
A primary in which any registered voter can vote (but must vote for candidates of only one party).

Front-Runner
The presidential candidate who appears to be ahead at a given time in the primary season.

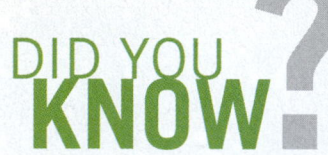
DID YOU KNOW?

That David Leroy Gatchell changed his middle name to None of the Above, but when he ran for the U.S. Senate representing Tennessee, a court ruled that he could not use his middle name on the ballot?

Front-Loading
The practice of moving presidential primary elections to the early part of the campaign to maximize the impact of these primaries on the nomination.

[18]*California Democratic Party v. Jones*, 530 U.S. 567 (2000).

Consequences of Early Primaries. Despite the apparent problems with the front-loaded primary season in 2000, the Democratic Party decided to hold some of its primaries even earlier in the 2007–2008 presidential election cycle. For example, the Democratic Iowa caucus was advanced to January 3, to be followed five days later by the New Hampshire primary. The Democrats' goal in moving up their primaries was obvious: settle on a candidate early so that she or he would have a long time during which to raise funds to win the presidency.

In 2005, a private commission headed by former president Jimmy Carter and former secretary of state James A. Baker III proposed a number of steps to avoid the consequences of early primaries. The Commission on Federal Election Reform was organized by American University. The commission argued in favor of keeping the Iowa caucuses and New Hampshire's early primary because "they test the candidates by genuine retail, door-to-door campaigning." After that, though, the commission had a radical suggestion—eliminate the state primaries and hold four regional presidential primaries. These regional primaries would be held at monthly intervals in March, April, May, and June, with the order rotated every four years.

The 2008 Primary Contest. The contest for the Democratic nomination drew a large and diverse field of candidates in 2008. Senator Hillary Rodham Clinton, former First Lady, started out as the strongest candidate due to her early fundraising and organizational strengths. Many observers saw former vice presidential candidate John Edwards of North Carolina as the real challenger to Clinton. Other candidates included Senators Joe Biden of Delaware and Chris Dodd of Connecticut, as well as first-term Senator Barack Obama of Illinois. Representative Dennis Kucinich renewed his perennial campaign. Governors Bill Richardson of New Mexico, Tom Vilsack of Iowa, and former Senator Mike Gravel of Alaska also entered the race.

The Iowa caucuses were front-loaded to January 3, 2008. After Iowans trudged through the snow for their local meetings, it became clear that Barack Obama, a senator of mixed race from Illinois, was the true victor and potentially new front-runner. Senator Clinton claimed New Hampshire in a victory not predicted by pollsters, but Obama claimed the most delegates in Nevada and won South Carolina decisively. Michigan and Florida held primaries that were judged illegitimate by the Democratic National Committee, so their votes for Clinton were not counted. Super Tuesday occurred on February 5, with 23 states and territories holding primary elections on that date. After the votes were counted, Clinton and Obama were the clear contenders for the nomination. Almost all of the other candidates dropped out and either endorsed one of the remaining candidates or kept silent. The two senators battled on through April and May, with Senator Clinton showing real strength in the midwestern "rust belt" states. Both campaigns pressured superdelegates to declare their preferences so that either Clinton or Obama would achieve the majority of the delegates. The Democratic Party leadership in Michigan and Florida continued to press the national party to allow their delegate votes to count, even though they had violated party rules in scheduling their respective primaries. Because of the rules for delegate selection, Senator Obama continued to gain delegates even in states where Senator Clinton won by a strong margin. By June it was clear that Senator Obama had the delegate votes to win the nomination, and Senator Clinton stepped aside.

In contrast to the Democratic race, the Republican nominating contest ended fairly early in the season. With winner-take-all rules for delegate counts, the candidate who won a state gained all the delegates at stake. The Republican contest began with a diverse field as well: Former Massachusetts governor Mitt Romney was a conservative favorite, along with Governor Mike Huckabee of Arkansas. Representative Ron Paul spoke for a libertarian perspective, while Representative Duncan Hunter was concerned about security. Senator John McCain had been working on his campaign for more than a year, but, at the beginning of the primary season, he barely had enough funds to keep his organization together. The most moderate Republican candidate was former New York mayor Rudy Giuliani, who was expected to do well in urban states.

Strategy made all the difference in the Republican race. While Huckabee and Romney sought out conservative Republican votes in Iowa, New Hampshire, and South Carolina, McCain concentrated on larger states. He was greatly advantaged by the new primary schedule, in that Independents and moderate Republican voters in states such as Florida could support him early in the campaign. Romney dropped out of the race after Super Tuesday and Huckabee after the mini–Super Tuesday in March, leaving McCain to build up his campaign war chest and public support for the rest of the spring and summer.

ON TO THE NATIONAL CONVENTION

MEMBERS OF THE ARIZONA delegation cheer as the convention ballots are counted and Barack Obama becomes the Democratic nominee for president in 2008. (John Moore/ Getty Images)

Presidential candidates have been nominated by the convention method in every election since 1832. The delegates are sent from each state and are apportioned on the basis of state representation. Extra delegates are allowed to attend from states that had voting majorities for the party in the preceding elections. Parties also accept delegates from the District of Columbia, the territories, and certain overseas groups.

Seating the Delegates. At the convention, each political party uses a **credentials committee** to determine which delegates may participate. The credentials committee usually prepares a roll of all delegates entitled to be seated. Controversy may arise when rival groups claim to be the official party organization for a county, district, or state. The Mississippi Democratic Party split along racial lines in 1964 at the height of the civil rights movement in the Deep South. Separate all-white and mixed white/African American sets of delegates were selected, and both factions showed up at the national convention. After much debate on party rules, the committee decided to seat the pro–civil rights delegates and exclude those who represented the traditional "white" party.

The 2008 election saw a similar intra-party conflict arise over the delegates from Florida and Michigan. The Clinton and Obama camps eventually agreed to a compromise that seated the delegates but gave each state only half of the votes they were normally entitled to. The issue was no longer important once Senator Obama had enough pledged delegates to win.

Credentials Committee
A committee used by political parties at their national conventions to determine which delegates may participate. The committee inspects the claim of each prospective delegate to be seated as a legitimate representative of his or her state

Convention Activities. The typical convention lasts only a few days. The first day consists of speech making, usually against the opposing party. During the second day, there are committee reports, and during the third day, there is presidential balloting. Because delegates generally arrive at the convention committed to presidential candidates, no convention since 1952 has required more than one ballot to choose a nominee, and since 1972, candidates have usually come into the convention with enough committed delegates to win. On the fourth day, a vice presidential candidate is usually nominated, and the presidential nominee gives the acceptance speech.

In 2008, the Democratic and Republican conventions were scheduled within one week of one another—one right before Labor Day and one immediately after. The Democratic National Convention was held in Denver, Colorado, and was meticulously planned to generate media coverage. Former candidate Senator Hillary Rodham Clinton gave a stirring speech on the second night of the convention, and on the third night, former president Bill Clinton spoke in support of the Obama–Biden ticket. The climax of the convention was Senator Obama's acceptance speech, which was delivered in a stadium to a crowd of more than 80,000 people. Those who wanted to attend lined up for seats hours before the event was to begin for the chance to witness the nomination of the first African American nominee for president.

The Republican convention was ready to kick off in St. Paul, Minnesota, when Hurricane Gustav took aim at Louisiana. The Republicans quickly canceled the first night of speeches to allow the news media to focus on the weather approaching New Orleans and the evacuations there. After it became clear that the hurricane would not be as serious as predicted, the Republican convention returned to normal with speeches by all the former presidential candidates. The high point of the convention, however, was vice presidential nominee Sarah Palin's acceptance speech. Because she was virtually unknown in the political world, commentators and politicians wondered how well she would do in her first speech. She exceeded all expectations and greatly increased the enthusiasm of all the delegates for their 2008 ticket.

ON TO THE GENERAL ELECTION

Even though the voters may think the presidential election process has gone on for years, the general election campaign actually begins after the two party conventions, when the nominees are officially proclaimed. The general election campaign strategies for each candidate are similar to those used during the primaries, except that each candidate now tries to articulate his or her differences from the opposition in terms of party issues. As noted in Chapter 6, voters respond to the campaigns on the basis of partisanship, the candidates' personalities, and the issues of the day.

Candidates plan their campaigns to use media advertising, debates, and Get Out the Vote (GOTV) campaigns. In addition, campaign strategists must constantly plan to win enough electoral votes to receive the majority. Campaign managers quickly identify those

Battleground State
A state that is likely to be so closely fought that the campaigns devote exceptional effort to winning the popular and electoral vote there.

states where their candidate will almost certainly win the popular vote. As illustrated in the endpapers of this book, certain states will quickly line up in the Republican or Democratic column. Those states see relatively light campaign activity and advertising. However, those states that are likely to be close in the popular vote have been tagged **battleground states** and will see intense campaigning up to the very day of the election.

In 2000 and 2004, Florida was such a state. States such as Ohio and Wisconsin, which have closely divided electorates, are often in the battleground column. However, it is important to note that the states that will be closely fought change with every presidential election, because the issues and appeals of the two candidates determine race dynamics. In any case, the votes will be counted, the exit polls will be tallied, and the commentators will be heard on election night. In 2008, many of the supposed battleground states were quickly declared Obama victories because so many of his supporters turned out. Some of these battleground states were won by Obama with large margins. Other states were too close to call for several days after the election. While many commentators and political consultants warned of faulty voting machines and the inevitability of voting fraud and discrimination, election day saw few reports of irregularities but very long voting lines.

YOU CAN MAKE A Difference

STUDENTS ON THE CAMPAIGN TRAIL

The U.S. Congress has 535 members; other elected officials across the nation include more than 7,000 state legislators; 53 governors, attorneys general, treasurers, and secretaries of state; and thousands of mayors and city council members. None of these leaders could run political campaigns without the volunteer efforts of students. What do you believe in? Some students view campaign work as a civic duty. Causes and candidates across the nation would benefit from a volunteer's time and talent.

WHY SHOULD YOU CARE?

The 2008 presidential race sparked interest in many young voters, with 70 percent of 18- to 24-year-olds following the campaign closely, according to a Harvard University survey. With the promise of change coming from all candidates in this presidential race, young voters seemed to be inspired to get involved. Turnout among young voters did increase a few percentage points although not as much as it increased (9%) between 2000 and 2004. Knocking on doors and manning phone banks may not be glamorous work, but these experiences can provide a glimpse into a community that you might not get even by living in the neighborhood. You can talk to people face to face about

issues that are important to them. Many students feel that college is the perfect time to work for a candidate or issue, when flexible school schedules and summers lend themselves to the time necessary to devote to a campaign.

You hear much discussion in the media concerning the youth vote but rarely find the opportunity for young people to speak for themselves concerning issues of the day. When you are volunteering for a campaign, opportunities to meet candidates, attend rallies, and engage in debate allow you to voice your opinion firsthand in the context of our political system. Opinions can be diverse even among volunteers with the same campaign affiliation, with some motivated by economic policy and fiscal issues and others by social issues.

WHAT CAN YOU DO?

Most people envision presidential races when first considering campaign volunteer work, but local elections or national hot-button issues such as gun control and local ballot initiatives in your own community feature some form of a campaign. How do you decide which campaign is right for you? Take into consideration how much time you can devote to the work, how close to home you want to stay, and how much responsibility you are willing to take on.

Campaign work can take many forms for first-time volunteers. You might help with fundraising, weekend door-to-door canvassing, or the effort to get people out to vote as election day approaches. You might work for one of the party organizations such as the Democratic National Committee or the Republican National Committee, or join a campus branch of College Democrats or College Republicans. These clubs host candidates to address students, hold voter registration drives, volunteer at local political events, and work phone banks for candidates and issues. You might also volunteer for an independent political entity, such as an issue-oriented nonprofit group or a 527 organization, advocating for candidates and voter mobilization.

Political campaigns offer many opportunities to develop a wide range of skills in a very fast-paced and exciting environment. You get a front-row seat to the electoral process; the work can be grueling but rarely boring. Satisfaction comes from working for a candidate or a cause that you respect and support and knowing that your individual efforts can make a difference.

For further information on volunteering for political campaigns, please contact one of the following organizations:

The Democratic National Committee
430 South Capitol Street SE
Washington, DC 20003
202-863-8000
www.democrats.org
College Democrats of America
430 South Capitol Street SE
Washington, DC 20003
202-863-8000
www.collegedems.com

The Republican National Committee
310 First Street, SE
Washington, DC 20003
202-863-8500
www.gop.com

College Republican National Committee
600 Pennsylvania Ave. SE, Suite 215
Washington, DC 20003
888-765-3564
www.crnc.org

REPUBLICAN PRESIDENTIAL

hopeful, Rudy Giuliani, greets campaign workers in his Florida headquarters before that state's primary in 2008. (AP Photo/ Gerald Herbert)

REFERENCES

Sharon Kelly, Justin Levitt, and Amanda Tammen Peterson, "One State, Two State, Red State, Blue State: A Quick Guide to Working on Political Campaigns," Cambridge, MA: Bernard Koteen Office of Public Interest Advising, Harvard Law School, 2007.

Mike Maciag, "BU Students Spread the Word for Candidates," *Peoria Journal Star*, May 4, 2008.

Emily Schultheis, "Students Plan to Hit the Campaign Trail," *Politico*, May 1, 2008.

Mercedes Suarez, "American College Students Embracing U.S. Political Process," America.gov, October 26, 2007.

KEY TERMS

CHAPTER SUMMARY

1. **What are the hallmarks of free and fair elections?** Free and fair elections are the basis for the continuation of a democratic form of government. To qualify as free and fair, elections should be fairly administered, information about the candidates and issues must be available through a free press, and voters must be free from coercion and intimidation.

2. People may choose to run for political office to further their careers, to carry out specific political programs, or in response to certain issues or events. The legal qualifications for holding political office are minimal at both the state and local levels, but holders of political office still are predominantly white and male and are likely to be from the professional class.

3. American political campaigns are lengthy and extremely expensive. In the last decade, they have become more candidate centered rather than party centered in response to technological innovations and decreasing party identification. Candidates have begun to rely less on the party and more on paid professional consultants to perform the various tasks necessary to wage a political campaign. The crucial task of professional political consultants is image building. The campaign organization devises a campaign strategy to maximize the candidate's chances of winning. Candidates use public opinion polls and focus groups to gauge their popularity and to test the mood of the country.

4. **Should all candidates have equal campaign financing?** The amount of money spent in financing campaigns is increasing steadily. A variety of corrupt practices acts have been passed to regulate campaign finance. The Federal Election Campaign Act of 1971 and its amendments in 1974 and 1976 instituted major reforms by limiting spending and contributions; the acts allowed corporations, labor unions, and interest groups to set up political action committees (PACs) to raise money for candidates. Additionally, public matching funds were made available to primary campaigns if certain criteria were met. The intent was to help candidates be competitive in the primaries. New techniques, including "soft money" contributions to the parties

and independent expenditures, were later developed. The Bipartisan Campaign Reform Act (BCRA) of 2002 banned soft money contributions to the national parties, limited advertising by interest groups, and increased the limits on individual contributions. By 2008, most of the major candidates refused public funding in the primary campaigns, as did the Obama campaign in the general election, resulting in very large differences between the campaigns in financial resources. The idea of "leveling the playing field" for candidates in either the primaries or the general election seemed to be obsolete.

5. **Should party members or the general public nominate the candidates for president?** After the Democratic Convention of 1968, the McGovern-Fraser Commission formulated new rules for primaries, which were adopted by all Democrats and by Republicans in many states. These reforms opened up the nomination process for the presidency to all voters. The new system effectively removed control of the nomination process from the political party members and gave it to the voting public. Sometimes this produces a great party leader, and other years it produces a candidate who is not well supported by party loyalists and who cannot win the election.

6. A presidential primary is a statewide election to help a political party determine its presidential nominee at the national convention. Some states use the caucus method of choosing convention delegates. The primary campaign recently has been shortened to the first few months of the election year.

7. The party conventions are held to finalize the nomination of a candidate for president. Normally, the convention is used to unite the party and to introduce the winning candidate to the public. It marks the beginning of the general election campaign. Contested conventions have been rare in the last 50 years.

8. The general election campaign begins after Labor Day in September. Presidential candidates and their campaign organizations use advertising, appearances, speeches, and debates to win support from voters. In recent years, attention has been lavished on battleground states where presidential contests were closely fought.

SELECTED PRINT, MEDIA, AND ONLINE RESOURCES

PRINT RESOURCES

Lau, Richard R., et al., eds. *How Voters Decide: Information Processing in Election Campaigns.* Cambridge, MA: Cambridge University Press, 2006. The researchers who wrote this book attempted to get "inside the heads" of citizens who confront huge amounts of information during modern presidential campaigns. The researchers argued that we should care not just about which candidates receive the most votes, but also about how many citizens voted "correctly"—that is, in accordance with their own interests.

MoveOn. *MoveOn's 50 Ways to Love Your Country: How to Find Your Political Voice and Become a Catalyst for Change.* Makawao, Maui, HI: Inner Ocean Publishing, 2004. This book contains 50 short chapters in which individuals describe how they sought to make a difference by getting involved in the political process. MoveOn has been called a "shadow party" to the Democrats. Nevertheless, the techniques described here could be used just as easily by Republicans. The volume is also available on audiotape.

Nelson, Michael, ed. *The Elections of 2008.* Washington, DC: CQ Press, 2009. This collection of essays by well-known political scientists comments on all aspects of the 2008 campaign, from the primaries through the general election.

Plouffe, David. *The Audacity to Win: The Inside Story and Lesson of Barack Obama's Historic Victory.* New York: Viking, 2009. David Plouffe, one of the president's closest advisers, and political consultants tell the inside story of the Obama campaign's strategy for winning in 2008. This is a good look at the inside of a high-powered campaign apparatus.

Smidt, Corwin, Kevin den Dulk, Bryan Froehle, James Penning, Stephen Monsma, and Douglas L. Koopman. *The Disappearing God Gap? Religion in the 2008 Presidential Election.* New York: Oxford University Press, 2010. After two elections in which religious conservatives seemed to have played a strong role, religion and religious views were much less important in the election of 2008. The authors examine the role of religion in American elections and comment on how that role changed in the Obama election.

Thurber, James A., and Candice J. Nelson, eds. *Campaigns and Elections American Style: Transforming American Politics.* New York: Westview Press, 2004. The articles in this book consider the basics of American campaigns and discuss practical campaign politics. They examine the evolution of campaigns over time, including town meetings, talk radio, infomercials, and focus groups. In this book, you will discover how campaign themes and strategies are determined.

Wayne, Stephen J. *The Road to the White House, 2008: The Politics of Presidential Elections.* Belmont, CA: Wadsworth Publishing, 2008. Stephen Wayne examines the changes in the election process since 1996 and provides an excellent analysis of the presidential selection process.

MEDIA RESOURCES

Bulworth—A 1998 satirical film starring Warren Beatty and Halle Berry. Jay Bulworth, a senator who is fed up with politics and life in general, hires a hit man to carry out his own assassination. He then throws political caution to the wind in campaign appearances by telling the truth and behaving the way he really wants to behave.

The Candidate—A 1972 film, starring a young Robert Redford, that effectively investigates and satirizes the decisions that a candidate for the U.S. Senate must make. It's a political classic.

If You Can't Say Anything Nice—Negative campaigning seems to have become the norm in recent years. This 1999 program looks at the resulting decline in popularity of politics among the electorate and suggests approaches to restoring faith in the process. It is part of the series *Politics as Usual,* available from the Films Media Group.

Money Talks: The Influence of Money on American Politics—Bill Moyers reports on the influence of money on our political system. Produced in 1994.

Primary Colors—A 1998 film starring John Travolta as a Southern governor who is plagued by a sex scandal during his run for the presidency.

ONLINE RESOURCES

Center for Responsive Politics a nonpartisan, independent, and nonprofit research group that tracks money in U.S. politics and its effect on elections and public policy: www.opensecrets.org

Federal Election Commission an independent regulatory agency created by Congress in 1975 to administer and enforce the Federal Election Campaign Act (FECA)—the statute that governs the financing of federal elections; contains detailed information about current campaign financing laws and the latest filings of finance reports: www.fec.gov

Project Vote Smart investigates voting records and campaign financing information: www.vote-smart.org

11

President Barack Obama gives a one-on-one interview in the White House with George Stephanopoulos of ABC This Week. (AFP PHOTO/Pete Souza/White House Photo/Handout/Newscom)

The Media and Cyberpolitics

QUESTIONS TO CONSIDER

What are the functions of the media in our society?

How do the media contribute to political dialogue about issues and candidates?

How do the "new media" influence politics?

CHAPTER CONTENTS

what if...

The Media Had to Reveal All Their Sources?

BACKGROUND

Reporters, whether they work for newspapers, newswire services, television stations, magazines, or Internet blogs, typically attempt to "protect their sources." Many of these sources are willing to talk to reporters only on the condition that they remain anonymous. Consequently, untold news stories include phrases such as "informed sources said . . ." or "an anonymous source revealed . . ." Typically, these sources are confident that their names will not be disclosed because so-called shield laws protect reporters from being forced to disclose their sources in court or in other judicial proceedings. In 1972, the U.S. Supreme Court stated that "news gathering is not without First Amendment protections."* The majority on the Court, though, did not see those protections as absolute and held, among other things, that the First Amendment did not protect reporters from federal grand jury subpoenas seeking their confidential sources. In response, state legislatures and courts created their own shield laws.

WHAT IF THERE WERE NO PROTECTION FOR NEWS SOURCES?

Assume that at both the federal and state levels, shield laws were abolished. In other words, imagine a world in which reporters could continue to cite anonymous sources but would be subject to subpoenas that legally would require them to reveal their sources. Clearly, news gatherers who could not guarantee confidentiality for many of their sources would find those sources refusing to provide information. In these circumstances, investigative reporting in general could "take a hit." Investigative reporters would discover that fewer individuals would be willing to talk to them, except about minor matters that were not controversial. Public officials might be more comfortable engaging in questionable deals or dealing unfairly with public employees if they knew their behavior could be protected by intimidating possible informants.

Many jurists have predicted the same outcome. One judge stated that compelling a reporter to disclose confidential sources "unquestionably threatens a journalist's ability to secure information that is made available to him only on a confidential basis." The judge continued by saying that the "negative effect of such disclosure on future undercover investigative reporting would be serious and threatens freedom of the press and the public's need to be informed."**

LET'S TAKE IT TO COURT

If news gatherers' sources were fair game without any shield law protection, there would probably be a big increase in litigation. Imagine a person who is unhappy about a story written about him or her. If that person were sufficiently motivated, he or she could go to court to demand the names of the anonymous sources who had provided the information on which the reporter based the detrimental story. The sources might then face a lawsuit.

Today, most people tend to rely on trusted news sources and dismiss what might be considered gossip. If trusted news sources engaged in less investigative reporting, though, anonymous bloggers who might or might not be accurate could become increasingly important.

FOR CRITICAL ANALYSIS

1. Is it fair that reporters can shield their sources today? If your answer is yes, under what circumstances might shielding sources be considered unfair?
2. Why do anonymous sources wish to keep their identities secret?

*Branzburg v. Hayes, 408 U.S. 665 (1972).

**Baker v. F & F Investment, 470 F.2d 778 (1972).

THE STUDY OF PEOPLE and politics—of how people gain the information they need to be able to choose among political candidates, to organize for their own interests, and to formulate opinions on the policies and decisions of the government—must take into account the role played by the media. Historically, the print media played the most important role in informing public debate. The print media developed, for the most part, our understanding of how news is to be reported. Traditional media separated "facts" and "opinion" by having opinion writing confined to editorial pages. Facts were to be laid out in a specific fashion in news columns. Today, however, more than 90 percent of Americans use television news as their primary source of information. In addition, the Internet has become a major source for political communication and fundraising. As Internet use grows, the system of gathering and sharing news and information is changing from one in which the media have a primary role to one in which the individual citizen may play a greater part.

Today's citizens use many sources of information, including social networking sites and YouTube videos, to gather information to make political decisions. In this chapter, we will look at the ways in which these contemporary outlets are similar and different from traditional sources of news.

THE MEDIA'S FUNCTIONS

The mass media perform several different functions in any country. In the United States, we can list at least six. Almost all of them can have political implications, and some are essential to the democratic process. These functions are as follows: (1) providing entertainment, (2) reporting the news, (3) identifying public problems, (4) socializing new generations, (5) providing a political forum, and (6) making profits.

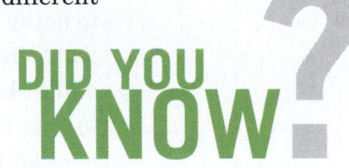

PROVIDING ENTERTAINMENT

By far, the greatest number of radio and television hours is dedicated to entertaining the public. The battle for prime-time and cable ratings indicates how important successful entertainment is to the survival of networks and individual stations. In recent years, the creation of reality shows such as *Survivor* and amateur talent shows including *American Idol* has underscored the importance of pure entertainment to the television industry.

Although there is no direct link between entertainment and politics, network dramas often introduce material that may be politically controversial and that may stimulate public discussion. Examples include the TV series *The West Wing* and *Commander in Chief,* which people believe promoted liberal political values, and *24,* which suggested more military tactics. Made-for-TV movies have focused on many controversial topics, including AIDS, incest, and spousal abuse. The growing number of documentary channels on cable—Discovery, History, National Geographic, and others—often tackle topics such as global warming or other environmental issues that are on the political agenda.

REPORTING THE NEWS

A primary function of the mass media in all their forms—newspapers and magazines, radio, television, cable, and online news services—is the reporting of news. The media provide words and pictures, sound and video about events, facts, personalities, and ideas. The protections of the First Amendment are intended to keep the flow of news as free as possible, because it is an essential part of the democratic process. If citizens cannot obtain unbiased information about the state of their communities and their leaders' actions, how can they make voting decisions? One of the most incisive comments about the importance of the media was made by James Madison, who said, "A people who mean to be their own governors must arm themselves with the power knowledge gives. A popular government without popular information or the means of acquiring it is but a prologue to a farce or a tragedy or perhaps both."[1]

---

[1]James Madison, "Letter to W. T. Barry" (August 4, 1822), in Gaillard P. Hunt, ed., *The Writings of James Madison* (New York: G.P. Putnam, 1910), Vol. 9, p. 103.

IDENTIFYING PUBLIC PROBLEMS

Public Agenda
Issues that are perceived by the political community as meriting public attention and governmental action.

The power of the media is important not only in revealing what the government is doing but also in determining what the government ought to do—in other words, in setting the **public agenda**. The mass media identify public issues, such as convicted sex offenders living in residential neighborhoods on their release from prison. The media then influence the passage of legislation, such as "Megan's Law," which requires police to notify neighbors about the release and/or resettlement of certain offenders. American journalists also work in a long tradition of uncovering public wrongdoing, corruption, and bribery and of bringing such wrongdoing to the public's attention. Closely related to this investigative function is that of presenting policy alternatives. Public policy is often complex and difficult to make entertaining, but programs devoted to public policy increasingly are being scheduled for prime-time television. Most networks produce shows with a "news magazine" format that sometimes include segments on foreign policy and other issues.

SOCIALIZING NEW GENERATIONS

As mentioned in Chapter 6, the media (particularly television) strongly influence the beliefs and opinions of Americans. Because of this influence, the media play a significant role in the political socialization of the younger generation, as well as immigrants to this country. Through the transmission of historical information (sometimes fictionalized), the presentation of American culture, and the portrayal of the diverse regions and groups in the United States, the media teach young people and immigrants about what it means to be an American. TV talk shows, such as *The Oprah Winfrey Show,* sometimes focus on controversial issues (such as abortion or assisted suicide) that relate to basic

THE REAL Hillary Clinton meets her stage double, Amy Poehler, during the March 1, 2008, edition of *Saturday Night Live.* What do candidates gain from appearing on a late night comedy show? (Dana Edelson/NBCU Photobank/AP Photos)

American values (such as liberty). Many children's shows are designed not only to entertain young viewers but also to instruct them in the traditional moral values of American society. In recent years, the public has become increasingly concerned about the level of violence depicted on children's programs and on other shows during prime time.

As more young Americans turn to the Internet for entertainment, they are also finding an increasing amount of social and political information there. America's youth today are the Internet generation. Young people do not use the Internet just for chat and e-mail. They also download movies and music, find information for writing assignments, gather news, visit social networking sites, and increasingly get involved in political campaigns and interact online with those campaigns.

PROVIDING A POLITICAL FORUM

As part of their news function, the media also provide a political forum for leaders and the public. Candidates for office use news reporting to sustain interest in their campaigns, while officeholders use the media to gain support for their policies or to present an image of leadership. Presidential trips abroad are an outstanding way for the chief executive to get colorful, positive, and exciting news coverage that makes the president look "presidential." The media also offer ways for citizens to participate in public debate, through letters to the editor, televised editorials, or electronic mail. As noted in the Making a Difference feature, 2008 saw the first YouTube live debate during the primaries, and candidates often posted video messages for their followers on their Web sites. The question of whether more public access should be provided will be discussed later in this chapter.

MAKING PROFITS

Most of the news media (including the Internet search engines) in the United States are private, for-profit corporate enterprises. One of their goals is to make profits for expansion and for dividends to the stockholders who own the companies. In general, profits are made as a result of charging for advertising. Advertising revenues usually are related directly to circulation or to listener/viewer ratings.

For the most part, the media depend on advertisers to obtain revenues to make profits. Media outlets that do not succeed in generating sufficient revenues from advertising either go bankrupt or are sold. Consequently, reporters may feel pressure from media owners and from advertisers. Media owners may take their cues from what advertisers want. If an important advertiser does not like the political bent of a particular reporter, the reporter could be asked to alter his or her "style" of writing. The Project for Excellence in Journalism discovered that 53 percent of local news directors said that advertisers try to tell them what to air and what not to air.[2]

Advertisers have been known to pull ads from newspapers and TV stations whenever they read or view negative publicity about their own companies or products. For example, CBS ran a *60 Minutes* show about Dillard's and other department stores that claimed store security guards used excessive force and racial profiling. In response, Dillard's pulled its ads from CBS. This example can be multiplied many times over.

Several well-known media outlets, in contrast, are publicly owned—public television stations in many communities and National Public Radio. These operate without

DID YOU KNOW?

That the first "wire" story transmitted by telegraph was sent in 1846?

---

[2]Project for Excellence in Journalism, "Gambling with the Future," *Columbia Journalism Review,* November/December 2001.

extensive commercials, are locally supported, and are often subsidized by the government and corporations. A complex relationship exists among the for-profit and nonprofit media, the government, and the public. Throughout the rest of this chapter, we examine some of the many facets of this relationship.

A HISTORY OF THE MEDIA IN THE UNITED STATES

Many years ago, Thomas Jefferson wrote, "Were it left to me to decide whether we should have a government without newspapers, or newspapers without a government, I should not hesitate a moment to prefer the latter."[3] Although the media have played a significant role in politics since the founding of this nation, they were not as overwhelmingly important in the past as they are today. For one thing, politics was controlled by a small elite who communicated personally. For another, during the early 1800s and before, news traveled slowly. If an important political event occurred in New York, it was not known until five days later in Philadelphia; 10 days later in the capital cities of Connecticut, Maryland, and Virginia; and 15 days later in Boston.

Roughly 3,000 newspapers were being published by 1860. Some of these, such as the *New York Tribune,* were mainly sensation mongers that concentrated on crimes, scandals, and the like. The *New York Herald* specialized in self-improvement and what today would be called practical news. Although sensational and biased reporting often created political divisiveness (this was particularly true during the Civil War), many historians believe that the growth of the print media also played an important role in unifying the country.

THE RISE OF THE POLITICAL PRESS

Americans may cherish the idea of an unbiased press, but in the early years of the nation's history, the number of politically sponsored newspapers was significant. The sole reason for the existence of such periodicals was to further the interests of the politicians who paid for their publication. As chief executive of our government during this period, George Washington has been called a "firm believer" in **managed news**. Although acknowledging that the public had a right to be informed, he believed that some matters should be kept secret and that news that might damage the image of the United States should be censored (not published). Washington, however, made no attempt to control the press.

THE DEVELOPMENT OF MASS-READERSHIP NEWSPAPERS

Two inventions in the 19th century led to the development of mass-readership newspapers. The first was the high-speed rotary press; the second was the telegraph. Faster presses meant lower per-unit costs and lower subscription prices. In addition, by 1848, the Associated Press had developed the telegraph into a nationwide apparatus for the dissemination of all types of information on a systematic basis.

Managed News
Information generated and distributed by the government in such a way as to give government interests priority over candor.

---

[3]Thomas Jefferson, "Letter to Edward Carrington" (1787), in Andrew A. Lipscomb and Albert E. Bergh, eds., *The Writings of Thomas Jefferson,* Memorial Edition (The Thomas Jefferson Memorial Association: Washington, DC, 1903–04), p. 57.

Along with these technological changes came a growing population and increasing urbanization. A larger, more urban population could support daily newspapers, even if the price per paper was only a penny. Finally, the burgeoning, diversified economy encouraged the growth of advertising, which meant that newspapers could obtain additional revenues from merchants who seized the opportunity to promote their wares to a larger public.

THE POPULAR PRESS AND YELLOW JOURNALISM

Students of the history of journalism have ascertained a change in the last half of the 1800s, not in the level of biased news reporting, but in its origin. Whereas politically sponsored newspapers had expounded a particular political party's point of view, the post–Civil War mass-based newspapers expounded whatever political philosophy the owner of the newspaper happened to have.

Even if newspaper owners did not have a particular political axe to grind, they often allowed their editors to engage in sensationalism and what is known as **yellow journalism**. The questionable or simply personal activities of a prominent businessperson, politician, or socialite were front-page material. Newspapers, then as now, made their economic way by maximizing readership. As the *National Enquirer* demonstrates with its current circulation of almost two million, sensationalism is still rewarded by high levels of readership.

THE AGE OF THE ELECTROMAGNETIC SIGNAL

The first scheduled radio program in the United States featured politicians. On the night of November 2, 1920, KDKA-Pittsburgh transmitted the returns of the presidential election race between Warren G. Harding and James M. Cox. The listeners were a few thousand people tuning in on primitive, homemade sets.

By 1924, there were nearly 1,400 radio stations. But it was not until 8 p.m. on November 15, 1926, that the electronic media came into their own in the United States. On that night, the National Broadcasting Company (NBC) made its debut with a four-hour program broadcast by 25 stations in 21 cities. Network broadcasting had become a reality.

Even with the advent of national radio in the 1920s and television in the late 1940s, many politicians were slow to understand the significance of the **electronic media**. The 1952 presidential campaign was the first to involve a real role for television. Television coverage of the Republican convention helped Dwight Eisenhower win over delegates and secure the nomination. His vice presidential running mate, Richard Nixon, put TV to good use. Accused of hiding a secret slush fund, Nixon replied to his critics with his famous "Checkers" speech. He denied the attacks, cried real tears, and said that the only thing he ever received from a contributor for his personal use was his dog, Checkers, and a "Republican cloth coat" for his wife, Pat. It was a highly effective performance.

Today, television dominates the campaign strategy of every would-be national politician, as well as that of every elected official. Politicians think of ways to continue to be newsworthy, thereby gaining free access to the electronic media. Attacking the president's programs is one way of becoming newsworthy; other ways include holding highly visible hearings on controversial subjects, going on "fact-finding" trips, and employing gimmicks (such as taking a walking tour of a state). In fact, the ideal way to get television coverage is to air a campaign advertisement that is so controversial or "talked about" that the news runs the ad over and over again for free.

Yellow Journalism
A term for sensationalistic, irresponsible journalism. Reputedly, the term is an allusion to the cartoon "The Yellow Kid" in the old *New York World,* a newspaper especially noted for its sensationalism.

Electronic Media
Communication channels that involve electronic transmissions, such as radio, television, and, to an increasing extent, the Internet.

" INTERESTING.....IT'S LIKE A PORTABLE 500K FILE and YOU DON'T HAVE TO WAIT FOR IT TO DOWNLOAD.... AND YOU SAY IT'S CALLED A NEWSPAPER ? "

THE REVOLUTION IN THE ELECTRONIC MEDIA

Just as technological change was responsible for the end of politically sponsored periodicals, technology is increasing the number of alternative news sources today. The advent of pay TV, cable TV, subscription TV, satellite TV, and the Internet has completely changed the electronic media landscape. With hundreds, if not thousands, of potential outlets for specialized programs, the electronic media are becoming more like the print media in catering to specialized tastes. This is sometimes referred to as **narrowcasting**. Cable and satellite television and the Internet offer the public unparalleled access to specialized information on everything from gardening and home repair to sports and religion. Most viewers are able to choose among several sources for their favorite type of programming.

In recent years, narrowcasting has become increasingly prevalent. The broadcast networks' audiences are declining. Between 1982 and 2008, their share of the audience fell from 72 percent to 29 percent. At the same time, the percentage of households having access to the Internet grew from zero to more than 70 percent.

TALK-SHOW POLITICS AND SATELLITE RADIO

Multiple news outlets have given rise to literally thousands of talk shows on television, radio, and the Internet. By 2007, there were more than two dozen national television talk shows; their hosts ranged from Jerry Springer, who is regarded as a sensationalist, to Jon Stewart whose comedy "news hour" draws in a younger audience. In 2003, Arnold Schwarzenegger actually announced his candidacy for governor of California on Jay Leno's *Tonight Show*. Higher-level talk shows like that of Charlie Rose on public television are seen as an important way for politicians to reach upper-income, well-educated audiences.

The real blossoming of "talk" has occurred on the radio. The number of radio stations that program only talk shows has increased from about 300 in 1989 to more than 1,200 today. The topics of talk shows range from business and investment to psychology and politics. There has been considerable criticism of the political talk shows, especially those hosted by Rush Limbaugh, Glenn Beck, and other conservatives, on the grounds that these shows focus on negative politics rather than policy issues. Critics contend that such shows increase the level of intolerance and irrationality in American politics.

Narrowcasting
Broadcasting that is targeted to one small sector of the population.

However, data from the Pew Center show that the audience for most of these talk shows is not very different from the general population.[4]

Responding to conservative dominance of "talk radio," liberal groups began considering the possibilities of left-of-center talk shows. In 2004, liberal comedian Al Franken went live on Air America Radio with his highly partisan take on the news. Franken was willing to match rhetoric with conservative talk-show hosts such as Rush Limbaugh, but the network went bankrupt in 2006. Air America programs were back on the air in 2007 with a new owner. Franken, however, entered politics and was elected senator from Minnesota in 2008.

Satellite radio has also become an important player in talk-show politics. Howard Stern, who was considered an outspoken force in both traditional radio and TV, moved to Sirius satellite radio in 2006. Though Stern spends much of his time on nonpolitical topics, he does interview political guests (whom he usually harasses). The satellite radio system XM, which has merged with Sirius, has its own political commentators, including Bob Edwards, who conducts interviews on XM Public Radio.

THE INTERNET, BLOGGING, AND PODCASTING

For at least 10 years, every politician has felt the necessity of having a Web site. On the national level, political Web sites were created for the two major-party candidates for president for the first time in 1996. Since then, even the lowliest local politician feels obligated to have a Web site that is updated at least on occasion. Political candidates have used the Internet to raise tens of millions of dollars. Howard Dean and John McCain were early adopters of the Internet to raise money, but Barack Obama became the leader in this practice in 2008. His Web site encouraged millions of supporters to donate small amounts to his primary campaign. His organization even allows individuals to sign up for automatic monthly donations with their credit cards.[5] The inexpensive nature of raising money through the Internet is a great advantage, particularly as compared to a traditional mailing.

Within the last few years, politicians have also felt obligated to post regular blogs on their Web sites. The word *blog* comes from "Web log," a regular updating of one's ideas at a specific Web site. Of course, many people besides politicians are also posting blogs. Not all of the millions of blogs posted daily are political in nature, but many are, and they can have a dramatic influence on events, giving rise to the term *blogosphere politics*. During the 2004 presidential campaign, CBS's Dan Rather reported on television that documents showed that President George W. Bush had failed to fulfill his obligations to the National Guard during the 1970s. Within four hours, a blogger on Freerepublic.com pointed out that the documents shown on CBS appeared to have been created in Microsoft Word, even though personal computers and Microsoft Word did not even exist in the 1970s. Another blogger, Charles Johnson (Littlegreenfootballs.com), showed that by using Word default settings he could create documents that matched those from CBS. Eleven days later, CBS admitted that an error had been made, and Dan Rather ultimately lost his job as a news anchor.

By 2004, politicians began to produce their own blogs. Howard Dean actually wrote his own blog, as did his staffers. They chronicled important campaign decisions as well as more mundane activities of the campaign. George Bush and John Kerry also posted blogs, but they were much more than campaign vehicles with galleries of pictures and audio clips. Analysis of these blogs indicated that although they encouraged citizen

[4]"News Audiences Increasingly Politicized," The Pew Research Center for the People and the Press, June 8, 2004, accessed at http://people-press.org/reports.
[5]Joshua Green, "The Amazing Money Machine," *The Atlantic*, June 2008, accessed at www.theatlantic.com/doc/200806.

RUSH LIMBAUGH, THE conservative radio talk show host, rallies his listeners on the air and through his Web site. (www.rushlimbaugh.com/ Clear Channel Communications, Inc.)

Podcasting
A method of distributing multimedia files, such as audio or video files, for downloading onto mobile devices or personal computers.

DID YOU KNOW?

That the number of people watching the television networks during prime time has declined by almost 25 percent in the last 10 years?

interaction, they tended to promote one-way communication, sending information from the candidate to the potential voter.[6]

Blogs are clearly threatening the mainstream media. They can be highly specialized, highly political, and highly entertaining—and they are cheap. *The Washington Post* requires thousands of employees, many reams of paper, and tons of ink to generate its offline product and incurs delivery costs to get its papers to readers. A blogging organization such as RealClearPolitics can generate its political commentary with fewer than 10 employees.

Once blogs—written words—became well established, it was only a matter of time before they would end up as spoken words. Enter **podcasting**, so-called because the first Internet-communicated spoken blogs were downloaded onto Apple's iPods. Podcasts, though, can be heard on one's computer or downloaded onto any portable listening device. Podcasting can also include videos. Hundreds of thousands of podcasts are now being generated every day. Basically, anyone who has an idea can easily create a podcast and make it available for downloading. Like blogs, podcasts threaten traditional media sources. Even video podcasting costs virtually nothing with today's inexpensive technology.

Although politicians were somewhat slow to adopt this form of communication, many now are using podcasts to keep in touch with their constituents. By the time you read this, there will be thousands, if not tens of thousands, of political podcasts. Certainly, the use of podcasts, blogs, and YouTube became a major part of campaigning during the 2007–2008 election cycle.

[6]Kaye D. Trammell, "The Blogging of the President," in Andrew Williams and John Tedesco, eds., *The Internet Election: Perspectives on the Web in Campaign 2004* (Lanham, MD: Rowman and Littlefield, 2006).

THE PRIMACY OF TELEVISION

Television is the most influential medium. It is also big business. National news TV personalities such as Katie Couric and Brian Williams earn millions of dollars per year from their TV contracts alone. They are paid so much because they command large audiences, and large audiences command high prices for advertising on national news shows. Indeed, news per se has become a major factor in the profitability of TV stations.

THE INCREASE IN NEWS-TYPE PROGRAMMING

In 1963, the major networks—ABC, CBS, and NBC—devoted only 11 minutes daily to national news. A 24/7 news cable channel—CNN—started operating in 1980. With the addition of CNN-Headline News, CNBC, MSNBC, FOX News, and other news-format cable channels since the 1980s, the amount of news-type programming has continued to increase. By 2008, the amount of time the networks devoted to news-type programming each day had increased to about three hours. In recent years, all of the major networks have also added Internet sites to try to capture that market, but they face hundreds of competitors on the Web.

TELEVISION'S INFLUENCE ON THE POLITICAL PROCESS

Television's influence on the political process today is recognized by all who engage in the process. Television news is often criticized for being superficial, particularly compared with the detailed coverage available in the print media, such as the *New York Times*. In fact, television news is constrained by its technical characteristics, the most important being the limitations of time—stories must be reported in only a few minutes.

The most interesting aspect of television is the fact that it relies on pictures rather than words to attract the viewer's attention. Therefore, the digital videos or slides that are chosen for a particular political story have exaggerated importance. Viewers do not know what other photos may have been taken or what other events may have been digitally recorded—they see only those appearing on their screens. Television news can also be exploited for its drama by well-constructed stories. Some critics suggest that there is pressure to produce television news that has a "story line," like a novel or movie. The story should be short, with exciting pictures and a clear plot. In the extreme case, the news media are satisfied with a **sound bite**, a several-second comment selected or crafted for its immediate impact on the viewer.

Sound Bite
A brief, memorable comment that can easily be fit into news broadcasts.

It has been suggested that these formatting characteristics—or necessities—of television increase its influence on political events. (Newspapers and news magazines are also limited by their formats, but to a lesser extent.) As you are aware, real life is usually not dramatic, nor do all events have a neat or an easily understood plot. Political campaigns are continuing events, lasting perhaps as long as two years. The significance of their daily turns and twists is only apparent later. The "drama" of Congress, with its 535 players and dozens of important committees and meetings, is also difficult for the media to present. Television requires dozens of daily three-minute stories.

Some commentators, including M. B. Zuckerman, editor in chief of *U.S. News and World Report,* claim that "policymaking is held hostage to imagery." Zuckerman argues that television networks "distort the meaning of events by failing to provide the context that would help us make sense of these images."[7] The TV newsroom cliché has been—and

---

[7]Mortimer B. Zuckerman, "Why TV Holds Us Hostage," *U.S. News and World Report,* February 20, 2005.

probably always will be—"if it bleeds, it leads." It is not news to show 100 rebuilt schools in Iraq, but it is news to show a car bombing that injures or kills civilians.

THE MEDIA AND POLITICAL CAMPAIGNS

All forms of the media—television, newspapers, radio, magazines, blogs, and podcasts—have a significant political impact on American society. Media influence is most obvious during political campaigns. News coverage of a single event, such as the results of the Iowa caucuses or the New Hampshire primary, may be the most important factor in having a candidate be referred to in the media as the front-runner in a presidential campaign. It is not too much of an exaggeration to say that almost all national political figures, starting with the president, plan every public appearance and statement to attract media coverage.

Because television is still the primary news source for the majority of Americans, candidates and their consultants spend much of their time devising strategies that use television to their benefit. Three types of TV coverage are generally employed in campaigns for the presidency and other offices: advertising, management of news coverage, and campaign debates.

ADVERTISING

Perhaps one of the most effective political ads of all time was a 30-second spot created by President Lyndon B. Johnson's media adviser in 1964. In this ad, a little girl stood in a field of daisies. As she held a daisy, she pulled the petals off and quietly counted to herself. Suddenly, when she reached number 10, a deep bass voice cut in and began a countdown: "10, 9, 8, 7, 6, . . ." When the voice intoned "zero," the unmistakable mushroom cloud of an atomic bomb began to fill the screen. Then President Johnson's voice was heard: "These are the stakes. To make a world in which all of God's children can live, or to go into the

PRESIDENT LYNDON JOHNSON'S "daisy girl" ad contrasted the innocence of childhood with the horror of an atomic attack. Johnson's opponent in the 1964 election was Senator Barry Goldwater, who was more likely to take a strong stance against the Soviet Union. (Democratic National Committee)

dark. We must either love each other or we must die." At the end of the commercial, the message read, "Vote for President Johnson on November 3."

To understand how effective this "daisy girl" commercial was, you must know that Johnson's opponent was Barry Goldwater, a Republican conservative candidate known for his expansive views on the role of the U.S. military. The ad's implication was that Goldwater would lead the United States into nuclear war. Although the ad was withdrawn within a few days, it has a place in political campaign history as the classic negative campaign advertisement. The ad's producer, Tony Schwartz, describes the effect in this way: "It was comparable to a person going to a psychiatrist and seeing dirty pictures in a Rorschach pattern. The daisy commercial evoked Goldwater's pro-bomb statements. They were like dirty pictures in the audience's mind."[8]

Since the daisy girl advertisement, negative advertising has come into its own. Candidates vie with one another to produce "attack" ads and then to counterattack when the opponent responds. The public claims not to like negative advertising, but as one consultant put it, "Negative advertising works." The most important effect of negative advertisements may not be to transfer votes from the candidate who is under attack to the candidate running the ads. Rather, the negative ads can demoralize the supporters of the candidate who is under attack. Some supporters, as a result, may not bother to vote. The widespread use of negative ads, therefore, can lead to reduced political participation and a general cynicism about politics.

Political advertising has become increasingly important for the profitability of television station owners. Hearst-Argyle Television, for example, obtains well over 10 percent of its revenues from political ads during an election year. Political advertising is not restricted to television, however. In addition to typical print ads, online political advertising has been on the rise. The Interactive Advertising Bureau estimates that during the 2008 presidential campaign, as much as $10 billion was spent on Internet advertising.

That the average length of a quote, or sound bite, for a candidate has decreased from 49 seconds in 1968 to less than 9 seconds today?

MANAGEMENT OF NEWS COVERAGE

Using political advertising to get a message across to the public is a very expensive tactic. Coverage by the news media, however, is free; it simply demands that the campaign ensure that coverage takes place. In recent years, campaign managers have shown increasing sophistication in creating newsworthy events for journalists to cover. As Doris Graber points out, "To keep a favorable image of their candidates in front of the public, campaign managers arrange newsworthy events to familiarize potential voters with their candidates' best aspects."[9]

The campaign staff uses several methods to try to influence the quantity and type of coverage the campaign receives. First, the campaign staff understands the technical aspects of media coverage—camera angles, necessary equipment, timing, and deadlines—and plans political events to accommodate the press. Second, the campaign organization is aware that political reporters and their sponsors—networks or newspapers—are in competition for the best stories and can be manipulated through the granting of favors, such as a personal interview with the candidate. Third, the scheduler in the campaign has the important task of planning events that will be photogenic and interesting enough

---

[8]As quoted in Kathleen Hall Jamieson, *Packaging the Presidency: A History and Criticism of Presidential Campaign Advertising*, 3rd ed. (New York: Oxford University Press, 1996), p. 200.
[9]Doris Graber, *Mass Media and American Politics*, 7th ed. (Washington, DC: Congressional Quarterly Press, 2005), p. 63.

for the evening news. A related goal, although one that is more difficult to attain, is to convince reporters that a particular interpretation of an event is correct.

Today, the art of putting the appropriate **spin** on a story or event is highly developed. Each candidate's or elected official's press advisers, often referred to as **spin doctors**, try to convince the journalists that their interpretations of the political events are correct. Each political campaign, and the president's own Office of Communication, send e-mails and faxes to all the major media, setting out their own version of an event virtually in real time. During the 2008 primary campaign, both the Obama campaign and the Clinton campaign spent endless hours "explaining" or "spinning" the results in a specific state or suggesting how the other candidate's "bowling score" or "gun handling" was pandering to voters. More recently, journalists have begun to report on the different spins used by candidates and elected officials to try to manipulate news coverage.

GOING FOR THE KNOCKOUT PUNCH—PRESIDENTIAL DEBATES

In presidential elections, perhaps just as important as political advertisements is the performance of the candidates in televised presidential debates. After the first such debate in 1960, in which John F. Kennedy, the young senator from Massachusetts, took on the vice president of the United States, Richard Nixon, candidates became aware of the great potential of television for changing the momentum of a campaign. In general, challengers have much more to gain from debating than do incumbents. Challengers hope that the incumbent will make a mistake in the debate and undermine his "presidential" image. Incumbent presidents are loath to debate their challengers because it puts their opponents on an equal footing with them, but the debates have become so widely anticipated that it is difficult for an incumbent to refuse.

Debates can affect the outcome of a race. Some people believe that Democrat Al Gore hurt himself during the 2000 debates by appearing arrogant. In 2008, the McCain and Obama campaigns agreed on three presidential debates and one vice presidential debate. With the addition of Sarah Palin to the Republican ticket and her stirring convention speech, almost as many Americans tuned in to her debate with Senator Joe Biden as they did to the presidential debates. Each of the presidential debates saw Senator Obama remain calm and composed and Senator McCain try to demonstrate his role as a reformer and cost-cutter. McCain was generally seen as being too assertive and lacking any humor, while Obama won over viewers with his presidential demeanor. Neither candidate made any mistakes, nor did either score a knockout punch. Postdebate commentary focused as much on the skill of the moderator as the performance of the candidates.

Although debates are justified publicly as an opportunity for the voters to find out how candidates differ on the issues, the candidates want to capitalize on the power of television to project an image. They view the debate as a strategic opportunity to improve their own images or to point out their opponents' failures. Candidates also know that the morning-after interpretation of the debate by the news media may play a crucial role in what the public thinks, so their staff bombards the news commentators with the "spin" they want on the event. Regardless of the risks of debating, the potential for gaining votes is so great that candidates undoubtedly will continue to seek televised debates. Of course, in today's Internet world, candidates also know that their performances will be "broadcast" on the Internet or posted on YouTube and that the bloggers will add their own interpretations to those of the mainstream media.

Spin
An interpretation of campaign events or election results that is favorable to the candidate's campaign strategy.

Spin Doctor
A political campaign adviser who tries to convince journalists of the truth of a particular interpretation of events.

A FAMILY WATCHES the 1960 Kennedy-Nixon debates on television. After the debate, TV viewers thought Kennedy had won, whereas radio listeners thought Nixon had won. (Time Life Pictures/National Archives/ Getty Images)

POLITICAL CAMPAIGNS AND THE INTERNET

Without a doubt, the Internet has become an important vehicle for campaign advertising and news coverage, as well as for soliciting campaign contributions. This was made clear during the 2004 presidential elections, when 7 percent of all Internet users participated in online campaign activities. (Internet users included about two-thirds of all American adults.) As pointed out previously, Democratic presidential hopeful Howard Dean (past head of the Democratic Party) used his Internet site and e-mailings to generate millions of dollars in campaign contributions, most of which were very small, such as $50 or $100. Barack Obama was able to raise millions of dollars each month during the primary season, with at least half being small contributions.

During the 2008 election campaigns, the Internet was used not only to advertise the candidates' positions, to solicit donations, and to podcast speeches and debates, but it also was used to target messages. Candidates sought e-mail lists sorted by age, gender, and other demographic variables. Then they e-mailed messages to targeted groups. Members of union households received, for example, messages about lowering the number of jobs going overseas. Candidates used the Internet to recruit volunteers for Get Out the Vote campaigns. They also used e-mail and blogs to instruct citizens on how to participate in the political caucuses and how to persuade others to support their candidate of choice.

Today, the campaign staff of every candidate running for a significant political office includes an Internet campaign strategist—a professional hired to create and maintain the campaign Web site, blogs, and podcasts. The work of this strategist includes designing a user-friendly and attractive Web site for the candidate, managing the candidate's e-mail communications, and tracking campaign contributions made through

POLITICS WITH A purpose

Have YouTube and Jon Stewart Changed How Politicians Campaign?

"Have you seen *that* video? You know that crazy one that's all over the Net? My friend just texted me the link." If this sounds familiar, you're in good company. "Viral videos" (video clips that spread from person to person via e-mail), share sites (such as YouTube), and social networking sites (Facebook and MySpace, for example) have become ubiquitous. The question for politics and politicians is whether these clips are a menace or yet another way to get out their message.

One of the most used share sites, YouTube, has been around since 2005. In the congressional elections of 2006, it took center stage as embarrassing and/or politically damaging videos surfaced. For example, at a campaign event, Senator George Allen (R.-Va.) called an Indian American staffer of his Democratic opponent (who was present at the event for opposition research) a "macaca," a racial slur. Not only was the moment captured on a cell phone video camera, but it was also uploaded onto YouTube. In addition to the hundreds of thousands of viewers who saw the video on that site, the "macaca moment" was widely covered by the mainstream media.[a] During the primary campaign in 2008, a remark that Barack Obama made about rural, white gun owners at a private fundraising dinner also made it to the Internet within hours. Hillary Clinton used that quote to bolster a win in the Pennsylvania primary.

In fact, the George Allen event has spawned its own nomenclature; the National Republican Senatorial Campaign Committee issued guidelines for its 2008 candidates to avoid their own "macaca moments": respect the importance of politically influential blogs; remember that you are always "live on film"; and "don't be antisocial," because social network sites such as MySpace can work for you.[b]

By the 2008 electoral cycle, candidates had become YouTube savvy and aware of the power of alternative news sources including Jon Stewart's satirical *The Daily Show* and Stephen Colbert's *The Colbert Report.* Senator John McCain, the Republican nominee for president, made more than nine appearances on Stewart's show. Senator Hillary Clinton, vying for the Democratic nomination, appeared on the show via satellite from Austin, Texas, the night before the nomination contests in that state. In advance of the Pennsylvania primary, Senator Barack Obama made his third appearance on the show.[c]

These candidates were wise to reach out to voters in this fashion. The Pew Research Center regularly conducts surveys on media consumption and news and information sources. Its 2004 survey found that 21 percent of those under age 30 reported getting campaign news from *The Daily Show.*[d] In a study two years later, in addition to being younger than the average TV viewer, *Daily Show* aficionados reported being more likely to self-identify as Democrats, be male, be more liberal, and be more knowledgeable about politics (though not as knowledgeable as Rush Limbaugh listeners).[e]

The Center also finds evidence for the emerging integration of YouTube into the public consciousness. Its January 2008 report showed that 48 percent of Internet users reported going to YouTube. Forty-two percent of younger people reported getting campaign news from the Internet, and 2 percent of those cited YouTube as a primary source. Three percent also said they went to MySpace and the Drudge Report for election news.[f]

As YouTube celebrates its five years of existence in 2010, the Web site has become a global resource for sharing videos of public events and political conflict. Supporters of the Tea Party movement posted videos to show off their large crowds, but others posted videos undercutting those estimates. Gulf Coast residents, environmentalists, and corporations posted videos reporting on the aftereffects of the 2010 oil rig explosion. Video of overseas conflicts, whether in Burma, Thailand, or Greece, is instantly available to the American public on YouTube. The question remains, however: In the absence of editing or video sources, which pictures can and should you believe?

[a] www.nytimes.com/2006/08/20/weekinreview/20lizza.html?partner=rssnyt&emc=rss, accessed April 18, 2008.
[b] www.politico.com/news/stories/0607/4483.html, accessed April 18, 2008.
[c] www.thedailyshow.com, accessed April 18, 2008.
[d] Its 2008 report saw a precipitous drop in this figure, down to 12 percent. However, the survey was conducted during a writers' strike that had a serious effect on TV viewership, and the authors of the study attribute the drop to the strike. www.pewinternet.org/pdfs/Pew_MediaSources_jan08.pdf, accessed April 18, 2008.
[e] http://people-press.org/reports/display.php3?ReportID=282, accessed April 18, 2008.
[f] www.pewinternet.org/pdfs/Pew_MediaSources_jan08.pdf, accessed April 18, 2008.

the site. Additionally, virtually all major interest groups in the United States now use the Internet to promote their causes. Prior to elections, various groups engage in issue advocacy from their Web sites. At little or no cost, they can promote positions taken by favored candidates and solicit contributions.

Is campaigning on the Internet the most important advance in politics? There are both advantages and disadvantages to a Web campaign. As noted by Robert J. Klotz, using the Internet for campaigning may be a double-edged sword for a candidate. Only individuals who want to look at a Web site will do so, which means few, if any, accidental viewers. This makes it easy to supply lots of information to those who are already interested but difficult to reach undecided voters. In addition, while the Internet may encourage blog posting and e-mail to the campaign, it raises expectations that cannot be met. No candidate can spend his or her time answering millions of e-mails. However, a great advantage to Internet campaigning for the candidate is that one minute of exposure costs the same as hours. Followers can view and interact with the Web for hours at a time for no additional cost to the campaign. Compare that strategy with spending millions on television prime-time advertising to a declining audience.[10]

THE MEDIA'S IMPACT ON THE VOTERS

The question of how much influence the media have on voting behavior is difficult to answer. Generally, individuals watch television, read newspapers, or log on to a Web site with certain preconceived ideas about political issues and candidates. These attitudes and opinions act as a kind of perceptual screen that filters out information that makes people feel uncomfortable or that does not fit with their own ideas.

Voters watch campaign commercials and news about political campaigns with "selective attentiveness"—that is, they tend to watch those commercials that support the candidates they favor and tend to pay attention to news stories about their own candidates. This selectivity also affects their perceptions of the content of a news story or commercial and whether it is remembered. Apparently, the media have the most influence on those persons who have not formed an opinion about political candidates or issues. Studies have shown that the flurry of television commercials and debates immediately before election day has the greatest impact on those voters who are truly undecided. Few voters who have already formed their opinions change their minds under the influence of the media.

THE ROLE OF THE MEDIA IN THE 2008 ELECTIONS

As in many past elections, broadcast television dominated media spending during the campaign. In the 2006 midterm elections, $912 million was spent on TV ads. In the 2008 elections, more than $2 billion was spent. The Obama and McCain campaigns produced numerous ads attacking the other's positions and, in some cases, his character. McCain's ads stressed Obama's lack of experience at high levels of office, while the Obama camp painted McCain as a strong supporter of President Bush. While the major media reported on the campaign, commentators and bloggers wrote about how the media treated the two candidates. Rarely have the media been so scrutinized in a presidential campaign. The major networks were frequently charged with being more positive toward Obama and more negative toward McCain in their news stories. Academic studies were published that seemed to back up such a claim. In their defense,

[10]Robert J. Klotz, *The Politics of Internet Communication* (Lanham, MD: Rowman and Littlefield, 2004).

the media responded that Obama's historic run for the presidency was more newsworthy then McCain's campaign and that they chose stories solely on news value. Both candidates sought to get beyond the prime-time news by appearing on late-night comedy shows. *Saturday Night Live* recorded some its highest ratings ever with its 2008 political coverage.

THE MEDIA AND THE GOVERNMENT

The mass media not only wield considerable power when it comes to political campaigns, but they also, in one way or another, can wield power over the affairs of government and over government officials. For example, in April 2004, President George W. Bush tried to keep Condoleezza Rice, then the national security adviser, from testifying before the bipartisan September 11 investigation commission by citing the doctrine of executive privilege. After several weeks, during which this decision was widely criticized in the print and electronic media, Bush reversed himself and allowed Rice to testify.

PREPACKAGED NEWS

In recent years, the public learned that the Bush administration had spent millions of dollars on public relations, including "news" programs that were often created specifically to be rebroadcast on television. In 2005, for example, the Bush administration had to acknowledge that it paid several conservative commentators to write in support of administration-backed programs. Specifically, conservative commentator Armstrong Williams received $240,000 to write favorably about the No Child Left Behind Act and the Department of Education. Additionally, the Bush administration created a video about the new education law that was designed to look like a legitimate news program. The administration used the same technique to promote the law providing a new prescription drug benefit for Medicare recipients.

Is the use of taxpayer dollars to create prepackaged news legal? Some argue that it is because the government is not forcing anyone to broadcast this "covert" propaganda.

WHITE HOUSE PRESS secretary Robert Gibbs briefs reporters at the White House in Washington, Tuesday, June 29, 2010. (AP Photo/ Charles Dharapak)

Others, however, question the ethical underpinnings of government advocacy at the expense of both unbiased journalism and taxpayers' dollars.

THE MEDIA AND THE PRESIDENCY

The relationship between the media and the president usually is reciprocal: Each needs the other to thrive. Because of this codependency, both the media and the president work hard to exploit one another. The media need news to report, and the president needs coverage. The political staff of the White House has as its goal constant and positive exposure of the president in the media. Presidential events and speeches are planned to the extent that the effort has been nicknamed "the presidential spectacle."

In the United States, the prominence of the president is accentuated by a **White House press corps** that is assigned full time to cover the presidency. These reporters even have a lounge in the White House where they spend their days, waiting for a story to break. Most of the time, they simply wait for the daily or twice-daily briefing by the president's **press secretary**. Because of the press corps' physical proximity to the president, the chief executive cannot even take a brief stroll around the Rose Garden without it becoming news. Perhaps no other nation allows the press such access to its highest government official. Consequently, no other democratic nation has its airwaves and print media so filled with absolute trivia regarding the personal lives of the chief executive and his or her family.

One of the first presidents to make truly effective use of the media was President Franklin D. Roosevelt (served 1933–1945), who brought new spirit to a demoralized country and led it through the Great Depression with his radio broadcasts. His "fireside chats" brought hope to millions. Through his speeches, Roosevelt was able to forge a common emotional bond among his listeners. His decisive announcement in 1933 on the reorganization of the banks, for example, calmed a jittery nation and prevented the collapse of the banking industry. (Nervous depositors were withdrawing their assets, which threatened to create a "run" on the banks.) His famous Pearl Harbor speech, following the Japanese attack on the U.S. Pacific fleet on December 7, 1941 ("a day that will live in infamy"), mobilized the nation for World War II.

President Barack Obama's White House truly has revolutionized the use of the media for getting the president's message to the public. While the president is famous for his skill in rhetoric, he has chosen to limit the free-for-all atmosphere of press conferences in favor of more intimate and controlled interviews with the major news anchors of virtually every network. The White House Web site (http://www.whitehouse.gov) is packed with position papers, speeches, presidential memos, and photo galleries. From the Web site, citizens can follow the president and his family on Twitter, Facebook, YouTube, and LinkedIn and download speeches and video via iTunes.

SETTING THE PUBLIC AGENDA

According to several studies, the media play an important part in setting the public agenda. Evidence is strong that whatever public problems receive the greatest media treatment will be cited by the public in contemporary surveys as the most important problems. Although the media do not make policy decisions, they do influence to a significant extent the policy issues that will be decided—and this is an important part of the political process. Because those who control the media are not elected representatives of the people, the agenda-setting role of the media necessarily is a controversial

White House Press Corps
The reporters assigned full time to cover the presidency.

Press Secretary
The presidential staff member responsible for handling White House media relations and communications.

DID YOU KNOW?

That Franklin D. Roosevelt held approximately 1,000 press conferences during his terms as president?

one. The relationship of the media to agenda setting remains complex, though, because politicians are able to manipulate media coverage to control some of its effects, as well as to exploit the media to further their agendas with the public.

INVESTIGATIVE REPORTING

Most major newspapers and many television networks devote some of their resources to investigative reporting. By finding a problem with a public policy or uncovering official wrongdoing, the media are alerting the public to important political information. Furthermore, the results of investigative reporting can have a very important impact on officeholders and, in the best case, bring about real change for the better. Richard Nixon, for example, barely avoided impeachment and resigned from office due to the investigative reporting of two *The Washington Post* reporters. Recently, the *Post* won a Pulitzer Prize for the investigative reporting that found very poor housing conditions at Walter Reed Army Medical Center for wounded veterans.

GOVERNMENT REGULATION OF THE MEDIA

The United States has one of the freest presses in the world. Nonetheless, regulation of the media does exist, particularly of the electronic media. Many aspects of this regulation were discussed in Chapter 4, when we examined First Amendment rights and the press.

The First Amendment does not mention electronic media, which did not exist when the Bill of Rights was written. For many reasons, the government has much greater control over the electronic media than it does over printed media. Through the Federal Communications Commission (FCC), which regulates communications by radio, television, wire, and cable, the number of radio stations has been controlled for many years, even though technologically we could have many more radio stations than now exist. Also, the FCC created a situation in which the three major TV networks dominated the airwaves.

IN JUNE 2010, President Barack Obama is briefed about the ongoing response to the BP oil spill by, from left, Carol Browner, assistant to the President for energy and climate change, National Incident Commander Admiral Thad Allen, and Senior Advisor Valerie Jarrett, aboard Air Force One en route to the Gulf Coast. (Pete Souza/White House/Sipa Press)

CONTROLLING OWNERSHIP OF THE MEDIA

Many FCC rules have dealt with ownership of news media, such as how many stations a network can own. In the past, the FCC auctioned off hundreds of radio frequencies, allowing the expansion of cellular telephone applications.

In 1996, Congress passed legislation that had far-reaching implications for the communications industry—the Telecommunications Act. The act ended the rule that kept telephone companies from entering the cable business and other communications markets. What this means is that a single corporation—whether Time Warner or Disney—can offer long-distance and local telephone services, cable television, satellite television, Internet services, and, of course, libraries of films and entertainment. The act opened the door to competition and led to more options for consumers, who now can choose among multiple competitors for all of these services delivered to the home. At the same time, it launched a race among competing companies to control media ownership.

Media Conglomerates. Many media outlets are now owned by corporate conglomerates. A single entity may own a television network, the studios that produce shows, news, and movies, and the means to deliver that content to the home via cable, satellite, or the Internet. The question to be faced in the future is how to ensure competition in the delivery of news so that citizens have access to multiple points of view from the media.

All of the prime-time television networks are owned by major American corporations, including such corporate conglomerates as General Electric (owner of NBC) and Disney (owner of ABC). The Turner Broadcasting/CNN network was also purchased by a major corporation, Time Warner. Later, Time Warner was acquired by America Online (AOL), a merger that combined the world's then-largest media company with the world's then-largest online company. FOX Television has always been a part of Rupert Murdoch's publishing and media empire. In addition to taking part in mergers and acquisitions, many of these companies have formed partnerships with computer software makers, such as Microsoft, for joint electronic publishing ventures.

The cast of *High School Musical* appears on the ABC show *Good Morning America*. *High School Musical* is a Disney creation and ABC is owned by the Disney company. (© Good Morning America/ABC News)

Increased Media Concentration. The FCC promulgates rules on what media conglomerates can own. One measure of a conglomerate's impact is "audience reach," or the percentage of the national viewing public that has access to the conglomerate's outlets. The FCC places an upper limit on audience reach, known as the "audience-reach cap." A few years ago, the FCC raised the national audience-reach cap from 35 percent to 45 percent and also allowed a corporation to own a newspaper and a television station in the same market. Congress rebelled against this new rule, however, and pushed the national audience-reach cap back below 40 percent. Nevertheless, a corporation can still own up to three TV stations in its largest market. The reality today is that there are only a few independent news operations left in the entire country.

This media concentration has led to the disappearance of localism in the news. Obviously, costly locally produced news cannot be shown anywhere except in that local market. In contrast, the costs of producing a similar show

DID YOU KNOW?

That a 30-second television advertisement shown during the Super Bowl costs more than $2.3 million?

for national broadcast can be amortized over millions and millions of viewers and paid for by higher revenues from national advertisers. Another concern, according to former media mogul Ted Turner, is that the rise of media conglomerates may lead to a decline in democratic debate. The emergence of independent news Web sites, blogs, and podcasts provides an offset to this trend, however. Consequently, the increased concentration of traditional media news organizations may not matter as much as in the past.

GOVERNMENT CONTROL OF CONTENT

On the face of it, the First Amendment would seem to apply to all media. In fact, the United States Supreme Court has often been slow to extend free speech and free press guarantees to new media. For example, in 1915, the Court held that "as a matter of common sense," free-speech protections did not apply to cinema. Only in 1952 did the Court find that motion pictures were covered by the First Amendment.[11] In contrast, the Court extended full protection to the Internet almost immediately by striking down provisions of the 1996 Telecommunications Act.[12] Cable TV also received broad protection in 2000.[13] (To learn about nations that exercise far more control over media content, see this chapter's Beyond Our Borders feature.)

Control of Broadcasting. While the Court has held that the First Amendment is relevant to radio and television, it has never extended full protection to these media. The Court has used several arguments to justify this stand—initially, the scarcity of broadcast frequencies. The Court later held that the government could restrict "indecent" programming based on the "pervasive" presence of broadcasting in the home.[14] On this basis, the FCC has the authority to fine broadcasters for indecency or profanity.

Indecency in broadcasting became a major issue in 2004. In the first three months of that year, the FCC levied fines that exceeded those imposed in the previous nine years combined. Including older fines, radio personality Howard Stern cost his employers almost $2 million. Another triggering episode was singer Janet Jackson's "wardrobe malfunction" during a 2004 Super Bowl halftime performance. Legislation was introduced in Congress to increase the maximum fine that the FCC can impose to $500,000 per incident.

Government Control of the Media during the Second Gulf War. During the First Gulf War in 1991, the U.S. government was strongly criticized for not providing accurate information to the media. Stung by this criticism, the Bush administration tried a two-pronged strategy during the Second Gulf (or Iraq) War in 2003. Every day, reporters at the central command post in Qatar were able to hear briefings from top commanders. (Reporters complained, however, that they did not hear enough about the true progress of the war.) The administration also allowed more than 500 journalists to travel with the combat forces as "embedded" journalists. Reports from the field were very favorable to the military. This was understandable, given that the journalists quickly identified with the troops and their difficulties. The Bush administration, however, was unable to control reports from foreign and Arab media.

The Government's Attempt to Control the Media during the Current War on Terrorism. Certainly, since September 11, 2001, government secrecy has increased, sometimes (apparently)

---

[11]*Joseph Burstyn, Inc. v. Wilson,* 343 U.S. 495 (1952).
[12]*Reno v. American Civil Liberties Union,* 521 U.S. 844 (1997).
[13]*United States v. Playboy Entertainment Group,* 529 U.S. 803 (2000).
[14]*FCC v. Pacifica Foundation,* 438 U.S. 230 (1978). In this case, the Court banned seven swear words (famously used by comedian George Carlin) during hours when children could hear them.

U.S. MARINES from the 3rd Battalion, 4th Regiment take up positions around Baghdad to capture a bridge in the east of the city. An embedded reporter (left) communicates with his newsroom during the attack. Are embedded reporters able to maintain their neutral point of view? (© Christophe Calais/ Corbis)

with the public's acceptance. Senator Patrick Leahy (D.-Vt.) argues that the First Amendment would have trouble winning ratification today if it were proposed as a constitutional amendment. He based this assertion on a Knight Foundation survey that found that almost 40 percent of 110,000 students believed that newspapers should have to get "government approval" of news articles before they are published.

In any event, the charter for the Department of Homeland Security, created soon after the September 11 terrorist attacks, includes a provision that allows certain groups to stamp "critical infrastructure information" on the top of documents when they submit information to Homeland Security. This information might include the maps of water-lines or the plans of nuclear power plants. The public has no right to see this information. Additionally, more and more government documents have been labeled "secret" so that they do not have to be revealed to the public.

Despite such measures, since the start of the war on terror and the second war in Iraq, there have been numerous intelligence leaks to the press. The public did find out about the government's monitoring of telephone calls to suspected terrorists abroad. The tension between needed intelligence secrecy and the public's "right to know" continues to create both legal and military problems.

THE PUBLIC'S RIGHT TO MEDIA ACCESS

Does the public have a right to **media access**? Both the FCC and the courts have gradually taken the stance that citizens do have a right of access to the media, particularly the electronic media. The argument is that because the airwaves are public, the government has the right to dictate how they are used. Congress could, for example, pass a law requiring the broadcast networks to provide free airtime to candidates, as is the case in some European nations. The 2008 Republican presidential nominee Senator John McCain of Arizona, a major proponent of campaign finance reform, proposed legislation that would provide such free airtime. Broadcast networks that make bigger profits in election years quietly oppose such a law.

Media Access
The public's right of access to the media. The Federal Communications Commission and the courts have gradually taken the stance that citizens do have a right to media access.

Beyond Our Borders

GOVERNMENT-CONTROLLED MEDIA ABROAD

The First Amendment to the Constitution guarantees freedom of expression in the United States. While there are certainly some restrictions on what Americans say on the radio and television, or even publish, those restrictions are few. This is not so in many other countries today, even though their constitutions may also guarantee freedom of expression.

IRAN'S CONTROL OF THE MEDIA

Broadcasting is run by the state in Iran. The state-run media reflect the views of President Mahmoud Ahmadinejad and those of his allies in the conservative clerical establishment. In Iran, there are no independent newspapers that can present views contrary to the government's conservative clerical views. Every newspaper has to be licensed. Virtually all reformist newspapers have been closed down. In a less-than-totally successful attempt to skirt such censorship, reformist journalists have gone to the Internet.

Because the Internet has become increasingly important as a source of news, Iran has one of the most sophisticated Internet censorship systems in the world, probably as good as or even better than the one used in China (see Chapter 4). Although Internet filtering is ostensibly used to prevent pornographic or immoral materials, the government in reality uses such blocking to censor political content.

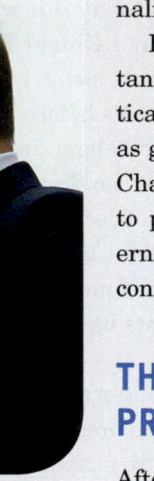

FORMER PRESIDENT AND CURRENT PRIME MINISTER

Vladimir Putin makes one of his many speeches, which are duly broadcast and rebroadcast on all available television channels throughout the country. There is virtually no independent television programming in Russia today. (Photo courtesy of Russian Presidential Press and Information Office/Sergeja Velichkina)

THE RUSSIANS HAVE LOST MANY PRESS FREEDOMS, TOO

After the end of communism in Russia, a thriving independent press arose. On television, radio, and in newspapers, Russians could read all sorts of political views. Since Vladimir Putin took over the presidency (he is now prime minister), though, virtually all opposition journalists have been silenced, in one way or another. During his tenure, Putin eliminated most privately owned television stations. In addition, private newspapers are frequently closed if they are too critical of the regime. More frightening to journalists has been the frequent murder of news reporters, especially those who were investigating government issues. By 2006, 13 well-known reporters had been murdered. Of course, the government claimed no involvement in these crimes. Russians are now fed a steady diet of Putin's pronouncements on TV. There is virtually no criticism of Putin's regime that the average Russian can view on TV or hear on the radio. Russians have to seek the foreign press to find out about the corruption that surrounds Putin's administration. Of course, the Internet and blogs still present a problem to the Russian political hierarchy, but Putin's government attempts to filter the Internet, although less successfully than in Iran or China.

THERE ARE WORSE EXAMPLES, OF COURSE

Currently, if you want to find the worst case of lack of freedom of expression, you have to examine North Korea. The country's dictator, Kim Jong Il, makes sure that North Korea's inhabitants have almost no knowledge of the outside world. Even radios are rigged so that they can only tune in to government channels. To a much lesser degree, there are various restrictions on freedom of the press in Cuba, Egypt, Lebanon, Myanmar (formerly Burma), Saudi Arabia, Syria, Venezuela, and Yemen. In short, the government controls the media in countries in which democracy is either unknown or weak.

FOR CRITICAL ANALYSIS

1. How has technology helped reduce various governments' control of the media?
2. How does the lack of a free press impact the views of citizens?

Technology is giving more citizens access to the electronic media and, in particular, to television. As more cable operators have more airtime to sell, some of it will remain unused and will be available for public access. At the same time, the Internet makes media access by the public very easy, although not everyone has the resources to take advantage of it.

BIAS IN THE MEDIA

Many studies have been undertaken to try to identify the sources and direction of **bias** in the media, and these studies have reached different conclusions. Some claim that the press has a liberal bias. Others conclude that the press shows a conservative bias. Still others do not see any notable partisan bias.

Bias
An inclination or a preference that interferes with impartial judgment.

DO THE MEDIA HAVE A PARTISAN BIAS?

In a classic study conducted in the 1980s, researchers found that media producers, editors, and reporters (the "media elite") exhibited a notably liberal and "left-leaning" bias in their news coverage.[15] Since then, the contention that the media have a liberal bias has been repeated time and again. Joining the ranks of those who assert that the media has a liberal bias is Bernard Goldberg, a veteran CBS broadcaster. Goldberg argues that liberal bias is responsible for the declining number of viewers who watch network news. He claims that this liberal bias, which "comes naturally to most reporters," has given viewers less reason to trust the big news networks.[16] Conservative journalist William McGowan also claims that the press exhibits a liberal bias. He maintains that most news reporters have liberal views on the issues they cover (he cites a

DID YOU KNOW?

That the average age of CNN viewers is 44 and that most people who watch the evening network news programs are over age 50?

---

[15]S. Robert Lichter, Stanley Rothman, and Linda S. Lichter, *The Media Elite* (New York: Adler and Adler, 1986).
[16]Bernard Goldberg, *Bias: A CBS Insider Exposes How the Media Distort the News* (Washington, DC: Regnery Publishing, 2001).

survey of journalists in which more than 80 percent of the respondents said that they were in favor of abortion rights) and that this bias prevents them from investigating and reporting on opposing viewpoints.[17]

In 2005, the University of Connecticut's Department of Public Policy surveyed 300 journalists nationwide. These journalists were asked whom they voted for in the 2004 presidential election. The Democratic challenger, John Kerry, received 52 percent of their votes, while Bush received only 19 percent (27 percent of those queried either refused to disclose their vote or did not vote).[18]

In that same year, there was heated debate about the liberal bias of the government-funded Public Broadcasting Service (PBS). President Bush had already named a Republican, Kenneth Y. Tomlinson, to chair the underlying Corporation for Public Broadcasting. Tomlinson contracted with an outside consultant to track PBS's political leanings on the program *Now with Bill Moyers*. Apparently, Tomlinson wanted proof that PBS had a liberal bias. To counter this supposed liberal bias, Tomlinson encouraged PBS officials to broadcast *The Journal Editorial Report,* a program hosted by Paul Gigot, editor of the conservative editorial page of the *Wall Street Journal*. In his defense, Tomlinson stated that "my goal here is to see programming that satisfies a broad constituency."[19]

A RACIAL BIAS?

Racial profiling is the act of routinely making negative assumptions about individuals based on race. The term was first used to describe the behavior of certain police officers who habitually stopped African American motorists more frequently than white ones, often on minor pretexts. African Americans have described these incidents as stops for "driving while black." Some observers have charged that the media—television in particular—engage in racial profiling in their reporting on minority group members.

Those who believe that the media engage in racial profiling point to common stereotypes that journalists often use when illustrating news stories. For example, a study found that while African Americans constituted 29 percent of the nation's poor, they made up 65 percent of the images of the poor shown on leading network news programs. In addition to being disproportionately portrayed as black, the poor were also largely represented by the persons least likely to command sympathy—unemployed adults. The elderly and the working poor were underrepresented.[20] Critics of racial profiling also argue that African Americans are regularly used to illustrate drug abusers or dealers, even though a majority of users are white, and that images of criminals in general are disproportionately black.

Americans of Middle Eastern ancestry have also complained about profiling. In this instance, the stereotype is of the Arab terrorist. Of course, such people exist, but like African American criminals, they make up a small part of the group's population.

Today's newsrooms are increasingly diverse. One survey revealed that minority group members made up 18 percent of the employees in television journalism, and African Americans made up 10 percent. Such a substantial minority presence may help prevent egregious examples of racial profiling. Some even argue that racial and ethnic

[17]William McGowan, *Coloring the News: How Political Correctness Has Corrupted American Journalism* (San Francisco: Encounter Books, 2003).
[18]University of Connecticut, "National Polls of Journalists and the American Public," May 16, 2005.
[19]"Republican Chairman Exerts Pressure on PBS, Alleging Biases," *Washington Times,* May 2, 2005, p. 7.
[20]Martin Gilens, "Race and Poverty in America: Public Misperceptions and the American News Media," *Public Opinion Quarterly,* Vol. 6 (1996).

diversity in the workforce leads television journalists to "pull their punches" when reporting on minority group members.

A COMMERCIAL BIAS?

According to Andrew Kohut, director of the Pew Research Center in Washington, D.C., however, the majority of those responding to Pew Research Center polls see no ideological or partisan pattern in media bias. Rather, what people mean when they say the press is biased in its political reporting is that it is biased toward its own self-interest—the need to gain higher ratings and thus more advertising revenues.

Interestingly, even though Bernard Goldberg, as just mentioned, argues that there is a liberal bias in the media, some of the examples he provides in his book would indicate that the bias in the press is more toward commercialism and elitism. For example, he states that during "sweeps" months (when ratings are important), the networks deliberately avoid featuring blacks, Hispanics, and poor or unattractive people on their prime-time news magazine shows. This, asserts Goldberg, is because such coverage might "turn off" the white, middle-class viewers that the networks want to attract so that they can build the ratings that advertisers want.

During the 2008 election, charges and countercharges flew when Hillary Clinton asserted that Barack Obama was receiving more favorable treatment from the media. As an example, Clinton complained that she was always asked the first question in debates, thus allowing Obama to think about the question and respond in a more thoughtful way. Investigation proved the facts of her allegation. A study by the Center for the Media and Public Policy at George Mason University found that the major networks gave much more positive coverage of Obama than of Clinton. Only the FOX network gave balanced coverage of all the candidates. Interestingly, this study was not reported by the other networks. The coverage of Obama most likely resulted from the fact that the success of his campaign was more newsworthy and that, as the first African American candidate to have a chance at the nomination, he was also more newsworthy as a personality.

YOU CAN MAKE A Difference

BEING A CRITICAL CONSUMER OF THE NEWS

Television and newspapers provide a wide range of choices for Americans who want to stay informed. Still, critics of the media argue that a substantial amount of programming and print is colored either by the subjectivity of editors and producers or by the demands of profit making. Few Americans take the time to become critical consumers of the news.

WHY SHOULD YOU CARE?

Even if you do not plan to engage in political activism, you have a stake in ensuring that your beliefs are truly your own and that they represent your values and interests. To guarantee this result, you need to obtain accurate information from the media and avoid being swayed by subliminal appeals, loaded terms, or outright bias. If you do not take care, you could find yourself voting for a candidate who is opposed to what you believe in or voting against measures that are in your interest.

Many media outlets are attempting to bridge this serious breach in the public's trust of their coverage with public editors or news ombudspersons. These journalists attempt to address their organization's coverage of hot-button issues that generate complaints from the public; to examine ethical issues, critical errors, or omissions; and to provide more accessibility to their audience. Dozens of newspapers across the country run regular columns from their public editors that deal with specific grievances or issues of broad public interest regarding coverage in their papers. Public editors may also coordinate public forums or reader advisory boards in an effort to reach out to readers.

WHAT CAN YOU DO?

Some media pundits would argue that you are already advocating for yourselves as media consumers, given the amount of information and access that is readily available on the Internet. In many cases, media blogs, or Web diaries updated daily, provide virtual warehouses of information that pull together stories from different media sources all over the world and allow instant comments from readers to be posted and shared. For example, Romenesko, www.poynter.org, is a media blog sponsored by the Poynter Institute (a school for journalists) that provides journalists and the public at large with brief commentary about, and links to, the big stories of the day, providing a worldwide platform for critical media consumption and comment. Some student-driven organizations like STAND encourage student participation. Their blog highlights news and events. You must remember that blogs are primarily focused on finding and linking stories, not verifying the original material, so critically evaluating the stories is even more important. Controversial news reports can be spun by the readers through blogs, not just by writers or editorial boards.

Watching the evening news can be far more rewarding if you look at how much the news depends on video effects. You will note that stories on the evening news tend to be no more than three minutes long, that stories with excellent videotape get more attention, and that considerable time is taken up with "happy talk," or human interest stories.

For example, you might compare the evening news with the daily paper. You will see that the paper is perhaps half a day behind television in reporting the news, but that the printed story contains far more information.

If you wish to obtain more information on the media, you can contact one of the following organizations:

National Association of Broadcasters
1771 N Street N.W.
Washington, DC 20036
202-429-5300
www.nab.org

National Newspaper Association
P.O. Box 7540
Columbia, MO 65205-7540
1-800-829-4NNA
www.nnaweb.org

Accuracy in Media (a conservative group)
4455 Connecticut Avenue N.W.
Suite 330
Washington, DC 20008
202-364-4401
www.aim.org

STAND is the student-led division of Genocide Intervention Network. (Courtesy of the Genocide Intervention Network, http://www.standnow.org)

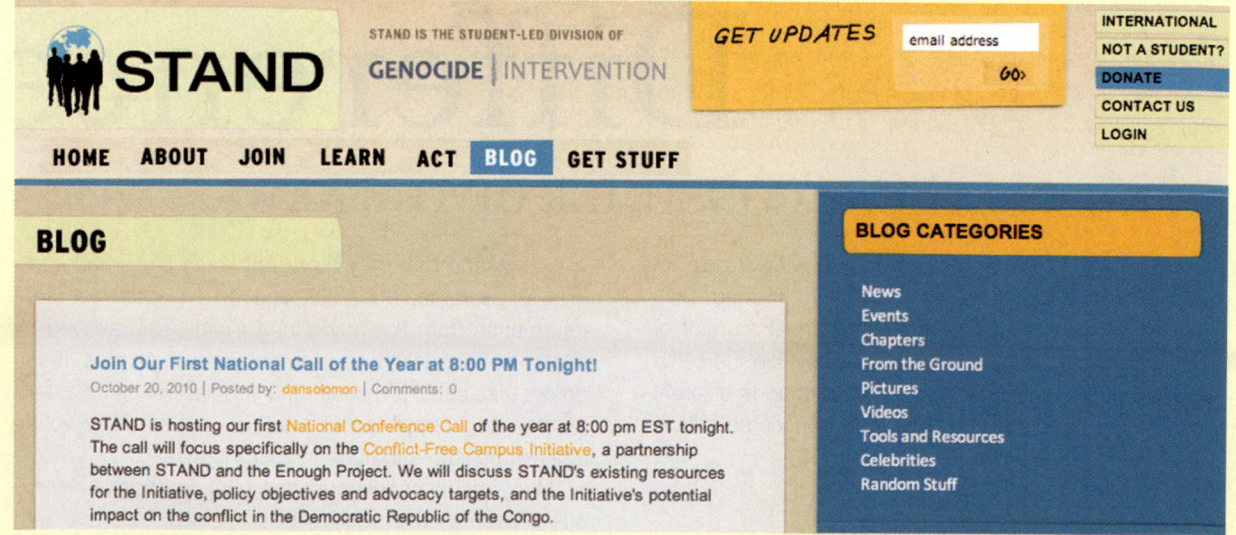

People for the American Way (a liberal group)
2000 M Street N.W., Suite 400
Washington, DC 20036
202-467-4999
www.pfaw.org

REFERENCES

"What is ONO?" *Organization of News Ombudsmen,* www. newsombudsmen.org/what.htm.

Simon Dumenco, "Is the Newspaper Ombudsman More or Less Obsolete?" *Advertising Age,* March 24, 2008.

KEY TERMS

bias 393
electronic media 375
managed news 374
media access 391
narrowcasting 376

podcasting 378
press secretary 387
public agenda 372
sound bite 379
spin 382

spin doctor 382
White House press corps 387
yellow journalism 375

CHAPTER SUMMARY

1. **What are the functions of the media in our society?** The media are enormously important in American politics today. They perform six main functions, including (1) providing entertainment, (2) reporting the news, (3) identifying public problems, (4) socializing new generations, (5) providing a political forum, and (6) making profits.

2. The media have always played a significant role in American politics. In the 1800s and earlier, however, news traveled slowly, and politics was controlled by small groups whose members communicated personally. The high-speed rotary press and the telegraph led to self-supported newspapers and mass readership.

3. Broadcast media (television and radio) have been important means of communication since the early 20th century. New technologies, such as cable television and the Internet, are giving broadcasters the opportunity to air a greater number of specialized programs.

4. **How do the media contribute to political dialogue about issues and candidates?** The media wield great power during political campaigns, including identifying the front-running candidate during the presidential primary season. Campaigns attempt to capitalize on news coverage by staging events for television as well as paying for extensive advertising on all networks. Better yet is free coverage of unusual or controversial campaign ads or candidate actions. During the general election,

campaign televised debates have come to play an important role in campaign strategy. Officeholders also try to get coverage for their initiatives and actions from the media, with the White House being the most energetic in maximizing press opportunities. While the media see their role as just reporting the news, candidates and their campaigns as well as officeholders see the media as a strong force in politics.

5. **How do the "new media" influence politics?** Today's campaigns rely much more heavily on the Internet to reach potential voters and donors. Candidates and their organizations use e-mail, podcasting, Web sites, blogs, and downloadable video and audio to involve people in campaigns. The use of these techniques does rely heavily on self-selection by the user, but the techniques are cheap and effective and may work to get the user to feel an attachment to the candidate or public official. Additionally, the new media serve as a counter to the mainstream media through investigations, leaks, and expression of alternative opinions. Today's younger citizens are much more likely to get information about politics from the Internet than are the older generations, although television continues to be a major source of news for Americans.

6. The relationship between the media and the president is close; each uses the other—sometimes positively, sometimes negatively. The media play an important role in investigating the government, in getting government

officials to understand better the needs and desires of American society, and in setting the public agenda.

7. The electronic media are subject to government regulation. Many Federal Communications Commission rules have dealt with ownership of TV and radio stations. Legislation has removed many rules about co-ownership of several forms of media, although the most recent steps taken by Congress have been to halt any further deregulation.

8. Studies of bias in the media have reached different conclusions. Some claim that the press has a liberal bias; others contend that the press shows a conservative bias. Still others conclude that the press is biased toward its own self-interest—the need to gain higher ratings and thus more advertising revenues. Other studies have found other types of biases, such as a bias in favor of the status quo or a bias against losers.

SELECTED PRINT, MEDIA, AND ONLINE RESOURCES

PRINT RESOURCES

Gillmor, Dan. *We the Media: Grassroots Journalism by the People, for the People.* Sebastopol, CA: O'Reilly, 2004. Blogs have become an increasingly important part of the media. In 2004, for the first time, bloggers were awarded press credentials to cover the national political conventions. Newspaper journalist Dan Gillmor, also a blogger, covers the new movement.

Goldberg, Bernard. *Arrogance: Rescuing America from the Media Elite.* New York: Warner, 2003. This is Goldberg's second book in which he argues that the media have a liberal bias and is a follow-up to *Bias: A CBS Insider Exposes How the Media Distort the News.* Goldberg argues that the media elite constitute an inbred, insular group.

Harfoush, Rahaf. *Yes We Did! An Inside Look at How Social Media Built the Obama Brand.* Berkeley, CA: New Riders Press, 2009. A young marketer enlists in the Obama presidential campaign with the goal of using the social media to win the election and then explains her strategy after the winning campaign ended.

Jones, Alex. *Losing the News: The Uncertain Future of the News That Feeds Democracy.* New York: Oxford University Press, 2008. Jones, a Pulitzer Prize–winning journalist at Harvard University, looks at how digital and electronic media are transforming journalism. He warns that the changes may be eroding the "iron core" of fact-based news, replacing it with openly biased opinion.

Kuypers, Jim. *Bush's War: Media Bias and Justification for War in a Terrorist Age.* Lanham, MD: Rowman & Littlefield, 2006. This researcher examines how the public understood President George W. Bush's justification of military actions since September 11, 2001, as that information was filtered through the news media. The author contends that the public perception of what the president says is shaped by media bias.

Mark, David. *Going Dirty: The Art of Negative Campaigning.* Lanham, MD: Rowman and Littlefield, 2006. Mark, editor in chief of *Campaigns and Elections* magazine, discusses the tactics and successes of negative campaigning.

Panagopoulos, Costas. *Politicking Online: The Transformation of Election Campaign Communications.* New Brunswick, NJ: Rutgers University Press, 2009. A political scientist systematically explores how the social media were used in the Obama campaign and others to reach voters and supporters.

Tremayne, Mark, ed. *Blogging, Citizenship, and the Future of Media.* Oxford: Routledge, 2006. This collection of essays examines the population's growing dependence on blogs for political information. Some of the essays also look at how blog readers differ from the rest of the population. Finally, the book explores the future of traditional media in light of the blogging phenomenon.

MEDIA RESOURCES

All the President's Men—A film, produced by Warner Brothers in 1976, starring Dustin Hoffman and Robert Redford as the two *Washington Post* reporters (Bob Woodward and Carl Bernstein) who broke the story on the Watergate scandal. The film is an excellent portrayal of *The Washington Post* newsroom and the decisions that editors make in such situations.

Citizen Kane—Based on the life of William Randolph Hearst and directed by Orson Welles, this 1941 film has been acclaimed as one of the best movies ever made. Welles stars as the newspaper tycoon. The film also stars Joseph Cotten and Alan Ladd.

Good Night, and Good Luck—A 2006 film about Edward R. Murrow, directed by George Clooney. Murrow's opposition to the tactics used by Senator Joe McCarthy's witch-hunters in the 1953–1954 provides a powerful example of integrity to reporters today.

Leveraging Technology for Your Legislative Campaigns: Effectively Using E-Newsletters, E-Mail Alerts, Podcasts, and Your Web Site—This is a series of audio compact discs and MP3 files created by Robert McLean and TheCapitol.net for Capitol Learning that gives you the ins and outs of how modern campaign managers use blogging and podcasts.

ONLINE RESOURCES

American Journalism Review national magazine that covers all aspects of print, television, radio, and online media: www.ajr.org

Drudge Report Posted by Matt Drudge, this site provides a handy guide to the Web's best spots for news and opinions. Its mission is one-click access to breaking news and recent columns: www.drudgereport.com

MediaChannel concerned with the political, cultural, and social impacts of the media, large and small. MediaChannel provides information and diverse perspectives; inspires debate, collaboration, action and citizen engagement; and includes links to news media around the world, including alternative media: www.mediachannel.org

12

Nancy Pelosi, Speaker of the House of Representatives from 2007 to 2011, calls a joint session of Congress to order for the State of the Union Address of President George W. Bush. Pelosi was the first woman in American history to hold this position. (© Jason Reed/Reuters/Corbis)

The Congress

QUESTIONS TO CONSIDER

Why is the Congress the most powerful branch of government?

Do members of Congress serve their constituents or the nation as a whole?

How do members of Congress decide their votes?

CHAPTER CONTENTS

what if...

Pork Were Banned?

BACKGROUND

Through *pork-barrel legislation,* members of Congress "bring home the bacon." Members directly help their constituents by adding into legislation projects that create more jobs and generate more profits locally. The official name for pork is *earmarked spending.* In recent years, from 11,000 to 15,000 earmarks yearly, worth from $15 billion to $69 billion, have passed through Congress. Most earmarks are never discussed on the floor. Many are "air-dropped" at the last minute into nonbinding conference reports that serve as "advice" to federal departments about where to allocate funds. The practice of earmarking is not new, but it has increased significantly over the last few decades. Consider that in 1987, President Ronald Reagan vetoed a bill because it included 157 earmarks valued at $1 billion. During 2009, Congress approved 10,160 earmarks worth $19.6 billion. Although the number of pork projects declined from the previous year, the spending increased by 14 percent.

Earmarking is a bipartisan activity. When the Democrats took control of Congress in 2007, they promised to "get tough" on special-interest groups and the earmarking that benefits such groups. While the volume of pork did decline slightly, massive quantities of pork continue to be routinely included in legislation.

WHAT IF PORK WERE BANNED?

Without pork, earmarks could not simply be slipped into bills sent to the president as amendments. Because Congress does not have an unlimited amount of time for debate, eliminating pork might reduce federal spending. Realize, though, that the federal budget is about $3.3 trillion, so eliminating pork would not change much.

Banning pork would mean that most spending projects coming before Congress would have to pass through the normal budget process. Ordinarily, the various executive agencies of government receive proposals for spending on various projects. They rank all the requests in order of "need" and choose the ones with the most merit, often within the constraints of formulas that ensure that funds will be spent in all parts of the country. The number of projects is limited by agency funding limits set by the president's Office of Management and Budget (OMB). The OMB submits that resulting budget to Congress.

Before the budget reaches Congress, however, the White House routinely adds its own laundry list of politically desirable projects that were never reviewed by the bureaucracy. The president may actually be the biggest single "porkmeister" in government.

If all pork were really banned, "legitimate pork" would be eliminated, too. After all, members of Congress may at times have a better understanding than does the bureaucracy of local spending needs for hospitals, infrastructure repairs, and the like. If true pork were banned, however, we would not see federal payments for a prison museum near Fort Leavenworth, Kansas. Federal funds would not be spent on the National Mule and Packers Museum in Bishop, California.

THE CHANGING WAYS OF CONGRESS

If pork were eliminated, Congress would have to change the way it goes about its business. Bills get passed in Congress through a process of *logrolling,* or "You scratch my back and I'll scratch yours." In other words, a member who does not favor a bill may be convinced by his colleagues to vote for it if they allow that member to add earmarked spending for his or her constituents. Much legislation gets passed in Congress in this manner. In the absence of pork, it would become harder to convince opposing members to vote in favor of certain legislation. Consequently, the absence of pork might result in less legislation from the halls of Congress.

THE IMPACT OF CAMPAIGNS AND CAMPAIGN CONTRIBUTIONS

Currently, many lobbyist groups are rewarded for their campaign contributions through pork-barrel legislation. Earmarks are a way to show a legislator's appreciation for campaign contributions made by a specific group. For example, management at a defense contractor might make the maximum campaign contributions for the reelection of the local representative. If that representative is reelected, she or he can earmark funds for a weapons system that the contractor manufactures in a local factory, even though the system was never officially requested by the Defense Department.

In the absence of pork, candidates for election or reelection would probably receive fewer campaign contributions from lobbying groups representing local interests. Why? Because those local groups would know they could not easily obtain something in return for their support. We could predict, then, that the number of registered lobbying groups would probably fall.

FOR CRITICAL ANALYSIS

1. In 2010, the Democrats campaigned on an "anti-pork" theme to wrest control of Congress from the Republicans. Nonetheless, pork-barrel legislation continues. Why?
2. If there were less legislation coming out of Congress, would Americans be better off or worse off? Explain your answer.

MOST AMERICANS VIEW Congress in a less than flattering light. In recent years, Congress has appeared to be deeply split, highly partisan in its conduct, and not very responsive to public needs. Polls show that public approval of the Congress rarely reaches more than 40 percent; many times, approval rates of the Congress are much lower than of the president. Yet individual members of Congress often receive much higher approval ratings from the voters in their districts. This is one of the paradoxes of the relationship between the people and Congress. Members of the public hold the institution in relatively low regard compared with the satisfaction they express with their individual representatives.

Part of the explanation for these seemingly contradictory appraisals is that members of Congress spend considerable time and effort serving their **constituents**. If the federal bureaucracy makes a mistake, the senator's or representative's office tries to resolve the issue. The members of the Congress spend considerable time and effort developing what is sometimes called a **"homestyle"** to gain the trust and appreciation of their constituents through service, local appearances, and the creation of local offices.

Congress, however, was created to work not just for local constituents but also for the nation as a whole. The representatives and senators in their Washington work are creating what might be called a **"hillstyle,"** which refers to their work on legislation and in party leadership to create laws and policies for our nation.[1] In this chapter, we describe the functions of Congress, including constituent service, representation, lawmaking, and oversight of the government. We review how the members of Congress are elected and how Congress organizes itself when it meets. We also examine how bills pass through the legislative process.

Constituent
One of the persons represented by a legislator or other elected or appointed official.

Homestyle
The actions and behaviors of a member of Congress aimed at the constituents and intended to win the support and trust of the voters at home.

Hillstyle
The actions and behaviors of a member of Congress in Washington, D.C., intended to promote policies and the member's own career aspirations.

THE FUNCTIONS OF CONGRESS

The founders of the American republic believed that the bulk of the power that would be exercised by a national government should be in the hands of the legislature because the members were elected by the people, or, in the case of the Senate, by the states. The leading role envisioned for Congress in the new government is apparent from its primacy in the Constitution. Article I deals with the structure, the powers, and the operation of Congress, beginning in Section 1 with an application of the basic principle of separation of powers: "All legislative Powers herein granted shall be vested in a Congress of the

---

[1]Richard Fenno, *Home Style: House Members in Their Districts* (Boston: Little, Brown, 1978).

Bicameralism
The division of a legislature into two separate assemblies.

United States, which shall consist of a Senate and House of Representatives." These legislative powers are spelled out in detail in Article I and elsewhere.

The **bicameralism** of Congress—its division into two legislative houses—was in part the result of the Connecticut Compromise, which tried to balance the large-state population advantage, reflected in the House, and the small-state demand for equality in policy making, which was satisfied in the Senate. Beyond that, the two chambers of Congress also reflected the social-class biases of the founders. They wished to balance the interests and the numerical superiority of the common citizens with the property interests of the less numerous landowners, bankers, and merchants. They achieved this goal by providing in Sections 2 and 3 of Article I that members of the House of Representatives should be elected directly by "the People," whereas members of the Senate were to be chosen by the elected representatives sitting in state legislatures, who were more likely to be members of the elite. (The latter provision was changed in 1913 by the passage of the Seventeenth Amendment, which provides that senators also are to be elected directly by the people.)

The logic of separate constituencies and separate interests underlying the bicameral Congress was reinforced by differences in length of tenure. Members of the House are required to face the electorate every two years, whereas senators can serve for a much more secure term of six years—even longer than the four-year term provided for the president. Furthermore, the senators' terms are staggered so that only one-third of the senators face the electorate every two years, along with all of the House members.

The bicameral structure of Congress was designed to enable the legislative body and its members to perform certain functions for the political system. These functions include the following: lawmaking, representation, service to constituents, oversight, public education, and conflict resolution. Of these, the two most important and the ones that are most often in conflict are lawmaking and representation.

THE LAWMAKING FUNCTION

Lawmaking
The process of establishing the legal rules that govern society.

The principal and most obvious function of any legislature is **lawmaking**. Congress is the highest elected body in the country charged with making binding rules for all Americans. Lawmaking requires decisions about the size of the federal budget, about health care reform and gun control, and about the long-term prospects for war or peace. This does not mean, however, that Congress initiates most of the ideas for legislation that it eventually considers. A majority of the bills that Congress acts on originate in the executive branch, and many other bills are traceable to interest groups and political party organizations. Through the processes of compromise and **logrolling** (offering to support a fellow member's bill in exchange for that member's promise to support your bill in the future), as well as debate and discussion, backers of legislation attempt to fashion a winning majority coalition to create policies for the nation.

Logrolling
An arrangement in which two or more members of Congress agree in advance to support each other's bills.

THE REPRESENTATION FUNCTION

Representation
The function of members of Congress as elected officials representing the views of their constituents.

Representation includes both representing the desires and demands of the constituents in the member's home district or state and representing larger national interests such as farmers or the environment. Because the interests of constituents in a specific district may be in conflict with the demands of national policy, the representation function is often at variance with the lawmaking function for individual lawmakers and sometimes for Congress as a whole. For example, although it may be in the interest of the nation to reduce defense spending by closing military bases, such closures are not

STATE REPRESENTATIVE Aaron Schock (R.-Ill.), left, greets a voter at a diner in Peoria, Illinois, after winning the Republican primary race for the Congressional nomination. Schock, who was only 26 at the time, became the youngest member of Congress when he won his seat in the November 2008 election. (AP Photo/Seth Perlman)

in the interest of the states and districts that will lose jobs and local spending. Every legislator faces votes that set representational issues against lawmaking realities.

How should the legislators fulfill the representation function? There are several views on how this should be accomplished.

The Trustee View of Representation. The first approach to the question of how representation should be achieved is that legislators should act as **trustees** of the broad interests of the entire society. They should vote against the narrow interests of their constituents if their conscience and their perception of national needs so dictate. For example, several Republican legislators have supported strong laws regulating the tobacco industry despite the views of some of their constituents.

The Instructed-Delegate View of Representation. Directly opposed to the trustee view of representation is the notion that the members of Congress should behave as **instructed delegates**; that is, they should mirror the views of the majority of the constituents who elected them to power in the first place. On the surface, this approach is plausible and rewarding. For it to work, however, we must assume that constituents actually have well-formed views on the issues that are decided in Congress and, further, that they have clear-cut preferences about these issues. Neither condition is likely to be satisfied very often.

Generally, most legislators hold neither a pure trustee view nor a pure instructed-delegate view. Typically, they combine both perspectives in a pragmatic mix that is often called the "politico" style.

SERVICE TO CONSTITUENTS

Individual members of Congress are expected by their constituents to act as brokers between private citizens and the imposing, often faceless federal government. This function of providing service to constituents usually takes the form of **casework**. As

Trustee
A legislator who acts according to her or his conscience and the broad interests of the entire society.

DID YOU KNOW?

That fewer than 3 in 10 people can name the House member from their district, and fewer than half can name even one of the two senators from their state?

Instructed Delegate
A legislator who is an agent of the voters who elected him or her and who votes according to the views of constituents regardless of personal beliefs.

Casework
Personal work for constituents by members of Congress.

noted previously, legislators make choices about their "hillstyle," deciding how much time they and their staff will spend on casework activities, such as tracking down a missing Social Security check, explaining the meaning of particular bills to people who may be affected by them, promoting a local business interest, or interceding with a regulatory agency on behalf of constituents who disagree with proposed agency regulations.

Legislators and many analysts of congressional behavior regard this **ombudsperson** role as an activity that strongly benefits the members of Congress. A government characterized by a large, confusing bureaucracy and complex public programs offers innumerable opportunities for legislators to assist (usually) grateful constituents. Morris P. Fiorina once suggested, somewhat mischievously, that senators and representatives prefer to maintain bureaucratic confusion to maximize their opportunities for performing good deeds on behalf of their constituents:

> Some poor, aggrieved constituent becomes enmeshed in the tentacles of an evil bureaucracy and calls upon Congressman St. George to do battle with the dragon. . . . In dealing with the bureaucracy, the congressman is not merely one vote of 435. Rather, he is a nonpartisan power, someone whose phone call snaps an office to attention. He is not kept on hold. The constituent who receives aid believes that his congressman and his congressman alone got results.[2]

Some members of Congress will go to great lengths to please their constituents. In 2006, for example, when gasoline prices increased to more than $3 per gallon, Senate Republicans argued in favor of sending $100 rebate checks to millions of taxpayers, while Senate Democrats campaigned for a 60-day gasoline tax holiday. The latter plan would have cut the price of gasoline by about 20 cents a gallon. Did members of Congress actually believe that a $100 rebate or a 60-day tax holiday would do anything to reduce high gasoline prices in the long run? Certainly not. In private, members of Congress who supported these schemes admitted that they would have

Ombudsperson
A person who hears and investigates complaints by private individuals against public officials or agencies.

FORMER CHIEF EXECUTIVE
officer of British Petroleum Tony Hayward listens to statements by members of the House Subcommittee on Oversight and Investigations after the oil spill in the Gulf of Mexico. (Jeff Malet/ Newscom)

[2]Morris P. Fiorina, *Congress: Keystone of the Washington Establishment,* 2nd ed. (New Haven, CT: Yale University Press, 1989), pp. 44, 47.

been little more than a gesture. Nevertheless, all members of Congress wanted to show their constituents that they were doing something about the problem.

THE OVERSIGHT FUNCTION

Oversight of the bureaucracy is essential if the decisions made by Congress are to have any force. **Oversight** is the process by which Congress follows up on the laws it has enacted to ensure that they are being enforced and administered in the way Congress intended. This is done by holding committee hearings and investigations, changing the size of an agency's budget, and cross-examining high-level presidential nominees to head major agencies. Sometimes Congress establishes a special commission to investigate a problem. For example, after Hurricane Katrina devastated New Orleans and parts of surrounding states in 2005, Congress created a commission to determine how and why the federal government, particularly the Federal Emergency Management Agency (FEMA), had mishandled government aid both during and after that natural disaster. Sometimes a commission may take several years to complete its work. This was the case with the so-called 9/11 Commission, which investigated why the United States was so unprepared for the terrorist attacks in 2001.

Senators and representatives increasingly see their oversight function as a critically important part of their legislative activities. In part, oversight is related to the concept of constituency service, particularly when Congress investigates alleged arbitrariness or wrongdoing by bureaucratic agencies.

Oversight
The process by which Congress follows up on laws it has enacted to ensure that they are being enforced and administered in the way Congress intended.

THE PUBLIC-EDUCATION FUNCTION

Educating the public is a function that is performed whenever Congress holds public hearings, exercises oversight over the bureaucracy, or engages in committee and floor debate on such major issues and topics as political assassinations, aging, illegal drugs, and the concerns of small businesses. In so doing, Congress presents a range of viewpoints on pressing national questions. In recent years, members of Congress and the committees of Congress have greatly improved access to information through their use of the Internet and Web sites. Congress also decides what issues will come up for discussion and decision; this agenda setting is a major facet of its public-education function.

THE CONFLICT-RESOLUTION FUNCTION

Congress is commonly seen as an institution for resolving conflicts within American society. Organized interest groups and representatives of different racial, religious, economic, and ideological interests look on Congress as an access point for airing their grievances and seeking help. This puts Congress in the position of trying to resolve the differences among competing points of view by passing laws to accommodate as many interested parties as possible. To the extent that Congress meets pluralist expectations in accommodating competing interests, it tends to build support for the entire political process.

THE POWERS OF CONGRESS

The Constitution is both highly specific and extremely vague about the powers that Congress may exercise. The first 17 clauses of Article I, Section 8, specify most of the **enumerated powers** of Congress—that is, powers expressly given to that body.

Enumerated Power
A power specifically granted to the national government by the Constitution. The first 17 clauses of Article I, Section 8, specify most of the enumerated powers of Congress.

POLITICS WITH A purpose

Keeping Tabs on Congress

What if we were to tell you that for every dollar you earned, we were going to take 28 cents and would decide how to spend it?[a] And that we could limit what you see on the Internet? And that our actions would influence how much it cost you to fill up your gas tank? You would probably think that if you gave us all this power, you should pay attention to see if we are making the "right" choices, especially since you have a say in whether we keep our jobs.

Congress has these kinds of powers. Along with the president, Congress sets tax law—including gas taxes—and regulates interstate commerce (the Internet), among many other activities. In fact, in any given week early in the legislative session, at least a hundred bills and resolutions are introduced in the U.S. Senate. How is the average citizen supposed to keep track of all of these pieces of potential legislation, any one of which may have an impact on his or her life? And, as you consider voting for your representative or the challenger, how can you know if your member voted in your best interest?

There are a variety of ways to assess substantive representation, the extent to which an elected official's actions match the interests of his or her constituency. The Congressional Record[b] is the official source of information on everything that has happened in Congress. The Library of Congress provides access to the Congressional Record and provides links to other data, such as congressional committees, government reports, and presidential nominations (http://thomas.loc.gov).

A quick perusal of these sites illustrates that in addition to the sheer volume of all the bills introduced, the legislative process is extremely complex. There are 22 House committees, 20 Senate committees, and four joint committees (where membership is shared between the chambers). These bodies all have subcommittees, where the real work of writing laws and holding hearings occurs. So how can you keep track of legislation that is important to you? You can become familiar with organizations that are vital to the democratic process by making sense of and tracking legislation. For example, certain nonprofit organizations gather information from advocacy groups, such as those discussed in Chapter 7.

These nonprofits examine the groups' preferences on legislation pending before Congress and then compare that with how the members of Congress vote. One nonprofit organization, Voter Information Services, hosts a Web site that allows users to create report cards on members of Congress by choosing from a list of advocacy groups.[c]

A closer examination of these report cards illustrates the differences in how particular groups assess the actions of members of Congress. Take, for example, the votes on which NARAL ProChoice America and the National Right to Life Committee (NRLC) "score" or record whether the member votes as the group wants. In 2006, Congress debated S. 403, the Child Custody Protection Act. NARAL described it as a bill making it a crime for anyone other than a parent "including a grandparent, adult sibling or religious counselor" to take a "young woman across state lines for abortion care." The NRLC described the same portion of the bill in very different terms, arguing that "abortion clinics' out-of-state advertising in non-notification states . . . frequently highlights the avoidance of parental notification as a selling point.

In other cases, young girls are subjected to tremendous pressure from much older males and others who do not have their best interests at heart."[d] Organizations like Voter Information Services allow you to examine these groups' assessments of members of Congress side-by-side. You can decide which groups' positions best match yours and whose assessments of members of Congress you most trust.

Whether you visit advocacy groups online or use the Congressional Record, journalistic sources such as *Congressional Quarterly* or *The National Journal,* or specialized tracking agencies like GalleryWatch.com or CongressNow.com, the information on what our Congress does is readily available. Our role as citizens is to pay attention.

[a]www.irs.gov/pub/irs-pdf/n1036.pdf
[b]http://thomas.loc.gov/home/r110query.html
[c]www.vis.org/crc/groupsincrc.aspx
[d]www.nrlc.org/Federal/CCPA/CCPASenateLetter092806.html

ENUMERATED POWERS

The enumerated, or expressed, powers of Congress include the right to impose taxes and import tariffs; borrow funds; regulate interstate commerce and international trade; establish procedures for naturalizing citizens; make laws regulating bankruptcies; coin (and print) money and regulate its value; establish standards of weights and measures; punish counterfeiters; establish post offices and postal routes; regulate copyrights and patents; establish the federal court system; punish illegal acts on the high seas; declare war; raise and regulate an army and a navy; call up and regulate the state militias to enforce laws, to suppress insurrections, and to repel invasions; and govern the District of Columbia.

The most important of the domestic powers of Congress, listed in Article I, Section 8, are the rights to collect taxes, to spend, and to regulate commerce. The most important foreign policy power is the power to declare war. Other sections of the Constitution allow Congress to establish rules for its own members, to regulate the electoral college, and to override a presidential veto. Congress may also regulate the extent of the Supreme Court's authority to review cases decided by the lower courts, regulate relations among states, and propose amendments to the Constitution.

Powers of the Senate. Some functions are restricted to one chamber. The Senate must advise on, and consent to, the ratification of treaties and must accept or reject presidential nominations of ambassadors, Supreme Court justices, and "all other Officers of the United States." But the Senate may delegate to the president or lesser officials the power to make lower-level appointments. In 2005, President George W. Bush faced two vacancies on the Supreme Court. After Justice Sandra Day O'Connor announced her retirement, President Bush nominated John Roberts to the Court, and the Senate appeared likely to approve the appointment. Then, when the death of Chief Justice William Rehnquist created a second vacancy, President Bush immediately changed Roberts' nomination to that of chief justice, and the Senate approved. When President Bush nominated a relatively inexperienced lawyer, Harriet Miers, however, it quickly became clear that the Senate would not approve her nomination. Therefore, President Bush named an experienced federal appeals court judge, Samuel Alito, who was confirmed.

Constitutional Amendments. Amendments to the Constitution provide for other Congressional powers. Congress must certify the election of a president and a vice president or choose these officers if no candidate has a majority of the electoral vote (Twelfth Amendment). It may levy an income tax (Sixteenth Amendment) and determine who will be acting president in case of the death or incapacity of the president or vice president (Twentieth Amendment and Twenty-fifth Amendment). In addition, Congress explicitly is given the power to enforce, by appropriate legislation, the provisions of several other amendments.

THE NECESSARY AND PROPER CLAUSE

Beyond these numerous specific powers, Congress enjoys the right under Article I, Section 8 (the "elastic" or "necessary and proper" clause), "[t]o make all Laws which shall be necessary and proper for carrying into Execution the foregoing Powers [of Article I], and all other Powers vested by this Constitution in the Government of the United States, or in any Department or Officer thereof." As discussed in Chapter 3, this vague statement of congressional responsibilities provided, over time, the basis for a greatly expanded national government. It also constituted, at least in theory, a check on the expansion of presidential powers.

CHECKS ON THE CONGRESS

When you consider all of the powers of Congress and its ability to override a presidential veto, there can be no doubt that it is the most powerful branch of government. However, because of the diversity of the United States and the corresponding diverse interests of members of the Congress, rarely is there enough unanimity to override presidential vetoes. So, one check on the Congress is the veto of the president. Another constitutional check is the power of the Supreme Court to hold a law passed by the Congress as unconstitutional. Additionally, the members of the House face election every two years. If the Congress were to exercise too much power in the eyes of the public, it is likely that many members would be voted out of office. And on the other side of Capitol Hill sits the Senate, which often curbs the House by not agreeing with proposals from the "other house."

HOUSE–SENATE DIFFERENCES

Congress is composed of two markedly different—but coequal—chambers. Although the Senate and the House of Representatives exist within the same legislative institution, each has developed certain distinctive features that clearly distinguish one from the other. A summary of these differences is given in Table 12–1.

TABLE 12–1 Differences between the House and the Senate

HOUSE*	SENATE*
Constitutional Differences	
Members chosen from local districts	Members chosen from an entire state
Two-year term	Six-year term
Originally elected by voters	Originally (until 1913) elected by state legislatures
May impeach (indict) federal officials	May convict federal officials of impeachable offenses
Process and Culture	
Larger (435 voting members)	Smaller (100 members)
More formal rules	Fewer rules and restrictions
Debate limited	Debate extended
Less prestige and less individual notice	More prestige and more media attention
More partisan	More individualistic
Specific Powers	
Originates bills for raising revenues	Has power to advise the president on, and to consent to, presidential appointments and treaties

*Some of these differences, such as the term of office, are provided for in the Constitution. Others, such as debate rules, are not.

SIZE AND RULES

The central difference between the House and the Senate is simply that the House is much larger than the Senate. The House has 435 representatives, plus delegates from the District of Columbia, Puerto Rico, Guam, American Samoa, and the Virgin Islands, compared with just 100 senators. This size difference means that a greater number of formal rules are needed to govern activity in the House, whereas correspondingly looser procedures can be followed in the less crowded Senate.

The effect of the difference in size is most obvious in the rules governing debate on the floors of the two chambers. The House operates with an elaborate system to control the agenda and allot time fairly in such a large assembly. For each major bill, the **Rules Committee** normally proposes a **Rule** for debate that includes time limitations for the debate, divides the time between the majority and the minority, and specifies whether amendments can be proposed. The House debates and approves the Rule, which will govern the debate on that specific legislation. As a consequence of its stricter time limits on debate, the House, despite its greater size, often is able to act on legislation more quickly than the Senate.

Rules Committee
A standing committee of the House of Representatives that provides special rules under which specific bills can be debated, amended, and considered by the House.

Rule
The proposal by the Rules Committee of the House that states the conditions for debate for one piece of legislation.

DEBATE AND FILIBUSTERING

In the Senate, the rules governing debate are much less limiting. In fact, for legislation to reach the floor of the Senate, the body must have approved the rules of debate by a **Unanimous Consent Agreement**, which means that the entire body agrees to the rules of debate. The Senate tradition of the **filibuster**, or the use of unlimited debate as a blocking tactic, dates back to 1790. In that year, a proposal to move the U.S. capital from New York to Philadelphia was stalled by such time-wasting maneuvers. This unlimited-debate tradition—which also existed in the House until 1811—is not absolute, however.

In 2009–2010, the use of the filibuster became the usual way of doing business in the Senate. At the beginning of the session, the Democratic majority plus the two independent senators (Sanders, Vt., and Lieberman, Conn.), could muster 60 votes to support President Obama's initiatives in health care reform and financial reform. The Republican strategy was to force a cloture vote against their filibuster on almost every issue, betting that some Democrats might not be able to support every initiative. The strategy forced the administration into deal-making on some votes, which may have increased public disapproval of some of the legislation. When Senator Scott Brown won election from Massachusetts in early 2010, Republicans had 41 seats and Democrats could be forced into more compromises to get the 60 votes to stop the filibuster. The use of such tactics has increased tremendously over the last two decades, leading to the concept of **unorthodox lawmaking**, meaning the use of obscure parliamentary procedures to get laws passed in the face of strong opposition.[3] Such tactics, however, are difficult to explain to the public and seem possibly undemocratic.

Unanimous Consent Agreement
An agreement on the rules of debate for proposed legislation in the Senate that is approved by all the members.

Filibuster
The use of the Senate's tradition of unlimited debate as a delaying tactic to block a bill.

Unorthodox Lawmaking
The use of out-of-the-ordinary parliamentary tactics to pass legislation.

Under Senate Rule 22, debate may be ended by invoking *cloture*. Cloture shuts off discussion on a bill. Amended in 1975 and 1979, Rule 22 states that debate may be closed off on a bill if 16 senators sign a petition requesting it and if, after two days have elapsed, three-fifths of the entire membership (60 votes, assuming no vacancies) vote

---

[3]Barbara Sinclair, *Unorthodox Lawmaking: New Legislative Processes in the U.S. Congress.* 3rd ed. (Washington, DC: CQ Press, 2007).

ORRIN HATCH, R.-Utah, spoke during the 39th hour of a marathon session organized by Republicans to protest Democratic filibusters. The Democrats were blocking Bush nominees for federal court judgeships. Why might senators seek to block a president's judicial candidates? (AP Photo/ Gerald Herbert)

for cloture. After cloture is invoked, each senator may speak on a bill for a maximum of one hour before a vote is taken.

In 1979, the Senate refined Rule 22 to ensure that a final vote must take place within 100 hours of debate after cloture has been imposed. It further limited the use of multiple amendments to stall post-cloture final action on a bill.

PRESTIGE

As a consequence of the greater size of the House, representatives generally cannot achieve as much individual recognition and public prestige as can members of the Senate. Senators are better able to gain media exposure and to establish careers as spokespersons for large national constituencies. To obtain recognition for his or her activities, a member of the House generally must do one of two things. He or she might survive in office long enough to join the ranks of the leadership on committees or within the party. Alternatively, the representative could become an expert on some specialized aspect of legislative policy, such as tax laws, the environment, or education.

CONGRESSPERSONS AND THE CITIZENRY: A COMPARISON

Members of the U.S. Senate and the U.S. House of Representatives are not typical American citizens. Members of Congress are older than most Americans, partly because of constitutional age requirements and partly because a good deal of political experience normally is an advantage in running for national office. Members of Congress are also disproportionately white, male, and trained in high-status occupations. Lawyers are by far the largest occupational group among congresspersons, although the proportion of lawyers in the House is lower now than it was in the past. Compared with the average American citizen, members of Congress are well paid. In 2010, annual congressional salaries were $174,000. Increasingly, members of Congress are also much wealthier than the average citizen. Whereas less than 1 percent of Americans have assets exceeding $1 million, about one-third of the members of Congress are millionaires. Table 12–2 summarizes selected characteristics of the members of Congress.

Compared with the composition of Congress over the past 200 years, however, the House and Senate today are significantly more diverse in gender and ethnicity than ever before. There are 74 women in the House of Representatives (17 percent) and 17 women in the U.S. Senate (17 percent). Minority group members fill over 17 percent of the seats in the

(© shutterstock.com)

TABLE 12–2 Characteristics of the 111th Congress, 2009–2011

	U.S. POPULATION, 2008	HOUSE	SENATE
Age (average)	36.8	57	63
Percent minority	25%	17.5%	7%
Religion			
Percent church members	61%	90.6%	99%
Percent Catholic	23.9%	31%	25%
Percent Protestant	51.3%	54.9%	55%
Percent Jewish	1.7%	13%	13%
Percent female	50.9%	17.8%	17%
Percent adv. degrees	5%	66.7%	76%
Lawyers	0.4%	38.6%	57%
Blue collar	30%	1.6%	3%
Percent earning more than $50,000	65%	100%	100%
Assets more than $1 million	0.7%	16%	33%

Sources: CIA World Factbook, 2010; Congressional Quarterly Weekly Report; Ethnic Majority Web site, http://www.ethnicmajority.com; author's update.

House; they include 42 African American members, 21 Hispanic members, 8 Asian or Pacific Islander Americans, and 1 Native American, Tom Cole of Oklahoma. There are 3 Hispanic members of the Senate but only 1 African American—Roland Burris of Illinois, who was appointed to fill the seat of Barack Obama after he won the presidential election. After the 2010 elections, it is unlikely that there will be any African American senators. The 111th Congress has significant numbers of members born in 1946 or later, the so-called Baby Boomers. A majority of House members and an even larger minority of the Senate belong to this postwar generation. This shift in the character of Congress may prompt consideration of the issues that will affect the Boomers, such as Social Security and Medicare.

CONGRESSIONAL ELECTIONS

The process of electing members of Congress is decentralized. Congressional elections are conducted by the individual state governments. The states, however, must conform to the rules established by the U.S. Constitution and by national statutes. The Constitution states that representatives are to be elected every second year by popular ballot, and the number of seats awarded to each state is to be determined every 10 years by the results of the census. It is important to note that the decennial census is viewed as crucial by members of Congress and by the states. If the census is not accurate, perhaps recording an undercount of individuals living in a state, then that state might lose a representative in Congress. Each state has at least one representative, with most congressional districts having about half a million residents. Senators are elected by popular vote (since the passage of the Seventeenth Amendment) every six years; approximately one-third of the seats are chosen every two years. Each state has two senators. Under Article I, Section 4, of the Constitution, state legislatures are given control over "[t]he Times, Places and Manner of holding Elections for Senators and Representatives"; however, "the Congress may at any time by Law make or alter such Regulations."

Only states can elect members of Congress. Therefore, territories such as Puerto Rico and Guam are not represented, though they do elect nonvoting delegates who sit in the House. The District of Columbia is also represented only by a nonvoting delegate. The District is not represented in the Senate at all. There have been several proposals to give D.C. voting representation in Congress. In 1978, Congress approved a constitutional amendment to give the District the representation it would have if it were a state, including two senators. The amendment was not ratified, however. More recently, District citizens have campaigned to make D.C. a state. New states can be admitted to the union without amending the Constitution. Another proposal is to allow District citizens to vote either with Maryland or Virginia, as they did in the 18th century. However, this solution would not give the citizens of the District the attention they believe is necessary to meet their interests. Democrats in Congress have generally supported more representation for the District because the majority of its citizens are African American and vote overwhelmingly Democratic. Republicans are generally not supportive of giving voting powers to D.C.'s representative.

CANDIDATES FOR CONGRESSIONAL ELECTIONS

Candidates for House and Senate seats may be self-selected. The qualifications for the two houses do differ: Members of the House must be at least 25 years old, a citizen for seven years, and live in the state they will represent; whereas senators must be 30 years old, a citizen for nine years, and a resident of the state they represent. In congressional districts where one party is very strong, however, there may be a shortage of candidates willing to represent the weaker party. In such circumstances, leaders of the weaker party must often actively recruit candidates. Candidates may resemble the voters of the district in ethnicity or religion, but they are also likely to be very successful individuals who have been active in politics before. House candidates are especially likely to have local ties to their districts. Candidates usually choose to run because they believe they would enjoy the job and its accompanying status. They also may be thinking of a House seat as a stepping-stone to future political office as a senator, governor, or president. Individuals who seek Senate seats may also have plans to run for governor in their home state or be considering a run for the presidency.

Congressional Campaigns and Elections. Congressional campaigns have changed considerably in the past two decades. Like all other campaigns, they are much more expensive, with the average cost of a winning Senate campaign now $8.5 million and a winning House campaign averaging more than $1.4 million. Campaign funds include direct contributions by individuals, contributions by political action committees (PACs), and "soft money" funneled through state party committees. As you read in Chapter 10, all of these contributions are regulated by laws, including the Federal Election Campaign Act of 1971, as amended, and most recently the Bipartisan Campaign Reform Act of 2002. Once in office, legislators spend time almost every day raising funds for their next campaign.

Most candidates for Congress must win the nomination through a **direct primary**, in which **party identifiers** vote for the candidate who will be on the party ticket in the general election. To win the primary, candidates may take more liberal or more conservative positions to get the votes of party identifiers. In the general election, they may moderate their views to attract the votes of independents and voters from the other party.

Presidential Effects. Congressional candidates are always hopeful that a strong presidential candidate on the ticket will have "coattails" that will sweep in senators and representatives of the same party. In fact, coattail effects have been quite limited, and in recent presidential elections have not materialized at all. One way to measure the coattail effect is to look at the subsequent midterm elections, held in the even-numbered years following the presidential contests. In these years, voter turnout falls sharply. In the past, the party controlling the White House normally lost seats in Congress in the midterm elections, in part because the coattail effect ceased to apply. Members of Congress who were from contested districts or who were in their first term were more likely not to be reelected.

Table 12–3 shows the pattern for midterm elections since 1942. The president's party lost seats in every election from 1942 to 1998. In that year, with President Bill Clinton under the threat of impeachment, voters showed their displeasure with the Republicans by voting in five more Democrats. In 2002, Republicans bucked the normal slump by winning five more Republican seats in the House. Most commentators believed that these midterm victories were based on public support for the president after the September 11 attacks. In 2006, the Republicans suffered a fairly normal midterm defeat, comparable to the midterm defeat in 1958, the sixth year of the Eisenhower presidency.

The 2010 midterm elections were a sweeping win by the Republicans aided by the newly energized members of the Tea Party movement. Republicans gained more than 60 seats in the House of Representatives, thus gaining majority control in that body. Although it is normal for the "out party" to gain seats in the midterms, the size of the Republican victory was the largest ever in modern times.

TABLE 12–3 Midterm Gains and Losses by the Party of the President, 1942–2010

SEATS GAINED OR LOST BY THE PARTY OF THE PRESIDENT IN THE HOUSE OF REPRESENTATIVES	
1942	−45 (D.)
1946	−55 (D.)
1950	−29 (D.)
1954	−18 (R.)
1958	−47 (R.)
1962	−4 (D.)
1966	−47 (D.)
1970	−12 (R.)
1974	−48 (R.)
1978	−15 (D.)
1982	−26 (R.)
1986	−5 (R.)
1990	−8 (R.)
1994	−52 (D.)
1998	+5 (D.)
2002	+5 (R.)
2006	−30 (R.)
2010	+62 (R.)

Direct Primary
An intraparty election in which the voters select the candidates who will run on a party's ticket in the subsequent general election.

Party Identifier
A person who identifies with a political party.

THE POWER OF INCUMBENCY

The power of incumbency in the outcome of congressional elections cannot be overemphasized. Once members are elected and survive the second election, they build up considerable loyalty among their constituents, and they are frequently reelected as long as they wish to serve. Table 12–4 shows that more than 90 percent of

TABLE 12–4 The Power of Incumbency

	ELECTION YEAR															
	1980	1982	1984	1986	1988	1990	1992	1994	1996	1998	2000	2002	2004	2006	2008	2010
HOUSE																
Number of incumbent candidates	398	393	411	394	409	406	368	387	384	402	403	393	404	405	389	393
Reelected	361	354	392	385	402	390	325	349	361	395	394	383	397	382	372	336
Percentage of total	90.7	90.1	95.4	97.7	98.3	96.0	88.3	90.2	94.0	98.3	97.8	97.5	98.3	94.3	95.6	85.4
Defeated	37	39	19	9	7	16	43	38	23	7	9	10	7	23	17	57
In primary	6	10	3	3	1	1	19	3	2	1	3	3	1	2	3	4
In general election	31	29	16	6	6	15	24	34	21	6	6	7	6	21	17	53
SENATE																
Number of incumbent candidates	29	30	29	28	27	32	28	26	21	29	29	28	26	29	32	25
Reelected	16	28	26	21	23	31	23	24	19	26	23	24	25	23	23	21
Percentage of total	55.2	93.3	89.6	75.0	85.2	96.9	82.1	92.3	90.5	89.7	79.3	85.7	96.2	79.3	81.3	84
Defeated	13	2	3	7	4	1	5	2	2	3	6	4	1	6	3	4
In primary	4	0	0	0	0	0	1	0	1	0	0	1	0	1*	0	2
In general election	9	2	3	7	4	1	4	2	1	3	6	3	1	6	3	2

*Joe Lieberman of Connecticut lost the Democratic primary but won the general election as an independent. He chose to organize with the Senate Democrats.
Sources: Norman Ornstein, Thomas E. Mann, and Michael J. Malbin, *Vital Statistics on Congress, 2001–2002* (Washington, DC: The AEI Press, 2002); and authors' update.

DID YOU KNOW?

That 2004 was the first time since 1866 that Republicans increased their majority in the House of Representatives in two consecutive elections?

representatives and a slightly smaller proportion of senators who decide to run for reelection are successful. This conclusion holds for both presidential-year and midterm elections. Several scholars contend that the pursuit of reelection is the strongest motivation behind the activities of members of Congress. The reelection goal is pursued in several ways. Incumbents develop their homestyle, using the mass media, making personal appearances with constituents, and sending newsletters—all to produce a favorable image and to make their name a household word. Members of Congress generally try to present themselves as informed, experienced, and responsive to people's needs. Legislators also can point to things that they have done to benefit their constituents—by fulfilling the congressional casework function or by bringing money for mass transit to the district, for example. Finally, incumbents can demonstrate the positions that they have taken on key issues by referring to their voting records in Congress.

PARTY CONTROL OF CONGRESS AFTER THE 2010 ELECTIONS

After the midterm elections, President Obama faces a divided Congress with Republicans having control of the House of Representatives and Democrats still holding a 53-47 majority in the Senate. Such a situation may result in "gridlock" if the two houses cannot agree on legislation. Even if the two houses can agree on legislation, the President, who campaigned strongly for his Democratic colleagues, may veto the bills if they do not support his policy agenda. Historically, there is evidence that divided government is not less effective than government controlled by one party so it is possible for the parties to collaborate to pass legislation that is acceptable to the president. Republicans expected, after the election, to curb some of the Obama Administration policies citing the public support made evident in the election. They also planned to seek votes in the Senate from Democratic senators who are facing election in 2012.

CONGRESSIONAL APPORTIONMENT

Two of the most complicated aspects of congressional elections are apportionment issues—**reapportionment** (the allocation of seats in the House to each state after each census) and **redistricting** (the redrawing of the boundaries of the districts within each state). In a landmark six-to-two vote in 1962, the United States Supreme Court made the apportionment of state legislative districts a **justiciable** (that is, a reviewable) **question**.[4] The Court did so by invoking the Fourteenth Amendment principle that no state can deny to any person "the equal protection of the laws." In 1964, the Court held that *both* chambers of a state legislature must be apportioned so that all districts are equal in population.[5] Later that year, the Court applied this "one person, one vote" principle to U.S. congressional districts on the basis of Article I, Section 2, of the Constitution, which requires that members of the House be chosen "by the People of the several States."[6]

Severe malapportionment of congressional districts before 1964 resulted in some districts containing two or three times the populations of other districts in the same state, thereby diluting the effect of a vote cast in the more populous districts. This system generally benefited the conservative populations of rural areas and small towns and harmed the interests of the more heavily populated and liberal cities. In fact, suburban areas have benefited the most from the Court's rulings, as suburbs account for an increasingly larger proportion of the nation's population, while cities include a correspondingly smaller segment of the population.

GERRYMANDERING

Although the general issue of apportionment has been dealt with fairly successfully by the one person, one vote principle, the **gerrymandering** issue has not yet been resolved. This term refers to the legislative boundary-drawing tactics that were used under Elbridge Gerry, the governor of Massachusetts, in the 1812 elections (see Figure 12–1). A district is said to have been gerrymandered when its shape is altered substantially by the dominant party in a state legislature to maximize its electoral strength at the expense of the minority party.

Reapportionment
The allocation of seats in the House of Representatives to each state after each census.

Redistricting
The redrawing of the boundaries of the congressional districts within each state.

Justiciable Question
A question that may be raised and reviewed in court.

Gerrymandering
The drawing of legislative district boundary lines to obtain partisan or factional advantage. A district is said to be gerrymandered when its shape is manipulated by the dominant party in the state legislature to maximize electoral strength at the expense of the minority party.

---

[4]*Baker v. Carr,* 369 U.S. 186 (1962). The term *justiciable* is pronounced "juhs-tish-a-buhl."
[5]*Reynolds v. Sims,* 377 U.S. 533 (1964).
[6]*Wesberry v. Sanders,* 376 U.S. 1 (1964).

FIGURE 12–1 The Original Gerrymander

The practice of "gerrymandering"—the excessive manipulation of the shape of a legislative district to benefit a certain incumbent or party—is probably as old as the Republic, but the name originated in 1812. In that year, the Massachusetts legislature carved out of Essex County a district that historian John Fiske said has a "dragonlike contour." When the painter Gilbert Stuart saw the misshapen district, he penciled in a head, wings, and claws and exclaimed, "That will do for a salamander!" Editor Benjamin Russell replied, "Better say a Gerrymander" (after Elbridge Gerry, then-governor of Massachusetts).

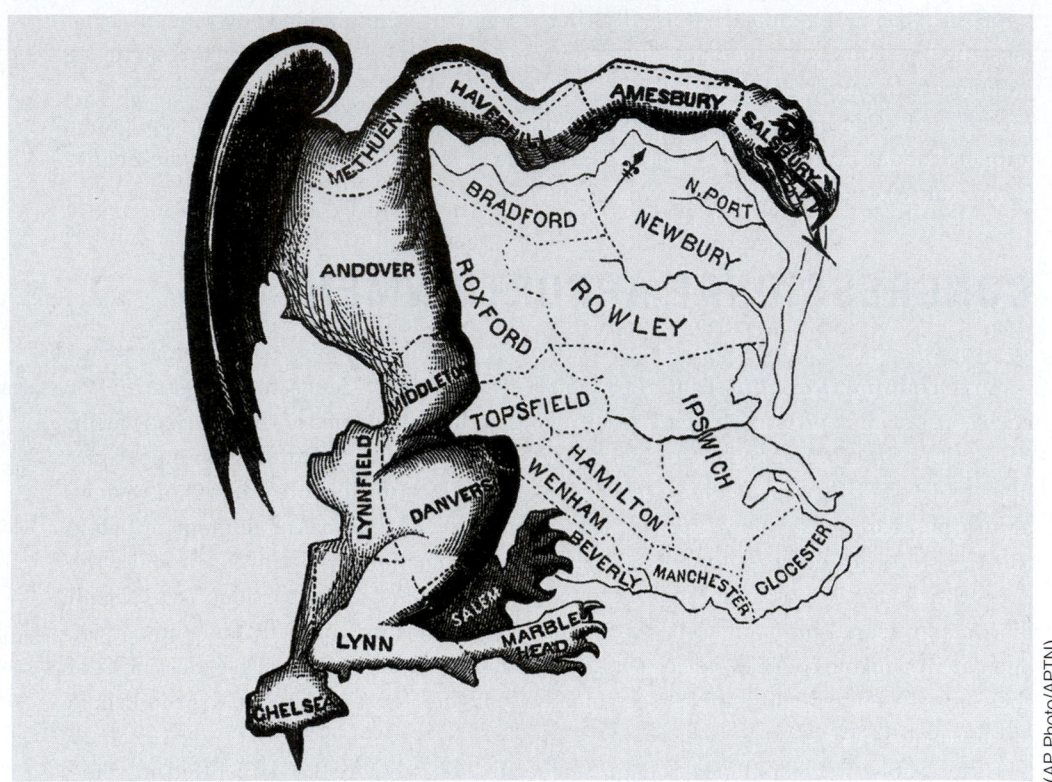

(AP Photo/APTN)

Source: *Congressional Quarterly's Guide to Congress*, 3rd ed. (Washington, DC: Congressional Quarterly Press, 1982), p. 695.

In 1986, the Supreme Court heard a case that challenged gerrymandered congressional districts in Indiana. The Court ruled for the first time that redistricting for the political benefit of one group could be challenged on constitutional grounds. In this specific case, *Davis v. Bandemer*,[7] however, the Court did not agree that the districts were drawn unfairly, because it could not be proved that a group of voters would consistently be deprived of influence at the polls as a result of the new districts.

REDISTRICTING AFTER THE 2000 CENSUS

In the meantime, political gerrymandering continues. For example, New York Democratic representative Maurice Hinchey's district, as shown in Figure 12–2, resembles a soup ladle. Why? That shape guarantees that he will always be able to pick up enough votes in Ithaca and Binghamton to win reelection.

----

[7]478 U.S. 109 (1986).

FIGURE 12–2 The 22nd Congressional District of NY

Congressional District 22

22 Congressional District

Sullivan County

New York (29 Districts)

Courtesy of The National Atlas of the United States of America

Redistricting decisions are often made by a small group of political leaders within a state legislature. Typically, their goal is to shape voting districts in such a way as to maximize their party's chances of winning state legislative seats as well as seats in Congress. Two of the techniques they use are called "packing" and "cracking." With the use of powerful computers and software, they *pack* voters supporting the opposing party into as few districts as possible or *crack* the opposing party's supporters into different districts. Consider that in Michigan, the Republicans who dominated redistricting efforts succeeded in packing six Democratic incumbents into only three congressional seats.

Clearly, partisan redistricting aids incumbents. The party that dominates a state's legislature will be making redistricting decisions. Through gerrymandering tactics such as packing and cracking, districts can be redrawn in such a way as to ensure that party's continued strength in the state legislature or Congress. As pointed out before, some have estimated that only between 30 and 50 of the 435 seats in the House of Representatives were open for any real competition in the most recent elections.

In 2004, the United States Supreme Court reviewed an obviously political redistricting scheme in Pennsylvania. The Court concluded, however, that the federal judiciary would not address purely political gerrymandering claims.[8] Two years later, the Supreme Court reached a similar conclusion with respect to most of the new congressional districts created by the Republicans in the Texas legislature in 2003. Again, except

[8]*Vieth v. Jubelirer,* 541 U.S. 267 (2004).

for one district in Texas, the Court refused to intervene in what was clearly a political gerrymandering plan.[9]

NONPARTISAN REDISTRICTING

Several states, including Arizona, Iowa, and Minnesota, have adopted nonpartisan redistricting procedures. As you will see if you compare the 22nd Congressional District of New York with the map of the Iowa districts (Figure 12–3), nonpartisan districts usually respect county lines and divide the state into fairly cleanly shaped districts that share geographic characteristics. Research has shown that nonpartisan districts tend

FIGURE 12–3 Congressional Districts of Iowa

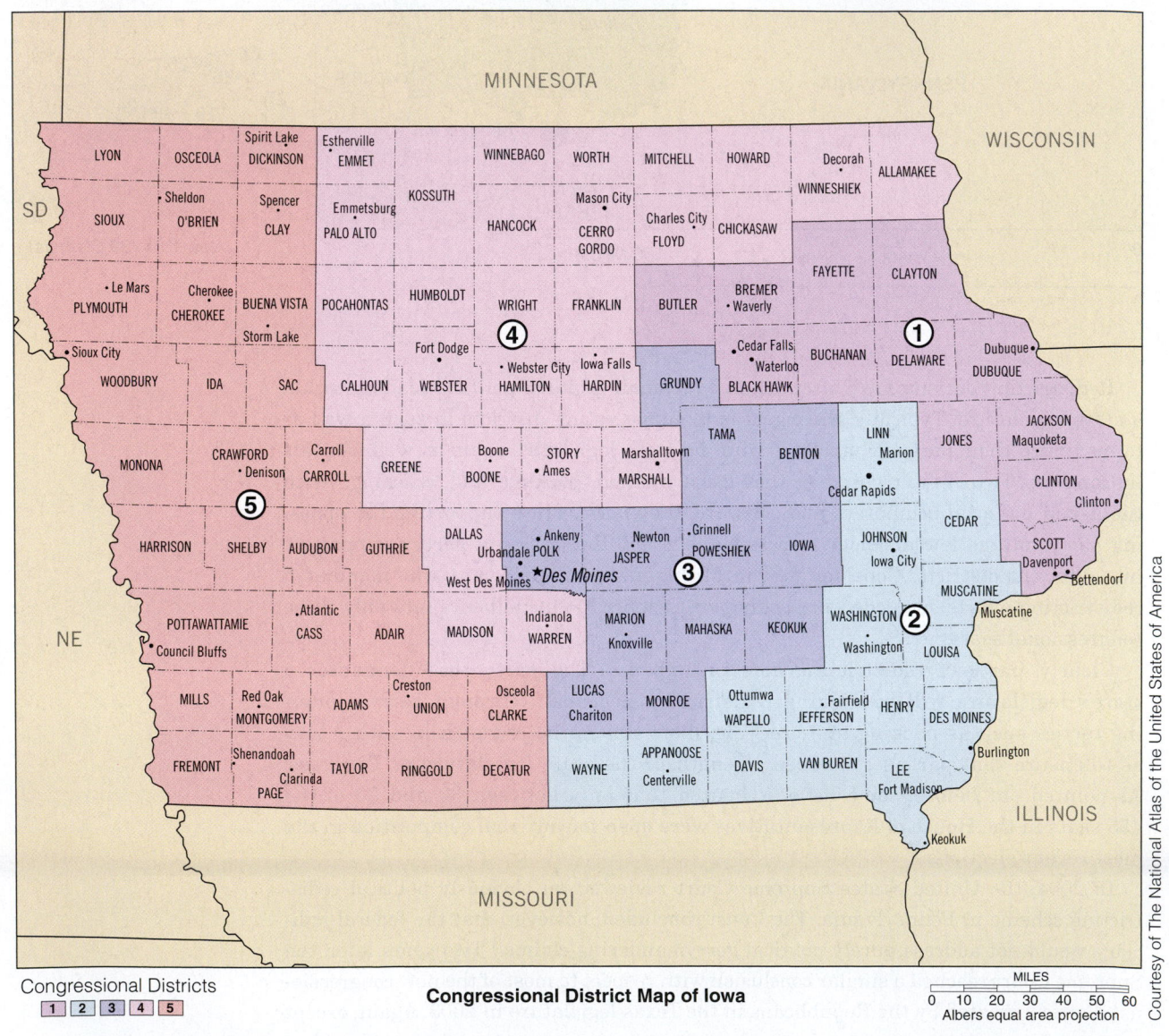

Congressional Districts
1 2 3 4 5

Congressional District Map of Iowa

MILES
0 10 20 30 40 50 60
Albers equal area projection

Courtesy of The National Atlas of the United States of America

---

[9]*League of United Latin American Citizens v. Perry*, 399 F.Supp. 2nd 756 (2006).

to be more competitive, no doubt because they have not been drawn to favor one party over the other.

"MINORITY-MAJORITY" DISTRICTS

In the early 1990s, the federal government encouraged a type of gerrymandering that made possible the election of a minority representative from a "minority-majority" area. Under the mandate of the Voting Rights Act of 1965, the Justice Department issued directives to states after the 1990 census instructing them to create congressional districts that would maximize the voting power of minority groups—that is, create districts in which minority voters were the majority. The result was several creatively drawn congressional districts—see, for example, the depiction of the Illinois Fourth Congressional District in Figure 12–4, which is commonly described as "a pair of earmuffs."

DID YOU KNOW?

That the most recently constructed dormitory for Senate pages cost about $8 million, or $264,200 per bed, compared with the median cost of a university dormitory of $22,600 per bed?

CONSTITUTIONAL CHALLENGES

Many of these "minority-majority" districts were challenged in court by citizens who claimed that creating districts based on race or ethnicity alone violates the equal protection clause of the Constitution. In 1995, the Supreme Court agreed with this argument when it declared that Georgia's new Eleventh District was unconstitutional. The district stretched from Atlanta to the Atlantic, splitting eight counties and five municipalities along the way. The Court referred to the district as a "monstrosity" linking "widely spaced urban centers that have absolutely nothing to do with each other." The Court went on to say that when a state assigns voters on the

FIGURE 12–4 The Fourth Congressional District of Illinois

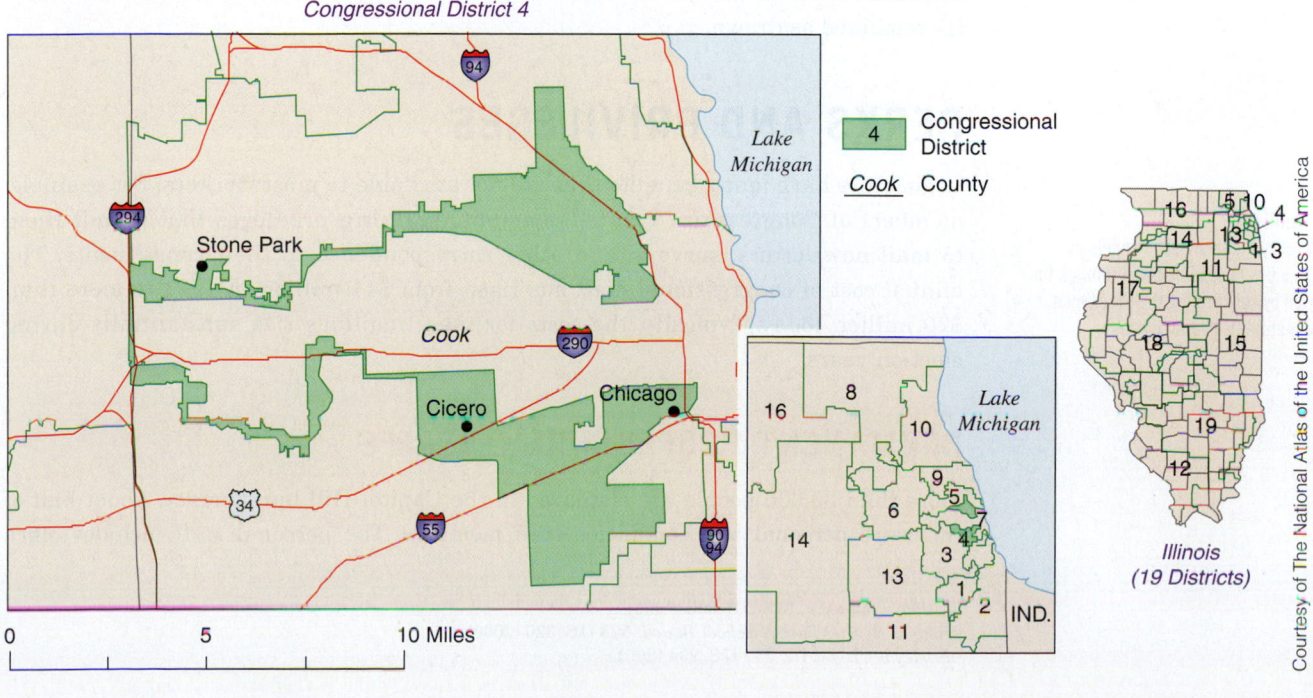

Courtesy of The National Atlas of the United States of America

basis of race, "it engages in the offensive and demeaning assumption that voters of a particular race, because of their race, think alike, share the same political interests, and will prefer the same candidates at the polls." The Court also chastised the Justice Department for concluding that race-based districting was mandated under the Voting Rights Act of 1965: "When the Justice Department's interpretation of the Act compels race-based districting, it by definition raises a serious constitutional question."[10] In subsequent rulings, the Court affirmed its position that when race is the dominant factor in the drawing of congressional district lines, the districts are unconstitutional.

DID YOU KNOW?

That before the Republicans reorganized House services in 1995, all members had buckets of ice delivered to their offices each day, at an annual cost of $500,000?

CHANGING DIRECTIONS

In the early 2000s, the Supreme Court seemed to take a new direction on racial redistricting challenges. In a 2000 case, the Court limited the federal government's authority to invalidate changes in state and local elections on the basis that the changes were discriminatory. The case involved a proposed school redistricting plan in Louisiana. The Court held that federal approval for the plan could not be withheld simply because the plan was discriminatory. Rather, the test was whether the plan left racial and ethnic minorities worse off than they were before.[11]

In 2001, the Supreme Court reviewed, for a second time, a case involving North Carolina's Twelfth District. The district was 165 miles long, following Interstate 85, for the most part. According to a local joke, the district was so narrow that a car traveling down the interstate highway with both doors open would kill most of the voters in the district. In 1996, the Supreme Court had held that the district was unconstitutional because race had been the dominant factor in drawing the district's boundaries. Shortly thereafter, the boundaries were redrawn, but the district was again challenged as a racial gerrymander. A federal district court agreed and invalidated the new boundaries as unconstitutional. In 2001, however, the Supreme Court held that there was insufficient evidence for the lower court's conclusion that race had been the dominant factor when the boundaries were redrawn.[12] The Twelfth District's boundaries remained as drawn.

PERKS AND PRIVILEGES

Legislators have many benefits that are not available to most workers. For example, members of Congress are granted generous **franking** privileges that permit them to mail newsletters, surveys, and other correspondence to their constituents. The annual cost of congressional mail has risen from $11 million in 1971 to more than $70 million today. Typically, the costs for these mailings rise substantially during election years.

Franking
A policy that enables members of Congress to send material through the mail by substituting their facsimile signature (frank) for postage.

PERMANENT PROFESSIONAL STAFFS

More than 30,000 people are employed in the Capitol Hill bureaucracy. About half of them are personal and committee staff members. The personal staff includes office

---

[10]*Miller v. Johnson,* 515 U.S. 900 (1995).
[11]*Reno v. Bossier Parish School Board,* 528 U.S. 320 (2000).
[12]*Easley v. Cromartie,* 532 U.S. 234 (2001).

clerks and secretaries; professionals who deal with media relations, draft legislation, and satisfy constituency requests for service; and staffers who maintain local offices in the member's home district or state.

The average Senate office on Capitol Hill employs about 30 staff members, and twice that number work on the personal staffs of senators from the most populous states. House office staffs typically are about half as large as those of the Senate. The number of staff members has increased dramatically since 1960. With the bulk of those increases coming in assistants to individual members, some scholars question whether staff members are really advising on legislation or are primarily aiding constituents and gaining votes in the next election.

Congress also benefits from the expertise of the professional staffs of agencies that were created to produce information for members of the House and Senate. For example, the Congressional Research Service, the Government Accountability Office, and the Congressional Budget Office all provide reports, audits, and policy recommendations for review by members of Congress.

That before the Republicans reorganized House services in 1995, all members had buckets of ice delivered to their offices each day, at an annual cost of $500,000?

PRIVILEGES AND IMMUNITIES UNDER THE LAW

Members of Congress also benefit from some special constitutional protections. Under Article I, Section 6, of the Constitution, they "shall in all Cases, except Treason, Felony and Breach of the Peace, be privileged from Arrest during their Attendance at the Session of their respective Houses, and in going to and returning from the same; and for any Speech or Debate in either House, they shall not be questioned in any other Place." The arrest immunity clause is not really an important provision today. The "speech or debate" clause, however, means that a member may make any allegations or other statements he or she wishes in connection with official duties and normally not be sued for libel or slander or otherwise be subject to legal action.

CONGRESSIONAL CAUCUSES: ANOTHER SOURCE OF SUPPORT

All members of Congress are members of one or more caucuses. The most important caucuses are those established by the parties in each chamber. These Democratic and Republican meetings provide information to the members and devise legislative strategy for the party. Other caucuses bring together members who have similar political views, such as the moderate Democratic Study Group, while some have a constituency focus, such as the Rust Belt Caucus or the Potato Caucus. Some of the most important and influential caucuses are those for minority and underrepresented groups in Congress.

The Congressional Women's Caucus has long provided support for the relatively few women who were elected to the Congress and has provided a forum for discussing issues that women members find important. Among the other minority or ethnic-based caucuses, two of the most important are the Congressional Black Caucus and the Hispanic Congressional Caucus. Both of these associations have grown in the last two decades as the numbers of African American and Hispanic members grew. These organizations, which are now funded by businesses and special interests, provide staff assistance and information for members of Congress and help them build support among specific groups of voters. Additionally, the caucuses provide internships and scholarships for students as a way to recruit political leaders for the future.

RETIRED NORTH CAROLINA
Supreme Court Chief Justice Henry Frye (left) swears in members of the Congressional Black Caucus of the 109th Congress on January 4, 2005. The Congressional Black Caucus has been an effective influence within Congress for several decades. (Alex Wong/ Getty Images)

THE COMMITTEE STRUCTURE

Most of the actual work of legislating is performed by the committees and subcommittees within Congress. Thousands of bills are introduced in every session of Congress, and no single member can possibly be adequately informed on all the issues that arise. The committee system is a way to provide for specialization, or a division of the legislative labor. Members of a committee can concentrate on just one area or topic—such as taxation or energy—and develop sufficient expertise to draft appropriate legislation when needed. The flow of legislation through both the House and the Senate is determined largely by the speed with which the members of these committees act on bills and resolutions.

THE POWER OF COMMITTEES

Sometimes called "little legislatures," committees usually have the final say on pieces of legislation.[13] Committee actions may be overturned on the floor by the House or Senate, but this rarely happens. Legislators normally defer to the expertise of the chairperson and other members of the committee who speak on the floor in defense of a committee decision. Chairpersons of committees exercise control over the scheduling of hearings and formal action on a bill. They also decide which subcommittee will act on legislation falling within their committee's jurisdiction.

Committees only very rarely are deprived of control over a bill—although this kind of action is provided for in the rules of each chamber. In the House, if a bill has been considered by a standing committee for 30 days, the signatures of a majority (218) of the House membership on a **discharge petition** can pry a bill out of an uncooperative

Discharge Petition
A procedure by which a bill in the House of Representatives may be forced (discharged) out of a committee that has refused to report it for consideration by the House. The petition must be signed by an absolute majority (218) of representatives and is used only on rare occasions.

---

[13]The term *little legislatures* is from Woodrow Wilson, *Congressional Government* (New York: Meridian Books, 1956 [first published in 1885]).

REPRESENTATIVE NYDIA M. VELAZQUEZ, D., N.Y., the first Puerto Rican woman elected to Congress praises the achievements of Supreme Court Justice Sonia Sotomayor who is the first Latina member of the Court. (AP Photo/J. Scott Applewhite)

committee's hands. From 1909 to 2007, however, although more than 900 such petitions were initiated, only slightly more than two dozen resulted in successful discharge efforts. Of those, 20 resulted in bills that passed the House.[14]

TYPES OF CONGRESSIONAL COMMITTEES

Over the past two centuries, Congress has created several different types of committees, each of which serves particular needs of the institution.

Standing Committees. By far the most important committees in Congress are the **standing committees**—permanent bodies that are established by the rules of each chamber of Congress and that continue from session to session. A list of the standing committees of the 111th Congress is presented in Table 12–5. In addition, most of the standing committees have created subcommittees to carry out their work. For example, in the 110th Congress, there were 68 subcommittees in the Senate and 88 in the House.[15] Each standing committee is given a specific area of legislative policy jurisdiction, and almost all legislative measures are considered by the appropriate standing committees.

Because of the importance of their work and the traditional influence of their members in Congress, certain committees are considered to be more prestigious than others. Seats on standing committees that handle spending issues are especially sought after because members can use these positions to benefit their constituents. Committees that control spending include the Appropriations Committee in either chamber and the Ways and Means Committee in the House. Members also normally seek seats on committees that handle matters of special interest to their constituents. A member of the House from an agricultural district, for example, will have an interest in joining the House Agriculture Committee.

Standing Committee
A permanent committee in the House or Senate that considers bills within a certain subject area.

That Samuel Morse demonstrated his telegraph to Congress in 1843 by stretching wire between two committee rooms?

[14]Congressional Quarterly, Inc., *Guide to Congress,* 5th ed. (Washington, DC: CQ Press, 2000); and authors' update.
[15]*Congressional Directory* (Washington, DC: U.S. Government Printing Office, various editions).

TABLE 12–5 Standing Committees of the 112th Congress, 2011–2013

HOUSE COMMITTEES	SENATE COMMITTEES
Agriculture	Agriculture, Nutrition, and Forestry
Appropriations	Appropriations
Armed Services	Armed Services
Budget	Banking, Housing, and Urban Affairs
Education and the Workforce	Budget
Energy and Commerce	Commerce, Science, and Transportation
Financial Services	Energy and Natural Resources
Government Reform	Environment and Public Works
Homeland Security	Finance
House Administration	Foreign Relations
International Relations	Governmental Affairs
Judiciary	Health, Education, Labor, and Pensions
Resources	Judiciary
Rules	Rules and Administration
Science	Small Business and Entrepreneurship
Small Business	Veterans Affairs
Standards of Official Conduct	
Transportation and Infrastructure	
Veterans Affairs	
Ways and Means	

Select Committee
A temporary legislative committee established for a limited time period and for a special purpose.

Joint Committee
A legislative committee composed of members from both chambers of Congress.

Conference Committee
A special joint committee appointed to reconcile differences when bills pass the two chambers of Congress in different forms.

Select Committees. In principle, a **select committee** is created for a limited time and for a specific legislative purpose. For example, a select committee may be formed to investigate a public problem, such as child nutrition or aging. In practice, a select committee, such as the Select Committee on Intelligence in each chamber, may continue indefinitely. Select committees rarely create original legislation.

Joint Committees. A **joint committee** is formed by the concurrent action of both chambers of Congress and consists of members from each chamber. Joint committees, which may be permanent or temporary, have dealt with the economy, taxation, and the Library of Congress.

Conference Committees. Special joint committees—**conference committees**—are formed to achieve agreement between the House and the Senate on the exact wording of legislative acts when the two chambers pass legislative proposals in different forms. The bill is reported out of the conference committee if it is approved by the majority of members from both houses who sit on the committee. It is then returned to the House and Senate for final votes. No bill can be sent to the White House to be signed into law unless it first passes both chambers in identical form. Sometimes called the "third house" of Congress, conference committees are in a position to make significant alterations to legislation and frequently become the focal point of policy debates.

The House Rules Committee. Because of its special "gatekeeping" power over the terms on which legislation will reach the floor of the House of Representatives, the House Rules Committee holds a uniquely powerful position. A special committee rule sets the time limit on debate and determines whether and how a bill may be amended. This practice dates back to 1883. The Rules Committee has the unusual power to meet while the House is in session, to have its resolutions considered immediately on the floor, and to initiate legislation on its own.

THE SELECTION OF COMMITTEE MEMBERS

In both chambers, members are appointed to standing committees by the Steering Committee of their party. The majority-party member with the longest term of continuous service on a standing committee can be given preference when the leadership nominates chairpersons. Newt Gingrich, during his time as Speaker in the House, restricted chairpersons' terms to six years. Additionally, he bypassed seniority to appoint chairpersons loyal to his own platform.

Respecting seniority is an informal, traditional process, and it applies to other significant posts in Congress as well. The **seniority system,** although it deliberately treats members unequally, provides a predictable means of assigning positions of power within Congress. The most senior member of the minority party is called the *ranking committee member* for that party.

The general pattern until the 1970s was that members of the House or Senate who represented **safe seats** would be reelected continually and eventually would accumulate enough years of continuous committee service to enable them to become the

Seniority System
A custom followed in both chambers of Congress specifying that the member of the majority party with the longest term of continuous service will be given preference when a committee chairperson (or a holder of some other significant post) is selected.

Safe Seat
A district that returns a legislator with 55 percent of the vote or more.

THREE SENATORS from the New York City area, Democrats Frank Lautenberg of New Jersey (far left), Charles Schumer of New York, and Robert Menendez of New Jersey hold a press conference about the Times Square bomber. (Bill Clark/Roll Call Photos/Newscom)

chairpersons of their committees. In the 1970s, a number of reforms in the chairperson selection process somewhat modified the seniority system. The reforms introduced the use of a secret ballot in electing House committee chairpersons and allowed for the possibility of choosing a chairperson on a basis other than seniority. The Democrats immediately replaced three senior chairpersons who were out of step with the rest of their party. The Republican leadership in the House has also taken more control over the selection of committee chairpersons.

THE FORMAL LEADERSHIP

The limited amount of centralized power that exists in Congress is exercised through party-based mechanisms. Congress is organized by party. When the Democratic Party, for example, wins a majority of seats in either the House or the Senate, Democrats control the official positions of power in that chamber, and every important committee has a Democratic chairperson and a majority of Democratic members. The same process holds when Republicans are in the majority.

Generally speaking, the leadership organizations in the House and the Senate look alike on paper. However, leaders in the House of Representatives have more control over the agenda of the body and, often, over their own party's members. Senate leaders, due to the power of individual members, must work closely with the other party's leaders to achieve success. Although the party leaders in both the House and the Senate are considered to be the most powerful members of the Congress, their powers pale compared to those given to the leaders in true "party government" legislatures. The differences between those legislatures and the U.S. Congress are detailed in the Beyond Our Borders feature.

LEADERSHIP IN THE HOUSE

The House leadership is made up of the Speaker, the majority and minority leaders, and the party whips.

The Speaker. The foremost power holder in the House of Representatives is the **Speaker of the House.** The Speaker's position is technically a nonpartisan one, but in fact, for the better part of two centuries, the Speaker has been the official leader of the majority party in the House. When a new Congress convenes in January of odd-numbered years, each party nominates a candidate for Speaker. All Democratic members of the House are expected to vote for their party's nominee, and all Republicans are expected to support their candidate. The vote to organize the House is the one vote in which representatives must vote with their party. In a sense, this vote defines a member's partisan status.

The influence of modern-day Speakers is based primarily on their personal prestige, persuasive ability, and knowledge of the legislative process—plus the acquiescence or active support of other representatives. In recent years, both the Republican and Democratic parties in the House have given their leaders more power in making appointments and controlling the agenda. The major formal powers of the Speaker include the following:

1. Presiding over meetings of the House.
2. Appointing members of joint committees and conference committees.
3. Scheduling legislation for floor action.

DID YOU KNOW?

That the Constitution does not require that the Speaker of the House of Representatives be an elected member of the House?

Speaker of the House
The presiding officer in the House of Representatives. The Speaker is always a member of the majority party and is the most powerful and influential member of the House.

4. Deciding points of order and interpreting the rules with the advice of the House parliamentarian.

5. Referring bills and resolutions to the appropriate standing committees of the House.

A Speaker may take part in floor debate and vote, as can any other member of Congress, but recent Speakers usually have voted only to break a tie. Since 1975, the Speaker, when a Democrat, has also had the power to appoint the Democratic Steering Committee, which determines new committee assignments for House party members.

In general, the powers of the Speaker are related to his or her control over information and communications channels in the House and the degree of support received from members. This is a significant power in a large, decentralized institution in which information is a very important resource. Since the Speakership of Newt Gingrich (R., Ga.) in 1994, the leadership of the House has held significant power to control the agenda and provide rewards to the members. During the same time period, the degree of polarization between the majority and minority parties has increased, and cohesion within each party has grown stronger. Scholars suggest that this is the result of increased ideological makeup within the congressional delegation of both parties and the election of fewer moderate or centrist members to the House of Representatives.

The Majority Leader. The **majority leader of the House** is elected by a caucus of the majority party to foster cohesion among party members and to act as a spokesperson for the party. The majority leader influences the scheduling of debate and acts as the chief supporter of the Speaker. The majority leader cooperates with the Speaker and other

Majority Leader of the House
A legislative position held by an important party member in the House of Representatives. The majority leader is selected by the majority party in caucus or conference to foster cohesion among party members and to act as spokesperson for the majority party in the House.

Beyond Our **Borders**

SHOULD PARTIES CONTROL LEGISLATURES (AND GOVERNMENTS)?

The Congress of the United States is, as you know, a bicameral legislature. The American-style legislature differs from most of the legislatures in the world in several significant ways. Because the U.S. government is composed of three branches, separate structures sharing powers, we frequently have "divided" government, meaning that the party that controls one or both houses of Congress does not control the presidency. Does this mean that the government is hopelessly deadlocked? Not usually. Members of Congress, especially in the House, frequently support their party leaders, but on many other votes, they "cross the aisle" to vote with members of the other side, thinking it best for their constituency or for their reelection.

Most Americans think that our legislature is modeled on the British parliament. However, the parliament of Great Britain, as well as that of many other Western nations, is based on the idea of "party government." No separation of powers exists between the legislature and the executive branch. What does this mean? When a political party wins a majority of seats in the House of Parliament (the lower and only powerful house), that party then selects the prime minister, who is also the party leader. The prime minister and his or her cabinet members actually sit in parliament during debates, where they play an active role. The party, which may have promised "lemonade in every drinking fountain" or a better welfare system, votes the new law into effect, and the prime minister implements the new policy.*

Similar systems with two major parties and some minor parties are in effect in Canada and other nations as well. Another variation on this type of party government occurs when a nation such as Germany, Italy, or Israel has a multiparty system. In that case, no party wins a majority of seats. The party with the plurality of the seats chooses the leader and then negotiates with other parties to form a coalition in order to constitute a government and pass new legislation. Governing as part of a coalition is much more difficult, however, because if one of the partners does not agree with the proposed policy, the coalition may fall apart, and new elections may be necessary.

Consider the important relationship between the executive (prime minister or president) and the legislature. In the U.S. system, even if the Congress and the president are of the same party, this does not guarantee that the president's agenda will be fully carried out. Although George W. Bush was able to get much of his legislation passed in the early years of his administration, he could not get support for reforming Social Security in 2005. Mr. Obama, who came into office with a very large majority in the House of Representatives, received speedy and cohesive support for his initiatives in his first year, but legislation often bogged down in the Senate due to its procedural rules. In fact, both the Democrats and the Republicans in the House were so cohesive throughout much of those years that some scholars believed it was a form of "conditional party government."** In a true party government system, everything on the Democrats' agenda would become law, and the president would be selected by the Congress.

DURING "QUESTION HOUR" in the British parliament, members may ask the prime minister directly about his government and its actions. In this picture, Deputy Prime Minister Nick Clegg and Prime Minister David Cameron, along with their fellow Cabinet ministers, take questions from members of the House of Commons. PA Wire URN:9031706 (Press Association via AP Images)

Although Americans complain bitterly about ineffective Congresses, they generally prefer divided government due to fear that one party will have too much power.

FOR CRITICAL ANALYSIS

1. Would the United States ever give the kind of power to the president to achieve his agenda that is given to the prime minister of Great Britain?
2. What is more important—controlling government power or having a more effective legislature?
3. How would the United States Congress be different if three or four parties were represented there?

*For information on the world's legislatures, go to the Web site of the Inter-Parliamentary Union at www.ipu.org.
**The "conditional party government" thesis has been developed by David Rohde, *Parties and Leaders in the PostReform House* (Chicago: University of Chicago Press, 1991).

party leaders, both inside and outside Congress, to formulate the party's legislative program and to guide that program through the legislative process in the House. The Democrats often recruit future Speakers from those who hold that position.

The Minority Leader. The **minority leader of the House** is the candidate nominated for Speaker by a caucus of the minority party. Like the majority leader, the leader of the minority party has as her or his primary responsibility the maintaining of cohesion within the party's ranks. The minority leader works for cohesion among the party's members and speaks on behalf of the president if the minority party controls the White House. In relations with the majority party, the minority leader consults with both the Speaker and the majority leader on recognizing members who wish to speak on the floor, on House rules and procedures, and on the scheduling of legislation. Minority leaders have no actual power in these areas, however.

Minority Leader of the House
The party leader elected by the minority party in the House.

Whips. The leadership of each party includes assistants to the majority and minority leaders, known as whips. The **whips** are members of Congress who assist the party leaders by passing information down from the leadership to party members and by ensuring that members show up for floor debate and cast their votes on important issues. Whips conduct polls among party members about the members' views on legislation, inform the leaders about whose vote is doubtful and whose is certain, and may exert pressure on members to support the leaders' positions. In the House, serving as a whip is the first step toward positions of higher leadership.

Whip
A member of Congress who aids the majority or minority leader of the House or the Senate.

LEADERSHIP IN THE SENATE

The Senate is less than one-fourth the size of the House. This fact alone probably explains why a formal, complex, and centralized leadership structure is not as necessary in the Senate as it is in the House.

The two highest-ranking formal leadership positions in the Senate are essentially ceremonial in nature. Under the Constitution, the vice president of the United States is the president (that is, the presiding officer) of the Senate and may vote to break a tie. The vice president, however, is only rarely present for a meeting of the Senate. The Senate elects instead a **president pro tempore** ("pro tem") to preside over the Senate in the vice president's absence. Ordinarily, the president pro tem is the member

President Pro Tempore
The temporary presiding officer of the Senate in the absence of the vice president.

**SENATE MAJORITY LEADER
HARRY REID** of Nevada, left, and
Senate Minority Leader Mitch
McConnell of Kentucky, arrive at
a meeting with the president on
health care reform. (AP Photo/
Pablo Martinez Monsivais)

Senate Majority Leader
The chief spokesperson of the majority
party in the Senate, who directs the
legislative program and party strategy.

Senate Minority Leader
The party officer in the Senate who
commands the minority party's opposition
to the policies of the majority party and
directs the legislative program and
strategy of his or her party.

Conservative Coalition
An alliance of Republicans and Southern
Democrats that can form in the House or
the Senate to oppose liberal legislation
and support conservative legislation.

of the majority party with the longest continuous term of service in the Senate. The president pro tem is mostly a ceremonial position. Junior senators take turns actually presiding over the sessions of the Senate.

The real leadership power in the Senate rests in the hands of the **Senate majority leader,** the **Senate minority leader,** and their respective whips. The Senate majority and minority leaders have the right to be recognized first in debate on the floor and generally exercise the same powers available to the House majority and minority leaders. They control the scheduling of debate on the floor in conjunction with the majority party's Policy Committee, influence the allocation of committee assignments for new members or for senators attempting to transfer to a new committee, influence the selection of other party officials, and participate in selecting members of conference committees. The leaders are expected to mobilize support for partisan legislative initiatives or for the proposals of a president who belongs to their party. The leaders act as liaisons with the White House when the president is of their party, try to obtain the cooperation of committee chairpersons, and seek to facilitate the smooth functioning of the Senate through the senators' unanimous consent. The majority and minority leaders are elected by their respective party caucuses.

Senate party whips, like their House counterparts, maintain communication within the party on platform positions and try to ensure that party colleagues are present for floor debate and important votes. The Senate whip system is far less elaborate than its counterpart in the House, simply because there are fewer members to track.

A list of the formal party leaders of the 110th Congress is presented in Table 12–6. Party leaders are a major source of influence over the decisions about public issues that senators and representatives must make every day.

HOW MEMBERS OF CONGRESS DECIDE

Each member of Congress casts hundreds of votes in each session. Each member compiles a record of votes during the years that he or she spends in the national legislature. There are usually several different reasons why any particular vote is cast. Research shows that the best predictor of a member's vote is party affiliation. Obviously, party members do have common opinions on some, if not all, issues facing the nation. In addition, the party leadership in each house works hard to build cohesion and agreement among the members through the activities of the party caucuses and conferences. In recent years, the increase in partisanship in both the House and the Senate has meant that most Republicans are voting in opposition to most Democrats.

THE CONSERVATIVE COALITION

Political parties are not always unified. In the 1950s and 1960s, the Democrats in Congress were often split between Northern liberals and Southern conservatives. This division gave rise to the **conservative coalition,** a voting bloc made up of conservative Democrats and conservative (which is to say, most) Republicans. This coalition was able to win many votes over the years. Today, however, most Southern conservatives are Republicans, so the

TABLE 12–6 Party Leaders in the 111th Congress, 2009–2011

POSITION	INCUMBENT	PARTY/STATE	LEADER SINCE
House			
Speaker	Nancy Pelosi	D.-Calif.	Jan. 2007
Majority leader	Steny Hoyer	D.-Md.	Jan. 2007
Majority whip	James Clyburn	D.-S.C.	Jan. 2007
Chair of the Democratic Caucus	Rahm Emanuel	D.-Ill.	Jan. 2007
Minority leader	John Boehner	R.-Ohio	Jan. 2007
Minority whip	Roy Blunt	R.-Mo.	Jan. 2007
Chair of the Republican Conference	Adam Putnam	R.-Fla.	Jan. 2007
Senate			
President pro tempore	Daniel Inouye	D.-Hawaii	June 2010
Majority leader	Harry Reid	D.-Nev.	Jan. 2007
Majority whip	Dick Durbin	D.-Ill.	Jan. 2007
Vice Chair of the Democratic Conference	Charles E. Schumer	D.-N.Y.	Jan. 2007
Minority leader	Mitch McConnell	R.-Ky.	Jan. 2007
Minority whip	Trent Lott	R.-Miss.	Jan. 2007
Chair of the Republican Conference	Jon Kyl	R.-Ariz.	Jan. 2007

coalition has almost disappeared. There are, however, some Democrats in Congress who represent more moderate states or districts. The votes of these members, who are known as **Blue Dog Democrats,** are frequently sought after by Republican leaders.

"CROSSING OVER"

On some votes, individual representatives and senators will vote against their party, "crossing over to the other side," because the interests of their states or districts differ from the interests that prevail within the rest of their party. In some cases, members vote a certain way because of the influence of regional or national interests. Other voting decisions are based on the members' religious or ideological beliefs. Votes on issues such as abortion or gay rights may be motivated by a member's religious views.

There are, however, far too many voting decisions for every member to be fully informed on each issue. Research suggests that many voting decisions are based on cues provided by trusted colleagues or the party leadership. A member who sits on the committee that wrote a law may become a reliable source of information about that law. Alternatively, a member may turn to a

Blue Dog Democrats
Members of Congress from more moderate states or districts who sometimes "cross over" to vote with Republicans on legislation.

DID YOU KNOW?

That in 2004, on the urging of representative Don Young (R., Alaska), the House approved a new bridge to connect a town of 7,845 people with an island of 50 residents—a $200 million structure with a longer span than the George Washington Bridge in New York?

colleague who represents a district in the same state or one who represents a similar district for cues on voting. Cues may also come from fellow committee members, leaders, and the administration.

LOGROLLING, EARMARKS, AND "PORK"

Sometimes, leaders on either side of the aisle will offer incentives to get needed votes for the passage of legislation. Even the president has been known to offer opportunities for the member to better serve his or her district through "bringing home the bacon." When a member "trades" his or her vote on a particular bill with another member in exchange for his or her vote on other legislation, the practice is known as logrolling, described earlier in the chapter. Often members request that special appropriations for projects back home are attached to a bill to gain their votes. If the actual project is named, this is referred to as an **earmark.** The term comes from the V-shaped mark that is cut in a pig's ear to identify the animal. The special projects that are so identified are often referred to as **pork,** as in bringing home the bacon or pork. Although the practice of special appropriations has a long history, the amounts now being earmarked equal more than $30 billion in most years. Efforts have been made to force lawmakers to reveal all of their special projects, but new methods have been found to hide these special appropriations from the public eye.

Politicians and reformers often rail against the practice of earmarks, and some projects seem absolutely silly to everyone except the people or state that will benefit. In some cases, earmarks truly are needed; in others, they are seen as the key to keeping a member of Congress in office. As the late Senator Robert Byrd of West Virginia has been known to remark, "One man's pork is another man's job."[16]

HOW A BILL BECOMES LAW

Each year, Congress and the president propose and approve many laws. Some are budget and appropriations laws that require extensive bargaining but must be passed for the government to continue to function. Other laws are relatively free of controversy and are passed with little dissension. Still other proposed legislation is extremely controversial and reaches to the roots of differences between Democrats and Republicans and between the executive and legislative branches.

As detailed in Figure 12–5, each law begins as a bill, which must be introduced in either the House or the Senate. Often, similar bills are introduced in both chambers. A "money bill," however, must start in the House. In each chamber, the bill follows similar steps. It is referred to a committee and its subcommittees for study, discussion, hearings, and rewriting ("markup"). When the bill is reported out to the full chamber, it must be scheduled for debate (by the Rules Committee in the House and by the leadership in the Senate). After the bill has been passed in each chamber, if it contains different provisions, a conference committee is formed to write a compromise bill, which must be approved by both chambers before it is sent to the president to sign or veto.

Another form of congressional action, the *joint resolution,* differs little from a bill in how it is proposed or debated. Once it is approved by both

FIGURE 12–5 How a Bill Becomes Law

This illustration shows the most typical way in which proposed legislation is enacted into law. Most legislation begins as similar bills introduced into the House and the Senate. The process is illustrated here with two hypothetical bills, House bill No. 100 (HR 100) and Senate bill No. 200 (S 200). The path of HR 100 is shown on the left, and that of S 200, on the right.

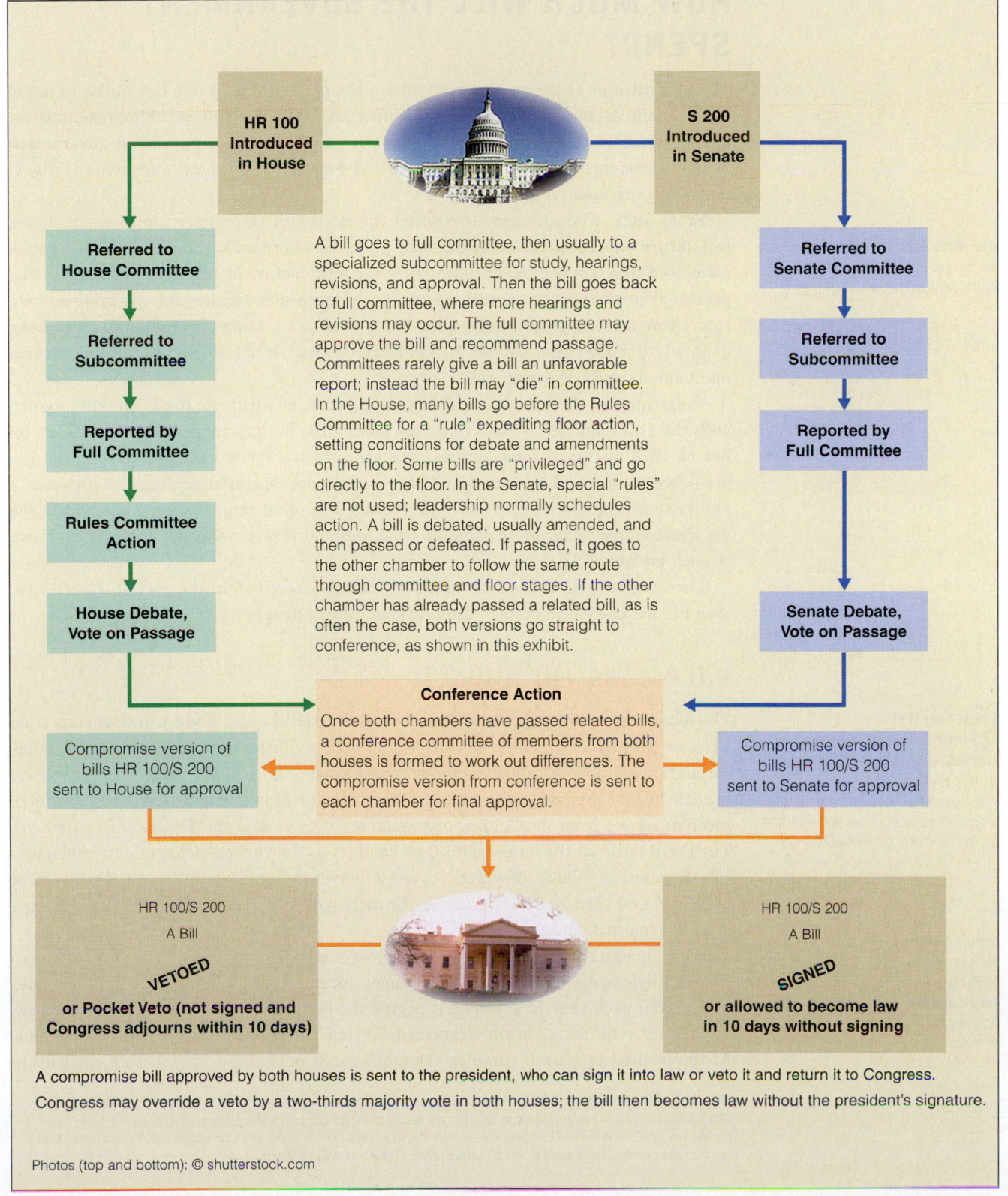

HR 100 Introduced in House

Referred to House Committee

Referred to Subcommittee

Reported by Full Committee

Rules Committee Action

House Debate, Vote on Passage

S 200 Introduced in Senate

Referred to Senate Committee

Referred to Subcommittee

Reported by Full Committee

Senate Debate, Vote on Passage

A bill goes to full committee, then usually to a specialized subcommittee for study, hearings, revisions, and approval. Then the bill goes back to full committee, where more hearings and revisions may occur. The full committee may approve the bill and recommend passage. Committees rarely give a bill an unfavorable report; instead the bill may "die" in committee. In the House, many bills go before the Rules Committee for a "rule" expediting floor action, setting conditions for debate and amendments on the floor. Some bills are "privileged" and go directly to the floor. In the Senate, special "rules" are not used; leadership normally schedules action. A bill is debated, usually amended, and then passed or defeated. If passed, it goes to the other chamber to follow the same route through committee and floor stages. If the other chamber has already passed a related bill, as is often the case, both versions go straight to conference, as shown in this exhibit.

Conference Action

Once both chambers have passed related bills, a conference committee of members from both houses is formed to work out differences. The compromise version from conference is sent to each chamber for final approval.

Compromise version of bills HR 100/S 200 sent to House for approval

Compromise version of bills HR 100/S 200 sent to Senate for approval

HR 100/S 200

A Bill

VETOED

or Pocket Veto (not signed and Congress adjourns within 10 days)

HR 100/S 200

A Bill

SIGNED

or allowed to become law in 10 days without signing

A compromise bill approved by both houses is sent to the president, who can sign it into law or veto it and return it to Congress. Congress may override a veto by a two-thirds majority vote in both houses; the bill then becomes law without the president's signature.

Photos (top and bottom): © shutterstock.com

chambers and signed by the president, it has the force of law.[17] A joint resolution to amend the Constitution, however, after it is approved by two-thirds of both chambers, is sent not to the president but to the states for ratification.

HOW MUCH WILL THE GOVERNMENT SPEND?

The Constitution is very clear about where the power of the purse lies in the national government: All taxing or spending bills must originate in the House of Representatives. Today, much of the business of Congress is concerned with approving government expenditures through the budget process and with raising the revenues to pay for government programs.

From 1922, when Congress required the president to prepare and present to the legislature an **executive budget,** until 1974, the congressional budget process was so disjointed that it was difficult to visualize the total picture of government finances. The president presented the executive budget to Congress in January. It was broken down into 13 or more appropriations bills. Some time later, after all of the bills had been debated, amended, and passed, it was more or less possible to estimate total government spending for the next year.

Frustrated by the president's ability to impound, or withhold, funds and dissatisfied with the entire budget process, Congress passed the Budget and Impoundment Control Act of 1974 to regain some control over the nation's spending. The act required the president to spend the funds that Congress had appropriated, ending the president's ability to kill programs by withholding funds. The other major accomplishment of the act was to force Congress to examine total national taxing and spending at least twice in each budget cycle.

The budget cycle of the federal government is described in the rest of this section. (See Figure 12–6 for a graphic illustration of the budget cycle.)

PREPARING THE BUDGET

The federal government operates on a **fiscal year (FY)** cycle. The fiscal year runs from October through September, so that fiscal 2009, or FY09, runs from October 1, 2008, through September 30, 2009. Eighteen months before a fiscal year starts, the executive branch begins preparing the budget. The Office of Management and Budget (OMB) receives advice from the Council of Economic Advisers and the Treasury Department. The OMB outlines the budget and then sends it to the various departments and agencies. Bargaining follows, in which—to use only two of many examples—the Department of Health and Human Services argues for more welfare spending, and the armed forces argue for more defense spending.

Even though the OMB has only 600 employees, it is one of the most powerful agencies in Washington. It assembles the budget documents and monitors federal agencies throughout each year. Every year, it begins the budget process with a **spring review,** in which it requires all of the agencies to review their programs, activities, and goals. At the beginning of each summer, the OMB sends out a letter instructing agencies to

Executive Budget
The budget prepared and submitted by the president to Congress.

Fiscal Year (FY)
A 12-month period that is used for bookkeeping, or accounting purposes. Usually, the fiscal year does not coincide with the calendar year. For example, the federal government's fiscal year runs from October 1 through September 30.

Spring Review
The annual process in which the Office of Management and Budget requires federal agencies to review their programs, activities, and goals and submit their requests for funding for the next fiscal year.

---

[17]In contrast, *simple resolutions* and *concurrent resolutions* do not carry the force of law, but rather are used by one or both chambers of Congress, respectively, to express facts, principles, or opinions. For example, a concurrent resolution is used to set the time when Congress will adjourn.

FIGURE 12–6 The Budget Cycle

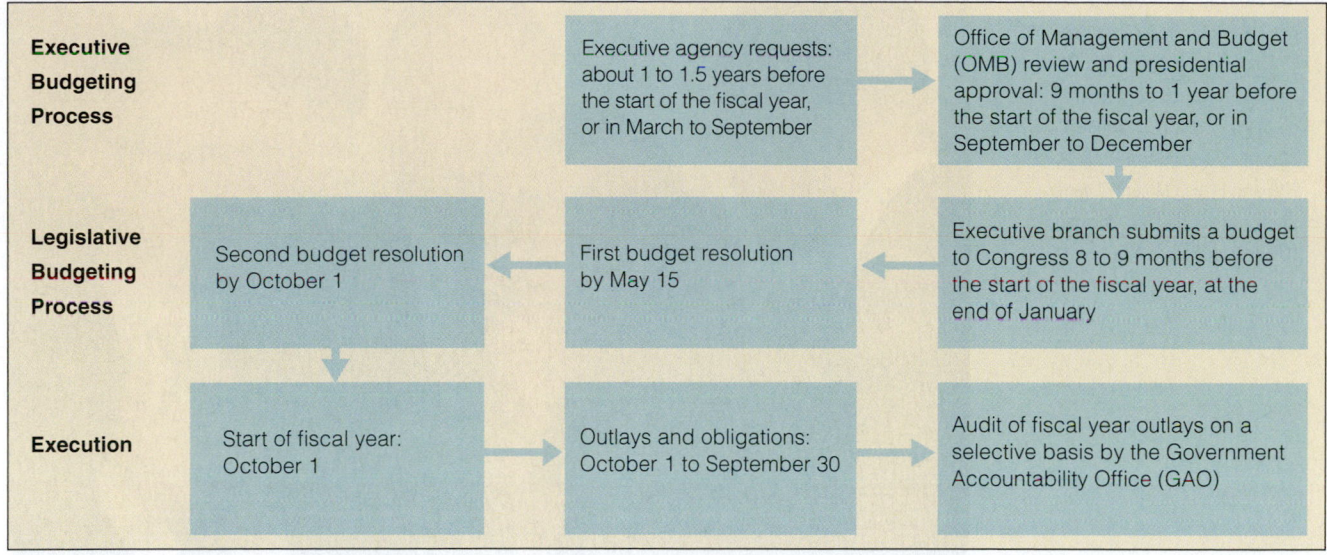

Executive Budgeting Process

| Executive agency requests: about 1 to 1.5 years before the start of the fiscal year, or in March to September | Office of Management and Budget (OMB) review and presidential approval: 9 months to 1 year before the start of the fiscal year, or in September to December |

Legislative Budgeting Process

| Second budget resolution by October 1 | First budget resolution by May 15 | Executive branch submits a budget to Congress 8 to 9 months before the start of the fiscal year, at the end of January |

Execution

| Start of fiscal year: October 1 | Outlays and obligations: October 1 to September 30 | Audit of fiscal year outlays on a selective basis by the Government Accountability Office (GAO) |

submit their requests for funding for the next fiscal year. By the end of the summer, each agency must submit a formal request to the OMB.

In actuality, the "budget season" begins with the **fall review.** At this time, the OMB looks at budget requests and, in almost all cases, routinely cuts them back. Although the OMB works within guidelines established by the president, specific decisions often are left to the OMB director and the director's associates. By the beginning of November, the director's review begins. The director meets with Cabinet secretaries and budget officers. Time becomes crucial. The budget must be completed by January so that it can be included in the *Economic Report of the President.*

Fall Review
The annual process in which the Office of Management and Budget, after receiving formal federal agency requests for funding for the next fiscal year, reviews the requests, makes changes, and submits its recommendations to the president.

CONGRESS FACES THE BUDGET

In January, nine months before the fiscal year starts, the president takes the OMB's proposed budget, approves it, and submits it to Congress. Then the congressional budgeting process takes over. The budgeting process involves two steps. First, Congress must authorize funds to be spent. The **authorization** is a formal declaration by the appropriate Congressional committee that a certain amount of funding may be available to an agency. Congressional committees and subcommittees look at the proposals from the executive branch and the Congressional Budget Office in making the decision to authorize funds. After the funds are authorized, they must be appropriated by Congress. The appropriations committees of both the House and the Senate forward spending bills to their respective bodies. The **appropriation** of funds occurs when the final bill is passed.

The budget process involves large sums. For example, President Barack Obama's proposed budget for fiscal year 2011 called for expenditures of $3.83 trillion, or $3,830,000,000,000. When forming the budget for a given year, Congress and the president must take into account revenues, primarily in the form of taxes, as well as expenditures to balance the budget. If spending exceeds the amount brought in by taxes, the government runs a budget deficit (and increases the public debt). For

Authorization
A formal declaration by a legislative committee that a certain amount of funding may be available to an agency. Some authorizations terminate in a year; others are renewable automatically, without further congressional action.

Appropriation
The passage, by Congress, of a spending bill specifying the amount of authorized funds that actually will be allocated for an agency's use.

example, although President Obama' proposed budget for fiscal year 2011 called for expenditures of approximately $3.83 trillion, projected revenues from taxes amounted to only about $2.56 trillion, leaving a deficit of $1.27 trillion.

With these large sums in play, representatives and senators who chair key committees find it relatively easy to slip spending proposals into a variety of bills. These proposals may have nothing to do with the ostensible purpose of the bill. Are such earmarked appropriations good policy?

BUDGET RESOLUTIONS

First Budget Resolution
A resolution passed by Congress in May that sets overall revenue and spending goals for the following fiscal year.

Second Budget Resolution
A resolution passed by Congress in September that sets "binding" limits on taxes and spending for the following fiscal year.

Continuing Resolution
A temporary funding law that Congress passes when an appropriations bill has not been decided by the beginning of the new fiscal year on October 1.

The **first budget resolution** by Congress is scheduled to be passed in May of each year. It sets overall revenue goals and spending targets. During the summer, bargaining among all the concerned parties takes place. Spending and tax laws that are drawn up during this period are supposed to be guided by the May congressional budget resolution.

By September, Congress is scheduled to pass its **second budget resolution,** one that will set "binding" limits on taxes and spending for the fiscal year beginning October 1. Bills passed before that date that do not fit within the limits of the budget resolution are supposed to be changed.

In actuality, between 1978 and 1996 Congress did not pass a complete budget by October 1. In other words, generally, Congress does not follow its own rules. Budget resolutions are passed late, and when they are passed, they are not treated as binding. In each fiscal year that starts without a budget, every agency operates on the basis of a **continuing resolution,** which enables the agency to keep on doing whatever it was doing the previous year with the same amount of funding. Even continuing resolutions have not always been passed on time.

YOU CAN MAKE A Difference

WHY SHOULD YOU CARE ABOUT CONGRESS?

The legislation that Congress passes can directly affect your life. Consider, for example, the major reform of American health policy and health insurance passed in 2010. For the time being, this bill will make it possible for young people under 26 to stay on their parents' health insurance policy. When you enter the workplace, the health insurance options that may be offered to you by your employer will be regulated by the new policies. If you have a medical condition that makes obtaining health insurance difficult, the new law will, eventually, prohibit discrimination against you in obtaining health insurance. And, finally, it is likely that these new rules will make health insurance more expensive than it is today.

Additionally, congressional legislation will affect the kind of car you buy, your use of the Internet, your access to cable or satellite TV, and how much you pay for gas for your car. Recent changes in law will make the federal government your source for student loans. So you had better pay attention to what Congress is doing and what your representative or senator is voting for.

You can make a difference in our democracy simply by going to the polls on election day and voting for the candidates you would like to represent you in Congress. It goes without saying, though, that to cast an informed vote, you need to know how your congressional representatives stand on the issues and, if they are incumbents, how they have voted on bills that are important to you.

WHAT CAN YOU DO?

To contact a member of Congress, start by going to the Web sites of the U.S. House of Representatives (www. house.gov) and the U.S. Senate (www.senate.gov). For the House, finding your representative is easy: Just type in your zip code and you will be directed to the member's Web site. For the Senate, look for your state.

Not all congressional Web sites are equally informative. Often, these Web sites post pictures of lawmakers, state flags, and pictures from their districts. Many sites contain congressional biographies, constituent services, sponsored legislation, and contact information. Some congressional Web sites have interactive polls and regularly updated blogs. In 2007, the Sunlight Foundation conducted the Congressional Web Site Investigation Project. This group wanted to examine how well members of Congress spend taxpayer money to maintain official Web sites. They used everyday citizens to evaluate their own congressional representatives' Web sites for transparency and accountability. Do these Web sites allow responsible citizens to exercise oversight over their representatives and hold them accountable for their performance? Go to www.sunlightlabs.com to find the project's results.

You can also contact your representatives using one of the following addresses or phone numbers:

United States House of Representatives
Washington, DC 20515
202-224-3121

United States Senate
Washington, DC 20510
202-224-3121

CONGRESSWOMAN SHEILA JACKSON LEE lists her voting record on her Web site making it easy for constituents to track her positions on issues they care about. (Courtesy of Congresswoman Sheila Jackson Lee)

Interest groups also track the voting records of members of Congress and rate the members on the issues. Project Vote Smart is supported by thousands of volunteers, conservative and liberal, who research the backgrounds and records of thousands of political candidates and elected officials to provide citizens with their voting records, campaign contributions, public statements, biographical data, and evaluations from more than 150 competing special-interest groups. You can contact Project Vote Smart at

> Project Vote Smart
> One Common Ground
> Philipsburg, MT 59858
> 1-888-VOTE-SMART (1-888-868-3762)
> www.votesmart.org

Nonpartisan, independent, and nonprofit, the Center for Responsive Politics (CRP) educates voters through research that tracks campaign contributions and lobbying data. They "count cash to make change" in government and strive to inform voters about how money in politics affects their lives. You can contact the CRP at

> The Center for Responsive Politics
> 1101 14th St. NW, Suite 1030
> Washington, DC 20005-5635
> 202-857-0044
> www.opensecrets.org

REFERENCES

Kelly McCormack, "Congressional Websites: The Bright, Bland and Bizarre," The Hill.com, accessed June 20, 2007.

Conor Kenny, "Participatory Democracy: Rate Your Senator's and Representative's Web Pages," PRWatch.org, accessed February 21, 2007.

"About Project Vote Smart," www.votesmart.org/program_about_pvs.php?q=print.

"Our Mission," www.opensecrets.org/about/index.php.

KEY TERMS

appropriation 437
authorization 437
bicameralism 404
Blue Dog Democrats 433
casework 405
conference committee 426
conservative coalition 432
constituent 403
continuing resolution 438
direct primary 415
discharge petition 424
earmarks 434
enumerated power 407
executive budget 436
fall review 437
filibuster 411
first budget resolution 438
fiscal year (FY) 436
franking 422

gerrymandering 417
hillstyle 403
homestyle 403
instructed delegate 405
joint committee 426
justiciable question 417
lawmaking 404
logrolling 404
majority leader of the House 429
minority leader of the House 431
ombudsperson 406
oversight 407
party identifier 415
pork 434
president pro tempore 431
reapportionment 417
redistricting 417

representation 404
Rule 411
Rules Committee 411
safe seat 427
second budget resolution 438
select committee 426
Senate majority leader 432
Senate minority leader 432
seniority system 427
Speaker of the House 428
spring review 436
standing committee 425
trustee 405
Unanimous Consent Agreement 411
unorthodox lawmaking 411
whip 431

CHAPTER SUMMARY

1. **Why is the Congress the most powerful branch of government?** The authors of the Constitution believed that the bulk of national power should be in the legislature because it represents the voters most directly. All legislative power rests in the Congress. The Constitution states that Congress will consist of two chambers. A result of the Connecticut Compromise, this bicameral structure established a balanced legislature, with the membership in the House of Representatives based on population and the membership in the Senate based on the equality of states.

2. **Do members of Congress serve their constituents or the nation as a whole?** Members of the House and the Senate cultivate votes in their constituencies through service, visits, and bringing home federal dollars for projects. At the same time, they must participate in debate and lawmaking for the nation as a whole, including casting votes for legislation that may be of no interest to their constituents or may, in fact, not be beneficial to them. The career of a legislator is determined both by his or her reelection and by the party leadership in Congress, so fulfilling both roles is necessary.

   The functions of Congress include (1) lawmaking, (2) representation, (3) service to constituents, (4) oversight, (5) public education, and (6) conflict resolution.

3. The first 17 clauses of Article I, Section 8, of the Constitution specify most of the enumerated, or expressed, powers of Congress, including the right to impose taxes, to borrow money, to regulate commerce, and to declare war. Besides its enumerated powers, Congress enjoys the right to "make all Laws which shall be necessary and proper for carrying into Execution the foregoing Powers, and all other Powers vested by this Constitution in the Government of the United States, or in any Department or Officer thereof." This is called the elastic, or necessary and proper, clause.

4. There are 435 members in the House of Representatives and 100 members in the Senate. Owing to its larger size, the House has more formal rules. The Senate tradition of unlimited debate (filibustering) dates back to 1790 and has been used over the years to frustrate the passage of bills. Under Senate Rule 22, cloture can be used to shut off debate on a bill.

5. Members of Congress are not typical American citizens. They are older and wealthier than most Americans, disproportionately white and male, and more likely to be trained in professional occupations.

6. Congressional elections are operated by the individual state governments, which must abide by rules established by the Constitution and national statutes. Most candidates for Congress must win nomination through a direct primary. The overwhelming majority of incumbent representatives and a smaller proportion of senators who run for reelection are successful. A complicated aspect of congressional elections is apportionment—the allocation of legislative seats to constituencies. The Supreme Court's "one person, one vote" rule has been applied to equalize the populations of congressional and state legislative districts.

7. Members of Congress are well paid and enjoy benefits such as franking privileges. Members of Congress have personal and committee staff members available to them and also receive many legal privileges and immunities.

8. Most of the actual work of legislating is performed by committees and subcommittees within Congress. Legislation introduced into the House or Senate is assigned to the appropriate standing committees for review. Select committees are created for a limited time for a specific purpose. Joint committees are formed by the concurrent action of both chambers and consist of members from each chamber. Conference committees are special joint committees set up to achieve agreement between the House and the Senate on the exact wording of legislative acts passed by both chambers in different forms. The seniority rule, which is usually followed, specifies that the longest-serving member of the majority party will be the chairperson of a committee.

9. The foremost power holder in the House of Representatives is the Speaker of the House. Other leaders are the House majority leader, the House minority leader, and the majority and minority whips. Formally, the vice president is the presiding officer of the Senate, with the most senior member of the majority party serving as the president pro tempore to preside when the vice president is absent. Actual leadership in the Senate rests with the majority leader, the minority leader, and their whips.

10. **How do members of Congress decide their votes?** A bill becomes law by progressing through both chambers of Congress and their appropriate standing and joint committees to the president. Members are usually most influenced in their voting decisions by their party affiliation, their constituency's interests, their own interests, and cues given by other legislators.

11. The budget process for a fiscal year begins with the preparation of an executive budget by the president. This is reviewed by the Office of Management and Budget and then sent to Congress, which is supposed to pass a final budget by the end of September. Since 1978, Congress generally has not followed its own time rules.

SELECTED PRINT, MEDIA, AND ONLINE RESOURCES

PRINT RESOURCES

Barone, Michael, and Grant Ujifusa. *The Almanac of American Politics, 2011.* Washington, DC: National Journal, 2011. This book, which is published biannually, is a comprehensive summary of current political information on each member of Congress, his or her state or congressional district, recent congressional election results, key votes, ratings by various organizations, sources of campaign contributions, and records of campaign expenditures.

Davidson, Roger H., and Walter J. Oleszek. *Congress and Its Members,* 11th ed. Washington, DC: CQ Press, 2008. This classic looks carefully at the "two Congresses," the one in Washington and the role played by congresspersons at home.

Just, Ward S. *The Congressman Who Loved Flaubert.* New York: Carrol and Graf Publishers, 1990. This fictional account of a career politician was first published in 1973 and is still a favorite with students of political science. Ward Just is renowned for his political fiction, and particularly for his examination of character and motivation.

Mann, Thomas B., and Norman J. Ornstein. *The Broken Branch: How Congress Is Failing America and How to Get It Back on Track.* New York: Oxford University Press, 2006. These two political scientists believe that Congress is more dysfunctional now than ever before. They argue that there is too much partisan bickering and internal rancor. These two scholars of government and politics present a blueprint for reform.

Rangel, Charles B., and Leon Wynter. *And I Haven't Had a Bad Day Since: The Memoir of Charles B. Rangel's Journey from the Streets of Harlem to the Halls of Congress.* New York: Scribner, 2007. This biographical account of one of Congress's most flamboyant members tells his story (obviously) from the streets of Harlem to the halls of Congress. Rangel, a high school dropout, became a lawyer and then a member of Congress. He helped create the earned-income tax credit for working families.

MEDIA RESOURCES

Charlie Wilson's War: One of the best movies of 2007, starring Tom Hanks and Julia Roberts. This hilarious film is based on the true story of how Wilson, a hard-living, hard-drinking representative from Texas, almost single-handedly won a billion dollars in funding for the Afghans, who were fighting a Russian invasion. When equipped with heat-seeking missiles, the Afghans win. Philip Seymour Hoffman steals the show portraying a rogue CIA operative.

The Congress—In one of his earliest efforts (1988), filmmaker Ken Burns profiles the history of Congress. Narration is by David McCullough, and those interviewed include David Broker, Alistair Cooke, and Cokie Roberts. PBS Home Video rereleased this film on DVD in 2003.

Congress: A Day in the Life of a Representative—From political meetings to social functions to campaigning, this 1995 program examines what politicians really do. Featured representatives are Tim Roemer (a Democrat from Indiana) and Sue Myrick (a Republican from North Carolina).

Mr. Smith Goes to Washington—A 1939 film in which Jimmy Stewart plays the naïve congressman who is quickly educated in Washington. A true American political classic.

Porked: Earmarks for Profit—A 2008 release from Fox News Channel that investigates congressional earmarks. Fox reporters contend that pork wastes tax dollars. Beyond that, the network also claims that some members of Congress have funded projects that benefited their own bank accounts.

The Seduction of Joe Tynan—A 1979 film in which Alan Alda plays a young senator who must face serious decisions about his political role and his private life.

ONLINE RESOURCES

Congressional Budget Office provides Congress with non-partisan analyses for economic and budget decisions and with estimates required for the congressional budget process: www.cbo.gov

Congressional Quarterly a publication that reports on Congress: www.cq.com

GPO Access a service of the U.S. Government Printing Office that provides free electronic access to a wealth of important information products produced by the federal government: www.gpoaccess.gov

The Hill a congressional newspaper that publishes daily when Congress is in session, with a special focus on business and lobbying, political campaigns, and goings-on on Capitol Hill: http://thehill.com/

Roll Call the newspaper of the Capitol that provides an inside view into what's going on in Washington, D.C.: www.rollcall.com

United States Congress To view the schedule of activities taking place in Congress and utilize a wealth of other resources, use the following Web sites: www.senate.gov and www.house.gov

13

President Barack Obama delivers a statement at the White House after a meeting about the oil spill with British Petroleum executives. (AP Photo/Manuel Balce Ceneta)

The President

QUESTIONS TO CONSIDER

What roles in American government does the President play?

How is presidential success judged?

What are the powers of the president as chief executive?

CHAPTER CONTENTS

what if...   There Were No Executive Privilege?

BACKGROUND

When a U.S. president wishes to keep information secret, he or she can invoke executive privilege. Although there is no mention of executive privilege in the Constitution, presidents from George Washington to George W. Bush invoked this privilege in response to perceived encroachments on the executive branch by Congress and by the judiciary. For example, in 2006, when two congressional committees were investigating the federal government's response to Hurricane Katrina, the Bush administration cited the need for confidentiality of executive-branch communications as justification for refusing to turn over certain documents, including e-mail correspondence involving White House staff members. The administration had previously refused to release the names of oil company executives who had advised Vice President Cheney on energy policy.

Nonetheless, Congress could try to prohibit the use of executive privilege by passing a law. Alternatively, the Supreme Court could hold that executive privilege is an unconstitutional exercise of executive power.

WHAT IF THERE WERE NO EXECUTIVE PRIVILEGE?

If there were no executive privilege, a president would have to be aware that all of his or her words, documents, and actions could be made public. We know from 20th century history that when a president does not have full executive privilege to protect information, the results can be devastating.

President Richard Nixon (served 1969–1974) had tape-recorded hundreds of hours of conversations in the Oval Office. During a scandal involving a cover-up (the Watergate scandal), Congress requested those tapes. Nixon invoked executive privilege and refused to turn them over. Ultimately, the Supreme Court ordered him to do so, however, and the tapes provided damning information about Nixon's role in the purported cover-up of illegal activities. Rather than face impeachment, Nixon resigned the presidency.

Clearly, if executive privilege were eliminated, it is unlikely that conversations between the president and other members of the executive branch would be recorded or otherwise documented. As a result, we would have fewer records of an administration's activities than we do today.

EXECUTIVE PRIVILEGE IN A WORLD FILLED WITH TERRORISM

Following the terrorist attacks on September 11, 2001, Attorney General John Ashcroft advised federal agencies "to lean toward withholding information whenever possible." Often, the Bush administration attempted to withhold information from Congress and the courts, not just the public. In one troubling example, a top civil servant was threatened with being fired if he told Congress the true projected cost of the administration's Medicare prescription drug bill. Of course, without executive privilege, the president might experience problems in waging a war on terrorism. While Congress has procedures that can be used to guard sensitive information, it is unaccustomed to keeping secrets and often finds it hard to do so. The very size of the Congress makes it difficult to keep secrets. There is a large number of members—or staff—who might leak information.

PAST, PRESENT, AND FUTURE PRESIDENTIAL PAPERS

The Bush administration attempted to control not only its own records but also those of former presidents, even against their wishes. Soon after September 11, 2001, President Bush signed Executive Order 13233, which provided that former presidents' private papers can be released only with the approval of both the former president in question and the current one. Former president Bill Clinton publicly objected, saying that he wanted all of his papers released to the public. Nevertheless, the Bush administration denied access to documents surrounding the 177 pardons that Clinton granted in the last days of his presidency.

If executive privilege were eliminated, the White House would have a difficult time regulating the flow of past presidential records into the public forum. The behavior of presidents and their administrations would certainly change. They might simply insist that there be no record of sensitive conversations. If so, future Americans would lose much of the historical background for America's domestic and international actions.

FOR CRITICAL ANALYSIS

1. The history of executive privilege dates back to 1796, when President George Washington refused a request by the House for certain documents. Given the changes that have taken place since that time, should executive privilege be eliminated—or is it even more necessary today than it was at that time?

2. What would be the costs to the nation if executive privilege were eliminated?

THE WRITERS OF the Constitution created the presidency of the United States without any models to follow. Nowhere else in the world was there a democratically selected chief executive. What the founders did not want was a king. In fact, given their previous experience with royal governors in the colonies, many of the delegates to the Constitutional Convention wanted to create a very weak executive who could not veto legislation. Other delegates, especially those who had witnessed the need for a strong leader in the Revolutionary army, believed a strong executive would be necessary for the new republic.

Overall, however, the delegates did not spend much time discussing the actual powers to be granted to the president, leaving those questions to the Committee on Detail. The delegates, in the end, created a chief executive who had enough powers granted in the Constitution to balance those of Congress.[1]

The power exercised by each president who has held the office has been scrutinized and judged by historians, political scientists, the media, and the public. The personalities and foibles of each president have also been investigated and judged by many. Indeed, it would seem that Americans are fascinated by presidential power and by the persons who hold the office. In this chapter, after looking at who can become president and at the process involved, we will examine closely the nature and extent of the constitutional powers held by the president, including whether the president can decide which records can be made public and which of his aides might testify before Congress, as discussed in the What If ... feature opening this chapter.

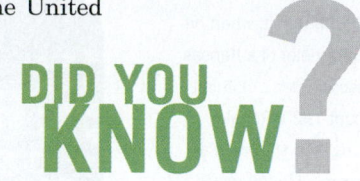

That George Washington's salary of $25,000 in 1789 was the equivalent of about $600,000 in today's dollars?

That the salary of the president did not increase from 1969 until 2001, when it was raised to $400,000?

WHO CAN BECOME PRESIDENT?

The requirements for becoming president, as outlined in Article II, Section 1, of the Constitution, are not overwhelmingly stringent:

> No person except a natural born Citizen, or a Citizen of the United States, at the time of the Adoption of this Constitution, shall be eligible to the Office of President; neither shall any Person be eligible to that Office who shall not have attained to the Age of thirty-five Years, and been fourteen Years a Resident within the United States.

The only question that arises about these qualifications relates to the term *natural-born citizen*. Does that mean only citizens born in the United States and its territories? What about a child born to a U.S. citizen (or to a couple who are U.S. citizens) visiting or living in another country? Although the Supreme Court has never directly addressed the question, it is reasonable to expect that someone would be eligible if her or his parents were Americans. The first presidents, after all, were not even American citizens at birth, and others were born in areas that did not become part of the United States until later. These questions were debated when George Romney, who was born in Chihuahua, Mexico, made a serious bid for the Republican presidential nomination in the 1960s.[2] Similar questions were raised about the 2008 Republican candidate, John McCain, who was born in Panama on an American military base. Those questions were quickly dismissed because it is clear that children born abroad to American citizens are considered natural-born Americans.

[1]Forrest McDonald, *The American Presidency: An Intellectual History* (Lawrence, KS: University Press of Kansas, 1994), p. 179.
[2]George Romney was governor of Michigan from 1963 to 1969. Romney was not nominated for the presidency, and the issue remains unresolved.

HARRY TRUMAN, left, when he was the proprietor of a Kansas City, Missouri, men's clothing store, about 1920. Ronald Reagan, right, is shown as a frontier marshal in the movie *Law and Order*, released in 1953. Compared to members of Congress, presidents have had a more varied background. How would varied life experiences benefit a president? (Truman, courtesy of Truman Presidential Library and Museum; Reagan, AP Photo/ Universal)

When Arnold Schwarzenegger became governor of California, many of his supporters suggested that he might be a potential presidential candidate. But Schwarzenegger, who was born in Austria, is a naturalized U.S. citizen and therefore is ineligible to become president under the Constitution. Early in his administration, a movement began to amend the Constitution to allow *naturalized* citizens to become president; however, as time passed, the idea lost support.

The American dream is symbolized by the statement that "anybody can become president of this country." It is true that in modern times, presidents have included a haberdasher (Harry Truman—for a short period of time), a peanut farmer (Jimmy Carter), and an actor (Ronald Reagan). But if you examine the list of presidents in the appendix, you will see that the most common previous occupation of presidents in this country has been that of lawyer. Out of 43 presidents, 26 have been lawyers, and many have been wealthy. (There have been fewer lawyers in the last century, in part because senators, who are likely to be lawyers, have had a difficult time being elected president. Senators have often faced the problem of defending their voting records.)

Although the Constitution states that the minimum-age requirement for the presidency is 35 years, most presidents have been much older than that when they assumed office. John F. Kennedy, at the age of 43, was the youngest elected president, and the oldest was Ronald Reagan, at age 69. The average age at inauguration has been 54. There has clearly been a demographic bias in the selection of presidents. Until 2009, all had been white, male, and from the Protestant tradition, except for John F. Kennedy, who was a Roman Catholic. The inauguration of Barack Obama, a man of mixed race—and, indeed, of Kenyan and American ancestry—was an extraordinary milestone in American history. Presidents have been men of great stature (such as George Washington) and men in whom leadership qualities were not so pronounced (such as Warren Harding; served 1921–1923). A presidential candidate usually has experience as a vice president, senator, or state governor. Former governors have been especially successful at winning the presidency, because they can make the legitimate claims to have executive experience and to be electable.

THE PROCESS OF BECOMING PRESIDENT

Major and minor political parties nominate candidates for president and vice president at national conventions every four years. As discussed in Chapter 9, the nation's voters do not elect a president and vice president directly, but rather cast ballots for presidential electors, who then vote for president and vice president in the electoral college.

Because winning the election requires winning the majority of electoral votes, it is conceivable that someone could be elected to the office of the presidency without having a majority of the popular vote cast. In four cases, candidates won elections even though their major opponents received more popular votes. One of those cases occurred in 2000, when George W. Bush won the electoral college vote and became president even though his opponent, Al Gore, won the popular vote. In elections when more than two candidates were running for office, many presidential candidates have won with less than 50 percent of the total popular votes cast for all candidates—including Abraham Lincoln, Woodrow Wilson, Harry Truman, John F. Kennedy, Richard Nixon, and, in 1992, Bill Clinton. Independent candidate Ross Perot garnered a surprising 19 percent of the vote in 1992. Remember from Chapter 9 that no president has won a majority of votes from the entire voting-age population.

Twice, the electoral college has failed to give any candidate a majority. At this point, the election is thrown into the House of Representatives. The president is then chosen from among the three candidates having the most electoral college votes, as noted in Chapter 9. Thomas Jefferson and Aaron Burr tied in the electoral college in 1800. This happened because the Constitution had not been explicit in indicating which of the two electoral votes were for president and which were for vice president. In 1804, the **Twelfth Amendment** clarified the matter by requiring that the president and vice president be chosen separately. In 1824, the House again had to make a choice, this time among William H. Crawford, Andrew Jackson, and John Quincy Adams. It chose Adams, even though Jackson had more electoral and popular votes.

Twelfth Amendment
An amendment to the Constitution, adopted in 1804, that specifies the separate election of the president and vice president by the electoral college.

THE MANY ROLES OF THE PRESIDENT

The Constitution speaks briefly about the duties and obligations of the president. Based on this brief list of powers and on the precedents of history, the presidency has grown into a very complicated job that requires balancing at least five constitutional roles: (1) head of state, (2) chief executive, (3) commander in chief of the armed forces, (4) chief diplomat, and (5) chief legislator of the United States. Here we examine each of these significant presidential functions, or roles. It is worth noting that one person plays all these roles simultaneously and that these roles may at times come into conflict.

HEAD OF STATE

Every nation has at least one person who is the ceremonial head of state. In most democratic governments, the role of **head of state** is given to someone other than the chief executive, who leads the executive branch of government. In Britain, for example, the head of state is the queen. In much of Europe, the prime minister is the chief executive, and the head of state is the president. But in the United States, the president is both chief executive and head of state. According to William Howard Taft, as head of state the president symbolizes the "dignity and majesty" of the American people.

Head of State
The role of the president as ceremonial head of the government.

PRESIDENT BARACK OBAMA
and Mexican president Felipe
Calderon walk through the
White House portico during the
state visit of the Mexican leader.
(bw2/ZUMA Press/Newscom)

As head of state, the president engages in many activities that are largely symbolic or ceremonial, such as the following:

- Decorating war heroes.
- Throwing out the first pitch to open the baseball season.
- Dedicating parks and post offices.
- Receiving visiting heads of state at the White House.
- Going on official state visits to other countries.
- Making personal telephone calls to astronauts.
- Representing the nation at times of national mourning, such as after the terrorist attacks of September 11, 2001; after the loss of the space shuttle *Columbia* in 2003; and after the destruction from Hurricane Katrina in 2005.

Some students of the American political system believe that having the president serve as both the chief executive and the head of state drastically limits the time available to do "real" work. Not all presidents have agreed with this conclusion, however—particularly those presidents who have skillfully blended these two roles with their role as politician. Being head of state gives the president tremendous public exposure, which can be an important asset in a campaign for reelection. When that exposure is positive, it helps the president deal with Congress over proposed legislation and increases the chances of being reelected—or getting the candidates of the president's party elected.

CHIEF EXECUTIVE

According to the Constitution, "The executive Power shall be vested in a President of the United States of America. ... [H]e may require the Opinion, in writing, of the principal Officer in each of the executive Departments, upon any Subject relating to the Duties of their respective Offices ... and he shall nominate, and by and with the Advice and Consent of the Senate, shall appoint ... Officers of the United States. ... [H]e shall take Care that the Laws be faithfully executed."

As **chief executive**, the president is constitutionally bound to enforce the acts of Congress, the judgments of federal courts, and treaties signed by the United States. The duty to "faithfully execute" the laws has been a source of constitutional power for presidents. Is the president allowed to reject certain parts of legislation if he or she believes that they are unconstitutional? This question relates to so-called **signing statements**, which are written declarations made by presidents that accompany legislation.

For at least 175 years, presidents have used signing statements to make substantive constitutional pronouncements on the bill being signed. In 1830, President Andrew Jackson created a controversy when he signed a bill and at the same time sent to Congress a message that restricted the reach of the statute. In 1842, President John Tyler expressed misgivings in a signing statement about the constitutionality and policy of an entire act. Presidents Abraham Lincoln, Andrew Johnson, Theodore Roosevelt, Woodrow Wilson, and Franklin Roosevelt all used signing statements.

As for the legality of the practice, the Department of Justice has advised the last four administrations that the Constitution provides the president with the authority to decline to enforce a clearly unconstitutional law. Four justices of the Supreme Court joined in an

That 21 presidents have served only one term in office?

Chief Executive
The role of the president as head of the executive branch of the government.

Signing Statement
A written declaration that a president may make when signing a bill into law. Usually, such statements point out sections of the law that the president deems unconstitutional.

opinion that the president may resist laws that encroach upon presidential powers by "disregarding them when they're unconstitutional."[3]

After George W. Bush took office, he issued signing statements on more than 800 statutes, more than all of the previous presidents combined. He also tended to use the statements for a different purpose. When earlier presidents issued signing statements, they were normally used to instruct agencies on how to execute the laws or for similar purposes. In contrast, many (if not most) of Bush's signing statements served notice that he believed parts of bills that he signed were unconstitutional or might violate national security.

Some members of Congress are not so concerned about Bush's signing statements. Senator John Cornyn (R.-Tex.) says that Bush's signing statements are only "expressions of presidential opinion" and carry no legal weight. According to Cornyn, federal courts would be unlikely to consider the statements when interpreting the laws with which they were issued.[4]

The Powers of Appointment and Removal. To assist in the various tasks of the chief executive, the president has a federal bureaucracy (see Chapter 14), which consists of more than 2.7 million federal civilian employees. You might think that the president, as head of the largest bureaucracy in the United States, wields enormous power. The president, however, only nominally runs the executive bureaucracy. Most government positions are filled by **civil service** employees, who generally gain government employment through a merit system rather than presidential appointment.[5] Therefore, even though the president has important **appointment power**, it is limited to Cabinet and sub-cabinet jobs, federal judgeships, agency heads, and several thousand lesser jobs. For example, of the more than 600,000 civilian jobs in the Department of Defense, the president may appoint fewer than 700. The largest number of jobs available for presidential appointments is in the State Department (more than 1,200), but many of those are ambassadorships, usually given to major donors and supporters of the president. Soon after each presidential election, the government publishes a list of these specific jobs in a volume titled, "The Plum Book: Policy and Supporting Positions." It is so-called because these have long been considered "plum jobs."

The president's power to remove from office those officials who are not doing a good job or who do not agree with the president is not explicitly granted by the Constitution and has been limited with regard to certain agencies. In 1926, however, a Supreme Court decision prevented Congress from interfering with the president's ability to fire those executive-branch officials whom the president had appointed with Senate approval.[6] There are 10 agencies whose directors the president can remove at any time, including the Arms Control and Disarmament Agency, the Commission on Civil Rights, the Environmental Protection Agency, the General Services Administration, and the Small Business Administration. In addition, the president can remove all heads of Cabinet departments, all individuals in the Executive Office of the President, and all political appointees.

Harry Truman spoke candidly of the difficulties a president faces in trying to control the executive bureaucracy. On leaving office, he referred to the problems that Dwight Eisenhower, as a former general of the army, was going to have: "He'll sit here and he'll

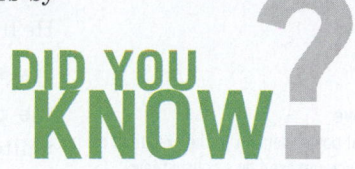

DID YOU KNOW?

That Thomas Jefferson was the first president to be inaugurated in Washington, D.C., where he walked to the Capitol from a boardinghouse, took the oath, made a brief speech in the Senate chamber, and then walked back home?

Civil Service
A collective term for the body of employees working for the government. Generally, civil service is understood to apply to all those who gain government employment through a merit system.

Appointment Power
The authority vested in the president to fill a government office or position. Positions filled by presidential appointment include those in the executive branch and the federal judiciary, commissioned officers in the armed forces, and members of the independent regulatory commissions.

---

[3]*Freytag v. C.I.R.,* 501 U.S. 868 (1991).
[4]T. J. Halstead, "Presidential Signing Statements: Constitutional and Institutional Implications" (Washington, DC: Congressional Research Service, September 17, 2007).
[5]See Chapter 14 for a discussion of the Civil Service Reform Act.
[6]*Meyers v. United States,* 272 U.S. 52 (1926).

say do this! do that! and nothing will happen. Poor Ike—it won't be a bit like the Army. He'll find it very frustrating."[7]

The Power to Grant Reprieves and Pardons. Section 2 of Article II of the Constitution gives the president the power to grant **reprieves** and **pardons** for offenses against the United States except in cases of impeachment. All pardons are administered by the Office of the Pardon Attorney in the Department of Justice. In principle, a pardon is granted to remedy a mistake made in a conviction.

The United States Supreme Court upheld the president's power to grant reprieves and pardons in a 1925 case concerning a pardon granted by the president to an individual convicted of contempt of court. The judiciary had contended that only judges had the authority to convict individuals for contempt of court when court orders were violated and that the courts should be free from interference by the executive branch. The Court simply stated that the president could grant reprieves or pardons for all offenses "either before trial, during trial, or after trial, by individuals, or by classes, conditionally or absolutely, and this without modification or regulation by Congress."[8]

The power to pardon can also be used to apply to large groups of individuals who may be subject to indictment and trial. In 1977, President Jimmy Carter extended amnesty to all of the Vietnam War resisters who avoided the military draft by fleeing to Canada. More than 50,000 individuals were allowed to come back to the United States, free from the possibility of prosecution. The power to reprieve individuals allows the president to extend clemency to federal prisoners, usually on humanitarian grounds. However, in 1999, President Bill Clinton extended a conditional offer of clemency to a group of Puerto Rican nationalists who had been tried for planning terrorist attacks in the United States. The condition was for them to renounce the use of terrorist tactics and to not associate with other nationalists who advocate violence. Twelve accepted the offer, while two refused to accept the conditions.

In a controversial decision, President Gerald Ford pardoned former president Richard Nixon for his role in the Watergate affair before any charges were brought in court. Just before George W. Bush's inauguration in 2001, President Clinton announced pardons for almost 200 persons. Some of these pardons were controversial and appeared to be political favors.

COMMANDER IN CHIEF

The president, according to the Constitution, "shall be Commander in Chief of the Army and Navy of the United States, and of the Militia of the several States, when called into the actual Service of the United States." In other words, the armed forces are under civilian, rather than military, control.

Wartime Powers. Certainly, those who wrote the Constitution had George Washington in mind when they made the president the **commander in chief**. The founders did not, however, expect presidents to lead the country into war without congressional authorization. Remember from Chapters 2 and 12 that Congress is given the power to declare war. As the United States grew in military power and global reach, presidents became much more likely to send troops into armed combat either in crisis situations or with

---

Reprieve
A formal postponement of the execution of a sentence imposed by a court of law.

Pardon
A release from the punishment for or legal consequences of a crime; a pardon can be granted by the president before or after a conviction.

Commander in Chief
The role of the president as supreme commander of the military forces of the United States and of the state National Guard units when they are called into federal service.

---

[7]Quoted in Richard E. Neustadt, *Presidential Power: The Politics of Leadership* (New York: Wiley, 1960), p. 9. Truman may not have considered the amount of politics involved in decision making in the upper echelon of the army.
[8]*Ex parte Grossman*, 267 U.S. 87 (1925).

an authorizing resolution short of a declaration of war. The last war to be fought under a congressional declaration was World War II.

Although we do not expect our president to lead the troops into battle, presidents as commanders in chief have wielded dramatic power. Harry Truman made the difficult decision to drop atomic bombs on Hiroshima and Nagasaki in 1945 to force Japan to surrender and thus bring World War II to an end. Lyndon B. Johnson ordered bombing missions against North Vietnam in the 1960s, and he personally selected some of the targets. Richard Nixon decided to invade Cambodia in 1970, which was widely condemned as going beyond his power as commander in chief.

The president is the ultimate decision maker in military matters and, as such, has the final authority to launch a nuclear strike using missiles or bombs. Everywhere the president goes, so too goes the "football"—a briefcase filled with all the codes necessary to order a nuclear attack. Only the president has the power to order the use of nuclear force.

The use of military force by presidents has raised some very thorny issues for the balance between Congress and the presidency. Harry Truman sent U.S. troops to Korea under a United Nations resolution, and Lyndon Johnson escalated the U.S. involvement in Vietnam under the quickly passed Gulf of Tonkin Resolution. George W. Bush invaded Iraq with congressional authorization. In none of these cases did Congress and the public expect extended wars with many casualties.

Presidents have also used military force without any congressional authorization, particularly in emergency situations. Ronald Reagan sent troops to Grenada to stop a supposedly communist coup, and Lyndon Johnson invaded the Dominican Republic. George H. W. Bush sent troops to Panama, and numerous presidents have ordered quick air strikes on perceived enemies.

The War Powers Resolution. In an attempt to gain more control over such military activities, in 1973 Congress passed the **War Powers Resolution**—over President Nixon's veto—requiring that the president consult with Congress when sending American forces into action. Once they are sent, the president must report to Congress within 48 hours. Unless Congress approves the use of troops within 60 days or extends the 60-day time limit, the forces must be withdrawn. The War Powers Resolution was tested in the fall of 1983, when Reagan requested that troops be left in Lebanon. The resulting compromise was a congressional resolution allowing troops to remain there for 18 months. Shortly after the resolution was passed, however, more than 240 sailors and marines were killed in a suicide bombing of a U.S. military housing compound in Beirut. That event provoked a furious congressional debate over the role that American troops were playing in the Middle East, and all troops were withdrawn shortly thereafter.

Despite the War Powers Resolution, the powers of the president as commander in chief have continued to expand. The attacks of September 11, 2001, were the first on U.S. soil since Pearl Harbor. The imminent sense of threat supported passage of legislation that gave the president and the executive branch powers that had not been seen since World War II. President Bush's use of surveillance powers and other powers granted by the PATRIOT Act have caused considerable controversy. However, as long as international terrorist groups threaten the United States, presidents are likely to have these enhanced powers.

> **War Powers Resolution**
> A law passed in 1973 spelling out the conditions under which the president can commit troops without congressional approval.

CHIEF DIPLOMAT

The Constitution gives the president the power to recognize foreign governments; to make treaties, with the **advice and consent** of the Senate; and to make special agreements

> **Advice and Consent**
> Terms in the Constitution describing the U.S. Senate's power to review and approve treaties and presidential appointments.

Chief Diplomat
The role of the president in recognizing foreign governments, making treaties, and effecting executive agreements.

Diplomatic Recognition
The formal acknowledgment of a foreign government as legitimate.

with other heads of state that do not require congressional approval. In addition, the president nominates ambassadors. As **chief diplomat**, the president dominates American foreign policy, a role that has been supported many times by the Supreme Court.

Diplomatic Recognition. An important power of the president as chief diplomat is that of **diplomatic recognition**, or the power to recognize—or refuse to recognize—foreign governments. In the role of ceremonial head of state, the president has always received foreign diplomats. In modern times, the simple act of receiving a foreign diplomat has been equivalent to accrediting the diplomat and officially recognizing his or her government. Such recognition of the legitimacy of another country's government is a prerequisite to diplomatic relations or treaties between that country and the United States.

Deciding when to recognize a foreign power is not always simple. The United States, for example, did not recognize the Soviet Union until 1933—16 years after the Russian Revolution of 1917. It was only after all attempts to reverse the effects of that revolution—including military invasion of Russia and diplomatic isolation—had proved futile that Franklin Roosevelt extended recognition to the Soviet government.

U.S. presidents faced a similar problem with the Chinese communist revolution. In December 1978, long after the communist victory in China in 1949, Jimmy Carter granted official recognition to the People's Republic of China.[9]

A diplomatic recognition issue that faced the Clinton administration involved recognizing a former enemy—the Republic of Vietnam. Many Americans, particularly those who believed that Vietnam had not been forthcoming in the efforts to find the remains of missing American soldiers or to find out about former prisoners of war, opposed any formal relationship with that nation. After the U.S. government had negotiated with the Vietnamese government for many years over the missing-in-action issue and engaged in limited diplomatic contacts for several years, President Clinton announced on July 11, 1995, that the United States would recognize the government of Vietnam and move to establish normal diplomatic relations.

DID YOU KNOW?

That John F. Kennedy was the youngest elected president, taking office at the age of 43, but that Theodore Roosevelt assumed office at the age of 42 after the assassination of President William McKinley?

PRESIDENT RICHARD NIXON
and First Lady Pat Nixon lead the way as they take a tour of China's famed Great Wall, near Beijing, February 21, 1972. Why was Nixon's visit to China so historic? (AP/Wide World Photos)

[9]The Nixon administration first encouraged new relations with the People's Republic of China by allowing a cultural exchange of Ping-Pong teams.

Proposal and Ratification of Treaties. The president has the sole power to negotiate treaties with other nations. These treaties must be presented to the Senate, where they may be modified and must be approved by a two-thirds vote. After ratification, the president can approve the senatorial version of the treaty. Approval poses a problem when the Senate has tacked on substantive amendments or reservations to a treaty, particularly when such changes may require reopening negotiations with the other signatory governments. Sometimes a president may decide to withdraw a treaty if the senatorial changes are too extensive, as Woodrow Wilson did with the Versailles Treaty in 1919. Wilson believed that the senatorial reservations would weaken the treaty so much that it would be ineffective. His refusal to accept the senatorial version of the treaty led to the eventual refusal of the United States to join the League of Nations.

President Carter was successful in lobbying for the treaties that provided for the return of the Panama Canal to Panama by the year 2000 and for neutralizing the canal. President Bill Clinton won a major political and legislative victory in 1993 by persuading Congress to ratify the North American Free Trade Agreement (NAFTA). In so doing, he had to overcome opposition from Democrats and most of organized labor. In 1998, he worked closely with Senate Republicans to ensure Senate approval of a treaty governing the use of chemical weapons. In 2000, President Clinton won another major legislative victory when Congress voted to normalize trade relations with China permanently.

Before September 11, 2001, President George W. Bush indicated his intention to steer the United States in a more unilateral direction on foreign policy. He rejected the Kyoto Agreement on global warming and proposed ending the 1972 Anti-Ballistic Missile (ABM) Treaty that was part of the first Strategic Arms Limitation Treaty (SALT I). After the terrorist attacks of September 11, 2001, however, President Bush sought cooperation from U.S. allies in the war on terrorism. Bush's return to multilateralism was exemplified in the signing of a nuclear weapons reduction treaty with Russia in 2002. Nonetheless, his attempts to gain international support for a war against Iraq to overthrow that country's government were not as successful as he had hoped. During the continuing occupation of Iraq, the Bush administration saw even more erosion in other countries' support of his actions.

The Obama administration quickly signaled a new outlook in foreign policy, with the president making multiple trips overseas, including to Egypt, in his first year in office. President Obama's stated goals in foreign policy included a more cooperative approach to world affairs and the reduction of nuclear weapons for all nations. In 2010, the president signed a treaty with Russia for a joint reduction of long-range nuclear weapons. The new START treaty was sent to the U.S. Senate for ratification in May 2010.

Executive Agreements. Presidential power in foreign affairs is enhanced greatly by the use of **executive agreements** made between the president and other heads of state. Such agreements do not require Senate approval, although the House and Senate may refuse to appropriate the funds necessary to implement them. Whereas treaties are binding on all succeeding administrations, executive agreements require each new president's consent to remain in effect.

Among the advantages of executive agreements are speed and secrecy. The former is essential during a crisis; the latter is important when the administration fears that open senatorial debate may be detrimental to the best interests of the United States or to the interests of the president.[10] There have been far more executive agreements (about 13,000) than treaties (about 1,300). Many executive agreements contain secret provisions

Executive Agreement
An international agreement made by the president, without senatorial ratification, with the head of a foreign state.

---

[10]The Case Act of 1972 requires that all executive agreements be transmitted to Congress within 60 days after the agreement takes effect. Secret agreements are transmitted to the foreign relations committees as classified information.

calling for American military assistance or other support. For example, Franklin Roosevelt (served 1933–1945) used executive agreements to bypass congressional isolationists when he traded American destroyers for British Caribbean naval bases and when he arranged diplomatic and military affairs with Canada and Latin American nations.

CHIEF LEGISLATOR

Chief Legislator
The role of the president in influencing the making of laws.

Constitutionally, presidents must recommend to Congress legislation that they judge necessary and expedient. Not all presidents have wielded their powers as **chief legislator** in the same manner. Some presidents have been almost completely unsuccessful in getting their legislative programs implemented by Congress. Presidents Franklin Roosevelt and Lyndon Johnson, however, saw much of their proposed legislation put into effect. Each year, the *Congressional Quarterly Weekly Review* publishes an analysis of presidential success in terms of legislation passed that the president has publicly supported. As illustrated by the graph in Figure 13-1, presidents tend to have a high success rate at the beginning of their administration, with a steep decline toward the end of their term. George W. Bush had more than a 70 percent success rate during the years he had a Republican-controlled Congress, but it fell to 34 percent after the Democrats won control of Congress in the 2006 elections. President Barack Obama found extraordinary support for his initiatives from the large Democratic majorities in both the House and the Senate, earning the highest success score ever recorded for a president in his first year, 96.7 percent.

FIGURE 13–1 Presidential Success Rate by Year of Presidency

The graph illustrates the president's success rate on bills on which he had taken a position. Note that presidents do very well at the beginning of their terms, especially when they have control of Congress. When the other party controls Congress, the presidential success rate falls.

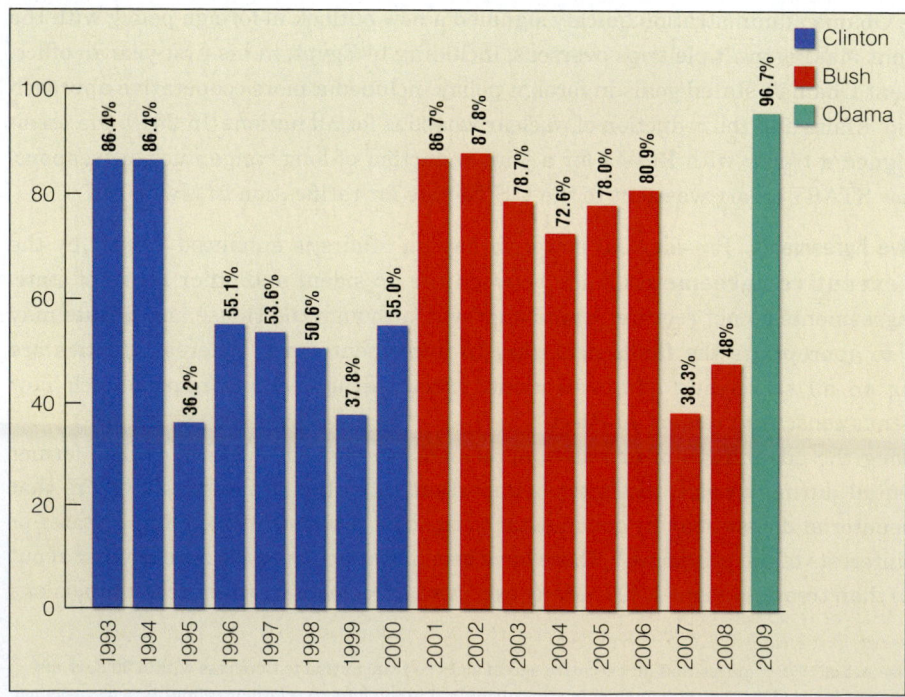

Source: *Congressional Quarterly Weekly Report*, January 14, 2008, p.137.

In modern times, the president has played a dominant role in creating the congressional agenda. In the president's annual **State of the Union message**, which is required by the Constitution (Article II, Section 3) and is usually given in late January, shortly after Congress reconvenes, the president, as chief legislator, presents a program. The message gives a broad, comprehensive view of what the president wishes the legislature to accomplish during its session. Originally, presidents simply sent a written memo to the Congress, which clearly satisfies the constitutional requirement. In modern times, however, presidents see the State of the Union address as a tool to advance their policy agenda. The president is able to command the media stage and set out his or her goals. President Ronald Reagan began the practice of referring to ordinary citizens and bringing the subjects of those stories to sit in the balcony during the speech. Today, the president, the opposition party, and the commentators all recognize the impact of the State of the Union message on public opinion.

Getting Legislation Passed. The president can propose legislation. Congress, however, is not required to pass—or even introduce—any of the administration's bills. How, then, does the president get those proposals made into law? One way is by exercising the power of persuasion. The president writes to, telephones, and meets with various congressional leaders; makes public announcements to influence public opinion; and, as head of the party, exercises legislative leadership through the congresspersons of that party. Most presidents also have an Office of Congressional Liaison within the White House Office. Such an office is staffed by individuals with extensive Washington experience, including former members of the Congress, who lobby the Congress on behalf of the president and monitor the progress of legislation on Capitol Hill. Presidents may also decide to use social events to lobby the Congress, inviting the members and their spouses to parties at the White House. A more negative strategy is for the president to threaten to veto legislation if it does not correspond to his or her position.

Saying No to Legislation. The president has the power to say no to legislation through use of the veto, by which the White House returns a bill unsigned to Congress with a **veto message** attached.[11] Because the Constitution requires that every bill passed by the House and the Senate be sent to the president before it becomes law, the president must act on each bill.

1. If the bill is signed, it becomes law.
2. If the bill is not sent back to Congress after 10 congressional working days, it becomes law without the president's signature.
3. The president can reject the bill and send it back to Congress with a veto message setting forth objections. Congress then can change the bill, hoping to secure presidential approval and pass it again. Or, Congress can simply reject the president's objections by overriding the veto with a two-thirds roll-call vote of the members present in both the House and the Senate.
4. If the president refuses to sign the bill and Congress adjourns within 10 working days after the bill has been submitted to the president, the bill is killed for that session of Congress. This is called a **pocket veto**. If Congress wishes the bill to be reconsidered, the bill must be reintroduced during the following session.

Presidents employed the veto power infrequently until after the Civil War, but it has been used with increasing vigor since then (see Table 13-1). The total number of vetoes

State of the Union Message
An annual message to Congress in which the president proposes a legislative program. The message is addressed not only to Congress but also to the American people and to the world.

DID YOU KNOW?

That one member of the Cabinet must not attend the State of the Union speech so that someone in the line of succession to the presidency would survive in case of an attack on the Capitol?

Veto Message
The president's formal explanation of a veto when legislation is returned to Congress.

Pocket Veto
A special veto exercised by the chief executive after a legislative body has adjourned. Bills not signed by the chief executive die after a specified period of time. If Congress wishes to reconsider such a bill, it must be reintroduced in the following session of Congress.

[11]*Veto* in Latin means "I forbid."

TABLE 13–1 Presidential Vetoes, 1789 to the Present

YEARS	PRESIDENT	REGULAR VETOES	VETOES OVERRIDDEN	POCKET VETOES	TOTAL VETOES
1789–1797	Washington	2	0	0	2
1797–1801	J. Adams	0	0	0	0
1801–1809	Jefferson	0	0	0	0
1809–1817	Madison	5	0	2	7
1817–1825	Monroe	1	0	0	1
1825–1829	J. Q. Adams	0	0	0	0
1829–1837	Jackson	5	0	7	12
1837–1841	Van Buren	0	0	1	1
1841–1841	W. Harrison	0	0	0	0
1841–1845	Tyler	6	1	4	10
1845–1849	Polk	2	0	1	3
1849–1850	Taylor	0	0	0	0
1850–1853	Fillmore	0	0	0	0
1853–1857	Pierce	9	5	0	9
1857–1861	Buchanan	4	0	3	7
1861–1865	Lincoln	2	0	5	7
1865–1869	A. Johnson	21	15	8	29
1869–1877	Grant	45	4	48	93
1877–1881	Hayes	12	1	1	13
1881–1881	Garfield	0	0	0	0
1881–1885	Arthur	4	1	8	12
1885–1889	Cleveland	304	2	110	414
1889–1893	B. Harrison	19	1	25	44
1893–1897	Cleveland	42	5	128	170
1897–1901	McKinley	6	0	36	42
1901–1909	T. Roosevelt	42	1	40	82
1909–1913	Taft	30	1	9	39
1913–1921	Wilson	33	6	11	44
1921–1923	Harding	5	0	1	6
1923–1929	Coolidge	20	4	30	50
1929–1933	Hoover	21	3	16	37
1933–1945	F. Roosevelt	372	9	263	635
1945–1953	Truman	180	12	70	250
1953–1961	Eisenhower	73	2	108	181
1961–1963	Kennedy	12	0	9	21
1963–1969	L. Johnson	16	0	14	30
1969–1974	Nixon	26*	7	17	43
1974–1977	Ford	48	12	18	66
1977–1981	Carter	13	2	18	31
1981–1989	Reagan	39	9	39	78
1989–1993	George H. W. Bush	29	1	15	44
1993–2001	Clinton	37**	2	1	38
2001–2008	George W. Bush	11	4	1	12
2009–2010	Obama	1	0	0	1
TOTAL		**1,496**	**110**	**1,067**	**2,564**

*Two pocket vetoes by President Nixon, overruled in the courts, are counted here as regular vetoes.

**President Clinton's line-item vetoes are not included.

Source: Office of the Clerk.

Beyond Our Borders

DO WE NEED A PRESIDENT *AND* A KING?

In the United States, the president is the head of state and the head of government. In many democratic societies, the government has a head of government, who actually guides government policy and is the political leader, and a head of state, who is the symbolic head of government. As noted in Chapter 12, in parliamentary systems the head of government is actually elected by his or her peers in the majority party in the legislature. In Great Britain, after the election, the leader of the majority party is asked by the queen of England (in her role as head of state) if he or she will serve as the prime minister. The queen has no political power whatsoever. She cannot refuse to name the leader of the majority party. When she opens the parliamentary session, she reads a speech written for her by the prime minister. Similar political systems with royal families and parliamentary leadership are found in Denmark, Sweden, Spain, and a few smaller European nations. The advantage of this system is that the head of state, the monarch, symbolically represents the nation. Public fascination with the royal family and the queen generally means that the prime minister can do his or her job without all the gossip and journalistic coverage that surrounds the president of the United States.

In other democracies, including Italy, France, and Germany, there are no royal families. The president of the nation is separately elected for a longer term but has little political power. He or she is the head of state and may counsel the head of the government, but political and executive power rests with the prime minister or premier. In some democratic states, the president and the premier are elected, although with different terms.

Until 2008, Vladimir Putin was the president of Russia, but his two terms were limited by the 1993 constitution. In the most recent election, his chosen successor, Dmitry Medvedev, won the election for president, and his party won 80 percent of the seats in the legislature. Some Russians who opposed Putin suggested that elections were not fair and that opposition leaders and journalists had been suppressed. Soon after the election, Medvedev named Putin as his premier. It seemed clear that Putin would still be running the government of Russia, even though his position had changed from head of government to head of state. So, in the case of Russia and some other states, the head of state is the president (who is elected) and who then can name the premier and the cabinet ministers. The intent of this system is for the president to be popularly elected and to exercise political leadership, while the premier runs the everyday operations of government and leads the legislative branch. But such a system can degenerate into a rivalry between the president and the premier. How can citizens know which one really has the power of the leader?

A RULER WITH only symbolic powers, King Juan Carlos I of Spain confers national honors on Spanish citizens. (EFE/Angel Diaz/Newscom)

FOR CRITICAL ANALYSIS

1. Why is it important to separate the roles of head of state and head of government?
2. Can the existence of a symbolic head of state, such as a monarch, make the elected leader more effective?
3. Is there too much burden put on the U.S. president, who is both head of state and head of government?

PRESIDENT DWIGHT D. EISENHOWER prepares for a nationwide radio and television address in 1959. In that address he called for new labor legislation "to protect the American people from the gangsters, racketeers, and other corrupt elements that have invaded the labor-management field." (AP Photo/Byron Rollins)

Line-Item Veto
The power of an executive to veto individual lines or items within a piece of legislation without vetoing the entire bill.

Constitutional Power
A power vested in the president by Article II of the Constitution.

Statutory Power
A power created for the president through laws enacted by Congress.

Expressed Power
A power of the president that is expressly written into the Constitution or into statutory law.

from George Washington through the middle of George W. Bush's second term in office was 2,552, with about two-thirds of those vetoes being exercised by Grover Cleveland, Franklin Roosevelt, Harry Truman, and Dwight Eisenhower.

Not since Martin Van Buren (served 1837–1841) has a president served a full term in office without exercising the veto power. George W. Bush, who had the benefit of a Republican Congress that passed legislation he was willing to sign, did not veto any legislation during his first term. Only in the summer of 2006 did Bush finally issue a veto, saying "no" to stem-cell research legislation passed by Congress. He occasionally threatened to use the veto and certainly used it when he was governor of Texas. After the Democrats took control of Congress in 2006, Bush used the veto more frequently, even on bills with bipartisan majorities.

The Line-Item Veto. Ronald Reagan lobbied strenuously for Congress to give to the president another tool, the **line-item veto**, which would allow the president to veto *specific* spending provisions of legislation that was passed by Congress. In 1996, Congress passed the Line Item Veto Act, which provided for the line-item veto. Signed by President Clinton, the law granted the president the power to rescind any item in an appropriations bill unless Congress passed a resolution of disapproval. Of course, the congressional resolution could be, in turn, vetoed by the president. The law did not take effect until after the 1996 election.

The act was soon challenged in court as an unconstitutional delegation of legislative powers to the executive branch. In 1998, by a 6-3 vote, the United States Supreme Court agreed and overturned the act. The Court stated that "there is no provision in the Constitution that authorizes the president to enact, to amend or to repeal statutes."[12]

Congress's Power to Override Presidential Vetoes. A veto is a clear-cut indication of the president's dissatisfaction with congressional legislation. Congress, however, can override a presidential veto, although it rarely exercises this power. Consider that two-thirds of the members of each chamber who are present must vote to override the president's veto in a roll-call vote. This means that if only one-third plus one of the members voting in one of the chambers of Congress do not agree to override the veto, the veto holds. Congress first overrode a presidential veto during the administration of John Tyler (served 1841–1845). In the first 65 years of American federal government history, out of 33 regular vetoes, Congress overrode only one, or about 3 percent. Overall, only about 7 percent of all regular vetoes have been overridden.

OTHER PRESIDENTIAL POWERS

The powers of the president just discussed are called **constitutional powers**, because their basis lies in the Constitution. In addition, Congress has established by law, or statute, numerous other presidential powers, such as the ability to declare national emergencies. These are called **statutory powers**. Both constitutional and statutory powers have been labeled the **expressed powers** of the president, because they are expressly written into the Constitution or into law.

---

[12]*Clinton v. City of New York*, 524 U.S. 417 (1998).

Presidents also have what have come to be known as **inherent powers**. These depend on the statements in the Constitution that "the executive Power shall be vested in a President" and that the president should "take Care that the Laws be faithfully executed." The most common example of inherent powers are those emergency powers invoked by the president during wartime. Franklin Roosevelt, for example, used his inherent powers to move the Japanese and Japanese Americans living in the United States into internment camps for the duration of World War II.

Clearly, modern U.S. presidents have many powers at their disposal. According to some critics, among the powers exercised by modern presidents are certain powers that rightfully belong to Congress but that Congress has yielded to the executive branch.

THE PRESIDENT AS PARTY CHIEF AND SUPERPOLITICIAN

Presidents are by no means above political partisanship, and one of their many roles is that of chief of party. Although the Constitution says nothing about the function of the president within a political party (the mere concept of political parties was abhorrent to most of the authors of the Constitution), today presidents are the actual leaders of their parties.

THE PRESIDENT AS CHIEF OF PARTY

As party leader, the president chooses the national committee chairperson and can try to discipline party members who fail to support presidential policies. One way of exerting political power within the party is through **patronage**—appointing political supporters to government or public jobs. This power was more extensive in the past, before the establishment of the civil service in 1883 (see Chapter 14), but the president retains important patronage power. As noted earlier, the president can appoint several thousand individuals to jobs in the Cabinet, the White House, and the federal regulatory agencies.

Perhaps the most important partisan role that the president played in the late 1900s and early 2000s was that of fundraiser. The president is able to raise large amounts for the party through appearances at dinners, speaking engagements, and other social occasions. President Clinton may have raised more than half a billion dollars for the Democratic Party during his two terms. President George W. Bush was even more successful than Clinton.

Presidents have other ways of exerting influence as party chief. The president may make it known that a particular congressperson's choice for federal judge will not be appointed unless that member of Congress is more supportive of the president's legislative program.[13] The president may agree to campaign for a particular program or for a particular candidate. Presidents also reward loyal members of Congress with support for the funding of local projects, tax breaks for regional industries, and other forms of "pork."

THE PRESIDENT'S POWER TO PERSUADE

According to political scientist Richard E. Neustadt, without the power to persuade, no president can lead very well. After all, even though the president is in the news

DID YOU KNOW?

That President William Henry Harrison gave the longest inaugural address (8,445 words) of any American president, lasting two hours (the weather was chilly and stormy, and Harrison caught a cold, got pneumonia and pleurisy, and died a month later)?

Inherent Power
A power of the president derived from the statements in the Constitution that "the executive Power shall be vested in a President" and that the president should "take Care that the Laws be faithfully executed"; defined through practice rather than through law.

Patronage
The practice of rewarding faithful party workers and followers with government employment and contracts.

DID YOU KNOW?

That 8 of the 44, or 18 percent, of U.S. presidents have been left-handed while less than 10 percent of the population is left-handed?

---

[13]"Senatorial courtesy" (see Chapter 15) often puts the judicial appointment in the hands of the Senate, however.

virtually every day, the Constitution gives Congress most of the authority in the U.S. political system. The Constitution does not give the executive branch enough constitutional power to keep the president constantly in a strong leadership position. Therefore, the president must establish a "professional reputation" that will convince Congress, the bureaucracy, and the public to support what the president wants. As Neustadt argues, "presidential power is the power to persuade."[14]

CONSTITUENCIES AND PUBLIC APPROVAL

All politicians worry about their constituencies, and presidents are no exception. Presidents with high approval ratings are able to leverage those ratings with the members of Congress who would prefer not to vote against the opinions of their own constituents.

Presidential Constituencies. According to Neustadt, presidents have not just one constituency, but many. In principle, they are beholden to the entire electorate—the public of the United States—even those who did not vote. They are certainly beholden to their party because its members helped to put them in office. The president's constituencies also include members of the opposing party whose cooperation the president needs. Finally, the president must take into consideration a constituency that has come to be called the **Washington community**. This community consists of individuals who—whether in or out of political office—are intimately familiar with the workings of government, thrive on gossip, and measure on a daily basis the political power of the president.

Washington Community
Individuals regularly involved with politics in Washington, D.C.

Public Approval. All of these constituencies are impressed by presidents who maintain a high level of public approval, partly because this is very difficult to accomplish. Presidential popularity, as measured by national polls, gives the president an extra political resource to use in persuading legislators or bureaucrats to pass legislation. As you will note from Figure 13-2, there are common patterns for almost all presidents. Presidential approval ratings tend to be very high when a new president takes office (the honeymoon period), and they certainly decline to a low in the last two years of the second term. Spikes in public approval apart from that cycle tend to occur when the United States sends troops in harm's way. This is called the "rally 'round the flag" effect. Take a look at George H. W. Bush's ratings. Popular approval of the president reached a new high at the beginning of the Persian Gulf War, but that approval had no staying power, and his ratings declined precipitously in the year following the victory. Bill Clinton defied all tradition by having high ratings even while he was fighting impeachment.

DID YOU KNOW?

That four United States presidents have been awarded the Nobel Prize for Peace—Theodore Roosevelt, Woodrow Wilson, Jimmy Carter, and Barack Obama?

George W. Bush and the Public Opinion Polls. The impact of popular approval on a president's prospects was placed in sharp relief by the experiences of President Bush. Immediately after September 11, 2001, Bush had the highest approval ratings ever recorded. His popularity then entered a steep decline that was interrupted only briefly by high ratings during the early phases of the Second Gulf War. During his second term, Bush's approval ratings reached new lows, falling to 31 percent before the midterm elections in 2006 and then declining further to less than 30 percent by 2008. Without doubt, the economic crisis of fall 2008 contributed to the final low ebb of his approval ratings.

[14]Richard E. Neustadt, *Presidential Power and the Modern Presidents: The Politics of Leadership from Roosevelt to Reagan,* rev. ed. (New York: Free Press, 1991).

FIGURE 13-2 Public Popularity of Modern Presidents

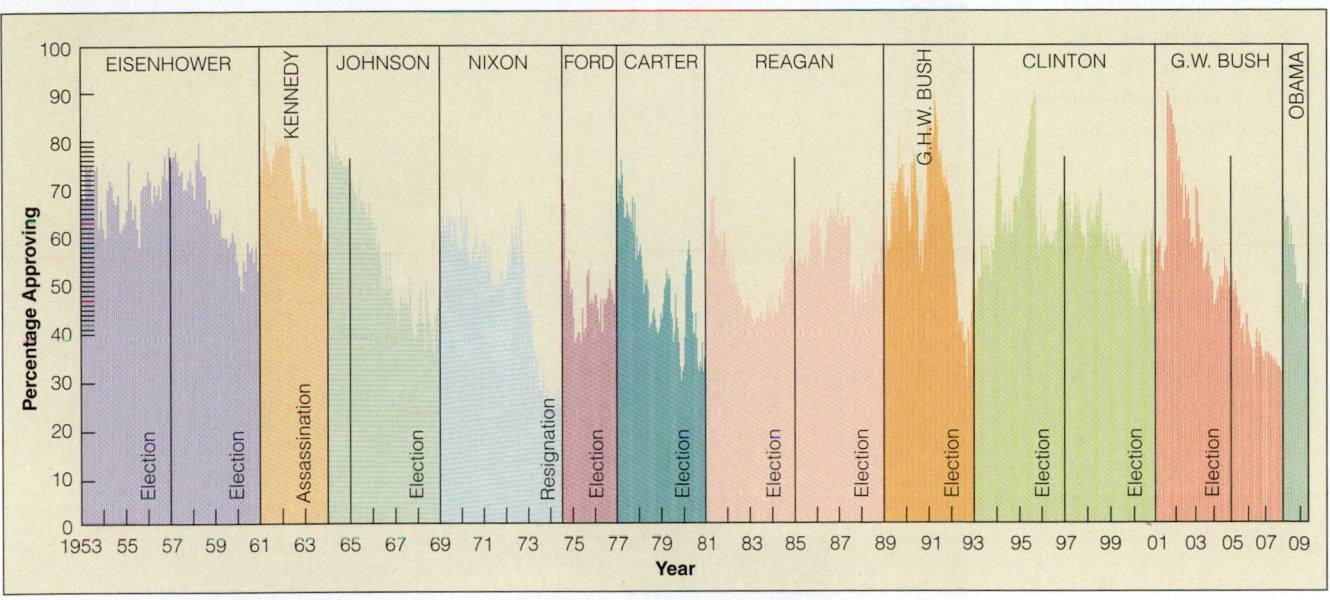

Sources: The Roper Center for Public Opinion Research; Gallup and USA Today/CNN Polls, March 1992 through September 2008.

BARACK OBAMA AND POPULAR APPROVAL

Like most presidents who win office with a substantial margin of victory, President Barack Obama entered the office with very high approval ratings. Voters, as usual, were willing to give the new president high marks for his first year in office. Additionally, Mr. Obama's youth, energy, and new outlook seemed to enhance his positive image. As the economic crisis deepened and various government measures failed to improve the unemployment figures, Mr. Obama began to experience some decline in his approval ratings. By the middle of his second year in office, his approval ratings had stabilized at about 50 percent, a level similar to that achieved by many other presidents in their first term in office.

"Going Public." Since the early 1900s, presidents have spoken more to the public and less to Congress. In the 1800s, only 7 percent of presidential speeches were addressed to the public; since 1900, 50 percent have been addressed to the public. One scholar, Samuel Kernell, has proposed that the style of presidential leadership has changed since World War II, owing partly to the influence of television, with a resulting change in the balance of national politics.[15] Presidents frequently go over the heads of Congress and the political elites, taking their cases directly to the people.

This strategy, which Kernell dubbed "going public," gives the president additional power through the ability to persuade and manipulate public opinion. By identifying their own positions so clearly, presidents make compromises with Congress much more difficult and weaken the legislators' positions. Given the increasing importance of the media as the major source of political information for citizens and elites, presidents will continue to use public opinion as part of their arsenal of weapons to gain support from Congress and to achieve their policy goals.

[15]Samuel Kernell, *Going Public: New Strategies of Presidential Leadership*, 3rd ed. (Washington, DC: Congressional Quarterly Press, 1997).

PRESIDENT JOHN F. KENNEDY discusses the Berlin crisis at a news conference in 1961. Kennedy continues to be considered the master of such events. (AP Photo/Bill Chaplis)

SPECIAL USES OF PRESIDENTIAL POWER

Presidents have at their disposal a variety of special powers and privileges not available in the other branches of the U.S. government: (1) emergency powers, (2) executive orders, and (3) executive privilege.

EMERGENCY POWERS

Emergency Power
An inherent power exercised by the president during a period of national crisis.

If you read the Constitution, you will find no mention of the additional powers that the executive office may exercise during national emergencies. The Supreme Court has indicated that an "emergency does not create power."[16] But it is clear that presidents have used their inherent powers during times of emergency, particularly in the realm of foreign affairs. The **emergency powers** of the president were first enunciated in the Supreme Court's decision in *United States v. Curtiss-Wright Export Corp.*[17] In that case, President Franklin Roosevelt, without authorization by Congress, ordered an embargo on the shipment of weapons to two warring South American countries. The Court recognized that the president may exercise inherent powers in foreign affairs and that the national government has primacy in these affairs.

---

[16]*Home Building and Loan Association v. Blaisdell*, 290 U.S. 398 (1934).
[17]299 U.S. 304 (1936).

Examples of emergency powers are abundant, coinciding with crises in domestic and foreign affairs. Abraham Lincoln suspended civil liberties at the beginning of the Civil War (1861–1865) and called the state militias into national service. These actions and his subsequent governance of conquered areas and even of areas of Northern states were justified by claims that they were essential to preserve the Union. Franklin Roosevelt declared an "unlimited national emergency" following the fall of France in World War II (1939–1945) and mobilized the federal budget and the economy for war.

President Harry Truman authorized the federal seizure of steel plants and their operation by the national government in 1952 during the Korean War. Truman claimed that he was using his inherent emergency power as chief executive and commander in chief to safeguard the nation's security, as an ongoing strike by steelworkers threatened the supply of weapons to the armed forces. The Supreme Court did not agree, holding that the president had no authority under the Constitution to seize private property or to legislate such action.[18] According to legal scholars, this was the first time a limit was placed on the exercise of the president's emergency powers.

After September 11, the Bush administration pushed several laws through the Congress that granted more power to the Department of Justice and other agencies to investigate possible terrorists. Many of these provisions of the PATRIOT Act and other laws have been reaffirmed by Congress in subsequent years, while others have been revised. In 2006, it became clear that President Bush had also authorized federal agencies to eavesdrop on international telephone calls without a court order when the party overseas was suspected of having information about terrorism or might be a suspect in a terrorist plot. This eavesdropping had not been authorized under the legislation. Many scholars claimed that this exercise of presidential power was far beyond what could be claimed an emergency power.[19] The Bush administration claimed that it was entirely within the president's power to make such an authorization, although it did not claim the authorization to be within the Supreme Court's definition of "emergency power." Following these disclosures, the administration pursued an expanded law to allow such wiretapping, but provisions of that new bill proved too controversial to pass in 2008.

"I don't think you can distance yourself from the White House on this one. After all, you are the President." (© 2002 The New Yorker Collection from cartoonbank.com. All rights reserved.)

DID YOU KNOW?

That the shortest inaugural address was George Washington's second one at 135 words?

EXECUTIVE ORDERS

Congress allows the president (as well as administrative agencies) to issue **executive orders** that have the force of law. These executive orders can do the following: (1) enforce legislative statutes, (2) enforce the Constitution or treaties with foreign nations, and (3) establish or modify rules and practices of executive administrative agencies.

An executive order, then, represents the president's legislative power. The only requirement is that under the Administrative Procedure Act of 1946, all executive orders must be published in the ***Federal Register***, a daily publication of the U.S.

Executive Order
A rule or regulation issued by the president that has the effect of law. Executive orders can implement and give administrative effect to provisions in the Constitution, to treaties, and to statutes.

Federal Register
A publication of the U.S. government that prints executive orders, rules, and regulations.

[18]*Youngstown Sheet and Tube Co. v. Sawyer,* 343 U.S. 579 (1952).
[19]Elizabeth Drew, "Power Grab," *New York Review of Books,* Vol. 53, No. 11, June 22, 2006.

POLITICS WITH A purpose

"For the Record" Versus "That's Privileged Information"

Do we have a right to know everything our government does? What circumstances might justify the president keeping his or her activities or those of the administration secret? These questions raise complex issues, and common sense says the answers lie somewhere in between the two extremes. How this balance is struck has been the subject of intense political debate.

After the Watergate scandal (see the "Abuses of Executive Power and Impeachment" section for an explanation of these events), Congress passed the Presidential Records Act of 1978 (PRA) to address control of the historical record of a presidential administration.[a] Immediately upon the inauguration of the successor, the National Archives physically takes control of all presidential and vice presidential records. For a period of 12 years, the National Archives is responsible for processing these papers and reviewing and examining each document for national security issues or other reasons that would preclude it from being made public. Under the PRA, after the 12-year period and as the archivists finish their work, the records are released to the presidential libraries. Each library—staffed by archivists employed by the federal government—houses all of the papers of that administration.[b] However, current or former presidents can request that certain documents not be released, claiming executive privilege (discussed in the "Special Uses of Presidential Power" section).[c]

President Reagan's records were the first to be processed under the PRA. In February 2001, President Bush was notified that one of the first batches of Reagan documents was scheduled for release, as the 12-year period was set to expire. The president's subsequent Executive Order (E.O. 13233) in November 2001 significantly altered the PRA. Under E.O. 13233, instead of the process described previously, the National Archives now cannot release documents until the current and former presidents have approved their release. Researchers who may want access to these records bear the burden of arguing before a federal court that there is no reason for the president to withhold the records. The burden of proof has shifted away from the current or former presidents, who formerly had to demonstrate a compelling reason to keep the public away from the

records. Now the burden is on the public to substantiate their need to know. A coalition of scholars, researchers, journalists, and public-interest lobby groups joined in a suit to stop the implementation of President Bush's executive order. Among the groups joining the 2002 suit filed by a public-interest group called Public Citizen were the Association of American University Presses (AAUP), the Association of American Publishers, the Society of American Historians, and the Society of Professional Journalists. The group won a partial victory in October 2007 when a federal court struck down the portion of E.O. 13233 allowing current and former presidents to screen the release of documents.[d]

In 2007, congressional partisan control reverted to the Democrats, and Representative Henry Waxman (D.-Ca.) became chair of the House Government and Oversight Committee. He coauthored The Presidential Records Act Amendments of 2007, which then passed the House and died in the Senate. Immediately after President Obama's inauguration, he signed an Executive Order that countermanded the Bush rules, although it did allow former presidents the opportunity to claim executive privilege for any requested documents. Around the same time, the House passed another, stronger version of the 2007 bill, but that bill has been delayed in the Senate for more than a year. The issue of executive privilege often comes into play when the Senate is considering nominations to the federal courts. In early 2010, President Obama nominated Elena Kagan for the Supreme Court. Immediately, the Senate Judiciary Committee requested access to memos that Ms. Kagan wrote as an aide in the Clinton White House. Although President Clinton's papers are not supposed to be available until 2013, the former president has raised no objection to releasing the Kagan memos. However, the Clinton library contains more than 77 million pages of documents, and most have not yet been catalogued.

---

[a]www.archives.gov/presidential-libraries/laws/1978-act.html.
[b]For a complete list of the presidential libraries, see www.archives.gov/presidential-libraries.
[c]If someone wants access to an unreleased document, the person can file a Freedom of Information Act (FOIA) request. Archivists trained with an understanding of the PRA, FOIA, and any other governing statutes determine whether to release the documents. This process remains in place today.

[d]http://aaupnet.org/news/press/PRAamicus.pdf.

government. Executive orders have been used to establish procedures to appoint non-career administrators, to implement national affirmative action regulations, to restructure the White House bureaucracy, to ration consumer goods and to administer wage and price controls under emergency conditions, to classify government information as secret, to regulate the export of restricted items, and to establish military tribunals for suspected terrorists.

It is important to note that executive orders can be revoked by succeeding presidents. George H. W. Bush issued an order to ban foreign aid to countries that included abortion in their family planning strategies, because that provision (known as the Hyde Amendment) could not make it through Congress as legislation. President Clinton revoked the order. The George W. Bush administration revoked many of the thousands of executive orders and regulations issued in the last months of the Clinton administration. Not surprisingly, the Obama administration revoked a number of the Bush orders and issued new orders in support of stronger environmental regulations, food safety, consumer safety, and many other areas.

Executive Privilege
The right of executive officials to withhold information from or to refuse to appear before a legislative committee.

EXECUTIVE PRIVILEGE

Another inherent executive power that has been claimed by presidents concerns the ability of the president and the president's executive officials to withhold information from or refuse to appear before Congress or the courts. This is called **executive privilege**, and it relies on the constitutional separation of powers for its basis.

Presidents have frequently invoked executive privilege to avoid having to disclose information to Congress on actions of the executive branch. For example, President George W. Bush claimed executive privilege to keep the head of the newly established Office of Homeland Security, Tom Ridge, from testifying before Congress. The Bush administration also resisted attempts by the congressional Government Accountability Office to obtain information about meetings and documents related to Vice President Dick Cheney's actions as chair of the administration's energy policy task force. Bush, like presidents before him, claimed that a certain degree of secrecy is essential to national security. Critics of executive privilege believe that it can be used to shield from public scrutiny actions of the executive branch that should be open to Congress and to the American citizenry.

Limiting Executive Privilege. Limits to executive privilege went untested until the Watergate affair in the early 1970s. Five men had broken into the headquarters of the Democratic National Committee and were caught searching for documents that would damage the candidacy of the Democratic nominee, George McGovern. Later investigation showed that the break-in was planned by members of Richard Nixon's campaign committee and that Nixon and his closest advisers had devised a strategy for impeding the investigation of the crime. After it became known that all of the conversations held in the Oval Office had been tape-recorded on a secret system, Nixon was ordered to turn over the tapes to the special prosecutor.

RICHARD NIXON says goodbye outside the White House after his resignation on August 9, 1974, as he prepares to board a helicopter for a flight to nearby Andrews Air Force Base. Nixon addressed members of his staff in the East Room prior to his departure. Was Nixon impeached? (AP Photo/Bob Daughtery)

Nixon refused to do so, claiming executive privilege. He argued that "no president could function if the private papers of his office, prepared by his personal staff, were open to public scrutiny." In 1974, in one of the Supreme Court's most famous cases, *United States v. Nixon,*[20] the justices unanimously ruled that Nixon had to hand over the tapes. The Court held that executive privilege could not be used to prevent evidence from being heard in criminal proceedings.

Clinton's Attempted Use of Executive Privilege. The claim of executive privilege was also raised by the Clinton administration as a defense against the aggressive investigation of Clinton's relationship with White House intern Monica Lewinsky by Independent Counsel Kenneth Starr. The Clinton administration claimed executive privilege for several presidential aides who might have discussed the situation with the president. In addition, President Clinton asserted that his White House counsel did not have to testify before the Starr grand jury due to attorney-client privilege. Finally, the Department of Justice claimed that members of the Secret Service who guard the president could not testify about his activities due to a "protective function privilege" inherent in their duties. The federal judge overseeing the case denied the claims of privilege, however, and the decision was upheld on appeal.

ABUSES OF EXECUTIVE POWER AND IMPEACHMENT

Impeachment
An action by the House of Representatives to accuse the president, vice president, or other civil officers of the United States of committing "Treason, Bribery, or other high Crimes and Misdemeanors."

Presidents normally leave office either because their first term has expired and they have not sought (or won) reelection or because, having served two full terms, they are not allowed to be elected for a third term (owing to the Twenty-second Amendment, passed in 1951). Eight presidents have died in office. But there is still another way for a president to leave office—by **impeachment** and conviction. Articles I and II of the Constitution authorize the House and Senate to remove the president, the vice president, or other civil officers of the United States for committing "Treason, Bribery, or other high Crimes and Misdemeanors." According to the Constitution, the impeachment process begins in the House, which impeaches (accuses) the federal officer involved. If the House votes to impeach the officer, it draws up articles of impeachment and submits them to the Senate, which conducts the actual trial.

In the history of the United States, no president has ever actually been impeached and also convicted—and thus removed from office—by means of this process.

President Andrew Johnson (served 1865–1869), who succeeded to the office after the assassination of Abraham Lincoln, was impeached by the House but acquitted by the Senate. More than a century later, the House Judiciary Committee approved articles of impeachment against President Richard Nixon for his involvement in the cover-up of the Watergate break-in of 1972. Informed by members of his own party that he had no hope of surviving the trial in the Senate, Nixon resigned on August 9, 1974, before the full House voted on the articles. Nixon is the only president to have resigned from office.

The second president to be impeached by the House but not convicted by the Senate was President Bill Clinton. In September 1998, Independent Counsel Kenneth Starr sent to Congress the findings of his investigation of the president on the charges of perjury and obstruction of justice. The House approved two charges against Clinton: lying to the grand jury about his affair with Monica Lewinsky and

[20]318 U.S. 683 (1974).

obstruction of justice. The articles of impeachment were then sent to the Senate, which acquitted Clinton.

THE EXECUTIVE ORGANIZATION

Gone are the days when presidents answered their own mail, as George Washington did. It was not until 1857 that Congress authorized a private secretary for the president, to be paid by the federal government. Woodrow Wilson typed most of his correspondence, even though he did have several secretaries. At the beginning of Franklin Roosevelt's long tenure in the White House, the entire staff consisted of 37 employees. With the New Deal and World War II, however, the presidential staff became a sizable organization.

Today, the executive organization includes a White House office staff of about 600, including some workers who are part-time employees and others who are borrowed from their departments by the White House. The more than 360 employees who work in the White House Office are closest to the president. The employees who work for the numerous councils and advisory groups are supposed to advise the president on policy and coordinate the work of departments. The group of appointees who perhaps are most helpful to the president is the Cabinet, each member of which is the principal officer of a government department.

THE CABINET

Although the Constitution does not include the word *cabinet,* it does state that the president "may require the Opinion, in writing, of the principal Officer in each of the executive Departments." Since the time of George Washington, there has been an advisory group, or **Cabinet**, to which the president turns for counsel.

Members of the Cabinet. Originally, the Cabinet consisted of only four officials—the secretaries of state, treasury, and war, and the attorney general. Today, the Cabinet numbers 14 department secretaries and the attorney general. (See Chapter 14 for a detailed discussion of these Cabinet departments.) The Cabinet may include others as well. The president can, at his or her discretion, ascribe Cabinet rank to the vice president, the head of the Office of Management and Budget, the national security adviser, the ambassador to the United Nations, or others.

Often, a president will use a **kitchen cabinet** to replace the formal Cabinet as a major source of advice. The term *kitchen cabinet* originated during the presidency of Andrew Jackson, who relied on the counsel of close friends who often met with him in the kitchen of the White House. A kitchen cabinet is a very informal group of advisors; usually, they are friends with whom the president worked before being elected.

Presidential Use of Cabinets. Because neither the Constitution nor statutory law requires the president to consult with the Cabinet, its use is purely discretionary. Some presidents have relied on the counsel of their Cabinets more than others. Dwight Eisenhower was used to the team approach to solving problems from his experience as supreme Allied commander during World War II, and therefore he frequently turned to his Cabinet for advice on a wide range of issues. More often, presidents have solicited the opinions of their Cabinets and then done what they wanted to do anyway. Lincoln supposedly said—after

Cabinet
An advisory group selected by the president to aid in making decisions. The Cabinet includes the heads of 15 executive departments and others named by the president.

Kitchen Cabinet
The informal advisers to the president.

a Cabinet meeting in which a vote was seven nays against his one aye—"Seven nays and one aye; the ayes have it." In general, few presidents have relied heavily on the advice of their Cabinet members.

It is not surprising that presidents tend not to rely on their Cabinet members' advice. Often, the departmental heads are more responsive to the wishes of their own staffs or to their own political ambitions than they are to the president. They may be more concerned with obtaining resources for their departments than with achieving the goals of the president. So there is often a strong conflict of interest between presidents and their Cabinet members.

THE EXECUTIVE OFFICE OF THE PRESIDENT

Executive Office of the President (EOP)
An organization established by President Franklin D. Roosevelt to assist the president in carrying out major duties.

When President Franklin Roosevelt appointed a special committee on administrative management, he knew that the committee would conclude that the president needed help. The committee proposed a major reorganization of the executive branch. Congress did not approve the entire reorganization, but it did create the **Executive Office of the President (EOP)** to provide staff assistance for the chief executive and to help coordinate the executive bureaucracy. Since that time, many agencies have been created within the EOP to supply the president with advice and staff help. These agencies include the following:

- White House Office
- White House Military Office
- Office of the Vice President
- Council of Economic Advisers
- Office of National Drug Control Policy
- Office of Science and Technology Policy
- Office of the United States Trade Representative
- Council on Environmental Quality

- President's Critical Infrastructure Protection Board
- Office of Management and Budget
- National Security Council
- President's Foreign Intelligence Advisory Board
- Office of National AIDS Policy

Several of the offices within the EOP are especially important, including the White House Office, the Office of Management and Budget, and the National Security Council.

White House Office
The personal office of the president, which tends to presidential political needs and manages the media.

The White House Office. The **White House Office** includes most of the key personal and political advisers to the president. Among the jobs held by these aides are those of legal counsel to the president, secretary, press secretary, and appointments secretary. Often, the individuals who hold these positions are recruited from the president's campaign staff. Their duties—mainly protecting the president's political interests—are similar to campaign functions. In fact, most observers of the presidency agree that contemporary presidents continue their campaigning after inauguration. The **permanent campaign** is a long-term strategy planned by the White House Office of Communications with the press secretary to keep the president's approval ratings high and to improve his support in Congress. The campaign includes staged events, symbolic actions, and controlled media appearances. In all recent administrations, one member of the White House

Permanent Campaign
A coordinated and planned strategy carried out by the White House to increase the president's popularity and support.

Office has been named **chief of staff**. This person, who is responsible for coordinating the office, is also one of the president's chief advisers.

The president may establish special advisory units within the White House to address topics the president finds especially important. Under George W. Bush, these units also included the Office of Faith-Based and Community Initiatives and the USA Freedom Corps. The White House Office also includes the staff members who support the First Lady.

In addition to civilian advisers, the president is supported by a large number of military personnel, who are organized under the White House Military Office. These members of the military provide communications, transportation, medical care, and food services to the president and the White House staff.

Employees of the White House Office have been both envied and criticized. The White House Office, according to most former staffers, grants its employees access and power. They are able to use the resources of the White House to contact virtually anyone in the world by telephone, cable, fax, or electronic mail, as well as to use the influence of the White House to persuade legislators and citizens. Because of this influence, staffers are often criticized for overstepping the bounds of the office. The appointments secretary is able to grant or deny senators, representatives, and Cabinet secretaries access to the president. The press secretary grants the press and television journalists access to any information about the president.

White House staff members are closest to the president and may have considerable influence over the administration's decisions. When presidents are under fire for their decisions, the staff is often accused of keeping the chief executive too isolated from criticism or help. Presidents insist that they will not allow the staff to become too powerful, but, given the difficulty of the office, each president eventually turns to staff members for loyal assistance and protection.

The Office of Management and Budget. The **Office of Management and Budget (OMB)** was originally the Bureau of the Budget, which was created in 1921 within the Department of the Treasury. Recognizing the importance of this agency, Franklin Roosevelt moved it into the White House Office in 1939. Richard Nixon reorganized the Bureau of the Budget in 1970 and changed its name to reflect its new managerial function. It is headed by a director, who must make up the annual federal budget that the president presents to Congress each January for approval. In principle, the director of the OMB has broad fiscal powers in planning and estimating various parts of the federal budget, because all agencies must submit their proposed budget to the OMB for approval. In reality, it is not so clear that the OMB truly can affect the greater scope of the federal budget. Rather, the OMB may be more important as a clearinghouse for legislative proposals initiated in the executive agencies.

The National Security Council. The **National Security Council (NSC)** is a link between the president's key foreign and military advisers and the president. Its members consist of the president, the vice president, and the secretaries of state and defense, plus other informal members. Included in the NSC is the president's special assistant for national security affairs. In 2001, Condoleezza Rice became the first woman to serve as a president's national security adviser.

Policy "Tsars." For many decades presidents have created positions within the Executive Office of the President that were focused on one special policy area. Many of these positions have been titled "senior policy coordinator" or "senior adviser," and most of them have been appointments that do not require Senate confirmation. In general, these

Chief of Staff
The person who is named to direct the White House Office and advise the president.

DID YOU KNOW?

That the 2008 presidential elections were the first since 1952 without an incumbent president or vice president running?

Office of Management and Budget (OMB)
A division of the Executive Office of the President. The OMB assists the president in preparing the annual budget, clearing and coordinating departmental agency budgets, and supervising the administration of the federal budget.

National Security Council (NSC)
An agency in the Executive Office of the President that advises the president on national security.

positions last only as long as the president. Each new president decides which domestic or foreign policy issues need special attention from an individual who can report directly to the chief executive. In recent administrations, the nickname **"policy tsar"** has been attached to these positions.

If the president has special councils on problems such as drugs or the environment and Cabinet departments or independent agencies designated to handle an area of government policy, why does he need yet another individual to supervise government action? What presidents expect when they appoint a policy tsar is a unique focus on the problem, along with the ability to coordinate the efforts of all the other government agencies that have some authority in that policy area. Additionally, the individuals who are named to these positions are often well-regarded experts who can bring an outsider's point of view both to the president and to the agencies involved in dealing with an issue. George W. Bush, over the two terms of his presidency, appointed more than 30 individuals to these positions. By the time Barack Obama was inaugurated, he had proposed more than 35 of these positions, leading to some criticism from Congress that there would be too much authority given to officials who had not been confirmed by the Senate.

THE VICE PRESIDENCY

The Constitution does not give much power to the vice president. The only formal duty is to preside over the Senate, which is rarely necessary. This obligation is fulfilled when the Senate organizes and adopts its rules and when the vice president is needed to decide a tie vote. In all other cases, the president pro tem manages parliamentary procedures in the Senate. The vice president is expected to participate only informally in senatorial deliberations, if at all.

THE VICE PRESIDENT'S JOB

Vice presidents have traditionally been chosen by presidential nominees to balance the ticket to attract groups of voters or appease party factions. If a presidential nominee is from the North, it is not a bad idea to have a vice presidential nominee who is from the South. If the presidential nominee is from a rural state, perhaps someone with an urban background would be most suitable as a running mate. Presidential nominees who are strongly conservative or strongly liberal would do well to have vice presidential nominees who are more in the middle of the political road.

Strengthening the Ticket. In recent presidential elections, vice presidents have often been selected for other reasons. Bill Clinton picked Al Gore to be his running mate in 1992, even though both were Southern and moderates. The ticket appealed to Southerners and moderates, both of whom were crucial to the election. In 2000, both vice presidential selections were intended to shore up the respective presidential candidates' perceived weaknesses. Republican George W. Bush, who was subject to criticism for his lack of federal government experience and his "lightweight" personality, chose Dick Cheney, a former member of Congress who had also served as secretary of defense. Democrat Al Gore chose Senator Joe Lieberman of Connecticut, whose reputation for moral integrity (as an Orthodox Jew) could help counteract the effects of Bill Clinton's sex scandals. In 2004, Democratic presidential candidate John Kerry made a more traditional choice in Senator John Edwards of North Carolina. Edwards provided regional balance and also a degree of socioeconomic balance because, unlike Kerry, he had been born into

Policy Tsar
A high-ranking member of the Executive Office of the President appointed to coordinate action in one specific policy area.

VICE PRESIDENT JOE BIDEN lays a wreath at the Tomb of the Unknowns in Arlington National Cemetery on Memorial Day, 2010. (AFP PHOTO/Jewel Samad/Newscom)

relatively humble circumstances. Both presidential candidates in 2008 sought to balance their perceived weaknesses with their vice presidential choices. Barack Obama chose Senator Joseph Biden to add experience and foreign policy knowledge to his ticket, and John McCain chose Sarah Palin to add youth and an appeal to the Christian right to his ticket.

Supporting the President. The job of vice president is not extremely demanding, even when the president gives some specific task to the vice president. Typically, vice presidents spend their time supporting the president's activities. During the Clinton administration (1993–2001), however, Vice President Al Gore did much to strengthen the position of vice president by his aggressive support for environmental protection policies on a global basis. He also took a special interest in areas of emerging technology and lobbied Congress to provide subsidies to public schools for Internet use.

Vice President Dick Cheney, as one of President George W. Bush's key advisers, clearly was an influential figure in the Bush administration. Although many of the Washington elite were happy to see Dick Cheney as vice president because of his intelligence and wide range of experience, he quickly became a controversial figure due to his outspoken support for a tough foreign and military policy and for having encouraged Bush to attack Iraq.

Vice President Joe Biden, the former senator from Delaware, was a popular choice for vice president among Democrats and voters. He had many years of experience in the Senate, thus balancing President's Obama's relative lack of experience on Capitol Hill. Once the Obama administration took office, Biden's role became somewhat clearer. His experiences in the Senate prepared him to be a senior adviser to the president on foreign policy issues, although he certainly was not as controversial a figure as Cheney had been. Of course, the vice presidency takes on more significance if the president becomes disabled or dies in office and the vice president becomes president.

Vice presidents sometimes have become elected presidents in their own right. John Adams and Thomas Jefferson were the first two vice presidents to do so. Richard Nixon was elected president in 1968 after he had served as Dwight D. Eisenhower's vice president from 1953 to 1961. In 1988, George H. W. Bush was elected to the presidency after eight years as Ronald Reagan's vice president.

PRESIDENTIAL SUCCESSION

Eight vice presidents have become president because of the death of the president. John Tyler, the first to do so, took over William Henry Harrison's position after only one month. No one knew whether Tyler should simply be a caretaker until a new president could be elected three and a half years later or whether he actually should be president. Tyler assumed that he was supposed to be the chief executive and he acted as such, although he was commonly referred to as "His Accidency." Since then, vice presidents taking over the position of the presidency because of the incumbent's death have assumed the presidential powers.

But what should a vice president do if a president becomes incapable of carrying out necessary duties while in office? When James Garfield was shot in 1881, he remained alive for two and a half months. What was Vice President Chester Arthur's role? This question was not addressed in the original Constitution. Article II, Section 1, says only that "[i]n Case of the Removal of the President from Office, or of his Death, Resignation, or Inability to discharge the Powers and Duties of the said Office, the same shall devolve on [the same powers shall be exercised by] the Vice President." There have been many instances of presidential disability. When Dwight Eisenhower became ill a second time in 1958, he entered into a pact with Richard Nixon specifying that the vice president could determine whether the president was incapable of carrying out his duties if the president could not communicate. John F. Kennedy and Lyndon Johnson entered into similar agreements with their vice presidents. Finally, in 1967, the **Twenty-fifth Amendment** was passed, establishing procedures in case of presidential incapacity.

THE TWENTY-FIFTH AMENDMENT

According to the Twenty-fifth Amendment, when a president believes that he or she is incapable of performing the duties of office, the president must inform Congress in writing. Then the vice president serves as acting president until the president can resume normal duties. When the president is unable to communicate, a majority of the Cabinet, including the vice president, can declare that fact to Congress. Then the vice president serves as acting president until the president resumes normal duties. If a dispute arises over the return of the president's ability, a two-thirds vote of Congress is required to decide whether the vice president shall remain acting president or whether the president shall resume normal duties.

In 2002, President George W. Bush formally invoked the Twenty-fifth Amendment for the first time by officially transferring presidential power to Vice President Dick Cheney while the president underwent a colonoscopy, a 20-minute procedure. He commented that he undertook this transfer of power "because we're at war," referring to the war on terrorism. The only other time the provisions of the Twenty-fifth Amendment have been used was during President Reagan's colon surgery in 1985, although Reagan did not formally invoke the Amendment.

DID YOU KNOW?

That President Richard Nixon served 56 days without a vice president, and that President Gerald Ford served 132 days without a vice president?

Twenty-fifth Amendment
A 1967 amendment to the Constitution that establishes procedures for filling presidential and vice presidential vacancies and makes provisions for presidential disability.

AN ATTEMPTED ASSASSINATION of Ronald Reagan occurred on March 31, 1981. In the foreground, two men bend over Press Secretary James Brady, who lies seriously wounded. In the background, President Reagan is watched over by a U.S. Secret Service agent with an automatic weapon. A Washington D.C. police officer, Thomas Delahanty, lies to the left after also being shot. (AP Photo/ Ron Edmonds)

WHEN THE VICE PRESIDENCY BECOMES VACANT

The Twenty-fifth Amendment also addresses the issue of how the president should fill a vacant vice presidency. Section 2 of the amendment simply states, "Whenever there is a vacancy in the office of the Vice President, the President shall nominate a Vice President who shall take office upon confirmation by a majority vote of both Houses of Congress." This is exactly what occurred when Richard Nixon's vice president, Spiro Agnew, resigned in 1973 because of his alleged receipt of construction contract kickbacks during his tenure as governor of Maryland. Nixon turned to Gerald Ford as his choice for vice president. After extensive hearings, both chambers of Congress confirmed the appointment. Then, when Nixon resigned on August 9, 1974, Ford automatically became president and nominated Nelson Rockefeller as his vice president. Congress confirmed Ford's choice. For the first time in the history of the country, neither the president nor the vice president had been elected to his position.

The question of who shall be president if both the president and vice president die is answered by the Succession Act of 1947. If the president and vice president die, resign, or are disabled, the Speaker of the House will become president, after resigning from Congress. Next in line is the president pro tem of the Senate, followed by the Cabinet officers in the order of the creation of their departments (see Table 13-2).

TABLE 13–2 Line of Succession to the Presidency of the United States

1.	Vice President
2.	Speaker of the House of Representatives
3.	Senate President Pro Tempore
4.	Secretary of State
5.	Secretary of the Treasury
6.	Secretary of Defense
7.	Attorney General (head of the Justice Department)
8.	Secretary of the Interior
9.	Secretary of Agriculture
10.	Secretary of Commerce
11.	Secretary of Labor
12.	Secretary of Health and Human Services
13.	Secretary of Housing and Urban Development
14.	Secretary of Transportation
15.	Secretary of Energy
16.	Secretary of Education
17.	Secretary of Veterans Affairs
18.	Secretary of Homeland Security

YOU CAN MAKE A Difference

WATCHING THE WHITE HOUSE

As our head of state, chief executive, commander in chief, and chief legislator, the president of the United States wields massive power over matters at home and abroad. However, the times we live in also present major challenges to this individual, and it is up to us as citizens to monitor our president's performance and balance our country's place in the world.

WHY SHOULD YOU CARE?

A recent panel convened at the Center for Public Leadership at Harvard's John F. Kennedy School of Government to discuss the challenges facing the president-elect in the 2008 election. Foreign policy issues topped concerns cited, with the continued U.S. presence in Iraq debated and the nuclear potential of Iran and North Korea studied. President Obama inherited the largest ongoing deployment of U.S. military forces in combat since the Vietnam War, while trying to overcome the unprecedented unpopularity of America in the world.

Domestically, five challenges were listed as needing resolution: (1) reforming America's financial institutions, (2) lessening inequality between society's richest 1 percent and the bottom 80 percent on the income scale, (3) improving the health care system, (4) creating a more open global economy, and (5) providing energy security while reducing climate change. This is a daunting to-do list for any president and, to make things even more complex, what needs to be done in each of these areas is not completely clear.

WHAT CAN YOU DO?

As you will remember, President Obama garnered a majority of votes from younger voters and more than expected from highly educated Americans. You can maintain a connection to the White House and keep informed on the president's initiatives by monitoring the home page of the White House, www.whitehouse.gov. This Web site has current news; links to the Web pages of the president, vice president, and First Lady; categories for public policy; pages for the president's Cabinet; and interactive links where you can register your comments. You can sign up for e-mail from the White House or the president's political campaign to receive constant updates on policy initiatives or appointments. You can also sign up for Facebook or Twitter updates. There is also a link to the White House's YouTube site, where you can watch videos from the president and other government officials. You can, of course, use "snail mail" to write to President Obama at this address:

The President of the United States
The White House
1600 Pennsylvania Avenue N.W.
Washington, DC 20500

Countless Web sites provide daily updates focusing on the president and the White House. White House Watch, www.washingtonpost.com/whitehousewatch, is published every weekday and includes White House–related items from newspapers, magazines, broadcast Web sites, and blogs. The White House Watch Links on the site include the latest White House salary list, a map of the West Wing, presidential approval polls, and a list of correspondents covering the White House for major news outlets. Politicalticker, a blog for CNNPolitics.com, features the latest political news and has a special category devoted to the president. BeltwayConfidential,

PRIME MINISTER JOHN HOWARD of Australia tries YouTube video-sharing while being observed by a journalist. (JEWEL SAMAD/AFP/Getty Images)

http://blogs.chron.com/beltwayconfidential, is a blog run by the *Houston Chronicle* that features "The President of America," with daily updates from media sources around the country and opportunities to post your comments.

Finally, if you would like to check the factual accuracy of statements made by the president or about him or her in the media, you can go to www.factcheck.org, a project of the Annenberg Public Policy Center (APPC) of the University of Pennsylvania. The APPC was established in 1994 to create a community of scholars to address public policy issues at the local, state, and federal levels.

What is most important is that you stay interested in the president and his or her initiatives whether you agree with them or not and keep up with the policy debates in Washington, D.C. By keeping up with the debates, you will be able to be an opinion leader among your friends and family and ensure their continued engagement with our political system.

REFERENCES

Glenn Greenwald, "Trust Us Government," Salon.com, accessed January 29, 2008, at www.salon.com.

Jeffrey Jones, "Low Trust in Federal Government Rivals Watergate Era Levels," Gallup News Service, accessed September 26, 2007, at www.gallup.com.

http://blogs.chron.com/beltwayconfidential/the_president_of_america.

http://politicalticker.blogs.cnn.com.

www.factcheck.org.

www.washingtonpost.com/whitehousewatch.

www.whitehouse.gov.

KEY TERMS

advice and consent 453
appointment power 451
Cabinet 469
chief diplomat 454
chief executive 450
chief legislator 456
chief of staff 471
civil service 451
commander in chief 452
constitutional power 460
diplomatic recognition 454
emergency power 464
executive agreement 455
Executive Office of the President (EOP) 470

executive order 465
executive privilege 467
expressed power 460
Federal Register 465
head of state 449
impeachment 468
inherent power 461
kitchen cabinet 469
line-item veto 460
National Security Council (NSC) 471
Office of Management and Budget (OMB) 471
pardon 452
patronage 461

permanent campaign 470
pocket veto 457
policy tsar 472
reprieve 452
signing statement 450
State of the Union message 457
statutory power 460
Twelfth Amendment 449
Twenty-fifth Amendment 474
veto message 457
War Powers Resolution 453
Washington community 462
White House Office 470

CHAPTER SUMMARY

1. The office of the presidency in the United States, combining as it does the functions of head of state and chief executive, was unique when it was created. The framers of the Constitution were divided over whether the president should be a weak or a strong executive.

2. **What roles are played by the president in American government?** The requirements for the office of the presidency are outlined in Article II, Section 1, of the Constitution. The president's roles include both formal and informal duties. The roles of the president include head of state, chief executive, commander in chief, chief diplomat, chief legislator, and party chief.

3. As head of state, the president is ceremonial leader of the government. As chief executive, the president is bound to enforce the acts of Congress, the judgments of the federal courts, and treaties. The chief executive has the power of appointment and the power to grant reprieves and pardons.

4. As commander in chief, the president is the ultimate decision maker in military matters. As chief diplomat, the president recognizes foreign governments,

negotiates treaties, signs agreements, and nominates and receives ambassadors.

5. The role of chief legislator includes recommending legislation to Congress, lobbying for the legislation, approving laws, and exercising the veto power. In addition to constitutional and inherent powers, the president has statutory powers written into law by Congress.

6. **How is presidential success judged?** Presidents are also the political leaders of their party, naming the leadership of the party and being the chief fundraiser for future elections. To become effective leaders and to gain support for their policies, presidents try to maintain strong approval ratings from the public, as measured by frequent polls. The White House Office works tirelessly to improve the president's image and reputation through its relationship with the media. Presidents who maintain their popularity are likely to have more success in their legislative programs.

7. Presidents have a variety of special powers that are not available to other branches of the government. These include emergency power and the power to issue executive orders and invoke executive privilege.

8. Abuses of executive power are dealt with by Articles I and II of the Constitution, which authorize the House and Senate to impeach and remove the president, vice president, or other officers of the federal government for committing "Treason, Bribery, or other high Crimes and Misdemeanors."

9. **What are the powers of the president as chief executive?** The president fulfills the role of chief executive by appointing individuals of his or her choice to positions in the departments and agencies of government, as well as various advisers in the White House Office and the Executive Office of the President. All appointees are supposed to be working for the president's initiatives and making sure that the larger bureaucracy is also supportive of the president's programs.

10. The vice president is the constitutional officer assigned to preside over the Senate and to assume the presidency in the event of the death, resignation, removal, or disability of the president. The Twenty-fifth Amendment, passed in 1967, established procedures to be followed in case of presidential incapacity and when filling a vacant vice presidency.

SELECTED PRINT, MEDIA, AND ONLINE RESOURCES

PRINT RESOURCES

Clinton, Bill. *My Life.* New York: Knopf, 2004. President Clinton's autobiography devotes ample space to illuminating stories from his childhood. In contrast, some may find the account of his presidential years excessively detailed. Still, the book is essential source material on one of the most important and controversial political figures of our time.

Crenson, Matthew, and Benjamin Ginsberg. *Presidential Power: Unchecked and Unbalanced.* New York: W. W. Norton, 2007. The authors return to the idea that the president has become too powerful and show how presidents over the last 30 years have expanded the power of the office.

Genovese, Michael A., and Lori Cox Han, eds. *The Presidency and the Challenge of Democracy.* Boston: Palgrave Macmillan, 2006. This collection of essays by leading scholars probes the current trend of expanding presidential powers.

Mann, James. *Rise of the Vulcans: The History of Bush's War Cabinet.* New York: Viking Books, 2004. This is a collective biography of the foreign policy team (not all of whom were actually in the Cabinet) during George W. Bush's first term. The self-described Vulcans included Donald Rumsfeld, secretary of defense; Vice

President Dick Cheney; Colin Powell, secretary of state; Paul Wolfowitz, deputy secretary of defense; Richard Armitage, deputy secretary of state; and Condoleezza Rice, national security adviser. While these individuals were never in perfect agreement, they shared basic values.

Skowronek, Stephen. *Presidential Leadership in Political Time: Reprise and Reappraisal.* Lawrence, KS: University Press of Kansas, 2008. In this updating of a well-known book, the author expands on his thesis that presidents' successes are, in part, constrained by the political events of the day. He includes both Bill Clinton and George W. Bush in his analysis.

MEDIA RESOURCES

Fahrenheit 9/11—Michael Moore's scathing 2004 critique of the Bush administration has been called "one long political attack ad." It is also the highest-grossing documentary ever made. While the film may be biased, it is—like all of Moore's productions—entertaining.

The Guns of October—This film explores the Cuban Missile Crisis of 1962. It portrays the Kennedy decision-making process in deciding not to attack Cuba.

LBJ: A Biography—An acclaimed biography of Lyndon Johnson that covers his rise to power, his presidency, and the events of the Vietnam War, which ended his presidency; produced in 1991 as part of PBS's *The American Experience* series.

Nixon—An excellent 1995 film exposing the events of Richard Nixon's troubled presidency. Anthony Hopkins plays the embattled but brilliant chief executive.

Sunrise at Campobello—An excellent portrait of one of the greatest presidents, Franklin Delano Roosevelt; produced in 1960 and starring Ralph Bellamy.

ONLINE RESOURCES

The American Presidency Project at the University of California at Santa Barbara a wonderful collection of presidential photographs, documents, audio, and video: www.presidency.ucsb.edu

Bartleby.com Internet publisher of literature, reference, and verse providing unlimited access to books and information. Includes inaugural addresses of American presidents from George Washington to Barack Obama: www.bartleby.com/124

Dave Leip's Atlas of U.S. Presidential Elections offers an excellent collection of data and maps describing all U.S. presidential elections: www.uselectionatlas.org

The White House extensive information on the White House and the presidency: www.whitehouse.gov

14

An aerial view of multiple federal buildings, including the IRS building and the Old Post Office Building. (© Hisham Ibrahim/Alamy)

The Bureaucracy

QUESTIONS TO CONSIDER

Why are government bureaucracies necessary?

What political decisions do bureaucrats make?

Why is it so difficult to manage the bureaucracy?

CHAPTER CONTENTS

what if...

The Public Graded Federal Bureaucracies?

BACKGROUND

Congress has repeatedly reformed the civil service since 1883. In addition, each modern administration has claimed that it would make bureaucrats more accountable. Despite all efforts, however, bureaucrats are far from accountable to their bosses in the executive branch, to Congress, and, least of all, to the public—the taxpayers who fund their salaries. Would bureaucrats be more accountable if report cards graded their efforts?

WHAT IF THE PUBLIC CREATED THE REPORT CARD?

Upon taking office, President George W. Bush implemented a plan known as "performance-based budgeting" to increase bureaucratic accountability. As part of this plan, the Office of Management and Budget (OMB) was to examine how well each agency met specific performance criteria and create a report card for each agency.

The government could also prepare report cards that summarized public input. Many commercial businesses actively solicit feedback from their customers on whether staff members were polite, whether problems were resolved quickly, and whether the customer was satisfied with the transaction overall. Similarly, the government could print evaluation forms to be distributed to citizens every time they interacted with the government. Taxpayers could add their comments to a Facebook page for the IRS or respond anonymously to a survey after completing their taxes.

THE PUBLIC'S IMPLICIT GRADING AFTER HURRICANE KATRINA

In one recent example, public opinion polls provided an actual evaluation of a federal agency's performance. In the immediate aftermath of Hurricane Katrina, residents of New Orleans were extremely critical of the assistance provided by FEMA. Criticism of FEMA's management led to a change in leadership at the agency. Interestingly, though, a Gallup Poll taken in October 2005, a month after the hurricane, found that half of the city's residents believed that FEMA had been very helpful to them.

USING THE EVALUATIONS

Under the Bush administration's plan for performance-based budgeting, budgetary payouts were to be linked to specific performance criteria for each program. Unfortunately, it is not always possible to cut the funding of a program that is performing poorly. The program may be so essential that it cannot be cut. It may be performing poorly because it is underfunded—and cutting back will only make matters worse.

Bad publicity might be a better tool for making bureaucrats more responsive. Already, numerous private groups are ridiculing the federal government by publicizing laughable programs and actions by federal bureaucrats that virtually no one could justify. If agencies were compared with other agencies and had to fear criticism if their performance fell below average, they might have an incentive to improve the quality of their work.

A BASIS FOR DISCIPLINE

Many observers believe that the greatest obstacle to making the federal bureaucracy responsive is that it is very difficult to fire federal bureaucrats. If bureaucrats in private businesses do not perform, their bosses simply fire them. The federal bureaucracy, in contrast, is so extensively governed by rules and regulations about firing that virtually no one is ever dismissed. Congress could make it easier for bureaucrats to be fired. If it did so, perhaps poor performance on a public report card could lead to discipline and, in due course, discharge.

FOR CRITICAL ANALYSIS

1. What specific items ought to be listed on a report card that is used to evaluate a federal bureaucracy?
2. Which agencies or departments do you think would get the worst grades?

FACELESS BUREAUCRATS—this image provokes a negative reaction from many, if not most, Americans. If they were to grade government bureaucracy as suggested in the What If ..., the grades would be low. Polls consistently report that the majority of Americans support "less government." The same polls, however, report that the majority of Americans support almost every specific program that the government undertakes. The conflict between the desire for small government and the benefits that only a large government can provide has been a constant feature of American politics. For example, the goal of preserving endangered species has widespread support. At the same time, many people believe that restrictions imposed under the Endangered Species Act violate the rights of landowners. Helping the elderly pay their medical bills is a popular objective, but hardly anyone enjoys paying the Medicare tax that supports this effort.

In addition, everyone complains about the inefficiency and wastefulness of government, in general and at federal, state, and local levels. The media regularly uncover examples of failures in governmental programs. Inadequate, slow, or bungling responses to crises such as Hurricane Katrina or the 2010 oil spill become the "face" of government through the news media. In this chapter, we describe the size, organization, and staffing of the federal bureaucracy. We review modern attempts at bureaucratic reform and the process by which Congress exerts ultimate control over the bureaucracy. We also discuss the bureaucracy's role in making rules and setting policy.

THE NATURE OF BUREAUCRACY

Every modern president, at one time or another, has proclaimed that his administration was going to "fix the government." All modern presidents also have put forth plans to end government waste and inefficiency. For instance, Bill Clinton's plan was called Reinventing Government, followed by Performance-Based Budgeting under George W. Bush. The success of plans such as these has been, in a word, underwhelming. Presidents generally have been powerless to affect the structure and operation of the federal bureaucracy significantly.

A **bureaucracy** is the name given to a large organization that is structured hierarchically to carry out specific functions. Generally, most bureaucracies are characterized by an organization chart. The units of the organization are divided according to the specialization and expertise of the employees.

Bureaucracy
A large organization that is structured hierarchically to carry out specific functions.

PUBLIC AND PRIVATE BUREAUCRACIES

We should not think of bureaucracy as unique to government. Any large corporation or university can be considered a bureaucratic organization. The fact is that the handling of complex problems requires a division of labor. Individuals must concentrate their skills on specific, well-defined aspects of a problem and depend on others to solve the rest of it.

Public or government bureaucracies differ from private organizations in some important ways, however. A private corporation, such as Microsoft, has a single set of leaders—its board of directors. Public bureaucracies, in contrast, do not have a single set of leaders. Although the president is the chief administrator of the federal system, all bureaucratic agencies are subject to Congress for their funding, staffing, and their continued existence. Furthermore, public bureaucracies supposedly serve the citizenry.

One other important difference between private corporations and government bureaucracies is that government bureaucracies are not organized to make a profit. Rather, they are supposed to perform their functions as efficiently as possible to conserve the taxpayers' dollars. Perhaps this ideal makes citizens hostile toward government bureaucracy when they experience inefficiency and red tape.

WORKERS LOAD OIL booms onto a boat to contain the oil spilling from the floor of the Gulf of Mexico after the explosion and collapse of the Deepwater Horizon oil drilling rig. (AP Photo/ Patrick Semansky)

MODELS OF BUREAUCRACY

Several theories have been offered to help us better understand the ways in which bureaucracies function. Each of these theories focuses on specific features of bureaucracies.

Weberian Model
A model of bureaucracy developed by the German sociologist Max Weber, who viewed bureaucracies as rational, hierarchical organizations in which decisions are based on logical reasoning.

Weberian Model. The classic model, or **Weberian model**, of the modern bureaucracy was proposed by the German sociologist Max Weber.[1] He argued that the increasingly complex nature of modern life, coupled with the steadily growing demands placed on governments by their citizens, made the formation of bureaucracies inevitable. According to Weber, most bureaucracies—whether in the public or private sector—are organized hierarchically and governed by formal procedures. The power in a bureaucracy flows from the top downward. Decision-making processes in bureaucracies are shaped by detailed technical rules that promote similar decisions in similar situations. Bureaucrats are specialists who attempt to resolve problems through logical reasoning and data analysis instead of instinct and guesswork. Individual advancement in bureaucracies is supposed to be based on merit rather than political connections. The modern bureaucracy, according to Weber, should be an apolitical organization.

Acquisitive Model
A model of bureaucracy that views top-level bureaucrats as seeking to expand the size of their budgets and staffs to gain greater power.

Acquisitive Model. Other theorists do not view bureaucracies in terms as benign as Weber's. Some believe that bureaucracies are acquisitive in nature. Proponents of the **acquisitive model** argue that top-level bureaucrats will always try to expand, or at least to avoid any reductions in, the size of their budgets. Although government bureaucracies are not-for-profit enterprises, bureaucrats want to maximize the size of their budgets and staffs, because these things are the most visible trappings of power in the public sector. These efforts are also prompted by the desire of bureaucrats to "sell" their products—national defense, public housing, agricultural subsidies, and so on—to both Congress and the public.

[1]Max Weber, *Theory of Social and Economic Organization,* Talcott Parsons ed. (New York: Oxford University Press, 1974).

Monopolistic Model. Because government bureaucracies seldom have competitors, some theorists have suggested that these bureaucratic organizations may be explained best by a **monopolistic model**. The analysis is similar to that used by economists to examine the behavior of monopolistic firms. Monopolistic bureaucracies—like monopolistic firms—essentially have no competitors and act accordingly. Because monopolistic bureaucracies usually are not penalized for chronic inefficiency, they have little reason to adopt cost-saving measures or to use their resources more productively. Some economists have argued that such problems can be cured only by privatizing certain bureaucratic functions.

Monopolistic Model
A model of bureaucracy that compares bureaucracies to monopolistic business firms. Lack of competition in either circumstance leads to inefficient and costly operations.

BUREAUCRACIES COMPARED

The federal bureaucracy in the United States enjoys a greater degree of autonomy than do federal or national bureaucracies in many other nations. Much of the insularity that is commonly supposed to characterize the bureaucracy in this country may stem from the sheer size of the government organizations needed to implement an annual budget that is about $3 trillion. Because the lines of authority often are not well defined, some bureaucracies may be able to operate with a significant degree of autonomy.

The federal nature of the American government also means that national bureaucracies regularly provide financial assistance to their state counterparts. Both the Department of Education and the Department of Housing and Urban Development, for example, distribute funds to their counterparts at the state level. In contrast, most bureaucracies in European countries have a top-down command structure so that national programs may be implemented directly at the lower level. This is due not only to the smaller size of most European countries but also to the fact that public ownership of such businesses as telephone companies, airlines, railroads, and utilities is far more common in Europe than in the United States.

The fact that the U.S. government owns relatively few enterprises does not mean, however, that its bureaucracies are comparatively powerless. Many **administrative agencies** in the federal bureaucracy—such as the Environmental Protection Agency, the Nuclear Regulatory Commission, and the Securities and Exchange Commission—regulate private companies.

DID YOU KNOW?

That the federal government spends more than $1 billion every five hours, every day of the year?

Administrative Agency
A federal, state, or local government unit established to perform a specific function. Administrative agencies are created and authorized by legislative bodies to administer and enforce specific laws.

THE SIZE OF THE BUREAUCRACY

In 1789, the new government's bureaucracy was minuscule. There were three departments—State (with nine employees), War (with two employees), and Treasury (with 39 employees)—and the Office of the Attorney General (which later became the Department of Justice). The bureaucracy was still small in 1798. At that time, the secretary of state had seven clerks and spent a total of $500 (about $8,545 in 2008 dollars) on stationery and printing. In that same year, the Appropriations Act allocated $1.4 million to the War Department (or $23.9 million in 2008 dollars).[2]

Times have changed, as we can see in Figure 14-1, which lists the various federal agencies and the number of civilian employees in each. Excluding the military, the federal bureaucracy includes approximately 2.7 million government employees. That number has remained relatively stable for the last several decades. It is somewhat deceiving, however, because many other individuals work directly or indirectly for the federal government as subcontractors or consultants and in other capacities. In fact,

---

[2]Leonard D. White, *The Federalists: A Study in Administrative History, 1789–1801* (New York: Free Press, 1948).

FIGURE 14–1 Federal Agencies and Their Respective Numbers of Civilian Employees

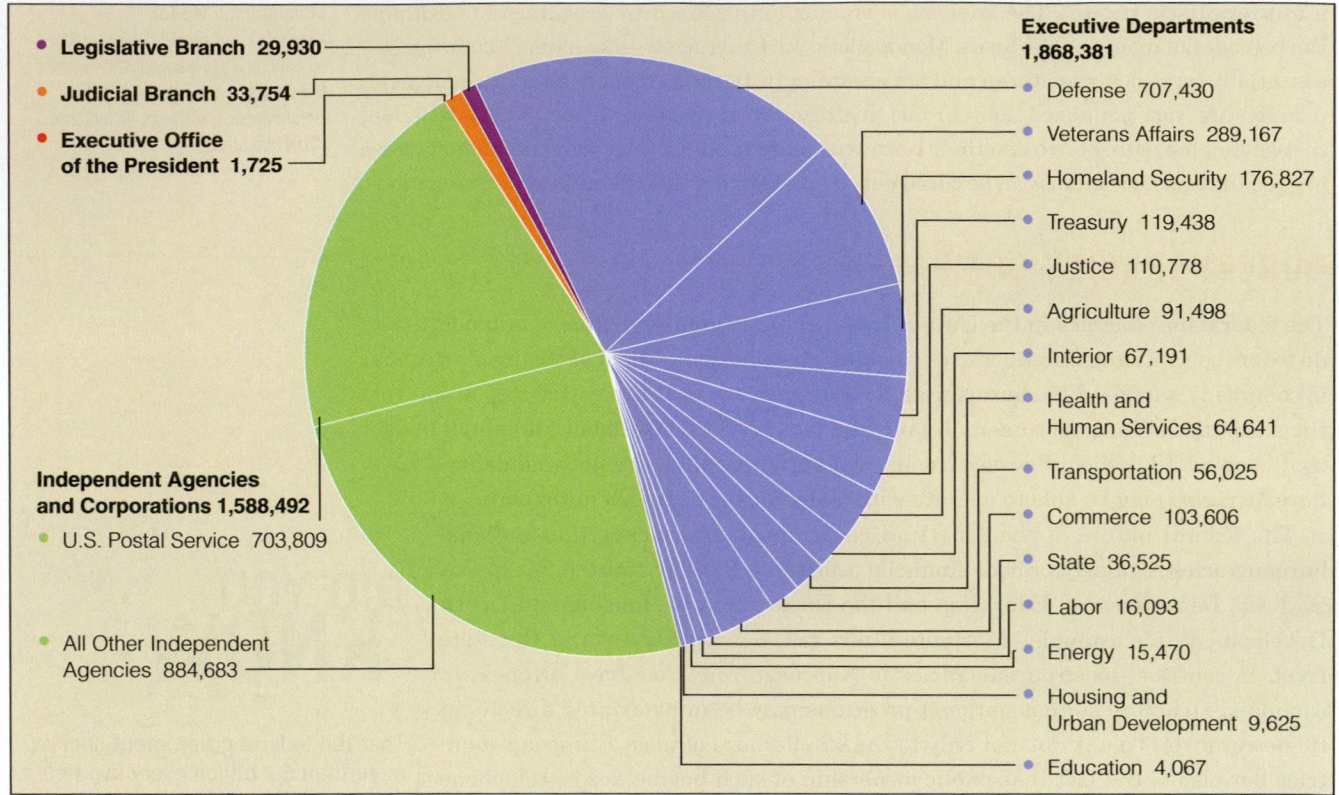

- **Legislative Branch 29,930**
- **Judicial Branch 33,754**
- **Executive Office of the President 1,725**

Independent Agencies and Corporations 1,588,492
- U.S. Postal Service 703,809
- All Other Independent Agencies 884,683

Executive Departments 1,868,381
- Defense 707,430
- Veterans Affairs 289,167
- Homeland Security 176,827
- Treasury 119,438
- Justice 110,778
- Agriculture 91,498
- Interior 67,191
- Health and Human Services 64,641
- Transportation 56,025
- Commerce 103,606
- State 36,525
- Labor 16,093
- Energy 15,470
- Housing and Urban Development 9,625
- Education 4,067

Source: U.S. Office of Personnel Management, Federal Employment Statistics, Table 14, http://www.opm.gov/feddata/html/2009/March/table14.asp, and authors' updates

FIGURE 14–2 Government Employment at the Federal, State, and Local Levels

There are more local government employees than federal or state employees combined.

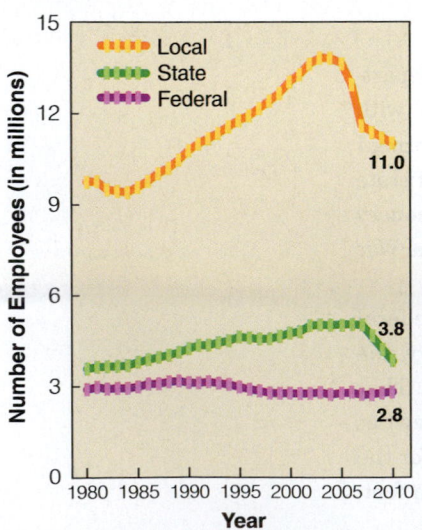

Source: Bureau of Labor Statistics, 2006.

according to some studies, the federal workforce vastly exceeds the number of official federal workers.[3]

The figures for federal government employment are only part of the story. Figure 14-2 shows the growth in government employment at the federal, state, and local levels. Since 1970, this growth has been mainly at the state and local levels. If all government employees are included, more than 16 percent of all civilian employment is accounted for by government. The costs of the bureaucracy are commensurately high. The share of the gross domestic product accounted for by all government spending was only 8.5 percent in 1929. Today, it exceeds 44 percent. Could we reduce the cost of government by eliminating unnecessary spending? We look at one example of questionable spending in the discussion of AMTRAK in the "Government Corporations" section.

THE ORGANIZATION OF THE FEDERAL BUREAUCRACY

Within the federal bureaucracy are several different types of government agencies and organizations. Figure 14-3 outlines the several bodies within the executive branch, as well as the separate organizations that provide

---

[3]See, for example, Paul C. Light, *The True Size of Government* (Washington, DC: Brookings Institution Press, 1999).

services to Congress, to the courts, and directly to the president. In Chapter 13, we discussed those agencies that are considered to be part of the Executive Office of the President.

The executive branch, which employs most of the government's staff, has four major types of structures: (1) Cabinet departments, (2) independent executive agencies, (3) independent regulatory agencies, and (4) government corporations. Each has a distinctive relationship to the president, and some have unusual internal structures, overall goals, and grants of power.

CABINET DEPARTMENTS

The 15 **Cabinet departments** are the major service organizations of the federal government. They can also be described in management terms as **line organizations.** This means that they are directly accountable to the president and are responsible for performing government functions, such as printing money and training troops. These departments were created by Congress when the need for each department arose. The first department to be created was State, and the most recent one was Homeland Security, established in 2003. The difficulties faced in creating that new department are discussed in the "Reorganizing to Stop Terrorism" section. A president might ask that a new department be created or an old one abolished, but the president has no power to do so without legislative approval from Congress.

Each department is headed by a secretary (except for the Justice Department, which is headed by the attorney general). Each also has several levels of undersecretaries, assistant secretaries, and so on.

Presidents theoretically have considerable control over the Cabinet departments, because presidents are able to appoint or fire all of the top officials. As discussed in Chapter 13, these positions are listed in the Plum Book. Even Cabinet departments do not always respond to the president's wishes, though. One reason that presidents are frequently unhappy with their departments is that the entire bureaucratic structure below the top political levels is staffed by permanent employees, many of whom are committed to established programs or procedures and who resist change. Table 14-1 on page 490 shows that each Cabinet department employs thousands of individuals, only a handful of whom are under the control of the president. The table also describes some of the functions of each of the departments.

INDEPENDENT EXECUTIVE AGENCIES

Independent executive agencies are bureaucratic organizations that are not located within a department but report directly to the president, who appoints their chief officials. When a new federal agency is created—the Environmental Protection Agency, for example—Congress decides where it will be located in the bureaucracy. In recent decades, presidents often have asked that a new organization be kept separate or independent rather than added to an existing department, particularly if a department may be hostile to the agency's creation. The Smithsonian Institution, which runs the government's museums and the National Zoo, was formed in 1846 and is an example of an independent executive agency. Another example is the Central Intelligence Agency (CIA). Formed in 1947, the CIA gathers and analyzes political and military information about foreign

Cabinet Department
One of the 15 departments of the executive branch (State, Treasury, Defense, Justice, Interior, Agriculture, Commerce, Labor, Health and Human Services, Homeland Security, Housing and Urban Development, Education, Energy, Transportation, and Veterans Affairs).

Line Organization
In the federal government, an administrative unit that is directly accountable to the president.

Independent Executive Agency
A federal agency that is not part of a Cabinet department but reports directly to the president.

SECRETARY OF THE TREASURY
Timothy Geithner testifies in 2009 before the Senate Banking Committee on the TARP (Troubled Assets Relief Program). (AP Photo/Manuel Balce Ceneta)

FIGURE 14–3 Organization Chart of the Federal Government

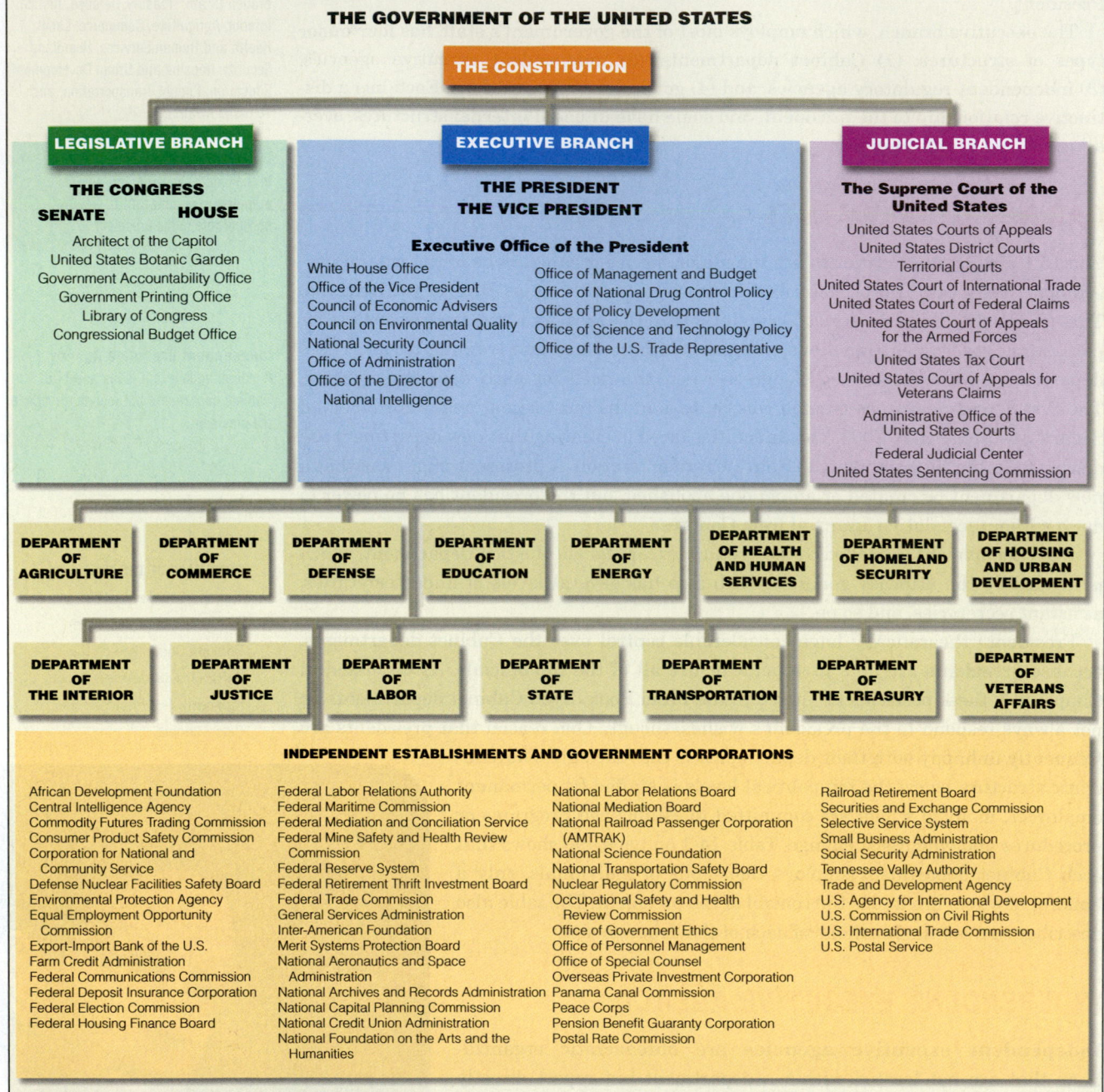

Source: United States Government Manual, 2007–2008 (Washington, DC: U.S. Government Printing Office, 2007).

countries and conducts covert operations outside the United States. You can read more about the CIA in Chapter 18.

INDEPENDENT REGULATORY AGENCIES

Independent Regulatory Agency
An agency outside the major executive departments charged with making and implementing rules and regulations.

The **independent regulatory agencies** are typically responsible for a specific type of public policy. Their function is to make and implement rules and regulations in a particular sphere of action to protect the public interest. The earliest such agency was the

Interstate Commerce Commission (ICC), which was established in 1887 when Americans began to seek some form of government control over the rapidly growing business and industrial sector. This new form of organization, the independent regulatory agency, was supposed to make technical, nonpolitical decisions about rates, profits, and rules that would benefit all and that did not require congressional legislation. In the years that followed the creation of the ICC, other agencies were formed to regulate communication (the Federal Communications Commission), nuclear power (the Nuclear Regulatory Commission), and so on. (The ICC was abolished on December 30, 1995.)

The Purpose and Nature of Regulatory Agencies. In practice, the regulatory agencies are administered independently of all three branches of government. They were set up because Congress felt it was unable to handle the complexities and technicalities required to carry out specific laws in the public interest. The regulatory commissions in fact combine some functions of all three branches of government—executive, legislative, and judicial. They are legislative in that they make rules that have the force of law. They are executive in that they enforce those rules. They are judicial in that they decide disputes involving the rules they have made.

Members of regulatory agency boards or commissions are appointed by the president with the consent of the Senate, although they do not report to the president. By law, the members of regulatory agencies cannot all be from the same political party. Members may be removed by the president only for causes specified in the law creating the agency. Presidents can influence regulatory agency behavior by appointing people of their own parties or individuals who share their political views when vacancies occur—in particular, when the chair is vacant. For example, President George W. Bush placed people on the Federal Communications Commission (FCC) who shared his belief in the need to curb obscene language in the media. Not surprisingly, the FCC soon thereafter started to "crack down" on obscenities on the air. One victim of this regulatory effort was Howard Stern, a nationally syndicated radio and television personality. His response was to switch from commercial radio and TV to unregulated satellite radio, where he can be heard every day on Sirius.

Agency Capture. Over the last several decades, some observers have concluded that these agencies, although nominally independent, may in fact not always be so. They contend that many independent regulatory agencies have been **captured** by the very industries and firms they were supposed to regulate. The results have been less competition rather than more competition, higher prices rather than lower prices, and less choice rather than more choice for consumers. One of the accusations made after the BP oil spill in 2010 was that the appropriate regulatory agency, the Minerals and Mining Administration, had become too lax in enforcing the safety regulations on the drilling rigs because it favored the oil companies.

Capture
The act by which an industry being regulated by a government agency gains direct or indirect control over agency personnel and decision makers.

Deregulation and Reregulation. During the presidency of Ronald Reagan (served 1981–1989), some significant deregulation (the removal of regulatory restraints—the opposite of regulation) occurred, much of which had started under President Jimmy Carter (served 1977–1981). For example, President Carter appointed a chairperson of the Civil Aeronautics Board (CAB), who gradually eliminated regulation of airline fares and routes. Then, under Reagan, the CAB was eliminated on January 1, 1985.

During the administration of George H. W. Bush (served 1989–1993), calls for reregulation of many businesses increased. During that administration, the Americans with Disabilities Act of 1990, the Civil Rights Act of 1991, and the Clean Air Act Amendments of 1991, all of which increased or changed the regulation of many businesses, were passed. Additionally, the Cable Re-regulation Act of 1992 was passed.

DID YOU KNOW?

That the Commerce Department's U.S. Travel and Tourism Administration gave away $440,000 in disaster relief to western ski resort operators because there hadn't been enough snow?

TABLE 14–1 Executive Departments

DEPARTMENT AND YEAR ESTABLISHED	PRINCIPAL FUNCTIONS
State (1789) (36,525 employees)	Negotiates treaties; develops foreign policy; protects citizens abroad
Treasury (1789) (119,438 employees)	Pays all federal bills; borrows money; collects federal taxes; mints coins and prints paper currency; supervises national banks
Interior (1849) (67,191 employees)	Supervises federally owned lands and parks; supervises Native American affairs
Justice (1870)* (110,778 employees)	Furnishes legal advice to the president; enforces federal criminal laws; supervises federal prisons
Agriculture (1889) (91,498 employees)	Assists farmers and ranchers; conducts agricultural research; works to protect forests
Commerce (1913)** (103,606 employees)	Grants patents and trademarks; conducts national census; monitors weather; protects interests of businesses (Note: The Commerce Department houses the Census Bureau, which increased its workforce from several thousand employees to more than a half million between early 2009 and summer 2010. Most of these workers are short-term temporary employees.)
Labor (1913)** (16,093 employees)	Administers federal labor laws; promotes interests of workers
Defense (1947)*** (707,430 employees)	Manages the armed forces; operates military bases; civil defense
Housing and Urban Development (1965) (9,625 employees)	Deals with nation's housing needs; develops and rehabilitates urban communities; oversees resale of mortgages
Transportation (1967) (56,025 employees)	Finances improvements in mass transit; develops and administers programs for highways, railroads, and aviation
Energy (1977) (15,470 employees)	Promotes energy conservation; analyzes energy data; conducts research and development
Health and Human Services (1979)*** (64,641 employees)	Promotes public health; enforces pure food and drug laws; conducts and sponsors health-related research
Education (1979)*** (4,067 employees)	Coordinates federal education programs and policies; administers aid to education; promotes educational research
Veterans Affairs (1988) (289,167 employees)	Promotes welfare of U.S. veterans
Homeland Security (2003) (176,827 employees)	Attempts to prevent terrorist attacks within the United States; controls U.S. borders; minimizes damage from natural disasters

*Formed from the Office of the Attorney General (created in 1789).

**Formed from the Department of Commerce and Labor (created in 1903).

***Formed from the Department of War (created in 1789) and the Department of the Navy (created in 1798).

****Formed from the Department of Health, Education, and Welfare (created in 1953).

Employment figures from U.S. Office of Personnel Management, Federal Employment Statistics, Table 14, http://www.opm.gov/feddata/html/2009/March/table14.asp, and authors' updates.

Under President Bill Clinton (served 1993–2001), the Interstate Commerce Commission was eliminated, and the banking and telecommunications industries, along with many other sectors of the economy, were deregulated. At the same time, extensive regulation protected the environment. In the wake of the mortgage crisis of

2007 and failure of several large investment houses in 2008, the administration and most members of Congress called for a bailout of the troubled firms and a return to more regulation.

GOVERNMENT CORPORATIONS

Another form of bureaucratic organization in the United States is the **government corporation**. Although the concept is borrowed from the world of business, distinct differences exist between public and private corporations.

A private corporation has shareholders (stockholders) who elect a board of directors, who in turn choose the corporate officers, such as president and vice president. When a private corporation makes a profit, it must pay taxes (unless it avoids them through various legal loopholes). It either distributes part or all of the after-tax profits to shareholders as dividends or plows the profits back into the corporation to make new investments.

A government corporation has a board of directors and managers, but it does not have any stockholders. We cannot buy shares of stock in a government corporation. If the government corporation makes a profit, it does not distribute the profit as dividends. Also, if it makes a profit, it does not have to pay taxes; the profits remain in the corporation.

Two of the best-known government corporations are the U.S. Postal Service and AMTRAK, the domestic passenger railroad corporation. Thirty-five years ago, after several private rail companies went bankrupt, Congress created a public railway system called AMTRAK. Today, AMTRAK links 500 American towns and cities in 46 states with more than 22,000 miles of rail. It has many critics both inside and outside of Congress.

During AMTRAK's existence, American taxpayers have subsidized it to the tune of more than $25 billion. Current subsidies typically exceed $1 billion per year—$1.8 billion was requested in 2006, and $2 billion was requested for 2007. As Republican Representative Harold Rogers of Kentucky has pointed out, "Every time a passenger boards a train, Uncle Sam writes a check for $138.71, on average." Those in favor of the AMTRAK subsidies argue that AMTRAK provides essential transportation for the poor. However, the majority of daily passengers are middle-class commuters on the eastern corridor routes.

For many years, critics of this government corporation have said that the benefits of AMTRAK, including reducing congestion on the highways, are less than the costs. Some have suggested that the passenger service be privatized—that is, sold to a private corporation. However, as the price of gasoline rose in 2008 and the issue of the future supply of oil became critical, AMTRAK became more popular with travelers. Faced with skyrocketing gas prices, rail transportation may see expansion rather than contraction in the next decade.

The U.S. Postal Service, which is the second largest employer in the United States (after Walmart), has more than 700,000 employees. On paper, the postal service appears to be "breaking even" in terms of costs and revenues. However, critics note that this government corporation has the right to borrow funds from the federal government at a very low interest rate and has borrowed about $10 billion so far to support its operations.

CHALLENGES TO THE BUREAUCRACY

With Cabinet departments, independent executive agencies, independent regulatory agencies, and government corporations, the federal bureaucracy is both complex and very specialized. Each agency, corporation, or line department has its own mission, its

Government Corporation
An agency of government that administers a quasi-business enterprise. These corporations are used when activities are primarily commercial.

That the Pentagon and the Central Intelligence Agency spent more than $11 million on psychics who were supposed to provide special insights regarding various foreign threats?

own goals, and, in many cases, its own constituents either at home or, in the case of the State Department, abroad. However, some problems and crises require the attention of multiple agencies. In these cases, overlapping jurisdictions can cause confusion, or there may be problems that no agency has the authority to solve.

There is a famous story about the Carter administration that makes this point: President Jimmy Carter believed he smelled something dead behind his Oval Office wall—probably a mouse. His staff called the General Services Administration, which has responsibility for the White House, but those bureaucrats claimed it was not their problem. They had fumigated recently, so the mouse must have come in from outside. The Department of the Interior, which has responsibility for the gardens and grounds, refused to help since the mouse was now inside. Eventually, an interagency task force was created to remove the mouse. If solving this small problem was complicated for the federal bureaucracy, consider larger issues such as terrorism and natural disasters.

REORGANIZING TO STOP TERRORISM

After September 11, 2001, the nation saw that no single agency was responsible for coordinating antiterrorism efforts. Nor was one person able to muster a nationwide response to a terrorist attack. Fighting terrorism involves so many different aspects—screening baggage at airports, inspecting freight shipments, and protecting the border, to name just a few—that coordinating them would be impossible unless all of these functions were combined into one agency.

The creation of the Department of Homeland Security (DHS) in 2003 was the largest reorganization of the U.S. government since 1947. Twenty-two agencies with responsibilities for preventing terrorism were merged into a single department. The Congress and the president agreed that combining the Federal Emergency Management Agency (FEMA), Customs and Border Protection, the Coast Guard, the Secret Service, and many other organizations into a single agency would promote efficiency and improve coordination. This sprawling agency now has more than 176,000 employees and an estimated budget of $55 billion (as of 2010).

One of the main challenges facing the new department was integrating agencies whose missions were very different. Some commentators suggested that the bureaucratic cultures of those agencies that were focused on law enforcement, such as the Secret Service and the Border Patrol, would have difficulty working with the agencies that focus on the problems faced by citizens in a time of natural disasters, such as the Federal Emergency Management Agency (FEMA). Indeed, when FEMA became part of the DHS, not only was its funding reduced, but more importantly, it received less attention because the focus of the DHS has been on fighting terrorism, not on responding to natural disasters.

Perhaps even more importantly, the DHS did not actually unify all U.S. antiterrorism efforts. The most important antiterrorist agencies are the Federal Bureau of Investigation (FBI) and the Central Intelligence Agency (CIA), but neither is part of the DHS. Many believe that the number-one problem in addressing terrorism is the failure of the FBI and CIA to exchange information with each other. To try to address this problem, President Bush created a Terrorist Threat Integration Center in *addition* to the DHS, the FBI, and the CIA. In 2004, Congress established the new Office of the Director of National Intelligence to coordinate the nation's intelligence efforts, and in 2005, President Bush appointed John Negroponte to be the director of national intelligence to try once again to coordinate the nation's intelligence agencies. This position, however, has been difficult to establish. By 2010, President Barack Obama was seeking to nominate the fourth director in five years after Dennis C. Blair was asked to resign. Many Washington insiders note that the authority of the director is often undercut by other appointees who may be closer to the president, including the director of the CIA and the national security adviser, making this a very difficult position to hold.

DEALING WITH NATURAL DISASTERS

As George H. W. Bush faced a tough reelection campaign in 1992, Hurricane Andrew struck southern Florida, one of only three Category 5 storms to hit the United States in the 20th century.

THE U.S. COAST GUARD patrols the waters of Boston Harbor in preparation for the 2004 Democratic convention. Since September 11, 2001, such precautions have become normal in the United States. (William B. Plowman/Reuters/ CORBIS)

Hurricane Andrew destroyed many communities south of Miami, Florida, leaving hundreds of thousands of people without power and without homes. Although the total death toll was only 65, the cost of the storm was more than $25 billion in damage and losses. The Bush administration was widely criticized for not getting aid to the victims quickly enough, and the president was chided for not putting in a personal appearance.

Supposedly, FEMA was strengthened and improved after Hurricane Andrew. FEMA did deal with hundreds of natural disasters in the years that followed, including tornados, floods, and blizzards. However, in 2005, a year in which five major hurricanes made landfall in the United States, FEMA again proved unable to meet the challenges of a massive natural disaster. When Hurricane Katrina headed toward New Orleans, all authorities warned of a possible flooding situation. No one dreamed of flooding that would trap thousands of residents in their homes for a week or more and destroy whole neighborhoods in New Orleans. No one had planned to evacuate thousands of people with no transportation of their own or to house them for years after the storm.

A natural disaster such as Hurricane Katrina can only be met by coordinated action from local, state, and federal authorities. Clearly, miscommunication occurred among all those levels of government in the case of Katrina. Responding to Hurricane Katrina involved the Army Corps of Engineers (responsible for the New Orleans levees), FEMA, the National Guard, the departments of Energy (oil rigs and refineries), Health and Human Services (hospitals, health services, vaccines), Housing and Urban Development (housing and rebuilding), and Education (schools destroyed throughout Louisiana). While FEMA is charged with emergency management, it does not have any direct control over these other federal agencies. The sitting president, George W. Bush, was severely criticized for not acting quickly enough in this crisis. In 2010, an oil drilling rig in the Gulf of Mexico exploded, triggering a massive oil spill. Again, within days, the media and local government officials were calling for faster and more effective federal government assistance even though the technology for dealing with such a spill is only available in the petroleum industry. President Barack Obama was accused of not visiting the region quickly enough and not demonstrating enough anger at the oil company.

What Hurricane Katrina illustrates is the huge challenge faced by bureaucracies when dealing with natural disasters. So many agencies and levels of government must be coordinated that sometimes responses are delayed and aid does not get to the victims in a timely way. Media coverage of these tragedies focuses on the struggles of citizens, while the struggles of the bureaucrats take place in back rooms as officials strive to find the right equipment and personnel to meet unique disasters. There may be no way that any president can be successful in dealing with the public relations aspect of these events.

STAFFING THE BUREAUCRACY

There are two categories of bureaucrats: political appointees and civil servants. As noted earlier, the president is able to make political appointments to most of the top jobs in the federal bureaucracy. The president can also appoint ambassadors to foreign posts. As noted in Chapter 13, these jobs are listed in the Plum Book. The rest of the national government's employees belong to the civil service and obtain their jobs through a much more formal process.

POLITICAL APPOINTEES

To fill the positions listed in the Plum Book, the president and the president's advisers solicit suggestions from politicians, businesspersons, and other prominent individuals. Appointments to these positions offer the president a way to pay off outstanding political debts. But the president must also consider such things as the candidate's work

SECRETARY OF STATE Hillary Clinton speaks during a joint press conference with her British counterpart, William Hague, at the State Department building in Washington, D.C. (AFP PHOTO/Mandel/Newscom)

experience, intelligence, political affiliations, and personal characteristics. Presidents have differed in the importance they attach to appointing women and minorities to plum positions. Presidents often use ambassadorships, however, to reward individuals for their campaign contributions.

We should note here that even though the president has the power to appoint a government official, this does not mean an appointment will pass muster. Before making any nominations, the administration requires potential appointees to undergo a detailed screening process and answer questions such as the following: What are your accomplishments? Did you ever *not* pay taxes for your nannies or housekeepers? What kinds of investments have you made? What have your past partisan affiliations been?

Such a process takes months, and after completing it, the appointees must be confirmed by the Senate. Even with such a screening process, the Bush administration made some serious errors. For example, the president's appointment of Michael Brown to head FEMA turned out to be a big mistake, because Brown had no experience in emergency planning and relief efforts. Several Obama appointees were either not confirmed or left the government quickly after difficulties with their resumes or political activities prior to taking office were uncovered.

The Aristocracy of the Federal Government. Political appointees are in some sense the aristocracy of the federal government. But their powers, although appearing formidable on paper, are often exaggerated. Like the president, a political appointee will occupy her or his position for a comparatively brief time. Political appointees often leave office before the president's term actually ends. In fact, the average term of service for political appointees is less than two years. As a result, most appointees have little background for their positions and may be mere figureheads. Often, they only respond to the paperwork that flows up from below. Additionally, the professional civil servants who make up the permanent civil service may not feel compelled to carry out their current boss's directives quickly, because they know that he or she will not be around for very long.

The Difficulty in Firing Civil Servants. This inertia is compounded by the fact that it is very difficult to discharge civil servants. In recent years, fewer than one-tenth of 1 percent of federal employees have been fired for incompetence. Because discharged employees may appeal their dismissals, many months or even years can pass before the issue is resolved conclusively. This occupational rigidity helps ensure that most political appointees, no matter how competent or driven, will not be able to exert much meaningful influence over their subordinates, let alone implement dramatic changes in the bureaucracy itself.

HISTORY OF THE FEDERAL CIVIL SERVICE

When the federal government was formed in 1789, it had no career public servants but rather consisted of amateurs who were almost all Federalists. When Thomas Jefferson took over as president, few people in his party were holding federal administrative jobs, so he fired more than 100 officials and replaced them with his own supporters. Then, for the next 25 years, a growing body of federal administrators gained experience and expertise, becoming in the process professional public servants. These administrators stayed in office regardless of who was elected president. The bureaucracy had become a self-maintaining, long-term element within government.

DID YOU KNOW?

That the average federal government civilian worker earns $106,579 per year in total compensation (wages plus health insurance, pension, etc.), whereas the average private-sector worker earns $53,289 a year in total compensation?

ON SEPTEMBER 19, 1881,
President James A. Garfield was assassinated by a disappointed office seeker, Charles J. Guiteau. The long-term effect of this event was to replace the spoils system with a permanent career civil service. This process began with the passage of the Pendleton Act in 1883, which established the Civil Service Commission. (Library of Congress, Prints & Photographs Division, Washington, D.C. [LC-USZ62-7622])

Spoils System
The awarding of government jobs to political supporters and friends.

Merit System
The selection, retention, and promotion of government employees on the basis of competitive examinations.

Pendleton Act (Civil Service Reform Act)
An act that established the principle of employment on the basis of merit and created the Civil Service Commission to administer the personnel service.

Civil Service Commission
The initial central personnel agency of the national government, created in 1883.

To the Victor Belong the Spoils. When Andrew Jackson took over the White House in 1828, he could not believe how many appointed officials (appointed before he became president, that is) were overtly hostile toward him and his Democratic Party. Because the bureaucracy was reluctant to carry out his programs, Jackson did the obvious: He fired federal officials—more than had all his predecessors combined. The **spoils system**—an application of the principle that to the victor belong the spoils—became the standard method of filling federal positions. Whenever a new president was elected from a different party, there would be an almost complete turnover in the staffing of the federal government.

The Civil Service Reform Act of 1883. Jackson's spoils system survived for several years, but it became increasingly corrupt. Also, as the size of the bureaucracy increased by 300 percent between 1851 and 1881, the cry for civil service reform became louder. Reformers began to look to the example of several European countries, Germany in particular, which had established a professional civil service that operated under a **merit system,** in which job appointments were based on competitive examinations.

In 1883, the **Pendleton Act**—or **Civil Service Reform Act**—was passed, placing the first limits on the spoils system. The act established the principle of employment on the basis of open, competitive examinations and created the **Civil Service Commission** to administer the personnel service. Initially, only 10 percent of federal employees were covered by the merit system. Later laws, amendments, and executive orders, however, increased the coverage to more than 90 percent of federal employees. The effects of these reforms were felt at all levels of government.

The Supreme Court strengthened the civil service system in *Elrod v. Burns*[4] in 1976 and *Branti v. Finkel*[5] in 1980. In those two cases, the Court used the First Amendment to forbid government officials from discharging or threatening to discharge public employees solely for *not* being supporters of the political party in power unless party affiliation is an appropriate requirement for the position. Additional enhancements to

[4] 427 U.S. 347 (1976).
[5] 445 U.S. 507 (1980).

the civil service system were added in *Rutan v. Republican Party of Illinois*[6] in 1990. The Court's ruling effectively prevented the use of partisan political considerations as the basis for hiring, promoting, or transferring most public employees. An exception was permitted, however, for senior policy-making positions, which usually go to officials who will support the programs of the elected leaders.

The Civil Service Reform Act of 1978. In 1978, the Civil Service Reform Act abolished the Civil Service Commission and created two new federal agencies to perform its duties. To administer the civil service laws, rules, and regulations, the act created the Office of Personnel Management (OPM), which is empowered to recruit, interview, and test potential government workers and determine who should be hired. The OPM makes recommendations to the individual agencies as to which persons meet the standards (typically, the top three applicants for a position), and the agencies then decide whom to hire. To oversee promotions, employees' rights, and other employment matters, the act created the Merit Systems Protection Board (MSPB), which evaluates charges of wrongdoing, hears employee appeals of agency decisions, and can order corrective action against agencies and employees.

Federal Employees and Political Campaigns. In 1933, when President Franklin D. Roosevelt set up his New Deal, a virtual army of civil servants was hired to staff the numerous new agencies that were created. Because the individuals who worked in these agencies owed their jobs to the Democratic Party, it seemed natural for them to campaign for Democratic candidates. The Democrats controlling Congress in the mid-1930s did not object. But in 1938, a coalition of conservative Democrats and Republicans took control of Congress and forced through the Hatch Act—or Political Activities Act—of 1939. The act prohibited federal employees from actively participating in the political management of campaigns. It also forbade the use of federal authority to influence nominations and elections and outlawed the use of bureaucratic rank to pressure federal employees to make political contributions.

The Hatch Act created a controversy that lasted for decades. Many contended that the act deprived federal employees of their First Amendment freedoms of speech and association. In 1972, a federal district court declared it unconstitutional. The United States Supreme Court, however, reaffirmed the challenged portion of the act in 1973, stating that the government's interest in preserving a nonpartisan civil service was so great that the prohibitions should remain.[7] Twenty years later, Congress addressed the criticisms of the Hatch Act by passing the Federal Employees Political Activities Act of 1993. This act, which amended the Hatch Act, lessened the harshness of the 1939 act in several ways. Among other things, the 1993 act allowed federal employees to run for office in nonpartisan elections, participate in voter-registration drives, make campaign contributions to political organizations, and campaign for candidates in partisan elections.

MODERN ATTEMPTS AT BUREAUCRATIC REFORM

As long as the federal bureaucracy exists, there will continue to be attempts to make it more open, efficient, and responsive to the needs of U.S. citizens. The most important actual and proposed reforms in the last several decades include sunshine and

DID YOU KNOW?

That federal officials spent $333,000 building a deluxe, earthquake-proof outhouse for hikers in Pennsylvania's remote Delaware Water Gap recreation area?

---

[6]497 U.S. 62 (1990).
[7]*United States Civil Service Commission v. National Association of Letter Carriers,* 413 U.S. 548 (1973).

sunset laws, privatization, incentives for efficiency, and more protection for so-called whistleblowers.

SUNSHINE LAWS BEFORE AND AFTER SEPTEMBER 11

Government in the Sunshine Act
A law that requires all committee-directed federal agencies to conduct their business regularly in public session.

In 1976, Congress enacted the **Government in the Sunshine Act**. It required for the first time that all multiheaded federal agencies—agencies headed by a committee instead of an individual—hold their meetings regularly in public session. The bill defined *meetings* as almost any gathering, formal or informal, of agency members, including a conference telephone call. The only exceptions to this rule of openness are discussions of matters such as court proceedings or personnel problems, and these exceptions are specifically listed in the bill. Sunshine laws now exist at all levels of government.

Information Disclosure. Sunshine laws are consistent with the policy of information disclosure that has been supported by the government for decades. For example, beginning in the 1960s, several consumer protection laws have required that certain information be disclosed to consumers when purchasing homes, borrowing funds, and so on. In 1966, the federal government passed the Freedom of Information Act, which required federal government agencies, with certain exceptions, to disclose to individuals, on their request, any information about them contained in government files.

Curbs on Information Disclosure. Since September 11, 2001, the trend toward government in the sunshine and information disclosure has been reversed at both the federal and state levels. Within weeks after September 11, 2001, numerous federal agencies removed hundreds, if not thousands, of documents from Internet sites, public libraries, and reading rooms found in various federal government departments. Information contained in some of the documents included diagrams of power plants and pipelines, structural details on dams, and safety plans for chemical plants. The military also immediately started restricting information about its current and planned activities, as did the FBI. These agencies were concerned that terrorists could use this information to plan attacks. The federal government has also gone back into the archives to remove an increasing quantity of not only sensitive information but also sometimes seemingly unimportant information.

"Who do I see to get big government off my back?" (© 2002 The New Yorker Collection from cartoonbank.com. All rights reserved.)

In making some public documents inaccessible to the public, the federal government was ahead of state and local governments, but they quickly followed suit. State and local governments control and supervise police forces, dams, electricity sources, and water supplies. Consequently, it is not surprising that many state and local governments followed in the footsteps of the federal government in curbing access to certain public records and information. Most local agencies, however, do include the public in their planning for emergencies.

SUNSET LAWS

Potentially, the size and scope of the federal bureaucracy can be controlled through **sunset legislation**, which places government programs on a definite schedule for congressional consideration. Unless Congress specifically reauthorizes a particular federally operated program at the end of a designated period, it is automatically terminated; that is, its sun sets.

The idea of sunset legislation was initially suggested by Franklin D. Roosevelt when he created the plethora of New Deal agencies in the 1930s. His assistant, William O. Douglas, recommended that each agency's charter should include a provision allowing for its termination in 10 years. Only an act of Congress could revitalize it. The proposal was never adopted. It was not until 1976 that a state legislature—Colorado's—adopted sunset legislation for state regulatory commissions, giving them a life of six years before their suns set. Today, most states have some type of sunset law.

Sunset Legislation
Laws requiring that existing programs be reviewed regularly for their effectiveness and be terminated unless specifically extended as a result of these reviews.

PRIVATIZATION

Another approach to bureaucratic reform is **privatization**, which occurs when government services are replaced by services from the private sector. For example, the government might contract with private firms to operate prisons. Supporters of

Privatization
The replacement of government services with services provided by private firms.

AN ARMED NUCLEAR SECURITY OFFICER patrols the coastal area of the Diablo Canyon nuclear power plant on May 5, 2004, in Avila Beach, California. Since September 11, all American utilities have increased the security at their facilities. Do you think that the increased awareness of a possible terrorist attack has actually prevented such an event? (AP Photo/ Michael A. Mariant)

privatization argue that some services could be provided more efficiently by the private sector. Another scheme is to furnish vouchers to "clients" in lieu of services. For example, instead of supplying housing, the government could offer vouchers that recipients could use to "pay" for housing in privately owned buildings.

The privatization, or contracting out, strategy has been most successful at the local level. Municipalities, for example, can form contracts with private companies for such things as trash collection. This approach is not a cure-all, however, as many functions, particularly on the national level, cannot be contracted out in any meaningful way. For example, the federal government could not contract out most of the Defense Department's functions to private firms. Nonetheless, the U.S. military has contracted out many services in Iraq and elsewhere, as you'll learn in this chapter's Beyond Our Borders feature.

Beyond Our Borders

Privatizing the U.S. Military Abroad

Privatization has been a hot topic for several decades now, at least domestically. All levels of government—federal, state, and local—have privatized at least some activities. Less well known, however, is that for more than a decade, the U.S. military has been employing private companies abroad to perform several functions that were previously done by military personnel. After the American military was downsized following the fall of the Berlin Wall in 1989, the military responded by outsourcing many functions to the private sector. Before the First Gulf War, the Pentagon was already spending about 8 percent of its overall budget on private companies.

Private Contractors Galore

Today, private contractors are everywhere in Iraq. By 2006, there were more than 100,000 private contractors/workers on the ground in Iraq employed in some capacity by the U.S. government. By 2008, the number reached almost 150,000, about as many as there are U.S. military personnel. What do all these private contractors actually do? They provide food and water for the troops, transport supplies for the coalition troops and for civilians stationed in Iraq, repair equipment, and are employed as guards for prisoners. In addition, most major construction on American bases and air fields is done by contractors.

The Numbers Tell it All

One of the reasons that the U.S. military has felt obligated to hire private contractors in Iraq and elsewhere is that the army in particular has been downsized. During the First Gulf War, active-duty troops in the army numbered 711,000. Today, that

CIVILIAN EMPLOYEES of the American firm, KBR, transport supplies in Iraq with a helicopter escort. A large proportion of such support activities are carried out by civilians employed by private contractors. (GERRY BROOME/KRT/Newscom)

number has been reduced by almost one-third, to only about 485,000. As a result, the Pentagon says that it has to fill ancillary jobs and programs by contracting with private companies that either send their workers abroad or hire workers there. The Army Corps of Engineers and the Navy Seabees did a great deal of the construction in World War II, but today, neither of these forces has the manpower to do similar work in Iraq.

Hiring private contractors to work in a combat zone has some real complications. First, private contractors are often subject to combat conditions resulting in the risk of capture, injury, or death. Several contractors, both American and European, have been captured and held as hostages. A few of these have been murdered. More than 1,100 civilian contractors have been killed in their line of work. In addition, private contractors can commit acts that are crimes against Iraqi civilians or against other contractors. In accordance with a recently approved amendment to the Uniform Code of Military Justice, contractors who are accused of crimes are tried in military court-martials.

Who is hiring these contractors, and where are they being hired? Large international firms, some of which are based in the United States, are the major employers. Kellogg, Brown and Root, a firm based in Houston, Texas, is the largest employer with more than 54,000 contractors in Iraq. Another firm, MPRI, has employees providing management services and technical training to Iraqis, while the 6,500 employees of Titan are linguists. You might wonder where Titan found 6,500 Americans who could be used as translators in Iraq. In fact, most of the civilian contractors are not Americans; only 27,000 of the 150,000 workers are Americans.[*] Many are Iraqis who are using their talents working for these firms and incurring the risks involved.

FOR CRITICAL ANALYSIS

Is there any national security argument against using private contractors to do U.S. military work?

---

[*]David Ivanovich, "Contractor Deaths Up 17 Percent across Iraq in 2007," *Houston Chronicle*, February 9, 2008.

INCENTIVES FOR EFFICIENCY AND PRODUCTIVITY

An increasing number of state governments are beginning to experiment with a variety of schemes to run their operations more efficiently and capably. They focus on maximizing the efficiency and productivity of government workers by providing incentives for improved performance.[8] For example, many governors, mayors, and city administrators are considering ways in which government can be made more entrepreneurial. Some of the most promising measures have included such tactics as permitting agencies that do not spend their entire budgets to keep some of the difference and rewarding employees with performance-based bonuses.

Government Performance and Results Act. At the federal level, the Government Performance and Results Act of 1997 was designed to improve efficiency in the federal workforce. The act required that all government agencies (except the CIA) describe their new goals and establish methods for determining whether those goals are met. Goals may be broadly crafted (e.g., reducing the time it takes to test a new drug before allowing it to be marketed) or narrowly crafted (e.g., reducing the number of times a telephone rings before it is answered).

The performance-based budgeting implemented by President George W. Bush took this results-oriented approach a step further. Performance-based budgeting links agency funding to actual agency performance. Agencies are given specific performance criteria to meet, and the Office of Management and Budget rates each agency to determine how well it has performed. In theory, the amount of funds that each agency receives in the next annual budget should be determined by the extent to which it has met the performance criteria.

Bureaucracy Has Changed Little, Though. Efforts to improve bureaucratic efficiency are supported by the assertion that although society and industry have changed enormously in the past century, the form of government used in Washington, D.C., and in most states has remained the same. Some observers believe that the nation's diverse economic base cannot be administered competently by traditional bureaucratic organizations. Consequently, the government must become more responsive to cope with the increasing demands placed on it. Political scientists Joel Aberbach and Bert Rockman take issue with this contention. They argue that the bureaucracy has changed significantly over time in response to changes desired by various presidential administrations. In their opinion, many of the problems attributed to the bureaucracy are, in fact, a result of the political decision-making process. Therefore, attempts to reinvent government by reforming the bureaucracy are misguided.[9] Public assessment of bureaucratic services would provide another way to get more feedback from the public.

Other analysts have suggested that the problem lies not so much with traditional bureaucratic organizations as with the people who run them. According to policy specialist Taegan Goddard and journalist Christopher Riback, what needs to be reinvented is not the machinery of government, but public officials. After each election, new appointees to bureaucratic positions may find themselves managing complex, multimillion-dollar enterprises, yet they often are untrained for their jobs. According to these authors, if we want to reform the bureaucracy, we should focus on preparing newcomers for the task of "doing" government.[10]

---

[8]See, for example, David Osborne and Ted Gaebler, *Reinventing Government: How the Entrepreneurial Spirit Is Transforming the Public Sector* (Reading, MA: Addison-Wesley, 1992); and David Osborne and Peter Plastrik, *Banishing Bureaucracy: The Five Strategies for Reinventing Government* (Reading, MA: Addison-Wesley, 1997).
[9]Joel D. Aberbach and Bert A. Rockman, *In the Web of Politics: Three Decades of the U.S. Federal Executive* (Washington, DC: Brookings Institution Press, 2000).
[10]Taegan D. Goddard and Christopher Riback, *You Won—Now What? How Americans Can Make Democracy Work from City Hall to the White House* (New York: Scribner, 1998).

Saving Costs through E-Government. Many contend that the communications revolution brought about by the Internet has not only improved the efficiency with which government agencies deliver services to the public but also helped reduce the cost of government. Agencies can now communicate with members of the public, as well as other agencies, via e-mail. Additionally, every federal agency now has a Web site to which citizens can go to find information about agency services instead of calling or appearing in person at a regional agency office. Since 2003, federal agencies have also been required by the Government Paperwork Elimination Act of 1998 to use e-commerce whenever it is practical to do so and will save on costs.

That each year, federal administrative agencies produce rules that fill 7,500 pages in the *Code of Federal Regulations?*

HELPING OUT THE WHISTLEBLOWERS

The term **whistleblower** as applied to the federal bureaucracy has a special meaning: It is someone who blows the whistle on a gross governmental inefficiency or illegal action. Whistleblowers may be clerical workers, managers, or even specialists, such as scientists.

Laws Protecting Whistleblowers. The 1978 Civil Service Reform Act prohibits reprisals against whistleblowers by their superiors, and it set up the Merit Systems Protection Board as part of this protection. Many federal agencies also have toll-free hotlines that employees can use anonymously to report bureaucratic waste and inappropriate behavior. About 35 percent of all calls result in agency action or follow-up.

Further protection for whistleblowers was provided in 1989, when Congress passed the Whistle-Blower Protection Act. That act established an independent agency, the Office of Special Counsel (OSC), to investigate complaints brought by government employees who have been demoted, fired, or otherwise sanctioned for reporting government fraud or waste. Congress is currently considering legislation that would extend whistleblower protections to civil servants at national security agencies, employees of government contractors, and federal workers who expose the distortion of scientific data for political reasons.

Some state and federal laws encourage employees to blow the whistle on their employers' wrongful actions by providing monetary incentives to the whistleblowers. At the federal level, the False Claims Act of 1986 allows a whistleblower who has disclosed information about a fraud against the U.S. government to receive a monetary award. If the government chooses to prosecute the case and wins, the whistleblower receives between 15 and 25 percent of the proceeds. If the government declines to intervene, the whistleblower can bring suit on behalf of the government, and if the suit is successful, will receive between 25 and 30 percent of the proceeds.

The Problem Continues. Despite these endeavors to help whistleblowers, there is little evidence that potential whistleblowers truly have received more protection. More than 40 percent of the employees who turned to the OSC for assistance in a recent three-year period stated that they were no longer employees of the government agencies on which they blew the whistle.

Additionally, in a significant 2006 decision, the U.S. Supreme Court placed restrictions on lawsuits brought by public workers. The case, *Garcetti v. Ceballos,*[11] involved an assistant district attorney, Richard Ceballos, who wrote a memo asking if a county sheriff's deputy had lied in a search warrant affidavit. Ceballos claimed that he was subsequently demoted and denied a promotion for trying to expose the lie. The outcome

Whistleblower
Someone who brings to public attention gross governmental inefficiency or an illegal action.

---

[11]126 S. Ct. 1951 (2006).

of the case turned on an interpretation of an employee's right to freedom of speech—whether it included the right to criticize an employment-related action. In a close (5-4) and controversial decision, the Supreme Court held that when public employees make statements relating to their official duties, they are not speaking as citizens for First Amendment purposes. The Court deemed that when he wrote his memo, Ceballos was speaking as an employee, not a citizen, and was thus subject to his employer's disciplinary actions. The ruling will affect millions of governmental employees.

BUREAUCRATS AS POLITICIANS AND POLICY MAKERS

Enabling Legislation
A statute enacted by Congress that authorizes the creation of an administrative agency and specifies the name, purpose, composition, functions, and powers of the agency being created.

Because Congress is unable to oversee the day-to-day administration of its programs, it must delegate certain powers to administrative agencies. Congress delegates the power to implement legislation to agencies through what is called **enabling legislation**. For example, the Federal Trade Commission was created by the Federal Trade Commission Act of 1914, the Equal Employment Opportunity Commission was created by the Civil Rights Act of 1964, and the Occupational Safety and Health Administration was created by the Occupational Safety and Health Act of 1970. The enabling legislation generally specifies the name, purpose, composition, functions, and powers of the agency.

In theory, the agencies should put into effect laws passed by Congress. Laws are often drafted in such vague and general terms, however, that they provide relatively little guidance to agency administrators as to how the laws should be implemented. This means that the agencies must decide how best to carry out the wishes of Congress.

The discretion given to administrative agencies is not accidental. Congress has long realized that it lacks the technical expertise and the resources to monitor the implementation of its laws. Hence, the administrative agency is created to fill the gaps. This gap-filling role requires the agency to formulate administrative rules (regulations) to put flesh on the bones of the law. But it also forces the agency to become an unelected policy maker.

THE RULE-MAKING ENVIRONMENT

Rule making does not occur in a vacuum. Suppose that Congress passes a new air pollution law. The Environmental Protection Agency (EPA) might decide to implement the new law through a technical regulation on factory emissions. This proposed regulation would be published in the *Federal Register,* a daily government publication, so that interested parties would have an opportunity to comment on it. Individuals and companies that opposed the rule (or parts of it) might then try to convince the EPA to revise or redraft the regulation. Some parties might try to persuade the agency to withdraw the proposed regulation altogether. In any event, the EPA would consider these comments in drafting the final version of the regulation following the expiration of the comment period.

Waiting Periods and Court Challenges. Once the final regulation has been published in the *Federal Register,* there is a 60-day waiting period before the rule can be enforced. During that period, businesses, individuals, and state and local governments can ask Congress to overturn the regulation. After that 60-day period has lapsed, the regulation can still be challenged in court by a party having a direct interest in the rule, such as a company that expects to incur significant costs in complying with it. The company could argue that the rule misinterprets the applicable law or goes beyond the agency's statutory purview. An allegation by the company that the EPA made a mistake in judgment probably would not be enough to convince the court to throw out the rule. The company instead would have to demonstrate that the rule was "arbitrary and capricious." To meet this standard, the company would have to show that the rule reflected a serious flaw in the EPA's judgment.

Controversies. How agencies implement, administer, and enforce legislation has resulted in controversy. Decisions made by agencies charged with administering the Endangered Species Act have led to protests from farmers, ranchers, and others whose economic interests have been harmed. For example, the government decided to cut off the flow of irrigation water from Klamath Lake in Oregon in the summer of 2001. That action, which affected irrigation water for more than 1,000 farmers in southern Oregon and northern California, was undertaken to save endangered suckerfish and salmon. It was believed that the lake's water level was so low that further use of the water for irrigation would harm these fish. The results of this decision were devastating for many farmers.

One of the agencies that seems to be most sensitive to a change in presidential administration is the Environmental Protection Agency, created by Congress in 1970. Over the years, Congress has passed several laws to improve air quality in the United States and given the EPA the authority to carry out this legislation. Presidents differ, however, in how they interpret these congressional mandates. During the George W. Bush administration, the EPA issued decisions that seemed to weaken the enforcement of air pollution laws. In 1999, several environmental groups petitioned the EPA to set new standards for automobiles to reduce greenhouse gas emissions. In 2003, the EPA refused to do so, claiming that it did not have the legal authority to do this. Massachusetts and other states that passed laws regulating automobiles in their own states sued the EPA. In 2007, the Supreme Court ruled, by a 5-4 majority, that the EPA cannot refuse to assess environmental hazards and issue appropriate regulations. As Justice John Paul Stevens wrote, "This is the Congressional design. EPA has refused to comply with this

THE FARMERS FROM KLAMATH LAKE, California, confronted the Bureau of Reclamation guards at the headgate of Canal A. The water was shut off to protect endangered sucker fish that live in Upper Klamath Lake and Coho salmon that live in the Klamath River downstream. (Peter Essick/ Aurora Photos)

clear statutory command."[12] This was an unusual situation in that the states actually challenged a regulatory agency to issue stronger regulations. Often, challenges to regulatory agencies are intended to weaken new regulations.

When Barack Obama became president, his administration took a much firmer stand on the enforcement of air pollution regulations. While the president was committed to the passage of a new energy bill that would reduce the United States' contribution to greenhouse gases, by spring of 2010 it seemed that major new legislation might not pass quickly. The Environmental Protection Administration issued new gas mileage requirements and new rules regulating tailpipe emissions for cars and trucks in April 2010. A Republican-led attempt in the Senate to veto these new regulations was defeated in June of that year. Under the Obama administration, the EPA also issued new regulations for coal mining and for emissions from coal-burning power plants. In all of these cases, the executive agency noted that it had the authority to issue such rules under prior legislation such as the Clean Air Act.

NEGOTIATED RULE MAKING

Since the end of World War II (1939–1945), companies, environmentalists, and other special-interest groups have challenged government regulations in court. In the 1980s, however, the sheer wastefulness of attempting to regulate through litigation became more and more apparent. Today, a growing number of federal agencies encourage businesses and public-interest groups to become directly involved in drafting regulations. Agencies hope that such participation may help prevent later courtroom battles over the meaning, applicability, and legal effect of the regulations.

Congress formally approved such a process, which is called *negotiated rule making,* in the Negotiated Rule-making Act of 1990. The act authorizes agencies to allow those who will be affected by a new rule to participate in the rule-drafting process. If an agency chooses to engage in negotiated rule making, it must publish in the *Federal Register* the subject and scope of the rule to be developed, the parties affected significantly by the rule, and other information. Representatives of the affected groups and other interested parties then may apply to be members of the negotiating committee. The agency is represented on the committee, but a neutral third party (not the agency) presides over the proceedings. Once the committee members have reached agreement on the terms of the proposed rule, a notice is published in the *Federal Register,* followed by a period for comments by any person or organization interested in the proposed rule. Negotiated rule making often is conducted under the condition that the participants promise not to challenge in court the outcome of any agreement to which they were a party.

BUREAUCRATS ARE POLICY MAKERS

Theories of public administration once assumed that bureaucrats do not make policy decisions but only implement the laws and policies promulgated by the president and legislative bodies. Many people continue to make this assumption. A more realistic view, which is now held by most bureaucrats and elected officials, is that the agencies and departments of government play important roles in policy making. As we have seen, many government rules, regulations, and programs are in fact initiated by bureaucrats, based on their expertise and scientific studies. How a law passed by Congress eventually is translated into concrete action—from the forms to be filled out to decisions about

[12]*Commonwealth of Massachusetts v. EPA,* 127 S. Ct. 1438 (2007).

who gets the benefits—usually is determined within each agency or department. Even the evaluation of whether a policy has achieved its purpose usually is based on studies that are commissioned and interpreted by the agency administering the program.

The bureaucracy's policy-making role has often been depicted by what traditionally has been called the "iron triangle." Recently, the concept of an "issue network" has been viewed as a more accurate description of the policy-making process.

Iron Triangles. In the past, scholars often described the bureaucracy's role in the policy-making process by using the concept of an **iron triangle**—a three-way alliance among legislators in Congress, bureaucrats, and interest groups. Consider as an example the development of agricultural policy. Congress, as one component of the triangle (as illustrated in Figure 14-4), includes two major committees concerned with agricultural policy, the House Committee on Agriculture and the Senate Committee on Agriculture, Nutrition, and Forestry. The Department of Agriculture, the second component of the triangle, has more than 95,000 employees, plus thousands of contractors and consultants. Agricultural interest groups, the third component of the iron triangle in agricultural policy making, include many large and powerful associations, such as the American Farm Bureau Federation, the National Cattleman's Association, and the Corn Growers Association. These three components of the iron triangle work together, formally or informally, to create policy.

For example, the various agricultural interest groups lobby Congress to develop policies that benefit their groups' interests. Members of Congress cannot afford to ignore the wishes of interest groups, because those groups are potential sources of voter support and campaign contributions. The legislators in Congress also work closely with the Department of Agriculture, which, in implementing a policy, can develop rules that benefit—or at least do not hurt—certain industries or groups. The Department of Agriculture, in turn, supports policies that enhance the department's budget and powers. In this way, according to theory, agricultural policy is created that benefits all three components of the iron triangle.

Iron Triangle
The three-way alliance among legislators, bureaucrats, and interest groups to make or preserve policies that benefit their respective interests.

FIGURE 14–4 Iron Triangle

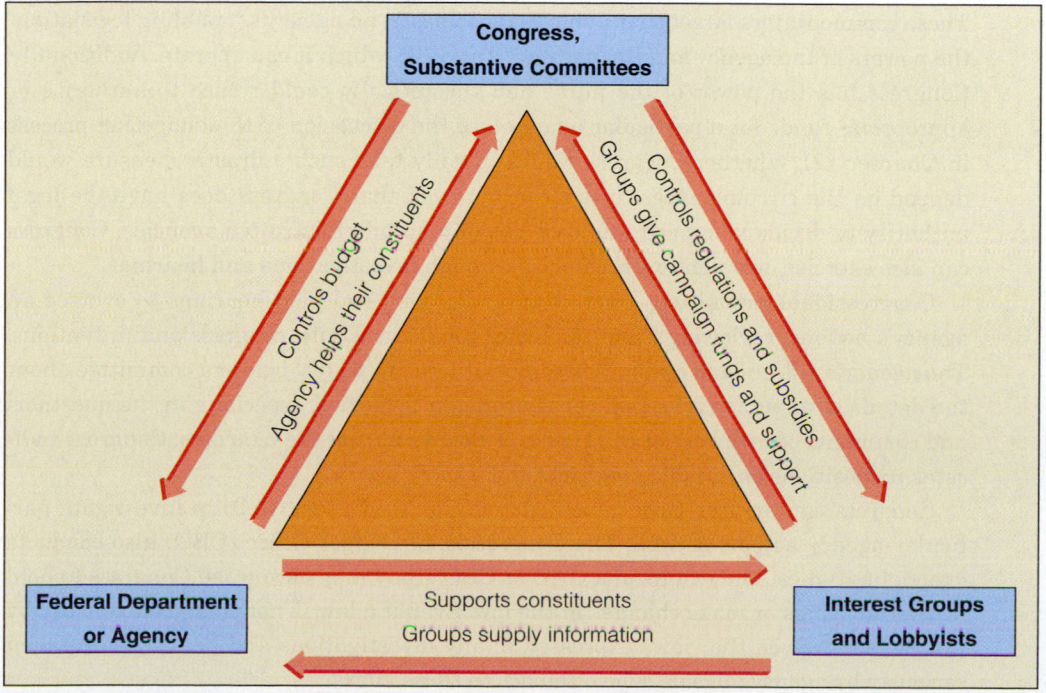

Issue Networks. To be sure, the preceding discussion presents a simplified picture of how the iron triangle works. With the growth in the complexity of government, policy making also has become more complicated. The bureaucracy is larger, Congress has more committees and subcommittees, and interest groups are more powerful than ever. Although iron triangles still exist, often they are inadequate as descriptions of how policy is actually made. Frequently, different interest groups concerned about a certain area of policy have conflicting demands, making agency decisions difficult. Additionally, divided government in some years has meant that departments are sometimes pressured by the president to take one approach and by Congress to take another.

Many scholars now use the term *issue network* to describe the policy-making process. An **issue network** consists of individuals or organizations that support a particular policy position on the environment, taxation, consumer safety, or some other issue. Typically, an issue network includes legislators and/or their staff members, interest groups, bureaucrats, scholars and other experts, and representatives from the media. Members of a particular issue network work together to influence the president, members of Congress, administrative agencies, and the courts to affect public policy on a specific issue. Each policy issue may involve conflicting positions taken by two or more issue networks. During the Obama administration, issue networks concerned with the health industry, the banking industry, and the energy industry ramped up their efforts to be influential in the sweeping legislation proposed by the president.

Issue Network
A group of individuals or organizations—which may consist of legislators and legislative staff members, interest group leaders, bureaucrats, the media, scholars, and other experts—that supports a particular policy position on a given issue.

CONGRESSIONAL CONTROL OF THE BUREAUCRACY

Many political pundits doubt whether Congress can meaningfully control the federal bureaucracy. Nevertheless, Congress does have some means of exerting control.

WAYS CONGRESS DOES CONTROL THE BUREAUCRACY

These commentators forget that Congress specifies in an agency's "enabling legislation" the powers of the agency and the parameters within which it can operate. Additionally, Congress has the power of the purse and theoretically could refuse to authorize or appropriate funds for a particular agency (see the discussion of the budgeting process in Chapter 12). Whether Congress would actually take such a drastic measure would depend on the circumstances. It is clear, however, that Congress does have the legal authority to decide whether to fund or not to fund administrative agencies. Congress can also exercise oversight over agencies through investigations and hearings.

Congressional committees conduct investigations and hold hearings to oversee an agency's actions, reviewing them to ensure compliance with congressional intentions. The agency's officers and employees can be ordered to testify before a committee about the details of an action. Through these oversight activities, especially in the questions and comments of members of the House or Senate during the hearings, Congress indicates its positions on specific programs and issues.

Congress can ask the Government Accountability Office (GAO) to investigate particular agency actions as well. The Congressional Budget Office (CBO) also conducts oversight studies. The results of a GAO or CBO study may encourage Congress to hold further hearings or make changes in the law. Even if a law is not changed explicitly by Congress, however, the views expressed in any investigations and hearings are taken seriously by agency officials, who often act on those views.

POLITICS WITH A purpose

Holding Government Accountable

If $17 million were stolen from the federal government, the thieves should be held to account.[a] If our nation's airport security system were not keeping pace with emerging terrorist threats, policy makers in a position to act should be informed.[b] If sensitive U.S. military equipment such as F-14 antennae, nuclear biological chemical gear, and pieces of body armor plates could be bought freely on Internet auction sites, an investigation should be launched to shut this practice down.[c] Keeping all aspects of government accountable and investigating possible fraud, waste, and abuse are among the key responsibilities of the Government Accountability Office (GAO).

Created by Congress in 1921, the GAO (originally named the General Accounting Office) was designed to audit and review executive branch agencies.[d] Sometimes called Congress's watchdog, GAO is part of the legislative branch and is headed by the comptroller general, who is appointed by the president and confirmed by the Senate for a 12-year, nonrenewable term. The size, responsibilities, and reach of GAO have changed over time, hitting their zenith in the early 1990s. In 2004, the agency's name was changed to the Government Accountability Office to reflect the way it had expanded from its original mission. The examples cited earlier are just a few of the many investigations it launches each year. With a staff of more than 3,100 people and a budget of more than $489 million, GAO conducts reviews, writes reports, and investigates (often undercover) alleged wrongdoing on the part of individuals within the federal government.[e]

One of the ways GAO keeps tabs on government is to list areas within the federal government that are at high risk for "fraud, waste, abuse, and mismanagement."[f] Some agencies, such as the Medicare Program and the Department of Defense Supply Chain Management, have remained on the list since 1990. An example of an agency recently removed from the list is the U.S. Postal Service. The Postal Service was originally added to the list because of concerns about its fiscal health. The GAO determined that significant changes, including retiring its debt and implementing $5 billion in cost savings, were made to justify removing it from the list.

The information GAO provides is critical in a democracy, where citizens need to be informed about the actions of government. The GAO issues many reports each year on such topics as understanding how the government spends taxpayers' dollars, the safety of our food supply, and successful strategies for monitoring convicted sex offenders. Many reports are available online, through your college or university library, or may be ordered directly from GAO (www.gao.gov/cgi-bin/ordtab.pl).

If this sort of investigative and analysis work sounds interesting, you might consider employment with GAO or another similar agency among the many you will discover in this chapter. Students can intern with these organizations to gain valuable work experience.[g] Those close to graduating should visit www.usajobs.opm.gov, which is a gateway to government employment opportunities. Whether you plan to be a chemist or are studying animal husbandry or criminal justice, the federal bureaucracy needs your talents.

[a]www.gao.gov/new.items/d07724t.pdf.
[b]http://oversight.house.gov/documents/20071114175647.pdf.
[c]www.gao.gov/new.items/d08644t.pdf.
[d]Frederick M. Kaiser, CRS Report for Congress (GAO: Government Accountability Office and General Accounting Office, 2007), updated June 22, 2007, Order Code RL30349, www.fas.org/sgp/crs/misc/RL30349.pdf, accessed May 15, 2007.

[e]www.gao.gov/about/gglance.html.
[f]www.gao.gov/new.items/d07310.pdf.
[g]www.studentjobs.gov/searchvol.asp.

In 1996, Congress passed the Congressional Review Act. The act created special procedures that can be employed to express congressional disapproval of particular agency actions. These procedures have rarely been used, however. Since the act's passage, the executive branch has issued more than 15,000 regulations. Yet only eight resolutions of disapproval have been introduced, and none of these was passed by either chamber.

REASONS WHY CONGRESS CANNOT EASILY OVERSEE THE BUREAUCRACY

Despite the powers just described, one theory of congressional control over the bureaucracy suggests that Congress cannot possibly oversee all of the bureaucracy. Consider two possible approaches to congressional control—(1) the "police patrol" and (2) the "fire alarm" approach. Certain congressional activities, such as annual budget hearings, fall under the police patrol approach. This regular review occasionally catches *some* deficiencies in a bureaucracy's job performance, but it usually fails to detect most problems.

In contrast, the fire alarm approach is more likely to discover gross inadequacies in a bureaucracy's job performance. In this approach, Congress and its committees react to scandal, citizen disappointment, and massive negative publicity by launching a full-scale investigation into whatever agency is suspected of wrongdoing. Clearly, this is what happened when Congress investigated the inadequacies of the CIA after the terrorist attacks of September 11, 2001. Congress was also responding to an alarm when it investigated the failures of FEMA after Hurricane Katrina. Fire alarm investigations will not catch all problems, but they will alert bureaucracies that they need to clean up their procedures before a problem arises in their own agencies.[13]

[13]Matthew D. McCubbins and Thomas Schwartz, "Congressional Oversight Overlooked: Police Patrols versus Fire Alarms," *American Journal of Political Science,* February 28, 1984, pp. 165–179.

YOU CAN MAKE A Difference

WHAT THE GOVERNMENT KNOWS ABOUT YOU

The federal government collects billions of pieces of information on tens of millions of Americans each year. These data are stored in files and sometimes are exchanged among agencies. You are probably the subject of several federal records (e.g., in the Social Security Administration, the Internal Revenue Service, and, if you are a male, the Selective Service).

WHY SHOULD YOU CARE?

Verifying the information that the government has on you can be important. On several occasions, the records of two people with similar names have become confused. Sometimes innocent persons have had the criminal records of other persons erroneously inserted into their files. Such disasters are not always caused by bureaucratic error. One of the most common crimes in today's world is identity theft, in which one person uses another person's personal identifiers (such as a Social Security number) to commit fraud. In some instances, identity thieves have been arrested or even jailed under someone else's name.

WHAT CAN YOU DO?

The 1966 Freedom of Information Act (FOIA) requires that the federal government release, at your request, any identifiable information it has about you or about any other subject. Ten categories of material are exempted, however (classified material, confidential material on trade secrets, internal personnel rules, personal medical files, and the like). To request material, write directly to the FOIA officer at the agency in question (say, the Department of Education). You must have a relatively specific idea about the document or information you want to obtain.

A second law, the Privacy Act of 1974, gives you access specifically to information the government may have collected about you. This law allows you to review records on file with federal agencies and to check those records for possible inaccuracies. If you want to look at any records or find out if an agency has a record on you, write to the agency head or Privacy Act officer, and address your letter to the specific agency. State that "under the provisions of the Privacy Act of 1974, 5 U.S.C. 522a, I hereby request a copy of (or access to) _____." Then describe the record that you wish to investigate.

The American Civil Liberties Union (ACLU) has published a manual, called *Your Right to Government Information,* that guides you through the steps of obtaining information from the federal government. You can order it online at www.aclu.org. Alternatively, you can order the manual from the ACLU at the following address:

ACLU Publications
P.O. Box 4713
Trenton, NJ 08650-4713
1-800-775-ACLU

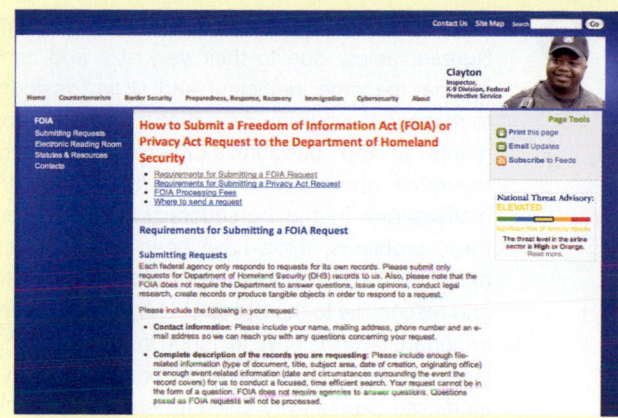

THE DEPARTMENT OF HOMELAND SECURITY Web site provides guidance on making an FOIA request. Visit www.dhs.gov/xfoia/editorial_0316.shtm.

KEY TERMS

acquisitive model 484
administrative agency 485
bureaucracy 483
Cabinet department 487
capture 489
Civil Service Commission 496
enabling legislation 504
government corporation 491

Government in the Sunshine Act 498
independent executive agency 487
independent regulatory agency 488
iron triangle 507
issue network 508
line organization 487

merit system 496
monopolistic model 485
Pendleton Act (Civil Service Reform Act) 496
privatization 499
spoils system 496
sunset legislation 499
Weberian model 484
whistleblower 503

CHAPTER SUMMARY

1. **Why are government bureaucracies necessary?** Bureaucracies are hierarchical organizations characterized by a division of labor and extensive procedural rules. Bureaucracy is the primary form of organization of most major corporations and universities as well as governments. These organizations are developed to carry out complex policies and procedures or to deliver multiple services or products in a fair, consistent, and effective manner.

2. Several theories have been offered to explain bureaucracies. The Weberian model posits that bureaucracies are rational, hierarchical organizations in which decisions are based on logical reasoning. The acquisitive model views top-level bureaucrats as pressing for ever-larger budgets and staffs to augment their own sense of power and security. The monopolistic model focuses on the environment in which most government bureaucracies operate, stating that bureaucracies are inefficient and excessively costly to operate because they have no competitors.

3. Since the founding of the United States, the federal bureaucracy has grown from 50 to about 2.7 million employees (excluding the military). Federal, state, and local employees together make up more than 16 percent of the nation's civilian labor force. The federal bureaucracy consists of 15 Cabinet departments, as well as a large number of independent executive agencies, independent regulatory agencies, and government corporations. These entities enjoy varying degrees of autonomy, visibility, and political support.

4. A federal bureaucracy of career civil servants was formed during Thomas Jefferson's presidency. Andrew Jackson implemented a spoils system through which he appointed his own political supporters. A civil service based on professionalism and merit was the goal of the Civil Service Reform Act of 1883. Concerns that the civil service be freed from the pressures of politics prompted the passage of the Hatch Act in 1939. Significant changes in the administration of the civil service were made by the Civil Service Reform Act of 1978.

5. What political decisions do bureaucrats make?

Bureaucracies, due to their very size and complexity, may become inefficient and slow. Presidents try to manage the bureaucracy through political appointments to top positions. Congress also becomes frustrated when it receives reports of corruption or malfeasance in the bureaucracy. To solve some of these problems, there have been many attempts to make the federal bureaucracy more open, efficient, and responsive to the needs of U.S. citizens. The most important reforms have included sunshine and sunset laws, privatization, strategies to provide incentives for increased productivity and efficiency, and protection for whistleblowers.

6. Why is it so difficult to manage the bureaucracy?

The bureaucracy has a complex relationship with the political branches of the government. While it reports to the president, the Congress oversees the bureaucracy and provides its budget. In addition, Congress delegates much of its authority to federal agencies when it creates new laws. The bureaucrats who run these agencies become important policy makers, because Congress has neither the time nor the technical expertise to oversee the administration of its laws. In the agency rule-making process, a proposed regulation is published. A comment period follows, during which interested parties may offer suggestions for changes. Because companies and other organizations have challenged many regulations in court, federal agencies now are authorized to allow parties that will be affected by new regulations to participate in the rule-drafting process.

7. Congress exerts ultimate control over all federal agencies because it controls the federal government's purse strings. It also establishes the general guidelines by which regulatory agencies must abide. The appropriations process may provide a way to send messages of approval or disapproval to particular agencies, as do congressional hearings and investigations of agency actions.

SELECTED PRINT, MEDIA, AND ONLINE RESOURCES

PRINT RESOURCES

Alexander, David. *The Pentagon: The People, the Building, and the Mission.* Osceola, WI: Zenith Press, 2008. Veteran defense writer and novelist David Alexander delivers the inside story on the people who have brought the Pentagon to life, from its initial construction during World War II to its restoration after the terrorist attacks on September 11, 2001.

Freeman, Jody, and Martha Minow. *Government by Contract: Outsourcing and American Democracy.* Cambridge, MA: Harvard University Press, 2009. Outsourcing raises questions about costs, quality, and democratic oversight. Harvard law professors Freeman and Minow describe the scope of government contracting and the issues that result.

Goodsell, Charles T. *The Case for Bureaucracy: A Public Administration Polemic,* 4th ed. Washington, DC: CQ Press, 2003. Goodsell argues for the excellence of the federal bureaucracy, introducing all types of performance measures and examining numerous public opinion polls that demonstrate satisfaction with government agencies.

Haymann, Philip, B. *Living the Policy Process.* New York: Oxford University Press, 2008. Haymann uses case studies to examine how policy makers struggle to affect governmental decisions. His detailed accounts range from the Cabinet level down to the middle tiers of the federal bureaucracy. Examples include providing support to anti-Soviet Afghan rebels and attempting to restrict smoking.

Meier, Kenneth J., and Lawrence J. O'Toole, Jr. *Bureaucracy in a Democratic State: A Governance Perspective.* Baltimore, MD: Johns Hopkins University Press, 2006. This study employs a governance approach to the bureaucracy. The authors examine the details of bureaucracy and demonstrate that bureaucracy can actually promote democracy.

Osborne, David, and Peter Plastrik. *Banishing Bureaucracy: The Five Strategies for Reinventing Government.* San Francisco: David Osborne Publishing, 2006. In 1992, David Osborne (with Ted Gaebler) wrote a best seller entitled *Reinventing Government. Banishing Bureaucracy* is his sequel, which goes one step further—it outlines specific strategies that can help transform public systems and organizations into engines of efficiency. The book focuses on clarifying a bureaucracy's purpose, creating incentives, improving accountability, redistributing power, and nurturing the correct culture.

Weiner, Tim. *Legacy of Ashes: The History of the CIA.* New York: Doubleday, 2007. The author has written a very readable account of the CIA with the general view that many of its directors and major players have been less than competent. The book provides real insight into the CIA's role in recent American history.

MEDIA RESOURCES

The Bureaucracy of Government: John Lukacs—In a 1988 Bill Moyers special, historian John Lukacs discusses the common political lament over the giant but invisible mechanism called bureaucracy.

King Corn—A 2007 documentary that demonstrates the impact of corn growing on modern America. Ian Cheney and Curt Ellis learn that corn is in almost everything they eat. They move to Iowa for a year to grow corn and find out what happens to it. Inevitably, they come face to face with America's farm policy and its subsidies.

When the Levees Broke: A Requiem in Four Acts—A strong treatment of Hurricane Katrina's impact on New Orleans by renowned African American director Spike Lee. We learn about the appalling performance of authorities at every level and the suffering that could have been avoided. Lee's anger at what he sees adds spice to the 2006 production.

Yes, Minister—A new member of the British cabinet bumps up against the machinations of a top civil servant in a comedy of manners. This popular 1980 BBC comedy is now available on DVD.

ONLINE RESOURCES

Federal Register the official publication for executive branch documents: www.gpoaccess.gov/fr/browse.html

The Plum Book lists the bureaucratic positions that can be filled by presidential appointment: www.gpoaccess.gov/plumbook/index.html

United States Government Manual describes the origins, purposes, and administrators of every federal department and agency: www.gpoaccess.gov/gmanual/index.html

USA.gov the United States government's official Web portal, which makes it easy for the public to get government information and services on the Web, such as telephone numbers for government agencies and personnel: www.USA.gov

15

Protestors demonstrate in front of the Supreme Court building during the International Day to Shut Down Guantánamo, January 11, 2007. (Paul J. Richards/AFP/Getty Images)

The Courts

what if...

Supreme Court Justices Had Term Limits?

BACKGROUND

The nine justices who sit on the Supreme Court are not elected officials. Rather, they are appointed by the president (and confirmed by the Senate). Barring gross misconduct, they also hold their offices for life. Given the long life span of Americans, it is not unusual for justices to be actively serving on the court after they turn 80 years old. Would the justices be more in tune with the ideas of Americans and less likely to use their power to make policy if they did not hold permanent seats? One way to make the justices even more responsive to public opinion might be to limit their tenure in office.

WHAT IF SUPREME COURT JUSTICES HAD TERM LIMITS?

If Supreme Court justices had term limits, what should be the length of the term? Perhaps an appropriate one would be the average time on the bench from the founding of our nation until 1970—15 years. In other words, after confirmation by the Senate, a person could serve only 15 years on the bench and then would have to retire. Perhaps the most important result of term limits would be a reduction in the rancor surrounding confirmation hearings. Today, the confirmation of a Supreme Court nominee—one chosen by the president to fit his or her views—is a major political event because that person may be on the Court for the next three decades.

Consider the current chief justice, John Roberts. When he took the Supreme Court bench at age 50, Americans could potentially anticipate that his conservative ideology would influence Supreme Court decisions for as long as 30 years. Knowing this, those who did not share his views or philosophy fought bitterly to prevent him from being confirmed. If term limits were in existence, in contrast, less would have been at stake—probably about half as many years of his influence.

TERM LIMITS WOULD PUT THE UNITED STATES IN LINE WITH OTHER DEMOCRACIES

In having no term limits for federal judges, the United States is somewhat out of step. Not only does just one state— Rhode Island—appoint state supreme court justices for life, but virtually every other major democratic nation has age or term limits for judges. Thus, term limits in the United States for federal judges would not be an anomaly. Even with term limits, Supreme Court justices would still be independent, which is what the framers of the Constitution desired.

MORE INFUSION OF NEW BLOOD

With term limits of, say, 15 years, vacancies would be created on a more or less regular basis. Consequently, Supreme Court justices would have less temptation to time their retirements for political purposes. Thus, liberal-leaning justices would not necessarily delay their retirements until a Democratic president was in office, and conservative-leaning justices would not necessarily wait for a Republican. In other words, fewer justices would follow the example of Justice Thurgood Marshall, who often said that he was determined to hang on to his judicial power until a Democratic president was in office to appoint his successor. After many years on the bench, he joked, "I have instructed my clerks that if I should die, they should have me stuffed—and continue to cast my votes."

In short, virtually every president, whether he or she was Republican or Democrat, would get a chance to fill a Supreme Court vacancy every few years. As a result, "new blood" would be infused into the Supreme Court more often. We would no longer face the risk of having Supreme Court justices who become less than enthusiastic about their work and less willing to examine new intellectual arguments. Term limits would also avoid the decrepitude that has occurred with several very old Supreme Court justices. In the last 30 years, some truly have stayed until the last possible minute. The public might prefer at least to have a mandatory retirement age.

FOR CRITICAL ANALYSIS

1. What are the benefits of having lifetime appointments to the Supreme Court?
2. Just because a president can appoint whomever he or she wishes to the Supreme Court, does that necessarily mean that the successful nominee will always reflect the president's political philosophy? Explain your answer.

THE JUSTICES OF the Supreme Court are not elected, but rather are appointed by the president and confirmed by the Senate. The same is true for all other federal court judges. It is a fact that many federal judges and Supreme Court justices sit on the bench for 30 years or more. As discussed in the What If . . . , some critics of the court suggest that lifetime appointments for judges guarantee that some will be out of touch with current political and social debates.

As Alexis de Tocqueville, a French commentator on American society in the 1800s, noted, "scarcely any political question arises in the United States that is not resolved, sooner or later, into a judicial question."[1] Our judiciary forms part of our political process. The instant that judges interpret the law, they become actors in the political arena—policy makers working within a political institution. The most important political force within our judiciary is the United States Supreme Court.

How do courts make policy? Why do the federal courts play such an important role in American government? The answers to these questions lie, in part, in our colonial heritage. Most of American law is based on the English system, particularly the English *common-law tradition.* In that tradition, the decisions made by judges constitute an important source of law. In the United States, the Supreme Court has extraordinary power to shape the nation's policies through the practice of **judicial review**, which was first explicated by Justice Marshall in the *Marbury v. Madison* case in 1803. We open this chapter with an examination of this tradition and of the various sources of American law. We then look at the federal court system—its organization, how its judges are selected, how these judges affect policy, and how they are restrained by our system of checks and balances.

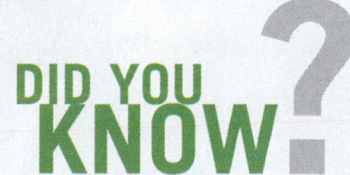

DID YOU KNOW?

That the Supreme Court was not provided with a building of its own until 1935, in the 146th year of its existence?

Judicial Review
The power of the Supreme Court or any court to hold a law or other legal action as unconstitutional.

SOURCES OF AMERICAN LAW

In 1066, the Normans conquered England, and William the Conqueror and his successors began the process of unifying the country under their rule. One of the ways they did this was to establish king's courts. Before the conquest, disputes had been settled according to local custom. The king's courts sought to establish a common or uniform set of rules for the whole country. As the number of courts and cases increased, portions of the most important decisions of each year were compiled in *Year Books.* Judges settling disputes similar to ones that had been decided before used the *Year Books* as the basis for their decisions. If a case was unique, judges had to create new laws, but they based their decisions on the general principles suggested by earlier cases. The body of judge-made law that developed under this system is still used today and is known as the **common law**.

The practice of deciding new cases with reference to former decisions—that is, according to **precedent**—became a cornerstone of the English and American judicial systems and is embodied in the doctrine of ***stare decisis*** (pronounced *ster*-ay dih-*si*-ses), a Latin phrase that means "to stand on decided cases." The doctrine of *stare decisis* obligates judges to follow the precedents set previously by their own courts or by higher courts that have authority over them.

For example, a lower state court in California would be obligated to follow a precedent set by the California Supreme Court. That lower court, however, would not be obligated to follow a precedent set by the supreme court of another state, because each state

Common Law
Judge-made law that originated in England from decisions shaped according to prevailing custom. Decisions were applied to similar situations and gradually became common to the nation.

Precedent
A court rule bearing on subsequent legal decisions in similar cases. Judges rely on precedents in deciding cases.

Stare Decisis
To stand on decided cases; the judicial policy of following precedents established by past decisions.

---

[1]Alexis de Tocqueville, *Democracy in America* (New York: Harper & Row, 1966), p. 248.

GEORGIA SUPREME COURT

Chief Justice Leah War Sears questions attorneys during oral arguments concerning Georgia's constitutional amendment to ban same-sex marriages. In 2006, the Georgia Supreme Court restored the state's constitutional ban on gay marriage, reversing a lower court judge's ruling.

(AP Photo/Ric Feld)

court system is independent. Of course, when the United States Supreme Court decides an issue, all of the nation's other courts are obligated to abide by the Court's decision, because the Supreme Court is the highest court in the land.

The doctrine of *stare decisis* provides a basis for judicial decision making in all countries that have common-law systems. Today, the United States, Britain, and several dozen other countries have common-law systems. Generally, those countries that were once British colonies, such as Australia, Canada, and India, have retained their English common-law heritage. An alternative legal system based on Muslim *sharia* is discussed in this chapter's *Beyond Our Borders* feature.

The body of American law includes the federal and state constitutions, statutes passed by legislative bodies, administrative law, and case law—the legal principles expressed in court decisions. The power of case law rests in the principle of judicial review.

CONSTITUTIONS

The constitutions of the federal government and the states set forth the general organization, powers, and limits of government. The U.S. Constitution is the supreme law of the land. A law in violation of the Constitution, no matter what its source, may be declared unconstitutional and thereafter cannot be enforced. Similarly, the state

Beyond Our Borders

THE LEGAL SYSTEM BASED ON *SHARIA*

Hundreds of millions of Muslims throughout the world are governed by a system of law called *sharia*. In this system, religious laws and precepts are combined with practical laws relating to common actions, such as entering into contracts and borrowing funds.

THE AUTHORITY OF *SHARIA*

It is said that *sharia,* or Islamic law, is drawn from two major sources and one lesser source. The first major source is the Qur'an (Koran) and the specific guidelines laid down in it. The second major source, called *sunnah,* is based on the way the Prophet Muhammad lived his life. The lesser source is called *ijma;* it represents the consensus of opinion in the community of Muslims. *Sharia* law is comprehensive in nature. All possible actions of Muslims are divided into five categories: obligatory, meritorious, permissible, reprehensible, and forbidden.

THE SCOPE OF *SHARIA* LAW

Sharia law covers many aspects of daily life, including the following:

- Dietary rules
- Relations between married men and women
- The role of women
- Holidays
- Dress codes, particularly for women
- Speech with respect to the Prophet Muhammad
- Crimes, including adultery, murder, and theft
- Business dealings, including the borrowing and lending of funds

WHERE *SHARIA* LAW IS APPLIED

The degree to which *sharia* is used varies throughout Muslim societies today. Several of the countries with the largest Muslim populations (e.g., Bangladesh, India, and Indonesia) do not have Islamic law. Other Muslim countries have dual systems of *sharia* courts and secular courts. In 2008, many British citizens were surprised by the remarks of the Archbishop of Canterbury, the religious leader of all Episcopalians, that there was a need for accommodation of *sharia* law in Great Britain.* He was referring to a system of *sharia* courts that has been functioning in Muslim neighborhoods for the last 20 years. The comments followed news that a *sharia* court had released some Somali youth who had stabbed another young man after ordering the assailants to compensate the victim and apologize. This incident led to national debate over whether the *sharia* court was performing functions that should be reserved for criminal and civil courts. In other parts of England, *sharia* courts deal mainly with Islamic laws regarding divorce and the rights of women, much in the same way the Catholic Church decides the status of its own members.**

Canada, which has a *sharia* arbitration court in Ontario, is the first North American country to establish a *sharia* court. Some countries, including Iran and Saudi Arabia, maintain religious courts for all aspects of jurisprudence, including civil and criminal law. Recently, Nigeria has reintroduced *sharia* courts.

A SHARIA COURT JUDGE in Great Britain confers with two Muslim women about their court case. (Ian Mcilgorm/Daily Mail/ Associated Newspapers Ltd./ Solo Syndication)

FOR CRITICAL ANALYSIS

1. Do you think that a nation can have two different systems of law at the same time?
2. How should decisions about religious law be regarded by civil legal systems?

*"Sharia Law Courts Are Already Dealing with Crime on the Streets of London, It Has Emerged," *Evening Standard,* London, February 8, 2008.
**"The View from Inside a Sharia Court," BBC News, February 11, 2008.

constitutions are supreme within their respective borders (unless they conflict with the U.S. Constitution or federal laws and treaties made in accordance with it). The Constitution thus defines the political playing field on which state and federal powers are reconciled. The idea that the Constitution should be supreme in certain matters stemmed from widespread dissatisfaction with the weak federal government that had existed previously under the Articles of Confederation adopted in 1781.

STATUTES AND ADMINISTRATIVE REGULATIONS

Although the English common law provides the basis for both our civil and criminal legal systems, statutes (laws enacted by legislatures) increasingly have become important in defining the rights and obligations of individuals. Federal statutes may relate to any subject that is a concern of the federal government and may apply to areas ranging from hazardous waste to federal taxation. State statutes include criminal codes, commercial laws, and laws covering a variety of other matters. Cities, counties, and other local political bodies also pass statutes, which are called ordinances. These ordinances may deal with such issues as zoning proposals and public safety. Rules and regulations issued by administrative agencies are another source of law. Today, much of the work of the courts consists of interpreting these laws and regulations and applying them to circumstances in cases before the courts.

CASE LAW

Case Law
Judicial interpretations of common-law principles and doctrines, as well as interpretations of constitutional law, statutory law, and administrative law.

Because we have a common-law tradition, in which the doctrine of *stare decisis* (described earlier) plays an important role, the decisions rendered by the courts also form an important body of law, collectively referred to as **case law**. Case law includes judicial interpretations of common-law principles and doctrines, as well as interpretations of the types of law just mentioned—constitutional provisions, statutes, and administrative agency regulations. As you learned in previous chapters, it is up to the courts—and particularly the Supreme Court—to decide what a constitutional provision or a statutory phrase means. In doing so, the courts, in effect, establish law.

JUDICIAL REVIEW

The process for deciding whether a law is contrary to the mandates of the Constitution is known as judicial review. This power is nowhere mentioned in the U.S. Constitution. Rather, this judicial power was first established in the famous case of *Marbury v. Madison* (as discussed in the *Politics with a Purpose* on the next page.). In that case, Chief Justice Marshall insisted that the Supreme Court had the power to decide that a law passed by Congress violated the Constitution:

> It is emphatically the province and duty of the Judicial Department to say what the law is. Those who apply the rule to a particular case must, of necessity, expound and interpret that rule. If two laws conflict with each other, the courts must decide on the operation of each.[2]

The Supreme Court has ruled parts or all of acts of Congress to be unconstitutional fewer than 200 times in its history. State laws, however, have been declared unconstitutional by the court much more often—more than 1,000 times. The court has been more active in declaring federal or state laws unconstitutional since the beginning of the 20th century.

[2]5 U.S. (1 Cranch) 137 (1803).

POLITICS WITH A purpose

Political Struggles Fought in the Court

Complaints about activist judges, a hotly contested election with partisan opponents hurling nasty insults, and debates about big government. One might argue that this is a description of politics in the 21st century. However, it also describes the presidential election of 1800, the aftermath of which led to *Marbury v. Madison,* one of the most important Supreme Court cases whose influence is felt today.

Marbury v. Madison established the doctrine of judicial review, or the ability of the Court to rule an act of government to be unconstitutional. It was precipitated by the presidential election of 1800, in which the incumbent president, John Adams, was defeated by his vice president, Thomas Jefferson. Not only did this event mark the first election where issues divided the emerging political parties, but the election was also intensely and personally fought. President Adams was a member of the Federalist Party, which had emerged victorious in the fights over ratification of the Constitution. Jefferson was an Anti-Federalist and the leader of the ascendant Jeffersonian Republicans. These two groups disagreed on the power of the federal government. In addition, the two men bitterly disagreed with each other's politics.

While Thomas Jefferson would eventually win the election, he would not take office until March 1801.[a] In the interim between the election and inauguration, the Federalist-controlled Congress passed a series of laws creating additional judicial positions that would be staffed with Federalist appointments. One of these positions was District of Columbia Justice of the Peace, a relatively low-level judicial appointment whose term would expire in five years. William Marbury was confirmed as one of these appointments. The day before inauguration, the appointment papers were signed and sealed, but not delivered. John Marshall was

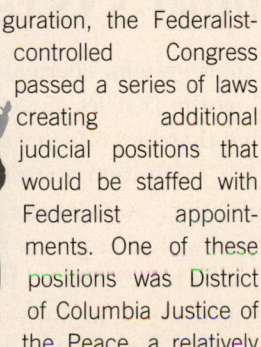

to deliver the appointment, but he had his own appointment to become chief justice of the Supreme Court. Upon taking office, President Jefferson ordered his secretary of state, James Madison, not to deliver the commissions. Marbury and two others brought suit to the Supreme Court, asking that the Court force Jefferson to deliver the commissions.

Some accounts argue that Marbury took this action, not because he wanted the appointment, but because he wanted to provoke a fight with Jefferson. Marbury was a committed Federalist who believed that the Jeffersonian argument to reduce federal government control and give power back to state governments was deeply flawed. These Federalists were very unhappy with the outcome of the election and were seeking mechanisms to remain influential.[b]

By then, the chief justice of the Supreme Court was John Marshall, a Federalist appointed by the former President Adams. Marshall had a real dilemma to resolve in this case. He knew that if he ordered Jefferson to honor the commission, the president would likely ignore the order, resulting in an unacceptably dangerous constitutional crisis for the young country, and the Supreme Court would be weakened. Marshall, writing for the Court, issued a decision that found Marbury's rights had been denied but that the law passed by Congress that would have granted the Court the power of redress was unconstitutional. In other words, Marshall said that the Supreme Court was not where Marbury should have sought a solution, arguing for the first time that the Court had the power to "say what the law is."[c]

There are many interpretations of John Marshall's role and of the legal arguments he used in deciding the case.[d] Without dispute, however, this case marked the formal articulation of judicial review, a power that in the 20th century would touch Americans' most basic liberties and rights. Even more significantly, the case illustrates that the intense battles waged by groups to make a difference in contemporary politics (e.g., *Roe v. Wade* and *Bush v. Gore*) are as old as the Republic.

---

[a]This election was also noteworthy for illustrating the flaw in the electoral college that resulted in a tie between Jefferson and his running mate, Aaron Burr. Breaking the tie in the House of Representatives took six days and 36 ballots. www.historynow.org/09_2004/historian4b.html, accessed May 16, 2008.

[b]www.claremont.org/publications/crb/id.1183/article_detail.asp#, accessed May 17, 2008.

[c]*Marbury v. Madison,* 5 U.S. 137 (1803).

[d]See, for example, Alexander M. Bickel, *The Least Dangerous Branch: The Supreme Court at the Bar of Politics* (New Haven, CT: Yale University Press, 1986); and William E. Nelson, *Marbury v. Madison: The Origins and Legacy of Judicial Review* (Lawrence, KS: University Press of Kansas, 2000).

FIGURE 15–1 Dual Structure of the American Court System

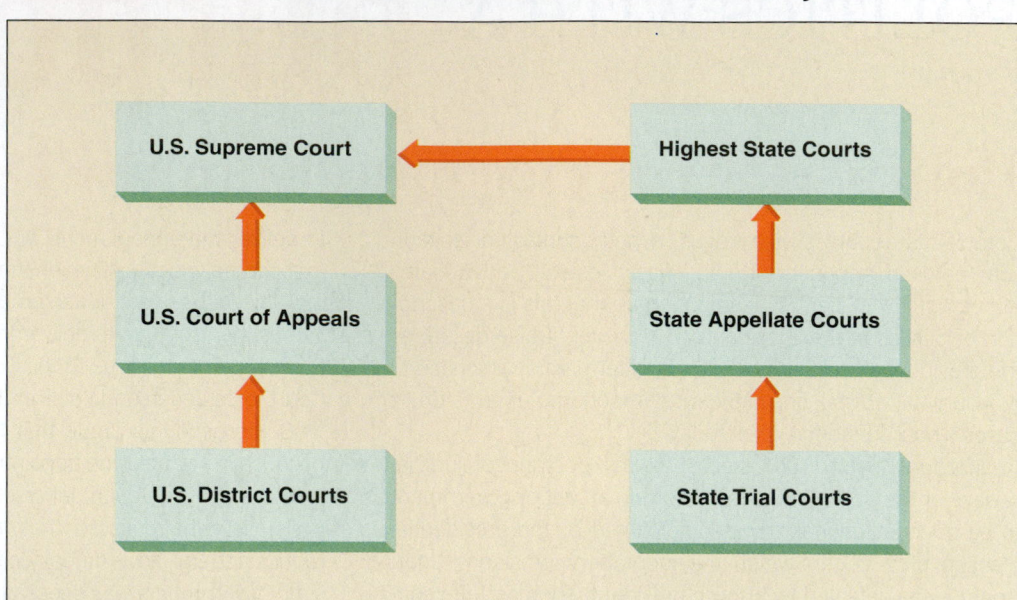

The Supreme Court, through its power of judicial review, can effectively define the separation of powers between the branches. In 1983, for example, the Court outlawed the practice of the legislative veto by which one or both chambers of Congress could overturn decisions made by the president or by executive agencies. This single decision overturned dozens of separate statutes and reinforced the Court's position as the arbiter of institutional power.

THE FEDERAL COURT SYSTEM

The United States has a dual court system. There are state courts and federal courts. Each of the 50 states, as well as the District of Columbia, has its own independent system of courts. This means that there are 52 court systems in total. The federal court derives its power from the U.S. Constitution, Article III, Section 1, and is organized according to congressional legislation. State courts draw their authority from state constitutions and laws. Court cases that originate in state court systems reach the Supreme Court only after they have been appealed to the highest possible state court. Figure 15-1 shows the basic components of the state and federal court systems.

BASIC JUDICIAL REQUIREMENTS

In any court system, state or federal, before a case can be brought before a court, certain requirements must be met. Two important requirements are jurisdiction and standing to sue.

Jurisdiction
The authority of a court to decide certain cases. Not all courts have the authority to decide all cases. Two jurisdictional issues are where a case arises as well as its subject matter.

Jurisdiction. A state court can exercise **jurisdiction** (the authority of the court to hear and decide a case) over the residents of a particular geographic area, such as a county or district. A state's highest court, or supreme court, has jurisdictional authority over all residents within the state. Because the Constitution established a federal government with limited powers, federal jurisdiction is also limited.

Article III, Section 1, of the U.S. Constitution limits the jurisdiction of the federal courts to cases that involve either a federal question or diversity of citizenship. A **federal question** arises when a case is based, at least in part, on the U.S. Constitution, a treaty, or a federal law. A person who claims that her or his rights under the Constitution, such as the right to free speech, have been violated could bring a case in a federal court. **Diversity of citizenship** exists when the parties to a lawsuit are from different states, or (more rarely) when the suit involves a U.S. citizen and a government or citizen of a foreign country. The amount in controversy must be at least $75,000 before a federal court can take jurisdiction in a diversity case, however.

Standing to Sue. Another basic judicial requirement is standing to sue, or a sufficient "stake" in a matter to justify bringing suit. The party bringing a lawsuit must have suffered a harm, or have been threatened by a harm, as a result of the action that led to the dispute in question. Standing to sue also requires that the controversy at issue be a justiciable controversy. A *justiciable controversy* is a controversy that is real and substantial, as opposed to hypothetical or academic. In other words, a court will not give advisory opinions on hypothetical questions.

TYPES OF FEDERAL COURTS

As you can see in Figure 15-2, the federal court system is basically a three-tiered model consisting of (1) U.S. district courts and various specialized courts of limited jurisdiction (not all of the latter are shown in the figure); (2) intermediate U.S. courts of appeals; and (3) the United States Supreme Court. Other specialized courts in the federal system are discussed in a later section. In addition, the U.S. military has its own system of courts, which are established under the Uniform Code of Military Justice. Cases from these other federal courts may also reach the Supreme Court.

U.S. District Courts. The U.S. district courts are trial courts. A **trial court** is what the name implies—a court in which trials are held and testimony is taken. The U.S. district courts are courts of **general jurisdiction**, meaning that they can hear cases involving

Federal Question
A question that has to do with the U.S. Constitution, acts of Congress, or treaties. A federal question provides a basis for federal jurisdiction.

Diversity of Citizenship
The condition that exists when the parties to a lawsuit are citizens of different states, or when the parties are citizens of a U.S. state and citizens or the government of a foreign country. Diversity of citizenship can provide a basis for federal jurisdiction.

Trial Court
The court in which most cases begin.

General Jurisdiction
Exists when a court's authority to hear cases is not significantly restricted. A court of general jurisdiction normally can hear a broad range of cases.

FIGURE 15–2 The Federal Court System

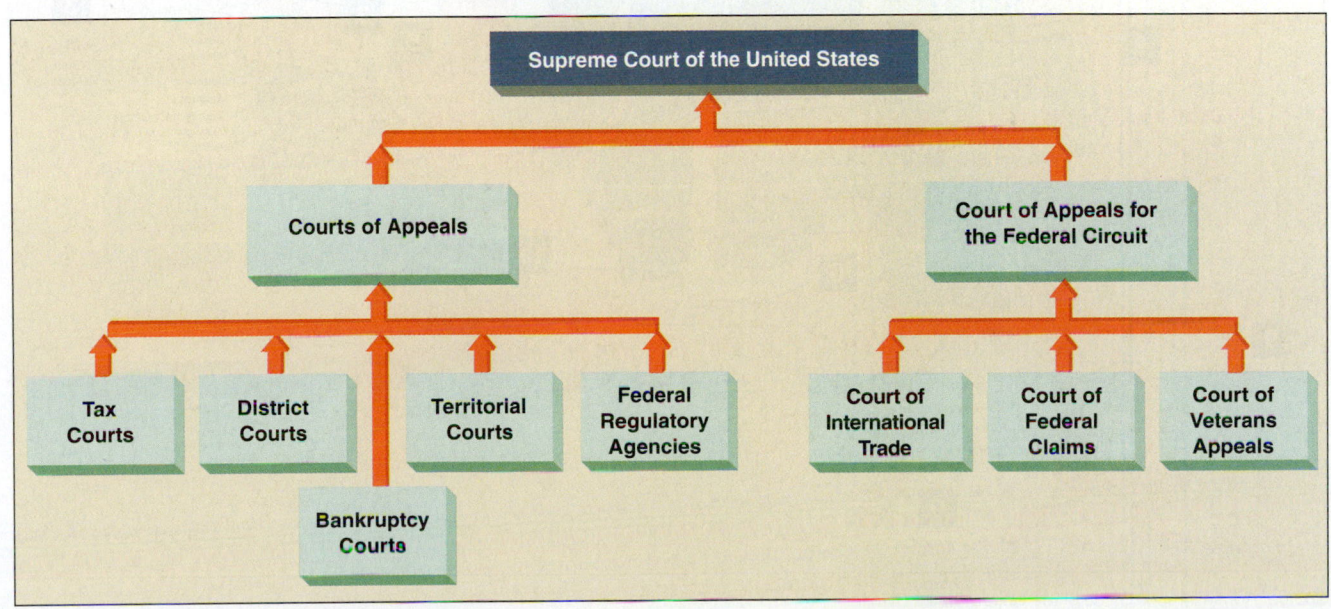

Limited Jurisdiction
Exists when a court's authority to hear cases is restricted to certain types of claims, such as tax claims or bankruptcy petitions.

Appellate Court
A court having jurisdiction to review cases and issues that were originally tried in lower courts.

a broad array of issues. Federal cases involving most matters typically are heard in district courts. The other courts on the lower tier of the model shown in Figure 15-2 are courts of **limited jurisdiction**, meaning that they can try cases involving only certain types of claims, such as tax claims or bankruptcy petitions.

There is at least one federal district court in every state. The number of judicial districts can vary over time as a result of population changes and corresponding case-loads. Currently, there are 94 federal judicial districts. A party who is dissatisfied with the decision of a district court can appeal the case to the appropriate U.S. court of appeals, or federal **appellate court**. Figure 15-3 shows the jurisdictional boundaries of the district courts (which are state boundaries, unless otherwise indicated by dotted lines within a state) and of the U.S. courts of appeals.

U.S. Courts of Appeals. There are 13 U.S. courts of appeals—also referred to as U.S. circuit courts of appeals. Twelve of these courts, including the U.S. Court of Appeals for the District of Columbia, hear appeals from the federal district courts located within their respective judicial circuits (geographic areas over which they exercise jurisdiction). The Court of Appeals for the Thirteenth Circuit, called the Federal Circuit, has national appellate jurisdiction over certain types of cases, such as cases involving patent law and those in which the U.S. government is a defendant.

Note that when an appellate court reviews a case that was decided in a district court, the appellate court does not conduct another trial. Rather, a panel of three or more judges reviews the record of the case on appeal, which includes a transcript of the trial proceedings, and determines whether the trial court committed an error. Usually, appellate courts do not look at questions of *fact* (such as whether a party did, in fact,

FIGURE 15–3 Geographic Boundaries of Federal District Courts and Circuit Courts of Appeals

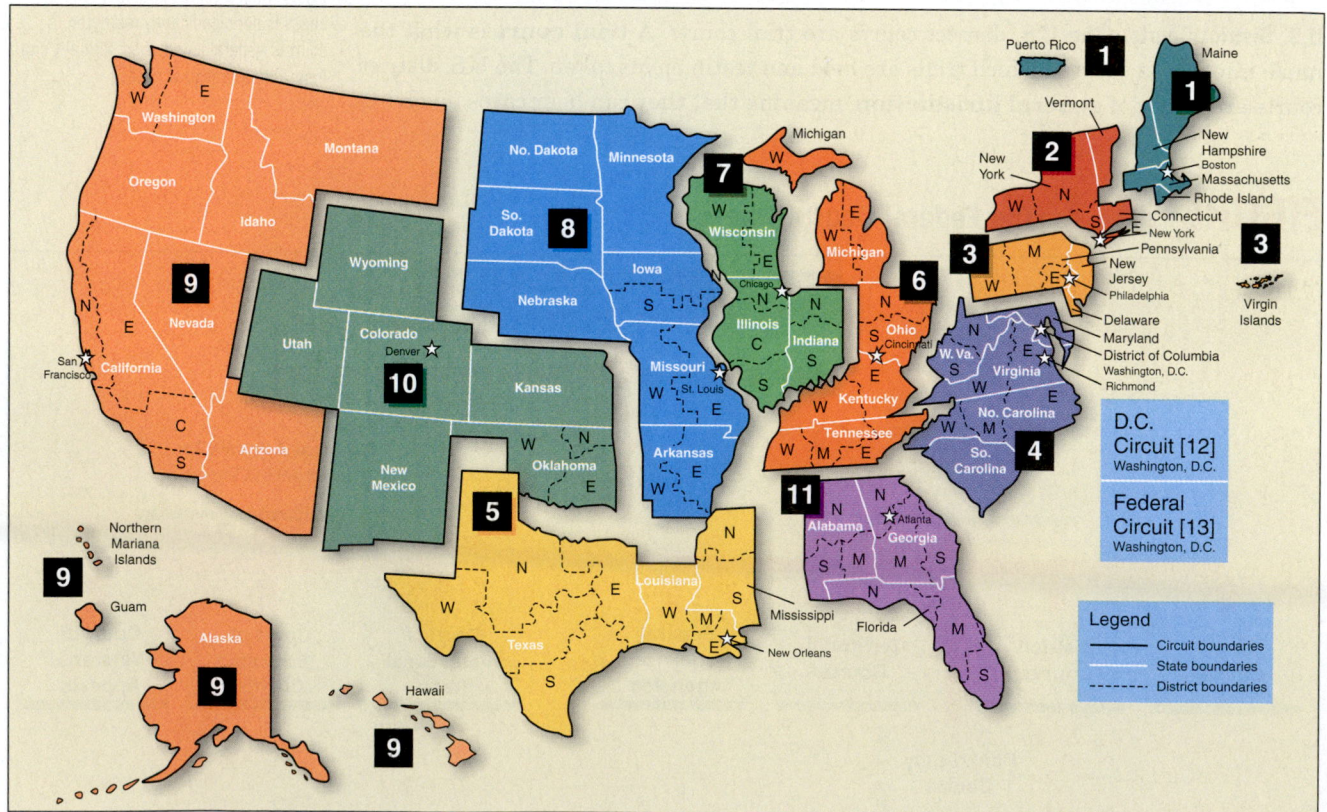

Source: Administrative Office of the United States Courts.

commit a certain action, such as burning a flag) but at questions of *law* (such as whether the act of burning a flag is a form of speech protected by the First Amendment to the Constitution). An appellate court will challenge a trial court's finding of fact only when the finding is clearly contrary to the evidence presented at trial or when no evidence supports the finding.

A party can petition the United States Supreme Court to review an appellate court's decision. The likelihood that the Supreme Court will grant the petition is slim, however, because the Court reviews very few of the cases decided by the appellate courts. This means that decisions made by appellate judges are usually final.

The United States Supreme Court. The highest level of the three-tiered model of the federal court system is the United States Supreme Court. When the Supreme Court came into existence in 1789, it had five justices. Congress passes laws that determine the number of justices and other aspects of the court. In the following years, more justices were added. Since 1869, there have been nine justices on the Court at any given time.

According to the language of Article III of the U.S. Constitution, there is only one national Supreme Court. All other courts in the federal system are considered "inferior." Congress is empowered to create other inferior courts as it deems necessary. The inferior courts that Congress has created include the district courts, the federal courts of appeals, and the federal courts of limited jurisdiction.

Although the Supreme Court can exercise original jurisdiction (that is, act as a trial court) in certain cases, such as those affecting foreign diplomats and those in which a state is a party, most of its work is as an appellate court. The Court hears appeals not only from the federal appellate courts but also from the highest state courts. Note, though, that the United States Supreme Court can review a state supreme court decision only if a federal question is involved. Because of its importance in the federal court system, we will look more closely at the Supreme Court in a later section.

SPECIALIZED FEDERAL COURTS AND THE WAR ON TERRORISM

As noted, the federal court system includes a variety of trial courts of limited jurisdiction, dealing with matters such as tax claims, patent law, Native American claims, bankruptcy, or international trade. The government's attempts to combat terrorism have drawn attention to certain specialized courts that meet in secret.

The FISA Court. The federal government created the first secret court in 1978. In that year, Congress passed the Foreign Intelligence Surveillance Act (FISA), which established a court to hear requests for warrants for the surveillance of suspected spies. Officials can request warrants without having to reveal to the suspect or the public the information used to justify the warrant. The FISA court has approved almost all of the thousands of requests for warrants that the U.S. attorney general's office and other officials have submitted. The seven judges on the FISA court (who are also federal district judges from across the nation) meet in secret, with no published opinions or orders. There is also no public access to the court's proceedings or records. Hence, when the court authorizes surveillance, most suspects do not even know that they are under scrutiny. Additionally, during the Clinton administration, the court was given the authority to approve physical as well as electronic searches, which means that officials may search a suspect's property without obtaining a warrant in open court and without notifying the subject.

In the aftermath of the terrorist attacks on September 11, 2001, the Bush administration expanded the powers of the FISA court. Previously, the FISA allowed secret domestic surveillance only if the target was spying by an agent of another nation. Post–September 11

THE PRISON AT GUANTÁNAMO BAY, Cuba, where the detainees from Afghanistan and Iraq are held until their military trials. While the number of prisoners has declined a great deal, many of the remaining detainees are from Yemen. To date, there has been no agreement between the United States and Yemen on how some of these men can be returned to that nation. Why did the United States create the prison at Guantánamo Bay? (BRENNAN LINSLEY/ ASSOCIATED PRESS)

amendments allow warrants if a "significant purpose" of the surveillance is to gather foreign intelligence and allow surveillance of groups who are not agents of a foreign government.

Alien "Removal Courts." The FISA court is not the only court in which suspects' rights have been reduced. In response to the Oklahoma City bombing in 1995, Congress passed the Anti-Terrorism and Effective Death Penalty Act of 1996. The act included a provision creating an alien "removal court" to hear evidence against suspected "alien terrorists." The judges rule on whether there is probable cause for deportation. If so, a public deportation proceeding is held in a U.S. district court. The prosecution does not need to follow procedures that normally apply in criminal cases. In addition, the defendant cannot see the evidence that the prosecution used to secure the hearing.

In some cases, the United States Supreme Court ruled against the George W. Bush administration's efforts to use secret legal proceedings in dealing with suspected terrorists. In 2004, the Supreme Court ruled that enemy combatants who are U.S. citizens and who have been taken prisoner by the United States cannot be denied due process rights. Justice Sandra Day O'Connor wrote that "due process demands that a citizen held in the United States as an enemy combatant be given a meaningful opportunity to contest the factual basis of that detention before a neutral decision maker. . . . A state of war is not a blank check for the president when it comes to the rights of the nation's citizens."[3] The Court also found that noncitizen detainees held at Guantánamo Bay in Cuba were entitled to challenge the grounds for their confinement.[4]

In response to the court rulings, the Bush administration asked Congress to enact a law establishing military tribunals to hear the prisoners' cases at Guantánamo. In 2006, the Court held that these tribunals did not meet due-process requirements for a fair hearing. The central issue in the case was whether the entire situation at the prison camp violated the prisoners' right of *habeas corpus*—the right of a detained person to challenge the legality of his or her detention before a judge or other neutral party. Congress then passed the Military Commissions Act of 2006, which eliminated federal court jurisdiction over *habeas corpus* challenges by enemy combatants. This law was also tested in court, but the Supreme Court refused to hear the case, so the law, as upheld by an appellate court, stands.[5]

Finally, in 2008, the Supreme Court, by a 5-4 majority, held that enemy combatants have the right to challenge their detention in front of a federal court if they have not been charged with a crime. This ruling essentially grants the detainees at Guantánamo Bay the right of *habeas corpus,* a right that the majority said Congress cannot restrict.[6] After President Obama took office in 2009, he announced that the prison at Guantánamo

[3]*Hamdi v. Rumsfeld,* 542 U.S. 507 (2004).
[4]Hamdi was eventually released following a settlement with the government under which he agreed to renounce his U.S. citizenship and return to Saudi Arabia.
[5]*Boumediene v. Bush,* 476 F.3d 981 (D.C. Cir. 2007).
[6]*Boumediene v. Bush,* 553 U.S. (2008).

would be closed within a year; however, Congress has been unwilling to fund a prison in the United States to hold suspected terrorists. In addition, it has been difficult to find countries to accept some of the remaining prisoners who might be released. As of 2010, about 200 prisoners remained in the Cuban facility awaiting either trial or release.

PARTIES TO LAWSUITS

In most lawsuits, the parties are the plaintiff (the person or organization that initiates the lawsuit) and the defendant (the person or organization against whom the lawsuit is brought). There may be numerous plaintiffs and defendants in a single lawsuit. In the last several decades, many lawsuits have been brought by interest groups (see Chapter 7). Interest groups play an important role in our judicial system, because they **litigate**— bring to trial—or assist in litigating most cases of racial or gender-based discrimination, virtually all civil liberties cases, and more than one-third of the cases involving business matters. Interest groups also file *amicus curiae* (pronounced ah-*mee*-kous *kur*-ee-eye) briefs, or "friend of the court" briefs, in more than 50 percent of these kinds of cases.

Sometimes interest groups or other plaintiffs will bring a **class-action suit**, in which whatever the court decides will affect all members of a class similarly situated (such as users of a particular product manufactured by the defendant in the lawsuit). The strategy of class-action lawsuits was pioneered by such groups as the National Association for the Advancement of Colored People (NAACP), the Legal Defense Fund, and the Sierra Club, whose leaders believed that the courts would offer a more sympathetic forum for their views than would Congress.

Litigate
To engage in a legal proceeding or seek relief in a court of law; to carry on a lawsuit.

Class-Action Suit
A lawsuit filed by an individual seeking damages for "all persons similarly situated."

PROCEDURAL RULES

Both the federal and the state courts have established procedural rules that shape the litigation process. These rules are designed to protect the rights and interests of the parties, to ensure that the litigation proceeds in a fair and orderly manner, and to identify the issues that must be decided by the court, thus saving court time and costs. Court decisions may also apply to trial procedures. For example, the Supreme Court has held that the parties' attorneys cannot discriminate against prospective jurors on the basis

A COURTROOM ARTIST'S rendering of the sentencing trial for Zacarias Moussaoui at the Federal Courthouse. The confessed September 11 conspirator testified he knew about the terrorist plot when he was arrested a month before the attacks and lied to FBI agents because he wanted the mission to go forward. (Art Lein/epa/ CORBIS)

of race or gender. Some lower courts have also held that people cannot be excluded from juries because of their sexual orientation or religion.

The parties must comply with procedural rules and with any orders given by the judge during the course of the litigation. When a party does not follow a court's order, the court can cite him or her for contempt. A party who commits *civil* contempt (failing to comply with a court's order for the benefit of another party to the proceeding) can be taken into custody, fined, or both, until the party complies with the court's order. A party who commits *criminal* contempt (obstructing the administration of justice or bringing the court into disrespect) also can be taken into custody and fined but cannot avoid punishment by complying with a previous order.

Throughout this book, you have read about how technology is affecting all areas of government. The judiciary is no exception. Today's courts continue to place opinions and other information online. Increasingly, lawyers are expected to file court documents electronically. There is little doubt that in the future we will see more court proceedings being conducted through use of the Internet.

JUSTICE RUTH BADER GINSBURG
being interviewed in 2008.
She noted the presence of two
Jewish justices on the court and
that their religion plays no role
in their decisions. (AP Photo/
Kevin Wolf, FILE)

THE SUPREME COURT AT WORK

The Supreme Court begins its regular annual term on the first Monday in October and usually adjourns in late June or early July of the next year. Special sessions may be held after the regular term ends, but only a few cases are decided in this way. More commonly, cases are carried over until the next regular session.

Of the total number of cases that are decided each year, those reviewed by the Supreme Court represent less than one-half of 1 percent. Included in these, however, are decisions that profoundly affect our lives. In recent years, the United States Supreme Court has decided issues involving capital punishment, affirmative action programs, religious freedom, assisted suicide, abortion, property rights, busing, term limits for congresspersons, sexual harassment, pornography, states' rights, limits on federal jurisdiction, and many other matters with significant consequences for the nation. Because the Supreme Court exercises a great deal of discretion over the types of cases it hears, it can influence the nation's policies by issuing decisions in some types of cases and refusing to hear appeals in others, thereby allowing lower court decisions to stand.

WHICH CASES REACH THE SUPREME COURT?

Many people are surprised to learn that in a typical case, there is no absolute right of appeal to the United States Supreme Court. The Court's appellate jurisdiction is almost entirely discretionary; the Court can choose which cases it will decide. The justices never explain their reasons for hearing certain cases and not others, so it is difficult to predict which case or type of case the Court might select. Former chief justice William Rehnquist, in his description of the selection process in *The Supreme Court: How It Was, How It Is*,[7] said that the decision of whether to accept a case "strikes me as a rather subjective decision, made up in part of intuition and in part of legal judgment."

[7]William H. Rehnquist, *The Supreme Court: How It Was, How It Is* (New York: Morrow, 1987).

Factors That Bear on the Decision. Factors that bear on the decision include whether a legal question has been decided differently by various lower courts and needs resolution by the highest court, whether a lower court's decision conflicts with an existing Supreme Court ruling, and whether the issue could have significance beyond the parties to the dispute.

Another factor is whether the solicitor general is pressuring the Court to take a case. The solicitor general, a high-ranking presidential appointee within the Justice Department, represents the national government before the Supreme Court and promotes presidential policies in the federal courts. He or she decides what cases the government should ask the Supreme Court to review and what position the government should take in cases before the Court.

Granting Petitions for Review. If the Court decides to grant a petition for review, it will issue a **writ of *certiorari*** (pronounced sur-shee-uh-*rah*-ree). The writ orders a lower court to send the Supreme Court a record of the case for review. More than 90 percent of the petitions for review are denied. A denial is not a decision on the merits of a case, nor does it indicate agreement with the lower court's opinion. (The judgment of the lower court remains in force, however.) Therefore, denial of the writ has no value as a precedent. The Court will not issue a writ unless at least four justices approve of it. This is called the **rule of four**.[8]

DECIDING CASES

Once the Supreme Court grants *certiorari* in a particular case, the justices do extensive research on the legal issues and facts involved in the case. (Of course, some preliminary research is necessary before deciding to grant the petition for review.) Each justice is entitled to four law clerks, who undertake much of the research and preliminary drafting necessary for the justice to form an opinion.[9]

The Court normally does not hear any evidence, as is true with all appeals courts. The Court's consideration of a case is based on the abstracts, the record, and the briefs. The attorneys are permitted to present **oral arguments**. All statements and the justices' questions are tape-recorded during these sessions. Unlike the practice in most courts, lawyers addressing the Supreme Court can be (and often are) questioned by the justices at any time during oral argument.

The justices meet to discuss and vote on cases in conferences held throughout the term. In these conferences, in addition to deciding cases currently before the Court, the justices determine which new petitions for *certiorari* to grant. These conferences take place in the oak-paneled chamber and are strictly private—no stenographers, tape recorders, or video cameras are allowed. Two pages used to be in attendance to wait on the justices while they were in conference, but fear of information leaks caused the Court to stop this practice.[10]

DECISIONS AND OPINIONS

When the Court has reached a decision, its opinion is written. The **opinion** contains the Court's ruling on the issue or issues presented, the reasons for its decision, the rules of law that apply, and other information. In many cases, the decision of the lower court is

Writ of *Certiorari*
An order issued by a higher court to a lower court to send up the record of a case for review.

Rule of Four
A United States Supreme Court procedure by which four justices must vote to grant a petition for review if a case is to come before the full court.

Oral Arguments
The verbal arguments presented in person by attorneys to an appellate court. Each attorney presents reasons to the court why the court should rule in her or his client's favor.

Opinion
The statement by a judge or a court of the decision reached in a case. The opinion sets forth the applicable law and details the reasoning on which the ruling was based.

---

[8]The "rule of four" is modified when seven or fewer justices participate, which occurs from time to time. When that happens, as few as three justices can grant *certiorari*.

[9]For a former Supreme Court law clerk's account of the role these clerks play in the high court's decision-making process, see Edward Lazarus, *Closed Chambers: The First Eyewitness Account of the Epic Struggles inside the Supreme Court* (New York: Times Books, 1998).

[10]It turned out that one supposed information leak came from lawyers making educated guesses.

Affirm
To declare that a court ruling is valid and must stand.

Reverse
To annul or make void a court ruling on account of some error or irregularity.

Remand
To send a case back to the court that originally heard it.

Unanimous Opinion
A court opinion or determination on which all judges agree.

Majority Opinion
A court opinion reflecting the views of the majority of the judges.

Concurring Opinion
A separate opinion prepared by a judge who supports the decision of the majority of the court but who wants to make or clarify a particular point or to voice disapproval of the grounds on which the decision was made.

Dissenting Opinion
A separate opinion in which a judge dissents from (disagrees with) the conclusion reached by the majority on the court and expounds his or her own views about the case.

affirmed, resulting in the enforcement of that court's judgment or decree. If the Supreme Court believes that a reversible error was committed during the trial or that the jury was instructed improperly, however, the decision will be **reversed**. Sometimes the case will be **remanded** (sent back to the court that originally heard the case) for a new trial or other proceeding. For example, a lower court might have held that a party was not entitled to bring a lawsuit under a particular law. If the Supreme Court holds to the contrary, it will remand (send back) the case to the trial court with instructions that the trial proceed.

The Court's written opinion sometimes is unsigned; this is called an opinion *per curiam* ("by the court"). Typically, the Court's opinion is signed by all the justices who agree with it. When in the majority, the chief justice assigns the opinion and often writes it personally. When the chief justice is in the minority, the senior justice on the majority side decides who writes the opinion.

When all justices unanimously agree on an opinion, the opinion is written for the entire Court (all the justices) and can be deemed a **unanimous opinion**. When there is not a unanimous opinion, a **majority opinion** is written, outlining the views of the majority of the justices involved in the case. Often, one or more justices who feel strongly about making or emphasizing a particular point that is not made or emphasized in the unanimous or majority written opinion will write a **concurring opinion**. That means the justice writing the concurring opinion agrees (concurs) with the conclusion given in the majority written opinion, but for different reasons. Finally, in other than unanimous opinions, one or more **dissenting opinions** are usually written by those justices who do not agree with the majority. The dissenting opinion is important because it often forms the basis of the arguments used years later if the Court reverses the previous decision and establishes a new precedent.

Shortly after the opinion is written, the Supreme Court announces its decision from the bench. At that time, the opinion is made available to the public at the office of the clerk of the Court. The clerk also releases the opinion for online publication. Ultimately, the opinion is published in the *United States Reports,* which is the official printed record of the Court's decisions.

Some have complained that the Court reviews too few cases each term, thus giving the lower courts less guidance on important issues. The number of signed opinions issued by the Court has dwindled notably since the 1980s. For example, in its 1982–1983 term, the Court issued signed opinions in 151 cases. By the early 2000s, this number dropped to between 80 and 100 per term.

Some scholars suggest that one of the reasons why the Court hears fewer cases today than in the past is the growing conservatism of the judges sitting on lower courts. More than half of these judges have now been appointed by Republican presidents. As a result, the government loses fewer cases in the lower courts, which lessens the need for the government to appeal the rulings through the solicitor general's office. Some support for this conclusion is given by the fact that the number of petitions filed by that office has declined by more than 50 percent since George W. Bush became president.

THE SELECTION OF FEDERAL JUDGES

All federal judges are appointed. The Constitution, in Article II, Section 2, states that the president appoints the justices of the Supreme Court with the advice and consent of the Senate. Congress has provided the same procedure for staffing other federal courts. This means that the Senate and the president jointly decide who shall fill every vacant judicial position, no matter what the level.

There are more than 850 federal judgeships in the United States. Once appointed to such a judgeship, a person holds that job for life. Judges serve until they resign, retire voluntarily, or die. Federal judges who engage in blatantly illegal conduct may be removed through impeachment, although such action is rare.

JUDICIAL APPOINTMENTS

Judicial candidates for federal judge-ships are suggested to the president by the Department of Justice, sena-tors, other judges, the candidates, and lawyers' associations and other inter-est groups. In selecting a candidate to nominate for a judgeship, the president considers not only the person's compe-tence but also other factors, including the person's political philosophy (as will be discussed shortly), ethnicity, and gender.

NOMINEE FOR THE SUPREME COURT, Judge Sonia Sotomayor takes questions from the Senate Judiciary Committee in July, 2009, before her nomination was confirmed by the full Senate. (AFP PHOTO/Karen BLEIER/Newscom)

Senatorial Courtesy
In federal district court judgeship nominations, a tradition allowing a senator to veto a judicial appointment in his or her state.

The nomination process—no matter how the nominees are obtained—always works the same way. The president makes the actual nomination, transmitting the name to the Senate. The Senate then either confirms or rejects the nomination. To reach a conclusion, the Senate Judiciary Committee (operating through subcommittees) invites testimony, both written and oral, at its various hearings. A practice used in the Senate, called **senatorial courtesy**, is a constraint on the president's freedom to appoint federal district judges. Senatorial courtesy allows a senator of the president's political party to veto a judicial appointment in her or his state by way of a "blue slip." Traditionally, the senators from the nominee's state are sent a blue form on which to make comments. They may return the "blue slip" with comments or not return it at all. Not returning the blue slip is a veto of the nomination.[11] During much of American history, senators from the "opposition" party (the party to which the president did not belong) also have enjoyed the right of senatorial courtesy, although their veto power has varied over time.

Federal District Court Judgeship Nominations. Although the president officially nominates federal judges, in the past the nomination of federal district court judges actually originated with a senator or senators of the president's party from the state in which there was a vacancy. In effect, judicial appointments were a form of political patron-age. President Jimmy Carter (served 1977–1981) ended this tradition by establishing independent commissions to oversee the initial nomination process. President Ronald Reagan (served 1981–1989) abolished Carter's nominating commissions and estab-lished complete presidential control of nominations.

Federal Courts of Appeals Appointments. Appointments to the federal courts of appeals are far less numerous than federal district court appointments, but they are more impor-tant. This is because federal appellate judges handle more important matters, at least from the point of view of the president, and therefore presidents take a keener interest in the nomination process for such judgeships. Also, the U.S. courts of appeals have become stepping-stones to the Supreme Court.

[11]Mitchell A. Sollenberger, "The Blue Slip Process in the Senate Committee on the Judiciary: Background, Issues, and Options," *Congressional Research Service,* November 21, 2003.

TABLE 15–1 Background of U.S. Supreme Court Justices to 2010 Number of Justices (112 = Total)

OCCUPATIONAL POSITION BEFORE APPOINTMENT	
Private legal practice	25
State judgeship	21
Federal judgeship	31
U.S. attorney general	7
Deputy or assistant U.S. attorney general	2
U.S. solicitor general	3
U.S. senator	6
U.S. representative	2
State governor	3
Federal executive post	9
Other	3
RELIGIOUS BACKGROUND	
Protestant	83
Roman Catholic	14
Jewish	7
Unitarian	7
No religious affiliation	1
AGE ON APPOINTMENT	
Under 40	5
41–50	34
51–60	59
61–70	14
POLITICAL PARTY AFFILIATION	
Federalist (to 1835)	13
Jeffersonian Republican (to 1828)	7
Whig (to 1861)	1
Democrat	46
Republican	44
Independent	1
EDUCATIONAL BACKGROUND	
College graduate	96
Not a college graduate	16
GENDER	
Male	108
Female	4
RACE	
White	109
African American	2
Hispanic American	1

Sources: Congressional Quarterly, *Congressional Quarterly's Guide to the U.S. Supreme Court* (Washington, DC: Congressional Quarterly Press, 1996); and authors' updates.

Supreme Court Appointments. As we have described, the president nominates Supreme Court justices.[12] As you can see in Table 15-1, which summarizes the background of all Supreme Court justices to 2008, the most common occupational background of the justices at the time of their appointment has been private legal practice or state or federal judgeship. Those nine justices who were in federal executive posts at the time of their appointment held the high offices of secretary of state, comptroller of the treasury, secretary of the navy, postmaster general, secretary of the interior, chairman of the Securities and Exchange Commission, and secretary of labor. In the "Other" category under "Occupational Position before Appointment" in Table 15-1 are two justices who were professors of law (including William H. Taft, a former president) and one justice who was a North Carolina state employee with responsibility for organizing and revising the state's statutes.

The Special Role of the Chief Justice. Although ideology is always important in judicial appointments, as described next, when a chief justice is selected for the Supreme Court, other considerations must also be taken into account. The chief justice is not only the head of a group of nine justices who interpret the law. He or she is also in essence the chief executive officer (CEO) of a large bureaucracy that includes all of the following: 1,200 judges with lifetime tenure, more than 850 magistrates and bankruptcy judges, and more than 30,000 staff members.

The chief justice is also the chair of the Judicial Conference of the United States, a policy-making body that sets priorities for the federal judiciary. That means that the chief justice also indirectly oversees the $5.5 billion budget of this group.

Finally, the chief justice appoints the director of the Administrative Office of the United States Courts. The chief justice and this director select judges who sit on judicial committees that examine international judicial relations, technology, and a variety of other topics.

PARTISANSHIP AND JUDICIAL APPOINTMENTS

Ideology plays an important role in the president's choices for judicial appointments. In most circumstances, the president appoints judges or justices who belong to the president's own political party. Presidents see their federal judiciary appointments as the one sure way to institutionalize their political views long after they have left office. By 1993, for example, presidents Ronald Reagan and George H. W. Bush together had

[12]For a discussion of the factors that may come into play during the process of nominating Supreme Court justices, see David A. Yalof, *Pursuit of Justices: Presidential Politics and the Selection of Supreme Court Nominees* (Chicago: University of Chicago Press, 1999).

appointed nearly three-quarters of all federal court judges. This preponderance of Republican-appointed federal judges strengthened the legal moorings of the conservative social agenda on a variety of issues, ranging from abortion to civil rights. Nevertheless, President Bill Clinton had the opportunity to appoint about 200 federal judges, thereby shifting the ideological makeup of the federal judiciary.

During the first two years of his second term, President George W. Bush was able to nominate two relatively conservative justices to the Supreme Court—John Roberts, who became chief justice, and Samuel Alito. Both are Catholics and have relatively, but not consistently, conservative views. In fact, during his first term as chief justice, Roberts voted most of the time with the Court's most conservative justices, Antonin Scalia and Clarence Thomas. Nonetheless, Roberts and Alito may not cause the Supreme Court to "tilt to the right" as much as some people anticipated. The reason is that the two newest Supreme Court members replaced justices who were moderate to conservative. Interestingly, some previous conservative justices have shown a tendency to migrate to a more liberal view of the law. Sandra Day O'Connor, the first female justice and a conservative, gradually shifted to the left on several issues, including abortion. In 1981, during her confirmation hearing before the Senate Judiciary Committee, she said, "I am opposed to it [abortion], as a matter of birth control or otherwise." By 1992, she was part of a 5-4 majority that agreed that the Constitution protects a woman's right to an abortion.

ON AUGUST 7, 2010, Elena Kagan is sworn in as the 112th U.S. Supreme Court justice and the Court's fourth woman ever. (SIPA USA/SIPA/Newscom)

Similarly, Justice John Paul Stevens, who was appointed by Gerald Ford, was expected to be a moderate or conservative in his views but, over time, became a member of the liberal bloc on the Court. Stevens, who retired in 2010, was renowned for his ability to find a compromise between the justices and to build a voting majority. President Obama nominated Solicitor General Elena Kagan, former dean of the law school at Harvard University, to fill Stevens's seat. His first nominee to the Court, Associate Justice Sonia Sotomayor, who replaced Justice David Souter, became the first Hispanic American to serve on the Court. Both of President Obama's appointments were to seats formerly held by more liberal justices, so the balance of ideology on the Supreme Court remained the same as it had been during the George W. Bush administration.

THE SENATE'S ROLE

Ideology also plays a large role in the Senate's confirmation hearings, and presidential nominees to the Supreme Court have not always been confirmed. In fact, almost 20 percent of presidential nominations to the Supreme Court have been either rejected or not acted on by the Senate. There have been many acrimonious battles over Supreme Court appointments when the Senate and the president have not seen eye to eye about political matters.

The U.S. Senate had a long record of refusing to confirm the president's judicial nominations extending from the beginning of Andrew Jackson's presidency in 1829 to the end of Ulysses Grant's presidency in 1877. From 1894 until 1968, however, only three nominees were not confirmed. Then, from 1968 through 1987, four presidential nominees to the highest court were rejected. One of the most controversial Supreme

Court nominations was that of Clarence Thomas, who underwent an extremely volatile confirmation hearing in 1991, replete with charges against him of sexual harassment. He was ultimately confirmed by the Senate, however, and has been a stalwart voice for conservatism ever since.

President Bill Clinton had little trouble gaining approval for both of his nominees to the Supreme Court: Ruth Bader Ginsburg and Stephen Breyer. President George W. Bush's nominees faced hostile grilling in their confirmation hearings, and various interest groups mounted intense media advertising blitzes against them. Bush had to forgo one of his nominees, Harriet Miers, when he realized that she could not be confirmed by the Senate. President Obama's two nominations, Sonia Sotomayor and Elena Kagan, while seen as too liberal by some senators, were eminently qualified for the Court and were approved by the Senate with little incident.

Both Clinton and Bush had trouble securing Senate approval for their judicial nominations to the lower courts. In fact, during the late 1990s and early 2000s, the duel between the Senate and the president aroused considerable concern about the consequences of the increasingly partisan and ideological tension over federal judicial appointments. On several occasions, presidents have appointed federal judges using a temporary "recess appointment." This procedure is always used for the same reason—to avoid the continuation of an acrimonious and perhaps futile Senate confirmation process.

Although the confirmation hearings on Supreme Court nominees get all of the media attention, the hearings on nominees for the lower federal courts are equally bitter, leading some to ask whether the politicization of the confirmation process has gone too far. According to Fifth Circuit Court Judge Edith Jones, judicial nominations have turned into battlegrounds because so many federal judges now view the courts as agents of social change. Jones argues that when judge-made law (as opposed to legislature-made law) enters into sensitive topics, it provokes a political reaction. Thus, the ideology and political views of the potential justices should be a matter of public concern and political debate.

Politics has played a role in selecting judges since the administration of George Washington. The classic case cited earlier, *Marbury v. Madison,* was rooted in partisan politics. Nonetheless, most nominees are confirmed without dispute. As of 2006, the vacancy rate on the federal bench was at its lowest point in 15 years. Those nominees who run into trouble are usually the most conservative Republican nominees or the most liberal Democratic ones. It is legitimate to evaluate a candidate's judicial ideology when that ideology is strongly held and likely to influence the judge's rulings.

POLICY MAKING AND THE COURTS

The partisan battles over judicial appointments reflect an important reality in today's American government: the importance of the judiciary in national politics. Because appointments to the federal bench are for life, the ideology of judicial appointees can affect national policy for years to come. Although the primary function of judges in our system of government is to interpret and apply the laws, inevitably judges make policy when carrying out this task. One of the major policy-making tools of the federal courts is their power of judicial review.

JUDICIAL REVIEW

If a federal court declares that a federal or state law or policy is unconstitutional, the court's decision affects the application of the law or policy only within that court's jurisdiction. For this reason, the higher the level of the court, the greater the impact of the decision on society. Because of the Supreme Court's national jurisdiction, its decisions have the greatest impact. For example, when the Supreme Court held that an Arkansas state constitutional amendment limiting the terms of congresspersons was unconstitutional, laws establishing term limits in 23 other states were also invalidated.[13]

Some claim that the power of judicial review gives unelected judges and justices on federal court benches too much influence over national policy. Others argue that the powers exercised by the federal courts, particularly the power of judicial review, are necessary to protect our constitutional rights and liberties. Built into our federal form of government is a system of checks and balances. If the federal courts did not have the power of judicial review, there would be no governmental body to check Congress's lawmaking authority.

"Do you ever have one of those days when everything seems un-Constitutional?" (© 2002 The New Yorker Collection from cartoonbank.com. All rights reserved.)

JUDICIAL ACTIVISM AND JUDICIAL RESTRAINT

Judicial scholars like to characterize different judges and justices as being either "activist" or "restraintist." The doctrine of **judicial activism** rests on the conviction that the federal judiciary should take an active role by using its powers to check the activities of Congress, state legislatures, and administrative agencies when those governmental bodies exceed their authority. One of the Supreme Court's most activist eras was the period from 1953 to 1969, when the Court was headed by Chief Justice Earl Warren. The Warren Court propelled the civil rights movement forward by holding, among other things, that laws permitting racial segregation violated the equal protection clause.

In contrast, the doctrine of **judicial restraint** rests on the assumption that the courts should defer to the decisions made by the legislative and executive branches, because members of Congress and the president are elected by the people, whereas members of the federal judiciary are not. Because administrative agency personnel normally have more expertise than the courts do in the areas regulated by the agencies, the courts likewise should defer to agency rules and decisions. In other words, under the doctrine of judicial restraint, the courts should not thwart the implementation of legislative acts and agency rules unless they are clearly unconstitutional.

Judicial activism sometimes is linked with liberalism, and judicial restraint with conservatism. In fact, though, a conservative judge can be activist, just as a liberal judge can be restraintist. In the 1950s and 1960s, the Supreme Court was activist and liberal. Some observers believe that the Rehnquist Court, with its conservative majority,

Judicial Activism
A doctrine holding that the Supreme Court should take an active role by using its powers to check the activities of governmental bodies when those bodies exceed their authority.

Judicial Restraint
A doctrine holding that the Supreme Court should defer to the decisions made by the elected representatives of the people in the legislative and executive branches.

---

[13]*U.S. Term Limits v. Thornton,* 514 U.S. 779 (1995).

became increasingly activist during the early 2000s. Some go even further and claim that the federal courts, including the Supreme Court, wield too much power in our democracy.

STRICT VERSUS BROAD CONSTRUCTION

Strict Construction
A judicial philosophy that looks to the "letter of the law" when interpreting the Constitution or a particular statute.

Broad Construction
A judicial philosophy that looks to the context and purpose of a law when making an interpretation.

Other terms that are often used to describe a justice's philosophy are *strict construction* and *broad construction*. Justices who believe in **strict construction** look to the "letter of the law" when they attempt to interpret the Constitution or a particular statute. Those who favor **broad construction** try to determine the context and purpose of the law.

As with the doctrines of judicial restraint and judicial activism, strict construction is often associated with conservative political views, whereas broad construction is often linked with liberalism. These traditional political associations sometimes appear to be reversed, however. Consider the Eleventh Amendment to the Constitution, which rules out lawsuits in federal courts "against one of the United States by Citizens of another State, or by Citizens or Subjects of any Foreign State." Nothing is said about citizens suing their *own* states, and strict construction would therefore find such suits to be constitutional. Conservative justices, however, have construed this amendment broadly to deny citizens the constitutional right to sue their own states in most circumstances. John T. Noonan, Jr., a federal appellate court judge who was appointed by a Republican president, has described these rulings as "adventurous."[14]

Broad construction is often associated with the concept of a "living constitution." Supreme Court Justice Antonin Scalia has said that "the Constitution is not a living organism, it is a legal document. It says something and doesn't say other things." Scalia believes that jurists should stick to the plain text of the Constitution "as it was originally written and intended."[15]

IDEOLOGY AND THE REHNQUIST COURT

William H. Rehnquist became the 16th chief justice of the Supreme Court in 1986, after 15 years as an associate justice. He was known as a strong anchor of the Court's conservative wing until his death in 2005. With Rehnquist's appointment as chief justice, it seemed to observers that the Court would necessarily become more conservative.

Indeed, that is what happened. The Court began to take a rightward shift shortly after Rehnquist became chief justice, and the Court's rightward movement continued as other conservative appointments to the bench were made during the Reagan and George H. W. Bush administrations. During the late 1990s and early 2000s, three of the justices (William Rehnquist, Antonin Scalia, and Clarence Thomas) were notably conservative in their views. Four of the justices (John Paul Stevens, David Souter, Ruth Bader Ginsburg, and Stephen Breyer) held moderate-to-liberal views. The middle of the Court was occupied by two moderate-to-conservative justices, Sandra Day O'Connor and Anthony Kennedy. O'Connor and Kennedy usually provided the swing votes on the Court in controversial cases.

Although the Court seemed to become more conservative under Rehnquist's leadership, its decisions were not always predictable. Many cases were decided by very close

[14]John T. Noonan, Jr., *Narrowing the Nation's Power: The Supreme Court Sides with the States* (Berkeley, CA: University of California Press, 2002).
[15]Speech given at the Woodrow Wilson Center, Washington, D.C., March 14, 2005.

votes, and results seemed to vary depending on the issue. For example, the Court ruled in 1995 that Congress had overreached its powers under the commerce clause when it attempted to regulate the possession of guns in schoolyards. According to the Court, the possession of guns in school zones had nothing to do with the commerce clause.[16] Yet in 2005, the Court upheld Congress's power under the commerce clause to ban marijuana use even when a state's law permitted such use.[17] In other areas such as civil rights, the Court generally issued conservative opinions.

THE ROBERTS COURT

In 2006, a new chief justice was appointed to the court. John Roberts had a distinguished career as an attorney in Washington, D.C. He had served as a clerk to the Supreme Court while in law school and was well-liked by the justices. The confirmation process had been quite smooth, and many hoped that he would be a moderate leader of the Court.

During John Roberts's first term (2005–2006) as chief justice, the Court ruled on several important issues, but no clear pattern was discernible in the decisions. Under Roberts, the Court ruled in 2006 that the due-process clause of the Constitution does not prohibit Arizona's use of an insanity test stated solely in terms of the accused's capacity to tell whether an act charged as a crime was right or wrong. In the same year, the Court held that federal courts can assess the procedures used in military tribunals when the accused is not a member of the military. With respect to capital punishment, the Roberts Court ruled that the capital sentencing statute in Kansas was constitutional.

In the years following his appointment, Roberts was more likely to vote with the conservative justices—Scalia, Thomas, and Alito—than with the moderate-to-liberal bloc. Thus, several important decisions were handed down with close votes. In an important case for environmentalist groups, the Court held that the Environmental Protection Agency (EPA) did have the power under the Clean Air Act to regulate greenhouse gases.

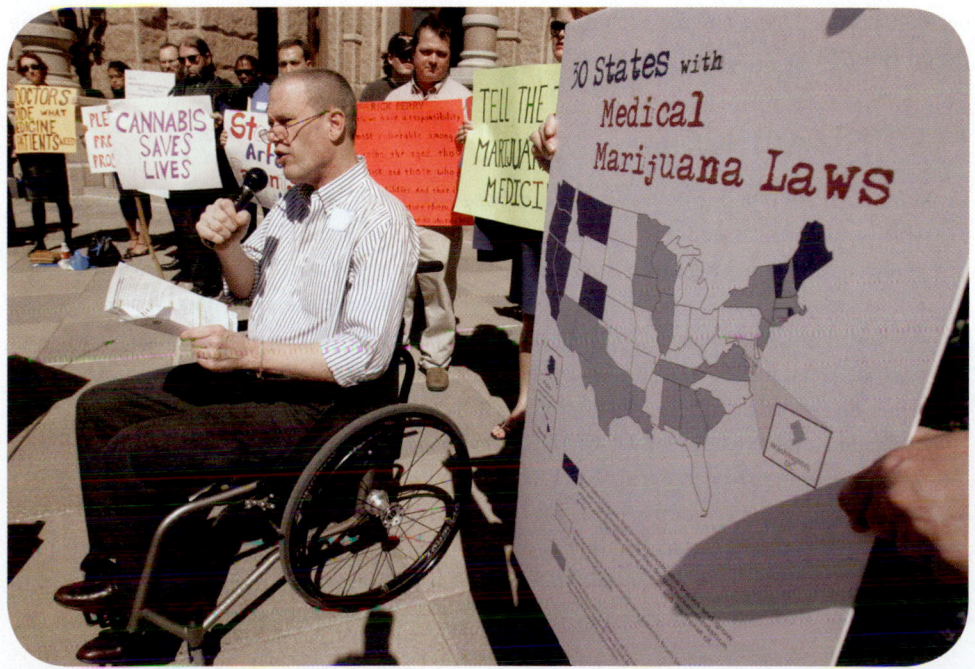

WHEELCHAIR BOUND due to multiple sclerosis, Tim Timmons speaks in favor of a medical marijuana law during a protest on the steps of the Capitol in Austin, Texas, Wednesday, February 21, 2007. Should a state be able to make the use of marijuana legal when the federal government does not? (AP Photo/LM Otero)

[16]*United States v. Lopez,* 514 U.S. 549 (1995).
[17]*Gonzales v. Raich,* 545 U.S. 1 (2005).

FEDERAL TROOPS were sent by President Eisenhower to guard Little Rock High School and to ensure the safety of the African American students who were going to attend that school. (Time & Life Pictures/Getty Images)

The vote was 5-4, with the chief justice on the minority side.[18] Similarly, when the Court upheld the 2003 federal law banning partial-birth abortions, Roberts was on the conservative side in a 5-4 vote.[19]

Later in 2007, the Supreme Court issued a very important opinion on school integration. By another 5-4 vote, the Court ruled that school district policies that included race as a determining factor in admission to certain schools were unconstitutional on the ground that they violated the equal protection clause of the Constitution.[20] These decisions of the Roberts Court suggest that there may often be a conservative majority on the Supreme Court, but the majority is razor thin, and swing votes can change the outcome in many cases.

WHAT CHECKS OUR COURTS?

Our judicial system is one of the most independent in the world, but the courts do not have absolute independence, for they are part of the political process. Political checks limit the extent to which courts can exercise judicial review and engage in an activist policy. These checks are exercised by the executive branch, the legislature, the public, and, finally, the judiciary.

EXECUTIVE CHECKS

Judicial Implementation
The way in which court decisions are translated into action.

President Andrew Jackson was once supposed to have said, after Chief Justice John Marshall made an unpopular decision, "John Marshall has made his decision; now let him enforce it."[21] This purported remark goes to the heart of **judicial implementation**—the enforcement of judicial decisions in such a way that those decisions are translated into policy. The Supreme Court simply does not have any enforcement powers, and whether a decision will be implemented depends on the cooperation of the other two branches of government. Rarely, though, will a president refuse to enforce a Supreme Court decision, as President Jackson did. To take such an action could mean a significant loss of public support because of the Supreme Court's stature in the eyes of the nation.

More commonly, presidents exercise influence over the judiciary by appointing new judges and justices as federal judicial seats become vacant. Additionally, as mentioned earlier, the U.S. solicitor general plays a significant role in the federal court system, and the person holding this office is a presidential appointee.

---

[18]*Massachusetts v. EPA,* 127 St. Ct. 1438 (2007).
[19]*Gonzales v. Carhart,* 127 St. Ct. 1610 (2007).
[20]*Parents Involved in Community Schools v. Seattle School District,* N. 1, 127 St. Ct. 2162 (2007).
[21]The decision referred to was *Cherokee Nation v. Georgia,* 30 U.S. 1 (1831).

Executives at the state level may also refuse to implement court decisions with which they disagree. A notable example of such a refusal occurred in Arkansas after the Supreme Court ordered schools to desegregate "with all deliberate speed" in 1955.[22] Arkansas Governor Orval Faubus refused to cooperate with the decision and used the state's National Guard to block the integration of Central High School in Little Rock. Ultimately, President Dwight Eisenhower had to federalize the Arkansas National Guard and send federal troops to Little Rock to quell the violence that had erupted.

LEGISLATIVE CHECKS

Courts may make rulings, but often the legislatures at local, state, and federal levels are required to appropriate funds to carry out the courts' rulings. A court, for example, may decide that prison conditions must be improved, but the legislature authorizes the funds necessary to carry out the ruling. When such funds are not appropriated, the court that made the ruling, in effect, has been checked.

Constitutional Amendments. Courts' rulings can be overturned by constitutional amendments at both the federal and state levels. Many of the amendments to the U.S. Constitution (such as the Fourteenth, Fifteenth, and Twenty-sixth Amendments) check the state courts' ability to allow discrimination, for example. Proposed constitutional amendments that were created in an effort to reverse courts' decisions on school prayer and abortion have failed.

Rewriting Laws. Finally, Congress or a state legislature can rewrite (amend) old laws or enact new ones to overturn a court's rulings if the legislature concludes that the court is interpreting laws or legislative intentions erroneously. For example, Congress passed the Civil Rights Act of 1991 in part to overturn a series of conservative rulings in employment-discrimination cases. In 1993, Congress enacted the Religious Freedom Restoration Act (RFRA), which broadened religious liberties, after Congress concluded that a 1990 Supreme Court ruling restricted religious freedom to an unacceptable extent.[23]

According to political scientist Walter Murphy, "A permanent feature of our constitutional landscape is the ongoing tug and pull between elected government and the courts."[24] Certainly, over the last few decades, the Supreme Court has been in conflict with the other two branches of government. Congress at various times has passed laws that, among other things, made it illegal to burn the American flag and attempted to curb pornography on the Internet. In each instance, the Supreme Court ruled that those laws were unconstitutional. The Court also invalidated the RFRA.

Whenever Congress does not like what the judiciary does, it threatens to censure the judiciary for its activism. One member of the Senate Judiciary Committee, John Cornyn (R.-Tex.), claimed that judges are making "political decisions yet are unaccountable to the public." He went on to say that violence against judges in the courtroom can be explained by the public's distress at such activism.

The states can also negate or alter the effects of Supreme Court rulings, when such decisions allow it. A good case in point is *Kelo v. City of New London*.[25] In that case, the Supreme Court allowed a city to take private property for redevelopment by private businesses. Since that case was decided, a majority of states have passed legislation limiting or prohibiting such takings.

----

[22]*Brown v. Board of Education*, 349 U.S. 294 (1955)—the second *Brown* decision.
[23]*Employment Division, Department of Human Resources of Oregon v. Smith*, 494 U.S. 872 (1990).
[24]As quoted in Neal Devins, "The Last Word Debate: How Social and Political Forces Shape Constitutional Values," *American Bar Association Journal*, October 1997, p. 48.
[25]545 U.S. 469 (2005).

PUBLIC OPINION

Public opinion plays a significant role in shaping government policy, and certainly the judiciary is not exempt from this rule. For one thing, persons affected by a Supreme Court decision that is noticeably at odds with their views may simply ignore it. Officially sponsored prayers were banned in public schools in 1962, yet it was widely known that the ban was (and still is) ignored in many Southern districts. What can the courts do in this situation? Unless someone complains about the prayers and initiates a lawsuit, the courts can do nothing. The public can also pressure state and local government officials to refuse to enforce a certain decision. As already mentioned, judicial implementation requires the cooperation of government officials at all levels, and public opinion in various regions of the country will influence whether such cooperation is forthcoming.

Additionally, the courts necessarily are influenced by public opinion to some extent. After all, judges are not isolated in our society; their attitudes are influenced by social trends, just as the attitudes and beliefs of all persons are. Courts generally tend to avoid issuing decisions that they know will be noticeably at odds with public opinion.[26] In part, this is because the judiciary, as a branch of the government, prefers to avoid creating divisiveness among the public. Also, a court—particularly the Supreme Court—may lose stature if it decides a case in a way that markedly diverges from public opinion. For example, in 2002, the Supreme Court ruled that the execution of mentally retarded criminals violates the Eighth Amendment's ban on cruel and unusual punishment. In its ruling, the Court indicated that the standards of what constitutes cruel and unusual punishment are influenced by public opinion and that there is "powerful evidence that today our society views mentally retarded offenders as categorically less culpable than the average criminal."[27]

JUDICIAL TRADITIONS AND DOCTRINES

Supreme Court justices (and other federal judges) typically exercise self-restraint in fashioning their decisions. In part, this restraint stems from their knowledge that the other two branches of government and the public can exercise checks on the judiciary, as previously discussed. To a large extent, however, this restraint is mandated by various judicially established traditions and doctrines. For example, in exercising its discretion to hear appeals, the Supreme Court will not hear a meritless appeal just so it can rule on the issue. Also, when reviewing a case, the Supreme Court typically narrows its focus to just one issue or one aspect of an issue involved in the case. The Court rarely makes broad, sweeping decisions on issues. Furthermore, the doctrine of *stare decisis* acts as a restraint because it obligates the courts, including the Supreme Court, to follow established precedents when deciding cases. Only rarely will courts overrule a precedent.

Hypothetical and Political Questions. Other judicial doctrines and practices also act as restraints. As already mentioned, the courts will hear only what are called justiciable disputes, which arise out of actual cases. In other words, a court will not hear a case that involves a merely hypothetical issue. Additionally, if a political question is involved, the Supreme Court often will exercise judicial restraint and refuse to rule on the matter. A **political question** is one that the Supreme Court declares should

Political Question
An issue that a court believes should be decided by the executive or legislative branch.

---

[26]One striking counterexample is the *Kelo v. City of New London* decision mentioned earlier.
[27]*Atkins v. Virginia*, 536 U.S. 304 (2002).

be decided by the elected branches of government—the executive branch, the legislative branch, or those two branches acting together. For example, the Supreme Court has refused to rule on the controversy regarding the rights of gays and lesbians in the military, preferring instead to defer to the executive branch's decisions on the matter. Generally, fewer questions are deemed political questions by the Supreme Court today than in the past.

The Impact of the Lower Courts. Higher courts can reverse the decisions of lower courts. Lower courts can act as a check on higher courts, too. Lower courts can ignore—and have ignored—Supreme Court decisions. Usually, this is done indirectly. A lower court might conclude, for example, that the precedent set by the Supreme Court does not apply to the exact circumstances in the case before the court; or the lower court may decide that the Supreme Court's decision was ambiguous with respect to the issue before the lower court. The fact that the Supreme Court rarely makes broad and clear-cut statements on any issue makes it easier for the lower courts to interpret the Supreme Court's decisions in a different way.

YOU CAN MAKE A Difference

VOLUNTEER IN THE COURTS

Almost everyone has a legal problem at some point in his or her life. As a student, you may be dealing with a traffic ticket, an accident citation, a drunk driving arrest, or a domestic dispute. Or you might have difficulty getting back a security deposit or forcing your landlord to fix your apartment. Every citizen has a right to be treated fairly when such issues bring him or her into the court system, whether it is a municipal court, a state court, or the federal district court. However, all court systems in the United States are overburdened with too many cases and too few employees to provide needed services. How can you make a difference in improving the court system and, perhaps, helping fellow students?

First, everyone should experience the courts at work. All local courts are open to the public to watch arraignments and first pleas. Check the Web site of your local court system and find out the place and time of municipal or other local court proceedings. Spend time as a visitor to the court to observe how individuals who are being charged with a crime are treated. Is it obvious that their rights are being respected? Are there attorneys to represent them in felony cases? Try to understand the wide variety of cases that come before a court.

HELP YOUR FELLOW STUDENTS

Most large universities have some type of office to help students who need legal services. Check your college's Web site for "Student Legal Services." These offices are often staffed

THIS YOUNG MAN may have been observing a court proceeding or volunteering in the court system. Explore such opportunities where you live or attend school. (iStockphoto.com/brocreative)

with attorneys who will consult with registered students if they are going to face charges either on campus or in the local community. Most of the student legal services offices also provide opportunities for student workers, either in paid positions or as volunteers, to assist students who need legal advice and counseling. This is an opportunity to become much more familiar with your rights as a student and the way to approach the legal system.

HELP IN YOUR COMMUNITY

Some American cities and states have volunteer opportunities and internships in the local court system for undergraduate students as well as for law students. In New York State, there are numerous volunteer opportunities in the court system helping victims and providing assistance in divorce and immigration court or other legal systems. San Diego, California, seeks student volunteers in its court system for such positions as helping at the information desk, providing services to jurors, working in the business office, providing tours, and assisting in the children's waiting rooms. In Los Angeles, California, where more than 300,000 litigants annually do not have lawyers, the courts seek college students from the southern California universities to become "volunteer lawyers," helping individuals in completing forms, applying to the right court, and dealing with court processes. Each student volunteer receives about 60 hours of training before he or she can become part of "the Justice Corps" of the Los Angeles courts.

Working in the court system will help you learn your own rights and, if you are interested in becoming an attorney, give you real experience in the field.

For information on campus-based student legal services, go to your university's Web site and search for "Legal Services" or "Student Legal Services."

For volunteer opportunities, check the Web site of your local court system.

KEY TERMS

affirm 530	**judicial activism** 535	**precedent** 517
appellate court 524	**judicial implementation** 538	**remand** 530
broad construction 536	**judicial restraint** 535	**reverse** 530
case law 520	**judicial review** 517	**rule of four** 529
class-action suit 527	**jurisdiction** 522	**senatorial courtesy** 531
common law 517	**limited jurisdiction** 524	*stare decisis* 517
concurring opinion 530	**litigate** 527	**strict construction** 536
dissenting opinion 530	**majority opinion** 530	**trial court** 523
diversity of citizenship 523	**opinion** 529	**unanimous opinion** 530
federal question 523	**oral arguments** 529	**writ of** *certiorari* 529
general jurisdiction 523	**political question** 540	

CHAPTER SUMMARY

1. **Why are appointed judges so powerful in a democracy?** American law is rooted in the common-law tradition, which is part of our heritage from England. Fundamental sources of American law include the U.S. Constitution and state constitutions, statutes enacted by legislative bodies, regulations issued by administrative agencies, and case law. The common-law doctrine of *stare decisis* (which means "to stand on decided cases") obligates judges to follow precedents established previously by their own courts or by higher courts that have authority over them. Precedents established by the United States Supreme Court, the highest court in the land, are binding on all lower courts. The justices of the Supreme Court as well as those in all federal courts are appointed for life terms, making them invulnerable to political pressure or the need for reelection. Thus, appointed judges are, in fact, able to make decisions that have a lasting impact on American society.

2. Article III, Section 1, of the U.S. Constitution limits the jurisdiction of the federal courts to cases involving (1) a federal question, which is a question based, at least in part, on the U.S. Constitution, a treaty, or a federal law; or (2) diversity of citizenship, which arises when parties to a lawsuit are from different states or when the lawsuit involves a foreign citizen or government. The

federal court system is a three-tiered model consisting of (1) U.S. district (trial) courts and various lower courts of limited jurisdiction; (2) U.S. courts of appeals; and (3) the United States Supreme Court. Cases may be appealed from the district courts to the appellate courts. In most cases, the decisions of the federal appellate courts are final because the Supreme Court hears relatively few cases.

3. The Supreme Court's decision to review a case is influenced by many factors, including the significance of the issues involved and whether the solicitor general is pressing the Court to take the case. After a case is accepted, the justices undertake research (with the help of their law clerks) on the issues involved in the case, hear oral arguments from the parties, meet in conference to discuss and vote on the issue, and announce the opinion, which is then released for publication.

4. **Why are judicial appointments so controversial?** Federal judges are nominated by the president and confirmed by the Senate. Once appointed, they hold office for life, barring gross misconduct. The nomination and confirmation process, particularly for Supreme Court justices, is often extremely politicized. Democrats and Republicans alike realize that justices may occupy seats on the Court for decades and naturally want to have persons appointed who share their basic views. Nearly 20 percent of all Supreme Court appointments have been either rejected or not acted on by the Senate.

5. In interpreting and applying the law, judges inevitably become policy makers. The most important policy-making tool of the federal courts is the power of judicial review. This power was not mentioned specifically in the Constitution, but John Marshall claimed the power for the Court in his 1803 decision in *Marbury v. Madison*.

6. **Should the Supreme Court make law?** Judges who take an active role in checking the activities of the other branches of government sometimes are characterized as "activist" judges, and judges who defer to the other branches' decisions sometimes are regarded as "restraintist" judges. The Warren Court of the 1950s and 1960s was activist in a liberal direction, whereas the Rehnquist Court became increasingly activist in a conservative direction. Several politicians and scholars argue that judicial activism has gotten out of hand. One of the criticisms of the Court is that it should not "make law" but should defer to the legislative branch in deciding policy issues. However, in the interpretation of previously written laws, it has often fallen to the Supreme Court to make a final determination. The Court has also taken on policy issues such as school segregation that no political branch would address.

7. Checks on the powers of the federal courts include executive checks, legislative checks, public opinion, and judicial traditions and doctrines.

SELECTED PRINT, MEDIA, AND ONLINE RESOURCES

PRINT RESOURCES

Baird, Vanessa. *Answering the Call of the Court: How Justices and Litigants Set the Supreme Court Agenda.* Charlottesville, VA: University of Virginia Press, 2006. The author attempts to relate the justices' political and philosophical priorities to the way the Court's agenda has expanded in recent years. This is one of the first studies of the Court's agenda-setting process.

Foskett, Ken. *Judging Thomas: The Life and Times of Clarence Thomas.* New York: William Morrow, 2004. Foskett, an Atlanta journalist, delves into the intellectual development of Justice Thomas, one of the nation's most prominent African American conservatives.

Greenburg, Jan Crawford. *Supreme Conflict: The Inside Story of the Struggle for the Control of the United States Supreme Court.* New York: Penguin Books, 2008. A newspaper and PBS reporter, Greenburg developed close relationships with justices and staff at the Supreme Court. She tells the inside story of which justices were really powerful and which were the followers.

Klarman, Michael J. *From Jim Crow to Civil Rights: The Supreme Court and the Struggle for Racial Equality.* New York: Oxford University Press, 2004. Klarman, a professor of constitutional law, provides a detailed history of the Supreme Court's changing attitudes toward equality. Klarman argues that the civil rights movement would have revolutionized the status of African Americans even if the Court had not outlawed segregation.

O'Connor, Sandra Day. *The Majesty of the Law: Reflections of a Supreme Court Justice.* New York: Random House, 2003. As the Supreme Court's most prominent swing vote during her years on the bench, Justice O'Connor may have been the most powerful member of that body. O'Connor gives a basic introduction to the Court, reflects on past discrimination against women in the law, tells amusing stories about fellow justices, and calls for improving the treatment of jury members.

Roosevelt, Kermit. *The Myth of Judicial Activism: Making Sense of Supreme Court Decisions.* New Haven, CT: Yale University Press, 2008. Roosevelt, a University of Pennsylvania professor, defends the Court against charges of undue judicial activism. Roosevelt finds the Court's decisions to be reasonable, although he disagrees with some of them.

Zimmerman, Joseph F. *Interstate Disputes: The Supreme Court's Original Jurisdiction.* Buffalo, NY: State University of New York, 2006. This well-researched study examines the role of the Court in settling disputes between the states. The author concludes that states should enter into more interstate compacts rather than taking their disputes to the Supreme Court.

MEDIA RESOURCES

Amistad—A 1997 movie, starring Anthony Hopkins, about a slave ship mutiny in 1839. Much of the story revolves around the prosecution, ending at the Supreme Court, of the slave who led the revolt.

Gideon's Trumpet—A 1980 film, starring Henry Fonda as the small-time criminal James Earl Gideon, which makes clear the path a case takes to the Supreme Court and the importance of cases decided there.

Justice Sandra Day O'Connor—In a 1994 program, Bill Moyers conducts Justice O'Connor's first television interview. Topics include women's rights, O'Connor's role as the Supreme Court's first female justice, and her difficulties breaking into the male-dominated legal profession. O'Connor defends her positions on affirmative action and abortion.

The Magnificent Yankee—A 1950 movie, starring Louis Calhern and Ann Harding, that traces the life and philosophy of Oliver Wendell Holmes, Jr., one of the Supreme Court's most brilliant justices.

Marbury v. Madison—A 1987 video on the famous 1803 case that established the principle of judicial review. This is the first in a four-part series, *Equal Justice Under Law: Landmark Cases in Supreme Court History,* produced by the Judicial Conference of the United States.

The Supreme Court—A four-part PBS series that won a 2008 Parents' Choice Gold Award. The series follows the history of the Supreme Court from the first chief justice, John Marshall, to the earliest days of the Roberts Court. Some of the many topics are the Court's dismal performance in the Civil War era, its conflicts with President Franklin D. Roosevelt, its role in banning the segregation of African Americans, and the abortion controversy.

truTV—This TV channel covers high-profile trials, including those of O. J. Simpson, the Unabomber, British nanny Louise Woodward, and Timothy McVeigh. (You can learn below how to access truTV from your area via its Web site.)

ONLINE RESOURCES

FindLaw searchable database of Supreme Court decisions since 1970: www.findlaw.com

Legal Information Institute at Cornell University Law School offers an easily searchable index to Supreme Court opinions, including some important historic decisions: www.law.cornell.edu/supct/index.html

The Oyez Project a multimedia archive devoted to the Supreme Court of the United States and its work: www.oyez.org/oyez/frontpage

Supreme Court of the United States Supreme Court decisions are available here within hours of their release: supremecourtus.gov

truTV.com Web site dedicated to the television station (formerly Court TV) that focuses on real-life stories told from a first-person perspective. The site offers the program lineup, which features six hours of daily trial coverage; a Crime Library, which includes case histories as well as selected documents filed with the court and court transcripts; and a link to CNN Crime for trial news: www.trutv.com

United States Courts The home page of the federal courts is a good starting point for learning about the federal court system in general. At this site, you can even follow the path of a case as it moves through the federal court system: www.uscourts.gov

16

Multiple boats combated the fires and petroleum leaks in the Gulf of Mexico after the explosion and destruction of the Deepwater Horizon oil drilling rig in 2010. (© Jim McKinley/Alamy)

Domestic Policy

QUESTIONS TO CONSIDER

How does the policy-making process reflect the will of the people?

Should the government provide health care to all Americans, or is the private sector better equipped to do so?

How do you balance the need to protect the environment with the need to sustain economic growth?

CHAPTER CONTENTS

what if...

We Had Universal Health Care?

BACKGROUND

In the United States, we have a private health care system with about 40 percent of Americans using government programs to pay for their health insurance. That includes the senior citizens under Medicare, the children who are insured under CHips, and Medicaid patients. The new U.S. health policy may end up as universal health care, meaning that access to health care will be made available to everyone, but for now, those who do not qualify for one of the government programs will be required to buy their own insurance. The government estimates that within 10 years, more than 90 percent of Americans will have health insurance.

WHAT IF WE HAD UNIVERSAL HEALTH CARE?

With universal health care, everyone in need of basic medical care would have access to physicians, clinics, and hospital services. Note that when we are referring to universal health care, we are not specifying how such a service would be funded—a major political issue. Nor have we specified how decisions would be made about health care. Would private insurance pay for more services than the government? Most wealthy nations other than the United States have universal, government-administered health insurance systems, but the United States so far has generally preferred a private insurance model.

THE SAN FRANCISCO EXPERIMENT

To understand how universal health care might work, we can go to San Francisco, California, where a universal health care plan was approved in the summer of 2006. The San Francisco Health Access Plan, as it is called, is financed by local government, mandatory contributions from employers, and income-adjusted premiums from users.

Enrollment fees range from $3 to $201, and most participants will pay $35 per month. Uninsured San Franciscans can then seek comprehensive primary care in the city's public and private clinics and hospitals. San Francisco Mayor Gavin Newsom described the city's historic undertaking as a "moral obligation."

Not everybody in the city is happy about the new plan, however. To offset the estimated annual price tag of more than $200 million, firms with 20 or more workers have to contribute about one dollar per hour worked by any employee. Those with more than a hundred workers have to pay $1.60 per hour, up to a monthly maximum of $180 per worker.

Many small-business owners in San Francisco predict that new businesses will no longer locate there. They also argue that goods and services within the city will become more expensive as employers pass on the added health care costs to customers.

THE RELATIONSHIP BETWEEN UNIVERSAL HEALTH CARE ACCESS AND THE NUMBER OF UNINSURED

Economic analysis yields a simple relationship between price and quantity demanded—the lower the price, the higher the quantity demanded. Medical care is a service like any other. If medical care is provided at a lower price to those who desire it, more medical care will be demanded.

We can predict that if a universal health care plan is implemented, the number of people without purchased health insurance will increase. To understand this, consider how people will behave if universal health care access becomes a reality. Over time, some individuals and families will choose not to renew their health insurance, because they will know that they can rely on universal health care access. Consequently, the existence of universal health care will actually increase the number of those who do not have private health insurance in the United States. As this happens, the burden on hospitals and clinics will increase, as will the costs to the government.

In essence, universal health care coverage is the equivalent of having a zero deductible for primary care. Note that this does not mean that people will become sicker if they have access to universal health care, but it does mean that they will make greater use of health care facilities. The United States does not, at the present time, have enough primary care doctors and clinics to provide the care that will be demanded by patients.

FOR CRITICAL ANALYSIS

1. What are the advantages and disadvantages of a universal health care system?
2. How could costs be controlled if a universal health care system is adopted?

WHEN PEOPLE ARE ASKED what the national government is supposed to do for them, generally they will answer that the government should defend our nation and solve our national problems. Americans expect the federal government to pay attention to the issues that impact the lives of American citizens. The legislation and regulations that are passed to address these problems are usually called "domestic policy." **Domestic policy** can be defined as all of the laws, government planning, and government actions that affect each individual's daily life in the United States. Consequently, the span of such policies is enormous. Domestic policies range from relatively simple issues, such as what the speed limit should be on interstate highways, to more complex ones, such as how best to reduce our nation's contribution to climate change or how to improve the performance of schools across the nation.

As noted in the *What If...* that opens this chapter, the question of providing health care to all Americans is a consuming national issue. In 2010, the United States adopted a major reform of our health policies, but the Congress did not adopt a universal health care system. The complex nature of the health policy reform legislation and the debate that accompanied that reform effort reflect the fact that the reform will touch virtually all Americans. Like many other domestic policies, this one was formulated and implemented by the federal government but will involve efforts of federal, state, and local governments.

In this chapter, we look at domestic policy issues involving health care, the environment and energy, poverty and welfare, immigration, and crime. Before we start our analysis, though, we must look at how public policies are made.

> **Domestic Policy**
> Public plans or courses of action that concern internal issues of national importance, such as poverty, crime, and the environment.

THE POLICY-MAKING PROCESS

How does any issue get resolved? First, the issue must be identified as a problem. Often, policy makers simply have to open their local newspapers—or letters from their constituents—to discover that a problem is brewing. On rare occasions, a crisis, such as that brought about by the terrorist attacks of September 11, 2001, creates the need to formulate policy. Like most Americans, however, policy makers receive much of their information from the national media. Finally, various lobbying groups provide information to members of Congress.

As an example of policy making, consider the Medicare reform bill. Medicare is a program that pays health care expenses for Americans age 65 and older. As initially created in the 1960s, Medicare did not cover the cost of prescription drugs. The new bill provided a direct drug benefit beginning in 2006. (Certain discounts were available immediately.)

No matter how simple or how complex the problem, those who make policy follow several steps. We can divide the process of policy making into at least five steps: agenda building, policy formulation, policy adoption, policy implementation, and policy evaluation (see Figure 16–1).

AGENDA BUILDING

First, the issue must get on the agenda. In other words, Congress must become aware that an issue requires congressional action. Agenda building may occur as the result of a crisis, technological change, or mass media campaigns, as well as through the efforts of strong political personalities and effective lobbying groups.

Advocates for the elderly, including AARP (formerly the American Association of Retired Persons), had demanded a Medicare drug benefit for years. Traditionally, liberals have advocated such benefits. Yet the benefit was created under President George W. Bush—a conservative Republican. Bush's advocacy of Medicare reform was essential to its success and shored up his support among more moderate voters.

FIGURE 16–1 The Policy Process

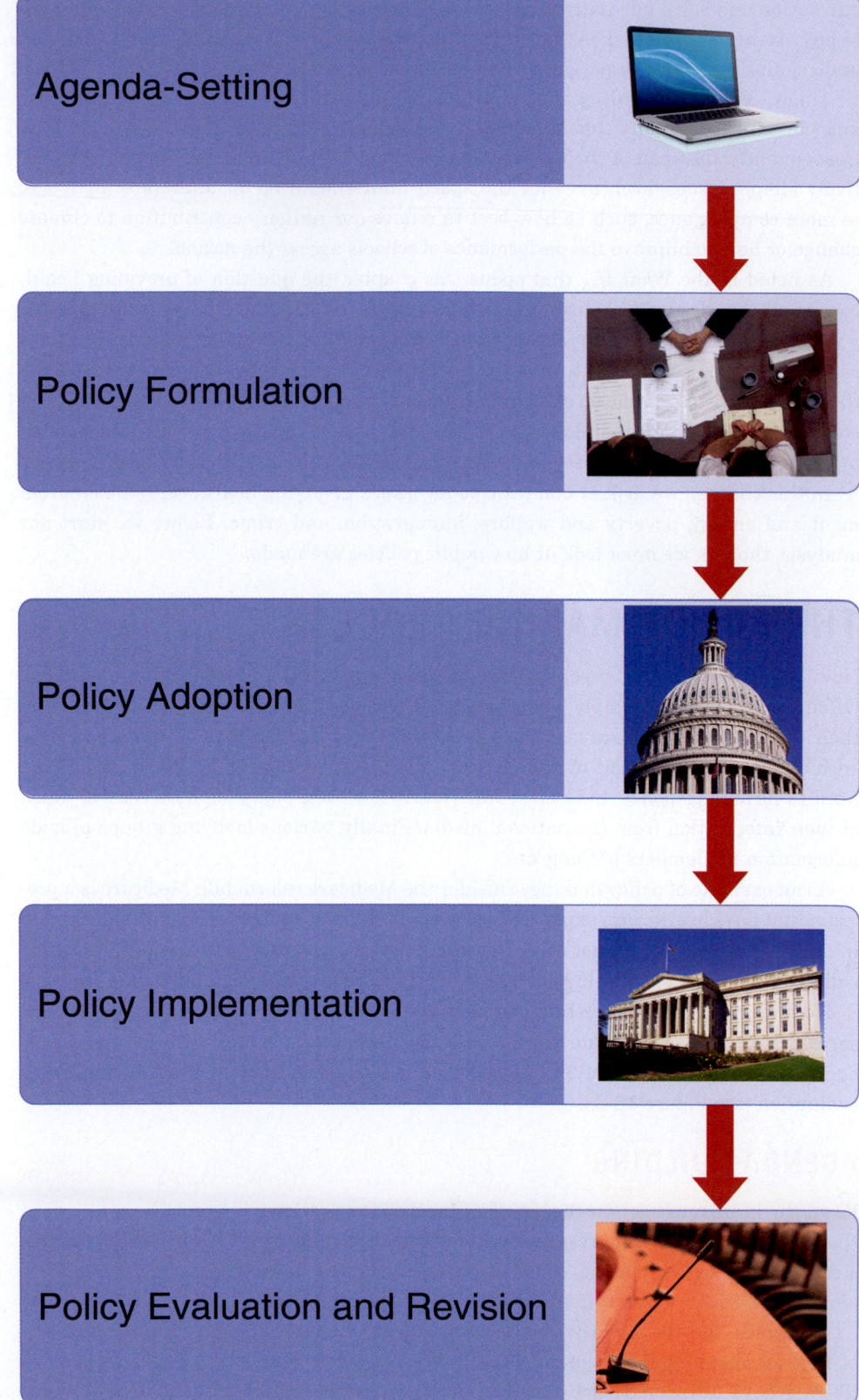

Agenda-Setting

Policy Formulation

Policy Adoption

Policy Implementation

Policy Evaluation and Revision

POLICY FORMULATION

During the next step in the policy-making process, various policy proposals are discussed among government officials and the public. Such discussions may take place in the printed media, on television, and in the halls of Congress. Congress holds hearings, the president voices the administration's views, and the topic may even become a campaign issue.

Many Republicans in Congress were opposed to any major new social-spending program, partly because they did not want to see more government control over the economy and partly because it would be very costly. Conservative members of Congress believed that insurance programs should be run by private businesses. To win their support, the Republican leadership advocated a degree of privatization. Under this plan, private companies would administer the drug benefit. The Republicans also proposed measures that would benefit the insurance and pharmaceutical industries. For example, the government would not use its immense bargaining power to obtain lower prices for Medicare drugs and would discourage the importation of lower-cost drugs from Canada. Finally, the Republicans proposed that to keep the cost of the bill down, not all drug expenses would be covered. To reduce costs, the Republican plan had a "doughnut hole" in which out-of-pocket drug expenses greater than $2,250 but less than $3,600 were not covered. Republicans argued that these limits would provide good, basic prescription coverage for most senior citizens but would require those with a certain level of income to pay a portion of their prescription costs. Poorer seniors were covered entirely. Democrats supported the plan, believing that they could increase coverage in the years to come.

DID YOU KNOW?

That in the mid-1930s, during the Great Depression, Senator Huey P. Long of Louisiana proposed that the government confiscate all personal fortunes of more than $5 million and all incomes of more than $1 million and use the funds to give every American family a house, a car, and an annual income of $2,000 or more (about $25,000 in today's dollars)?

POLICY ADOPTION

The third step in the policy-making process involves choosing a specific policy from among the proposals that have been discussed. In the end, the Republican proposals were adopted, and the bill passed by the narrowest of margins. The progress of the bill through Congress revealed some of the intense partisan behavior that has become common in recent years. For example, the Republicans refused to allow any Democrats from the House to participate in the conference committee that reconciled the House and Senate versions of the bill—a startling departure from tradition. Of course, Democrats then did the same thing in passing the health reform legislation of 2010.

Almost at the last minute, AARP endorsed the bill, which may have guaranteed its success. A significant minority of the Democratic members of Congress broke with their party to support the bill, and that was enough to balance out the Republicans who refused to vote for it.

POLICY IMPLEMENTATION

The fourth step in the policy-making process involves the implementation of the policy alternative chosen by Congress. Government action must be implemented by bureaucrats, the courts, police, and individual citizens. In the example of the Medicare reform bill, the main portion of the legislation was not to come into effect until 2006. For the most part, therefore, implementation did not begin immediately. Some sections of the bill did become effective in 2004, however. These included a series of drug discount cards, sponsored by the government in cooperation with various insurance companies, which would provide some savings on prescription drugs right away and an advertising campaign to educate seniors about the program.

POLITICS WITH A purpose

Defining Problems and Finding Solutions in Education

What's in a name? Policy makers often choose names for legislation as a way of directing attention to a particular policy problem. For example, President George W. Bush's No Child Left Behind (NCLB) landmark education bill[a] was designed to focus on specific problems the president had identified: inadequate accountability of schools to the public; tax dollars not having their intended effect on education; and disturbing trends showing disparate rates of success in school among children of different socioeconomic groups.

As governor of Texas, President Bush had been a proponent of the reforms that had grown in popularity during the late 1980s and early 1990s. Accountability advocates favored standardized testing throughout a child's educational career to measure concretely the progress schools were making toward specific educational goals. The results of these tests would factor significantly into teacher raises and funding for particular schools and school districts across the state.[b]

The president also identified what he called the "soft bigotry of low expectations," referring to the lower test scores of specific groups of children.[c] In an effort to close these gaps, NCLB mandates that test scores must be reported separately for specific racial and ethnic groups, for low-income children, for children for whom English is a second language, and for children with disabilities. States are charged with setting educational goals, assessing how close to the goals schools were at the time of passage of the law, and using the differential to determine "adequate yearly progress" (AYP) benchmarks the schools must hit each year. If any one of the subgroups listed does not make AYP, the entire school is listed as "needs improvement"; NCLB allows children in these schools to transfer to better-performing schools.

NCLB passed Congress with bipartisan support and without major opposition from teachers' groups and unions. Interestingly, these groups had been an active part of the dialogue on school reform for several decades. For example, in 1983, the Department of Education issued a report entitled "A Nation at Risk," in which it asserted that "the educational foundations of our society are presently being eroded by a rising tide of mediocrity that threatens our very future   as a Nation and a

people."[d] One group, the American Federation of Teachers (AFT), was more supportive of the call for reform than another, the National Education Association (NEA). The AFT's immediate response to NCLB was similar to its response in the 1980s—to embrace goals to close the gaps between groups of children. The NEA, on the other hand, has been vocal in its opposition to NCLB, even threatening to sue to overturn the law.[e] In recent years, both groups have been critical of the testing, arguing that its high-stakes nature drives curriculum, creating a "teaching to the test" mentality.

These teacher groups have been joined by others in opposition to the implementation of the law. Disability and immigration advocates argue that NCLB does not meet the special needs of children with disabilities and immigrant children.[f] Some conservative groups are frustrated by what they see as an inappropriate growth of federal government  power.[g] All of these criticisms have been voiced in the debate over the bill's reauthorization in the 2007–2008 congressional session.

With the election of President Barack Obama, a number of groups believed that they had an ally in the White House. The teachers' unions, the AFT and NEA, were surprised to see the president choose Arne Duncan, former superintendent of the Chicago schools, as secretary of education. Duncan had been the chief administrator for the Chicago schools and an outspoken supporter of teacher accountability and school reform. The Obama administration has continued the push for more accountability for teachers, for charter schools, and for improvements in student learning. A billion-dollar fund was established for competitive grants to states for improvement. To even qualify to compete for the grants, teachers, administrators, and boards of education must agree to support the innovations funded by the grants. So far, only two states have qualified for grant funding.

---

[a]Signed by the president on January 8, 2002, PL 107–110.
[b]E. DeBray, K. McDermott, and P. Wohlstetter, "Introduction to the Special Issue on Federalism Reconsidered: The Case of the No Child Left Behind Act," *Peabody Journal of Education*, Vol. 80, 2005, pp. 1–18.
[c]The president used this phrase many times in the lead-up to the legislation and during its implementation. An example of the latter is in a speech made to the National Association for the Advancement of Colored People (NAACP) in June 2006, available at www.whitehouse.gov/news/releases/2006/07/20060720.html.

[d]www.ed.gov/pubs/NatAtRisk/risk.html
[e]J. Koppich, "A Tale of Two Approaches—The AFT, the NEA, and NCLB," *Peabody Journal of Education*, Vol. 80, 2005, pp. 137–155.
[f]www.ncd.gov/newsroom/news/2003/r03-419.htm; www.urban.org/publications/411469.html
[g]www.heritage.org/Press/Commentary/ed031707a.cfm
[h]An alternative to NCLB proposed by a coalition of Republican lawmakers; www.heritage.org/Press/Commentary/ed031707a .cfm, accessed May 25, 2008.

POLICY EVALUATION

After a policy has been implemented, it is evaluated. Groups inside and outside the government conduct studies to determine what actually happens after a policy has been in place for a given period of time. Based on this feedback and the perceived success or failure of the policy, a new round of policy-making initiatives will be undertaken to improve on the effort. Given that the new prescription drug benefit was the most significant expansion of Medicare since its creation 40 years ago, there was certain to be mixed feedback. In this instance, much of the initial feedback was negative because of the multiplicity of plans and confusion over which drugs would be covered. As the program was fully implemented, both Congress and the Bush administration began to propose changes, including increasing premiums for higher-income beneficiaries to help pay for the program. Overall, the program became very popular with senior citizens, with more than one million prescriptions filled every day. And, in the 2010 legislation, the Democratic Congress began to improve the benefit for all seniors.

HEALTH CARE

Undoubtedly, one of the most important problems facing the nation is how to guarantee affordable health care for all Americans at a cost the nation can bear. Spending for health care is estimated to account for almost 20 percent of the total U.S. economy. In 1965, about 6 percent of our income was spent on health care, and that percentage has been increasing ever since, exceeding 15 percent by 2005 and projected to reach 18 percent by 2010. Per capita spending on health care is greater in the United States than almost anywhere else in the world. Measured by the percentage of the gross domestic product (GDP) devoted to health care, America spends almost twice as much as Australia or Canada (see Figure 16–2). (The GDP is the dollar value of all final goods and services produced in a one-year period.)

FIGURE 16–2 Cost of Health Care in Economically Advanced Nations

Cost is given as a percentage of total gross domestic product (GDP).

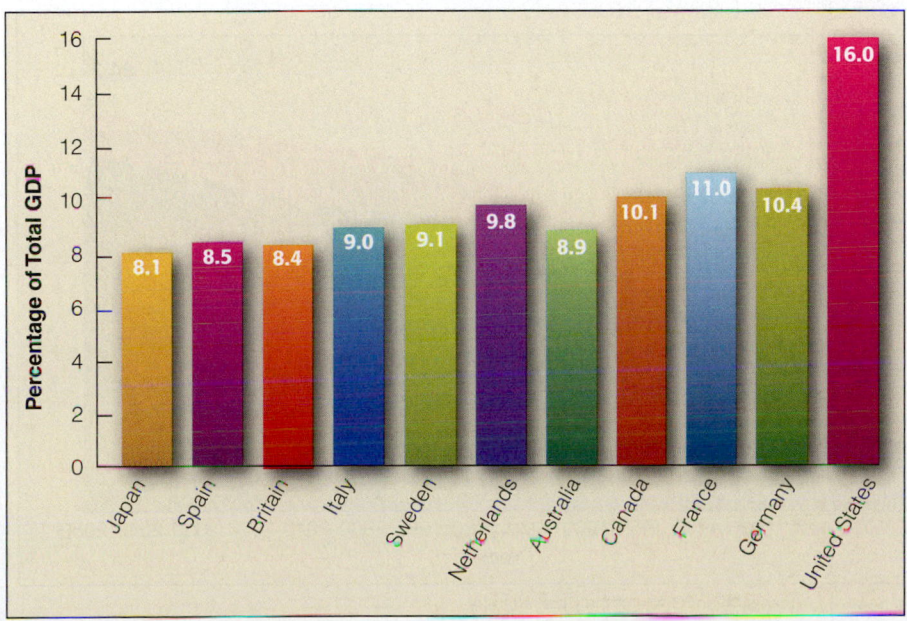

Source: Organization for Economic Cooperation and Development, *OECD Health Data*, 2009.

THE RISING COST OF HEALTH CARE

Numerous explanations exist for why health care costs have risen so much. At least one has to do with changing demographics—the U.S. population is getting older. Life expectancy has gone up, as shown in Figure 16–3. The top 5 percent of those using health care incur more than 50 percent of all health care costs. The bottom 70 percent of health care users account for only 10 percent of health care expenditures. Not surprisingly, the elderly make up most of the top users of health care services, including nursing home care and long-term care for those suffering from debilitating diseases.

Advanced Technology. Another reason why health care costs have risen so dramatically is advancing technology. A computerized tomography (CT) scanner costs around $1 million. A magnetic resonance imaging (MRI) scanner can cost more than $2 million. A positron emission tomography (PET) scanner costs approximately $4 million. All of these machines have become increasingly available in recent decades and are in demand around the country. Typical fees for procedures using these scanners range from $300 to $500 for a CT scan to as high as $2,000 for a PET scan. The development of new technologies that help physicians and hospitals prolong human life is an ongoing process in an ever-advancing industry. New procedures and drugs that involve even greater costs can be expected in the future. It is also true that these advanced procedures are more readily available in the United States than anywhere else in the world.

The Government's Role in Financing Health Care. Currently, government spending on health care constitutes about 45 percent of total health care spending. Private insurance accounts for about 35 percent of payments for health care. The remainder—less than 20 percent—is paid directly by individuals or by philanthropy. Medicare and Medicaid have been the main sources of hospital and other medical benefits for 35 million U.S. residents, most of whom are age 65 and older.

FIGURE 16–3 Life Expectancy in the United States

Along with health-care spending, life expectancy has gone up. Therefore, we are presumably getting some return for our spending.

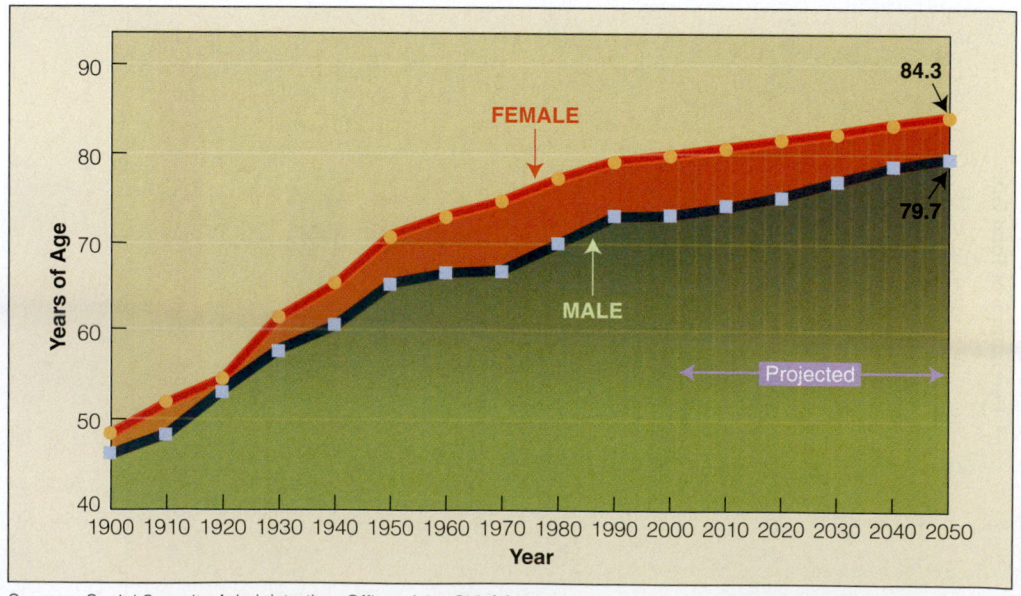

Sources: Social Security Administration, Office of the Chief Actuary.

Medicare is specifically designed to support the elderly, regardless of income. **Medicaid**, a joint state–federal program, is in principle a program to subsidize health care for the poor. In practice, it often provides long-term health care to persons living in nursing homes. (To become eligible for Medicaid, these individuals must first exhaust their financial assets.) Medicare, Medicaid, and private insurance companies are called *third parties*. Caregivers and patients are the two primary parties. When third parties pay for medical care, the demand for such services increases; health care recipients have no incentive to restrain their use of health care. One result is some degree of wasted resources.

MEDICARE

The Medicare program, which was created in 1965 under President Lyndon B. Johnson (served 1963–1969), pays hospital and physicians' bills for U.S. residents age 65 and older. As already mentioned, beginning in 2006, Medicare also pays for at least part of the prescription drug expenses of the elderly. In return for paying a tax on their earnings (currently set at 2.9 percent of wages and salaries) while in the workforce, retirees are ensured that the majority of their hospital and physicians' bills will be paid for with public funds.

Over the past 40 years, Medicare has become the second-largest domestic spending program, after Social Security. Government expenditures on Medicare have routinely turned out to be far in excess of the expenditures forecast at the time the program was put into place or expanded. In Chapter 17, you will learn about Medicare's impact on the current federal budget and the impact it is likely to have in the future. For now, consider only that the total outlays on Medicare are high enough to create substantial demands to curtail its costs.

One response by the federal government to soaring Medicare costs has been to impose arbitrary reimbursement caps on specific procedures. To avoid going over Medicare's reimbursement caps, however, hospitals have an incentive to discharge patients quickly. The government has also cut rates of reimbursement to individual physicians and physician groups, such as health maintenance organizations (HMOs). One consequence has been a nearly 15 percent reduction in the amount the government pays for Medicare services provided by physicians. As a result, physicians and HMOs have become reluctant to accept Medicare patients. Several of the nation's largest HMOs have withdrawn from certain Medicare programs.

MEDICAID

In a few short years, the joint federal–state taxpayer-funded Medicaid program for the "working poor" has generated one of the biggest expansions of government entitlements in the last 50 years. In 1997, Medicaid spending was around $150 billion. Ten years later, it exceeded $300 billion. At the end of the last decade, 34 million people were enrolled in the program. Today, there are more than 46 million. The increase in unemployment after the financial crisis of 2008 added almost 4 million people to the Medicaid program. When you add Medicaid coverage to Medicare and the military and federal employee health plans, the government has clearly become the nation's primary health insurer. More than 100 million people—one in three—in the United States have government coverage.

Why Has Medicaid Spending Exploded? One of the reasons Medicaid has become such an important health insurance program is that the income ceiling for eligibility has

Medicare
A federal health insurance program that covers U.S. residents age 65 and older. The costs are met by a tax on wages and salaries.

Medicaid
A joint state–federal program that provides medical care to the poor (including indigent elderly persons in nursing homes). The program is funded out of general government revenues.

increased to more than $44,000 per year in most states. In other words, a family of four can earn around $44,000 and still obtain health insurance through Medicaid for its children. Indeed, many low-income workers choose Medicaid over health insurance offered by employers. Why? The reason is that Medicaid is less costly and sometimes covers more medical expenses. For most recipients, Medicaid is either free or almost free.

Medicaid and the States. On average, the federal government pays almost 60 percent of Medicaid's cost; the states pay the rest. Certain states, particularly in the South, receive even higher reimbursements. In general, such states are not complaining about the expansion of Medicaid. Other states, however, such as New York, have been overwhelmed by the rate of increase in Medicaid spending. Even with the federal government's partial reimbursement, the portion paid by the states has increased so rapidly that the states are becoming financially strapped. Florida, for example, had to drastically revise its Medicaid eligibility rules to reduce the number of families using Medicaid. Otherwise, the state projected a budget deficit that it would not be able to handle.

THE UNINSURED

More than 45 million Americans—15 percent of the population—do not have health insurance. The proportion of the population that is uninsured varies from one part of the country to another. In Hawaii and Minnesota, only 7 percent of working adults lack coverage. In Texas, however, the figure is 27 percent. According to the Congressional Black Caucus Foundation, African Americans, Hispanics, and Asian/Pacific Islanders make up more than half of the year-round uninsured, even though they constitute only 29 percent of the total U.S. population. Hispanic Americans are the most likely to be uninsured, with only 35 percent of working Hispanic adults having coverage.

According to surveys, being uninsured has negative health consequences. People without coverage are less likely to get basic preventive care, such as mammograms; less likely to have a personal physician; and more likely to rate their own health as only poor or fair.

The Uninsured Employed. The uninsured population is relatively young, in part due to Medicare, which covers almost everyone age 65 or older. Also, younger workers are more likely to be employed in entry-level jobs that do not come with health insurance benefits so, to maximize their income, they choose not to buy health insurance. The current system of health care in the United States assumes that employers will provide health insurance. Many small businesses, however, simply cannot afford to offer their workers health insurance. Insurance costs are now approaching an average of $10,000 per year for each employee.

Shifting Costs to the Uninsured. A further problem faced by the uninsured is that when they do seek medical care, they must usually pay much higher fees than would be paid on their behalf if they had insurance coverage. Large third-party insurers, private or public, normally strike hard bargains with hospitals and physicians over how much they will pay for procedures and services. The uninsured have less bargaining power. As a result, hospitals attempt to recover from the uninsured the revenues they lost in paying third-party insurers.

In any given year, most people do not require expensive health care. Young, healthy people in particular can be tempted to do without insurance. One benefit of insurance coverage, however, is that it protects the insured against catastrophic costs resulting from unusual events. Medical care for life-threatening accidents or diseases can run into thousands or even hundreds of thousands of dollars. An uninsured person who requires this kind of medical care may be forced into bankruptcy.

THE 2010 HEALTH CARE REFORM LEGISLATION

On March 23, 2010, after a long and intense battle in Congress, President Obama signed the Patient Protection and Affordable Care Act, the biggest reform of the American health care and health insurance system since the approval of Medicare in 1965. The new legislation relies on a combination of private insurance, public programs such as Medicare and Medicaid, and new state-based nonprofit health exchanges to provide health insurance coverage to almost all Americans. The program, as it passed the Congress, is not like the types of programs adopted in many European countries or in Canada.

Western Europe, Japan, Canada, and Australia all provide systems of universal coverage. Such coverage is provided through **national health insurance**. In effect, the government takes over the economic function of providing basic health care coverage. Private insurers are excluded from this market. The government collects premiums from employers and employees on the basis of their ability to pay and then pays physicians and hospitals for basic services to the entire population. Because the government provides all basic insurance coverage, national health insurance systems are often called **single-payer plans**. National health insurance systems are also sometimes called *socialized medicine*. It should be noted, though, that only health insurance is socialized. The government does not employ most physicians, and in many countries the hospitals are largely private as well.[1]

What are the major provisions of the new health policy legislation? The new act requires all Americans who earn wages to have a health insurance policy either through their employer or through one of the new non-profit health exchanges. Taxpayers who do not have health insurance may face a fine if they do not qualify for government help

National Health Insurance
A plan to provide universal health insurance under which the government provides basic health care coverage to all citizens. In most such plans, the program is funded by taxes on wages or salaries.

Single-Payer Plan
A plan under which one entity has a monopoly on issuing a particular type of insurance. Typically, the entity is the government, and the insurance is basic health coverage.

---

[1]Britain is an exception. Under the British "National Health," most (but not all) physicians are employed by the government.

to buy insurance. Employers may purchase private insurance as they do currently or, by 2017, participate in the state-based exchanges as well. However, the types of insurance that employers may offer employees will be regulated to ensure certain coverage and to limit employee contributions. Additionally, eligibility for Medicaid will be expanded, as will insurance options for children of low-income families. Prescription costs for seniors will be discounted gradually until all their costs are covered. The health insurance industry also received new mandates to insure younger Americans, up to age 26, on their parents' policies, to not drop coverage for those who become ill, and to eliminate lifetime limits on coverage. The legislation also includes more than 100 new programs to improve the delivery of health services to patients and to make medical systems more efficient.

The legislation faced strong opposition from a number of different groups: Republicans and economic conservatives charged that the program would cost a great deal of money and raise the federal deficit; some doctors and medical providers opposed the regulations that will imposed on them; many employers and small businesses forecast an increase in their costs, along with more regulation of their benefit plans. Democrats and the president believe that the new taxes on wealthier Americans and savings on Medicare expenses will pay for any new costs, while other groups believe that the new programs will surely add to the federal deficit. Both the plan benefits and the new taxes are scheduled to be phased in over a 10-year period, so it is not possible to know at this time what the costs will actually be.[2]

ENVIRONMENTAL POLICY

Americans have paid increasing attention to environmental issues in the last three decades. A major source of concern for the general public has been the emission of pollutants into the air and water. Each year, the world atmosphere receives 20 million metric tons of sulfur dioxide, 18 million metric tons of ozone pollutants, and 60 million metric tons of carbon monoxide. A majority of climate scientists believe that these pollutants are the cause of global climate change and that global warming will represent a major threat to human survival on the planet. International efforts to limit the output of pollutants, especially carbon dioxide from vehicles and power plants, have been controversial but are widely supported by citizens throughout the world.

ENVIRONMENTALISM

Environmental issues are not limited to concerns about pollution. A second major concern is the protection of the natural environment. The protection of endangered species is an example of this type of issue. The movement to protect the environment has been based on two major strands of thought since its beginnings in the early 1900s. One point of view calls for *conservation*—that is, a policy under which natural resources should be used, but not abused. A second view advocates *preservation*. Under this policy, natural preserves are established that are isolated from the effects of human activity.

The Environmentalist Movement. In the 1960s, an environmentalist movement arose that was much more focused on pollution issues than the previous conservation movement. A series of high-profile events awoke environmental interest. In 1962, Rachel Carson of the U.S. Fish and Wildlife Service published the

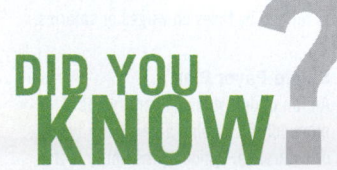

DID YOU KNOW?

That some economists estimate that the Environmental Protection Agency's new ozone standards, when fully implemented, will cost nearly $100 billion per year?

---

[2]There are many good summaries of the new legislation. Among these is one provided by the Georgetown University Health Institute, http://ccf.georgetown.edu; and the Kaiser Family Foundation, http://kff.org.

THE CUYAHOGA RIVER in 1969—firefighters extinguish a fire that started on the river and spread to a wooden trestle bridge. (Photo courtesy of the Environmental Protection Agency)

book *Silent Spring,*[3] in which she detailed the injurious effects of pesticides on a variety of wild species. In 1969, an oil spill off the coast of Santa Barbara, California, drew national attention. That same year, the Cuyahoga River in Cleveland actually caught fire due to flammable chemicals floating on top of the water.

In 1970, the environmental movement organized the first Earth Day (April 22), which proved to be very successful in drawing attention to environmentalism and its concerns. Pollution control was a popular goal, and during the 1960s and 1970s, Congress passed numerous bills aimed at cleaning up the nation's air and water. We will describe some of these efforts in greater detail shortly.

Ecology. In the 1970s, many environmental activists began to advocate policies that were more controversial than pollution control. These policies represented a radical elaboration of the older preservationist philosophy and a rejection of the conservationist principle of wise use. Not only did the new line of thought reject the conservation of natural resources for use by people, but some activists also argued that the human race itself was the problem. Along with the new thinking came a new label—the ecology movement. *Ecology* refers to the total pattern of relationships between organisms and their environment.

CLEANING UP THE AIR AND WATER

The government has been responding to pollution problems since before the American Revolution, when the Massachusetts Bay Colony issued regulations to try to stop the pollution of Boston Harbor. In the 1800s, states passed laws controlling water pollution after scientists and medical researchers convinced most policy makers that dumping sewage into drinking and bathing water caused disease. At the national level, the Federal Water Pollution Control Act of 1948 provided research and assistance to the states for pollution-control efforts, but little was done.

[3]Boston: Houghton Mifflin, 1962; repr., Boston: Mariner Books, 2002.

The National Environmental Policy Act. The year 1969 marked the start of the most concerted national government involvement in solving pollution problems. As mentioned, in that year, the conflict between oil exploration interests and environmental interests literally erupted when an oil well six miles off the coast of Santa Barbara, California, exploded, releasing 235,000 gallons of crude oil. The result was an oil slick that covered an area of 800 square miles and washed up on the city's beaches and killed plant life, birds, and fish. Hearings in Congress revealed that the Interior Department had no guidance in the energy-environment trade-off. Congress soon passed the National Environmental Policy Act of 1969. This landmark legislation established, among other things, the Council on Environmental Quality. It also mandated that an **environmental impact statement (EIS)** be prepared for all major federal actions that could significantly affect the quality of the environment. The act gave citizens and public-interest groups who were concerned with the environment a weapon against the unnecessary and inappropriate use of natural resources by the government.

Curbing Air Pollution. Beginning in 1975, the government began regulating tailpipe emissions from cars and light trucks in an attempt to curb air pollution. In 1990, after years of lobbying by environmentalists, Congress passed the Clean Air Act of 1990. The act established tighter standards for emissions of nitrogen dioxide (NO_2) and other pollutants by newly built cars and light trucks. California was allowed to establish its own, stricter standards. By 1994, the maximum allowable NO_2 emissions (averaged over each manufacturer's "fleet" of vehicles) were about one-fifth of the 1975 standard. The "Tier 2" system, phased in between 2004 and 2007, reduced maximum fleet emissions by cars and light trucks to just over 2 percent of the 1975 standard. In 2008–2009, the standards were extended to trucks weighing between 6,000 and 8,500 pounds.

Stationary sources of air pollution were also subjected to more regulation under the 1990 act. The act required 110 of the oldest coal-burning power plants in the United States to cut their emissions by 40 percent by 2001. Controls were placed on other factories and businesses in an attempt to reduce ground-level ozone pollution in 96 cities to healthful levels by 2005 (except in Los Angeles, which has until 2010 to meet the standards). The act also required that the production of chlorofluorocarbons (CFCs) be stopped completely by 2002. CFCs are thought to deplete the ozone layer in the upper atmosphere and increase the levels of harmful radiation reaching the earth's surface. CFCs were formerly used in air-conditioning and other refrigeration units.

In 1997, in light of evidence that very small particles (2.5 microns, or millionths of a meter, across) of soot might be dangerous to our health, the Environmental Protection Agency (EPA) issued new particulate standards for motor vehicle exhaust systems and other sources of pollution. The EPA also established a more rigorous standard for ground-level ozone, which is formed when sunlight combines with pollutants from cars and other sources. Ozone is a major component of smog.

Water Pollution. One of the most important acts regulating water pollution is the Clean Water Act of 1972, which amended the Federal Water Pollution Control Act of 1948. The Clean Water Act established the following goals: (1) make waters safe for swimming; (2) protect fish and wildlife; and (3) eliminate the discharge of pollutants into the water. The act set specific time schedules, which were subsequently extended by further legislation. Under these schedules, the EPA establishes limits on discharges of types of pollutants based on the technology available for controlling them. The 1972 act also required municipal and industrial polluters to apply for permits before discharging wastes into navigable waters.

The Clean Water Act also prohibits the filling or dredging of wetlands unless a permit is obtained from the Army Corps of Engineers. The EPA defines *wetlands* as

Environmental Impact Statement (EIS)
A report that must show the costs and benefits of major federal actions that could significantly affect the quality of the environment.

"those areas that are inundated or saturated by surface or ground water at a frequency and duration sufficient to support, and that under normal circumstances do support, a prevalence of vegetation typically adapted for life in saturated soil conditions." In recent years, the broad interpretation of what constitutes a wetland that is subject to the regulatory authority of the federal government has generated substantial controversy.

Perhaps one of the most controversial regulations concerning wetlands was the "migratory-bird rule" issued by the Army Corps of Engineers. Under this rule, any bodies of water that could affect interstate commerce, including seasonal ponds or waters "used or suitable for use by migratory birds" that fly over state borders, were "navigable waters" subject to federal regulation under the Clean Water Act as wetlands. In 2001, after years of controversy, the United States Supreme Court struck down the rule. The Court stated that it was not prepared to hold that isolated and seasonal ponds, puddles, and "prairie potholes" become "navigable waters of the United States" simply because they serve as a habitat for migratory birds.[4]

COST-EFFECTIVE SOLUTIONS

Before the mid-1980s, environmental politics seemed to be couched in terms of "them against us." "Them" was everyone involved in businesses that cut down rain forests, poisoned rivers, and created oil spills. "Us" was the government, and it was the government's job to stop "them." Today, particularly in the United States, more people are aware that the battle lines are blurred.

According to the EPA, the United States is spending about $210 billion annually to comply with federal environmental rules. There is a bright side, however. A report issued by the Office of Management and Budget in 2003 concluded that the health and social benefits of enforcing tough new clean-air regulations are five to seven times greater than the costs of compliance. The government has become interested in how to solve the nation's environmental problems at the lowest cost. Moreover, U.S. corporations are becoming increasingly engaged in producing recyclable and biodegradable products, as well as helping to solve some environmental problems.

The Costs of Clean Air. Cost concerns clearly were on the minds of the drafters of the Clean Air Act of 1990 when they tackled the problem of sulfur emissions from electric power plants. Rather than tightening the existing standards, the law simply limited total sulfur emissions. Companies had a choice of either rebuilding old plants or buying rights to pollute. The result was that polluters had an incentive to not even attempt to deal with exceptionally dirty plants. When closing down such plants, they could sell their pollution rights to those who valued them more. The law is straightforward: An electric utility power plant is allowed to emit up to one ton of sulfur dioxide into the air in a given year. If the plant emits one ton of sulfur dioxide, the allowance disappears. If a plant switches to a fuel low in sulfur dioxide, for example, or installs "scrubbing equipment" that reduces sulfur dioxide, it may end up emitting less than one ton. In this circumstance, it can sell or otherwise trade its unused pollution allowance, or it can bank it for later use.

These rights to pollution allowances are being traded in the marketplace. Indeed, a well-established market in "smog futures" is offered on the Chicago Board of Trade and the New York Mercantile Exchange.

There Have Been Improvements. The United States is making fairly substantial strides in the war on toxic emissions. According to the EPA, in the last 30 years U.S. air pollution

---

[4]*Solid Waste Agency of Northern Cook County v. U.S. Army Corps of Engineers,* 531 U.S. 159 (2001).

has been cut in half. Airborne lead is 3 percent of what it was in 1975, and the lead content of the average American's blood is one-fifth of what it was in that year. Airborne sulfur dioxide concentrations are one-fifth of the levels found in the 1960s. Carbon monoxide concentrations are one-quarter of what they were in 1970. Water pollution is also down. Levels of six persistent pollutants in U.S. freshwater fish are about one-fifth of their 1970 levels. One reason for these successes is the increased awareness of the American public of the need for environmental protection. To a large extent, this increased awareness has been brought about through the efforts of various environmental interest groups, which have also exerted pressure on Congress to take action.

THE ENDANGERED SPECIES ACT

Inspired by the plight of disappearing species, Congress passed the Endangered Species Preservation Act in 1966. In 1973, Congress passed a completely new Endangered Species Act (ESA), which made it illegal to kill, harm, or otherwise "take" a species listed as endangered or threatened. The government could purchase habitat critical to the survival of a species or prevent landowners from engaging in development that would harm a listed species.

The ESA proved to be a powerful legal tool for the ecology movement. In a famous example, environmental groups sued to stop the Tennessee Valley Authority from completing the Tellico Dam on the grounds that it threatened habitat critical to the survival of the snail darter, a tiny fish. In 1978, the United States Supreme Court ruled in favor of the endangered fish.[5] Further controversy erupted in 1990, when the Fish and Wildlife Service listed the spotted owl as a threatened species. The logging industry blamed the ESA for a precipitous decline in national forest timber sales in subsequent years.

The ESA continues to be a major subject of debate. There are signs, however, that the government and environmentalists may be seeking common ground. Both sides are shifting toward incentives for landowners who participate in protection programs.

IN 1978, construction on the multimillion dollar Tellico Dam was stopped dead in its tracks when a group of environmentalists argued that it endangered the snail darter fish, shown on the right. Several years later, the snail darter was found to be thriving in other locations, and shortly thereafter, it was removed from the government's endangered species list. How does a society balance environmental issues with economics ones? (Courtesy of the Tennessee Valley Authority and the U.S. Fish and Wildlife Service)

---

[5]*Tennessee Valley Authority v. Hill,* 437 U.S. 153 (1978). In 1979, Congress exempted the snail darter from the ESA. In 1980, snail darters were discovered elsewhere, and the species turned out not to be in danger.

Beyond Our Borders

HOW GREEN IS EUROPE?

The European Community has shown a remarkable ability to agree on energy conservation and environmental goals for all of its members and make considerable progress towards attaining these goals. Following the publication of the European Commission's report on sustainable energy in 2006, the European Parliament began considering the situation and acting upon it in 2007. This confederation of nations agreed to cut greenhouse gases by 20 percent by 2020 and to work for a new treaty to follow the Kyoto accords that would further decrease such emissions by 2020. In addition, the European Community has taken a number of steps to help its citizens to make "green decisions" to conserve energy in the home and on the road.

All appliances of almost every type that are sold in Europe are tagged with an Energy Efficiency Rating. These easy-to-read tags grade the appliance on a scale of A to G on energy efficiency and carbon dioxide impact. The nations agreed that all new buildings and those undergoing substantial remodeling should be more energy efficient and install the most energy-efficient heating and air conditioning systems available. In future years, Europeans will be able to buy cars and trucks that are increasingly efficient and better for the environment as well. The agreement among the nations sets carbon dioxide emissions standards for all new cars and requires manufacturers to further cut emissions by 1 percent per year every year until 2020.

What about the day-to-day habits of European citizens? Countries have differing standards, but all of the European Union members have agreed to try to reduce waste and increase recycling. If you live in Germany, for example, your neighbors have strong expectations that you will reuse, recycle, and sort your garbage. Virtually every German neighborhood or apartment building has five different bins outside, all color-coded to help you dispose of your waste properly. You will use the yellow bin for any kind of food packaging, the blue bin for paper and cardboard, the "bio" bin for leftover food waste, and separate bins for clear, brown, and green glass. There will also be a black bin for those who are too lazy to separate or have something that doesn't fit the system. Switzerland and Denmark also have extremely high rates of recycling waste products from households. In some nations, there are complaints that the government does not provide enough bins for trash or does not pick up the materials properly while in other nations, citizens are fined for not separating their trash.

THESE RECYCLING BINS IN WALES, United Kingdom, are typical of those found in many European countries. Citizens are asked, at the minimum, to sort their waste into paper, plastic, glass, and compostable food items. (© Stephen Dorey ABIPP/Alamy)

Not only do the European nations pride themselves on their "green" habits, but the European Commission makes public everyone's results on the various measures it has adopted. For example, if you go to the Web site Europe's Energy Portal, http://www.energy.eu/, you will find scorecards for gas and oil prices, energy dependency, CO_2 emissions, and renewable energy production for each nation. Imagine a report card on the American states that would give the same kind of measures!

FOR CRITICAL ANALYSIS

1. Why do you think the European nations have been able to agree on such progressive measures in energy efficiency and environmental protections?
2. Do you think government regulations and fines are the best way to gain citizen compliance with energy and environmental goals?

"Regulatory incentives really do result in landowners doing good things for their land," said William Irvin of the World Wildlife Fund.[6] Still, environmental groups accused the Bush administration of underfunding the act and undermining the species-listing process by shifting control from the Fish and Wildlife Service to the secretary of the interior.

GLOBAL WARMING

In the 1990s, scientists working on climate change began to conclude that average world temperatures will rise significantly in the 21st century. Gases released by human activity, principally carbon dioxide, may produce a "greenhouse effect," trapping the sun's heat and slowing its release into outer space. In fact, many studies have shown that global warming has already begun, although the effects of the change are still modest. Christine Todd Whitman, who headed the EPA from 2001 to 2003, called global warming "one of the greatest environmental challenges we face, if not the greatest."

The Kyoto Protocol. In 1997, delegates from around the world gathered in Kyoto, Japan, for a global climate conference sponsored by the United Nations. The conference issued a proposed treaty aimed at reducing emissions of greenhouse gases to 5.2 percent below 1990 levels by 2012. Only 38 developed nations were mandated to reduce their emissions, however—developing nations including China and India faced only voluntary limits. The U.S. Senate voted unanimously in 1997 that it would not accept a treaty that exempted developing countries, and in 2001 President Bush announced that he would not submit the Kyoto protocol to the Senate for ratification. By 2007, 124 nations had ratified the protocol. Its rejection by the United States, however, raised the question of whether it could ever be effective.

Even in those European countries that most enthusiastically supported the Kyoto protocol and signed it, the results have not been overly positive. Thirteen of the 15 original European Union signatories will miss their 2010 emission targets. For

---

[6]"Endangered Species Act Turns 30 as Environmental Strategy Shifts," *The Charleston Post and Courier,* Charleston, SC, January 2, 2004.

BJØRN LOMBORG, the director of the Copenhagen Consensus Center at the Copenhagen Business School, wrote a book called *Cool It: The Skeptical Environmentalist's Guide to Global Warming.* In his book, Lomborg argues that limiting emissions of carbon dioxide and other greenhouse gases is not a cost-effective policy today. He also argues that global warming, while a significant issue, is not as serious as other problems facing the world. (Bloomberg via Getty Images)

example, Spain will miss its target by 33 percentage points. Denmark had agreed to reduce its levels of greenhouse gas emissions by 21 percent, but so far its emissions have *increased* by more than 6 percent since 1990. Greece has seen its greenhouse gas emissions increase by 23 percent since 1990. Closer to home, Prime Minister Paul Martin of Canada lambasted the United States for its lack of a "global conscience." But since 1990, Canada's emissions have risen by 24 percent, much faster than the U.S. rate.

The Global Warming Debate. While the majority of scientists who perform research on the world's climate believe that global warming will be significant, there is considerable disagreement as to how much warming will actually occur. It is generally accepted that world temperatures have already increased by at least 0.6 degree Celsius over the last century. Scenarios by the United Nations Intergovernmental Panel on Climate Change predict increases ranging from 2.0 to 4.5 degrees Celsius by the year 2100. More conservative estimates, such as those by climate experts James Hansen and Patrick Michaels, average around 0.75 degree Celsius.[7]

Global warming has become a major political football to be kicked back and forth by conservatives and liberals. Some conservatives have seized on the work of scientists who believe that global warming does not exist at all. (Some of these researchers work for oil companies.) If this were true, there would be no reason to limit emissions of carbon dioxide and other greenhouse gases. A more sophisticated argument by conservatives is that major steps to limit emissions in the near future would not be cost effective. Bjørn Lomborg, a critic of the environmental movement, believes that it would be more practical to take action against global warming later in the century, when the technology to do so is better and when renewable energy sources have become more competitive in price.[8]

[7]J. E. Hansen, "Can We Defuse the Global Warming Time Bomb?" *Scientific American,* March 2004, pp. 69–77. This article is also online at www.sciam.com/media/pdf/hansen.pdf.
[8]Bjørn Lomborg, *The Skeptical Environmentalist* (Cambridge, England: Cambridge University Press, 2001), pp. 258–324.

THE WATER SEEPING from an abandoned coal mine on Kayford Mountain in West Virginia contains sulphur and other waste products that pollute local streams such as this one. (AFP PHOTO/Mandel NGAN/Newscom)

ENERGY POLICY

The United States has always had enormous energy resources, whether from coal, oil, natural gas, or alternative sources such as wind or solar power. However, the American economy depends almost totally on fossil fuel, namely oil, coal, and natural gas. **Energy policy**—that is, laws that are concerned with how much energy is needed and used—and the regulation of energy producers tend to become important only during a crisis. In 1973, the Organization of Petroleum Exporting Countries (OPEC), the cartel of oil-producing nations, instituted an embargo on shipments of petroleum to the United States because of our support of Israel in the Arab–Israeli conflict of that year. President Nixon declared that the United States would achieve energy independence through reducing speed limits and meeting Corporate Average Fuel Economy (CAFE) standards by a certain time.

In 1977, President Carter also found himself facing shortages of oil and natural gas. The Department of Energy was created, and numerous programs were instituted to assist citizens in buying more energy-efficient appliances and improving the energy profile of their homes. In addition, legislation created the National Petroleum Reserve, and incentives for researching alternative forms of energy were instituted. However, over time, Americans sought to replace their smaller, more efficient cars with sport utility vehicles (SUVs) and light trucks. Airline traffic grew. Suburbs were built farther from cities and jobs. America's dependence on foreign oil has grown, as has the nation's overall appetite for energy.

In 2007, the United States consumed about 20 million barrels of petroleum per day, with half of this used as gasoline for transportation. Of those 20 million barrels per day, more than 65 percent was imported. As shown in Figure 16–4, the United States is the third largest producer of oil but the largest consumer among the major producers. As shown in Figure 16–5, the price of gasoline closely tracks the price per barrel for crude oil. When the price for crude began to rise after 2003, the gasoline price rose quickly as well. The figure also shows the earlier eras of oil shortages in 1981 and 1990. The rapid increase in the price of crude since 2003 appears to be caused by the loss of Iraqi oil

Energy Policy
Laws concerned with how much energy is needed and used.

FIGURE 16–4 Oil Consumption and Production for Top 15 Producers, 2009

The United States is by far the largest consumer of petroleum products and the third largest producer. The only other producer in this list that consumes more than it produces is China.

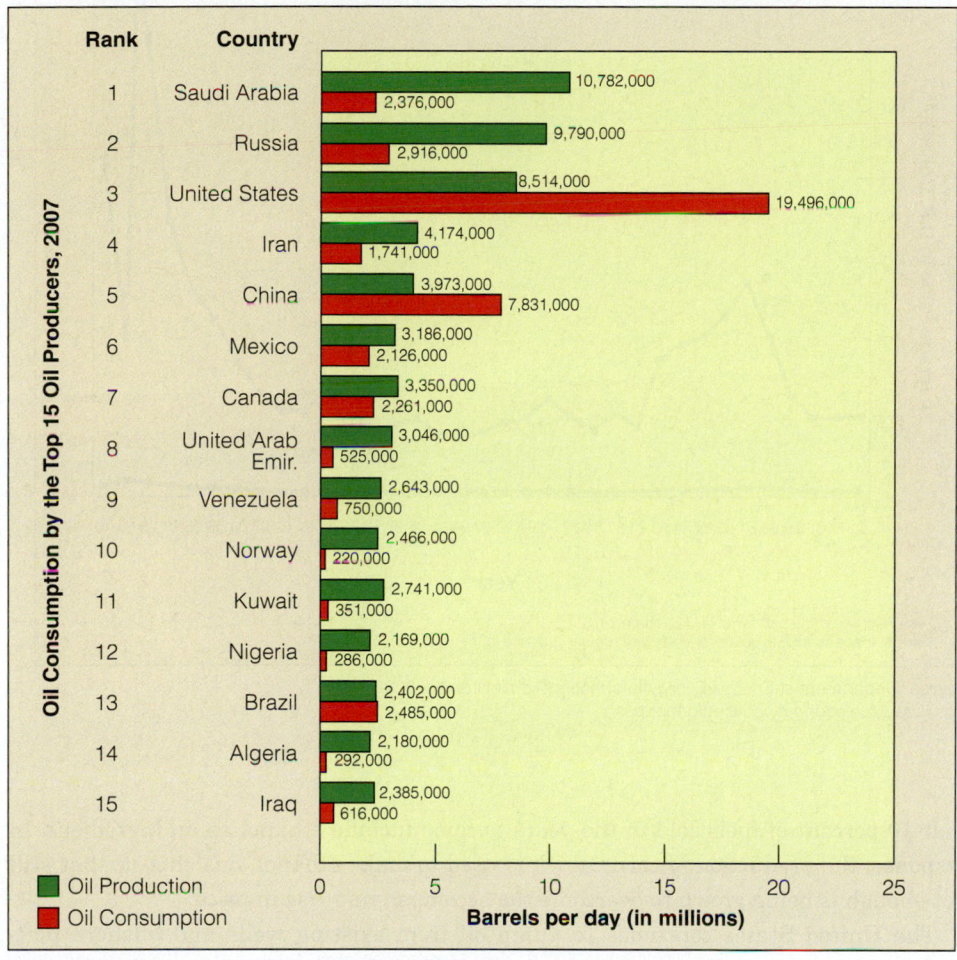

Rank	Country	Oil Production	Oil Consumption
1	Saudi Arabia	10,782,000	2,376,000
2	Russia	9,790,000	2,916,000
3	United States	8,514,000	19,496,000
4	Iran	4,174,000	1,741,000
5	China	3,973,000	7,831,000
6	Mexico	3,186,000	2,126,000
7	Canada	3,350,000	2,261,000
8	United Arab Emir.	3,046,000	525,000
9	Venezuela	2,643,000	750,000
10	Norway	2,466,000	220,000
11	Kuwait	2,741,000	351,000
12	Nigeria	2,169,000	286,000
13	Brazil	2,402,000	2,485,000
14	Algeria	2,180,000	292,000
15	Iraq	2,385,000	616,000

Oil Consumption by the Top 15 Oil Producers, 2007

Barrels per day (in millions)

Source: Department of Energy, Energy Information Administration, 2009.

fields during the war, the growing demand for oil (especially by India and China), and speculation on future prices. There was an enormous spike in the price in the summer of 2008, followed by a drop during that fall's financial crisis. Even with the BP oil spill in the Gulf of Mexico, oil prices stabilized at about $80 per barrel during 2010.

ENERGY AND THE ENVIRONMENT

Because of the effects of producing energy and burning fuels, energy policy is deeply entangled with environmental policy.[9] Using gasoline to power a car is the normal practice. However, burning gasoline produces serious emissions that contribute to the buildup of smog in the atmosphere. As noted previously, through a series of laws passed over the last 20 years, the EPA has forced cities to implement procedures to reduce smog and to require cleaner-burning gasoline. In addition, Congress has mandated

[9]For a comprehensive look at all energy resources in the United States, go to the Web site of the Department of Energy: www.energy.gov/energysources.

FIGURE 16–5 U.S. Crude Oil and Retail Gasoline Prices, 1976–2008

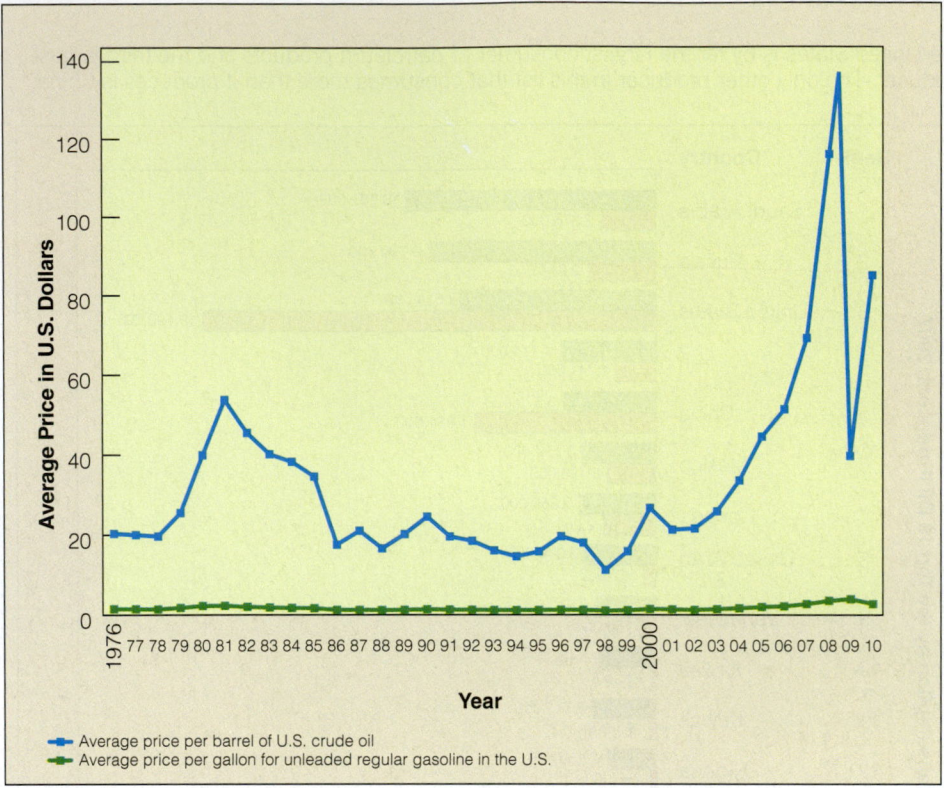

Source: Department of Energy, Energy Information Administration, 2008;
http://www.fueleconomy.gov/feg/gasprices/

that 10 percent of fuels sold in the years to come include ethanol as an ingredient. In response, the production of corn, which is used to make ethanol, has shot up, but still not enough is being grown to overcome the accompanying rise in price.

The United States continues to pump oil from existing wells and offshore platforms. However, more areas exist where oil could be found and extracted, but in most cases, environmental risks would be incurred. Following the oil spill in Santa Barbara, California, from an offshore drilling rig, most Americans welcomed laws that forbade drilling in new areas off Florida, Louisiana, Texas, and California. In addition, large areas of the Arctic National Wilderness Reserve (ANWR) have also been protected from oil exploration. Drilling in the ANWR is an extremely controversial issue because of the pristine nature of the land and the potential danger to native wildlife in that area of Alaska. In 2010, the clash between environmental protection and the need for energy sources came to a head in the Gulf of Mexico at a drilling rig named the Deepwater Horizon. The rig, leased by British Petroleum, was drilling for oil more than a mile deep in the ocean when a "blowout" of oil and gas occurred. The blowout preventer—a multimillion-dollar, five-story apparatus on the sea floor—failed, and the rig exploded. In the weeks and months that followed, millions of gallons of oil and gas spewed from the well as attempts to cap it met limited success. President Obama made a number of trips to the Gulf coast to see the cleanup attempts for himself. He convinced BP to set aside $20 billion in a fund to compensate Gulf residents for losses in wages and business revenues. Gulf state governors and mayors expressed great anger at the inefficiency of the federal response and the perceived neglect of their states' polluted beaches and economic losses. The president was criticized for not seeming to be more "involved" in the crisis, although the Coast Guard commander on the site noted that the guard and BP were doing all they could in the situation.

Another dilemma facing the United States involves domestic power production and the need for cleaner air. The majority of electric power generated in the United States comes from coal-fired plants in the Midwest and central regions of the nation. For many years, these plants spewed carbon emissions into the air. As scientists became aware of the impact of these emissions on the environment, new laws required the plants to reduce their emissions by installing scrubbers or, after reaching the legal "cap" on their carbon emissions, buying or trading for the right to produce more. The EPA, under the Bush administration, issued regulations for coal-burning plants that reduced their burden of meeting the standards. States that felt they received the most damage from some of these emissions sued to make the EPA issue standards that meet the letter of the Clean Air Act. The Supreme Court agreed with these states, and the EPA began to prepare stricter standards. After President Obama was elected, the EPA moved ahead with great energy to enforce stricter standards both for power plants and for the emissions of cars and trucks, including a mandate for average fuel efficiency of 35 miles per gallon for cars and light trucks by 2019.

NUCLEAR POWER PLANTS such as this one on the Rhone River in France operate throughout Europe producing clean electricity. (Walter Bibikow/DanitaDelimont.com/Newscom)

NUCLEAR POWER—AN UNPOPULAR SOLUTION

One strategy for reducing carbon emissions of coal-fired plants and also the environmental and human risks of coal mining is to increase the number of nuclear power plants in the United States. Nuclear power plants are very efficient and emit very low levels of greenhouse gases.[10] However, the accident at the Three Mile Island plant in Pennsylvania in 1979 and the disaster at Chernobyl in the Soviet Union in 1986 have almost destroyed any support for nuclear power in the United States. Not only do people fear the possibility of an accident at such a plant, but nuclear plants also provide a superb target for terrorist attacks.

Finally, nuclear plants produce spent fuel, which must be stored until it is safe. No state wants to be the repository for nuclear waste, and few citizens want the waste trucked through their neighborhoods. The United States, though, is alone among industrialized nations in its fear of nuclear power. While Europe depends on oil, gas, coal, and nuclear power for electricity, hundreds of nuclear plants in

---

[10]Larry Parker and Mark Holt, "Nuclear Power: Outlook for New U.S. Reactors" (Washington, DC: Congressional Research Service, March 9, 2007).

MANY ENVIRONMENTALISTS and commentators suggest that a much greater use of wind power could reduce the nation's dependence on fossil fuels. This California windmill farm produces energy for Palm Springs. However, windmill farms cannot be successful everywhere in the United States. (Jim Corwin)

Europe and the former states of the Soviet Union have operated safely for decades, and hundreds more are planned throughout the world. As the United States has become more concerned about carbon emissions, attention has begun to turn to nuclear power again, and permits have been issued to plan a few new plants.

ALTERNATIVE APPROACHES TO AN ENERGY CRISIS

Several alternative sources of energy can be used to reduce the nation's dependence on fossil fuels. Huge wind farms in California generate energy for cities there. Research continues on harnessing the power of the ocean waves to produce electricity and the most efficient ways to use geothermal energy from below the surface of the earth.[11] However, the technology does not yet exist to use any of these sources to produce the quantity of energy needed to replace our coal plants or other current energy sources. And, in some areas, citizens consider wind farms as extremely disturbing to the environment and area wildlife.

The rising price of gasoline in 2008 spurred a much greater demand for hybrid automobiles and for smaller, more fuel-efficient cars. In addition, people began to ride motor scooters for city commutes and increased their use of mass transit. Homes closer to the city center became somewhat more attractive, although it will be many years before the trend of living in the suburbs will be reversed. Both political parties seemed supportive of new legislation encouraging energy efficiency in home building, using energy-efficient light bulbs, and giving incentives to buy hybrid vehicles. The Obama administration has sought comprehensive energy legislation from the Congress since the president's inauguration. Members of the administration and of Congress realize that both energy needs and environmental concerns must be addressed in the same legislation. Proponents of a "cap and trade" system want industries to account for their carbon emissions through a market system as is in place in Europe and described in the *Beyond Our Borders* in this chapter. The opponents of such a system believe that it will drive up energy costs for everyone because costs will be passed down to the ultimate consumer. Energy legislation remained stalled in the Congress in 2010.

POVERTY AND WELFARE

Throughout the world, poverty has historically been accepted as inevitable. The United States and other industrialized nations, however, have sustained enough economic growth in the past several hundred years to eliminate mass poverty. In fact, considering

---

[11]For a discussion of these new technologies, see Jay Inslee and Bracken Henricks, *Apollo's Fire* (Washington, D.C.: Island Press, 2007).

the wealth and high standard of living in the United States, the persistence of poverty here appears bizarre and anomalous. How can so much poverty exist in a nation of so much abundance? And what can be done about it?

A traditional solution has been **income transfers**. These are methods of transferring income from relatively well-to-do to relatively poor groups in society, and as a nation, we have been using such transfers for a long time. Before we examine these efforts, let us look at the concept of poverty in more detail and at the characteristics of the poor.

Income Transfer
A transfer of income from some individuals in the economy to other individuals. This is generally done by government action.

THE LOW-INCOME POPULATION

We can see in Figure 16–6 that the number of people classified as poor fell steadily from 1961 to 1968—that is, during the presidencies of John Kennedy and Lyndon Johnson. The number remained level until the recession of 1981–1982, during Ronald Reagan's presidency, when it increased substantially. The number fell during the Internet boom of 1994–2000, but then it started to rise again. Over the last 50 years, the number of Americans who are classified as poor has ranged from a high of 40 million in 1959 to a low of 25 million. The percentage has remained fairly low. In 2010, about 39.8 million Americans, or about 13.2 percent, were classified as poor. The economic downturn and increase in unemployment sent the rate to the highest it has been since 1997.

The threshold income level that is used to determine who falls into the poverty category was originally based on the cost of a nutritionally adequate food plan designed by the U.S. Department of Agriculture in 1963. The threshold was determined by multiplying the food-plan cost times three, on the assumption that food expenses constitute approximately one-third of a poor family's expenditures. Until 1969, annual revisions of the threshold level were based only on changes in food prices. After 1969, the adjustments were made on the basis of changes in the consumer price index (CPI). The CPI is based on the average prices of a specified set of goods and services bought by wage earners in urban areas.

FIGURE 16–6 The Official Number of Poor in the United States

The number of individuals classified as poor fell steadily from 1961 through 1968. It then increased during the 1981–1982 recession. After 1994, the number fell steadily until 2000, when it started to rise again. The recession that began in 2008 spurred an increase to a fifty-year high in the number of poor Americans.

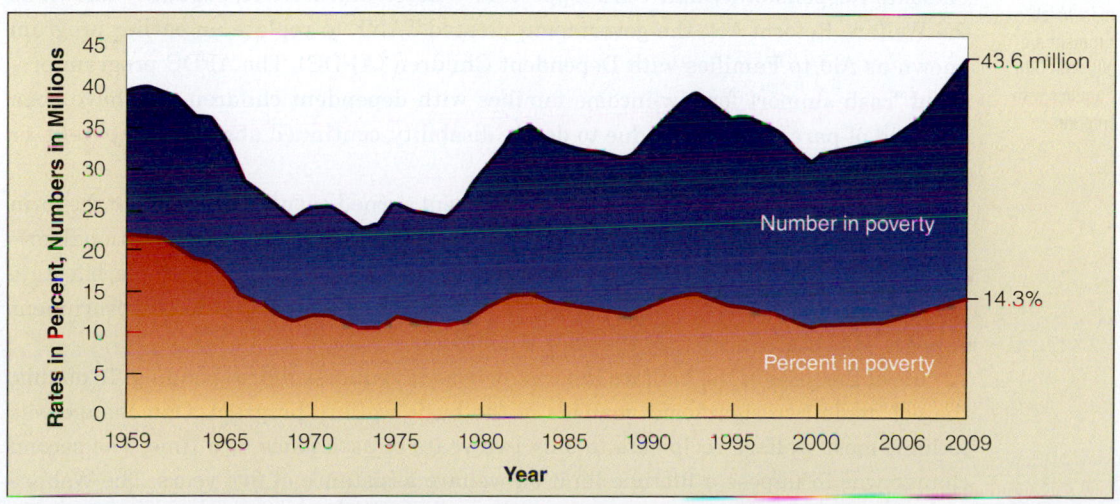

Note: The data points represent the midpoints of the respective years.
Source: U.S. Census Bureau, Current Population Reports, *Income, Poverty, and Health Insurance Coverage in the United States: 2007*, Washington, D.C.: Government Printing Office (2007).

The low-income poverty threshold thus represents the income needed to maintain a specified standard of living as of 1963, with the purchasing-power value increased year by year to reflect the general increase in prices. For 2009, for example, the official poverty level for a family of four was about $22,000.

The official poverty level is based on pretax income, including cash but not **in-kind subsidies**—food stamps, housing vouchers, and the like. If we correct poverty levels for such benefits, the percentage of the population that is below the poverty line drops dramatically. To put the official U.S. poverty level in perspective, consider that this income level for the United States is twice as high as the world's average per capita income level. According to the World Bank, only 26 countries have per capita incomes higher than the poverty income threshold defined by the U.S. government.

In-Kind Subsidy
A good or service—such as food stamps, housing, or medical care—provided by the government to low-income groups.

THE ANTIPOVERTY BUDGET

It is not always easy to determine how much the government spends to combat poverty. In part, this is because it can be difficult to decide whether a particular program is an antipoverty program. Are grants to foster parents an antipoverty measure? What about job-training programs? Are college scholarships for low-income students an antipoverty measure?

President Obama's 2010 budget allocated about $700 billion, or about one-fourth of all federal expenditures, to federal programs that support persons of limited income (scholarships included).[12] Of this amount, $275 billion was for Medicaid, which funds medical services for the poor, as discussed earlier. The states were expected to contribute an additional $150 billion to Medicaid. Medical care is by far the largest portion of the antipoverty budget. One reason why medical spending is high is the widespread belief that everyone should receive medical care that at least approximates the care received by an average person. No such belief supports spending for other purposes, such as shelter or transportation. Elderly people receive 60 percent of Medicaid spending.

BASIC WELFARE

The program that most people think of when they hear the word *welfare* is now called **Temporary Assistance to Needy Families (TANF)**. With the passage in 1996 of the Personal Responsibility and Work Opportunity Reconciliation Act, popularly known as the Welfare Reform Act, the government created TANF to replace an earlier program known as Aid to Families with Dependent Children (AFDC). The AFDC program provided "cash support for low-income families with dependent children who have been deprived of parental support due to death, disability, continued absence of a parent, or unemployment."

Temporary Assistance to Needy Families (TANF)
A state-administered program in which grants from the national government are used to provide welfare benefits. The TANF program replaced the Aid to Families with Dependent Children (AFDC) program.

Under the TANF program, the U.S. government turned over to the states, in the form of block grants, funds targeted for welfare assistance. The states, not the national government, now bear the burden of any increased welfare spending. For example, if a state wishes to increase the amount of TANF payments over what the national government supports, the state has to pay the additional costs.

One of the aims of the Welfare Reform Act was to reduce welfare spending. To do this, the act made two significant changes in the basic welfare program. One change was to limit most welfare recipients to only two years of assistance at a time. The second change was to impose a lifetime limit on welfare assistance of five years. The Welfare

---

[12]This sum does not include the earned-income tax credit, which is not part of the federal budget.

Reform Act has largely met its objectives. During the first five years after the act was passed, the number of families receiving welfare payments was cut in half. The 2010 federal budget allocated $22 billion to the TANF block grants.

WELFARE CONTROVERSIES

Whether known as AFDC or TANF, the basic welfare program has always been controversial. Conservative and libertarian voters often object to welfare spending as a matter of principle, believing that it reduces the incentive to find paid employment. Because AFDC and TANF have largely supported single-parent households, some also believe that such programs are anti-marriage. Finally, certain people object to welfare spending out of a belief that welfare recipients are "not like us." In fact, non-Hispanic whites made up only 30 percent of TANF recipients in the mid-2000s. As a result of all these factors, basic welfare payments in the United States are relatively low when compared with similar payments in other industrialized nations. In 2010, the average monthly TANF payment nationwide was about $700, with a national maximum of $1,500 for a family of four.

OTHER FORMS OF GOVERNMENT ASSISTANCE

The **Supplemental Security Income (SSI)** program was established in 1974 to provide a nationwide minimum income for elderly persons and persons with disabilities who do not qualify for Social Security benefits. The 2010 budget allocated $44 billion to this program.

The government also issues **food stamps**, benefits that can be used to purchase food; they are usually provided electronically through a card similar to a debit card. Food stamps are available to low-income individuals and families. Recipients must prove that they qualify by showing that they have a low income (or no income at all). Food stamps go to a much larger group of people than do TANF payments. President Obama's 2010 budget allocated $72 billion to the food stamp program. The food stamp program has become a major part of the welfare system in the United States, although it was started in 1964 mainly to benefit farmers by distributing surplus food through retail channels.

The **earned-income tax credit (EITC) program** was created in 1975 to help low-income workers by giving back part or all of their Social Security taxes. Currently, about 15 percent of all taxpayers claim an EITC, and an estimated $49 billion per year is rebated to taxpayers through the program.

HOMELESSNESS—STILL A PROBLEM

The plight of the homeless remains a problem. Some observers argue that the Welfare Reform Act of 1996 has increased the number of homeless persons. No hard statistics on the homeless are available, but estimates of the number of people without a home on any given night in the United States range from a low of 230,000 to as many as 750,000 people.

It is difficult to estimate how many people are homeless because the number depends on how the homeless are defined. There are *street people*—those who sleep in bus stations, parks, and other areas. Many of these people are youthful runaways. There are also the so-called *sheltered homeless*—those who sleep in government-supported or privately funded shelters. Many of these individuals used to live with their families or

DID YOU KNOW?

That the Greenville County Department of Social Services in South Carolina wrote to a food stamp recipient, "Your food stamps will be stopped ... because we received notice that you passed away. May God bless you. You may reapply if there is a change in your circumstances."?

Supplemental Security Income (SSI)
A federal program established to provide assistance to elderly persons and persons with disabilities.

Food Stamps
Benefits issued by the federal government to low-income individuals to be used for the purchase of food; originally provided as coupons, but now typically provided electronically through a card similar to a debit card.

Earned-Income Tax Credit (EITC) Program
A government program that helps low-income workers by giving back part or all of their Social Security taxes.

friends. Whereas street people are almost always single, the sheltered homeless include many families with children. Homeless families are the fastest-growing subgroup of the homeless population. The homeless problem pits liberals against conservatives. Conservatives argue that there are not really that many homeless people and that most of them are alcoholics, drug users, or the mentally ill. Conservatives contend that these individuals should be dealt with by either the mental health system or the criminal justice system. In contrast, many liberals argue that homelessness is caused by a reduction in welfare benefits and by excessively priced housing.

Some cities have "criminalized" homelessness. Many municipalities have outlawed sleeping on park benches and sidewalks, as well as panhandling and leaving personal property on public property. In some cities, police sweeps remove the homeless, who then become part of the criminal justice system. In general, northern cities have assumed a responsibility to shelter the homeless in bad weather. Cities in warmer climates are most concerned with a year-round homeless problem. No new national policies on the homeless have been initiated, in part because of disagreement about the causes of and solutions for the problem.

Since 1993, the U.S. Department of Housing and Urban Development has spent billions of dollars on programs designed to combat homelessness. Yet because of the intense disagreement about the number of homeless persons, the reasons for homelessness, and the possible cures for the problem, no consistent government policy has resulted. Whatever policies have been adopted usually have been attacked by one group or another.

IMMIGRATION

Time and again, this nation has been challenged and changed—and culturally enriched—by immigrant groups. All of these immigrants have faced the problems involved in living in a new and different political and cultural environment. Most of them have had to overcome language barriers, and many have had to deal with discrimination in one form or another because of their skin color, their inability to speak English fluently, or their customs. The civil rights legislation passed during and since the 1960s has done much to counter the effects of prejudice against immigrant groups by ensuring that they obtain equal rights under the law.

One of the questions facing Americans and their political leaders today is the effect of immigration on American politics and government. Other issues are whether immigration is having a positive or negative impact on the United States and the form immigration reform should take.

THE CONTINUED INFLUX OF IMMIGRANTS

Today, immigration rates are among the highest they have been since their peak in the early 20th century. Every year, more than one million people immigrate to this country, and people who were born on foreign soil now constitute more than 10 percent of the U.S. population—twice the percentage of 30 years ago.

Minority Groups' Importance on the Rise. Since 1977, four out of five immigrants have come from Latin America or Asia. Hispanics have overtaken African Americans as the nation's largest minority. If current immigration rates continue, by the year 2060, minority groups collectively will constitute the "majority" of Americans. If Hispanics, African Americans, and perhaps Asians were to form coalitions, they could increase their political power dramatically and would have the numerical strength to make significant changes. According to Ben Wattenberg of the American Enterprise Institute, in the future the "old guard" white majority will no longer dominate American politics.

The Advantages of High Rates of Immigration. Some regard the high rate of immigration as a plus for America, because it offsets the low birthrate and aging population. Immigrants expand the workforce and help support, through their taxes, government programs that benefit older Americans, such as Medicare and Social Security. If it were not for immigration, contend these observers, the United States would be facing even more serious problems than it already does with funding these programs (see Chapter 17). In contrast, nations that do not have high immigration rates, such as Japan, are experiencing serious fiscal challenges due to their aging populations.

ATTEMPTS AT IMMIGRATION REFORM

A significant number of U.S. citizens, however, believe that immigration—both legal and illegal—negatively affects America. They argue, among other things, that the large number of immigrants seeking work results in lower wages for Americans, especially those with few skills. They also worry about the cost of providing immigrants with services such as schools and medical care.

Not surprisingly, before the 2006 elections, members of Congress were in favor of enacting a sweeping immigration reform bill, but the two houses could not agree on what it should do. Some versions of the bill in the House would have made every illegal immigrant in the United States a felon. The Senate, in contrast, came up with a much softer immigration reform system, one that was similar to a proposal made by President Bush. The Senate bill in its various forms in 2006 would have allowed illegal immigrants to gradually become citizens. None of these immigration reform bills came to fruition. Later in the year, however, Congress did pass legislation authorizing the construction of a 700-mile-long fence between the United States and Mexico. The fence is to be a real fence in some areas and a "virtual fence" using cameras and surveillance technologies in other areas. In 2007, some members of Congress indicated that Congress, then under Democratic leadership, might review that legislation when working on a comprehensive immigration reform bill.

Conservative radio talk show hosts took up the cause of defeating the Senate's comprehensive immigration bill because it was seen to offer "amnesty" for illegal immigrants. Members of Congress were content to let the bill die rather than face unhappy constituents in an election year. By 2008, the debate seemed to have changed, with virtually all of the candidates for president, except the most

ARIZONA GOVERNOR JAN BREWER talks to the media about her approval of the Arizona immigration enforcement law. (Art Foxall/ART FOXALL/Newscom)

LOOKING WEST OVER THE HILLS, the continuing U.S./Mexico border fence construction can be seen near Palominas, Arizona, in 2007. Congress has approved construction of the fence, although environmentalists claim it will have a serious impact on wildlife while doing little to contain illegal immigration. (AP Photo/John Miller)

conservative, supporting legislation that would tighten the borders, force employers to check the papers of their workers, and eventually build a path to citizenship. In the meantime, many illegal workers were "swept up" by law enforcement and deported, while others quietly left the country to avoid arrest. Some states and cities enacted laws making it illegal for undocumented residents to access public services or to get drivers' licenses.

In 2010, Arizona passed a law requiring state and local police and law enforcement officers to check individuals' citizenship or residency papers if they had been stopped on suspicion of an offense. The law, which requires local officials to enforce federal law, sparked a national debate. President Obama ordered the Justice Department to investigate whether the Arizona law was constitutional, and demonstrations against the law took place in many cities. Public opinion, however, strongly supported the Arizona law, while the governor claimed that the law was necessary to limit crime and violence related to illegal border crossings. In July 2010, Federal District Court Judge Susan Bolton issued a preliminary injunction blocking the most controversial parts of the law while allowing others to take effect, including one that bans cities from refusing to cooperate with federal immigration officials. The injunction was in response to a legal challenge brought against the law by the Obama administration.

CRIME IN THE 21ST CENTURY

In 2006, overall crime rates in the United States dropped below those in many other countries, such as Britain. Nonetheless, virtually all polls taken in the United States in the last 10 years have shown that crime remains one of the public's major concerns. A related issue that has been on the domestic policy agenda for decades is controlling the use and sale of illegal drugs—activities that are often associated with crimes of violence. Additionally, finding ways to deal with terrorism has become a priority for the nation's policy makers.

CRIME IN AMERICAN HISTORY

In every period in the history of this nation, people have voiced apprehension about crime. Some criminologists argue that crime was probably as frequent around the time of the American Revolution as it is today. During the Civil War, mob violence and riots erupted in several cities. After the Civil War, people in San Francisco were told that "no decent man is in safety to walk the streets after dark; while at all hours, both night and day, his property is jeopardized by incendiarism [arson] and burglary."[13] From 1860 to 1890, the crime rate rose twice as fast as the population.[14] In 1910, one author stated that "crime, especially in its more violent forms and among the young, is increasing steadily and is threatening to bankrupt the Nation."[15]

From 1900 to the 1930s, social violence and crime increased dramatically. Labor union battles and race riots were common. Only during the three-decade period from the mid-1930s to the early 1960s did the United States experience, for the first time in its history, stable or slightly declining overall crime rates.

What most Americans are worried about is violent crime. From the mid-1980s to 1994, its rate rose relentlessly. The murder rate per 100,000 people in 1964 was 4.9, whereas in 1994 it was estimated at 9.3, an increase of almost 100 percent. Between 1995 and 2004, violent crime rates declined. Some argue that this decline was a result of the growing economy the United States has generally enjoyed since about 1993. Others claim that the $3 billion of additional funds the federal government has spent to curb crime in the last few years has led to less crime. Still others claim that an increase in the number of persons who are jailed or imprisoned is responsible for the reduction in crime. Some have even argued that legalized abortion has reduced the population that is likely to commit crimes. You can see changes in the rate of violent crimes in Figure 16–7.

Many people have heard that the United States has the highest crime rates in the world. This is not actually true. Total crime rates are higher in some other countries, including Britain, Denmark, and Sweden, than in the United States. You are much more likely to be robbed in London than in New York City. What the United States has is not a high total crime rate, but a *murder* rate that is unusually high for an advanced industrialized nation. Explanations for this fact vary from easy access to firearms to a cultural predisposition for settling disputes with violence. It is worth noting, however, that many countries in Asia, Africa, and Latin America have much higher homicide rates than the United States.

DID YOU KNOW?

That a University of Southern California evaluation of a gang prevention program discovered that when the program lost funding, the gang broke up and the gang's crime rate declined?

CRIMES COMMITTED BY JUVENILES

A disturbing aspect of crime is the number of serious crimes committed by juveniles, although the number of such crimes is also dropping. The political response to this rise in serious juvenile crimes has been varied. Some cities have established juvenile curfews. Several states have begun to try more juveniles as adults, particularly juveniles who have been charged with homicides. Still other states are operating "boot camps" to try to "shape up" less violent juvenile criminals. Additionally, victims of juvenile crime and victims' relatives are attempting to pry open the traditionally secret juvenile court system.[16]

---

[13]President's Commission on Law Enforcement and Administration of Justice, *Challenge of Crime in a Free Society* (Washington, DC: Government Printing Office, 1967), p. 19.

[14]Richard Shenkman, *Legends, Lies, and Cherished Myths of American History* (New York: HarperCollins, 1988), p. 158.

[15]President's Commission, *Challenge of Crime*, p. 19.

[16]See Chapter 5 for details on the rights of juveniles in our legal system.

FIGURE 16–7 Violent Crime Rates

Violent crime rates have declined since 1994, reaching the lowest level ever recorded in 2002. The crimes included in this chart are rape, robbery, aggravated and simple assault, and homicide.

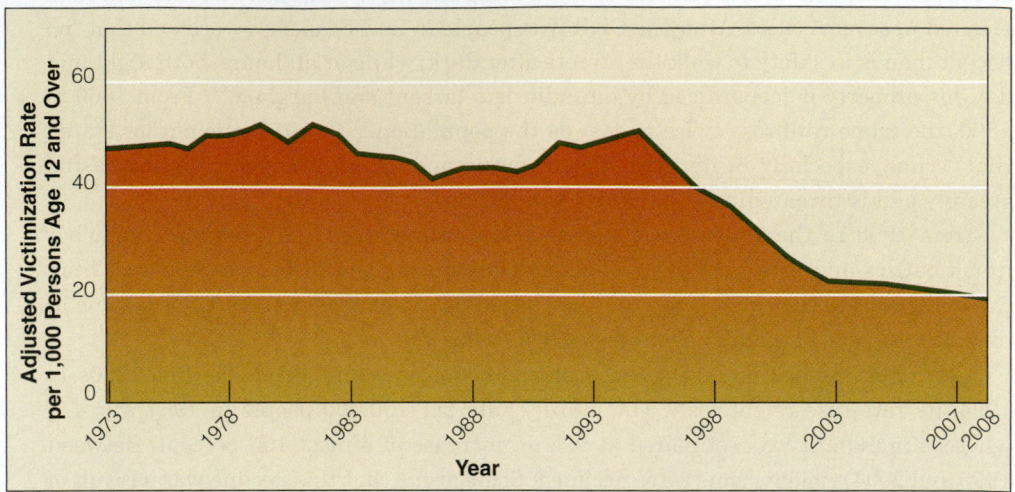

Sources: U.S. Department of Justice; rape, robbery, and assault data are from the *National Crime Victimization Survey*; the homicide data are from the Federal Bureau of Investigation's *Uniform Crime Reports*.

Some worry that the decline in serious juvenile crimes is only temporary. The number of youths between the ages of 15 and 17 will rise from about 9 million today to almost 13 million in the year 2010. As a result, the grave concern about preventing an even worse juvenile crime problem in the years to come is understandable.

SCHOOL SHOOTINGS

School shootings are a form of violent crime that, for most people, is particularly shocking and difficult to understand. Perhaps the most widely publicized of all school shootings in the United States occurred in 1999 in Littleton, Colorado. In what has become known as the Columbine High School massacre, two teenaged students went on a shooting rampage, killing 12 students and a teacher, and wounding 24 others, before committing suicide.

School shootings occur not only in secondary schools but also in elementary schools and on college campuses. Even a one-room school in Lancaster County, Pennsylvania, was not immune from such violence: In October 2006, a milk-truck driver held 10 Amish girls hostage before shooting five of them and then himself at the small schoolhouse. The deadliest school shooting to date, however, occurred on a college campus. On April 16, 2007, the nation was stunned to learn that a South Korean student at Virginia Polytechnic Institute and State University (Virginia Tech) in Blacksburg, Virginia, had killed 32 students and wounded some 29 others before killing himself.

The perception of school shootings as a growing form of violence is reinforced, to some extent, by the extraordinary media attention that such killings receive. Even while homicide rates in the schools were declining from 1993 to 2002, media attention increased in 2007 due to the many victims at the Virginia Tech campus. Overall, it remains true that students continue to face less risk of being victims of serious violent crimes while at school than while out of school. According to the National School Safety

STUDENTS, FAMILY AND SUPPORTERS attend a silent vigil in honor of the 32 victims of the shooting on the campus of Virginia Tech in Blacksburg, Virginia, on April 23, 2007. Many campuses have installed new warning systems for such incidents. Do you think such measures will make campuses and schools safer? (KEVIN DIETSCH/UPI/Landov)

Center, the annual probability of a school experiencing a student-perpetuated homicide is about 1 in 11,520.[17]

THE COST OF CRIME TO AMERICAN SOCIETY

For the perpetrator, crime may pay in certain circumstances—a successful robbery or embezzlement, for example—but crime certainly costs the American public. One study suggests that when everything is added up, including the expenses of the legal system, the costs of private deterrence, losses by victims, and the value of time wasted by criminals and victims, the annual burden of crime in the United States exceeds a trillion dollars each year.[18]

The Office for Victims of Crime, a unit of the U.S. Department of Justice, has estimated that the direct tangible costs to crime victims, including the costs of medical expenses, lost earnings, and victim assistance, are $105 billion annually. Pain, suffering, and reduced quality of life increase the cost to $450 billion annually. Check fraud costs an estimated $10 billion each year. Fraud involving stocks, bonds, and commodities costs about $40 billion per year. Telemarketing fraud costs another $40 billion (though the recently established "do not call" list may have curbed this expense somewhat). Insurance fraud costs about $80 billion per year.[19]

THE PRISON POPULATION BOMB

Many Americans believe that the best solution to the nation's crime problem is to impose stiff prison sentences on offenders. Such sentences, in fact, have become national policy.

[17]National School Safety Center, *Indicators of School Crime and Safety, 2006* (Washington, DC: Bureau of Justice Statistics, 2006).
[18]David A. Anderson, "The Aggregate Burden of Crime," *Journal of Law and Economics*, Vol. 42, No. 2, October 1999.
[19]These estimates are online at www.ojp.usdoj.gov/ovc/ncvrw/2006/welcome.html.

By 2008, U.S. prisons and jails held 2.3 million people. About two-thirds of the incarcerated population was in state or federal prisons, with the remainder held in local jails. About 60 percent of the persons held in local jails were awaiting court action. The other 40 percent were serving sentences.

The number of incarcerated persons has grown rapidly in recent years. In 1990, for example, the total number of persons held in U.S. jails or prisons was still only 1.1 million. From 1995 to 2002, the incarcerated population grew at an average of 3.8 percent annually. The rate of growth has slowed since 2002, however. You might ask why the prison population has grown so much when the crime rate was declining in the last decade. As noted previously, many states and localities have increased the list of crimes for which a criminal may receive a mandatory sentence. In addition, many individuals who are in prison were convicted of drug offenses. Many states operate under a "three strikes" law, which means that on the third drug conviction, even if it involves possession of a small amount of drugs, the individual is automatically sentenced to prison for a specified length of time.

The Incarceration Rate. Some groups of people are much more likely to find themselves behind bars than others. Men are more than 10 times more likely to be incarcerated than women. Prisoners are also disproportionately African American. To measure how frequently members of particular groups are imprisoned, the standard statistic is the **incarceration rate**. This rate is the number of people incarcerated for every 100,000 persons in a particular population group. To put it another way, an incarceration rate of 1,000 means that 1 percent of a particular group is in custody. Using this statistic, we can say that U.S. men have an incarceration rate of 1,403, compared to a rate of 135 for U.S. women. Table 16-1 shows selected incarceration rates by gender, race, and age. Note the very high incarceration rate for African Americans between the ages of 25 and 29—at any given time, more than 10 percent of this group is in jail or prison.

International Comparisons. The United States has more people in jail or prison than any other country in the world. That fact is not necessarily surprising, because the United States also has one of the world's largest total populations. More to the point, the United

Incarceration Rate
The number of persons held in jail or prison for every 100,000 persons in a particular population group.

TABLE 16–1 Incarceration Rates per 100,000 Persons for Selected U.S. Population Groups

	MEN	WOMEN
Non-Hispanic white, total	727	93
Non-Hispanic white, aged 25–29	1,550	225
Non-Hispanic black, total	4,777	349
Non-Hispanic black, aged 25–29	10,408	691
Hispanic, total	1,760	147
Hispanic, aged 25–29	3,792	326
All groups	1,403	145

Source: U.S. Department of Justice, "Prison and Jail Inmates at Midyear 2008," *Bureau of Justice Statistics Bulletin*, 2009.

States has the highest reported incarceration rate of any country on earth.[20] Figure 16–8 compares U.S. incarceration rates, measured by the number of prisoners per 100,000 residents, with incarceration rates in other major countries.

Prison Construction. To house a growing number of inmates, prison construction and management have become sizable industries in the United States. Ten years ago, prison overcrowding was a major issue. In 1994, for example, state prisons had a rated capacity of about 500,000 inmates but actually held 900,000 people. The prisons were therefore operating at 80 percent above capacity. Today, after a major prison construction program, state prisons are operating between 1 and 16 percent above capacity, although the federal prison system is still 31 percent above capacity. Since 1980, Texas has built 120 new prisons, Florida has built 84, and California has built 83. In 1923, there were only 61 prisons in the entire United States.

Effects of Incarceration. When imprisonment keeps truly violent felons behind bars longer, it prevents them from committing additional crimes. The average predatory street criminal commits 15 or more crimes each year when not behind bars. But most prisoners are in for a relatively short time and are released on parole early, often because of prison overcrowding. Then many ex-convicts find themselves back in prison because they have violated parole, typically by using illegal drugs. Of the more than 1.5 million people who are arrested each year, the majority are arrested for drug offenses. Given that from 20 million to 40 million Americans violate one or more drug laws each year, the potential supply of prisoners seems virtually limitless. Consequently, it may not matter how many prisons are built; overcrowding will remain as along as we maintain the same legislation on illegal drugs.

FEDERAL DRUG POLICY

Illegal drugs are a major cause of crime in America. A rising percentage of arrests are for illegal drug trafficking. The latest major illegal drug has contributed to an increase in the number of drug arrests. That drug is methamphetamine, sometimes known as meth or speed. Methamphetamine is often made in small home laboratories using toxic household chemicals. Raids on meth labs around the country have become common news stories. The violence that often accompanies the illegal drug trade occurs for several reasons. One is that drug dealers engage in "turf wars" over the territories in which drugs can be sold. Another is that when drug deals go bad, drug

FIGURE 16–8 Incarceration Rates Around the World, 2008

Incarceration rates of major nations measured by the number of prisoners per 100,000 residents. Some authorities believe that the estimate for China is too low.

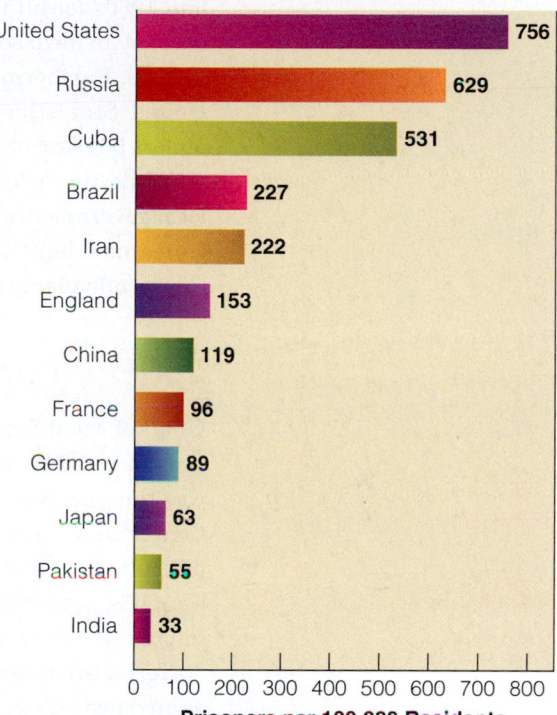

Country	Prisoners per 100,000 Residents
United States	756
Russia	629
Cuba	531
Brazil	227
Iran	222
England	153
China	119
France	96
Germany	89
Japan	63
Pakistan	55
India	33

Source: Kings College, London, International Centre for Prison Studies, 2008.

That the odds are 1 in 20 that an American born today will wind up in jail or prison at some point during his or her lifetime?

---

[20]North Korea probably has a higher incarceration rate than the United States, but that nation does not report its incarceration statistics. The incarceration rate for political prisoners alone is estimated to be between 650 and 900 per 100,000 inhabitants. North Korea also holds an unknown number of prisoners as common criminals. See Pierre Rigoulot, "Comparative Analysis of Concentration Camps in Nazi Germany, the Former Soviet Union, and North Korea," 2002. This article is online at the Web site of Human Rights without Frontiers. Go to www.hrwf.net/north_korea/cf_north_korea_political_pri.html.

dealers cannot turn to the legal system for help, so they resort to violence. Finally, drug addicts who do not have the income to finance their habits often engage in crime—assault, robbery, and sometimes murder.

The war on drugs and the increased spending on drug interdiction over the years have had virtually no effect on overall illegal drug consumption in the United States. Mandatory sentences, which have been imposed by the federal government since the late 1980s for all federal offenses, including the sale or possession of illegal drugs, are also not an ideal solution. Mandatory sentences lead to a further problem—overcrowded prisons. Furthermore, almost half of the 1.5 million people arrested each year in the United States on drug charges are arrested for marijuana offenses—and of these, almost 90 percent are charged with possession only.

While the federal government has done little to modify its drug policy, state and local governments have been experimenting with new approaches to the problem. Many states now have special drug courts for those arrested for illegal drug use. In these courts, offenders typically are sentenced to a rehabilitation program.

CONFRONTING TERRORISM

Of all of the different types of crimes, terrorism can be the most devastating. The victims of terrorist attacks can number in the hundreds—or even in the thousands, as was the case when hijacked airplanes crashed into the Pentagon and the World Trade Center on September 11, 2001. Additionally, locating the perpetrators is often extremely difficult. In a suicide bombing, the perpetrators have themselves been killed, so the search is not for the perpetrators, but for others who might have conspired with them in planning the attack.

Terrorism is certainly not a new phenomenon in the world, but it is a relatively new occurrence on U.S. soil. And certainly, the September 11 attacks made many Americans aware for the first time of the hatred of America harbored by some foreigners—in this case, a network of religious fundamentalists in foreign countries. As you have read elsewhere in this text, the U.S. government took many actions immediately after September 11, including launching a war in Afghanistan as part of a war on terrorism. Congress quickly passed new legislation to fund these efforts, as well as many other acts, such as the Aviation Security Act.

Some of the actions taken in the wake of September 11, such as the war in Afghanistan, were widely supported by the public. Others, such as the enactment of the USA PATRIOT Act and President Bush's executive order establishing military tribunals, have been criticized for infringing too much on Americans' civil liberties. Worldwide, terrorists' acts have continued since September 11. Among others, they include bomb attacks on the subway system and a bus in London, which killed more than 50 people, and bomb attacks on the public transportation system in Madrid, which killed more than 200 people. In the summer of 2006, the British government foiled what could have been one of the worst terrorist attacks yet. Ten or more individuals had prepared to take clear liquids into planes departing for the United States. These liquids were in fact bomb materials, and they were going to be detonated with electronic devices, such as MP3 players (or what appeared to be these devices). Isolated terrorist incidents have continued in the United States as well, with one suspect carrying bomb material in his underwear on a flight to Detroit and another attempting to detonate a homemade bomb in Times Square. Certainly, at this point no end is in sight to the war on terrorism. As with all policies, the nation's policy with respect to terrorism will be evaluated—and perhaps modified—over time.

YOU CAN MAKE A Difference

DOING YOUR PART: GLOBAL WARMING

While debate continues over the causes of global warming, consensus exists among most scientists and climate researchers that global warming is here and will make an enormous impact on our planet. Sea levels, rainfall patterns, and snow and ice cover are all changing as a result of increasing greenhouse gas levels in the atmosphere. Human beings probably are tipping the ecological balance in the atmosphere with increased population, deforestation, cars, factories, and power plants.

WHY SHOULD YOU CARE?

Global warming is changing the earth's climate and is already affecting people, animals, and plants in different ways. The seas are rising, the glaciers are shrinking, trees are blooming earlier, and ice on lakes and rivers is freezing later and breaking up earlier. In the United States, scientists believe that most areas will continue to warm, with increased precipitation and evaporation. Drier soil is predicted for the middle parts of the country. Northern regions, including Alaska, are forecast to experience the most drastic warming. Extreme periods of heat, cold, and storms can affect human health; climate-related diseases will increase, and smog episodes will rise. Doctors at the Harvard Medical School have linked recent U.S. outbreaks of dengue fever, malaria, and hantavirus to our changing climate. The eight warmest years on record (official records date to 1850) have all happened since 1998.

Some of the world's most respected climate scientists believe that we have a single decade, until today's college students will be in their thirties, to slow the growth of carbon emissions. Your generation will have to live with the consequences, and global warming is a defining issue on college campuses today.

WHAT CAN YOU DO?

Thinking about global problems can be overwhelming, but acting locally lets everyone participate and contribute to a solution.

Action that starts at home can set the stage for national policy change. Tell your representatives in Congress and the Senate that you want to see a national plan to address global warming. Find out about all political candidates' positions on energy and global warming before voting.

Here are 10 actions we can all take to reduce our own carbon imprint on the planet:

1. Save energy at home by switching to Energy Star fluorescent lightbulbs. If every household in the United States replaced five conventional bulbs in the most frequently used fixtures, we would prevent greenhouse gas emissions equivalent to those from nearly 10 million cars.
2. Every gallon of gas burned emits 20 pounds of carbon dioxide; that's several times your car's weight every year. Try walking, taking public transportation, or riding a bike.
3. Recycle as much as possible; any reduction in trash going to the landfill makes a difference.

AT THE 2009 POWER SHIFT Rally in Washington, D.C., young people demonstrated in support of legislation addressing climate change and clean energy. (Alex Wong/Getty Images)

4. Buy recycled products; in some cases, products made from recycled materials require less energy to produce. Also look for goods with less packaging that will create less waste going to the landfill.

5. Many utilities are offering the choice to buy green electricity, generated by wind or solar power. Support this or any renewable energy development.

6. Make informed choices about the products and services you buy. Use businesses that make an effort to protect the climate, and let them know why you chose their services. Buy local produce whenever possible, because this food does not have to be shipped great distances, burning more fossil fuel to get to your table (and often tastes better, too!).

7. Educate yourself about global warming and climate change; many sources of information confuse the issues, and the ability to think critically is important when reading the paper or watching the news.

8. Let your elected representatives know you care about global warming; urge them to support actions to reduce pollution and save energy.

9. Create a climate-friendly environment on your college campus by working with school administrators to increase energy efficiency, develop an inventory of the school's greenhouse gas emissions, and create a campus climate action plan.

10. Seek out and support nonprofit groups that support green legislation and offer positions on environmental issues.

The EPA's Web site, www.epa.gov, provides details on actions by states and local agencies to address global warming. Find out what your region's or state's climate action plan is all about.

Clean Air–Cool Planet has partnered with several universities in the northeastern United States to develop a Campus Climate Action Plan Toolkit, available to anyone who is interested in making colleges more climate-friendly. For more information, please go to www.cleanair-coolplanet.org.

Focus the Nation is a national effort to focus attention on global warming issues at American college campuses. A 2008 national teach-in provided a climate change seminar with more than 10,000 volunteers on more than 1,300 campuses. About one million people participated across the nation; another teach-in was held in 2009. Focus the Nation's Web site offers opportunities to blog with other students and educators, events to get your campus involved, contests promoting creative solutions, and dozens of ways to participate politically. For more information, contact:

Focus the Nation Headquarters
4160 SW Haven St.
Lake Oswego, OR 97035
503-200-2313
www.focusthenation.org

REFERENCES

Daniel Horgan, "College Students Seeing Green as the Way to Go," *USA Today,* accessed March 12, 2008, at www.usatoday.com.

Bryan Walsh, "Changing the Climate on Campus," *Time,* accessed February 8, 2008, at www.time.com.

www.clearnair-coolplanet.org.

www.epa.gov/climatechange.

www.focusthenation.org.

www.stopglobalwarming.org.

KEY TERMS

CHAPTER SUMMARY

1. Domestic policy consists of all of the laws, government planning, and government actions that affect the lives of American citizens. Policies are created in response to public problems or public demand for government action. Major policy problems discussed in this chapter include health care, poverty and welfare, immigration, crime, and the environment.

2. **How does the policy-making process reflect the will of the people?** The policy-making process is initiated when policy makers become aware—through the media or from their constituents—of a problem that needs to be addressed by the legislature and the president. The process of policy making includes five steps: agenda building, policy formulation, policy adoption, policy implementation, and policy evaluation. As the proposed policy is formulated and debated during the adoption process, the views of the public, interest groups, and the government are heard. All policy actions necessarily result in both costs and benefits for society.

3. Health care spending is about 15 percent of the U.S. economy and is growing. Reasons for this growth include the increasing number of elderly persons, advancing technology, and higher demand because costs are picked up by third-party insurers. A major third party is Medicare, the federal program that pays health care expenses of U.S. residents age 65 and older. The federal government has tried to restrain the growth in Medicare spending, but it has also expanded the program to cover prescription drugs.

4. **Should the government provide health care to all Americans, or is the private sector better equipped to do so?** About 15 percent of the population does not have health insurance—a major political issue. Most uninsured adults work for employers that cannot afford to offer health benefits. Hospitals tend to charge the uninsured higher rates than they charge insurance companies or the government. One proposal for addressing this problem is a national health insurance system under which the government provides basic coverage to all citizens. The United States has chosen to continue with a plan that combines government-required health insurance, private and public insurers, and private provision of services. Most Americans prefer this approach because they wish to choose their own medical providers. Whether this approach will result in cost control and better health for Americans is yet to be seen.

5. Pollution problems continue to plague the United States and the world. Since the 1800s, several significant federal acts have been passed in an attempt to curb the pollution of our environment. The National Environmental Policy Act of 1969 established the Council on Environmental Quality. That act also mandated that environmental impact statements be prepared for all legislation or major federal actions that might significantly affect the quality of the environment. The Clean Water Act of 1972 and the Clean Air Act amendments of 1990 constituted the most significant government attempts at cleaning up our environment. With the recent Gulf oil spill, the conflict between protecting the environment and keeping energy cheap in the United States has become more intense.

6. **How do you balance the need to protect the environment with the need to sustain economic growth?** Energy policy in the United States has generally sought to stabilize the supply of cheap energy to meet the demands of Americans. When energy sources are threatened, new policies have been adopted, increasing efficiency standards for automobiles, funding research on new technologies, and supporting the use of alternative energy. All energy policies are deeply interconnected with environmental issues, because the use of fossil fuels contributes to air pollution and climate change. Reducing the use of energy and using new technologies for cleaner energy make all energy more expensive for Americans. However, reduced future supplies are likely to mean more reforms in the future. Whether Americans will choose to pay more for their everyday needs to provide for a cleaner environment is a question that will be resolved in the future.

7. Despite the wealth of the United States as a whole, a significant number of Americans live in poverty or are homeless. The low-income poverty threshold represents the income needed to maintain a specified standard of living as of 1963, with the purchasing-power value increased year by year based on the general increase in prices. The official poverty level is based on pretax income, including cash, and does not take into consideration in-kind subsidies (food stamps, housing vouchers, and so on).

8. The 1996 Welfare Reform Act transferred more control over welfare programs to the states, limited the number of years people can receive welfare assistance, and imposed work requirements on welfare recipients. The act succeeded in reducing the number of welfare recipients in the United States by at least 50 percent.

9. America has always been a land of immigrants and continues to be so. Today, more than one million immigrants from other nations enter the United States each year, and more than 10 percent of the U.S. population

consists of foreign-born persons. The civil rights legislation of the 1960s and later has helped immigrants to overcome some of the effects of prejudice and discrimination against them. Today, the controversy centers on a reform of our immigration legislation that will improve our system for temporary workers and enable undocumented immigrants to have a path to citizenship.

10. There is widespread concern in this country about violent crime, particularly the large number of crimes that are committed by juveniles. However, the overall rate of violent crime, including crimes committed by juveniles, declined between 1995 and 2004. In response to crime concerns, the United States has incarcerated an unusually large number of persons. Crimes associated with illegal drug sales and use have also challenged policy makers. A pressing issue facing Americans and their government today is terrorism—one of the most devastating forms of crime. Government attempts to curb terrorism will no doubt continue for some time to come.

SELECTED PRINT, MEDIA, AND ONLINE RESOURCES

PRINT RESOURCES

Blundell, Katherine, and Fraser Armstrong. *Energy ... Beyond Oil.* Cambridge, England: Oxford University Press, 2007. Written by two British scientists, the book reviews all of the major new technologies for energy generation and discusses whether or when the technologies can make a contribution to world energy needs.

Ehrenreich, Barbara. *Nickel and Dimed: On (Not) Getting By in America.* New York: Owl Books, 2002. Released on audio CD in 2004. What is life like for the working poor? Commentator and humorist Barbara Ehrenreich sought to live for a few months working at minimum-wage jobs. Here, she describes her experiences.

Hage, Dave. *Reforming Welfare by Rewarding Work: One State's Successful Experiment.* Minneapolis, MN: University of Minnesota Press, 2004. Hage describes the Minnesota Family Investment Program, a pilot program in welfare reform. He illustrates the story with firsthand accounts of three families.

Laufer, Peter, and Markos Kounalakis. *Calexico: Hope and Hysteria in the California Borderlands.* Sausalito, CA: PoliPointPress, 2009. Calexico is a news-gathering travelogue that explores the California-Mexico border region, a land of its own inhabited by people who experience the immigration crisis in all its dimensions, every day. Laufer is a foreign affairs journalist and radio commentator; Kounalakis is the editor of the *Washington Monthly.*

Miller, Roger LeRoy, et al. *The Economics of Public Issues,* 15th ed. Reading, MA: Addison-Wesley, 2005. Chapters 4, 8, 11, 13, 19, 20, 22, 24, and 27 are especially useful. The authors use short essays of three to seven pages to explain the purely economic aspects of numerous social problems, including health care, the environment, and poverty.

Schellenberger, Michael, and Ted Nordhaus. *Break Through: From the Death of Environmentalism to the Politics of Possibility.* New York: Houghton-Mifflin, 2007. The authors argue that the environmentalist movement is no longer useful nor effective. A new approach to policy embracing research and societal needs will succeed, in their view.

Sered, Susan Starr, and Rushika Fernandopulle. *Uninsured in America: Life and Death in the Land of Opportunity.* Berkeley, CA: University of California Press, 2006. Based on interviews with 120 uninsured individuals and numerous policy makers and medical providers, this book looks at the growing ranks of Americans lacking health insurance and the problems with the nation's current health care policies.

Zuberi, Dan. *Differences That Matter: Social Policy and the Working Poor in the United States and Canada.* Ithaca, NY: Cornell University Press, 2006. The author takes a comparative approach to the lives of the working poor in the United States and Canada, looking at vital issues ranging from health care to labor policies.

MEDIA RESOURCES

A Day's Work, A Day's Pay—This 2002 documentary by Jonathan Skurnik and Kathy Leichter follows three welfare recipients in New York City from 1997 to 2000. When forced to work at city jobs for well below the prevailing wage and not allowed to go to school, the three fight for programs that will help them get better jobs.

The Age of Terror: A Survey of Modern Terrorism—A four-part series, released in 2002, that contains unprecedented interviews with bombers, gunmen, hijackers, and kidnappers. The interviews are combined with photos from police and news archives. The four tapes are *In the Name of Liberation, In the Name of Revolution, In the Name of God,* and *In the Name of the State.*

America's Promise: Who's Entitled to What?—A four-part series that examines the current state of welfare.

An Inconvenient Truth—A 2006 Paramount Classics production of former vice president Al Gore's Oscar-winning documentary on global warming and actions that can be taken in response to this challenge.

Sicko—Michael Moore's 2007 effort, which takes on the U.S. health care industry. Rather than focusing on the plight of the uninsured, Moore addresses the troubles of those who have been denied coverage by their insurance companies. In his most outrageous stunt ever, Moore assembles a group of 9/11 rescue workers who have been denied proper care and takes them to Cuba, where the government, perfectly aware of the propaganda implications, is more than happy to arrange for their treatment.

Traffic—A 2001 film, starring Michael Douglas and Benicio Del Toro, that offers compelling insights into the consequences of failed drug policies. (*Authors' note:* Be aware that this film contains material of a violent and sexual nature that may be offensive.)

Young Criminals, Adult Punishment—An ABC program that examines the issue of whether the harsh sentences given out to adult criminals, including capital punishment, should also be applied to young violent offenders.

ONLINE RESOURCES

Federal Bureau of Investigation has been tasked with collecting, publishing, and archiving statistics from the Uniform Crime Reporting (UCR) Program since 1930: www.fbi.gov/ucr/ucr.htm

Institute for Research on Poverty offers information on poverty in the United States and the latest research on this topic: www.ssc.wisc.edu/irp

National Governors Association The bipartisan organization of the nation's governors promotes visionary state leadership, shares best practices, and speaks with a unified voice on national policy, such as the current status of welfare reform: www.nga.org

U.S. Census Bureau reports current statistics on poverty in the United States: www.census.gov/hhes/www/poverty.html

17

This is just one of many homes abandoned by its owners because they were unable to make their mortgage payments. (Justin Sullivan/Getty Images)

Economic Policy

QUESTIONS TO CONSIDER

How much can Congress and the president do to manage the economy?

Is trade with other nations good or bad for the United States?

What is the goal of our federal taxation system?

CHAPTER CONTENTS

what if...

The Federal Government Were Required To Balance Its Budget?

BACKGROUND

Except for the wartime periods of the Civil War and World War II, the United States government budget normally ran a very low deficit. Of course, up until the Great Depression, the number of government spending programs was very low. Although the government has normally run a deficit budget for the last 50-plus years, all states are required by constitutions to balance their budgets. To understand the ramifications of a balanced federal budget, you first have to consider how it would be balanced. Let's assume that an amendment requiring a balanced budget is added to the U.S. Constitution. Initially, the two possible ways to balance the federal budget would be to raise taxes and increase user fees or to reduce the amount of federal government spending. Alternatively, a combination of these two actions could be undertaken.

INCREASED TAXES

On the revenue side of the equation, one way to balance the budget is to increase taxes on individuals and corporations. If the government did this by increasing taxes on individuals, then the tax rates paid by the middle class would have to rise significantly. Why? The reason is simply that the middle class is the source of most tax revenues for the federal government. The rich and the super-rich pay a more-than-proportionate share in taxes, but not enough households in that group exist to increase the revenues enough to balance the budget. Thus, middle-class Americans would see their taxes go up rather dramatically.

Taxes on corporations might increase significantly, too. Corporations, though, exist only as legal entities. Therefore, increased corporate taxes would mean reduced income for owners of corporate stock, lower salaries for employees of corporations, and higher prices for consumers on all the products they produce.

It would also be possible to increase user fees for all federal government services, perhaps to keep them more in line with the actual costs of the federal government. The fees to visit national parks would likely be raised, as one example.

REDUCED FEDERAL GOVERNMENT SPENDING

On the spending side of the equation, a reduction in federal government spending could mean dramatic changes for many Americans. Fewer pork-barrel spending projects would be available for members of Congress to get for their states and districts, but these projects actually make up a very small proportion of the federal budget.

Much more spending would have to be reduced to balance the budget (unless taxes were raised at the same time). So there might be across-the-board cuts of, say, 6 percent in every department. Each department would then have to decide how much to cut from its own programs. Even more drastic would be cuts in entitlement programs such as Social Security, Medicare and Medicaid, and veterans' benefits. Obviously, the public would be outraged as popular programs were either cut back substantially or eliminated altogether.

FOREIGN OWNERSHIP OF U.S. TREASURY BONDS

Another effect of a balanced federal budget would be a reduction in the amount of U.S. Treasury bonds held by foreign residents and governments. When the federal government runs a deficit, it creates debt obligations, usually in the form of U.S. Treasury bonds. Currently, foreigners buy a significant portion of those bonds, up to 50 percent. If the government had to balance its budget, foreigners would no longer be able to buy U.S. debt. Many Americans are uncomfortable knowing that foreigners own so much of our accumulated federal deficit and would therefore view this change as beneficial.

FOR CRITICAL ANALYSIS

1. Of the two methods of reducing the deficit to zero—raising taxes or decreasing government spending—which method do you believe would be perceived by most people to be less painful? Why?
2. How can the federal government spend more than it receives every year, whereas a family would have a hard time doing the same thing year in and year out?

NOWHERE ARE THE principles of public policy making more obvious than in the economic decisions made by the federal government. The president and Congress (and to a growing extent, the judiciary) are constantly faced with questions of economic policy. A major economic policy issue is how to maintain stable economic growth without falling into either excessive unemployment or **inflation** (rising prices). Inflation is defined as a sustained upward movement in the average level of prices. Excessive unemployment and the decline of economic growth are the symptoms of recession. Americans certainly became aware of the problems brought by recession after the financial industry meltdown in the fall of 2008 and the long period of rising unemployment that followed the crisis. The federal government, led in 2008 by President George W. Bush and then from 2009 onwards by President Barack Obama, initiated a number of efforts to prop up the American economy, but the recovery proved to be very slow and difficult to predict.

The federal dollars spent to shore up American banks and industries such as the automobile manufacturers generated huge federal budget deficits in 2008, 2009, and 2010, with more deficits predicted for future years. The prospect of a federal budget that will be in deficit for the next decade increased the controversy over whether the federal government should have a balanced budget, as discussed in this chapter's opening *What If . . .* The budget and deficit spending, the government's tools to manage the economy, taxes, trade, and Social Security will be discussed in this chapter.

Inflation
A sustained rise in the general price level of goods and services.

GOOD TIMES, BAD TIMES

Other than the fundamental tasks of maintaining law, order, and national security, no governmental objective is more important than the maintenance of economic stability. Like any economy that is fundamentally capitalist, the U.S. economy experiences ups and downs. Good times—booms—are followed by lean years. If a slowdown is so severe that the economy actually shrinks for six or more months, it is called a **recession**. Recessions—in part because they bring increased unemployment—are political poison for a sitting president, even though a president's power to control the economy is actually not that great. The government tries to moderate the effects of such downturns. In contrast, booms are historically associated with another economic problem that the government must address: rising prices, or inflation. We will turn to the topic of inflation shortly. First, we consider the problem of excessive unemployment.

Recession
Two or more successive quarters in which the economy shrinks instead of grows.

UNEMPLOYMENT

One political goal of any administration is to keep the rate of unemployment down. **Unemployment** is the inability of those who are in the workforce to find jobs. Individuals may become unemployed for several reasons. Some people enter the labor force for the first time and have to look for a job. Some people are fired or laid off and have to look for a job. Others just want to change occupations. **Full employment** is defined as a level of unemployment that makes allowances for normal movement between jobs. Full employment is widely considered to be a desirable state of affairs, but the nation does not always have it. During recessions, unemployment rises well above the full-employment level. For example, during the business slowdown of 2001–2002, following the 9/11 attack, the rate of unemployment increased from 4 to 6.5 percent. By late 2005, the unemployment rate fell to less than 5 percent and stayed there until spring 2008, when it reached 5.5 percent. As the financial crisis of 2008 grew in size and scope, the stock markets plunged and business activity throughout the world weakened. The average unemployment rate for 2009 was more than 9 percent and the rate showed little sign of decreasing in 2010.

Unemployment
The inability of those who are in the labor force to find a job; defined as the total number of those in the labor force actively looking for a job but unable to find one.

Full Employment
An arbitrary level of unemployment that corresponds to "normal" friction in the labor market. In 1986, a 6.5 percent rate of unemployment was considered full employment. Today, it is assumed to be around 5 percent.

Unemployment Becomes an Issue. For much of American history, unemployment was not a problem that the federal government was expected to address. In the early years of the Republic, most people would have thought that the national government could not do much about unemployment. By the late 1800s, many people had come to believe that as a matter of principle, the government should not fight unemployment. This belief followed from an economic philosophy that was dominant in those years—*laissez-faire economics*. (You learned about the concept of *laissez-faire*—French for "let it be"—in Chapter 1.) Advocates of this philosophy believed then (and believe now) that government intervention in the economy is almost always misguided and likely to lead to negative results. A second barrier to any federal government action against unemployment was the doctrine of *dual federalism*, which was described in Chapter 3. Under this theory, *only* state governments had the right to address a problem such as unemployment. For the most part, however, ups and downs in the economy were a matter of the capitalist system and not a matter for government.

The Great Depression of the 1930s ended popular support for dual federalism and *laissez-faire* economics. As the Depression took hold, unemployment initially exceeded 25 percent. Relatively high rates of unemployment—more than 15 percent—persisted for more than 10 years. One of the methods that the Roosevelt administration adopted to combat the effects of the Depression was direct government employment of those without jobs through such programs as the Civilian Conservation Corps and the Works Progress Administration.

Since the passage of the Social Security Act of 1935, the federal government has also offered a program of unemployment insurance. The program is the government's single most important source of assistance to the jobless. Not all unemployed workers are eligible, however. In fact, only about one-third of the unemployed receive benefits. Benefits are not available to employees who quit their jobs voluntarily or are fired for cause (for example, constantly showing up late for work). They are also not paid to workers who are entering the labor force for the first time but cannot find a job. Unemployment insurance is a joint state–federal program and the state portion is paid for by a tax on employers. In 2009 and 2010, facing the highest unemployment rate in decades, Congress extended the benefits to 99 weeks for some of the most affected states and pumped more federal dollars into the fund.

Measuring Unemployment. Estimates of the number of unemployed are prepared by the U.S. Department of Labor. The Bureau of the Census also generates estimates using survey research data. Figure 17–1 shows how unemployment has fluctuated over the course of American history.

Critics of the published unemployment rate calculated by the federal government believe that it fails to reflect the true numbers of discouraged workers and "hidden unemployed." Although no exact definition of discouraged workers or a way to measure them exists, the Department of Labor defines them as people who have dropped out of the labor force and are no longer looking for a job because they believe that the job market has little to offer them.

INFLATION

Rising prices, or inflation, can also be a serious political problem for any sitting administration, especially if prices are rising fast. As previously stated, inflation is a sustained upward movement in the average level of prices. Inflation can also be defined as a decline in the purchasing power of money over time. The government measures inflation using the **consumer price index (CPI)**. The Bureau of Labor Statistics (BLS)

Consumer Price Index (CPI)
A measure of the change in price over time of a specific group of goods and services used by the average household.

FIGURE 17–1 More than a Century of Unemployment

Unemployment reached lows during World Wars I and II of less than 2 percent and a high during the Great Depression of more than 25 percent.

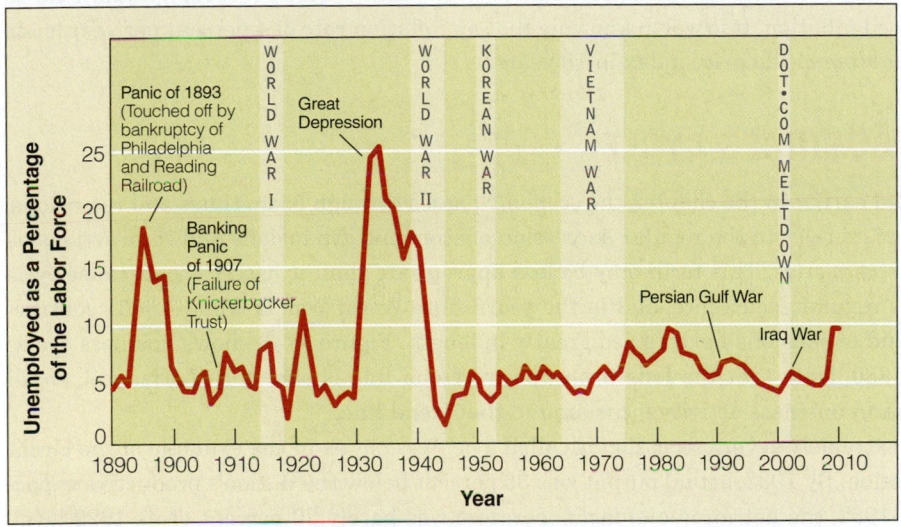

Source: U.S. Department of Labor, Bureau of Labor Statistics.

FIGURE 17–2 Changing Rates of Inflation, 1860 to the Present

From the Civil War until World War II, the United States experienced alternating inflation and deflation.(Deflation is a sustained decrease in the average price level.) Since World War II, deflation has not been a problem. The vertical yellow bars represent wartime.

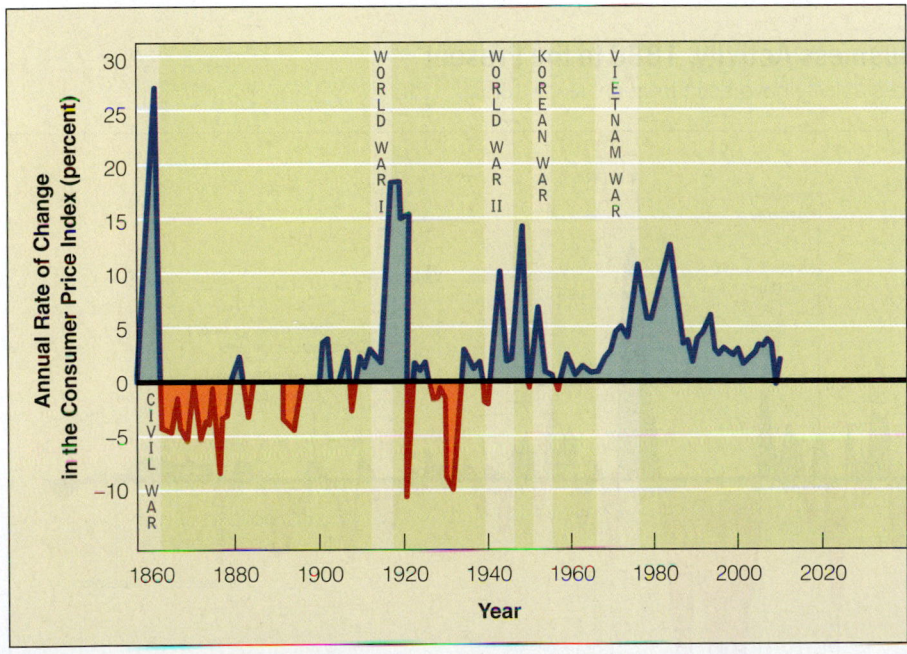

Source: U.S. Department of Labor, Bureau of Labor Statistics.

identifies a market basket of goods and services purchased by the typical consumer and regularly checks the price of that basket. Over a period of many years, inflation can add up. For example, today's dollar is worth (very roughly) one-twentieth of what a dollar was worth a century ago. Figure 17–2 shows the changing rates of inflation in the United States since 1860. While interest rates have not increased very much in the mid-2000s, the increase in the price of oil and, thus, all transportation costs, has begun to drive up all prices of consumer goods. Inflation is always a concern for the nation; however, the recession of 2008–2010 has seen very low or negative inflation, mostly due to very low interest rates. Economists worry that a quick recovery would lead to increased inflation. It is worth knowing that an inflation rate of 4 percent per year leads to a *doubling* of the price index in 18 years.

THE BUSINESS CYCLE

As noted earlier in the chapter, the economy passes through boom times and recessions. Economists refer to the regular succession of economic expansions and contractions as the *business cycle*. This term may be less appropriate than it used to be, because *cycle* implies regular recurrence, and in the years since World War II (1939–1945), contractions and expansions have varied greatly in length. Figure 17–3 shows business cycles since 1880. Note that the long-term upward trend line is shown as horizontal, so all changes in business activity focus around that trend line.

An extremely severe recession is called a *depression*, as in the example of the Great Depression. By 1933, actual output was 35 percent below the nation's productive capacity. By 1932, the net income of farm operators was barely 20 percent of its 1929 level, even though total farm output had risen by 3 percent in the interim. Between 1929 and 1932, more than 5,000 banks (one out of every five) failed, and their customers' deposits vanished. Compared to that catastrophe, most modern recessions have been mild. However, the bank failures of 2008 and the stock market plunge may lead to another worldwide depression. The United States government, as well as the governments of every major power, try to prevent such economic disasters by every means available.

FIGURE 17–3 National Business Activity, 1880 to the Present

Variations around the trend of U.S. business activity have been frequent since 1880.

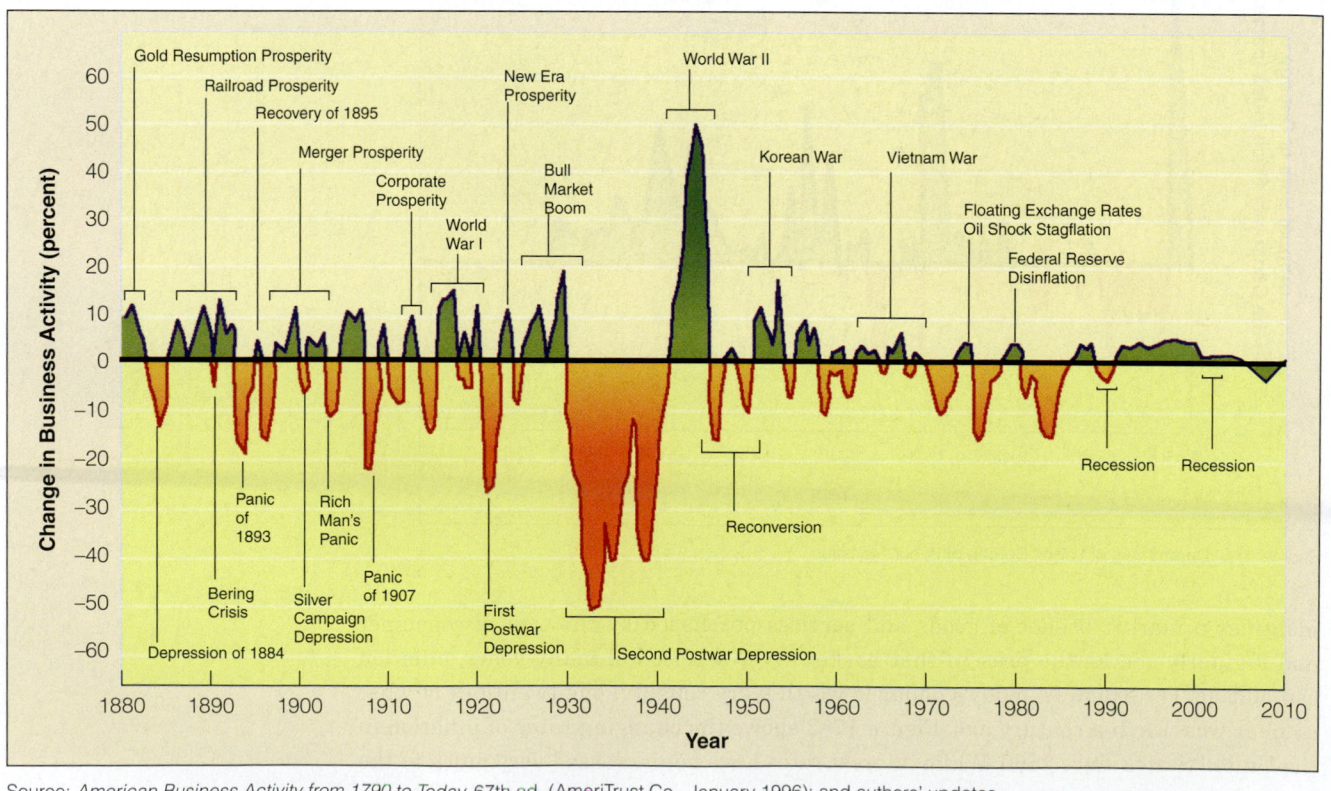

Source: *American Business Activity from 1790 to Today,* 67th ed. (AmeriTrust Co., January 1996); and authors' updates.

For example, in 2008 the Congress passed the first TARP (Troubled Asset Relief Program) fund to bail out major financial houses and banks with loans to cover their obligations. By 2010, many of those institutions had repaid those loans with interest, although the recession continued. Other actions taken by the government to stem the crisis included taking over and restructuring the General Motors Corporation and Chrysler Corporation; providing financial aid and assistance to homeowners who faced foreclosure on their homes; and passing a huge stimulus package to aid states in paying public workers, increase research in medicine and health, and provide funding for public infrastructure projects such as the rebuilding of roads and bridges.

FISCAL POLICY

To smooth out the ups and downs of the national economy, the government has several policy options. One is to change the level of taxes or government spending. The other possibility involves influencing interest rates and the money side of the economy. We will examine taxing and spending, or **fiscal policy**, first. Fiscal policy is the domain of Congress and the president. Generally, the incumbent president and his party are blamed by the public for an economic downturn. However, any real changes in fiscal policy are likely to be initiated by the president and then passed by the Congress. A fiscal policy approach to stabilizing the economy is often associated with a 20th-century economist named John Maynard Keynes.

Keynesian Economics. The British economist John Maynard Keynes (1883–1946) originated the school of thought called **Keynesian economics**, which supports the use of government spending and taxing to help stabilize the economy. (*Keynesian* is pronounced *kayn*-zee-un.) Keynes believed that a need for government intervention in the economy existed, in part because after falling into a recession or depression, a modern economy may become trapped in an ongoing state of less than full employment.

Government Spending. Keynes developed his fiscal policy theories during the Great Depression. He believed that the forces of supply and demand operated too slowly on their own in such a serious recession. Unemployment meant people had less to spend, and because they could not buy things, more businesses failed, creating additional unemployment. It was a vicious cycle. Keynes's idea was simple: In such circumstances, the government should step in and undertake the spending that is needed to return the economy to a more normal state.[1]

Government Borrowing. Government spending can be financed in several ways, including increasing taxes and borrowing. For government spending to have the effect Keynes wanted, however, it was essential that the spending be financed by borrowing, and not by taxes. In other words, the government should run a **budget deficit**, which is discussed in the *Politics with a Purpose* feature—it should spend more than it receives. If the government financed its spending during a recession by taxation, the government would be spending funds that would, for the most part, otherwise have been spent by taxpayers.

Normally, businesses constantly borrow funds to expand future production and invest in equipment. Consumers also borrow to finance items that cannot be paid for out of current income, such as a house or a car. In a recession, however, borrowing slows down. Businesses may not believe that they can sell the new goods or services that would allow them to repay the funds they might borrow. Consumers may be fearful of incurring long-term obligations at a time when their jobs might be threatened.

Fiscal Policy
The federal government's use of taxation and spending policies to affect overall business activity.

Keynesian Economics
A school of economic thought that tends to favor active federal government policy making to stabilize economy-wide fluctuations, usually by implementing discretionary fiscal policy.

Budget Deficit
Government expenditures that exceed receipts.

---

[1] Robert Skidelsky, *John Maynard Keynes: The Economist as Savior, 1920–1937: A Biography* (New York: Penguin USA, 1994).

When the government borrows during a recession, this borrowing replaces the borrowing that businesses and consumers would normally undertake. By running a budget deficit, therefore, the government makes up not only for reduced spending by businesses and consumers, but for reduced private borrowing as well.

Discretionary Fiscal Policy. Keynes originally developed his fiscal theories as a way of lifting an economy out of a major disaster such as the Great Depression. Beginning with the presidency of John F. Kennedy (served 1961–1963), however, policy makers have attempted to use Keynesian methods to fine-tune the economy. This is discretionary fiscal policy—*discretionary* meaning left to the judgment or discretion of a policy maker. For example, President George W. Bush pushed his tax cuts of 2001 and 2003 as a method of stimulating the economy to halt the economic slowdown of those years. During 2006, Bush repeatedly pointed out that since his tax cuts had been put into effect, the economy had grown so much that federal tax revenues increased more than anticipated, thereby reducing the federal budget deficit below the level that had been predicted. As Bush approached the end of his second term, he noted that the 2008 budget submitted to Congress would reduce the budget deficit and, if his proposals were followed, the budget would produce a surplus by 2012. However, the financial crisis of 2008 intervened and the government increased its deficit spending at a rapid rate, producing the likelihood of unbalanced budgets for the next decade.

Kennedy was the first American president to explicitly adopt Keynesian economics. In 1963, during a mild business slowdown, Kennedy proposed a tax cut. Congress did not actually pass the necessary legislation until early 1964, after Kennedy had been assassinated. The economy picked up—and the tax cut was a success.

Discretionary Fiscal Policy Failures. Subsequent presidents did not have the same success as Kennedy with their fiscal policies. Lyndon B. Johnson, Kennedy's successor, presided over a boom that was partially fueled by spending on the Vietnam War (1964–1975). In principle, Johnson should have asked for a tax increase to pay for the war. He was afraid of the political consequences, however; the Vietnam War was unpopular enough already. Instead of raising taxes, Congress borrowed and ran a budget deficit. This is the exact opposite of what Keynes would have recommended. One of the results seemed to be inflation.

Ending an inflationary spiral can be politically dangerous. It may result in a recession. Johnson's successors, presidents Richard Nixon, Gerald Ford, and Jimmy Carter, were reluctant to take that risk and, in any event, may have lacked the political support needed for serious anti-inflationary measures. Nixon, in particular, chose to fight inflation not with fiscal or monetary policies but by instituting a comprehensive system of **wage and price controls**. Eventually, Nixon had to lift the controls, and when he did, measured inflation came roaring back stronger than ever. In the end, inflation was halted through the use of monetary policy, which you will read about shortly.

THE THORNY PROBLEM OF TIMING

Attempts to fine-tune the economy face a timing problem. Have you ever taken a shower, turned on the hot water, and had the water come out cold? And then, in frustration, given the hot water faucet another turn and gotten scalded? What happened was a lag between the time you turned on the faucet and the time the hot water actually reached the showerhead. Policy makers concerned with short-run stabilization face similar difficulties.

DID YOU KNOW?

An aide to President George W. Bush gave this succinct description of federal priorities: "It helps to think of the government as an insurance company with an army"?

Wage and Price Controls
Government-imposed controls on the maximum prices that may be charged for specific goods and services, plus controls on permissible wage increases.

It takes a while to collect and assimilate economic data. Time may go by before an economic problem can be identified. After an economic problem is recognized, a solution must be formulated. There will be an action time lag between the recognition of a problem and the implementation of policy to solve it. Getting Congress to act can easily take a year or two. Finally, after fiscal policy is enacted, it takes time for the policy to act on the economy. Because fiscal policy time lags are long and variable, a policy designed to combat a recession may not produce results until the economy is already out of the recession.

AUTOMATIC STABILIZERS

Not all changes in taxes or in government spending require new legislation by Congress. Certain automatic fiscal policies—called **automatic, or built-in, stabilizers**—include the tax system and government transfer payments such as unemployment insurance.

You know that if you work less, you are paid less, and therefore you pay lower taxes. The amount of taxes that our government collects falls automatically during a recession. Some economists consider this an automatic tax cut. Like other tax cuts, it may help reduce the extent of a recession.

Similar to the tax system, unemployment compensation payments may boost total economy-wide demand. When business activity drops, many laid-off workers automatically become eligible for unemployment compensation from their state governments. They continue to receive income, although certainly it is less than they earned when they were employed.

Automatic, or Built-in, Stabilizers
Certain federal programs that cause changes in national income during economic fluctuations without the action of Congress and the president. Examples are the federal income tax system and unemployment compensation.

DEFICIT SPENDING AND THE PUBLIC DEBT

The federal government typically borrows by selling **U.S. Treasury bonds**. The sale of these federal government bonds to corporations, private individuals, pension plans, foreign governments, foreign businesses, and foreign individuals adds to this nation's *public debt*. In the last few years, foreigners have come to own about 50 percent of the U.S. public debt. Thirty years ago, the share of the U.S. public debt held by foreigners was only 15 percent.

U.S. Treasury Bond
Debt issued by the federal government.

AN UNEMPLOYED WORKER
applies for benefits at the Los Angeles, California, Job Service office. Many construction workers lost their jobs as the subprime mortgage crisis continued in 2008. (Damian Dovarganes/ AP Photo)

Gross Public Debt
The net public debt plus interagency borrowings within the government.

Net Public Debt
The accumulation of all past federal government deficits; the total amount owed by the federal government to individuals, businesses, and foreigners.

Gross Domestic Product (GDP)
The dollar value of all final goods and services produced in a one-year period.

The Public Debt in Perspective. Did you know that the federal government has accumulated trillions of dollars in debt? Does that scare you? It certainly would if you thought that we had to pay it back tomorrow, but we do not.

There are two types of public debt—gross and net. The **gross public debt** includes all federal government interagency borrowings, which really do not matter. This is similar to your taking an IOU ("I owe you") out of your left pocket and putting it into your right pocket. Currently, federal interagency borrowings account for close to $3 trillion of the gross public debt. What is important is the **net public debt**—the public debt that does not include interagency borrowing. Table 17–1 shows the net public debt of the federal government since 1940.

This table does not consider two very important variables: inflation and increases in population. A better way to examine the relative importance of the public debt is to compare it to the **gross domestic product (GDP)**, as is done in Figure 17–4. (The *gross domestic product* is the dollar value of all final goods and services produced in a one-year period.) There you see that the public debt reached its peak during World War II and fell thereafter. Since about 1960, the net public debt as a percentage of GDP has ranged between 30 and 50 percent; however, the recent spending to combat the financial crisis and new federal programs such as the health care reform bill suggest that our future net public debt could reach 70 percent of the GDP. This is a level that would lead to a weakening of the nation's credit in the world and serious economic problems.

Are We Always in Debt? From 1960 until the last few years of the 20th century, the federal government spent more than it received in all but two years. Some observers consider these ongoing budget deficits to be the negative result of Keynesian policies. Others

TABLE 17–1 Net Public Debt of the Federal Government

YEAR	TOTAL (BILLIONS OF CURRENT DOLLARS)	YEAR	TOTAL (BILLIONS OF CURRENT DOLLARS)
1940	$42.7	1998	$3,870.0
1945	235.2	1999	3,632.9
1950	219.0	2000	3,448.6
1960	237.2	2001	3,200.3
1970	284.9	2002	3,528.7
1980	709.3	2003	3,878.4
1990	2,410.1	2004	4,295.0
1992	2,998.6	2005	4,592.0
1993	3,247.5	2006	4,895.0
1994	3,432.1	2007	5,035.0
1995	3,603.4	2008	5,788.6
1996	3,747.1	2009	7,532.6
1997	3,900.0	2010	9,136.9*

*Estimate.
Source: Congressional Budget Office.

POLITICS WITH A purpose

Managing Your Money

Have you ever worried that your paycheck will not cover your monthly expenses, about how you are going to pay your bills, or about repaying your college loans? Most of us experience these concerns at one time or another and are forced to find solutions. Maybe we become more fiscally disciplined and stick to a budget. Maybe we find a way to increase revenue. Maybe one of your motivations for going to college is economic security.

The federal government faces similar dilemmas, only on a much larger and more complicated scale. As you will learn in this chapter, the federal government has, at various times, engaged in deficit spending—that is, spending more on services and programs than it has generated in tax revenue. Prolonged periods of deficit spending cumulate to the federal debt.

Many organizations track deficit spending and the national debt carefully out of concern for the health and stability of the national economy. The Concord Coalition (www.concordcoalition.org) is a bipartisan organization advocating a "generationally responsible fiscal policy." As an advocacy group (see Chapter 7), its mission involves creating public awareness and lobbying government for reduced spending, fiscal discipline, and balanced budgets.

The Concord Coalition encourages public awareness of government spending.[a] Imagine if you had 100 pennies. Think about how you would divide those pennies among the various categories of spending: defense, education, interest on the debt, foreign aid, Social Security, welfare, health, the environment, and other programs such as homeland security and agriculture. Each penny represents 1 percent of all federal spending. Interest on the federal debt alone is almost 10 percent.

So is it a problem that the government often spends more money than it takes in? Conflicting opinions exist. The Concord Coalition clearly advocates against deficit spending. At a 2004 forum, then–Federal Reserve Board Governor Edward M. Gramlich argued, "When the government runs deficits, it siphons off private savings . . . leaving less available for capital investment."[b]

By contrast, some argue that keeping tax rates low will have the most positive impact on the economy, regardless of the effect on the government. Some are openly hostile to the deficit hawks, calling them representative of the "Chicken Little deficit reduction myopia that was once the rage in the Republican Party."[c] These "supply siders" argue that taxes need to be held to a minimum in order for businesses to keep a maximum amount of their profits to reinvest in the economy. Some among them who also advocate for a smaller government that engages in fewer programs would also argue that lower taxes are a way to "starve" the federal government into being leaner and more efficient.[d] These conservatives argue that a "budget with Federal spending at 15 percent of GDP [gross domestic product], and a deficit of 3 percent of GDP, is far preferable to a balanced budget with Federal spending at 35 percent of GDP."[e] In other words, they prioritize low government spending over

a balanced budget. Similarly, they point to rising costs of entitlement programs as a major threat to economic growth.

As a candidate, Senator Obama's platform included fiscal reform, citing the debt and deficit spending as barriers to "responsible fiscal policies." However, upon becoming president, he was faced with an extraordinary economic crisis and needed to use the fiscal tools of stimulus spending and aid to the unemployed to stabilize the economy. The resulting increase in the deficit will, in turn, support the president's call to increase taxes on the wealthiest Americans to help support these programs.[f]

[a]www.concordcoalition.org/learn/educators/penny-game, accessed October 10, 2008.

[b]www.concordcoalition.org/issues/primers/fiscal-responsibility.html, accessed May 28, 2008.

[c]www.nationalreview.com/moore/moore121102.asp, accessed May 28, 2008.

[d]www.businessweek.com/print/magazine/content/04_52/b3914021_mz007.htm?chan=gl, accessed May 28, 2008.

[e]www.spectator.org/dsp_article.asp?art_id=13277, accessed May 28, 2008.

[f]www.barackobama.com/issues/fiscal, accessed June 2, 2008.

FIGURE 17–4 Net Public Debt as a Percentage of the
Gross Domestic Product

During World War II, the net public debt as a percentage of GDP grew dramatically. It fell
thereafter but rose again from 1975 to 1995. The percentage fell after 1995, began to
rise again after the events of September 11, 2001, and then fell again, starting in 2004.

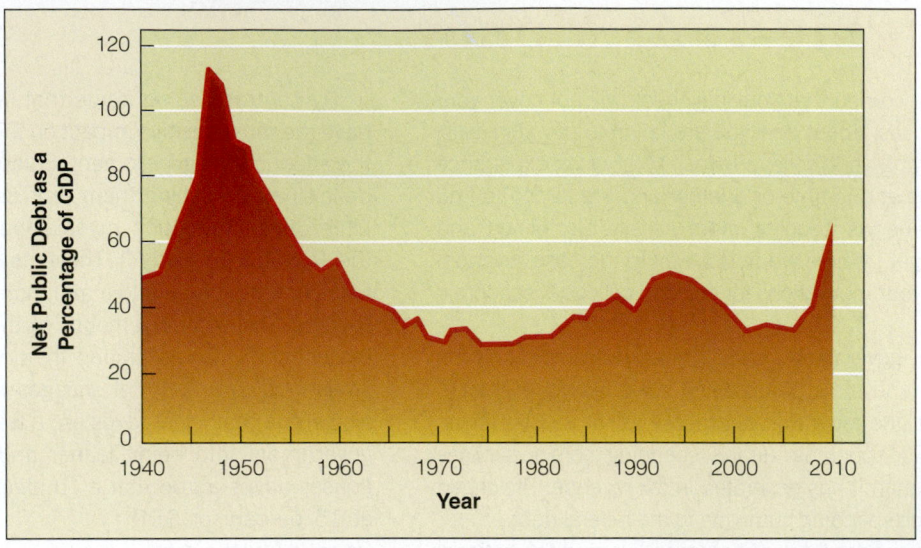

Source: U.S. Department of Labor, Bureau of Labor Statistics.

argue that the deficits actually result from the abuse of Keynesianism. Politicians have
been more than happy to run budget deficits in recessions, but they have often refused to
implement the other side of Keynes's recommendations—to run a budget surplus during
boom times.

In 1993, however, President Bill Clinton (served 1993–2001) obtained a tax increase
as the nation emerged from a mild recession. For the first time, the federal government
implemented the more painful side of Keynesianism. In any event, between the tax
increase and the dot-com boom, the United States had a budget surplus each year from
1998 to 2002. Some commentators predicted that we would be running federal government surpluses for years to come. All of those projections went by the wayside because of
several events.

One event was the dot-com bust, followed by the 2001–2002 recession, which was
caused by the terrorist attacks on September 11, 2001. These events lowered not
only the rate of growth of the economy but also the federal government's tax receipts.
Another event was a series of large tax cuts passed by Congress in 2001 and 2003 at the
urging of President George W. Bush. Finally, the government had to pay for the war in
Iraq in 2003 and the occupation of that country thereafter, which turned out to be far
more costly than ever imagined. The federal budget deficit for 2007 was close to $270
billion. Then the financial crisis of 2008 occurred, plunging the nation into recession
and unemployment. Congress reacted by creating bailout funds and passing stimulus
spending, thus increasing the debt.

MONETARY POLICY

Federal Reserve System (the Fed)
The agency created by Congress in 1913
to serve as the nation's central banking
organization.

Controlling the rate of growth of the money supply is called *monetary policy*. This policy
is the domain of the **Federal Reserve System**, also known simply as **the Fed**. The Fed
is the most important regulatory agency in the U.S. monetary system.

The Fed performs several important functions. Perhaps the Fed's most important ability is that it is able to regulate the amount of money in circulation, which can be defined loosely as checkable account balances and currency. The Fed also provides a system for transferring checks from one bank to another. In addition, it holds reserves deposited by most of the nation's banks, savings and loan associations, savings banks, and credit unions.

ORGANIZATION OF THE FEDERAL RESERVE SYSTEM

A board of governors manages the Fed. This board consists of seven full-time members appointed by the president with the approval of the Senate. The 12 Federal Reserve district banks have 25 branches. The most important unit within the Fed is the **Federal Open Market Committee**. This is the body that actually determines the future growth of the money supply and other important economy-wide financial variables. This committee is composed of the members of the Board of Governors, the president of the New York Federal Reserve Bank, and presidents of four other Federal Reserve banks, rotated periodically.

Federal Open Market Committee
The most important body within the Federal Reserve System. The Federal Open Market Committee decides how monetary policy should be carried out.

The Board of Governors of the Federal Reserve System is independent. The president can attempt to influence the board, and Congress can threaten to merge the Fed into the Treasury Department, but as long as the Fed retains its independence, its chairperson and governors can do what they please. Hence, any talk about "the president's monetary policy" or "Congress's monetary policy" is inaccurate. To be sure, the Fed has, on occasion, yielded to presidential pressure, and for a while the Fed's chairperson had to observe a congressional resolution requiring him to report monetary targets over each six-month period. But now more than ever before, the Fed remains one of the truly independent sources of economic power in the government.[2]

LOOSE AND TIGHT MONETARY POLICIES

The Federal Reserve System seeks to stabilize nationwide economic activity by controlling the amount of money in circulation. Changing the amount of money in circulation is a major aspect of **monetary policy**. You may have read a news report in which a business executive complained that money is "too tight." This means that the Federal Reserve has increased the interest rate that it charges banks, making it more expensive to borrow money. You may have run across a story about an economist who has warned that money is "too loose." In this instance, the Fed has lowered the interest rate in hopes of stimulating borrowing by businesses and individuals. The businesses will then use that money to invest in new equipment and create new jobs. When the interest rate is lowered, it is easier, theoretically, for businesses and individuals to borrow money, thus stimulating the economy.

Monetary Policy
The utilization of changes in the amount of money in circulation to alter credit markets, employment, and the rate of inflation.

How do the actions of the Federal Reserve affect the life of the ordinary citizen? The answer to that question depends on what kinds of loans an individual might have. If you have a 30-year fixed-rate mortgage on your home, for example, nothing the Fed does will change the interest rate of your loan. However, if you have a low adjustable-rate mortgage, the rate will increase as the Fed increases the prime rate. This happened to millions of homeowners and investors between 2005 and 2007, with payments increasing so much that many homes were foreclosed on by the banks. Generally, interest on

---

[2]Axel Krause, "The American Federal Reserve System: Functioning and Accountability" (Paris, France: Groupement d'études et de recherches, Notre Europe, Research and Policy Paper No. 7, 1999). This paper is available online at www.notre-europe.eu/en/axes.

Loose Monetary Policy
Monetary policy that makes credit
inexpensive and abundant, possibly
leading to inflation.

Tight Monetary Policy
Monetary policy that makes credit
expensive in an effort to slow the economy.

credit cards remains high no matter what the Fed does. It is important to remember that the Fed is more interested in stimulating business activity than it is in stimulating individuals to buy more homes.[3]

If the Fed implements a **loose monetary policy** (often called an "expansionary" policy), the supply of credit increases and its cost falls. If the Fed implements a **tight monetary policy** (often called a "contractionary" policy), the supply of credit falls and its cost increases. A loose money policy is often implemented as an attempt to encourage economic growth. You may be wondering why any nation would want a tight money policy. The answer is to control inflation. If money becomes too plentiful too quickly, prices (and ultimately the price level) increase, and the purchasing power of the dollar decreases.

TIME LAGS FOR MONETARY POLICY

You learned earlier that policy makers who implement fiscal policy—the manipulation of budget deficits and the tax system—experience problems with time lags. The Fed faces similar problems when it implements monetary policy. Sometimes accurate information about the economy is not available for months. Once the state of the economy is known, time may elapse before any policy can be put into effect. Still, the time lag when implementing monetary policy is usually much shorter than the lag involved in fiscal policy. The Federal Open Market Committee meets eight times per year and can put a policy into effect relatively quickly. Nevertheless, a change in the money supply may not have an effect for several months.

Time lags were a major reason why the Fed's implementation of monetary policy had dismal results for much of the 20th century. Researchers point out that until the last two decades or so, the Fed's policies turned out to be procyclical rather than anticyclical—that is, by the time the Fed started pumping money into the economy, it was usually

---

[3]For data on Federal Reserve prime rates and mortgage rates, see the Historical Data series from the Federal Reserve Board of Governors at www.federalreserve.gov.

time to do the opposite. By the time the Fed started reducing the rate of growth of the money supply, it was usually time to start increasing it.

The Fed's greatest blunder occurred during the Great Depression. The Fed's policy actions at that time resulted in an almost one-third decrease in the amount of money in circulation. Some economists believe that the Fed was responsible for turning a severe recession into a full-blown depression.

In the early years of the 21st century, the United States experienced a housing boom and a rapid increase in the values of homes and condominiums. Credit was easily available, and the Fed, seeking to keep the economy growing, kept rates low. Then rates began to increase to stop inflation, and many millions of Americans found themselves with mortgages that were becoming more expensive. The housing market declined, values of homes declined, and people ended up owning homes that were not worth the mortgage value. Some people lost their homes, whereas others simply let the bank take over their investments. As the crisis continued, Congress struggled to create legislation to help homeowners who found themselves in this situation. Some analysts criticized the Fed for lowering interest rates too far and stimulating borrowing, whereas other commentators blamed the lending institutions and financial houses that borrowed funds against overvalued mortgages. The mortgage crisis was not limited to the United States: European banks shared the banking crisis.[4]

THE WAY FEDERAL RESERVE POLICY IS ANNOUNCED

Whatever the Fed's intentions, it signifies its current monetary policy by announcing an interest rate target. Nevertheless, when the chair of the Fed states that the Fed is lowering the interest rate from, say, 4.75 percent to 4.50 percent, something else is really meant. The interest rate referred to is the *federal funds rate*, or the rate at which banks can borrow excess reserves from other banks. The direct impact of this interest rate on the economy is modest. To have a significant effect on interest rates throughout the economy, the Fed must increase or restrain the growth in the money supply.

DID YOU KNOW?

That it costs the U.S. Mint 1.4 cents to make a penny and 7.8 cents to make a nickel?

MONETARY POLICY VERSUS FISCAL POLICY

A tight monetary policy is effective as a way of taming inflation. (Some would argue that, ultimately, a tight monetary policy is the only way that inflation can be fought.) If interest rates go high enough, people *will* stop borrowing. How effective, though, is a loose monetary policy at ending a recession?

Under normal conditions, a loose monetary policy will spur an expansion in economic activity. At any given time, many businesses are considering whether to borrow. If interest rates are low, the businesses are more likely to do so. Low interest rates also reduce the cost of new houses or cars and encourage consumers to spend.

Recall from earlier in the chapter, however, that in a serious recession like that of 2008–2009, businesses may not want to borrow no matter how low the interest rate falls. Likewise, consumers may be reluctant to make major purchases even if the interest rate is zero. In these circumstances, monetary policy is ineffective. Using monetary policy in this situation has been described as "pushing on a string," because the government has no power to *make* people borrow. Here is where fiscal policy becomes important. The borrowing *can* take place—if the government does it itself.

[4]"CSI: Credit Crunch," *The Economist*, October 18, 2007, www.economist.com/specialreports.

WORLD TRADE

Most of the consumer electronic goods you purchase—flat-screen television sets, portable media players, cell phones, and digital cameras—are made in other countries. Many of the raw materials used in manufacturing in this country are also purchased abroad. For example, more than 90 percent of bauxite, from which aluminum is made, is brought in from other nations.

World trade, however, is a controversial topic. Since 1999, meetings of major trade bodies such as the World Trade Organization have been marked by large and sometimes violent demonstrations against "globalization." Opponents of globalization often refer to "slave" wages in developing countries as a reason to restrict imports from those nations. Others argue that we should restrict imports from countries that do not follow the same environmental standards as the United States.

Although economists of all political persuasions are strong believers in the value of international trade, this is not true of the general public. In 2009, both the CNN/Opinion Research Corporation Poll and the CBS/New York Times Poll showed a majority of Americans believing that foreign trade is good for the economy. However, when asked whether restrictions on trade are necessary to protect American industries, 60 percent supported such restrictions.[5]

IMPORTS AND EXPORTS

Imports
Goods and services produced outside a country but sold within its borders.

Imports are those goods (and services) that we purchase from outside the United States. Today, imports make up about 15 percent of the goods and services that we buy. This is a significant share of the U.S. economy, but actually it is quite small in comparison with many other countries.

Exports
Goods and services produced domestically for sale abroad.

We not only import goods and services from abroad, but we also sell goods and services abroad, called **exports**. Each year we export more than $1.2 trillion worth of goods. In addition, we export about $300 billion worth of services. The United States exports about 13 percent of the GDP. Like our imports, our exports are a relatively small part of our economy compared with those of many other countries.

Back in the 1950s, imports and exports comprised only about 4 percent of the U.S. GDP. In other words, international trade has become more important for the United States. This is also true for the world as a whole. Since the 1950s, world trade has increased by more than 22 times, although the output of all nations has only increased by eight times.

DID YOU KNOW?

That the largest car-producing country is China, which produced more than twice as many vehicles as the United States in 2009?

THE IMPACT OF IMPORT RESTRICTIONS ON EXPORTS

What we gain as a country from international trade is the ability to import the things we want. We must export other things to pay for those imports. A fundamental proposition for understanding international trade is the following: *In the long run, imports are paid for by exports.*

In the short run, imports can also be paid for by the sale (or export) of U.S. assets, such as title to land, stocks, and bonds, or through an extension of credit from other countries. Other nations, however, will not continue to give us credit forever for the goods and services that we import from them.

---

[5] http://www.pollingreport.com/trade.htm. June 2010.

Economists point out that if we restrict the ability of the rest of the world to sell goods and services to us, then the rest of the world will not be able to purchase all of the goods and services that we want to sell to them. This argument runs contrary to the beliefs of people who want to restrict foreign competition to protect domestic jobs. Although it is certainly possible to preserve jobs in certain sectors of the economy by restricting foreign competition, there is evidence that import restrictions actually reduce the total number of jobs in the economy. Why? The reason is that ultimately such restrictions lead to a reduction in employment in export industries.

Protecting American Jobs. When imports are restricted to save jobs, one effect is to reduce the supply of a particular good or service, and thus to raise its price to consumers. Economists calculate that restrictions on imports of clothing have cost U.S. consumers $45,000 *per year* for each job saved. In the steel industry, the cost of preserving a job has been estimated at approximately $750,000 per year.

One of the best examples of how import restrictions raise prices to consumers has been in the automobile industry, where "voluntary" restrictions on Japanese car imports were in place for more than a decade. Due in part to the enhanced quality of imported cars, sales of domestically produced automobiles fell from 9 million units per year in the late 1970s to an average of 6 million units annually between 1980 and 1982. The U.S. automakers and the United Automobile Workers demanded protection from import competition.

The United States and Japan entered into a "voluntary agreement" to reduce imports of Japanese cars from 1981 into the late 1990s. The result was more demand for Japanese cars than supply, and their prices went up. Domestic carmakers then increased their prices to match those of the imported cars. The estimated cost in one year to consumers was $6.5 billion, or $250,000 for each of the 26,000 American jobs saved. The price was paid by American consumers. In addition, the major Japanese and Korean car companies now assemble cars in the United States, employing thousands of Americans in their plants.

Quotas and Tariffs. The U.S. government uses two key tools to restrict foreign trade: import quotas and tariffs. An **import quota** is a restriction imposed on the value or the number of units of a particular good that can be brought into the United States. **Tariffs** are taxes specifically on imports. Tariffs can be set as a particular dollar amount per unit—say, 10 cents per pound—or as a percentage of the value of the imported commodity.

Tariffs have been a part of the import landscape for two centuries. One of the most famous examples of the use of tariffs was the Smoot-Hawley Tariff Act of 1930. It included tariff schedules for more than 20,000 products, raising taxes on affected imports by an average of 52 percent. The Smoot-Hawley Tariff Act encouraged similar import-restricting policies by the rest of the world. Britain, France, the Netherlands, and Switzerland soon adopted high tariffs, too. The result was a massive reduction in international trade. According to many economists, this worsened the ongoing Great Depression.

Free-Trade Areas and Common Markets. To lower or even eliminate restrictions on free trade among nations, some nations and groups of nations have created free-trade areas, sometimes called common markets. The oldest and best-known common market is today called the European Union (EU). As of 2008, the EU consisted of 27 member nations. These countries have eliminated almost all restrictions on trade in both goods and services among themselves.

On our side of the Atlantic, the best-known free-trade zone consists of Canada, the United States, and Mexico. This free-trade zone was created by the North American Free Trade Agreement (NAFTA), approved by Congress in 1993. A more recent trade

Import Quota
A restriction imposed on the value or number of units of a particular good that can be brought into a country. Foreign suppliers are unable to sell more than the amount specified in the import quota.

Tariffs
Taxes on imports.

DID YOU KNOW?

That the United States imports more than 17 million containers of goods each year and that 1 in 25 goes to Walmart?

agreement is the Central American–Dominican Republic Free Trade Agreement (CAFTA-DR), which was signed into law by President George W. Bush in 2005. This agreement was formed by Costa Rica, the Dominican Republic, El Salvador, Guatemala, Honduras, Nicaragua, and the United States. CAFTA-DR was implemented on a rolling basis as the trade partners agreed to various provisions. By 2007, almost all of the nations were part of the agreement. The CAFTA agreement is still opposed by many members of American textile workers' unions, which see the agreement as a threat to their jobs.

THE WORLD TRADE ORGANIZATION

Since 1997, the principal institution overseeing tariffs throughout the world has been the World Trade Organization (WTO). The goal of the nations that created the WTO was to lessen trade barriers throughout the world, so that all nations can benefit from freer international trade.

What the WTO Does. The WTO's many tasks include administering trade agreements, acting as a forum for trade negotiations, settling trade disputes, and reviewing national trade policies. Today, the WTO has more than 140 member nations, accounting for more than 97 percent of world trade. Another 30 countries are negotiating to obtain membership. Since the WTO came into being, it has settled many trade disputes between countries, sometimes involving the United States.

For example, a few years ago, the United States, backed by five Latin American banana-exporting nations, argued before the WTO that the banana import rules of the European Union (EU) favored former European colonies in Africa and the Caribbean at the expense of Latin American growers and U.S. marketing companies. Specifically, Chiquita Banana claimed that its earnings had fallen because its competitors' bananas received preferential treatment from the EU. Because the EU would not back down, the United States imposed a 100 percent tariff on almost $200 million worth of EU items in nine categories. The right of the United States to impose the tariffs was backed by the WTO. Finally, the WTO brokered a deal between the United States and the EU. The EU agreed to dismantle its banana import policy that favored European multinationals and former European colonies. The United States agreed to drop the 100 percent tariff.

The WTO and Globalization. Opponents of globalization have settled on the WTO as the embodiment of their fears. As noted in Chapter 7, WTO meetings in recent years have been the occasion for widespread and sometimes violent demonstrations. The WTO raises serious political questions for many Americans. Although the WTO has arbitration boards to settle trade disputes, no country has veto power. Some people claim that a vetoless America will be repeatedly outvoted by the countries of Western Europe and East Asia. Some citizens' groups have warned that the unelected WTO bureaucrats based in Geneva, Switzerland, might be able to weaken environmental, health, and consumer safety laws, if such laws affect international trade flows.

The work of the WTO has met opposition in many regions of the world. During the 2003 meetings in Cancun, Mexico, African nations walked out of the "Doha Round" of negotiations because they disagreed with the more-developed nations over new rules for investments and cross-border transfers. One of the areas of the greatest disagreement in the WTO is the treatment of agriculture. Most developed nations subsidize their own farmers and want to protect them from competition from other countries. Doha negotiations continue within the G20 nations, with some hope of resolution in 2010.[6]

THE BALANCE OF TRADE AND THE CURRENT ACCOUNT BALANCE

You may have heard on the news that the U.S. **balance of trade** is "negative" by some large figure. What does this announcement mean? To begin with, a negative balance of trade exists when the value of goods imported into a country is greater than the value of its exports. This situation is called a *trade deficit*. The United States has consistently had a large trade deficit since the late 1970s.

The Current Account Balance. The balance of trade is limited to trade in goods. A broader concept is the **current account balance**, which includes trade in services and several other items. The United States has enjoyed a positive balance of trade in *services* for a long time. (Does the recent practice of outsourcing service jobs abroad change this fact? We examine this question in this chapter's *Beyond Our Borders* feature.) Like the balance of trade, however, the current account balance is negative and has been growing more negative for years. Figure 17–5 shows the growth in the current account deficit.

Are We Borrowing Too Much from Other Countries? If we run a current account deficit, as we have in recent years, we can finance it only by increasing our obligations to other countries. The increasing current account deficit shown in Figure 17–5 can also be viewed as an increase in the claims that foreigners have on our economy. These obligations to other countries can take a variety of forms. Foreigners can buy stocks on Wall Street. They can buy American businesses or real estate. Above all, they can buy U.S. Treasury bonds issued by the government to fund the federal budget deficit.

Have our obligations abroad, which by 2010 were increasing by more than $700 billion per year, become too large? It is true that during the last 20 years, the United States has enjoyed a larger share of the world's economic growth than any country other than China. Many people in other nations therefore consider the United States an attractive place to invest. While foreign appetites for investment in America are not unlimited, the rise in the current account deficit suggests that foreigners are still willing to invest in the United States.

Balance of Trade
The difference between the value of a nation's exports of goods and the value of its imports of goods.

Current Account Balance
The current account balance includes the balance of trade in services, unilateral transfers, and other items. This is a wider concept than the balance of trade.

---

[6]Jonathan Lynn, "Doha Round Negotiators Bear Down in Hopes of Deal This Year," *International Herald Tribune*, March 9, 2008.

FIGURE 17–5 The Current Account Deficit

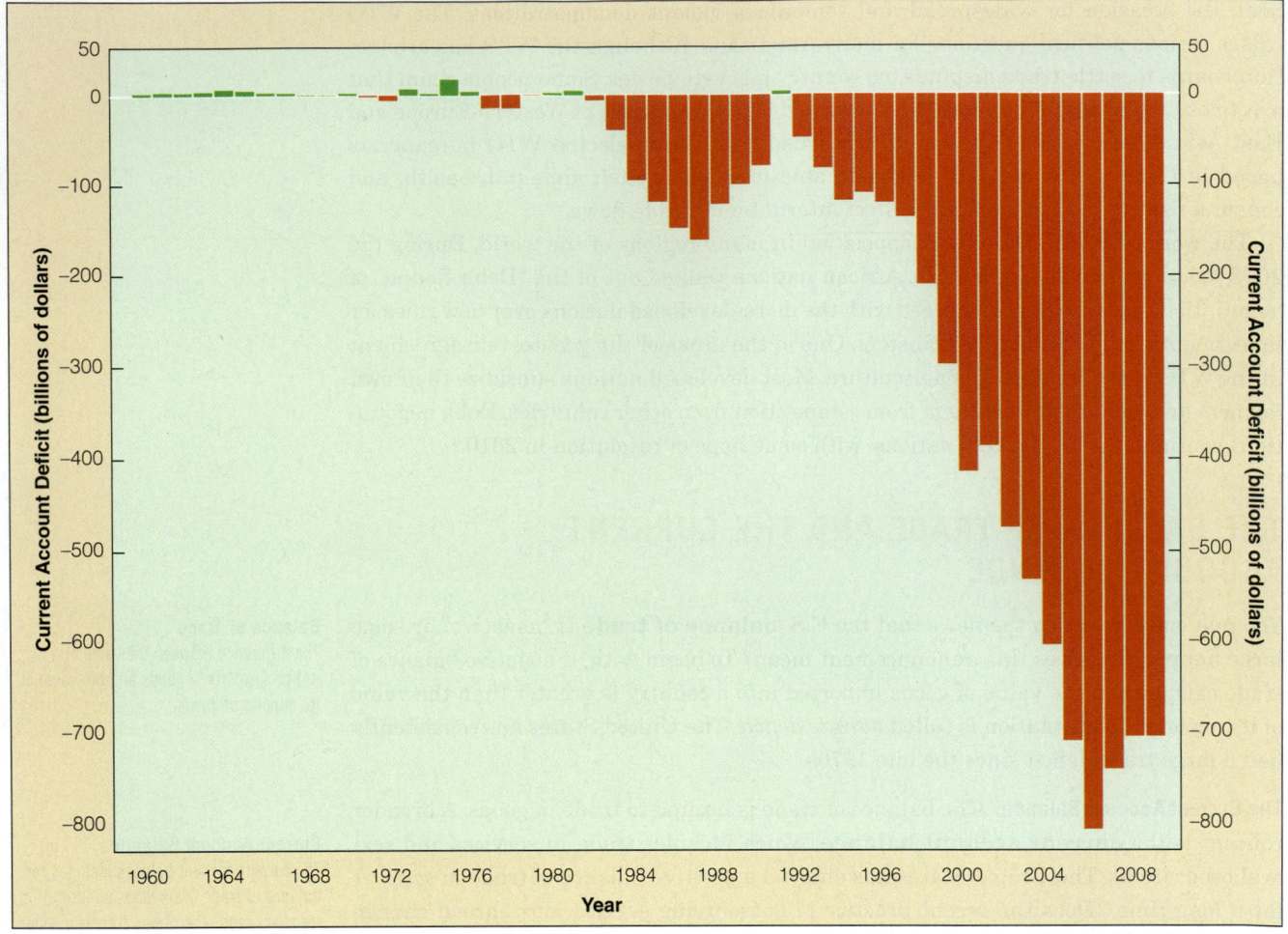

Source: U.S. Department of Commerce, Bureau of Economic Analysis, U.S. International Transactions Accounts Data, Table 1, June 18, 2010.

Beyond Our Borders

SENDING WORK OVERSEAS

For hundreds of years, nations have bought goods and services from abroad. Nonetheless, Americans have always perceived the purchase of services from other countries as a way of allowing those countries to "steal" American jobs. Today, such activity is called either *offshoring* or *outsourcing*. During the 2008 presidential election campaigns, outsourcing continued to be a hot topic, particularly as factories continue to close in the United States.

OUTSOURCING PROBABLY EXAGGERATED

The latest data about outsourcing from the McKinsey Global Institute show that about 300,000 jobs per year are lost to overseas outsourcing firms. This may sound like a lot, but we must put that number in perspective: The U.S. labor market has close to 140 million workers! In any one month, more than 4 million U.S. residents start new jobs with new employers. Also, consider that from 1999 to 2003, according to the Institute for International Economics, the United States lost 125,000 programming jobs to foreign outsourcing, but it added 425,000 jobs for higher-skilled software analysts and engineers.

OUTSOURCING CHANGES TO MEET THE TIMES

Outsourcing is here to stay, but the countries to which jobs are outsourced may change. India and China were the leading "villains" in the outsourcing debate a few years ago, but other countries may soon take their place. Why? Wages for outsourcing services are rising rapidly in both of those countries. This means that other low-wage countries, such as the Philippines and Indonesia, may become larger providers of services.

Outsourcing service providers in India and China have seen the handwriting on the wall. In response, they are attempting to move into higher-tech activities. In India, for example, calls for customer service are increasingly being handled by automated systems, thereby reducing the demand for low-cost Indian workers in this low-tech field. A recent report suggested that Indian business sees legal processing as a profitable target for outsourcing. Legal processing would employ white-collar, highly trained individuals to do legal investigations, prepare contracts, write patents, and perform legal research for clients in other English-speaking, common law countries such as the United States, Canada, and Australia.*

AN EMPLOYEE at a Bangalore, India, call center provides telephone support to international clients. (© Sherwin Crasto/Reuters/Corbis)

FOR CRITICAL ANALYSIS

1. Do you think that outsourcing of jobs is an economic threat to the United States?
2. Will legal documents prepared abroad be an advantage in an American court or not?

*www.washingtonpost.com/wp-dyn/content/article/2008/05/10/AR2008051002355.html

THE POLITICS OF TAXES

Taxes are enacted by members of Congress. Today, the Internal Revenue Code encompasses thousands of pages, thousands of sections, and thousands of subsections—our tax system is very complex.

Americans pay a variety of different taxes. At the federal level, the income tax is levied on most sources of income. Social Security and Medicare taxes are assessed on wages and salaries. There is an income tax for corporations, which has an indirect effect on many individuals. The estate tax is collected from property left behind by those who have died. State and local governments also assess taxes on income, sales, and land. Altogether, the value of all taxes collected by the federal government and by state and local governments is about 30 percent of GDP. This is a substantial sum, but it is less than what many other countries collect, as you can see in Figure 17–6.

FEDERAL INCOME TAX RATES

Individuals and businesses pay taxes based on tax rates. Not all of your income is taxed at the same rate. The first few dollars you make are not taxed at all. The highest rate is imposed on the "last" dollar you make. This highest rate is the *marginal* tax rate. Table 17–2 shows the 2010 marginal tax rates for individuals and married couples. The higher the tax rate—the action on the part of the government—the greater the public's reaction to that tax rate. If the highest tax rate you pay on the income you make is 15 percent, then any method you can use to reduce your taxable income by one dollar saves you 15 cents in tax liabilities that you owe the federal government. Individuals paying a 15 percent rate have a relatively small incentive to avoid paying taxes, but consider the individuals who faced a marginal tax rate of 94 percent in the 1940s. They had a tremendous incentive to find legal ways to reduce their taxable incomes. For every dollar of income that was somehow deemed nontaxable, these taxpayers would reduce tax liabilities by 94 cents.

LOOPHOLES AND LOWERED TAXES

Loophole
A legal method by which individuals and businesses are allowed to reduce the tax liabilities owed to the government.

Individuals and corporations facing high tax rates will adjust their earning and spending behavior to reduce their taxes. They will also make concerted attempts to get Congress to add **loopholes** to the tax law that allow them to reduce their taxable

FIGURE 17–6 Total Amount of Taxes Collected as a Percentage of Gross Domestic Product (GDP) in Major Industrialized Nations

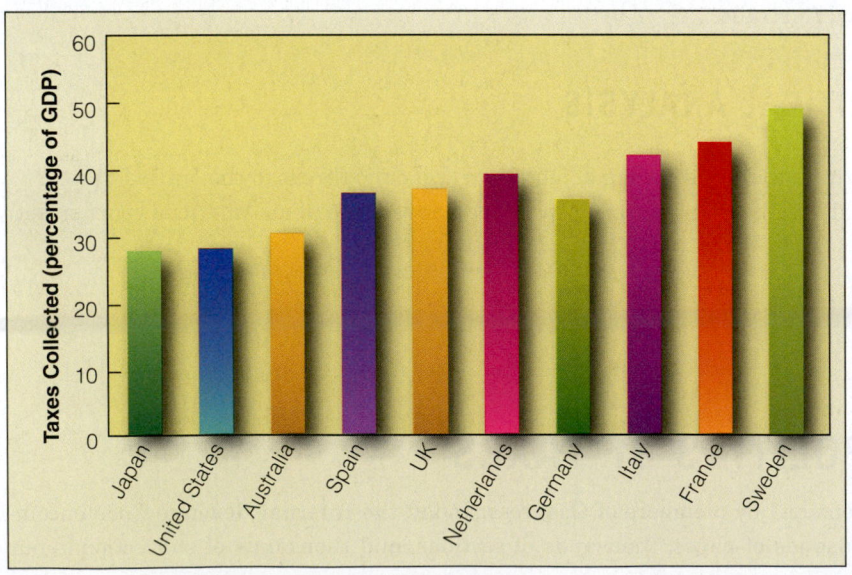

Source: OECD Revenue Statistics, 1965-2007, 2008 edition.

TABLE 17–2 Marginal Tax Rates for Single Persons and Married Couples (2010)

SINGLE PERSONS		MARRIED FILING JOINTLY	
MARGINAL TAX BRACKET	**MARGINAL TAX RATE**	**MARGINAL TAX BRACKET**	**MARGINAL TAX RATE**
$0–$8,375	10%	$0–$16,750	10%
$8,375–$34,000 plus $837.50	15%	$16,750–$68,000, plus $1,675	15%
$34,000–$82,400, plus $4,681	25%	$68,000–$137,300, plus $9,362	25%
$82,400–$171,850, plus $16,781	28%	$137,300–$209,250, plus $26,687.50	28%
$171,850–$373,650, plus $41,827	33%	$209,250–$373,650, plus $46,833	33%
$373,650, plus $108,085	35%	$373,650, plus $101,085	35%

incomes. When Congress imposed very high tax rates on high incomes, it also provided for more loopholes than it does today. For example, special provisions enabled investors in oil and gas wells to reduce their taxable incomes.

In 2001, President George W. Bush fulfilled a campaign pledge by persuading Congress to enact new legislation lowering tax rates for a period of several years. In 2003, rates were lowered again, retroactive to January 2003; these rates are reflected in Table 17–2. As a result of other changes contained in the new tax laws, the U.S. tax code became even more complicated than it was before. President Bush tried several times to renew his tax rate cuts on a permanent basis, but after Democrats took over Congress in 2006, the possibility of the cuts becoming permanent was gone. President Barack Obama has announced his intention to let the tax cuts expire for the wealthiest taxpayers while keeping some of the cuts for middle-income and lower-income Americans.

Progressive and Regressive Taxation. As Table 17–2 shows, the greater your income, the higher the marginal tax rate. Persons with large incomes pay a larger share of their income in income tax. A tax system in which rates go up with income is called a **progressive tax** system. The federal income tax is clearly progressive.

The income tax is not the only tax you must pay. For example, the federal Social Security tax is levied on wage and salary income at a flat rate of 6.2 percent. (Employers pay another 6.2 percent, making the total effective rate 12.4 percent.) In 2008, however, there was no Social Security tax on wages and salaries in excess of $102,000. (This threshold changes from year to year.) Persons with very high salaries therefore pay no Social Security tax on much of their wages. In addition, the tax is not levied on investment income (including capital gains, rents, royalties, interest, dividends, or profits from a business). The wealthy receive a much greater share of their income from these sources than do the poor. As a result, the wealthy pay a much smaller portion of their income in Social Security taxes than do the working poor. The Social Security tax is therefore a **regressive tax**.

Who Pays? The question of whether the tax system should be progressive—and if so, to what degree—is subject to vigorous political debate. Democrats in general and liberals in particular favor a tax system that is significantly progressive. Republicans and conservatives are more likely to prefer a tax system that is proportional or even regressive. For example, President Bush's tax cuts made the federal system somewhat less progressive, largely because they significantly reduced taxes on nonsalary income. If you look at Figure 17–7, you will see that almost half of all American households pay no federal income

Progressive Tax
A tax that rises in percentage terms as incomes rise.

Regressive Tax
A tax that falls in percentage terms as incomes rise.

FIGURE 17–7 Federal Tax Burden by Income Group, 2007

Percentage of federal taxes paid as compared to percentage of gross national income earned by tiers, 2007.

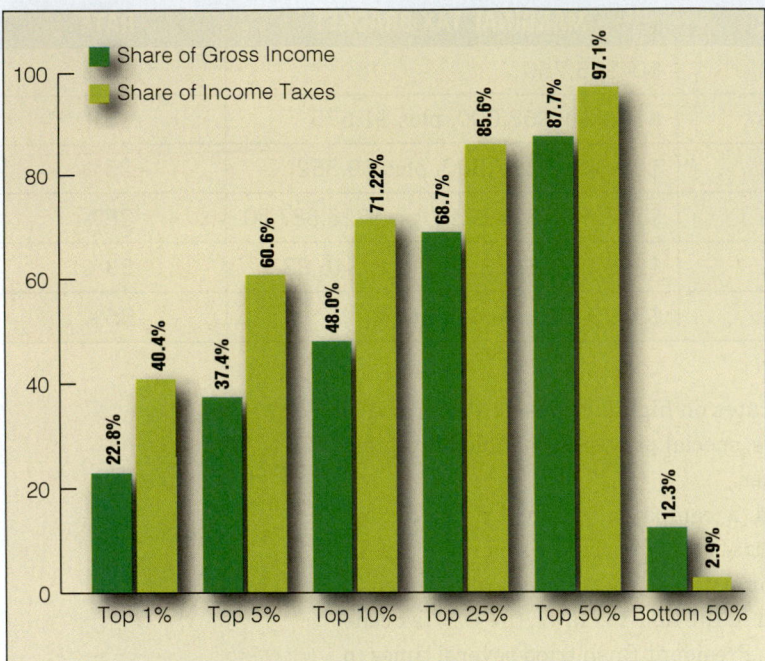

Source: The Tax Foundation, 2007. http://www.taxfoundation.org.

taxes at all, while the top 25 percent of all households pay more than 85 percent of all income taxes. Thus, the federal income tax is progressive, but the tax burden overall is much more complicated.

Overall, what kind of tax system do we have? The various taxes Americans pay pull in different directions. The Medicare tax, as applied to wages and salaries, is entirely flat—that is, neither progressive nor regressive. Because it is not levied on investment income, however, it is regressive overall. Sales taxes are regressive because the wealthy spend a relatively smaller portion of their income on items subject to the sales tax. Table 17–3 lists the characteristics of major taxes. Add everything up, and the tax system as a whole is probably slightly progressive.[7]

THE SOCIAL SECURITY PROBLEM

Closely related to the question of taxes in the United States is the viability of the Social Security system. Social Security taxes came into existence when the Federal Insurance Contribution Act (FICA) was passed in 1935. Social Security was established as a means of guaranteeing a minimum level of pension benefits to all persons. Today, many people regard Social Security as a kind of "social compact"—a national promise to successive generations that they will receive support in their old age.

To pay for Social Security, as of 2010, a 6.2 percent rate is imposed on each employee's wages up to a maximum of $106,800. Employers must pay in ("contribute") an equal percentage. In addition, a combined employer/employee 2.9 percent tax rate is assessed for Medicare on all wage income, with no upper limit. (Medicare is a federal program, begun in 1965, that pays hospital and physicians' bills for persons age 65 and older. See Chapters 7 and 16.)

TABLE 17–3 Progressive versus Regressive Taxes

PROGRESSIVE TAXES	REGRESSIVE TAXES
Federal income tax	Social Security tax
State income taxes	Medicare tax
Federal corporate income tax	State sales taxes
Estate tax	Local real estate taxes

[7]Brian Roach, "GDAE Working Paper No. 03–10: Progressive and Regressive Taxation in the United States: Who's Really Paying (and Not Paying) Their Fair Share?" (Medford, MA: Global Development and Environment Institute, Tufts University, 2003). This paper is online at www.ase.tufts.edu/gdae/Pubs/wp/03-10-Tax_Incidence.pdf.

SOCIAL SECURITY IS NOT A PENSION FUND

One of the problems with the Social Security system is that people who pay into Social Security think that they are actually paying into a fund, perhaps with their name on it. This is what you do when you pay into a private pension plan. It is not the case, however, with the federal Social Security system, which is basically a pay-as-you-go transfer system in which those who are working are paying benefits to those who are retired.

Currently, the number of people who are working relative to the number of people who are retiring is declining. Therefore, those who continue to work will have to pay more in Social Security taxes to fund the benefits of those who retire. In 2025, when the retirement of the Baby Boomer generation is almost complete, benefits are projected to cost almost 25 percent of taxable payroll income in the economy, compared with the current rate of 16 percent. In today's dollars, that amounts to more than $1 trillion of additional taxes annually.

WORKERS PER RETIREE

One way to think about the future bill that today's college students (and their successors) could face in the absence of fundamental changes in Social Security is to consider the number of workers available to support each retiree. As you can see in Figure 17–8, roughly three workers now provide for each retiree's Social Security, plus his or her Medicare benefits. Unless the current system is changed, by 2030 only two workers will be available to pay the Social Security and Medicare benefits due each recipient.

The growing number of people claiming the Social Security retirement benefit may pose less of a problem than the ballooning cost of Medicare. In the first place, an older population will require greater expenditures on medical care. In addition, however, medical expenditures *per person* are also increasing rapidly. Given continuing advances in medical science, Americans may logically wish to devote an ever-greater share of the national income to medical care. This choice puts serious pressure on federal and state budgets, however, because a large part of the nation's medical bill is funded by the government. With the adoption of the new health care reform legislation and the increase in the number of Americans who will likely be covered either by Medicaid or a state-sponsored program, it is very difficult to predict the future expenditures for these three programs. It is possible that the three combined will total more than 20 percent of the nation's gross domestic product, with a corresponding increase in taxes to fund the benefits provided.

WHAT WILL IT TAKE TO SALVAGE SOCIAL SECURITY?

The facts just discussed illustrate why efforts to reform Social Security and Medicare have begun to dominate the nation's public agenda. What remains to be seen is how the government ultimately will resolve the problem. What, if anything, might be done?

Raise Taxes. One option is to raise the combined Social Security and Medicare payroll tax rate. A 2.2 percentage point hike in the payroll tax rate, to an overall rate of 17.5 percent, would yield an $80 billion annual increase in contributions. Such a tax increase would keep current taxes above current benefits until 2020, after which the system would again technically be in "deficit." Another option is to eliminate the current cap on the level of wages to which the Social Security payroll tax is applied; this measure would also generate about $80 billion per year in additional tax revenues. Nevertheless, even a combined policy of eliminating the wage cap and implementing a 2.2 percentage point tax increase would not keep tax collections above benefit payments over the long run.

FIGURE 17–8 Workers per Social Security Retiree

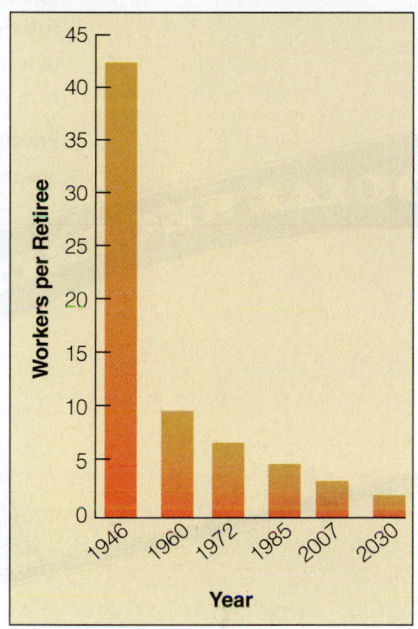

Sources: Social Security Administration; and authors' estimates.

Consider Other Options. Proposals are also on the table to increase the age of full benefit eligibility, perhaps to as high as 70. In addition, many experts believe that increases in immigration offer the best hope of dealing with the tax burdens and workforce shrinkage of the future. Unless Congress changes the existing immigration system to permit the admission of a much larger number of working-age immigrants with useful skills, however, immigration is unlikely to relieve fully the pressure building due to our aging population.

Privatize Social Security. Still another proposal calls for partially privatizing the Social Security system in the hope of increasing the rate of return on individuals' retirement contributions. Privatization would allow workers to invest a specified portion of their Social Security payroll taxes in the stock market and possibly in other investment options, such as bonds or real estate. Although such a solution would have been unthinkable in past decades, today there is some support for the idea. If the economy is good and the stock market grows, then the increased value of these investments would provide more benefits to individuals when they retire. Indeed, President George W. Bush's proposal that Social Security be partially privatized in this way drew significant support from younger Americans but total opposition from most members of Congress and the AARP.

Several groups oppose the concept of partial privatization. These groups fear that the diversion of Social Security funds into individual investment portfolios could jeopardize the welfare of future retirees, who could be at the mercy of the volatile stock market. Opponents of partial privatization point out that such a plan might mean that workers would have to pay for two systems for many years—the benefits for today's retirees cannot simply be abolished.

Obviously, solving the problem of increasing Social Security and Medicare obligations is a task for future presidents and Congresses. While it will be a controversial issue, most Americans are aware that it must be solved.

YOU CAN MAKE A Difference

HOW TO PLAN FOR YOUR FUTURE

If you are between 20 and 40 today, you may likely live to be 100 years old. That might sound incredible, but how do you plan for a retirement that could last 40 years? Retirement is probably the last thing on your mind right now, with college loans and credit card debt to be paid. Today's college graduates kick off their careers more than $20,000 in debt, on average. College costs have soared; tuition has increased 28 percent for private colleges and 38 percent for public colleges in the past 10 years. Meanwhile, average earnings have not kept pace; men with a bachelor's degree today earn only 5.45 percent more than they did a decade ago, with women earning about 10.4 percent more.

WHY SHOULD YOU CARE?

As the common saying goes, a comfortable retirement is based on a "three-legged stool" of Social Security, pensions, and savings. Several trends are working against today's college graduates. Unless reforms are enacted to shore up the system, Social Security benefits for future retirees, who are now in their twenties, could be cut by more than 20 percent and be reduced every year thereafter. The traditional pension is disappearing from the workplace, with more employers favoring 401(k) plans that allow you to save with pretax contributions. Today's young employees are expected to invest in these employer-sponsored retirement plans, which allow them to choose from a mix of investment options and may have employers matching contributions. You may also choose to save through individual retirement accounts (IRAs), stocks, bonds, mutual funds, and cash accounts such as bank savings accounts, certificates of deposit (CDs), and money market funds.

The point of this is that when it comes to retirement, young workers are on their own and need a plan for future financial security.

FINANCIAL ADVISOR WORKING with a young couple to plan their future. (istockphoto.com/Kurhan)

WHAT CAN YOU DO?

Money compounds over time, so the earlier you invest, the greater your yield will be. Compound interest means that you earn interest on the original amount you've saved, and you continue to earn interest on the interest. The longer your money is invested, the more compounding can work for you. The earlier you start, the less you have to save to reach your goal. The longer you wait, the harder it is to make up for lost interest earnings. For example, if you have a goal to save $100,000 and have 20 years to do so, at a conservative 4 percent rate of return, you would need to invest $3,272 per year; compounding will do the rest of the work for you. If you needed to save the same $100,000 and only had 10 years to do so, you would have to save more and take more risk. Even with an 8 percent rate of return, you would need to save $6,559 each year.

When you make saving money a part of your lifestyle at a young age, it will become a habit, not an option. As you begin your career, make sure you take advantage of all savings options at your disposal. Here are a few key questions you should ask any potential or current employer:

- Is there a traditional benefit pension plan?
- Is there a 401(k) or other contribution plan and, if so, are your contributions matched?
- How soon can you join the plan?
- What are the plan's vesting rules, and what happens to your money if you leave the company?

Your employer may have plans to help you save for your future, but the responsibility really lies with you. Financial experts agree on a few simple rules to keep you on track to reach your goals: avoid credit card debt, track expenses and spend within a monthly budget, maintain three to six months of savings equivalent to living expenses in a short-term account, contribute the maximum allowed to your 401(k), take advantage of any "free money" company matches, and maintain savings beyond employer-sponsored plans, such as individual retirement accounts (IRAs).

Choose to Save, a program of the nonprofit Employee Benefit Research Institute and the American Savings Education Council, was created in 1996 to promote individual savings. Its Web site, www.choosetosave.org, provides free savings tools and information to help plan for financial security. Retirement planning worksheets, interactive financial calculators, DVDs, and other materials are available. You can also contact this organization at:

Choose to Save
1100 13th St. NW, Suite 878
Washington, DC 20005
202-659-0670

To monitor reforms in Social Security, contact:

Social Security Administration
Office of Public Inquiries
Windsor Park Bldg.
6401 Security Blvd.
Baltimore, MD 21235
800-772-1213
www.ssa.gov

REFERENCES

Aleksandra Todorova, "What Will Retirement Be Like for Gens X and Y?" *Smart Money*, May 15, 2007. www.smartmoney.com.
www.choosetosave.org.
www.ssa.gov.

KEY TERMS

automatic, or built-in, **stabilizers** 597
balance of trade 607
budget deficit 595

consumer price index (CPI) 592
current account balance 607
exports 604

Federal Open Market Committee 601
Federal Reserve System (the Fed) 600

CHAPTER SUMMARY

 1. **How much can Congress and the president do to manage the economy?** One of the most important policy goals of the federal government is to maintain economic growth without falling into either excessive unemployment or inflation (rising prices). Inflation is commonly measured using the Consumer Price Index (CPI) published by the U.S. Bureau of Labor Statistics. The regular fluctuations in the economy are called business cycles. If the economy fails to grow for six months or more, the nation is experiencing a recession. The president, the Congress, and the Federal Reserve System all have tools to help stabilize the economy. Generally, the two major strategies are fiscal policy and monetary policy.

2. Fiscal policy is the use of taxes and spending to affect the overall economy. Economist John Maynard Keynes is credited with developing a theory under which the government should run budget deficits during recessions to stimulate the economy. Keynes also advocated budget surpluses in boom times, but political leaders have been reluctant to implement this side of the policy. Time lags in implementing fiscal policy can create serious difficulties.

3. The federal government has run a deficit in most years since the 1930s. The deficit is met by U.S. Treasury borrowing. This adds to the public debt of the U.S. government. Although the budget was temporarily in surplus from 1998 to 2002, deficits now seem likely for many years to come.

4. Monetary policy is controlled by the Federal Reserve System, or the Fed. Monetary policy involves changing the rate of growth of the money supply in an attempt to either stimulate or cool the economy. A loose monetary policy, in which more money is created, encourages economic growth. A tight monetary policy, in which less money is created, may be the only effective way of ending an inflationary spiral. Monetary policy may, however, be ineffectual in pulling the economy out of a severe recession—fiscal policy may be required.

 5. **Is trade with other nations good or bad for the United States?** World trade has grown rapidly since 1950. The United States imports and exports goods as well as services. While economists of all persuasions strongly support world trade, the public is less enthusiastic. Restrictions on imports to protect jobs are often popular. Ultimately, however, imports are paid for by exports. Restricting imports restricts exports as well, with resulting loss of employment in export industries. Trade restrictions also increase the cost of the affected goods to consumers.

6. Groups of nations have established free-trade blocs to encourage trade among themselves. Examples include the European Union and the North American Free Trade Association (NAFTA). The World Trade Organization (WTO) is an international organization that oversees trade disputes and provides a forum for negotiations to reduce trade restrictions. The WTO has been a source of controversy in American politics.

7. The current account balance includes the balance of trade, which is limited to goods, and also the balance in the trade of services and other items. A possible problem for the future is the growing size of the U.S. current account deficit, which is funded by foreign investments in the United States.

8. **What is the goal of our federal taxation system?** The various types of taxes levied by the federal, state, and local governments have different goals and different impacts on citizens. U.S. taxes amount to about 30 percent of the gross domestic product, which is not particularly high by international standards. Individuals and corporations that pay taxes at the highest rates will try to pressure Congress into creating exemptions and tax loopholes, which allow high-income earners to reduce their taxable incomes. The federal income tax is progressive; that is, tax rates increase as income increases. Some other taxes, such as the Social Security tax and state sales taxes, are regressive—they take a larger share of the income of poorer people. As a whole, the tax system is slightly progressive.

9. Closely related to the question of taxes is the viability of the Social Security and Medicare systems. As the number of people who are retired increases relative to the

number of people who are working, those who are working may have to pay more for the benefits of those who retire. Proposed solutions to the problem include raising taxes, reducing benefits, allowing more immigration, and partially privatizing the Social Security system in hopes of obtaining higher rates of return on contributions.

SELECTED PRINT, MEDIA, AND ONLINE RESOURCES

PRINT RESOURCES

Bernstein, Michael. *A Splendid Exchange: How Trade Shaped the World.* New York: Atlantic Monthly Press, 2008. The author does a superb job of tracing the history of trade between nations and demonstrates how trade changed the way societies live.

Friedman, Milton, and Walter Heller. *Monetary versus Fiscal Policy.* New York: Norton, 1969. This is a classic presentation of the pros and cons of monetary and fiscal policy given by a noninterventionist (Friedman) and an advocate of federal government intervention in the economy (Heller).

Hira, Ron, and Anil Hira. *Outsourcing America: The True Cost of Shipping Jobs Overseas and What Can Be Done about It.* New York: AMACON, 2008. The authors look closely at the effects of outsourcing on the American economy and make suggestions to political leaders on how to bring jobs back to the United States.

Kotlikoff, Laurence J., and Scott Burns. *The Coming Generational Storm: What You Need to Know about America's Economic Future.* Cambridge, MA: MIT Press, 2004. The authors explain how an aging population will create a crisis in Social Security and Medicare funding. One possible flaw in the authors' argument is their unquestioning use of very long-term demographic projections, which are inherently uncertain.

Lewis, Michael. *The Big Short: Inside the Doomsday Machine.* New York: Norton, 2010. A former Wall Street investor and longtime financial reporter explains the derivative business and the reasons for the financial crisis.

Phillips, Kevin. *Bad Money, Reckless Finance, Failed Politics, and the Global Crisis of American Capitalism.* New York: Viking, 2008. This best-selling author and former reporter for the *New York Times* investigates the deterioration of U.S. influence in the world and the causes of the subprime mortgage crisis.

Sorkin, Andrew Ross. *Too Big to Fail: How Washington and Wall Street Fought to Save the Financial System and Themselves.* New York: Viking, 2009. This absorbing book traces the day-to-day decisions that led to the government bailout of the major banks and averted a worldwide depression.

MEDIA RESOURCES

Alan Greenspan—This rather laudatory biography of the former chair of the Federal Reserve was released in 1999. Using Greenspan as an example, the film looks at factors that influence the world and national economies.

Enron: The Smartest Guys in the Room—The risk-taking culture of the Enron Corporation led to its fall and the trials of many of its executives, even though, as this 2005 documentary shows, they were the smartest guys in the room.

Frontline: The Warning—This 2010 *Frontline* program interviews many individuals from the 1980s onward to analyze decisions that led to the mortgage crisis of 2008.

Outsourced—A 2008 satiric comedy starring Josh Hamilton that examines the experience of an American manager who is sent to India to manage a call center.

ONLINE RESOURCES

Federal Reserve Bank of San Francisco keeps up with actions taken by the Federal Reserve: www.frbsf.org

Office for Management and Budget at the White House OMB's predominant mission is to assist the president in overseeing the preparation of the federal budget and to supervise its administration in executive branch agencies. Visit OMB's Web site to view recent budgets and budget factsheets: www.whitehouse.gov/omb/budget/fy2009

Social Security Administration delivers services through a nationwide network of over 1,400 offices. Information and services available online: www.ssa.gov

Tax Foundation The mission of the Tax Foundation is to educate taxpayers about sound tax policy and the size of the tax burden borne by Americans at all levels of government. Read about federal tax policy, including several studies on its impact, at the Web site of this nonpartisan educational organization: www.taxfoundation.org

World Trade Organization provides a set of rules and a negotiating forum for trade between nations at a global or near-global level: www.wto.org

18

American soldiers meet with Afghan tribal leaders to seek their support in repelling attacks by the Taliban fighters. (MANPREET ROMANA/AFP/ Getty Images/Newscom)

Foreign Policy and National Security

QUESTIONS TO CONSIDER

What should be the goals of American foreign policy?

Can nuclear weapons be eliminated from the world?

Who formulates foreign policy: the president, the bureaucracy, or Congress?

CHAPTER CONTENTS

what if... The United States Disposed of All of Its Nuclear Weapons?

BACKGROUND

At the height of the Cold War, both the United States and the Soviet Union possessed more than 10,000 nuclear warheads ready for missile launch. In addition to land-based missiles, both nations had fleets of submarines fully armed with nuclear missiles that could be launched in a matter of minutes. As you will read in this chapter, efforts to limit these weapons began in the Nixon administration and, following the fall of the Soviet Union, several agreements have been signed by the United States and Russia to destroy significant numbers of these weapons.

WHAT IF THE UNITED STATES DISPOSED OF ALL OF ITS NUCLEAR WEAPONS?

According to the Arms Control Association, the United States still maintains about 5,000 active and inactive nuclear warheads and more than 4,000 "retired" warheads waiting for disposal in some form or another. The Soviet Union has about 2,600 active warheads and more than 8,000 "retired" warheads. What would happen if the United States declared unilaterally that it was proceeding to dismantle and destroy all of its nuclear weapons? It is likely that the other major Western nations that have nuclear weapons—the United Kingdom and France— would do likewise. Russia, which has agreed to a mutual plan for destroying part of its arsenal, might agree, in principle, to do so as well. China, which is estimated to hold 250 warheads, may or may not agree to do so. The nations thought to have nuclear arms but which do not admit to such include Israel, India, and Pakistan. Iran, North Korea, and Syria are developing or have developed the capacity to make such weapons.

Why wouldn't China, Russia, India, Pakistan, and Israel be quick to dispose of their weapons and thus reduce the possibility of a nuclear war that would threaten the existence of all life on earth? The answer lies in each nation's perception of its most immediate threat. Israel fears attacks from neighboring Arab nations, attacks that would be devastating if a nuclear weapon were used. Pakistan, India, China, and Russia share common borders and also are concerned about being vulnerable to attack. The nations that are secretly developing weapons are doing so, supposedly, for self-defense and protection against their enemies. For these

nations to dispose of their weapons requires the establishment of peace in their respective regions of the globe.

CAN WE EASILY DISPOSE OF THESE WEAPONS?

In 2010, the United States and Russia agreed to dispose of a large proportion of their stockpiles of nuclear material in addition to reducing their actual warheads. This agreement follows up on a 2000 agreement between the nations to get rid of 34 tons of plutonium each. That amount of plutonium is enough to make 17,000 bombs. Imagine how much other "spare" nuclear material is available around the world! The material has not been disposed of to date because other nations had not donated the promised $2 billion to help Russia fulfill its end of the bargain. Disposing of nuclear materials and dismantling nuclear warheads is an extremely expensive and difficult business.

Some of the ways that nuclear material can be destroyed include "burning" it as fuel for energy, diluting it with waste from nuclear power plants, destroying the material in accelerators, disposing of waste in deep holes bored in the earth, burying it beneath the seabed, or sending it to outer space. At the present time, any excess material from the destruction of nuclear warheads is "capsulized" in secure containers for permanent storage. Each method entails enormous problems involving the transport and secure storage of the material at every step. It would take several decades to actually dismantle and destroy all the material currently owned by the United States alone.

WHAT ARE THE POLITICS OF THIS PROPOSAL?

Some arms control advocates have been pushing for a nuclear-free world for many decades. In 2007, four prominent American statesmen including George Shultz and Henry Kissinger, both former secretaries of state, called for more effort to eliminate nuclear weapons globally. They noted that the "rogue" states and those worried about their own security might be convinced to give up their weapons if the United States and the world's strongest nations agreed to a multilateral approach that reduced the threat of nuclear weapons and provided a secure way to get rid of them together. Arms control advocates point to such an essay as the right idea but suggest that the American nuclear industry and the weapons industry are dragging their feet and slowing down the process of agreeing to the end of the nuclear era because it would destroy their businesses. Conservatives who believe that a strong military posture is essential to American foreign policy point to dangers in the world to the United States and support keeping some nuclear capability. All in all, there does not seem to be enough trust in the world to begin this process.

FOR CRITICAL ANALYSIS

1. Do you think the United States would be safe from attack if it disposed of its nuclear arsenal?
2. How can the United States and Russia be sure that they have each disposed of all their weapons and that other nations have done so as well?

ON SEPTEMBER 11, 2001, Americans were forced to change their view of national security and of our relations with the rest of the world—literally overnight. No longer could citizens of the United States believe that national security issues involved only threats overseas or that the American homeland could not be attacked. No longer could Americans believe that regional conflicts in other parts of the world had no direct impact on the United States.

Within a few days, it became known that the attacks on the World Trade Center and on the Pentagon had been planned and carried out by a terrorist network named al Qaeda that was funded and directed by the radical Islamist leader Osama bin Laden. The network was closely linked to the Taliban government of Afghanistan, which had ruled that nation since 1996.

Americans were shocked by the complexity and the success of the attacks. They wondered how our airport security systems could have failed so drastically. How could the Pentagon, the heart of the nation's defense, have been successfully attacked? Shouldn't our intelligence community have known about and defended against this network? And, finally, how could our foreign policy have been so blind to the anger voiced by Islamist groups throughout the world?

In this chapter, we examine the tools of foreign policy and national security policy in light of the many challenges facing the United States in the world today, including the threat of nuclear weapons, as discussed in the opening *What If* … .

FACING THE WORLD: FOREIGN AND DEFENSE POLICY

The United States is only one nation in a world with more than 200 independent countries, each of which has its own national goals and interests. What tools does our nation have to deal with the many challenges to its peace and prosperity? One tool is **foreign policy**. By this term, we mean both the goals the government wants to achieve in the world and the techniques and strategies used to achieve them. For example, if one national goal is to achieve stability in the Middle East and to encourage the formation of pro-American governments there, U.S. foreign policy in that area may be carried out through **diplomacy, economic aid, technical assistance**, or military intervention. Sometimes foreign policies are restricted to statements of goals or ideas, such as

Foreign Policy
A nation's external goals and the techniques and strategies used to achieve them.

Diplomacy
The process by which states carry on political relations with each other; settling conflicts among nations by peaceful means.

Economic Aid
Assistance to other nations in the form of grants, loans, or credits to buy the assisting nation's products.

Technical Assistance
The practice of sending experts in such areas as agriculture, engineering, or business to aid other nations.

helping to end world poverty, whereas at other times foreign policies are comprehensive efforts to achieve particular objectives, such as changing the regime in Iraq.

As you will read later in this chapter, in the United States, the **foreign policy process** usually originates with the president and those agencies that provide advice on foreign policy matters. Congressional action and national public debate often affect foreign policy formulation.

Foreign Policy Process
The steps by which foreign policy goals are decided and acted on.

NATIONAL SECURITY POLICY

As one aspect of overall foreign policy, **national security policy** is designed primarily to protect the independence and the political integrity of the United States. It concerns itself with the defense of the United States against actual or potential (real or imagined) enemies, domestic or foreign.

U.S. national security policy is based on determinations made by the Department of Defense, the Department of State, and many other federal agencies, including the National Security Council (NSC). The NSC acts as an advisory body to the president, but it has increasingly become a rival to the State Department in influencing the foreign policy process.

Defense policy is a subset of national security policy. Generally, defense policy refers to the set of policies that direct the scale and size of the U.S. armed forces. Among the questions defense policy makers must consider is the number of major wars the United States should be prepared to fight simultaneously. Defense policy also considers the types of armed forces units we need to have, such as Rapid Defense Forces or Marine Expeditionary Forces, and the types of weaponry that should be developed and maintained for the nation's security. Defense policies are proposed by the leaders of the nation's military forces and the Secretary of Defense and are greatly influenced by congressional decision makers.

National Security Policy
Foreign and domestic policy designed to protect the nation's independence and political and economic integrity; policy that is concerned with the safety and defense of the nation.

Defense Policy
A subset of national security policies having to do with the U.S. armed forces.

DIPLOMACY

Diplomacy is another aspect of foreign policy. Diplomacy includes all of a nation's external relationships, from routine diplomatic communications to summit meetings among heads of state. More specifically, diplomacy refers to the settling of disputes and conflicts among nations by peaceful methods. Diplomacy is the set of negotiating techniques by which a nation attempts to carry out its foreign policy.

Diplomacy can be carried out by individual nations, by groups of nations, or by international organizations. The United Nations often spearheads diplomatic actions in the interests of maintaining peace in certain areas. For example, in 2006, several incidents set off an ever-escalating war between Israel and Hezbollah, a militant Shiite Islamist group that attempts to control Lebanon. While Israeli aircraft bombed Hezbollah's positions and Hezbollah fighters shelled Israeli cities, diplomatic efforts persisted at the United Nations, eventually reaching a peace settlement.

Over the past 50 years, American presidents have often exercised diplomacy to encourage peace in the Middle East. The most successful example was President Jimmy Carter's efforts in 1978 to get Israel and Egypt to agree to a path to peaceful relations. The Camp David Accords were negotiated in the United States by the leaders of Egypt and Israel, with the direct mediation of President Carter. The two countries agreed to work toward peace between them, including mutual recognition.[1]

---

[1]To read the text of the Camp David Accords, go to: www.jimmycarterlibrary.org/documents/campdavid/accords/phtml.

AN AMERICAN PEACE CORPS volunteer works with students in a Kenyan school. (Courtesy of the Peace Corps Press Office)

Diplomacy can be successful only if the parties are willing to negotiate. Diplomacy clearly failed before the First Gulf War and perhaps before the second (some observers believe that the United States did not give diplomacy a long enough time to work to avoid the Second Gulf War). The United States continues to work with European allies to pressure Iran to reject the development of nuclear weapons and—through talks including Russia, China, Japan, South Korea, and North Korea—to persuade North Korea to end its weapons development. In the summer of 2008, North Korea agreed to hand over its long-awaited nuclear program declaration (description of its program) to Chinese officials, and it blew up a cooling tower at one of its nuclear facilities to demonstrate its desire to move forward in ending its weapons program. However, in the spring of 2009, North Korea proceeded to test a nuclear weapon and has rejected all further talks.

MORALITY VERSUS REALITY IN FOREIGN POLICY

From the earliest years of the republic, Americans have felt that their nation had a special destiny. The American experiment in democratic government and capitalism, it was thought, would provide the best possible life for men and women and be a model for other nations. As the United States assumed greater status as a power in world politics, Americans came to believe that the nation's actions on the world stage should be guided by American political and moral principles. As Harry Truman stated, "The United States should take the lead in running the world in the way that it ought to be run."

MORAL IDEALISM

This view of America's mission has led to the adoption of many foreign policy initiatives that are rooted in **moral idealism**. This philosophy sees the world as fundamentally benign and assumes that most nations can be persuaded to take moral considerations

Moral Idealism
A philosophy that sees nations as normally willing to cooperate and to agree on moral standards for conduct.

into account when setting their policies.[2] In this perspective, nations should come together and agree to keep the peace, as President Woodrow Wilson (served 1913–1921) proposed for the League of Nations. Many of the foreign policy initiatives taken by the United States have been based on this idealistic view of the world. The Peace Corps, which was created by President John Kennedy in 1961, is one example of an effort to spread American goodwill and technology that has achieved some of its goals. In fact, Kennedy once said that the United States would "pay any price" and "bear any burden" to further liberty in the world.

POLITICAL REALISM

Political Realism
A philosophy that sees each nation as acting principally in its own interest.

In opposition to the moral perspective is **political realism**, often called *realpolitik* (a German word meaning "realistic politics"). Realists see the world as a dangerous place in which each nation strives for its own survival and interests regardless of moral considerations. The United States must also base its foreign policy decisions on cold calculations without regard for morality. Realists believe that the United States must be prepared to defend itself militarily, because all other nations are, by definition, out to improve their own situations. A strong defense will show the world that the United States is willing to protect its interests. The practice of political realism in foreign policy allows the United States to sell weapons to military dictators who will support its policies, to support American business around the globe, and to repel terrorism through the use of force.

AMERICAN FOREIGN POLICY—A MIXTURE OF BOTH

It is important to note that the United States has never been guided by only one of these principles. Instead, both moral idealism and political realism affect foreign policy making. President George W. Bush drew on the tradition of morality in foreign policy when he declared that the al Qaeda network of Osama bin Laden was "evil" and that fighting terrorism was fighting evil. To actually wage war on the Taliban in Afghanistan, however, U.S. forces needed the right to use the airspace of India and Pakistan, neighbors of Afghanistan. The United States had previously criticized both of these South Asian nations because they had developed and tested nuclear weapons. In addition, the United States had taken the moral stand that it would not deliver certain fighter aircraft to Pakistan as long as it continued its weapons program. When it became absolutely necessary to work with India and Pakistan, the United States switched to a realist policy, promising aid and support to both regimes in return for their assistance in the war on terrorism.

The Second Gulf War that began in 2003 also revealed a mixture of idealism and realism. While the primary motive for invading Iraq was realistic (the interests of U.S. security), another goal of the war reflected idealism—the liberation of the Iraqi people from an oppressive regime and the establishment of a democratic model in the Middle East. The reference to the war effort as Operation Iraqi Freedom emphasized this idealistic goal.

In 2008, Secretary of State Condoleezza Rice wrote about the future of American foreign policy, noting that "The old dichotomy between realism and idealism has never really applied to the United States, because we do not really accept that our national

[2] Eugene R. Wittkopf, Charles W. Kegley, and James M. Scott, *American Foreign Policy*, 6th ed. (Belmont, CA: Wadsworth Publishing, 2002).

interest and our universal ideals are at odds. … Even when our interests and our ideals come into tension in the short run, we believe that in the long run they are indivisible."[3]

THE MAJOR FOREIGN POLICY THEMES

Although some observers might suggest that U.S. foreign policy is inconsistent and changes with each occupant of the White House, the long view of American diplomatic ventures reveals some major themes underlying foreign policy. In the early years of the nation, presidents and the people generally agreed that the United States should avoid foreign entanglements and concentrate instead on its own development. From the beginning of the 20th century until today, however, a major theme has been increasing global involvement. The theme of the post–World War II years was the containment of communism. One of the themes for the first decade of the 21st century has been the battle against terrorism and, under President Obama, another is the United States' effort to end the presence of nuclear weapons in the world.

THE FORMATIVE YEARS: AVOIDING ENTANGLEMENTS

Foreign policy was largely nonexistent during the formative years of the United States. Remember that the new nation was operating under the Articles of Confederation. The national government had no right to levy or collect taxes, no control over commerce, no right to make commercial treaties, and no power to raise an army (the Revolutionary army was disbanded in 1783). The government's lack of international power was made clear when Barbary pirates seized American hostages in the Mediterranean. The United States was unable to rescue the hostages and ignominiously had to purchase them in a treaty with Morocco.

The founders of this nation had a basic mistrust of European governments. George Washington said it was the U.S. policy "to steer clear of permanent alliances," and Thomas Jefferson echoed this sentiment when he said America wanted peace with all nations but "entangling alliances with none." This was also a logical position at a time when the United States was so weak militarily that it could not influence European development directly. Moreover, being protected by oceans that took weeks to traverse certainly allowed the nation to avoid entangling alliances. During the 1800s, therefore, the United States generally stayed out of European conflicts and politics. In this hemisphere, however, the United States pursued an actively expansionist policy. The nation purchased Louisiana in 1803, annexed Texas in 1845, gained substantial territory from Mexico in 1848, purchased Alaska in 1867, and annexed Hawaii in 1898.

The Monroe Doctrine. President James Monroe, in his message to Congress on December 2, 1823, stated that the United States would not accept foreign intervention in the Western Hemisphere. In return, the United States would not meddle in European affairs. The **Monroe Doctrine** was the underpinning of the U.S. **isolationist foreign policy** toward Europe, which continued throughout the 1800s.

The Spanish-American War and World War I. The end of the isolationist policy started with the Spanish-American War in 1898. Winning the war gave the United States possession of Guam, Puerto Rico, and the Philippines (which gained independence in 1946). On the

Monroe Doctrine
A policy statement made by President James Monroe in 1823, which set out three principles: (1) European nations should not establish new colonies in the Western Hemisphere; (2) European nations should not intervene in the affairs of independent nations of the Western Hemisphere; and (3) the United States would not interfere in the affairs of European nations.

Isolationist Foreign Policy
A policy of abstaining from an active role in international affairs or alliances, which characterized U.S. foreign policy toward Europe during most of the 1800s.

[3]Condoleezza Rice, "Rethinking the National Interest: American Realism for a New World," *Foreign Affairs*, July/August 2008.

heels of that war came World War I (1914–1918). In his reelection campaign of 1916, President Woodrow Wilson ran on the slogan "He kept us out of war." Nonetheless, the United States declared war on Germany on April 6, 1917, because that country refused to give up its campaign of sinking all ships headed for Britain, including passenger ships. (Large passenger ships of that time commonly held more than a thousand people, so the sinking of such a ship was a disaster comparable to the attack on the World Trade Center.)

In the 1920s, the United States went "back to normalcy," as President Warren G. Harding urged it to do. U.S. military forces were largely disbanded, defense spending dropped to about 1 percent of total annual national income, and the nation returned to a period of isolationism.

THE ERA OF INTERNATIONALISM

Isolationism was permanently shattered by the bombing of the U.S. naval base at Pearl Harbor, Hawaii, on December 7, 1941. The surprise attack by the Japanese caused the deaths of 2,403 American servicemen and wounded 1,143 others. Eighteen warships were sunk or seriously damaged, and 188 planes were destroyed at the airfields. The American public was outraged. President Franklin Roosevelt asked Congress to declare war on Japan immediately, and the United States entered World War II. This unequivocal response was certainly due to the nature of the provocation. American soil had not been attacked by a foreign power since the occupation of Washington, D.C., by the British in 1814.

The United States was the only major participating country to emerge from World War II with its economy intact, and even strengthened. Britain, France, Germany, Italy, Japan, the Soviet Union, and several minor participants in the war were economically

BRITISH PRIME MINISTER, Winston Churchill, U.S. President Franklin Roosevelt, and Soviet leader Joseph Stalin met at Yalta from February 4 to 11, 1945, to resolve their differences over the shape that the international community would take after World War II. (Library of Congress Prints & Photographs Division, Washington, D.C. [LC-USZ62-7449])

devastated. The United States was also the only country to have control over operational nuclear weapons. President Harry Truman had made the decision to use two atomic bombs, on August 6 and August 9, 1945, to end the war with Japan. (Historians still argue over the necessity of this action, which ultimately killed more than 100,000 Japanese and left an equal number permanently injured.) The United States truly had become the world's superpower.

The Cold War. The United States had become an uncomfortable ally of the Soviet Union after Adolf Hitler's invasion of that country. Soon after World War II ended, relations between the Soviet Union and the West deteriorated. The Soviet Union wanted a weakened Germany, and to achieve this, it insisted that Germany be divided in two, with East Germany becoming a buffer against the West. Little by little, the Soviet Union helped install communist governments in Eastern European countries, which began to be referred to collectively as the **Soviet bloc.** In response, the United States encouraged the rearming of Western Europe. The **Cold War** had begun.[4]

In Fulton, Missouri, on March 5, 1946, Winston Churchill, in a striking metaphor, declared that from the Baltic to the Adriatic Sea "an iron curtain has descended across the [European] continent." The term **iron curtain** became even more appropriate when Soviet-dominated East Germany built a wall separating East Berlin from West Berlin in August 1961.

Containment Policy. In 1947, a remarkable article was published in *Foreign Affairs*. The article was signed by "X." The actual author was George F. Kennan, chief of the policy-planning staff for the State Department. The doctrine of **containment** set forth in the article became—according to many—the bible of Western foreign policy. The author, "X," argued that whenever and wherever the Soviet Union could successfully challenge the West, it would do so. He recommended that our policy toward the Soviet Union be "firm and vigilant containment of Russian expansive tendencies."[5]

The containment theory was expressed clearly in the **Truman Doctrine**, which was enunciated by President Harry Truman in his historic address to Congress on March 12, 1947. In that address, he announced that the United States must help countries in which a communist takeover seemed likely. Later that year, he backed the Marshall Plan, an economic assistance plan for Europe that was intended to prevent the expansion of communist influence there. By 1950, the United States had entered into a military alliance with the European nations commonly called the North Atlantic Treaty Organization (NATO). The combined military power of the United States and the European nations worked to contain Soviet influence to Eastern Europe and to maintain a credible response to any Soviet military attack on Western Europe. Figure 18–1 shows the face-off between the U.S.–led NATO alliance and the Soviet-led Warsaw Pact.

SUPERPOWER RELATIONS

During the Cold War, there was never any direct military conflict between the United States and the Soviet Union. Rather, confrontations among "client" nations were used to carry out the policies of the superpowers. Only on occasion did the United States directly enter a conflict in a significant way. Two such occasions were in Korea and in Vietnam.

Soviet Bloc
The Soviet Union and the Eastern European countries that installed communist regimes after World War II and were dominated by the Soviet Union.

Cold War
The ideological, political, and economic confrontation between the United States and the Soviet Union following World War II.

Iron Curtain
The term used to describe the division of Europe between the Soviet bloc and the West; coined by Winston Churchill.

Containment
A U.S. diplomatic policy adopted by the Truman administration to contain communist power within its existing boundaries.

Truman Doctrine
The policy adopted by President Harry Truman in 1947 to halt communist expansion in southeastern Europe.

---

[4]See John Lewis Gaddis, *The United Nations and the Origins of the Cold War* (New York: Columbia University Press, 1972).
[5]X, "The Sources of Soviet Conduct," *Foreign Affairs*, July 1947, p. 575.

FIGURE 18–1 Europe during the Cold War

This map shows the face-off between NATO (led by the United States) and the Soviet bloc (the Warsaw Pact). Note that France was out of NATO from 1966 to 1996, and Spain did not join until 1982.

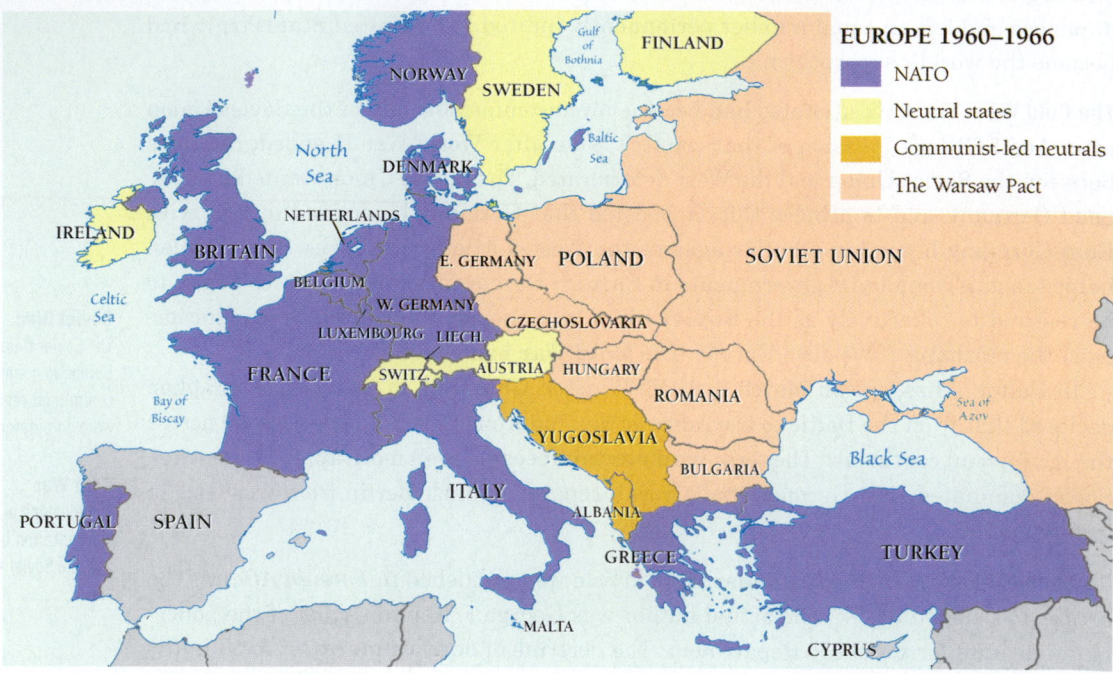

After the end of World War II, northern Korea was occupied by the Soviet Union, and southern Korea was occupied by the United States. The result was two rival Korean governments. In 1950, North Korea invaded South Korea. Under United Nations authority, the United States entered the war, which prevented an almost certain South Korean defeat. When U.S. forces were on the brink of conquering North Korea, however, China joined the war on the side of the North, resulting in a stalemate. An armistice signed in 1953 led to the two Koreas that exist today. U.S. forces have remained in South Korea ever since.

The Vietnam War (1964–1975) also involved the United States in a civil war between a communist North Vietnam and pro-Western South Vietnam. When the French army in Indochina was defeated by the communist forces of Ho Chi Minh and the two Vietnams were created in 1954, the United States assumed the role of supporting the South Vietnamese government against North Vietnam. President John Kennedy sent 16,000 "advisers" to help South Vietnam, and after Kennedy's death in 1963, President Lyndon B. Johnson greatly increased the scope of that support. More than 500,000 American troops were in Vietnam at the height of the U.S. involvement. More than 58,000 Americans were killed and 300,000 were wounded in the conflict. A peace agreement in 1973 allowed U.S. troops to leave the country, and in 1975 North Vietnam easily occupied Saigon (the South Vietnamese capital) and unified the nation. The debate over U.S. involvement in Vietnam became extremely heated and, as mentioned previously, spurred congressional efforts to limit the ability of the president to commit forces to armed combat. The military draft was also a major source of contention during the Vietnam War.

The Cuban Missile Crisis. Perhaps the closest the two superpowers came to a nuclear confrontation was the Cuban missile crisis in 1962. The Soviets installed missiles in Cuba, 90 miles off the U.S. coast, in response to Cuban fears of an American invasion and to try to balance an American nuclear advantage. President Kennedy and his advisers rejected the option of invading Cuba and set up a naval blockade around the island instead. When Soviet vessels appeared near Cuban waters, the tension reached its height. After intense negotiations between Washington and Moscow, the Soviet ships turned around on October 25, and on October 28, the Soviet Union announced the withdrawal of its missile operations from Cuba. In exchange, the United States agreed not to invade Cuba in the future and to remove some of its own missiles that were located near the Soviet border in Turkey.

A Period of *Détente*. The French word ***détente*** means a relaxation of tensions. By the end of the 1960s, it was clear that some efforts had to be made to reduce the threat of nuclear war between the United States and the Soviet Union. The Soviet Union gradually had begun to catch up in the building of strategic nuclear delivery vehicles in the form of bombers and missiles, thus balancing the nuclear scales between the two countries. Each nation acquired the military capacity to destroy the other with nuclear weapons.

As the result of lengthy negotiations under Secretary of State Henry Kissinger and President Nixon, the United States and the Soviet Union signed the **Strategic Arms Limitation Treaty (SALT I)** in May 1972. That treaty "permanently" limited the development and deployment of antiballistic missiles (ABMs) and limited the number of offensive missiles each country could deploy. To further reduce tensions, new scientific and cultural exchanges were arranged with the Soviets, as well as new opportunities for Jewish emigration out of the Soviet Union.

The policy of *détente* was not limited to the U.S. relationship with the Soviet Union. Seeing an opportunity to capitalize on increasing friction between the Soviet Union and the People's Republic of China, Kissinger secretly began negotiations to establish a new relationship with that nation. President Nixon eventually visited China in 1972. The visit set the stage for the formal diplomatic recognition of that country, which occurred during the Carter administration (1977–1981).

The Reagan–Bush Years. President Ronald Reagan took a hard line against the Soviet Union during his first term, proposing the strategic defense initiative (SDI), or "Star Wars," in 1983. The SDI was designed to serve as a space-based defense against enemy missiles. Reagan and others in his administration argued that the program would deter nuclear war by shifting the emphasis of defense strategy from offensive to defensive weapons systems.

In November 1985, however, President Reagan and Mikhail Gorbachev, the Soviet leader, began to work on an arms reduction compact. The negotiations resulted in a historic agreement signed by Reagan and Gorbachev in Washington, D.C., on December 8, 1987. The terms of the Intermediate-Range Nuclear Force (INF) Treaty, which was ratified by the Senate, required the superpowers to dismantle a total of 4,000 intermediate-range missiles within the first three years of the agreement.

Beginning in 1989, President George H. W. Bush continued the negotiations with the Soviet Union to reduce the number of nuclear weapons and the number of armed troops in Europe. Subsequent events, including developments in Eastern Europe, the unification of Germany, and the dissolution of the Soviet Union (in December 1991), changed the world order. American and other Western leaders now worked to find and control the weapons that had formerly been in the inventory of the Soviet Union. Agreements were signed with Russia and with other former Soviet republics to reduce the weapons threat.

The Dissolution of the Soviet Union. After the fall of the Berlin Wall in 1989, it was clear that the Soviet Union had relinquished much of its political and military control over the states of Eastern Europe that formerly had been part of the Soviet bloc. Figure 18–2 shows the current alliances in Europe. No one expected the Soviet Union to dissolve into separate states as quickly

Détente
A French word meaning a relaxation of tensions. The term characterized U.S.-Soviet relations as they developed under President Richard Nixon and Secretary of State Henry Kissinger.

Strategic Arms Limitation Treaty (SALT I)
A treaty between the United States and the Soviet Union to stabilize the nuclear arms competition between the two countries. SALT I talks began in 1969, and agreements were signed on May 26, 1972.

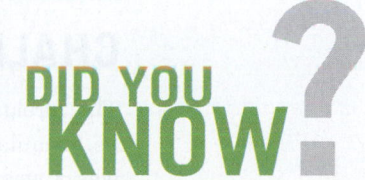

DID YOU KNOW?

That Russia suffered more battle deaths in putting down the rebellion in Chechnya than the Soviet Union experienced in its decades-long attempt to subdue Afghanistan?

FIGURE 18–2 Europe after the Fall of the Soviet Union

This map shows the growth in European unity as marked by the participation in transnational organizations. The United States continues to lead NATO (and would be orange if it were on this map). Note the reunification of Germany and the creation of new states from former Yugoslavia and the former Soviet Union.

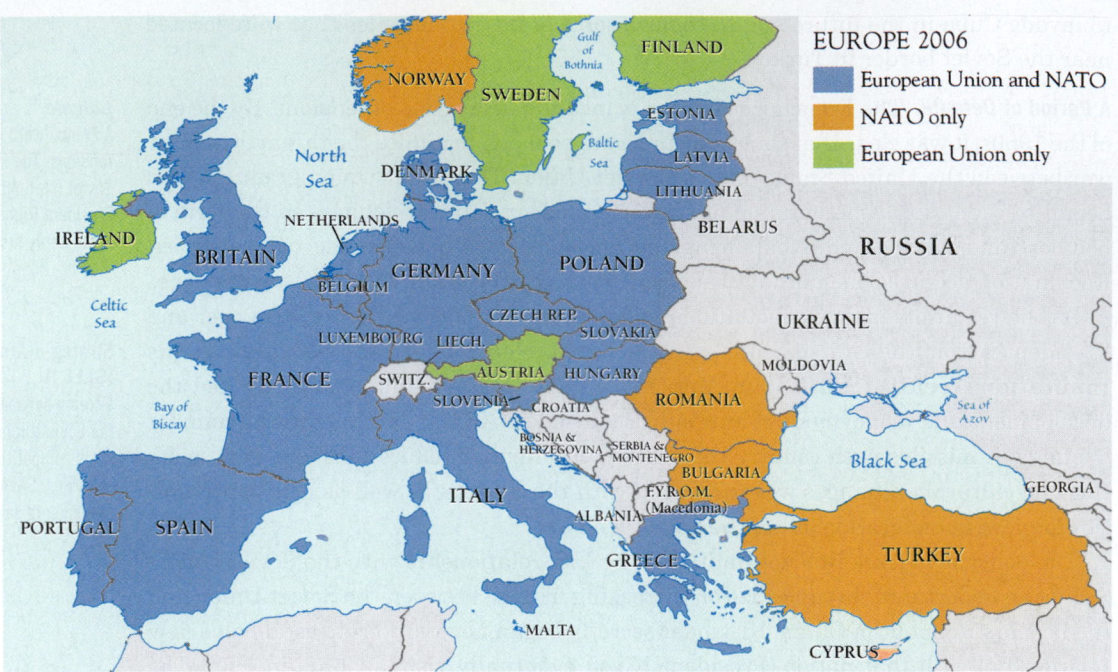

as it did, however. Though Gorbachev tried to adjust the Soviet constitution and political system to allow greater autonomy for the republics within the union, demands for political, ethnic, and religious autonomy grew. Since 1991, Russia has struggled to develop a democratic system of government. Boris Yeltsin, president of Russia from 1991 to 1999, attempted to lead needed reforms of the government and electoral system. In 2000, Yeltsin, whose health was failing, named Vladimir Putin as acting president. After completing his terms as an elected president, Putin became the premier of Russia in 2008.

Although Putin has claimed that Russia's most important task is to "develop as a free and democratic state," his actions belie his words. Throughout his time in office, he has slowly but surely limited freedom of the press and freedom of speech. Most strangely, quite a few opposition journalists have been murdered in Russia with no arrests for their assassins. In addition, he has reduced the number of political offices that are filled by free elections. Some argue that without the huge revenues that the Russian government is obtaining as a result of the high price of oil, Putin would face popular discontent and would be unable to carry out his antidemocratic actions.[6]

CHALLENGES IN WORLD POLITICS

The foreign policy of the United States, whether moralistic, realistic, or both, must be formulated to deal with world conditions. Early in its history, the United States was a weak, new nation facing older nations well equipped for world domination. In the 21st century, the United States faces different challenges. Now it must devise foreign and defense policies that will enhance its security in a world in which it is the

[6]Martha Brill Olcott, "Vladimir Putin and Russia's Oil Policy," Carnegie Moscow Center, Issue 1, 2005.

global superpower and has no equal. Among the challenges that must be faced are the growth of new economic and military powers, the threat of terrorism, war in Iraq and Afghanistan, the proliferation of nuclear weapons, and numerous regional conflicts, including the ongoing violence in the Middle East.

THE EMERGING WORLD ORDER

From 1945 until 1989, the world watched as two superpowers, the United States and the Soviet Union, dueled for power in the world. Both nations had their allies and fought wars through their surrogates. Both nations built up huge arsenals of nuclear weapons and were militarily prepared to destroy each other and the world itself. After the Berlin Wall fell in 1989, the entire Soviet bloc disintegrated with surprising speed. East Germany, one of the strongest allies of the Soviet Union, merged with West Germany to become one nation, democratic and capitalistic. The United States was quick to establish strong relationships with Estonia, Latvia, and Lithuania, the three Baltic states that were occupied by the Soviet Union after World War II. All of the other Eastern bloc nations became truly independent states, and the Soviet Union was divided into Russia and several other states that are part of the Russian Federation.

The U.S. military and U.S. nuclear scientists worked closely with their Russian counterparts to account for the nuclear arsenal of the Soviet Union and to try to control these weapons. For a time, as Russia held democratic elections, U.S. political consultants were hired to help Russian candidates market their campaigns just as in the United States. Moscow quickly developed into a major capital with luxury shops and condominiums. Russia supported the U.S. war against terrorism, even as it fought terrorists within Chechnya.

After the Persian Gulf War in 1991, it was clear that the American military was the finest in the world and that U.S. advances in technology and weaponry were far superior to those of any other nation. What this meant was that the United States was the sole military global superpower. Under the Clinton administration, the Pentagon tried to plan for a post–Cold War world. What should be the objectives of the nation in terms of national security? How should the military be structured? How many wars should the United States be equipped to handle at one time? What kinds of intelligence gathering would now be important if the Soviets were no longer a threat? All of these questions and more needed to be answered in terms of American foreign and national security policy.

The Clinton administration, with the approval of Congress, began to change the size and scope of the American military. By 2001, the active-duty military was one-third less than it had been in 1990, dropping from 2.1 million in 1989 to 1.4 million in 1999.[7] Fewer appropriations were made to build new ships and acquire new equipment. The Central Intelligence Agency was ordered to focus more on economic intelligence and less on military intelligence. However, the United States continued to lead NATO and maintain this military alliance of European nations. Russia objected on the grounds that this alliance was no longer needed. Instead, many of the former Soviet bloc nations, beginning with Poland, expressed interest in joining NATO and, by 2008, the alliance included the 27 members who joined at the beginning of or before the fall of the Soviet Union, as well as the Czech Republic, Hungary, Poland, Bulgaria, Estonia, Latvia, Lithuania, Romania, Slovakia, and Slovenia, all former allies of Russia.

[7]Edward F. Bruner, "Military Forces: What is the Appropriate Size for the United States?" *Congressional Research Service Report for Congress*, updated February 10, 2005.

At the same time, other developments in the world challenged American policy. The European Union became a single economic unit, competing with American exports around the world. China began to become an economic force in the world and, a few years later, India followed suit. By 2008, China was a major trading partner of the United States and, with its newly generated cash, a major holder of the securities of the U.S. government. China became a major military power as well, with nuclear weapons and missile capabilities. Other nations such as Brazil and Australia became important economic players in the world.

By 2001, when terrorists attacked the World Trade Center in New York, the United States was focused more on economic growth and economic competition in the world. The United States military was prepared for crisis situations and technologically sophisticated warfare, but not for a long engagement on the ground. The wars in Iraq and Afghanistan have drained our military resources. One of the questions that Americans must face in the future is whether to plan for strengthening the military to face global threats or to place our hopes in a more peaceful world.

THE THREAT OF TERRORISM

Dissident groups, rebels, and other revolutionaries have long engaged in terrorism to gain attention and to force their enemies to the bargaining table. Over the last two decades, however, terrorism has increasingly threatened world peace and the lives of ordinary citizens.

Terrorism and Regional Strife. Terrorism can be a weapon of choice in regional or domestic strife. The conflict in the Middle East between Israel and the Arab states is an example. Until recently, the conflict had been lessened by a series of painfully negotiated agreements between Israel and some of the Arab states. Those opposed to the peace process, however, have continued to disrupt the negotiations through assassinations, mass murders, and bomb blasts in the streets of major cities within Israel. Other regions have also experienced terrorism. In September 2004, terrorists acting on behalf of Chechnya, a breakaway republic of Russia, seized a school at Beslan in the nearby Russian republic of North Ossetia. In the end, at least 330 people—most of them children—were dead.

In Colombia, the Farc terrorist group, supported in some part by the Venezuelan president, Hugo Chavez, continues to capture civilians, both Colombians and foreigners, and hold them as hostages. By the spring of 2008, more than 700 hostages were being held in the jungle, including a former candidate for president, Ingrid Betancourt, and at least three Americans. President Chavez of Venezuela assisted in getting two hostages released in January 2008 and four former legislators released one month later. Betancourt, the Americans, and several other hostages were freed on July 13, 2008, in a daring raid conducted by the Colombian army. Hundreds of hostages are still being held, some for ransom and others to exchange for Farc guerrillas who have been arrested and imprisoned.[8]

Terrorist Attacks against Foreign Civilians. In other cases, terrorist acts are planned against civilians of foreign nations traveling abroad to make an international statement. One of the most striking attacks was that launched by Palestinian terrorists against Israeli athletes at the Munich Olympics in 1972, during which 11 athletes were murdered. Other attacks have included ship and airplane hijackings, as well as bombings of embassies. For example, in 1998, terrorist bombings of two American embassies in Africa killed 257 people, including 12 Americans, and injured more than 5,500 others.

---

[8]"Colombian Hostages Freed by Farc," *BBC News*, February 28, 2008, www.bbbc.co.uk.

September 11. In 2001, terrorism came home to the United States in ways that few Americans could have imagined. In a well-coordinated attack, 19 terrorists hijacked four airplanes and crashed three of them into buildings—two into the World Trade Center towers in New York City and one into the Pentagon in Washington, D.C. The fourth airplane crashed in a field in Pennsylvania, after the passengers fought the hijackers. Why did the al Qaeda network plan and launch attacks on the United States? Apparently, the leaders of the network, including Osama bin Laden, were angered by the presence of U.S. troops on the soil of Saudi Arabia, which they regard as sacred. They also saw the United States as the primary defender of Israel against the Palestinians and as the defender of the royal family that governs Saudi Arabia. The attacks were intended to so frighten and demoralize the American people that they would convince their leaders to withdraw American troops from the Middle East.

London Bombings. On July 7, 2005, terrorists carried out synchronized bombings of the London Underground (subway) and bus network. Four suicide bombers, believed to have been of Middle Eastern descent, claimed the lives of 52 people and wounded hundreds more in the attacks. On July 21, a second group of bombers attempted to carry out a similar plot, but no one was killed. Following the attacks, security was heightened in Britain and elsewhere (including New York City).

In August 2006, British authorities foiled a plot to bring down 10 planes scheduled to leave London's Heathrow Airport for the United States. If successful, it would have been the largest terrorist attack since September 11. The alleged bombers planned to blow up the airplanes with liquid chemicals that could be combined to make a bomb. The chemicals were to be carried onboard in containers for bottled water and other ordinary liquids, mixed together on the plane, and then ignited using triggers installed in what appeared to be MP3 players and other small electronic devices. After the suspects were arrested, the London airport was shut down, flights to the United States were canceled, and travel by air was extremely difficult in England for a few days. Travel in the United States was severely disrupted, too, as carry-on luggage was given extra screening.

THE WAR ON TERRORISM

After September 11, President George W. Bush implemented stronger security measures to protect homeland security and U.S. facilities and personnel abroad. The president sought and received congressional support for heightened airport security, new laws allowing greater domestic surveillance of potential terrorists, and new funding for the military. The Bush administration has also conducted two military efforts as part of the war on terrorism.

Military Responses. The first military effort was directed against al Qaeda camps in Afghanistan and the Taliban regime, which had ruled that country since 1996. In late 2001, after building a coalition of international allies and anti-Taliban rebels within Afghanistan, the United States defeated the Taliban and fostered the creation of an interim government that did not support terrorism. However, by 2008, it was clear that the Taliban were still active in the mountainous regions of the nation, and attacks on coalition forces were escalating.

Then, during 2002 and early 2003, the U.S. government turned its attention to the threat posed by Saddam Hussein's government

The wreckage of a bus with its seats open to the elements and its roof blown off after an explosion in London in 2005. Nearby, simultaneous explosions rocked the London subway and a double-decker bus during the morning rush hour, causing 52 deaths and sending bloodied victims fleeing from debris-strewn blast sites. (AP Photo/ Sang Tan/FILE)

in Iraq. (The war in Iraq and the subsequent occupation of that country will be discussed in detail later in this chapter under "The Iraq Wars.")

A New Kind of War. Terrorism has posed a unique challenge for U.S. foreign policy makers. The Bush administration's response was unique. In September 2002, President Bush enunciated what has since become known as the "Bush doctrine," or the doctrine of preemption:

> We will . . . [defend] the United States, the American people, and our interests at home and abroad by identifying and destroying the threat before it reaches our borders. While the United States will constantly strive to enlist the support of the international community, we will not hesitate to act alone, if necessary, to exercise our right of self-defense by acting preemptively against such terrorists, to prevent them from doing harm against our people and our country.[9]

The concept of "preemptive war" as a defense strategy is a new element in U.S. foreign policy. The concept is based on the assumption that in the war on terrorism, self-defense must be *anticipatory*. As President Bush stated on March 17, 2003, just before launching the invasion of Iraq, "Responding to such enemies only after they have struck first is not self-defense, it is suicide."

The Bush doctrine was not without its critics. Some pointed out that preemptive wars against other nations have traditionally been waged by dictators and rogue states—not democratic nations. By employing such tactics, the United States would seem to be contradicting its basic values. In his campaign for president, Barack Obama repudiated this approach to national security policy and, in the first year of his presidency, made a number of speeches abroad in which he signaled a new, more conciliatory approach to other nations.

THE IRAQ WARS

On August 2, 1990, the Persian Gulf became the setting for a major challenge to the international system set up after World War II (1939–1945). President Saddam Hussein of Iraq sent troops into the neighboring oil sheikdom of Kuwait, occupying that country. This was the most clear-cut case of aggression against an independent nation in half a century.

The Persian Gulf—The First Gulf War. At the formal request of the king of Saudi Arabia, American troops were dispatched to set up a defensive line at the Kuwaiti border. After the United Nations (UN) approved a resolution authorizing the use of force if Saddam Hussein did not respond to sanctions, the U.S. Congress reluctantly also approved such an authorization. On January 17, 1991, two days after a deadline for Hussein to withdraw, U.S.–led coalition forces launched a massive air attack on Iraq. After several weeks, the ground offensive began. Iraqi troops retreated from Kuwait a few days later, and the First Gulf War ended, although many Americans criticized President George H. W. Bush for not sending troops to Baghdad to depose Saddam Hussein.

As part of the cease-fire that ended the Gulf War, Iraq agreed to abide by all UN resolutions and to allow UN weapons inspectors to search for and oversee the destruction of its medium-range missiles and all weapons of mass destruction, including any chemical and nuclear weapons, and related research facilities. Economic sanctions were to be imposed on Iraq until the weapons inspectors finished their work. In 1999, however, Iraq placed so many obstacles in the path of the UN inspectors that they withdrew from the country.

---

[9]George W. Bush, September 17, 2002. The full text of the document from which this statement is taken can be accessed at www.whitehouse.gov/nsc/nssall.html.

The Iraq War. After the terrorist attacks on the United States on September 11, 2001, President George W. Bush called Iraq and Saddam Hussein part of an "axis of evil" that threatened world peace. In 2002 and early 2003, Bush called for a "regime change" in Iraq and began assembling an international coalition that might support further military action in Iraq.

Having tried and failed to convince the UN Security Council that the UN should take action to enforce its resolutions, Bush decided to create a coalition of 35 other nations, including Britain, to join the United States to invade Iraq. Within three weeks, the coalition forces had toppled Hussein's decades-old dictatorship and were in control of Baghdad and most of the other major Iraqi cities.

The process of establishing order and creating a new government in Iraq turned out to be extraordinarily difficult, however. In the course of the fighting, the Iraqi army, rather than surrendering, disbanded itself. Soldiers simply took off their uniforms and made their way home. As a result, the task of maintaining law and order fell on the shoulders of a remarkably small coalition expeditionary force that faced disorder across the nation. Saddam Hussein was found and later tried and executed by an Iraqi court for crimes against the Kurdish people, but that did not stop the insurgent resistance movement against the coalition forces.

Occupied Iraq. The people of Iraq are divided into three principal groups by ethnicity and religion. The Kurdish-speaking people of the north, who had in practice been functioning as an American-sponsored independent state since the First Gulf War, were overjoyed by the invasion. The Arabs adhering to the Shiite branch of Islam live principally in the south and constitute a majority of the population. The Shiites were glad that Saddam Hussein, who had murdered many thousands of Shiites, was gone. They were deeply skeptical of U.S. intentions, however. The Arabs belonging to the Sunni branch of Islam live in the center of the country, west of Baghdad. Although the Sunnis constituted only a minority of the population, they had controlled the government under Hussein. Many of them considered the occupation to be a disaster. Figure 18–3 shows the distribution of major ethnic and religious groups in Iraq.

The Situation Worsens. In April 2004, four non-Iraqi civilian security personnel were murdered in the Sunni city of Fallujah, and their bodies were publicly defiled. U.S. Marines entered the city to locate and arrest the perpetrators. In the months and years that followed, sectarian violence between the various ethnic and religious groups continued. Some sectors of Iraq fell under the control of local clerics such as Muqtada al Sadr, who had his own militia.

To make matters worse, in May 2004, graphic photographs were published showing that U.S. guards at Abu Ghraib prison in Baghdad had subjected prisoners to physical and sexual abuse.

While coalition forces were able to maintain control of the country, they were now suffering monthly casualties comparable to those experienced during the initial invasion. Casualties continued to increase in the years that followed, and the unpopularity of the war among the American people dragged President Bush's approval rating to historic lows.

The Continuing Insurgency. Certainly, establishing a stable Iraqi government did prove difficult, particularly because of the problems with Sunni participation.

By 2007, it was clear that al Qaeda terrorist cells were also participating in the attacks both against coalition forces and the emerging Iraqi government. In spring 2007, President Bush and his commanders in the field requested additional troops for a "surge" of military activity to defeat the insurgency. Although many in Congress and

FIGURE 18–3 Ethnic/Religious Groups in Iraq

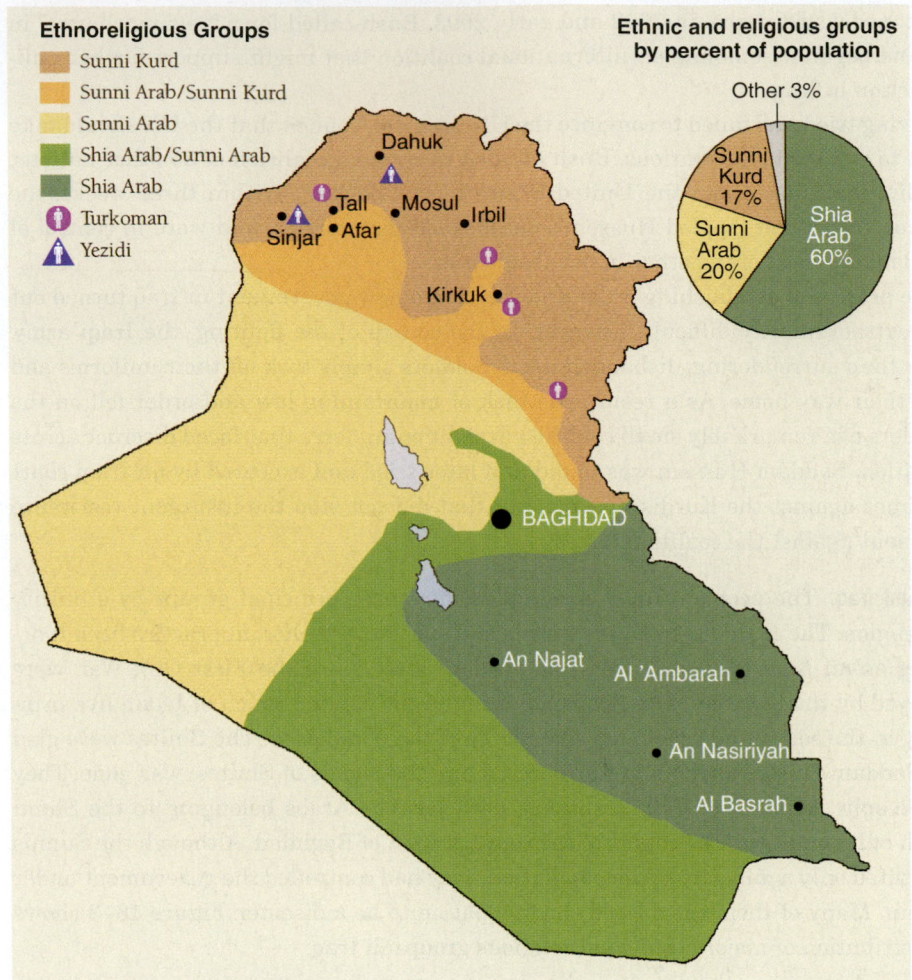

the public did not believe that the surge would be successful, by late 2007, violence in many parts of Iraq had decreased, and the Iraqi military forces were taking the lead in operations against the insurgents. By 2009, it was clear that the new strategy, which encouraged field commanders to establish good relations with local leaders who helped root out insurgents, had worked and the Iraqi government continued to strengthen its control over the nation.

While the Bush administration stood firm in its commitment to defeating the insurgents in 2008 and made few promises of bringing the troops home, the question of how to exit Iraq was a major issue in the primary campaigns. By the time that President Obama was inaugurated, the success of the surge made the creation of a reasonable timetable for Americans to leave Iraq possible. However, the situation in Afghanistan began to worsen as the Taliban regrouped in the provinces and corruption spread through the government. President Obama had campaigned on the premise that Afghanistan was a "necessary" war, so he was faced, in 2009, with a serious decision on how to proceed with the American mission in that nation. After several months of internal discussions, the administration agreed to a type of "surge" in Afghanistan and a planned beginning to withdrawal in 2011. Policy seemed to be in disarray, however, in 2010, when the commanding officer, General Stanley McChrystal, was fired and General David Petraeus was asked to take over the situation in the theater of war.

NUCLEAR WEAPONS

In 1945, the United States was the only nation to possess nuclear weapons. Several nations quickly joined the "nuclear club," however, including the Soviet Union in 1949, Great Britain in 1952, France in 1960, and China in 1964. Few nations have made public their nuclear weapons programs since China's successful test of nuclear weapons in 1964. India and Pakistan, however, detonated nuclear devices within a few weeks of each other in 1998, and North Korea conducted an underground nuclear explosive test in October 2006. Several other nations are suspected of possessing nuclear weapons or the capability to produce them in a short time.

The United States and the Soviet Union. More than 32,000 nuclear warheads are known to be stocked worldwide, although the exact number is uncertain, because some countries do not reveal the extent of their nuclear stockpiles. Although the United States and Russia have dismantled some of their nuclear weapons systems since the end of the Cold War and the dissolution of the Soviet Union in 1991, both still retain sizable nuclear arsenals. Even more troublesome is nuclear proliferation—that is, the development of nuclear weapons by additional nations.

Nuclear Proliferation. The United States has attempted to influence late arrivals to the nuclear club through a combination of rewards and punishments. In some cases, the United States has promised aid to a nation to gain cooperation. In other cases, such as those of India and Pakistan, it has imposed economic sanctions as a punishment for carrying out nuclear tests. In the end, Pakistan demonstrated its ability to explode nuclear bombs in 1998. Despite the United States' disagreement with these countries, President Bush signed a new nuclear pact with India in March 2006.

In 1999, President Bill Clinton presented the Comprehensive Nuclear Test Ban Treaty to the Senate for ratification. The treaty, formed in 1996, prohibits all nuclear test explosions worldwide and established a global network of monitoring stations. Ninety-three nations have ratified the treaty. Among those that have not are China, Israel, India, and Pakistan. In a defeat for the Clinton administration, the U.S. Senate rejected the treaty in 1999.

The United States has suspected for some time that nations such as North Korea and Iran might supply nuclear materials to terrorists or to nations that want to have nuclear capability. In addition, Israel is known to possess more than 100 nuclear warheads. South Africa developed six nuclear warheads in the 1980s but dismantled them in 1990. In 2003, Libya announced that it was abandoning a secret nuclear weapons program. Also, since the dissolution of the Soviet Union in 1991, the security of its nuclear arsenal has declined. There have been reported thefts, smugglings, and illicit sales of nuclear material from the former Soviet Union in the past 15 years.

For years, the United States, the European Union, and the UN have tried to prevent Iran from becoming a nuclear power. Today, though, many observers believe that Iran has already developed nuclear capability or is close to doing so. Continued diplomatic attempts to at least slow down Iran's quest for a nuclear bomb have proved ineffectual at best.

With nuclear weapons, materials, and technology available worldwide, it is conceivable that terrorists could develop a nuclear device and use it in a terrorist act. In fact, a U.S. federal indictment filed in 1998, after the attack on the American embassies in Kenya and Tanzania, charged Osama bin Laden and his associates with trying to buy components for a nuclear bomb "at various times" since 1992.

DID YOU KNOW?

That including the Civil War, more than one million Amerian soldiers have been killed in the nation's wars?

REGIONAL CONFLICTS

The United States has played a role—sometimes alone, sometimes with other powers—in many regional conflicts during the 1990s and 2000s.

Cuba. Tensions between the United States and Cuba have frequently erupted since Fidel Castro took power in Cuba in 1959. Relations with Cuba continue to be politically important in the United States, because the Cuban American population can influence election outcomes in Florida, a state that all presidential candidates try to win. When Fidel Castro became seriously ill and underwent surgery in the summer of 2006, his brother, Raul, temporarily assumed power. In 2008, Fidel named his brother as his official successor. Although no major changes have occurred in relationships with the United States, Raul Castro immediately legalized cell phones for Cuban citizens. Other reforms in Cuban society seem likely, although no one knows when relations with the United States might be normalized.

Beyond Our Borders

CHINA: A SUPERPOWER UNDER THE SPOTLIGHT

China has experienced rapid economic growth for the last 30 years and today is one of the world's great economic powers. Adjusted for purchasing power, China's gross domestic product (GDP) is now second only to that of the United States and is almost double that of Japan. This fact does not mean that all Chinese are rich. Per capita income in China is well below that of the United States and Europe.

Between 2001 and 2007, China's industrial output increased by almost 50 percent. China now produces more steel than America and Japan combined. Such rapid growth requires massive amounts of raw materials. China consumes 40 percent of the world's output of cement, for example. China's growing demand for raw materials has contributed to dramatic increases in the world prices of many commodities, including oil. Although the worldwide recession of 2008–2009 had some impact on China's economy, mostly because consumers in Western nations purchased fewer Chinese exports, the Chinese economy held steady throughout the entire period.

CHINA'S ECONOMIC PROSPECTS

Goldman Sachs, a U.S. investment firm, has projected that China's GDP will surpass that of the United States by 2039, making China's economy the largest in the world. In fact, this projection may underestimate China's prospects, because it uses substantially lower growth rates than the actual rates China has posted during the last 30 years.

CHINESE-AMERICAN RELATIONS

Since Richard Nixon's visit to China in 1972, American policy has been to gradually engage the Chinese in diplomatic and economic relationships in the hope of turning the nation in a more pro-Western direction. In 1989, however, when Chinese students engaged in extraordinary demonstrations against the government, the Chinese government crushed the demonstrations, killing several students and protesters and imprisoning others. The result was a distinct chill in Chinese-American relations.

After initially criticizing the administration of George H. W. Bush (served 1989–1993) for not being hard enough on China, President Bill Clinton came around to a policy of diplomatic outreach to the Chinese. An important reason for this change was the large and growing trade ties between the two countries. China was granted *most-favored-nation status* for tariffs and trade policy on a year-to-year basis. In 2001, Congress granted China permanent **Normal Trade Relations (NTR) status**, thus endorsing China's admission to the World Trade Organization (WTO). For a country that is officially communist, China already permits a striking degree of free enterprise, and the rules China must follow as a WTO member will further increase the role of the private sector in China's economy.

Normal Trade Relations (NTR) Status
A status granted through an international treaty by which each member nation must treat other members at least as well as it treats the country that receives its most favorable treatment. This status was formerly known as most-favored-nation status.

In recent years, China did support the American efforts against terrorists but did not support the war in Iraq. Although the two nations have had diplomatic differences, China has joined the six-party talks, working with the United States, Japan, Russia, South Korea, and North Korea to negotiate with North Korea to end its pursuit of nuclear weapons.

CHINA IN THE SPOTLIGHT

In 2008, China became the center of world attention. First, an enormous earthquake struck the area near Chengdu, causing thousands of deaths and billions of dollars of destruction. For the first time since World War II, the Chinese government chose to be open to the media and to allow foreign journalists to report the tragedy. The Chinese government used every resource possible to help the people in the region and to encourage truthful reporting. The openness shown by China in this situation may well have been related to China's pride in hosting the 2008 Olympics in Beijing. Although already an economic and military superpower, the Chinese government and the Chinese people placed a great deal of importance on enhancing the nation's standing in the world by producing the most successful Olympic games ever seen.

THE CITY OF SHANGHAI, China, is known for its beautiful skyline. New buildings are constructed each year in this growing metropolis. (Image copyright Eclaudio zaccherini 2010. Used under license from Shutterstock.com)

FOR CRITICAL ANALYSIS

1. Can China truly be recognized as a superpower if it does not become more democratic?
2. What are some of the issues involving trade that have tarnished China's image in recent years?

Israel and the Palestinians. As a longtime supporter of Israel, the United States has undertaken to persuade the Israelis to negotiate with the Palestinian Arabs who live in the territories occupied by the state of Israel. The conflict, which began in 1948, has been extremely difficult to resolve. The internationally recognized solution is for Israel to yield the West Bank and the Gaza Strip to the Palestinians in return for effective security commitments and abandonment by the Palestinians of any right of return to Israel proper. Unfortunately, the Palestinians have been unable to stop all terrorist attacks on Israel, and Israel has been unwilling to dismantle all of its settlements in the occupied territories. Furthermore, the two parties have been unable to come to an agreement on how much of the West Bank should go to the Palestinians and on what compensation (if any) the Palestinians should receive for abandoning all claims to settlement in Israel proper.

In December 1988, the United States began talking directly to the Palestine Liberation Organization (PLO), and in 1991, under great pressure from the United States, the Israelis opened talks with representatives of the Palestinians and other Arab states. In 1993, both parties agreed to set up Palestinian self-government in the West Bank and the Gaza Strip. The historic agreement, signed in Cairo on May 4, 1994, put in place a process by which the Palestinians would assume self-rule in the Gaza Strip and in the town of Jericho. In the months that followed, Israeli troops withdrew from much of the occupied territory, the new Palestinian Authority assumed police duties, and many Palestinian prisoners were freed by the Israelis.

The Collapse of the Israeli–Palestinian Peace Process. Although negotiations between the Israelis and the Palestinians resulted in more agreements in Oslo, Norway, in 2000, the agreements were rejected by Palestinian radicals, who began a campaign of suicide bombings in Israeli cities. In 2002, the Israeli government responded by moving tanks and troops into Palestinian towns to kill or capture the terrorists. One result of the Israeli reoccupation was an almost complete collapse of the Palestinian Authority. Groups such as Hamas (the Islamic Resistance Movement), which did not accept the concept of peace with Israel even in principle, moved into the power vacuum.

TO PROTECT ISRAELI civilians from terrorism, Israel has built a wall to separate Palestinian settlements from Jewish neighborhoods. (© Picture Contact BV/Alamy)

In 2003, President Bush attempted to renew Israeli-Palestinian negotiations by sponsoring a "road map" for peace. First, the road map called for an end to terrorism by the Palestinians. Later, it held out hopes for a Palestinian state alongside Israel. In its weakened condition, however, the Palestinian Authority was unable to make any commitments, and the road map process ground to a halt. In February 2004, Israeli Prime Minister Ariel Sharon announced a plan under which Israel would withdraw from the Gaza Strip regardless of whether a deal could be reached with the Palestinians. Sharon's plan met with strong opposition within his own political party, but ultimately the withdrawal took place.

After the death of Palestinian leader Yasir Arafat in 2004, a moderate prime minister was elected. In January 2006, however, the militant group Hamas won a majority of the seats in the Palestinian legislature. American and European politicians hoped that after it became part of the legitimate government, Hamas would agree to rescind its avowed desire to destroy Israel, but so far, it has not done so.

Wars and AIDS in Africa. The continent of Africa presents many extremely serious challenges to the United States and the rest of the world. Many African nations are still underdeveloped, with enormous health problems and unstable regimes. Tribal rivalries lead to civil wars and, in the worst cases, genocide. The United States has worked with the United Nations to try to end conflicts and improve the situation on the continent.

During the early 2000s, the disease AIDS (acquired immune deficiency syndrome) spread throughout southern Africa. This disease infects one-fourth of the populations of Botswana and Zimbabwe and is endemic in most other nations in the southernmost part of the continent. Millions of adults are dying from AIDS, leaving orphaned children. The epidemic is taking a huge economic toll on the affected countries because of the cost of caring for patients and the loss of skilled workers. The disease may be the greatest single threat to world stability emanating from Africa. The Bush administration put in place a special aid package directed at this problem amounting to $15 billion over five years.

The year 1994 brought disaster to the African nation of Rwanda. Following the death of that country's president, members of the Hutu tribe launched a campaign of genocide against the Tutsi tribe. More than half a million people were killed in a matter of weeks. The genocide campaign ended abruptly as a Tutsi guerrilla force, sponsored by neighboring Uganda, overthrew the Rwandan government. A large number of Hutus then fled from Rwanda. The United States played almost no part in this crisis until small military and civilian contingents were sent to assist the Hutu refugees.

That the United States invaded and occupied part of Russia in 1919?

In Angola, wars dating back as far as 1961 ended in 2002 with the death of rebel leader Jonas Savimbi, who had received U.S. support for several years in the 1970s. In 1996, civil war broke out in Zaire (now named the Democratic Republic of the Congo; also known as Congo-Kinshasa). Rebels were aided by Rwandan and Ugandan forces, while Angolan and Zimbabwean forces entered the country to support the government. The civil war officially ended in 2002, and a coalition government was established in 2003. Several million deaths, primarily due to disease and malnutrition, have been attributed to the war. At the present time, more than 17,000 United Nations peacekeepers are trying to keep the coalition government stabilized.

In 2004, the world woke up to a growing disaster in Darfur, a western province of Sudan. In the spring of 2004, Sudan had reached a tenuous agreement with rebels in the southern part of the country, but the agreement did not cover a separate rebellion in Darfur. Government-sponsored militias drove more than a million inhabitants of Darfur from their homes and into refugee camps, where they faced starvation. Despite a cease-fire, fighting renewed during the summer of 2006 and continued to plague the region.

WHO MAKES FOREIGN POLICY?

Given the vast array of challenges in the world, developing a comprehensive U.S. foreign policy is a demanding task. Does this responsibility fall to the president, to Congress, or to both acting jointly? There is no easy answer to this question, because, as constitutional authority Edwin S. Corwin once observed, the U.S. Constitution created an "invitation to struggle" between the president and Congress for control over the foreign policy process. Let us look first at the powers given to the president by the Constitution.

CONSTITUTIONAL POWERS OF THE PRESIDENT

The Constitution confers on the president broad powers that are either explicit or implied in key constitutional provisions. Article II vests the executive power of the government in the president. The presidential oath of office given in Article II, Section 1, requires that the president "solemnly swear" to "preserve, protect and defend the Constitution of the United States."

War Powers. In addition, and perhaps more importantly, Article II, Section 2, designates the president as "Commander in Chief of the Army and Navy of the United States." Starting with Abraham Lincoln, all presidents have interpreted this authority dynamically and broadly. Since George Washington's administration, the United States has been involved in at least 125 undeclared wars that were conducted under presidential authority. For example, in 1950, Harry Truman ordered U.S. armed forces in the Pacific to counter North Korea's invasion of South Korea. Dwight Eisenhower threatened China and North Korea with nuclear weapons if the Korean peace talks were not successfully concluded. Bill Clinton sent troops to Haiti and Bosnia. In 2001, George W. Bush authorized an attack against the al Qaeda terrorist network and the Taliban government in Afghanistan. As described earlier, in 2003, after receiving

DISPLACED CHILDREN in Kalma camp near Nyala in South Darfur wait in the shade while their mother works in nearby fields for income. This work is very dangerous, as relief workers report that women who venture from the camps are often targets of Jingaweit attacks, including rape and murder. Why have the continued killings in Darfur not created more outrage throughout the world? (Photo courtesy of USAID)

authorization to use force from Congress, Bush sent military forces to Iraq to destroy Saddam Hussein's government.

Treaties and Executive Agreements. Article II, Section 2, of the Constitution also gives the president the power to make treaties, provided that two-thirds of the senators present concur. Presidents usually have been successful in getting treaties through the Senate. In addition to this formal treaty-making power, the president uses executive agreements (discussed in Chapter 13). Since World War II (1939–1945), executive agreements have accounted for almost 95 percent of the understandings reached between the United States and other nations.

Executive agreements have a long and important history. During World War II, Franklin Roosevelt reached several agreements with the Soviet Union and other countries. One agreement with long-term results was concluded at Yalta in the Soviet Crimea. In other important agreements, Presidents Eisenhower, Kennedy, and Johnson all promised support to the government of South Vietnam. In all, since 1946, more than 8,000 executive agreements with foreign countries have been made. There is no way to obtain an accurate count, because perhaps as many as several hundred of these agreements have been secret.

Other Constitutional Powers. An additional power conferred on the president in Article II, Section 2, is the right to appoint ambassadors, other public ministers, and consuls. In Section 3 of that article, the president is given the power to recognize foreign governments by receiving their ambassadors.

INFORMAL TECHNIQUES OF PRESIDENTIAL LEADERSHIP

Other broad sources of presidential power in the U.S. foreign policy process are tradition, precedent, and the president's personality. The president can employ a host of informal techniques that give the White House overwhelming superiority within the government in foreign policy leadership.

First, the president has access to information. The Central Intelligence Agency (CIA), the State Department, and the Defense Department make more information available to the president than to any other governmental official. This information carries with it the ability to make quick decisions—and the president uses that ability often. Second, the president is a legislative leader who can influence the funds that are allocated for different programs. Third, the president can influence public opinion. President Theodore Roosevelt once made the following statement:

> People used to say to me that I was an astonishingly good politician and divined what the people are going to think. ... I did not "divine" how the people were going to think; I simply made up my mind what they ought to think and then did my best to get them to think it.[10]

Presidents are without equal with respect to influencing public opinion, partly because of their ability to command the media. Depending on their skill in appealing to patriotic sentiment (and sometimes fear), they can make people believe that their course in foreign affairs is right and necessary. Public opinion often seems to be impressed by the president's decision to make a national commitment abroad. President George W. Bush's speech to Congress shortly after the September 11 attacks rallied the nation and brought new respect for his leadership. It is worth noting that presidents normally, although certainly not always, receive the immediate support of the American people in a foreign policy crisis.

Finally, the president can commit the nation morally to a course of action in foreign affairs. Because the president is the head of state and the leader of one of the most powerful nations on earth, once the president has made a commitment for the United States, it is difficult for Congress or anyone else to back down on that commitment.

DID YOU KNOW?

That it is estimated that the Central Intelligence Agency has more than 16,000 employees, with about 5,000 in the clandestine services?

OTHER SOURCES OF FOREIGN POLICY MAKING

In addition to the president, there are at least four foreign policy-making sources within the executive branch: (1) the Department of State, (2) the National Security Council, (3) the intelligence community, and (4) the Department of Defense.

The Department of State. In principle, the State Department is the executive agency that has primary authority over foreign affairs. It supervises U.S. relations with the more than 200 independent nations around the world and with the United Nations and other multinational groups, such as the Organization of American States. It staffs embassies and consulates throughout the world. It has about 32,000 employees. This number may sound impressive, but it is small compared with, say, the 67,000 employees of the Department of Health and Human Services. Also, the State Department had an annual budget of only $9.1 billion in fiscal year 2009, one of the smallest budgets of the Cabinet departments.

Newly elected presidents usually tell the American public that the new secretary of state is the nation's chief foreign policy adviser. Nonetheless, the State Department's preeminence in foreign policy has declined since World War II. The State Department's image within the White House Executive Office and Congress (and even with foreign governments) is quite poor—a slow, plodding, bureaucratic maze of inefficient, indecisive individuals. Reportedly, Premier Nikita Khrushchev of the Soviet Union urged President John F. Kennedy to formulate his own views rather than rely on State Department officials who, according to Khrushchev, "specialized in why something had not worked forty years ago."[11] In any event, since the days of Franklin Roosevelt, the State Department has often been bypassed or ignored when crucial decisions are made.

[10]Sidney Warren, *The President as World Leader* (New York: McGraw-Hill, 1964), p. 23.
[11]Theodore C. Sorensen, *Kennedy* (New York: Harper & Row, 1965), pp. 554–555.

POLITICS WITH A **purpose**

Think Tanks

Why is the price of gasoline so high? What is the effect of the demand for oil from emerging markets like China? Should the United States empty out its Strategic Petroleum Reserves to combat the low production from oil-producing nations?[a] Would that have a detrimental effect on our ability to respond should we need to send troops and ships into a military situation? Can the United States meet the oil price crisis alone, or would a coalition of nations have more influence on oil producers?

Policy makers need experts to help them answer these questions, and they often turn to think tanks for this expertise. Former State Department adviser Richard Haass called the influence of these "idea factories" "among the most important and least appreciated."[b] Emerging at the beginning of the 20th century, think tanks were named for the small rooms in which research scientists and military strategists plotted the conduct of World War II. They have proliferated; more than 2,000 of these organizations are based in the United States alone. Most are nonprofit and nonpartisan, although many advocate particular ideological perspectives. Some are so-called legacy organizations, like the Carter Center, the Hoover Institute, or the Nixon Center for Peace and Freedom. Some are attached to universities, like the Harvard Kennedy School, and some are independent, like the RAND Corporation.[c] Throughout the 1960s and 1970s, advocacy think tanks emerged, such as the conservative Heritage Foundation (1973) and the libertarian Cato Institute (1977), named for the libertarian pamphlets written during the American Revolution.[d]

In addition to governments' seeking ideas from think tanks, there is a revolving door between think tanks and government.[e] Many U.S. government officials have worked for think tanks, often after having served as officials in previous presidential administrations. For example, Zbigniew Brzezinski, who was President Carter's national security adviser, is a counselor for the Center for Strategic and International Studies. Lee Feinstein has been a senior fellow for U.S. Foreign Policy and International Law at the Council on Foreign Relations and was a senior official in President Clinton's Department of State. James Baker was the secretary of state under George H. W. Bush and now is the honorary head of the James A. Baker III Institute for Public Policy at Rice University.[f] Aside from providing personnel for executive branch policy positions, think tanks also try to influence opinion through publications, press releases, opinion editorials (op-eds), and media appearances.

Returning to the questions posed earlier about rising oil prices, in a 2006 op-ed in the *Washington Times*, an analyst for RAND argued that the United States has little control over oil prices and that the government should encourage alternative fuels such as ethanol and increase supply by opening up drilling in the protected Arctic National Wildlife Reserve (ANWR),[g] a move opposed by some environmental groups. Similarly, in 2008, representatives from the Cato Institute recommended drilling in ANWR as well as opening up federally protected land in the Mountain West to oil

shale development. Cato also advocates draining the Strategic Petroleum Reserves, arguing that threats to our national security from worldwide oil embargoes against us are exaggerated.[h] While the American Enterprise Institute places the "blame" for high oil prices on increased demand from emerging markets,[i] George Soros (whose foundation has funded several advocacy groups and think tanks) has argued the cause involves the complex relationship among competing and complicated factors.[j] As the Obama administration made appointments to powerful positions in national security and defense, scholars and commentators from several think tanks moved into the administration, while other Republican-connected or more conservative thinkers moved back to the private sector.

[a]The Strategic Petroleum Reserves is a large stockpile of emergency petroleum, controlled by the U.S. Department of Energy, created after the 1973–1974 oil embargo. www.fossil.energy.gov/programs/reserves/#Strategic%20 Petroleum%20Reserve, accessed June 4, 2008.
[b]Richard Haass, "Think Tanks and U.S. Foreign Policy: A Policy-Maker's Perspective," *U.S. Foreign Policy Agenda, An Electronic Journal of the U.S. Department of State*, Vol. 7, 2000, pp. 5–8, accessed June 1, 2008, at http://usinfo.state.gov/journals/itps/1102/ijpe/ijpe1102.pdf.
[c]Donald E. Abelson, "Think Tanks and U.S. Foreign Policy: An Historical View," *U.S. Foreign Policy Agenda, An Electronic Journal of the U.S. Department of State*, Vol. 7, 2000, pp. 9–12.
[d]www.cato.org/about.php, accessed June 5, 2008.
[e]*U.S. Foreign Policy Agenda, An Electronic Journal of the U.S. Department of State*, Vol. 7, 2000, pp. 39–40, accessed June 1, 2008, at http://usinfo.state.gov/journals/itps/1102/ijpe/ijpe1102.pdf.

[f]*Ibid.*
[g]www.rand.org/commentary/051906WT.html.
[h]www.cato.org/pub_display.php?pub_id=9438.
[i]www.aei.org/publications/pubID.27426,filter.all/pub_detail.asp.
[j]He argues that subsidies foreign countries place on their production of oil, the profit margins on oil exploration and development, and speculative buying on world commodities markets have all driven the price of oil upward. www.salon.com/tech/htww/2008/06/03/soros_oil_bubble_2/, accessed June 3, 2008.

Negative Constituents
Citizens who openly oppose the
government's policies.

It is not surprising that the State Department has been overshadowed in foreign policy. It has no natural domestic constituency as does, for example, the Department of Defense, which can call on defense contractors for support. Instead, the State Department has what might be called **negative constituents**—U.S. citizens who openly oppose the government's policies. One of the State Department's major functions, administering foreign aid, often elicits criticisms. There is a widespread belief that the United States spends much more on foreign aid than it actually does. For 2007, President Bush's budget request allocated $25 billion to foreign economic aid, or about 88 cents for every 100 dollars of federal spending.

The National Security Council. The job of the National Security Council (NSC), created by the National Security Act of 1947, is to advise the president on the integration of "domestic, foreign, and military policies relating to the national security." Its larger purpose is to provide policy continuity from one administration to the next. As it has turned out, the NSC—consisting of the president, the vice president, the secretaries of state and defense, the director of emergency planning, and often the chairperson of the joint chiefs of staff and the director of the CIA—is used in just about any way the president wants to use it.

The role of national security adviser to the president seems to adjust to fit the player. Some advisers have come into conflict with heads of the State Department. Henry A. Kissinger, Nixon's flamboyant and aggressive national security adviser, rapidly gained ascendancy over William Rogers, the secretary of state. More recently, Condoleezza Rice played an important role as national security adviser during George W. Bush's first term. Rice eventually became secretary of state.

The Intelligence Community. No discussion of foreign policy would be complete without some mention of the **intelligence community**. This consists of the 40 or more government agencies or bureaus that are involved in intelligence activities. They are as follows:

Intelligence Community
The government agencies that gather
information about the capabilities and
intentions of foreign governments or that
engage in covert actions.

1. Central Intelligence Agency (CIA)
2. National Security Agency (NSA)
3. Defense Intelligence Agency (DIA)
4. Offices within the Department of Defense
5. Bureau of Intelligence and Research in the Department of State

6. Federal Bureau of Investigation (FBI)
7. Army intelligence
8. Air force intelligence
9. Drug Enforcement Administration (DEA)
10. Department of Energy
11. Directorate of Information Analysis and Infrastructure Protection in the Department of Homeland Security
12. Office of the Director of National Intelligence

The CIA, created as part of the National Security Act of 1947, is the lead organization of the intelligence community.

Covert Actions. Intelligence activities consist mostly of overt information gathering, but covert actions also are undertaken. Covert actions, as the name implies, are carried out in secret, and the American public rarely finds out about them. The CIA covertly aided in the overthrow of the Mossadegh regime of Iran in 1953 and the Arbenz government of Guatemala in 1954. The agency was instrumental in destabilizing the Allende government in Chile from 1970 to 1973.

During the mid-1970s, the "dark side" of the CIA was partly uncovered when the Senate undertook an investigation of its activities. One of the major findings of the Senate Select Committee on Intelligence was that the CIA had routinely spied on American citizens domestically—supposedly a prohibited activity. Consequently, the CIA was scrutinized by oversight committees within Congress, which restricted the scope of its operations. By 1980, however, the CIA had regained much of its lost power to engage in covert activities.

Criticisms of the Intelligence Community. By 2001, the CIA had come under fire for several lapses, including the discovery that one of its agents was spying on behalf of a foreign power, the failure to detect the nuclear arsenals of India and Pakistan, and, above all, the failure to obtain advance knowledge about the September 11 terrorist attacks. With

AN AERIAL VIEW of the Pentagon, the headquarters of the U.S. Department of Defense (DoD), located between the Potomac River and Arlington National Cemetery. The Pentagon employs approximately 23,000 military and civilian personnel and is one of the world's largest office buildings, with three times the floor space of the Empire State Building in New York City. In the background, the obelisk of the Washington Monument is visible. When the media refer to The Pentagon, what do they mean? (Johnny Bivera, U.S. Navy)

the rise of terrorism as a threat, the intelligence agencies have received more funding and enhanced surveillance powers, but these moves have also provoked fears of civil liberties violations. In 2004, the bipartisan September 11 Commission called for a new intelligence czar to oversee the entire intelligence community, with full control of all agency budgets. After initially balking at this recommendation, President Bush eventually called for a partial implementation of the commission's report. Legislation enacted in 2004 established the Office of the Director of National Intelligence to oversee the intelligence community. In 2005, Bush appointed John Negroponte to be the first director. In 2009, President Obama named the fourth director in five years to the position. It seemed apparent that infighting with the CIA chief and other national security advisers makes this a very difficult position to hold.

The Department of Defense. The Department of Defense (DoD) was created in 1947 to bring all of the various activities of the American military establishment under the jurisdiction of a single department headed by a civilian secretary of defense. At the same time, the joint chiefs of staff, consisting of the commanders of the various military branches and a chairperson, was created to formulate a unified military strategy.

Although the Department of Defense is larger than any other federal department, it declined in size after the fall of the Soviet Union in 1991. In the subsequent 10 years, the total number of civilian employees was reduced by about 400,000, to about 665,000. Military personnel were also reduced in number. The defense budget remained relatively flat for several years, but with the advent of the war on terrorism and the use of military forces in Afghanistan and Iraq, funding has again been increased.

CONGRESS BALANCES THE PRESIDENCY

A new interest in the balance of power between Congress and the president on foreign policy questions developed during the Vietnam War (1964–1975). Sensitive to public frustration over the long and costly war and angry at Richard Nixon for some of his other actions as president, Congress attempted to establish limits on the power of the president in setting foreign and defense policy. In 1973, Congress passed the War Powers Resolution over President Nixon's veto. The act limited the president's use of troops in military action without congressional approval (see Chapter 13). Most presidents, however, have not interpreted the "consultation" provisions of the act as meaning that Congress should be consulted before military action is taken. Instead, Presidents Ford, Carter, Reagan, George H. W. Bush, and Clinton ordered troop movements and then informed congressional leaders. Critics note that it is quite possible for a president to commit troops to a situation from which the nation could not withdraw without incurring heavy losses, whether or not Congress is consulted.

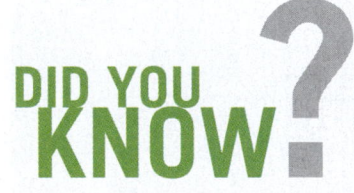

DID YOU KNOW?

That in the name of national security, the United States spends at least $5.6 billion annually to keep information classified?

Congress has also exerted its authority by limiting or denying presidential requests for military assistance to various groups (such as Angolan rebels and the government of El Salvador) and requests for new weapons (such as the B-1 bomber). In general, Congress has been far more cautious in supporting the president in situations in which military involvement of American troops for a long period of time is possible. Like most members of the American public, members of Congress do not want to see American troops in harm's way unnecessarily.

Congress has its limits, of course, and often these are based on political considerations about election campaigns. Prior to the 2006 elections, Democrats found that antiwar platforms could be very effective during their campaigns. Certainly, the Iraq War and the future foreign policy direction of the United States were very important issues in the presidential and congressional elections of 2008; however, when the Democratic

Party won control of the Congress and the presidency in 2008, it then assumed leadership of our national security policy. As is normally the case, the party of the president tends to support the commander in chief even when its members may have personal doubts about the use of military force.

DOMESTIC SOURCES OF FOREIGN POLICY

The making of foreign policy is often viewed as a presidential prerogative because of the president's constitutional power in that area and the resources of the executive branch that the president controls. Foreign policy making is also influenced by various other sources, however, including elite and mass opinion and the *military-industrial complex*, described in a following section.

ELITE AND MASS OPINION

Public opinion influences the making of U.S. foreign policy through several channels. Elites in American business, education, communications, labor, and religion try to influence presidential decision making through several strategies. A number of elite organizations, such as the Council on Foreign Relations and the Trilateral Commission, work to increase international cooperation and to influence foreign policy through conferences, publications, and research. The members of the American elite establishment also exert influence on foreign policy through the general public by encouraging debate about foreign policy positions, publicizing the issues, and using the media.

Generally, the efforts of the president and the elites are most successful with the segment of the population called the **attentive public** . This sector of the mass public, which probably constitutes 10 to 20 percent of all citizens, is more interested in foreign affairs than are most other Americans, and members of the attentive public are likely to transmit their opinions to the less interested members of the public through conversation and local leadership.

Attentive Public
That portion of the general public that pays attention to policy issues.

DID YOU KNOW?

That the Pentagon's stockpile of strategic materials includes 1.5 million pounds of quartz crystals used in pre–Great Depression radios and 150,000 tons of tannin used in tanning cavalry saddles?

THE MILITARY-INDUSTRIAL COMPLEX

Civilian fear of the relationship between the defense establishment and arms manufacturers (the **military-industrial complex**) dates back many years. During President Eisenhower's eight years in office, the former five-star general of the army experienced firsthand the kind of pressure that could be brought against him and other policy makers by arms manufacturers. Eisenhower decided to give the country a solemn and—as he saw it—necessary warning of the consequences of this influence. On January 17, 1961, in his last official speech, he said:

Military-Industrial Complex
The mutually beneficial relationship between the armed forces and defense contractors.

> In the councils of government, we must guard against the acquisition of unwarranted influence, whether sought or unsought, by the military-industrial complex. The potential for the disastrous rise of misplaced power exists and will persist. . . . Only an alert and knowledgeable citizenry can compel the proper meshing of the huge industrial and military machinery of defense with our peaceful methods and goals, so that security and liberty may prosper together.[12]

The Pentagon has supported a large sector of our economy through defense contracts. It has also supplied retired army officers as key executives to large defense-contracting firms. Perhaps the Pentagon's strongest allies have been members of Congress whose

[12]*Congressional Almanac* (Washington, DC: Congressional Quarterly Press, 1961), pp. 938–939.

districts or states benefit economically from military bases or contracts. After the Cold War ended in the late 1980s, the defense industry looked abroad for new customers. Sales of some military equipment to China raised serious issues for the Clinton administration. The war on terrorism provoked a new debate about what types of weaponry would be needed to safeguard the nation in the future. When President George W. Bush proposed legislation in 2002 to increase the Defense Department's budget substantially, weapons manufacturers looked forward to increased sales and profits.

YOU CAN MAKE A Difference

WORKING FOR HUMAN RIGHTS

In many countries throughout the world, human rights are not protected. In some nations, people are imprisoned, tortured, or killed because they oppose the current regime. In other nations, certain ethnic or racial groups are oppressed by the majority population. Monks in Myanmar, lawyers in Pakistan, food rioters in Bangladesh, Egypt, and Haiti, and women activists in Iran have all landed on the front pages of our newspapers in the past year, fighting for the basic human rights of millions of people in the world. More than 200,000 people in Darfur alone have died since 2003, as a direct result of the Sudanese government's actions to displace an entire population.

STUDENT MEMBER of Amnesty International. (© Kathy deWitt/ Alamy)

WHY SHOULD YOU CARE?

The strongest reason for involving yourself with human rights issues in other countries is simple moral altruism—unselfish regard for the welfare of others. The defense of human rights is unlikely to put a single dollar in your pocket. A broader consideration, however, is that human rights abuses are often associated with the kind of dictatorial regimes that are likely to provoke wars. To the extent that the people of the world can create a climate in which

human rights abuses are unacceptable, they may also create an atmosphere in which national leaders believe that they must display peaceful conduct generally. This, in turn, might reduce the frequency of wars, some of which could involve the United States. Fewer wars would mean preserving peace and human life, not to mention reducing the financial burden of warfare.

WHAT CAN YOU DO?

What can you do to work for the improvement of human rights in other nations? One way is to join an organization that attempts to keep watch over human rights violations. Two such organizations are listed at the end of this feature, and several support student chapters on college campuses. By publicizing human rights violations, such organizations try to pressure nations into changing their practices. Sometimes, these organizations are able to apply enough pressure and cause enough embarrassment that victims may be freed from prison or allowed to emigrate.

Another way to work for human rights is to keep informed about the state of affairs in other nations and to write personally to governments that violate human rights or to their embassies, asking them to cease these violations.

If you want to receive general information about the position of the United States on human rights violations, you can contact the State Department:

U.S. Department of State
Bureau of Democracy, Human Rights, and Labor
2201 C St. NW
Washington, DC 20520
202-647-4000
www.state.gov/g/drl/hr

The following organizations are well known for their watchdog efforts in countries that violate human rights for political reasons:

Amnesty International U.S.A.
5 Penn Plaza
New York, NY 10001
212-807-8400
www.amnestyusa.org

American Friends Service Committee
1501 Cherry St.
Philadelphia, PA 19102
215-241-7000
www.afsc.org

KEY TERMS

attentive public 649
Cold War 627
containment 627
defense policy 622
détente 629
diplomacy 621
economic aid 621
foreign policy 621
foreign policy process 622

intelligence community 646
iron curtain 627
**isolationist foreign
   policy** 625
**military-industrial
   complex** 649
Monroe Doctrine 625
moral idealism 623
national security policy 622

negative constituents 646
**Normal Trade Relations
   (NTR) status** 639
political realism 624
Soviet bloc 627
**Strategic Arms Limitation
   Treaty (SALT I)** 629
technical assistance 621
Truman Doctrine 627

CHAPTER SUMMARY

1. **What should be the goals of American foreign policy?** Foreign policy includes national goals and the techniques used to achieve them. National security policy, which is one aspect of foreign policy, is designed to protect the independence and the political and economic integrity of the United States. Diplomacy involves the nation's external relationships and is an attempt to resolve conflict without resort to arms. U.S. foreign policy is sometimes based on moral idealism and sometimes on political realism. The goals of U.S. foreign policy have shifted over the two centuries of the nation's existence as our place in global affairs also changed from minor ex-colony to superpower.

2. Three major themes have guided U.S. foreign policy. In the early years of the nation, isolationism was the primary strategy. With the start of the 20th century, isolationism gave way to global involvement. From the end of World War II through the 1980s, the major goal was to contain communism and the influence of the Soviet Union.

3. During the 1800s, the United States had little international power and generally stayed out of European conflicts and politics, and so these years have been called the period of isolationism. The Monroe Doctrine of 1823 stated that the United States would not accept foreign intervention in the Western Hemisphere and would not meddle in European affairs. The United States pursued an actively expansionist policy in the Americas and the Pacific area, however.

4. The end of the policy of isolationism toward Europe started with the Spanish-American War of 1898. U.S. involvement in European politics became more extensive when the United States entered World War I on April 6, 1917. World War II marked a lasting change in American foreign policy. The United States was the only major country to emerge from the war with its economy intact and the only country with operating nuclear weapons.

5. Soon after the close of World War II, the uncomfortable alliance between the United States and the Soviet Union ended, and the Cold War began. A policy of containment, which assumed an expansionist Soviet Union, was enunciated in the Truman Doctrine. Following the frustrations of the Vietnam War and the apparent arms equality of the United States and the Soviet Union, the United States adopted a policy of *détente*. Although President Reagan took a tough stance toward the Soviet Union during his first term, his second term saw serious negotiations toward arms reduction, culminating in the signing of the Intermediate-Range Nuclear Force Treaty in 1987. After the fall of the Soviet Union, Russia emerged as a less threatening state and signed the Strategic Arms Reduction Treaty with the United States in 1992. The United States and Russia have agreed on some issues in recent years, such as the fight against terrorism, but have disagreed on other matters, such as the war against Iraq in 2003.

6. After the dissolution of the Soviet Union, the United States assumed the position of global superpower without a military competitor. However, the United States has maintained the NATO alliance with its European

allies and has added several former Soviet bloc states to the alliance. Russia has remained a powerful nation, one that is becoming increasingly a one-party state. The European Union continues to increase its influence as an economic superpower and competitor to the United States, while the rapidly developing economies of India and China continue to push those nations into the global power structure.

7. Terrorism has become a major challenge facing the United States and other nations. The United States waged war on terrorism after the September 11 attacks. U.S. armed forces occupied Afghanistan in 2001 and Iraq in 2003.

? 8. **Can nuclear weapons be eliminated from the world?** Nuclear proliferation continues to be an issue as a result of the breakup of the Soviet Union and loss of control over its nuclear arsenal, along with the continued efforts of other nations to gain nuclear warheads. More than 32,000 nuclear warheads are known to exist worldwide. The United States is a signatory to the Nuclear Non-proliferation Treaty and the Comprehensive Test Ban Treaty and works actively with other nations to reduce the threat of nuclear arms. Recently, the United States and Russia signed a treaty to further reduce each nation's supply of nuclear missiles.

9. Ethnic tensions and political instability in many regions of the world provide challenges to the United States. In the Caribbean, Cuba requires American attention because of its proximity. Civil wars have torn apart Rwanda and other countries. The Middle East continues to be a hotbed of conflict despite efforts to continue the peace process. In 1991 and again in 2003, the United States sent combat troops to Iraq. The Second Gulf War in 2003 succeeded in toppling the decades-long dictatorship in Iraq.

10. **Who formulates foreign policy: the president, the bureaucracy, or Congress?** The formal power of the president to make foreign policy derives from the U.S. Constitution, which designates the president as commander in chief of the army and navy. Presidents have interpreted this authority broadly. They also have the power to make treaties and executive agreements. In principle, the State Department is the executive agency with primary authority over foreign affairs. The National Security Council also plays a major role. The intelligence community consists of government agencies engaged in activities varying from information gathering to covert operations. In response to presidential actions in the Vietnam War, Congress attempted to establish some limits on the power of the president to intervene abroad by passing the War Powers Resolution in 1973.

SELECTED PRINT, MEDIA, AND ONLINE RESOURCES

PRINT RESOURCES

Chomsky, Noam, and Gilbert Achcar. *Perilous Power: The Middle East and U.S. Foreign Policy Dialogues on Terror, Democracy, War, and Justice.* Boulder, CO: Paradigm, 2006. Chomsky is one of the most vocal critics of U.S. foreign policy, and he shows it in the essays in this book. Achcar is a specialist in Middle Eastern affairs who has lived in the region. These authors examine key questions relating to terrorism, conspiracies, democracy, anti-Semitism, and anti-Arab racism. This book can serve as an introduction to understanding the Middle East today.

Hoffmann, Stanley. *Chaos and Violence: What Globalization, Failed States, and Terrorism Mean for U.S. Foreign Policy.* Lanham, MD: Rowman & Littlefield, 2006. What is the proper place of the United States in a world that has been defined by the terrorist acts of September 11, 2001? What are the ethics of intervention, and what is the morality of human rights? These are questions the author answers. He also attempts to show how our broken relationship with Europe can be repaired. He believes that America has engaged in too much unilateralism.

Hook, Steven W. *U.S. Foreign Policy: The Paradox of World Power,* 3rd ed. Washington, DC: CQ Press, 2010. In his third edition of this survey of American foreign policy, Hook adds the first two years of the Obama administration and its initiatives in foreign policy to his account.

Kang, David. *China Rising: Peace, Power, and Order in East Asia.* New York: Columbia University Press, 2007. Kang examines the history of China and suggests that the ascendance of China to great power status is not a destabilizing force in the world, but that the Chinese rise to power will be peaceful and an asset to other Asian nations.

O'Hanlon, Michael, and Mike M. Mochizuki. *Crisis in the Korean Peninsula: How to Deal with a Nuclear North Korea.* New York: McGraw-Hill, 2003. The authors provide a comprehensive introduction to the dangers posed by North Korea, which could become a greater threat to world peace than the current terrorist movements. They also offer a possible "grand bargain" to defuse the crisis.

Power, Samantha. *A Problem from Hell: America and the Age of Genocide.* New York: HarperCollins, 2007. This well-known former journalist, who is now the executive director of Harvard's Carr Center for Human Rights, looks at U.S. responses to genocide in Rwanda, Darfur, and other areas of the world during the last century. She argues that U.S. intervention has been woefully inadequate.

Ricks, Thomas E. *The Gamble: General David Petraeus and the American Military Adventure in Iraq, 2006–2008.* New York: Penguin Press, 2009. In 2007, Ricks released *Fiasco: The American Military Adventure in Iraq, 2003 to 2005.* This was one of the most well received and scathing accounts of disastrous U.S. policies and practices in that country and became a number-one *New York Times* best seller. In *The Gamble,* Ricks returns to Iraq to find out whether America's new counterinsurgency strategy can rescue a seemingly impossible situation.

Zakaria, Fareed. *The Post-American World.* New York: W. W. Norton, 2008. Zakaria, a *Newsweek* editor and television commentator, does not write about the decline of America, but about the rise of other nations, especially China and India. An optimist despite the current terror crisis, Zakaria contends that the world is richer and more peaceful than it has ever been and that these trends are likely to continue. He concludes with a critique of the U.S. foreign policy process, which he believes is designed for partisan battles rather than problem solving.

MEDIA RESOURCES

Black Hawk Down—This 2002 film recounts the events in Mogadishu, Somalia, in October 1993, during which two U.S. Black Hawk helicopters were shot down. The film, which is based on reporter Mark Bowden's best-selling book by the same name, contains graphic scenes of terrifying urban warfare.

The Fall of Milosevic—A highly acclaimed 2003 documentary by Norma Percy and Brian Lapping, this film covers the final years of the crisis in former Yugoslavia, including the war in Kosovo and the fall of Slobodan Milosevic, the Serb nationalist leader and alleged war criminal. Except for Milosevic, almost all top Serb and Albanian leaders are interviewed, as are President Bill Clinton and British prime minister Tony Blair.

The 50 Years War—Israel and the Arabs—This is a two-volume PBS Home Video released in 2000. More balanced than some accounts, this film includes interviews with many leaders involved in the struggle, including (from Israel) Yitzhak Rabin, Shimon Peres, Benjamin Netanyahu, and Ariel Sharon; (from the Arab world) Egypt's Anwar al-Sadat, Jordan's King Hussein, and Yasir Arafat; and (from the United States) Presidents Jimmy Carter, George H. W. Bush, and Bill Clinton.

The Hurt Locker—This Academy Award–winning film traces the work of an American bomb squad in Iraq and brings home the intensity of these soldiers' work in identifying Iraqi attackers.

No End in Sight: Iraq's Descent into Chaos—Packed with interviews of officials, generals, and soldiers, this 2007 film argues that insufficient troop levels, the disbanding of Iraq's army, and the dismantling of the Iraqi government led to the insurgency and chaos that have bedeviled the country. *No End in Sight* is a shocking portrait of arrogance and incompetence, laced with terrifying war footage.

Senator Obama Goes to Africa—A documentary of Barack Obama's 2006 trip to Kenya, South Africa, and Chad. Despite the many questions Americans have had about Barack Obama, he has been more open about his unusual past than most politicians. One source of information is this film, which shows some of the advantages and disadvantages of Obama's international fame. In the end, he can do little about the suffering that he sees.

United 93—A 2006 documentary about the fourth airplane hijacked on 9/11. When they learned the fate of the other three planes through cell phones, the passengers decided to fight back, with the result that the flight crashed in a Pennsylvania field, far from its intended target. *United 93* takes places in real time and is almost unbearably moving. Several critics named it the best film of the year.

ONLINE RESOURCES

Arms Control Association a national nonpartisan membership organization dedicated to promoting public understanding of and support for effective arms control policies. The Web site of the ACA lists each country's status in terms of signing arms control treaties and its inventory of weapons: http://www.armscontrol.org

Brookings a nonprofit public policy organization based in Washington, D.C. Access the research reports of this think tank: www.brookings.edu

Center for Security Studies (CSS) an academic institute at ETH Zurich specialized in research, teaching, and the provision of services in international and national security policy. Provides information about human rights, national security, and other issues from a European point of view: http://www.css.ethz.ch/index_EN

Central Intelligence Agency created in 1947 with the signing of the National Security Act by President Harry S. Truman. Learn more about this independent agency responsible for providing national security intelligence to senior U.S. policy makers: www.cia.gov

Freedom House an organization that promotes its vision of democracy around the world and rates all nations on their democratic practices: www.freedomhouse.org

U.S. Department of State provides access to hundreds of Web sites on foreign and defense policies of the U.S. government and the governments of other nations and includes information about visas, passports, and individual countries: www.state.gov

19

The Alamo in San Antonio symbolizes the state's rich political history. (Larry Brownstein/Getty Images)

Texas History and Culture

QUESTIONS TO CONSIDER

What action did female, African American, and Latino Texans take to change the state laws that relegated them to second-class citizenship? What might your lives be like today if they had simply accepted that "life is unfair"?

Does your cultural region reflect the conclusions of Meinig and Elazar?

What social changes are most likely to dominate Texas's political future?

CHAPTER CONTENTS

what if...

Texas Became Five States?

BACKGROUND

Every day, every schoolchild in every public school in Texas pledges from memory: "Honor the Texas flag; I pledge allegiance to thee, Texas, one and indivisible." This pledge is wrong, wrong, wrong! In fact, Texas is "divisible."

A provision of the Articles of Annexation, which admitted Texas into the Union, granted her the privilege of "creating . . . new states, of convenient size, not exceeding four in number, in addition to said State of Texas."[1] Thus, present-day Texans can politically carve Texas's geographic territory into a total of five states. This "privilege" was part of a political strategy to ensure an equal number of slave and free states in the existing Union. Although free-state representatives outnumbered slave-state members in the U.S. House, senators from slave states could block any federal legislation they deemed detrimental to their states' interests. It was assumed that the five states created from Texas would all be slave states, and their senators might be needed to maintain the tenuous balance between senators from free and slave states. As it turned out, the Senate remained balanced without dividing Texas for another 15 years, until slave states began withdrawing from the Union in 1860.

THE PLAN

The provision suggests fascinating possibilities for modern-day Texans, however. If the territory that is now the state of Texas consisted of five states instead of one, the geographic area would have 10 U.S. senators instead of two and eight more votes in the electoral college. Modern Texans would thereby gain influence in the U.S. Senate, as well as in presidential politics.

It can also be argued that with five states, the political, ethnic, and historical diversity of Texas could be respected, and various cultural groups would be given better representation. Such a plan is shown in Figure 19–1. Lubbock would be West Texas's economic

[1] The Annexation of Texas, Joint Resolution of Congress, March 1, 1845, *U.S. Statutes at Large*, Vol. 5, pp. 797–798. This document can be found online at http://www.lsjunction.com/docs/annex.htm.

FIGURE 19–1 The Plan

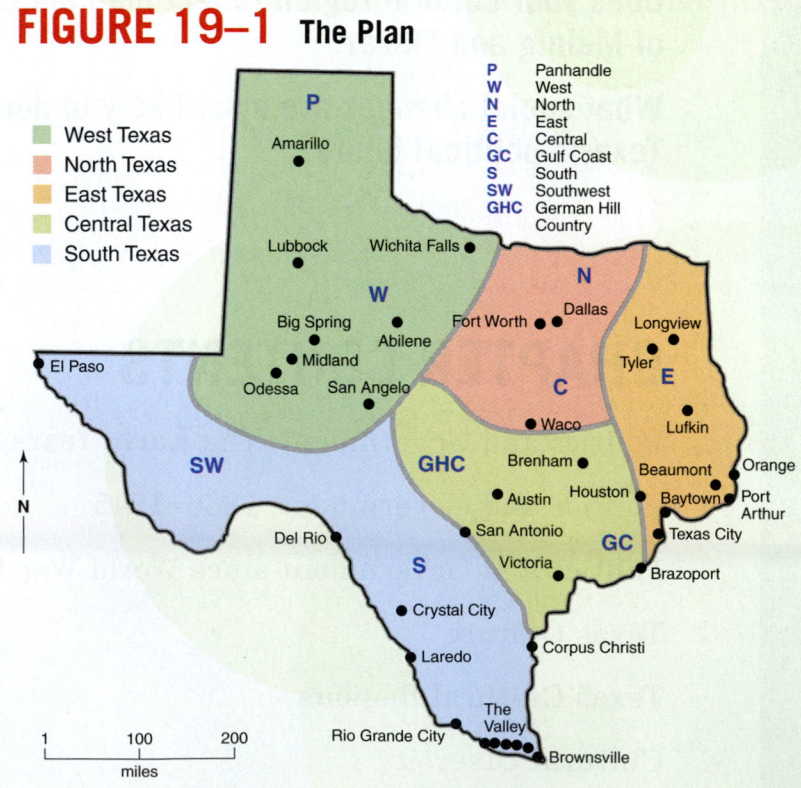

and political capital and include the oil-producing areas around Midland and Odessa. North Texas's capital would be the Dallas–Fort Worth Metroplex, with its western border along a line east of Abilene and Wichita Falls and including Waco to the south. East Texas would comprise the easternmost area of the state from Oklahoma to the Gulf of Mexico, including the eastern part of Houston and Texas City. Central Texas would include the western part of Houston, Victoria, northern San Antonio, and the Hill Country. South Texas would be bracketed by Brownsville and Corpus Christi on the east and El Paso on the west and include southern San Antonio.

OPPOSITION TO THE PLAN

Modern Texans, however, seem uninterested in the prospect of carving four additional states from Texas. Republicans could oppose the plan because South Texas, and possibly Central Texas and East Texas, could vote Democratic. Various interests would vie to be placed in one state or the other, and compromise boundaries would be difficult to achieve. Such a deal would require at least as much wily political talent as was needed to gerrymander Texas legislative and congressional districts. More importantly, the question of which state would have the Dallas Cowboys football team and the Alamo seems beyond resolution. So Texans will probably continue to be clustered in just one state, with only two U.S. senators and one governor.

FOR CRITICAL ANALYSIS

1. What arguments would you make against Texas becoming five states? Do Texans benefit from the combined economic and political power of being in a single state?
2. What are your arguments that favor five states? Should states be carved out to represent ethnic, cultural, and political groups?
3. Would you be more or less satisfied with your new state than you are with the present single-state arrangement? Why?

ALMOST 500 YEARS ago Spanish explorer Alonzo Alvarez de Pineda first set foot on what was to become Texas. During the next three centuries, land-hungry settlers pushed the Cherokees and the Caddos from the eastern pine forests; the Karankawas from the sands of the coast; and the Comanches, Apaches, and Kiowas from the western plains. Texas culture and history have been made under 37 Spanish governors, 15 Mexican governors, five presidents of the Republic of Texas, and 48 state governors.[2]

The successful end of the Texas Revolution in 1836 saw the English/Scotch-Irish culture, as it had evolved in its migration through the southern United States, become the dominant culture of the state. Anglo Americans were the most numerous population group and controlled most of the political and economic systems in Texas.[3]

Latinos and Native Americans stood in the way of the Anglo-Saxon concept of "Manifest Destiny" and, by various methods, hundreds of old Latino families throughout Texas were driven from their property as waves of Anglo settlers poured into the new republic. Even Latino heroes of the Texas Revolution with names like Navarro, Seguin, de Zavala, and de Leon lost much of their property.

San Antonio Latinos were spared the worst of this onslaught due to the opposition by the city's strong German community, which considered such actions to be contrary to republican values. Still, by 1856 half the city's Latino population was gone.[4]

DID YOU KNOW?

That Sam Houston, David Crockett, and Jim Bowie were of Scotch-Irish descent and culture? Scotch-Irish immigrants from the Scotish–English border, by way of northern Ireland, led the Anglo American movement west and had a major impact on the development of modern mid-American culture.

---

[2]The information in this and subsequent sections depends heavily on Seymour V. Connor, *Texas: A History* (New York: Thomas Y. Crowell, 1971); Rupert N. Richardson, *Texas: The Lone Star State*, 3rd ed. (Englewood Cliffs, NJ: Prentice Hall, 1970); and T. R. Fehrenbach, *Lone Star: A History of Texas and the Texans* (New York: Collier Books, 1980).

[3]To read a copy of the Texas Declaration of independence from Mexico, see the Lone Star Junction, http://www.lsjunction.com/docs/tdoi.htm.

[4]David Montejano, "Anglos and Mexicans in the Making of Texas, 1836–1986," University of Texas Press, 1987, pp. 26–29.

THIS PAINTING OF SAM HOUSTON shows him in the prime of life. Houston was the commander in chief of the armies of Texas during the war for independence from Mexico and subsequently was elected the first president of the Republic of Texas. His lifelong friendship with the Native Americans and his opposition to secession set him apart from other Texans of his generation. He died in 1863 during the American Civil War. (Courtesy Huntsville Arts Commission)

Anglo American Protestant sects also became the dominant religious groups in Texas. As evidence of the dominance of this Anglo-Scotch culture, all the presidents of the republic and the governors of the state have been Protestant and had surnames linked to the British Isles.

Although women could neither serve on juries nor vote, unmarried women retained many of the rights that they had enjoyed under Spanish law, which included control over their property. Married women also retained some Spanish law benefits for, unlike under Anglo-Saxon law, Texas marriage laws did not create one legal person with the husband as the head. Married women could own inherited property, share ownership in community property, and legally make a will. However, the husband legally had control of all the property, both separate and community (including earned income), and an employer could not hire a wife without her husband's consent.[5]

Divorce laws were restrictive on both parties, but a husband could win a divorce due to the wife's "amorous or lascivious conduct with other men, even short of adultery," or if she had committed adultery only once, although he could not gain a divorce for concealed premarital fornication. On the other hand, a wife could gain a divorce only if "the husband had lived in adultery with another woman." Physical violence was not grounds for divorce unless the wife could prove a "serious danger" that might happen again. In practice, physical abuse was tolerated if the wife behaved "indiscreetly" or had "provoked" her husband. Minority and poor wives had little legal protection from beatings, as the woman's "station in life" and "place in society" were also legal considerations.[6]

POLITICS AND GOVERNMENT: THE EARLY YEARS

Politics in the Republic of Texas was simpler than politics in Texas today. There were no political parties, and conflict revolved around pro-Houston and anti-Houston policies. Sam Houston, the hero of the battle of San Jacinto (1836), advocated peaceful relations with the eastern Native Americans and U.S. statehood for Texas. The anti-Houston forces were led by Mirabeau B. Lamar, who believed that Native American and Anglo American cultures could not coexist, and in 1839 drove the Cherokees and other tribes from Texas. In his version of Manifest Destiny, Lamar envisioned Texas as a great nation extending from the Sabine River to the Pacific.

JOINING THE UNION

Annexation
The incorporation of a territory into a larger political unit, such as a country, state, county, or city.

Texas voters approved **annexation** to the United States in 1836, almost immediately after Texas achieved independence from Mexico. However, because owning human property was legal in the Republic and would also be legal in Texas once it became a state, the annexation of Texas would upset the tenuous balance in the U.S. Senate between pro- and anti-slavery senators. This and several other political issues, primarily relating to slavery, postponed Texas's annexation until December 29, 1845, when it officially became the 28th state.

Several articles of annexation were more or less peculiar to Texas. Most important was that Texas retained ownership of its public lands because the U.S. Congress

---

[5]Handbook of Texas Online: Women and the Law.
[6]Ibid.

refused to accept them in exchange for payment of the republic's $10 million public debt. Although many millions of acres were eventually given away or sold, the remaining public lands continue to produce hundreds of millions of dollars in state revenue, mostly in royalties from the production of oil and natural gas. Today, this revenue primarily benefits the Permanent University Fund and the Permanent School Fund. The annexation articles also granted Texas the privilege of "creating . . . new states, of convenient size, not exceeding four in number, in addition to said State of Texas."[7]

EARLY STATEHOOD AND SECESSION: 1846–1864

The politics of early statehood immediately began to revolve around pro-Union and secessionist forces. Sam Houston, a strong Unionist, was alarmed at the support for **secession** in Texas, resigned his seat in the U.S. Senate, and in 1857 ran for the office of governor of Texas. He was defeated, primarily because secessionist forces controlled the dominant Democratic Party. He was elected governor two years later, however.

After Abraham Lincoln was elected president of the United States in 1860, a Texas secessionist convention voted to secede from the Union. Governor Sam Houston used his considerable political skills in the vain attempt to keep Texas in the Union. He declared the convention illegal, but it was upheld as legitimate by the Texas legislature. Although only about 5 percent of white Texans owned slaves, the electorate ratified the actions of the convention by an overwhelming 76 percent majority. Although defeated by the secessionists, Houston adamantly continued to fight what he considered Texans' determination to self-destruct. Reluctantly accepting the vote to secede, Houston tried to convince secessionist leaders to return to republic status rather than joining the newly formed Confederate States of America—a plan that might have saved Texas from the tragedy of the U.S. Civil War. Texas's convention rejected this political maneuver and petitioned for membership in the new Confederacy. Houston refused to accept the actions of the convention, which summarily declared the office of governor vacant and ordered the lieutenant governor into the position. Texas was then admitted to the Confederacy.[8]

The politics during the Civil War primarily concerned the military. Besides supplying large numbers of (primarily Confederate but also Union) troops to the conflict, Texas was responsible for the defense of the frontier and the Mexican border. Thus, the state—not the central Confederate government—filled the military vacuum created by the withdrawal of federal troops.

> **Secession**
> The separation of a territory from a larger political unit. Specifically, the secession of Southern states from the Union in 1860 and 1861.

POST–CIVIL WAR TEXAS: 1865–1885

Following the collapse of the Confederacy, relative anarchy existed in Texas until it was occupied by federal troops on June 19, 1865. Only then were government functions and stability restored to the state.

Radical Republicans gained control of the U.S. Congress and enacted punitive legislation that strictly limited both voter registration and eligibility to hold public office for former Confederate soldiers and officials. This restriction even included former mayors and school board members.

The Reconstruction of Texas under E. J. Davis. From 1865 through 1869, Texas government was under the military rule of the U.S. Army. Following the adoption of the constitution

DID YOU KNOW?

That Juneteenth, or Emancipation Day, long celebrated by Texas African Americans, only became an official state holiday in 1979?

---

[7]The Annexation of Texas, Joint Resolution of Congress, March 1, 1845, *U.S. Statutes at Large*, Vol. 5, pp. 797–798. This document can be found online at http://www.lsjunction.com/docs/annex.htm.
[8]Connor, p. 194. See *Texas Ordinance of Secession (February 2, 1861)* at http://lsjunction.com/docs/secession.htm.

RECONSTRUCTION GOVERNOR

E. J. Davis (Edmund J. Davis
1989.16; Courtesy State
Preservation Board; Austin, TX;
Photographer: Bill Kennedy
8/31/92 pre conservation/Texas
State Preservation Board)

of 1869, E. J. Davis, a Texan and Radical Republican who had fought for the Union in the Civil War, was elected governor of Texas in an election in which the former slaves could vote—but the former leaders of the state could not. Texas was then readmitted to the Union and governed by civilian authority under Davis, who served for one four-year term from 1870 through 1873. Under the 1869 Texas Constitution, political power was centralized in the office of the governor, and the state police and the militia were placed under his direct control.

Charges of corruption were common during the Davis administration, and state indebtedness drastically increased. Regardless of the accuracy of these allegations, Republican domination of Texas politics was "a world turned upside down" for most white Texas citizens.

The Fall of Governor Davis. The perception of the Davis administration as a government imposed on a defeated people in itself made it unpopular and prompted a strong anti-Republican reaction. In 1873, former Confederates were allowed to vote, and in 1874, Democrat Richard Coke was overwhelmingly elected governor in a hotly contested campaign. The Texas Supreme Court, handpicked by Davis, invalidated the election based on a technicality.

Davis locked himself in the capitol, surrounded it with the state police, requested the support of federal troops from President Ulysses S. Grant, and refused to leave office. In the predawn hours of January 13, 1874, however, Democratic legislators managed to gain access to the unoccupied legislative chambers, declared a quorum present, and officially validated the election of Coke as governor of Texas. Despite Grant's refusal to send in troops and with tension mounting, Davis still refused to leave the capitol. Only when serious violence seemed imminent between the state police and the numerically superior Coke forces did Davis withdraw.

The End of Republicanism. The new Texas officials immediately began to remove the last vestiges of radical Republicanism. One of the first steps was to rewrite the state constitution. A constitutional convention of 90 members was elected (75 Democrats and 15 Republicans) that included many former officials of both the Union and Confederate governments. Forty members of the 1875 convention also belonged to the Grange, a nonpartisan organization of farmers. Ratified in 1876, the new constitution cut expenditures, decentralized state government, and strictly limited the flexibility of elected officials. Although often amended, it is still in use. Davis established a law practice in Austin and continued to head the Republican Party and control patronage from Washington until his death in 1883. He remained unpopular with most Texans, and his death created a racial division between black and white Republicans. The African American forces, under Norris Wright Cuney of Galveston, gained control of both the state party machinery and party patronage from Washington. The political consequence of Reconstruction and the policies of E. J. Davis was one-party dominance by an all-white Democratic Party with the numerically smaller, predominantly black Republican Party in opposition.

POLITICS AND GOVERNMENT: 1886–1945

After 1886, increasing demands for change forced the Democratic Party to make political adjustments. Many reform measures were enacted and enforced in Texas in the 1880s, especially **antitrust legislation**. The election of James Stephen Hogg as attorney general in 1886 ensured the vigorous enforcement of the new laws against abuses by insurance companies, railroads, and other corporate interests.

Antitrust Legislation
Legislation directed against economic monopolies.

GOVERNOR HOGG

Hogg, who had strong support among small East Texas farmers, played an important reformist role in Texas politics and rapidly developed a reputation as a champion of the common people. Feeling that he needed more power to regulate the railroad interests that dominated many state governments, Hogg ran for governor. The 1890 Democratic state convention nominated him as its candidate for governor in spite of opposition from powerful political and corporate business interests. A major issue in the campaign that followed was a proposed amendment giving the Texas legislature the power to establish a commission to regulate railroads. The voters gave both Hogg and the amendment a clear victory.

The Railroad Commission. As governor, Hogg was able to persuade the legislature to establish a three-member Railroad Commission, in spite of intense opposition from special-interest legislators. His appointment of respected political figures to the commission, notably John H. Reagan as chairman, enabled it to become one of the most important railroad regulatory bodies in the United States.

The constitutionality of a railroad commission still had to be tested in the federal courts, but it was upheld after two years of litigation. The commission was later given the power to regulate the production and transportation of oil and natural gas and to regulate rubber-tired vehicles used in intrastate commerce. In 1994, however, the U.S. Congress determined that the commission's *intrastate* trucking regulations were an obstacle to *interstate* commerce and mandated gradual deregulation of the trucking industry in Texas.

Edward M. House. In 1894, an early Hogg supporter, Edward M. House, was able to take control of the Democratic Party from Hogg on a "promote unity" platform. House established himself as a behind-the-scenes political power in Texas for the next 40 years. House also wielded significant influence in national politics, first as a supporter and later as chief confidant of President Woodrow Wilson (1913–1921). Although he never sought elective office, he was one of the most astute politicians ever to operate in Texas.

Throughout the early 1900s, programs enacted by the legislature continued to identify Texas as one of the most progressive states in the nation. Texas pioneered the regulation of monopolies, railroads, child labor, and other employer abuses, as well as reform of prisons, taxes, and insurance companies. In 1905, state conventions were replaced with direct primaries to nominate major-party candidates.

FARMER JIM: 1914–1918

James E. Ferguson entered the Texas political scene in 1914 and was a controversial and powerful force in Texas politics for the next 20 years. He had worked as a migrant laborer in California, Nevada, Colorado, and Texas. Although Ferguson had little formal education and only a few months' study of law, he was admitted to the Texas bar in 1897.

By 1914, when he announced his candidacy for governor, Ferguson owned varied business interests and was the president of the Temple State Bank. Ferguson was an anti-prohibitionist ("wet") at a time when **Prohibition** was a major political issue, and although his strongest opponent in the Democratic primary was a prohibitionist ("dry"), Ferguson tried to ignore the liquor issue. Although sensitive to the problems and interests of the business community, Ferguson called himself "Farmer Jim" to emphasize his rural background and focused his campaign on the difficulties of the numerous **tenant farmers** in Texas.

JAMES STEPHEN HOGG was a progressive newspaperman, a politician, and the first Texas-born governor of Texas. (Frontispiece, Speeches and State Papers of James Stephen Hogg, C. W. Raines, editor. The State Publishing Company, Austin, Texas, 1905. The University of Texas at Austin, Center for American History)

That Governor Hogg's daughter, Ima Hogg (Miss Ima), was a major benefactor and philanthropist to Texas institutions and charities? (Contrary to popular belief, Governor Hogg did not have a daughter named Ura Hogg.)

Prohibition
Outlawing of the production, sale, and consumption of alcoholic beverages.

Tenant Farmer
A farmer who does not own the land that he or she farms but rents it from a landowner.

A PHOTOGRAPH OF Minnie Fisher Cunningham, a Texas suffragist (1882–1964). (© Bettmann/CORBIS)

Progressive Movement
A political movement within both major parties in the early 20th century. Progressives believed that the power of the government should be used to restrain the growing power of large corporations, as well as to provide services for its citizens.

Item Veto
The power to veto particular sections or items of an appropriations bill while signing the remainder of the bill into law. The governors of most states have this power.

Farmer Jim as Governor. The legislature was unusually receptive to Ferguson's programs, which were in the best tradition of the **progressive movement**, and enacted legislation designed to help alleviate problems of tenant farmers, rural schools, and state courts. Governor Ferguson was reelected in 1916, and although rumors of financial irregularities in the office had begun to gain credibility, his progressive legislative programs were again successful. This was especially true in the areas of public school and college education and the proposal to create a state highway commission. The latter agency was formed to take the construction and maintenance of state roads away from the counties, where there was great variation in quality and consistency.

The Fall of Farmer Jim. Rumors of financial irregularities such as bribery and embezzlement continued during Ferguson's second term. His fatal step, however, may have been "declaring war" on the University of Texas. After the legislature had adjourned, Ferguson issued an **item veto** of the entire appropriation for the university, apparently because the board of regents had refused to remove certain faculty members whom the governor found objectionable. This step alienated many politically powerful graduates. They immediately demanded action, and Ferguson was indicted by the Travis County grand jury for illegal use of public funds.

Women also joined in the groundswell of opposition to Ferguson. Led by Minnie Fisher Cunningham, Texas suffragists had organized, spoken out, marched, and lobbied for the right to vote during the Ferguson years but gained no real political traction, as Farmer Jim strongly opposed their cause. Suffragists effectively lobbied state legislators "through the back door" and organized rallies advocating his impeachment.[9]

Ultimately, Farmer Jim was impeached on 21 charges. In August 1917, following three weeks of hearings by the state senate, Ferguson was convicted on 10 of the charges, removed from office, and barred from holding public office in Texas.

Ferguson was found guilty of accepting funds from secret sources, tampering with state officials, depositing state funds in the Temple State Bank (which he partly owned), and using public funds for personal gain. His successor was Lieutenant Governor W. P. Hobby, Sr.

Again women actively participated in the political arena although they lacked the right to vote. William P. Hobby, considered receptive to women's suffrage, was touted as "The Man Whom Good Women Want." This tactic ultimately proved successful and women, after some delay, won the legislative battle and gained the right to vote in the 1918 Texas primaries.[10]

National suffrage momentum precipitated a proposed constitutional amendment establishing the right of women to vote throughout the United States. Having endured over five years of "heavy artillery" by Cunningham and the Texas Equal Suffrage Association, legislative opposition crumbled and Texas became one of the first Southern states to ratify the Nineteenth Amendment. Texas women received full voting rights in 1920.[11]

The same legislature, in another called session, ratified the Eighteenth Amendment to the U.S. Constitution, establishing national Prohibition. The prohibitionists had won.

WORLD WAR I, THE TWENTIES, AND THE RETURN OF FARMER JIM: 1919–1928

As did the rest of the nation, Texas saw boom years during World War I. Its favorable climate and the Zimmerman Note (in which Germany allegedly urged Mexico to invade

[9]Women of the West Museum: Western Women's Suffrage—Texas.
[10]Ibid.
[11]Ibid.

Texas) prompted the national government to station additional troops in the state. Texas became an important training area for the military, and many of the training camps later became permanent bases.

Progressive political programs, however, suffered during the war. Governor Hobby's proposals to use the state's credit to help individuals purchase homes and to write a new constitution were defeated either by the legislature or by the voters.

In 1921, Pat M. Neff became governor of Texas. His proposals to reorganize the executive branch to eliminate duplication and waste and to rewrite the Texas Constitution both failed. Meanwhile, bootleggers—traffickers in illegal alcohol—often circumvented Prohibition. Governor Neff, an avid prohibitionist, used the Texas Rangers to find and destroy private stills used to produce illegal spirits. The Rangers were too few in number to be effective and the legislature refused to give Neff the police powers necessary to enforce Prohibition effectively. Crime, education, and the **Ku Klux Klan (KKK)** emerged as issues that demanded attention from the politicians and voters.

Progressive measures enacted during this period included free textbooks for public schools, the establishment of several colleges, and the beginning of the state park system.

Civil Rights. Civil rights for racial minorities remained an elusive concept during this period. African American Texans were legally denied the right to vote in the Democratic **white primary** and public facilities, theaters, restaurants, beaches, and so forth were segregated by race. Segregation laws were enforced both by official law enforcement agents and unofficial organizations using terror tactics.

Although these laws were not specifically directed at Latinos, who were legally white, they were effectively enforced against them through social custom and coercion. The Ku Klux Klan, local law officers, and the Texas Rangers actively participated in violence and intimidation of both Latinos and African American Texans to keep them "in their segregated place." Lynching was also used against both groups, often after torture.[12]

The Ku Klux Klan (first organized in the late 1860s to intimidate freed African slaves) was reborn in the 1920s with a somewhat modified mission. The new Klan saw itself as a patriotic, Christian, fraternal organization for native-born white Protestants. Its members perceived both a general moral decline in society, precipitated by "modern" young people, and a basic threat to the Protestant white Christian "race" and its values by African Americans, Jews, Catholics, Latinos, German Americans, and other "foreigners." Acting on its paranoia, the 1920s Klan set out to force society to comply with its version of fundamentalist Christian morality. It used intimidation, violence, and torture—tarring and feathering, branding, beating, threats of castration—as means of coercion. As many as 80,000 Texans may have joined the "invisible empire" in an effort to make the world more to their liking. Many elected officials—U.S. and state legislators as well as county and city officials—were either avowed Klansmen or friendly neutrals. In fact, the Klan influenced Texas society to such an extent that its power was a major political issue from 1921 through 1925.

In response to this racially charged atmosphere, a number of organizations committed to equality were founded or grew larger during the 1920s. Among these were the National Association for the Advancement of Colored People (NAACP), established in 1909, and the League of United Latin American Citizens (LULAC), which was formed in Corpus Christi in 1929.

When Dr. L. H. Nixon, an African American citizen of El Paso, was denied the right to vote in the Democratic primary, the NAACP instituted legal action and the U.S. Supreme Court found in *Nixon v. Herndon*[13] that the Texas white primary law was

Ku Klux Klan (KKK)
A white supremacist organization. The first Klan was founded during the Reconstruction era following the Civil War.

White Primary
The practice of excluding African Americans from Democratic party primary elections in Texas. First enforced by law and later by party rules, this practice was found unconstitutional in *Smith v. Allwright*, 321 U.S. 649 (1944).

DID YOU KNOW?

The University of Texas changed the names of Simkins Hall and Simkins Park on July 15, 2010, to Creekside Hall and Park. The dorm and park were named after former UT law professor William S. Simkins and former UT system regent Eldred J. Simkins. The brothers were active organizers and members of the Ku Klux Klan. The dorm was built and named in the 1950s.

---

[12]*The Handbook of Texas Online*, tshaonline.org/handbook/online/.
[13]273 U.S. 536 (1927).

unconstitutional. However, the Texas legislature transferred control of the primary from the state to the Democratic State Executive Committee and the discrimination continued. Dr. Nixon again sought justice in the courts, and the U.S. Supreme Court in 1931 also ruled the new scheme unconstitutional. Texas Democrats then completely excluded African American Texans from party membership. In *Grovey v. Townsend,*[14] the U.S. Supreme Court upheld this ploy, and the Texas Democratic primary remained all white. Although it had suffered a temporary setback in the episode, the NAACP had proven its potential as a viable instrument for African Americans to achieve justice.[15]

The Return of the Fergusons. The strongest anti-Klan candidate in the gubernatorial election of 1924 was Miriam A. "Ma" Ferguson, wife of the impeached (and convicted) Farmer Jim. Running successfully on a platform of "Two Governors for the Price of One," she became the first female governor of Texas. Ma's election indicated that Texas voters had forgiven Farmer Jim. Her success in getting legislation passed that prohibited wearing a mask in public led to the end of the Klan as an effective political force in Texas. Ma was criticized, however, for her lenient pardoning policy (occasionally a convicted felon was pardoned before reaching prison) and a highway scandal. In the 1926 election, she was defeated by Attorney General Dan Moody, also a reformer and an anti-Klan candidate.

In 1928, national politics exerted more influence than usual on Texas politics when Al Smith became the Democratic nominee for president. Smith was a Roman Catholic, a "wet," and a big-city politician; Herbert Hoover, the Republican nominee, was a Protestant, a "dry," and an international humanitarian. Hoover won the electoral votes from Texas—the first Republican ever to do so.

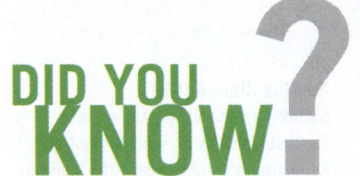

DID YOU KNOW?

That "Ma" Ferguson was governor in name only, and that Farmer Jim exercised the real power of the office?

THE GREAT DEPRESSION: 1929–1939

When the stock market crashed in 1929, Texas, along with the entire nation, was crushed under the blow. Almost overnight, prices dropped, farm products could not be sold, mortgages and taxes could not be paid, and many jobs ceased to exist. Numerous businesses and bank accounts were wiped out.

The Independent Oil Crisis. The discovery of the East Texas oil field near Kilgore in 1930 helped to alleviate the situation until overproduction of oil forced the price to drop to as low as 10 cents a barrel (about $1.60 in today's currency). Unlike earlier discoveries, the East Texas field was developed and controlled largely by "independents"—oil producers not associated with the major oil companies. The "majors" owned the oil refineries, however, and because of the oil surplus, they often refused to purchase oil from independents for refining. Independents requested assistance from Governor Ross Sterling, but instead he ordered the East Texas field closed because of its threat to the entire oil industry. Outraged independents claimed that he had overreacted and refused to stop production.

Sterling declared martial law and sent in the National Guard. Eventually, the Railroad Commission (RRC) was given the power to control production of oil in Texas (first by executive order, later by law). To give the RRC some authority, the Texas Rangers were pressed into service in 1933 in an attempt to enforce the RRC guidelines. Despite the work of the Rangers, some East Texas independents still circumvented RRC orders by building their own refineries for processing illegal ("hot") oil and selling gasoline through independent retail outlets. A legislative act in 1934 that required refineries to divulge

14 295 U.S. 45 (1935).
15 Connor, pp. 378–379.

their sources of crude oil eventually ended the expansion of independent operators and refiners. The whole enforcement question soon became unimportant, however, because by 1938 the major oil companies had gained control of 80 percent of the production in the East Texas fields.

"Ma" Ferguson Again. In 1932, Ma Ferguson, using economy in government as her campaign issue, was reelected governor.

In 1933, the ratification of the Twenty-first Amendment to the U.S. Constitution brought an end to nationwide Prohibition. Prohibition ended in Texas two years later with the adoption of local option elections, although selling liquor by the drink was still forbidden statewide. A board was established to administer taxing and licensing of liquor dealers.

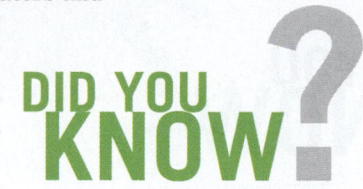

DID YOU KNOW?

That Governor Sterling was one of the founders of Humble Oil Company (later Exxon), and that the commander of the Texas National Guard was employed by Texaco Oil Company as an attorney?

"PASS THE BISCUITS, PAPPY": 1938–1945

W. Lee O'Daniel, certainly one of the most colorful and unusual characters in Texas politics, entered the Democratic gubernatorial primary in 1938. "Pappy" O'Daniel was a highly successful flour salesman and the host of a radio hillbilly music show that was liberally sprinkled with homespun poetry and moral advice. O'Daniel's show had more daily listeners than any show in the history of Texas radio. The leader of O'Daniel's band, the Light Crust Doughboys, was Bob Wills.

In his gubernatorial campaign, O'Daniel used the slogan, "Pass the biscuits, Pappy!" Touring Texas in a bus with the Light Crust Doughboys, O'Daniel ran on a platform of the Ten Commandments, the Golden Rule, and increased old-age pensions.

He had never run for public office, had never voted in Texas, had never paid a poll tax (saying that no politician was worth $1.75), and admitted that he knew nothing about politics. With no campaign manager and no campaign headquarters, and without a runoff, he defeated 13 candidates in the Democratic primary—some of whom were well-known, prominent political figures.

"PAPPY" O'DANIEL and the Hillbilly Boys—Pappy is on the right. For all his failings politically and personally, "Pappy" O'Daniel was an important figure in the development of western swing music. Because of his talent for publicity and his business acumen, his bands, the Light Crust Doughboys and the Hillbilly Boys, became nationally recognized performers. (Courtesy of the Texas State Library and Archives)

"Pappy" as Governor. Governor O' Daniel was not successful as a legislative leader, but he was reelected easily in 1940 against strong opposition in the Democratic primary. Again, he was notably unsuccessful in getting his proposals passed by the legislature. When a U.S. senator from Texas died, O'Daniel appointed Andrew Jackson Houston, the last surviving son of Sam Houston. Houston, at age 87, became the oldest man ever to enter the U.S. Senate. Indeed, there was some question as to whether he could survive the trip to Washington! He did, but he died 18 days later.

"Pappy" as Senator. Pappy then entered the special election for the Senate seat and won, defeating 29 other candidates. (His closest competitor was a young congressman from Central Texas, Lyndon B. Johnson.) Lieutenant Governor Coke R. Stevenson succeeded Pappy as governor. O'Daniel served with a notable lack of distinction in the Senate but was reelected to a full six-year term in 1942. His ineffectiveness in Washington was possibly related to his habit of making derogatory remarks about other politicians, such as "Washington is the only lunatic asylum in the world run by its own inmates."

POLITICS AND GOVERNMENT SINCE WORLD WAR II

Beauford Jester easily won the gubernatorial election of 1946 after an especially bitter primary victory over Homer P. Rainey, the former president of the University of Texas. A major campaign issue was university autonomy and academic freedom.

The 1948 senatorial campaign for the seat of the retiring Pappy O'Daniel is worth special note. Several qualified people announced their candidacies for the position. The runoff in the Democratic primary pitted former governor Coke R. Stevenson against U.S. congressman Lyndon B. Johnson.

The campaign was especially controversial, and the election was the closest in the state's history, with both candidates charging election fraud. At first, the election bureau gave the unofficial count as 494,330 votes for Stevenson and 493,968 for Johnson; then the revised returns for counties began to be reported, most of which favored Johnson. The final official election results were 494,191 for Johnson and 494,104 for Stevenson—a difference of 87 votes.

"Box 13" in Jim Wells County, one of several "machine" counties dominated by political boss George Parr (the "Duke of Duval"), was particularly important in these new figures. This box revised Johnson's vote upward by 202 votes and Stevenson's upward by only one. Box 13 was also late in reporting. In the end, after various bitter political and judicial battles, Johnson was certified the victor.

CIVIL RIGHTS REVISITED: LATINO TEXANS

Returning World War II veterans, fresh from fighting to make the world safe for democracy, found discrimination still existed in the homeland. A decorated veteran, Major Hector Garcia, settled in Corpus Christi and became convinced by conditions in the Latino American community in South Texas that still another battle was yet to be fought—and in his own backyard. Garcia, a medical doctor, found farm laborers enduring inhuman

[16]Fehrenbach, *Lone Star*, p. 659.

living conditions; deplorable medical conditions in slums; disabled veterans starving, sick, and ignored by the Veteran's Administration; and an entrenched unapologetic Anglo Texan elite maintaining public school segregation.

To begin his war, Dr. Garcia needed recruits for his "army." With other World War II veterans, Dr. Garcia organized the American GI Forum in a Corpus Christi elementary school classroom in March 1948. This organization spread throughout the United States and played a major role in giving Latino Americans full citizenship and civil respect.[17]

One of the most incendiary sparks to ignite Latino Texans to fight for civil rights was Felix Longoria's funeral. Private Longoria was a decorated casualty of World War II whose body was returned to Three Rivers for burial in the "Mexican section" of the cemetery, which was separated from the white section by barbed wire. But an obstacle developed—the funeral home's director refused the Longoria family's request to use the chapel because "whites would not like it." Longoria's widow asked Dr. Hector Garcia for support, but the director also refused his request. Dr. Garcia then sent a flurry of telegrams and letters to Texas congressmen protesting the actions of the funeral director. Senator Lyndon B. Johnson immediately responded and arranged for Private Longoria to be buried at Arlington National Cemetery.[18]

African American Texans. The Texas branch of the NAACP remained active during this period and served as a useful vehicle for numerous legal actions to protect African American civil rights. African American Texans at last won the right to participate in the Texas Democratic primary when the U.S. Supreme Court ruled in *Smith v. Albright* (1944)[19] that primaries were a part of the election process and that racial discrimination in the electoral process is unconstitutional. Twenty years later, the first African American Texans since Reconstruction were elected to the Texas legislature.

World War II veteran Herman Sweatt applied for admission to the University of Texas Law School, which by Texas law was segregated. State laws requiring segregation were constitutional so long as facilities serving blacks and whites were equal. Since Texas had no African American law school, the Texas legislature hurriedly sought to establish a law school for Sweatt—conveniently located in his hometown of Houston. Although the new law school was established, it lacked faculty and a library, and the NAACP sued Texas. Ruling that the new law school was indeed not equal, the U.S. Supreme Court ordered Sweatt admitted to the University of Texas. It is worth noting that "separate but equal" facilities remained legal since the Court did not overturn *Plessy v. Ferguson,* which granted the constitutional sanction for legal segregation. Instead the Court simply ruled that the new law school was not equal to the University of Texas.[20]

THE 1950s: SHIVERCRATS AND THE SEEDS FOR A REPUBLICAN TEXAS

Lieutenant Governor Allan Shivers became governor in 1949 following the death of Governor Jester. He was easily elected governor in 1950, setting the stage for the 1952 Texas political extravaganza in which a president, the governor, and a U.S. senator would be elected.

DR. HECTOR P. GARCIA was a civil rights activist, founder of the American GI Forum, and the first Mexican American to receive the Presidential Medal of Freedom. (Dr. Hector P. Garcia Papers, Special Collections and Archives, Texas A&M University Corpus Christi Bell Library)

PRIVATE FELIX LONGORIA was a hero and casualty of World War II. (Dr. Hector P. Garcia Papers, Special Collections and Archives, Texas A&M University Corpus Christi Bell Library)

[17] http://www.justiceformypeople.com/drhector2.html.
[18] *Handbook of Texas Online.*
[19] 321 U.S. 649 (1944).
[20] *Sweatt v. Painter,* 339 U.S. 629 (1950); *Plessy v. Ferguson,* 163 U.S. 537 (1892).

HERMAN SWEATT successfully integrated Texas public law schools after the U.S. Supreme Court began to chip away at the "separate but equal" doctrine in the landmark case *Sweatt v. Painter*, 339 U.S. 629 (1950). (Joseph Scherschel/Time & Life Pictures/Getty Images)

Tidelands
A submerged area that extends three leagues (about 10 miles) off the Texas coast. The tidelands controversy developed when offshore oil was discovered and the federal government contended that Texas's jurisdiction extended only three miles into the Gulf of Mexico.

Shivercrat
A follower of Governor Allan Shivers of Texas (1949–1957). Shivercrats split their votes between conservative Democrats for state office and Republicans for the U.S. presidency.

Both state and national political issues captured the interest of the 1952 Texas voters. Harry Truman, a Democrat, had succeeded to the presidency in 1945 following the death of Franklin Roosevelt. Several scandals marred the Truman administration, and many conservative Texas Democrats were disillusioned with the New Deal and Fair Deal policies of the Roosevelt-Truman era.

The Tidelands Controversy. Another major issue was the **tidelands** question. Following the discovery of oil in the Gulf of Mexico, a jurisdictional conflict arose between the government of the United States and the governments of the coastal states.

Texas claimed three leagues (a Spanish unit of measure equal to about 10 miles) as its jurisdictional boundary; the U.S. government said that Texas had rights to only three miles. At stake were hundreds of millions of dollars in royalty revenue.

Governor Shivers and Attorney General Price Daniel, who were campaigning for the U.S. Senate, both attacked the national Democratic administration as being corrupt and soft on communism, eroding the rights of states, and being outright thieves in attempting to steal the tidelands oil from the schoolchildren of Texas. State control would direct much of the oil income to the Permanent School Fund used for public education and would mean a lower school tax burden for Texans. The Democratic presidential nomination of Adlai Stevenson of Illinois, who disagreed with the Texas position on the tidelands, only intensified this opposition.

Loyalists and Shivercrats. The Republicans nominated Dwight Eisenhower, a World War II hero who was sympathetic to the Texas position on the tidelands issue. Eisenhower was born in Texas (but reared in Kansas), and his supporters used the campaign slogan "Texans for a Texan." The presidential campaign crystallized a split in the Texas Democratic Party that lasted for the next 40 years. The conservative "Texas Democrats" faction of the party, led by Shivers and Daniel, advocated "splitting the ticket"—voting for Eisenhower for president and for Texas Democrats for state offices (for some time afterward adherents of this sort of split voting came to be known as **"Shivercrats"**). The liberal faction, or "Loyalist Democrats of Texas," led by Judge Ralph "Raff" Yarborough, campaigned for a straight Democratic ticket.

Texas voted for Eisenhower, and the tidelands dispute was eventually settled in favor of Texas. Shivers was reelected governor, and Daniel succeeded in entering the U.S. Senate. Shivers, Daniel, and the Democratic candidates for several other statewide offices (including those of lieutenant governor and attorney general) were also nominated by the Republican Party. Running as Democrats, these candidates defeated themselves as Republicans in the general election.

Governor Shivers also sought and won an unprecedented third term in 1954, but the fallout from the U.S. Supreme Court's *Brown v. Board of Education* (1954) public school desegregation decision would loom large during the Shivers term.[21] In 1956, when Mansfield school district, just southeast of Fort Worth, was ordered to integrate, angry whites surrounded the school and prevented the enrollment of three African American children. Governor Shivers declared the demonstration an "orderly protest" and sent the Texas Rangers to support the protestors. Since the Eisenhower administration took no action, the school remained segregated. The Mansfield school desegregation incident "was the first example of failure to enforce a federal court order for the desegregation of

---

[21]*Brown v. Board of Education of Topeka*, 347 U.S. 483 (1954).

a public school." Only in 1965, when facing a loss of federal funding, did Mansfield desegregate.[22]

Important to Latino Americans and ultimately other whites facing discrimination was *Hernandez v. State of Texas* (1954). Pete Hernandez was convicted of murder in Edna, Jackson County, Texas, by an all-Anglo jury. Latino attorneys Gustavo (Gus) Garcia, Carlos Cadena, John Herrera, and James DeAnda challenged the conviction, arguing that the systematic exclusion of Latinos from jury duty in Texas violated their rights to equal protection of the law guaranteed by the Fourteenth Amendment of the U.S. Constitution. Texas courts ruled that Latinos were white, so all-Anglo (white) juries could not be discriminatory. To change the system, the Latino team of lawyers would have to change the interpretation of the U.S. Constitution. The stakes were high, for if they failed, Latino discrimination throughout the southwestern United States could legally continue for decades. Garcia argued that Latinos, though white, were "a class apart" and suffered discrimination based on their "class." The U.S. Supreme Court agreed, overturned the Texas courts, and ruled that Latinos were protected by the Constitution from discrimination by other whites. The Hernandez decision established the precedent of constitutional protection by class throughout the United States and was a forerunner for future decisions prohibiting discrimination based on gender, disability, and sexual orientation.

The veterans' land and insurance scandals also surfaced to mar Shivers's administration and scandals continued well into the administration of his successor, Price Daniel, Sr. Lobbyists' use of the "three Bs" of lobbying ("booze, beefsteak, and babes"), campaign contributions, and all-expense-paid vacations for influential administrators and legislators continued to buy weak laws and lax regulation. In 1959, public outrage forced the legislature to adopt (minimal) controls on lobbyists. During the Daniel administration, Texas's first broadly based tax, the general sales tax, was enacted.

THE 1960s: TEXAS HAS A PRESIDENT AND DISCOVERS THE EQUAL PROTECTION CLAUSE

When Lyndon B. Johnson, majority leader of the U.S. Senate and one of the most powerful men in Washington, lost his bid for the Democratic

GOVERNOR SHIVERS WAS KNOWN for being all business. This photo shows him making a rare exception. To what extent might Shivers's hostility to the national Democratic Party have been the result of its refusal to give Texas the royalties from oil in the tidelands? (Texas State Library and Archives)

GUS GARCIA WAS THE LEAD attorney in the U.S. Supreme Court decision, Hernandez v. Texas that established Latinos as a "class apart," thereby establishing the precedent of Constitutional protection for various other classes of Americans. (Dr. Hector P. Garcia Papers, Special Collections and Archives, Texas A&M)

[22]See: Mansfield School Desegregation Incident, *Handbook of Texas Online*, http://www.tshaonline.org/handbook/online/articles/MM/jcm2.html.

presidential nomination to John F. Kennedy in 1960, he accepted the nomination for vice president. By the grace of the Texas legislature, Johnson was on the ballot of the general election as both vice presidential and senatorial nominee. When the Democratic ticket was successful, he was elected to both positions, and a special election was necessary to fill the Senate seat he chose to vacate. In the special election, Republican John Tower was elected to fill Johnson's vacated seat in the Senate—the first Republican since Reconstruction to serve as a U.S. senator from Texas.

Following the assassination of President Kennedy in 1963, Lyndon B. Johnson became president and was then easily elected for a full term in 1964. He chose not to run again in 1968, however, largely because of urban race riots, anti–Vietnam War sentiment, and poor health. In 1962, John B. Connally, the secretary of the navy in the John F. Kennedy administration, returned to Texas and was elected governor. Connally became a dominant force in Texas politics and was easily reelected to second and third terms. He did not seek reelection for a fourth term and, in 1969, was succeeded by Lieutenant Governor Preston Smith.

The 1960s are known for the victories of the national civil rights movement. Texan James Farmer was cofounder of the Congress of Racial Equality (CORE), and along with Dr. Martin Luther King Jr., Whitney Young, and Roy Wilkins, was one of the "Big

PRESIDENT LYNDON JOHNSON GIVES Texas civil rights activist and Director of the Congress of Racial Equality James Farmer the pen used to sign the Voting Rights Act of 1965. (© akg-images/Newscom)

Four" African Americans who shaped the civil rights struggle in the 1950s and 1960s. Farmer, who followed the nonviolent principles of Mahatma Gandhi, initiated both sit-ins as a means of integrating public facilities and freedom rides as a means of registering African Americans to vote.

The first sit-in to protest segregation in Texas was organized with CORE support by students from Wiley and Bishop colleges in the rotunda of the Harrison County courthouse in Marshall, Texas. The founder of CORE, James Farmer was himself a graduate of Wiley College and was a member of its 1935 national champion debate team, which served as the inspiration for the popular movie *The Great Debaters* starring Denzel Washington.[23]

Most African Americans and Mexican Americans were relegated to the lowest-paid jobs as either service workers or farmworkers. The fight to organize into labor unions was the primary focus for much of the Mexican American civil activism in the 1960s. In rural areas, large landowners controlled the political as well as the economic system and were largely united in opposition of labor unions. The United

TEXAS SOUTHERN UNIVERSITY students stage a sit-in at a Houston supermarket lunch counter, 1960. (AP Photo)

[23] For more information see CORE-online.org.

THE PAINTING "LOS TRABAJADORES" by artist Jesse Trevino honors the farm workers march to Austin in 1977 to draw attention to their grievances. The painting is owned by San Antonio Attorney Frank Herrera, Jr. (Courtesy of Frank Herrera, Jr.)

Farm Workers (UFW) led a strike against melon growers and packers in Starr County in the 1960s, demanding a minimum wage and the solution of other grievances. Starr County police officers, the local judiciary, and the Texas Rangers were accused of brutality as they arrested and prosecuted strikers for minor offenses.

On February 26, 1977, members of the Texas Farm Workers Union (TFWU), strikers, and other supporters began a march to Austin to demand the $1.25 minimum wage and other improvements for farmworkers. Press coverage intensified as the marchers made their way north in the summer heat. Politicians, members of the AFL-CIO, and the Texas Council of Churches accompanied the protestors. Governor John Connally, who had refused to meet them in Austin, traveled to New Braunfels with then–house speaker Ben Barnes and attorney general Waggoner Carr to intercept the march and inform strikers that their efforts would have no effect. Ignoring the governor, the marchers continued to Austin and held a 6,500-person protest rally at the state capitol. The rally was broken up by Texas Rangers and law enforcement officers. Legal action was taken against the Rangers for their part in the strike and the protest. The eventual ruling of the Supreme Court held that the laws the Rangers had been enforcing were in violation of the U.S. Constitution.[24] The Rangers were reorganized as a part of the Texas Department of Public Safety.

Women were given the right to serve on juries in 1954. The 1972 ratification of Texas's Equal Rights Amendment, together with the passage of a series of laws titled the Marital Property Act, amounted to a revolution for women. The act granted married women equal rights in insurance, banking and real estate, contracts, divorce, child custody, and property ownership. This was the first such comprehensive family law in the United States.[25]

In 1972, Texas's Equal Rights Amendment was ratified by the voters. Also, *Roe v. Wade,* a Texas case tried by Texas lawyer Sarah Weddington before the U.S. Supreme Court, still stands in the center of national debate. The *Roe* decision overturned Texas statutes that criminalized abortions and in so doing established a limited, national right of privacy for women to terminate a pregnancy. *Roe* followed a 1965 Connecticut privacy case that overturned a state law that criminalized the use of birth control.[26]

THE 1970s: SCANDAL AND REFORM

The Sharpstown scandal erupted in 1971. It began when attorneys for the U.S. Securities and Exchange Commission (SEC) filed a suit alleging stock fraud against a series of elected Texas officials. The SEC also filed suit against Frank Sharp, owner of the Sharpstown State Bank. Buried in the SEC's supporting material was the allegation that several prominent politicians, including Governor Smith and House Speaker Gus Mutscher, had accepted bribes to support legislation favorable to Sharp. Although

[24]See Robert E. Hall, "Pickets, Politics and Power: The Farm Worker Strike in Starr County," *Texas Bar Journal* 70(5); *Allee v. Medrano,* 416 U.S. 802 (1974), and Texas Farm Workers Union; *Handbook of Texas Online.*
[25]*Handbook of Texas Online* – Women and the Law.
[26]*Handbook of Texas Online–Roe v. Wade,* 410 U.S. 558 (1973); *Griswold v. Connecticut,* 381 U.S. 479 (1965).

Governor Smith was not found guilty of any wrongdoing, Mutscher, along with others, was convicted of conspiracy to accept a bribe.[27]

In the wake of the scandal, a large number of "reform" advocates were elected in 1972. Dolph Briscoe, a wealthy Uvalde rancher and banker, won the governorship by a plurality of less than 100,000 votes over his Republican and Raza Unida opponents—the first general election since the institution of the party primary in 1906 in which the Democratic gubernatorial candidate did not receive a majority of the votes. Briscoe was easily reelected in 1974.

In 1974, state legislators served as delegates to a constitutional convention but failed to propose a new constitution to the voters, primarily because of conflict over a proposed *right-to-work* provision. (Under right-to-work laws passed in many states, union membership cannot be a requirement for employment.) The legislature in the next regular session proposed an extensive revision of the Texas Constitution in the form of amendments, but voters rejected them by a margin of almost three to one.

In 1979 William P. Clements became the first Republican governor of Texas since E. J. Davis had vacated the office in 1874. The election of a Republican governor did not affect legislative-executive relations, however, since Clements received strong political support from conservative Democrats.

THE 1980s: EDUCATION REFORM

In 1982, Democratic Attorney General Mark White displaced incumbent governor Bill Clements despite Clements's unprecedented campaign spending. Teachers overwhelmingly supported White, who promised them salary increases and expressed support for education. Clements opposed the salary increases and was perceived as unsympathetic to education.

In 1984, House Bill 72, the first comprehensive educational reform since 1949, became law. The reform increased teachers' salaries, made school district revenue somewhat more equitable, and—controversially—raised standards for students and teachers. Public school teachers were required to pass a competency test to continue to teach ("no pass, no teach"), and students who failed a course were barred from extracurricular activities for six weeks ("no pass, no play").

In 1986, voter unhappiness with education reform, a sour economy, and decreased state revenue was enough to return Republican Bill Clements to the governor's office in a sweeping victory over Democrat Mark White. In 1988, three Republicans were elected to the Texas Supreme Court and one to the Railroad Commission—the first Republicans elected to statewide office (other than governor or U.S. senator) since Reconstruction.

In 1989, the Texas Supreme Court unanimously upheld an Austin district court's ruling in *Edgewood v. Kirby*[28] that the state's educational funding system violated the Texas constitutional requirement of "an efficient system" for the "general diffusion of knowledge." After several reform laws were also declared unconstitutional, the legislature in 1993 enacted a complex law that left the property tax as the basic vehicle for school funding but required wealthier school districts to share their wealth with poorer districts. Critics called the school finance formula a "Robin Hood" plan.

---

[27]For further discussion of the Sharpstown scandal, see Charles Deaton, *The Year They Threw the Rascals Out* (Austin: Shoal Creek Publishers, 1973), and Sam Kinch, Jr., and Ben Procter, *Texas under a Cloud: Story of the Texas Stock Fraud Scandal* (Austin and New York: Jenkins, 1972).
[28]777 S.W.2d 391 (Tex. 1989).

THE 1990s: TEXAS ELECTS A WOMAN GOVERNOR AND BECOMES A TWO-PARTY STATE

In 1990, the State Board of Education adopted the first elementary and high school biology texts since the 1960s that contained a thorough explanation of Darwin's theory of evolution. In 1994, however, the board removed pictures of male and female reproductive systems and discussions of changes that occur at puberty from high school health books.

With the 1990 election of Dan Morales (attorney general), Kay Bailey Hutchison (treasurer), and Rick Perry (agriculture commissioner), Texas elected the first Hispanic ever, and the first Republicans since Reconstruction, to **down-ticket** executive offices. (You will learn more about such offices in Chapter 25.) Austin voters elected the first openly gay legislator in 1991.

Texans also elected Ann Richards as their first female governor since Miriam "Ma" Ferguson. Through her appointive powers, she opened the doors of state government to unprecedented numbers of women, Latinos, and African Americans. In 1992, Texas elected Kay Bailey Hutchison as its first female U.S. senator. She joined fellow Republican Phil Gramm, and they became the first two Republicans to hold U.S. Senate seats concurrently since 1874.

Two-Party Politics. When the smoke, mud, and sound bites of the 1994 general election settled, a new political age had dawned—Texas had truly become a two-party state. Republican candidates won victories from the top to the bottom of the ballot. For the first time since Reconstruction, with the election of George W. Bush, Republicans held the governor's office and both U.S. Senate seats.

Although both Democratic and Republican incumbents were reelected to down-ticket administrative positions, Republicans held all the Railroad Commission seats and a majority on the State Board of Education and the Texas Supreme Court.

In 1996, Republicans won a majority in the Texas Senate for the first time since Reconstruction. The 1997 legislature failed to enact campaign finance reform, nonpartisan election of judges, and Governor Bush's tax initiative to reduce public schools' reliance on local property taxes. The state's first comprehensive water management plan was enacted, however, along with voluntary surgical castration for child molesters, prohibition of tobacco possession by minors, and authorization for patients to sue health maintenance organizations (HMOs) for malpractice. Voters also ratified an amendment to the Texas Constitution that allows them to use their *home equity* (the current market value of a home minus the outstanding mortgage debt) as collateral for a loan.

Republican Dominance. The 1998 general election was a sweep year for Republicans, who won every statewide elective office. This overwhelming achievement also positioned Governor George W. Bush as the front-runner for the Republican nomination for president in 2000. In the seventy-sixth Texas legislature (1999), however, Democrats narrowly retained control of the state house of representatives, and Republican control of the state senate was diminished to a one-vote margin.

Legislators deregulated electric companies in Texas and required parents' permission for underage girls to obtain an abortion or have their bodies (except for ears) pierced. Physicians were also given the right to collectively bargain with HMOs. The legal blood-alcohol level for driving drunk was reduced to 0.08 percent; cities and counties were prohibited from suing gun manufacturers; and the state's city annexation law was made more restrictive.

Public school teachers received a pay raise, but not enough to bring them up to the national average. A plan for taxpayer-funded vouchers to be used by families to pay for their children's private school education failed. To take advantage of federal grants that

Down-ticket
Describes a candidate for political office relative to others located higher on the ballot.

had been made available, Texas adopted a program to provide basic health insurance to some of the state's children who lacked health insurance coverage. Despite passage of this Children's Health Insurance Program (CHIP), more than 20 percent of children remain uninsured today.

THE 2000s: TEXAS BECOMES A REPUBLICAN STATE

The 2001 legislature enacted a "hate crimes" law that strengthened penalties for crimes motivated by a victim's race, religion, color, gender, disability, sexual orientation, age, or national origin. The legislature also criminalized open alcohol containers in most motor vehicles, established partial funding for health insurance for public school employees, and made it easier for poor children to apply for health care coverage under Medicaid. With little conflict, the legislature increased subsidies to corporations by agreeing to reimburse school districts that grant **tax abatements** to corporations. A Republican proposal to redraw U.S. congressional districts preoccupied the 2001 legislature as major state issues were left unresolved.

The Republicans Consolidate Their Power. The Republicans swept Texas statewide offices and both chambers of the legislature in the 2002 elections. A Republican governor, lieutenant governor, and speaker of the house ensured Republican proposals a sympathetic hearing in the 2003 legislative session. A nonpartisan policy, however, remained in effect in the legislature, as the lieutenant governor and speaker appointed some Democrats to committee chair and vice chair positions.

A projected $10 billion budget deficit created an uncomfortable environment for the Republicans. Politically and ideologically opposed to both new taxes and state-provided social services, the legislature and the governor chose to reduce funding for most state programs but especially education, health care, children's health insurance, and social services for the needy.

Attempts to close some tax loopholes failed. For example, businesses and professions of all sizes continued to organize as "partnerships" to avoid the state corporate franchise tax. The legislature did place limits on pain-and-suffering jury awards for injuries caused by physician malpractice and hospital incompetence and made it more difficult to sue the makers of unsafe, defective products.

The legislature's social agenda was ambitious. It outlawed civil unions for same-sex couples and barred recognition of such unions even when they are registered by other states. In addition, a 24-hour wait to be "educated" about the fetus is now required before a woman can have an abortion.

The Redistricting Controversy. Although the districts for electing U.S. representatives in Texas had been redrawn by a panel of one Democratic and two Republican federal judges following the 2000 census, Texas Congressman and U.S. House Majority Leader Tom DeLay was unhappy that more Texas Republicans were not elected to Congress. Governor Rick Perry agreed to call a special session in order to further redraw the new court-approved districts to increase Republican representation. Minority party Democrats argued that the districts had already been drawn to accommodate the decade's population shifts and that the Republicans were only trying to gerrymander Texas voters. (See Chapter 6 for a further discussion of the gerrymander.)

During Special Session One (June 30, 2003), most house Democrats (dubbed the Killer Ds) left the state for Oklahoma to deny the state house of representatives the required two-thirds quorum necessary to conduct its business.

Special Session Two (July 28, 2003) saw Republican Lieutenant Governor David Dewhurst change the senate rule that had required a two-thirds majority vote for bills

Tax Abatement
A reduction of or exemption from taxes (usually real estate taxes); typically granted by a local government to businesses in exchange for bringing jobs and investments to a community.

to be heard on the senate floor. This denied the minority senate Democrats a procedural tool to block congressional redistricting. In response, most senate Democrats left the state for New Mexico so that the Texas Senate would not have the required quorum. For Special Session Three (September 15, 2003), senate Democrats were unable to muster enough members to block the quorum, and the new district lines were drawn. The redistricting generated numerous lawsuits challenging its legality, but the U.S. Supreme Court refused to overturn most of the actions of the Texas legislature, affirming that states could redistrict more than once each decade and rejecting the argument that the redistricting was an illegal partisan gerrymander.

Congressman Tom DeLay was indicted for money laundering and forced to resign his seat in Congress. The voters elected a former Democratic congressmen, Nick Lampson, to DeLay's old seat. The 2007 legislature saw almost continuous battle between the house and the speaker, the senate and the lieutenant governor, the senate and the house, and the legislature and the governor. Legislators did find time to restore some 127,000 poor children to the Children's Health Insurance Program (CHIP).

The 2009 legislature seemed almost placid following the unprecedented house revolt against Speaker Tom Craddick and election of Joe Straus as new speaker. However, consideration of the contentious voter identification bill caused conflict in the senate and a parliamentary shutdown of the Texas House of Representatives in the last days of the legislative session. The house adjourned without a voter ID resolution, leaving several important matters to be resolved by special session. Other bills that failed included proposals to legalize casino gambling, increase the legal age to purchase tobacco products, and allow needle exchange programs, guns on campus, medical marijuana, and increased strip club fees. The legislature passed new laws including limited restrictions on using a cell phone when driving through a school zone and a tax increase on smokeless tobacco.

Much of the state's political attention was focused on disputes about Texas's acceptance of federal funds. Texas accepted federal stimulus money to help balance the state's budget, but turned down over $500 million in federal stimulus money for unemployed Texans. The state declined to apply for up to $700 million in federal grant money linked to Race to the Top, a program to improve education quality and results. Governor Perry believed that the money would result in a federal takeover of Texas's education. Texas also joined Alaska as the only states refusing to participate in a National Governors Association effort to rewrite national curriculum standards.

TEXAS CULTURE

A political culture reflects the political values and beliefs of a people. It explains how people feel about their government—their expectations of what powers it should have over their lives and what services it should provide. A political culture is largely developed through agents of socialization such as family, religion, peer group, and education and is characterized by its levels of ethnic and religious diversity and political tolerance. Shaped by culture, individual participation in the political system depends on people's view of their place within it.

MORAL, TRADITIONAL, AND INDIVIDUALISTIC CULTURES

A number of different approaches have been used to study diversity in nations, regions, states, and communities. One popular approach is that of Daniel J. Elazar, who depicted American political culture as a mix of three distinct subcultures, each prevalent in at least one area of the United States.

Elazar used the term *moralistic* to describe a culture whose adherents are concerned with "right and wrong" in politics. *Moralistic culture* views government as a positive force, one that values the individual but functions to the benefit of the general public. Discussion of public issues and voting are not only rights but opportunities to better the individual and society alike. Furthermore, politicians should not profit from their public service. Moralistic culture is strongest in New England, and although a product of Puritan religious values, it is associated with more secular (nonreligious) attitudes.

Individual culture embodies the view that government is practical, its prime objective being to further private enterprise, but that its intervention into people's lives should be strictly limited. Blurring the distinction between economic and political life, individualistic culture sees business and politics as appropriate avenues by which an individual can advance her or his interests. Accordingly, business interests play a very strong role and running for office is difficult without their support. Conflicts of interest are fairly commonplace, and political corruption may be expected as a natural political activity. The individualistic culture predominates in the commercial centers of the Middle Atlantic states, moving west and south along the Ohio River and its tributaries.

Widespread throughout America, *traditional culture* in Texas derives primarily from the plantation society of the Old South and the patron system of northern Mexico and South Texas. Government is seen to have an active role, but primarily to maintain the dominant social and religious values. Government should also help maintain accepted class distinctions and encourage the beliefs of the dominant religion. Traditionalistic culture views politics as the special preserve of the social and economic elite—as a process of maintaining the existing order. Believing in personal rather than public solutions to problems, it views political participation as a privilege and accepts social pressure and restrictive election laws that limit participation.[29]

POLITICAL CULTURE AND POLITICAL PARTICIPATION

Elazar considered Texas a mix of traditional and individualistic cultures. The traditional overrides the individualistic in East Texas, which was initially settled by immigrants from the Upper Old South and Mexican border areas, where the patron system dominated early Texas. The individualistic supersedes the traditional throughout the rest of the state. As a result, in Texas participation in politics is not as highly regarded as in those states with a moralistic culture. Voter turnout in Texas is in fact well below the national average. Texans see politics largely as the domain of economic interests, and most tend to ignore the significance of their role in the political process and how it might benefit them.[30]

TEXAS CULTURAL REGIONS

D. W. Meinig found that the cultural diversity of Texas was more apparent than its homogeneity and that no unified culture has emerged from the various ethnic and cultural groups that settled Texas. He believed that the "typical Texan," like the "average American," does not exist but is an oversimplification of the more distinctive social, economic, and political characteristics of the state's inhabitants.[31]

[29]Daniel J Elazar, *American Federalism: A View from the States*, 3rd ed. (New York: Harper & Row, 1984).
[30]Ibid.
[31]Information for this section is adapted from D. W. Meinig, *Imperial Texas: An Interpretive Essay in Cultural Geography* (Austin and London: University of Texas Press, 1969).

Both Meinig and Elazar see modern regional political culture as largely determined by migration patterns, for people take their culture with them as they move geographically. Meinig believed that Texas had evolved into nine fairly distinct cultural regions. However, whereas political boundaries are distinct, cultural divisions are often blurred and transitional. For example, the East Texas region shares political culture with much of the Upper South, while West Texas shares a similar culture with eastern New Mexico, and so forth. (See Figure 19–2.)

The effects of mass media, the mobility of modern Texans statewide and beyond, and immigration from Mexico also blur the cultural boundaries within Texas, between it and its bordering states, and with Mexico. Although limited because they do not take into account these modern-day realities, both Meinig's and Elazar's explanations are useful guides to a general understanding of contemporary Texas culture, attitudes, and beliefs.

EAST TEXAS

East Texas is a social and cultural extension of the Old South. It is basically rural and biracial. In spite of the changes brought about by civil rights legislation, black "towns" still exist alongside white "towns," as do many segregated social and economic institutions, such as churches, fraternal lodges, and chambers of commerce.

East Texas counties and towns are often dominated by old families, whose wealth is usually based on real estate, banking, construction, and retail merchandising. Cotton—once "king" of agriculture in the region—has been replaced by beef cattle, poultry, and timber. Owing to a general lack of economic opportunity, young East Texans migrate to

FIGURE 19–2 Texas Political Culture

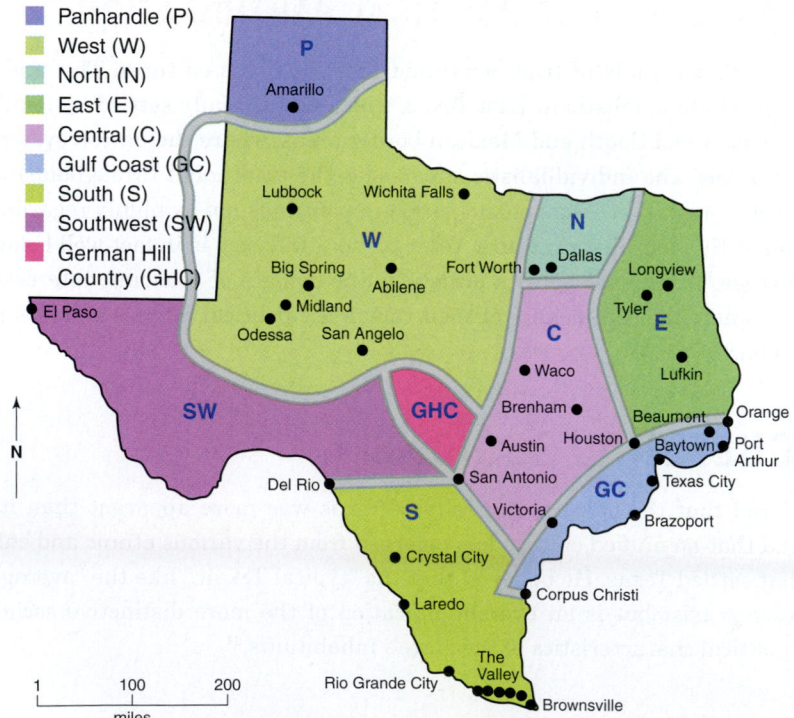

Source: Adapted from D. W. Meinig, *Imperial Texas: An Interpretive Essay in Cultural Geography* (Austin and London: University of Texas Press, 1969). Reproduced by permission of the publisher. © 1969 D. W. Meinig. All rights reserved.

metropolitan areas, primarily Dallas–Fort Worth and Houston. Seeking more tranquility and solitude, retiring urbanites have begun to revitalize some small-town and rural communities that lost population to the metropolitan areas. The region is dominated spiritually by fundamentalist Protestantism, which permeates its political, social, and cultural activities.

THE GULF COAST

Before 1900, Texas was an economic colony; it sold raw materials to the industrialized North and bought northern manufactured products. In 1901, however, an oil well named **Spindletop** was drilled near Beaumont, and the Texas economy began to change. Since Spindletop, the Gulf Coast has experienced almost continuous growth, especially during World War II, the Cold War defense buildup, and the various energy booms of the late 20th and early 21st centuries.

In addition to being an industrial and petrochemical center, the Gulf Coast is one of the most important shipping centers in the nation. Spindletop was backed by out-of-state investors, largely from the northeastern states, and its success stimulated increased out-of-state investment. Local wealth was also generated and largely reinvested in Texas to promote long-range development. Nevertheless, much of the economy is still supported by the sale of raw materials.

Spindletop
A major oil discovery in 1901 near Beaumont that began the industrialization of Texas.

A BOOM BASED IN HOUSTON

Through boom and bust, the petrochemical industry, which is concentrated on the Gulf Coast, has experienced unprecedented growth, producing a boomtown psychology. Rapid growth has fed real estate development and speculation throughout the region. The Houston area especially has flourished, and Harris County (Houston) has grown to become the third most populous county in the United States.

The initial growth of Houston was fueled by the influx of job seekers from East Texas and other rural areas of the state after World War II. This tended to give the Gulf Coast the flavor of rural Texas in an urban setting. Houston's social and economic elite was generally made up of second- and third-generation rich persons whose wealth came from oil, insurance, construction, land development, or banking. This rural flavor diminished, however, as migration to Texas from the Frost Belt (Great Lakes and Mid-Atlantic states) occurred. Frost Belt migration was, to a large extent, a result of the economic difficulty resulting in the metamorphosis of the U.S. economy from an industrial to a service base. This migration included both skilled and unskilled workers and added large numbers of well-educated young executives and professionals to the Houston elite pool. The Gulf Coast economy also attracts heavy immigration from the Americas, Africa, Europe, and Asia, giving modern Houston a culture as international as that of Los Angeles or New York. In fact, modern Houston has street signs in Vietnamese, Chinese, and English in areas with large Vietnamese and Chinese populations.

There are still many large ranches and plantations in the Gulf Coast region. They are owned either by wealthy business executives who live in the large cities or by "old families." The collapse of the oil boom and drastic declines in the price of oil and other petroleum products in the 1980s and 1990s struck especially hard at the Gulf Coast economy, which relies heavily on the petrochemical industry. Conversely, rising prices in the 2000s have resulted in another oil-based boom for the region.

The implosion of Houston-based Enron Corporation in the early 2000s affected financial markets and political attitudes nationwide, but it was

DID YOU KNOW?

That Texas has the second largest population of any state in the country—an estimated 23,507,783 in 2006?

DID YOU KNOW?

That the Houston Astros baseball team changed the name of its stadium from Enron Field to Minute Maid Park after Enron's embarrassing collapse?

especially damaging to Houston's economy, labor force, and national image. Enron was intertwined with the fabric of Houston's political, social, cultural, and financial existence to an extent rarely seen in corporate America. A dynamic corporate citizen, Enron made significant contributions to almost every aspect of Houston life. Its collapse left many Houstonians with dramatically decreased retirement incomes and investments. Despite the Enron collapse, the Gulf Coast continues to be a remarkably vibrant and energetic region. Houston, the worldwide oil and gas capital, boasts many corporate headquarters.

Although negatively affected, the Texas economy weathered the 2008 economic and financial meltdown much better than other urban states. Texas real estate also suffered fewer home foreclosures, primarily because the state did not experience a housing boom comparable to the booms on the West Coast, East Coast, and in Nevada and Arizona.

SOUTH TEXAS

The earliest area settled by Europeans, South Texas developed a **ranchero culture** based on livestock production that was similar to the feudal institutions in far-away Spain. **Creoles,** who descended from Spanish immigrants, were the economic, social, and political elite, while the first Texas cowboys, the **Mestizos** and the Native Americans, did the ranch work. Anglo Americans first became culturally important in South Texas when they gained title to much of the real estate in the region following the Texas Revolution of 1836. However, modern South Texas still retains elements of the ranchero culture, including some of its feudal aspects. Large ranches, often owned by one family for several generations, are prevalent; yet wealthy and corporate ranchers and farmers from outside the area are becoming common.

SOUTH TEXAS AGRICULTURE TODAY

Because of the semitropical South Texas climate, **The Valley (of the Rio Grande)** and the **Winter Garden** around Crystal City became major producers of citrus and vegetable products. These areas were developed by migrants from the northern United States in the 1920s and continue to be important multiuse agricultural assets.

The development of citrus and vegetable enterprises required intensive manual labor, which brought about increased immigration from Mexico. Modern South Texas Latinos can usually trace their U.S. roots to the 1920s or later because much of the Latino population was driven south of the Rio Grande after the Texas Revolution.

SOUTHWEST TEXAS

Southwest Texas exhibits many of the same **bicultural** characteristics as South Texas. Its large Mexican American population often maintains strong ties with relatives and friends in Mexico. The Roman Catholic Church strongly influences social and cultural attitudes on both sides of the border.

Southwest Texas is a major commercial and social passageway between Mexico and the United States. El Paso, the "capital city" of Southwest Texas and the fifth largest city in Texas, is a military, manufacturing, and commercial center. El Paso's primary commercial partners are Mexico and New Mexico. The economy of the border cities of Southwest Texas, like that of South Texas, is closely linked to Mexico and has also benefited from the economic opportunities brought about by NAFTA. The agricultural economy of much of the region depends on sheep, goat, and cattle production, although there is some irrigated row-crop agriculture. Most of the labor on ranches, as well as in manufacturing and commerce, is Latino.

Ranchero Culture
A quasi-feudal system whereby a property's owner, or patron, gives workers protection and employment in return for their loyalty and service. The rancher and workers all live on the *ranchero*, or ranch.

Creole
A descendant of European Spanish (or in some regions, French) immigrants to the Americas.

Mestizo
A person of both Spanish and Native American lineage.

The Valley (of the Rio Grande)
An area along the Texas side of the Rio Grande River known for its production of citrus fruits.

Winter Garden
An area of South Texas known for its vegetable production.

Bicultural
Encompassing two cultures.

DID YOU KNOW?

The *La Raza Unida* (literally "A United People") political movement of the 1960s began in Crystal City? The party organized to encourage Mexican Americans to unite politically and identify ethnically as one people. Its name is inspired by Mexican intellectual Jose Vasconcelos, who argued that the mixed-heritage Mestizos constituted a new race and should unite regardless of national boundaries.

La Raza Unida
A party organized in the late 1960s as a means of getting Mexican Americans to unite politically and to identify ethnically as one people.

POLITICS WITH A purpose

When Art and History Clash

Texas has a long and rich history, one that is filled with heroes and villains. Efforts to commemorate these figures with art can sometimes stir up public opinion concerning who is a villain and who is a hero. Such has been the case in El Paso. In 2007, the city of El Paso erected the world's largest equestrian statue. The work was created by the sculptor John Sherrill Houser, son of Ivan Houser, who worked on Mount Rushmore, and took a decade to complete.

The sculpture is of Juan de Onate, who explored the region that is now the southwestern United States in the late 1500s and early 1600s. The 36-foot-tall statue honored the man who led an expedition that claimed the northern region of the Rio Grande for Spain. Onate would also help found Santa Fe, New Mexico. While Onate's stated mission in traveling to this region was to spread Catholicism, like other Spanish colonists he sought to mine minerals in the area. However, he is remembered by many as being particularly cruel to Native Americans, namely the Acoma Indians. After a skirmish with the Acoma that left Onate's nephew dead, Onate demanded that the left foot of every male Indian over the age of 25 be amputated.

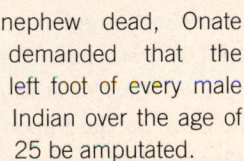

This and other tyrannical actions against the Native American population were deemed so cruel that Onate was recalled back to Mexico City, where he was convicted of cruelty and other offenses. Eventually he would clear his name, but many descendants of the early Native Americans in West Texas have not forgotten his offenses. In New Mexico, for instance, a smaller equestrian statue of Onate had its right foot removed in an act of vandalism. And in El Paso, the Native American population put pressure on the city council to name the statue simply "the Equestrian." Onate's name does not appear on his statue.

Native Americans in the region are offended that the city would honor someone who had committed such atrocities. Protesters carried signs reading, "Onate butcher of 800 Acoma men, women and children," "A monument to a war criminal," and "Onate fue asesino" (Onate was an assassin). Native American populations protest that such a work is an insult to them because it honors the legacy of someone who did much harm to their people. Such insensitivity from the broader public is an affront to both the Native American and Mestizo populations. Supporters of the sculpture argue that Onate must be seen in a bigger picture. His exploration led people into areas previously unknown by Spanish colonists. In doing so, he brought new technology and ideas to the Southwest.

What do you think? Should Onate be honored in this way? What about other such individuals? When artistic decisions are made, how much consideration should be given to descendants of long-dead victims? What roles do time and forgiveness play in a situation like this? How long is enough time for people to forgive and forget?

THE TEXAS BORDER

South and Southwest Texas together make up the area known as the "Texas Border." A corresponding "Mexico Border" includes parts of the Mexican states of Chihuahua, Coahuila, Nuevo León, and Tamaulipas. It can be argued that the Texas Border and the Mexico Border are two parts of an economic, social, and cultural region with a substantial degree of similarity that sets it off from the rest of the United States and Mexico. The Border region, which is expanding in size both to the north and to the south, has a **binational**, bicultural, and bilingual subculture in which **internationality** is commonplace and the people, economies, and societies on both sides constantly interact.[32]

Binational
Belonging to two nations.

Internationality
Having family and/or business interests in two or more nations.

[32]John Sharp, Texas Comptroller of Public Accounts, "Bordering the Future: Challenge and Opportunity in the Texas Border Region," July 1998, p. 3; Jorge Bustamante, "A Conceptual and Operative Vision of the Population Problems on the Border," in *Demographic Dynamics on the U.S.–Mexico Border*, ed. John R. Weeks and Roberto Ham Chande (El Paso: Texas Western Press, 1992), cited in Sharp, "Bordering the Future."

DID YOU KNOW?

That among the states in 2010, only Tennessee and Arkansas had a lower cost of living than Texas?

Maquiladora
A factory in the Mexican border region that assembles goods imported duty-free into Mexico for export. In Spanish, it literally means "twin plant."

North American Free Trade Agreement (NAFTA)
A treaty between Canada, Mexico, and the United States that calls for the gradual removal of tariffs and other trade restrictions. NAFTA came into effect in 1994.

South and Southwest Texas are "mingling pots" for the Latino and Anglo American cultures. Roman Catholic Latinos often retain strong links with Mexico through extended family and friends in Mexico and through Spanish-language newspapers. Many Latinos continue to speak Spanish; in fact, Spanish is also the commercial and social language of choice for many of the region's Anglo Americans.

The Texas Border cities are closely tied to the Mexican economy, on which their prosperity depends. Although improving economically, these regions remain among the poorest in the United States. The economy of the Texas Border benefits economically from *maquiladoras*, which are Mexican factories through which U.S. corporations employ inexpensive Mexican labor for assembly and piecework. Unfortunately, lax environmental and safety standards result in high levels of air, ground, and water pollution in the general area. In fact, the Rio Grande is now one of America's most ecologically endangered rivers.

The ongoing **North American Free Trade Agreement (NAFTA)**, which has helped remove trade barriers between Canada, Mexico, and the United States, is an economic stimulus for the Texas Border because it is a conduit for much of the commerce with Mexico.

Immigration and National Security. Poverty, military conflicts, crime, political disorder, and suppression of civil liberties in Central America and Mexico have driven hundreds of thousands of immigrants into the border regions of the United States. This flow of immigrants continues in spite of the tightened security measures and fence construction following the September 11, 2001, terror attack on New York. The Texas border is a major staging ground for the migration of both legal and illegal immigrants into the interior of Texas and the rest of the United States. The governments' immigration control expenditures economically benefit the regions.

Military expenditures by the U.S. government are also important to the economy of the region. A decision by the U.S. Navy to station a contingent of naval vessels in Ingleside has been an economic boost to the upper South Texas coast, and Fort Bliss continues to economically benefit the El Paso area.

A SECTION OF THE U.S.–MEXICO BORDER fence under construction in Granjeno, Texas. February 4, 2009. (AP Photo/ Eric Gay)

The American craving for illegal, mind-altering, addictive chemicals provides a steady flow of American capital through the Texas Border into Mexico and South America. Basically, the drug traffic is uncontainable as long as its U.S. market exists, but newspapers and other media virtuously trumpet feel-good headlines about "record drug busts" and arrests while the drug trade continues unabated.

This "invisible trade," because of its illegal status, inevitably results in violence as surely as did the American experiment prohibiting the sale and consumption of alcoholic beverages from 1919 to 1933. The collateral damage of the drug trade is readily visible and all too common as stories of death and destruction lead the evening news and provide villains and endless plots for movies and television detective programs. Although the worst of the violence is confined to the border areas of Mexico and the United States, its political, economic, lawless, and violent extension is increasingly evident throughout both countries.

Collateral to the drug traffic and its companion violence is a reverse cash flow from Mexico to the United States for weapons purchases. This illegal traffic moves easily obtained weapons, ammunition, and explosives from Texas and other states into Mexico and South America, minimally balancing the outflow of capital from the United States to Mexico and South America for drugs.

When the expenditures by the Mexican, Texas, and U.S. governments for narcotics and immigration agents, prison construction and operation, related military operations, and increased police employment are combined with the expenses, wages, and bribe money spent by drug, weapons, and immigrant traffickers, the result is increased employment and a significant but dangerous and unwholesome economic infusion to both sides of the border. Immigration, illegal traffic, and border security will be major political issues for both Democrats and Republicans in future election campaigns.

GERMAN HILL COUNTRY

The Hill Country was settled primarily by immigrants from Germany but also by immigrants who were Czech, Polish, and Norwegian. Although they mixed with Anglo Americans, Central European culture and architecture were dominant well into the 20th century. Skilled artisans were common in the towns; farms were usually moderate in size, self-sufficient, and family owned and operated. Most settlers were Lutheran or Roman Catholic, and these remain the most common religious affiliations for modern residents.

The German Hill Country is still a distinct cultural region. Although its inhabitants have become "Americanized," they still cling to many of their Central European cultural traditions. Primarily a farming and ranching area, the Hill Country is socially and politically conservative and has long been a stronghold of the Texas Republican Party.

Migration into the region, primarily by Anglo Americans and Latinos, is increasing. The most significant encroachment into the Hill Country is residential growth from rapidly expanding urban areas, especially San Antonio and Austin. Resorts, country homes, and retirement villages for well-to-do urbanites from the Gulf Coast and Dallas–Fort Worth area are also contributing to the cultural transformation of the German Hill Country.

DID YOU KNOW?

That immigration and border security were major political issues for both Democrats and Republicans in the 2010 primaries and in the general election?

DID YOU KNOW?

That Comfort, Texas, was settled by German "Freethinkers" seeking freedom *from* religion? They were both abolitionists and opponents of secession, and many were massacred by pro-Confederate raiders during the U.S. Civil War?

WEST TEXAS

The defeat of the Comanches in the 1870s opened West Texas to Anglo American settlement. Migrating primarily from the southern United States, these settlers passed their social and political attitudes and southern Protestant fundamentalism on to their descendants.

There are relatively few African Americans in modern West Texas, but Latinos migrated into the region in significant numbers, primarily to the cities and the intensively farmed areas. West Texas is socially and politically conservative, and its religion is Bible Belt fundamentalism. West Texas voters traditionally supported conservative Democrats but today favor the Republican Party. Indeed, this is true of most conservative Texans throughout the state.

The southern portion of the area emphasizes sheep, goat, and cattle production. In fact, San Angelo advertises itself as the "Sheep and Wool Capital of the World." Southern West Texas, which is below the Cap Rock Escarpment, is the major oil-producing area of Texas. The cities of Snyder, Midland, and Odessa owe their existence almost entirely to oil and related industries.

Northern West Texas is part of the Great Plains and High Plains and is primarily agricultural, with cotton, grain, and feedlot cattle production predominating. In this part of semiarid West Texas, the outstanding agricultural production is due to extensive irrigation from the **Ogallala Aquifer**. The large amount of water used for irrigation is gradually depleting the Ogallala. This not only affects the present economy of the region through higher costs to farmers but also serves as a warning signal for its economic future.

Ogallala Aquifer
A major underground reservoir and a source of water for irrigation and human consumption in northern West Texas and the Texas Panhandle, as well as other states.

THE PANHANDLE

Railroads advancing from Kansas City through the Panhandle brought midwestern farmers into this region, and wheat production was developed largely by migrants from Kansas. Because the commercial and cultural focus of the region was Kansas City, the early Panhandle was basically midwestern in both character and institutions.

The modern Texas Panhandle shares few cultural attributes with the American Midwest. Its religious, cultural, and social institutions function with little discernable difference from those of northern West Texas. The Panhandle economy is fed through extensive irrigation of cotton and grains from the Ogallala Aquifer. Feedlots for livestock and livestock production were established due to their proximity to the region's grain production but are major economic enterprises in their own right. Effective conservation of the Ogallala Aquifer is critical to the economic future of both northern West Texas and the Panhandle.

DID YOU KNOW?

That the median age of Texans is 32.7 years and that only one state (Utah) has a younger population?

NORTH TEXAS

Located between East and West Texas, North Texas exhibits many characteristics of both regions. Early North Texas benefited from the failure of the French socialist colony of **La Réunion**, which included many highly trained professionals in medicine, education, music, and science. (La Réunion was located on the south bank of the Trinity River, across from modern downtown Dallas.) The colonists and their descendants helped give North Texas a cultural and commercial distinctiveness. North Texas today is dominated by the Dallas–Fort Worth **Metroplex**. Dallas is a banking and

La Réunion
A failed French socialist colony of the 1800s located within the city limits of modern Dallas. Its skilled and educated inhabitants benefited early Dallas.

Metroplex
The greater Dallas–Fort Worth metropolitan area.

commercial center of national importance, and Fort Worth is the financial and commercial center of West Texas.

When railroads came into Texas from the North in the 1880s, Dallas became a rail center, and people and capital from the North stimulated its growth. Fort Worth became a regional capital that looked primarily to West Texas. The Swift and Armour meatpacking companies, which moved plants to Fort Worth in 1901, became the first national firms to establish facilities close to Texas's natural resources. More businesses followed, and North Texas began its evolution from an economic colony to an industrially developed area.

North Texas experienced extraordinary population growth after World War II, with extensive migration from the rural areas of East, West, and Central Texas. The descendants of these migrants are now third- and fourth-generation urbanites and tend to have urban attitudes and behavior. Recently, migration from other states, especially from the North, has been significant. Many international corporations have established headquarters in North Texas. Their executive and support staffs contribute to the region's diversity and cosmopolitan environment.

Although North Texas is more economically diverse than most other Texas regions, it relies heavily on the defense and aerospace industries. It also produces electronic equipment, computer products, plastics, and food products.

CENTRAL TEXAS

Central Texas is often called the "core area" of Texas. It is roughly triangular in shape, with its three corners being Houston, Dallas–Fort Worth, and San Antonio. The centerpiece of the region is Austin, one of the fastest-growing metropolitan areas in the nation. Already a center of government and education, the Austin metropolitan area has become the "Silicon Valley" of high-tech industries in Texas. Although the worldwide downturn in the high-tech sector after 2000 dealt a serious blow to the area's economy, high-tech industries still make a major economic contribution.

Austin's rapid growth is a result of significant migration from the northeastern United States and the West Coast, as well as from other regions in Texas. The influx of well-educated persons from outside Texas has added to the already substantial pool of accomplished Austinites, making it the intellectual and political capital of the state, as well as the economic center of Central Texas. The cultural and economic traits of all the other Texas regions mingle here, with no single trait being dominant. Central Texas is a microcosm of Texas culture.

CULTURAL DIVERSITY

Texas is one of the fastest-growing states in the nation. No longer predominantly rural and agrarian, Texas is becoming more culturally diverse than ever as immigrants continue to find it a desirable place to call home.

The 2000 census showed a significant trend toward greater ethnic diversity. Over the 10-year period, the Anglo majority declined from 60.7 to 53.1 percent, while Hispanics increased from 25.5 to 32.0 percent and the rapidly growing "Other" classification (primarily Asians, Pacific Islanders, Middle Easterners, and Native Americans) grew from 2.1 to 3.3 percent. The African American percentage of the total population also fell marginally, from 11.7 to 11.6 percent.

The Texas State Population Estimates and Projections Program aids government and corporate planners by developing estimates of Texas's future population growth.

FIGURE 19–3 Texas Population, Midrange Scenario

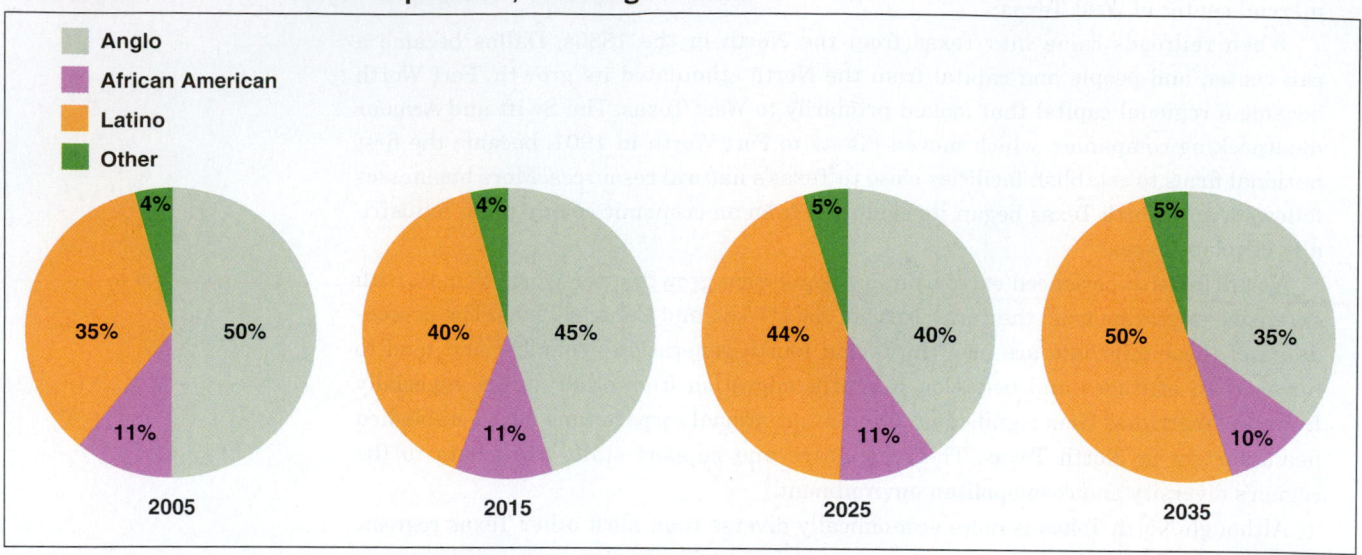

Source: Data from Population Estimates and Projections Program, "Projections of Texas and Counties in Texas by Age, Sex, and Race/Ethnicity for 1990–2040" (San Antonio: Texas State Data Center, Office of the State Demographer, 2004). Methodology and data are online at http://txsdc.utsa.edu/tpepp/2006projections/. Click on "Population Projections for the State of Texas."

This group of researchers has proposed a number of possible population scenarios. The middle-of-the-road scenario shown by the pie charts in Figure 19–3 is the one Texas statisticians recommend for long-range business and governmental planning. This scenario assumes a moderate degree of immigration and predicts a Texas population of slightly more than 35 million by 2040, with a Latino plurality by 2025 and a Latino majority by 2035.

In contrast, a high-immigration scenario projects a Texas population of more than 51 million by 2040. Hispanics achieve plurality status by 2015 and majority status by 2030. The "Other" classification surpasses African Americans and collectively becomes the third largest group by 2040. All scenarios show Anglo Texans losing their numerical majority by 2010.

Clearly, Texans are becoming more diverse and now have the opportunity to continue to build on their already rich cultural pluralism. Increasing diversity could also have a significant impact on the political culture of Texas, because the interests of more groups will have to be seriously considered as public policy is formulated and implemented.

A downside of Texas diversity is an unequal distribution of wealth and social services. As shown in Figures 19–4, 19–5, and 19–6, Latino Americans, African Americans, and others are more likely to live in poverty, have significantly lower family income, and have lower levels of health insurance than the more favored Anglo Americans.

POLITICS AND DIVERSITY

Voter participation in Texas is historically low, even by United States standards. Social scientists argue that this is due to political conditioning as well as social and economic reality. And Latino participation is low even by Texas standards. However, Latino voter

FIGURE 19–4 Net Family Income in Texas

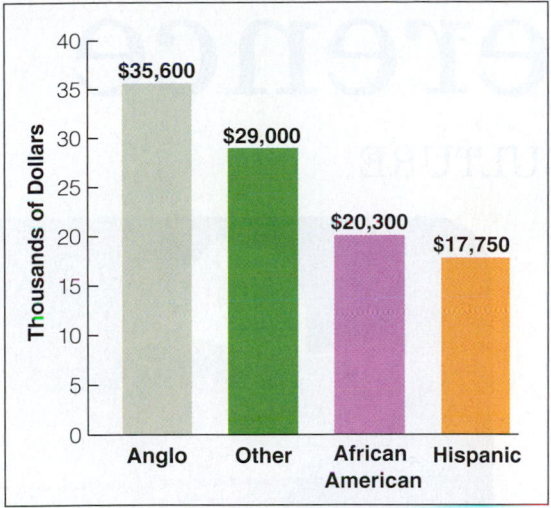

Source: The Henry J. Kaiser Family Foundation, "State Health Facts Online," www.statehealthfacts.kff.org.

FIGURE 19–5 Percentage of Persons in Poverty in Texas

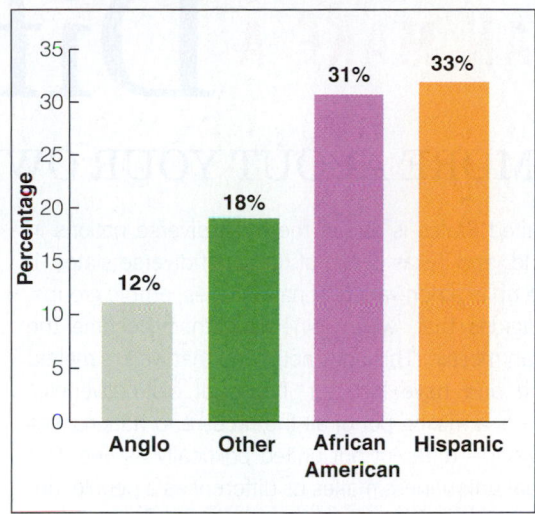

Source: The Henry J. Kaiser Family Foundation, "State Health Facts Online," www.statehealthfacts.kff.org.

FIGURE 19–6 Health Insurance Status of Persons Under the Age of 65 in Texas

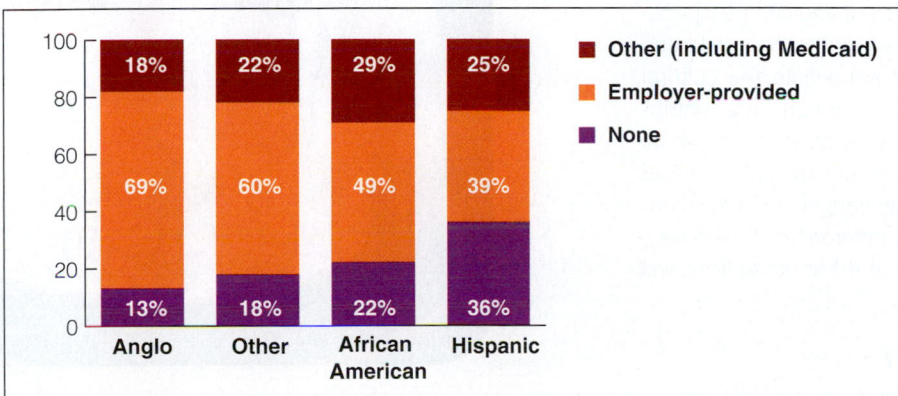

Source: The Henry J. Kaiser Family Foundation, "State Health Facts Online," www.statehealthfacts.kff.org.

turnout surged during the 2008 primary and November election. Is this sleeping political giant really awake, or was this level of political participation simply an anomaly? How would substantial Mexican American political participation affect public policy and the Texas political system?

YOU CAN MAKE A Difference

LEARN MORE ABOUT YOUR OWN CULTURE

The United States is one of the most diverse nations in the world, and Texas is one of the most diverse states. It is made up of a rich variety of nationalities, ethnic groups, and religions that, when joined together, become the American mosaic. This does not mean that we are melted into one and have lost our individual distinctiveness. America is a mixing pot of all the races and nationalities of the world—different but united politically as one. Our individual uniqueness makes us different as a people; our unity in diversity makes us different as a nation.

WHY SHOULD YOU CARE?

Our individual cultural and ethnic histories are, in a sense, who we are. Gaining knowledge of this history adds to your understanding of your own uniqueness. What you learn about your cultural and ethnic history will become a part of your understanding of yourself and can be a priceless gift to pass on to your children and to their children.

Learning to understand and appreciate the cultural and ethnic histories of others as well can only contribute to our understanding and appreciation of who we all are, both as individuals and as Americans. We can find both our national strength and the danger of internal conflicts among us in our individual differences. Collectively, our choice will determine which of these possibilities will predominate.

WHAT CAN YOU DO?

Talk to your grandparents, parents, and uncles and aunts to learn what they know about your culture and family history. Record as much oral history as you can about their personal lives, experiences, and political recollections, as well as family myths and traditions. You may find this information priceless as you someday talk to your own children and grandchildren about their culture. Broaden your cultural and political experiences. Participate in activities and organizations of ethnic, religious, and ideological groups that are different from your own. This will help you better understand and appreciate the rich diversity of modern American life.

THE MODEL OF A MEMORIAL honoring pioneer Texas Latinos by Laredo sculptor Armando Hinojosa. The memorial is to stand on the south lawn of the Capitol Building in Austin. (Courtesy of Dr. Cayetano E. Barrera, http://www.tejanos.com/artists.htm)

KEY TERMS

annexation 658	La Réunion 684	secession 659
antitrust legislation 660	maquiladora 682	Shivercrat 668
bicultural 680	Mestizo 680	Spindletop 679
binational 681	Metroplex 684	tax abatement 675
Creole 680	North American Free Trade	tenant farmer 661
down-ticket 674	Agreement (NAFTA) 682	tidelands 668
internationality 681	Ogallala Aquifer 684	The Valley (of the Rio
item veto 662	progressive movement 662	Grande) 680
Ku Klux Klan (KKK) 663	Prohibition 661	white primary 663
La Raza Unida 680	ranchero culture 680	Winter Garden 680

CHAPTER SUMMARY

1. Originally part of Mexico, Texas was largely settled by migrants from the American South. Texas declared its independence from Mexico in 1836 and joined the United States in 1845. Early politics revolved around the slavery issue and the possibility of secession from the Union, which was strongly opposed by Sam Houston, one of the founders of the Texas Republic and the hero of the battle of San Jacinto (1836). After the election of Abraham Lincoln as U.S. president, Texas left the Union and joined the Confederacy. The collapse of the Confederacy meant anarchy until Union troops occupied Texas in June 1865.

2. After a period of military occupation, radical Republican E. J. Davis (1870–1873) became governor in an election in which African Americans could vote but many former Confederates could not. The Davis administration was enormously unpopular with the white majority in Texas, and after the former Confederates regained the franchise, Davis was swept from office. The Democratic Party was to control Texas politics for more than a hundred years.

3. While conservatives normally dominated the Democratic Party, Texas experienced a degree of progressive reform with the election of several progressive governors between 1890 and 1939, including James Hogg (1891–1895) and both "Farmer Jim" and "Ma" Ferguson (1915–1917, 1925–1927, and 1933–1935). Another colorful governor was radio announcer W. "Pappy" Lee O'Daniel, a popular figure who nonetheless had little legislative success.

4. A key figure in the era following World War II (1939–1945) was Governor Allan Shivers (1949–1957). A conservative Democrat, Shivers advocated voting for Republican presidents and conservative Democrats for all other offices. In 1960, Lyndon B. Johnson, U.S. senator from Texas and the Senate majority leader, became vice president under John F. Kennedy. In a special election in 1961, Republican John Tower filled Johnson's seat. Tower was the first Republican since Reconstruction to be elected to an important position in Texas, but he would not be the last. In 1963, following Kennedy's assassination, Johnson became president of the United States.

5. Civil rights have always been an issue for both African Americans and Mexican Americans in Texas, who were seen by the dominant Anglo Americans as sources of cheap labor. Modern Texans can take no pride in the historical treatment of both these groups, who, undereducated and exploited for their labor, lived under a state-enforced caste system. The enduring consequences of discrimination are still with us, as illustrated by their lower levels of health care, education, and income.

6. The election of Republican William Clements as governor in 1979 was a sign of the growing importance of the Republican Party. By 1994, Texas was clearly a two-party state. By 2002, the Republicans were in complete control of all levels of state government, including both chambers of the legislature. Texas seemed headed toward a one-party system again, but under a different party. In 2003, the Republicans consolidated their power by redistricting the U.S. House seats. As a result, in 2004 they gained control of the Texas delegation to the U.S. House.

7. **What action did female, African American, and Latino Texans take to change the state laws that relegated them to second-class citizenship? What might your lives be like today if they had simply accepted that "life is unfair"?** Legal discrimination against female, African American, and Latino Texans during the latter half of the 19th century and the first half of the 20th century was considered normal, if not necessary, for the protection of family values and the economic development of the state.

All of these groups began their struggle through organizations that lobbied, protested, and filed legal action for protection from prejudiced individuals, family members, and the state itself. Women's groups gained the right to vote through legislative action, but the courts were the primary venue for all the groups to achieve equal rights. Although dramatic, the reward of judicial or legislative success was achieved only after decades of struggle and group action by motivated, courageous members of these mistreated groups.

8. **Does your cultural region reflect the conclusions of Meinig and Elazar?** Texas can be divided into a series of cultural regions with differing characteristics and traditions: (1) East Texas, (2) the Gulf Coast, (3) South Texas, (4) Southwest Texas, (5) the German Hill Country, (6) West Texas, (7) the Panhandle, (8) North Texas, and (9) Central Texas. These regions display varying combinations of moralistic, traditionalistic, and individualistic culture.

9. **What social changes are most likely to dominate Texas's political future?** Projections of population growth and immigration predict a gradual shift in Texas's population away from an Anglo American majority toward a Hispanic American majority. Increased political clout can come with increased population, and Hispanic Americans could begin to challenge the political and economic dominance of Anglo Americans. Regardless of the political outcome of population shifts, Texas is becoming more culturally diverse and now has an opportunity to build on its already rich cultural pluralism.

SELECTED PRINT, MEDIA, AND ONLINE RESOURCES

PRINT RESOURCES

Brammer, Billy Lee. *The Gay Place.* Austin: University of Texas Press, 1995. This work is really three interlocking novels that use Texas politics as the setting and Texas politicians as the primary characters.

Campbell, Randolph B. *Gone to Texas: A History of the Lone Star State.* New York: Oxford University Press, 2003. A leading Texas historian, Campbell sets early Texas history firmly within the history of Mexico and also keeps African Americans, both slave and free, at the center of his story. Much of the book concerns the state's lively political history. Campbell exhibits considerable skepticism about claims that Texas is unique among the states.

Davidson, Chandler. *Race and Class in Texas Politics.* Princeton, NJ: Princeton University Press, 1992. The author examines the forces that shape Texas politics. The book is recommended by *The American Political Science Review.*

Farmer, James. *Lay Bare the Heart.* Fort Worth: Texas Christian University Press, 2005. James Farmer describes the battles, heroes, and knaves associated with the civil rights movement in the 1950s and 1960s.

Lind, Michael. *Made in Texas: George W. Bush and the Southern Takeover of American Politics.* New York: Basic Books, 2003. This book looks at how the political tradition of Texas is shaping U.S. and world politics.

Montejano, David. *Anglos and Mexicans in the Making of Texas, 1836–1986.* University of Texas Press, 1987. Montejano chronicles Anglo-Latino relations from the beginning of the Republic. An excellent read.

Rogers, Mary Beth (with an introduction by Bill Moyers). *Cold Anger: A Story of Faith and Power Politics.* Denton: University of North Texas Press, 1990. Rogers writes the story of Ernesto Cortes, who employs religion and other tools to develop grassroots Mexican American movements in South Texas.

Shabazz, Amilcar. *Advancing Democracy: African Americans and the Struggle for Access and Equity in Higher Education in Texas.* Chapel Hill: University of North Carolina Press, 2004. Shabazz chronicles the expansion of higher-education opportunities for African Americans.

Soltero, Carlos R. *Latinos and American Law: Landmark Supreme Court Cases.* Austin: University of Texas Press, 2006. This work documents major civil rights cases expanding the rights of Latinos.

MEDIA RESOURCES

The American Experience: A Class Apart—This PBS documentary highlights the U.S. Supreme Court decision *Hernandez v. Texas* (1954) that became a landmark civil rights case successfully challenging Jim Crow–style discrimination against Latinos. The documentary also discusses the challenges faced by the Latino legal team as well as the high cost that their failure would bring for the Latino population. A must-see for those interested in the evolution of civil rights.

The American Experience: Remember the Alamo—This PBS program is available in both Spanish and English versions. The documentary explores the life of prominent Mexican Texan José Antonio Navarro and the Latinos who fought alongside Anglo Texans for Texas independence.

Justice for My People: The Dr. Hector P. Garcia Story—This KEDT-TV public television production chronicles the rise of the Mexican American civil rights movement from the 1920s to the 1980s, as lived by Dr. Hector Garcia.

Lone Star—Producer/director John Sayles explores the cultural and social interaction among Mexicans, Mexican Americans, African Americans, and Anglo Americans along the Texas-Mexico border.

Mexican American Legislative Caucus: The Texas Struggle for Equality and Opportunity—A product of a team at Texas State University–San Marcos, this documentary was first aired by KLRN, a PBS station. Through interviews with several retired and present-day Tejano legislators, the story of the caucus and its increasing influence on state affairs unfolds from its founding in the early 1970s to the present. The documentary also traces the role of Tejanos from Texas independence through the period of political exclusion to the modern struggle for full citizenship.

Traffic—Director Steven Soderbergh examines the impact of the "war against drugs" on the people, institutions, and social structures along the Mexican border.

Two Towns of Jasper—Another PBS production, from 2002, this program explores the separate reactions and viewpoints of the white and black communities of Jasper, Texas, following the murder of James Byrd, a black man who was dragged to his death while chained to a pickup truck by three white men.

ONLINE RESOURCES

The Handbook of Texas Online A great source for information on Texas history, culture, and geography. A joint project of the Texas State Historical Association and the University of Texas at Austin, it is an encyclopedia of all things Texan: www.tshaonline.org

Lone Star Junction This nonprofit organization chartered by the state of Texas provides an online resource about Texas and its early history: www.lsjunction.com

Texas Fact Book 2008 Factual information and statistics can be found in this resource written by Bob Bullock of the Texas State History Museum for the Legislative Budget Board: www.lbb.state.tx.us/Fact_Book/Texas_Factbook_2008.pdf

Texas.gov The state of Texas home page offers information on Texas history, early native populations, historical events and dates, historic sites, and population information, projections, and demographics: www.texas.gov

Texas Monthly chronicles life in contemporary Texas, reporting on vital issues such as politics, the environment, industry, education, and the leisure and cultural scene: www.texasmonthly.com

University of Texas at Austin Perry-Castañeda Library Map Collection houses historical maps of Texas including "State of Origin of the Old Stock Anglo-American Population"; "Black Slaves as a Percentage of Total Population, 1840 and 1860"; "German Element, 1850"; "Spanish and French Surnames, 1850"; and the "Vote on Secession, 1861": www.lib.utexas.edu/maps/historical/history_texas.html

20

The Texas seal on the floor of the
capitol building. (AP Photo)

The Texas Constitution

QUESTIONS TO CONSIDER

How do cultural and political forces help shape a state's constitution?

How do constitutional restrictions hinder the effective and efficient operation of government?

What are the major criticisms of the Texas Constitution?

CHAPTER CONTENTS

what if...

Texas Used the U.S. Constitution as a Model?

BACKGROUND

Some reformers criticize and even ridicule the Texas state constitution. In contrast, Americans have come to revere their national constitution, and it is respected among scholars around the world. While it establishes basic liberties that have become the standard for international human rights advocates and the envy of people suffering oppression in many other countries, it also establishes fundamental governing institutions that balance power and thwart tyrants. It has endured world wars, civil wars, and depressions and has served the nation well as it transformed from a fledgling rural nation of 4 million in 1789 to a dominant world power of more than 300 million today.

USING THE U.S. CONSTITUTION AS A TEMPLATE

While a new Texas Constitution based on national constitutional provisions would be 91 percent shorter than today's and would have 94 percent fewer amendments, many provisions would be surprisingly controversial. Even using the U.S. Bill of Rights would generate opposition. For example, 22 state representatives voted against these first 10 amendments when Representative Jake Johnson introduced them in the Texas legislature as "an act to protect our fundamental liberties." Other U.S. constitutional provisions would generate much more opposition.

THE LEGISLATURE

The Texas legislature would meet annually instead of biennially (once every two years) as it does now. More frequent sessions would allow the legislature to pass an annual budget instead of a two-year budget, and as a result, it would not need to predict the state's financial needs a full two years in advance. Rather than being limited to 140 days, the legislature could meet as long as it chose and could spend more time on legislative tasks.

Many Texans would vigorously resist these changes because they hold the concept of a "citizen legislature" in high regard. They believe legislators should be ordinary citizens who work at other professions, and who set aside their day-to-day responsibilities for five months every other year to serve out of a sense of public duty. Some Texans believe legislators should not spend so much time in Austin that they become government insiders. They fear that longer and more frequent sessions would give the legislature too much opportunity to pass new regulations, to create new programs, and to pass higher taxes to pay for them. In short, many Texans hold to the old adage that "no one's life or liberty is safe while the legislature is in session."

THE GOVERNOR

Although the governor could be elected to no more than two terms, the powers of the office would dramatically increase. The governor, like the president, would appoint all major executives, direct a cabinet, and be able to issue orders to coordinate, supervise, and eliminate duplication among state agencies.

Texas would replace the long ballot in which Texans elect the attorney general, comptroller of public accounts, commissioner of the general land office, commissioner of agriculture, three railroad commissioners, and 15 members of the board of education. With a short ballot, Texans would cast only one vote for a governor and lieutenant governor as a team. The governor would not need to compete with many other elected officers who have their own ambitions. However, any attempt to take away their right to elect major executives would outrage voters. Furthermore, Texans have feared the concentration of executive power since the time of E. J. Davis, and an attempt to increase the power of the governor would be seen as a "power grab."

THE COURTS

Although reformers can make some convincing arguments for reforming Texas's legislative and executive branches along these lines, they would find it impossible to persuade the state to remodel the Texas courts after the federal courts. Few would argue that the governor should appoint judges for terms of good behavior (amounting to life terms). If state courts had the power to interpret broad language in the constitution, politicians would charge Texas judges with arrogance and judicial activism, and they would accuse judges of making law rather than interpreting it.

FOR CRITICAL ANALYSIS

1. How would Texans react if their legislature, like Congress, had unlimited borrowing power and the authority to adopt a personal income tax?

2. How can Texans admire the national constitution and, at the same time, harbor so many doubts about applying its provisions to Texas? Is there a fundamental difference between governing a state and governing a nation?

THE REAL CHARACTER of a government is determined less by the provisions of its constitution than by the minds and hearts of its citizens. Government is a process of decision making conditioned by a state's history, its people, and the pressures exerted by individuals, interest groups, and political parties.

Still, our national, state, and local governments would be vastly different were it not for their constitutions. Although the exact meaning of constitutional provisions may be disputed, there is general agreement that a constitution should be respected as the legal basis controlling the fundamentals of government decision making. A constitution serves as a rationalization for actions by courts, legislatures, executives, and the people. The very idea of having a written constitution has become part of the basic system of political beliefs in the United States—our political culture.

Constitutions establish major governing institutions, assign them power, and place both implicit and explicit limits on the power that has been assigned. And, because Americans respect constitutions, they promote *legitimacy*, a concept we discussed in Chapter 1. Texans' reactions to Reconstruction (1864–1877) led to the adoption of a constitution designed to curb government power. The legislature is hampered by numerous limitations on salary, sessions, and activities; power in the executive branch is fragmented; appeals courts are divided; and judges are elected rather than appointed. A rigid structure and ceilings on debt and tax restrictions limit local government, especially county government.

Therefore, it is difficult for the Texas state government to develop new programs without first amending the constitution. Amendments have been adopted for such seemingly minor purposes as abolishing the office of county surveyor in Jackson County and clearing some land titles in Fort Bend County. The division of executive power, which makes it difficult for the governor or any other official to become an effective leader, also obstructs problem solving. Although Texas has had some powerful governors, such as Allan Shivers, John Connally, and George W. Bush, they were effective despite the constitution, not because of it.

THE ORIGINAL CONSTITUTION OF TEXAS was adopted in 1876 by a rural society in the aftermath of Reconstruction. What historical factors led to the writing of the Texas Constitution? What should Texans do to modernize and streamline it? (Courtesy of the Texas State Library and Archives)

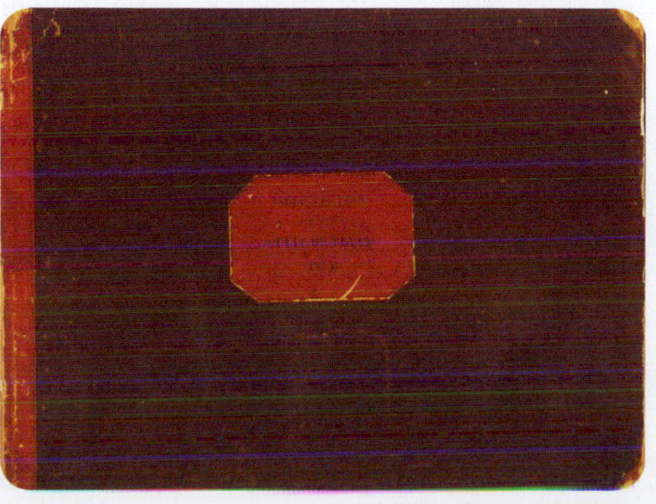

THE TEXAS CONSTITUTION IN HISTORY

Why has Texas adopted one of the longest, most frequently amended, and most restrictive state constitutions? Like all other state constitutions, the Texas Constitution reflects the interests and concerns of those who wrote and amended it. Some of its history parallels the histories of other state constitutions, but much of it is unique to Texas.

THE FIRST TEXAS CONSTITUTIONS

The first constitution of Texas was written in 1836 after Texas had gained its independence from Mexico and become an independent republic. The constitutional convention established a *unitary*, as opposed to a *federal*, government (see Chapter 3). Several other provisions were direct reactions to policies experienced under the government of Mexico. The convention provided a constitution with strict separation of church and state, forbidding clergy of any faith from holding office. It reversed the antislavery policies of the old Mexican government by forbidding masters from freeing their slaves without consent of the Republic's congress. Remembering the abuses of Mexican president Santa Anna, Texans limited the terms of their presidents to three years and prohibited them from serving consecutive terms.

Aside from these provisions, the Texas Constitution was almost a word-for-word copy of the U.S. Constitution and those of several Southern states. It was clearly the product of the political culture from which the early Texans came—the Anglo-American traditions of Southern planters.

The Constitution of 1845. The constitution of 1845 was written in preparation for Texas's admission into the United States. Although similar to other Southern state constitutions, it also incorporated certain elements of Spanish political culture (some of which would later be adopted by other states). The constitution of 1845 exempted homesteads from **foreclosure**, protected a wife's property rights, and provided for **community property**, meaning that a husband and wife would equally own property acquired during their marriage. It also required a two-thirds vote in the Texas house to establish any corporation and made bank corporations illegal altogether. The governor served a two-year term, and legislative sessions were held once every two years.

The Constitution of 1861. The constitution of 1861 was basically the same as that of 1845, except for changes required by the fact that Texas had become one of the Confederate states at war with the United States. It increased the debt ceiling and prohibited the emancipation of slaves.

CONSTITUTIONS AFTER THE CIVIL WAR

Following the Civil War, the U.S. Army occupied Texas, as well as other Confederate states. Texans wrote the constitution of 1866, which they believed would permit the restoration of civilian government under President Andrew Johnson's mild Reconstruction program. The new constitution nullified secession, abolished slavery, and renounced Confederate war debts. Still, it did not fully satisfy the few requirements set down by President Johnson for the following reasons:

- It did not declare that secession was unconstitutional.
- It failed to ratify the Thirteenth Amendment (abolishing slavery).
- It did not adequately establish the civil status and rights of African Americans.

Texans, however, were correct in assuming that Johnson would accept it. Under its terms, a civilian government was elected and operated for several months despite some interference from the **Freedmen's Bureau** of the national government, which had responsibility for the former slaves.

Foreclosure
The legal process by which a lender takes possession of a mortgaged property when the borrower defaults on the loan.

Community Property
Any property that a married couple has acquired during their marriage. In certain states, it is divided equally between them in the event of a divorce.

Freedmen's Bureau
The Bureau of Refugees, Freedmen and Abandoned Lands, a federal bureau established in 1865 to aid refugees of the Civil War (including former slaves) and to administer confiscated property. Among other tasks, it sought to provide education to the former slaves. It was disbanded in 1872.

IN THIS 1868 drawing, a man representing the Freedman's Bureau stands between armed whites and African Americans. (Library of Congress Prints & Photographs Division, Washington, D.C. [LC-USZ62-105555])

Johnson's lenient policies were unacceptable to the Republican-controlled U.S. Congress, which took control of Reconstruction in 1867. Under the authority of the Reconstruction Act, the U.S. military purged the civilian-elected authorities and imposed military rule. Texas would be under military occupation until the Reconstruction era ended.

The Constitution of 1869. Under congressional Reconstruction, top former Confederates and persons who refused to swear an "ironclad oath" of loyalty to the Union were temporarily barred from participation in politics. While those barred made up only about 10 percent of the population, they included almost the entire former leadership of Texas politics and society. The remaining voters, including newly enfranchised African Americans, elected 81 whites and nine blacks to the constitutional convention in 1868. The convention produced a document that centralized state power in the hands of the governor, lengthened the chief executive's term to four years, and allowed the governor to appoint all major state officers, including judges. It provided for annual legislative sessions; weakened local government, which was controlled by traditional elites; and centralized the public school system. The convention in 1868 reflected little of the fear of centralized government power that was later to become the hallmark of Texas government. The constitution it proposed was ratified in 1869.

Reconstruction under the Constitution of 1869. The constitution of 1869 served as the instrument of government for an era that white Texans would regard as the most abusive in the state's history. An **enabling act** allowed Republican Governor E. J. Davis to fill about 8,500 jobs in state government that had been left vacant by enforcement of the ironclad oath. The legislature authorized a state police force that had the authority to operate anywhere in the state, overruling local law enforcement officials. The state police were hated by the white majority, because blacks made up a sizable portion of the force and because the force was used to put down violent opposition to Reconstruction. In four counties where law and order broke down, Governor Davis declared martial law and sent in the state police to regain state control. Davis also took control of voter registration, intimidated unsupportive newspapers, and arrested several political opponents.

Enabling Act
Legislation that confers on appropriate officials the power to implement or enforce the law.

The economic policies of the Davis administration were also unlike anything that had ever been seen in Texas. Both taxes and spending increased dramatically, in part to fund railroads and public schools. High taxes led to widespread tax evasion, and lavish government spending led to a large state debt. Subsidies to railroad companies, along with other legislation that financially benefited Republican-oriented interests, helped inspire the widespread view that the Davis administration was the most corrupt in Texas history. In 1874, Democrat Richard Coke was elected governor in a landslide. The Republican-dominated state supreme court, however, invalidated the election. Davis wired President Ulysses S. Grant to send federal troops to thwart the Democratic victory. Grant refused, and Democrats gathered in the legislative chambers to form the new government.

The Fall of Davis. According to legend, Davis was determined not to give up his office and surrounded himself with armed state police in the capitol. Only when a well-armed group of Coke supporters marched toward the capitol singing "The Yellow Rose of Texas" did Davis finally vacate his offices.

That the Texas Supreme Court invalidated the 1874 election based on the placement of a semicolon in the state constitution?

For most white Texans, Reconstruction left a bitter memory of a humiliating, corrupt, extravagant, and even tyrannical government. Some recent historians, however, writing in the wake of the modern civil rights movement, have argued that Davis was not personally corrupt and that during Reconstruction an activist government attempted to play a positive role in people's lives while protecting the civil and political rights of former slaves. Whichever historical view is more accurate, it is clear that the period that followed was a conservative white reaction to the policies of the Davis administration.

DEMOCRAT RICHARD COKE was elected governor in 1874 to replace the highly controversial governor E. J. Davis. (Library of Congress Prints & Photographs Division, Washington, D.C. [LC-BH826-3220])

THE CONSTITUTION OF 1876

Most Texans were determined to strip power away from state government by writing a new constitution. The Texas Grange (whose members were called Grangers) organized in 1873. Campaigning on a platform of "retrenchment and reform," it managed to elect at least 40 of its members to the constitutional convention of 1875. Like most of the 90 delegates, they were Democrats who were determined to strike at the heart of big government.

Retrenchment. To reduce expenses, the convention did not publish a journal, reflecting the frugal tone of the final constitution. When the convention ended, some of the funds appropriated for its expenses remained unspent. The constitution created by the convention cut salaries for governing officials, placed strict limits on property taxes, and restricted state borrowing. The new regime was also miserly with the power it granted to government officials. Most of the governor's powers were stripped, the term of office was reduced from four to two years, and the salary was cut. In addition, the new constitution required that the attorney general and state judges be elected rather than appointed by the governor.

Restrictions on the Legislature. The legislature did not escape the convention's pruning. Regular legislative sessions were to be held only once every two years, and legislators were encouraged to limit the length of the sessions. Legislative procedure was detailed in the constitution of 1876, with severe restrictions placed on the kinds of policies the legislature might enact. In fact, several public policies were written directly into the Texas Constitution. Local government was strengthened, and counties were given many of the administrative and judicial functions of the state.

Ratification. The convention had largely reacted to the abuse of state power by attempting to abolish it. Despite opposition from blacks, Republicans, most cities, and railroad interests, voters ratified the constitution in 1876, and it remains in effect today.

THE TEXAS CONSTITUTION TODAY

Many students begin their examination of state constitutions with an ideal or model constitution in mind. Comparisons with this ideal then leave them with the feeling that if only this or that provision were changed, state government would somehow find its way to increased honesty, efficiency, and effectiveness. But in truth, no ideal constitution could serve well in each of the diverse 50 states. Nor is it possible to write a state constitution that could permanently meet the dynamically changing needs and concerns of the state's citizens. Further, because government is much more than its constitution, honest and effective government must be commanded by the political environment—by leaders, citizens, parties, and interest groups. Constitutions alone cannot guarantee good government. Scoundrels will be corrupt and unconcerned citizens will be apathetic under even the best constitution.

This pragmatic view of the role of state constitutions, however, should not lead to the conclusion that these documents are only incidental to good government. A workable constitution is necessary for effective government even if it is not sufficient to guarantee it. Low salaries may discourage independent, high-caliber leaders from seeking office. Constitutional restrictions may make it virtually impossible for government to meet the changing needs of its citizens. Institutions may be set up so that they will operate inefficiently and irresponsibly.

The events preceding the adoption of the current Texas Constitution in 1876 did not provide the background for developing a constitution capable of serving well under the pressures and changes that would take place in the century to follow. The decade of the 1870s was an era of paranoia and reaction, and the constitution it produced was directed more toward solving the problems arising from Reconstruction than toward meeting the challenges of generations to follow. It was literally a reactionary document.

SEPARATION OF POWERS

Like the Bill of Rights, Article 2 of the Texas Constitution limits government. To prevent the concentration of power in the hands of any single institution, the national government and all states have provided for a *separation of powers* among three branches: legislative, executive, and judicial branches (see Chapter 2).

Because any of these three branches can still potentially abuse whatever powers it has been given, the Texas Constitution also follows American tradition in subsequent constitutional articles—it sets up a system of *checks and balances*. So that each branch of government can check the others, functions normally assigned to one branch of government are given to another. For example, the veto power that deals with lawmaking (a legislative function) is given to the governor (an executive). Impeachment and conviction, which deal with determining guilt (a judicial function), are given to the legislature. The state senate (a chamber of the legislature) confirms appointments made by the governor in the executive branch.

Despite the separation of powers, the checks-and-balances system requires that each branch have the opportunity to influence the others. The three branches specialize in separate functions, but they share some powers as well.

LEGISLATIVE BRANCH

The legislative article (Article 3) is by far the longest in the Texas Constitution. It assigns legislative power to a bicameral (two-chamber) legislature consisting of the 31-member senate and the 150-member house of representatives. Elected for a four-year term from a single-member district, each senator must be:

- at least 26 years old.
- a U.S. citizen.
- a resident of the state for five years and of the district for one year.

A representative serves only two years and must be:

- at least 21 years old.
- a U.S. citizen.
- a resident of the state for two years and of the district for one year.

The Texas constitutional provisions concerning bicameralism, number of members of the legislature, and length of terms are typical of state constitutions (see Table 20–1). Minimum qualifications for Texas senators, however, are somewhat more restrictive than average.

THE POSTER SHOWS delegates to the Texas constitutional convention of 1875. The convention severely limited the powers of the state government. Why might Texans traditionally have been so resistant to strong government—an attitude that dates back to well before the Civil War? (Courtesy of Prints and Photographs Collection, The Center for American History, The University of Texas at Austin, CN 01063)

DID YOU KNOW?

That although many of the framers of the constitution of 1876 opposed the idea of public education, they were persuaded to allow it only if segregated schools were established by local governments?

TABLE 20–1 Requirements for Election to Various Legislatures: How Does Texas Compare?

CONSTITUTIONAL AND STATUTORY PROVISIONS FOR LEGISLATIVE BODIES	TEXAS LEGISLATURE	U.S. CONGRESS	THE 50 STATE LEGISLATURES
Bicameral	Yes	Yes	Only Nebraska's legislature is unicameral.
Number of members			
Senate	31	2 per state	39.4 is average.
House	150	435 by statute	108.2 is average.
Term			
Senate	4 years; no limit on number of terms	6 years; no limit on number of terms	4 years in 38 states; 2 in the remainder. Fifteen states impose term limits.
House	2 years; no limit on number of terms	2 years; no limit on number of terms	2 years in all but 5 states, which have extended it to 4 years. Fifteen states impose term limits.
Qualifications			
Senate			
Age	26 years	30 years	Only 6 states set higher age requirements than Texas.
Residence in state	5 years	Citizen 9 years and current resident of state	Three years or less in 42 states; 2 states require more than 5 years.
Residence in district	1 year	—	Three states require more than 1 year.
House			
Age	21 years	25 years	Only 6 states set higher age requirements than Texas, while 17 states allow 18-year-olds to serve.
Residence in state	2 years	Citizen 7 years and current resident of state	Only 11 states require more than 2 years.
Residence in district	1 year	None	Only 2 states require more than 1 year.

Source: Council of State Governments, *Book of the States 2009.*

DID YOU KNOW?

That Texas's 2009 legislature spent $1.3 billion for every day in session—more than any in modern history?

Salaries of Legislators. The Texas Constitution sets annual salaries at $7,200, unless the Texas Ethics Commission recommends an increase and voters approve it. The commission has made no such recommendation but has exercised its power to increase the *per diem* allowance (for daily expenses) to $139 while the legislature is in session. No other large state sets legislative salaries so low. Table 20–2 lists legislative salaries in the 50 states, along with limitations on the length and frequency of legislative sessions.

TABLE 20–2 State Legislative Sessions and Annual Salaries: How Does Texas Compare?

STATE△	FREQUENCY OF REGULAR SESSION	LIMIT ON SESSION LENGTH	SALARY*
Alabama	Annual**	Yes	$10(d)†
Alaska	Annual	Yes	24,012†
Arizona	Annual	No	24,000†
Arkansas	Annual	Yes	15,060†
California	**Annual**	**No**	**116,208†**
Colorado	Annual	Yes	30,000†
Connecticut	Annual	Yes	28,000
Delaware	Annual	Yes	42,750
Florida	**Annual**	**Yes**	**30,336†**
Georgia	**Annual**	**Yes**	**17,342†**
Hawaii	Annual	Yes	48,708†
Idaho	Annual	No	16,116†
Illinois	**Annual**	**No**	**67,836†**
Indiana	Annual	Yes	22,616†
Iowa	Annual	No	25,000†
Kansas	Annual	Yes	88.66(d) †
Kentucky	Annual	Yes	186.73(d)†
Louisiana	Annual	Yes	16,800†
Maine	Annual	Yes	13,526†
Maryland	Annual	Yes	43,500†
Massachusetts	Annual	Yes	58,237†
Michigan	**Annual**	**No**	**79,650†**
Minnesota	Annual	Yes	31,141†
Mississippi	Annual	Yes	10,000†
Missouri	Annual	Yes	31,915†
Montana	Biennial	Yes	82.64(d)†
Nebraska"	Annual	Yes	12,000†
Nevada	Biennial	Yes	137.90(d)†
New Hampshire	Annual	Yes	200
New Jersey	**Annual**	**No**	**49,000**
New Mexico	Annual	Yes	0†
New York	**Annual**	**No**	**79,500†**
North Carolina	**Biennial††**	**No**	**13,951†**

(Continued)

TABLE 20–2 (continued)

STATE△	FREQUENCY OF REGULAR SESSION	LIMIT ON SESSION LENGTH	SALARY*
North Dakota	Biennial	Yes	135(d)†
Ohio	**Annual**	**No**	**60,584**
Oklahoma	Annual	Yes	38,400†
Oregon	Biennial	No	21,612†
Pennsylvania	**Annual**	**No**	**78,315†**
Rhode Island	Annual	No	13,089
South Carolina	Annual	Yes	10,400†
South Dakota	Annual	Yes	12,000†
Tennessee	Annual	Yes	19,009†
Texas	**Biennial**	**Yes**	**7,200†**
Utah	Annual	Yes	130(d)†
Vermont	Annual	No	625.36(w)†
Virginia	**Annual**	**Yes**	**18,000‡‡**
Washington	Annual	Yes	42,106†
West Virginia	Annual	Yes	20,000†
Wisconsin	Annual	No	49,943†
Wyoming	Annual	Yes	150(d)†

△Twelve most populated states in bold.

*Salaries annual unless otherwise noted as (d)—per day, (b)—biennium, or (w)—per week.

†Plus *per diem* living expenses.

"Unicameral (single-house) legislature.

**Includes legislative sessions that convene every year and those that meet in continuous sessions.

††Annual at option of legislature.

‡‡Senate; House is $17,640.

Source: Council of State Governments, *Book of the States 2009.*

Regular Session
A legislative session scheduled by the constitution. Texas regular sessions are biennial (once every two years) rather than annual, as in most states and in Congress.

Special Session
Any legislative session that is not specifically scheduled by the constitution or by statute. In some states, the legislature may call itself into special session, but in Texas only the governor may call the legislature into special session.

Limited Sessions. Texas is one of very few states that have a constitution restricting their legislatures to biennial **regular sessions**. Most other major populous states, with large budgets and complicated issues to deal with, allow annual legislative sessions and do not limit their length. In contrast, because Texas's infrequent legislative sessions are limited to 140 days, important legislation may receive inadequate consideration, and many bills are ignored altogether. The 2009 legislature introduced an incredible 12,238 bills, concurrent resolutions, and joint resolutions (87 per day). It passed 5,910 (49 percent) of these legislative proposals, and it spent $1.3 billion for every day in session—more than any in history.

Unlike legislatures in most states, the Texas legislature may not call itself into **special sessions** or determine the issues to be decided in such sessions. Special sessions are convened by the governor to consider only the legislative matters he or she presents, and the length of a special session is limited to 30 days. Special sessions are more restricted than in any other state.

Ironically, in 1917, Governor James E. Ferguson called the special session that would impeach and convict him. Despite the governor's ordinary power to call special sessions and limit their purpose, the courts later held that impeachment powers were so broad they could be exercised beyond the limits imposed by the governor. The legislature has also adopted laws to permit it to call itself into special session for the sole purpose of impeachment.

Setting Legislative Procedures. The Texas Constitution establishes more specific procedural requirements than most other state constitutions. Although the provision is often suspended, the Texas Constitution requires that a bill must be read on three separate days unless four-fifths of the legislature set aside the requirement. It stipulates when bills may be introduced and how they will be reported out of committee, signed, and entered into the **house and senate journals** once enacted. It even specifies how the enacting clause will read. (The enacting clause is formal language in any bill that gives the bill the force of law if it is approved.)

Mandating a Balanced Budget. Most states legally require a balanced budget, but the restrictions imposed by the Texas Constitution seem more effective than most. Article 3 (Section 49) prohibits the legislature from authorizing state debt except under rare conditions. The comptroller of public accounts is required to certify that funds are available for each appropriations measure adopted. Although specific constitutional amendments have authorized the sale of bonds for such purposes as veterans' real estate programs, student loans, cancer prevention, parks, highways, water projects, and prison construction, per capita state debt remains among the lowest in the nation.

Statute-Like Details. The Texas Constitution further confines the legislature by establishing detailed policies on subjects that normally would be handled by legislative statute. Much of the length of Article 3 results from its in-depth description of the veterans' land program, Texas park and water development funds, student loans, welfare programs, a grain warehouse self-insurance fund, and the municipal donation of outdated firefighting equipment. The Texas Constitution establishes the design of the great seal of Texas and authorizes the legislature to pass laws concerning fences. Article 16 authorizes the legislature to regulate cattle brands; Article 11 permits the building of seawalls. The Texas Constitution even explains how the state must purchase stationery.

By including such **statute-like details** in the Texas Constitution, its framers guaranteed that even relatively unimportant decisions that might easily be handled by the legislature could instead be changed only by constitutional amendment. Events may outstrip detailed constitutional provisions, leaving behind **deadwood**—provisions that are no longer functional. For example, Article 9, Section 14, provides for establishment of county poorhouses. Only by amending the constitution can Texans remove such provisions. In brief, basic distrust of the legislature—however much it may have been deserved in 1876— put a straitjacket on the state's ability to cope with the challenges of the 21st century.

House and Senate Journals
The official public records of the actions of the two chambers of the Texas legislature. The two journals are issued daily during sessions.

That Texas's per capita state debt was lower in 2007 than in any state except Tennessee?

That Texas's constitution even explains how the state must purchase stationery?

Statute-Like Details
Detailed state constitutional provisions characterized by the narrow scope usually found in statutory law.

Deadwood
In the context of state government, constitutional provisions made inoperative by changing circumstances or by conflicting federal constitutional or statutory law.

EXECUTIVE BRANCH

Article 4 establishes the executive branch, with the governor as its head. The governor must be

- a citizen.
- at least 30 years of age.
- a resident of the state for five years preceding his or her election.

Since the passage of a constitutional amendment in 1974, the governor is elected to a four-year term. The governor's salary is no longer constitutionally limited; according to statute, it is $150,000. Table 20–3 compares the governor of Texas with other governors and the U.S. president.

TABLE 20–3 Constitutional Provisions for Chief Executives' Qualifications: How Does Texas Compare?

CONSTITUTIONAL PROVISIONS	TEXAS GOVERNOR	U.S. PRESIDENT	THE 50 STATES' GOVERNORS
Age	30 years	35 years	Thirty-four states set the minimum age at 30.
Residence	5 years	14 years	5 years or less in 37 states
Term	4 years with no limit on the number of terms	4 years (limited to 2 terms or 10 years)	Forty-eight states allow a 4-year term, but, unlike Texas, 36 states impose term limits.

Source: Council of State Governments, *Book of the States 2009.*

Plural Executive
An executive branch with power divided among several independent officers and a weak chief executive.

DID YOU KNOW?

That, in most states, Governor Rick Perry would not have been allowed to run for reelection in 2010 because they impose term limits similar to those on the president of the United States?

Removal Power
The power to dismiss government officials. In Texas, the governor can remove an official that he or she appointed only with the consent of two-thirds of the state senate.

Indirect Appointive Power
In Texas, the power of the governor to appoint supervisory boards (but not operational directors) for most state agencies. The supervisory boards and commissions usually appoint the actual heads of most state agencies in Texas.

Directive Authority
The power to issue binding orders to state agencies. This power is severely limited for the governor of Texas.

Budgetary Power
The power to propose a spending plan to the legislature. The governor of Texas has limited budgetary power because of the competing authority of the Legislative Budget Board.

A Plural Executive. Provisions for terms, qualifications, and salary may be somewhat less restrictive than in most states, but other constitutional provisions restrict the power of the office more severely. The governor of Texas remains among the weakest in the nation. Although the Texas Constitution provides that the governor is the chief executive, it actually establishes a **plural executive** by dividing executive powers among several independently elected officers—the governor, the lieutenant governor, the attorney general, the comptroller of public accounts, the commissioner of the general land office, and three railroad commissioners. There are also provisions for a state board of education to be either elected or appointed.

Few states elect as many officials as Texas. Seven states have abolished the office of lieutenant governor as an executive elected statewide, and a few have made offices as important as the attorney general appointive rather than elective. Comptrollers and land, educational, and agricultural officers are rarely elected in states other than Texas.

In the tradition of the constitutional plural executive, the legislature by statute has established an elected commissioner of agriculture and has exercised its option to have the state board of education elected independently of the governor. Most of the remaining agencies the legislature establishes to administer state programs are headed by appointed multimember boards with substantial independence from the governor. Generally, the governor appoints only supervisory boards for the agencies, with the approval of two-thirds of the state senate. Each board in turn appoints the agency's director. The governor does not appoint the agency administrator directly. Texas is one of eight states lacking a formal cabinet.

The Governor's Powers over the Executive Branch. The governor has narrow **removal powers** to supplement the **indirect appointive powers** described in the preceding paragraph. Officers appointed by the current governor (but not by her or his predecessors) may be fired, but only if two-thirds of the senators agree—making firing almost as difficult as impeachment and conviction. **Directive authority** (to issue binding orders) is quite restricted, and **budgetary power** (to recommend to the legislature how much it should appropriate for various executive agencies) is limited by the competing influence of the Legislative Budget Board. (We will describe the Legislative Budget Board in depth in Chapter 24. This board, which is controlled by the presiding officers of the two chambers of the legislature, prepares a draft of the state budget that is often more important than the draft prepared by the governor.) Weak control by the chief executive can lead to duplication of functions and to lack of planning, coordination, and accountability.

The Governor's Veto Powers. The statutes and the constitution combine to make the governor a relatively weak executive; however, the veto gives the governor effective influence over legislation. The legislature has not mustered the two-thirds vote necessary to override a governor's veto in more than 40 years. The Texas legislature often lacks the opportunity to override a veto because major legislation may be adopted during the last days of the session. Once the legislature delivers a bill to the governor, the governor must either sign it or veto it within 10 days. If the bill is passed during the last 10 days of the session, the governor can simply wait until the legislature adjourns before vetoing it. The governor has 20 days to act after the legislature adjourns.

Texas is among 43 states that give the governor *item veto* (see Chapter 19) power to strike out particular sections of an appropriations bill without vetoing the entire bill. (Several states—but not Texas—also allow the item veto to be used on matters other than appropriations.) The governor of Texas lacks both the **reduction veto** (to reduce appropriations without striking them out altogether) and the pocket veto (to kill bills simply by ignoring them after the end of the session).

Reduction Veto
The power of governors in some states (but not Texas) to reduce amounts in an appropriations bill without striking them out altogether.

THE COURTS

Just as the Texas Constitution limits the power of the chief executive, it also fragments the court system, which is governed by Article 5. Texas is the only state other than Oklahoma that has two courts of final appeal. The highest court for civil matters is the nine-member Texas Supreme Court; the other, for criminal matters, is the nine-member Court of Criminal Appeals. Leaving some flexibility as to number and jurisdiction, the constitution also creates intermediate courts of appeals and district, county, and justice of the peace courts. (The structure of the Texas court system is displayed in Figure 20–1.) The same article describes the selection of grand and trial juries and such administrative officers as sheriff, county clerk, and county and district attorney.

Judicial Problems. The number and variety of courts confuse the average citizen, and coordination among courts is minimal, as is supervision of lower-level judges. Some have also claimed that the state courts lack qualified judges. The Texas Constitution specifies only general qualifications for county judges and justices of the peace, who need not be lawyers. There may have been good reason for nonlawyers to serve as judges in a simple, rural setting, but today such judges may be an anachronism.

FIGURE 20–1 The Texas Court System

Texas is the only state, other than Oklahoma, with two "supreme courts," or courts of final appeal.

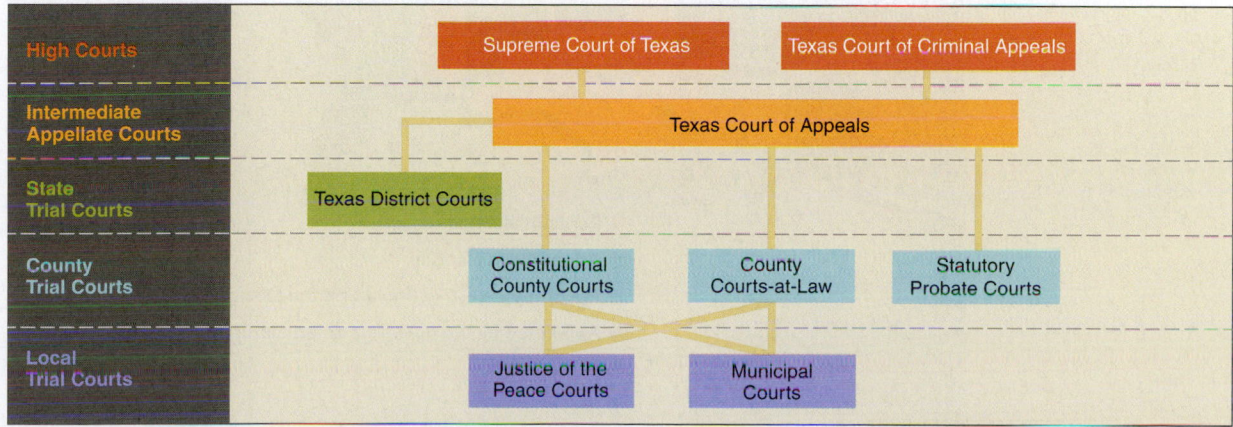

Source: University of North Texas libraries.

Partisan Election
An election between candidates who are nominated by their parties and whose party affiliation is designated on the ballot. In Texas, all state and county officials (including judges) are selected in this manner. Only municipal and some special district elections are nonpartisan in Texas.

Missouri Plan
A method of selecting judges that combines appointment and election. Under the plan, the state governor or another official selects judges from nominees chosen by a nonpartisan committee. After a year on the bench, the judges face a popular election to determine whether the public wishes them to remain in office.

Partisan Election of Judges. The manner of selecting judges is another factor that affects their qualifications. Texas judges are chosen in **partisan elections** in which they run as Democrats or Republicans. Trial judges are elected to four-year terms and appeals court judges to six-year terms, but the governor has frequent opportunities to fill temporary vacancies when judges leave office before the end of their terms—opportunities that give the governor enormous influence over the makeup of the courts because, once in office, judges are usually returned to office without serious challengers in the next election.

Although a majority of states elect their judges, some critics regard this effort at popular control as undesirable. A judge may become too much the politician and too little the independent magistrate needed to apply the law uniformly. Several states have attempted to solve these problems by providing for nonpartisan election of judges. Other states make their judges independent of electoral politics altogether by giving their governors or legislators the power to appoint and reappoint high court judges without direct voter input.

Still others have attempted to combine the advantages of appointment with benefits of election by allowing the governor to make an appointment for an initial term, after which voters decide whether to retain the appointed judge based on his or her record. Many of those using an appointive-elective system require the governor to make an initial appointment from a list nominated by a judicial qualifying commission—a merit system also commonly known as the **Missouri Plan**. Figure 20–2 shows the methods used to select supreme court judges in various states.

FIGURE 20–2 State-by-State Selection Methods of Supreme Court Judges

This figure shows that states use a variety of methods to select their supreme court judges. Each method of selection has some advantages and some disadvantages.

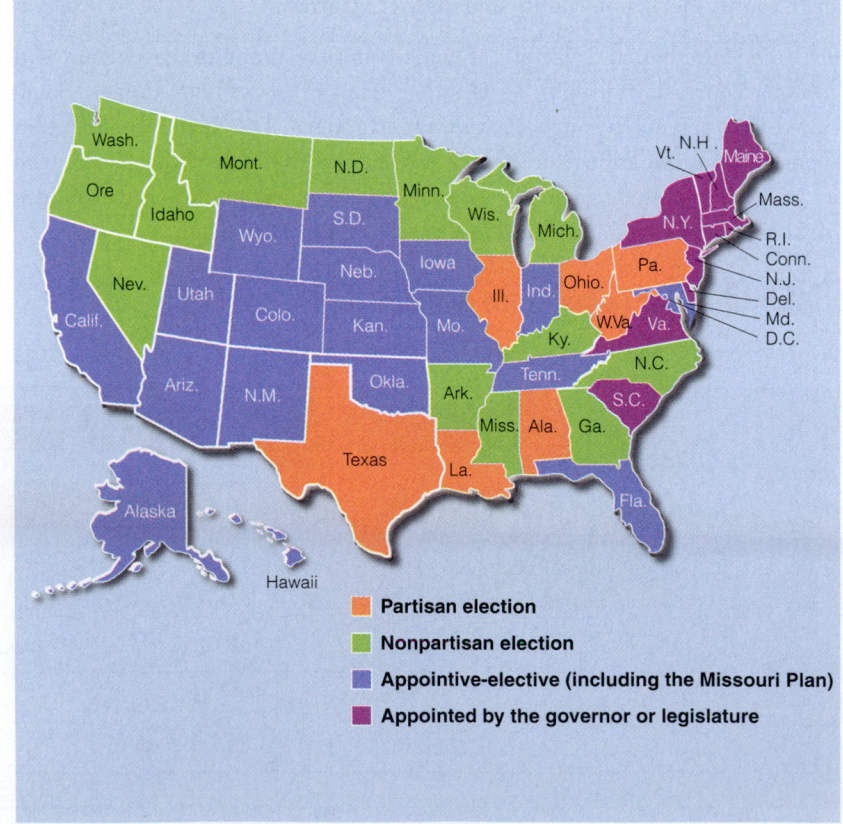

Partisan election
Nonpartisan election
Appointive-elective (including the Missouri Plan)
Appointed by the governor or legislature

Source: American Judicature Society.

LOCAL GOVERNMENT

The Texas Constitution decentralizes governmental power by assigning many functions to units of local government, especially counties. Much of the counties' rigid organizational structure is set down in Articles 9 and 16. As a result of these provisions, voters of the entire state were once required to approve constitutional amendments to allow individual counties to abolish unneeded offices such as treasurer, weigher, and surveyor. The Texas Constitution now authorizes county voters to abolish some offices, but there is no provision for county **home rule**. As in state government, the constitution divides and diffuses county powers through a plural executive system.

The legislature, which has the power to set up structures for city governments, has offered municipalities several standard alternative **general-law charters**. Cities with populations of more than 5,000 may adopt home-rule charters and establish any organizational structure or program that does not conflict with state law or the Texas Constitution.

Generally, the legislature has the power to establish limited-purpose local governments known as **special districts**. Numerous special districts are also established by the Texas Constitution, and to eliminate one of them requires a constitutional amendment. Many of the districts have been created to perform functions that general-purpose local governments, such as counties and cities, cannot afford because of constitutional tax and debt limits. Special districts have multiplied taxing and spending authorities and, except for school districts, operate largely outside the public's view.

THE CONSTITUTION AND THE PEOPLE

The Texas Constitution defines the relationship between the state's government and its people, and in doing so it reflects basic American political culture. For example, its bill of rights contains provisions similar to those found in other state constitutions and the U.S. Constitution. Important areas in which the constitution affects the people of Texas include civil rights and liberties and voting rights.

CIVIL RIGHTS AND LIBERTIES

As you learned in Chapter 4, the United States Supreme Court has interpreted the Fourteenth Amendment to extend most national constitutional guarantees to the states. The U.S. Constitution establishes only minimum standards for the states, however. The Texas Bill of Rights (Article 1) guarantees additional rights not specifically mentioned by the U.S. Constitution.

Texans' Rights under the State Constitution. Notably, Texas has adopted an amendment to prohibit discrimination based on gender. Similar guarantees were proposed as an Equal Rights Amendment to the U.S. Constitution, but it was never ratified by the states (see Chapter 5). The Texas Constitution also guarantees victims' rights and forbids imprisonment for debt. A person who is mentally ill may not be committed for an extended period without a jury trial. The constitution also prohibits the suspension of the writ of *habeas corpus* under any circumstances. Article 16 protects homesteads and prohibits garnishment of wages except for court-ordered child support. There is general agreement that the Texas bill of rights and other provisions guarantee the average citizen a greater variety of protections than most other state constitutions.

Rights Established by the Courts and the Legislature. Texas courts have interpreted some state constitutional provisions in a way that broadens basic rights beyond the minimum standards set by the U.S. Constitution. While the United States Supreme Court has

DID YOU KNOW?

That although no country has elected a country inspector of hides and animals in modern times, the office was not removed from the Texas Constitution until 2007?

Home Rule
The right of a local government to write a charter establishing any organizational structure or program that does not conflict with state law. The Texas Constitution reserves home rule for municipalities with populations of 5,000 or more.

General-Law Charter
A city structure established by statute. Most smaller Texas cities choose among several available options allowed by the state legislature.

Special Districts
Local governments that provide services to a jurisdiction that are not provided by general-purpose governments. Examples are municipal utility districts, hospital authorities, and transit authorities.

POLITICS WITH A purpose

Defending the Innocent

The bill of rights in the Texas Constitution takes elaborate steps to promise fairness to those accused of crime. The constitution carefully guarantees the "due process" of law during arrest, through trial, and after conviction. Unfortunately, these guarantees are too often a statement about how the system ideally ought to function rather than a description of how it actually functions in practice. For years, the judicial system has relied on faulty evidence to convict individuals of crimes. Because the judicial system relies on jailhouse snitches, eyewitness misidentification, inadequate scientific techniques, and overworked lawyers, many innocent people have been convicted of crimes they did not commit.[a] Whether deserved or not, the Texas judicial system is perceived as being particularly harsh toward indigent and minority defendants accused of crimes.

As you read in the *Politics with a Purpose* box in Chapter 4, the work of the Innocence Project has spread throughout the United States and to some foreign countries. There are now 54 affiliated projects, mostly at law schools, and centers in 45 states, one of them being Texas. Part of the Innocence Project of Texas (IPOT), Jeff Blackburn, an Amarillo lawyer, and a team of university students, lawyers, and friends have reviewed the cases of hundreds of individuals convicted of crimes where faulty evidence or poor procedures may have been used. In 2007, Texas prison inmate Jerry Wayne Johnson sent IPOT a letter admitting to being the "Tech Rapist" who had terrorized the Texas Tech University campus by abducting at least five women including Michele Mallin in parking lots near campus, driving them to a vacant location, and raping them. IPOT learned that the Lubbock County District Attorney's office had not only located physical DNA evidence from the case but also tested that evidence, which revealed that Jerry Wayne Johnson had actually attacked Michele Mallin.

IPOT took a special interest in the case because Texas had long ago wrongfully convicted Timothy Cole for these crimes,

but unfortunately, Cole had died in prison from a heart attack at age 39. Austin District Judge Charlie Baird heard the case of Cole's innocence and emphatically exonerated him. In response to Cole's tragic wrongful conviction, the Texas legislature passed the most generous exoneree compensation law in the nation[b] and created the Timothy Cole Advisory Panel on Wrongful Convictions to investigate the causes of wrongful convictions and to make recommendations on how to prevent them in the future.[c] And, Governor Rick Perry issued the first posthumous pardon in Texas history.[d]

University professors are using participation in the Innocence Project of Texas as a learning tool to provide university students real-world experience that has a meaningful impact in the lives of others. Professor and attorney Nicole Casarez, who teaches a course on investigative journalism at the University of Saint Thomas, states, "I felt the Innocence Project was an excellent way to teach students about investigative reporting. It involves interviewing witnesses, searching public records, reviewing case files, public information requests, and reading court transcripts. These are all  elements of investigative reporting."[e] The success of the Innocence Project of Texas depends in large part on the contributions of university students who contribute their time to review the evidence in court cases.

[a]Texas leads the nation, with more than 40 DNA exonerations. Innocence Project of Texas http://ipoftexas.org/texas-cases/texas-exonerations/.

[b]http://innocenceprojectoftexas.org/pdf/TimothyColeAdvisoryPanel.pdf.
[c]http://innocenceprojectoftexas.org/pdf/TimColeAct.pdf.
[d]http://www.aolnews.com/nation/article/texas-issues-tim-cole-who-died-in-prison-its-first-posthumous-pardon/19379566.
[e]University of Saint Thomas, "Investigative Journalism: The UST Innocence Project," at www.stthom.edu.

refused to interpret the Fourteenth Amendment as guaranteeing equal public school funding,[1] the Texas Supreme Court interpreted the efficiency clause of the Texas Constitution (Article 7, Section 1) to require greater equality in public school funding between rich and poor school districts.[2]

[1]*San Antonio Independent School District v. Rodriguez*, 411 U.S. 1 (1973).
[2]*Edgewood v. Kirby*, 777 S.W. 2d 391 (Texas 1989).

Using Texas constitutional and **statutory law** (law passed by the legislature), Texas courts have struck down polygraph (lie-detector) tests for public employees, required workers' compensation for farmworkers, expanded free-speech rights of private employees, and affirmed free-speech rights at privately owned shopping malls.

Statutory Law
Law passed by legislatures and eventually compiled in law codes.

SUFFRAGE

A major way in which state and local governments determine the character of our democracy is by setting suffrage requirements and administering elections. Article 6 of the Texas Constitution deals with suffrage requirements. It denies the right to vote to persons under age 18, to certain convicted felons, and to those found mentally incompetent by a court of law.

Although constitutional restrictions on the qualifications of voters are now as minimal in Texas as in any other state, Texas voters still lack certain opportunities to participate in state government. The *initiative* (a vote on statutory or constitutional changes brought about by petition), the referendum (a vote on laws submitted to the people by the legislature or by initiative), and the recall (a special election to remove an official before his or her term expires) are available in many other states and even in some Texas cities, but not for statewide issues in Texas. Texas limits voters to ratifying constitutional amendments, approving a state income tax, and increasing legislative salaries. Political parties in Texas sometimes place referenda on their primary ballots, but they are not legally binding.

AMENDING AND REVISING THE CONSTITUTION

Given the level of detail in the Texas Constitution, the ability to amend that document is of great importance. It is much easier to amend the Texas Constitution than the U.S. Constitution.

RULES FOR AMENDING THE CONSTITUTION

The Texas Constitution provides that constitutional amendments must be proposed by two-thirds of the total membership of each chamber of the legislature (at least 21 senators and 100 representatives). Ratification requires approval by a majority of those persons voting on the amendment in either a general or a special election. Because an extraordinary majority of legislators must agree merely to propose constitutional amendments, many are relatively uncontroversial. Historically, voters have approved more than 70 percent of proposed constitutional amendments. Since 1876, Texans have amended their constitution 467 times, more than twice as frequently as the average state. Only three states have amended their constitutions more than Texas: Alabama (807), California (518), and South Carolina (493). Table 20–4 compares the process of amending the Texas Constitution with the methods used to amend the constitutions of the federal government and the other states.

DIFFICULTIES IN REVISING THE CONSTITUTION

Although the Texas Constitution has been frequently amended, successive attempts to revise it have met with failure. Ironically, in 1972, Texas voters had to amend the constitution in order to provide for its revision. Under the provisions of that amendment, the legislature established a constitutional revision commission of 37 members appointed by the governor, lieutenant governor, speaker of the house, attorney general, chief justice of the supreme court, and presiding judge of the Court of Criminal Appeals.

TABLE 20-4 Procedures for Amending Constitutions: How Does Texas Compare?

AMENDING PROCEDURES	TEXAS CONSTITUTION	U.S. CONSTITUTION	THE 50 STATES' CONSTITUTIONS
Proposal	Two-thirds of the entire membership of both chambers of the legislature	(1) Two-thirds of those voting in both chambers of Congress or (2) a national convention called by petition of two-thirds of the states	Twenty-one states require a two-thirds vote, but 9 permit a three-fifths vote, and 20 permit a simple majority vote; 18 permit proposal by initiative.
Ratification	A majority of those voting on the amendment	(1) Three-fourths of state legislatures or (2) three-fourths of state ratifying conventions	Forty-three other states have the same requirement as Texas; 4 require a majority of those voting in the entire election; New Hampshire and Florida require more than a simple majority; Delaware requires no ratification by voters; and some states allow alternative methods.

Source: Council of State Governments, *Book of the States 2009*.

DID YOU KNOW?

That the Texas Constitution even mentions public notaries—who are not elected—making them constitutional officers?

The Proposed Constitution of 1975. The commission made several proposals for revising the constitution. Meeting in 1974, the legislature acted as a constitutional convention and agreed to many of these recommendations. Ultimately, though, the convention divided over the issue of a right-to-work provision (under which workers have the right not to join labor unions), and supporters could not muster the two-thirds vote needed to submit the final document to the electorate.

The New Constitution Goes to the People. The proposed revision remained alive, however, in another form. In the 1975 regular session, the legislature proposed eight constitutional amendments to the voters. Together, these amendments were substantially the same as the proposal defeated in the convention. If the amendments had been adopted, they would have shortened the constitution by 75 percent through reorganization and through elimination of statute-like detail and deadwood. The legislature would have been strengthened by annual sessions, and a salary commission would have set the legislators' salary. Although limited to two terms, the governor would have been designated as the chief planning officer and given removal powers and certain powers of fiscal control. The court system would have been unified and its administrative procedure simplified. Local governments would have operated under broader home-rule provisions, and counties would have been authorized to pass ordinances and abolish offices.

The People Turn It Down. Opponents' chief arguments against the amendments focused on fear that they would result in more power for the legislature, greater government costs, and the possibility of an income tax—all of which are serious issues for many Texans. Because the legislature had written the proposals, it was easy for Texas voters to see such things as annual sessions and changes in legislative salaries as a "grab for power" that would substantially increase government expenditures. Despite an emotional campaign, only 23 percent of registered voters cast ballots in the election, and they overwhelmingly rejected the proposed amendments.

THE TEXAS CONSTITUTION COMPARED

The U.S. Constitution is widely regarded as a model and is revered by most scholars. State constitutions, including the Texas Constitution, have attracted more criticism. Here, we compare the various constitutions and examine the reasons that many state constitutions have been so frequently criticized.

THE NATIONAL CONSTITUTION

As of 2011, the U.S. Constitution has been in effect for 222 years but has been formally amended only 27 times. It has endured mammoth and fundamental changes in government and society largely because it does not lock government into a rigid framework. Because the U.S. Constitution deals only with the most basic elements of government and leaves much to Congress, the president, and the courts, few formal amendments have been necessary.

Although the U.S. Constitution provides for a representative government, the nation's government was hardly democratic in the earliest years. During the Jeffersonian and Jacksonian eras, it became more democratic as political parties developed, states lowered suffrage requirements, and voters were allowed to choose electors in the electoral college.

The 1800s saw the growth of the new nation from 13 fledgling agricultural states on the Atlantic coast to a vast industrial nation stretching across a continent. In the modern era, America moved from the position of a third-rate international power to a dominant role in the world. Since the New Deal of the 1930s, government has increasingly provided a safety net for disadvantaged Americans. Much of the nature of the national government is determined by statute, executive order, and court interpretation, so these changes did not require changing the language of the U.S. Constitution.

DID YOU KNOW?

That the Texas Constitution has more amendments (467) than 46 other state constitutions?

CRITICISMS OF STATE CONSTITUTIONS

Although state constitutions vary considerably (see Table 20–5), most are much longer than the national Constitution, and they frequently deal with details of both structure and policy. Consequently, as changing political and social conditions require changes in government structure and policy, formal constitutional amendments are necessary. Critics of existing state constitutions have advanced several reasons for both the amount of detail in these constitutions and the frequency with which they are amended:

1. Public officials, interest groups, and voters seem to view their state constitutions as more than the basic law of the state. They fail to make a clear distinction between

TABLE 20–5 State Constitutions' Length and Number of Amendments: How Does Texas Compare?

CONSTITUTIONAL CHARACTERISTICS	TEXAS CONSTITUTION	U.S. CONSTITUTION	AVERAGE FOR STATE CONSTITUTION*
Length (words)	90,000	7,575	38,288
Amendments	467	27	144
Age (years)	135	222	109
Frequency of amendment	3.5 per year	Once every 8 years	1.3 per year

*Source: Council of State Governments, *Book of the States 2009.*

Organic Law
The superior law that establishes governing institutions and organizes their formal power relationships.

what ought to be and what ought not to be in the constitution. Thus, critics claim, all sorts of inappropriate details are included in the documents. A constitution is fundamental law; it deals with the basic principles of government. It is **organic law**—the superior law that establishes governing institutions and organizes their formal power relationships. Accordingly, constitutions ideally should describe how decisions will be made but should not actually establish policies that must change with political and social conditions.

2. States have added detailed amendments to block the effects of controversial court interpretations of general constitutional provisions. For example, supreme courts in Hawaii, Massachusetts, Iowa, New Jersey, and Vermont found that denying the benefits of marriage to same-sex couples was a violation of their state constitutions. As a result, Hawaii and a majority of other states (including Texas) added amendments to define marriage as an exclusively heterosexual right.

3. Institutions and interest groups frequently feel safer when their interests are protected in a constitution, which is usually more difficult to change than ordinary law. As a result, many state constitutions include long lists of protections for vested interests.

4. State governments have a peculiar position in the federal system. They are presumed to have all the powers that have not been explicitly denied them. Thus, citizens fearing strong governments have felt the need to impose detailed constitutional restrictions.

5. When state governments misuse their powers, the response is usually to place constitutional limitations and restrictions on such powers. The result is a longer constitution but—it is argued—not a more responsible government. A government bound by a rigid constitution may be unable to respond effectively to changing needs. Excessive restrictions might actually guarantee unresponsive, and thus irresponsible, government.

6. Critics maintain that state constitutions are poorly written and arranged. Some provisions are so ambiguously drafted that they are interpreted to be even more restrictive than the constitution's framers intended, and as a result, new amendments must be added to authorize states to perform vital functions in a modern society.

CRITICISMS OF THE TEXAS CONSTITUTION

The Texas Constitution has been characterized as an example of poor writing. Only two state constitutions are as concise as the U.S. Constitution (fewer than 10,000 words). Nevertheless, at about 90,000 words, the Texas Constitution is one of the least concise in the nation. One sentence rambles on for 765 words, and several approach 300 words in length. The document is ambiguous, overlapping, and poorly organized. For example, the provisions dealing with local government are scattered throughout Articles 3, 5, 8, 9, 11, and 16. This poor draftsmanship has led to a restrictive interpretation of the constitution's provisions and, on the part of Texas citizens, ignorance of its contents and confusion as to its intentions.

The continuing need to amend a detailed and restrictive state constitution means that citizens are frequently called to pass judgment on proposed amendments. Although some maintain that giving Texas voters the opportunity to express themselves on constitutional amendments reaffirms popular control of government, there is little voter interest in amendment elections. Faced with trivial, confusing, or technical amendments, often as few as 10 to 15 percent of the voting-age population vote on constitutional amendments, and turnout has occasionally dropped even lower.

DID YOU **KNOW?**

That only Alabama's state constitution is longer than Texas's?

YOU CAN MAKE A Difference

AMENDING THE TEXAS CONSTITUTION

The Texas Constitution is often criticized because it is so frequently amended. On the one hand, as you know, frequent amendment of the constitution has drawbacks. On the other hand, it gives you an extraordinary opportunity to participate in the continual rewriting of the state's fundamental law.

WHY SHOULD YOU CARE?

Because so many detailed provisions of Texas law are spelled out in the state constitution, much legislative business is of necessity placed before the voters at large. This gives you and other Texas citizens a degree of control over legislation that may affect your life. Such control is not possible at the national level and is available in few other states to the same extent as in Texas.

WHAT CAN YOU DO?

You can express your approval or disapproval of proposed constitutional amendments by voting in general and special elections, by writing letters to the local newspaper or other publications, or by participating in campaigns for or against an amendment. Although many amendments deal with technicalities and details, they will be explained in local newspapers, and summaries are available through the Texas Legislative Council, a research body set up by the legislature. Constitutional amendment analyses can be found in Texas Legislative Council publications and at the council's Web site at **www.tlc.state.tx.us**. The Legislative Reference Library (**www.lrl.state.tx.us**) is another good resource for reading about constitutional amendments. The League of Women Voters (**www.lwvtexas.org**) often provides good analyses as well. Be aware that special-interest groups often pay for television and newspaper ads on amendments, and their ads often reflect their biases.

JESSE DANIEL AMES, a graduate of Southwestern University of Georgetown, fought against the lynching of African Americans in Texas and battled for women's right to vote. After the Nineteenth Amendment was ratified she helped found the Texas League of Women Voters in 1919 as an organization dedicated to keeping the general public informed about public affairs. Today, the League's nonpartisan *Voters Guides* provide reliable explanations of proposed state constitutional amendments and other public issues. (Research & Instructional Services Department, Louis Round Wilson Special Collections Library, The University of North Carolina at Chapel Hill)

1920

KEY TERMS

CHAPTER SUMMARY

1. **How do constitutional restrictions hinder the effective and efficient operation of government?** A constitution sets forth fundamental law that establishes basic governing principles and structures. Some constitutions, like that of Texas, also establish many details of routine government and require frequent amendment to reflect new realities. In such circumstances, it is difficult for the state government to develop effective programs without first amending the constitution. Numerous amendments dealing with minor issues are added, like patches, to the constitution.

2. **How do cultural and political forces help shape a state's constitution?** Constitutions are always the result of a political process in which framers reflect their values, hopes, and fears. The current Texas Constitution was written in the period following Reconstruction after the U.S. Civil War. Most white Texans viewed the Reconstruction state government as extravagant, tyrannical, and abusive. In 1875, an elected state constitutional convention reacted to the Reconstruction regime by limiting state government in almost every imaginable way. Voters overwhelmingly approved the convention's work in 1876.

3. The Texas Constitution strictly limits the sessions and salaries of state legislators and includes many statute-like details that the legislature cannot change without a constitutional amendment. Special sessions are especially restricted, and procedures in both regular and special sessions are circumscribed.

4. The governor of Texas is limited in his or her role as chief executive, because Texas has a plural executive system that includes many independently elected executives over which the governor has no control. The governor lacks most of the powers of typical executives to hire, fire, direct, and budget. Although Texas has had some powerful governors, such as Allan Shivers and

John Connally (discussed in Chapter 19), they were effective despite the constitution, not because of it.

5. The power of the courts to interpret the Texas Constitution is limited by its detail. Texas divides its final court of appeal into two bodies—the Court of Criminal Appeals and the Texas Supreme Court—and also establishes intermediate courts of appeals and district, county, and justice of the peace courts. Judges are chosen in partisan elections. Critics say that judges elected in this way may become too concerned with political matters.

6. County and special district governments are particularly limited by constitutional and statutory requirements. Only large cities have the considerable flexibility of home rule. All local governments face debt and tax restrictions.

7. The Texas Constitution includes a bill of rights that is more expansive than that in most constitutions. At the state level, the constitution does not provide for the initiative, referendum, or recall, though such mechanisms may be available at the municipal level.

8. **What are the major criticisms of the Texas Constitution?** Critics find the Texas Constitution confusing. It contains not only the fundamentals of government but also detailed provisions concerning matters that might better be left to the ongoing institutions of government. It is long, it contains much deadwood, and many say that it is poorly drafted and disorganized. Reformers argue that a constitution should include only organic law; that is, it should organize responsible institutions of government. If it goes beyond fundamentals, it becomes a rigid legislative code, difficult to change and baffling to voters.

9. Texas has one of the longest, most detailed, and most frequently amended state constitutions in the United States, but it does reflect Texans' general political culture and their skeptical view of government. It is clear why Texans wrote such a constitution and have held to its principles for so long.

SELECTED PRINT, MEDIA, AND ONLINE RESOURCES

PRINT RESOURCES

Angell, Robert H. *A Compilation and Analysis of the 1998 Texas Constitution and the Original 1876 Text.* Lewiston, NY: Edwin Mellon Press, 1998. This work contains a version of the Texas Constitution with amendments placed in appropriate spots and obsolete text deleted, thus yielding a more coherent document. In his thoroughgoing analysis of the text, Angell argues against assertions that the original 1876 constitution was excessively limited.

Campbell, Randolph B. *Grass-Roots Reconstruction in Texas, 1865–1880.* Baton Rouge: Louisiana State University Press, 1998. Campbell, who later authored *Gone to Texas: A History of the Lone Star State*, uses statistics and case studies to determine the actual impact of Reconstruction at the county level. Campbell notes that the counties with the largest number of freed slaves experienced the greatest degree of political controversy and armed violence.

May, Janice C. *The Texas State Constitution: A Reference Guide.* Reference Guides to the State Constitutions of the United States, no. 26. Westport, CT: Greenwood Press, 1996. May, of the University of Texas, is an expert on the Texas Constitution. Her work analyzes Texas constitutional and political history from Spanish and Mexican rule to the present. An analytical commentary on the current constitution, with amendments, makes up the heart of the book.

Moneyhon, Carl H. *Texas after the Civil War: The Struggle of Reconstruction.* College Station: Texas A&M University Press, 2004. This new account of Reconstruction in Texas may become a standard. Moneyhon argues that the Civil War shook, but did not destroy, antebellum society. He pays due attention to the violence that accompanied the end of Reconstruction.

MEDIA RESOURCE

The American Experience: Reconstruction, The Second Civil War—This dramatic PBS miniseries recounts the aftermath of the Civil War and the social and political struggles that set the stage for the Texas Constitution.

ONLINE RESOURCES

Findlaw links to compare 50 state constitutions: www.findlaw.com/11stategov/indexconst.html

League of Women Voters of Texas A nonpartisan political organization that encourages informed and active participation in government and influences public policy through education and advocacy. Find voters' guides discussing amendment proposals: www.lwvtexas.org/

Tarleton Law Library offers searchable texts of Texas's constitutions through history through the Texas Constitutions Digitization Project: http://tarlton.law.utexas.edu/constitutions/constitutions.html

Texas Legislative Council provides professional, nonpartisan service and support to the Texas legislature and the other legislative agencies; find a history of proposed amendments and analyses of recently proposed constitutional amendments at its Web site: www.tlc.state.tx.us/

Texas Legislative Reference Library A search engine for constitutional amendments proposed by the state legislature: www.lrl.state.tx.us/

Texas Legislature Online The online home of the Texas legislature offers the text of the current Texas Constitution as amended: www.legis.state.tx.us/

Texas State Library and Archives Commission provides the original Texas Constitution as it was written in 1876: www.tsl.state.tx.us/treasures/constitution/index.html

21

Tax protesters march in Austin after a rally at the Capitol on April 15, 2009. Earlier, Governor Perry fired up another anti-tax "tea party" with his stance against the federal government and for states' rights, saying that officials in Washington have abandoned the country's founding principles.
(AP Photo/Harry Cabluck)

Texas Interest Groups

QUESTIONS TO CONSIDER

What are the positive and negative effects of interest groups in Texas politics? How can the negative effects be controlled?

What techniques do interest groups use to influence state policies?

What factors determine the relative power of interest groups in Texas?

CHAPTER CONTENTS

what if...

Former Texas Lawmakers Were Banned from Lobbying?

BACKGROUND

In recent years, a peculiar practice has developed among many former members of state legislative bodies. Many ex-lawmakers are becoming lobbyists for the very interest groups they once regulated. To be certain, few people would be better suited to serve as lobbyists than ex-lawmakers. Former legislators are intricately familiar with the legislative process, many are policy experts, and they often have friendships with lawmakers who are still in office. Their familiarity with the policy-making process, their policy expertise, and their kinship with other lawmakers make them very attractive candidates for the lobbying profession.

Despite their fitness to serve as lobbyists, there are some dangers to permitting former lawmakers to serve as lobbyists. *Ex*-lawmakers, after all, were once *lawmakers*. That is to say, they were once in the position of creating legislation, regulating industry, and providing oversight of government agencies. Lawmakers planning their next career move might feel compelled to reward their future employers with favorable public policy. Ex-lawmakers might author bills that help the industries that they hope to lobby for once they leave office. Ex-lawmakers might remove onerous legislation, or be less diligent in their oversight responsibilities, when they plan to become lobbyists.

Unlike the federal government and many other states, Texas does not ban former lawmakers from becoming lobbyists. While 26 other states have some ban on lobbying immediately after leaving office, Texas has no such restrictions. Furthermore, Texas pays its citizen legislators a mere $7,200 per year. A legislator's poor pay does not compare to the salaries of successful lobbyists. In a recent study conducted by the Center for Public Integrity, 70 former members of the Texas legislature were working as lobbyists—the largest number of any state. California and New York, which have full-time legislative bodies, reported only 35 and 19 ex-lawmakers-turned-lobbyists, respectively.*

WHAT'S WRONG WITH FORMER LAWMAKERS LOBBYING?

If ex-lawmakers were banned from lobbying, the legislator's freedom to choose a career path would be denied

for the sake of assumed improved representation. Many ex-lawmakers leave public office with financial obligations. They have mortgage payments, their kids' college tuition, and many other expenses they must attend to. As former lawmakers, these individuals have developed skills that can be parlayed into a lobbying career that could allow them to address the personal needs that they were unable to fully address as public servants. As it stands, Texas lawmakers are poorly compensated for their public service. The public expects legislators to represent them fully. When a legislator does so, that legislator compromises personal finances for public service.

Unfortunately, the risk of affording lawmakers the freedom to choose lobbying careers upon leaving office creates a more sinister outcome. Lawmakers are in a position to exploit their positions for the sake of future returns. Unscrupulous lawmakers can sponsor legislation that rewards those interest groups that will provide such lawmakers employment upon leaving the legislature. Although it is difficult to gauge the extent to which *quid pro quo* occurs, the coincidences can be troubling. In 2003, State Representative Jamie Capelo coauthored a bill that capped medical liability lawsuits. Shortly after leaving office, Capelo was a lobbyist for interest groups that benefited from his earlier legislation. Such connections between public policy and the interest-group beneficiaries that would later employ the sponsors of the public policy are common.

Others are critical that the use of public service as a stepping stone to a more lucrative career as a lobbyist is simply unseemly. Public service should be its own reward. Most public servants do not enter public service because it is lucrative, but because they care about creating good public policy.

ONE- OR TWO-YEAR BAN?

A ban on lobbying would limit the career paths of many public servants. It would also ensure that ex-lawmakers do not seek personal gain from their positions upon leaving office.

A compromise that many state legislative bodies have reached, and one upon which the federal government relies, is a one- or two-year ban on lobbying. Ex-lawmakers must wait either one or two years before they can lobby their former colleagues. This still does not avoid the problems mentioned previously, but some

---

*Center for Public Integrity, "Ex-legislators Registered to Lobby 2005," accessed March 1, 2008, at www.publicintegrity.org/hiredguns/reg.aspx.

believe that a one- or two-year ban reduces the number of ex-lawmakers who become lobbyists. Relying on the Center for Public Integrity's data for 2005, one can gauge the effectiveness of these programs. While states with no ban on lobbying produced an average of 29 ex-lawmakers who became lobbyists, states with a one-year ban averaged 22 lawmakers who became lobbyists, and the six states with a two-year ban averaged 28 lawmakers who became lobbyists. The differences among the states are even smaller when one considers that some states have much smaller legislative bodies, thus producing fewer ex-lawmakers.

Further contributing to the number of former lawmakers who become lobbyists is the number of states that have set term limits for lawmakers. Term limits help produce more *ex*-lawmakers in need of employment—employment that ex-lawmakers tend to find as lobbyists. A complete ban on post-legislative service would ensure that ex-lawmakers do not use their public service as a stepping-stone to a more lucrative lobbying career. Such a ban, however, would deny the ex-lawmaker the liberty to choose a career after public service.

FOR CRITICAL ANALYSIS

1. What other factors might explain why ex-lawmakers become lobbyists?
2. Is the cost of denying a lawmaker the freedom to choose a lobbying career outweighed by the public's expectation for good public policy?

PEOPLE IN THE United States endorse participation in the political process without hesitation. Constitutions and laws guarantee the right to do so. Public education encourages it, yet many citizens fail to participate. Whether people choose to be involved depends on a host of factors, including their personality types, the time they have available, their degree of understanding of government's impact on their lives, their confidence in themselves, their trust in government, and their concern for others. People also differ in their concepts of **civic duty**.

Participation is most effective when it is undertaken collectively—that is, by interest groups—rather than by isolated individuals. This chapter identifies what interest groups are and what they do, explores the constitutional protections for interest groups, classifies groups by type, and discusses the craft of lobbying and the interaction that occurs between the public and government in policy making.

Civic Duty
A citizen's understood obligation to register, to vote, to be knowledgeable, and to take action to make the community a better place.

WHAT ARE INTEREST GROUPS?

Individuals may act alone to influence government, and millions do. As discussed in Chapter 7, when individuals join with others in an organizational structure designed to express their preferences to government, however, they act as an *interest group*. The media frequently speak of the interests of women, minorities, or employers, but individuals who share an interest must unite in a cooperative effort to promote some policy objective before they can be thought of as an interest group.

In summary, interest groups are collections of individuals having shared interests who are organized to influence government decision makers. Usually, they hire *lobbyists* to represent them to public officials. Many interest groups are private institutions pursuing public-policy goals on behalf of their members. Government agencies also may function as interest groups. The concerns of interest groups are narrower than those of political parties. Unlike parties, they do not nominate candidates for office, but because the individuals who hold office affect what government does, interest groups often endorse and support candidates who are favorable to their cause. At the same time, they often work with members of both parties to secure their goals.

Interest groups are also sometimes called *pressure groups*. The two terms basically mean the same thing. The term *pressure group* comes from the fact that interest groups try to apply pressure on decision makers as they seek favorable policy outputs. Pressure on the officeholder can come from the voting power of the group and the value of its endorsement, campaign contributions, and volunteer help in elections.

CONSTITUTIONAL GUARANTEES

The constitutions of the United States and of Texas guarantee to citizens the right to political participation through voting, speaking, writing, and petitioning government "for redress of grievances." To peaceably assemble *for political expression* is likewise clearly encouraged. The Texas constitution says it very well:

> The citizens shall have the right . . . to . . . apply to those invested with the powers of government for redress of grievances or other purposes, by petition, address or remonstrance [formal protest]. (Article I, Section 27)

The First Amendment to the U.S. Constitution makes our liberties even more clear:

> Congress shall make no law . . . abridging the freedom of speech, or of the press; or the right of the people peaceably to assemble, and to petition the Government for a redress of grievances.

In these constitutional expressions, free speech, a free press, and the right to join together in political parties and interest groups "to petition the government" are guaranteed. These guarantees and the right to vote are essential to democracy. Representative democracy, however, creates dangers. The liberty that comes with it requires citizens to inform themselves about political issues and involve themselves in the choices to be made. Both extreme zealousness and apathy can present dangers to democracy. Highly organized and active groups can threaten the well-being of the unorganized majority. The organized and zealous can be expected to triumph over the apathetic or unorganized. Hence, small factions of the population, rather than the majority, may control selected policy areas.

WHAT INTEREST GROUPS DO

The primary goal of interest groups is to influence the branches of government to produce policies favorable to their members. It follows that groups also seek to block policies harmful to their members. Very few, if any, government policies affect all classes of citizens equally. Some benefit, some suffer inconvenience, and others experience economic loss from any policy adopted.

States like Texas, which have a diverse and complex economic system, tend to produce a greater diversity of interest groups. The diversity of interest groups that exist in Texas makes it difficult for any one special-interest group to dominate Texas politics. And, as a result, the public is protected from public policy that benefits one group. The agricultural, energy, legal, banking, medical, religious, racial, ethnic, and educational interest groups are just a few organized interests in Texas, and all compete with one another for favorable legislation. Because there are so many interest groups in Texas, no one group is the sole recipient of public goods.

Interest groups are instrumental in drawing citizens into political participation to influence public policies, but most often they draw in *selected* citizens in a way that promotes interests that may be narrow and selfish. There are two views of interest groups, one positive and one negative.

Positive Views of Interest Groups. Interest groups have the ability to draw citizens into the political processes of communicating with public officials and voting. Certainly, democracy calls for politically attentive and active citizens. From this perspective, interest groups educate their members about issues and mobilize them to participate in constitutionally approved ways. Simultaneously, interest groups inform and educate public officials.

Interest groups also provide policy makers with valuable information. This information is often provided in the form of testimony before committees. Because state law makes it a crime to share knowingly false information with state lawmakers,[1] most special-interest groups are careful to provide truthful, albeit one-sided, information. The information provided by interest groups can be costly to gather both in terms of time and money. Because interest groups provide the information free of cost, taxpayers are spared the expense.

Negative Views of Interest Groups. Critics, in contrast, focus on the harm that can result when powerful groups demand that public policy reflect their values. Private meetings with public officials present no opportunity for rebuttal of the views that are advanced. Critics worry about corruption and intimidation of public officials by what they call "special-interests." The need for campaign contributions, they believe, makes elected officials especially vulnerable to pressure.

A **conflict of interest** is a situation that arises when a legislator, bureaucrat, executive official, or judge can make an official decision that results in a personal economic advantage. The result is a potential or real conflict between the personal interests of the officeholder and the general interests of the public.

An illustration of this type of activity occurred on February 2, 2007, when Governor Rick Perry issued an executive order to vaccinate preteen girls against the sexually transmitted human papilloma virus (HPV), which causes cervical cancer in women. Fearing opposition from members of his own party, Governor Perry issued the executive order to circumvent the Texas legislature completely. He expected opposition from conservative groups that believe such a vaccine would give young girls tacit consent to have sex.

Shortly after he issued the executive order, it was revealed that Governor Perry's chief of staff, Deirdre Delisi, met with other members of the governor's team for an "HPV Vaccine for Children Briefing" on October 16, 2006.[2] That same day, Merck and Company's political action committee contributed $5,000 to the Perry campaign. Merck and Company is the only manufacturer of Gardasil, the vaccine that is believed to fend off the virus. One of Merck and Company's lobbyists at the time was Mike Toomey, Rick Perry's former chief of staff and Deirdre Delisi's predecessor.

In early March 2007, the Texas legislature passed a bill rescinding the executive order, which Governor Perry grudgingly allowed to become law without his signature. While the governor's office claims that the connection between the campaign contribution and the meeting held by his chief of staff was merely a coincidence, critics contend that the coincidence at the very least sheds light on the conflicts of interest that can occur between elected officials in need of raising campaign contributions, on the one hand, and the need of special-interest groups for public policy that provides them with direct benefits, on the other hand.

Conflict of Interest
A situation that arises when a legislator, bureaucrat, executive official, or judge can make an official decision that results in a personal economic advantage. The result is a potential or real conflict between the personal interests of the officeholder and the general interests of the public.

---

[1] Texas Government Code, 305.021.
[2] Liz Austin Peterson, "Perry's Staff Discussed Vaccine on Day Merck Donated to Campaign," Associated Press, February 22, 2007.

TABLE 21–1 Positive and Negative Aspects of Interest Groups

POSITIVE	NEGATIVE
Increased political representation	Narrow interests
Political participation and mobilization	Secret communications with officials
Education of their members	Corruption or intimidation of public officials
Shared information and data	
Reduced cost to taxpayers	

Special-interest groups are also powerful enough to determine the outcome of elections. Interest groups are in a position to make significant campaign contributions that will elect candidates that hold positions that are favorable to their interests. In some cases, interest groups are powerful enough to have their own employees selected for public office. Several of the state's major law firms, which also have powerful lobbying arms in Texas government, boast members of the Texas legislature and executive branch as current or former members. Similarly, senior administrators with powerful corporations or special-interest groups tend to be successful in being selected to serve on government boards and commissions.

The bottom line for critics is their concern that special-interests will prevail over the desires of the general public. As Bob Stein, the Lena Gohlman Fox Professor of Political Science at Rice University, has said, "Long before the legislature sits down and writes a bill, the lobbyists are there."[3] Table 21–1 summarizes the positive and negative aspects of interest groups.

TYPES OF INTEREST GROUPS

Interest groups can be classified in a multitude of ways. The most simple is to categorize them as economic, noneconomic, or mixed. Table 21–2 provides classification and examples of Texas interest groups.

Economic. Economic interests operating at the state level include business and the professions, education, local government, agriculture, and labor. Each interest seeks financial advantages for its members. Business and agriculture are always interested in keeping their taxes low, securing benefits called **subsidies**, avoiding regulation, and obtaining government contracts. Labor unions seek legislation to obtain workers' compensation and workplace safety benefits and to make it easier to organize (unionize) labor.

Subsidies
Grants or special tax exemptions provided by the government to individuals or businesses in the private sector.

Noneconomic. Noneconomic groups seek the betterment of society as a whole or reform of the political, social, or economic system in ways that do not directly affect their members' pockets. Such groups are difficult to form because the groups work for goods that everyone benefits from. This creates an incentive for individuals who will benefit from the work of a noneconomic interest group to become what Mancur Olson calls a *free rider*.[4] A free rider is an individual who benefits from the work of an interest group, but who does not participate in the collective actions that made the benefits possible. Environmental and political reformers maintain that society in general benefits from

---

[3]Clay Robison, "Weak State Government Paved Way for Lobbyists," *Houston Chronicle*, December 29, 2002, p. A1.
[4]Mancur Olson (1971) [1965], *The Logic of Collective Action: Public Goods and the Theory of Groups* (revised ed.) (Cambridge, MA: Harvard University Press).

TABLE 21–2 Examples of Texas Interest Groups

ECONOMIC TYPE OF GROUP	EXAMPLES	NONECONOMIC TYPE OF GROUP	EXAMPLES	MIXED TYPE OF GROUP	EXAMPLES
Agriculture	Texas Farm Bureau	Patriotic	American Legion	Education	Texas State Teachers Association Texas Association of School Administrators
Business	Texas Association of Business and Chambers of Commerce	Public interest	Texas Common Cause Texans for Public Justice	Race and ethnicity	League of United Latin American Citizens NAACP (African Americans)
Labor	American Federation of Labor–Congress of Industrial Organizations (AFL-CIO)	Religious	Texas Christian Life Commission	Local government	Texas Municipal League Texas County Judges and Commissioners Association
Occupations and professions	Texas Association of Realtors Texas Trial Lawyers Association	Environment and recreation	Texas Nature Conservatory Texas Committee on Natural Resources		

their programs. Clean air, clean water, and fair elections are said to promote the well-being of all. Many individuals who join noneconomic interest groups are motivated to participate by two or three things—intense passion, selective incentives, and social pressures. Individuals who join the Texas Right to Life movement are motivated by strong beliefs about conception and when life begins. The intensity of passion that these individuals possess motivates them to join. Other organizations recruit members by offering selective incentives such as T-shirts, coffee mugs, and newsletters as a way of attracting members. Still other noneconomic interest groups rely on social pressure to attract members to join. Neighborhood organizations can pressure neighbors to join the local civic association. Failing to join a neighborhood group makes one auspiciously absent from civic life in the community. The threat of ostracism leads many to join such groups. Noneconomic interest groups benefit from large memberships because they translate into greater political clout in the Texas legislature. Group members can write letters, call, and even vote for or against members of the Texas legislature. What some noneconomic interest groups lack in financial resources they make up for in group membership.

Government. Levels and branches of government also lobby. They are not generally recognized as interest groups, but they are affected by what other political institutions and jurisdictions decide. Governors have staffs that promote their political agenda in the legislature. Cities, school districts, and other local governments are seriously affected by legislative decisions on finances and local government authority. They are also affected by rules set by state executive-branch agencies. Therefore, they must protect and/or promote their interests by employing lobbyists or reassigning employees to be lobbyists as needed.

In recent years, the public has criticized governmental agencies for hiring lobbyists. Critics argue that the public elects representatives to represent their interests. The hiring of lobbyists is simply an added cost to taxpayers. But cities, universities, and other public agencies respond that they are at a tremendous disadvantage when they do not have the additional assistance of lobbyists. When the Texas Department of Transportation hired a lobbyist, Robert Black, a spokesman for Governor Rick Perry defended the action by saying, "The fact of the matter is the transportation bureaucracy in Washington, D.C., is incredibly extensive and to have people on the ground who can traverse that bureaucratic maze is highly valuable."[5] Cities and other local governments that do not hire lobbyists to represent their interests can find themselves at a disadvantage.

Mixed. Many groups do not fit neatly into economic or noneconomic classifications because they pursue social goals that have clear economic effects. For example, discrimination on the basis of age, disability, ethnicity, gender, or native language is a social problem that also has negative consequences on wages and promotion within the workplace. Groups pursuing equality in society and the workplace can thus be classified as mixed or hybrid organizations.

Similarly, education and local government groups want economic benefits such as greater state support and increased salaries and benefits for their employees. In addition, blocking **unfunded mandates** imposed by the state and obtaining more local control over their affairs are often objectives. Many of the goals of such groups can also be characterized as noneconomic. Improvements to the educational system, for example, can be seen as contributing to the betterment of persons other than the educators.

Unfunded Mandate
A requirement imposed on a lower level of government by a higher level of government. The requirement is not accompanied by the funds to pay for the resulting expenses.

WHY PEOPLE JOIN INTEREST GROUPS

As explained in Chapter 7, people join interest groups for many reasons. To influence government, you need to be a joiner. Most individuals lack the status, knowledge, political skills, and funds to operate alone and be successful. Joining together creates a network of like-minded people who can pool their talents and other resources to obtain their political ends. Furthermore, work and family obligations leave little time for most people to become experts on the complexities of policy issues. The solution is to create or "hire" an organization to advocate or protect their economic, recreational, social, or political interests. The organization can monitor activities in the capital and alert its members to the need to call or write public officials and influence decisions relevant to the members. A group with many members contacting officials at the same time has a better chance of obtaining favorable results.

That among the 50 states, Texas has the nation's highest rate of cervical cancer: 10.1 for every 100,000?[6]

The Benefits of Socializing. Joining a group can advance career and social goals as well. Certainly, belonging to a collectivity that meets periodically will increase your circle of friends and business contacts. Getting to know people in your trade or profession can lead to job offers, knowledge exchange, and enjoyment of others who share your interests. Hence, active membership leads to networking that has economic, social, and political benefits.

[5]Michelle Mittelstadt, "Democrats Rip State Agency for Hiring D.C. Lobbyists," *Houston Chronicle*, February 2, 2007, Sec. A1.
[6]The Henry J. Kaiser Family Foundation, "Cervical Cancer Incidence Rate per 100,000 Women, 2003," Statehealthfacts.org, accessed March 15, 2008.

Other Benefits. Sometimes people in a particular profession join a group because the culture of the profession requires membership— that is, it may be seen as unprofessional not to be a member. People are expected to stay current in their fields, and participation in a professional group may help meet this goal. All organizations exist to disseminate information or knowledge, but an organization may also offer other tangible benefits. For example, malpractice insurance is available to teachers, attorneys, and medical personnel through organizational memberships. A monthly or quarterly magazine or newsletter may attract membership. Publications of nature and conservation groups are often so beautiful that one might join simply to enjoy such groups' magazines. Such benefits are referred to as selective incentives, and they are often offered by interest groups only to those who join the group.

GOVERNOR RICK PERRY signs House Bill 3011, authorizing creation of the Houston Ship Channel Security District in 2007. (Courtesy of the Office of the Governor, Austin, Texas)

Selective incentives are used to get around the *free-rider* problem. A free rider is a person who benefits from the work of others without incurring much cost for the benefit. The free-rider problem is most common among groups that provide benefits to everyone. Environmental groups might fight for clean air. Given that everyone who breathes benefits from clean air, the environmental group has a large pool of potential members. But the actual number of people who become members of the environmental group is much smaller than the group that benefits. Joining a group means that the member of the interest group will incur some costs. The cost could come in the form of time, money, or other resources. An individual might conclude that if the environmental group lobbies for clean air, everyone benefits, even the nonmembers. Being rational, most people choose to be free riders and benefit from the environmental work of others. To mitigate the free-rider problem, interest groups offer selective incentives such as T-shirts, coffee mugs, or magazines to their members.

The Ultimate Goal. Whatever people's reasons for joining interest groups, we should not be surprised to learn that their ultimate goal is to influence government. After all, the government regulates our occupations and professions. It decides who pays how much in taxes and who receives the benefits of those tax dollars through public spending programs. Few aspects of life are untouched by the political system. Those who do not pay attention to what is going on in Washington, Austin, and city hall will nonetheless feel the effects of what occurs there.

INFLUENCING GOVERNMENT

As you learned in Chapter 7, the techniques used by interest groups can be divided into direct and indirect techniques. With *direct techniques*, groups attempt to influence government officials by dealing with them personally. With *indirect techniques*, groups attempt to influence officials by influencing other parties, such as the electorate at large.

DIRECT TECHNIQUES OF EXERCISING INFLUENCE

Using lobbyists to contact government officials is the most obvious direct technique. Lawsuits and demonstrations can also fall under this heading.

Lobbying the Legislative and Executive Branches. Lobbying is direct contact between an interest-group representative and a legislative- or executive-branch official or employee to influence a specific public-policy outcome.[7] Most people understand that the legislature creates, finances, and changes government programs. Therefore, it comes as no surprise that individuals and groups affected by these decisions attempt to participate in the lawmaking process by lobbying legislators. Awareness that privilege, prestige, and funds are at stake in the executive decision-making process that follows the lawmaking is not so common.

The executive branch, or the administration, is charged with the **implementation** of legislative policy. The legislature delegates a great deal of **discretion** to executive agencies, both directly and indirectly. This freedom allows the administrative agencies to complete the policy-making process by issuing rules or regulations that specify how the law will be applied to actual situations. Interest groups seek to shape the regulations that will apply to them.

In short, because what government does is not simply a function of legislative decisions, lobbyists must actively monitor and seek to influence executive branch rule making and enforcement as well. The importance of this is revealed in the Texas Ethics Commission Report of 2006—a year when the legislature was not in regular session—which showed that nearly 1,500 registered lobbyists were at work in Texas.

Filing Suit in Court. There are several reasons why organized interests use the courts to further their causes. Lack of funds or public support often motivates interest groups to file lawsuits. It can be less expensive to file a suit than to successfully influence the legislature. Furthermore, public opinion is supposed to be irrelevant to judicial outcomes.

A second reason for using the courts is to seek a more favorable interpretation of the law than the one employed by the enforcing agency. "More favorable" can mean less costly to the profession, business, or individuals who must obey the rules set by the overseeing agency. Additionally, an interest group that has lost the political struggle may be able to challenge the constitutionality of the law or the means of enforcement selected by the administering agency.

A third reason is to delay the implementation of a new law or rule. Courts often postpone implementation of the law or rule while the case is pending. The members of the group bringing the litigation can then continue to operate as before, in (presumably) a more profitable and unrestrained manner. Filing suit, even when one expects to lose, may delay application of costly rules. If the interest group does prevail in court, two positive outcomes for the interest are possible: (1) the previous way of doing things may be restored, or (2) the state may have to wait until the next session of the legislature to take action.

A fourth reason to file suit is to gain public attention. Media coverage of the suit brings the issue to the attention of the branch or level of government that has the power to produce the change the group seeks. The publicity that results from being sued may provide an incentive for the government to enter into negotiation with the lawsuit's filer to change the policy without the necessity of judicial action. Suits, then, can be utilized to delay, stop, or start action. The goal depends on the needs of the interest group.

Advising and Serving on State Boards. State law in Texas generally requires that a majority of the members of appointed boards come from the profession, occupation, business, or activity the board is regulating. The mere existence of such a requirement is testimony to the power of special-interest groups to shape government decisions in Texas. The board members and commissioners appointed as a result of this

Implementation
The carrying out of laws by executive officials and the bureaucrats who work for them.

Discretion
An official's power to make decisions based on personal judgment rather than on the specific requirements of the law; the freedom to decide or make choices.

---

[7]Texas Government Code Section 305.003a.

requirement are part-time officials but full-time practitioners of the activity they have the power to regulate. They simultaneously exercise power as state officials and function as members of a special-interest group that may testify and present information to the agency.

We can call this blurring of the line between the state and the special-interest **co-optation**. Critics of interest groups believe that the public interest is endangered when state officials can act as representatives of the group the agency regulates. As mentioned earlier, a conflict of interest exists when the decision maker is personally affected by the decision she or he makes.

The newly created Texas Residential Construction Commission (2003) is testimony to the power of Texas home builders to create an agency to protect themselves, for the law requires home buyers to take complaints to mediation rather than to the courts. The law requires that four members come from the home-building industry and the remainder represent "citizens." Governor Rick Perry has filled four citizen seats with supporters who have ties to the construction industry. Thus, the nine-member commission has eight members with ties to either home building or construction, even though the job of the commission is to be an "impartial" judge of complaints against the home builder.

Co-optation
The "capturing" of an agency by members of an interest group. In effect, governmental power comes to be exercised by a private interest.

Public Demonstrations. Marches and demonstrations are used periodically to obtain publicity for a cause. Press coverage is all but guaranteed. This sort of "theater" is especially suited to television news. In 2006, Governor Rick Perry fast-tracked approval to build several coal-fired power plants in Texas. To bring attention to these plans, several environmental groups protested in the streets of Austin in December 2006, asking passersby to sign their names to envelopes of coal that would be delivered to the governor just in time for Christmas. This stunt, although comical, garnered serious media attention.[8] The challenge for interest groups using this method of pressuring the state is to simultaneously enlist enough members to be impressive and still control their activity. One solution to the challenge has been found in the development of **astroturf lobbying**, or the fabrication of public support for issues supported by industry and special-interest groups to give the impression of widespread public support. Violating the law, forging signatures on letters sent to lawmakers, blocking traffic, damaging property, and using obscenities are usually counterproductive. Such conduct may antagonize fellow citizens or public officials who have the power to change the conditions at which the protest is aimed.

FACULTY, STAFF, AND STUDENTS from the University of Texas at Austin and UT Hearts of Texas volunteers form the "Heart of Texas" on the main mall of the campus in Austin. The UT Hearts of Texas promotes charitable giving and volunteerism and participates in the Texas State Employee Charitable Campaign. Organizations affiliated with UT and other large universities are important interest groups. (AP Photo/UT Austin)

INDIRECT TECHNIQUES OF INFLUENCING GOVERNMENT

Attempts to influence the voting public are the most obvious indirect technique used by interest groups. We can also characterize as indirect those interactions with government officials that are not specific attempts to address a particular piece of legislation or a particular administrative rule. Socializing at parties and other recreational events may allow lobbyists to create a positive impression on officials they may later seek to influence.

---

[8] See video of protest on YouTube, "Austin Sends Dirty Coal Back to Gov. Perry," December 19, 2006, www.youtube.com/watch?v=DEGlbXGKnDw, accessed March 15, 2008.

POLITICS WITH A purpose

Tuition Deregulation and Public Universities

In 2003, the state of Texas deregulated tuition rates, allowing university regents to raise tuition as they saw fit. Since this time, designated tuition has risen by 113 percent.[a] Students at the University of Texas at Dallas watched their tuition rise from $690 in 2003 to $2,022 in the fall of 2007—a 193 percent increase for 15 semester credit hours.[b] Such dramatic increases ignore the fact that Texas university students pay an average of $2,952 in mandatory fees and course fees.[c] In the end, middle-class students are feeling the pinch most directly. Not wealthy enough to afford the increase and not poor enough to qualify for grants, middle-class students are finding themselves having to make difficult choices. Many of these students find their way to community colleges, which have their own sources of revenue such as taxing property owners in their jurisdictions; others are organizing. In doing so, they are letting lawmakers know how they feel.

The legislature supported the idea of tuition deregulation because it meant that the state would not have to come up with more revenue to adequately fund public universities. Governor Rick Perry continues to support tuition deregulation, arguing that universities can be more efficient,[d] but lawmakers are feeling the pressure from their constituents. Senator Rodney Ellis reports receiving phone calls, e-mails, and letters asking for some kind of protection from tuition increases.[e]

University students have begun to organize to protect their interests. They are demanding that the legislature rein in state universities and the authority granted to university regents to raise tuition rates. At the University of Texas, the Tuition Accountability Coalition has brought students from disparate groups together to protest tuition increases. Across the state, the Texas Student Association has been revived after years of dormancy. Among the issues it hopes to bring to the forefront is tuition deregulation.

Editorial boards of many local newspapers have been reading angry letters from students and parents. In many opinion pieces, local papers are asking the state to repeal tuition deregulation. While many state lawmakers have followed the strategy of rebuking boards of regents, recent attempts to repeal the law have not been very successful. If university students are successful at organizing, they may very well force the legislature to repeal the law.

Do you think that the law should be repealed? How much of the burden of funding public universities should fall on the state?

[a]Texas Higher Education Coordinating Board, "Academic Charges (Tuition, Mandatory Fees, and Average College and Course Fees) Fall 2002–Fall 2007," July 10, 2008, www.thecb.state.tx.us/reports.
[b]Ibid.
[c]Ibid.
[d]Christy Hoppe, "Higher Education—Perry Asks Regents to Shift Their Thinking—Proposals Include Giving Students, Not Schools, Public Money," *Dallas Morning News*, May 22, 2008, p. 3A.

[e]Jeannie Kever, "Complaints Rising Right Along with Tuition, Fees: Legislators Feel the Heat, Wonder if Deregulation Needs New Look," *Houston Chronicle*, July 10, 2008, p. A1.

Electioneering. Although interest groups do not nominate candidates for office, one candidate may be more favorable to their cause than another. The organization may endorse that candidate and recommend that its members vote for that person. The organization's newsletter or magazine will be used to carry this message.

A second means of helping candidates who are favorable to the group's interests is to create a political action committee (PAC). This structure, separated from the interest group legally, is solely intended to funnel funds to candidates for office.

MORE THAN 40 organizations gathered outside the Texas capitol in February 2007 asking the Texas legislature to pass a resolution on coal-fired generating plants and supporting cleaner energy solutions. (AP Photo/Harry Cabluck)

Educating the Public. An interest group clearly benefits from providing the general public with messages that build a positive image of the interest the group supports. Industry interest groups may employ the services of public relations people to enhance the industry's reputation for honesty, satisfactory products and services, concern for the well-being of customers, and good citizenship. Organizational magazines, annual reports to stockholders, and press releases to newspapers are some of the ways to build a reputation and educate the public about the wisdom of policy proposals supported by the organization. Occasionally, a group purchases advertisements on radio and television and in magazines and newspapers to shape and mobilize public opinion on behalf of the interest group or to neutralize opposition to what the interest group wants to do.

Those who seek government action must articulate the need or problem in exactly the right language. Their goal must be to evoke a favorable response and to stay in control of the definition of the problem. It is advantageous to educate public officials before an issue becomes public. Once an issue is public, opponents may try to reverse the interest group's definition—that is, to redefine the issue and put the interest group's position in a negative light. For example, those who favor vouchers that can be used to pay for tuition at private schools, including church-sponsored schools, may emphasize their belief that vouchers will improve the education of children who are ill-served by the existing system. Opponents may attempt to convince the voters that such aid violates the principle of separation of church and state. Most political struggles are group-against-group battles, and words are the weapons of political combat.

Socializing. Interest-group representatives know that friendships can be formed at social functions. Informal occasions allow people to interact in comfortable settings. A lobbyist may invite a public official to lunch or to a social gathering to establish a positive relationship. Formal occasions designed to honor a person can also build positive relationships. Invitations to speak before a group are another way to cultivate relationships with public officials.

The purpose of social invitations is to establish a positive impression that pays off in favorable votes or other friendly decisions by government officials. Interest groups view socializing with public officials as a good investment, whether or not there is an immediate need for the official's support.

Access to public officials is the prerequisite for influencing public decisions. Lobbyists seek to "get in the door" to discuss a matter of concern in time to shape the public-policy outcome. Indirect techniques of influencing government often pave the road for direct techniques. Groups that have established good relations with public officials are more likely to enjoy access, but even the most successful groups can expect to lose sometimes.

Access
The ability to contact an official either in person or by telephone. Campaign contributions are often given in hopes of gaining access to elected officials.

WHICH INTERESTS ARE POWERFUL?

Twenty years ago, businesses and the professions tended to be the most powerful interests in Texas. They still are, despite an explosion in the number of interest groups in recent years. Generally speaking, the newer interest groups, such as environmentalists, have not supplanted the old. In conservative, pro-business Texas, that is not surprising. For many corporations, the power of interest groups waxes and wanes depending on the political environment. If an industry feels that it stands to gain or lose from government action, it will lobby the legislature.

Although it is not the best measure of the strength of an interest group, one can gauge the strength of a lobbying effort by the amount of money spent to lobby. Table 21–3 lists the 27 groups that spent $1 million or more on lobbying in 2009. Note the frequency of times that groups from the energy and natural resources sector appear. Eighteen percent (or up to $62 million) of all lobbying contracts in 2009 were made on behalf of the energy and natural resources sector of the economy.[9] In 2009, the energy sector, led by Energy Future's Holding Corporation, lobbied for a piece of the $5 billion Texas Public Utility Commission bid request to build power lines that would move wind power energy from north and west Texas to the urban centers.[10] Such a huge energy contract brought a lot of energy sector lobbyists to the capitol. Oncor, which is a subsidiary of Energy Future's Holding Corporation, and American Electric Power received the biggest awards.[11]

The power of interest groups is in part a function of the lobbying campaigns they organize. The National Institute on Money in State Politics identifies the major industries in Texas by the amount of money they contribute. In 2008, those industries were:

---

[9]Texans for Public Justice, "Austin's Oldest Profession: Texas's Top Lobby Clients and Those Who Support Them," 2010 Edition, available at http://info.tpj.org/reports/austinsoldest09/facts.html.
[10]Ibid.
[11]Ibid.

Lawyers and lobbyists	$22,539,424
Oil and gas	$ 8,358,558
Real estate industry	$ 6,788,562
Health professionals	$ 5,729,622
Liberal policy organizations	$ 4,958,016
Home builders	$ 4,195,487
Party committees	$ 4,126,629
Business associations	$ 3,532,973
Beer, wine, and liquor	$ 3,203,543
Candidate committees	$ 2,994,129
Electric utilities	$ 2,968,513
Other/Single-issue groups	$ 2,681,052
Securities and investments	$ 2,399,476
Insurance	$ 2,331,257
General contractors	$ 2,304,550[12]

These sectors of the economy have strong membership associations, such as the Texas Association of Realtors, Texas Medical Association, and the Texas State Teachers Association, which have the funds to maintain permanent headquarters in Austin and to employ clerical and research staff, as well as lobbyists, to make their presence felt. These resources, when competently managed, enable some interest groups to create a need for themselves within the halls of government. Research shows that the number-one element determining the political power of a group is how much public officials need the group. Officials may need the group's expertise to help the state solve problems. They may depend on the group for campaign contributions. Perhaps the state's economy depends on the economic sector the group represents. There are many explanations of public officials' need for a particular interest group.[13]

GOVERNOR RICK PERRY, right, listens while receiving the endorsement of the political arm of the Texas Medical Association November 2, 2009, in Austin, Texas. TMA President Dr. William H. Fleming, III, is on the left.
(AP Photo/Harry Cabluck)

[12]National Institute on Money in State Politics, "Top 15 Industries," 2008, http://www.followthemoney.org/database/state_overview.phtml?y=2008&s=TX, accessed June 20, 2010.
[13]Ronald Hrebenar and Clive Thomas, "Who's Got Clout? Interest Group Power in the States," *State Legislatures*, April 1999.

THE STRENGTH OF THE BUSINESS LOBBY

Records of registered lobbyists kept by the Texas Ethics Commission show that two-thirds of the registered groups represent some form of business. Business is a comprehensive category. Therefore, we should not think of all business interests as being alike. There are both powerful and weak interests within this classification. Furthermore, independent and small businesses frequently seek policy outcomes opposed by larger enterprises. This diversity within the business sector ensures that no one business group dominates other groups.

The number of lobbyists by subject-matter category, shown in Table 21–3, reflects the importance of business interests. Unraveling the lobbyist registration reports to determine the number of lobbyists representing specific trade groups, business associations, or other interests is challenging. Many organizations listed may be supported by the same benefactors and represent the same industry, business, or activity. It is easier to identify the lobbyists representing a particular company, profession, union, or employee association. Among business interests, 57 percent are associated with an identifiable company. Many companies, however, are also represented through **umbrella organizations**, in which industries, wholesalers, producers, retailers, and others join together to promote their collective interests. In other words, a firm may employ lobbyists directly and also through these umbrella organizations.

Umbrella Organization
An organization created by interest groups to promote common goals. Several interest groups may choose this mechanism to coordinate their efforts to influence government when they share the same policy goals. The umbrella organization may be temporary or permanent.

THE EFFECTS OF POVERTY

Not all interests are well represented in the political system. Low levels of political participation in Texas are associated with the below-average educational attainment of many Texas citizens. Education and income are also related. Compared with the rest of the country, Texas has a relatively high proportion of poor people in its population. The poor and marginalized do not participate actively in politics. These factors bias the political system toward the upper-middle and upper classes. For the most part, people in these classes have the income to obtain education that pays off economically and socially.

HOW GROUPS USE THEIR POWER

A well-organized interest group will attempt to inform its membership, through newsletters or other means, about important matters likely to come before the legislature and executive agencies. Groups also seek to organize their membership into telephone chains or mail chains, or both. When a "hot" issue is about to come to a vote, an "action alert" can be dispatched. Members are asked to contact public officials and express the group's position on the issue. The intent is to apply outside (grassroots) pressure, while lobbyists work inside with public officials in Austin.

Special-interests with full-time staffs and multiple lobbyists that also disperse sizable sums of money in campaign contributions achieve more than interests that cannot support such activities. There are, however, additional factors involved in interest-group success. The media can sway the opinions of the public and of government officials on many issues. The governor may intervene in affairs before executive agencies or in legislative issues and change the outcome. Access and goodwill "bought" by campaign contributions can be nullified by media exposure, public opinion, and the countervailing power of rival interest groups. Thus, as we observed earlier, powerful groups may win more often than they lose, but they are not guaranteed success.

IRON TRIANGLES AND ISSUE NETWORKS

Political scientist Ernest Griffin observed nearly 70 years ago that the relationships and interactions among members of the legislature are generally weaker than the

TABLE 21–3 The Biggest Spenders on Lobbyists in Texas

CLIENT	MAXIMUM VALUE OF LOBBYING CONTRACT	INDUSTRY
AT&T Corp.	$9,250,000	Communications
Energy Future Holdings Corp.	$3,240,000	Energy/Natural Resources
Reliant Energy, Inc.	$2,540,000	Energy/Natural Resources
McGinnis, Lochridge & Kilgore	$2,175,000	Lawyers/Lobbyists
Texas Trial Lawyers Assn.	$1,850,000	Lawyers/Lobbyists
American Electric Power	$1,800,000	Energy/Natural Resources
Texas Assn. of Realtors	$1,770,000	Real Estate
Texas Medical Assn.	$1,720,000	Health
TXU Energy Retail Co.	$1,495,000	Energy/Natural Resources
CenterPoint Energy	$1,485,000	Energy/Natural Resources
Oncor Electric Delivery Co.	$1,470,000	Energy/Natural Resources
Assn. of Electric Companies of Texas	$1,425,000	Energy/Natural Resources
City of Houston	$1,315,000	Ideological/Single Issue
Wholesale Beer Distributors of Texas	$1,305,000	Misc. Business
Baker Botts	$1,285,000	Lawyers/Lobbyists
ExxonMobil Corp.	$1,260,000	Energy/Natural Resources
El Paso County	$1,250,000	Ideological/Single Issue
Texas Cable & Telecom. Assn.	$1,245,000	Communications
Linebarger Heard Goggan Blair	$1,200,000	Lawyers/Lobbyists
Verizon	$1,115,000	Communications
Luminant Holding Co.	$1,110,000	Energy/Natural Resources
RRI Energy, Inc.	$1,050,000	Energy/Natural Resources
City of Austin	$1,045,000	Ideological/Single Issue
Atmos Energy Corp.	$1,015,000	Energy/Natural Resources
Henderson Global Investors	$1,002,000	Finance
Locke Lord Bissell & Liddell	$1,000,000	Lawyers/Lobbyists
UnitedHealth Group	$1,000,000	Health

Source: Texans for Public Justice, "Austin's Oldest Profession: Texas's Top Lobby Clients and Those Who Support Them," 2010 Edition, available at http://info.tpj.org/reports/austinsoldest09/facts.html (accessed June 21, 2010).

relationships between the legislators and the lobbyists, academics, and high-ranking bureaucrats who interact to address specific needs and solve specific problems.[14] When these participants are active, they become a subsystem of the legislative or administrative decision-making process.

Iron Triangles. In the literature of political science, a stable interaction pattern among legislative committee members, high-ranking bureaucrats, and representatives of special-interests is called an *iron triangle*, which we first discussed in Chapter 14. The members of such a triangle can be very powerful when they operate out of public view; they may even control policy outcomes. This is especially likely if the policy issue is very narrow and affects only a small segment of society.

Issue Networks. The iron triangle arrangement does not describe the environment of all or even most decision making. Another kind of arrangement, called an *issue network*, was also discussed in Chapter 14. Participants in a network are interested in a general policy area, such as health, transportation, or rural economic development, but as the specific topics change, the participants may change. For example, some participants concerned about health care focus on cost and access to services, whereas others are concerned more with professionalism and the supply of health care providers. Thus, people representing interests move into and out of the subsystem as the issue focus changes.[15]

Another key difference between issue networks and iron triangles is that, typically, networks exist that are opposed to each other on policy issues. As a result, more players are drawn into issue networks than are likely to participate in an iron triangle. While issue networks have more participants than iron triangles, the numbers involved are still small. The general public is absent from most public policy-making and policy-implementing events.

Broad and Narrow Concerns. Iron triangles are most likely to control rather routine decisions. Economic concerns dominate their agenda. Often, what motivates the actors is subsidies in the form of grants or tax deductions that favor specific economic interests.

Issue networks are broader in their interests and, hence, have more participants. Their focus may be economic, social, or both. The participants may be members of professional and social organizations that are national in scope and that distribute information through newsletters and other publications. They may strive to bring legislative and bureaucratic actors together in agreement on an approach to a problem.

FACTORS THAT AFFECT INTEREST GROUP POWER

The Texas political environment has its peculiarities, and it differs from the national political environment and the environments in many other states. The special characteristics of Texas politics affect organized interest groups in several ways. Here, we look at a variety of factors that determine the strength of interest groups in general relative to other players in the political game.

---

[14]Ernest Stacey Griffin, *The Impasse of Democracy* (New York: Harrison-Hilton Books, 1939), p. 182.
[15]Hugh Heclo, "Issue Networks and the Executive Establishment," in Anthony King, ed., *The New American Political System*, 2nd ed. (Washington, DC: American Enterprise Institute Press, 1990).

A CULTURE OF NONPARTICIPATION

One hundred and fifty years of one-party politics has probably given many Texans less incentive to participate in political affairs than citizens living in states with competitive parties. The absence of two competitive parties has also helped empower elites and strengthen special-interests. Historically, conservative Texas political elites used their control of state government to enact laws that discouraged mass political participation. The poll tax, annual voter registration, and the white primary were examples. These barriers to participation promoted a culture of nonparticipation by the masses that has yet to be undone.

PARTY COMPETITION

Studies by political scientists consistently show that where political parties are weak, interest groups are strong. States with a long history of two-party competition have weaker interest groups than states with weak party development.[16] Parties in competitive states must appeal to the majority of the population to have a chance of winning elections. They cannot limit themselves to one issue or a limited number of issues, as interest groups do, and expect to win a majority of the votes.

In Texas, one-party politics has left the parties weak. In the 1990s, the growth of the Republican Party raised the possibility that Texas would, for the first time, enjoy competition between two strong parties. The elections since 2002, however, suggest that Texas has simply been in transition from one dominant party (Democratic) to another (Republican). The two-party system in Texas may simply have been a passing fancy. As of the summer of 2010, Republican Party control now extends to the two highest courts in the state, both houses of the legislature, and all elected officers in the executive branch. We can expect that a one-party Republican system will be as vulnerable to interest-group domination as a one-party Democratic system.

THE PART-TIME LEGISLATURE

With more than 24 million people, Texas is the second most populous state in the Union. It is the only large state with legislative sessions that are limited in length and frequency. In addition, legislative pay is very low, and member turnover is fairly high. The result is a legislative body that is easily influenced by special-interest groups. Professor Cal Jillson of Southern Methodist University has put it this way: "If you meet only occasionally, get paid little and have weak staffs, you are at the disposal of the lobby because you have to go to them to get information."[17]

There is no question that the quality of staff in the legislative and executive branches has significantly improved since the 1950s. Better sources of information and research are now available within the government. Therefore, public officials may depend somewhat less on special-interests for information. Still, this change may be nullified by the dependence of elected officials on campaign funds. The Center for Public Integrity claims that the percentage of Texas legislators with financial ties to special-interests is the highest in the United States.[18] The author of this report suggests that the low pay of Texas legislators makes them highly vulnerable to interest-group pressure. While that may be true, it is also clear that in the political culture of Texas, politicians accept large campaign contributions as "the way it is done," and the public is resigned to this system.

[16]Ronald Hrebenar and Clive Thomas, "Who's Got Clout? Interest Group Power in the States," *State Legislatures*, April 1999.
[17]Clay Robison, "Weak State Government Paved Way for Lobbyists," *Houston Chronicle*, December 29, 2002, p. A1.
[18]John Dunbar, "Low-Paid Texas Lawmakers Tops in Connections to Lobbyists: Is Their Pay a Factor?" The Center for Public Integrity, October 28, 2000.

WARREN D. CHISUM, R-PAMPA
(front), makes a point on the
House floor regarding school
finance and property taxes as
behind him House Speaker
Tom Craddick (right) talks with
Representative Dwayne Bohac
of Houston. (John Davenport/
ZUMA Press/Newscom)

THE DECENTRALIZATION OF EXECUTIVE-BRANCH POWER

Texas has a plural executive. Power is divided among numerous independently elected executives—the governor, the lieutenant governor, the attorney general, the comptroller, an agricultural commissioner, a land commissioner, and the multiple members of the Railroad Commission and the State Board of Education.

Government by Commission. The **fragmentation**, or division of power, within the executive branch is enhanced by the practice of establishing independent boards and commissions as structures for implementing the law. The governor appoints the membership of most unelected boards and commissions—usually one-third of the membership every two years—but has little power to remove those appointed. Reformists have argued that if each agency were headed by a single executive who was appointed and removable by the governor, agencies would be more responsive to the broader values represented by the governor rather than those of the specific clientele the agencies serve.

Fragmentation and Interest Group Power. The plural executive and fragmentation of authority mean that no strong central executive authority has the legal power to control the executive branch of government. This situation increases the vulnerability of each executive agency to special-interest influence. The result may be policies established with less regard for the general public interest than for special-interests. Increasing this likelihood is the requirement (previously discussed) that a majority of members on many boards and commissions be engaged in the profession, business, or activity that the board or commission regulates.

LAWS

Reformers have long advocated laws to regulate the relationship between public officials and private parties who seek special favors from government. Texas, as we will see later in this chapter, does have laws that define lobbying and require reporting of information about the lobbyist, his or her employer, and the expenses associated with trying to influence government decisions. The Texas Ethics Commission makes this information generally available. The press has a special obligation to examine this information and report it to the public in a usable form. If the voters receive this information, they may be able to act on it.

Fragmentation
In state government, a division of power among separately elected executive officials. A plural executive is a fragmented executive.

THE MEDIA

The media are essential to the democratic system. Radio, television, Internet, and print journalists serve as watchdogs of government. Public officials and bureaucrats know that every decision they make, as well as their general conduct, is fair game for the news media. In a democracy, the public has a right to know what public officials are doing, and the public relies on the media to tell it.

The media not only relay the activities of government to the people but also transmit the people's moods and messages to the state leaders. In addition, members of the media communicate their own opinions to both the public and the government. The media are a link between the people and the government, but they are not necessarily a neutral one.

The Media and Open Government. The media's interests are allied with the interests of the people when the media demand that the government's business be conducted in public view. The media work to promote open meetings, open records, and recorded votes on policy decisions in the legislature and in administrative boards and commissions. Openness is the enemy of conflicts of interest and other questionable conduct, and the press delights in exposing such behavior to the public. Thus, the interaction of lobbyists and public officials is a matter of interest to the media.

Coverage of News from the Capital. The media, however, labor under self-imposed restraints on reporting. These restraints may be based on the fact that newspapers, news magazines, and radio and television stations are businesses concerned with making a profit. Austin, the state capital, is not the home of the largest newspapers or broadcasting channels in Texas. It is costly for media outlets not located in the capital to employ journalists stationed in Austin, and declining newspaper readership has led to the closing of several Austin news bureaus. In 2004, the last of the TV news bureaus, A. H. Belo Corporation (owner of the *Dallas Morning News* and WFFA), "destaffed" its Austin operation. KHOU Houston and KENS San Antonio had previously closed their operations, except for the presence of the local Austin news manager.

This has affected TV coverage of state government as well, because media chains generally own newspapers as well as radio and TV stations in their market areas. Increasingly, local station managers deemphasize coverage of the legislature, governor, and high courts, saying that members of the public are uninterested.

Duplication of Effort. Some observers argue that if the media combined their staffs and worked cooperatively, there would be sufficient press personnel to cover many more aspects of state government. Breadth and depth of reporting could be improved by pooling staffs, and there would be no increase in cost to the individual media companies.

The Media versus the Government. The media thrive on scandals, corruption, inefficiencies, mistakes, and conspiracies in the public sector. Money in politics and cozy relationships between public officials and interest groups make good news stories. This seems true even though most of the Texas mass-distribution dailies appear to share the conservative politics that are dominant in Texas. It is true even though competition between newspapers and broadcast media is limited because major newspapers own radio stations and can own at least one key television station in their market area.

NEW TECHNOLOGIES

Perhaps the biggest change affecting existing power relationships in the state in recent years is the increasing use of the computer as a political tool. Databases allow groups to keep track of members and finances more easily than in the past. Also, interest groups that are starved for economic resources now have a medium—the Internet—

DID YOU KNOW?

That in terms of per capita federal support for homeland security, only one state (California) received less than Texas in 2006?

that connects them to their members and to state decision makers. Contacting public officials has never been easier. The Internet cannot completely overcome the disadvantages of scarce funds and other resources, but it does make possible the raising of new and underrepresented voices.

It is too early to know whether the Internet will compensate for the increasing concentration of ownership in print and electronic media. The Internet's political uses are rapidly increasing, nonetheless. The giant media empires will continue to play the major role as news suppliers, but countless individuals and independent opinion and news sources may use the emerging technologies to engage in the political arena.

CONSTITUENT INFLUENCE

Interest-group strength on any issue is affected by the values, attitudes, and beliefs of the voters. No elected official can consistently ignore the "folks back home." Most state representatives and senators have lived in their districts for a long time and may have been born and raised there. They know the culture of their home regions. On many issues before the legislature, they know what the voters would want them to do. In other words, even in the absence of public input, legislators may understand the preferences of their constituents.

Constituent Influence and the Part-Time Legislature. Texas has a part-time legislature that is only in regular session for 140 days every odd-numbered year. Hence, members are home in their districts 590 days out of 730 in every two-year period. Furthermore, they are home almost every weekend during the four and a half months of the session. Members do not have to exert much effort to find out what their constituents want (presuming that the constituents *know* what they want).

When District Opinion Is Clear. To please a special-interest, would an elected representative vote against the desires of his or her constituents when these desires are clear and known? The answer is "probably not." Further, if an experienced interest group knows that the voters in a legislator's district disagree with the interest group's positions, it probably will not seek to punish the legislator for representing her or his district. In contrast, when the voters back home have no consensus on an issue, then interest groups, fellow legislators, the governor, and the legislator's party may struggle for the legislator's vote.

INTEREST GROUPS AS CHECKS ON OTHER INTEREST GROUPS

On issues of major public importance, an interest group is likely to be confronted by one or more other interests that do not want the same outcome. In such circumstances, the groups may offset each other's influence. On more obscure issues, a group may be fortunate enough to find itself without opposition. Whether one or many special-interests are involved in the policy-making process, however, the status, resources, size, reputation, and lobbying skills of a group affect its ability to influence legislators and agency heads. These factors, plus the substance of what the group is seeking and the financial condition of the state, combine to shape policy outcomes.

Obscure Issues. When the outcome a special-interest seeks is very narrow or specific, the general public and other interest groups may not be aware of the issue. Even if they are aware, they may see no reason to intervene; the matter may simply be of no concern to them. Under such circumstances, the special-interest that is concerned may need to persuade only a few key people, such as legislative committee chairs and presiding officers, to win its objective. If the committee approves, the vote on the floor will most likely be favorable.

Broad or Controversial Issues. When a special-interest seeks a policy change that affects the political, social, or economic balance of power, however, there will be much greater participation and conflict. Group will be pitted against group, and the general public may be drawn in, because the media will transmit stories of conflict to their readers, listeners, and viewers.

As the number of participants in any political debate increases, the possibilities for conflict increase, and the influence of each participating interest group diminishes. Many groups and ordinary citizens are interested in broad or controversial issues, such as tax policy, education, campaign-finance reform, gun control, and abortion. Such issues may generate substantial political conflict. The challenge for the public officials involved is to lead the warring groups to a compromise. Without that, no policy output will be produced. How to defend homeland security without damaging the border economy is one example of an issue that pits interest groups against each other at the national level. For most Texas interests, however, the health of the border economy is the greater value.

CAMPAIGN CONTRIBUTIONS

Money in politics is a hot topic, in part because of a startling increase in the amount of funds raised and spent by candidates for elective office at all levels. A candidate for state representative in a metropolitan area of Texas may spend more than $200,000 to win an office that pays $7,200 per year.

Campaign contributions for legislative and statewide offices often come from large donors. These donors may represent banks, insurance companies, the petrochemical industry, physicians, trial lawyers, real estate agents, teachers, and others who use political action committees (PACs) to funnel money to candidates. These donors participate because the state legislature, the governor, the Railroad Commission, and other agencies and officers make decisions that affect their economic well-being. Donors contribute to gain access to public officials. A substantial contribution may create a sense of obligation on the part of an elected official to listen when the contributor calls. Ordinary citizens may find access more difficult.

According to Texans for Public Justice, statewide and legislative candidates raised $95 million in the 2008 election cycle. An estimated $70 million was raised by the 281 major candidates vying for a seat in the Texas house, and an estimated $25 million raised by the 31 candidates vying for seats on the Texas senate.[19] Sixty-five percent of the dollars raised by house candidates went to incumbents, and 58 percent of money raised by senate candidates went to incumbent senators.[20]

Texans for Public Justice reports that 126 individual donors contributed over $100,000 in 2008. These 126 donors contributed $45.5 million. The top 143 institutional donors that contributed over $150,000 gave $89.8 million during the 2008 election cycle.[21] PACs and businesses contributed $51.9 million. Individuals contributed $43 million.[22] Even when candidates face little or no opposition, they raise large amounts of money. Their success in raising campaign contributions is indicative of the state's economic and political importance.

---

[19]Texans for Public Justice, "Money in PoliTex: A Guide to Money in the 2008 Texas Elections," September 29, 2009, at http://info.tpj.org/reports/politex08/index08.html, accessed June 20, 2010.
[20]Ibid.
[21]Ibid.
[22]Ibid.

A MEMBER OF TEXANS for Public Justice, a group that monitors money in Texas politics, shows a report entitled "Ain't Nobody's Business." The report concluded that few politicians and officials in Texas fully report lobbyists' payments. How might Texas do a better job of tracking lobbying activities? (AP Photo/ Harry Cabluck)

"LATE-TRAIN" CONTRIBUTIONS

One of the biennial rituals in Austin occurs after each election when special-interest groups hold fundraising events to honor selected legislators. State law forbids giving and accepting campaign contributions 30 days before the start of a legislative session and throughout the session, causing a rush of fundraising activity during the five weeks following election day. Note that the fundraising occurs after the election, not before. The reason, as one lobbyist has said, is to "pay the price of admission," or to obtain good access to legislators. Post-election contributions, or **"late-train" contributions**, are commonly given to the winning candidates in the executive branch as well. Losers are rarely the beneficiaries of such largesse.

THE EFFECT OF CONTRIBUTIONS ON THE SYSTEM

Do campaign contributions buy sponsorship of bills and special favors? The press—and much of the public—thinks that they do.[23] Lobbyists and legislators claim they do not. The increasing volume of campaign contributions noted earlier, and the 16 percent increase in the number of lobbyists from 1998 to 2009, are evidence that would tend to support the perceptions of the press and the public.[24] In 2007, there were 9.8 lobbyists for every legislator.[25] Records of the 2009 legislative session show that lobbyists earned $344 million trying to influence decisions of the Texas legislature.[26]

THE REGULATION OF LOBBYING

Lobbyists and organizations that spend more than a specified amount attempting to shape public decisions are required to register and file reports with the Texas Ethics Commission. Appropriate behavior of both lobbyists and public officials is spelled out in Chapter 305 of the Government Code of Texas.

WHO MUST REGISTER AND REPORT LOBBYING COSTS?

Not all lobbyists are required by state law to register and report their activities. Classes of lobbyists not required to register and report include state officials and state employees who lobby, even if lobbying is their principal function. Also exempt are individuals

---

[23]James Gibbons, "Officials Come and Go; the Lobby Rules," *Austin American-Statesman*, January 27, 2003.
[24]The Texas Ethics Commission listed 1,561 registered lobbyists in 1999. In 2009, the number of registered lobbyists increased to 1,861. See Texas Ethics Commission, "Lobby Lists and Reports," www.ethics.state.tx.us/ dfs/loblists.htm, accessed June 20, 2010.
[25]The ratio of lobbyists to lawmakers is calculated by dividing the number of registered lobbyists in 2007 (1,780) by 18—the number of legislators in the Texas house and senate.
[26]Texans for Public Justice, "Austin's Oldest Profession: Texas's Top Lobby Clients and Those Who Support Them," 2010 Edition, http://info.tpj.org/reports/austinsoldest09/facts.html.

from the private sector who are not paid for their services and do not directly spend any money to influence legislative or administrative action.

Those who do have to register and report are private-sector lobbyists who pass the "compensation threshold" of $1,000 in salary per quarter-year or the "expenditure threshold" of $500 per quarter-year. These rules seem simple and straightforward, but an examination of the law reveals that not all compensation and expenditures are counted as lobbying. Exempted from reporting are the following:

- Compensation received to prepare for lobbying.
- Office expenses, including telephone, fax, copying, office supplies, postage, dues and subscriptions, transportation, and the costs of clerical help.
- Costs associated with events to which all members of the legislature are invited.[27]

These and other exemptions in the law mean that an incomplete picture of the investment in lobbying by interest groups is made available to the people.

WHAT MUST A LOBBYIST REPORT?

The lobbyist registration form requires the lobbyist to reveal the following:

- For whom he or she lobbies—information about these clients and employers.
- The policy areas of concern.
- The compensation category into which the salary or reimbursement received falls.
- The name of, and information about, anyone who assists the principal lobbyist through direct contact with public officials.

Activity reports must be filed by the tenth day of each month for any lobbyist who foresees expending more than $1,000 per year. Those who spend less need only file annually.[28]

Reporting on Clients. A firm or entity often represents multiple clients before the state legislature and administrative agencies. The reporting law requires a lobbyist working for a lobbying firm to report who pays the firm to represent its interests to the government. Without such a requirement, those who wanted to influence legislative and executive officials anonymously could simply hire someone else to lobby on their behalf. For many years, in fact, this guarantee of anonymity existed in Texas.

Financial Reporting. As noted, the lobbyist's compensation and expenditures are reported in broad categories rather than in actual amounts. Some believe that this practice understates the influence of money on policy making. We consider two examples of financial reports to illustrate the problem.

One report was filed with the Texas Ethics Commission by Electronic Data Systems Corporation (EDS) of Dallas in 1995. Forty-two lobbyists were identified in four pay categories: 31 were paid from $0 to $9,999.99; two received from $50,000 to $99,999.99; seven obtained from $150,000 to $199,999.99; and one was paid from $200,000 to $999,999.99. EDS, in other words, spent somewhere between $1,400,000 and $3,008,990,

DID YOU KNOW?

That during the 2008 election cycle, Texas house Republicans raised 57 percent of the money contributed to campaigns, Democrats 43 percent?[29]

---

[27]Texas Ethics Commission, "Texas Ethics Commission Rules: Chapter 34. Regulation of Lobbyists," 2007, www.ethics.state.tx.us/legal/ch34.html, accessed March 16, 2008.
[28]Ibid.
[29]Texans for Public Justice, "Money in PoliTex: A Guide to Money in the 2008 Texas Legislative Elections," http://info.tpj.org/reports/politex08/index.html, accessed June 20, 2010.

but the exact amount is unknown.[30] (In 1999, EDS reported using 28 lobbyists and paying between $1.8 million and $2.5 million. Why the difference? Issues before the legislature were of less concern to EDS four years later.[31])

As another example, in 2003, Southwestern Bell Telephone reported having 12 paid and 14 unpaid lobbyists at the time of filing, and 65 "prospective" lobbyists with salaries set but not paid. The payroll for the session was between $3,935,000 and $7,600,000. Again in 2005, Southwestern Bell, renamed AT&T, led all others in lobby contracts and expenditures.[32]

Criticisms of the Reporting Standards. Some critics of the law maintain that its provisions continue to leave the public ill-informed about the extent of lobbying. One area of concern, as already indicated, is financial reporting. Critics have suggested that the actual compensation and expenditures of a lobbyist should be disclosed, rather than broad categories. This additional detail would require little effort, because the lobbyist must have the actual figures to know which category to mark on the form.

Reporting on which policy area a lobbyist seeks to influence can also be rather vague. The lobbyist, again, need only check a box on the form. Such a requirement may hide as much as it reveals. Requiring lobbyists to reveal more specifically what they are lobbying about would enable the public to see where corporations, trade associations, labor unions, and individuals were concentrating their efforts.

To provide a clear picture of lobbying activity, Texas could require lobbyists to list the numbers of the bills they have lobbied for and the rule-making hearings before executive agencies at which they have testified. This would require more time and expense in filling out the activity forms. Many believe that Texas does not require this additional information because special-interests have successfully lobbied the legislature to keep the lobbying law relatively weak.

What We Know about Lobbying. Thanks to the research of Texans for Public Justice and the Texas Ethics Commission, several interesting facts about the lobbying industry in Texas are clear:

- Special-interests entered into 8,125 lobby contracts with 1,690 lobbyists in 2009.[33]
- Fourteen identifiable industry groupings spent more than $5 million each to have their interests protected or advanced.[34]
- Most lobbyists are affiliated with law firms in Texas.

Table 21–4 shows details on the industries spending the most money to influence Texas state government and the number of lobby contracts entered into by each. We also have information about expenditures in a few categories that do require detailed reporting. Expenditures of more than $50 per day on members of the state legislature for food, drink, transportation, or lodging or in the form of a gift must be reported by name, date, place, and purpose.[35] Expenditures for broadcast or print advertisements, mass mailings, and other communications designed to support or oppose legislation or administrative actions also must be identified.

Late-train Contribution
A contribution given to a candidate in the period that begins after an election and ends 30 days before a regular legislative session.

What Is Not Reported as Lobbying. Campaign and **late-train contributions** to public officials are not lobbying expenses as defined by law, even though the state recognizes

---

[30]Texas Ethics Commission, *List of Employers and Clients*, 1995, pp. 63–65.
[31]Texas Ethics Commission, *List of Employers / Clients with Lobbyists Sorted by Employer / Client Name*, 1999, pp. 59–60.
[32]Texans for Public Justice, "Austin's Oldest Profession: Texas's Top Lobby Clients and Those Who Service Them," at http://info.tpj.org/reports/austinsoldest09/index.html, 2010.
[33]Ibid.
[34]Ibid.
[35]Texas Ethics Commission, *Lobbying in Texas*, Part IVB.

TABLE 21–4 NUMBER AND MAXIMUM VALUE OF CONTRACTS SIGNED BY SELECTED LOBBY INDUSTRY GROUPS: 2009

Industry Group	NUMBER OF CONTRACTS Number of Contracts	MAXIMUM VALUE OF CONTRACTS Maximum Value of Contracts
Energy/Natural Resources/Waste	1,228	$62,315,000
Ideological/Single Issue	1,768	$55,221,570
Health	986	$41,770,000
Miscellaneous Business	830	$37,600,000
Communications	378	$20,380,000
Lawyers & Lobbyists	341	$19,365,000
Real Estate	461	$18,735,000
Finance	413	$16,177,000
Construction	293	$13,341,000
Insurance	260	$12,495,000
Computers & Electronics	283	$12,485,000
Transportation	349	$12,385,000
Other	176	$ 6,640,000
Agriculture	142	$ 6,335,000
Labor	123	$ 5,760,000
Unknown	94	$ 2,635,000
TOTALS:	**8,125**	**$ 343,639,570**

their potential to influence policy making. As noted earlier, such contributions cannot be made fewer than 30 days before a legislative session or during the session. This restriction is intended to prevent corruption or the appearance of corruption. Campaign contributions are thus reported to the Texas Ethics Commission separately from lobbying expenses.

REGISTRATION AND THE LEGISLATURE

Members of the Texas legislature are provided with a list of registered lobbyists and their clients by February 1 of each legislative (odd-numbered) year.[36] The public may obtain copies of registration and activity reports from the Texas Ethics Commission. Much of the information is available from the Ethics Commission on the Internet or on paper.

[36]Texas Government Code, Section 305.011.

REP. SYLVESTER TURNER (D-HOUSTON), center, is approached by clean air and renewable energy lobbyists Dan Hinkle, left, and Tom "Smitty" Smith outside the Texas House of Representatives Thursday, May 11, 2006, in Austin. Hinkle is a lobbyist for the solar industry. Smith is with the watchdog group Public Citizen. (AP Photo/ Harry Cabluck)

There is much evidence that lawmakers' regulation of lobbying remains, in the public's mind, unfinished business and controversial. The legislature tweaks the laws frequently in response to suspected or verifiable scandal. In 2001, for example, a new conflict-of-interest statute directed the Ethics Commission to write rules requiring lobbyists to provide written notice to the commission and to their clients when they represent multiple clients who may have incompatible legislative goals. It is a common practice for a lobbyist in Texas to represent multiple clients. Because many firms represent many clients, the possibility of a conflict exists when different people in the firm represent clients with opposing legislative objectives. It can be argued that this change to the law benefits the interests that hire lobbyists more than it does the general public.

THE CRAFT OF LOBBYING

Those who directly contact public officials to influence their behavior will find their work easier if they are extroverted and enjoy socializing. The lobbyist's first job is to become known and recognized by members of the legislature and by any executive officials relevant to the interest he or she represents.

LOBBYING BEFORE THE LEGISLATIVE SESSION BEGINS

Before a legislative session begins, a lobbyist must have successfully completed several tasks:

- Learn who is predisposed to support the lobbyist's cause, who is on the other side, and which members can be swayed.

- Memorize the faces of the members, their nonlegislative occupations, the counties they represent, and a little about their families.

- Establish rapport through personal contact with the members of the legislature.

- Get to know the staffs of legislators, because the members can be influenced through them.

- Know the legislative issues, including the arguments of opponents.

Honesty Is the Best Policy. To maintain relationships with legislators, the lobbyist must provide sound, accurate information about the legislation the lobbyist's group supports or opposes. This includes off-the-record admission of the pluses and minuses of the legislation. Honesty is, in fact, often the best policy for a lobbyist when dealing with a public official.

Wining and Dining Also Helps. A lobbyist can befriend a legislator in several ways that may eventually pay off in support. Lobbyists have information that may be valuable to a legislator, and they may be able to help draft an important piece of legislation for her or him. Providing an occasional free meal or acknowledging a helpful legislator at a banquet in his or her honor also has merit from the lobbyist's perspective. All of these actions are necessary to create and maintain goodwill, without which nothing is possible.

Approaching the Legislators. How does a lobbyist approach a member of the legislature or a member of the leadership? How do you get in the door, and what do you say when you get in? How important is the staff of a legislator to a lobbyist? Is it necessary to see all 181 members of the legislature, the lieutenant governor, and the governor?

Given that there are only 140 days in a session, lobbying must precede the convening of the legislature. The 18-month period between regular sessions leaves ample time to do the following:

- Work on relationships.
- Learn what proposals have a chance of receiving favorable responses.
- Draft legislation.
- Line up sponsors to introduce bills in the house and senate at the beginning of the next session.

Key Endorsements. Not all members of the legislature are equal. Establishing rapport with, and obtaining feedback from, the powerful presiding officers—the speaker of the house and the lieutenant governor, who presides over the senate—are especially useful. No endorsements are more important to an interest group than those of the presiding officers. If an endorsement for the group's legislative proposal is not forthcoming, the lobbyist must at least persuade the presiding officers to remain neutral in the legislative struggle.

Securing the endorsement of the chairs of committees through which the legislation must pass before it can go to the floor for a vote is an advantage second only to that of securing the support of the presiding officers. In addition, legislation sought by a local government must have the endorsement of the members representing the relevant legislative districts, or it is doomed to fail.

LOBBYING ADMINISTRATIVE AGENCIES

Administrators and interest-group representatives seek each other out to provide and obtain information. For example, the Texas Educational Diagnosticians Association (TEDA) and the state colleges of education may wish to know whether the examination for the certification of diagnosticians is scheduled for revision. They will therefore contact the State Board for Educator Certification to obtain an answer. The issue is important to the TEDA, because the content and difficulty of the exam affect the number of recruits to the profession. Colleges of education know that changes in the state exam mean changes in the curriculum. Inquiries about the exam also allow the interest groups to communicate their professional opinion about the current exam and suggest any changes.

Administrators seek to discover the impact of their programs and rules on the clientele they serve. They may well seek input from those they serve about present and planned programs. In so doing, they surrender some of their power to the clientele to maintain the political support that is in turn necessary to retain the support of the legislature and governor. An agency's clientele is especially interested in influencing the rules and guidelines that control how they do business, because these rules directly affect profits.

The Rule-Making Process. Agencies issue formal rules that prescribe the standards of conduct to be followed by citizens who are subject to the law. Agencies also issue guidelines to govern the actions of their staffs in applying the law. The rule-making process in Texas gives all interested parties an opportunity to influence an agency's decision. Notice of intent to make a rule must be published in the **Texas Register**. A time for written public comment on the proposed rule is established. At the close of the comment period, the agency analyzes the public's views. It then publishes a "final rule" having the force of law.

While all citizens have the right to participate in the rule-making process, it is obvious that only those who are aware of, and interested in, the proposed rule will participate. Ordinary citizens do not subscribe to the *Texas Register*. Corporations, labor unions, law firms, and interest groups do. Hence, they know when to mobilize their members to influence decision making.

The Co-optation of Agencies. There is a natural linkage from agency to clientele and clientele to agency. As you learned earlier in this chapter, most state agencies are headed by boards and commissions drawn from the industry, trade, profession, or activity the agency regulates. It is normal for individuals who engage in an economic activity to join the state board or commission regulating that activity and then return to the private sector and resume the regulated activity.

The purpose of this staffing system is to fill the need for expertise in board membership. The question is how the interests of the larger society can be protected when roles become so blurred. Can those regulating an economic activity be objective public servants when they have been, and will be, participants in that activity? Many observers argue that such arrangements endanger the public interest and benefit only special-interests. The *Economist* has noted that, in Texas, "the state's business and political elites are hopelessly intertwined."[37]

DID YOU KNOW?

That for a brief period in 2006 and 2007, it was permissible for the policy makers who were given gifts in the form of checks to simply report the check as a gift without having to disclose the amount that the check was made out for?

LOBBYING THE COURTS

Filing suit to affect government activities is not lobbying or pressure politics. Rather, it involves using a long-established set of legal procedures to challenge the substance of laws, administrative rules, or other government actions. Only persons licensed to practice law can handle cases in the state's major trial courts.

Grounds for Lawsuits. Anyone negatively affected by a law, an administrative rule, or a government action may seek relief from the courts. The challenge may be made on the ground that the agency failed to follow proper procedures in making the rule or that it misinterpreted the law in writing guidelines or rules. The allegation that the laws or rules are applied unfairly is another basis for suit.

Using the courts is typically a last resort. Nevertheless, major corporations, labor unions, interest groups, and local governments employ staff attorneys to protect their interests. Smaller and less wealthy organizations may keep attorneys on retainer or use attorneys on their boards of directors to represent their interests as needed.

The Impact of Judicial Elections. In a state that elects judges, the question arises as to whether wealthy corporations and other interest groups can influence judicial decisions through campaign contributions. Between 1994 and 2006, CBS ran programs about "justice for sale" on *60 Minutes*, alleging that the Texas Supreme Court overwhelmingly identifies with specific interests. These reports have led to demands for campaign-finance regulations to reduce any possible conflicts of interest caused by justices accepting campaign contributions. In the 2008 elections for the Texas Supreme Court, the incumbents and their challengers "took approximately two-thirds of their political funds from contributors

---

[37]"The Future Is Texas," *The Economist*, December 19, 2002.

with business before the court."[38] Thus far, however, the legislature has resisted enactment of anything but voluntary compliance standards for judicial campaigns.[39] The U.S. Supreme Court steered clear of restricting campaign contributions in the 2009 *Caperton v. A.T. Massey Coal Company* case. In this case, the Supreme Court ruled as follows:

> We conclude that there is a serious risk of actual bias—based on objective and reasonable perceptions—when a person with a personal stake in a particular case had a significant and disproportionate influence in placing the judge on the case by raising funds or directing the judge's election campaign when the case was pending or imminent. The inquiry centers on the contribution's relative size in comparison to the total amount of money contributed to the campaign, the total amount spent in the election, and the apparent effect such contribution had on the outcome of the election.[40]

While the decision begins to set parameters for the most egregious examples of conflicts of interest, *Caperton v. A.T. Massey* does not ban campaign contributions made by litigants or attorneys. If greater restrictions are to be established, it will be up to the Texas legislature to set those restrictions.

Large campaign contributions to judicial candidates are newsworthy, because judges are held to a higher standard than elected legislators and executives. Legislators and elected executives are expected to be highly partisan. Judges are expected to be as impartial as humanly possible. Currently, Texas is one of 15 states that elects its judges in partisan elections. Even though most voters do not know who the judicial candidates are, they prefer to elect their judges rather than allow an independent commission or some other body to nominate nonpartisan judges. Political parties and campaign consultants also have a vested interest in maintaining the status quo. Reformers, however, will continue to seek changes in the method of selecting judges, even when they do not advocate changes in the other branches of government.

DAN LAMBE, executive director of Texas Watch, displays what he calls the ten most harmful Texas Supreme Court decisions for consumers. He says that the Texas Supreme Court routinely favors business over consumer and family rights in deciding cases. Does this type of campaign have any chance of influencing the Texas court? (AP Photo/Harry Cabluck)

---

[38] Texans for Public Justice, "Courtroom Contributions Stain Supreme Court Campaigns: October 2008," http://info.tpj.org/reports/courtroomcontributions/index.html, accessed June 20, 2010.

[39] Clay Robison, "Campaign 96: 'Justice for Sale' Charges Leveled Anew," *Houston Chronicle*, September 22, 1996, p. 1A.

[40] *Caperton v. A.T. Massey* 129 U.S. 2264 (2009).

YOU CAN MAKE A Difference

GETTING INVOLVED BY JOINING AN INTEREST GROUP

The Texas legislature decided in 2003 to allow each university to set tuition, rather than having it set by the legislature. This decision has led to rapidly rising tuition costs in Texas. Were you represented during the policy formulation and policy adoption stages of that policy-making event? Probably not. Many students may not know why tuition has risen.

WHY SHOULD YOU CARE?

The new tuition policy in Texas affects how many people can go to the state universities and which institutions they can afford to attend. Zack Hall, shown here, organized protests to speak out about the proposed tuition increases late in 2007. We can see similar effects in other policy areas. State policies, in other words, affect the quality of life of every citizen. That is why groups organize to control the political agenda and policy outcomes. Those who do not participate do not have a say about what rules apply to them or how state programs may benefit or harm them.

WHAT CAN YOU DO?

Time is precious. Working, studying, sleeping, and socializing consume the lion's share of any student's time. Citizens, however, still have the opportunity to become informed and use their knowledge to influence the decisions of their state and local governments. How? Become a joiner. Allow an organization that shares your values to monitor government activities and represent you at the state capitol and city hall.

Organizations can analyze the political environment and summarize the information that you need to know to understand the political situation. The organization you join can notify you whenever a phone call, e-mail, or letter from you could help affect the outcome of votes and rule-making activities. Such participation will not take much of your time.

ZACK HALL, a recent graduate from the University of Texas, lobbied against tuition hikes on campus and started a social networking page for the cause. "Everybody standing up and saying 'Enough is enough' really meant something. I think a combination of student and legislative pressure led to this. And it just shows you that if you stand up for what you believe in, you can accomplish change," Zack explained. (Courtesy of Zack C. Hall)

Almost every organized interest has a Web site that you can locate using popular search engines. Size and wealth are assets that help groups to become powerful, but good leadership and good issues are also important. One group that you might consider is Common Cause of Texas. Founded more than 30 years ago, it has never had a membership in excess of 6,000 or a budget in excess of $100,000, yet it is constantly called on for advice by the Texas Ethics Commission and the state legislature. Why? Because of the consistency of its opinions, the length of time it has spent in the political arena, the stability of its leadership, and its focus on "good government" issues. You can contact Common Cause at:

Common Cause of Texas
603 W. 13th, Suite 2-D
Austin, TX 78701
512-474-2374
e-mail: commoncause@ccsi.com
www.commoncause.org
Click on "State Organizations" and then on Texas on the U.S. map.

KEY TERMS

access 730	**discretion** 726	**subsidies** 722
civic duty 719	**fragmentation** 736	*Texas Register* 746
conflict of interest 721	**implementation** 726	**umbrella organization** 732
co-optation 727	**late-train contribution** 742	**unfunded mandate** 724

CHAPTER SUMMARY

1. Interest groups are organizations of people who agree on policy issues that affect their members. Interest groups do not nominate candidates for office but do care about the ideologies of those who stand for election. They therefore may form political action committees (PACs) to support candidates favorable to their causes.

2. The constitutions of the United States and Texas promote political expression. The right to organize to petition officials is explicit. This right recognizes that representatives of the people can represent their constituents only when they are informed of their wishes. Interest groups are therefore constitutionally protected.

3. **What are the positive and negative effects of interest groups in Texas politics? How can the negative effects be controlled?** Positive effects include increased political representation, political participation and mobilization, education of membership, shared information and data, and reduced cost to taxpayers for acquiring such information. Negative effects include a narrowing of interests considered, private meetings presenting no opportunity for rebuttal of views, and corruption and intimidation of public officials. These negative effects can be controlled through laws regulating lobbyists' activities and campaign contributions and requiring registration and reports; the media's role as watchdog, as well as conveyor of public opinion to the government; and interest groups acting as a check on other interest groups.

4. Groups with sufficient resources employ staff to monitor the government. They proactively bring issues before decision makers and reactively move into the political process to stop or alter proposals that negatively affect their membership.

5. **What techniques do interest groups use to influence state policies?** Direct techniques for influencing policy include lobbying the legislative and executive branches, filing suit in court, advising and serving on state boards, and public demonstrations. Indirect techniques include electioneering, educating the public, and socializing with public officials.

6. Business groups are among the strongest interests. Large corporations lobby decision makers both through umbrella organizations and directly. It is not uncommon for large interests to have more than 20 paid lobbyists working for them during a legislative session. Between sessions, groups conduct research, draft proposed legislation for the next session, and monitor and influence the executive branch, which writes the rules to carry out laws.

7. **What factors determine the relative power of interest groups in Texas?** The number one element determining the political power of a group is how much public officials need the group. For example, officials may need the group's expertise to help the state solve problems, they may depend on the group for campaign contributions, or the state's economy may depend on the economic sector the group represents.

8. Interest groups have been powerful in Texas due to the historical absence of competitive two-party politics, restrictive election laws, low voter turnout, and the below-average educational attainment of many citizens.

9. As happens at the national level, "iron triangles" often form in Texas. These triangles unite interest groups that represent a particular industry or activity with the

bureaucracy that regulates the activity and with the members of the legislative committee that oversees the bureaucracy. Iron triangles are especially potent in Texas, because regulatory boards and commissions are required to have members who actively participate in the regulated activity. This requirement almost guarantees conflicts of interest. Looser alliances called *issue networks* also form. These may consist of legislators, legislative staff members, interest-group leaders, bureaucrats, journalists, scholars, and others who support a particular policy position on a given issue.

10. The media, a few nonprofit and officially nonpartisan special-interests, and the Texas Ethics Commission are the sources of most of the information we have about the relationship between interest groups and public officials in Texas. Most lobbyists are required to file reports with the Ethics Commission, which in turn publishes the names, addresses, employers, expenditures, and salaries (in broad categorical ranges) of lobbyists. The media and the nonpartisan interests "blow the whistle" about conflicts of interest and official behavior that is suspect.

SELECTED PRINT, MEDIA, AND ONLINE RESOURCES

PRINT RESOURCES

Hrebenar, Ronald, and Clive Thomas. *Interest Group Politics in the Southern States.* Tuscaloosa: University of Alabama Press, 1992 (reprinted in 2002). This is one of four regional analyses of special-interest power in the United States by these authors. It gives a comprehensive look at power structures, types of interests, lobbying tactics, and state regulations. It contains very good, although somewhat dated, information.

Hrebenar, Ronald, and Clive Thomas. "Who's Got Clout? Interest Group Power in the States." *State Legislatures*, April 1999. This article serves to update the authors' previous works. The title pinpoints the focus.

Prindle, David. *Petroleum Politics in Texas and the Texas Railroad Commission.* Austin: University of Texas Press, 1981. This work looks inside one of the most powerful regulatory agencies in the United States, the Texas Railroad Commission. Internal politics, conflicts of interest, external pressure groups and their agents, methods of operation, and consequences of the commission's policy choices are all examined.

Texans for Public Justice. *Austin's Oldest Profession: Texas's Top Lobby Clients and Those Who Service Them.* Austin: Texans for Public Justice, published annually. Through this publication, Texans for Public Justice compiles information from the Texas Ethics Commission and disseminates it widely throughout the state in press releases, in publications, and electronically. Registered lobbyists in Texas are identified, along with their employers. Lobbyists are grouped by interests, such as energy and natural resources, ideological and single issues, health, and miscellaneous business.

Texas Ethics Commission. *Lobbying in Texas.* Austin: Texas Ethics Commission, published annually. This document defines lobbying and summarizes the law governing lobbying. Information on who should register, how to fill out reports, and dates of submission is included. Available in paper and online.

MEDIA RESOURCES

Willmar 8—This documentary that tells the story of eight female bank employees in a small-town bank in Minnesota who rebel at being kept at entry-l positions because of their gender. The film shows how ordinary people become politically active and how others view their political activity.

Saul Alinsky: Leader of Social Reform—In this video, the late Saul Alinsky outlines his approach for organizing the powerless.

ONLINE RESOURCES

American Federation of Labor–Congress of Industrial Organizations (AFL-CIO) A state federation of labor unions representing 220,000 members in Texas: www.texasaflcio.org

Center for Public Policy Priorities A nonpartisan, nonprofit 501(c)(3) policy institute committed to improving public policies to better the economic and social conditions of low- and moderate-income Texans. Here you can find Web sites of selected think tanks: www.cppp.org

Center for Responsive Politics Find out who made major campaign contributions on a state-by-state or even ZIP-code-by-ZIP-code basis: www.opensecrets.org

FreedomWorks (formerly Texas Citizens for a Sound Economy) Founded by Koch Industries, this organization recruits, educates, trains, and mobilizes millions of volunteer activists to fight for less government, lower taxes, and more freedom: www.freedomworks.org/texas

League of United Latin American Citizens (LULAC) Group who states as its mission to advance the economic condition, educational attainment, political influence, health, and civil rights of the Hispanic population of the United States: www.tx-lulac.org

Texas Association of Business Employer organization that works to improve the Texas business climate and help strengthen the state's economy: www.txbiz.org

Texas Association of Mexican-American Chambers of Commerce (TAMACC) A private, nonprofit corporation, with headquarters in Austin, Texas, acting as an organizational umbrella providing advocacy, technical support, programs, and services to the network of local Hispanic chambers: www.tamacc.org

Texas Association of School Boards (TASB) Created in 1949, the Texas Association of School Boards is a voluntary, nonprofit, statewide educational association that serves and represents local Texas school districts: www.tasb.org

Texas Farm Bureau Founded in 1933, this organization provides a voice for farmers, ranchers, rural citizens, and everyone interested in preserving and protecting the farming way of life: www.txfb.org

Texas Public Policy Foundation A nonprofit, nonpartisan research institute: www.texaspolicy.com

Texas State Teachers Association (TSTA) The Texas affiliate of the National Education Association. Since 1857, NEA has crusaded for the rights of educators and children: www.tsta.org

Texas Trial Lawyers Association A member organization comprised of plaintiff's attorneys founded in 1949 to protect the rights of Texas's families: www.ttla.com/tx

22

Governor Rick Perry speaks to the first general session of the Republican Party of Texas convention in Dallas, in June, 2010. (AP Photo/LM Otero)

Political Parties in Texas

QUESTIONS TO CONSIDER

Why was Texas politics dominated by the Democratic Party until the early 1990s?

Why have a majority of Texans come to identify with the Republican Party?

What developments could lead to a resurgence of support for the Texas Democratic Party?

CHAPTER CONTENTS

what if...

Texas Nominated its Candidates by Conventions?

BACKGROUND

In Texas and most other states, political parties use the direct primary election for selecting nominees to national, state, and some local offices. This method of selecting party nominees through elections is unique to the American political system. In most Western democracies, party leaders and delegates meeting in conventions or caucuses select party candidates; rank-and-file voters do not participate in the nomination process.

In the early 20th century reformers, disenchanted with the autocratic and corrupt influence of party leaders, pressed for more involvement of ordinary voters in the nomination process. In addition, in states where there was very little party competition, the primary election helped ensure meaningful popular participation. This was certainly the case in Texas, which, like the South in general, was dominated by the Democratic Party.

NOMINATION BY CONVENTION

Nominating by convention allows parties much more control over the nomination. Party leaders can ensure that candidates are those loyal to the party's platform; they can also select nominees they believe will be stronger candidates in the general election. For example, in Great Britain, the national party organization sends a list of approved party nominees to the local party organization. The local party organization then interviews the potential nominees and selects them based on several factors, including the candidate's loyalty to party goals and his or her potential for winning. The party is able to concentrate its resources behind its nominee and play a dominant role in organizing the campaign.

Although the prospect of this kind of party control seems unthinkable to Texans and most other Americans, there are consequences of the convention nomination process that appeal to some, particularly party activists. Texas parties would be able to exercise more control over those who bear their party label. For example, a Republican candidate in Texas who supports abortion rights would have little chance of being the GOP nominee (the GOP's official position is prolife). Others argue that it is easier to assign credit or blame to the party in power if nominees are closely tied to the party and the party's program. That is, a convention system may result in greater accountability in government, particularly if both the executive and legislative branches are controlled by the same party. Some observers maintain that there would be less need for the massive amounts of funding that characterize competitive primary races.

Although every state in the United States allows for nomination by the direct primary, some states either permit or require conventions to nominate candidates for governor or U.S. senator. For example, in New York, primaries are not mandatory and are held only if two or more candidates receive 25 percent of the convention delegates' votes. Some states, such as Massachusetts and Minnesota, allow for preprimary endorsements by party conventions.

As long as the Republican Party continues to dominate Texas politics at the state level, a formal role for state conventions in the nominating process is not likely. As this chapter points out, for many offices in Texas, the Republican primary may be the only competitive election. However, if the state moves toward two truly competitive parties, there may be incentives for the Democratic and Republican party leaders to exert more influence over the nomination process.

FOR CRITICAL ANALYSIS

1. Other than GOP dominance, what other factors would make it difficult for Texas to adopt a convention system of nominating candidates?
2. Describe the major issue positions of Democrats or Republicans in Texas. How would a convention system of nominating candidates make it easier for the state party to enact its positions into law?

THE AMERICAN FOUNDERS created our complicated federal system and provided for the election of a president and Congress. But the U.S. Constitution makes no mention of political parties. Indeed, early American leaders held negative attitudes about parties. George Washington warned of the "baneful effects of the spirit of party" in his farewell address. James Madison, in *Federalist Paper* No. 10 (see Appendix B), criticized parties or "factions" as divisive, although he admitted they were inevitable. Madison and others thought that parties would encourage conflict and undermine consensus on public policy. Yet despite their condemnation of parties, these early American politicians engaged in partisan politics and initiated a competitive two-party system, as described in Chapter 8.

Parties, then, are apparently something we cannot live without. They have been with us from the start of this country and will be with us for the foreseeable future, influencing our government and public policy. It is important, therefore, to gain an understanding of what they are all about.

HOW POLITICAL PARTIES OPERATE

What is a political party? This question conjures up various stereotypes: smoke-filled rooms where party leaders or bosses make important behind-the-scenes decisions; activists or regulars who give time, funding, and enthusiastic support to their candidates; and voters who proudly identify themselves as Democrats or Republicans. Essentially, though, a political party is simply a broad-based coalition with the primary purpose of winning elections. Gaining control of government through popular elections is the most important goal for political parties, and most of the activities parties pursue are directed toward this purpose. Parties recruit and nominate their members for public office. They form coalitions of different groups and interests to build majorities so that they can elect their candidates.

Political parties are vital to democracy in that they provide a link between the people and government. Parties make it possible for the ordinary citizen and voter to participate in the political system. They provide the means for organizing support for particular candidates. In organizing this support, parties unify various groups and interests and mobilize them on behalf of candidates who support the parties' positions.

Political parties developed and survived because they perform important functions. We described these functions in Chapter 8 and review them here. The functions of parties are as follows:

1. *Nominate and elect their members to public office.* Except for many local elections in which parties are forbidden by law to participate, political parties nominate candidates, and parties run the election process.
2. *Simplify the issues for voters so that there are fewer positions on a question of public policy.* In other words, parties educate the public. They help make sense of the issues and provide voters with cues on how to vote.
3. *Mobilize voters by encouraging participation in the electoral process.* Individuals are persuaded to become active in support of party candidates. Contributing funds to campaigns, telephoning, and door-to-door canvassing are all examples of how parties mobilize supporters. The more organized the party, the more effective it becomes in getting out the vote for its candidates.
4. *Run the government.* The president, members of Congress, governors, state representatives, and (in Texas) state judges are all elected to public office under the party label. Once elected, these officials try to promote the positions of their party. In our political system, however, it is often difficult for parties to manage the government, because the same party may not capture all of the separate branches of government.

CHARACTERISTICS OF AMERICAN POLITICAL PARTIES

In examining American political parties, we must look at three distinct characteristics not always found in parties elsewhere in the world: (1) pragmatism, (2) decentralization, and (3) the effects of the two-party system.

PRAGMATISM

Pragmatism

The philosophy that ideas should be judged by their practical results rather than on an ideological basis. American political parties are usually pragmatic because they are typically more interested in winning elections than in taking clear stands on issues.

Pragmatism in politics means that ideas should be judged on the basis of their practical results rather than on an ideological basis. In other words, a pragmatist is interested in what works. American parties are willing to compromise principles to appeal successfully to a majority of voters and gain public office. They willingly bargain with most organized groups and take stands that appeal to a large number of interests to build a winning coalition.

Pragmatism often means taking clear-cut positions only on issues for which there is broad agreement. The natural outcome of a campaign strategy designed to attract all groups (and to repel none) is that the party's ideology is not easily brought into sharp focus. Taking clear-cut stands on controversial issues may alienate potential members of the party's electoral coalition. Political parties and their candidates, including those in Texas, thus prefer to deemphasize issues and instead attempt to project a positive but vague image. Broad, fuzzy campaign themes that stress leadership potential, statesmanship, family life, and personality often take precedence over issues.

It would be a mistake, nonetheless, to assume that parties do not differ from one another. Indeed, many observers feel that American parties have become more programmatic in recent years. To succeed, they must satisfy their traditional supporters—voters, public-opinion leaders, interest groups, and campaign contributors. The candidates are not blank slates but have their own beliefs, prejudices, biases, and opinions. In most elections, broad ideological differences are apparent. Voters in Texas who participated in the presidential elections of 2008 could easily identify the conservative and liberal orientations of Republican John McCain and Democrat Barack Obama.

DECENTRALIZATION

Decentralization

In American party politics, distribution of power to state and local party organizations rather than concentration of power in the national organization. In government, distribution of authority to local and regional governments rather than concentration of authority in a central government.

Grassroots

The lowest organizational level of a political party.

At first glance, American party organizations may appear to be neatly ordered and hierarchical, with power flowing from national to state to local parties. In reality, American parties are not nearly so hierarchical. Instead, they reflect the American federal system, with its **decentralization** of power to national, state, and local levels. Political party organizations operate at the precinct, or **grassroots**, level; the local government level (city, county, or district); the state level; and the national level.

Figure 22–1 illustrates the nature of power in American political parties. State and local party organizations are semi-independent actors that exercise considerable discretion on most party matters. The practices that state and local parties follow, the candidates they recruit, the campaign funds they raise, the innovations they introduce, the organized interests to which they respond, the campaign strategies they create, and, most importantly, the policy orientations of the candidates who run under their labels are all influenced by local and state political cultures, leaders, traditions, and interests.

The Service Role of the National Parties. We have seen that the American party system is decentralized. Observers have argued, though, that in recent years power has shifted to the national party organizations. Both the Democratic and Republican national parties have become stronger and more involved in state and local party activities. By using new campaign technologies—computer-based mailing lists, direct-mail solicitations, and the Internet—the national parties have raised millions of dollars. Thus, the national party organizations have assumed a greater service role by providing unprecedented levels of assistance to state parties and candidates. This assistance includes a variety of services—candidate recruitment, research, public-opinion polling, computer networking, production of radio and television commercials, direct mailing, and consultation on redistricting issues. As national parties provide more funds and services to state and local parties, they exercise more influence over state and local organizations, issues, and candidates.[1]

THE TWO-PARTY SYSTEM

In a majority of states, political competition usually comes down to competition between the two major parties: the Democrats and the Republicans. As mentioned earlier in Chapter 8, we call this the *two-party system*. Third parties have often tried to gain office but have had little success, because the major parties make a pragmatic, conscientious effort to absorb them by adopting their platforms. (Consider, for example, how the original Populist Party was absorbed by the Democratic Party, as described in Chapter 8.) Voters, potential campaign contributors, and political activists also behave pragmatically; they tend to avoid supporting losing causes. Our electoral system—the **single-member district system**—encourages this pragmatic behavior. If only one representative can be elected in a district, voters normally will cast their ballots for the candidates who have the best chance of winning. Third parties face the problem of historical inertia, too. Voters usually vote for the major parties because they have always done so.

The national campaign for the presidency in 1992 by Texas billionaire Ross Perot illustrates the difficulty faced by third-party or independent candidates in American politics. Perot was able to appear on the ballots of all 50 states only because his supporters organized mass petition drives in every state. In the 1992 presidential election, Perot received 19 percent of the national vote and 22 percent of the vote in his home state of Texas. Nonetheless, both nationally and in Texas, Perot's support was diffuse. His support was not concentrated enough in any one state to win that state's electoral votes, the votes needed to actually win the presidency.

In Texas, third parties, such as the Libertarian and Green parties, must have received at least 5 percent of the vote in the previous election to be automatically included on the ballot in the current election. A party that fails to gain this 5 percent can appear on the ballot only by launching petition drives to collect the signatures of a specified number of registered voters who did not vote in the primary of either major party. (We discussed primaries in Chapters 8 and 9 and describe them again in the following section.) Independent candidates must also meet this standard. For example, in order to compete against incumbent governor Rick Perry in the November 2006 gubernatorial election, independent candidates Carole Keeton Strayhorn and Kinky Friedman were forced to collect 45,000 signatures from eligible voters who had not voted in the March 7 primary.

FIGURE 22–1 The Decentralized Nature of American Political Parties and the Strengthening of the National Party's Service Function

This chart represents intraparty relationships during the era of soft money. Since the passage of the McCain-Feingold Act of 2002 (see Chapter 10), the influence of the national parties has been diminished.

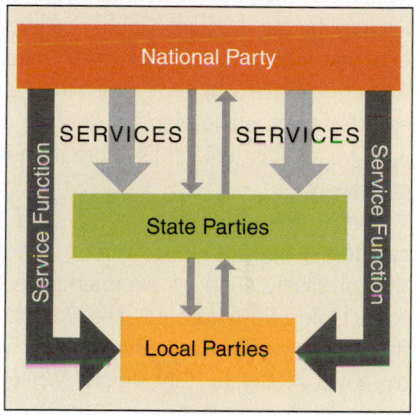

Single-Member District System
A system that allows only one candidate to be elected from each electoral district. This system discourages the formation of third parties.

That in the 1890s, the journalist O. Henry wrote, "We have only two or three laws [in Texas], such as against murder before witnesses and being caught stealing horses and voting the Republican ticket"?

[1] Marjorie Hershey, *Party Politics in America*, 13th ed. (New York: HarperCollins, 2009), pp. 70–71.

POLITICS WITH A purpose

Crystal City High School and the Creation of the Raza Unida Party

Political parties have generally been viewed with suspicion by the American people. In spite of that trepidation, they formed as soon as the country was founded. Except for a brief period known as the "Era of Good Feelings," when the country experimented with one party, the United States has operated under a two-party system. Given that candidates are generally selected from single-member districts and must win a plurality of votes, it is difficult for more than two parties to compete effectively.

Every now and then, however, a third party develops, causing a restructuring among the larger parties. Texas had precisely such an experience in the 1970s, when the Raza Unida Party formed. The Raza Unida Party arose from the ethnic conflicts experienced by Mexican Americans in the town of Crystal City, Texas. While the town had served as an internment camp for German, Japanese, and Italian Americans during World War II, by the 1960s its spinach fields had attracted a growing Mexican American population. This group had long been denied political power. Poll taxes and intimidation were used to dissuade Hispanics from voting in the town.[a] In 1963, the Hispanic population organized, getting a substantial number to pay the poll tax and vote. The result was a turnover in control of the city council from white to Hispanic.

A few years later, Hispanic students at Crystal City High School, led by José Ángel Gutiérrez, protested the unequal treatment Hispanic students experienced at the school. After several walkouts, protests, and even federal intervention, the Mexican American population was successful in electing Hispanics to the school board.[b] The movement also led to the creation of the Mexican American Youth Organization (MAYO), which led to the creation of the Raza Unida Party in 1970. The leaders of MAYO—Mario Compean, José Ángel Gutiérrez, Ignacio Pérez, and Willie Velásquez—would lead the Raza Unida Party into other states. They would field candidates for office, having their greatest electoral success at the local level.[c]

Twice the Raza Unida Party fielded Ramsey Muñiz as its gubernatorial candidate. In 1972, he ran a campaign with a focus on improving the lives of Mexican Americans. In 1974, he expanded the focus of the campaign to include improved transportation, education, and health care[d] but attracted less support.

While the Raza Unida Party was unsuccessful in electing statewide officeholders, it was successful in electing school board members and city and county officials. More importantly, the party mobilized thousands of previously disenfranchised voters. Young Hispanics became politically involved in ways not seen before. The Raza Unida Party's influence would wane, but its efforts demonstrate the influence young people can have on politics. Moreover, the party accomplished what many third parties can do—bringing the issues of a previously ignored population to the forefront. The Raza Unida Party brought the concerns of Mexican Americans to the attention of the two major political parties. These concerns would become part of the Democratic Party's platform.

What were some of the ramifications of creating a third party like the Raza Unida Party? Why is it that third parties have such a difficult time winning elections? What would have to change for the United States to have a multiparty system?

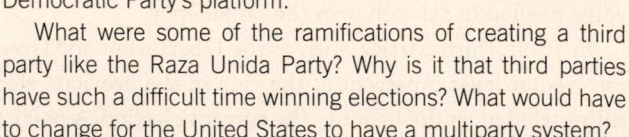

[a]John Staples Shockley, *Chicano Revolt in a Texas Town* (Notre Dame, IN: University of Notre Dame Press, 1974).
[b]Ibid.

[c]Ignatio M. Garcia, *United We Win: The Rise and Fall of La Raza Unida Party* (Tucson: University of Arizona Mexican American Studies Research Center, 1989).
[d]Teresa Palomo Acosta, "Raza Unida Party," in The Handbook of Texas Online, www.tshaonline.org/handbook/online/articles/RR/war1.html, accessed May 21, 2008.

DEVELOPMENT OF THE TEXAS PARTY SYSTEM

Although the two-party system characterizes American politics, many states and localities—Texas, for one—have been dominated by just one party at various times in history. Texas was formerly a one-party Democratic state, but that is no longer the case. To understand political parties in Texas, it is necessary to examine the history of one-party dominance by the Democratic Party, the emergence of two-party competition in the state, and the emerging Republican Party domination of Texas, which can be expected to last years into the future.

THE ONE-PARTY TRADITION IN TEXAS

Under the Republic of Texas, there was little party activity. Political divisions were usually oriented around support of, or opposition to, Sam Houston (a leading founder of the Republic). After Texas became a state, however, the Democratic Party dominated Texas politics until the 1990s. This legacy of dominance was firmly established by the Civil War and the era of Reconstruction, as described in Chapters 19 and 20. During this period, Northern troops occupied the South under the direction of a Republican U.S. Congress. From the time Republican and former Union soldier Edmund J. Davis's single term as governor ended in 1874 until Republican Bill Clements's surprising victory in the 1978 gubernatorial election, the Democrats exercised almost complete control over Texas politics.

The Populist Challenge. The Democratic Party was, at times, challenged by the emergence of more liberal third parties. The most serious of these challenges came in the late 1800s with the Populist revolt. The Populist Party grew out of the dissatisfaction of small farmers, who demanded government regulation of rates charged by banks and railroads, as well as an end to the gold standard they felt caused a deflation in agricultural prices.

These farmers—joined by sharecroppers, laborers, and African Americans—mounted a serious election bid in 1896 by taking 44 percent of the vote for governor. Eventually, however, the Democratic Party diffused the threat of the Populists by co-opting many of the issues of the new party. The Democrats also effectively disenfranchised African Americans and poor whites in 1902 with the establishment of a poll tax.

The Democratic Primary. Two events in the early 20th century solidified the position of the Democrats in Texas politics. The first was the institution of party primary reforms in 1906. For the first time, voters could choose the party's nominees by a vote in a **direct primary**. Thereafter, the Democratic primary became the substitute for the two-party

Direct Primary
An intraparty election in which the voters select the candidates who will run on a party's ticket in the subsequent general election. In Texas, nominees must win a majority of the votes, which often means that there are primary runoff elections between the top two candidates.

OFFICIAL PHOTOGRAPH of the 1928 Democratic National Convention, held in Houston. Holding the convention in Texas did little to help the Democratic nominee, Governor Al Smith of New York. Smith was the first Catholic ever nominated as a presidential candidate by a major party, and he lost many Southern states, including Texas. Why might many Protestants have been unwilling to accept a Catholic presidential candidate in those days? (Calvin Wheat Studio, Library of Congress Prints & Photographs Division, Washington, D.C. [LC-USZ62-128459])

OFFICIAL PHOTOGRAPH
NATIONAL DEMOCRATIC CONVENTION
HOUSTON, TEXAS 1928
© CALVIN WHEAT STUDIO

contest—the general election. In the absence of Republican competition, the Democratic primary was the only game in town, and it provided a competitive arena for political differences within the state.

The Great Depression. The second event that helped the Democrats was the Great Depression. Although Republican presidential candidate Herbert Hoover carried Texas in 1928, the Republicans were blamed for failing to do enough to combat the Great Depression of the 1930s. The effect of this crisis, added to the effects of the Civil War and Reconstruction, ensured Democratic dominance in state government until the early 1990s.

IDEOLOGICAL BASIS OF FACTIONALISM: CONSERVATIVES AND LIBERALS

Although members of a political party may be similar in their views, *factions*, or divisions, within the party inevitably develop. These conflicts may involve a variety of different personalities and issues, but the most important basis for division is ideology.

To understand the ideological basis for factionalism in political parties in Texas, it is necessary to define the terms *conservative* and *liberal*—a difficult task, because the meanings change with time and may mean different things to different people. You learned about conservative and liberal ideologies in Chapter 1; we review these concepts here.

Conservatives. Modern conservatives typically combine support for the free market with support for traditional values. Conservatives believe that individuals should be left alone to compete in a free market unfettered by government control; they prefer that government regulation of the economy be kept to a minimum. Conservatives, though, often support government subsidies and promotion of business. They may favor construction of highways, tax incentives for investment, and other government aids to business. The theory is that these aids will encourage economic development and hence prosperity for the entire society. In contrast, conservatives are likely to oppose government programs that involve redistribution of wealth, such as welfare, health care assistance, and unemployment compensation.

As the label suggests, conservatives may view change suspiciously. They may tend to favor the status quo—things as they are now and as they have been in the recent past. They emphasize traditional values associated with the family and close communities, and they often favor government action to preserve what they see as the proper moral values of society. Because conservatives hold a more skeptical view of human nature than do liberals, they are more likely to be tougher on perceived threats to personal safety and the public order. For example, conservatives are more likely to favor stiffer penalties for criminals, including capital punishment.

Liberals. Modern liberals believe that it is often necessary for government to regulate the economy. They point to concentrations of wealth and power that have threatened to control government, destroy economic competition, and weaken individual freedom. Government power, they believe, should be used to protect the disadvantaged and to promote equality. Liberals generally support the social-welfare programs that conservatives oppose. They are also more likely to favor *progressive* taxes, which increase in percentage terms as incomes increase (see Chapter 17). The best example of a progressive tax is the federal tax on individual incomes.

Liberals possess a more optimistic view of human nature than conservatives. They tend to believe that individuals are essentially rational and, therefore, that consciously planned change will ultimately bring improvements in the human condition. Liberals want government to protect the civil rights and liberties of individuals and are critical of interference with the exercise of constitutional rights of free speech, press, religion, assembly, association, and privacy. They are often suspicious of conservatives' attempts to "legislate morality" because of the potential for interference with individual rights.

CONSERVATIVE AND LIBERAL FACTIONS IN THE DEMOCRATIC PARTY

For many years, factions within the Texas Democratic Party resembled a two-party system, and the election to select the Democratic Party's nominees—the primary—was the most important election in Texas. Until the 1990s, conservative Democrats were much more successful than their liberal counterparts in these primaries, in part because Republican voters, facing no significant primary race of their own, regularly "crossed over" and supported conservative Democratic candidates. Voters in the general elections, faced with a choice between a conservative Democrat and a conservative Republican, usually went with the traditional party—the Democrats. These Republican crossover votes enabled conservative Democrats, with few exceptions, to control the party and state government for many years—until 1978, when Bill Clements was elected as the first Republican governor of Texas in 105 years.

Conservative Democrats. Conservative Democrats in Texas provided a good example of the semi-independent relationship of national, state, and local party organizations (as illustrated in Figure 22–1). Texas conservatives traditionally voted Democratic in state and local races but often refused to support the national Democratic candidates for president. The development of the conservative Democratic faction in Texas was an outgrowth of conservative dissatisfaction with many New Deal proposals of Franklin D. Roosevelt in the 1930s and Fair Deal proposals of Harry Truman in the late 1940s. Conservative Democrats in Texas continued their cool relationship with the national party when many of them supported Republican presidential candidates Dwight D. Eisenhower in 1952 and 1956, Richard Nixon in 1968 and 1972, and Ronald Reagan in 1980 and 1984.

The Success of the Conservative Democrats. In the past, the conservative wing of the Democratic Party enjoyed almost continuous success in Texas politics. This faction supplied almost every governor elected from the mid-1930s to the 1970s. These governors included Allan Shivers (served 1949–1957), John Connally (served 1963–1969), and Preston Smith (served 1969–1973), all of whom later switched to the Republican Party. It also included governors Dolph Briscoe (served 1973–1979) and Mark White (served 1983–1987). Until recently, conservative Democrats held almost all of the state's congressional seats; they also dominated both chambers of the Texas legislature.

Several factors accounted for this success, but the most important were the power and resources of the conservative constituency. Conservatives have traditionally made up the state's power elite and represent such interests as the oil, gas, and sulfur industries; other large corporations; bigger farms and ranches, or "agribusiness"; owners and publishers of most of the state's major daily newspapers; and veterans. In other words, the most affluent persons in the state have been able and willing to contribute their considerable resources to the campaigns of like-minded politicians. These segments of the population are also the most likely to turn out to vote in elections. This was a significant advantage to conservative Democrats competing in the party primaries, where turnout has generally been low.

The Impact of Governor Shivers. As described in Chapter 19, Governor Allan Shivers, elected in 1948, did more than any individual to establish the dominance of the conservative faction of the Democratic Party. The Shivers faction (labeled *Shivercrats* by liberals) announced its support for the 1952 Republican presidential nominee, Dwight

GOVERNOR ALLAN SHIVERS

(right) was nationally known for his break with the Democratic Party over the tidelands issue. Shivers endorsed Dwight Eisenhower's presidential candidacy in 1952 and was instrumental in delivering the electoral votes of Texas to the Republicans. A few months after taking office, Eisenhower signed a law that endorsed the state's claim to the tidelands. (Texas State Library and Archives)

D. Eisenhower, and urged Texas Democrats to vote Republican for president and Democratic for state offices. That same year, Shivers, along with all other Democratic state officeholders at the time (with the exception of state agriculture commissioner John White), received the nomination of both the Democratic and Republican parties. This dual nomination was a unique situation in Texas politics.

Liberal Democrats. Liberals in the Texas Democratic Party consist of those groups that have supported the national Democratic Party ticket and its presidents (Roosevelt, Truman, Kennedy, Johnson, Carter, Clinton, and Obama). These groups include the following:

- Organized labor, in particular the AFL-CIO.
- African American groups, such as the National Association for the Advancement of Colored People (NAACP).
- Mexican American groups, such as the American G.I. Forum, the League of United Latin American Citizens (LULAC), Mexican American Democrats (MAD), and the Mexican American Legal Defense and Educational Fund (MALDEF).
- Various professionals, teachers, and intellectuals.
- Small farmers and ranchers, sometimes belonging to the Texas Farmers Union.
- Environmental groups, such as the Sierra Club.
- Abortion-rights groups, such as the Texas Abortion Rights Action League.
- Trial lawyers—that is, lawyers who represent plaintiffs in civil suits and defendants in criminal cases.

Success for liberal Democratic politicians in Texas has been infrequent and has rarely persisted for more than a few years. The heyday of Texas liberalism came in a period from the 1890s through the 1930s with the election of several progressive governors. The latter included governors James Hogg (served 1891–1895), "Pa" and "Ma" Ferguson (served 1915–1917, 1925–1927, and 1933–1935), Dan Moody (served 1927–1931), and James V. Allred (served 1935–1939). Since the Great Depression of the 1930s, liberals have been able to capture a U.S. Senate seat only once, in 1957, with the election of Ralph Yarborough. In 1970, Yarborough was defeated for reelection by the moderate-to-conservative Democrat Lloyd Bentsen, who held the seat until he became President Bill Clinton's treasury secretary in 1992.

Today, liberal Texas Democrats enjoy more success in capturing their party's nomination, largely because conservatives are voting in the Republican primary. In recent years, liberal or moderate Democrats have been routinely nominated for all statewide offices. This presents an irony for liberal Democrats: Although they have gained strength within the party from the defection of conservatives, this very defection has permitted the Republicans to dominate Texas politics.

DID YOU KNOW?

That when Texas voted for Republican presidential candidate George H. W. Bush in 1992, it was the first time in history that Texas voted for a Republican presidential candidate who was unable to win nationally?

THE RISE OF THE REPUBLICAN PARTY

Before the presidential election of 1988, only three modern-day Republicans had won statewide races in Texas: U.S. Senator John Tower (served 1961–1985), Governor Bill Clements (served 1979–1983 and 1987–1991), and U.S. Senator Phil Gramm (served 1985–2003). Why had the Republican Party failed to compete in Texas in the past? As we have seen, the most important reason was the bitter memory that was left by the state's experience in the Civil War and during Reconstruction. The Republican administration of Governor E. J. Davis (served 1870–1874) was widely considered by the white majority to be the most corrupt and abusive in Texas history. Only in the last few years has the Republican Party been able to shake its image as "the party of Reconstruction."

The Republicans Become Competitive. The revival of the Republican Party was foreshadowed in the 1950s by the development of the so-called presidential Republicans (those who vote Republican for national office but Democratic for state and local office). Conservative Democrats objected to the liberal policies of the national Democratic Party and often voted for Republican presidential candidates.

The first major step in the rejuvenation of the Republican Party in Texas came in 1961, when John Tower, a Republican, was elected to the U.S. Senate. Tower won a special nonpartisan election held when Lyndon B. Johnson gave up his Senate seat to assume the vice presidency. Tower initially won with the help of many liberal Democrats and was reelected until he retired in 1984. The Republicans retained his seat with the election of former congressman Phil Gramm over his liberal Democratic opponent Lloyd Doggett in 1984. In November 2002, John Cornyn, a Republican and the state's former attorney general, was elected to replace Gramm.

In November 1978, the Republicans achieved their most stunning breakthrough when Republican Bill Clements defeated Democrat John Hill in the race for governor. After losing the governor's seat to moderate-to-conservative Democrat Mark White in 1982, the Republicans regained their momentum in 1986, when Clements turned the tables on White and recaptured the governor's chair.

The Republicans Become Dominant. Developments in the 1990s and early 2000s transformed Texas into Republican country. With the election in 1992 of U.S. Senator Kay Bailey Hutchison, Republicans held both U.S. Senate seats for the first time since Reconstruction. In 1994, Republican George W. Bush (son of former president George H. W. Bush) defeated incumbent Democratic governor Ann Richards.

By far the most impressive gains for the Republicans came in the November 1998 elections, when incumbent governor George W. Bush led the Republicans to victory in every statewide election. For the first time in living memory, no Democrats occupied any statewide executive or judicial office. Republicans have continued to maintain their monopoly on statewide offices. In 2004, after a successful effort at congressional redistricting, the GOP captured a majority in Texas's congressional delegation.

The Republican Party is also extremely competitive in lower-level offices in the state, where Democrats have been most firmly entrenched. In 1974, the GOP held only 53 offices at the county level; they now hold more than 2,000 county offices. In 1996, the Republicans gained a majority of seats in the state senate, the first time in 126 years that Republicans had held a majority in either chamber of the legislature; and in 2002, they captured the state house of representatives.

Table 22–1 shows the dramatic increases by Republicans in the Texas legislature and the Texas delegation to the U.S. House of Representatives. The extent to which these gains signal a Republican-dominated party system in Texas is discussed later in this chapter.

Sources of Republican Strengths and Weaknesses. Republican voting strength in recent years has been concentrated in several clusters of counties (see Figure 22–2):

- The Houston area.
- The Dallas–Fort Worth area.
- The Midland-Odessa area.
- The Northern Panhandle.
- The East Texas oil field counties of Smith, Rusk, and Gregg.
- The Hill Country–Edwards Plateau area.

TABLE 22–1 Changes in the Number of Republican and Democratic Officeholders in Texas

	1973		2011	
	DEMOCRATS	**REPUBLICANS**	**DEMOCRATS**	**REPUBLICANS**
Texas House of Representatives	132	17	51	99
Texas Senate	28	3	12	19
U.S. House of Representatives	20	4	9	23
U.S. Senate	1	1	0	2

Results from the 2008 presidential race reveal that the Republican Party is weaker in the following areas:

- Large urban cities: Houston, Dallas, San Antonio, El Paso, Austin.
- South and South Central Texas.
- Far West Texas.
- Far pockets of East Texas.

FIGURE 22–2 Presidential Candidates with Most Votes

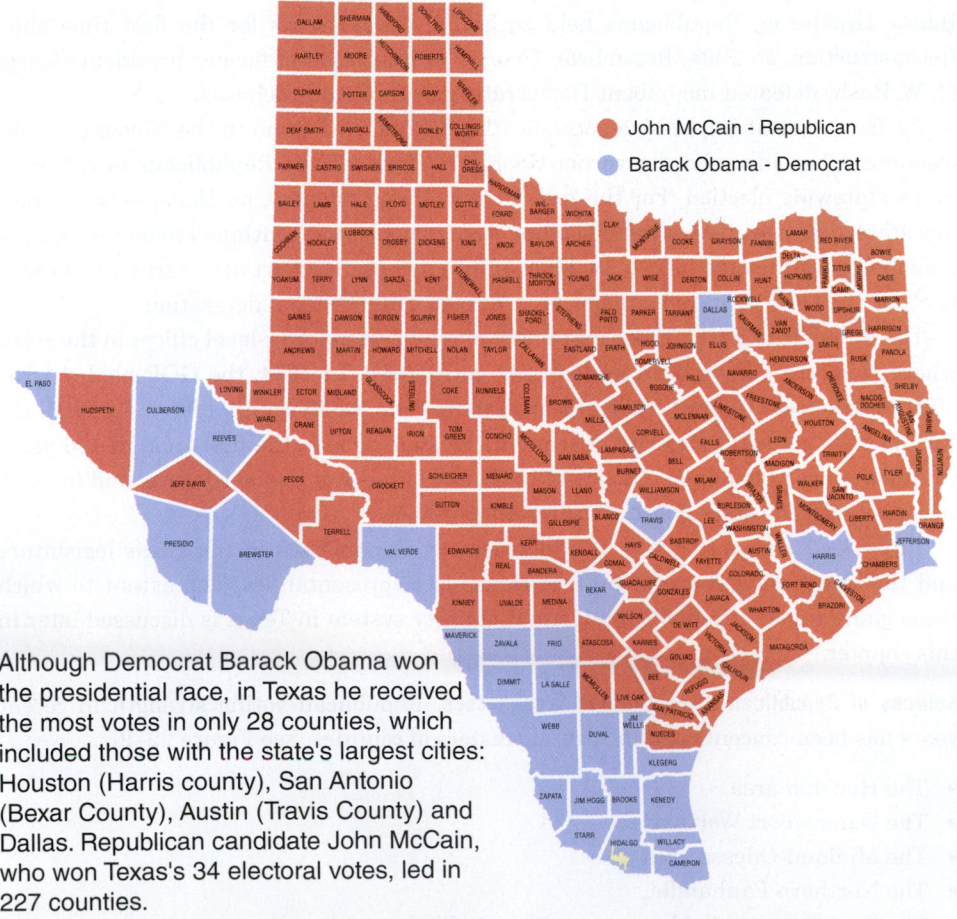

John McCain - Republican

Barack Obama - Democrat

Although Democrat Barack Obama won the presidential race, in Texas he received the most votes in only 28 counties, which included those with the state's largest cities: Houston (Harris county), San Antonio (Bexar County), Austin (Travis County) and Dallas. Republican candidate John McCain, who won Texas's 34 electoral votes, led in 227 counties.

Source: Texas Almanac, 2010–2011, Denton, TX: Texas State Historical Association, copyright 2010.

The Republican Party seems to appeal primarily to the following groups:

- Middle- and upper-class individuals in urban and suburban communities.
- Rural, high-income ranchers.
- White Anglo-Saxon Protestants.
- German Americans whose ancestors were strong supporters of the Union during the Civil War.
- Active and retired military officers.
- Traditional conservatives who find themselves in a new suburban setting.

The party has benefited from the economic growth and prosperity that occurred in Texas from the end of World War II to the early 1980s. During this period, newcomers from more Republican parts of the country were lured to the state by a sympathetic business climate or by the promise of jobs. These transplanted Texans joined more prosperous native Texans to provide a political climate more conducive to Republican Party politics.

CONSERVATIVE AND MODERATE FACTIONS WITHIN THE REPUBLICAN PARTY

As the Republican Party becomes dominant in Texas politics, it is experiencing some of the factional differences that characterized the Democratic Party in Texas for years. For example, a bloc of conservative Christians, sometimes loosely referred to as **evangelical** or fundamentalist Christians, has increasingly dominated the Texas Republican Party.[2] This group is concerned with such issues as family, religion, and community morals, and it has been effective in influencing the *party platform*.

The Success of the Conservative Christian Bloc. In 1992, conservative Christians in the Texas Republican Party easily gained control of the Republican state convention and strengthened the antiabortion and antihomosexuality planks in the party's platform. They also captured more than half the seats on the Republican State Executive Committee. Since 1994, the state party chair and a majority of the members of the state executive committee have been conservative Christians. This dominance of leadership positions has given the conservative Christians a degree of control of the party machinery that continues today.

Republican Moderates. The control of the state's Republican Party by the conservative, or right, wing is opposed by the more moderate, or centrist, wing. Many of these moderates fear that the radicalism of the right will interfere with the party's ability to win elections. Many moderates represent business interests, and they are more concerned with keeping taxes low and limiting the government's interference in business decision making than with moral issues. The conservative faction of the Republican Party scored a major victory in the 2010 GOP primary when incumbent governor Rick Perry received his party's nomination with more than 50 percent of the vote over incumbent U.S. senator Kay Bailey Hutchison. Perry campaigned vigorously against President Obama's health care and other federal government initiatives and avoided a runoff with his opponent.

Evangelical
Having to do with a broad spectrum of Protestant Christianity that emphasizes salvation and traditional values. Evangelical voters are likely to support culturally conservative politics.

[2]Actually, a majority of American Protestants can be characterized as evangelical. Not all are politically conservative. Some are politically liberal, such as former Democratic presidents Jimmy Carter and Bill Clinton. Conservative Protestants are also sometimes referred to as *fundamentalists*. Fundamentalists are a subset of evangelicals who believe in several doctrines not held by all evangelicals. In particular, fundamentalists believe in *biblical inerrancy*—that is, that every word of the Bible is literally true. In politics, fundamentalists are notably more conservative than other evangelicals; liberal fundamentalists are rare. See George M. Marsden, *Understanding Fundamentalism and Evangelicalism* (Grand Rapids, MI: Eerdmans Publishing, 1991); and Karen Armstrong, *The Battle for God* (New York: Ballantine Books, 2001).

REPUBLICANS AND MINORITIES

In general, the Republican Party has failed to generate much support among the state's minority voters. African American identification with the Republicans consistently hovers around 5 percent. Party strategists have made no great effort to attract African Americans, believing they are unlikely to switch parties.

Although George W. Bush received almost half of the "Tejano" vote in the 2004 presidential elections, Mexican Americans in Texas have traditionally identified with the Democratic Party. In 2008, Barack Obama captured 63 percent of the Hispanic vote in Texas. Democrats typically capture elections in heavily Hispanic counties, such as those found in the southern and southwestern areas of the state. Nevertheless, observers note that a substantial number of Hispanic voters are *swing voters* (see Chapter 8) not bound by party identification. The Democratic Party cannot afford to take this portion of the electorate for granted, and the Republican Party cannot assume that Hispanic party identification will trend its way. Do the Republicans have a chance of winning enough of the Hispanic vote to maintain their dominance in the state?

A LAWN SIGN supporting Bob Smither, the Libertarian Party's candidate for District 22 in the 2006 elections. This district was vacated by the scandal-plagued Tom DeLay. Smither received 6 percent of the vote, breaking the Texas Libertarian Party's record for a congressional candidate. (Nick Lampson won.) In total, the Libertarian Party of Texas had 168 candidates on the ballot, its highest count ever. (Photo courtesy of Advocates for Self-Government and Bob Smither's campaign)

AN EXAMPLE OF A THIRD PARTY: THE LIBERTARIAN PARTY

Chances are, if you have voted in a Texas election, you have seen many Libertarian candidates on the ballot. In recent years, the Libertarian Party has become an active, if not always influential, force in Texas politics. The Libertarian Party has a hands-off philosophy of government that combines the conservative emphasis on free markets with the liberal skepticism toward legislating morality. The party's general philosophy is one of individual liberty and personal responsibility. Applying their doctrine to the issues, Libertarians oppose Social Security, campaign finance reform, and military intervention abroad. The Libertarian Party faces the same hurdles as other third parties: poor financing, a lack of media coverage, and in some states, getting access to the ballot. A key problem for the Libertarians is that some of their ideas may be taken over by one of the major parties, in particular the Republicans. They have managed, however, to elect more than 300 Libertarians to public office at the local and state levels throughout the country.

HOW THE PARTY MACHINERY IS ORGANIZED IN TEXAS

To better understand how political parties are organized in Texas, we can divide the party machinery into two parts: the *temporary*, consisting of a series of short-lived conventions at various levels; and the *permanent*, consisting of people elected to continuing leadership positions in the party (see Figure 22–3).

TEMPORARY PARTY ORGANIZATION

Conventions are held at all levels of party organization in Texas. Conventions draw in a much larger number of party members than the ongoing permanent bodies can mobilize.

The Precinct Convention. The voting precinct is the starting point of party activity, for it is the scene of the precinct convention, a gathering of the faithful that is open to all who voted earlier in the day in that party's primary. It is also the key to getting involved in politics. (See the *You Can Make a Difference* feature at the end of this chapter.)

On a Tuesday early in March in even-numbered years, both the Democratic and the Republican parties hold conventions in almost all the voting precincts in the state. The ticket of admission is usually a voter-registration card stamped to indicate that the holder voted in the party's primary earlier in the day. The agenda of the precinct convention includes the following:

- Adoption of resolutions to be passed on to the county or state senatorial district convention.
- Selection of delegates to the county or senatorial district convention.

Although eligibility for participation in this grassroots level of democracy is open to all who vote in the first primary election, the attendance is low—usually only 2 or 3 percent of those who vote. This low attendance makes it possible for a small, determined minority of the electorate to assume control of the precinct convention and dominate its affairs.

FIGURE 22–3 Texas Political Party Organization

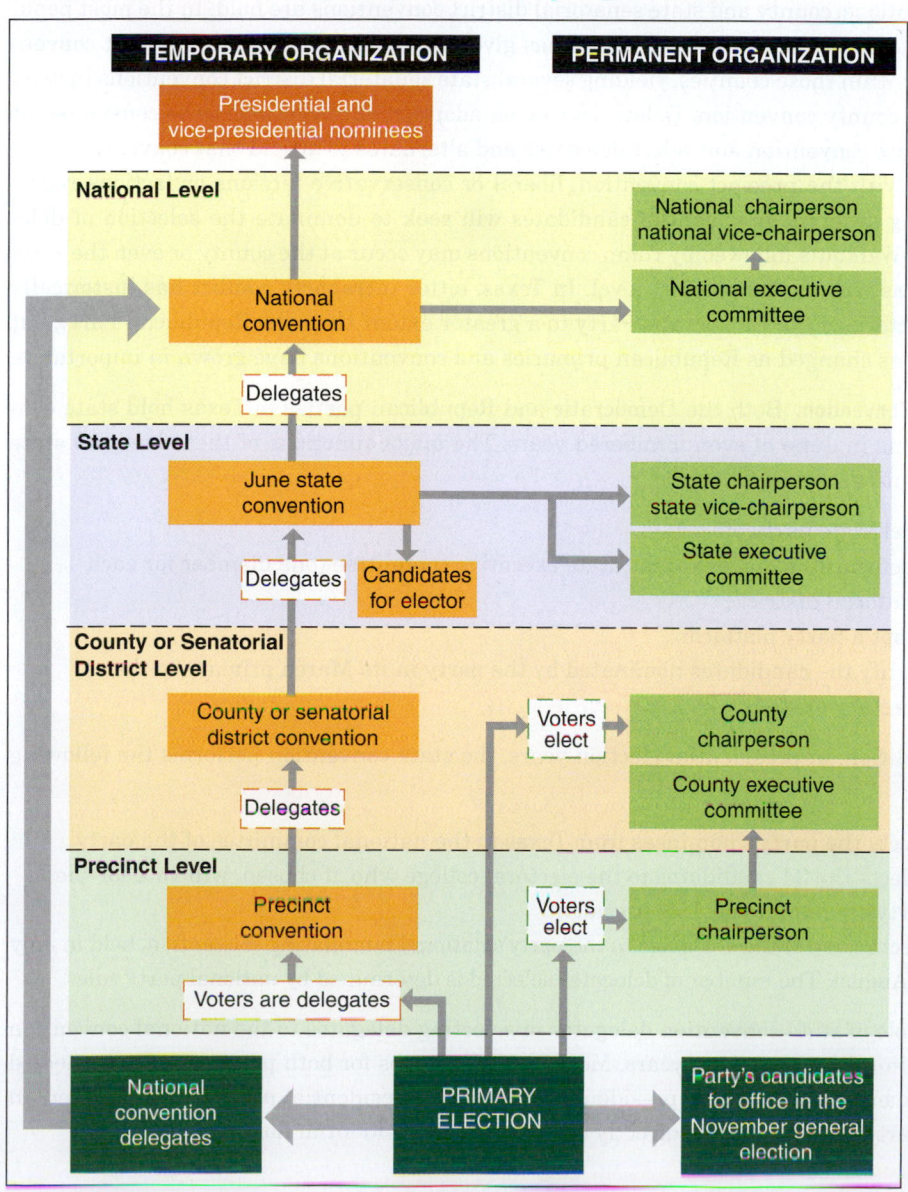

Political Divisions at the Precinct Level. A precinct convention normally starts with signing in those present and certifying that they voted in the party's primary. In presidential election years, those signing in also indicate their preference for a presidential candidate, while in nonpresidential election years, delegates may organize themselves in different ways, such as by indicating support for a "conservative caucus," "moderate-progressive caucus," and so forth. The preferences are used to evaluate the strength of support for each candidate or caucus. Those factions with the largest numbers present are able to dominate the selection of delegates to the county convention.

If contending factions in a precinct are closely divided, one side or the other may walk out if it loses a key vote and claim a grave injustice was done. Such a group may conduct its own convention, called a **rump convention**, going through the same procedures; then both precinct groups will appeal to a credentials committee appointed by the county executive committee. The credentials committee will decide which set of rival delegates is to be officially seated at the county convention. Although fairness and justice sometimes determine the results, the decision on which group to seat usually depends on which faction is in the majority on the credentials committee.

County and Senatorial District Conventions. In the weeks following the primary and precinct conventions, county and state senatorial district conventions are held. In the most populous counties, the county convention has given way to state senatorial district conventions within those counties, yielding several state senatorial district conventions instead of one county convention. Delegates vote on adoption of resolutions to be considered at the state convention and select delegates and alternates to attend that convention.

As with the precinct convention, liberal or conservative factions or factions representing different presidential candidates will seek to dominate the selection of delegates. Walkouts followed by rump conventions may occur at the county or even the state level, as well as the precinct level. In Texas, bitter intraparty conflict has historically characterized the Democratic Party to a greater extent than the Republican Party, but that has changed as Republican primaries and conventions have grown in importance.

State Convention. Both the Democratic and Republican parties in Texas hold state conventions in June of even-numbered years. The major functions of these biennial state conventions are as follows:

- Elect state party officers.
- Elect the 62 members of the state executive committee (one member for each senatorial district).
- Adopt a party platform.
- Certify the candidates nominated by the party in its March primary to the secretary of state.

In addition, in presidential election years, the state convention performs the following tasks:

- Elects the party's nominees from Texas to the national committee of the party.
- Selects the 34 candidates to the electoral college who, if chosen, will vote for the party's candidate for U.S. president.
- Elects some of the delegates to the party's national nominating convention, held in July or August. The number of delegates selected is determined by national party rules.

The role of state convention delegates in selecting delegates to the national convention has diminished in recent years. Most of the delegates for both parties are now selected on the basis of the party's presidential primary. A presidential primary allows voters in the party primary to vote directly on the party's presidential nominee.

Rump Convention
A meeting of members from a larger convention who secede and organize their own convention elsewhere.

In 2008, Texas held its presidential primary on March 4. Both Democrats and Republicans, voting in their separate primaries, indicated their selections for presidential candidates, as well as candidates for state and local offices. Texas Democrats were given the opportunity to express their preference for either Senator Hillary Clinton or Senator Barack Obama—twice. Dubbed the "Texas Two-Step" by the national press, Democrats voted once in the presidential primary election, and, if they chose, voted again in the precinct convention or caucus held in the evening after polls had closed. Democrats were allocated 228 delegates to the Democratic national convention, 126 of whom were chosen by the primaries, 67 by precinct conventions or caucuses, and 35 by unpledged superdelegates or party leaders. The assignment of delegates to candidates at the precinct convention distinguishes the Democratic from the Republican party in Texas. The GOP also holds precinct conventions, but only to choose who gets to attend the higher-level party conventions. Texas Republicans were allocated 140, all but three of whom were determined by the primary vote. The rules for selecting delegates to the respective parties' national conventions are somewhat complex; each state party organization describes these rules in detail on its Web site.

For the Democrats, the 67 "pledged" caucus-chosen delegates are assigned based on who shows up to the precinct conventions after the polls close in the evening. When Democrats established this system in 1988, the sentiment was that the caucuses would give party regulars an opportunity to exert some influence over both the nominating process and the party platform. The system was supposed to encourage turnout by rewarding those who had participated in the primary.

In the past, the precinct conventions had very few attendees, even in presidential election years. With the stakes so much higher in 2008, an estimated 1.1 million people turned out for the precinct convention-caucuses, four times what party officials were expecting. The unprecedented numbers caused a myriad of problems. Hundreds of people were squeezed into child-sized cafeterias or other small spaces. Some even caucused outside. Voters who arrived at 7:15 P.M. were kept waiting for hours while party officials tried to figure out obtuse procedures (including a curious rule that no one is in charge when the event begins). Some left because of the time it took to sign in, figure out the rules, and find a place to caucus. In some polling places, the police were called to address clashes between highly charged supporters of both candidates. The confusion drew the attention of the national media and complaints from the candidates, particularly the Clinton campaign, which threatened to file suit over irregularities. It took weeks to finalize the final results.

DID YOU KNOW?

The number of votes cast in the 2008 presidential primaries in Texas was almost 4.3 million, breaking the previous record of 2.8 million set in 1988?

STATE PARTY CONVENTIONS write the parties' platforms to represent their views on the issues. Because convention delegates are often intense partisans with the most strident positions, party candidates usually find it necessary to distance themselves from platform positions to win support from more centrist voters. (AP Photo/The Daily Texan, Tamir Kalifa)

Those who defended the caucuses claimed that the process energized the party and attracted those who had never participated in the past. Still, the negative publicity had many party activists calling for changes in the system.

PERMANENT PARTY ORGANIZATION

The permanent structure of the party consists of people selected to lead the party organization and provide continuity between election campaigns.

Precinct-Level Organization. At the bottom, or grassroots, level of the party structure is the precinct chair. Voters in the precinct's primary election choose the precinct chair for a two-year term. Often the position is uncontested, and in some precincts the chair is elected by write-in votes. The chair's role is to serve as party organizer in the precinct, regularly contacting known and potential party members. He or she may help organize party activities in the neighborhood, such as voter-registration drives. The precinct chair is responsible for arranging and presiding over the precinct convention and serving as a member of the county executive committee.

County-Level Organization. The county chair has a much more active and important role than the precinct chair. The voters choose the county chair for a two-year term in the party primary. The chair presides over the county executive committee, which is composed of all precinct chairs.

The county chair determines where the voting places will be for the primaries and appoints all primary **election judges**. (These choices must later be approved by the county commissioners court.) Accepting candidates for places on the primary ballot and printing paper ballots or renting voting machines are also the chair's responsibilities. Finally, the chair, along with the county executive committee, must certify the names of official nominees of the party to the secretary of state's office.

The county executive committee has three major functions:

1. Assemble the temporary roll of delegates to the county convention.
2. Canvass (that is, examine and certify) the returns from the primary for local offices.
3. Help the county chair prepare the primary ballot, accept filing fees, and determine the order of candidates' names on the ballot. The order of names is an important consideration if there is a great deal of "blind voting" in which ill-informed voters opt for the first name they come to on the ballot.

State-Level Organization. Delegates to the state convention choose the state chair—the titular head of the party—for a two-year term. The duties of the chair are to:

- preside over meetings of the state executive committee;
- call the state convention to order;
- handle the requests of statewide candidates on the ballot; and
- certify any runoff primary election winners to the state convention.

Each party's state executive committee has 64 members and is led by a chair and a vice chair (who must be of opposite genders). In addition, the Democratic and Republican state convention delegates choose one man and one woman from each of the 31 state senate districts. The main legal duties of the state executive committee are as follows:

- Determine the site of the next state convention—sometimes a crucial factor in determining whose loyal supporters can attend, since the party does not pay delegates' expenses.
- Canvass statewide primary returns and certify the nomination of party candidates.

Election Judge
A public official who is responsible for enforcing election rules at a polling place on election day.

The state executive committee also has some political duties, including issuing press releases and other publicity, encouraging organizational work in precincts and counties, raising money, and coordinating special projects. The state committee may work closely with the national party. These political chores are so numerous that the executive committees of both parties now employ full-time executive directors and staff assistants.

A NEW ERA OF REPUBLICAN DOMINANCE

Even with a national political climate that led to Democratic Party control of both houses of Congress and the presidency in 2006 and 2008, the Republican Party continues its dominance in Texas state politics. Republicans hold 99 of the 150 seats in the Texas house and 19 of the 31 seats in the Texas senate. In 1978, the Republicans held just 92 elected offices across all of Texas. Today the total is over 2,000. Clearly, the old pattern of Texans' voting Republican at the top of the ticket and Democratic at the bottom of the ticket is no longer true.

Most observers now agree that Texas has experienced a political *realignment*—that is, a transition from one stable party system to another. After 100 years of Democratic Party domination following the Civil War, the pendulum has swung to the Republican Party. (We discussed realignment in Chapter 8.)

EMERGENCE OF REPUBLICAN PARTY DOMINANCE

Realignment involves more than just casting a vote for a Republican Party candidate. It refers to a shift in *party identification*. Evidence that Texas is becoming a two-party or even a Republican-dominated state comes from public opinion polls that show more Texans are identifying with the Republican Party than in the past. Table 22–2 indicates that in 1952, an overwhelming percentage of those who identified with a political party in Texas were Democrats. In 2008, polls showed that the number of voters who identified with the Republican Party exceeded the number who identified with the Democratic Party.

The Slow Progress of Realignment in Texas. As we have already suggested, there are several reasons for the rise of Republican Party dominance in Texas. The first was the shift among existing voters as conservative middle- and upper-class white Democrats gradually switched their allegiance to the Republican Party during the decades following 1968. After years of voting Republican in presidential elections but identifying themselves as Democrats, these conservatives began thinking of themselves as Republicans. Many white voters defected to the Republican Party because they were alienated by the national Democratic Party's emphasis on civil rights in the 1960s and 1970s. The existence of popular and powerful Democratic leaders from Texas, such as President Lyndon B. Johnson (served 1963–1969), may have slowed the transition briefly but could not stop it.

TABLE 22–2   Democratic and Republican Party Identifiers

	DEMOCRATS(%)	REPUBLICANS (%)	TOTAL (%)
1952	66	6	72
1972	57	14	71
1990	34	30	64
2008	35	37	72

Sources: Statewide polls in 1952 and 1972 conducted by Belden Associates of Dallas and archived at the Roper Center. Data for 1990 from the Texas poll, Texas A&M University Policy Resources Laboratory, Harte-Hanks Communications. Data for 2008 from University of Texas, Austin, Texas Politics Poll.

This shift in partisan identification was also spurred, in part, by the election of an extremely popular Republican president. Ronald Reagan, elected in 1980 and reelected in 1984, combined clearly conservative positions with a charismatic personality that attracted conservative Democrats into the Republican camp. The impact of Reagan's leadership was reinforced by the election of George W. Bush to the presidency in 2000 and 2004. Bush had been a very popular governor, and his election to the presidency helped solidify the Republican realignment in Texas.

Interstate Immigration, Industrialization, and Urbanization. Party switching by native Texans has not been the only cause of realignment. Another factor involves newcomers to the state. A majority of recent migrants to Texas from other states have been Republicans or independents. These newcomers, who came to Texas in large numbers in the 1970s and 1980s, have helped break down traditional partisan patterns.

Finally, long-term economic trends have provided opportunities for political change. Texas has slowly become an industrialized and urbanized state, a pattern that accelerated after the 1940s. Industrialization, urbanization, and the rise of an affluent middle class have created a new environment for many Texans, and many Texans have been willing to adopt a new party as part and parcel of their new lives. In some parts of the country, urbanization and affluence have been associated with support for the Democratic Party, but in Texas these phenomena may have benefited the Republicans.

CAN THE DEMOCRATS STILL BE COMPETITIVE?

Some observers believe that Texas will emerge as a competitive two-party state. They note that Democrats still have considerable resources in many local governments, especially in some central cities and South and Southwest Texas. For example, in 2006, Democrats swept every contested countywide race in Dallas County. Democrats also seem poised to make significant inroads in Houston. In 2006, they won back six legislative seats to bring them much closer in number to Republicans in the Texas House of Representatives.

Democratic strategists are also encouraged by the state's growing population of ethnic minorities, particularly Hispanics. These voters tend to support Democratic candidates. In spring 2008 many Hispanics and African Americans were energized by the race for the Democratic presidential nominee and turned out in record numbers. Ethnic minorities now make up a majority of the state's population. The growing number of Hispanics could cause the phenomenon of **tipping**, in which growing numbers of a demographically significant group cause significant changes in the electorate. If Hispanic voters' energy and commitment to politics continue, a significant Democratic resurgence could occur.

Tipping
A phenomenon that occurs when a group that is becoming more numerous over time grows large enough to change the political balance in a district, state, or county.

DEALIGNMENT

There is also speculation that what is occurring in Texas is not realignment but *dealignment*, meaning that the voters are refusing to identify with either political party and are more inclined to call themselves independents. Evidence for dealignment comes from evaluating the percentage of voters engaging in *ticket splitting*—that is, voting for candidates of both parties in the general election rather than voting for all the candidates of one party or the other (a straight ticket). Increased numbers of ticket splitters suggest that dealignment is occurring. In 2008, perhaps in part because of the hotly contested presidential election between Barack Obama and John McCain, party identification increased. These figures could indicate that while some voters are becoming more independent, others are becoming more closely identified with one party or the other.

YOU CAN MAKE A Difference

GRASSROOTS POLITICS AT THE PRECINCT LEVEL

Have you ever wondered how politicians get their start? Chances are they become involved with a political party at the grassroots level. In Texas, as in many other states, the most basic level of partisan participation is the party precinct. Precincts are this country's smallest political unit and are generally composed of about 2,000 to 3,000 voters. Political activity at the precinct level involves personal face-to-face activity, such as registering voters in your precinct, attending the precinct conventions, and getting voters to the polls on election day.

WHY SHOULD YOU CARE?

Political participation is one of the most important principles of democracy. The American federal system provides many access points for participation; some would say the most important point of access is the local level. Through your involvement, you influence the leadership and activities of your party and, ultimately, the issues that directly affect your life. In a practical sense, a strong and vital precinct organization is a key component in building the success of your county or district and state party organizations.

WHAT CAN YOU DO?

Participating at the precinct level can include several activities, but one of the most important is participating in the precinct convention. In early March, during even-numbered years, both the Democratic and Republican parties in Texas hold their primary elections. Voters in the party primary may attend their party's precinct convention or caucus, which begins around 7:15 P.M. after the polls close at 7:00 P.M. Resolutions are passed, and delegates to the next level of party conventions (the county or senate district level) are selected. Because attendance is often sparse (2008 was an exception), an individual has a good chance of being heard and even being elected as a delegate. Delegates at the county or district level will pass more resolutions and will elect delegates to the state level. If you are persistent and lucky, you may be selected as a delegate to the state party convention. At this point, you will have become a significant player in politics.

For further information on Texas party conventions and events, leaders, rules, and issue positions, you can check the Web sites of both state political parties at:

Texas Democratic Party
www.txdemocrats.org

Texas Republican Party
www.texasgop.org

PRECINCTS ARE SMALL and few people attend party precinct conventions. You and a few of your neighbors can easily take control of them, elect delegates and pass resolutions to send to county or district conventions. (AP Photo/Harry Cabluck)

KEY TERMS

decentralization 756
direct primary 759
election judges 770
evangelical 765

grassroots 756
pragmatism 756
rump convention 768

single-member district
system 757
tipping 772

CHAPTER SUMMARY

1. Despite the hostility of the founders to them, political parties have become an important part of American political life. This is because parties perform critically important functions in a democracy. They nominate and elect their members to public office, educate and mobilize voters and provide them with cues on how to vote, and run the government at whatever level (local, state, or national) they are active.

2. In discussing political parties in the United States, we must look at three fundamental characteristics: (1) pragmatism, (2) decentralization, and (3) the effects of the two-party system. Pragmatism follows from the major goal of American parties, which is to build majority coalitions and win elections. This means that both Republican and Democratic Party candidates are often fuzzy on issues. The candidates try to accommodate many different interests and viewpoints and alienate as few voters as possible. Because there are few voters on the extremes, left or right, serious third parties have great difficulty developing and surviving, and they are often co-opted by one of the two major parties.

3. Parties are relatively decentralized, with much of the control of the nominating process (the primary) and party machinery in the hands of state and local voters and their leaders. In the recent past, however, both the Democratic and Republican national party organizations have increased their control over state and local parties because of their capacity to raise large amounts of money and provide various services. The McCain-Feingold Act of 2002 may end this trend by cutting off the flow of "soft money" to the major parties.

4. For much of its history, Texas was a one-party, Democratic state. Until recently, one-party dominance meant that the election to select the Democratic Party's nominees—the Democratic primary—was the most important election in Texas. Moderate and conservative factions within the Democratic Party became the key political players.

5. **Why was Texas politics dominated by the Democratic Party until the early 1990s?** Following the Civil War, the era of Reconstruction meant Northern troops occupied the South under the direction of a Republican Congress. Reacting to the occupation of federal troops and an unpopular Republican governor, E. J. Davis, Texans developed long-term ties to the Democratic Party. These ties were reinforced by the development of the direct primary as the method for nominating candidates and by the Great Depression of the 1930s.

6. **Why have a majority of Texans come to identify with the Republican Party?** After years of domination by the Democratic Party, Texas began to experience strong two-party competition. As a result, both parties strengthened their party machinery and made aggressive appeals to their traditional constituencies. The Republican Party rose to dominance in Texas in the 1970s and 1980s because of white conservative reaction to the civil rights policies of the national Democratic Party, the election of Ronald Reagan in 1980, the migration of Republican immigrants to Texas from other states, and the development of a more affluent middle class spurred by industrialization and urbanization. By the late 1990s, the Republicans had become the dominant party in Texas. The transition from a party system in which the Democrats were overwhelmingly dominant to a new system in which the Republicans have a clear edge can be described as a political realignment. The realignment process was foreshadowed in the 1950s by the Shivercrats—Democrats who advocated voting for Republican presidential candidates and conservative Democrats at the state level. After the 1960s, the Republicans slowly but surely gained strength at the state level. In 1978, they gained the governorship. By 2002, they controlled both chambers of the state legislature, and in 2004 they captured a majority in the state's congressional delegation. The Republicans will no doubt remain dominant in the foreseeable future.

7. **What developments could lead to a resurgence of support for the Texas Democratic Party?** Republicans have attracted voters in the expanding suburban areas of the state and have increased their appeal to white voters in rural areas. Democrats have attracted votes in inner cities and among ethnic minorities. The state's increasing ethnic diversity, specifically the increase in the Hispanic population, could thus augur well for the Democratic Party.

8. A second political mechanism that may be at work, in addition to realignment, is political dealignment. In this process, voters become detached from both political parties and begin to see themselves as independents.

SELECTED PRINT, MEDIA, AND ONLINE RESOURCES

PRINT RESOURCES

Black, Earl, and Merle Black. *The Rise of Southern Republicans*. Cambridge, MA: Harvard University Press, 2002. This book discusses the slow but sure rise of Republican strength in the previously solid Democratic South over the past five decades.

Burnham, Walter Dean. *Critical Elections and the Mainsprings of American Politics*. New York: W. W. Norton, 1970. This classic work develops the concept of critical elections and electoral realignments. According to Burnham, critical elections establish new dominant parties. Burnham's theories have been criticized on the ground that political realignments are not always tied to specific elections.

Davidson, Chandler. *Race and Class in Texas Politics*. Princeton, NJ: Princeton University Press, 1992. This work on Texas politics explores the complicated relations between the politically disorganized Texas blue-collar class and the wealthy elite and illustrates the tactics used by the latter to largely control policy making in the state.

Keefe, William J., and Marc J. Hetherington. *Parties, Politics, and Public Policy in America.* Washington, DC: Congressional Quarterly Press, 2003. This fine, up-to-date textbook examines the two-party system in America. The authors discuss how parties have changed and what role partisanship plays among the elites and among ordinary voters.

Key, V. O. *Southern Politics*. New York: Knopf, 1949. This classic work describes the one-party Democratic system that existed in the South until recent years.

Richards, David. *Once Upon a Time in Texas: A Liberal in the Lone Star State*. Austin: University of Texas Press, 2002. This is a lively account of the experiences of Texas liberals from the 1950s to the 1990s. It includes a description of policy battles and profiles of prominent politicians and journalists.

MEDIA RESOURCES

Giant—A 1956 film that tells the story of rival ranchers in Texas in the middle years of the 20th century. It stars Elizabeth Taylor, Rock Hudson, James Dean, and Carroll Baker.

Last Man Standing: Politics Texas Style—A 2004 PBS video that documents the successful challenge to a Republican incumbent legislator by a 24-year-old Democratic "upstart." It features comments by such important figures as George W. Bush strategist Karl Rove, former Democratic governor Ann Richards, and former president Bill Clinton appointees Henry Cisneros and Paul Begala.

Lone Star—A 1996 film that offers a realistic portrait of the political machine in a South Texas border town. The story involves characters from the middle and younger generations of three ethnic communities who uncover and confront the surprising truth about their elders' past.

ONLINE RESOURCES

Blog Search Engine indexes the blogosphere: www.blogsearchengine.com

Fagan Finder is intended as a gateway to the Internet with searching capability and acts as an exclusive directory only to high-quality Web sites and blogs. Like a guide, it tries to help you in your search experience: www.faganfinder.com/blogs

Home Pages of the Democratic and Republic Parties The two major political parties have Web sites both nationally and in Texas. Republicans in Texas: www.texasgop.org; Republicans nationally: www.gop.com; Democrats in Texas: www.txdemocrats.org; Democrats nationally: www.democrats.org.

Postcards: Texas Government and Politics Blog Many newspapers have political blogs. For example, Austin's *Statesman's* blog regularly discusses Texas government and politics: www.statesman.com/blogs/content/shared-gen/blogs/austin/politics/

Texas Politics The University of Texas offers an excellent Web site describing Texas politics in general. The unit on Texas political parties includes the history and functions of political parties in the state, as well as features such as graphs and video clips: texaspolitics.laits.utexas.edu

23

A December, 2009 rally in Houston for Democratic gubernatorial candidate Bill White. (AP Photo/David J. Phillip)

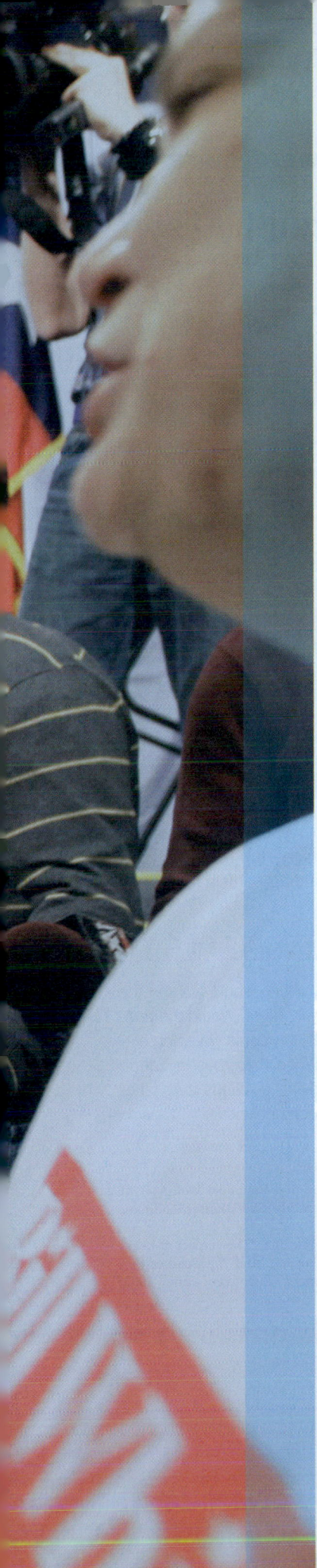

Voting and Elections in Texas

QUESTIONS TO CONSIDER

Why is voter turnout in Texas lower than it is in most other states?

What is the majority election rule, and why do we use it in Texas primaries?

Why are some candidates more likely than others to win elections in Texas?

CHAPTER CONTENTS

what if...

Voting Were Required by Law?

BACKGROUND

The 2008 presidential elections were fairly close. Nationally, Barack Obama received a 6.4 percent larger share of the votes than John McCain (or about 8 million more votes). Only about 61.6 percent of those who were eligible to vote actually did so, however. In Texas, about 54.4 percent of the eligible population turned out to vote.

In the United States and most other countries, voting is voluntary, and people can decide whether or not to go to the polls. In some countries, however, voting is mandatory. In Australia, for example, all citizens are required to vote. Those who do not vote risk a fine and even imprisonment. The same is true in a handful of other countries, including Belgium. Turnout in these countries (not surprisingly) is high.

POSSIBLE CHANGES RESULTING FROM MANDATORY VOTING

Suppose voting had been required by law in the 2008 presidential election. Would it have made a difference at the national level? In other words, would John McCain have emerged victorious? What about in Texas? John McCain took 55 percent of the Texas vote in 2008, but what would have happened if the 45.4 percent of the eligible population that did not vote had turned out?

Voters and nonvoters are different. Voters are on average better educated. They also tend to have better jobs and higher incomes. Not surprisingly, voters tend to be more Republican than nonvoters. It would seem to follow that if everyone voted, Democratic candidates would do better on election day. But is this true? Do Democrats stand to gain and Republicans to lose? We cannot be sure what would happen if everyone voted. Based on what we know about how people with certain characteristics vote, however, we can simulate how nonvoters would behave. Such an analysis suggests that most of the time, Democrats would gain more than Republicans, but by only a small margin.

There are two main reasons for this prediction. First, the differences in the preferences of voters and nonvot-

ers are actually not very great.* Second, nonvoters are more likely to be influenced by short-term forces such as the state of the economy.** Therefore, their support might go disproportionately to the victor. Expanding the voting population might merely widen the winner's margin. Some evidence for this argument comes from the presidential election of 2004, where voter turnout was up significantly from 2000. Democrat John Kerry received about 8 million more votes nationally in 2004 than Democrat Al Gore did in 2000, but George W. Bush received about 11.5 million more votes than he did four years previously.

WHAT IF EVERYONE VOTED IN TEXAS?

Even if the partisan balance at the national level remained largely unchanged, it might conceal some measure of variance among individuals, states, and localities. This may be especially true in states such as Texas. It would take a very large change to overcome the current state-level Republican dominance. In state legislative races, however, the parties are often more closely balanced, and turnout is much lower. In local races, turnout tends to be lower still. In such races, expanding participation could have significant effects.

FOR CRITICAL ANALYSIS

1. Consider whether mandatory voting would work in the United States and specifically in Texas. Would the public support mandatory voting? How could we enforce it?
2. Would mandatory voting change the types of candidates who run for office and the positions they take? Might it ultimately change public policies?

---

*See the report by Benjamin Highton and Raymond Wolfinger at www.igs.berkeley.edu/publications/par/July1999/HightonWolfinger .html.
**Glenn Mitchell II and Christopher Wlezien, "The Impact of Legal Constraints on Voter Registration, Turnout, and the Composition of the American Electorate," *Political Behavior*, June 1995, pp. 179–202.

DEMOCRACY MAKES DEMANDS on its citizens in terms of both time and finances. It takes time for voters to inform themselves about the large number of candidates who compete in the spring for nomination in the party primaries. Then in the November general election, roughly 4,200 of these nominees ask the Texas voters to elect them to local, state, and national offices.

Voting in elections is the most basic and common form of political participation, but other forms of participation exist as well. Many people discuss political issues with friends and coworkers, write letters to local representatives or to newspaper editors, distribute campaign literature, make contributions to campaigns, or place bumper stickers on their cars. Some people are members of interest groups, such as neighborhood or trade associations, or serve on political party committees or as delegates to conventions. Voting is fundamental, yet not everyone votes, as we point out in this chapter's *What If . . .* feature at the beginning of this chapter.

POLITICAL PARTICIPATION

Elections are a defining characteristic of representative democracies. We hold elected officials accountable through our votes. Votes are what matter to politicians, at least those interested in winning and holding office. If we vote—and thereby reward or punish elected officials for what they do while in office—politicians have an incentive to do what we want. If we do not vote, elected officials are largely free to do what they want. Clearly, voting is important in a representative democracy.

THE PARTICIPATION PARADOX

A problem with voting is that a single individual's vote usually does not make a difference in an election. Imagine that you voted in the 2010 Texas gubernatorial election. Did your vote matter? In other words, did your vote swing the election, ensuring Rick Perry's victory or dooming him to defeat? It did not. Governor Perry won reelection despite your vote.

Our individual votes rarely have any effect on the outcome, yet people still vote. Among political scientists, this is known as the **participation paradox**. The purpose for mentioning this paradox is not to say that you or other people should not vote. Rather, it is to point out that people vote for other reasons (and chiding people to vote because their votes "make a difference" probably is not very effective).

Participation Paradox
The fact that people vote even though their individual votes rarely influence the outcome of an election.

WHO VOTES?

Over the years, political scientists have learned much about why people go to the polls. It now is clear that a relatively small number of demographic and political variables are especially important.[1]

Education, Income, and Age. The most important demographic variables are education, income, and age. The more education a person has, the more likely the person is to vote. The same is true for income, regardless of how much education a person has. Age also matters. As people grow older, they are more likely to vote, at least until they become very old. Why do these factors matter? The answer is straightforward: People who are educated, have high incomes, and are older are more likely to care about, and pay attention to, politics. Thus, they are more likely to vote.

---

[1] Raymond E. Wolfinger and Steven Rosenstone, *Who Votes?* (New Haven, CT: Yale University Press, 1980). Also see Sydney Verba and Norman H. Nie, *Participation in America* (New York: Harper & Row, 1972).

A VOTER EXERCISING her right, together with a future voter. Children of voters also are likely to vote. Is this true in your case? Are your parents voters or nonvoters? Do you think it influences what you do? (AP Photo/La Salle News Tribune, Kemp Smith)

Interest in Politics and Partisan Identification. In addition to demographic factors, certain political factors influence the likelihood of voting, especially a person's expressed interest in politics and intensity of identification with a political party. The greater the interest in politics, the more likely a person is to vote. The effect is obvious but nevertheless quite important. A person who does not have much education or income still is very likely to vote if she or he has an intense interest in politics.

Identification with either of the political parties also makes a person more likely to vote. People who are strong partisan identifiers, on average, care much more about politics than those who do not identify with the parties. Parties also attempt to mobilize their identifiers—that is, the more you identify with a party, the more likely it is that you will be contacted by the party and its candidates during election campaigns.

Deciding to Vote. In one sense, deciding to vote is much like deciding to attend a sporting event such as a professional baseball game. We do not go to a game to affect the outcome. We go for other reasons, because we like baseball and care about it or the team(s) playing. The same is true for voting: Education, income, age, interest, and party identification are important indicators of our desire to participate.

While other factors may contribute to electoral participation, the small group of demographic and political variables just discussed tells us quite a bit. With this information, we can make a good prediction as to whether a person will or will not vote in a particular election. We also can account for most of the differences in turnout among different groups, such as African Americans, Asian Americans, Mexican Americans, and Anglo Americans.

THE PRACTICE OF VOTING

The legal qualifications for voting in Texas are surprisingly few and simple. Anyone who meets the following requirements is eligible to register and vote in Texas:

1. Be a citizen of the United States.
2. Be at least 18 years of age.
3. Be a resident of the state.

The only individuals prohibited from voting in Texas are those who have been declared "mentally incompetent" in formal court proceedings and those convicted of a felony whose civil rights have not been restored by a pardon or by the passage of two calendar years from the completion of the sentence.

Registration. Meeting these qualifications does not mean that a person can simply walk into the voting booth on election day. To vote, a person must be registered. As a result of the Voting Rights Acts of 1965 and 1970, several United States Supreme Court rulings, and recent congressional action, the registration procedure is almost as simple as voting itself. A person may register in person or by mail at any time of the year up to 30 days before the election. Since the passage of federal "motor voter" legislation, a person can also register when renewing a driver's license; every person renewing a driver's license is asked whether he or she wants to register. Spouses, parents, or offspring also can register the applicant, provided they are qualified voters.

The present Texas registration system is as open and modern as that of any other state that requires advance registration. (Note that a number of states, including Maine, Minnesota, and Wisconsin, permit election day registration, while North Dakota requires no registration at all. There, you simply walk in, show your identification, and vote.) The Texas system, established by law in 1975, provides for the mailing of a new two-year voter-registration certificate to every registered voter by January 1 in even-numbered years. The system is permanent; once a voter is on the rolls, he or she will not be removed unless the nonforwardable certificate is returned. Since 1977, Texas law requires the secretary of state to make postage-free registration applications available at any county clerk's office. They are also available at various other public offices.

The "Strike List." Names on returned certificates are stricken from the list of eligible voters and placed on a "strike list." The strike list is attached to the list of voters for each precinct. What if you move? For three months, registered voters who have moved and whose names are therefore on the strike list can vote in their old precincts—provided they have filled out a new voter-registration card for the new residence. They can vote, however, only for those offices that both residences have in common. Coroner's death reports, lists of felony convictions, and adjudications of mental incompetence are also used to purge the list of eligible voters.

Residency Requirements. Establishing residence for voting is no longer a matter of living at a place for a specified time. Residence is defined primarily in terms of intent (that is, people's homes are where they intend them to be). No delay in qualifying to vote is permitted under United States Supreme Court rulings, except for a short period of time during which the application is processed and the registrant's name is entered on the rolls. Under a federal court ruling, that delay in Texas is fixed at 30 days.[2]

Voting. Once a person is registered, voting is easy. This is especially true in Texas, which has passed laws to make voting easier. In 1975, for example, the legislature required that all ballots and election materials be printed in Spanish as well as English in counties with a Hispanic population of 5 percent or more. In 1991, the legislature established early voting, which allows people to vote at several different sites before election day.[3]

VOTER TURNOUT IN THE UNITED STATES AND TEXAS

Easier registration and voting was expected to result in increased *voter turnout*—that is, the proportion of Americans who vote. Many people believe that, instead, voter turnout has fallen during recent decades. Political scientists and pundits alike have made this claim. Some commentators have blamed the falling turnout on negative campaigning and broad public cynicism about the political process. The upturn in voter turnout during the 2004 presidential elections has tended to put this issue to rest, at least for now.

---

[2]*Beare v. Smith*, 321 F.Supp. 1100 (1971). In later cases—*Burns v. Fortson*, 410 U.S. 686 (1973) and *Martson v. Lewis*, 410 U.S. 679 (1973)—the United States Supreme Court upheld delays of up to 50 days in Georgia and Arizona.
[3]Texas was one of the first states to institute early voting for all voters.

IS VOTER TURNOUT DECLINING?

Voting-Age Population (VAP)
The total number of persons in the United States or a state who are 18 years of age or older, regardless of citizenship, military status, felony conviction, or mental state.

Is it true that voter turnout had been declining in the years before 2004? If you look at the percentage of the **voting-age population (VAP)** that actually cast a ballot, there seems to be some evidence of this decline. The national voter turnout as measured by the voting-age population is shown by the green bars in Figure 23–1.

One problem with using the VAP figure to gauge voter turnout is that it is not a very accurate measure of the number of *eligible voters*. The VAP figure includes felons who have lost the right to vote. Above all, it includes new immigrants who are not yet citizens. Finally, it does not include Americans living abroad, who can cast absentee ballots. As we stated in Chapter 9, the national voting-age population in 2008 was 231 million people. The number of eligible voters, however, was only 213 million. We call this second, more accurate figure the **vote-eligible population (VEP)**. Using the VEP measure, voter turnout in 2008 was not 56.9 percent, as it is sometimes reported, but 61.6 percent.

Vote-Eligible Population (VEP)
The total number of persons actually eligible to cast a ballot, excluding noncitizens, felons, and other ineligible persons but including citizens who are temporarily abroad (and who may vote absentee).

As you read in Chapter 1, the United States has experienced high rates of immigration in recent decades. Political scientists Michael McDonald and Samuel Popkin argue that the apparent decline in voter turnout since 1972 is entirely a function of the increasing size of the ineligible population, chiefly due to immigration. Voter turnout as measured by McDonald and Popkin using VEP figures that they have calculated is shown by the upper (orange) bars in Figure 23–1. (Even if voter turnout has not declined in the United States, however, it is low by international standards, as we explain in this chapter's *Beyond Our Borders* feature.)

Midterm Elections. The national elections that take place halfway between presidential elections are called *midterm elections*. Voter turnout for midterm elections is substantially lower than for presidential elections, even though many states—including Texas—choose their governors in these elections. As measured by VEP, presidential election turnout has fluctuated around an average of 55 percent since 1972. Turnout for the midterm elections has been more constant, rarely moving very far from an average of 40 percent.[4]

Young Voters. As we have observed, young people are much less likely to vote than the average American. Since 1972, citizens in the 18- to 20-year-old age group have rarely posted turnout rates as high as 40 percent, even in a presidential year. In fact, there is some evidence that turnout rates among the youngest voters have fallen since 1972, reaching a low point of 30 percent in 2000. Young citizens increased their turnout markedly in 2004, however (as did all other groups). In 2004, turnout among the 18- to 24-year-old age group rose by almost 6 percentage points over 2000.[5] It was up another 2 points in 2008.

VOTER TURNOUT IN TEXAS

In past years, voter turnout in Texas (and in most of the South) has been consistently lower than the turnout nationwide. Figure 23–3 on page 785 shows that turnout in Texas (as measured by VEP) has tracked national turnout but has regularly been 6

---

[4]Michael P. McDonald and Samuel Popkin, "The Myth of the Vanishing Voter," *American Political Science Review*, Vol. 95, No. 4, 2001, p. 966.
[5]Ibid. For 2004 figures, see reports issued by the Center for Information and Research on Civic Learning and Engagement (CIRCLE) at www.civicyouth.org.

FIGURE 23–1 U.S. Voter Turnout in Presidential Elections Since 1948

This figure shows voter turnout in presidential elections based both on the vote-eligible population (VEP) and on the voting-age population (VAP). Note that a drop-off in voter turnout took place in 1972, in part because the minimum voting age was lowered to 18 and young people are less likely to vote. As measured by the more accurate VEP figure, turnout since then has gone up and down but has shown no consistent tendency to drop.

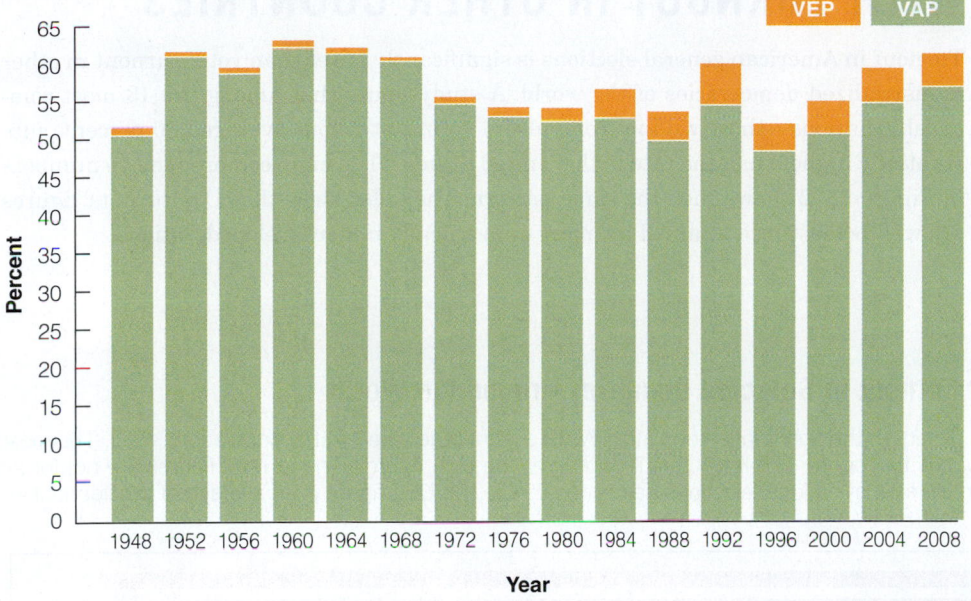

Sources: Data through 2000 are from Michael P. McDonald and Samuel Popkin, "The Myth of the Vanishing Voter," *American Political Science Review*, Vol. 95, No. 4, 2001, p. 963–974. The 2004 and 2008 figures are from the United States Elections Project and are available at elections.gmu.edu/voter_turnout.htm

to 7 percentage points lower than the national number. In 2004, only two states posted lower turnout rates than Texas, and the same was true in 2008.

Turnout for midterm elections in Texas shows a greater amount of variation. Since 1982, it has fluctuated between 30 and 40 percent. The turnout rate was especially good in 1990 and 1994, at 36.2 percent and 38.9 percent, respectively. These relatively high figures may have resulted from fierce competition between Republicans and Democrats at the state level in those years.[6] In 2006, turnout actually dropped to 31% despite the open field of four candidates, which included not only Republican governor Perry and Democrat challenger Chris Bell but two independent candidates as well— Republican state comptroller Carole Keeton Strayhorn (who ran as an independent) and singer-writer Kinky Friedman. In 2010 voter participation rose just slightly to 32.2 percent.

REASONS FOR LOW VOTER TURNOUT IN TEXAS

Most Texans probably think that Texas is in the mainstream of American society. Why, then, is there such a difference between Texas and other urbanized and industrialized

[6]Michael P. McDonald, "State Turnout Rates among Those Eligible to Vote," *State Politics and Policy Quarterly*, Vol. 2, No. 2, 2002. The 2002 and 2004 figures are from the United States Elections Project and are available at elections.gmu.edu/voter_turnout.htm.

Beyond Our Borders

AMERICAN VOTER TURNOUT COMPARED WITH TURNOUT IN OTHER COUNTRIES

Turnout in American general elections is significantly lower than voter turnout in other industrialized democracies of the world. A study found that among the 13 most comparable nations—those without compulsory voting—turnout averaged 80 percent, substantially higher than the rate in the United States.* The more comprehensive numbers in Figure 23–2 show much the same pattern. They also show that U.S. turnout figures are well below those attained by many economically underdeveloped nations.

FIGURE 23–2 Voter Turnout in Selected Countries Around the World

The turnout figures given here are based on the voting-age population (VAP) and not the vote-eligible population (VEP). The extent to which this makes a difference varies by country (we know that it depresses the U.S. figure). The turnout figures are not for any particular election but represent an average of national elections held since 1945. The U.S. figure is an average of presidential and midterm elections.

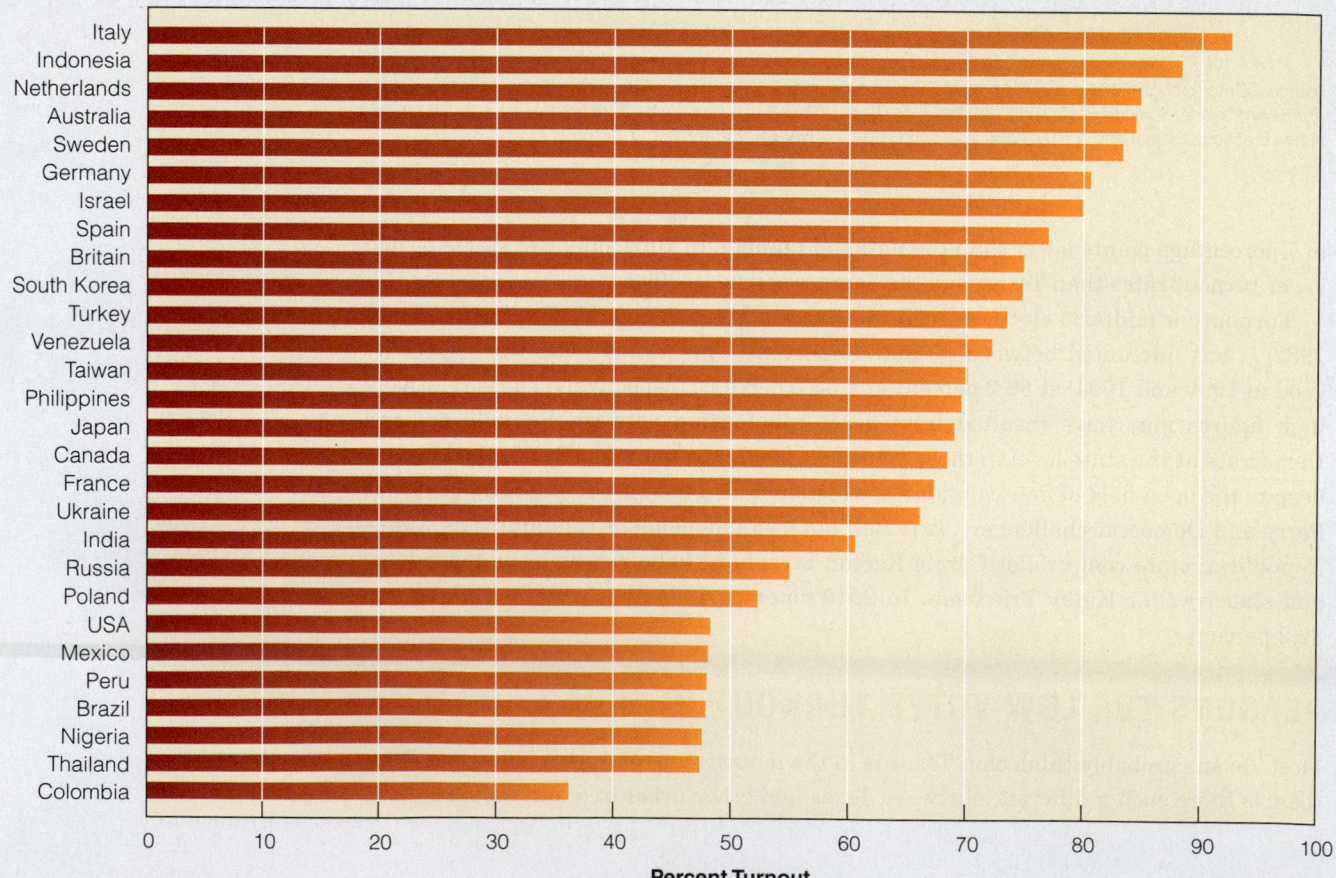

Source: International Institute for Democracy and Electoral Assistance, *Voter Turnout since 1945: A Global Report* (Stockholm, Sweden, 2002). The specific data shown above are available at www.idea.int/vt/index.cfm.

Some have argued that Americans are less likely to vote than Europeans because welfare spending is much lower (on a per capita basis) in the United States than in most European countries. Because low-income persons in the United States are less likely to depend on government spending than low-income persons in Europe, they have less of an incentive to follow politics and may find it easier to believe that election results are irrelevant to their lives. As we have seen, low-income persons are less likely to vote than high-income individuals.

FOR CRITICAL ANALYSIS

Political observers often wonder about whether who votes matters. We know that low-income citizens are less likely to vote in the United States than in other countries and less likely in Texas than in other states.

1. What consequences does this have for policy?
2. Do politicians in the United States and especially Texas have much incentive to represent the interests of the poor?

*G. Bingham Powell, Jr., "American Voter Turnout in Comparative Perspective," *American Political Science Review*, Vol. 80, March 1986, pp. 17, 23.

FIGURE 23–3 Texas Versus National Voter Turnout

The chart shows turnout in presidential election years since 1980. The figures do not appear to show any long-term trend upward or downward, though some elections have clearly been more interesting to the voters than others. The difference between the Texas voting-age population (VAP) and vote-eligible population (VEP) figures has grown, primarily because of a growing number of noncitizen residents.

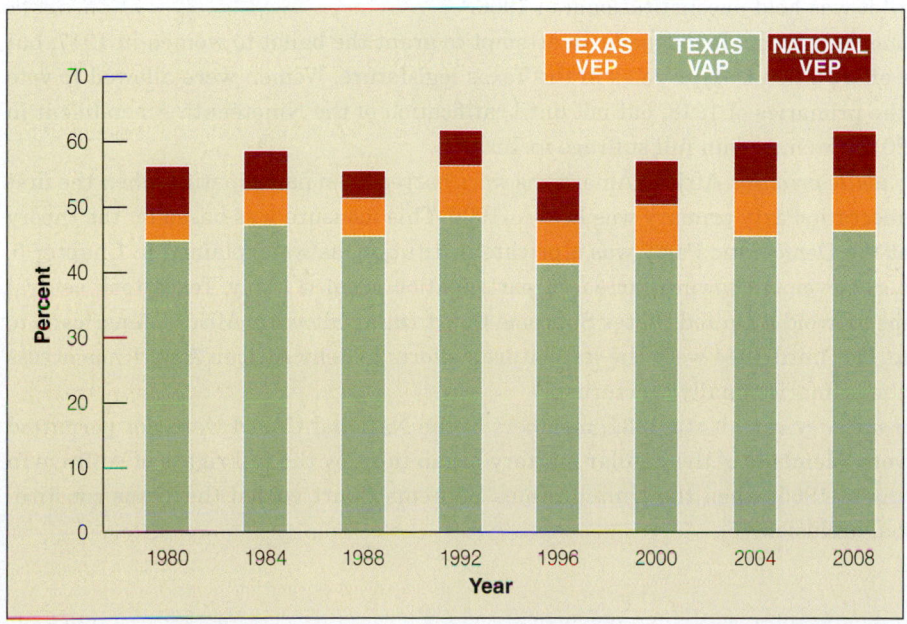

Sources: National VEP figures through 2000 are from Michael P. McDonald and Samuel Popkin, "The Myth of the Vanishing Voter," *American Political Science Review*, Vol. 95, No. 4, 2001, p. 963–974. Texas VEP and VAP figures are from Michael P. McDonald, 'State Turnout Rates among Those Eligible to Vote,' *State Politics and Policy Quarterly*, Vol. 2, No. 2, 2002. All 2004 figures are from the United States Elections Project and are available at elections.gmu.edu/voter_turnout.htm

states in political behavior? Why is Texas closer to the states of the Deep South in voter turnout? The answer may lie in its laws, socioeconomic characteristics, political structure, and political culture.

Legal Constraints. Traditionally, scholars interested in the variation in turnout across the American states have focused on laws regulating registration and voting. Clearly, the most important of these laws were restrictions on who was allowed to vote, such as the poll tax, property ownership requirements, and the outright exclusion of African Americans and women.

Although these restrictions disappeared some time ago, other barriers to registration and voting persisted, and some remain in effect today.[7] We can ask: Does a state promote political participation by setting the minimum necessary limitations and making it as convenient as possible for the individual to vote? Or does a state repeatedly place barriers on the way to the polls, making the act of voting physically, financially, and psychologically as difficult as the local sense of propriety will allow? There is no doubt into which category Texas once fell; the application has been uneven, but historically Texas was among the most restrictive states of the Union in its voting laws.

Today, nearly all of these restrictions have been abolished by amendments to the U.S. Constitution, changes to state and national laws, rulings by the U.S. Department of Justice, and judicial decisions. Even a cursory examination of the restrictions and the conditions under which they were removed makes us appreciate the extent to which Texas elections were at one time closed. Consider these changes in Texas voting policies:

1. *Poll tax.* The payment of a poll tax was made a prerequisite for voting in 1902. The cost was $1.75 ($1.50 plus $0.25 optional for the county) and represented more than a typical day's wages at that time. Many poor Texans were therefore kept from voting. When the Twenty-fourth Amendment was ratified in 1964, it voided the poll tax in national elections. Texas was one of only two states to keep it for state elections, until it was held unconstitutional in 1966.[8]

2. *Women's suffrage.* Texas made an attempt to grant the ballot to women in 1917, but the effort failed by four votes in the Texas legislature. Women were allowed to vote in the primaries of 1918, but not until ratification of the Nineteenth Amendment in 1920 did women gain full suffrage in Texas.

3. *The white primary.* African Americans were barred from participating when the first Democratic Party primary was held in 1906. This measure was based on the theory that the Democratic Party was a private institution, as we explained in Chapter 5. When movement toward increased participation seemed likely, Texas took several steps to avoid a United States Supreme Court ruling allowing African Americans to vote. Not until 1944 were the legislature's efforts to deny African Americans access to the primaries finally overturned.[9]

4. *The military vote.* Until 1931, members of the National Guard were not permitted to vote. Members of the regular military began to enjoy the full rights of suffrage in Texas in 1965, when the United States Supreme Court voided the Texas constitutional exclusion.[10]

[7]See Glenn Mitchell II and Christopher Wlezien, "The Impact of Legal Constraints on Voter Registration, Turnout, and the Composition of the American Electorate," *Political Behavior*, June 1995, pp. 179–202.
[8]*U.S. v. Texas*, 384 U.S. 155 (1966).
[9]*Smith v. Allwright*, 321 U.S. 649 (1944).
[10]*Carrington v. Rash*, 380 U.S. 89 (1965).

5. *Long residence requirement.* The Texas residency requirement of one year in the state and six months in the county was modified slightly by the legislature to allow new residents to vote in the presidential part of the ballot, but not until a United States Supreme Court ruling in 1972 were such requirements abolished altogether.[11]

6. *Property ownership.* Texas required property ownership for voting in bond elections until the United States Supreme Court ruled out property ownership as a requirement for revenue bond elections in 1969[12] and for tax elections in 1969 and in 1975.[13]

7. *Annual registration.* Even after the poll tax was voided, Texas continued to require voters to register every year until annual registration was prohibited by the federal courts in 1971.[14]

8. *Early registration.* Texas voters were required to meet registration requirements by January 31, earlier than the cutoff date for candidates' filings and more than nine months before the general election. This restriction was also voided in 1971.[15]

9. *Jury duty.* Texas law provided that the names of prospective jurors must be drawn from the voting rolls. Some Texans did not want to serve on juries, and not registering to vote ensured against a jury summons. (Texas counties now use driver's licenses for jury lists.)

Texas used almost every technique available except the literacy test and the grandfather clause[16] to deny the vote to some citizens or to make voting time consuming, expensive, and psychologically difficult. This is not the case today. Most barriers to voting in Texas have been removed. In fact, as mentioned previously, the legislature has instituted provisions that make voting easier than in most states. Thus, the laws in Texas may help us understand why turnout was low in the past and, with the relaxing of restrictions, why turnout has increased somewhat since 1960. The current laws do not help us understand why turnout in Texas remains low today. For this, we need to look elsewhere.

DID YOU KNOW?

That Texas has the nation's eighth largest percentage of people living in poverty—more than 16 percent in 2007?

Socioeconomic Factors. Texas, with its cattle barons and oil tycoons, is known as the land of the "big rich." What is not so well known is that Texas is also the land of the "big poor." While nationally the proportion of people living below the poverty level in 2007 was 13 percent, in Texas the proportion was 16.3 percent. More than 25 percent of African American and Mexican American Texans have incomes below the poverty level. Nearly 4 million individuals in Texas live in poverty, and more than 1 million of these are children. Understandably, formal educational achievement also is low. Of all Texans who are older than age 25, one out of four has not graduated from high school. Among African Americans, the ratio is slightly less than one out of three, and among Mexican Americans it is almost one out of two.[17]

Given that income and education are such important determinants of electoral participation, low voter turnout is exactly what we should expect in Texas. Because income and education levels are particularly low among African Americans and especially Mexican Americans, turnout is particularly low for these groups. Voting by Texas minorities is on the rise, however, and this has led to much greater representation of both groups in elected offices, as we will see. These trends should continue as income and education levels among minorities increase.

[11]*Dunn v. Blumstein*, 405 U.S. 330 (1972).

[12]*Kramer v. Union Free District*, No. 15, 395 U.S. 621 (1969).

[13]*Cipriano v. City of Houma*, 395 U.S. 701 (1969); and *Hill v. Stone*, 421 U.S. 289 (1975).

[14]*Beare v. Smith*, 321 F.Supp. 1100 (1971).

[15]Ibid.

[16]Grandfather clauses were found unconstitutional by the United States Supreme Court in *Guinn v. United States*, 238 U.S. 347 (1915).

[17]U.S. Census Bureau. The definition of poverty depends on the size and composition of the family. For a family of four, two of whom are children, the poverty-level threshold in 2007 was $21,027.

Political Structure. Another deterrent to voting in Texas is the length of the ballot and the number of different elections. Texas uses a long ballot that provides for the popular election of a large number of public officers. (Critics believe that some of these officers should be appointed rather than elected.) In an urban county, the ballot may call for the voter to choose among 150 and 200 candidates vying for 50 or more offices. The frequency of referendums on constitutional amendments also contributes to the length of the ballot in Texas. In addition, voters are asked to go to the polls for various municipal, school board, bond, and special district elections. Government simply is far more fragmented in Texas than in other states, and this makes particular elections less meaningful and perhaps more frustrating to voters.

Political Culture. Low voter turnout in Texas may be partly due to the state's political culture. Texas citizens may be less likely to vote than citizens of other states because many Texans do not value political participation in itself and tend to think that they have little role to play in politics.

PRIMARY, GENERAL, AND SPECIAL ELECTIONS IN TEXAS

Winning an office typically is a two-stage process. First, the candidate must win the Democratic or Republican nomination in the primary election. Second, the candidate must win the general election against the nominee of the other party. It is possible for a candidate to get on the general-election ballot without winning a primary election (as we explain shortly), but this is rare. As in most other states, elections in Texas are dominated by the Democratic and Republican parties.

PRIMARY ELECTIONS

Three devices for selecting political party nominees have been used in U.S. history, each perceived as a cure for the ills of a previous system that was considered corrupt, inefficient, or inadequate. The first was the *caucus*, consisting of the elected party members serving in the legislature. The "insider" politics of the caucus room motivated the reformers of the Jacksonian era to institute the party convention system in 1828. In this system, ordinary party members select delegates to a party convention, and these delegates then nominate the party's candidates for office and write a party platform. The convention system was hailed as a surefire method of ending party nominations by the legislative bosses.

The Direct Primary. By 1890, however, the backroom politics of the convention halls again moved reformers to action, and the result was the direct primary, which most states adopted between 1890 and 1920. The first direct primary in Texas was held in 1906, under the Terrell Election Law (passed in 1903). This law enables party members to participate directly in their party's selection of candidates to represent them in the general election.

The White Primary. Traditionally regarded as private activities, primaries were at one time largely beyond the concern of legislatures and courts. Costs of party activities, including primaries, were paid through donations and through assessments of candidates who sought a party's nomination. Judges attempted to avoid suits among warring factions of the parties in the same way that they avoided those suits involving church squabbles over the division of church property. On the basis of the theory that primaries were private activities, the United States Supreme Court in 1935 upheld the decision of the Texas Democratic Party convention to continue barring African Americans from participating in the Democratic Party primary.[18]

Recognizing that political party activities were increasingly circumscribed by law, the Court reversed itself in 1944 and threw out the white primary system.[19] The Court argued that in a one-party state, which Texas was at the time, the party primary may be the only election in which any meaningful choice is possible. Because the Democratic Party seldom had any real opposition in the general election, winning the nomination was, for all practical purposes, winning the office. Therefore, African Americans could not constitutionally be prevented from participating in the primary.

Who Must Hold a Primary? Texas, like most other states, has for decades required that major political parties—those whose candidates for governor received a fixed minimum number of votes in the last general election—select their nominees through the primary. Other parties, however, were at one time allowed to nominate candidates by primary or convention, whichever they chose. In 1973, the Texas legislature amended the Texas election code to provide that any party receiving 20 percent or more of the gubernatorial vote must hold a primary, and that all other parties must use the convention system.[20]

Limits on New Parties. New parties must meet additional requirements if their nominees are to be on the general-election ballot. In addition to holding a convention, these parties must file with the secretary of state a list of supporters equal to 1 percent of the total vote for governor in the last general election. The list may consist of the names of those who participated in the party's convention, those who signed a nominating petition, or a combination of the two groups. Persons named as supporters must be registered voters who have not participated in the activities (primaries or conventions) of either of the two major parties. Each page (though not each name) on the nominating petition must be notarized. This requirement is, as intended, difficult to meet and therefore inhibits the creation of new political parties.

Financing the Primaries. From their beginning in 1906 through 1970, the Texas political party primaries were financed under the **user-benefit theory**, in which users paid the cost through fees or assessments. The users were those who sought to become their party's nominees for public office. For all statewide and some local offices, nominal fixed-dollar fees were assessed. The major costs of the primaries were borne by candidates for district, county, and precinct offices. The county executive committees assessed candidates on the basis of the estimated costs of the primaries in their respective counties.

Since 1971, however, primary elections have been funded mostly from the state treasury. State and county executive committees initially make the expenditures, but the secretary of state reimburses each committee for the difference between the filing fees collected and the actual cost of the primary. To get on the primary ballot, a candidate need only file an application with the state or county party chair and pay the prescribed fee. The categories of fees, applicable also for special elections, are summarized in Table 23–1.

Getting on the Ballot through a Petition. So that no person is forced to bear an unreasonable expense when running for political office, the legislature (prodded by the federal courts) provided the petition as an alternative to the filing fee. For those seeking nomination to statewide office, the petition must bear the names of 5,000 voters. For district and lesser

User-Benefit Theory
The principle that the people who benefit from certain types of governmental services should also be the ones to pay the costs for those services.

---

[18]*Grovey v. Townsend*, 295 U.S. 45 (1935).
[19]*Smith v. Allwright*, 321 U.S. 649 (1944).
[20]La Raza Unida Party challenged this limitation. The U.S. Justice Department and federal courts sustained the challenge, but only as applied to La Raza Unida, which was permitted to conduct a primary in 1978. Otherwise, the law stands as written.

TABLE 23–1 Fees for Appearing on a Party Primary Ballot in Texas

OFFICE	FEE SCHEDULE
U.S. senator	$5,000
Texas statewide officers	$3,750
U.S. representative	$3,125
State senator	$1,250
State representative	$750
County commissioner	$750–$1,250
District judge	$1,500–$2,500
Justice of the peace, constable	$375–$1,000
County surveyor	$75

offices, the number of signatures must equal 2 percent of the votes cast for the party's candidate for governor in the last election, up to a maximum of 500 required signatures. A sample county primary ballot is reproduced in Figure 23–4.

Administering Primaries. In a county primary, the chair and the county executive committee of each party receive applications and filing fees and hold drawings to determine the order of names on the ballot for both party and government offices. They then certify the ballot, select an election judge for each voting precinct (usually the precinct chair), select the voting devices (paper ballots, voting machines, or punch cards), and arrange for polling places and for printing. After the primary, the county chair and the executive committee canvass (count) the votes and certify the results to their respective state executive committees.

In the state primaries, the state party chair and the state executive committee of each political party receive applications of candidates for state offices, conduct drawings to determine the order of names, certify the ballot to the county-level officials, and canvass the election returns after the primary.

The Dual Primary. In Texas, as in other Southern states that once had a Democratic one-party system (except Tennessee and Virginia), nominations are decided by a majority (50 percent plus one) of the popular vote. If no candidate receives a majority of votes cast for a particular office in the first primary, a second **runoff primary** is required, in which the two candidates receiving the highest number of votes are pitted against each other.

Primary elections in Texas usually are held on the second Tuesday in March of even-numbered years. The runoff primary is scheduled for the second Tuesday in April, roughly a month after the initial primary election. Although there are earlier presidential primaries, no other state schedules primaries to nominate candidates for state offices so far in advance of the general election in November.

Presidential Aspirations and Early Primaries. Until 1960, the primaries were held much later in the year, on the fourth Saturday in July and the fourth Saturday in August. The dates were moved up so that presidential aspirant Lyndon B. Johnson could "lock up" his renomination to the U.S. Senate before the Democratic National Convention began in Los Angeles.

Runoff Primary
A second primary election that pits the two top vote-getters from the first primary against each other. Such an election is held in states such as Texas when the winner of the first primary did not receive a majority of the votes.

FIGURE 23–4 Sample Ballot for 2006 Republican Party Primary Election

Vote Both Sides   *Vote en Ambos Lados de la Página*

March 7, 2006 Joint Primary Election
Elección Primaria Junta 7 de marzo de 2006
Travis County
Condado de Travis
March 07, 2006 - *07 Marzo 2006*   **Precinct** *Precinto* **REP SAMPLE**

Instruction Note:
Use a BLUE or BLACK pen to mark your ballot. To vote, completely fill in the square to the left of your candidate or proposition choice. To vote for a write-in candidate, completely fill in the square to the left of "Write-in" and enter the name of the certified write-in candidate on the line provided.

Nota de Instruccion:
Marque su boleta con una pluma negra o azul. Para votar, llene completamente el espacio cuadrado a la izquierda del nombre del candidato o selección de proposición de su preferencia. Para votar por un candidato por voto escrito, llene completamente el espacio cuadrado a la izquierda de Voto Escrito y escriba el nombre del candidato certificado en la linea provista.

UNITED STATES SENATOR - REP
SENADOR DE LOS ESTADOS UNIDOS - REP
☐ Kay Bailey Hutchison

DISTRICT 10, UNITED STATES REPRESENTATIVE - REP
DISTRITO NÚM. 10, REPRESENTANTE DE LOS ESTADOS UNIDOS - REP
☐ Michael T. McCaul

DISTRICT 21, UNITED STATES REPRESENTATIVE - REP
DISTRITO NÚM. 21, REPRESENTANTE DE LOS ESTADOS UNIDOS - REP
☐ Lamar Smith

GOVERNOR - REP
GOBERNADOR - REP
☐ Rhett R. Smith
☐ Larry Kilgore
☐ Rick Perry
☐ Star Locke

LIEUTENANT GOVERNOR - REP
GOBERNADOR TENIENTE -REP
☐ David Dewhurst
☐ Tom Kelly

ATTORNEY GENERAL - REP
PROCURADOR GENERAL - REP
☐ Greg Abbott

COMPTROLLER OF PUBLIC ACCOUNTS - REP
CONTRALOR DE CUENTAS PÚBLICAS - REP
☐ Susan Combs

COMMISSIONER OF THE GENERAL LAND OFFICE - REP
COMISIONADO DE LA OFICINA GENERAL DE TIERRAS - REP
☐ Jerry Patterson

COMMISSIONER OF AGRICULTURE - REP
COMISIONADO DE AGRICULTURA - REP
☐ Todd Staples

RAILROAD COMMISSIONER - REP
COMISIONADO DE FERROCARRILES - REP
☐ Major Buck Werner
☐ Elizabeth Ames Jones

CHIEF JUSTICE, SUPREME COURT, UNEXPIRED TERM - REP
JUEZ PRESIDENTE, CORTE SUPREMA, DURACIÓN RESTANTE DEL CARGO - REP
☐ Wallace Jefferson

PLACE 2, JUSTICE, SUPREME COURT - REP
LUGAR NÚM. 2, JUEZ, CORTE SUPREMA - REP
☐ Steve Smith
☐ Don Willett

PLACE 4, JUSTICE, SUPREME COURT - REP
LUGAR NÚM. 4, JUEZ, CORTE SUPREMA - REP
☐ David M. Medina

PLACE 6, JUSTICE, SUPREME COURT - REP
LUGAR NÚM. 6, JUEZ, CORTE SUPREMA - REP
☐ Nathan Hecht

PLACE 8, JUSTICE, SUPREME COURT, UNEXPIRED TERM - REP
LUGAR NÚM. 8, JUEZ, CORTE SUPREMA, DURACIÓN RESTANTE DEL CARGO - REP
☐ Phil Johnson

PRESIDING JUDGE, COURT OF CRIMINAL APPEALS - REP
JUEZ PRESIDENTE, CORTE DE APELACIONES CRIMINALES - REP
☐ Sharon Keller
☐ Tom Price

PLACE 7, JUDGE, COURT OF CRIMINAL APPEALS - REP
LUGAR NÚM. 7, JUEZ, CORTE DE APELACIONES CRIMINALES - REP
☐ Barbara Parker Hervey

PLACE 8, JUDGE, COURT OF CRIMINAL APPEALS - REP
JUEZ, CORTE DE APELACIONES CRIMINALES, LUGAR NÚM. 8 - REP
☐ Robert W. Francis
☐ Charles Holcomb
☐ Terry Keel

DISTRICT 5, MEMBER, STATE BOARD OF EDUCATION - REP
DISTRITO NÚM. 5, MIEMBRO DE LA JUNTA ESTATAL DE EDUCACIÓN PÚBLICA - REP
☐ Ken Mercer
☐ Mark Loewe
☐ Dan Montgomery

DISTRICT 10, MEMBER, STATE BOARD OF EDUCATION - REP
DISTRITO NÚM. 10, MIEMBRO DE LA JUNTA ESTATAL DE EDUCACIÓN PÚBLICA - REP
☐ Tony Dale
☐ Cythnia Dunbar

STATE SENATOR, DISTRICT 25 - REP
SENADOR ESTATAL, DISTRITO NÚM. 25 - REP
☐ Jeff Wentworth

DISTRICT 47, STATE REPRESENTATIVE - REP
DISTRITO NÚM. 47, REPRESENTANTE ESTATAL - REP
☐ Dick Reynolds
☐ Bill Welch
☐ Rich Phillips
☐ Terry Dill
☐ Alex Castano

DISTRICT 48, STATE REPRESENTATIVE - REP
DISTRITO NÚM. 48, REPRESENTANTE ESTATAL - REP
☐ Ben Bentzin

Sample Ballot   Sample Ballot

Vote Both Sides   *Vote en Ambos Lados de la Página*

(Courtesy of Travis County, Texas)

The presidential ambitions of another Texan, vice president George H. W. Bush, contributed to the adoption of an even earlier primary. Believing an early primary victory in Texas would benefit their candidate, Bush's Republican supporters joined conservative Democrats in urging Texas to join most other Southern states holding a regional primary on Super Tuesday. In a special session in 1986, the Texas legislature rescheduled the primary to nominate all state officials on the second Tuesday in March in both presidential and midterm election years. In 1996, Super Tuesday included primary elections in Florida, Louisiana, Mississippi, Oklahoma, Oregon, Tennessee, and Texas. (In later years, several states made further changes to their primary schedules, and these changes broke up the Super Tuesday primary.) By 2008, most states already had their primaries before March, but Texas (and Ohio, which held its primary on the same day) may have had a bigger impact on the process than in previous years. Both Texas and Ohio went for Hillary Clinton, temporarily disrupting Barack Obama's path to the Democratic nomination. The states also sealed the nomination for Republican presidential candidate John McCain.

Turnout in Primaries. Turnout in Texas primaries is much lower than in general elections. Take 2002, for example: Although 4.5 million Texans voted in the general election, only 1.6 million participated in either the Democratic or the Republican primary—that is, approximately 12 percent of the vote-eligible population. Matters were even worse in 2006, when 1.2 million people, less than 10 percent of the eligible population, voted in either primary. Turnout in presidential election years is higher but still averages below 30 percent. Participation was up in 2008, especially for the Democrats, as 2.9 million citizens turned out to support either Obama or Clinton. Another 1.4 million voted in the much-less-competitive Republican primary in that year. The people who vote in primary elections are not representative of the overall population: They tend to be better educated, more affluent, and more ideologically extreme.

Open versus Closed Primaries. Party primaries are defined as either open or closed. These terms specify whether or not participation is limited to party members. Because the purpose of a primary is to choose the party's nominee, it would seem logical to exclude anyone who is not a party member. Not every state accepts this argument, however. Alaska and Washington used to have a blanket primary, in which voters could "mix and match" among the various parties' candidates, but the United States Supreme Court declared it unconstitutional in 2004. Seven states have an *open primary*, in which voters decide at the polls in which primary they will participate. Texas and the remaining 40 states use what is called a *closed primary*.

The Closed Primary in Texas. Although Texas is classified technically as a closed-primary state, it operates as an open-primary state in practice. As in other closed-primary states, the primary voter is morally—but not legally—bound to vote only in his or her own party's elections. This means that people can participate in either the Democratic or the Republican primary whether they are party members or not. Only two minor legal restrictions make Texas technically a closed-primary state:

1. A person is forbidden to vote in more than one primary on the day of the primary elections.
2. Once a person has voted in the first primary, he or she cannot switch parties and participate in the runoff election or convention of any other party.

Closed Primaries in Other States. In contrast, the closed primary used in many other states requires that when registering to vote, a person must specify a party preference. The party's name is then stamped on the registration card at the time it is issued. A voter may change his or her party registration between elections, up to a set time (often 30 days) before the primary or convention. Voters are limited to participating in the activities of the party for which they have registered. Furthermore, an individual who registers as an independent (no party preference) is excluded from the primaries and conventions of all parties. Note that how a person votes (or fails to vote) in any type of primary does not limit in any way that person's choice in the general election in November.

Crossover Voting. The opportunity always exists in Texas for members of one political party to invade the other party's primary. This is called **crossover voting**. It is often done to increase the chances that the nominee from the other party will be someone whose philosophy is similar to that of the invader's own party. For example, if Republicans can ensure the nomination of a strong conservative in the Democratic primary, either of the two major parties' candidates may be quite acceptable to them in November.

Crossover Voting
A circumstance in which members of one political party vote in the other party's primary to influence which nominee is selected by the other party.

In the past, the Republican Party "institutionalized" crossover voting to a degree by not holding a Republican primary in some counties. In those counties, Republicans had no place to go except to the Democratic primary. The decision to forgo the primary was not necessarily based on a lack of support for Republican candidates. Although that was true in some counties, it was certainly not true of all. Of the 22 counties that did not hold a Republican primary in 1980, President Ronald Reagan carried 10; in 1984, he carried 18 of 26. This is because a large number of Democrats voted for Reagan in the general election.

The Effects of Crossover Voting. Crossover voting has long been the liberal Democrat's nemesis in Texas, because many persons who will vote for Republicans in the general election cross over to support conservatives in the Democratic primary. The candidacy of Lloyd Bentsen for the U.S. Senate in 1970 illustrates the point. In the Democratic primary, Bentsen outpolled Senator Ralph Yarborough, the liberal incumbent, in 87 voting precincts in Dallas County, the great majority of which were located in the affluent areas of northern Dallas. In the general election, though, Bentsen received a far smaller share of the votes in these precincts and lost most of them to the Republican candidate, George H. W. Bush. In another twist, there is some evidence that Republicans in other parts of the state voted for Yarborough because they believed he would be easier to defeat.

That while Texas does not limit the number of terms for either legislators or the governor, most neighboring states, including Arkansas, Colorado, Louisiana, and Oklahoma, limit both?

Crossover voting is a two-edged sword, as the Republicans learned in 1976 when Texas Democrats apparently crossed over in many areas to vote for Ronald Reagan in the presidential primary. The result was that Republican President Gerald Ford was shut out. With the help of conservative Democrats, the Reaganites captured all 100 delegates to the Republican National Convention. Many were startled that this could happen to an incumbent president (Ford). Mindful thereafter of the hazards of cross-over voting, many Republicans have supported a "party-purity" law that would require voters to register their party affiliation and be limited to participating in the primaries of that party.

In 2008, exit polls show that about 9 percent of the Democratic primary voters identified themselves as Republicans.[21] Despite encouragement from conservative talk show hosts to vote for Clinton, 53 percent reported voting for Obama. If anything, then, crossover voting narrowed the margin of Clinton's victory in Texas.

GENERAL ELECTIONS

The purpose of party primaries is to choose each party's candidates from among the competing intraparty factions. General elections, in contrast, allow the voters

[21]Wayne Slater and Gromer Jeffers, Jr., "Elections '08 President: Many Obama Voters Skipped Other Texas Races, Could Be No-Shows Without Him," *Dallas Morning News*, accessed March 9, 2008, at www.dallasnews. com/sharedcontent/dws/news/politics/national/stories/DN-demvoters_09pol.ART.North.Edition1.446fbfd.html.

PRESIDENT RONALD REAGAN
and First Lady Nancy Reagan are joined on the podium by his vice-presidential running mate, George H. W. Bush, and his wife, Barbara, at the Republican National Convention in Dallas, Texas, in 1984. How much of a benefit do you think the Republicans gained from holding the convention for Reagan's nomination to his second term in Texas? How much might Reagan have benefited from having a Texan—George H. W. Bush—as his vice-presidential running mate? (Courtesy of the Ronald Reagan Presidential Library)

to choose the people who will actually serve in national, state, and county offices from among the competing political party nominees and write-in candidates. General elections differ from primaries in at least two other important ways. First, general elections are administered completely by public (as opposed to party) officials of state and county governments. Second, unlike Texas primaries, in which a majority vote is required, the general election is decided by plurality vote, in which the winning candidate only need receive at least one more vote than any opponent.

Scheduling General Elections. General elections in Texas are held biennially on the same day as national elections—the first Tuesday after the first Monday in November of even-numbered years. In years divisible by four, Americans elect the president, the vice president, all U.S. representatives, and one-third of the U.S. senators. In Texas, the voters elect all 150 members of the state house in these elections and roughly half (15 or 16) of the 31 senators. Texas voters also elect the winners of a number of board and court positions at the state level, as well as about half of the county positions.

Most major state executive positions (governor, lieutenant governor, attorney general, and others) are not filled until the midterm election, when all U.S. representatives and one-third of U.S. senators (but not the president) again face the voters. All state house representatives and half of the state senators are elected in these years. Some board members, judges, and county officers are chosen as well.

The Effects of Simultaneous State and National Elections. Holding simultaneous national and state elections has important political ramifications. During the administration of Andrew Jackson, parties first began to tie the state and the national governments together politically. A strong presidential candidate and an effective candidate for state office can benefit significantly by cooperating and campaigning under the party label. This usually works best if the candidates are in fundamental agreement on political philosophy and the issues.

In Texas, which is more politically conservative than the average American state, such fundamental agreement has often been lacking. This has been especially true for the Democrats. Popular Democrats in the state have often disassociated themselves from the more liberal presidential nominee of the party. As you learned in Chapter 19, Democratic governor Allan Shivers openly endorsed and worked for the election of the Republican candidate for president in 1952 and again in 1956. In 1980, four former governors (all Democrats) joined Republican governor Bill Clements in endorsing Ronald Reagan for president. State leaders are often hesitant to be identified with a presidential nominee who may "drag them down" because the candidate is less popular with the Texas voters than they are.

The Effects of Separating State and National Elections. When the Texas Constitution was amended in 1972 to extend the terms of the governor and other major administrative officials from two years to four years, the elections for these offices were scheduled for the midterm election years. This change had two major effects. First, the separation of presidential and state campaigns insulates public officials from the ebb and flow of presidential politics and allows them to disassociate themselves from the national political parties. Elections for statewide office now largely reflect Texas issues and interests.

Second, the separation reduces voter turnout in statewide elections and makes the outcomes much more predictable. As was shown earlier, turnout is much lower in midterm elections than in presidential elections, when many people are lured to the polls by the importance and the visibility of the presidential campaign. Independent and marginal voters are more likely to turn out, and election results for congressional and state-level offices are less predictable. In midterm election years, however, the less informed and the less predictable voters are more likely to stay home, and the contest is largely confined to party regulars. Most incumbent state politicians prefer to cast their lot with this more limited and predictable midterm electorate.

SPECIAL ELECTIONS

As the name implies, special elections are held to meet special or emergency needs, such as to ratify a constitutional amendment or to fill a vacant office. Special elections are held to fill vacancies only in those legislative bodies having general (rather than limited) lawmaking power. Legislative bodies with general power are the U.S. Senate and House of Representatives, state legislatures, and city councils in home-rule cities. All other vacancies, including judgeships and county commissioner seats, are filled by appointment. The special election fills a vacancy only until the end of the regular term or until the next general election, whichever comes first.

Special elections are nonpartisan, and so the process of getting on the ballot is relatively easy and does not involve a primary.[22] All that is required is the filing of the application form in a timely and appropriate manner and the payment of the designated filing fee. Unlike the winner of a general election, the winner of a special election must receive a majority of the votes. Thus, a runoff special election may be necessary when no candidate wins an absolute majority the first time around.

Senator Yarborough. The runoff requirements for special elections in Texas have been enacted in piecemeal fashion—an illustration of how public policy is often established for the political advantage of a particular candidate or political ideology. Before 1957, all special elections could be won with a plurality vote. During a special election in 1957, however, liberal Democratic candidate Ralph Yarborough appeared likely to win. Therefore, the Texas House of Representatives (controlled by conservative Democrats) quickly passed a bill requiring a runoff in any election to fill a vacant U.S. Senate seat whenever the top candidate fails to win a majority.

A few liberal legislators, however, were able to delay the bill in the state senate until after the special election, in which Yarborough led the field of 23 candidates. Given that Yarborough received only 38 percent of the popular vote, it is possible that he would have lost in a runoff. Sixteen days after the

TEXAS'S SENIOR SENATOR KAY BAILEY HUTCHISON challenged Governor Rick Perry in the 2010 Republican primary and lost, receiving 31 percent to Perry's 53 percent. The rest of the vote went to Tea Party activist Debra Medina. (AP Photo/ David J. Phillip)

---

[22]Here, *nonpartisan* means only that the party label does not appear on the ballot, and certification by the party is not necessary. Special elections are, in fact, often partisan because regular party supporters work for their candidates.

election, the state senate passed the runoff bill, and it was signed into law by the governor—too late to prevent Yarborough's victory. Once in office, Yarborough was able to capitalize on his incumbency and served for 13 years.

Senator Hutchison. In 1993, after U.S. Senator Lloyd Bentsen was nominated to serve as secretary of the treasury by President Bill Clinton, a special election was necessary to fill the vacancy. Democratic governor Ann Richards appointed Robert Krueger, a former member of Congress and ambassador-at-large, to fill in until the special election, in which he was the Democratic candidate. Republican Kay Bailey Hutchison ultimately won the special election, however, becoming the first woman elected to represent Texas in the U.S. Senate.

THE CONDUCT AND ADMINISTRATION OF ELECTIONS

Texas has entered a new era in the administration of elections. Gone are the days of almost complete decentralization of responsibility for elections. In the past, some Texas counties did not include certain contests on their ballots or refused to hold elections at all. Because of the problem of local officials ignoring state law, in 1967 the Texas legislature designated the secretary of state as the chief election officer of Texas. In this capacity, the secretary of state interprets legislation and issues guidelines. Under the Voting Rights Act, the U.S. Department of Justice must approve these decisions, so they appear to carry the weight of federal authority as well.

Since 1973, the secretary of state has had the responsibility for disbursing funds to the state and county party executive committees to pay for the primary elections. The secretary of state is the keeper of election records, both party and governmental. The secretary also receives certificates of nomination from parties that have conducted primaries and conventions and uses these certificates to prepare the ballot for statewide offices. The governor, the secretary of state, and a gubernatorial appointee are the members of a three-person board that canvasses election returns for state and district offices.

COUNTY-LEVEL ADMINISTRATION

Except for the preparation of the statewide portion of the ballot, county-level officials actually conduct general elections. In 1977, the legislature created three options from which the counties may choose when administering general elections.

The Traditional System. The first option is to maintain the decentralized system that the counties have used for decades. Under this system, the major responsibility rests with the county clerk. By the time the clerk receives the state portion of the ballot from the secretary of state, she or he will have certified the candidates' names for the county-level and precinct-level portions of the ballot. The board of elections—consisting of the county judge, sheriff, and clerk and the chairs of the county executive committees of the two major parties—arranges for polling places and for the printing of ballots. The county tax assessor-collector processes all voter applications and updates the voting rolls. The county commissioners' court draws precinct voting lines, appoints election judges, selects voting devices, canvasses votes, and authorizes payment of all election expenses from the county treasury.

Alternative County Options. The two other options are designed to promote efficiency. One is for the county commissioners' court to transfer the voter-registration function from the office of the tax assessor-collector to that of the county clerk, thus removing the assessor-collector from the electoral process.

The third option, available for the first time in 1979, involves more extensive changes and may represent the direction that election administration will take in the future. It calls for all election-related duties of both the assessor-collector and the county clerk to be transferred to a county election administrator. This officer is appointed for a term of two years by the county elections commission, which, in counties that choose this option, replaces the board of elections. (The membership of the commission is the same as that of the board, except that the sheriff is not included.)

BALLOT CONSTRUCTION

Like so many other features of an election system, ballot construction reflects both practical and political considerations. Two basic types of general-election ballots are available: the party-column ballot and the office-block ballot.

The Party-Column Ballot. In the *party-column ballot* (which we first described in Chapter 9), the names of all the candidates of each party are listed in parallel columns. This is the type of ballot that has traditionally been used in Texas. The ballot itemizes the offices as prescribed by law in descending order of importance, and the candidates are listed in each row. Beside each name is a box (on paper ballots) or lever (on voting machines) that the voter must mark or pull if she or he wishes to vote a split ticket. At the top of each column is the party's name and a box or lever. To vote a straight ticket, the voter need only mark the box or pull the lever for the party of his or her choice.

The Office-Block Ballot. In the *office-block ballot* (which we also described in Chapter 9), the names of the candidates for each office are listed underneath the title of the office. To vote a straight party ticket, a voter must pick his or her party's candidate for each office. Several states use the office-block ballot, which also is called the Massachusetts ballot because it originated there. Minor parties in Texas (which once included the Republican Party) and independent voters advocate the use of this ballot type because it makes straight-ticket voting for the major parties more difficult.

The Politics of Ballot Construction. Understandably, supporters of the major Texas political parties strongly support the use of the party-column ballot. It enables lesser-known candidates to ride on the coattails of the party label or of a popular candidate running for major office. There also may be an extra advantage in the use of this type of ballot for the party that is listed in the first column.

In the past, candidates of the once-dominant Democratic Party were always listed first, and the practice was accepted without challenge. In 1963, however, the legislature enacted a requirement that the parties be slated from left to right on the ballot according to the proportion of votes that each party's candidate for governor received in the most recent gubernatorial election. Next come candidates of parties that were not on the ballot in the last election, and last come independents. After the election of Governor Bill Clements in 1979, the Republicans achieved the favored ballot position.

Beginning with the 2002 elections, many Texas counties moved away from a strict party-column ballot. Partly because of the adoption of electronic voting systems (discussed later), ballots in these counties combine features of the office-block and party-column designs. As with the office-block ballot, candidates are listed underneath each office. As with the party-column ballot, however, one can vote a straight party ticket with a single mark; that is, before turning to specific offices, voters are first given the option to vote a straight ticket.

GETTING ON THE BALLOT

For a candidate to get his or her name on the general-election ballot, the candidate must be either a party nominee or an independent. If a party received at least 5 percent of the vote for any statewide office in the previous general election, its full slate of candidates is placed on the ballot automatically. Thus, the Democratic and Republican parties have no problems, and certification by the appropriate party officials of the winner of a primary or convention is routine.

Making Life Hard for Third Parties and Independents. Minor parties have a more difficult time. For instance, neither the Libertarian Party nor the Green Party received the necessary votes in 2002, and both had to petition to get their candidates on the ballot in 2004. Independent candidates for president have the most difficult challenge, for they must present a petition with signatures equaling 1 percent of the total state vote for president in the last election. For John Anderson, an independent candidate who ran in 1980, that meant a minimum of 40,719 names on the petition. In 1992, Ross Perot's supporters presented 54,275 signatures to get his name on the ballot.

For all offices except president, the total vote for governor is the basis for determining the required number of signatures for both independents and third-party candidates. A candidate for statewide office needs signatures equaling 1 percent of the total gubernatorial vote in the entire state. For multicounty district offices, the requirement is 3 percent of the gubernatorial vote in the district. For all other district and local offices, it is 5 percent of the gubernatorial vote in the district (a maximum of 500 signatures at the local level). Further requirements add to the difficulty of gaining access to the ballot by petition. Signers must be registered voters and must not have participated in the selection of a nominee for that office in another party's primary. In addition, each page of the petition must be notarized.[23]

As a general rule, candidates using the petition route seek twice the required number of signatures to ensure the petition's certifiability. For example, in 1980, the Libertarian Party submitted 55,000 signatures, and the Socialist Workers Party (SWP) turned in 30,000 to ensure that each had 23,698 persons who were legally qualified to sign. Only the Libertarians succeeded in placing their candidates' names on the ballot, however. The SWP fell below the minimum when almost half of the petitioners' signatures were found to be those of persons not qualified to sign.[24]

Write-in Candidates. Write-in candidates are not listed on the ballot—voters must write them in. These candidates often are individuals who have entered and lost in a party primary. A different type of write-in candidacy developed in 1976 when Charles W. Barrow, chief justice of the Fourth Court of Civil Appeals in San Antonio, was thought to be virtually unopposed for the Democratic nomination for associate justice of the Texas supreme court. The legal establishment was stunned when Don Yarbrough, a young Houston attorney involved in a number of legal entanglements, upset Barrow in the quest for the Democratic nomination. Apparently, the voters had confused the young attorney's name with that of former gubernatorial candidate Don Yarborough. No one had filed in the Republican primary, so there was no Republican candidate to challenge Yarbrough in the general election. Yarbrough appeared to be a shoo-in.

---

[23]In 1976, the secretary of state interpreted the law as requiring that each signature be notarized. The next year, the legislature specified that a notary need only sign each page of the petition. Difficulties involving technical aspects of the law and adverse interpretations of the law represent only part of the harassment that minor parties and independents have traditionally encountered in their quest for a place on the ballot. See Ernest Crain, et al., *Understanding Texas Politics*, 12th ed. (Belmont, CA: Wadsworth Publishing Company, 2006).
[24]The SWP was founded in 1938 by followers of the Russian Communist leader Leon Trotsky, who was Joseph Stalin's chief opponent in the struggle for control of the Soviet Union. (Trotsky lost.) In recent decades, the SWP has looked less to Trotsky for inspiration and more to former Cuban leader Fidel Castro.

Embarrassed, the legal establishment sought to have the primary winner disqualified from the ballot. Failing that, they mounted a write-in campaign supported strongly by the leaders of both political parties. Playing the name game themselves, they chose as their candidate District Judge Sam Houston Jones. The write-in campaign failed miserably. Don Yarbrough's victory was short-lived, however. Under threat of removal by the legislature, he resigned after serving approximately six months. He was replaced through gubernatorial appointment by Charles W. Barrow—his opponent in the Democratic primary. (Some reformers have advocated a system under which all judges would be appointed by the governor, at least initially.)

Write-in candidates have had an easier time as a result of a law subsequently passed by the legislature. It requires a candidate to register with the secretary of state prior to the beginning of absentee voting in general elections and 45 days before a primary election. The names of write-in candidates must be posted at the election site, possibly in the election booth. A candidate not properly registered cannot win, regardless of the votes he or she receives. Even when registered, write-in candidates are seldom successful.

THE SECRET BALLOT AND THE INTEGRITY OF ELECTIONS

Most people believe that the right to vote includes the rights to cast a ballot in secret, have the election conducted fairly, and have the ballots counted correctly. These rights have not always been available, however. The *Australian ballot* (see Chapter 9), adopted by Texas in 1892, includes names of the candidates of all political parties on a single ballot printed at public expense and available only at the voting place.[25] Given a reasonably private area in which to mark the ballot, the voter was offered a secret ballot for the first time.

Election Judges and Poll Watchers. Protection of the integrity of the electoral process in Texas is primarily addressed through political remedies. As a result, minor parties have reason to be concerned that irregularities in elections administered by members of the majority parties may not be observed and, if observed, may not be reported.

[25]Optional at first, the Australian ballot was made mandatory in 1903.

Traditional practice has been that, in general and special elections, the county board of elections appoints as election judges the precinct chairs of the political party that has a majority on the elections board. Since 1967, each election judge has been required to select at least one election clerk from each of the lists submitted by the county chairs of the two major political parties. Moreover, law now recognizes the status of "poll watchers," and both primary candidates and county chairs are authorized to appoint them. These oversight options mark a significant improvement over the days when the only possible (and usually ineffective) remedy was to go to court.

Rechecks and Recounts. If there is a question about the election results, candidates can ask for either a recheck or a recount of the ballots. A recheck applies primarily to voting machines. It checks for counting errors and costs $3 per precinct. The loser of an election also can ask for a recount (this is discussed in greater detail in the section on "Voting Problems"). The candidate who requests a recount must put up a deposit and is liable for the entire cost unless she or he wins or ties in the recount. Moreover, a recount (but not a recheck) must include all precincts. In a large county, the cost of a recount can be prohibitive.

MULTILINGUALISM

Ballots in most Texas counties are printed in English. In more than 100 counties, the ballot is printed in both English and Spanish. In some parts of the United States, other languages are required, including Chinese, Eskimo, Filipino, Japanese, and Korean. In Los Angeles County alone, ballots are printed in seven different languages.

Vietnamese Ballots in Houston. In 2002, the U.S. Department of Justice ordered several counties around the country, including Harris County (which contains Houston), to provide ballots and voting materials in Vietnamese as well as Spanish. Harris County was the only county in Texas required to provide Vietnamese ballots and the only county outside California to face this requirement. The requirement was due to the Voting Rights Act of 1965 and its 1992 amendments. According to Section 203 of the act, a political subdivision (typically a county) must provide such help if significant numbers of voting-age citizens are members of a single-language minority who do not speak or understand English "well enough to participate in the electoral process."

When Are Multilingual Ballots Required? Specifically, the legal requirement is triggered when more than 5 percent of the voting-age citizens or 10,000 of these citizens meet the criteria. The 2000 census showed that more than 55,000 people living in Harris County identified themselves as Vietnamese. The Department of Justice determined that at least 10,000 of them were old enough to vote and not proficient in English. Thus, the requirement was triggered. Given the current record levels of immigration into the United States, the number of ballot languages is almost certain to increase. We show a sample multilingual ballot in Figure 23–5.

VOTING ABSENTEE AND VOTING EARLY

All states allow members of the U.S. armed forces to vote absentee, and Texas, along with 40 other states, also permits absentee voting for reasons such as illness or anticipated absence from the county. Traditionally, absentee voting in Texas (and other states) was mostly a convenience for the middle class and served as a boost for conservative candidates.

Current Rules for Absentee Voting. In 1987, the legislature made changes that appear to have far-ranging effects:
- To vote absentee in person (rather than by mail), you need not swear that you intend to be out of the city or county on election day.
- Absentee ballots can be cast in substations in the urban counties.

FIGURE 23–5 English-Vietnamese Language Ballot Used in Harris County for the 2008 General Election

The general election ballot shown here is an example of the kind of ballot arrangement most voters actually encounter on electronic voting machines in Texas. Notice that the candidates are not arranged in columns under party labels, but the candidates are consistently arranged in the order of their parties' performance in the last election for governor thereby giving the Republicans the preferred first position. Voters are given the opportunity to vote a straight ticket by making a single ballot mark. What are the arguments for and against bilingual ballots such as the one shown here?

SAMPLE BALLOT **LÁ PHIẾU MẪU**

Official Ballot Phiếu Bầu Chính Thức
General and Special Elections
Các Cuộc Tổng Tuyển Cử và Bầu Cử Đặc Biệt
Harris County, Texas
Quận Harris, Texas
November 04, 2008 - *Ngày 4 tháng Mười Một, 2008* Precinct *Phân Khu Bầu Cử* *All*

Instruction Text:
TO VOTE: Mark the ballot by placing an "X" in the square beside the candidate of your choice. You may vote for a write-in candidate by placing an "X" in the square beside the write-in choice and writing the name of the write-in candidate of your choice. You may vote straight-party (that is, cast a vote for all the candidates of one party), by placing an "X" by the party of your choice. Voting straight-party automatically cast a vote for all of that party's candidates. If you change a vote to an opposing party candidate, your vote for the opposing party candidate will be counted as well as your vote for all other candidates of the party of the straight-party vote which was cast.

Ghi chủ hướng dẫn:
BỎ PHIẾU: Điền lá phiếu bằng cách đánh dấu "X" vào ô vuông bên cạnh tên ứng cử viên mà quý vị lựa chọn. Quý vị có thể bỏ phiếu cho một ứng cử viên ghi thêm bằng cách đánh dấu "X" vào ô vuông bên cạnh lựa chọn ghi thêm và ghi vào tên của ứng cử viên mà quý vị muốn bầu chọn. Quý vị có thể bỏ phiếu bầu cho một chính đảng [nghĩa là, bầu cho tất cả ứng cử viên của cùng một đảng] bằng cách đánh dấu "X" vào ô vuông bên cạnh tên của đảng mà quý vị muốn bầu chọn. Bỏ phiếu theo cách bầu đảng thì tất cả các ứng cử viên của đảng đó sẽ tự động được bầu. Nếu quý vị đổi để bỏ phiếu cho đối thủ của một ứng cử viên của đảng đó, lá phiếu bầu cho đối thủ kia sẽ được tính cũng như lá phiếu bầu cho tất cả các ứng cử viên khác của một đảng mà quý vị bầu chọn.

SPECIAL ELECTION
CUỘC BẦU CỬ ĐẶC BIỆT

State Senator, District 17, Unexpired Term
Thượng Nghị Sĩ Tiểu Bang, Khu Vực 17, Nhiệm Kỳ Vô Thời Hạn
- Austen Furse — Republican Party, Đảng Cộng Hòa
- Ken Sherman — Republican Party, Đảng Cộng Hòa
- Stephanie E. Simmons — Democratic Party, Đảng Dân Chủ
- Grant Harpold — Republican Party, Đảng Cộng Hòa
- Joan Huffman — Republican Party, Đảng Cộng Hòa
- Chris Bell — Democratic Party, Đảng Dân Chủ

GENERAL ELECTION
CUỘC TỔNG TUYỂN CỬ

Straight Party
Bỏ phiếu cho các ứng cử viên của cùng một đảng
- Republican Party — *Đảng Cộng Hòa*
- Democratic Party — *Đảng Dân Chủ*
- Libertarian Party — *Đảng Tự Do*

President and Vice President
Tổng Thống và Phó Tổng Thống
- John McCain / Sarah Palin — Republican Party, Đảng Cộng Hòa
- Barack Obama / Joe Biden — Democratic Party, Đảng Dân Chủ
- Bob Barr / Wayne A. Root — Libertarian Party, Đảng Tự Do
- Write-in — *Bầu chọn ứng cử viên không có tên trong lá phiếu*

United States Senator
Thượng Nghị Sĩ Hoa Kỳ
- John Cornyn — Republican Party, Đảng Cộng Hòa
- Richard J. (Rick) Noriega — Democratic Party, Đảng Dân Chủ
- Yvonne Adams Schick — Libertarian Party, Đảng Tự Do

United States Representative, District 2
Dân Biểu Hoa Kỳ, Khu vực số 2
- Ted Poe — Republican Party, Đảng Cộng Hòa
- Craig Wolfe — Libertarian Party, Đảng Tự Do

United States Representative, District 7
Dân Biểu Hoa Kỳ, Khu vực số 7
- John Culberson — Republican Party, Đảng Cộng Hòa
- Michael Skelly — Democratic Party, Đảng Dân Chủ
- Drew Parks — Libertarian Party, Đảng Tự Do

United States Representative, District 9
Dân Biểu Hoa Kỳ, Khu vực số 9
- Al Green — Democratic Party, Đảng Dân Chủ
- Brad Walters — Libertarian Party, Đảng Tự Do

United States Representative, District 10
Dân Biểu Hoa Kỳ, Khu vực số 10
- Michael T. McCaul — Republican Party, Đảng Cộng Hòa
- Larry Joe Doherty — Democratic Party, Đảng Dân Chủ
- Matt Finkel — Libertarian Party, Đảng Tự Do

United States Representative, District 18
Dân Biểu Hoa Kỳ, Khu vực số 18
- John Faulk — Republican Party, Đảng Cộng Hòa
- Sheila Jackson Lee — Democratic Party, Đảng Dân Chủ
- Mike Taylor — Libertarian Party, Đảng Tự Do

United States Representative, District 22
Dân Biểu Hoa Kỳ, Khu vực số 22
- Pete Olson — Republican Party, Đảng Cộng Hòa
- Nick Lampson — Democratic Party, Đảng Dân Chủ
- John Wieder — Libertarian Party, Đảng Tự Do

United States Representative, District 29
Dân Biểu Hoa Kỳ, Khu vực số 29
- Eric Story — Republican Party, Đảng Cộng Hòa
- Gene Green — Democratic Party, Đảng Dân Chủ
- Joel Grace — Libertarian Party, Đảng Tự Do

Railroad Commissioner
Ủy Viên Ngành Hỏa Xa
- Michael L. Williams — Republican Party, Đảng Cộng Hòa
- Mark Thompson — Democratic Party, Đảng Dân Chủ
- David Floyd — Libertarian Party, Đảng Tự Do

Chief Justice, Supreme Court
Chánh Thẩm, Tối Cao Pháp Viện
- Wallace B. Jefferson — Republican Party, Đảng Cộng Hòa
- Jim Jordan — Democratic Party, Đảng Dân Chủ
- Tom Oxford — Libertarian Party, Đảng Tự Do

Justice, Supreme Court, Place 7
Chánh Án, Tối Cao Pháp Viện, Vị Trí số 7
- Dale Wainwright — Republican Party, Đảng Cộng Hòa
- Sam Houston — Democratic Party, Đảng Dân Chủ
- David G. Smith — Libertarian Party, Đảng Tự Do

Justice, Supreme Court, Place 8
Chánh Án, Tối Cao Pháp Viện, Vị Trí số 8
- Phil Johnson — Republican Party, Đảng Cộng Hòa
- Linda Reyna Yanez — Democratic Party, Đảng Dân Chủ
- Drew Shirley — Libertarian Party, Đảng Tự Do

Judge, Court of Criminal Appeals, Place 3
Chánh Án, Tòa Kháng Án Hình Sự, Vị Trí số 3
- Tom Price — Republican Party, Đảng Cộng Hòa
- Susan Strawn — Democratic Party, Đảng Dân Chủ
- Matthew E. Eilers — Libertarian Party, Đảng Tự Do

Judge, Court of Criminal Appeals, Place 4
Chánh Án, Tòa Kháng Án Hình Sự, Vị Trí số 4
- Paul Womack — Republican Party, Đảng Cộng Hòa
- J.R. Molina — Democratic Party, Đảng Dân Chủ
- Dave Howard — Libertarian Party, Đảng Tự Do

Sample Ballot

Sample Ballot

(Courtesy of Harris County, Texas)

Since 1989, the absentee-voting period has begun 22 days before the election and ended on the sixth day before the election. Moreover, substation voting places now remain open 12 hours a day Monday through Friday, with shorter hours on Saturdays and Sundays. As a result, absentee voting has increased tremendously. Whether cast by mail or in person, on paper ballots or by punch card or electronic machines, absentee votes are not counted until election day.

Early Voting. In 1991, the Texas legislature instituted early voting.[26] All Texas voters now are able to cast their ballots before election day. Unlike absentee voting, early voting is available to any registered voter. In addition to traditional election day voting sites, such as schools and fire stations, there are other places to vote early, including grocery and convenience stores.

This innovation clearly has made voting easier in Texas, and people are taking advantage of it. In 1992, for example, about 25 percent of all votes were cast before election day. In 1996, approximately 33 percent of votes were cast early. In 2000, the number was slightly less than 39 percent. In 2004, over 50 percent voted early, and in 2008, two out of every three did so. Although people are voting earlier, turnout has not increased greatly. Still, the tendency to vote early may have important implications for when and how politicians campaign, as late campaign activities cannot influence those whose votes have already been cast.

VOTING PROBLEMS

We take for granted that when we vote, the system will work correctly. As we learned in Florida in the 2000 presidential elections, this is not always ensured. The first machine count of ballots in Florida showed George W. Bush with a 1,725-vote lead. In a mandatory machine recount of the same ballots, the same machines cut his lead to 327. We also learned that some ballots were not counted because they were defective, and other ballots were so poorly designed that they may have led voters to pick the wrong candidate. Claims were also raised that some ineligible persons (typically, former felons) cast votes. What does this mean? The answer is simple: Even machines make mistakes. Some ballots are not counted. Some votes may be counted for the wrong candidate. Some people vote who are not supposed to do so. Experts have known for a long time that voting involves a degree of error. By most accounts, the error rate averages from 1 to 2 percent, although it can be higher, depending on the system used.

The Punch-Card Ballot Problem. The error rate is largest for punch-card ballots, which have commonly been used in big cities in Texas and other states. To vote, you insert the ballot into a slot in the voting booth and then punch holes corresponding to candidates' names, which are printed on lists, usually in the form of a booklet.

There are two sources of error with these ballots. First, some voters do not fully punch out the pieces of paper from the perforated holes—that is, these pieces of paper, which are called **chad**, remain attached to the ballot. Second, even where the chad are completely detached, machines do not read every ballot. This is of importance to voters. It typically is of little consequence for election outcomes, however. Counting errors tend to cancel out, so that no candidate gains a great number of votes. Thus, the errors are important only when elections are very close—within half a percentage point or less, which is not very common. When it does happen, the losing candidate can request a recount.

Chad
A small fragment of paper produced by the punching of a data card, such as a punch-card ballot.

---

[26]For a description of early voting and a preliminary assessment of its effects, see Robert M. Stein and Patricia A. Garcia-Monet, "Voting Early but Not Often," *Social Science Quarterly*, Vol. 78, December 1997, pp. 657–671. For a more recent evaluation, see Paul Gronke, Eva Galanes-Rosenbaum, and Peter A. Miller, "Early Voting and Turnout," *PS: Political Science and Politics*, Vol. 40, 2007, pp. 639–645.

Recounts. Texas has specific laws about recounts. A candidate can request a recount if he or she loses by less than 10 percent. This is a fairly generous rule compared with other states. The candidate who requests the recount does have to pay for it, however, which means that most candidates do not request a recount unless the margin is much closer, say, 1 percentage point.

The Texas election code states that "only one method may be used in the recount [and] a manual recount shall be conducted in preference to an electronic recount." The procedures are fairly detailed. What may be most interesting is the set of rules for how chad should be interpreted. Canvassing authorities are allowed to determine whether "an indentation on the chad from the stylus or other object is present" and whether "the chad reflects by other means a clearly ascertainable intent of the voter to vote."[27] This leaves ample room for discretion on the part of canvassing authorities in the various Texas counties.

Electronic Voting. Partly in response to the events in Florida in the 2000 presidential elections—and the potential for similar problems in Texas—several counties introduced electronic voting in the 2002 midterm election. Instead of punching holes in ballots or filling in empty circles on sheets that can be read by machine, voters in Dallas, Houston, and San Antonio voted by touching screens.

The technology is similar to what is used for e-ticket check-in at many airports and promises an exact count of votes. Electronic voting is being used in many jurisdictions throughout the United States. As with any new technology, however, problems have occurred with the new systems in Texas and elsewhere.[28]

UNDER TEXAS ELECTION LAW, hand recounts include "hanging chad." Here, an election worker holds a ballot filled with undetached chad (squares of paper that are pushed out of punch-card ballots) that will have to be manually removed before the ballot can be counted. Why might some states refuse to count ballots unless they are perfectly formed? (AP Photo/ Ted S. Warren)

ELECTION CAMPAIGNS IN TEXAS

The aim of party activity is to nominate candidates in the party primary or convention and then get them elected in the general election. The pattern in Texas before 1978 was for Republicans and other minor parties to run only token, poorly financed candidates for most contested offices, so the real choices were made in the Democratic primary. Today, the battle has moved from the Democratic primary to the general election.

WHO GETS ELECTED

It is useful to think of the elective offices in Texas as a pyramid. At the bottom of the pyramid are the most local of offices, and at the top is the governor. Moving from bottom to top, the importance of the office increases, and the number of officeholders decreases. It thus becomes increasingly difficult for a politician to ascend higher up the pyramid, and only the best politicians rise to the top. This tells us much about candidates and elections in Texas and elsewhere.

---

[27]Texas Code 127.130. Also see Carlos Guerra, "Texas Is Far Friendlier to All Our Chad," *San Antonio Express-News*, November 25, 2000, p. B1.

[28]Rachel Konrad, "Reports of Electronic Voting Trouble Top 1,000," *USA Today*, accessed November 4, 2004, at www.usatoday.com/tech/news/techpolicy/evoting/2004-11-04-1000-reports_x.htm.

A LINEUP OF PEOPLE voting electronically. This fairly recent voting technology promises to be more accurate than paper ballots. Some argue that this is not correct. What do you think? Does electronic voting solve the problems with paper ballots? How can you tell? (Bob Daemmrich/Image Works)

Candidates for Statewide Office. In the most local elections, the pool of candidates is diverse. Contenders may vary in educational background, income, and profession. As we move up the pyramid, however, candidates become more homogeneous. For statewide office, the typical candidate is middle or upper class, is from an urban area, and has strong ties to business and professional interests in the state. Most officers who are elected statewide, including the governor, lieutenant governor, and attorney general, must be acceptable to the state's major financial and corporate interests and to its top law firms. These interests help a statewide candidate to raise the large volume of funds that is critical to a successful race.

Successful candidates for statewide office in Texas traditionally have been white Protestant males. Before 1984, when Raul Gonzalez was elected to the state supreme court, no Mexican American or African American had been elected to statewide office, although these two ethnic groups combined represent half of the state's population. The only female governor had been Miriam A. "Ma" Ferguson, who in the 1920s served as surrogate for her husband, Jim. In 1982, Ann Richards was elected state treasurer, becoming the second woman ever to be elected to statewide office in Texas.

Gains by Women and Minorities. Since then, women and minority group members have made substantial gains in statewide offices. In 1990, Democrat Ann Richards (1933–2006) became the first woman elected governor in her own right. That same year, Republican Kay Bailey Hutchison captured the state treasurer's office. In 1993, Hutchison won a special election to become the first woman from Texas elected to the U.S. Senate. Dan Morales became the first Mexican American to win a state executive office when he was elected attorney general in 1990.[29] More history was made in 1992 when Morris Overstreet of Amarillo won a seat on the Texas Court of Criminal Appeals and became the first African American elected to a statewide office.

Women and ethnic groups are starting to make inroads in other elected offices in Texas as well. In the seventy-ninth legislature (2005–2006), 32 women were elected to the 150-member house and four to the 31-member senate. Women have also held the post of

[29]Morales was convicted of mail and tax fraud in 2003 and was sentenced to four years in prison.

POLITICS WITH A purpose

Who Can Run for Office?

Members of the Texas legislature must meet a few minimum constitutional requirements to hold office. House members must be at least 21 years old, and senators must be at least 26. House members must also have lived in the state for at least two years. Senators must have lived in the state for at least five. All members of the Texas legislature must be U.S. citizens, qualified voters, and residents of the district they will represent for at least one year. Any individual who meets these requirements can run for office.

Overcoming the cost of an election to the Texas legislature can seem quite daunting to many. After all, an average Texas house race can cost as much $153,000. Senate races can be even more costly, averaging more than $452,000. While it is true that most lawmakers are older, many young, ambitious candidates have successfully won seats in the Texas leg-islature. Countless members of the Texas legislature got there while they were either still in college or recent college gradu-ates. Many spent modest amounts of money to win seats that they have turned into powerful positions, making meaningful contributions to the state of Texas. Many have won these seats in races in which a few thousand votes were cast. Others have won with no real competition. Some races for elective offices can be costly, challenging, and highly competitive; many oth-ers are not. Many highly ambitious, smart young people have run successful campaigns.

Representative Jessica Farrar was a 27-year-old engineer-ing student at the University of Houston when she first ran for office in 1994. She spent some $10,000 to purchase door knockers and yard signs. She then took to pounding the pave-ment and meeting as many constituents as she could. Fourteen years later, she serves on the powerful House Committee on State Affairs and the House Committee on Juvenile Justice and Family Issues. In 1997, Representative Dennis Bonnen was only 24 years old when he was elected to the Texas house. He is now in his sixth term.

Do you think it is a good idea or a bad idea to elect young people to the Texas house or senate? Why?

---

mayor in five of the state's largest cities—Austin, Dallas, El Paso, Houston, and San Antonio. Mexican Americans hold 35 seats in the state legislature, and African Americans occupy 16 seats. Among the state's 32 U.S. congressional representatives are three women, six Mexican Americans, and three African Americans. Clearly, Texas politics has changed quite a bit.

THE GENERAL-ELECTION CAMPAIGN

To a large extent, election outcomes are predictable. Despite all the media attention paid to conventions, debates, advertising, and other elements of political campaigns, certain factors powerfully structure the vote in national and state elections.[30] In state elections, two factors predominate: party identification and incumbency.

Party Identification. First, if the voters in a state tend to identify more with one politi-cal party than the other, the candidates of the favored party have an advantage in

---

[30]Most of the research has focused on presidential elections. See Christopher Wlezien, "On Forecasting the Presidential Vote," *PS: Political Science and Politics*, Vol. 34, March 2001, pp. 25–31, available at www. apsanet.org/imgtest/CJ312-ElectionIntro%5B23-24%5D.pdf. There is some research on state gubernatorial and legislative elections. See, for example, Mark E. Tompkins, "The Electoral Fortunes of Gubernatorial Incumbents," *Journal of Politics*, Vol. 46, May 1984, pp. 520–543; and Ronald E. Weber, Harvey J. Tucker, and Paul Brace, "Vanishing Marginals in State Legislative Elections," *Legislative Studies Quarterly*, Vol. 16, February 1991, pp. 29–47.

general elections. When most Texans identified with the Democratic Party, Democratic candidates dominated elected offices throughout the state. As Texans have become more Republican in their identification, Republican candidates have done very well. As we pointed out in Chapter 22, Republicans now hold every statewide elective office.

Party identification varies considerably within Texas, however, and this has implications for state legislative elections. In some parts of the state, particularly in urban districts, a majority of the voters identify with the Democratic Party. Democratic candidates typically represent those areas in the state house and senate. Thus, party identification in the state and in the various districts has much to do with which candidates win general elections. How the boundaries of the various districts are drawn also has an important effect on the outcome.

Incumbency. Second, incumbent candidates—those who hold office and are up for reelection—are more likely to win in general elections. This is particularly true in state legislative elections, where the districts are fairly homogeneous and the campaigns are not very visible, but incumbency also is important in elections for statewide office. Incumbents have several advantages over challengers, the most important of which is that they have won before. To become an incumbent, a candidate has to beat an incumbent or win in an open-seat election, which usually includes strong candidates. By definition, therefore, incumbents are good candidates. In addition, incumbents have the advantages of office. They are in a position to do things for their constituents, and thus increase their support among voters.

While party identification and incumbency are important in Texas elections, they are not the whole story. What they really tell us is the degree to which candidates are advantaged or disadvantaged as they embark on their campaigns. Other factors also matter on election day, and we consider some of those factors next.[31]

Mobilizing Groups. Groups play an important role in elections for any office. A fundamental part of campaigns is getting out the vote among those groups that strongly support the candidate. To a large extent, candidates focus on groups aligned with the political parties.[32] At the state level, business interests and teachers are particularly important; Republican candidates tend to focus their efforts on the former and Democratic candidates on the latter.

Candidates also attempt to mobilize other groups, including African Americans and Mexican Americans. Traditionally, Democratic candidates emphasized these minority groups, although Governor George W. Bush broke somewhat with this tradition and focused substantial attention on the Hispanic community in Texas. Mobilizing groups does not necessarily involve taking strong public stands on their behalf. Mobilization of such groups may be conducted quietly, often through targeted mailings and phone calls.

Choosing Issues. Issues play a role in any campaign. In campaigns for state office, the issues of taxes, education, and crime are relevant, and the abortion issue is important in many states. As with the mobilization of groups, the issues that candidates select tend to reflect their party affiliations, but issue stands are often not so clear-cut. Very few candidates, after all, are in favor of higher taxes and less spending on education and crime prevention.

[31]For a detailed analysis of election campaigns in Texas in a single election year, see Richard Murray, "The 1996 Elections in Texas," in Kent L. Tedin, Donald S. Lutz, and Edward P. Fuchs, eds., *Perspectives on American and Texas Politics*, 5th ed. (Dubuque, IA: Kendall/Hunt, 1998), pp. 247–286.

[32]For an analysis of how membership in various demographic groups influences voting behavior, see Robert S. Erikson, Thomas B. Lancaster, and David W. Romero, "Group Components of the Presidential Vote, 1952–1984," *Journal of Politics*, Vol. 50, May 1988, pp. 337–346. For an analysis of how identification with various social groups influences voting behavior, see Christopher Wlezien and Arthur H. Miller, "Social Groups and Political Judgments," *Social Science Quarterly*, Vol. 78, December 1997, pp. 625–640.

Where candidates do differ is in their emphasis on particular issues and their policy proposals. Their choices depend heavily on carefully crafted opinion polls. Using polls, candidates attempt to identify the issues that the public considers important and then develop policy positions to address those issues. The process is ongoing, and candidates pay close attention to changes in public opinion and, perhaps most important, to the public's response to the candidates' own positions. Polling is thus fundamental in modern political campaigns in America.

The Campaign Trail. Deciding where and how to campaign is a critical part of campaign strategy. Candidates spend countless hours "taking the stump," or traveling around the state or district to speak before diverse groups. In a state as large as Texas, candidates for statewide office must pick and choose areas to maximize their exposure. This means that candidates spend most of their time in urban areas.

Today, no candidate is elected by stumping alone. The most direct route to the voters is through the media. There are some 17 media markets in Texas. These include approximately 200 television and cable stations and more than 500 radio stations. In addition, there are 79 daily and 403 weekly papers dispersed throughout the state's 254 counties.[33] Candidates hire public relations firms in their effort to take advantage of all these media outlets, and media consultants and advertising play a large role.

These days, a successful campaign often relies on **negative campaigning**, in which candidates attack opponents' issue positions or character. As one campaign consultant said, "Campaigns are about definition. Either you define yourself and your opponent or they do. . . . Victory goes to the aggressor."[34] While many consider negative campaigning an unfortunate part of American politics, such campaigning can provide voters with information about the candidates and their issue positions.

Negative Campaigning
A strategy in political campaigns of attacking the opposing candidate's issue positions or—especially—his or her character.

Timing. The timing of the campaign effort can be very important. Unlike presidential campaigns, campaigns for state offices, including the governorship, begin fairly late in the election cycle. It is common to hear little from gubernatorial candidates until after Labor Day and not much from candidates for the legislature until a month before the election.

Candidates often reserve a large proportion of their campaign advertising budget for a last-minute media blitz. Early voting may affect this strategy, however. In 2008, two-thirds of the votes in Texas were cast early, which means that any final campaign blitz came far too late to have any effect on those voters. Because of this trend, in the future candidates may be less likely to concentrate their efforts on the final days of the campaign.

FINANCING POLITICAL CAMPAIGNS

Political campaigns are expensive, which means that candidates need to raise substantial funds to be competitive. The amount a candidate raises can be the deciding factor in the campaign. How much a candidate needs depends on the level of the campaign and the competitiveness of the race. High-level campaigns for statewide office are usually multimillion-dollar affairs.

In recent years, the race for governor has become especially expensive. George W. Bush spent almost $15 million to defeat Ann Richards in 1994. In 2002, Tony Sanchez spent almost $70 million, mostly his own funds, but lost to incumbent governor Rick Perry, who spent slightly less than $30 million. In 2006, the four candidates vying spent about $46 million, with Perry leading the way at $23 million.[35]

[33]*Gale Directory of Publications and Broadcast Media*, Vol. 2, 129th ed. (Detroit, MI: Gale Research, 1997).
[34]Quoted in Dave McNeely, "Campaign Strategists Preparing Spin Systems," *Austin American-Statesman*, October 21, 1993, p. A11.
[35]See http://www.statesman.com/news/content/region/legislature/stories/04/06/0406perryrga.html.

Although lower-level races in Texas are usually not million-dollar affairs, they too can be expensive. This is certainly true if a contested office is an open seat (where the incumbent is not running for reelection) or if the district is a marginal one (where the incumbent won office with less than 55 percent of the vote). It is not unusual for a candidate in a competitive race for the state house to spend between $100,000 and $200,000.

Where Does the Funding Come From? Where do contributions of this size come from? Candidates often try to solicit small individual contributions through direct-mail campaigns. But to raise the millions required for a high-level state race, they must solicit "big money" from wealthy friends or from business and professional interests that have a stake in the outcome of the campaign. Banks, corporations, law firms, and professional associations—such as those representing physicians, real estate agents, or teachers—organize and register their political action committees (PACs) with the secretary of state's office. PACs serve as the vehicle through which interest groups collect donations and then contribute them to political candidates. (You learned about PACs at the national level in Chapter 10.) Another source of big money is loans. Candidates often borrow heavily from banks or wealthy friends or even from themselves.[36]

Where Do the Contributions Go? Today's political campaign involves a multitude of different expenses. Newspaper ads, billboards, radio messages, bumper stickers, yard signs, and phone banks are all staples in the traditional campaign. Candidates for statewide and urban races must rely on media advertising, particularly television, to get the exposure they need in the three- or four-month campaign period. These candidates are likely to hire consulting firms to manage their campaigns. Consultants contract with public opinion pollsters, arrange advertising, and set up direct-mail campaigns that can target certain areas of the state.

We can get some idea about spending in campaigns from what candidates pay for advertising and political consultants in Houston (and Harris County):[37]

- A 30-second TV spot costs about $1,500 for a daytime ad, $2,000 to $5,000 for an ad during the evening news, and $5,000 to $20,000 for an ad during a prime-time show, depending on the show's popularity rating. For some very popular programs, such as *CSI*, the cost can be even higher, as much as $25,000.
- Prime time for most radio broadcasting corresponds with "drive time" (5:00 A.M. to 10:00 A.M. and 3:00 P.M. to 8:00 P.M.), when the largest number of people are driving to or from work. Drive-time rates range from $250 to $2,000 per 60-second spot.
- Billboards can run anywhere from $600 to $15,000 per month, depending on the location. Understandably, billboards on busy freeways are the most expensive.
- Newspaper ads cost from $300 to $500 per column inch in the Sunday paper and $250 per column inch in the daily paper. In November 2004, a half-page ad in the *Houston Chronicle* run on the day before the election cost about $15,000. Advertising rates for political campaigns actually are higher than the rates charged to commercial customers because campaigns are not given the discounts that regular advertisers receive.
- Hiring a professional polling organization to conduct a poll in Harris County costs $15,000 to $30,000.
- Hiring a political consulting firm to manage a campaign in Harris County costs up to $50,000, plus a percentage of the media buys. (Technically, the latter cost is paid by the television and radio stations.) Most firms also get a bonus ranging from $5,000 to $25,000 if the candidate wins.

---

[36]For a comprehensive treatment of campaign finance, see Frank J. Sorauf, *Inside Campaign Finance: Myths and Realities* (New Haven, CT: Yale University Press, 1992).

[37]Nancy Sims of Pierpont Communications, with offices in both Austin and Houston, graciously provided this information.

Clearly, finance is important in political campaigns. While the candidate who spends the most does not always win, a certain amount of spending is necessary for a candidate to be competitive. Speaking with his tongue halfway in his cheek, one prominent politician noted, in regard to high-level statewide races in Texas, that even if "you don't have to raise $10 million, you have to raise $8 million."[38]

Controlling Campaign Finance. Prompted by the increasing use of television in campaigns and the increasing amount of funds needed to buy television advertisements, the federal government and most state governments passed laws regulating campaign finance in the early 1970s. (We first discussed campaign finance in Chapter 10.) The Federal Elections Campaign Act of 1971, substantially amended in 1974, established regulations that apply only to federal elections (president, vice president, and members of Congress). It provided for public financing of presidential campaigns through tax dollars, limited the size of the contributions that individuals and PACs could make to campaigns, and required disclosure of campaign donations. In 1976, the United States Supreme Court declared that it was unconstitutional to set spending limits for campaigns that are not publicly funded. This means there are no spending limits for congressional races.[39]

Growing Campaign Expenditures. Not surprisingly, expenditures in election campaigns continue to increase. The Federal Election Commission reported that $211.8 million was spent in the 1976 election of the president and members of Congress, with $122.8 million spent in the presidential race alone. Of the $60.9 million spent in the elections of the 435 House members, more was spent on behalf of candidates in Texas ($4.5 million) than on those of any other state except California. Such expenditure levels appear modest by today's standards. In 1998, outlays for all congressional races (House and Senate combined) totaled $740 million.[40] In the same year, candidates for the 30 U.S. House seats allocated to Texas spent $27 million in their election efforts, an average of almost $1 million per seat. In 2002, spending totaled over $40 million, more than $1.25 million on average for the 32 seats Texas holds. In 2006 the average ballooned again to over $1.75 million per seat and the level of campaign spending is likely to continue to rise. Costs of campaigns for state offices in Texas are at least proportionately high, and Texas has joined other states in enacting legislation designed to control the flow of funds.

Current Texas Campaign Law. The most important provisions of current Texas law on campaign finance are as follows:

1. Candidates may not raise or spend funds until an official campaign treasurer is appointed.
2. Candidates and PACs may not accept contributions in currency for more than an aggregate of $100.
3. Direct contributions from corporations and labor unions are prohibited.
4. Candidates and treasurers of campaign committees are required to file sworn statements listing all contributions and expenditures for a designated reporting period to the Texas secretary of state's office.
5. Both criminal and civil penalties are imposed on those who violate the law's provisions. Primary enforcement of campaign regulations is the responsibility of the Texas Ethics Commission.

DID YOU KNOW?

That PACs active in Texas include AQUAPAC (the Water Quality Association), NUTPAC (the Nut Processors Association), SIX-PAC (the National Beer Wholesalers Association), WAFFLEPAC (Waffle House, Inc.), and WHATAPAC (Whataburger Corporation of Texas)?

---

[38]Interview with Jim Hightower, "The Senate Can Wait," in *The Texas Observer*, January 27, 1989, p. 6.
[39]*Buckley v. Valeo*, 424 U.S. 1 (1976).
[40]Federal Election Commission data, reported in *Congressional Quarterly Almanac 1977* (Washington, DC: Congressional Quarterly, 1977), p. 35A; and *Congressional Quarterly Weekly Report*, March 5, 1989, p. 478. Since 1976, the federal government actually has expanded the role of contributions in elections.

Although these provisions may sound imposing, in fact raising and spending funds in Texas campaigns still is fairly wide open. For example, while corporations and labor unions may not give directly to a candidate, they may give through their PACs. Note that the amount a candidate may spend of his or her own funds is unlimited. Probably the most important effect of the campaign-finance law in Texas comes from the disclosure requirements. How much a candidate raises, who makes contributions, and how campaign funds are spent are matters of open record. This information may be newsworthy to reporters or other individuals motivated to inform the public.

Soft Money and Independent Expenditures. In 1979, amendments to the Federal Elections Campaign Act made it legal for political parties to raise and spend unlimited amounts of *soft money*. Party funds could be used to help candidates in a variety of ways, especially through voter-registration and Get Out the Vote drives. The United States Supreme Court further opened up spending in 1985 by deciding that *independent expenditures* could not be limited.[41] As a result, individuals and organizations can spend as much as they want to promote a candidate so long as they are not working or communicating directly with the candidate's campaign organization. (Soft money and independent expenditures were discussed in Chapter 10.) The 2002 Campaign Reform Act limited independent expenditures by corporations and labor unions, but this was overturned by the Supreme Court in its 2010 decision in *Citizens United v. Federal Election Commission*.[42] This may have implications for state and local races that have bans on corporate spending, including Texas. The 2002 act also deprived the parties of their soft money resources, but activists simply set up nonparty organizations to collect and disperse such funds. Understandably, it has been very difficult to effectively control money in political campaigns.

[41]Federal Election Commission (www.fec.gov).
[42]*Citizens United v. Federal Election Commission*, 558 U.S. (2010).

YOU CAN MAKE A Difference

"THINK GLOBALLY, ACT LOCALLY"

"Think globally, act locally" is a common slogan in American politics. The phrase reflects a simple and well-known logic. While it may be a good thing to care about the really big issues, such as global warming and the war in Iraq, it makes more sense to act locally, where the effects of our actions are much greater. The math is quite convincing. If I am one of 100 million, my contribution is likely to be a small share of the total. If I am one of 50, however, I can make a noticeable difference. Ironically, we are much more likely to vote in national-level elections, where we have an almost imperceptible effect, than in local-level elections, where we can make a big impact. To have really tangible effects, we should play a bigger role in local politics.

WHY SHOULD YOU CARE?

Elections for local office seem much less important than national elections, and there is truth in this perception. Whether we go to war in Iraq is a question decided by our national politicians. The largest taxes are collected nationally. Social Security is a federal program. The states are the next biggest players. Much of the funding for higher education and welfare comes from the states.

Counties and cities still have a big role to play, however, as do other local governing bodies. They are largely responsible for streets and garbage collection. These services may seem basic, but they are important, as you probably know all too well. Take roads, for instance. Poorly designed roads can create unnecessary gridlock. Badly managed traffic lights can have the same effect. Potholes have an obvious impact on our cars and our patience. Local governments also largely fund and oversee our schools. Do we tax a lot or a little for education? Do we fund classrooms or teachers or athletic facilities?

These are big decisions, obviously, and they are largely in the hands of local governments. In addition to basic services and schools, local governments are responsible for policing the streets where we live, work, and shop. Whether the police are well trained, well equipped, and properly managed clearly matters. Indeed, it can be a matter of life or death.

WHAT CAN YOU DO?

The obvious thing to do is to get involved in local elections. First, find out more about local politics. Newspapers are a good source, and the Internet is, too, but do not forget about your family and your fellow students. They also can be sources of information. You might be surprised by how much of what happens locally is not only interesting but also important. You may find yourself getting involved in an election campaign or an interest group. There, you could really make a difference.

A WOMAN DISTRIBUTES FLIERS on a college campus. This is one way to get people to think about issues that are not receiving much attention in the mainstream media. How much effect do you think it has? (AP Photo/Bob Child)

KEY TERMS

chad 802
crossover voting 793
negative campaigning 807

participation paradox 779
runoff primary 790
user-benefit theory 789

vote-eligible population (VEP) 782
voting-age population (VAP) 782

CHAPTER SUMMARY

1. Elections are the defining characteristic of representative democracy. We hold elected officials accountable through our votes.

2. A small number of demographic and political variables are important in predicting who will vote. The most important demographic variables are education, income, and age. Certain political factors also influence the likelihood of voting, especially a person's level of interest in politics and intensity of identification with a political party. Other factors are important as well, but with this small set of demographic and political variables, we can pretty well predict whether a person will vote in a particular election.

3. Voting in Texas (and most other states) is a two-stage process. Before you can vote, you must first register. Traditionally a barrier for women and minorities, the registration procedure today is as simple as voting—perhaps even simpler. Since the passage of federal "motor voter" legislation, a person can register when renewing a driver's license.

4. Traditionally, voter turnout was measured as a percentage of the voting-age population (VAP). That figure has become increasingly inaccurate, mainly because it includes a growing number of noncitizens, who cannot vote. We can use estimates of the vote-eligible population (VEP) instead. By that measure, national turnout in presidential elections has fluctuated around 55 percent in recent years. In midterm elections, turnout is around 40 percent. These numbers are significantly lower than what we find in other advanced democracies. Voter turnout in Texas is even below the U.S. national average.

5. **Why is voter turnout in Texas lower than it is in most other states?** Low voter turnout in Texas may be partly related to the state's socioeconomic characteristics. A comparatively large percentage of the population lives below the poverty level. An even larger percentage has not graduated from high school, and these people are not very likely to vote. Income and education levels are low for African Americans and Mexican Americans, so turnout is particularly low for these groups. Political factors, such as political structure and political culture, may also play a role in low turnout.

6. **What is the majority election rule, and why do we use it in Texas primaries?** In Texas, as in other Southern states that once were predominantly Democratic, a majority rule is used in primary elections. If no candidate receives a majority of the votes cast for a particular office in the first primary, a second, runoff primary is used to determine the winner. Outside the South, only a plurality of the votes is typically required.

7. Ballot design is an important factor in elections. Texas traditionally has used the party-column ballot, in which the names of all the candidates of each party are listed in parallel columns. The main alternative is the office-block ballot, in which the names of candidates are listed underneath each office. Beginning with the 2002 election, many Texas counties adopted electronic voting systems, which combine features of the office-block and party-column designs.

8. Texas is a diverse state, and the pool of candidates for local offices reflects this diversity. As we move up the pyramid of elected offices, however, the candidates become much more homogeneous. Successful candidates for statewide office traditionally have been white males. While this remains true today, women and minorities have made substantial gains, which are likely to continue as more women and minorities enter politics.

9. **Why are some candidates more likely than others to win elections in Texas?** In state elections, two factors predominate: party identification and incumbency. As Texans have become more Republican in their identification, Republican candidates have done very well, currently holding every statewide elective office. Party identification varies considerably in Texas, however, and in some parts of the state, particularly urban districts, voters identify with the Democratic Party and Democratic candidates typically represent those areas in the state house and senate.

Second, incumbent candidates—those who hold office and are up for reelection—are more likely to win in general elections. They have the advantages of holding office, being in a position to do things for their constituents, and having won before, proving themselves as strong candidates.

10. In a state as large as Texas, media advertising, political consultants, and polling are required for any candidate seeking to win statewide office or the most competitive state legislative and local elections. These services are expensive.

11. Without a certain amount of funding, it is impossible to be competitive in Texas elections. The high and rising cost of campaigns means that serious candidates must collect contributions from a variety of sources. Most candidates must rely on PACs and wealthy individuals. Although the Texas legislature has passed laws regulating campaign finance in state races, raising and spending funds is still fairly wide open.

SELECTED PRINT, MEDIA, AND ONLINE RESOURCES

PRINT RESOURCES

Brischetto, Robert, David Richards, Chandler Davidson, and Bernard Grofman. "Texas." In Chandler Davidson and Bernard Grofman, eds., *Quiet Revolution in the South: The Impact of the Voting Rights Act, 1965–1990.* Princeton, NJ: Princeton University Press, 1994. This chapter chronicles how the Voting Rights Act influenced Texas elections and politics in the 25 years after its enactment.

Davidson, Chandler. *Race and Class in Texas Politics.* Princeton, NJ: Princeton University Press, 1992. This wide-ranging book by a Texas sociologist highlights the power of business interests in Texas politics.

Murray, Richard. "The 1996 Elections in Texas." In Kent L. Tedin, Donald S. Lutz, and Edward P. Fuchs, eds., *Perspectives on American and Texas Politics,* 5th ed. Dubuque, IA: Kendall/Hunt, 1998. In this article, a leading analyst of Texas elections and politics offers a view of Texas campaigns through the prism of the 1996 elections.

Murray, Richard, and Sam Attlesey. "Texas: Republicans Gallop Ahead." In Alexander Lamis, ed., *Southern Politics in the 1990s*. Baton Rouge: Louisiana State University Press, 1999. This very accessible chapter traces the rise of Republicans in Texas state politics during the 1990s.

Stein, Robert M. "Early Voting." *Public Opinion Quarterly*, Vol. 62, No. 1 (1998), pp. 57–69. This article by a well-known Texas political scientist analyzes the effects of early voting in Texas on both the level of turnout and the composition of the electorate.

Tolleson-Rinehart, Sue, and Jeanie Ricketts Stanley. *Claytie and the Lady: Ann Richards, Gender, and Politics in Texas*. Austin: University of Texas Press, 1994. The authors of this book examine the influence of gender in Texas politics, focusing especially on the 1990 gubernatorial election, in which Ann Richards defeated Clayton Williams after a truly fascinating campaign.

MEDIA RESOURCES

Hispanic Voters **on Cengage's Texas Political Theatre 2008**—This is a feature on the Houston mayoral election, during which a Hispanic conservative, with strong support from the party establishment, nearly defeated a black Democrat. The election, according to political observers, demonstrates that both parties have an opportunity to gain strength by promoting Hispanic candidates.

Populism **on Cengage's Texas Political Theatre 2008**—During an interview, Kinky Friedman, an unsuccessful candidate for governor in 2006, discusses unusual political stances, his friendship with former president Bush, and his attempt to challenge the two-party system.

ONLINE RESOURCES

Election Law Blog Follow Professor Rick Hasen's popular and well-respected election law blog: electionlawblog.org/

Federal Election Commission created in 1975 by Congress to administer and enforce the Federal Election Campaign Act (FECA), the statute that governs the financing of federal elections. Find a wide array of campaign finance data at the FEC's Web site: www.fec.gov

Localvoter—Learn about current elections and get information about candidates and issues in your community, ways to get involved, and links to other resources: www.localvoter.com

Pew Center on the States works to advance state policies that serve the public interest; provides an up-to-date digest of election reform developments in Texas and other states: www.electionline.org

Politifact A project of the *St. Petersburg Times* to help identify the truth in politics, where you can fact-check Texas politicians' claims: www.politifact.com/texas

PollingReport.com A resource on trends in American public opinion including public opinion in Texas: www.pollingreport.com/

Rasmussen Reports An electronic media company specializing in the collection, publication, and distribution of public opinion polling information; generates a daily cycle of news reports based on original survey results and what are referred to as Media Meters: www.rasmussenreports.com/public_content/politics/general_state_surveys/texas/

Southwest Voter Registration Education Project This organization is specifically interested in enrolling Hispanic Americans: www.svrep.org

Texas Secretary of State At the Texas secretary of state's election page, you can register to vote or check out election results: www.sos.state.tx.us

24

The Texas State Capitol Building in downtown Austin. (Brandon Seidel/Shutterstock.com)

The Texas Legislature

QUESTIONS TO CONSIDER

How does the political and legal environment affect the way Texas's legislature operates?

What are the main power structures in the Texas legislature?

What are the major steps by which laws are passed?

CHAPTER CONTENTS

what if...

The Texas Legislature Were a Full-Time Legislature?

BACKGROUND

State legislatures are often described as either part-time or full-time legislative bodies. While the Texas legislature does not always fit neatly into either one of the two categories,[a] it does share some characteristics that are found in part-time legislatures. Part-time legislatures tend to meet for shorter periods of time, their members tend to be paid less for their service than the members of full-time legislatures, and they tend to have smaller legislative staffs.

For its part, the Texas legislature meets for 140 days on odd-numbered years, unless the governor calls a special session. Members of the Texas legislature are paid $7,200 per year plus a *per diem* (daily allowance) for days when the legislature is in session. Members of the Texas house average a staff of about three people, while senators average a staff of a little more than seven. The Texas legislature is considered a part-time legislative body.

Texas legislators often must depend on outside sources of income to earn a living, making them vulnerable to the temptations of special-interest groups. Some lawmakers will work in areas in which their clients are the very interest groups that also lobby these lawmakers when the legislature is in session.[b] Legislators who are not paid adequately are also more likely to leave their posts after a short period of service, leading to greater instability in the legislative body.[c] As lawmakers leave the legislature, they take with them policy and political expertise that is necessary to adequately represent the public.

WHAT IF THE TEXAS LEGISLATURE WERE A FULL-TIME LEGISLATIVE BODY?

If the Texas legislature were a full-time legislative body, one would expect to see improvements in the quality of representation that Texans receive. Legislators would certainly receive better salaries if the Texas legislature were a full-time legislative body. Better pay would attract more qualified individuals to run for public office, and better pay would help retain experienced legislators who would otherwise seek higher office.

BETTER LEGISLATION

Some have argued that a part-time legislature is better because it governs less, but in Texas, this is not always the case. In the 140 days of the 80th legislative session, more than 1,400 bills became law.[d] The 109th Congress, by contrast, produced 482 laws in twice as many days. With fewer resources and less time, the Texas legislature produces many more pieces of legislation than does the U.S. Congress. While the Texas legislature is certainly not governing less (as measured by legislative activity), some have speculated about the quality of so much legislation produced in such a short period of time.

As it stands, legislators rely on lobbyists to write bills that lawmakers then introduce. Because of time constraints, it is difficult for lawmakers to properly vet bills. As a result, legislators are often not familiar with the legislation on which they are asked to vote. A full-time legislative body would provide lawmakers with the necessary resources to better represent the public.

CAN WE EXPECT THE TEXAS LEGISLATURE TO CHANGE TO A FULL-TIME LEGISLATIVE BODY?

It is unlikely that the Texas legislature will be reformed any time soon. Current lawmakers have been successful under this system and are unlikely to want to change the legislature to a system that would bring uncertainty into their lives. The public is also unlikely to want to go along with such a change because of assumptions that the public has about lawmakers and lawmaking. The public assumes that Texas legislators are compensated more than adequately. Or, when it is familiar with the part-time nature of the Texas legislature, the public assumes that the Texas legislature governs best when it governs least. Such assumptions from the public, and concerns about the future from legislators, make it unlikely that the Texas legislature will be reformed anytime soon.

FOR CRITICAL ANALYSIS

1. What other reasons would lawmakers have for not wanting to reform the legislature from a part-time to a full-time legislative body?
2. In what ways does a part-time or full-time legislative body improve representation?

[a]NCSL, "NCSL Backgrounder: Full- and Part-Time Legislatures," accessed February 15, 2008 at www.ncsl.org/programs/press/2004/backgrounder_fullandpart.htm.
[b]Center for Public Integrity, "Low-Paid Texas Lawmakers Tops in Connections to Lobbyists," accessed February 15, 2008, at projects.publicintegrity.org/hiredguns.
[c]Peverill Squire, "Career Opportunities and Membership Stability in Legislatures," *Legislative Studies Quarterly,* Vol. 13, February, pp. 65–82.

[d]House Research Organization, "Focus Report: Major Issues of the 80th Legislature, Regular Session," accessed February 25, 2008, at www.hro.house.state.tx.us/focus/major80.pdf.

THE LEGISLATURE IS one of the basic components of the three-branch concept of government and is often considered to be the branch closest to the people. In this chapter, we examine the organization, structure, and processes of the Texas legislature.

The Texas legislature, like the U.S. Congress and all other state legislatures, except that of Nebraska, is a bicameral (two-chamber) legislature composed of a senate and a house of representatives. Although the two chambers have approximately equal power, the smaller, 31-member Texas senate is more prestigious, and its individual members generally exercise greater power and influence than the 150 members of the Texas house. The Texas legislature has several unusual features. One such feature is the great power of the **presiding officers** in each body. A second is the no-party system of organizing the two chambers, which allows each presiding officer to recruit members of the other party to his or her team. Texas is also one of the few large states that relies on a **part-time legislature**.

THE LIMITED SESSION

The Texas legislature meets on the second Tuesday in January in odd-numbered years for a 140-day session. It is the only legislature among those of the 10 most populous states that meets biennially—every two years. Although 43 states have instituted annual sessions to conduct state business, Texas has refused to do so. Many Texans believe that the legislature does more harm than good when it is in session and that a longer session would simply give legislators more time to make mischief.

In these short, infrequent sessions, the volume of legislation can overwhelm legislators. Most bills are passed or killed with little consideration. As a result, many important bills are never granted a legislative hearing.

SPECIAL SESSIONS

The short biennial sessions and the increasingly complex problems of a modern society make 30-day special sessions, which can be called only by the governor, more frequent. They are, however, usually unpopular with both the general public and the legislators. The public tends to see the added expense as wasteful, and legislators may be distressed by calls away from their homes, families, and primary occupations. Furthermore, any interest that was able to get the legislature to kill an item of legislation during the regular session will strongly oppose a special session to reconsider the item that has already been killed.

TIME PRESSURES

Because most of the legislative work is done during the regular session, time is valuable. Legislators, lacking adequate staff support, find it difficult to obtain even rudimentary knowledge of the content of much of the legislation that must be considered, whether in committee or on the *floor*, which will be discussed later in this chapter. The time constraints dictated by the limited session tend to isolate individual legislators and deepen their reliance on the information provided by lobbyists, administrators, and the legislative leadership. Thus, bills that lack interest-group, administrative agency, or legislative leadership support have no chance of passage or even serious consideration.

Presiding Officers
In Texas, the chief officers of the state senate and house. They are the lieutenant governor, who presides over the senate, and the speaker of the house.

Part-Time Legislature
A legislative body that meets for short periods of time. Its members are often provided limited resources, including small salaries.

DID YOU KNOW?

That the Texas legislature passed a bill during the 80th legislative session that allows school districts to offer classes in Bible studies to students in high school?

LAWMAKERS AND FAMILY

MEMBERS crowded the chamber of the Texas House of Representatives as the 79th Texas legislature began its regular session in January 2005. What is special about Texas legislative sessions? (AP Photo/ Harry Cabluck)

Historically, much questionable legislation was passed in the last days of the session. In 1993, the house adopted new rules to address the end-of-session legislative crunch. During the last 17 days of the session, the house may consider only bills that originated in the senate or that received previous house approval. The new rules also give house members 24 hours to study major legislation before taking floor action. These reforms diminish the volume of last-minute legislation and give legislators time to become better acquainted with bills.

QUALIFICATIONS, TERMS, AND COMPENSATION OF MEMBERS

Texas has citizen legislators who meet for only 140 days every other year and receive most of their income from outside sources. It is reasonable to expect the lawmakers to be more focused on their full-time careers and outside sources of income than on the Texas public's business. Texas lawmakers are not constrained in the amount of outside sources of income they can have. As a result, entrepreneurial lawmakers will often work as consultants for special-interest groups that have issues pending before the committees on which the lawmakers serve.

FORMAL QUALIFICATIONS

Although an individual must meet legal, or formal, qualifications before he or she can serve in the Texas legislature, the criteria are broad enough to allow millions of Texas residents the opportunity to run. To be a state senator, a person must be a U.S. citizen, a qualified voter, at least 26 years of age, and must have lived for the previous five years in the state and one year in the district in which he or she seeks election. Qualifications for house membership are even more easily met. To be a representative, an individual must be a U.S. citizen, a qualified voter of the state, at least 21 years of age, and have lived in Texas for the two previous years and in the district for one year prior to being elected.

TERMS

Texas senators are elected for four-year staggered terms; representatives are elected for two-year terms. This means that the entire house and half the senate are elected every two years.

Redistricting, which is based on the census, takes place every 10 years and triggers a special senate procedure in the first election following redistricting. The next such election will take place in 2012. Because of redistricting, the entire senate will be up for election. At the start of the first session after the redistricting, senators will draw lots to determine who will serve a four-year term and who will serve for two years. Unlucky senators face reelection in 2014, while the lucky ones will not have to run for reelection until 2016. Thereafter, all senators will serve four-year terms until the election that follows the next census

DID YOU KNOW?

That in the 140 days of the 2007 regular session 1,481 bills were enacted into law? With 6,190 bills filed, nearly one-quarter of the bills became law.

(in 2022). The relative competitiveness of a senator's district determines whether the result of the lottery is only an inconvenience or an incident of major significance.

Texas legislators experience a more rapid turnover than their counterparts in the U.S. Congress, where seniority brings political power. Frustrated by low salaries and the inability to achieve legislative goals that are not supported by powerful interests or the presiding officers, many house members leave office to pursue full-time careers or to seek higher political office. Senators and the members of the house power structure tend to serve longer. Redistricting also brings significant legislative turnover when district lines are redrawn and power bases shift. The median length of service for senators is about 12 years and for house members about seven.

COMPENSATION

Legislators receive an annual salary of $7,200 plus $168 *per diem* (per day) for expenses during both regular and special sessions. They also have a travel allowance on a reimbursement basis when the legislature is in session. The **Texas Ethics Commission** is constitutionally empowered to propose salary increases, subject to voter approval, for legislators and the lieutenant governor. Lawmakers have not received a pay increase since 1975, when Texas voters approved a pay raise for lawmakers. An attempt to increase their salaries failed in 1991. As a result, lawmakers often rely on campaign contributions to offset the cost of public service. Texas lawmakers are among the worst-paid legislators in the country, but the law allows them to rely on campaign contributions to offset their living expenses while living and working in Travis County. The Travis County seat is Austin, Texas, the capital of Texas.

Texas Ethics Commission
A constitutionally authorized body that has the power to investigate ethics violations and to penalize violators of Texas ethics laws.

The Texas Ethics Commission. The eight-member Texas Ethics Commission enforces state ethics and campaign finance law. The governor, lieutenant governor, and speaker appoint the commission from a list provided by the Democratic and Republican legislative caucuses. Legislators are excluded from serving on the commission.

Conflicts of Interest. There is little motivation for a Texas legislator to keep his or her position solely for the salary. Present legislative salaries are so low that legislators must receive their primary income from other sources. While Texans require that their legislators seek additional income to subsist, they rarely question the nature of this income. People tend to be responsible to those who pay them, and the public does not furnish most of the legislators' income.[1]

The potential for conflict between the public interest and the interests of a lawmaker's business or employer is obvious. Some legislators recognize the dilemma. For example, Bob Bullock faced it in 1991 when he left the comptroller's office, which paid $74,698 per year, and became the lieutenant governor for a salary of $7,200. Although many employers were eager to hire the lieutenant governor, the appearance of a conflict of interest concerned Bullock enough that he rejected several lucrative offers and accepted employment as a counselor and consultant with View Point Recovery Centers, a network of alcohol rehabilitation hospitals. His salary from View Point, his state employees' retirement income, and his salary as lieutenant governor gave Bullock approximately the same income he had received as comptroller. Many Texas officials have not shared Bullock's desire to avoid even the appearance of impropriety. (Bullock retired in 1998 and died in 1999. The Texas State History Museum is named in his honor.)

---

[1]See Chapter 25 for a further discussion of the interaction among administrators, lobbyists, and legislators.

LEGISLATIVE DISTRICTS

The members of the Texas house of representatives, like the members of the Texas senate, are elected from single-member districts—one member per house district (see Figure 24–1) and one senator per senate district (see Figure 24–2). These districts are required by the U.S. Constitution to be approximately equal in population.[2] Following every 10-year census, each state must undertake a redistricting process to correct for changes in the populations of the districts. Today, the average population of an electoral district for the Texas house exceeds 160,000. State senators represent an average of about 800,000 people. Members of the Texas senate now represent more people than the Texas members of the U.S. House of Representatives (see Figure 24–3).

In Texas, as in most other states, the state legislature redraws its own districts, as well as those of the state's delegation to the U.S. Congress. In the event the Texas legislature fails to redistrict, the state constitution provides for the function to be performed by the Legislative Redistricting Board. The board is **ex officio**, which means that members hold other offices. It is made up of the lieutenant governor, the speaker of the house, the attorney general, the comptroller, and the commissioner of the General Land Office.

Ex Officio
Having a position by virtue of holding a particular office. For example, the lieutenant governor of Texas serves *ex officio* as the presiding officer of the Texas senate.

FIGURE 24–1   State House Districts, 82nd Legislature, 2011–2013

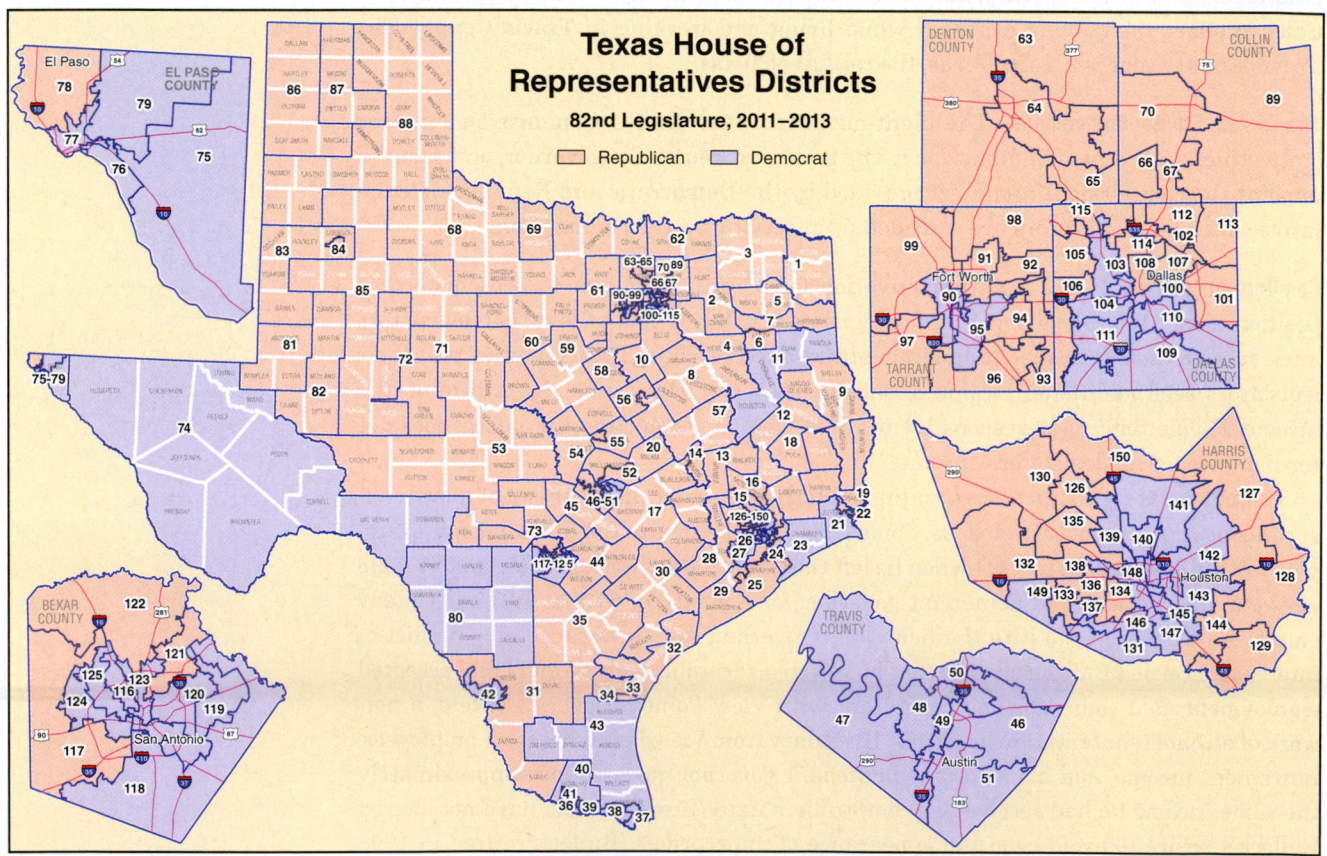

Source: Texas Legislative Council.

[2]*Reynolds v. Sims*, 377 U.S. 533 (1964).

GERRYMANDERING

The once-per-decade ritual of redistricting may take place with little notice by the casual observer of politics. For the political practitioner and the political activist, however, it may resemble a life-or-death struggle. The way districts are drawn at any level of government to a large extent determines the political, ideological, and ethnic makeup of the legislative body. When districts are subject to *gerrymandering*, political careers may be made or broken, public policy determined for at least a decade, and the power of ethnic or political minorities enhanced or diminished. Three gerrymandering techniques are common: cracking, packing, and pairing.

Cracking and Packing. One technique is to diffuse a concentrated political or ethnic minority among several districts so that its votes within any one district are negligible (*cracking*). A second tactic is used if the minority's numbers are great enough when diffused to affect the outcome of elections in several districts. In this circumstance, the minority is concentrated within the smallest possible number of districts (*packing*), thereby ensuring that it will influence the fewest possible elections and that its influence within the legislature as a whole will be minimal. (See Figure 24–4 on page 823.)

Pairing Incumbents. A third tactic is the **pairing** technique, which redistricts in such a way that two or more **incumbent** legislators must run in the same district, thereby ensuring that one will be defeated. Pairing can be used to punish legislators who have fallen from grace with the legislative leadership.

Pairing
In political redistricting, placing two incumbent officeholders from the same party in the same district. (Only one of these officeholders can be reelected.)

Incumbent
The current holder of an office.

FIGURE 24–2 State Senate Districts, 82nd Legislature, 2011–2013

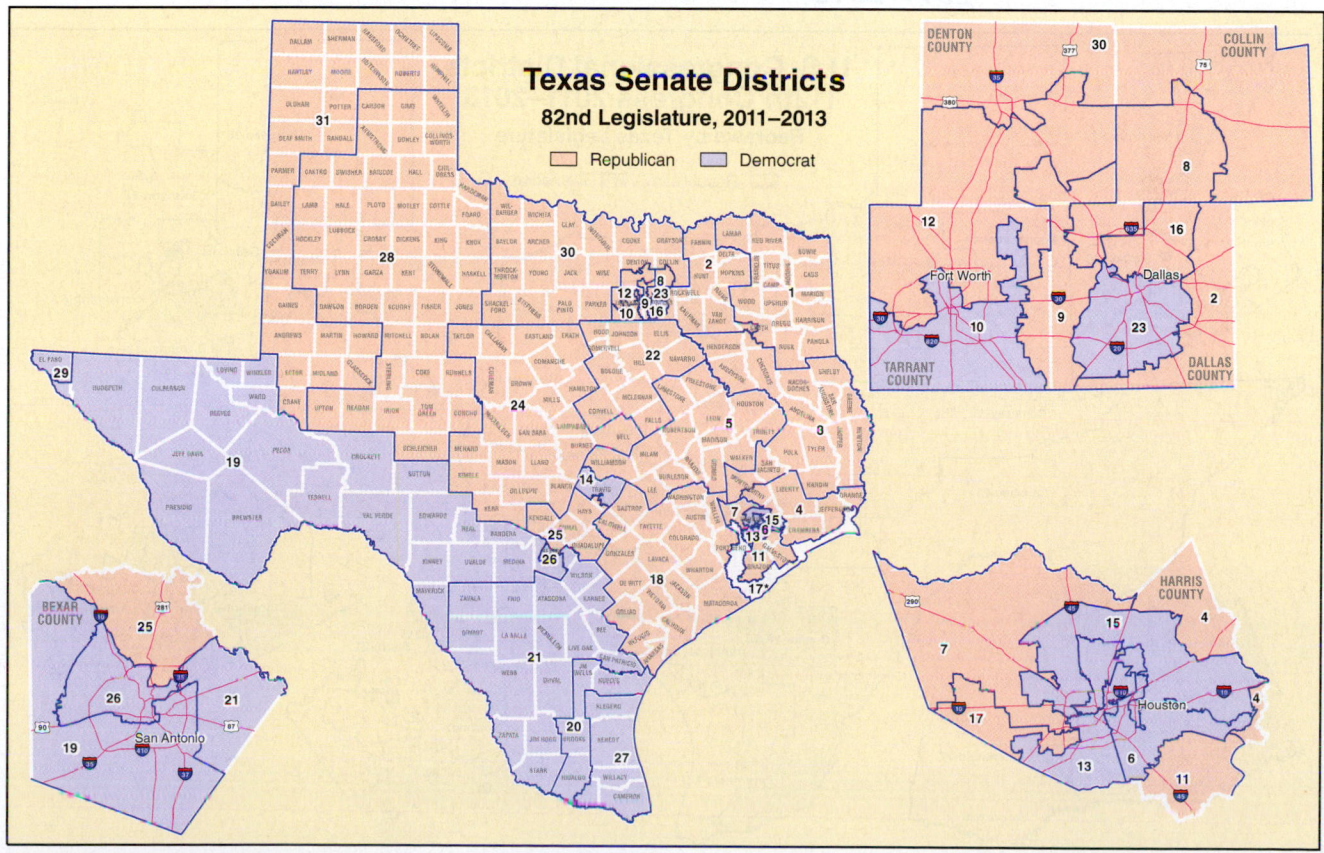

Source: Texas Legislative Council.
*At the time of publication, the winner of District 17 had not yet been decided.

REDISTRICTING AFTER THE 1990 AND 2000 CENSUSES

Redistricting after the last two censuses substantially changed the makeup of both the Texas legislature and the Texas delegation to the U.S. House of Representatives.

Redistricting after 1990. Following the 1990 census, it took a special session of the Texas legislature, 11 lawsuits, and various other legal actions in both state and federal courts from 1990 through 1994 to settle the placement of district boundaries. Republican membership in the Texas senate immediately increased from nine in 1991 to 13 in 1993. By 1996, Republicans controlled the Texas senate, although Democrats continued to be the majority in the house.

State House and Senate Redistricting after 2000. Controversy flared again after the 2000 census. Because of the state's dramatic population growth, driven by the growth in the Latino population, Texas picked up two additional congressional seats from the previous decade. In the 1990s, Texas was awarded 30 seats to the U.S. House of Representatives. After the 2000 census, 32 House seats were allocated to Texas. These two additional seats, in conjunction with shifts in the population, meant that districts would have to be redrawn so that they would be equal in size. Republican lawmakers refused to accept the legislative redistricting that followed the census and forced the redistricting effort into the Legislative Redistricting Board, where Republicans enjoyed a four-to-one

FIGURE 24–3 U.S. Congressional Districts, 112th Congress, 2011–2013

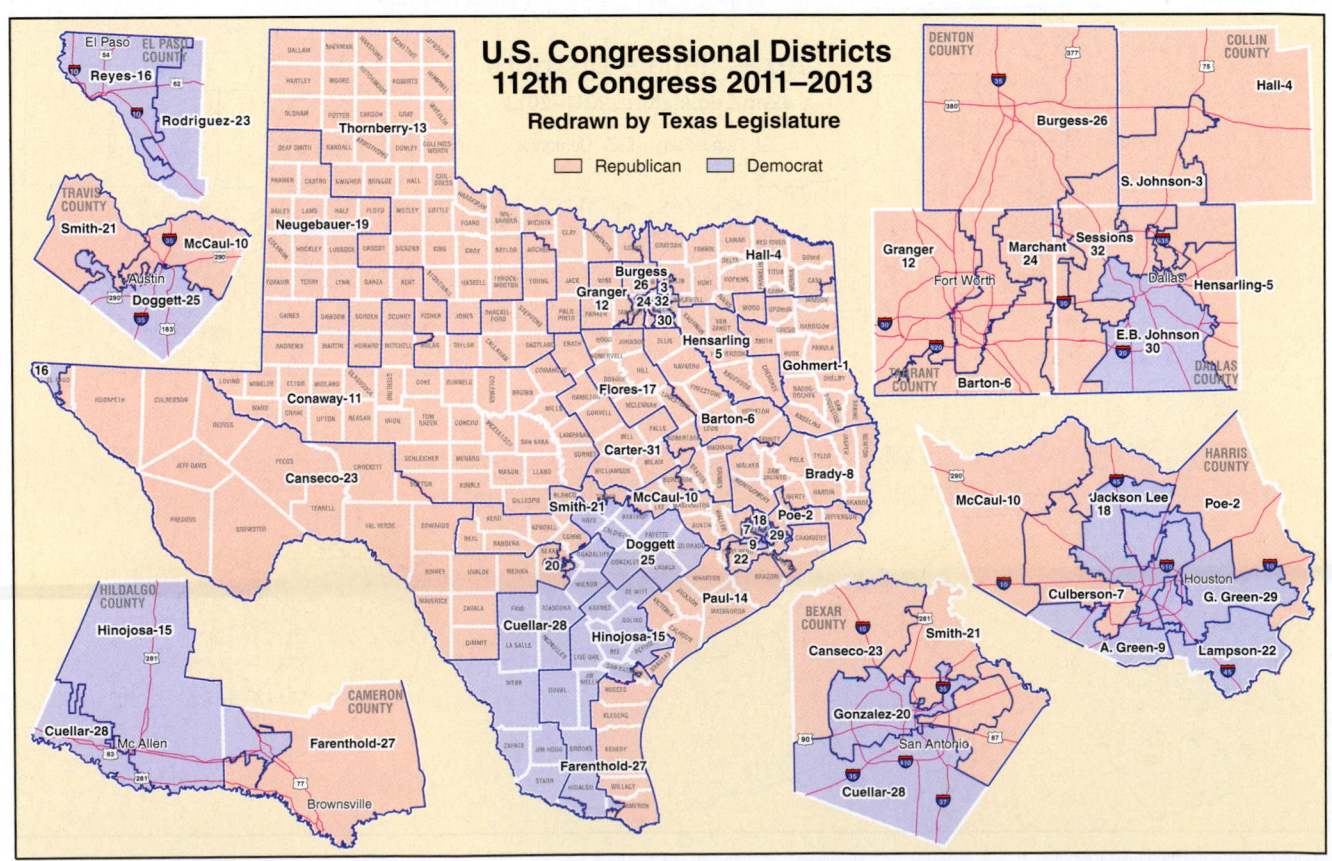

FIGURE 24–4 Cracking and Packing

The diagram at the top is balanced, having eight red "voters" and eight blue "voters" represented by the dots in each of the four "districts." Redrawing the electoral districts in the lower example results in a guaranteed three-to-one advantage in representation for the blue voters. Here, 14 red dots are "packed" into the green-tinted district and the remaining 18 are "cracked" across the three gray-tinted districts.

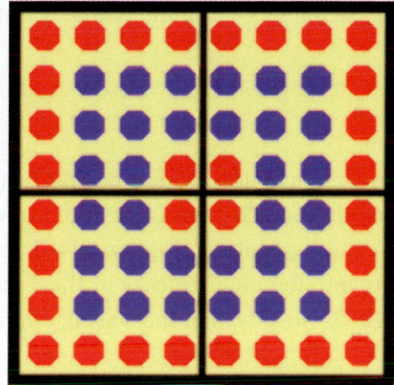
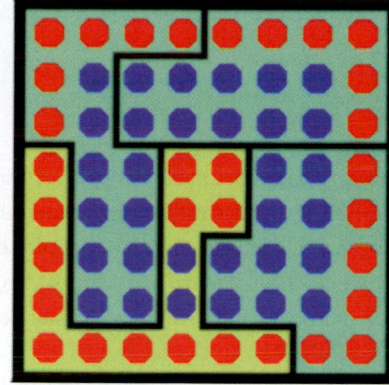

majority. Subsequent to the board's redistricting, the 2002 election increased the senate Republican majority to 19 and gave Republicans a majority in the Texas house for the first time since Reconstruction.

Redistricting for the U.S. Congress after 2000. Following a series of lawsuits, the Texas districts that elect members of the U.S. House were redesigned in 2000 by a panel of one Democratic and two Republican U.S. district judges. Despite the political tendencies of the judges, the Democrats still maintained a 17-to-15 majority in the Texas congressional delegation after the 2002 elections. Given the narrow majority that the Republicans possessed in the U.S. House, its former majority leader, Tom DeLay (a Texan), encouraged Republican-controlled legislatures in Texas, Colorado, and other states to redraw congressional districts before the 2010 census to favor Republican candidates.

In Texas, Governor Rick Perry called a special session to revise the 2000 judicial plan. The first two special sessions were unsuccessful, because first the house and then the senate Democrats fled the state. The congressional district boundaries were finally redrawn in a third special session in 2003.

As shown by the irregular district shapes in Figure 24–3, the Republican majority in the third legislative special session used classic gerrymandering techniques to redraw the boundaries for the Texas congressional districts. Although the federal courts prohibit racial gerrymandering, they are reluctant to become involved in **partisan gerrymandering**.[3]

Following the 2006 elections, the Texas congressional delegation still had a Republican majority. Anglo American Democratic members of Congress and rural constituents appear to have been the principal losers. Armed with new census data and gains in congressional district seats, the Texas legislature will begin the process of redrawing its congressional district lines in 2011.

Partisan Gerrymandering
The drawing of district lines for the purpose of providing electoral advantage to members of one political party.

[3]The United States Supreme Court, by a 6-3 vote, refused to hear an appeal from Colorado Republicans following a Colorado Supreme Court ruling that nullified political gerrymandering similar to that in Texas. The gerrymandering was found by the state court to be in conflict with the Colorado Constitution.

WHO CAN BECOME A MEMBER OF THE LEGISLATURE?

We have already described the legal requirements for holding legislative office in Texas. The most important requirements, though, are not the legal ones but the informal ones. Political, social, and economic criteria largely determine who is elected not only to the state legislature but also to offices at all levels of government—national, state, county, city, and special district.

RACE AND GENDER

In 2004, Texas became a majority-minority state.[4] Texas is a state where no one racial or ethnic group accounts for the majority of the population. The change in the state's demographics has impacted the makeup of the Texas legislature. Figures 24–5 and 24–6 track the increase of Latino, African American, and female members of the Texas house of representatives and Texas senate since 1963—just before the Voting Rights Act of 1965.

Latinos make up 37 percent of the Texas population but hold just over 20 percent of the seats in the Texas house and 23 percent in the Texas senate. It is important to note that many Latinos are not eligible to vote because they are not U.S. citizens. As Latino immigrants become U.S. citizens and vote, their levels of representation are expected to

FIGURE 24–5 Percentage of Hispanic, African American, and Female Members of the Texas House of Representatives, 1963–2011

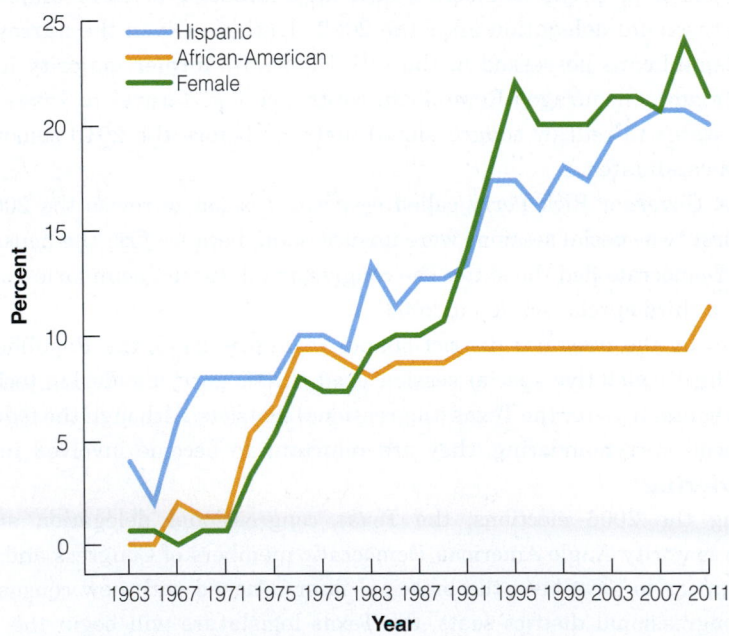

[4]Robert Bernstein, "Texas Becomes Nation's Newest 'Majority-Minority' State, Census Bureau Announces," *U.S. Census Bureau News*, accessed February 24, 2008, at www.census.gov/PressRelease/www/releases/archives/population/005514.html.

FIGURE 24–6 Percentage of Hispanic, African American, and Female Members of the Texas Senate, 1963–2011

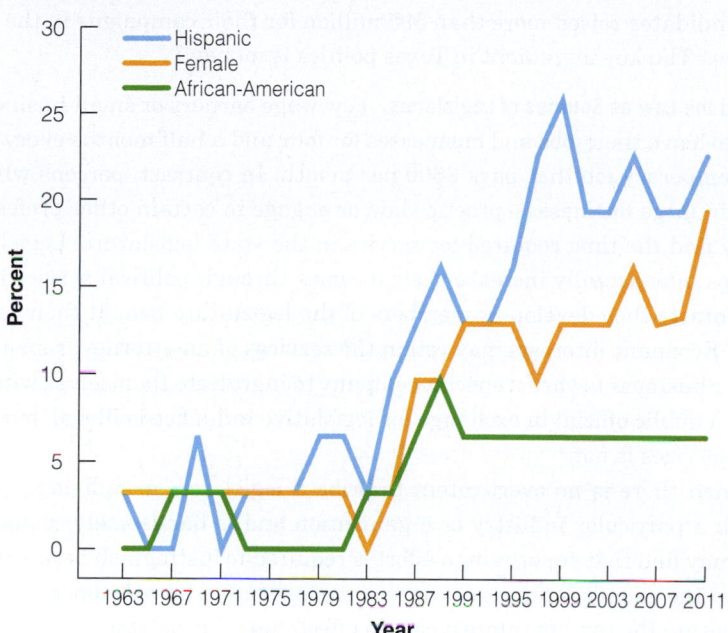

improve. African Americans, with just over 12 percent of the population, are represented by about 11 percent of the seats in the Texas house and 6 percent in the Texas senate. Asian Americans, accounting for 4 percent of the population, are represented by two Asian Americans in the Texas house and none in the Texas senate. During the 82nd legislative session, two Asian Americans served in the Texas house: Republican Angie Chen Button and Democrat Hubert Vo. Martha Wong, who also served in the Texas house, was defeated in 2006.

The female population is perhaps the most underrepresented of the major groups. Although females account for slightly more than half of the state's population, only 21 percent of the members of the Texas house and 19 percent of Texas senators are female. As the number of female candidates increases, one can expect to see more women serving in the Texas legislature.

The Anglo population in the state is 46 percent of the total population, but accounts for 67 percent of the members of the Texas house and 71 percent of the Texas senate. Anglo males account for a larger percentage of the members of the Texas legislature than their numbers in the population would indicate.

That the Institute for Women's Policy Research ranked Texas 49th among the 50 states in women's voter turnout?

CAMPAIGN FUNDING

Another qualification for winning legislative office is access to campaign funds. Many competent, motivated individuals who want to serve are excluded because they are unable to raise the funds necessary to finance an adequate campaign. Thus, the voters' pool of potential candidates may be limited to persons who can appeal to the economic interests that provide most campaign contributions. Securing office space, printing campaign literature, buying postage stamps, building a campaign organization, and purchasing advertisements are all among the necessary ingredients for a successful campaign—and all are expensive. In 2008, the National Institute on Money in State

Politics found that the 361 candidates who ran for the Texas house raised an average of $197,415 for their campaigns. In 2006, the candidates raised an average of $153,706 for their campaigns. In two years, the average amount raised increased by more than $43,000. The Texas senate candidates raised an average of $478,530 for their campaigns.[5] Candidates raised more than $95 million for their campaigns in the house and senate races.[6] The key ingredient in Texas politics is money![7]

Business and the Law as Sources of Legislators. Few wage earners or small-business owners can afford to leave their jobs and businesses for four and a half months every other year to take a temporary job that pays $600 per month. In contrast, persons who serve as executives in large businesses, practice law, or engage in certain other professions may more easily find the time required for service in the state legislature. Legislators from these groups may actually increase their incomes through political service if the prestige and contacts they develop as members of the legislature benefit their law firms or companies. Economic interests may retain the services of an attorney from a particular firm or steer business toward a specific company to ingratiate themselves with a legislator. Paying a public official in exchange for legislative influence is illegal, but paying for goods and services is not.[8]

Even when there is no overt intent to bribe a legislator, an individual who works closely with a particular industry or organization and is handsomely compensated for that work may find that superhuman effort is required to distinguish between the public interest and the client's interest. Because some legislators do not appear to strive very hard to separate the two, an interest can, in effect, "buy a legislator."

When Legislators Appear before Boards and in Court. Legislators who are lawyers may also be employed to represent clients in adversary proceedings before the various state administrative boards and commissions. The legislature is responsible for the appropriations to state boards and commissions, and the fact that the concerned agency may be generous in evaluating the legal arguments of a lawyer-legislator is not lost on the litigants. In this instance, both the lawyer and her or his client may benefit from the lawyer's legislative position.

A state judge may also grant a trial delay in civil or criminal litigation to a lawyer serving in the legislature. This right of delay lasts from 30 days before a legislative session begins until 30 days after it ends. Either the plaintiff or the defendant may benefit from such a delay. Thus, when either party to a suit seeks a delay, and the legislature is in session, that party may find a lawyer-legislator desirable as a counsel.

ORGANIZATION OF THE TEXAS LEGISLATURE

The Texas legislative system places an unusual degree of power in the hands of the presiding officers of each chamber. As in most legislative bodies, the house and senate committees do much of the actual work of the legislature. The presiding officers appoint the chairpersons of committees and most of the committee members. In the Texas legislature, committees are often seen as extensions of the presiding officers' power.

---

[5]National Institute on Money in State Politics; "Election Summary," http://www.followthemoney.org/.
[6]Texans for Public Justice, "Money in PoliTex: A Guide to Money in the 2008 Texas Elections." September 29, 2009 at http://info.tpj.org/reports/politex08/index08.html.
[7]See http://www.followthemoney.org for comprehensive information on Texas campaign contributions.
[8]See John Dunbar, "Public Service, Personal Gain in Texas," Center for Public Integrity, available at www.publicintegrity.org/oi/iys.aspx?st=TX&sub=pub.

THE PRESIDING OFFICERS

The presiding officers in the Texas legislature are the lieutenant governor in the senate and the speaker of the house of representatives. Although these are primarily legislative offices, their holders exercise significant influence throughout Texas government.

Lieutenant Governor. The presiding officer in the Texas senate is the lieutenant governor, who serves as its president. Although not a senator, the lieutenant governor is in the unique situation of being a member of both the legislative branch and the executive branch. The lieutenant governor is elected in a statewide, partisan election, and can have a party affiliation that is different from that of the governor or other members of the Texas executive branch. In the event the office becomes vacant through death, disability, or resignation, the senate elects one of its members to serve as acting lieutenant governor until the next regular election. The senators have adopted rules that grant the lieutenant governor extensive legislative, organizational, procedural, administrative, and planning authority.

TEXAS LIEUTENANT GOVERNOR David Dewhurst and Speaker of the House Joe Straus. A bipartisan coalition in the Texas House of Representatives elected Republican Joe Straus as its speaker in January, 2009. Straus, however, had to deal with new political realities as the 2010 election boosted the Republican majority to an unprecedented level. (AP Photo/Harry Cabluck)

The election of the lieutenant governor, who serves a four-year term, attracts far less public attention than the power of the office merits; the lieutenant governor is one of the most influential officials in Texas government. Organized interests are well aware of the importance of the office and contribute sizable sums to influence the election.

Although lieutenant governors in many states exercise a hybrid executive-legislative function, their influence rarely approaches that of the lieutenant governor of Texas. The political power of the lieutenant governor of Texas is largely based on senate rules and could be weakened by a majority of the senate. Therefore, the lieutenant governor must maintain a working relationship with the majority of the senators. The Republican-dominated 79th senate (2005), however, enacted rules that maintained the power of the Republican lieutenant governor.

Speaker of the House. The Texas house of representatives, by a majority vote of its membership, chooses its presiding officer from among its members by a recorded vote. The actual campaign can be very competitive and may attract candidates from all parts of the ideological spectrum. Yet because the vote for speaker is not secret, the successful candidate may take punitive action against opponents and their supporters. As a result, incumbent speakers have rarely faced serious opposition. When Republicans gained a majority in the Texas house in 2002, however, they ousted the Democratic incumbent and elected the first Republican speaker since Reconstruction, Tom Craddick.

During the 80th legislative session, Speaker Craddick faced an open challenge from members of his own party who were critical of Craddick's autocratic style. House Republicans attempted to oust the speaker, but the speaker refused to recognize motions that would lead to him being unseated. In legislative bodies, when majority parties hold a significant majority over the minority party, party leaders such as Tom Craddick enjoy centralized party control. Under centralized party control, the party leadership maintains strong control over the activities of the chamber. When the majority party loses seats, however, the party leadership loses control of the legislative agenda; that is, the legislative body becomes decentralized. When the Republicans took control of the Texas house, they enjoyed an 88 to 62 majority. In 2008, the house Republicans lost an additional four seats, giving Republicans a 76 to 74 majority over Democrats. Since taking over the Texas house, Republicans have lost 12 seats, even when the senate Republicans gained seats. Figure 24–7 shows the percentage of Democratic and Republican officeholders in the Texas house since the Republicans took control of the chamber. When such losses occur, rank-and-file party members tend to punish their leadership. The 12 lost seats, in conjunction with Speaker Craddick's autocratic leadership style, led many of his fellow Republicans to turn on him. In 2009, Republicans and Democrats joined together to elect Joe Straus as their new speaker. Joe Straus is a more moderate Republican from San Antonio, called by some members of his own party a RINO (Republican in Name Only).[9] Although speakers generally do not attract a lot of opposition, Speaker Straus's moderate views have continued to attract opponents from within his own party.[10] The 2010 elections gave Republicans 65 percent of the seats in the Texas house, a significant increase that will help the republican leadership.

House members who support the winning candidate can become part of the speaker's team, even if they are members of the opposition party. As mentioned earlier, this Texas legislative idiosyncrasy is known as the no-party system. The speaker appoints team members to serve on prestigious committees and selects her or his most reliable supporters as committee chairs. Tom Craddick, the Republican speaker of the Texas house of representatives, has relied on Democrats to chair or vice chair committees. Of the 40 standing committees in

DID YOU KNOW?

That in Texas, a state legislator cannot legally receive a campaign contribution 30 days before the start of a regular legislative session or 20 days after its adjournment?

FIGURE 24–7 Percentage of Democrat and Republican House Members since 2003 (the Year Republicans Won Control of the House)

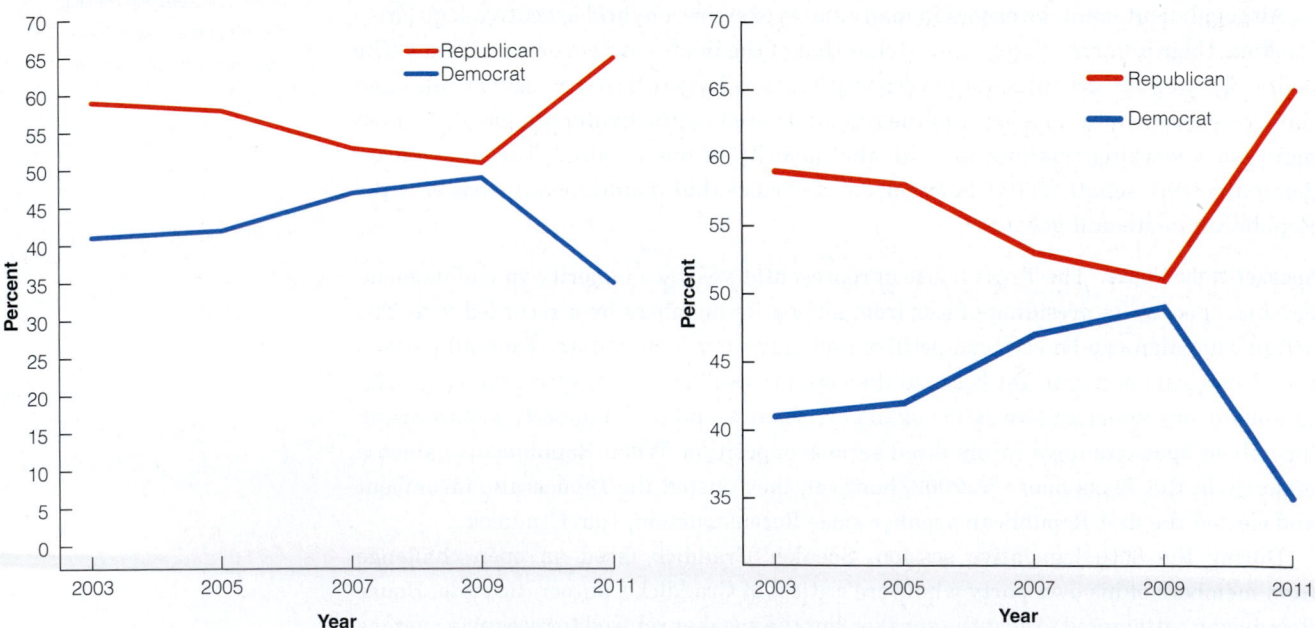

[9]Leo Berman, in a television interview, claimed that the Republican Party had been "taken over by 11 people last session that we call RINOs, Republicans in Name Only." Representative Berman counts Speaker Straus as one of the 11 RINOs. Watson, Brad (2010, June 20). *Inside Texas Politics* [Television Broadcast], Dallas/Fort Worth, WFAA News 8, http://www.wfaa.com/video?id=96754954&sec=552937.

[10]Jason Embry, "Former Party Leader Tries to Rally Republicans Against Straus," *Austin American Statesman*, http://www.statesman.com/blogs/content/sharedgen/blogs/austin/politics/entries/2010/06/12/former_party_leader_tries_to_r.html?cxntfid=blogs_postcards.

the Texas house, 10 were headed by Democrats during the 80th legislature. Another 15 vice chairs were Democrats. Lobbyists attempt to form alliances with powerful team members by making campaign contributions and supporting their legislative agendas.

Running for Speaker. Funds raised and spent during a campaign for the speakership are part of the public record. Candidates for speaker are required to file a complete statement of loans, campaign contributions, and expenditures with the secretary of state. No corporation, labor union, or organization may contribute, and individual contributions are limited to $100. All expenditures over $10 must be reported. These requirements represent an attempt to reduce the influence of lobbyists and interest groups on the speaker's race by limiting and making public their campaign contributions. Still, the support of **"The Lobby"** (the major Texas economic interests) remains necessary to become speaker. In an attempt to curtail abuses of power, a law against "legislative bribery" prohibits the use of threats or promises of important appointments during the campaign to become speaker. The law is difficult to enforce, and it is simply understood that the speaker's supporters will be appointed to important committees.

LEGISLATIVE COMMITTEES

Because several thousand bills are introduced into the Texas legislature each session, a division of labor is necessary for an orderly operation. The committee system exists to carry out this distribution of tasks. Each committee has a chair and a vice chair. The chair controls the committee's agenda, its schedule of hearings, the witnesses to be called, and the voting schedule.

Types of Committees. There are several types of committees in the Texas house and Texas senate: standing, conference, joint, and select committees. The latter of these are also referred to as special committees and can have features of joint committees. Committees are classified based on function, membership, and longevity. The function of some committees is to draft legislation (standing and conference committees), while others are charged with a specific purpose, such as studying a problem or making recommendations (select and joint committees). The membership of some committees may only include members of one chamber (standing and select committees), while others may consist of members from both chambers (conference and joint committees). Some special committees may even include members of the public. Some tend to be temporary or ad hoc committees (conference and select committees), while others are more permanent (standing and joint committees). Table 24–1 summarizes the characteristics of each type of committee.

Standing Committees. There are two types of standing committees—substantive and procedural committees. All of the standing committees are listed in Table 24–2. Substantive and procedural committees are marked accordingly. Most committees are standing substantive committees. Each committee of this type is given authority over a subject of political interest, such as education, taxes, appropriations, or agriculture. Each committee also may have subcommittees with authority over specific topics within the general subject area of the committee. Substantive committees have been called "little legislatures," because they normally conduct the real legislative business of conflict, compromise, and accommodation.

Each bill brought before the Texas legislature is assigned to a substantive standing committee in each chamber, where witnesses—both for and against the proposal—may be heard, debates held, and bills **marked up** (changed) or killed. Successful bills are seldom reported out of a committee in their original form. Because standing committees do the basic legislative work, the general membership relies heavily on them for

"The Lobby"
Collectively, the most politically and economically powerful special-interest groups in Texas.

Mark up
In legislation, to amend, change, or rewrite bills while they are in committee.

TABLE 24–1 Types of Committees in Texas Legislature

	STANDING	CONFERENCE	JOINT	SELECT
FUNCTION	Lawmaking authority	Lawmaking authority	Advisory	Advisory
LONGEVITY	Permanent	Temporary	Permanent	Temporary
MEMBERSHIP	From one chamber only	From both the house and senate	From both the house and senate	May include members of one chamber, both chambers, or members of the legislature and non-legislators
EXAMPLES	House: Agriculture and Livestock Committee Senate: Criminal Justice Committee		Legislative Budget Board	House Select Committee Emergency Preparedness

guidance on how to vote on a bill being considered on the floor. In fact, attempting to amend some bills, or even questioning the work of the committee, violates the norms of the Texas senate.

The most important standing procedural committee is the **Calendars Committee** in the Texas house of representatives. It controls the flow of legislation from the substantive committees to the floor of the house. No bill can reach the floor of the house without authorization from the Calendars Committee (or the much less important Local and Consent Calendars Committee).

Pigeonholing Bills. An important function of committees in the Texas legislature is to serve as a burial ground for bills. A legislator may introduce a bill as a favor to some group or constituent who feels very strongly about the matter, even though the legislator knows full well that the bill will be killed, or **pigeonholed**, in committee (and that the committee will take the blame). Other bills may be assigned to hostile committees with the expectation that they will be totally rewritten, if not pigeonholed.

Killing legislation by denying it a hearing is a convenient method of affecting public policy. Legislators do not have to go on record as being in opposition to a bill and thereby provide campaign fodder for political opponents. They can claim that they simply never had a chance to vote on the measure, even though they may have been instrumental in presiding over the bill's death in a substantive committee or subcommittee or in one of the calendars committees.

Expertise. Where a seniority system is used, committee members and committee chairs are usually returned to the same committee posts each session, and legislators can thus become reasonably well informed, if not expert, on a given subject. This expertise is important, because members must hear interest-group lobbyists and administrative officials and evaluate their arguments on the merits of proposed legislation.

Calendars Committee
The committee in the Texas house of representatives that assigns bills to the calendars for floor action. (The less important Local and Consent Calendars Committee also performs this function.)

Pigeonhole
The action by which a legislative committee tables a bill and then ignores it.

TABLE 24–2 List of Substantive and Procedural Standing Committees in the Texas House and Senate Committees (81st Legislature)

HOUSE COMMITTEES	SENATE COMMITTEES
Agriculture & Livestock	Administration (Procedural)
Appropriations	Agriculture & Rural Affairs
Border & International Affairs	Business & Commerce
Business & Industry	Criminal Justice
Calendars (Procedural)	Economic Development
Corrections	Education
County Affairs	Finance
Criminal Jurisprudence	Government Organization
Culture, Recreation, & Tourism	Health & Human Services
Defense and Veterans' Affairs	Higher Education
Elections	Intergovernmental Relations
Energy Resources	International Relations and Trade
Environmental Regulation	Jurisprudence
General Investigating & Ethics (Procedural)	Natural Resources
Higher Education	Nominations (Procedural)
House Administration (Procedural)	State Affairs
Human Services	Transportation & Homeland Security
Insurance	Veteran Affairs & Military
Judiciary & Civil Jurisprudence Land & Resource Management	
Licensing & Administrative Procedures	
Local & Consent Calendars (Procedural)	
Natural Resources	
Pensions, Investments & Financial Services	
Public Education	
Public Health	
Public Safety	
Redistricting (Procedural)	
Rules & Resolutions (Procedural)	
State Affairs	
Technology, Economic Development & Workforce	
Transportation	
Urban Affairs	
Ways & Means	

Compared with the U.S. Congress and most other state legislatures, the Texas legislature operates under a very limited seniority system. Therefore, the expertise of committee members may come from their occupational backgrounds rather than from legislative experience. As a result, many Texas legislators are *preference outliers*. These are legislators who self-select into one particular committee. Texas legislators, as we have seen, are seldom politicians to the exclusion of other occupations, and their interest in their primary occupations may create conflicts with the public interest. For example, if the primary occupation of a legislator is banking, then that lawmaker may be more sensitive to the interests of the banking industry than to the interests of the public. The same problem arises with any occupation.

Bureaucratic Oversight. In the United States, legislatures function as watchdogs over the executive branch; that is, the legislature oversees the administrative bureaucracy as it executes the law and implements public programs. The vehicle for oversight is usually the legislative committee. Legislators wish to determine whether the bureaucrats are administering the laws in the way the legislature intended. They also must determine if new or revised legislation is needed. Accordingly, committees hold hearings and ask bureaucrats under their jurisdiction about the laws and programs that they are implementing.

Ostensibly, the committees are watching out for the public good by checking on whether the bureaucrats perform their duties in ways consistent with the public interest. More often than not, however, the committees serve as legislative advocates for the bureaucrats and the interests and viewpoints of their clientele. Therefore, a committee may not undertake a truly critical scrutiny of the agencies under its jurisdiction.

LEGISLATIVE STAFF

The Texas legislature has seen fit to provide only minimal funds for hiring competent staff. Monthly staff allotments are about $13,250 for house members and $35,623 for senators, who also receive reimbursement for other "reasonable and necessary" office expenses. These funds are not for personal use, but for staff salaries, office expenses, and official travel. House members have about three or four staff people, while in the senate, the average staff size is slightly more than seven. Some senators have as many as 14 staff members, while others have as few as four.[11]

The Consequences of Limited Staff Support. As a result of limited funds, neither individual legislators nor legislative committees have professional staff comparable to that of special-interest groups. With minimal staff support, individual legislators and committees have no way of challenging the expert testimony and arguments of interest-group lobbyists and agency liaisons. Powerful interests and administrative agencies have a distinct advantage when they alone possess information and expertise, and legislators become dependent on them for research data, advice, and other services. Some house and senate members with shared political views have pooled their expense allocations to hire staff personnel. This tactic provides the participants with a rudimentary level of independent information.

Barriers to Greater Staff Funding. Whenever the legislature considers larger appropriations to hire competent staff members, both the general public and special interests voice strong opposition. Members of the public are usually swayed by arguments against increased government spending and do not recognize the potential benefits of an informed legislature. Special interests understand very well how limited staff resources work to their benefit.

DID YOU KNOW?

That the most powerful Texas house committees are Appropriations, Ways and Means, and State Affairs, and that the most powerful Texas senate committees are Finance, Jurisprudence, and State Affairs?

---

[11]The data was calculated using the following report: House Research Organization, "Legislative Staff: 80th Legislature," *Focus Report No. 80-4,* March 1, 2007, accessed February 29, 2008, at www.hro.house.state.tx.us/focus/staff80.pdf.

POLITICS WITH A purpose

University Students as Legislative Aides

Members of the Texas legislature are given a monthly stipend to run their offices that is generally not enough to be an effective representative. As a result, state lawmakers depend heavily on interns for assistance to run their offices while the legislature is in and out of session. Many interns are involved in reviewing bills before the legislature. Interns are asked to provide lawmakers feedback on bills, meet with lobbyists, address constituency concerns, and work with the staff of other legislators. These very important functions are often assigned to university students with little or no experience with legislative work.

Some lobbyists complain that interns are given too many responsibilities and are underprepared for the important work assigned to them. Others believe that the use of interns creates an unstable environment where office staff members come and go with such frequency that it is difficult to develop institutional memory, or the know-how and experiences learned over many years. With the exception of lawmakers, who have longer tenures, few lawmakers retain their interns or their staff for a very long period of time, diminishing the experience of legislative office staff.

Nevertheless, the internship experience has a profound impact on the lives of university students who take part in such programs. Christopher Smith, an associate with Thompson and Knight, LLP, an international law firm with four Texas offices, writes that his internship experience provided him "an unparalleled opportunity to understand the legislative process by being part of the legislative process. The insight I gained and the relationships I developed as a TLIP intern are assets that will serve me well in my legal career."[1] Similarly, Chris Lopez, an associate attorney with Weil, Gotshal and Manges, LLP, another of Texas's largest firms, writes, "The Texas Legislative Internship Program provided me with the best opportunity to enhance my understanding of the Texas Legislature and contributed to my success as an attorney."[2] Young people who serve as interns develop a sense of self confidence in their ability to make a difference in public policy and in the lives of others.

Many find their way back into public service after having served as interns in Austin. Before Texas State Representative Ana Hernandez served in Austin as a lawmaker, she served as an intern. Similarly, Shelley Davis, who now serves as an assistant to the Reverend Jesse Jackson, credits his internship experience for preparing him for public office as a Georgetown city council member.[3]

Every year, thousands of university students who are interested in politics get involved in politics in a truly fundamental way—by serving as interns in the offices of state lawmakers. Such involvement has a direct impact in the enactment of public policy and in the casework assigned to interns. But, most importantly, such service has a meaningful and positive impact in the lives of those young people who serve as interns. What do you think about the role of interns in the Texas legislature? Is this something you think you could do?

[a]Texas Legislative Internship Program, accessed August 3, 2008, at www.rodneyellis.com/tlip/.

[b]Ibid.
[c]Ibid.

THE PRESIDING OFFICERS AND THE LEGISLATIVE COMMITTEES

To understand how the Texas legislature works, one must understand the powers exercised by the lieutenant governor in the Texas senate and the speaker in the Texas house of representatives. These powers can be roughly divided into two general categories: procedural powers, which are directly related to the legislative process, and institutional powers, which cover administrative policies such as budgeting, planning, and management.

A SUMMARY OF THE POWERS OF THE PRESIDING OFFICERS

Both state law and the rules of each chamber, formal and informal, give the presiding officers the procedural power to do the following:

1. Appoint most committee members.
2. Appoint committee chairs.
3. Assign bills to committees.
4. Schedule legislation for floor action.
5. Recognize members on the floor for amendments and points of order.
6. Interpret the procedural rules when conflict arises.
7. Appoint the chairs and members of conference committees.

In addition, laws or legislative rules grant the presiding officers nonprocedural, institutional power to do the following:

1. Serve as joint chairs and appoint the other members of the Legislative Budget Board.
2. Serve as joint chairs and appoint the other members of the Legislative Council.
3. Serve on and appoint the members of the Legislative Audit Committee.
4. Serve on and appoint the members of the Sunset Advisory Commission.

Power in the Texas legislature is thus concentrated in the offices of the lieutenant governor and the speaker of the house. In the rest of this chapter, we describe the powers just summarized in greater detail.

CONTROL OF COMMITTEES

Committees are central to the legislative process. Those who have the authority to name a committee's members are able to influence the policy decisions of the legislative body. In Texas, this authority belongs to the lieutenant governor and the speaker. Control of committees also provides a degree of control over scheduling, though the presiding officers have additional tools to control scheduling.

Committee Membership in the House. In the house, the speaker appoints the total membership as well as the chairs and vice chairs of the procedural committees. The speaker also appoints all members of the powerful Appropriations Committee, whose members serve as *ex officio* chairs of the subcommittees for budget and oversight of the substantive committees. Thus, the speaker's appointees to the Appropriations Committee also control the budget requests of the other committees. The Appropriations Committee strongly influences funding for all divisions of state government.

The House Calendars Committee controls the flow of legislation from the committees to the house floor. The speaker uses his or her influence with this procedural committee to determine if and when bills are heard on the house floor.

For all substantive committees other than Appropriations, a limited seniority system in the house determines up to one-half of the membership; the speaker appoints the other half. The speaker also appoints the committee's chair and vice chair, which ensures that the committee leadership, as well as a numerical majority of each substantive committee, will be speaker appointees. The standing committee chairs appoint the membership and the chairs and vice chairs of the subcommittees.

Committee Membership in the Senate. The lieutenant governor officially appoints the total membership, as well as the chairs and vice chairs, of all senate committees and permanent subcommittees. In practice, an informal seniority system allows the most senior senators to choose the committee on which they wish to serve until one-third of the committee's positions are filled. This ensures that senior senators will serve on the more powerful committees. The chairs of the standing committees, at their discretion, may appoint subcommittees from the committee membership.

Results of Control by the Presiding Officers. The appointive power of the presiding officers means that the action of a committee on specific legislation is usually predictable. The presiding officers can also use the power of appointment to reward friends and supporters as well as to punish opponents. Interest groups often attempt to influence the presiding officer's decision to their advantage. Interest groups need to have sympathetic members on a committee that reviews legislation important to their interests.

The relative power of the committee and the legislator's position on it (as committee or subcommittee chair) can largely determine that person's influence with administrators, lobbyists, and other legislators. Members actively seek appointments to committees that consider taxes, spending, or legislation for powerful economic interests or control the house calendar.

There is no way to determine precisely all the coalitions, compromises, and bargains that can relate to a desirable committee appointment. Negotiations for committee positions are intense, and conflicts over committee appointments arise in all legislative bodies. Concentrating the power over committee selection in the presiding officers is one way to resolve such conflicts.

That the house legislative calendars are Emergency, Major State, Constitutional Amendments, General State, Local Consent and Resolutions, and Congratulatory and Memorial Resolutions?

Selection of Committee Chairs. Because the chairs of legislative committees play an important role in determining the ultimate success or failure of legislation, conflict over their selection must be resolved. In some states, the majority of the committee selects the committee chair. In others, a seniority system is used. In Texas, as already explained, the presiding officers make these decisions. Owing to the power of each chair over the committee's organization, procedure, and subcommittees, the fate of much public policy can be determined when the chair is selected.

The presiding officers, by virtue of their power to appoint the chairs of all committees, have a tool that works like a magnet to attract legislators to their teams. If legislators want to get along in the legislature, they go along (with the presiding officers). This power also increases the bargaining position of the presiding officers relative to interest groups. The lobbyist who can help get a sympathetic legislator appointed as chair of an important committee has earned the salary paid by the interest group that employs her or him. At the same time, the lobbyist owes the presiding officer a real favor for appointing the "right" committee chair.

The appointive power of the presiding officers, although significant, does not provide absolute power over the legislature. The presiding officers may also appoint to important positions legislators who have political power in their own right, such as legislators with close ties to powerful special-interest groups. The presiding officers may then have the support of some of the most powerful members of the legislature in a reciprocally beneficial relationship. The presiding officers can usually count on the loyalty of the chairs, who in turn can usually depend on support from the presiding officers.

The No-Party System. The Texas legislature has historically been organized on the basis of ideology, rather than political party, with a coalition of Republicans and conservative-to-moderate Democrats usually in control. Under this no-party system, party affiliation has less significance than ideology and interest-group ties.

Historically, the conservative Democratic speakers appointed mostly Democrats—but some Republicans—to committee chair positions. Today, the no-party system has been modified and continued under conservative Republican leadership. In 2009, for example, under a Republican-controlled house, 53 percent of standing committees were chaired by Democrats, and 44 percent were vice-chaired by Democrats. The chairs of the most powerful committees are usually, but not always, appointed from the presiding officers' party.

It is important to understand that although the Texas legislature is organizationally a no-party system, party differences are important on matters of policy. Political party caucuses do not fill the positions of power as they do in the U.S. Congress, and members of the minority party may join the presiding officers' team, serve on important committees, and become committee chairs. Differences on public-policy issues are sometimes intense, however, and are becoming increasingly partisan.

COMMITTEE ACTION

Committee members can deliver to the leadership such things as substantial changes in bills, support for legislation favored by the leadership team, and opposition to legislation the leadership wants to defeat. A politically knowledgeable leadership that astutely uses its power over committee members can thus consolidate support for its policies.

Committee Jurisdiction. The presiding officers in the Texas legislature are responsible for assigning bills to particular committees. Because committee jurisdiction in the Texas legislature is often poorly defined, the officers have considerable discretion when making these assignments. The speaker may even reconsider a bill's assignment and change its committees during the legislative session.

The presiding officers do not hesitate to assign a bill they oppose to a committee they know will act unfavorably on the bill—and likewise, to assign a bill they support to a committee that will report on it positively. Because the presiding officers can stack the committees to their liking, this is a simple process.

Killing Bills. There are several reasons why a presiding officer may oppose a specific bill (other than that the bill is simply bad public policy):

1. The backers and financial supporters of the presiding officer may view the bill as a threat to their economic or political well-being.
2. The presiding officer and his or her team may feel that supporters of the bill have been uncooperative in the past and should be punished.
3. The supporters of the bill may be outbargained by the bill's opponents.
4. The presiding officer and his or her supporters may believe that the bill, if it became law, would take funds away from programs that they favor.

When a legislator who does not serve on the committee opposes a bill, the legislator may bargain with the members of the committee to pigeonhole it. There are several reasons for this. The most obvious is that the legislator—or an interest that she or he represents—is ideologically opposed to the substance of the bill. In addition, a legislator may want to kill a bill on which his or her political supporters are evenly divided, for no matter how the legislator voted, he or she would lose political support and face political or economic repercussions from angered interest groups or constituents.

Tagging

In the Texas senate, a rule that allows a senator to halt a standing committee's consideration of a bill for 48 hours.

Tagging in the Senate. The Texas senate also practices **tagging**. Once each session, any senator may require the chair of a senate committee to give that senator 48 hours' advance notice as to when the committee will hold hearings on a bill. This means that, in effect, the senator can delay the hearings for 48 hours. The tagging procedure is not debatable; any committee action on the bill within the 48-hour period is void. If the bill's sponsors can get the senator to remove the tag, however, the bill can be immediately cleared for committee hearings. The effect of tagging would be minimal if it were not for the limited legislative session. Under the existing system, tagging late in the session enables a single senator to kill or force the modification of a bill.

The Discharge Petition. All legislative bodies have some procedure whereby bills can be extracted from reluctant committees, but it is usually difficult to accomplish. Even though they may support a bill that is buried in a committee, legislators are reluctant to vote to discharge it. They see the discharge petition as a threat to the privileges of the entire committee system—privileges that they too enjoy.

The Relative Weakness of Committees in Texas. The importance of legislative committees within the political system varies from state to state. In Texas, the power of legislative committees is proportionately less, and the power of the bureaucracy and special interests is proportionately more, than in some other political jurisdictions. The reasons include the following:

1. Because legislative sessions are infrequent and short, committees seldom meet and cannot provide ongoing oversight.
2. Members often move from one committee to another, hampering the development of expertise and long-term working relationships.
3. Texas legislators serve for relatively short periods compared with top administrators and lobbyists.

RESTRAINTS ON THE POWERS OF THE PRESIDING OFFICERS

Although taken together, the organizational, procedural, and institutional powers of the speaker and the lieutenant governor seem to be—and at times are—overwhelming, certain restraints curtail arbitrary and absolute use of these powers.

Personality. The personalities of the individual presiding officers and the way they view their offices determine their approach to legislative leadership. They may use their powers to develop strong, aggressive leadership, ruthlessly overpowering opposition, or they may be accommodating and compromising, accomplishing the desired results with only the implied possibility of reprisal.

The Team. The presiding officers require a strong coalition of legislative support to accomplish their aims, despite the concentration of powers they enjoy. Support from other legislators may come because of friendship or ideological agreement. Legislators may believe that it is in the best interest of their constituents and supporters for them to be team players and back the presiding officers. The speaker and the lieutenant governor are usually able to build on, and add cohesiveness to, this support through use of their powers to reward or punish.

The Lobby and the Bureaucracy. The relationship between the presiding officers, The Lobby, and their bureaucratic allies is of great importance in determining the chance of success for specific legislation. When the lieutenant governor, the speaker, bureaucrats, and powerful lobbyists all agree and work together toward a common goal, legislative victory is almost ensured.

In the event of conflict between the lobby-bureaucracy coalition and the speaker or the lieutenant governor, the program of the presiding officer may be either diluted or defeated, depending on such complex factors as the amount of support that can be mustered from the governor, other interest groups, and other legislators. Against a strong coalition of an interest group and the bureaucracy, all of the formal and informal powers of the presiding officers may not be enough to control the legislation. A conflict of this nature is unusual, however, and the presiding officers are usually in basic agreement with the more powerful interests, which often have given political and financial support to their campaigns.

The Governor. Veto power and influence with lobbyists are the most useful instruments the governor has to achieve changes in the substance of bills while they are still in the legislature. The veto powers given to the governor by the Texas Constitution are among her or his most important powers. They include the veto over legislative acts and the item veto over appropriations. These formal powers place the governor in a strong bargaining position, and the governor's support for or opposition to specific programs is an important determinant of their success.

The governor also has the support of friendly interest groups, which can often be enlisted to exert pressure on the presiding officers and other legislators. Interest-group support complements the governor's formal legislative power and enhances his or her influence. A governor who tends toward activism can exercise substantial influence over legislation and thereby moderate the powers of the presiding officers. In fact, successful legislation usually requires a coalition among the governor, the lieutenant governor, and the speaker, with each affecting the content of legislation. Of course, the governor has lost a battle with the legislative leadership if forced to veto a bill after attempting to influence it. If the governor chooses a passive legislative role, her or his influence is significantly decreased—inaction or restraint affects public policy as profoundly as does activist leadership.

The Political Climate. The general public is seldom aware of events that take place in Austin. Rare exceptions arise when news of a scandal spreads across the state, as in the examples of the veterans' land scandals of the 1950s, the Sharpstown bank scandal of the 1970s, and the delinquent property tax scandal of the 1990s. Although public interest is stimulated by a scandal, most citizens seem content to find and punish a few "bad apples" instead of demanding serious institutional inquiry and the systemic reform of government procedures and regulations.

Scandal does make the presiding officers aware of public scrutiny and temporarily more aware of public criticism. In fact, the political climate following both the Sharpstown and the delinquent property tax scandals resulted in ethics reform legislation. Without scandal, the legislative leadership is all but free from public attention, with only interest groups, administrators, a few concerned citizens, some members of the press, and the governor monitoring legislative activity.

If two-party competition ever returns to Texas, the competition might weaken the authority of the presiding officers, especially the lieutenant governor. It is true that if partisan politics dominated the house, the house majority might simply choose a member of the majority party as speaker and retain the somewhat authoritarian house rules. In contrast, if a lieutenant governor were elected who belonged to a different party than the senate majority, that majority might change the senate rules to seriously reduce the lieutenant governor's powers. In this event, the senate majority would have to institute other mechanisms to broker power and resolve conflict.

Political or Economic Ambition. Through effective management of the press, accumulation of political credits to be cashed in at some future date, and consolidation of interest-group support, the offices of speaker and lieutenant governor can serve as stepping-stones for advancement in politics. The presiding officers must not, however, antagonize powerful economic and political forces in the process. Consequently, ambition can serve as a very real restraint on their independence.

DID YOU KNOW?

That in 1965, 22 members of the Texas house voted against a bill that was a word-for-word copy of the U.S. Bill of Rights when it was introduced as "an act to protect our fundamental liberties" by Representative Jake Johnson, a liberal from San Antonio?

Interest-group support, campaign finances, and the backing of established politicians are all necessary for political advancement. Presiding officers must play their political cards right if they want to build an economic and political base solid enough to attain higher office.

Other Legislators. Many committee chairs and other legislators exercise a political influence in their own right through their mastery of the intricacies of legislative rules and procedures, strong support of powerful interest groups, and the respect or fear they can generate in other legislators. Because of the ties these individuals have built through the years with administrators, interest groups, and other legislators, the presiding officers may need to solicit their backing on key legislation. Generally, however, these individuals are the exception in an environment that is heavily influenced by the lieutenant governor or speaker.

THE CALENDAR AND THE FLOOR

The instrument for controlling the flow of legislation from the committees to the floor is the **calendar**. Control of the calendar of bills is important in any legislative body. In Texas, it is of paramount importance because of the short biennial sessions.

With the calendar schedules, as with other important aspects of the legislative process, power in the Texas legislature is centralized in the offices of the presiding officers. Unlike many of their other organizational and procedural powers, however, the ability of the speaker and the lieutenant governor to control scheduling is based as much on their influence with other legislators as on the formal powers of the offices.

Because timing a bill for consideration on the floor is critical to its eventual passage or defeat, control of the schedule is a powerful weapon that can be used to aid or to hinder legislation, to reward allies, or to punish enemies. For example, any of the following situations may occur:

1. Supporters may want floor consideration of a bill delayed until they can muster the necessary votes to get it passed. (Opponents, in contrast, may favor quick action because they have the necessary votes to defeat the bill but believe those votes could erode if the supporters are given time to consolidate their forces.)
2. Conversely, supporters may want early consideration of a bill because the opposition appears to be gaining strength. (Opponents would want delay under these circumstances.)
3. If a bill has been placed far down on the calendar, opponents can kill it through the filibuster, tagging, or parliamentary maneuvers even if they are in the minority.

HOUSE CALENDARS

The speaker of the house exercises no formal control over the house calendars. The Calendars Committee (and the much less important Local and Consent Calendars Committee) performs this function. This apparent decentralization of power, however, is more illusion than reality. The members and the chairs of the two committees are appointed by the speaker, are allies of the speaker, and can usually be persuaded to be amenable to the speaker's wishes.

There are several calendars for different kinds of bills. Unimportant or trivial bills are placed on special schedules and are usually disposed of promptly with little debate by the body of the house. The process is not so automatic for major or controversial legislation, however. In fact, the speaker and the committee chair often use the Calendars Committee as a black hole into which bills simply disappear. The process was once even

Calendar
In the Texas legislature, the schedule that serves as a conduit for legislation between the committees and the primary legislative body.

more opaque than it is today. In a much-applauded action, the 1993 house, under the leadership of Speaker Pete Laney, adopted rules making the process more open to the general house membership.

THE SENATE CALENDAR

Unlike the house, the senate has only one calendar. Officially, the senate has a rule that requires bills to be placed on the calendar and then considered on the senate floor in the same chronological order in which they were reported from the committees. In practice, bills are taken off the calendar for senate consideration only by a suspension of this rule. The **suspension of the rule** requires a two-thirds majority vote of the entire membership of the senate.

Suspension of the Rule
Setting aside of the rules of a legislative body so that another set of rules can be used.

Blocking Bill
In Texas, a bill placed early on the senate calendar that will never actually be considered. A rule—which can be suspended by a two-thirds vote—requires that the senate address bills in chronological order. The blocking bill ensures that a measure must win the vote of two-thirds of the senate even to be considered.

The Blocking Bill. The procedure for consideration goes something like this: The first bill placed on the senate calendar each session is called a **blocking bill**. It is usually a bill dealing with a proposed horticultural change somewhere around the state capitol. It will never be taken off the calendar. It does, however, block all other bills' access to the floor except by the two-thirds vote to suspend the rule.

A Two-Thirds Majority for Action. This senate practice affects the senate's entire legislative process. The irony is that while only a simple majority is necessary for final passage in the senate, a two-thirds majority is necessary to get the bill to the floor for consideration. It can be said that this process protects the minority from the majority. It is also a means whereby the senate can kill a bill without having a floor vote for or against—the bill simply fails to reach the floor and so dies on the calendar. Although lobbyists are keenly interested in which bills die for lack of two-thirds support in a consideration vote, the general public and some members of the press are often unaware that an important vote has even occurred.

During the 81st legislative session, the senate changed its rules for one bill and one bill only. In 2009, Republicans in the state legislature, fearing voter fraud, wanted to pass a bill that would require voters to show a picture identification card when they cast their votes. Democrats, fearing that the bill would prevent low-income and elderly populations from voting (because they are less likely to have a picture identification card), objected to such a law. The senate Democrats held 12 of the 31 seats (or 39 percent of the seats). These 12 votes effectively prevented the senate from moving the voter ID bill to the senate floor. Because of the two-thirds rule, Republicans needed 21 votes, or two-thirds of the votes, to pass the voter ID bill. To permit this, they changed the rules for this one bill, allowing the voter ID bill to come up for a floor vote with a simple majority, rather than the two-thirds votes typically needed.

The bill would eventually die in the house, however, but only after Democrats in the Texas house slowed down the work of the chamber to such an extent that the session would end before the house would get to the voter ID bill. The house Democrats used a tactic known as *chubbing*, in which house members pepper bill sponsors with questions on seemingly innocuous bills for nine minutes and 30 seconds, having the effect of delaying the legislative process, and essentially killing bills that the chamber does not get to because the session has ended.

The two-thirds rule is a tool that can be used to enhance the powers of the presiding officer. By using this requirement, the lieutenant governor can keep a bill from reaching the floor of the senate by simply persuading 11 members to vote against it. The bill then lacks the necessary two-thirds majority and cannot advance to the floor of the senate. Any coalition of 11 senators can achieve the same result—occasionally, against the wishes of the lieutenant governor.

THE QUORUM REQUIREMENT

At least two-thirds of the members of each chamber must be present to conduct business. Absence of 11 or more senators brings any senate action to a halt, as does the absence of 51 or more house members. The quorum rule is written into the state constitution, and lack of a quorum is an absolute bar to legislative action. This fact has led to a series of incidents in which members have absented themselves to halt business. Texas has an unusually high figure for a legislative quorum. Half the membership is a more common rule, and the U.S. Constitution establishes that quorum for the U.S. House and Senate.

THE FLOOR

The Texas Constitution requires that bills must be "read on three consecutive days in each house." The purpose of this action on the **floor** is to ensure that laws are not passed without adequate opportunity for debate. Bills are read once on being introduced before the presiding officer assigns them to a committee. In practice, the entire bill is seldom read at this time. Instead, a caption, or brief summary, is read to acquaint the members of the legislature with the subject of the bill. The bill is read the second time before floor debate in each chamber, and if an entire bill is to be read, it is usually on this second reading. The third reading usually occurs at least one day after floor passage.

> **Floor**
> The place where a legislative body debates, amends, votes on, enacts, and defeats proposed legislation; the entire house or senate acting as a whole.

Bills containing a statement that they are "cases of imperative public necessity" may be read for the third time on the same day as floor passage, as long as four-fifths of the membership agree. All bills now routinely contain this provision and usually receive the third reading immediately following floor passage. A simple majority is required for passage on the third reading, while a two-thirds majority is necessary for the addition of an amendment.

The House Floor. As bills reach the floor of the house, a loudspeaker system allows the members and visitors to follow the debate. **Floor leaders** usually stand at the front of the chamber, answer questions, and speak in favor of or against the bill. Microphones located elsewhere in the house chamber serve opponents of the bill and other concerned lawmakers as they argue against the bill, speak for the bill, or simply ask questions.

> **Floor Leaders**
> Legislators who are responsible for getting party members to vote for or against particular legislation.

The consideration of bills on the floor of the house would seem to be a study in confusion and inattention. Throughout the process, members of the house may be laughing, talking, reading papers, or sleeping at their desks. Because many members often know very little about a bill under consideration, however, this is an excellent opportunity for both proponents and opponents of the legislation to seek support for their positions. Eloquent speeches seldom change votes. In fact, many members vote for or against legislation based on who is supporting it or who is against it and only then ask what the bill was all about. This practice is especially true of specialized bills that have generated little statewide interest. Voting time usually brings both supporters and opponents of the bill up and down the aisles pleading with either one finger (vote yes) or two fingers (vote no).

Electronic Voting in the House. House members insert cards into a voting panel on their desks that allows them to push buttons to record a vote of yes, no, or present but not voting. The tallies are displayed on a large electronic scoreboard with green, red, and white bulbs next to each legislator's name. (Green means yes, red means no, and white means present but not voting.)

Although the use of the electronic voting machine in the Texas house is a major innovation, it has made the practice of "ghost voting" more visible. The house rules prohibit ghost voting, whereby legislators cast votes for absent colleagues. The practice, however,

REPRESENTATIVE JIM KEFFER
urges an "aye" vote on the floor of the Texas House of Representatives. (AP Photo/ Harry Cabluck)

Points of Order
A formal question to the chairperson about the legitimacy of a parliamentary process. A successful point of order can result in the postponement or defeat of legislation.

Committee of the Whole
An entire legislative body (such as the Texas senate) acting as a committee. The committee's purpose is to allow the body to relax its rules and thereby expedite legislation.

Cloture
An action by which legislative debate is ended so that a floor vote must be taken.

persists. Nanci Wilson, an Austin reporter for CBS Channel 42, caught many lawmakers casting votes for absent colleagues.[12] The practice has real implications. Suspecting that the defeat of a 1993 bill to increase the penalties for having drugs or weapons near schools was a result of ghost voting, the bill's supporters requested a roll-call vote. Ten members, eight of whom had voted against the bill, had been present only in spirit. The bill was then passed 65 to 58 by the roll-call vote.

Points of Order in the House. Throughout the voting, the speaker recognizes members from the floor, rules on **points of order**, and so forth. If a point of order is sustained late in the session, there may not be time to correct the error, and in that case the bill dies.

Although raising a point of order is not uncommon, it seldom has the impact that it did during the 1997 legislature. Representative Debra Danburg, a Democrat from Houston, raised a point of order that killed a bill requiring parental notification before a minor could have an abortion. In reaction, Arlene Wohlgemuth, a Republican representative from Burleson and a proponent of the antiabortion bill, raised points of order that killed some 80 pending bills, many of which were supported by Governor George W. Bush and other Republican legislators.[13]

The Senate Floor. The senate scene may be similar to that in the house in one sense—usually, few members are paying attention to the debate. Senate debates on even important bills are usually much shorter than debates in the house, primarily due to the all-important rule that requires a two-thirds vote before a bill can be brought to the floor out of its calendar sequence. Bringing a bill to the floor requires the cooperation of the lieutenant governor (who can recognize senators from the floor) and at least 21 senators. Such support suggests that compromises have been made and deals have been brokered well before the legislation ever reaches the floor.

The senate may also form itself into a **committee of the whole**, at which time the lieutenant governor appoints a senator to preside. Only a simple majority rather than the usual two-thirds is necessary to consider legislation, and the lieutenant governor may debate and vote on all questions. Otherwise, the senate rules are observed. No journal is kept of the proceedings.

Filibustering in the Senate. The *filibuster*, which was discussed in Chapter 12, is a threat to bills in the Texas senate, just as it is in the U.S. Senate. The difference in the Texas senate is that a member may not give the floor to other senators who also want to filibuster. In Texas, the lieutenant governor controls the floor, so in effect only one senator may filibuster for as long as he or she can physically last. Then the vote is taken. **Cloture** to force a vote is not an option in the Texas senate.

The purpose of a filibuster is either to attract public attention to a bill that is sure to pass without the filibuster or to delay legislation in the closing days of the session. In fact, the mere threat of a filibuster may be enough to compel a bill's supporters to change the content of the bill to reach a compromise with the disgruntled senator. If a filibuster does

[12]Nanci Wilson, "One Lawmaker, Many Votes?" *CBS 42 Investigates*, May 14, 2007. The video can be seen on YouTube under "Texas Politicians' multiple voting breaks legislature rules."
[13]"In Session: Notes on the Legislature," *Austin American-Statesman*, May 30, 1997, p. B7.

occur, it means that no compromise was possible—usually because the senators who favor the bill, by virtue of their numbers, refuse to be intimidated by the threat of a filibuster.

Senator Bill Meier set the world record for a filibuster in the 1977 legislative session by talking for 43 hours. This feat broke the old record of 42 hours and 33 minutes set in 1972 by Senator Mike McKool. There have been several other notable filibusters in the Texas senate. In 1993, Senator Gonzalo Barrientos filibustered for 17 hours and 50 minutes in an attempt to kill legislation that overturned an Austin ordinance designed to protect the Barton Springs watershed from development. During the filibuster, Barrientos was required to stand and was restricted to a three-square-foot area. The bill eventually passed by 22 to 7.[14]

Finally, the Senate Votes. Following the debate, the senators usually vote by hand signals directed toward a recording clerk—one finger for a yes vote and two fingers for a no. During the voting process, senators plead for their colleagues' votes using the same hand signals directed toward the senators. Only a simple majority is necessary for passage.

CONFERENCE COMMITTEES

A unique by-product of bicameralism is the need to resolve differences in similar bills passed by the two chambers. A temporary (or ad hoc) committee known as a *conference committee* is appointed for each bill to resolve these differences. To determine the acceptability of proposed compromises, the membership of this committee remains in contact with interested legislators, lobbyists, administrators, and the presiding officers.

Conference Committee Membership. In Texas, conference committees are composed of five members from each chamber (known as conferees), appointed by each chamber's presiding officer. At least two of the senate conferees must be from the standing committee that heard the bill, and the chair of the senate conferees is either the author or sponsor of the bill for which the conference committee is called. The compromise proposal must win the support of a majority of the committee members from each chamber to be reported out of the conference committee. Because the members of the committee may alter or even kill a bill, the attitudes of the legislators appointed to the committee are of crucial concern to the various interests involved. Bargaining before the selection of the committee is common, and bargaining continues among the committee members during deliberations. Both the presiding officers and the conference committee members are well placed to affect the outcome.

Conference Committee Reports. After a bill has been reported from the conference committee, it cannot be amended by either chamber but must be accepted or rejected as written or sent back to the conference committee for further compromise. In practice, because of the volume of legislation that must be considered and the limited time available, the Texas legislature tends to accept conference committee reports on most legislation.

GOVERNOR PERRY (center, hand to chin), works with the conference committee meeting on House Bill 2, on July 15, 2005, in Austin. Lieutenant Governor David Dewhurst is standing on the left. (AP Photo/ Harry Cabluck)

[14]Diana R. Fuentes, *San Antonio Express-News*, May 1, 1993, p. 17A.

HOW A BILL BECOMES A LAW

Bills may be introduced in either chamber or, to speed the process, in both chambers at the same time. Consider as an example a bill that is introduced in the senate before it is sent to the house. The numbers in Figure 24–8 on page 845 correspond to the numbers in the following discussion.

1. *Introduction in the Senate.* A senator must introduce a bill in the senate. It is not difficult to find a legislator who is willing to perform this somewhat clerical function. More difficult is finding a sponsor who will use her or his political skills and bargaining prowess to help get the bill through the intricacies of the legislative process. On introduction, the bill is assigned a number—for example, Senate Bill 13 (SB 13).

2. *Assignment to a Senate Committee.* The lieutenant governor assigns bills to committees in the senate and can, for many bills, choose between two or more committees. It is very important to proponents of the bill that the chosen committee not oppose the spirit of the bill. If possible, proponents of the bill and their allies will gain the lieutenant governor's support and receive a friendly committee assignment. This may be granted in exchange for their support of or opposition to some other bill of particular interest to the lieutenant governor.

3. *Senate Committee Action.* In the relevant subcommittee, supporters and opponents of the bill are allowed to testify. Witnesses are often lobbyists or concerned bureaucrats affected by the bill. The subcommittee then marks up (makes changes to) the bill and sends it to the whole committee. The committee may hear additional testimony and further mark up the bill. Some senate committees do not have subcommittees. In that circumstance, the entire committee initially hears testimony and marks up the bill. The committee may then report on the bill favorably or unfavorably or may refuse to report on it at all.

4. *The Senate Calendar.* The senate has only one calendar of bills, and it is rarely followed. In the usual procedure, as described earlier, a senator makes a motion to suspend the regular calendar order and consider a proposed bill out of its sequence. For this parliamentary maneuver to succeed, prior arrangements must be made for the lieutenant governor to recognize the senator who will make the motion. If two-thirds of the senators agree to the motion, the bill, with the blessings of the lieutenant governor, is ready for action on the senate floor.

5. *The Senate Floor.* The president of the senate (the lieutenant governor) has the power to recognize senators who wish to speak and to interpret rules and points of order. Rarely does the senate overrule these interpretations. Unlimited debate is the rule in the Texas senate. This does not mean that the Texas senate is a deliberative body, for it is not; such luxury is not possible in the short legislative session. Unlimited debate could, however, lead to a filibuster—an attempt to either "talk the bill to death" or force a compromise. If a bill is successful in reaching the senate floor, it has already cleared its major obstacle (the two-thirds majority necessary for senate consideration) and will usually pass in some form. A simple majority is necessary for a bill to pass. The lieutenant governor may vote only to break ties.

6. *Introduction to the House.* Following senate passage, the bill is sent to the house. A procedure similar to that in the senate is followed there.

7. *Assignment to a House Committee.* The speaker of the house assigns each bill to a committee. The speaker, like the lieutenant governor, has some freedom of choice in selecting a committee, because the jurisdiction of house committees is vague.

8. *House Committee Action.* Committee action in the house is similar to that in the senate. Each bill is assigned to a committee and then to a subcommittee, which may hold public hearings. The subcommittee as well as the committee may amend, totally rewrite, pigeonhole, or report favorably or unfavorably on a bill.

9. *House Calendars.* A bill that is reported favorably by a standing committee, or receives a favorable minority report by the required number of committee members, is placed on one of the eight house calendars by one of the two calendars committees. This establishes the approximate order in which the whole house will consider the legislation. If a calendars committee fails to assign the bill to a calendar, it can be forced to do so by the action of a simple majority of the house. If a bill has the blessings of the speaker, however, it is sure to be promptly placed on the appropriate calendar.

10. *The House Floor.* The speaker of the house has the power to recognize representatives on the house floor and also to interpret the rules and points of order. Although the speaker may be overruled, he or she seldom is. The size of the house necessitates

FIGURE 24–8 How a Bill Becomes a Law in Texas

The procedure shown in this figure follows a bill that is first introduced in the Texas senate and eventually reaches the governor's desk. If a bill is first introduced in the Texas house of representatives, the procedure is much the same, but the diagram would be a mirror image of what you see here, and the bill would be introduced as HB 13.

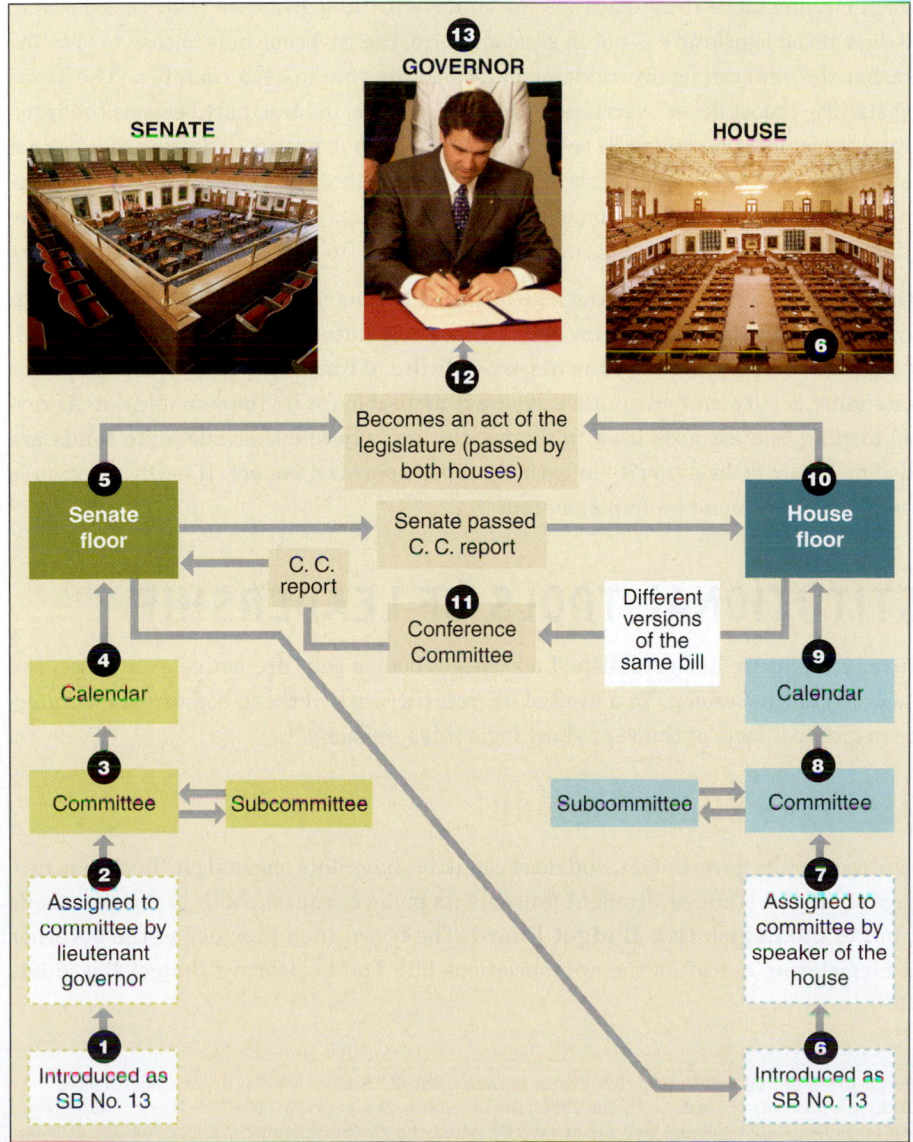

All photos courtesy of the Governor's Office, Austin, TX.

that debate be more limited than in the senate—usually each member is allowed 10 minutes. A bill may be amended, **tabled** (which usually kills the measure), defeated, or sent back to committee. The "yes" votes of only a simple majority of members present and voting are necessary for a bill to pass.

11. *Conference Committee.* If the house makes a change in the senate-passed version of a bill, a conference committee is necessary to reconcile the differences between the two versions of the bill. The lieutenant governor appoints five senators and the speaker appoints five representatives to sit on the committee. The compromise bill must be approved by a majority of both the senators and the representatives before it can be reported out of the conference committee.

12. *Final Passage.* A bill reported out of a conference committee is sent first to the chamber where it originated and then to the other chamber for final approval. Neither one may amend the reported bill but must accept it, reject it, or send it back to the conference committee. If both the senate and the house pass the conference committee version of the bill, it becomes an act of the legislature and is sent to the governor.

13. *The Governor.* The governor has several options for dealing with an act of the legislature. First, she or he may sign it into law. Second, he or she may choose not to sign it, in which circumstance it becomes law in 10 days if the legislature is in session or in 20 days if the legislature is not in session. Third, the governor may choose to veto the act, but the veto can be overridden by a two-thirds vote in each chamber. (The Texas legislature almost never overrides a governor's vetoes, in large part because the legislature typically is no longer in session when the veto is issued.) The governor cannot veto a portion of an act unless it is a clause that actually appropriates funds. This is the power known as line-item veto power. The governor may strike out an item of appropriation, but he or she does not have a reduction veto (to reduce spending for an item).

If the governor signs an act of the legislature, it becomes a law in 90 days—or sooner if it is an appropriations act or an act that the legislature has designated as emergency legislation. If the act requires the expenditure of funds, the comptroller of public accounts must certify that adequate revenue is available for its implementation. If revenue is lacking, the act goes back to the legislature, where either adequate funds are provided or a four-fifths majority in each chamber approves the act. If neither option is successful, the act cannot be implemented.

INSTITUTIONAL TOOLS OF LEADERSHIP

The Texas legislature has established a series of bodies that are active even when the legislature is not in session. To a limited degree, the work of these bodies may counteract the negative effects of the very short legislative sessions.[15]

LEGISLATIVE BUDGET BOARD

Most states, the U.S. government, and most countries have only one budget. Texas has two. Each agency in the state government presents its budget requests both to the governor's office and to the **Legislative Budget Board**. The board then provides to the governor and the legislature a draft of the appropriations bill. The Legislative Budget Board has

---

[15]Sources for this material are *Guide to Texas State Agencies*, 9th ed. (Austin: Lyndon B. Johnson School of Public Affairs, University of Texas at Austin, 1996); the Legislative Budget Board Web site at www.lbb.state.tx.us; the Texas Legislative Council Web site at www.tlc.state.tx.us; the State Auditor's Office Web site at www.sao.state.tx.us; and the Sunset Advisory Commission Web site at www.sunset.state.tx.us.

also been given broad authority over strategic planning for the state, bill analyses, and policy and impact analyses affecting education, criminal justice, and other policy areas.

The Legislative Budget Board operates continuously, even when the legislature is not in session. It is made up of the lieutenant governor and the speaker (who serve as joint chairs), as well as four members from each chamber who are appointed by their presiding officers. These 10 members include the chairs of the senate Finance Committee and the house Ways and Means and Appropriations committees. The board appoints an administrative director.

Clearly, the control of the board is in the hands of the two presiding officers, who are in a position to strongly influence state government from the budgeting stage through the final appropriations stage. The board staff assists the appropriating committees and their chairs, and it also has the watchdog function of overseeing to some extent the expenditures of the executive agencies and departments. Thus, in this critical area of finance, the concentration of power in the hands of the presiding officers is even greater than in other legislative areas.

LEGISLATIVE COUNCIL

Another instrument of influence is the 14-member **Legislative Council**, which includes six senators, the chair of the house Administration Committee, five other representatives, and the lieutenant governor and the speaker of the house, who serve as joint chairs. The lieutenant governor appoints the senate members, and the speaker appoints the house members. A director and staff who serve at the pleasure of the council perform the administrative work.

The Legislative Council functions as a source of information and support to the legislature, state agencies, and other governmental institutions. It provides research support to legislators and helps draft legislative proposals.

Legislative Council
In Texas, a body that provides research support, information, and bill-drafting assistance to legislators.

LEGISLATIVE AUDIT COMMITTEE

The primary function of the **Legislative Audit Committee** is to audit (formally check) the expenditures of the state agencies and departments. The committee is composed of the presiding officers and the chairs of the taxing committees, the house Appropriations Committee, and the senate State Affairs Committee. The state auditor, who serves at the pleasure of the committee, heads the State Auditor's Office. Here, too, management of the fiscal affairs of the Texas government is firmly under the influence of the presiding officers.

Legislative Audit Committee
In Texas, a committee that performs audits of state agencies and departments for the legislature.

SUNSET ADVISORY COMMISSION

The Texas Sunset Act requires that most state agencies undergo reevaluation, usually on a 12-year cycle, to determine the need for their continuance. Agencies are automatically terminated if they are not renewed—that is, the "sun sets" on those agencies not specifically renewed by the legislature. Reauthorization may result in altered scope and authority for the agency.

The 12-member **Sunset Advisory Commission** enforces the act. The lieutenant governor appoints five senators and one public member, and the speaker appoints five representatives and one public member. The presiding officers may also serve on the commission as one of the legislative appointees. Public members are appointed for two-year terms and legislators for four-year staggered terms. The commission appoints the agency's executive director.

In the Sunset Advisory Commission's more than 33-year history, the commission has abolished more than 52 state agencies, saving taxpayers hundreds of millions of dollars.

Sunset Advisory Commission
In Texas, a body that periodically evaluates most government agencies and departments. The commission may recommend the restructuring, abolition, or alteration of the jurisdiction of an agency.

YOU CAN MAKE A Difference

CITIZEN PARTICIPATION

A democratic republic such as ours is a unique form of government. Under most other forms of government, citizen participation is neither important nor encouraged, but a democratic republic does not function well without the participation of its citizens. All of us have interests and issues that concern us directly, and it is important for us to become informed and to support the legislators and interest groups that are our allies.

WHY SHOULD YOU CARE?

What is your opinion of your legislators' positions on the issues? Do your elected representatives work in your best interest? In our political system, it is our business to find out where our legislators stand on the issues. If you raise your voice—and if those who share your views raise their voices as well—you may be able to sway your legislator on an issue of concern to you.

Learn who finances the campaigns of your elected representatives. Go to "Follow the Money: The Institute on Money in State Politics" at **www.followthemoney.org**. Under "State-at-a-Glance," scroll to Texas, and use the date of the last election. In the "Election Summary" section, click on "House" or "Senate," and then click on your representative or senator. You will find a list of his or her top contributors, along with contributions by industry, by economic interest, and by geographic location. This information can help you understand who has access to your representative and, to a large extent, where she or he stands on various issues.

WHAT CAN YOU DO?

You can follow legislation. The best time to learn how the legislature works is when the legislature is in session. By going to **www.capitol.state.tx.us**, you can find a bill that affects you personally. Click on "Legislation," then scroll to and click on "Bills by Subject." Now click on the legislative session desired and then on your subject of interest. There will be a list of bills from which to choose.

1. Adopt a bill as your project, and follow the bill through the legislative process. Did your bill pass, or was it killed? If it was killed, where did it die?
2. Try to determine what interest groups favored or opposed your bill. Why did they take these positions? Most interest groups have Web pages, and you can go to a group's Web page to learn about the group and its view on the issues before the legislature.
3. What action did the governor take on the bill? If your bill became law, which agency is responsible for its administration?

ANA HERNANDEZ, the youngest female member of the Texas legislature, is shown on the floor of the Texas House of Representatives in April 2006.
(AP Photo/Harry Cabluck)

KEY TERMS

blocking bill 840
calendar 839
Calendars Committee 830
cloture 842
committee of the
whole 842
ex officio 820
floor 841
floor leaders 841
incumbent 821

Legislative Audit Committee 847
Legislative Budget
Board 846
Legislative Council 847
"The Lobby" 829
mark up 829
pairing 821
partisan gerrymandering 823
part-time legislature 817

pigeonhole 830
point of order 842
presiding officers 817
Sunset Advisory
Commission 847
suspension of the rule 840
table 846
tagging 836
Texas Ethics Commission 847

CHAPTER SUMMARY

1. The Texas legislature meets on odd-numbered years for 140 days. Texas alone, among the large states, has such a restricted period of time in which to conduct legislative business. The Texas legislator tends to be a white, male, Protestant businessperson or lawyer with enough personal wealth or interest-group support to adequately finance a campaign.

2. **What are the main power structures in the Texas legislature?** There are 31 senators and 150 representatives. The Texas two-chamber legislature is presided over by the lieutenant governor in the senate and the speaker in the house of representatives. Actual power in the legislative process rests with these presiding officers. Through appointive, jurisdictional, and other procedural powers, they are able to strongly influence state policy.

3. **How does the political and legal environment affect the way Texas's legislature operates?** Historically, Texas government has been dominated by a coalition of conservative Democrats and Republicans. This coalition dominated the legislature through ideology rather than by using party membership as the basis for control. Under Republican control of the legislature, the no-party system of legislative organization remains superficially intact, and Democrats continue to be appointed to chair committees under Republican leadership. The viability of the no-party system may be nearing its end as state politics becomes more partisan.

4. **What are the major steps by which laws are passed?** Bills may be introduced in either chamber or in both chambers at the same time, where they will be assigned to committee. In committees and subcommittees, supporters and opponents are allowed

to testify and the bill is marked up. The bill is placed on the calendar or a motion is made to consider the bill and the bill is debated and voted on the floor. If the bill receives a simple majority, the bill is passed to the other chamber and it goes through the process again. If one chamber makes a change to the version passed in the first chamber, a conference committee is necessary to reconcile the differences between the two versions of the bill. The compromise bill must be approved by a majority of both house and senate. If approved, the bill is sent to the governor, who may sign it into law, not sign and let it pass into law within a number of days, or veto the bill. A veto can only be overridden by a two-thirds vote in each chamber.

5. Legislative action is based on the committee system. The presiding officers appoint the committee chairs and many of the committee members. The officers assign bills to committees and have discretion over which committee to use. If a committee does not report on a bill (but instead pigeonholes or tables it), the measure is most likely dead for the session.

6. To reach the floor of the house, a bill must also be placed on a calendar by one of the two calendar committees. These committees are firmly under the control of the speaker. A bill that does not receive a calendar assignment is probably out of the running.

7. The senate calendar is an artificial device. The first item on the calendar is a "blocking bill," which is never brought to the floor. Actually bringing a bill to the floor requires a vote by two-thirds of the senators to "suspend the rule" and vote on the bill out of its calendar order. Given that two-thirds of the senate must vote in the affirmative even to bring a measure to the floor, most bills that reach the floor are approved.

8. To become an act of the legislature, a bill must pass both chambers with identical language. To iron out any differences, bills are sent to a conference committee, a special joint committee with members from both chambers. The presiding officers appoint these committees. Once a conference committee report is accepted by both chambers, the bill is sent to the governor.

9. The governor can sign or refuse to sign a bill (in which circumstance it eventually becomes law without the governor's signature). The governor can also veto a bill. If the bill contains an appropriations clause, the governor can strike it out with an item veto. In theory, the legislature could override a veto, but by the time the veto is issued, the legislature is usually no longer in session.

10. The institutional powers of the presiding officers include control over legislative boards and commissions that manage the budgeting function of state government (the Legislative Budget Board), the auditing function (the Legislative Audit Committee), and policy research (the Legislative Council).

SELECTED PRINT, MEDIA, AND ONLINE RESOURCES

PRINT RESOURCES

Bickerstaff, Steve. *Lines in the Sand: Congress Redistricting in Texas and the Downfall of Tom Delay.* Austin: University of Texas Press, 2007. This book provides a detailed account of the redistricting controversy in 2003, often through the personal stories of members of both parties and of minority activist groups. It examines the political aftermath and criminal prosecution of Delay.

Crawford, Ann Fears, and Frances "Sissy" Farenthold. *Frankie: Mrs. R. D. Randolph and Texas Liberal Politics.* Austin, TX: Eakin Press, 1999. This book describes the life and political impact of Mrs. Randolph, the founder of the *Texas Observer*, a patron of liberal Democratic candidates, and an unelected leader of liberal Democrats in their conflicts with Shivercrats and Republicans.

Hanna, Betty Elliott. *Ladies of the House: How to Survive as the Wife of a Texas Legislator.* Austin, TX: Eakin Press, 1993. This book describes Texas politics from the spousal viewpoint.

Jones, Nancy Baker. *Capitol Women: Texas Female Legislators, 1923–1999.* Austin: University of Texas Press, 2000. The lives, memories, and political strategies of 87 female Texas legislators.

Kinch, Sam, and Anne Marie Kilday. *Too Much Money Is Not Enough: Political Power and Big Money in Texas Politics.* Austin, TX: Campaigns for People, 2001. This book includes interviews with Texas legislators and commentary about Texas's campaign finance system and the resulting concentration of political power in the hands of wealthy contributors.

Spaw, Patsy McDonald, ed. *Texas Senate, Volume 1: Republic to Civil War, 1836–1861;* and *Texas Senate, Volume 2: Civil War to the Eve of Reform, 1861–1889.* College Station: Texas A&M University Press, 1991 and 1999. Written by the Senate Engrossing and Enrolling Department, this two-volume set is a narrative account of issues, personalities, and events that shaped the economy, politics, and personality of the state.

MEDIA RESOURCES

Last Man Standing: Politics—Texas Style—In a documentary shown on the PBS program *POV* in 2004, Paul Stekler highlights two 2002 election campaigns. One pits the Democratic "dream team" of Tony Sanchez, Ron Kirk, and John Sharp against Rick Perry and the Republican political operatives of President George W. Bush and Karl Rove for, as Stekler says, "the future of Texas politics." The second campaign pits an Anglo American Republican against an Anglo American Democrat in a race for the Texas house of representatives. The documentary is available in DVD format through Netflix.com.

NOW with Bill Moyers— In the May 16, 2003, episode, Moyers interviews columnist Molly Ivins about the redistricting conflict in the Texas legislature.

Tussle in Texas—In a 2003 interview available on PBS's *Online NewsHour*, Tom Bearden reports on Texas congressional redistricting designed to increase the number of Republicans in the U.S. Congress.

ONLINE RESOURCES

Legislative Budget Board helps the legislature to prepare the budget: www.lbb.state.tx.us

Legislative Reference Library of Texas another good source of information about the Texas legislature: www.lrl.state.tx.us

Office of the Lieutenant Governor Read up on the duties of the office, the major issues facing the state, and the activities of the legislative committees: http://www.ltgov.state.tx.us/

refdesk.com lists and provides the links to all Texas newspapers: www.refdesk.com/tx.html

Sunset Advisory Commission Created by the Texas legislature in 1977 to identify and eliminate waste, duplication, and inefficiency in government agencies: www.sunset.state.tx.us

Texas House of Representatives Learn about and access the speaker of the house, house membership, bills, and happenings: www.house.state.tx.us/speaker/welcome.htm

Texas Legislative Council A nonpartisan legislative agency that provides bill drafting, computing, research, publishing, and document distribution services to the Texas legislature and the other legislative agencies: www.tlc.state.tx.us

Texas Legislature Online A comprehensive resource: www.capitol.state.tx.us

Texas State Auditor's Office The independent auditor for Texas state government: www.sao.state.tx.us

Texas State Library A source for legislative, administrative, and judicial research, as well as general information about many political, economic, and social aspects of Texas: www.tsl.state.tx.us

25

The Governor's Mansion,
(AP Photo/Harry Cabluck)

The Texas Executive Branch

QUESTIONS TO CONSIDER

What is the basic function of the executive branch of government?

How does the structural organization of the Texas administration compare with that of the United States government?

How can the formal powers of the governor be strengthened by his informal powers?

CHAPTER CONTENTS

what if...

Texas Used Private Contractors to Administer State Government?

BACKGROUND

The 21st century is seeing a movement away from the concept of government employees administering the laws and policies of government. Private contractors are prevalent at all levels of the U.S. government. One well-known example is the use of private contractors in the logistics, administration, and fighting of the Iraq and Afghanistan wars.

Private contractors in Texas government are also common. Operation of prisons and jails, highway construction and repair, management of the Children's Health Insurance Program (CHIP), and various education services are just a few examples of private contractors performing state functions.

WHAT IF TEXAS DISBANDED THE STATE'S ADMINISTRATION?

State services might be run more cheaply by private contractors than by the state. Contractors could hire employees for the lowest wage and not be bound by the more restrictive concept of government employee pay grades. Work could also be outsourced to subcontractors from developing countries, providing even greater savings. The worrisome and expensive need for employee medical care and retirement benefits could also be disregarded by private contractors.

USING FEES INSTEAD OF TAXES

State services could be funded by fees, which would be charged by the contractor to defray expenses and make a profit. User fees could simply replace the need for taxes, removing the need for tax collectors, appraisers, and so forth. Because fee-for-service is already an integral part of Texas government, it need only be expanded to ensure a profit and to cover the expense of providing the service.

Some may not be able to afford to pay for the cost of services. For example, some parents could have a problem paying the full cost for educating their children. The state could remedy this by giving contracts to lending institutions that would then lend money to the parents so they could fund their children's education. Something similar to the former college student loan program could be reinstituted and expanded to finance public school and other services.

SELLING GOVERNMENT ASSETS

Existing physical assets could be sold to corporations and individuals. This would be a financial boon to Texas, because these proceeds could be placed in an emergency fund in the event of a future economic or environmental catastrophe and to pay the elected officials still necessary to award and administer the contract program. The state could save millions of tax dollars presently used to maintain offices, schools, highways, dams, bridges, and so forth by shifting the burden of upkeep and operation to private contractors.

DEVELOPING A CONTRACT SPOILS SYSTEM

Contracting out the state administration would also provide politicians with a way to reward political supporters. People are often reluctant to invest their time or resources in political campaigns unless they see personal gain. President Andrew Jackson solved this problem by hiring supporters to government positions, popularizing the slogan "to the victors belong the spoils!" Since modern political campaigns rely less on block walking and more on advertising, campaigns depend heavily on private financial contributions. Politicians could simply reward their contributors with contracts to provide public services, thereby encouraging political participation. To paraphrase Jackson, "to the victor belong the contract spoils!"

OPPOSITION TO PRIVATIZATION

Opponents of privatization could argue that one of the basic functions of a political system is to provide services to its citizens. Others might contend that with profit as a motive, corporations could not be trusted to provide adequate services when no regulatory oversight is in place. With a fee-for-service system, many citizens with moderate incomes might be unable to afford or reluctant to seek necessary services, such as police and fire protection or garbage disposal, which are critical for the continuation of a civilized society.

FOR CRITICAL ANALYSIS

1. What is your opinion of the present private contractor system?
2. Do you think private contractors should replace government employees?
3. What problems might develop with privatization?

THE LEGISLATIVE FUNCTION is to create law, and the executive function is to carry it out. For example, the legislative function is to determine who will pay how much in taxes, but the executive function is to actually collect those taxes. The legislative function is to determine how much will be appropriated for each agency and to set financial priorities, but the executive function is to actually spend the appropriations—write the checks and make the contracts. The legislative function is to define crime and prescribe punishment, but the executive function is to arrest, prosecute, and punish criminals. The legislative function is to determine which services will be provided, but the executive function is to actually provide those services—to hire personnel and manage their day-to-day conduct. The executive function is basically to do what the government does. Although more executive functions are now being outsourced (as we discuss in the *What If . .* section), almost all of a citizen's contacts with the government are with the executive branch.

The administrators' function is to see that the law is enforced, but also embedded within this function are elements of functions of the other branches of government. Administrators make law when they write rules and regulations that are designed to clarify and specify the more general wording of the actual statute. In other words, the bureaucracy interprets the meaning of the law (a **quasi-judicial function**) and then writes the rules and regulations (a **quasi-legislative function**) that are used to implement the enforcement.

Quasi-Judicial Functions
Actions by a branch other than the courts that involve interpreting the law.

Quasi-Legislative Functions
Legislative actions by entities other than the legislature; for example, executive branch agencies' adoption of rules and regulations that are binding on citizens.

STRUCTURE AND POLITICS OF THE GOVERNOR'S OFFICE

More than 200 state agencies (the bureaucracy) administer Texas public policy. The state constitution designates the governor as the chief executive (chief bureaucrat) but then proceeds to systematically deny him or her the power to control state agencies. The executive branch of the Texas government is divided into many elective and appointive offices, primarily because Texans traditionally have feared concentration of power anywhere in government, particularly in the executive branch. The effect of this fear is compounded by legislators' reluctance to pass laws that would increase the powers of the chief executive relative to their own powers. As a result, the Texas executive branch has evolved into a mixture of elective offices, boards, and commissions, most separate from, and largely independent of, the governor.

Despite these constitutional and statutory restrictions, the governor can influence state policy by persuading and bargaining with others. The governor's legislative powers, media access, party influence, and appointive powers to boards and commissions enable an astute, politically savvy officeholder to exert meaningful influence on both legislative and administrative decisions.

WHO CAN BECOME GOVERNOR?

As is usual with elective offices, the legal requirements for becoming governor are minimal: A candidate must be (1) 30 years of age, (2) an American citizen, and (3) a citizen of Texas for five years before election. While the formal qualifications for governor are easily met, the informal criteria are more restrictive.

White Protestant. Since the Texas Revolution, governors have all been white Protestants, usually Methodists or Baptists. They have also been Anglo, with family names originating in the British Isles.

Male. The governor is historically male. The only female governor of Texas before Ann Richards (served 1991–1995) was Miriam A. Ferguson, who served for two nonconsecutive terms (1925–1927 and 1933–1935). Ferguson ran on the slogan "Two Governors for the Price of One" and did not really represent a deviation from male domination of Texas politics, because it was clear that her husband, former governor James E. Ferguson, actually exercised the power of the office.[1] Only Ann Richards was a female governor in her own right.

Middle-Aged Businessperson or Attorney. The governor will probably be successful in business or law—more than half of the governors who have served in the last 100 years have been lawyers. The governor will most likely be between 40 and 60 years old; have a record of elective public service in state government or some other source of name recognition; and be a participant in service, social, and occupational organizations.

Today, a Republican. Democrats historically dominated Texas politics. Between 1952 and 1988, the Republicans became competitive in top-of-the-ticket elections—president, U.S. senator, and governor—but the state was basically Democratic for most other offices. Texas became an authentic two-party state with the 1990 election of two Republicans to the down-ticket offices of state treasurer and commissioner of agriculture.

Fourteen years later, Texas had completed its evolution into a strongly Republican state. Republicans first swept statewide offices in 1998, electing the governor, lieutenant governor, and all elected down-ticket administrators, including members of the Texas Railroad Commission. The down-ticket Republican victories have additional political significance. Statewide elective offices can provide political experience and name recognition. They also can serve as a springboard to higher office, as Kay Bailey Hutchison demonstrated by moving from state treasurer to the U.S. Senate. In 1998, Rick Perry rose from commissioner of agriculture to lieutenant governor, and in 2002 he was elected governor. That same year, Texas Attorney General John Cornyn was elected to the U.S. Senate. As with most states from the Old South, Texas's electorate now strongly favors Republican candidates for public office.

DID YOU KNOW?

That when Ann Richards was elected state treasurer in 1982, she was the first woman to win a statewide election to *any* post in Texas since "Ma" Ferguson was elected governor in 1932?

TEXAS GOVERNOR RICK PERRY delivers his State of the State address at the state capitol in Austin. As the most prominent leader in the state, the governor has the opportunity to supplement his or her rather limited formal powers by appealing to the people. How might the governor turn popular support to his or her advantage when seeking new legislation? (Photo courtesy of the Governor's Office)

[1]Rupert N. Richardson, *Texas: The Lone Star State*, 2nd ed. (Englewood Cliffs, NJ: Prentice Hall, 1958), p. 317.

The Democrats' Problem. The Democratic gubernatorial primary is usually a match among moderate-to-liberal candidates. The Democratic nominee must forge an unlikely coalition of business leaders, central cities, ethnic minorities, unions, intellectuals, teachers, and consumer advocates. To win the general election, Democrats would have to win a substantial number of rural votes. Traditionally Democratic rural voters, however, are largely deserting the Democrats, giving the Republicans a distinct advantage in all statewide elections. It is unlikely that a Democrat will win any major statewide elective office in the near future. The Republican primary will continue to nominate the near-certain winner. This primary is a joust between conservative-to-moderate candidates, with the more conservative candidate usually winning.

Support by Interest Groups. Most successful candidates for governor have substantial interest-group support. For example, the expenses of the 2003 inauguration of Governor Perry and Lieutenant Governor David Dewhurst were mostly paid by large corporations, including AT&T, Philip Morris, SBC Communications, Sprint, insurance companies, and the state's primary Medicaid contractor. Consumer lobbyists and liberals voiced concern about the likely impact on the pending agenda for insurance, health care, and other legislation facing the 2003 legislature. The festivities cost about $1.5 million, of which $500,000 was raised by ticket sales to the event.[2]

Well-Funded Campaigns. In the general election, Republican gubernatorial candidates usually have the campaign funds to outspend their Democratic opponents. This allows them to develop the necessary political image and name recognition and also to identify and define the issues of the campaign. Candidates who spend the most usually win in competitive races. Paul Taylor, executive director of the Alliance for Better Campaigns, has said that "the legacy is a political culture in which we auction off the right to free speech 30 seconds at a time to the highest political bidder."[3]

A hefty bankroll is necessary even for serious consideration. Challengers usually must spend more than incumbents to buy name recognition. Spending does not buy all elections, however. In the 2002 Texas gubernatorial election, Democrat Tony Sanchez and Republican Rick Perry together spent $95 million to win a job that paid $115,345 per year. The incumbent, Perry, spent $29.9 million, and the challenger, Sanchez, spent a record $67.2 million, including $60 million of his own personal wealth. Sanchez spent $36 per vote and lost; Perry spent $9 per vote and won. Regardless of campaign spending, Texans seem to strongly favor Republican issues and values.

TENURE, REMOVAL, AND SUCCESSION

Texas governors serve a four-year term, as do governors in 47 other states. Unlike most states, however, Texas imposes no limit on the number of terms a governor may serve. The governor may be removed from office before the end of his or her term only by impeachment by the Texas house of representatives and conviction by the Texas senate. Impeachment is the legislative equivalent of **indictment** and requires only a simple majority of members present. Conviction requires a two-thirds majority.

If the governor is removed or vacates the office, the lieutenant governor becomes governor for the remainder of the elected term. The Texas senate then elects a senator as acting lieutenant governor, who also serves as president pro tem until the next general election.

Indictment
A formal accusation issued by a grand jury against a party charged with a crime when the jury determines that there is sufficient evidence to bring the accused to trial.

[2]Associated Press, *Dallas Morning News*, January 2, 2003, available at www.dallasnews.com; and J. Taylor Rushing, "One Big Party," *Fort Worth Star-Telegram*, January 21, 2003, available at www.dfw.com.
[3]Colleen McCain Nelson, "For Sanchez, More Wasn't Better," *Dallas Morning News*, November 7, 2002.

COMPENSATION

The governor's annual salary is set by the legislature. Now at $150,000, it stands in marked contrast to the low salaries paid to legislators. However, nine other Texas state officials earn more than the governor.

The governor receives free use of the governor's mansion, and there is an expense account to keep it maintained and staffed. The governor has a professional staff with offices in the capitol. This is important, because a modern chief executive depends heavily on staff personnel to carry out the duties of office.

STAFF

The growing role of the executive in legislative affairs, the need to make appointments, and increased demands on government by the general public have placed greater claims on the time and resources of the executive branch. The Texas governor—like all executives in modern government—depends on others for advice, information, and assistance when making decisions and recommendations. A good staff is a key resource for a successful chief executive.

Assisting the Governor. Some administrative assistants head executive offices that compile and write budget recommendations and manage and coordinate activities within the governor's office. Staff personnel also exercise administrative control over the governor's schedule of ceremonial and official duties. The governor's staff, although primarily designed to assist in the everyday duties of the office, also attempts to persuade legislators, administrators, and the representatives of various local governments to follow the governor's leadership in solving common problems.

Evaluating Appointees. Among the most important concerns of the governor's staff are political appointments. Each year, the governor makes several hundred appointments to various boards, commissions, and executive agencies. He or she also fills newly created judicial offices and those vacated because of death or resignation. Staff evaluation of potential appointees is necessary, because the governor may not personally know many of the individuals under consideration.

Legislative Liaison. Legislative assistants act as liaisons between the office of the governor and the legislature. Their job is to stay in contact with key legislators, committee chairs, and the legislative leadership. These assistants are, in fact, the governor's lobbyists. They keep legislators informed and attempt to persuade them to support the governor's position on legislation. Often, the success of the governor's legislative program rests on the ability and political expertise of the staff.

Informal Powers
Powers not directly granted by law. The governor's informal powers may follow from powers granted by law but may also come from the governor's persuasive abilities, which are affected by the governor's personality, popularity, and political support.

Formal Powers
Legal powers granted to the governor by constitution or statute. Powers of this type, when exercised by the U.S. president, are called *expressed powers*.

THE GOVERNOR'S POWERS OF PERSUASION

A governor's ability to influence the creation and execution of government policy depends in part on his or her bargaining skills, persuasiveness, and ability to broker effectively among competing interests—the tools of persuasion. Thus, the **informal powers** of office are as important as the **formal powers** (those granted by the constitution or by law). The ability to use informal powers is largely determined by the extent of the formal powers.

Compared with the governors of other states (especially other populous, industrialized states), the governor of Texas has weak formal administrative powers. Yet some Texas governors have been able to exert significant influence on policy formulation and execution. Generally, this occurs when the governor's formal and informal powers are enhanced by a blending of other conditions, such as the following:

- a strong personality.
- political expertise.
- prestige.
- a knack for public relations and political drama.
- good relations with the press.
- supporters with political and economic strength.
- a favorable political climate.

THE GOVERNOR AS CHIEF OF STATE

The governor, as the first citizen of Texas, serves as a symbol of Texas as surely as the bluebonnet or the pecan tree. A significant part of the governor's job is related to the pomp and ceremony of the office. These ceremonial duties include throwing out the first baseball of the season; greeting Boy Scout troops at the state capitol; visiting disaster areas; and riding in parades for peanut festivals, county fairs, and cow chip–throwing contests.

The ceremonial role of **chief of state** is important because it can contribute indirectly to the governor's leadership effectiveness through increased popularity and prestige. The governor also broadens the image of first citizen to that of first family of Texas whenever possible. Voters identify with the governor's family, and the governor's spouse often is included in photo opportunities, particularly if the spouse is photogenic and articulate.

Chief of State
Nationally, the head of state—the president of the United States, for example. In Texas and other states, the governor—who serves as the symbol of the state and performs ceremonial duties—is the chief of state.

THE GOVERNOR AS PARTY CHIEF

The governor usually maintains the leadership of his or her party by controlling the membership of its executive committee (though there may be varying degrees of competition from other elected officials and from political activists). The chair and a majority of the executive committee of the party are formally elected at the party's state convention but are typically selected by the governor.

Control of the party is a useful channel of influence for a governor. It permits what many consider to be one of the most effective tools of gubernatorial persuasion—rewarding supporters with political patronage. Influential party members who support the governor's party choices and proposals and who contribute to his or her election may be permitted to influence the several hundred appointments the governor makes each year.

The Governor as National Party Leader. The Texas governor can also be a major player in national politics if she or he is so inclined. Unless the governor suffers from serious public relations problems, any candidate for president would want the support of the governor of the nation's second most populous state. The large number of electoral votes that Texas casts also makes the governor an attractive candidate for president or vice president. A governor's support for a winning presidential candidate provides influence over the political patronage that flows from Washington to the state. Of course, patronage can be dramatically increased if a Texas governor actually becomes president.

Taking Positions on National Issues. National politics also affords the governor an opportunity to build a clear public image within Texas. The governor can take positions on political issues that do not involve the Texas government and that the governor cannot control (such as foreign aid and national defense), but that nevertheless are of great concern to the voters. State government issues are often difficult for voters to understand (because of the complexities of the issues or inadequate reporting by the media). As a result, the electorate can more easily make political identifications through national issues.

LEGISLATIVE TOOLS OF PERSUASION

Ironically, the governor's most important bargaining tools are often legislative. How these tools are used frequently determines the governor's effectiveness.

The Veto. One of the most powerful formal legislative tools of the governor is the veto. After a bill has passed both chambers of the legislature (as described in Chapter 24), it is sent to the governor. If the governor signs the bill, it becomes law. If the governor vetoes the bill, it is sent back to the legislature with a message stating the reasons for the governor's opposition. The legislature has the constitutional power to override a veto by a two-thirds vote, but in practice vetoes are usually final.

Because legislative sessions in Texas are short, the vast majority of important bills are passed and sent to the governor in the final days of the session. The governor need take no action on the legislation for 10 days when the legislature is in session (20 days when it is not in session), so he or she can often wait until the legislature has adjourned, and thereby ensure that a veto will not be overridden. In fact, it is so difficult to override a veto that this has happened only once since World War II (1939–1945). Thus, the veto gives the Texas governor a strong bargaining position with legislators.

No Pocket Veto. The Texas governor lacks the pocket veto that is available to many other chief executives, including the president of the United States. A pocket veto permits an executive to kill legislation passed at the end of a session by ignoring it. If the Texas governor neither signs nor vetoes a bill, it becomes law without her or his signature. By not signing a bill and allowing it to become law, the governor may register protest against the bill or some of its sections.

The Item Veto. The single most important bill that the legislature passes is the appropriations bill. If it should be vetoed in its entirety, funds for the operation of the government would be cut off, and a special session would be necessary. Thus, Texas, like most other states, allows the governor an *item veto*, which can be used to veto funds for specific items or projects without killing an entire bill.

The item veto is potentially a very effective legislative tool. Funding is necessary to administer laws, so by vetoing an item or a category of items, the governor can, in effect, kill either programs or classes of programs. Because the appropriations bill is normally passed at the end of the session, the governor usually employs the item veto after the legislature has adjourned. As a result, there is no opportunity for an override.

The Threat of a Veto. An informal legislative power of the governor that is not mentioned in the constitution or the law is the **threat to veto**. This power nevertheless is a very real and effective tool, which depends on the formal power of the veto. Both the veto and the item veto are negative tools that simply kill bills or programs; they do not help the governor shape legislation. Threatening a veto is effective in this regard, however, because the legislature knows how difficult it is to override a veto, and usually lawmakers will at least partially meet the governor's wishes in response to such a threat.

The governor can also use the threat of an item veto to influence bureaucrats who seek funding for programs and projects. The governor may influence the administration of existing agency programs by threatening to veto funds or other bills actively supported by the agency. In addition, the governor can use the threat of an item veto to pressure the agency's legislative liaison personnel (its lobbyists) to support the governor's legislative program.

Finally, the threat of a veto can be used to consolidate support for the governor's legislative proposals among lobbyists in general. Lobbyists may offer to support the governor's position on legislation if the governor will agree not to veto a particular bill that is considered vital to the interests of the lobbyists' employers. The governor can thus bargain with both supporters and opponents of legislation to gain political allies.

Threat to Veto
An informal power by which a state governor (or the U.S. president) threatens to veto legislation so as to affect the content of the legislation while it is still in the legislature.

GOVERNOR RICK PERRY signs legislation providing $22 million to encourage television production in Texas. Standing, left to right: Rep. Dawanna Dukes, actor Dennis Quaid, and Texas Motion Picture Alliance president Hector Garcia. (AP Photo/ Harry Cabluck)

We give an example of how Governor Perry has affected policy through the threat of a veto in this chapter's *Beyond Our Borders* feature.

Bargaining. The governor's bargaining with legislators, lobbyists, and administrators is often intense. These other political forces may attempt to convince the governor to support, oppose, or maintain neutrality toward certain legislation. If the governor or the governor's political and financial supporters have not made this legislation an explicit part of their legislative program, avenues are left open for political bartering. Whoever seeks the governor's support must be willing to give something of real political value in return. All sides of the negotiation want to gain as much as possible and give as little as they can. There is, of course, a vast difference in political resources among politicians, just as there is among interest groups.

Presession Bargaining. If, before the legislative session begins, the governor, the legislative leadership, concerned administrators, and special-interest groups can arrive at successful bargains and compromises, the prospect for passage of the agreed-on proposals is greatly enhanced. **Presession bargaining** is a way of seeking compromises, but harmonious relationships seldom develop immediately.

Representatives of powerful competing political forces may continue bargaining throughout the legislative session. Failure to reach an amicable settlement usually means either defeat of a bill in the legislature or a veto by the governor.

Advance agreement on a given bill can result in several advantages:

1. The advocates of the bill are assured that both the legislative leadership and the governor are friendly to the legislation.
2. The governor need not threaten a veto to influence the content of the bill. This keeps the chief executive on better terms with the legislature.
3. The legislative leaders can guide the bill through their respective chambers, secure in the knowledge that the legislation will not be opposed or vetoed by the governor.

The magnitude and intensity of presession bargaining depend on several factors, including the degree of support for a particular proposal shown by the governor, the members of the legislature, and interest groups. We summarize the elements that go into determining the intensity of the bargaining in Figure 25–1.

Presession Bargaining
In Texas and other states, negotiation that lets the governor and legislative leaders reach compromises on particular bills before the beginning of the legislative session. This usually ensures the passage of the bills.

Beyond Our Borders

SHOULD TEXAS RECOGNIZE IDENTITY CARDS ISSUED BY MEXICO?

Mexico issues an identity card called the *matrícula consular* (consular registration) to its citizens in the United States. Applicants for the card must appear in person at a Mexican consular office and present a Mexican birth certificate or an official Mexican identification document that contains a photograph. The *matrícula* card resembles a U.S. state driver's license and has many security features to prevent forgery.

The state of Texas currently does not accept the *matrícula* card as a valid form of identification, but 13 other states do accept it, as do several dozen Texas cities, counties, and police departments, including those of Dallas and Houston. At least 85 bank systems accept the card as identification for opening an account.*

PROPOSALS IN TEXAS

In 2003, lawmakers unsuccessfully introduced several bills that would have required the Texas Department of Public Safety to accept the *matrícula* card as proof of identity for obtaining a Texas driver's license. Then—Mexican President Vicente Fox lobbied Governor Rick Perry on behalf of the card in 2003, but Perry continued to object to it based on questions about its security and reliability. In 2001, Perry vetoed a bill that would have recognized Mexican birth certificates, and he appeared poised to veto recognition of the *matrícula* card should such a measure ever pass the legislature.

HOW SECURE IS THE *MATRÍCULA* CARD?

Opponents of the card have claimed that it is insufficiently secure, that it can be forged, that Mexican officials do not adequately check the documents used to obtain it, and that no unified database of cardholders can be checked by Texas officials. Supporters of the card claim that it meets the same standards as U.S. driver's licenses, which can also be forged, and point out that Mexico instituted a centralized database to track the cards in 2004. Supporters also argue that it is better if as many Texans as possible have acceptable, official identification. If cardholders can obtain driver's licenses, there will be fewer unlicensed, uninsured drivers on the road. Use of the card would make it easier for police agencies and other government bodies to carry out their functions.

THE ISSUE OF ILLEGAL IMMIGRATION

Technically, recognition of the *matrícula* card has no effect on a cardholder's immigration status. There is little question, however, that recognition of the card would make

---

*See Texas House of Representatives, House Research Organization, *"Matrícula Consular:* Should Texas Recognize Mexican-Issued Identity Cards Held by Immigrants?" by Kellie Dworaczyk, *Interim News,* No. 78–2, January 20, 2004.

life much easier for undocumented—illegal—immigrants. Legal immigrants do not need the card because they have other acceptable forms of identification.

Card advocates argue that enforcement of the immigration laws is a federal responsibility in which the state government should not involve itself. In contrast, opponents believe that Texas has both the right and the responsibility to uphold national law and that allowing illegal immigrants to readily integrate themselves into mainstream society is poor policy. The belief that the *matrícula* card may facilitate illegal immigration could, in fact, be the most powerful argument against recognizing the card, although many politicians may be reluctant to make the case for fear of appearing anti-Hispanic.

FOR CRITICAL ANALYSIS

The *matrícula consular* and the methods used for issuing it appear to match the standards of an American driver's license. Those who argue to the contrary seem to be grasping at straws. Yet there is ample evidence that, historically, Mexican officials have been much more susceptible to bribery and corruption than American ones. Even if the technical standards of the card are high, therefore, it is possible to raise questions about the staff administering the program. Why might elected officials be reluctant to make this point explicitly?

FIGURE 25–1 Factors That Determine the Governor's Flexibility and Intensity in Bargaining

1 The depth of the governor's commitment to a bill.	If the governor is committed to a position, because of either a political debt or ideological belief, his or her position may not be open to negotiation.
2 Timing.	Politicians often try to be the ones to tip the scales for the winning side.
3 Political and financial support given the governor during a campaign.	This does not mean that all campaign contributions buy political decisions, but they do increase the chances that contributors will get a favorable hearing.
4 Future campaign support.	Bargaining may involve financial or political support for the reelection or advancement of an ambitious politician.
5 The identity of a bill's supporters and opponents.	The governor may not want to align with a group that is unpopular either with the governor's financial supporters or with the general electorate. Examples of unpopular groups include advocates for the legalization of marijuana or a graduated state income tax.
6 The amount of firm legislative support for or opposition to a proposal.	Even if the chief executive is inclined toward a particular position, backing a losing cause could mean a loss of prestige.
7 The political benefits to be gained.	Some groups may be more willing or able than others to pay a high price for the governor's support. Thus, an important consideration is the relative strength of the supporters and the opponents of a bill and their ability to pay their political and financial debts. For example, because medical patients in Texas have no organization and few political allies, their interests are not as well represented as those of the Texas Medical Association, health-maintenance organizations, or insurance companies. These interests have strong organizations and political and financial resources.
8 The attitude of interests that could provide postgubernatorial economic opportunities	Some governors have extensive investments and are unlikely to make political decisions that could mean personal financial loss.

Limits of Presession Bargaining. Presession bargaining does not always help the governor. Legislative sources revealed that in late 2002, Governor Rick Perry, Lieutenant Governor David Dewhurst, and Tom Craddick, who was expected to become speaker of the Texas house, were negotiating the extent of influence that the governor's office would have on the 2003–2004 state budget. Past budgets had been written largely by the Legislative Budget Board, which is controlled by the lieutenant governor and the speaker. Perry's argument was that because all officers were Republicans, the governor should have more input into the process. The specific decision made in these negotiations is not known, but Governor Perry either declined or was denied the opportunity to contribute to the budget process. He therefore submitted a "budget" in 2003 with no monetary recommendations.[4]

Special Sessions. As mentioned in Chapter 24, the constitution gives the governor exclusive power to call the legislature into *special session* and to determine the legislative subjects to be considered by the session. The legislature may, however, consider nonlegislative subjects, such as confirmation of appointments, resolutions, impeachment, and constitutional amendments, even if the governor does not include them in the call. Special sessions are limited to 30 days' duration, but the governor may call them as often as he or she wants.

When coalitions of legislators and lobbyists request a special session so that a "critical issue" can be brought before the legislature, other coalitions of legislators and interests often oppose consideration of the issue and therefore oppose calling the special session. Because there is seldom any legislation that does not hurt some interests and help others, the governor has an opportunity to use the choice of whether to call a special session as a bargaining tool. He or she may or may not call a special session based on some concession or support to be delivered in the future. The supporters and opponents of specific legislation may also have to bargain with the governor over the inclusion or exclusion of specific policy proposals in the special session.

Of course, if the governor has strong feelings about the proposal and is determined to call (or not to call) a special session, this position may not be open to negotiation. If the governor does think that an issue is critical, the attention of the entire state can be focused on the proposal during the special session much more effectively than during the regular session.

Message Power. As a constitutional requirement, the governor must deliver a State of the State message at the beginning of each legislative session. This message includes the outline for the governor's legislative program. Throughout the session, the governor may also submit messages calling for action on individual items of legislation. The receptiveness of the legislature to the various messages is influenced by the governor's popularity, the amount of favorable public opinion generated for the proposals, and the governor's political expertise.

The **message power** of the governor is a formal power that is enhanced by the visibility of the office. Through the judicious use of the mass media (an informal power), the governor can focus public attention on a bill when it might otherwise be buried in the legislative maze. He or she must not overuse the mass media, however, for too many attempts to urge legislative action can result in public apathy toward all gubernatorial appeals. An effective governor "goes to the people" only for legislation considered vital to the interest of the state or to her or his political and financial supporters.

Message Power
The ability of a governor (or a U.S. president) to focus the attention of the press, legislators, and citizens on legislative proposals that he or she considers important. The visibility of the office gives the chief executive instant public attention.

[4]W. Gardner Selby, "Pair May Back Perry's Budget," *San Antonio Express-News,* December 18, 2002, p. 5B; and John Moritz, *Fort Worth Star-Telegram*, January 18, 2003.

Fact-Finding Commissions. Governors sometimes appoint **blue-ribbon commissions** consisting of influential citizens, politicians, and members of concerned special-interest groups. Such commissions can serve either as trial balloons to measure public acceptance of a proposal or as a means to provide information and increase public and interest-group support for a proposal. Blue-ribbon commissions are also commonly used to delay the actual consideration of a political "hot potato" until it has cooled. Politicians know that the attention span of the public is short and that other personally important issues, such as the Dallas Cowboys, jobs, and families, draw people's attention away from politics.

Blue-Ribbon Commission
A commission composed of public personalities or authorities on the subject that is being considered. In Texas, such a commission may have both fact-finding and recommending authority.

THE GOVERNOR AS CHIEF EXECUTIVE

The Texas Constitution charges the governor, as the chief executive, with broad responsibilities. Yet it systematically denies the governor the power to meet these responsibilities through direct executive action. In fact, four other important elective executive offices are established in the same section of the constitution and are legally independent of the governor, thus undermining his or her executive authority:

1. the lieutenant governor.
2. the comptroller of public accounts.
3. the attorney general.
4. the commissioner of the General Land Office.

Other provisions in the constitution further fragment executive power. For example, the constitution establishes the Railroad Commission and states that its members are to be elected. It provides that the State Board of Education can be either elected or appointed. (It is elected independently of the governor.) Moreover, the Texas legislature, by statute, has systematically continued to assume executive functions such as budgeting and auditing. The legislature has also created the Department of Agriculture and a multitude of boards and commissions that are independent of direct gubernatorial control to administer state laws. Elected officials in Texas are shown in Figure 25–2. Given the present fragmented executive branch in Texas, few executive bargaining tools are available to the governor, making that officer one of the weakest state chief executives in the nation.

APPOINTIVE POWERS

An effective governor will use the power of appointment to the maximum. Probably the most important appointments the governor makes are to certain independent **boards and commissions**. The members of these boards establish general administrative and regulatory policy for state agencies or institutions and choose the top administrators to carry out these policies.

Boards and Commissions
In Texas, bodies consisting of three to 18 members that supervise most state agencies.

The governor's ability to affect board policy through appointments is not immediate, however, because the boards are usually appointed for fixed, six-year staggered terms. Because only one-third of these positions become vacant every two years, the governor will have appointed a majority of the members of most boards only in the second half of his or her term.

Interest-Group Concerns. Interest groups in Texas are vitally concerned with seeing that the right kind of appointees are selected to serve on boards and commissions. In the present age of consumerism, industry interest groups are particularly anxious to have industry advocates (often former lobbyists or industry executives) appointed to the boards that oversee and set policy for their agencies. Appointment of a consumer advocate could disturb the close relationship that usually exists between an industry and

FIGURE 25–2 Elected Administrative Officials in Texas

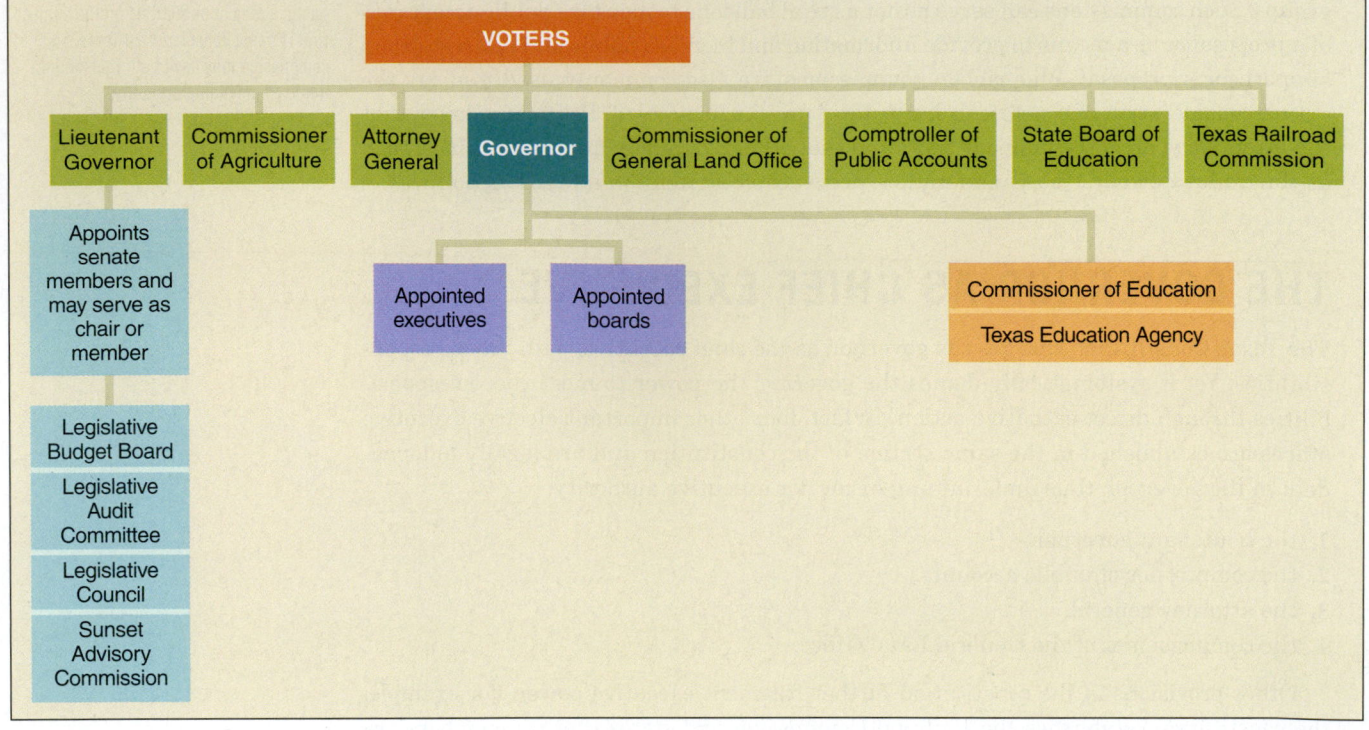

its agency. Furthermore, competing interest groups within one industry may bargain individually with the governor, each promoting an appointee who is favorable to its particular viewpoint. Thus, appointments to important boards often result in intense lobbying by special-interest groups, which gives the governor opportunities to develop support for policies and to help secure funds for future political campaigns.

The Influence of the Senate. The Texas senate must confirm appointments, and individual senators have some influence over appointments from their districts as a result of the practice of *senatorial courtesy*. The senate will usually refuse to vote for confirmation if a senator announces that an appointee from his or her district is "personally obnoxious." The senators thereby show courtesy to the disgruntled senator by refusing to confirm his or her political enemy.

Bureaucratic Concerns. Administrators also want commissioners appointed to their agency who are sympathetic to their problems and who share their goals. Appointments friendly to the administrators' interests can strengthen a governor's influence with these administrators.

Judicial Appointments. The governor can exert a great deal of influence on the state's judiciary. It is common for judges to retire or resign before their terms end. The governor is empowered to fill these vacancies until the next general election. The result is that the governor is able to repay political supporters with judicial appointments, and the appointees enjoy the advantage of incumbency in the general election.

REMOVAL POWERS

Although the governor possesses broad powers of appointment, powers of removal are limited. She or he may remove members of the executive office and a few minor administrators. The governor may also remove—for cause and with the consent of two-thirds of the senate—his or her own appointees to boards and commissions. (The governor cannot remove those appointed by previous governors even through this difficult procedure.)

In general, the governor cannot issue directives or orders to state agencies, nor remove executive officials who do not abide by her or his wishes. If the governor believes that an official is administering the law so as to violate its spirit, there is no official way to force that official to administer the law differently. Only by focusing public attention on the agency and garnering public support can the governor force an administrator to change positions or resign.

PLANNING POWERS

Mostly because of national government requirements concerning federal grants, the governor has gained some powers to engage in planning for state and local governments. With federal encouragement, the state government developed rudimentary coordination and cooperation activities to link the various government units and subunits in the state. The natural center for such statewide planning is the governor's office, which is in a position to determine whether grant requests are in accord with statewide plans. The result is some centralization of planning in the governor's office. The governor also serves as a member of (or appoints representatives to) many multistate organizations and conferences that work to coordinate relations between Texas and other states.

Texas created the Office of State-Federal Relations in Washington, D.C., to facilitate the governor's job of coordinating the activities of state agencies and local governments with the federal government. The governor appoints (and may remove) the director. The office provides information to state officials about federal initiatives and also advocates for the interests of the Texas government with Congress, the administration, and federal agencies. The governor may request federal aid when the state has suffered disaster, drought, or economic calamity. As chief of state, he or she often flies over or visits a disaster area to personally assess the damage—and also to show the unfortunate victims that the governor is concerned for their welfare.

BUDGET POWERS

Many state executives find their power to propose a budget to the legislature important in dealing with state agencies. The Texas governor also is legally designated as the state's chief budget officer, and each biennium the various agencies and institutions submit their appropriation requests to the governor's staff and to the staff of the Legislative Budget Board (LBB). Working from these estimates, the governor and staff may prepare a budget based on both the state's estimated income and the estimated cost of program proposals. When completed, the budget is submitted to the legislature.

The independent Legislative Budget Board also submits a plan for state spending, however. Because the LBB includes the legislature's most powerful officers, the governor's budget may be largely ignored in favor of the LBB proposals.

LAW ENFORCEMENT POWERS

The governor has little law enforcement power. In the basic tradition of Texas government, law enforcement is decentralized. The governor does have the power to extradite fugitives from Texas law and to grant or refuse such requests from other states.

At the state level, the Texas Rangers and the Highway Patrol conduct law enforcement. Both agencies are under the administrative direction of a director of public safety, who is appointed by an independent board, the Public Safety Commission. At the local level, police functions are under the jurisdiction of county sheriffs and constables (who are elected) and city chiefs of police (who are appointed by city officials).

Criminal acts are prosecuted either by elected district or county attorneys or by appointed city attorneys. The judiciary, which tries and sentences criminals, is elective (except for municipal judges, who are appointed by city officials).

MILITARY POWERS

The governor is commander in chief of the state militia, which has two basic parts: the Texas National Guard and the Texas State Guard. The governor appoints (and can remove) an **adjutant general**, who exercises administrative control over both units.

The governor may send units of the militia to keep the peace and protect public property (usually following a natural disaster). She or he may also employ the militia to "execute the laws of the state, suppress insurrection and repel invasions." The governor does not have the power to order evacuations in the event of terrorist attacks, hurricanes, or other natural disasters; only county judges have that power.

The Texas National Guard is made up of both army and air force components and is financed by the U.S. government. It must meet federal standards and may be called to active duty by the president. In the event the Guard is nationalized, command passes from the governor to the president.

The Texas State Guard was established during World War II and serves as a backup organization in the event the National Guard is called to active duty by the president. It cannot be called into active duty by the federal government, and its members receive no pay unless mobilized by the governor.

CLEMENCY POWERS

The 1876 constitution granted the governor virtually unlimited power to pardon, parole, and grant reprieves. Several governors were very generous with these powers, resulting in a 1936 constitutional amendment that established the Board of Pardons and Paroles. Many of the powers that had been held by the governor were transferred to the board, which grants, revokes, and determines the conditions for parole and makes **clemency** recommendations to the governor. The governor appoints the board's membership and can grant less clemency than recommended by the board, but not more. He or she can no longer exercise a check on the parole process by blocking early releases from prison. The governor can postpone executions for 30 days.

THE TEXAS BUREAUCRACY

The most distinctive characteristic of the Texas administration is that no one is really in charge of the administrative apparatus. As in many other states, the administration of laws in Texas is fragmented into several elective and many appointive positions. No single official in the Texas government bears the ultimate responsibility for the actions of the Texas bureaucracy, and no single official can coordinate either planning or program implementation among the many agencies, commissions, and departments. The Texas bureaucracy can be visualized as more than 200 separate entities, each following its own path, often oblivious to the goals and ambitions of other agencies. Texas, in other words, has a *plural executive* system.

We can categorize the various divisions of the executive branch according to whether they have as their top policy maker or policy makers:

Adjutant General
The principal staff officer of an army, who passes communications to the commanding general and distributes the general's orders to subordinates. In the example of the Texas National Guard and Texas State Guard, the "commanding general" is the governor. *Adjutant* comes from a Latin word meaning "helper."

Clemency
Relief from criminal punishment granted by an executive. In Texas, the power of the governor to grant clemency is strictly limited.

1. a single elected administrator.
2. a single appointed executive.
3. a multimember board or commission, which may be elected, appointed, or serve *ex officio* (serve automatically—discussed further in a later subsection).

ELECTED EXECUTIVES

The constitutional and statutory requirement that several administrators (in addition to the governor) be elected was a deliberate effort to decentralize administrative power and prevent any one official from gaining control of the government. Under the Texas plural executive system, the governor shares executive power with several other independently elected executives and boards. These elected officials are directly responsible to the people rather than to the governor. The fact that few Texans can name the individuals who hold these offices, much less judge their competence or honesty, tends to challenge the theory that the popular election of multiple administrators enhances democracy.

Lieutenant Governor. Although the lieutenant governor technically is part of the executive branch, the source of his or her power comes from the legislative branch. The lieutenant governor, as president of the senate, is the *ex officio* cochair of the Legislative Budget Board, the Legislative Council, and the Legislative Audit Board and, if he or she desires, exercises considerable personal influence in the Sunset Advisory Commission and the Legislative Criminal Justice Board. (You learned about most of these bodies in Chapter 24.) These legislative boards and commissions are not part of the bureaucracy, but they conduct continuing studies of administrative policies and make recommendations to the legislature.

TEXAS LIEUTENANT GOVERNOR DAVID DEWHURST, right, and Texas Attorney General Greg Abbott, left, speak to members of the Senate Criminal Justice Committee in Austin, Texas. (AP Photo/Harry Cabluck)

Attorney General. The attorney general is elected for a four-year term and holds one of the four most powerful offices in Texas government. The attorney general is the lawyer for all officials, boards, and agencies in state government. The legal functions of the office range from antitrust actions and consumer protection to activities concerning insurance, banking, and securities. A broad spectrum of the state's business—oil and gas, law enforcement, environmental protection, highways, transportation, and charitable trusts, to name only a few—is included under the overall jurisdiction of the attorney general.

The attorney general performs two major functions: (1) to give advisory opinions to state officers and (2) to represent the state in major civil actions. Because Texas courts, like other American courts, will not issue advisory opinions or rule on hypothetical cases, the attorney general's opinions perform this function. As the state's lawyer, the attorney general advises his or her clients on the meaning of the constitution, state law, and administrative regulations. Although these **attorney general's opinions** are no more than legal advice, they are in effect a quasi-judicial opinion that fills the gap between legislative statute or administrative regulation and judicial interpretation. Although the opinion lacks official enforcement authority, the fact that the attorney general will not defend ignored opinions in court usually ensures compliance by legislators and administrators.

The attorney general also represents the state and the state government in civil litigation, including conflicts with the national government. The attorney general has defended Texas positions on such past issues as the poll tax and segregation and on current issues such as:

- abortion.
- obscenity laws.
- challenges to state legislative districts.
- affirmative-action programs.

Attorney General's Opinion
An interpretation of the state's constitution or laws by the state attorney general. Officials may request such opinions, and although the opinions are not legally binding, they are usually followed.

SUSAN COMBS is the Texas state comptroller. As manager of the state's financial activities, she holds a powerful position. (AP Photo/Harry Cabluck)

The attorney general also initiates suits in cooperation with the governments of other states on antitrust violations or consumer protection. For example, the Texas attorney general, along with the attorneys general from most other states, sued the tobacco industry to recover the state's Medicaid expenses for tobacco-related injuries. The attorney general's power to prosecute crimes is relatively narrow, however, because the primary responsibility for criminal prosecution in Texas lies with the locally elected district and county attorneys.

Comptroller of Public Accounts. The comptroller, who has become one of the state's most powerful officials, is elected for a four-year term to manage most financial activities of state government. She or he is the state's chief tax collector and accountant. The constitution requires that the comptroller certify the estimated two-year state revenue, and the state legislature may not constitutionally appropriate more than the comptroller certifies.

The comptroller also certifies the financial condition of the state at the close of each fiscal year. The governor and legislature are anxious to learn if they must reduce spending or increase taxes. (Unlike the federal government, Texas cannot simply balance the books by borrowing.) In recent years, the economy has forced them to do both.

Commissioner of the General Land Office. The commissioner of the General Land Office is elected for a four-year term. Principal duties of the commissioner are managing public lands and leasing mineral rights beneath them and overseeing riverbeds, tidelands, bays, and inlets.

The land commissioner also serves *ex officio* on several boards and chairs the important Veterans' Land Board and the School Land Board, whose programs are administered by the General Land Office. The Veterans' Land Board lends sums to veterans for land purchases and home purchases and improvements. The School Land Board oversees approximately 20 million acres of public land and mineral rights properties, a large portion of which are dedicated to the **Permanent School Fund** (for public schools) and the Permanent University Fund, which benefits the University of Texas and Texas A&M University.

Permanent School Fund
In Texas, a fund that provides support to the public school system. Leases, rents, and royalties from designated public school lands are deposited into the fund.

Commissioner of Agriculture. The commissioner of agriculture is elected for a four-year term to oversee the Texas Department of Agriculture. The department has more than 500 employees and is responsible for the administration of all laws relating to agriculture, as well as research, educational, and regulatory activities. The duties of the department range from checking the accuracy of scales in meat markets and gas pumps at service stations to determining labeling procedures for pesticides and promoting Texas agricultural products in national and world markets. The commissioner also administers the Texas Agricultural Finance Authority, which provides grants and low-interest loans to businesses that produce, process, market, and export Texas agricultural products. The possibility of conflict between the interests of producers and the interests of consumers is ever present in the department's activities.

APPOINTED EXECUTIVES

The governor of Texas does have the power to appoint a limited number of officials. In general, these officials are less powerful than the ones who are directly elected by the public.

Secretary of State. The governor appoints the secretary of state with confirmation by the state senate. The secretary of state is keeper of the seal of the state. She or he serves as the chief election officer for Texas, administers Texas election laws, maintains voter-registration records, and receives election results. The office of the secretary of state provides a repository for official, business, and commercial records required to be filed with the office. The secretary publishes government rules and regulations and commissions notaries public. By executive order, Governor Rick Perry has also directed the secretary of state to serve as his liaison for Texas border and Mexican affairs and to represent him and the state at international and diplomatic occasions.

Adjutant General. The adjutant general is appointed by the governor with the consent of the senate for a two-year term. The adjutant general serves as the state's top-ranking military officer and exercises administrative jurisdiction over the Texas National Guard and Texas State Guard. These are among the few state agencies under the direct administrative control of the governor.

Commissioner of Health and Human Services. The office of commissioner of health and human services was created in the first special session in 1991 and is filled by the governor with the consent of the senate for a two-year term. The commissioner heads an umbrella agency that oversees and manages 11 health and welfare agencies.

Insurance Commissioner. The commissioner of insurance is appointed directly by the governor for a two-year term, subject to senate confirmation. The commissioner oversees the Department of Insurance, which monitors and regulates the Texas insurance industry. The department provides consumer information; monitors corporate solvency; prosecutes violators of insurance law; licenses agents and investigates complaints against them; develops statistics for rate determination; and regulates specific lines of insurance such as property, liability, and life insurance.

BOARDS AND COMMISSIONS

Texas government includes at least 200 boards and commissions. These administrative bodies may be elective, appointive, *ex officio*, or some combination of the three. Members may be salaried or may serve only for reimbursement of expenses. Boards differ considerably in their political power. Generally speaking, the most important boards are those that affect the largest number of people and have the largest budgets. Other important boards charter or regulate the state's business, industrial, and financial powers. Their rules and regulations, which often have the force of law, are called **administrative law**.

Administrative Law
Rules and regulations written by administrators to implement laws. The effectiveness of a law is often determined by how the corresponding administrative law is written.

Elective Boards—The Railroad Commission. One of the most important state regulatory boards in the United States has been the Texas Railroad Commission, a constitutionally authorized elective board whose three members serve for overlapping six-year terms. The governor fills any midterm vacancies on the board, and these appointees serve until the first election, at which time they may win election to the board in their own right.

The board is politically partisan, and its members must first win their party's nomination before running in the general election. The chair position is rotated so that each member becomes the chair during the last two years of his or her term. This forces any candidate who is challenging an incumbent commissioner to run against the chair of the commission.

The commission regulates gas utilities, oil and gas pipelines, oil and gas drilling and pumping activities, and intrastate railroad transportation. It is also responsible for regulation of waste disposal by the oil and gas industry and the protection of both surface and subsurface water supplies from oil- or gas-related residue. Formerly, the Railroad Commission (RRC) regulated **intrastate** truck freight in Texas, but the national government preempted the commission's powers in this area because the RRC's rules of regulation interfered with **interstate** commerce.

Intrastate
Within the state.

Interstate
Between two or more states.

Elective Boards—The State Board of Education. The elected State Board of Education (SBOE) sets policy for the Texas Education Agency (TEA), which oversees and regulates the Texas public school system below the college level and administers national and state education law and SBOE rules and regulations. The TEA writes regulations for and compels local compliance with legislative and judicial mandates and reforms, dispenses state funds, serves as a conduit for some funds from the national government to the local schools, and approves the textbooks to be purchased at state expense for use by local districts.

Members of the SBOE are elected on a partisan basis from 15 single-member districts and serve four-year staggered terms. The governor appoints the chair for a two-year term from the SBOE membership. The SBOE establishes policy, implements policy established by law, and, as mentioned, oversees the TEA. The board also recommends three nominees for commissioner of education (the TEA's chief executive officer), who is appointed by the governor with the senate's consent to a four-year term.

***Ex Officio* Boards.** A number of boards have memberships that are completely or partially *ex officio*—that is, some or all of their members belong automatically because of other offices they hold. There are two basic reasons for creating such boards. One is that when travel to Austin was expensive and time consuming, it seemed logical to establish a board consisting of persons already in Austin. Another reason is that *ex officio* members may have relevant subject-matter expertise.

The Texas Bond Review Board is an example of an *ex officio* board. It has four *ex officio* members—the governor, the lieutenant governor, the speaker of the house, and the comptroller of public accounts—and has 12 full-time employees. It reviews and approves all bonds and other long-term debt issued by state agencies and universities. It also engages in various other functions pertaining to state and local long-term debt.

A number of agencies' boards have some *ex officio* members. The Agriculture Resources Protection Authority (15 members, nine *ex officio*), the Texas Cosmetology Commission (seven members, one *ex officio*), and the Texas Turnpike Authority (12 members, three *ex officio*) are examples of such boards.

Appointive Boards. Appointive boards vary extensively in importance, administrative power, and salary. The members of these boards, who are usually not salaried, set the policies for their agencies and appoint their own chief administrators. The governor, with the consent of the senate, usually appoints board members, but there are many mixed boards whose members are appointed by the governor or by some other official or whose membership is partially *ex officio*. Due to the usual practice of appointing members to staggered terms, six years may lapse before a governor can appoint a complete board.

DID YOU KNOW?

Texas incumbent Texas Railroad Commission Chair Victor Carrillo was defeated in the Republican primary by political unknown David Porter, who won a resounding 60 percent of the vote? Commissioner Carrillo outspent the challenger $600,000 to $30,000 and had the backing of the Texas Republican establishment.

TEXAS RAILROAD COMMISSIONER ELIZABETH A. JONES IS SHOWN with Governor Perry, and the image to the right shows Commissioner Michael L. Williams. The third commissioner, David Porter (not shown here), was elected into office in November 2010. See the Did You Know? above. To what extent may declining production of oil and natural gas reduce the importance of the commission in the future? (Photos courtesy of the Texas Railroad Commission and the Governor's Office)

Board appointees are often representatives of groups that have an economic interest in the rules and policies of the board. Appointments may be either a reward for political support or an attempt to balance competing interest groups whose economic well-being is affected by board rules and policies.

The governor can remove board members before the expiration of their terms only if he or she appointed those board members, and then only with the concurrence of two-thirds of the senate. The governor may encourage board members to resign, however, by publicly criticizing the members or policies of a board.

THE BUREAUCRACY AND PUBLIC POLICY NEUTRALITY

Texans have not only decentralized public functions, but they have also attempted to depoliticize the bureaucracy by establishing the independent board and commission system. This is an attempt to insulate the bureaucracy from the politics of the legislature and the governor.

Attempts to depoliticize the bureaucracy, however, have simply replaced one kind of politics with another. Most political observers today agree that the Texas bureaucracy is deeply engaged in politics, that politics strongly affects public policy, and that policy formulation cannot be separated from policy administration. Public administration is "in politics" because it operates in a political environment and must seek political support from somewhere if it is to accomplish goals, gain appropriations, or even survive. The result of strong political support for an agency is increased size, jurisdiction, influence, and prestige. The less successful agency may suffer reduced appropriations, static employment, narrowed administrative jurisdiction, and possibly extinction. Where, then, does a unit of the bureaucracy look for the political support so necessary for its well-being? It may look to clientele interest groups, the legislature, the chief executive, and the public. Political power also comes from factors within the bureaucracy, such as expertise, control of information, and discretion in the interpretation and administration of laws.

PUBLIC SUPPORT

Good public relations benefits any agency, both in appropriations and jurisdictional battles with other agencies. Favorable propaganda, myth, and literature create broad-based public support for such agencies as the Texas Department of Criminal Justice, the Texas Rangers, and to some extent, the Texas Highway Patrol.

Clientele
Persons represented by a government agency or a politician.

Clientele Groups. The most natural allies for an agency are its **clientele** (or constituent) interest groups—the private groups that benefit directly from agency programs. At the national level, examples of close-knit alliances of interest groups and agencies are defense contractors and the Department of Defense, agribusiness and the Department of Agriculture, and the airlines and the Federal Aviation Administration. In Texas, close bedfellows include the Texas Good Roads and Transportation Association and the Texas Department of Transportation; the oil, gas, and transportation industries and the Texas Railroad Commission; the banking industry and the Department of Banking; and the Texas Medical Association and the Department of Health.

The Agency-Clientele Alliance. Agitation by interest groups often leads to the establishment of a state agency, and the agency's power and importance may be directly related to the power and influence of its clientele groups and the intensity of their support. The agency and its clientele groups are therefore usually allied from the very beginning, and this alliance continues to grow and mature as mutual convenience, power, and prosperity increase. Economic and political ties are cemented by mutual self-interest. Agencies and clients share information, have common attitudes and goals, exchange employees, and lobby together with the legislature for both agency appropriations and government policies that favor the interest groups.

Reciprocity. Mutual accommodation has become so accepted that clientele groups often speak of "our agency" and devote considerable time and funds to lobbying for it. The agency reciprocates by protecting its clients within the administration. Of course, both the bureaucracy and the various clientele groups are made up of many entities, and there is often competition for appropriations, so both agencies and special interests seek allies in the legislative branch.

THE LEGISLATURE, THE LIEUTENANT GOVERNOR, AND THE SPEAKER

Bureaucratic power is enhanced by the support of powerful legislators, often including the chairperson of the committee that exercises legislative oversight over the agency. The agency depends on legislative allies for laws that expand its powers, increase the scope of its duties, protect it from unfriendly interests, and appropriate the funds for its operation. Therefore, administrators seek the favor of influential lawmakers.

Although the committee chairs are important in the Texas legislature, the short session and the power of the presiding officers limit their influence. For this reason, an agency seeks the support of the lieutenant governor and the speaker of the house, as well as members of the finance and appropriations committees, the Legislative Budget Board, and the Legislative Council.

Campaigns for the Leadership. The importance of legislative support explains the intense lobbying activity that surrounds the appointment of legislators to powerful committees and the campaign activity that precedes election to positions of legislative leadership. If an interest group and its agency are unable to get allies appointed or elected to positions of influence in the legislature, they are forced to try to win support after the influential legislators are chosen—a more difficult endeavor.

The Revolving Door. Relationships among interest groups, agencies, and lawmakers can be enhanced by the exchange of personnel. The practice by which corporations employ former administrators and legislators as executives, lobbyists, or consultants is known as the **revolving door**. A government employee may resign and accept lucrative employment with an individual, a corporation, or some other organization that has profited financially by that employee's actions. In this environment, legislators, administrators, and regulators often become promoters of the regulated industry. The revolving door negatively affects public perception of public servants and prompts cynicism toward government.

Revolving Door
The interchange of employees among the legislature, government agencies, and related private special-interest groups.

THE GOVERNOR

Although the governor has few direct administrative powers, agencies still need support from the governor. The governor's cooperation is especially important because of his or her power to appoint policy-making boards and commissions. Moreover, the governor's support gives the agency greater bargaining power with legislators and interest groups. The Texas governor can influence and shape agency programs and success through veto power as well as through appointments.

Agency employees develop shared attitudes, an esprit de corps, and a sense of communality with the employees of the agency's clientele interest groups. Because an agency's interests are usually similar to those of its clientele, both want the governor to appoint board members who will advance their mutual political goals.

PUBLIC POLICY AND THE IRON TEXAS STAR

The explanation of how public policy is made and implemented is a complex endeavor. Teachers and writers often use models as a generalization to help explain the process. A model is a simplification of reality to explain reality. One such model, the **Iron Texas Star**, is depicted in Figure 25–3. It attempts to explain the relationships between the political actors in Texas government that make legislative and administrative public policy happen.

Iron Texas Star
A policy-making coalition that includes interest groups; the lieutenant governor and the speaker of the house; standing committees of the legislature; the governor; and administrators, boards, and commissions.

The Five Points of the Star. The coalitions that make policy in Texas can be thought of as consisting of the following five players:

1. and 2. *Presiding officers and the legislative institutions and committees that they control.* Due to the hands-on authority exercised by the lieutenant governor and the speaker of the house of representatives, each of the presiding officers and the legislative institutions and committees that they control warrant a point on the Texas star. Although individual legislators often have independent political support, the power of the lieutenant governor and the speaker to select most of the membership and all of the chairs of the standing committees, the conference committees, and the legislative boards and commissions gives each presiding officer undeniable influence within both the legislature and the bureaucracy.

3. *Elected and appointed boards and elected administrators.* These individuals are also important players in the Texas political process. Usually appointed or elected with the support of economic special interests, these administrators and board members often possess political support independent of the legislature and the governor. Their influence within the bureaucracy itself is amplified due to the virtual absence of a civil service system for Texas government employees, making them especially vulnerable to political influence.

4. *The governor.* Strong legislative, appointive, and other powers ensure the inclusion of the governor as the fourth point on the Texas star.

5. *Economic interest groups.* These groups provide campaign funds for elected officials, political and financial support for friendly legislators and administrators, and employment and investment opportunities for former, present, and future state officials. Economic special interests provide both the plans and the mortar that builds and holds together the five-cornered coalition that we call the Texas government.

Acquiring "Friends." The basic goal for special interests is to accumulate "friends" in the policy-making and regulatory areas of government. It is equally critical for political operatives to acquire friends among economically powerful individuals and special-interest groups. The members of the coalition also support the friends of their friends at the other points of the iron star, and thereby develop a system of mutual support from which all can benefit.

Legislators, administrators, the presiding officers, and the governor rely to varying degrees on the support of their interest-group friends for campaign contributions, supplemental income, political advancement, financial advice and opportunity, and after-office employment and income. As time passes and members of the coalition become more interdependent, each looks to the others for support. Legislators bargain for the

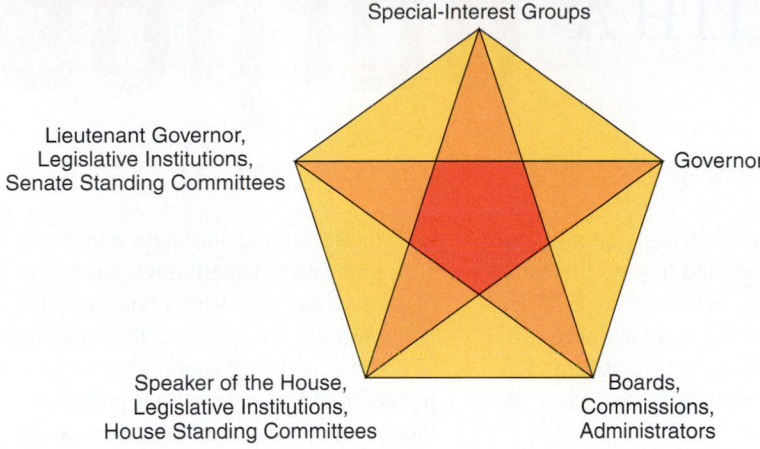

FIGURE 25–3 The Iron Texas Star Model

interest of the coalition in the legislature. Administrators issue favorable regulations and support their friends' viewpoints in administrative decisions. The presiding officers may shepherd the proposals of their friends through the legislative process and also place the friends of economic special interests on powerful legislative committees and legislative boards and commissions. Finally, the governor appoints friends and friends of friends to various boards and commissions that make policy affecting these same friends. Other government officials may also broker with political operatives for decisions favorable to their friends in the iron star coalition.

Again, the Revolving Door. Appointees to boards and administrative positions are usually chosen from the industry concerned, and the policy decisions they make tend to benefit the most influential operatives in the industry. In turn, when government employees leave government service, many find jobs in the industry where their expertise lies. This interchange of employees between the public and private sectors is the revolving door we mentioned earlier in this chapter, and it undermines the independence of government employees. Literally hundreds of former administrators and legislators work for special interests as lobbyists, consultants, and executives.

BUREAUCRATIC ACCOUNTABILITY

Throughout the history of the United States, people have tried to hold government responsible for its policies. The rise of the modern state is the most recent challenge to responsible government. The growing size and political power of modern bureaucracy make the problem of administrative accountability ever more acute. Various organizational arrangements and legal restrictions have been used in attempts to make the bureaucracy accountable to the citizenry, or at least to someone whom the citizens can hold responsible.

ELECTIVE ACCOUNTABILITY

The simplest approach has been to make the bureaucracy directly accountable to the people through the democratic process—a system of **elective accountability**. In Texas, this plan was established through election of the governor, lieutenant governor, attorney general, treasurer, comptroller of public accounts, commissioner of the General Land Office, commissioner of agriculture, Railroad Commission, and State Board of

Elective Accountability
A condition in which officials are directly accountable to the voters for their actions.

POLITICS WITH A purpose

Lobbying for Very Personal Interests

Interest groups influence public policy at every step of the political process. Groups work for and help finance the campaigns for candidates who are friendly to their interests. They influence and educate politicians during the legislative process and then lobby administrators to get a favorable rendering of the policy as the regulations are written and again as they are implemented.

What if you were injured in high school athletics and lost the use of your legs? After months of physical therapy, you found that the world had changed. Activities that had been routine were now difficult or impossible. Commercial and public facilities often lacked accommodations for wheelchairs, denying you and others like you the access necessary to live an independent life. To try to change this, you joined an organization that worked on the state level to educate commercial enterprises, contractors, and the government to be more aware of the issues of customers and citizens with disabilities. Before long you were employed by this group to lobby and educate state legislators and administrators as to the daily problems faced by people with disabilities. You worked at this job while earning your bachelor's degree. Upon graduation, you joined the Coalition of Texans with Disabilities as director of advocacy and community organizing. You became quite well known around the state capitol for both your lobbying skills and your tenacious advocacy for people with disabilities. In the process, you were a finalist for the 2008 Austin Under Forty Awards. The governor then appointed you to the Board of Architectural Examiners, which licenses and regulates the members of the architectural profession. If you had done all this, you might be Chase Bearden—and you would be making a difference.

Readers and students, join an advocacy group that works to influence those who have power over your life. The economic and political forces that determine your life's environment can be educated and influenced by organized group action. Although you have little power as an individual, when joined with others you can make a difference in those things that affect your life.

Education. The reasoning was that the public, if given an opportunity, would keep a close watch on elected administrators and refuse to reelect those who were incompetent or dishonest. Administrators, therefore, would be sensitive to the wishes of the voters and would administer the laws only in the interest of the general public.

Difficulties of Applying the Concept. Several problems exist with the application of elective accountability. Perhaps the most obvious is the difficulty an elected official faces in determining the will of the people or even in determining the public interest. Texas is made up of many divergent groups, each with its own interests, and these interests are often incompatible. Frequently, pleasing one group means displeasing another.

The Invisibility of Many Elected Officials. Another major problem is the relative invisibility of elected executives. As shown in Figure 25–2, the list of elected executives is long enough that few voters are even aware of the names of many officeholders, much less their administrative competence. Ineptitude, inefficiency, corruption, and incompetence go unnoticed by the public and the press. Administrators, once elected, are usually returned to office until they die, retire, anger powerful special interests, or commit an act so flagrantly unethical that the voters finally "throw the rascals out."

Elective accountability may be practical for local offices, especially in rural areas, where voters are more likely to be acquainted with their elected officials. In an increasingly urban society, however, elective accountability seems an ineffective method of either influencing administrative behavior or making administrators more responsive to the public.

LEGISLATIVE ACCOUNTABILITY

Some advocates of administrative reform argue that the bureaucracy should be accountable to the legislature, because the legislature is the branch of government closest to the people. According to this argument, because the legislature is elected to protect constituent interests, and because legislators establish policies, elected representatives should determine whether those policies are being administered according to legislative intent. This principle has been implemented in Texas by establishing various auditing, budgeting, and oversight boards as well as legislative committees to try to hold administrators accountable.

The Sunset Advisory Commission. As an important oversight step, the Texas legislature established the Sunset Advisory Commission in 1977 to make recommendations on whether to alter, terminate, or continue most state boards, commissions, and agencies. Currently, about 150 state administrative entities and their operations are reviewed periodically, usually in 12-year cycles. At the end of its cycle, an agency ceases to exist unless the legislature takes specific action to renew it. If an agency is renewed, the Sunset Commission evaluates its compliance with legislative directives. In addition, agency functions may be expanded, diminished, or reassigned to other agencies by legislative action. The state auditor also evaluates any management changes recommended by the commission. Some argue that periodic legislative evaluation together with agency self-evaluation should result in better, more efficient administration.

Problems with Legislative Accountability. In practice, accountability to the legislature also has limited effectiveness. The assumption that the legislative branch best represents the people is debatable. Legislators' independent judgment may be compromised by financial conflicts of interest, campaign contributions from special-interest groups, and political ambition. Although legislative oversight may serve the purposes of individual legislators and special interests, the general public does not necessarily benefit. Another problem is the invisibility of committee hearings and decision-making processes in the legislature. The public is not aware of many policy decisions that are made in its name by the legislature.

Finally, because the Texas legislature is seldom in session, permanent legislative institutions, such as the Legislative Budget Board and the Legislative Council, are given the task of overseeing the administration. These institutions, by themselves, cannot enforce accountability on autonomous agencies in Texas government, and they also lack the visibility necessary for effective operation in the public interest. A major problem of responsible government is knowing who is "watching the watchers."

ACCOUNTABILITY TO THE CHIEF EXECUTIVE

Some reformers advocate a Texas administration patterned after the cabinet system of the federal government. As shown in Figure 25–4, establishing a **cabinet system** would entail reorganizing the executive branch. Existing departments would be consolidated into larger departments, and the governor would have the power to appoint and remove top administrators and to control the budget. Administrative authority would be concentrated at the top. Advocates argue that this is only proper, because the governor usually receives the blame for administrative blunders anyway and would have a powerful incentive to hold the appointed bureaucrats accountable for their actions.

Cabinet System
At the state government level, a form of executive organization that allows the governor to appoint and remove top-level administrators, giving the governor more control over the administration.

FIGURE 25-4
The Usual Cabinet System

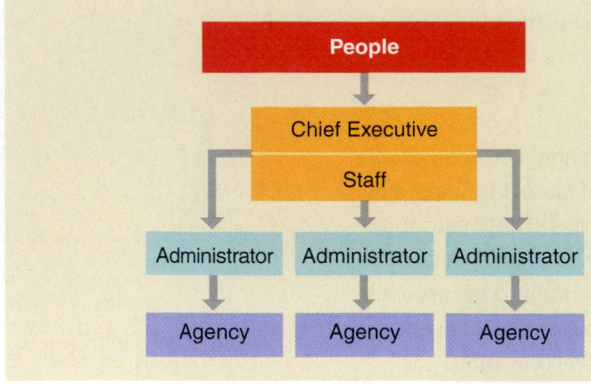

Theoretically, several benefits could result from accountability to the governor. The office is visible to the general public, so the problem of who watches the watchers would be solved. There would be no question of who has the ultimate responsibility for any corruption or incompetence in the administration. Administrative control could be simplified, resulting in coordinated planning and policy implementation. Waste and duplication could be reduced.

The Need for an Executive Office. Clearly, no single person can control dozens of agencies, their chiefs, and their thousands of employees. Analysis of the national government, however, demonstrates that one means by which the president can hold the bureaucracy accountable is through the Executive Office of the President—in particular, the Office of Management and Budget. If public administration in Texas were reorganized on the federal model, the governor would need similar staff organizations. The governor's executive staff, although relatively invisible to the public, would nevertheless be accountable to the governor.

Continued Problems under a Cabinet System. This chain of accountability—administrative agency, to appointed executive, to staff, to governor, to the people—is weakened by the close ties usually found among administrators, constituent interest groups, and legislators. Interest groups would continue to influence administrative appointments and removals in "their agencies" just as they influence appointments to boards and commissions under the present system. Even under a cabinet system, the governor would have problems enforcing the accountability of agencies that have allies among powerful interest groups and legislators.

BUREAUCRATIC RESPONSIBILITY

To whom is a Texas administrator really responsible? The answer may well be to the economic interest groups that benefit from the programs that the officer administers. Politics works on the basic principles of mutual accommodation among allies, conflict among opponents, coalition building, and compromise. Agency officials are often obligated to administer the laws and make policy decisions in ways that support the goals and aspirations of their political allies among private economic interests.

Open Meetings and Open Records. How, then, can the Texas administration be made more accountable to the public? There is no single answer. More openness in government offers one possibility. A basic concept of democratic government is that policy made in the name of the public should be made in full view of the public. Texas has made great strides in this area.

Open-meetings laws require that meetings of government bodies at all levels be open to the general public, except when personnel, land acquisition, and litigation are discussed. The laws further prohibit holding unannounced sessions and splitting up to avoid a quorum, and they require that public notice be posted for both open and closed sessions. These laws are continuously being tested by policy makers, however, who feel more comfortable operating in secret.

Openness is further encouraged by the state's **open-records law**, which requires that records of all government proceedings and decisions be available to the public. The only cost in obtaining such records is the expense involved in assembling and reproducing them, which is low when using the Internet.

Open-Meetings Law
A law that requires meetings of government decision-making bodies to be open to public scrutiny (with some exceptions).

Open-Records Law
A law requiring that records of all government proceedings and decisions are made available to the public.

Whistle-blowers and Ombudspersons. Another source of openness is whistle-blowers—government employees who expose bureaucratic excesses, blunders, corruption, or favoritism. These employees could be commended and protected from retribution, but too often they are instead exiled to the minor agencies or fired for their effort. To its credit, the Texas whistle-blowers' law prohibits governments from acting against employees who report law violations. Enforcement is difficult and time consuming, however. Whistle-blowers must often hire attorneys at great expense and lose years of their careers.

Still another option is for government to provide an ombudsperson, an official who hears and investigates complaints by private individuals against public officials or agencies. The appointment of ombudspersons at every level of government would give individuals increased access to the bureaucracy and a single, impartial office with which to lodge complaints against administrative decisions.

YOU CAN MAKE A Difference

BECOME A SMART CONSUMER OF STATE SERVICES

The state's executive branch follows many antiquated traditions, but state agencies are beginning to join the information age and provide a wealth of information and conveniences to residents. Some agency Web sites are not user friendly, but many provide information that can serve as an excellent original source for academic research. Quite a few of these sites also offer online services that can make life easier for Texans.

WHY SHOULD YOU CARE?

Democracy depends on an informed electorate. In addition, Texas state agencies provide vital services, and students may benefit directly from many of those services. Some of the best information about crime is available online at the Texas Department of Public Safety site, for example. The most comprehensive analyses of tax and spending issues are available through the Texas Office of the Comptroller of Public Accounts and the Legislative Budget Board.

WHAT CAN YOU DO?

You can browse through the Legislative Budget Board's latest *Fiscal Size-Up, 2006–2007* at **www.lbb.state.tx.us** to see what services the state offers. From which of these services can you benefit? Guaranteed student loans and grants are one possibility.

You can contact the Consumer Protection Division of the Office of the Attorney General to learn about your rights and how to exercise them. Also available are copies of the Deceptive Practices Act and consumer brochures.

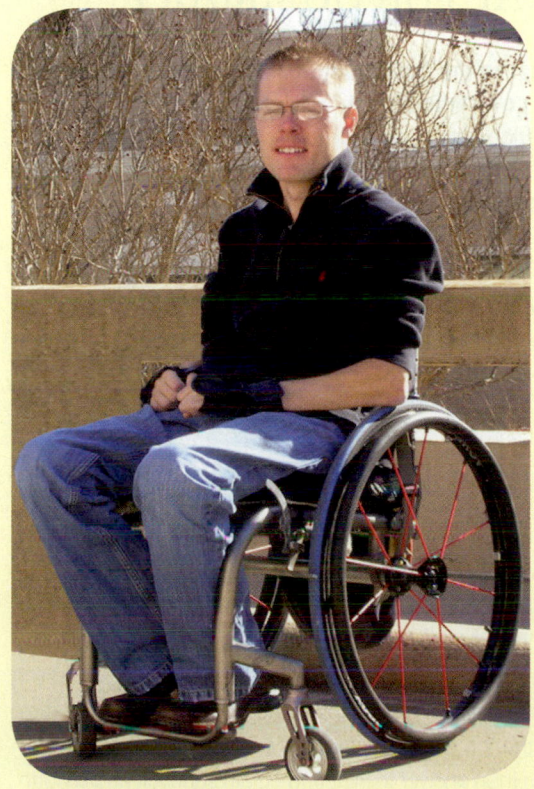

BY BEING an informed and vocal Texas citizen, Chase Bearden, discussed in the *Politics with a Purpose feature* on p. 878, has made a major impact on disability issues facing Texans and now serves on a state agency supporting his cause. (Courtesy of Chase Bearden)

The office provides instructions on how to file a complaint, along with a copy of a consumer complaint form. You can contact the office at:

Consumer Protection Division Office
of the Attorney General
P.O. Box 12548
Austin, TX 78711-2548
www.oag.state.tx.us/consumer/index.shtml

Complaints against health care professionals can be lodged with the Health Professions Council at 800-821-3205.

Privately owned electric utility rates will no longer be set by the Texas Public Utility Commission. In the new competitive environment, shop for lower utility bills at **www.powertochoose.org**.

KEY TERMS

adjutant general 868
administrative law 872
attorney general's opinion 870
blue-ribbon commission 865
boards and commissions 865
cabinet system 879
chief of state 859
clemency 868

clientele 874
elective accountability 877
formal powers 858
indictment 857
informal powers 858
interstate 872
intrastate 872
Iron Texas Star 876
message power 864

open-meetings law 880
open-records law 880
Permanent School Fund 871
presession bargaining 861
quasi-judicial functions 855
quasi-legislative functions 855
revolving door 875
threat to veto 860

CHAPTER SUMMARY

1. **What is the basic function of the executive branch of government?** The basic function of the executive branch is to see that the laws are administered. In this process the administrators influence policy formation, legislation, and adjudication. In the process of performing their duties, it is the administrator who is most likely to be in direct contact with the average citizen.

2. The government of Texas was conceived in the post-Reconstruction era, following an unfortunate and unhappy experience with a centralized, unpopular government. Distrust of the chief executive's power led the constitution's authors to establish a weak governorship as part of a plural executive system in which executive power is shared among many independently elected officers, as well as appointed boards and commissions.

3. **How does the structural organization of the Texas administration compare with that of the United States government?** The structural organization of the United States government is hierarchical, constructed something like a pyramid. At the top is the president, to whom most of the top administrators answer. Lower-level administrators then answer to their immediate superior, and so forth.

   The Texas administration operates under the plural executive concept, with several top administrators, including the governor. The Texas administration could be viewed as hundreds of little pyramids, each

similar in function to the U.S. administration, but without the single office at the top. This is evidenced by the other elected administrators and 200 state agencies headed by elected and appointed boards and commissions. The boards and commissions make general rules and appoint chief administrative directors. The governor usually does not appoint the actual administrators of state agencies.

4. The governor lacks meaningful removal, budgetary, or directive powers (to issue executive orders to state agencies). The result is an executive branch that is fragmented, uncoordinated, and insufficiently supervised. The governor is not a true chief executive.

5. **How can the formal powers of the governor be strengthened by his informal powers?** The governor can reclaim some powers by using the threat to veto (a legislative power); bargaining with legislators, administrators, and lobbyists; and using message power to gain the attention of the general population. A long-serving governor can also enhance the power of the office by his or her appointments to boards, commissions, and the judiciary.

6. In the absence of effective gubernatorial power, interest groups and legislative leaders usually fill the power vacuum. Bureaucrats and agency heads have greater latitude to follow their own agendas.

7. Important elected officials other than the governor include the following: (1) the lieutenant governor, who has a powerful role as the presiding officer in the senate; (2) the attorney general, who serves as the lawyer for the state and can issue opinions on the legality of various measures and practices in response to official requests; (3) the comptroller of public accounts, who handles tax collection and state accounting tasks; (4) the commissioner of the General Land Office, who manages state-owned land and mineral rights; and (5) the commissioner of agriculture, who both serves the agricultural industry and oversees consumer protection laws.

SELECTED PRINT, MEDIA, AND ONLINE RESOURCES

PRINT RESOURCES

Gantt, Fred, Jr. *The Chief Executive in Texas.* Austin: University of Texas Press, 1964. This is the classic study of the governor's office in Texas.

Gantt, Fred, Jr. *The Impact of the Texas Constitution on the Executive.* Houston: Institute for Urban Studies, University of Houston, 1973. This book presents an analysis of the state constitution as it affects the executive branch and provides some insights by comparing the Texas governor with governors of other states. Some provisions in the Texas Constitution have been changed since the book was written.

Gray, Virginia, and Russell L. Hanson. *Politics of the American States: A Comparative Analysis.* Washington, DC: Congressional Quarterly, 2003. This publication offers an interesting comparison of politics in the various states.

Prindle, David F. *Petroleum Politics and the Texas Railroad Commission.* Austin: University of Texas Press, 1981. This book offers perhaps the best description available of relations between a Texas agency and its clientele group.

MEDIA RESOURCES

The Best Little Whorehouse in Texas—A lighthearted play and later a movie starring Dolly Parton and Burt Reynolds. It shows the governor's frustration with Texas values and the tradition of local control. Although based partly on fact, neither the play nor the movie reveals that the Texas attorney general finally closed the house with a public-nuisance civil suit.

ONLINE RESOURCES

Attorney General of Texas The lawyer for the state of Texas, Green Abbott, is charged by the Texas Constitution to defend its laws, represent the state in litigation, and approve public bond issues: www.oag.state.tx.us

Comptroller of Public Accounts The comptroller is the chief steward of the state's finances, acting as tax collector, chief accountant, chief revenue estimator, and chief treasurer for all of state government: www.cpa.state.tx.us

Governor's Appointments Learn about the governor's appointive power: http://governor.state.tx.us/appointments/positions/

Governor's Initiatives Since taking office in 2000, Governor Perry has followed a deliberate course of action to transform the state of Texas. Focusing on areas that are most essential to an improved quality of life, Perry has pursued improvements in safety, education, economic development, infrastructure, resource management, and personal well-being. Read about these legislative initiatives: http://governor.state.tx.us/priorities/

Governor's Mansion The governor's mansion, which is open to the public, is displayed online: www.governor.state.tx.us/about/governors_mansion

Lieutenant Governor Read up on the duties of the office, the major issues facing the state, and the activities of the legislative committees: www.senate.state.tx.us/75r/LtGov/Ltgov.htm

Office of the Governor The governor's Web site: www.governor.state.tx.us

State of Texas For a list of all state agencies and almost anything about Texas: info.texas.gov

Texas Department of Agriculture A state agency established by the Texas legislature in 1907, currently headed by Commissioner Todd Staples: www.agr.state.tx.us

Texas Education Agency Comprises the commissioner of education and agency staff. The TEA and the State Board of Education (SBOE) guide and monitor activities and programs related to public education in Texas: www.tea.state.tx.us

Texas General Land Office Since its founding in 1836, the GLO's duties have evolved, but its core mission is still the management of state lands and mineral-right properties totaling 20.3 million acres: www.glo.state.tx.us

Texas Military Forces For the governor's commander-in-chief powers, visit the site of the Texas adjutant general: www.agd.state.tx.us

Texas Railroad Commission Established in 1891 under a constitutional and legislative mandate to prevent discrimination in railroad charges and establish reasonable tariffs: www.rrc.state.tx.us

Texas Secretary of State One of six state officials named by the Texas Constitution to form the Executive Department of the State. The secretary is appointed by the governor, with confirmation by the senate, and serves at the pleasure of the governor: www.sos.state.tx.us

26

The Texas Supreme Court (Courtesy of the
Supreme Court of Texas)

The Texas Judiciary, Law, and Due Process

QUESTIONS TO CONSIDER

What are the differences between the kinds of cases tried in Texas's criminal courts and those tried in its civil courts?

How does due process in Texas's courts balance the rights of individuals and the mores of the community as a whole?

What are the criticisms of Texas's judicial selection process?

CHAPTER CONTENTS

Civil Law and Criminal Law

Issues in Civil Law

Issues and Elements in Criminal Law

Due Process of Law

Texas Court Organization

Selection of Judges

what if...

Texas Abolished the Death Penalty?

BACKGROUND

Although the national execution rate has been declining and New Mexico has recently abolished the death penalty altogether, the South is likely to remain the region where most executions take place. Between 1976 and 2009, Southern states carried out over 80 percent of all executions in the United States. Texas led the nation (437), and Virginia ranked second (103). By 2009, Texas accounted for 38 percent of all executions nationwide. Texas juries are actually no more likely to impose the death penalty in a murder case than juries in other states, but Texas does follow through to execute a larger share of its death row prisoners.

By 2010, 331 offenders remained on Texas's death row—31 percent of them were white, 38 percent were black, 30 percent were Hispanic, and 1 percent were members of other ethnic groups.

EVALUATING THE DEATH PENALTY

One way of evaluating what might happen if capital punishment were abolished in Texas is to run down the list

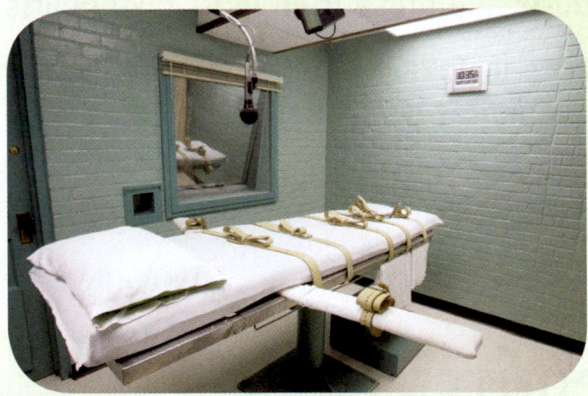

TEXAS WAS THE FIRST STATE to use lethal injection in executions. Today, it is an option for execution in all 35 states with the death penalty. Critics have argued that the lethal drug cocktail can cause excruciating pain in still-conscious subjects who show few signs of discomfort because of drug-induced paralysis. Despite these arguments, the U.S. Supreme Court ruled in 2008 that lethal injection does not violate the Eighth Amendment ban on cruel and unusual punishment.* (AP Photo/ Pat Sullivan)

*Baze et al. v. Rees et al., 553 U.S. 35 (2008).

of reasons why the state punishes criminals. One goal of any punishment is to remove the guilty from society to prevent further crimes. Obviously, the death penalty accomplishes this, but Texas now allows an effective alternative—a life sentence without parole.

A second goal is to deter future crimes through the fear of punishment. Death penalty supporters argue that capital punishment prevents crime because no penalty is more frightening to potential criminals than death itself. Opponents believe that the death penalty is not a strong deterrent because murderers either commit their crimes in the passion of the moment or do not consider the possibility of punishment. Even in Texas, such a small portion (about 2 percent) of murderers are sentenced to death that it is impossible to evaluate these arguments about the possible deterrent effect of capital punishment. Because the murder rates are higher in states with the death penalty than in those without it, many believe that the murder rate would not go up if Texas abolished the death penalty.

A third goal is rehabilitation to allow the convict to return to society as a productive citizen. This goal is irrelevant to the death penalty because the condemned are never meant to return to society. However, death penalty critics argue that even a person serving a life sentence as an alternative to execution may experience redemption.

A fourth goal is justice—settling accounts with those who have violated society's norms. Supporters of the death sentence find it the only appropriate punishment for outrageous crimes such as mass murder and serial killings. Supporters argue that without the sentence, there would be no chance for appropriate social vengeance, and victims' families would be denied closure.

MISCARRIAGES OF JUSTICE

Critics of the Texas death penalty argue that its abolition would reduce the danger of miscarriages of justice. Some death row inmates have later been proved innocent through the use of such methods as DNA testing. By early 2010, 11 wrongfully convicted persons had been released from death row, and substantial evidence of Cameron Todd Willingham's innocence has only developed since he was executed in 2004. Although it is uncertain how many innocent persons Texas may have executed, it is certain that the death penalty has the potential to result in an irreversible error.

FOR CRITICAL ANALYSIS

1. Should other states with capital punishment follow Texas's lead in expediting the death penalty or New Mexico's lead in abolishing it?

2. Texas has one of the highest execution rates in the nation, but it also has one of the highest murder rates. Why do states with the death penalty have a higher murder rate than those without?

AMERICAN SOCIETY HAS increasingly turned to the judiciary to find answers to personal, economic, social, and political problems. Courts are often asked to determine our rights. Important legal questions touch almost every aspect of our lives. For example, what level of privacy should we expect in our cars, offices, and homes? What level of safety and reliability should consumers expect from the merchandise they buy? Should manufacturers be responsible for work hazards and pollution at their factories? How about accountability for incompetence and neglect in hospitals? Should workers feel safe from discrimination at their workplaces? When should a person go to jail, and if so, for how long? What about the death penalty, which is discussed in the *What If . . .* section? These are among the thousands of questions asked and answered daily by courts in the United States.

In this chapter, our focus will be the Texas judicial system and general attributes of American legal procedure and *due process*. What will quickly become clear is the sheer size and complexity of the Texas court system. We describe political influences on the courts and examine how those influences create controversy about how we choose Texas judges.

CIVIL LAW AND CRIMINAL LAW

America is often considered the most litigious (willing to go to court to settle differences) society in the world. We have approximately one-quarter of the world's lawyers.[1] There are more than 1 million attorneys in the United States today.[2] In 1951, one out of every 700 people was a lawyer; today, that figure is now about one out of 260 people.[3] Cases in American courts have included, for example, a legal action by parents blaming McDonald's food for obesity in teens, a $54 million lawsuit by a judge against dry cleaners for losing his suit pants, a case in which a wife sued her husband for not shoveling the snow in front of their home, and a lawsuit in which a woman asked for $12 million because she was "pawed" and "humiliated" when a fur-costumed actor interacted with her during a Broadway performance of the musical *Cats*.[4] You should understand, though, that even if people file outrageous-sounding suits, it does not guarantee that they will win in court. There are few restrictions on what kinds of suits Americans can bring, even if they have little or no chance of success.

[1]G. Alan Tarr, *Judicial Process and Judicial Policymaking*, 3rd ed. (Belmont, CA: Wadsworth Publishing, 2003), p. 107.
[2]American Bar Association, "Lawyer Demographic," accessed February 2, 2008, at www.abanet.org.
[3]U.S. Department of State, "Outline of the United States Legal System: Lawyers, Litigants, and Interest Groups in the Judicial Process," accessed April 2, 2006, at usinfo.state.gov/products/pubs/legalotln/lawyers.htm.
[4]"Civil Wars," *Newsweek*, December 15, 2003, p. 45; "Scenes from a Maul: Suit Targets 'Cats,'" *Dallas Morning News*, January 23, 2003, p. 4A, and February 8, 1997, p. C6.

IN PRACTICE, judges determine our legal rights. Indeed, a large part of our system of laws is judge-made and dates back before the Texas Revolution—or even the American Revolution. This system is the "common law," and it can be traced back to medieval England, when judges began codifying standard answers to legal questions. When a state legislature or the U.S. Congress passes a law, the new statute takes precedence over the common law. Judges must also interpret the meaning of every new statute whenever there is a question that bears on a case. (AP Photo/Irwin Thompson)

LITIGATION IN TEXAS

Texas clearly fits into this general pattern of using the courts often. The Chamber of Commerce ranks Texas as having the 15th worst litigation environment in America.[5] In 2000, it had one attorney for every 337 people.[6] Texas also has more than 2,700 courts and approximately 3,300 justices or judges.[7] These courts dealt with more than 12 million cases in 2009—on average, about one case for every two residents of the state.[8] In addition, in recent years, Texas courts have heard important or controversial cases involving topics such as flag-burning, the death penalty, school desegregation, school finance, sexual orientation, and the freedom-of-association rights of the Ku Klux Klan, as well as a case involving two large oil companies, in which one was found liable for more than $10 billion.

CIVIL LAW VERSUS CRIMINAL LAW

In the American legal system, court actions are generally classified as cases under either the civil law or the criminal law. Civil law concerns private rights and remedies and usually involves private parties or organizations (for example, *Smith v. Jones*), although the government may be involved. A personal-injury suit, a divorce case, a child-custody dispute, a breach of contract case, a challenge to utility rates, and a dispute over water rights are all examples of civil suits.

Criminal law involves violations of laws established by the government. If convicted, the lawbreaker may be punished by a fine or imprisonment, or both. The action is taken by the state against the accused (for example, *State of Texas v. Smith*). Typical examples of grounds for prosecution are arson, rape, murder, armed robbery, speeding, jaywalking, and embezzlement. With exceptions, the characteristics laid out in Figure 26–1 generally distinguish civil and criminal cases.

[5]Institute for Legal Reform, "Lawsuit Climate 2010," at http://instituteforlegalreform.com/lawsuit-climate.html.
[6]American Bar Association, "National Lawyer Population by State," accessed February 2, 2008, from www.abanet.org; figures from the census of 2000, quickfacts.census.gov.
[7] *Annual Statistical Report for the Texas Judiciary, Fiscal Year 2009* (Austin: Office of Court Administration, Texas Judicial Council, 2009), p. 3.
[8]Ibid., pp. 31, 34, 37.

FIGURE 26–1 Civil Law Versus Criminal Law

Civil Law	Criminal Law
1 Deals primarily with individual or property rights. Civil law involves a concept of responsibility but not guilt.	**1** Deals with public concepts of proper behavior and morality as defined in law. The case is initiated by a government prosecutor on behalf of the public.
2 The plaintiff, or petitioner, is often a private party, as is the defendant, or respondent.	**2** Specific charges of wrongdoing are spelled out in a grand jury indictment or a writ of information.
3 A dispute is usually set out in a petition.	**3** On arraignment, the defendant enters a plea of guilty or not guilty.
4 A somewhat more relaxed procedure is used to weigh the evidence than in criminal law; the side with the preponderance of the evidence wins the suit.	**4** Strict rules of procedure are used to evaluate evidence. The standard of proof is guilt beyond a reasonable doubt.
5 The final court remedy is relief from or compensation for the violation of legal rights.	**5** Determination of guilt results in punishment.

One of the most important distinctions between civil and criminal cases involves the issue of **burden of proof**. In civil cases, the standard used is a "preponderance of the evidence." This means that whichever party has more evidence or proof on its side should win the case. In a criminal case, however, the burden of proof falls heavily on the government, or prosecution. The prosecution must prove that the defendant is guilty "beyond a reasonable doubt." The evidence must overwhelmingly (without serious question or doubt) point to the defendant's guilt, or the defendant should be found not guilty.

Burden of Proof
In a court case, a party's duty to convince a judge or jury that the party's version of the facts is true. The standard of proof is higher in a criminal case than in a civil one.

ISSUES IN CIVIL LAW

Some argue that society has become too litigious. These people claim that frivolous lawsuits overcrowd court **dockets**, and excessive damages awards unnecessarily drive up insurance premiums and other business costs. When then–Texas governor George W. Bush urged **tort reform** to limit awards for injury, he was supported by groups representing conservatives and defendants in civil actions, by the Texas Civil Justice League, by insurance companies, and by a wide range of business and medical interest groups.

As a result, the Texas legislature passed bills to restrict lawsuits by prison inmates, reduce frivolous lawsuits, limit liability in civil cases involving multiple defendants and government employees, enforce residency requirements for plaintiffs, and cap **punitive damages awards**. Texans narrowly approved a constitutional amendment to allow the legislature to limit all medical malpractice and other damages, such as those for pain and suffering, except actual economic damages. Are allegedly frivolous lawsuits sometimes more serious than one might gather from media reports?

Dockets
The schedule of court activity.

Tort Reform
In civil law, a tort is a wrong or injury (other than a breach of contract). Tort reform is an effort to limit liability in tort cases.

Punitive Damages Awards
A financial payment that may be awarded to a plaintiff in a civil case to punish the defendant and deter similar conduct in the future.

ISSUES AND ELEMENTS IN CRIMINAL LAW

Crime is a national issue, but despite the popularity of "law and order" as a campaign slogan in national elections, only 5 percent of crimes are prosecuted under federal law. The activities of the criminal justice system are primarily state, not federal, functions.

Congress has made the following crimes, among many others, federal offenses:

1. Those committed on the high seas.
2. Those committed on federal property, territories, and reservations.
3. Those that involve the crossing of state or national boundaries.
4. Those that interfere with interstate commerce.
5. Those committed against the national government or its employees while they are engaged in official duties.

Otherwise, most crimes are violations of state rather than federal law.

THE CRIME

As commonly used, the word *crime* refers to an act that violates whatever an authorized body (usually a state legislature) defines as the law. Many people obey the law simply because it is the law; others may obey out of fear of punishment. Attitudes and values usually determine whether a person will respect or disobey a law. If a law reflects the values of most of society, as the law against murder does, then it is usually obeyed. If, however, a large part of society does not accept the values protected by law, as happened with the national prohibition of alcoholic beverages in the 1920s, then violations become widespread.

Felonies are serious crimes. *Murder* is the illegal, willful killing of another human being. *Robbery* is attempting to take something from a person by force or threat of force. It is inaccurate to say that "a house was robbed"—only people can be robbed. Buildings are *burglarized*—unlawfully entered for the purpose of committing a felony or theft.

Theft (larceny) is simply taking property from the rightful possession of another. Grand larceny—taking something valued at more than $1,500—is a felony. In Texas, regardless of value, livestock rustling is a felony.

In Texas, it is a crime for a commercial fisher to possess a flounder less than 12 inches in length. Minors may not possess alcohol. Most traffic violations are crimes, and the resulting fine is a form of punishment. Such minor crimes are called **misdemeanors**,

Felony
A crime—such as arson, murder, rape, or robbery—that carries the most severe sanctions, usually ranging from one year in prison to death.

Misdemeanor
A lesser crime than a felony, punishable by a fine or imprisonment for up to one year.

TABLE 26–1 Crime and Punishment under the Texas Penal Code

OFFENSE	TERMS*	MAXIMUM FINE
Capital Murder Including murder of a police officer, firefighter, prison guard, or child under age six; murder for hire; murder committed during certain other felonies; and mass murder.	Life sentence or execution	
First-Degree Felony Including aggravated sexual assault, theft of more than $200,000, robbery, noncapital murder, and sale of more than four grams of "hard" drugs such as heroin	5 to 99 years	$10,000
Second-Degree Felony Including theft of more than $100,000 and burglary of a habitation	2 to 20 years	$10,000
Third-Degree Felony Including theft of more than $20,000, drive-by shootings (that do not result in murder), and involuntary manslaughter	2 to 10 years	$10,000
State Jail Felony Including theft of more than $1,500, burglary of a building other than a habitation, sale of less than one gram of narcotics, auto theft, and forgery	180 days to 2 years	$10,000
Class A Misdemeanor Including theft of more than $500, driving while intoxicated, resisting arrest, and stalking	1 year maximum	$4,000
Class B Misdemeanor Including theft of more than $50, possession of small amounts of marijuana, and reckless conduct (such as pointing a gun at someone)	180 days maximum	$2,000
Class C Misdemeanor Including theft of less than $50, smoking on a public elevator, and disorderly conduct (such as indecent exposure)	None	$500

*Punishments may be reduced for murder committed in "sudden passion" or may be enhanced to the next level if gang activity (involving three or more persons) or the use of deadly weapons is involved, if the person who committed the crime has had previous convictions, or if the murder is a hate crime (motivated by bias based on ethnicity, religion, or sexual orientation).

punishable by a sentence in a county jail, a fine, or both. We list the various types of felonies and misdemeanors in Texas in Table 26–1.

THE CRIMINAL

What causes people to commit crimes? What leads them to adopt values different from those reflected in the criminal laws of society? Persons who become criminals vary across the broad spectrum of human personality and may come from any socioeconomic class. Yet the persons who commit most serious crimes are similar. For one reason or another, they are unwilling to accept the *mores* (beliefs about "right" and "wrong") of those who write the laws. Lawbreakers are disproportionately young and poor; many have acute emotional and social problems. They have little stake in the values that lawmakers hold dear.

With the decline of traditional family life and the rise of single-parent households, many young people are inadequately socialized by adults and do not have useful and rewarding roles in society. They lack the sense of responsibility that usually accompanies a job or a family. A young person who has dropped out of school or who is unemployed has difficulty functioning in legitimate society.

DID YOU KNOW?

That in 2008, Texas had the nation's ninth-highest crime rate—4,494 crimes per each 100,000 in population?

DID YOU KNOW?

That Texas's crime rate was twice as high as New Hampshire's and higher than 41 other states' in 2008?

Street Gangs. In some neighborhoods, street gangs offer the only center for social life and capitalistic endeavor. Gangs may be the only source of approval, protection, and a sense of belonging for their members, and they become traditional neighborhood training grounds in crime for successive generations. Lessons not learned on the streets may be picked up from the thousands of demonstrations of crime seen in movies and on television.

Juvenile Crime. Whether as gangs or individuals, persons under age 17 commit a disproportionate share of crime. In Texas, juveniles (under age 17) accounted for 17 percent of all arrests for theft in 2008, 23 percent of all arrests for burglary, and 31 percent of all arrests for arson.[9] Americans under the age of 18 accounted for 23 percent of all arrests nationwide for **FBI index crimes**.[10] Used as the barometer for the crime rate, the FBI index crimes are murder and non-negligent manslaughter, forcible rape, robbery, aggravated assault, burglary, theft, and motor vehicle theft.

> **FBI Index Crimes**
> A set of crimes reported by the FBI and commonly used as a way of measuring the overall crime rate. The index crimes are murder and non-negligent manslaughter, forcible rape, robbery, aggravated assault, burglary, theft, and motor vehicle theft.

Some people may refuse to recognize that the young are major contributors to crime, and others are convinced that young offenders "will grow out of it." In fact, disproportionate numbers of young people commit crimes, and rather than growing out of it, many graduate to more serious crimes. Nevertheless, little is done to rehabilitate juveniles early in their criminal careers. Juvenile courts in Texas provide only limited social services for delinquents, and many of these young offenders have no access to vocational training, employment placement, emergency shelter, foster homes, or halfway houses. Because they are limited in resources, Texas juvenile facilities not only fail to correct, but also serve as breeding grounds for adult crime.

Men and Crime. Far more men than women are arrested for crimes. In 2008, males accounted for 90 percent of Texans arrested for burglary, 87 percent of those arrested for robbery, and 79 percent of those arrested for aggravated assault.[11] Perhaps the traditional male social roles and the accompanying psychological attitudes make it difficult for men to accept certain of society's mores. Aggressive and assertive attitudes, violent sports, protectiveness, and working for pay are often regarded as essentials of a boy's training for manhood. Apparently, many young men fail to learn the distinction between the kind of assertiveness that society approves of and the kind it condemns.

Crime and Minority Groups. Minority group members are arrested disproportionately for crimes. In 2008, 44 percent of Texans arrested for robbery, 33 percent of those arrested for murder, and 25 percent of those arrested for rape were African American. Hispanics accounted for 39 percent of the arrests for murder, 40 percent for rape, and 36 percent for robbery.[12] Prejudice among members of law enforcement agencies may account for some minority arrests, but the actual crime rate is clearly higher among minority group members.

ELLIS UNIT IN HUNTSVILLE, Texas, holds the state's death row inmates. Since 1976, the state of Texas has led the nation in state-sanctioned executions. What is at least one reason why this is so? (Greg Smith/Corbis)

[9] *Texas Crime Report for 2008* (Austin: Texas Department of Public Safety, 2009), pp. 30–36.
[10] Calculated based on data from Federal Bureau of Investigation, *Uniform Crime Reports: Crime in the United States 2008—Persons Arrested* (Washington, DC: U.S. Government Printing Office, 2009), Table 38.
[11] *Texas Crime Report for 2008*, pp. 26–30.
[12] Ibid., pp. 18–26.

Poverty. Ethnic minorities are disproportionately poor, but poverty is by no means unique to them. Perhaps more important, poverty is often accompanied by low educational attainment and psychological problems. The poor, regardless of racial or ethnic background, are more likely to commit violent crimes than are the middle and upper classes.

Urbanization. Crime is more likely in large metropolitan areas. More than three-fourths of all Texans live in metropolitan areas of more than 50,000 people. The character of urban life may contribute to crime. Cities are more anonymous than rural areas and small towns, and social sanctions seem less effective in this setting. Not only is there greater freedom in the city to act criminally, but gangs and other organizations may openly encourage criminal activity. A majority of inmates in Texas prisons are from the San Antonio, Dallas, and Houston areas.

Illegal Drugs. Drug addiction contributes to crime in a variety of ways. In 2008, 144,953 Texans were arrested for narcotics violations,[13] and it is impossible to estimate what percentage of robberies, burglaries, and thefts are committed to finance illegal habits. Narcotics and alcohol also reduce inhibitions, and at least one-third of crimes are committed under their influence.

White-Collar Crime. Most violent crimes are committed by those who in one way or another are on the fringes of society. In many instances, these perpetrators simply live in an environment that promotes despair, low self-esteem, and weak emotional ties to the "legitimate" society. Some criminals consciously identify themselves as victims and rationalize their conduct based on their supposed victim status.

In contrast, few think of successful businesspersons or professionals as being criminals, yet these people may violate federal income tax laws, keep fraudulent business accounts, or pollute the environment. Because they seldom rob, rape, murder, or commit other violent acts, however, these white-collar criminals are often punished less severely. Crimes such as bribery, tax fraud, business fraud, price fixing, and embezzlement are committed largely by white-collar criminals, who have often benefited from the very best that society has to offer.

THE VICTIM

The American people have paid the costs of white-collar crime for centuries, but the recent near collapse of the economy has focused the public's attention, as never before, on white-collar crime. Fraud committed by Bernie Madoff, R. Allen Sanford, and Enron and the resulting loss in confidence in the economy and stock values likely cost victims many times more than all robberies, burglaries, and thefts. Still, the outrage against crime is directed largely toward violent crimes such as murder, rape, and robbery, as well as certain property crimes such as burglary, larceny, and auto theft. In general, the public is more concerned about physical security than financial loss. Figure 26–2 shows that rates of both violent crime and property crime continue their historic decline in Texas. However, Figure 26–3 shows that the frequency of serious crime remains a continuing cause for concern.

Such crimes as prostitution, gambling, and illegal drug possession are sometimes called **victimless crimes**, because they do not have an obvious victim; the primary

DID YOU KNOW?

That Tennessee makes it illegal for anyone except a zoo to import skunks; West Virginia makes it illegal to taunt someone fighting a duel; Texas makes it illegal to libel vegetables; Rhode Island requires that a driver must make a loud noise when passing on the left; North Carolina limits bingo games to five hours; New Jersey and Texas make it illegal to wear a bulletproof vest while committing murder; in Wisconsin, it is a crime for restaurants to serve margarine unless requested by the customer; and in Texas, it is a crime to disturb hunters?

Victimless Crime
A crime in which there does not appear to be a victim—a consensual crime. (Alternatively, the person breaking the law may be considered the primary victim.) Examples often cited include prostitution, gambling, and illegal drug possession.

---

[13] *Annual Statistical Report for the Texas Judiciary, Fiscal Year 2009*, p. 37.

FIGURE 26–2 Texas Crime Rates since 1991

This figure shows that the violent crime rate and total index crime rate per 100,000 population in Texas have declined over most of the past two decades. Why do news media continue to focus on a problem that is becoming less severe?

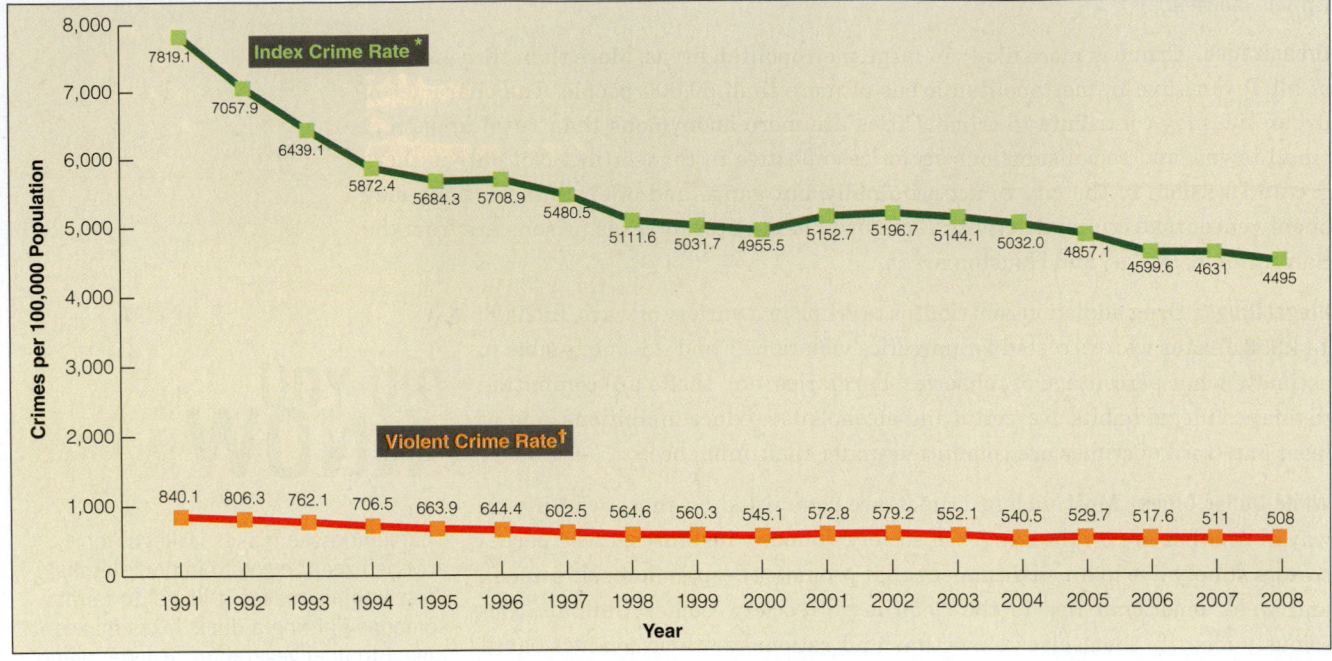

*Total of violent and property crimes (burglary, theft, and motor vehicle theft) per 100,000 population.
†Murder, rape, robbery, and aggravated assault.
Source: Texas Crime Report for 2008 (Austin: Texas Department of Public Safety, 2009), p. 10.

victims may be the criminals themselves. The families of these criminals and society at large also pay a price for these activities, however, and victimless crimes are often linked to more serious crimes.

Even though more-affluent areas of the state and nation sometimes are victimized by crime, police reports continue to demonstrate that the highest rates of victimization are in the poor areas of our cities. Crime is largely a neighborhood affair and is often committed against friends and families of the criminal. Acquaintance rape, or date rape, has been well publicized. Moreover, at least 46 percent of Texas killers are acquainted with their victims, and 15 percent of all murders occur within the family. Minorities and young people suffer most from crime—in a typical recent year, 39 percent of Texas murder victims were Hispanics, and 35 percent were African Americans.[14]

Victims have the right to be informed of investigations and court proceedings against the accused and to have their victim-impact statements taken into account during sentencing and **parole** actions. The Crime Victims' Compensation Fund is administered by the attorney general and financed by small fees collected from criminals when they are convicted. These meager funds are available to victims who have suffered extreme personal hardship resulting from physical injury during a crime. Most victims are not eligible, however, nor is there compensation for the billion dollars' worth of property stolen each year.

Parole
Early release from prison under official supervision.

[14]Ibid., p. 21.

FIGURE 26–3   The Texas Time Clock: Crime Observations, 2008

One murder every 6 hours and 23 minutes; one theft every 48 seconds; other data remains the same.

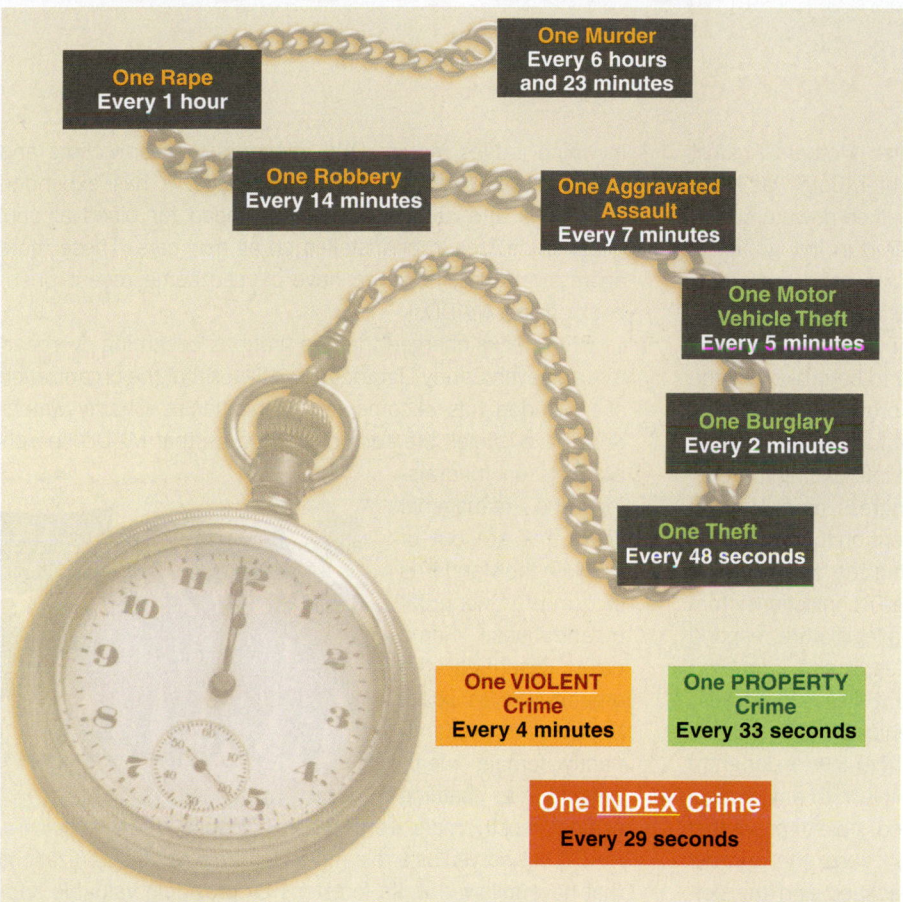

Source: Texas Crime Report 2008 (Austin: Texas Department of Public Safety, 2009), p. 13.

DUE PROCESS OF LAW

The courts enforce the most general concepts of justice and the broadest norms of society against specific individuals. The courts must blend two conflicting goals of society:

1. To protect society according to the state's legal concepts of right and wrong.
2. To protect the rights of the individual charged with wrongdoing.

As a result of these conflicting goals, elaborate traditions of court process and procedure have developed over the centuries, dating back to when the American states were still colonies of Britain. Many of these traditional procedures derive from the English experience, whereas others were developed more recently in the American states. Some court procedures have been written into state and national constitutions and statutes; others are included in written and unwritten traditional codes of court process. Such procedures are designed to promote justice and protect the individual from the government, and together they constitute what is called **due process**.

Unfortunately, the guaranteed rights of the accused are very nearly meaningless unless courts, prosecutors, and law enforcement agents protect them. Sometimes,

That Texas's violent crime rate has declined 39 percent since 1991?

Due Process
Established rules and principles for the administration of justice designed to safeguard the rights of the individual. The right to due process of law is provided by the U.S. Constitution and state constitutions.

POLITICS WITH A purpose

Advocating for Victims' Rights

Candice (Candy) Lightner helped organize Mothers Against Drunk Driving after her 13-year-old daughter, Cari, was killed by a drunken hit-and-run driver as she walked down a suburban street in California. Now headquartered in Irving, Texas, MADD has become one of the most successful grassroots victims' advocacy groups in history.[a] Capitalizing on the dedicated motivation of members and public sympathy for drunk-driving victims and their families, it came to be ranked as the most credible and popular charity or nonprofit in the nation.[b]

MADD, with the help of much of the auto insurance industry, has been extraordinarily successful in influencing the U.S. Congress and the Texas legislature. Congress made federal highway funding for states partly dependent on increasing the minimum drinking age to 21 and reducing the blood alcohol content for DWI (driving while intoxicated) convictions from 0.1 to .08 percent. Not only did the Texas legislature respond by complying with these federal mandates, it also increased penalties for DWI convictions and made it illegal to possess an open alcohol container in a moving vehicle. The legislature enacted a DUI (driving under the influence) law making it a crime for a minor to operate a motor vehicle with any alcohol in the blood whatsoever. Although it is impossible to prove that these changes in the laws were the only cause, the number of motor vehicle fatalities has steadily declined and the percentage of fatalities involving drunk drivers has also decreased dramatically since these laws were passed.[c]

Today, MADD continues to advocate for strict alcohol enforcement, sobriety checkpoints, and victim impact panels in which judges require DWI offenders to hear victims and their relatives describe their experiences. It has expanded its agenda and has even begun to plead for blood alcohol interlock devices to be installed on all new cars. These more aggressive goals, however, have caused some recent pushback against MADD.

Critics have charged that the group is becoming overbearing, and even Candy Lightner now alleges that the organization she founded has become neo-prohibitionist. Charity watchdogs have leveled the additional criticism that MADD spends amounts on fundraising and managerial costs that are out of line with the standards of most nonprofit organizations.[d] Some have described the organization as sexist because its predominantly female membership is battling

against mostly male perpetrators. Despite these criticisms, MADD has served as a role model for the several organizations that have followed in its footsteps by providing valuable support for crime victims in Texas today.[e]

[a]Funding Universe at http://www.fundinguniverse.com/company-histories/Mothers-Against-Drunk-Driving-MADD-Company-History.html.
[b]"The Charities Americans Like Most and Least," *The Chronicle of Philanthropy*, December 13, 1996, at http://philanthropy.com.
[c]National Highway Transportation Safety Administration data reported at http://www.alcoholalert.com/drunk-driving-statistics-texas.html.

[d]Jayne O'Donnell, "MADD Enters 25th Year with Change on Its Mind," *USA Today*, September 29, 2005, at http://www.usatoday.com/money/2005-09-28-madd-change-usat_x.htm; see also The Charity Navigator at http://www.charitynavigator.org/index.cfm?bay=search.summary&orgid=4129.
[e]Murder Victims Families for Reconciliation Texas provides a list of public resources for victims of all crimes at http://mvfr-texas.tripod.com/resources/resources.htm; access MADD victim services at http://www.madd.org/Victim-Services.aspx.

due process becomes more a philosophy of how justice should be carried out than a description of what really happens.

PRETRIAL COURT ACTIVITIES

Following arrest, the suspect is jailed while reports are completed and the district attorney's office decides whether to file charges and what bail to recommend. As soon as is practical, the accused is presented before a justice of the peace or other magistrate for arraignment, at which time the court performs the following actions:

1. It explains the charges against the accused.
2. It reminds the suspect of the rights to remain silent, to be represented by counsel, and to request a written acknowledgment that the *Miranda* warning (see Chapter 4) was given and understood.
3. It sets bail.
4. It informs the accused of the right to an **examining trial**.

The Right to Know the Nature of the Accusation. The suspect is usually told the charges (1) on arrest, (2) in the arraignment, and (3) again in subsequent proceedings. One of the most fundamental requirements of due process is telling the prisoners why they are being held. Because the states have governments of "laws and not men," no one should be held in custody on a whim, but only for legal cause. Although a person need not necessarily be guilty of a crime to be held, there must be "probable cause" for the confinement. If it is determined that a person is being held unlawfully, counsel may secure release by a writ of *habeas corpus* (a court order requiring that the prisoner be presented in person and legal cause shown for imprisonment, discussed in Chapter 4).

The Right to Legal Counsel. The right to counsel is vital to the accused. Aside from clearly understanding the constitutional rights of an accused person, an attorney will be familiar with the baffling intricacies of the law. So important is the assistance of counsel that many suspects will contact an attorney before they appear in front of a magistrate. Yet this right to counsel has never been absolute.

Guaranteed in both the U.S. and Texas constitutions, the right to counsel was traditionally interpreted to mean that a person had a right to counsel if he or she could afford it. In 1932, the United States Supreme Court ruled that the Sixth Amendment requires state courts to appoint counsel for the poor, but only in capital cases.[15] Later, the Court extended the indigent's right to counsel to other felony cases and serious misdemeanor cases in which imprisonment might be involved, but the right does not extend to petty offenses such as traffic violations.[16]

The right to court-appointed counsel does not necessarily guarantee equal justice for the poor. An indigent defendant usually is not assigned an attorney until a district judge can respond to the defendant's written request. Some counties use an assigned counsel system in which judges appoint indigents' attorneys on a case-by-case basis. Some lawyers who specialize in civil matters may be appointed to defend indigents in criminal cases. Indigents therefore may not receive the kind of expert defense they would have if they could choose among attorneys who specialize in criminal cases. The attorney's fee, paid by the county, is considerably less than most attorneys receive from paying clients. Although some lawyers may be diligent in indigent cases, other lawyers will act on the assumption that time spent defending poor people does not significantly advance either their practices or their incomes.

Some Texas counties have reformed their system for providing legal representation by adopting public defender systems. These counties employ full-time salaried professional attorneys who specialize in criminal matters. Such reforms have not solved all of the problems of unequal representation for the poor—public defenders often have heavy workloads and inadequate staffing.

Examining Trial
A relatively uncommon procedure that may be requested by felony defendants in Texas. In an examining trial, a justice of the peace reviews the facts and decides whether a defendant should have to face trial in criminal court.

DID YOU KNOW?

That in 1999, the federal Fifth Circuit Court of Appeals reversed the death penalty conviction of Calvin Burdine because his attorney had slept during much of the trial?

---

[15] *Powell v. Alabama,* 287 U.S. 45 (1932).
[16] *Gideon v. Wainwright,* 372 U.S. 335 (1963); and *Argersinger v. Hamlin,* 407 U.S. 25 (1972).

The Right to Bail. Bail is the security required for the release of a suspect awaiting trial. When the suspect appears at trial, the bail is refunded. Some persons released on bail fail to appear in court, and their security is forfeited. Others commit still more crimes while on bail. The legal system presumes, however, that an individual is innocent unless convicted, and bail supports this assumption by permitting the accused to resume his or her professional and social life while preparing a defense.

The Texas Constitution guarantees the right to bail immediately after arrest, except when proof is "evident" in capital cases or when the defendant is being charged with a third felony after two prior felony convictions. The state constitution allows bail to be denied if the defendant is charged with committing a felony while released on bail or under indictment for another felony.

In practice, the right to bail exists only for those who can afford it. Private licensed bonding companies may be willing to post bond for a fee (usually 10 to 50 percent of the bail as set by the court), which, unlike bail, is not refunded. Many cannot afford even this fee, and unless these prisoners are released on **personal recognizance** (their personal promise to appear), they will await trial in jail. In our criminal justice system, bail procedures may create more problems for the poor than any other single practice.

Personal Recognizance
A defendant's personal promise to appear in court.

The Right to an Examining Trial. Although few defendants request one, in Texas the accused has the right to an examining trial in felony cases, as mentioned earlier. In an examining trial, a justice of the peace reviews the facts and decides whether the case should be recommended for criminal proceedings. If the facts warrant, the charges may be dismissed or bail adjusted.

FORMAL CHARGES

Although an *indictment*, or formal charge, sometimes precedes arrest, a felony case is usually bound over to a **grand jury** for indictment following arraignment. A grand jury should not be confused with a petit, or trial, jury. Grand juries do not determine a person's guilt or innocence, as trial juries do. Often, the accused does not even appear before the grand jury. The grand jury primarily weighs the evidence in the hands of the prosecutor to determine whether the case will be taken to trial. If the grand jury determines that the evidence could be sufficient to convict, it issues an indictment, which constitutes a formal charge that enables the case to go to trial.

Grand Jury
A jury that sits in pretrial proceedings to determine if sufficient evidence exists to try an individual and, therefore, approve an indictment.

A determination that the evidence is sufficient to convict is necessary, because if the prosecutor does not have enough evidence to convict, there is no point in bringing the case to trial. Trying a case on flimsy evidence not only costs the taxpayers financially, but it also costs the accused in terms of needless expense, lost time, and damaged reputation. The right to a grand jury indictment is guaranteed in both the Texas and the federal courts to protect innocent citizens against harassment on unjustified charges.

In practice, the grand jury is often made up of untrained citizens, who frequently cannot critically evaluate a case. A grand jury usually acts as a rubber stamp for the prosecutor. Some states have abolished the grand jury in favor of **writs of information**, in which a judge evaluates the evidence to determine if it is sufficient to go to trial. Texas guarantees the right to a grand jury indictment in all felony cases but uses the writ of information to charge people with misdemeanors.

Writ of Information
In criminal law, a formal accusation filed by a prosecutor against a party charged with a crime. It is an alternative to an indictment and does not involve a grand jury.

PRETRIAL HEARINGS

After the indictment, the defendant has the right to another hearing, sometimes called the second arraignment. A district judge (rather than a justice of the peace) presides as the formal indictment is read and the defendant enters a plea. If the plea is guilty, a later hearing is scheduled to set punishment. Most often, the defendant pleads not guilty at this point, and the case is placed on the docket (schedule of court activity) for subsequent trial. A variety of motions may be presented, including a motion for delay or for the suppression of certain evidence.

The Insanity Defense. Another subject of pretrial hearings concerns possible insanity. A person cannot be held morally and criminally responsible for a crime if, at the time of the offense, mental disorder made it impossible for him or her to recognize that it was wrong. There is considerable controversy regarding the effects of mental disorder, so professional testimony may be necessary to establish legal insanity, and psychiatric opinion is frequently divided. The courts rarely find a defendant not guilty by reason of insanity.

Change of Venue. A change in the site of a trial (a **change of venue**) may be necessary when the news media have so publicized a case that an unbiased jury cannot be selected or when inflamed public opinion may prevent a fair trial. A real tension exists between the rights of the free press and the rights of the accused.

Change of Venue
A change in the site of a trial.

PLEA BARGAINING

Ideally, the trial is the final step in society's elaborate guarantees of due process. Yet for most of those who are accused of a crime, the final day in court never comes. In fact, the system is designed to discourage and even punish those who choose to exercise the right to a trial. Most cases end in a secret bargaining session with the prosecutor (**plea bargaining**).

Faced with overcrowded dockets and limited staffs, prosecuting attorneys usually meet with the accused and offer a deal in exchange for a plea of guilty, which eliminates the necessity of a trial. The usual deal is to offer to drop some of the charges, to recommend probation or a lighter sentence, or to charge the accused with a lesser

Plea Bargaining
Negotiations that take place between the prosecution and the defense in a criminal case in which the defendant normally is offered a lighter sentence or other benefits in return for a guilty plea.

ANDREA YATES drowned her five children in a bathtub after discontinuing antipsychotic drugs for 13 days. A second trial resulted in a verdict of not guilty by reason of insanity—an exceedingly rare outcome in Texas. Like most insane convicts, Yates will spend most, if not all, of her life in a mental institution operated by the Texas prison system. (Steve Ueckert/AP Photo/Pool)

Deferred Adjudication
A procedure that allows a judge to postpone final sentencing in a criminal case; charges are dismissed if the defendant completes a satisfactory probationary period.

crime. The prosecutor may agree to delay prosecution (**deferred adjudication**) and later drop charges if the defendant agrees to meet certain probation-like conditions. Such agreements cut costs and court time, and may be useful to law enforcement when defendants are given a lighter sentence in exchange for acting as witnesses and testifying against fellow criminals.

The guilty obviously benefit from plea bargaining because they are not punished for the full measure of their crimes. Defense attorneys frequently encourage their clients to accept the bargain to save them the effort of a courtroom trial, and some become as much implicit agents for the prosecution as advocates for the defense. The innocent and those who are unwilling to trade their rights for a secret backroom bargain take the chance of being punished more severely for demanding trial.

THE TRIAL

Unless the defense waives the right to a trial by jury, the first major step in the trial is the selection of a jury. The right to a jury trial is often regarded as one of the most valuable rights available in the U.S. criminal justice system. In fact, every state provides for trial by jury in all but the most minor cases, and Texas goes even further, providing for the right to trial by jury in every criminal case.[17]

Nevertheless, the right to trial by jury in a criminal case is one of the most frequently waived rights, especially in cases in which the defendant is an object of community prejudice (a member of an unpopular political group or ethnic minority) or in which the alleged crime is particularly outrageous. If the right to a jury trial is waived, the presiding judge determines the verdict. Regardless of whether a person chooses to exercise the right to trial by jury, this right remains a valuable alternative to decisions by possibly arbitrary judges.

Selecting the Jurors. During an initial questioning, prospective jurors may be asked about possible biases, their prior knowledge of the case, or any opinions they may have formed about the case. Either the prosecution or the defense may challenge a prospective juror for reason of prejudice, and the presiding judge will evaluate that challenge.

In addition to asking the judge to dismiss a prospective juror on the ground that he or she is prejudiced, both the prosecution and the defense may dismiss several jurors by *peremptory challenges* (challenges without cause). Experienced attorneys and prosecutors use peremptory challenges to eliminate jurors who may be hostile to their side of the case. The defense and the prosecution may consider the occupations, social status, and attitudes of possible jurors. In principle, race and gender are not legitimate grounds for peremptory challenges, but bias is hard to prove. Some lawyers have been known to employ psychologists to assist in the selection process, and lucrative consulting businesses have developed to assist attorneys in jury selection.

Adversary System
A legal system in which parties to a legal action are opponents and are responsible for bringing the facts and law related to their case before the court.

The Adversary System. The United States has an **adversary system**, in which two parties to the case (the prosecution and the defense in criminal cases) arm themselves with whatever evidence they can muster and battle in court, under the rules of law, to final judgment. An adversary system cannot operate fairly unless both the defense and the prosecution have an equal opportunity to influence the decision of the court. Hence, procedural guarantees are designed to ensure that both sides have equal access to (1) knowledge of the law and (2) the evidence. So that equal knowledge of the law is guaranteed, the legal knowledge of the prosecution is balanced by the right of the defendant to have legal counsel. Because the government (in the person of the prosecutor)

[17]The United States Supreme Court held, in the case of *Duncan v. Louisiana*, 391 U.S. 145, 149 (1968), that trial by jury is an essential part of due process when state criminal proceedings involve more than petty offenses.

has the power to seize evidence and to force witnesses to testify under oath, the defense must be given that same power (called *compulsory process*).

Presenting Evidence. In the adversary system, each side can challenge the material evidence and cross-examine the witnesses presented by the opposition. Only evidence that is presented can be evaluated in court. The fact that both parties to a case have opposite biases means that each has an interest in concealing evidence that could benefit the opposition.

As it is the legal responsibility of the prosecutor to prove guilt beyond reasonable doubt (the burden of proof lies with the state), the counsel for the defense has no responsibility to present evidence of the defendant's guilt, nor can the defendant be forced to take the stand to testify. Because the prosecutor has the responsibility to convict the guilty rather than the innocent, however, it is a violation of due process for the government to withhold evidence that could benefit the accused—but it happens. There is no way of knowing how many unjust verdicts have been handed down because not all of the evidence was presented.

In jury trials, once the evidence has been presented, the presiding judge reads the charge to the jury; this charge constitutes the judge's instructions and the law that applies in the case. He or she will instruct the jurors to ignore such things as hearsay testimony and other illegal evidence to which they may have been exposed during the course of the trial. (Still, it is difficult for jurors to erase from their minds the impact of illegal testimony.) The judge is supposedly neutral and cannot comment on the weight of the evidence that has been presented.

Concluding the Trial. Following the judge's charge to the jury, the prosecution and defense are allowed to summarize the case. During their summary remarks, the prosecutor will argue that the evidence points toward guilt, and the defense will conclude that the evidence is insufficient to prove guilt beyond a reasonable doubt.

The jury then retires to decide between verdicts of guilty and not guilty. Texas law requires that all the jurors agree on the verdict in criminal cases. If the jury cannot agree, it is said to be a *hung jury*, and the judge will declare a **mistrial**, but the defendant may be tried again.

Sentencing. Regardless of whether the judge or the jury determines guilt, the judge usually prescribes a sentence, unless the defendant demands that the jury do so. After considering the character of the defendant, any past criminal record, and the circumstances surrounding the crime, the judge may assess a penalty between the minimum and maximum provided by law.

A first offender may be given **probation**, which allows her or him to serve the sentence in free society according to specific terms and restrictions and under the supervision of a probation officer. Similarly, deferred adjudication allows judges to postpone final sentencing in criminal cases; and after a satisfactory probationary period, the charges are dismissed. Judges have a great deal of latitude in assessing penalties, so the fate of a defendant will depend in large part on the attitudes of the presiding judge. Different judges sometimes assess vastly different penalties for similar crimes committed under similar circumstances.

After sentencing, the prisoner may be sent to one of the state's penal institutions. Time served in jail before and during trial is usually deducted from the sentence of the guilty. (For the innocent, however, the time served awaiting trial is a casualty of an imperfect system of justice—underlining the necessity for care in accusing and trying our citizens.)

That it costs more (about $1.2 million) merely to try a death penalty case than it does to imprison a murderer for 40 years (about $700,000)?

That Texas imprisons a larger percentage of its population than China, Russia, Cuba, or Iran?

Mistrial
A trial judged to be invalid because of fundamental error. When a mistrial is declared, the trial may start again, beginning with the selection of a new jury.

Probation
A sentencing alternative to imprisonment in which the court releases convicted defendants under supervision as long as certain conditions are observed.

POSTTRIAL PROCEEDINGS

Acquitted
Found not guilty.

To protect the accused from double jeopardy, a person who is **acquitted** (found not guilty) cannot be tried again for the same offense. Protection from double jeopardy is much more limited than many citizens realize. In the event of a mistrial or an error in procedure, the trial may end in neither a conviction nor an acquittal. The defendant may then be tried for the same offense on the theory that he or she was never put in jeopardy by the first trial.

Multiple Charges. A person found not guilty of one crime may be tried for a related offense. For example, a person accused of driving 75 miles per hour through a school zone, going the wrong way on a one-way street, striking down a child in the crosswalk, and then leaving the scene of the accident may have committed several crimes. Being acquitted for speeding does not free the defendant of possible charges for each of the other offenses—they were separate crimes.

Likewise, such acts as bank robbery and kidnapping may violate both federal and state law, and the accused may be tried by both jurisdictions. Finally, even if a person is found not guilty of a crime, a victim of that crime can sue the defendant under civil law. Because the standards of proof under civil law are lower than under criminal law, an acquitted individual may still be forced to pay monetary damages to the alleged victim or the alleged victim's heirs.

Appeals. A defendant may appeal a guilty verdict. Although the state cannot appeal a not-guilty verdict, because doing so would constitute double jeopardy, prosecutors may appeal the reversal of a guilty verdict by a higher court. Appellate procedure is designed to review the law as applied by lower courts. In most cases, the appellate court will not assess the evidence. Its major concern is procedure. If serious procedural errors are found, the appellate court may return the case to a lower court for retrial. Such a retrial does not constitute double jeopardy.

Having exhausted the rights of appeal in the Texas courts, a very few defendants appeal their cases to the federal courts, which have jurisdiction in federal law. A ground for appeal to federal courts is the assertion that the state courts have violated the U.S. Constitution or other federal laws.

DID YOU KNOW?

That only three states had a higher incarceration rate (number of prison inmates per 100,000 population) than Texas in 2009?

TEXAS COURT ORGANIZATION

Figure 26–4 outlines the organizational structure of the Texas court system. This figure shows the various types and levels of courts in the system. It should be noted that some courts within this rather large and complicated system have overlapping jurisdiction.

MUNICIPAL COURTS

Although *municipal courts* are authorized by state statute, they are set up by incorporated cities and towns. Their status and organization are normally recognized in the city charter or municipal ordinances.

Legally, the municipal courts have exclusive jurisdiction to try violations of city ordinances. They also handle minor violations of state law—class C misdemeanors, for which the punishment is a fine of $500 or less and does not include a jail sentence. (Justice of the peace courts have overlapping jurisdiction to handle such minor violations.) Approximately 82 percent of the cases disposed in municipal courts involve traffic violations.[18]

---

[18] *Annual Report for the Texas Judiciary, 2009*, p. 53; Texas Judiciary Online, accessed February 1, 2010, at www.courts.state.tx.us/pubs/AR2009/AR09.pdf.

FIGURE 26–4 Court Structure of Texas

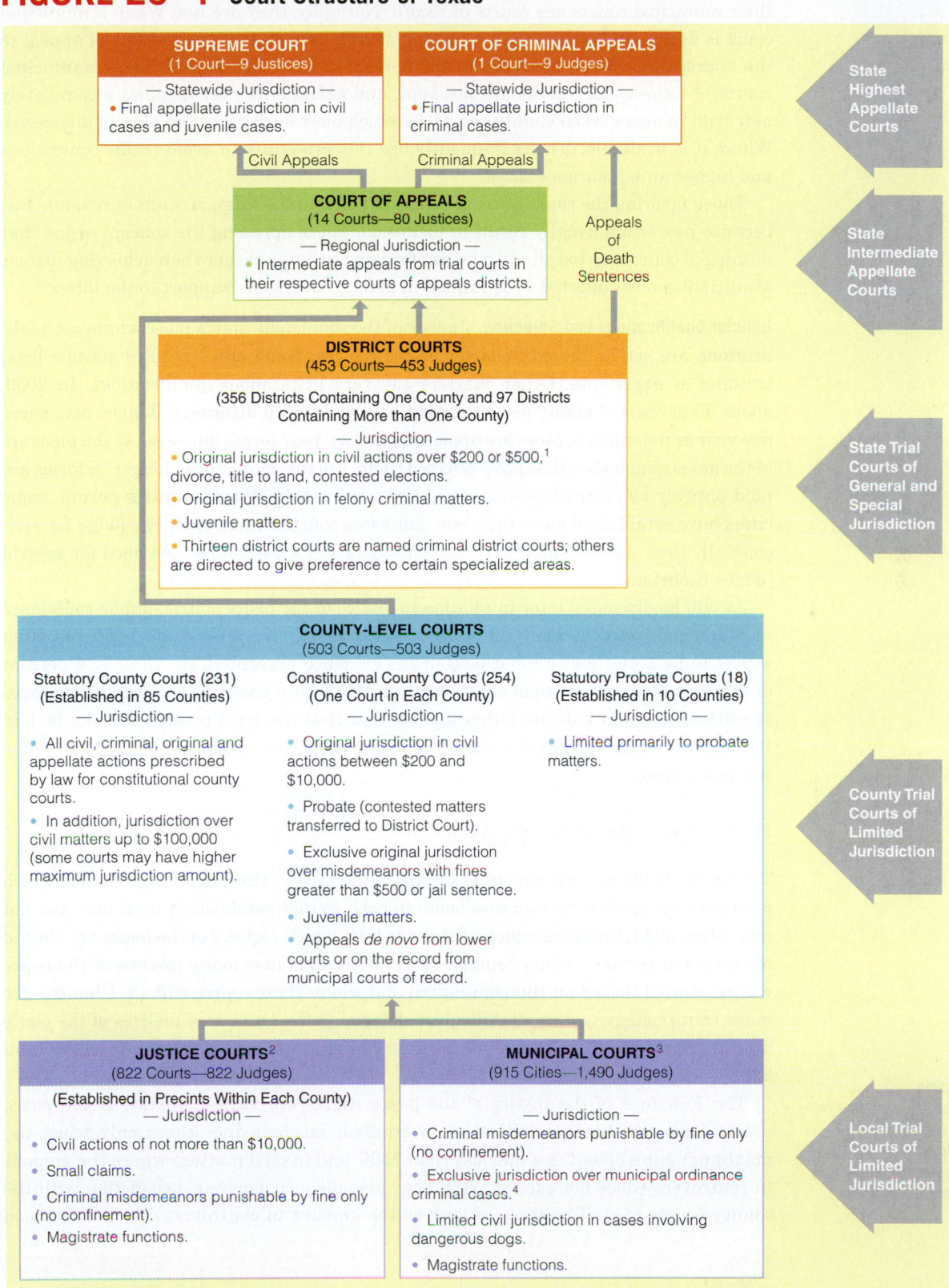

SUPREME COURT
(1 Court—9 Justices)

— Statewide Jurisdiction —
• Final appellate jurisdiction in civil cases and juvenile cases.

COURT OF CRIMINAL APPEALS
(1 Court—9 Judges)

— Statewide Jurisdiction —
• Final appellate jurisdiction in criminal cases.

State Highest Appellate Courts

Civil Appeals   Criminal Appeals

COURT OF APPEALS
(14 Courts—80 Justices)

— Regional Jurisdiction —
• Intermediate appeals from trial courts in their respective courts of appeals districts.

Appeals of Death Sentences

State Intermediate Appellate Courts

DISTRICT COURTS
(453 Courts—453 Judges)

(356 Districts Containing One County and 97 Districts Containing More than One County)
— Jurisdiction —
• Original jurisdiction in civil actions over $200 or $500,[1] divorce, title to land, contested elections.
• Original jurisdiction in felony criminal matters.
• Juvenile matters.
• Thirteen district courts are named criminal district courts; others are directed to give preference to certain specialized areas.

State Trial Courts of General and Special Jurisdiction

COUNTY-LEVEL COURTS
(503 Courts—503 Judges)

Statutory County Courts (231)
(Established in 85 Counties)
— Jurisdiction —

• All civil, criminal, original and appellate actions prescribed by law for constitutional county courts.
• In addition, jurisdiction over civil matters up to $100,000 (some courts may have higher maximum jurisdiction amount).

Constitutional County Courts (254)
(One Court in Each County)
— Jurisdiction —

• Original jurisdiction in civil actions between $200 and $10,000.
• Probate (contested matters transferred to District Court).
• Exclusive original jurisdiction over misdemeanors with fines greater than $500 or jail sentence.
• Juvenile matters.
• Appeals *de novo* from lower courts or on the record from municipal courts of record.

Statutory Probate Courts (18)
(Established in 10 Counties)
— Jurisdiction —

• Limited primarily to probate matters.

County Trial Courts of Limited Jurisdiction

JUSTICE COURTS[2]
(822 Courts—822 Judges)

(Established in Precints Within Each County)
— Jurisdiction —

• Civil actions of not more than $10,000.
• Small claims.
• Criminal misdemeanors punishable by fine only (no confinement).
• Magistrate functions.

MUNICIPAL COURTS[3]
(915 Cities—1,490 Judges)

— Jurisdiction —

• Criminal misdemeanors punishable by fine only (no confinement).
• Exclusive jurisdiction over municipal ordinance criminal cases.[4]
• Limited civil jurisdiction in cases involving dangerous dogs.
• Magistrate functions.

Local Trial Courts of Limited Jurisdiction

1. The dollar amount is currently unclear.
2. All justice courts and most municipal courts are not courts of record. Appeals from these courts are by trial *de novo* in the county-level courts, and in some instances in the district courts.
3. Some municipal courts are courts of record—appeals from those courts are taken on the record to the county-level courts.
4. An offense that arises under a municipal ordinance is punishable by a fine not to exceed: (1) $2,000 for ordinances that govern fire safety, zoning, and public health or (2) $500 for all others.

Courts of Record? The legislature has authorized city governments to determine whether their municipal courts are courts of record. Normally, they are not. When a municipal court is designated as a court of record, however, its records are the basis of appeal to the appropriate county court. (Only 0.2 percent of cases are appealed from municipal courts.)[19] Otherwise, records are not kept, and defendants may demand a completely new trial in overworked county courts, in which most such cases are simply dismissed. Where it is available, drivers frequently use this procedure to avoid traffic convictions and higher auto insurance rates.

Those favoring the court-of-record concept point to the large amount of revenue lost because new trials usually result in dismissal. Those opposing the concept argue that municipal courts are too often a means of raising revenue rather than achieving justice. Municipal courts collected $734 million in 2009, giving some support to the latter.[20]

Judicial Qualifications and Selection. Judges of the municipal courts meet whatever qualifications are set by the city charter or ordinances. Some cities require specific legal training or experience. Other charters say very little about qualifications. In 2009, about 50 percent of municipal court judges were licensed attorneys. Judges may serve one year or indefinitely. Most are appointed for two-year terms but serve at the pleasure of the governing bodies that have selected them. Furthermore, these judges' salaries are paid entirely by their respective cities and vary widely. Where statutes permit, some cities have established more than one municipal court or more than one judge for each court. In view of the volume of cases pending before these courts, the need for several judges is obvious.

As will be discussed later in relation to justice of the peace courts, public confidence in municipal courts is low. Out-of-town, out-of-county, or out-of-state residents often expect to be found guilty regardless of the evidence presented. In 2009, 36.4 percent of all cases filed in municipal courts were settled before trial.[21] Such large percentages of settlement could indicate either guilt or fear that the legal process will not be fair. It could also indicate people's desire to avoid the inconvenience or expense of going through a trial.

JUSTICES OF THE PEACE

The justice of the peace courts in Texas are authorized by the Texas Constitution, which requires that the county commissioners in each county establish at least one, and not more than eight, justice precincts (the areas from which justices of the peace are elected for four-year terms). County commissioners determine how many justices of the peace will be elected (based on the population) and where their courts will sit. Changes are made continuously, making it difficult to determine the number of justices of the peace at any given time. The Texas Judicial Council determined that there were more than 820 justices of the peace during 2009.[22]

The functions of the justice of the peace courts are varied. Justice of the peace courts have **original jurisdiction** in criminal misdemeanor cases only when the maximum punishment is a fine less than $500, and in civil matters where the amount in controversy does not exceed $200. They also have concurrent jurisdiction with the county courts in civil matters as long as the amount in controversy does not exceed

Original Jurisdiction
The authority of a court to consider a case in the first instance; the power to try a case, as opposed to appellate jurisdiction, which involves the power to review cases decided by other courts.

---

[19]Ibid., p. 55.
[20] *Annual Report for the Texas Judiciary, Fiscal Year 2009*, p. 62; Texas Judiciary Online, accessed February 1, 2010, at www.courts.state.tx.us/pubs/AR2009/AR09.pdf.
[21]Ibid., p. 61.
[22]Ibid., p. 13; Texas Judiciary Online, accessed February 1, 2010, at http://www.courts.state.tx.us/pubs/AR2009/AR09.pdf.

$10,000. Justices of the peace may issue warrants for search and arrest, serve *ex officio* as notaries public, conduct preliminary hearings, perform marriages, serve as coroners in counties having no medical examiner, and hear cases involving small claims. Approximately 87.5 percent of cases filed in justice courts are criminal, and most involve traffic violations.[23]

Qualifications. All the functions just mentioned are performed by an official whose only qualification is to be a registered voter. No statutory or constitutional provisions require that a justice of the peace be a lawyer, and only about 7 percent of Texas's justices of the peace are lawyers.

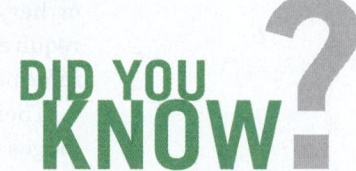

When a justice of the peace is not a licensed attorney, he or she is required by statute to take a 40-hour course in the performance of the duties of the office, plus a 20-hour course each year thereafter, at an accredited state-supported institution of higher education. Some people have questioned the constitutionality of this provision, because it adds a qualification for the office not specified in the constitution.

Compensation. For many years, counties in Texas varied widely as to whether they paid their justices of the peace a specific salary or paid them fees based on services performed. Some counties had a mixed system, wherein some justices were salaried while others were paid according to a fee system. Since January 1973, all justices of the peace have been paid a salary,[24] but the salary may vary a great deal from county to county and from justice to justice within the same county.

The Negative Image of Justices of the Peace. The public's perception of justices of the peace is often not flattering. Many justices are regarded as biased, untrained in the law, and incompetent. The average citizen is skeptical about getting a fair trial, which may be a major factor in the settlement of a high percentage of cases before trial (34 percent of criminal cases in 2009).[25] What about a person who goes before a justice of the peace in a county in which he or she does not live? The general assumption is that fairness and decency in this situation are the exception rather than the rule.

There are justices of the peace who are conscientious, objective, and fair, but they find it difficult to overcome the stereotype just described. This negative image is reinforced by the activities of justices of the peace who act as coroners. The function of the coroner is to determine the cause of death in specified cases. For decades, stories have been told about coroners' verdicts that left more questions than answers.

Thus, despite changes in the qualifications, salaries, and responsibilities of justices of the peace, they still do not inspire confidence in many people. Defenders of the system traditionally refer to the justice of the peace courts as the "people's courts" and maintain that elimination of the justice courts would remove the close contact between officials and the public that many treasure. Eliminating these courts, defenders say, would limit judicial power to professionals and would ignore the value of amateur status and commonsense law. This position is in line with the view, widely held in Texas, that government is best when it is closest to the people. Critics counter that incompetence and bias are not justified simply because these courts are close to the people.

[23]Ibid., p. 58; Texas Judiciary Online, accessed January 29, 2010, at www.courts.state.tx.us/pubs/AR2009/AR09.pdf.
[24]Article 16.61 of the Texas Constitution, as amended in November 1972.
[25]*Annual Report for the Texas Judiciary, 2009,* p. 58; Texas Judiciary Online, accessed February 1, 2010, at www.courts.state.tx.us/pubs/AR2009/AR09.pdf.

COUNTY COURTS

Each of the 254 counties in Texas has a county court presided over by the county judge. (The county judge is sometimes referred to as the constitutional county judge, and his or her court may be called the constitutional county court.) The Texas Constitution requires that county judges be elected by voters for four-year terms and be "well informed in the law of the state," which can mean almost anything.

Their salaries are paid by the county and vary greatly. About 12 percent of county judges are licensed to practice law. County courts handle probate and other civil matters in which the amount in dispute is between $200 and $10,000. Their criminal jurisdiction is confined to serious misdemeanors for which punishment is a fine of more than $500, a jail sentence not to exceed one year, or both.

County Courts-at-Law. Because the constitutional county judge also has administrative responsibilities as presiding officer of the commissioners court (the governing body for Texas counties and not a judicial entity at all), the judge may have little time to handle judicial matters. The legislature has responded by establishing **county courts-at-law** in certain counties to act as auxiliary, or supplemental, courts. Their judges are elected for four-year terms. There are 222 of these statutory courts-at-law in 84 Texas counties.[26] They have either civil or criminal jurisdiction or a combination of both, as determined by the legislative act that established them. Their civil jurisdiction includes cases involving claims of less than $100,000. Their criminal jurisdiction includes misdemeanors that are more serious than those tried by the justice of the peace and municipal courts, or misdemeanors that include a jail sentence or a fine in excess of $500.

County Courts-at-Law
In Texas, county courts in addition to the constitutional county court. They are established by the legislature in all but the smallest Texas counties and may have criminal or civil jurisdiction. They form a level of courts superior to justice of the peace and municipal courts but inferior to district courts.

THESE PHOTOS SHOW four of the 254 county courthouses in Texas. Clockwise from the upper left are the courthouses that serve Tarrant County, Somervell County, Hood County, and Anderson County. In 1999, the Texas legislature and then-governor George W. Bush established the Texas Historic Courthouse Preservation Program. The program provides partial matching grants to Texas counties for the restoration of their historic county courthouses. The legislature has approved $145 million for the program since it began. (Photos courtesy of Texas Historical Commission)

[26]Texas Judiciary Online, "Court Structure of Texas," accessed October 1, 2008, at www.courts.state.tx.us.

The qualifications of the judges of the statutory county courts-at-law vary according to the statute that established the particular court. In addition to residence in the county, a court-at-law judge usually must have four years' experience as a practicing attorney or judge.

More than two-thirds of cases disposed in county-level courts are criminal. Cases involving theft and driving while intoxicated or under the influence of drugs are the most common. Civil cases include probate matters and suits to collect debt.

Popular Perceptions of County Judges. Administration of justice in Texas county courts is widely considered to be uneven. Many of the judges are competent and run their courts in an orderly manner, but others regard their courts and official jurisdictions as personal fiefdoms, paying little attention to finer points of law or accepted procedures. If the county judge is performing as a judicial officer as well as the chief administrative officer of the county, the opportunities for arbitrary action are compounded.

DISTRICT COURTS

The district courts are often described as the chief trial courts of the state, and as a group these courts are called the *general trial courts*. The names of the courts and their jurisdictions vary. There are constitutional district courts, civil district courts, criminal district courts, and so on, throughout more than 40 other jurisdictions.

Texas has 444 district courts, all of which are single-judge courts.[27] Each judge must be at least 25 years of age, a resident of the district for two years, and a citizen of the United States and a judge or a licensed practicing attorney for a combined four years. Judges are elected for four-year terms by voters in their districts. The state of Texas pays $125,000 of the salary of each district judge. Each county may supplement the state salary up to a maximum of $140,000.

Jurisdiction of the District Courts. District courts have jurisdiction in felony cases, which make up about one-third of their caseloads. Civil cases in which the claim exceeds $200 may also be tried in district courts, and such cases constitute the greatest share of their workload (approximately 69 percent). Juvenile cases are usually tried in district courts. While most district courts exercise both criminal and civil jurisdiction, there is a tendency for courts in metropolitan areas to specialize in criminal, civil, or family law matters.

Plea Bargaining. The caseload for district courts is heavy, and plea bargaining is often used to dispose of criminal cases at this level. Plea bargaining saves the state a great amount of time and expense. It is estimated that about 90 percent of criminal cases in district courts are disposed of in this way.[28] If plea bargaining were not used in many urban areas, court delays would be increased by months, if not years. While efficient, plea bargaining raises serious issues concerning equity and justice; it often encourages innocent people to plead guilty and allows guilty people to escape with less punishment than the law provides.

Civil Settlements. Similarly, many civil lawsuits are resolved through negotiated settlements between the parties. At times, settlements may be appropriate and just. In many urban areas, however, there is such a backlog of civil cases before the courts that it can take years for a matter to be heard and settled. Therefore, litigants often choose to settle their cases out of court for reasons other than justice.

DID YOU KNOW?

That Harris County Criminal Court-at-Law Judge Michael Peters sentenced a woman who starved her horses to "thirty days in jail and to have a diet restricted to bread and water for the first three days." The judge was later officially admonished for such "creative sentencing."

---

[27]Ibid.
[28] *Texas Crime, Texas Justice* (Austin: Comptroller's Office, 1994), p. 51.

COURTS OF APPEALS

Fourteen courts of appeals hear immediate appeals in both civil and criminal cases from district- and county-level courts in their areas. These courts are said to have **appellate jurisdiction**. Only a small percentage of trial court cases are appealed. For example, during 2009, the courts of appeals disposed of 11,286 cases.[29] In these cases, the appeals courts reversed, at least in part, the decision of the trial court 9.2 percent of the time.[30]

The state pays each chief appeals justice $140,000 and each associate justice $137,500. Counties may pay a supplement to appeals judges, but the total salary cannot exceed $147,500 for the chief appeals justice and $145,000 for an associate justice. Appeals judges are elected from their districts for six-year terms. They must be at least 35 years of age, with at least 10 years' experience as a lawyer or judge.

COURT OF CRIMINAL APPEALS

An 1891 constitutional amendment established the present system of dual courts of last resort. The Texas Supreme Court is the highest state appellate court in civil matters, and the Court of Criminal Appeals is the highest state appellate court in criminal matters. Only Oklahoma has a similar system.

Although most criminal cases decided by the 14 courts of appeals go no further, some are heard by the Court of Criminal Appeals, which consists of a presiding judge and eight other judges. In 2009, Criminal Appeals Court judges wrote 447 opinions, of which more than 76 percent were "determinative opinions" that disposed of cases, and the remainder were dissents, concurrences, or opinions on rehearings.[31]

Criminal Appeals Court judges are elected statewide in partisan elections for six-year overlapping terms. They must be at least 35 years old and be lawyers or judges with 10 years' experience. The presiding judge of the Court of Criminal Appeals receives a salary of $152,500; the other judges receive $150,000.

TIMOTHY COLE. On March 1, 2010, he became the first person to receive a posthumous pardon from Texas's governor. Using DNA evidence, Texas Tech law students like Sarah Hegi helped establish Cole's innocence. His case is discussed in the *Politics with a Purpose* feature in Chapter 20.
(AP Photo/Harry Cabluck)

---

[29] *Annual Report for the Texas Judiciary, 2009*, p. 31; Texas Judiciary Online, accessed February 1, 2010, at www.courts.state.tx.us/pubs/AR2009/AR09.pdf.
[30] Ibid., p. 31.
[31] Ibid., p. 29.

Reversing Criminal Verdicts. Historically, the Texas Court of Criminal Appeals has generated a large measure of public controversy due to its alleged coddling of criminals. Between 1900 and 1927, the court reversed 42 percent of all the cases it reviewed. As early as 1910, the court was cited by the American Institute of Criminal Law as being "one of the foremost worshippers, among the American appellate courts, of the technicality." In the 1940s, largely in response to both professional and public criticism, the reversal rate began to drop, and by 1966 it was only 3 percent.[32] Today's Court of Criminal Appeals reverses a very small percentage of the cases that it takes on appeal.

The nature of its work makes the Court of Criminal Appeals a highly visible court, even if its individual members are not so visible. When the court reverses convictions based on inadmissible arguments by prosecutors or the introduction of unacceptable or tainted evidence, protests are sure to follow from prosecutors, newspaper editorial writers, Internet bloggers, and civic club luncheon speakers. Remarks concerning legal technicalities are frequent when a conviction is overturned, even though the real reason for the reversal might be the overkill of a zealous prosecutor or other inappropriate behavior by the state. Ordinarily, a reversal means only that the case will be retried.

The Court of Criminal Appeals and the Texas Bill of Rights. The Court of Criminal Appeals has been involved in another controversy. Previously criticized for its nit-picking opinions, the court has recently been accused of unfounded interpretations of the Texas Bill of Rights. For example, in a 1991 decision, *William Randolph Heitman v. State*, the court ruled that the Texas Constitution provides criminal defendants more protection against illegal searches and seizures than the U.S. Constitution does.[33] Critics argue that the court should guarantee the accused no broader rights than those protected by the U.S. Constitution. Those supporting the court's decisions point out that the bill of rights in the Texas Constitution is not identical to the Bill of Rights in the U.S. Constitution and therefore lends itself to different interpretations.

That Michael Richard was executed because Texas Court of Criminal Appeals Judge Sharon Keller refused to take his appeal after 5 p.m.?

The Death Penalty. The Court of Criminal Appeals has exclusive jurisdiction over automatic appeals in death penalty cases. In 2009, the court received 19 death penalty appeals.[34] Since the United States Supreme Court restored the use of capital punishment in 1976, Texas has executed far more individuals than any other state. By March 2010, the state had executed 450 convicted murderers (more than three times as many as the state with the second-highest total). For several years, the rate of executions averaged approximately 25 to 30 per year (including a record of 40 in 2000).[35] This rate has recently been dropping, however (24 individuals were executed in 2009).[36] Death penalty cases have led to headline stories, including controversies over the use of lethal injections, executing a woman (Karla Faye Tucker), a 66-year-old man, persons who were juveniles when they committed the crimes for which they were sentenced to death, individuals who were mentally retarded or mentally ill, those who had received poor

[32]Paul Burka, "Trial by Technicality," *Texas Monthly*, April 1982, p. 131.
[33]815 S.W. 2d 681 (1991).
[34] *Annual Report for the Texas Judiciary, 2009*, p. 52; Texas Judiciary Online, accessed February 1, 2010, at www.courts.state.tx.us/pubs/AR2009/AR09.pdf.
[35]"Retarded Man's Impending Execution Prompts Scrutiny of Death-Penalty Laws," *Dallas Morning News*, February 15, 2000; "Who Really Deserves to Die?," *Fort Worth Star-Telegram*, January 14, 2001.
[36]Texas Department of Criminal Justice, "Executions: December 7, 1982 through March 2, 2010," accessed March 2, 2010, at http://www.tdcj.state.tx.us/stat/annual.htm.

legal counsel (including a sleeping attorney), and persons who might actually have been innocent of the crimes (Cameron Todd Willingham).[37]

THE STATE SUPREME COURT

The Texas Supreme Court is the final court of appeals in civil and juvenile cases. The court has original jurisdiction over issuing writs and conducting proceedings for involuntary retirement or removal of judges. In its other cases, the court has appellate jurisdiction. The court also has the power to make rules for the administration of justice—rules of civil practice and procedure for courts having civil jurisdiction. In addition, it makes rules governing licensing of members of the state bar.

The Texas Supreme Court consists of one chief justice and eight associate justices. All are elected statewide after being nominated in party primaries. Three of the nine justices are elected every two years for six-year terms. The Texas Constitution specifies that a justice must be at least 35 years of age and a citizen of the United States and of Texas and must have been a lawyer or judge of a court of record for at least 10 years. The salary of the chief justice is $152,500, and the salary of associate justices is $150,000.

The Supreme Court's Workload. During 2009, the court acted on 3,247 matters.[38] The justices wrote 165 opinions, of which 125 (75.7 percent) were deciding opinions that disposed of cases.[39] The court also reversed (at least in part) approximately 67 percent of the cases that came to it from the 14 courts of appeals on petitions for review (formerly "applications for writs of error").[40]

The Role of the Texas Supreme Court. The Texas Supreme Court spends much of its time deciding which petitions for review will be granted, because not all appeals are heard. Generally, it only takes the cases it views as presenting the most significant legal issues. It should also be noted that the Texas Supreme Court plays a policy-making role in the state. As discussed in Chapter 20, for example, in 1989 the court unanimously decided the *Edgewood v. Kirby* case.[41] In this decision, the court ordered major changes in how public schools were financed in Texas. It found unacceptable the huge disparities between rich and poor school districts in the state.

SELECTION OF JUDGES

Officially, Texas elects its judges (except municipal court judges) in partisan elections. This statement oversimplifies the process, however, and can be somewhat misleading. Former chief justice Robert W. Calvert referred many times to the system as an

[37]"High Court Looks at Lethal Injections," *Dallas Morning News*, September 26, 2007; "Karla Faye Tucker Executed," *Dallas Morning News*, February 4, 1998; "Questions of Competence Arise in Death Row Appeal," *Dallas Morning News*, September 11, 2000; "Man Denied New Trial Despite Sleeping Lawyer," *Fort Worth Star-Telegram*, October 28, 2000; "Death-Penalty Trials Rife with Errors, Study Finds," *Dallas Morning News*, June 12, 2000; "Man Executed for 1988 Revenge Killing," *Fort Worth Star-Telegram*, November 21, 2002; "Death Penalty Debate Reopens," *Fort Worth Star-Telegram*, November 8, 2002; "At Last Name Is Cleared," *Dallas Morning News*, October 6, 2004; "Supreme Court, 5–4, Forbids Execution in Juvenile Crime," *The New York Times*, March 2, 2005, p. A1; "Trial by Fire: Did Texas Execute an Innocent Man?" *The New Yorker*, September 7, 2009, accessed online March 1, 2010 at www.newyorker.com/reporting/2009/09/07/090907fa_fact_grann.
[38] *Annual Report for the Texas Judiciary, 2009*, p. 31; Texas Judiciary Online, accessed February 1, 2010, at www.courts.state.tx.us/pubs/AR2009/AR09.pdf.
[39]Ibid., p. 31.
[40]Ibid., p. 29.
[41]777 S.W. 2d 391 (Tex. 1989).

"appointive-elective" one. Approximately 45 percent of the trial judges (those who serve in district courts, criminal district courts, county courts-at-law, and probate courts) first assume office through appointment to fill vacancies created when judges leave office before their terms expire.[42] Likewise, about 40 percent of the judges of the appellate courts first assume office through appointment. These appointments between elections are made by the governor with the advice and consent of the senate. In the elections for judicial offices, approximately 80 percent of all Texas judges are reelected unopposed. Even when there is no incumbent running for reelection, serious competition for judicial posts is uncommon.

The system of judicial selection in Texas, and practices related to it, have been under attack. Some critics have alleged that Texas has the "best justice that money can buy." In fact, the court system has received negative national exposure on the TV program *60 Minutes*. In the following sections, we explain the reasons for the criticisms and outline the essentially political nature of the system.

AN UNINFORMED ELECTORATE

Because Texas elects judges, a natural question arises: How knowledgeable are voters in these judicial elections? In other words, do voters know who the candidates are and what their records in office look like? Research on the United States Supreme Court has repeatedly shown that the vast majority of the public knows little about its rulings and actions.[43] If most Americans know very little about the United States Supreme Court,

[42]"Profile of Appellate and Trial Judges," *Texas Judicial System Annual Report, 2002* (Austin: Office of Court Administration), p. 54.

[43]For example, see John Kessel, "Public Perceptions of the Supreme Court," *Midwest Journal of Political Science*, Vol. 10, 1966, pp. 167–191; Kenneth Dolbeare, "The Public Views the Supreme Court," in Herbert Jacob, ed., *Law, Politics, and the Federal Courts* (Boston: Little, Brown, 1967); Gregory Casey, "Popular Perceptions of Supreme Court Rulings," *American Politics Quarterly*, Vol. 4, 1976, pp. 3–45; *Gallup Report*, Vol. 264, 1987, pp. 29–30; Thomas Marshall, *Public Opinion and the Supreme Court* (New York: Longman, 1989); and Lee Epstein et al., *The Supreme Court Compendium* (Washington, DC: CQ Press, 2003).

the court that receives the most media attention in this country, how much can we expect voters to know about state and local courts?

A voter in Texas could be asked to vote for candidates running for the Texas Supreme Court, the Court of Criminal Appeals, a court of appeals, a district court, and a county court, as well as justice of the peace. Not surprisingly, polls and research indicate that most voters enter the voting booth with scant knowledge of the candidates running for various judicial posts.[44] For example, a poll taken in Texas after a presidential general election found that only 14.5 percent of voters could recall the name of one of the candidates for either the Texas Supreme Court or the Court of Criminal Appeals.

In addition to systematic research, anecdotal evidence also indicates that most voters in Texas are unaware of candidates' qualifications or experience. Thus, name recognition of any sort can lead people to cast their votes for a candidate. Consequently, candidates with names the same as or similar to those of movie stars, historical figures, or public personages are often candidates for judicial positions.

In 1976, for example (as discussed earlier in this text), Don Yarbrough, an unknown attorney, was elected to the Texas Supreme Court. It is believed that many voters confused him with former Senator Ralph Yarborough or with Don Yarborough, who had run for governor. Soon after winning a seat on the court, Yarbrough resigned because criminal charges had been filed against him. He was later convicted of perjury and, after fleeing the country, was eventually apprehended and imprisoned in Texas.

PARTY IDENTIFICATION

Because voters know so little about individual candidates, they may use party identification as a cue to determine how to vote. In other words, if a voter has no knowledge of the views or backgrounds of the candidates on the ballot, he or she may make a choice based on the candidates' political party affiliation. In Texas, this appears to be a common way for voters to make selections in judicial elections.

The Rise of the Republicans. Historically, Texas was part of the "Solid South," and as in other Southern states, the Democratic Party monopolized politics. This monopoly was reflected in the judicial posts throughout the state. When Texas became a competitive two-party state in the 1980s, many Republicans were elected to judicial positions. One researcher noted, "In one decade the Republican party moved from a position of being locked out of power in the court house to controlling 36 of 37 district seats" in the city of Dallas.[45] This dramatic change included both the Texas Supreme Court and the Court of Criminal Appeals. Both high courts are entirely Republican; not a single Democrat serves as a justice on either court. Republican successes led many incumbent Democratic judges to switch to the Republican Party in hopes of continuing their judicial careers.[46] In the 2006 and 2008 elections, however, the Democratic Party began to show some renewed signs of life. In 2006 in Dallas County, Democratic candidates won all 42 of

[44]For example, see Philip Dubois, *From Ballot to Bench: Judicial Elections and the Quest for Accountability* (Austin: University of Texas Press, 1980); and Anthony Champagne and Gregory Thielemann, "Awareness of Trial Court Judges," *Judicature*, Vol. 74, 1991, pp. 271–276.

[45]Champagne and Thielemann, "Awareness of Trial Court Judges."

[46]Office of the Secretary of State, *Race Summary Report for the 2006 General Election*, accessed at elections.sos.state.tx.us/elchist.exe.

the contested judicial races, and in Harris County in 2008, Democratic candidates won 22 of 26 contested judicial positions.[47] The 2010 elections reversed Democratic gains in Harris County, however, as Republican judicial candidates won every countywide race as a result of straight-ticket voting.

The Effects of Partisan Voting. It has been argued that because judges, especially at the appellate level, make significant policy decisions, it is reasonable for voters to select judges on the basis of political party affiliation.[48] Party affiliation may provide accurate information concerning the general ideology and, thus, the decision-making patterns of judges. Even if this is true, voting based solely on a candidate's political party can lead to controversial results. Some critics point to the 1994 election of Steve Mansfield to the Texas Court of Criminal Appeals as evidence of what can happen when voters do not educate themselves about a candidate's qualifications or background. During the campaign, it was revealed that Mansfield had very limited legal experience and that he had lied in his campaign literature about his experience and his personal and political background. He won nonetheless, apparently because many voters supported every Republican on the ballot (that is, they voted a *straight ticket*).

JUDICIAL CAMPAIGN SPENDING

Because voters often look for simple voting cues (such as name familiarity or party identification), candidates often want to spend as much money as possible to make their names or candidacy well known. In recent years, spending in judicial races has risen dramatically. Candidates need to win two elections: their party's nomination and the general election. This can be an expensive endeavor. In the 1988 races for six open seats on the Texas Supreme Court, the candidates spent more than $10 million.[49] In the 1996 races for the same seats, three of four incumbent Republican candidates raised about $1 million each (the fourth incumbent received about $700,000, although he was running unopposed).[50] None of the three Democrats in the race raised even $100,000. For example, Chief Justice Tom Phillips received more than $1.1 million, while his challenger raised a little more than $15,000.[51] Not surprisingly, all four Republicans were reelected. In the three races in 1998 in which the Republicans mostly outspent their rivals, the funding ratio was 15 to one (nearly $2.9 million collected compared with $190,000 for the Democrats).[52] In 2002 and 2008, the results were similar. In 2002, the Republicans won or held on to all five seats that were up for election and outspent Democrats approximately three to one (even with Chief Justice Phillips accepting no new

[47]"Dallas County Judges Lose Seats in Democratic Deluge," *Dallas Morning News*, November 8, 2006, accessed online February 20, 2010 at www.dallasnews.com/sharedcontent/dws/news/politics/local/stories/DN-dems_08tex.ART.State.Edition2.3e326fb.html; "Sweep Revives Debate on Election of Judges," *Houston Chronicle*, November 8, 2008, accessed February 20, 2010 at www.chron.com/disp/story.mpl/front/6102615.html.
[48]Dubois, *From Ballot to Bench*.
[49]Anthony Champagne, "Campaign Contributions in Texas Supreme Court Races," *Crime, Law, and Social Change*, Vol. 17, 1992, pp. 91–106; Kyle Cheek and Anthony Champagne, "Money in Texas Supreme Court Elections: 1980–1998," *Judicature*, Vol. 84, 2000, pp. 20–25.
[50] "Republican Judges Lead Money Race," *Dallas Morning News*, October 27, 1996, p. A45.
[51]Ibid.
[52]"Justice Spector Hopes to Win Tough Race against Well-Financed Republican O'Neill," *Dallas Morning News*, October 18, 1998, p. A47.

campaign contributions).[53] In 2008, the three Republican incumbents raised over $2.8 million while their Democratic challengers raised just over $1 million.[54] The incumbents were easily reelected.

An Appearance of Impropriety. Campaign finances have raised questions concerning fairness and the advantages of incumbency. In addition, many (including *60 Minutes*) have asked whether justice is for sale in Texas. More precisely, individuals and organizations often appear before judges after having contributed to their election campaigns. Do such contributions affect a judge's impartiality in deciding a case? If nothing else, such a system gives the appearance of possible impropriety or bias.

A notable example was the *Pennzoil v. Texaco*[55] case. This lawsuit involved billions of dollars, and it was decided by justices on the Texas Supreme Court, who had received hundreds of thousands of dollars in campaign contributions from the opposing attorneys and their respective law firms. Research has indicated that 40 percent of campaign contributions to Texas Supreme Court justices came from those with cases before the court.[56] In 2008, Texas Supreme Court incumbents running for reelection received half their support from lawyers, law firms, and lobbyists.[57] A public advocacy group once sued Texas over this system, claiming it violates due process and the right to a fair trial.[58] The group cited surveys indicating that 83 percent of the Texas public, 79 percent of Texas lawyers, and 48 percent of Texas judges believe that campaign contributions significantly affect judicial decisions.[59]

In 2009, the United States Supreme Court weighed in on the question of judicial bias where litigants significantly influence the election of judges hearing their cases. In *Caperton* v. *A.T. Massey Coal Co., Inc.*, the court held that the chairman of Massey Coal had created such a question by donating $3 million to help finance the successful election of a new justice to the Supreme Court of Appeals of West Virginia. The possible conflict of interest arose because Massey Coal Company had a $50 million civil suit appeal pending before the court at the time; it was later decided in their favor by a 3-2 vote with the new justice voting with the majority. A 5-4 Supreme Court majority reversed and remanded the case, holding "there is a serious risk of actual bias . . . when a person with a personal stake in a particular case had a significant and disproportionate influence in placing the judge on the case."[60]

Consumer Lawsuits. Part of this debate about possible impropriety involves the battle between plaintiffs' attorneys and defense attorneys in civil cases. Texas has traditionally been a conservative, pro-business state. This perspective has usually been reflected in the decisions of the judiciary, which have often favored big business and professional groups (such as the medical profession).

Plaintiffs' lawyers and their related interest group, the Texas Trial Lawyers Association, have made a concerted effort in the past few decades to

DID YOU KNOW?

That only 2.8 percent of Texas district judges are African Americans?

[53]"Report: Justice Candidates Raise about $3 Million," *Fort Worth Star-Telegram*, August 28, 2002.

[54]Texans for Public Justice, *Interested Parties: Who Bankrolled Texas' High-Court Justices in 2008?*, October 2009: http://info.tpj.org/reports/supremes08/InterestedParties.oct09.pdf.

[55]748 S.W. 2d 631 (Tex. App. 1988).

[56]"Lawyers Give Most to High Court Hopefuls," *Dallas Morning News*, February 28, 1998, p. A26. Texans for Public Justice keeps current track of litigants' campaign contributions to Texas Supreme Court judges in its "Dollar Track" at http://www.tpj.org/publication_list.jsp?typeid=1.

[57]Texans for Public Justice, *Interested Parties: Who Bankrolled Texas' High-Court Justices in 2008?*, Oct. 2009. http://info.tpj.org/reports/supremes08/InterestedParties.oct09.pdf.

[58]"State Sued over Judicial Elections," *Fort Worth Star-Telegram*, April 4, 2000.

[59]Ibid.

[60]*Caperton v. A.T. Massey Coal Co., Inc.*, 556 U.S.__2009.

make the judiciary more open to consumer suits. Such suits are often filed against businesses, physicians, and their insurance companies. The plaintiffs' lawyers have poured millions of dollars into the political funds of candidates they believed would be more favorable to their perspective. Defense and business attorneys have responded with millions of dollars of their own contributions. Plaintiff and defense lawyers alike then often appear before the very judges to whom they have given these large sums.

MINORITY REPRESENTATION

A final major criticism of the current partisan elective system involves questions about diversity and minority representation. In 1988, African American and Hispanic groups challenged in federal court the way judges were elected in urban areas of Texas, citing the Voting Rights Act of 1965, as amended. They argued that the at-large (countywide) election of district and county court judges in Bexar, Dallas, Ector, Harris, Jefferson, Lubbock, Midland, Tarrant, and Travis counties made the election of minority candidates difficult because it diluted minority voting strength. Attorney General Dan Morales pointed out that African Americans and Hispanics made up 40 percent of Texas's population but held only 5 percent of state district judgeships. In August 1993, the full federal Court of Appeals for the Fifth Circuit upheld the current system. In January 1994, the United States Supreme Court rejected an appeal of the decision without comment.

In recent decades, however, minority judicial candidates have won several high-profile victories. For example, in 1984, Raul A. Gonzalez became the first Hispanic to serve on the Texas Supreme Court. In 1990, Morris Overstreet became the first African American to serve on the Texas Court of Criminal Appeals. In 2001, Governor Rick Perry filled two vacancies on the Texas Supreme Court with minorities—and one of these individuals, Wallace Jefferson, was appointed chief justice in 2004.[61] Nevertheless, these changes have been modest, and ethnic minorities are still underrepresented among trial court judges. Their judges are elected for four-year terms. There are 222 of these statutory courts-at-law in 84 Texas counties.[62]

---

[61]"First Black Named to Texas High Court," *Fort Worth Star-Telegram*, March 15, 2001.
[62] *Annual Report for the Texas Judiciary, 2009*, p. 13; Texas Judiciary Online, accessed February 17, 2010, at www.courts.state.tx.us/pubs/AR2009/AR09.pdf. The authors wish to thank Adrianna Brosovic, Jason Knaumann, and Bhavik Pradipkumar for their invaluable research assistance.

YOU CAN MAKE A Difference

DEALING INTELLIGENTLY WITH LAW ENFORCEMENT OFFICERS IN TEXAS

Many students may become involved in the criminal justice process as victims, witnesses, or perpetrators. (Legally, traffic offenses are crimes.) As a victim or witness of crime, you must decide whether to report it. Many criminals get away with their crimes because many citizens (especially in minority communities) fear dealing with law enforcement. Others fear that crime reports will increase their insurance rates. Some fail to report crimes

A LAW ENFORCEMENT agent conducts a field sobriety test. Learn to deal intelligently with the law. You can access alcohol-related regulations at http://www.tabc.state.tx.us. (Yellowdog Productions/Jane Sob/ Getty Images)

because the perpetrator is a friend or relative. Still others fear the perpetrator's vengeance. Some (especially rape victims) are embarrassed by the fact they have become victims. Failure to report crime, however, creates an environment that supports it. The individual must personally evaluate the costs and benefits of filing a report.

WHY SHOULD YOU CARE?

Sooner or later, many of us will be arrested—if only through a traffic stop. Do not take such an arrest lightly. In some instances, your life, liberty, property, and reputation may be at stake. Even a traffic ticket can affect your insurability, and accumulating several tickets may now result in a large annual state fee to keep your driver's license.

WHAT CAN YOU DO?

Let's consider how you might deal with traffic violations. The best advice is to avoid them. Law enforcement officers do not often ticket drivers traveling less than 10 miles per hour above the posted speed limit except in school zones—there, 20 miles per hour means exactly that, and absolutely no more! Regardless of posted speed limits, Texas law provides that you must travel at safe and reasonable speeds, and this provision is usually taken to mean that about one-sixth of the traffic will pass you.

Since 1998, it has been illegal to possess open alcoholic beverages in a car in Texas. Therefore, keep any opened alcoholic beverage containers in the trunk of the car or, if the vehicle has no trunk, behind the last seat.

If you are arrested for a traffic violation or any other crime, be respectful and obey the officer or officers. Sometimes a polite, reasoned explanation can prevent the ordeal of a traffic ticket. Do not confess guilt or argue your innocence—these matters will be settled in court later. If you believe a police order is unlawful, you should politely state that you believe the order is unlawful. For example, it is not legal for an officer to demand that you open any locked compartment without probable cause.

If you ultimately are given a ticket, take advantage of the opportunity to take a safe-driving course to absolve your responsibility. Other alternatives include hiring a lawyer to have the ticket dismissed or obtaining a plea bargain with the prosecutor or judge to plead guilty to the crime of "failure to appear" in exchange for having the ticket dismissed. Deferred adjudications are also a real possibility. Good drivers may get help finding lower insurance rates through the Texas Department of Insurance.

KEY TERMS

acquitted 902
adversary system 900
appellate jurisdiction 908
burden of proof 889
change of venue 899
county courts-at-law 906
deferred adjudication 900
docket 889

due process 895
examining trial 897
FBI index crimes 892
felony 890
grand jury 898
misdemeanor 890
mistrial 901
original jurisdiction 904

parole 894
personal recognizance 898
plea bargaining 899
probation 901
punitive damages award 889
tort reform 889
victimless crime 893
writ of information 898

CHAPTER SUMMARY

1. **What are the differences between the kinds of cases tried in Texas's criminal courts and those tried in its civil courts?** Within the American legal system, cases are classified as either civil or criminal. Civil cases primarily involve the rights of private parties or organizations (e.g., *Smith v. Jones*). Resolution of the conflicts between these parties may result in compensation or relief based on the concept of responsibility rather than guilt. Disputes are usually set out in a petition, and the side with the preponderance of the evidence wins the suit.

   In contrast to civil cases, criminal cases deal with public concepts of proper behavior and morality as defined by law. Punishment for a conviction ranges from a fine to imprisonment to a combination of both. Initiated by a government prosecutor on behalf of the public, a criminal case is brought by the state against the accused (e.g., *State of Texas v. Smith*). Specific charges of wrongdoing are spelled out in a grand jury indictment or a writ of information. In addition, in criminal cases the prosecutor must prove that the defendant is guilty beyond a reasonable doubt, a much higher standard than in civil cases.

2. Tort actions involving personal injuries are common in civil law as plaintiffs' lawyers usually representing injured patients, workers, consumers, and insurance policy holders bring suits against corporations, employers, health care providers, and insurance companies. Support for limiting personal and corporate liability in such personal injury cases is widespread in Texas, and the Texas legislature has enacted tort reform to reduce the number of lawsuits and to cap damage awards. Liability issues also affect judicial campaigns, as trial lawyers and corporate defense attorneys provide campaign contributions to candidates who reflect their positions on corporate liability.

3. More serious crimes are called felonies and minor crimes are called misdemeanors. Although crime rates have been declining in recent years, the people most likely to be arrested are younger, less educated members of ethnic minorities living in cities.

4. **How does due process in Texas's courts balance the rights of individuals and the mores of the community as a whole?** The court procedures that constitute due process aim to promote justice and protect individuals from the government. These procedures are generally either written into state and national constitutions and statutes or included in written and unwritten traditional codes of court process. Court procedures have been greatly influenced by tradition. Unfortunately, the goal of due process is often an ideal rather than a reality. It is largely through due process, though, that the courts aim to blend two conflicting goals of society: (1) to protect society according to the state's legal concepts of right and wrong and (2) to protect the rights of the individual charged with wrongdoing.

5. The Texas court system is a large and complicated structure. There are many municipal courts, fewer county-level courts, still fewer district courts and courts of appeals, and only one Texas Supreme Court and one

Court of Criminal Appeals. With jurisdictions frequently overlapping, the organization of courts in Texas is often confusing. Reformers have often urged streamlining Texas's courts and improving their professionalism.

? 6. **What are the criticisms of Texas's judicial selection process?** Although Texas judges are selected by partisan election, judges often retire before their terms expire, giving the governor frequent opportunities to fill vacancies until the next election. The system has come under attack due to its political nature. For example, voters are often ignorant of the candidates and their records in office, qualifications, and experience. Many vote along party lines. Finally, individuals or organizations often appear before judges after contributing large amounts to their election campaigns, thereby fueling perceptions of apparent or real conflicts of interest.

SELECTED PRINT, MEDIA, AND ONLINE RESOURCES

PRINT RESOURCES

Abraham, Henry. *The Judicial Process*, 7th ed. New York: Oxford University Press, 1998. This work is a comparative review of courts and court systems throughout the world.

Abramsky, Sasha. *Vengeance in the Age of Mass Imprisonment*. New York: Beacon Press, 2007. This provocative book argues against the conventional wisdom that a "get tough" approach to crime can reduce crime rates.

Abramson, Jeffrey. *We, the Jury*. New York: Basic Books, 1994. Abramson reviews various issues surrounding the jury system and its connection to democracy.

Baum, Lawrence. *American Courts: Process and Policy*, 5th ed. Boston: Houghton Mifflin, 2001. This volume is a broad review of lawyers, judges, and U.S. courts.

Dubois, Philip. *From Ballot to Bench: Judicial Elections and the Quest for Accountability*. Austin: University of Texas Press, 1980. Dubois discusses the concepts of competition and accountability in judicial elections.

Epstein, Lee, ed. *Contemplating Courts*. Washington, DC: CQ Press, 1995. This edited collection of essays in political science deals with the law, the courts, and the judicial process.

Marquart, James W., Sheldon Ekland-Olson, and Jonathan R. Sorensen. *The Rope, the Chair, and the Needle: Capital Punishment in Texas, 1923–1990*. Austin: University of Texas Press, 1994. James W. Marquart, now director of the Crime and Justice Studies Program at The University of Texas at Dallas, and his coauthors explore the history of the death penalty in Texas and discuss some of the most interesting issues surrounding it.

Segal, Jeffrey, and Harold Spaeth. *The Supreme Court and the Attitudinal Model*. New York: Cambridge University Press, 1993. This research attempts to show how the behavior and decision making of justices are affected by their personal policy preferences and attitudes.

Zimbardo, Philip. *The Lucifer Effect: Understanding How Good People Turn Evil*. New York: Random House, 2007. Using a classic Stanford psychology experiment, the author shows that prison roles are toxic to both prisoners and guards.

MEDIA RESOURCES

A Class Apart—PBS's *American Experience* presents the stirring story about *Hernandez v. Texas* in which Latinos win a victory in the struggle for equality as they earn the right to serve on Texas juries.

Dead Man Walking—A movie starring Susan Sarandon and Sean Penn that examines both sides of the death penalty issue.

The Executed—A PBS *Frontline* case study of an execution in Texas.

The Exonerated—A play by Jessica Blank and Erik Jenson that brings together characters whose lives were affected by wrongful death sentences, including some that occurred in Texas. It is based on real-life interviews.

Justice for Sale—A provocative film that critically examines the election of judges in three states, including Texas. It is available from the Center for Investigative Reporting and the WGBH Education Foundation.

Not Guilty by Reason of Insanity—An A&E production that questions why the mentally ill find their way into the criminal justice system and whether it is difficult to get out of it.

The Plea—A video produced by PBS *Frontline* that focuses on the judicial process and trial by jury.

ONLINE RESOURCES

The Bureau of Justice Statistics A rich source of national data about crime, victims, prosecution, prison, probation, and capital punishment: www.ojp.usdoj.gov/bjs/

The Federal Bureau of Investigation allows you to compare Texas crime figures with the national index crime figures in the Uniform Crime Reports: www.fbi.gov/ucr/ucr.htm

Texas Attorney General's Office provides access to services for crime victims: www.oag.state.tx.us/victims

The Texas Bar helps with family law, tenants' rights, and small claims court suits: www.texasbar.com/template. cfm?section=pamphlets

Texas Civil Justice League works with corporate legal departments to support tort reform to limit civil court awards: www.tcjl.com

Texas Judicial Server provides access to the Texas courts: www.courts.state.tx.us

Texas Law Help provides tips on low-cost and do-it-yourself civil legal strategies: http://texaslawhelp.org/

Texas Legislature Online gives access to all of Texas's laws (statutes): www.capitol.state.tx.us

The Texas Supreme Court features Webcasts of oral arguments: www.supreme.courts.state.tx.us

Texas Trial Lawyers Association presents the position of plaintiffs' attorneys, who argue cases for consumers, patients, and the insured: www.ttla.com

27

Texas students rally for their public policy interests as they oppose tuition hikes. (AP Photo/Pat Roque)

Texas Public Policy

QUESTIONS TO CONSIDER

What kinds of taxes does Texas collect?

In the politics of taxation, how are different groups' views of the "public interest" affected by their social and economic positions?

Which political values do Texas public policy priorities reflect?

CHAPTER CONTENTS

what if...

Texas Denied Illegal Immigrants Access to State Services?

BACKGROUND

The United States generally followed a policy of unlimited immigration until 1924, when Congress responded to a wave of anti-immigrant fervor by establishing numerical limits on total immigration for the first time. Today, over 11 million unauthorized immigrants live in this country—more than one million of them in Texas.* While immigration control is primarily the responsibility of the national government, some critics of national policies have urged states to pursue their own efforts to resist illegal immigration.

STATE EFFORTS TO CONTROL IMMIGRATION

Several states have adopted laws to restrict access to state services to citizens and resident aliens, but many of these state laws have been found unconstitutional. In 1975, Texas's legislature passed a law to cut off state funds for educating illegal immigrant children and to authorize local school districts to deny them the right to enroll. The U.S. Supreme Court held that Texas law was discriminatory and in violation of the Fourteenth Amendment in the U.S. Constitution.** California voters passed Proposition 187 in 1994 to deny publicly funded health care, social welfare, and educational services to those who had not been legally admitted but, like the Texas law, it too was found unconstitutional. In 2010, Arizona tried another approach by simply making it a crime to be an undocumented alien in the state, but federal courts initially ruled this approach to be an unconstitutional intrusion on the national government's powers.

DENYING STATE SERVICES

Despite these legal setbacks, Texans fighting illegal immigration argue that Texas should vigorously enforce policies that deny illegal immigrants access to public welfare and health care wherever federal law permits. Some contend that the state should also maintain a list of illegal immigrants attending public schools and ban in-state tuition to undocumented aliens in state colleges and universities. Immigration opponents contend that federal policies have not worked to stem the tide of illegal immigration and that states should refuse state services to illegal immigrants as a way of reducing incentives for them to cross the U.S. border. State services for undocumented aliens are costly, and taxpayers should not reward foreigners who have violated U.S. laws.***

Others argue that denying state services would have very little effect on illegal immigration because immigrants do not come to Texas expressly to take advantage of state services. Instead, the flow of immigrants has been driven by job availability, and the rate of immigration has already declined as a result of economic recession. Denying state services to illegal immigrants who remain in Texas would create an underclass of unhealthy and uneducated residents who would be unable to fully participate in society or contribute fully to its future economic development. Many public health and social welfare services are already denied to illegal immigrants who, nevertheless, pay Texas state and local governments quite a bit in the form of sales taxes and property taxes.****

FOR CRITICAL ANALYSIS

1. What are the practical implications of denying state services to undocumented immigrants? How does their access to these state services impact the state's future?
2. What economic, cultural, and political issues drive the debate over illegal immigration?

---

*Pew Hispanic Center, "U.S. Unauthorized Immigration Flows Are Down Sharply Since Mid-Decade," September 1, 2010, p. 3, http://pewhispanic.org/files/reports/126.pdf.
**Plyler v. Doe, 457 U.S. 202 (1982).

***Jack Martin and Ira Mehlman, The Cost of Illegal Immigration to Texans, Federation for American Immigration Reform, April 2005.
****Texas Comptroller of Public Accounts, "Special Report—Undocumented Immigrants in Texas: A Financial Analysis of the Impact to the State Budget and Economy," December 2006.

AT THE END of its 2009 session, the Texas legislature passed and sent to the governor the largest budget in the state's history—a total of almost $182.2 billion for fiscal years 2010 and 2011. Texas has the third largest state budget, exceeded only by those of California and New York.

In a sense, though, the size of the most recent Texas budget is not surprising. Each successive budget over the past several years has been larger than the preceding one, resulting in a long succession of record expenditures, as shown in Figure 27–1.

Inflation alone explains some of the rise in government spending, as you can see in the figure. Just as the cost of what individuals and families buy has increased, the cost of what government buys has increased as well. Nevertheless, inflation has also driven up the salaries and profits with which residents pay their taxes.

Population growth also has played a role in the growth in state spending. Texas's population has grown more rapidly than that of most other states. Each new person must be served, protected, and educated. Of course, the demands of a larger population for increased state services are offset by the fact that more people are also paying taxes to support them. Adjusted for population and inflation, state spending has grown at an average annual rate of 1.6 percent during the past 14 years.

REVENUES

What are the sources of the funds that the state spends? Surprisingly, much state revenue comes from sources other than state taxes. In 2010–2011, less than half of the state's revenues (43 percent) would come from various state taxes. Federal funding, mostly

FIGURE 27–1 Trends in Texas State Expenditures, All Funds, by Biennial Budget Periods, 1996–2011 (in millions of dollars)

This figure shows that state expenditures have grown considerably, but after adjusting for inflation and population growth, state spending has increased only modestly. Which of these measures of government spending is most meaningful? Why?

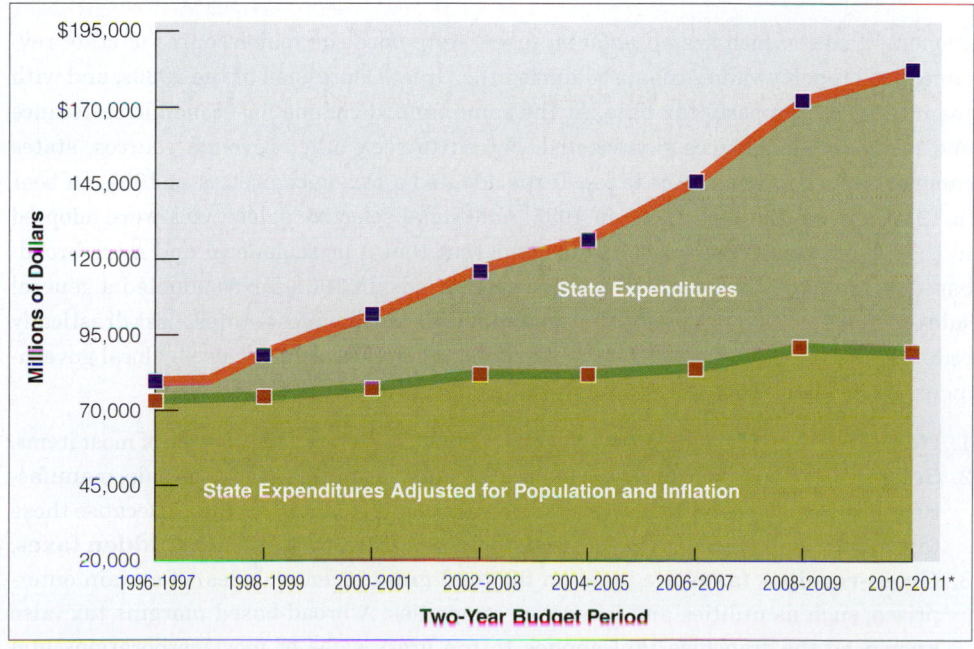

*Estimated.

Source: Legislative Budget Board, *Fiscal Size-Up, 2010–2011* (Austin: Legislative Budget Board, 2009), p. 9.

FIGURE 27–2 Sources of Estimated Revenues, 2010–2011 Budget Period

This figure shows that Texas's largest single revenue source is federal funding and the largest state tax is the general sales tax. Which of the other state taxes could also be considered sales taxes?

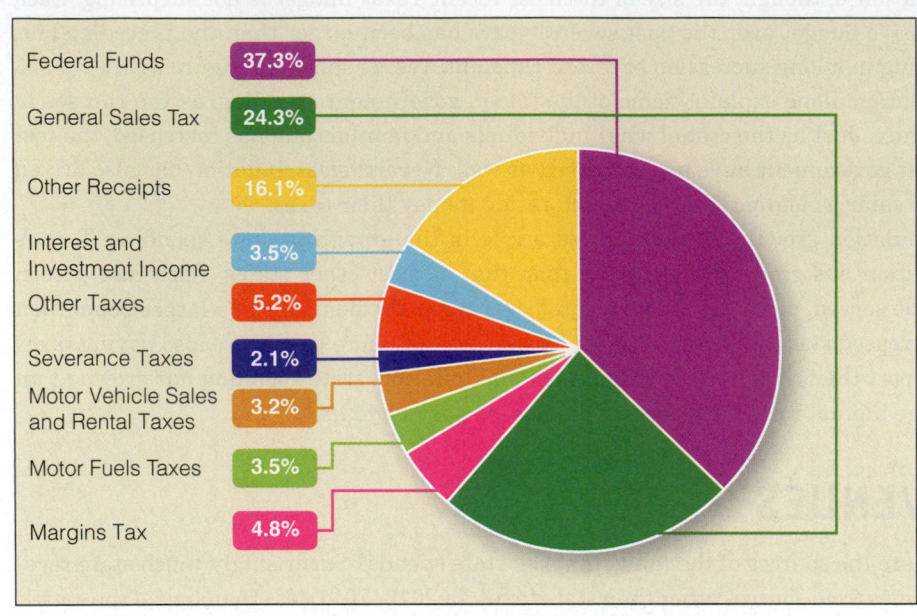

Federal Funds	37.3%
General Sales Tax	24.3%
Other Receipts	16.1%
Interest and Investment Income	3.5%
Other Taxes	5.2%
Severance Taxes	2.1%
Motor Vehicle Sales and Rental Taxes	3.2%
Motor Fuels Taxes	3.5%
Margins Tax	4.8%

Source: Legislative Budget Board, *Fiscal Size-Up, 2010–2011*, p. 21.

grants-in-aid, accounted for 37 percent, interest and investment income for 3.5 percent, and other nontax revenues for the remaining 16 percent, as shown in Figure 27–2. In addition, the Texas legislature has some limited ability to borrow funds.

TAXATION

Property taxes (which are *ad valorem taxes*) were once the major source of state revenue, but property values collapsed during the Great Depression of the 1930s, and with them went the property tax base. At the same time, demands for economic assistance and other public services skyrocketed. Forced to seek other revenue sources, states came to rely on various sales taxes. Texas adopted a tax on cigarettes in 1931, on beer in 1933, and on distilled spirits in 1935. Additional selective sales taxes were adopted in the 1940s and 1950s, but it became apparent that a more general and more broad-based tax would be necessary to meet revenue needs. In 1961, Texas adopted a general sales tax on most items sold. At the same time, Texas, like most states, first drastically reduced its property taxes, and then abandoned them for exclusive use by local governments. Texas has adopted several types of sales taxes:

General Sales Tax
A broad-based tax collected on the retail price of most items.

Selective Sales Tax, or Excise Tax
A tax levied on specific items only.

Hidden Tax
A tax that is reflected in higher prices of the goods and services sold.

Gross-Receipts Tax
A tax on the gross revenues of certain enterprises.

1. **General sales taxes** are broad-based taxes collected on the retail price of most items.
2. **Selective sales taxes**, also known as **excise taxes**, are levied on the sale, manufacture, or use of particular items, such as liquor, cigarettes, and gasoline. Because these taxes are usually included in the items' purchase price, they are often **hidden taxes**.
3. **Gross-receipts taxes** are taxes on the total gross revenue (sales) of certain enterprises, such as utilities and insurance companies. A broad-based margins tax (also known as the franchise tax) applies to the gross sales of most corporations and limited partnerships after taking a deduction for cost of goods or personnel. Small companies, sole proprietorships, and general partnerships are exempt.

Figure 27–2 shows that most state tax revenue in 2010–2011 came from various sales tax collections. The general sales tax (6.25 percent on retail sales of most items) yielded 24.2 percent of the state's revenues; margins tax, 4.8 percent; motor fuels taxes, 3.5 percent; and motor vehicle sales and rental taxes, 3.2 percent. Once a major source of state revenue, *severance taxes* (production taxes on oil and natural gas) now account for only 2.1 percent. Texas also collects special taxes on a range of items and activities, such as tobacco, alcohol, registration of motor vehicles, hotel and motel occupancy, and insurance company operations.

Most states, like Texas, rely heavily on sales and gross-receipts taxes, but few are as dependent on them as Texas. Texas is one of seven states without a personal income tax, and it is one of only four states without a corporate income tax. In 21 states, income taxes account for the largest share of revenues.

State taxes remain low in Texas compared with those in other states. Whereas the average state collects 6.4 percent of its residents' incomes in taxes, Texas collects 4.6 percent. Including local taxes and even the taxes that Texans pay in other states, the Tax Foundation calculated that Texans paid only 8.4 percent of personal income in all state and local taxes in 2009—residents of only seven states paid less.

THE POLITICS OF TAXATION

As with all other public policies, elected politicians, in response to pressure from various interests, design a state's tax policy. Tax policies are hotly debated, and these debates often refer to the public interest, but in reality, taxes are evaluated according to the way particular taxes affect various groups in society.

In the battle over taxation, one of the most volatile issues is what should be taxed. The decision about *what* to tax is really a decision about *whom* to tax and how heavily to tax them. Those with influence on decision makers try to get special tax treatment for themselves and other taxpayers in their group. What seems to motivate almost every group is the principle that the best tax is the one somebody else pays. In the following discussion, we examine what Texas has decided to tax and how those tax choices affect various groups.

Broad-based versus Narrow-based Taxes. Not all taxes are equally effective in raising funds for the public till. **Tax rates** (the tax per unit on a given item or activity) may be raised or lowered, but simply raising the tax rate may not guarantee increased revenues. That is because tax rates affect the **tax base** (the object taxed). Excessive property taxes discourage construction and repair of buildings, for example. High income taxes can discourage general economic activity and individual initiative, undermining the tax base. High tax rates on a narrow base tend to destroy the base and thus make the tax ineffective as a source of revenue. To raise necessary revenue, then, a tax must not discourage too much of the activity that produces the revenue. Instead, most governments tax a wide variety of items and activities, having found that **broad-based taxes** (those paid by a large number of taxpayers)—such as taxes on property, general sales taxes, and income taxes—are most effective at raising revenue.

Regulatory Taxes. Taxes do more than simply pay for the services of government; they often serve as a tool for social or economic control. Rewarding approved behavior with lower taxation or punishing socially undesirable action with a higher tax can have a definite effect on conduct. Many federal tax loopholes (discussed in Chapter 17) are designed to reward particular economic choices, such as saving and investing. Because higher-income taxpayers have more discretionary income, they are financially better able to spend in ways favored by the federal tax structure. Low- and middle-income taxpayers must spend most of their after-tax income on consumption as they buy the essentials of life.

DID YOU KNOW?

That Texans have the third lowest state taxes (as a percentage of income) in the nation?

Tax Rate
The amount of tax per unit of taxable item or activity.

Tax Base
The object or activity taxed.

Broad-Based Tax
A tax designed to be paid by a large number of taxpayers.

DID YOU KNOW?

That, for each admission to an adult business, Texans pay a $5 tax called a "pole tax" (a reference to a prominent stage prop in strip clubs) dedicated to benefit sexual assault victims? The legality of the pole tax is now being challenged in the courts.

Benefits-Received Tax
A tax assessed according to the services received by the payers.

Ability-to-Pay Tax
A tax apportioned according to taxpayers' financial capacity.

Most state **regulatory taxes** are designed to control isolated individual choices, especially those with moral overtones, and are sometimes called "sin taxes." The most prominent example of such state regulatory taxation is the "use" tax to discourage the consumption of such items as alcohol and tobacco. Texas has an excise tax (selective sales tax) on alcoholic beverages, and its cigarette tax is among the highest in the nation.

Texans continue to drink and smoke, so high state use taxes do not entirely prevent "sin," but they place a substantial share of the tax burden on the "sinner." Indeed, the regulatory intent of use taxes may be a rationalization. A large part of the motive behind such taxes may be to place the tax burden on others, since the most vocal advocates of alcohol and tobacco taxes are those who abstain. Proponents, however, argue that regulatory taxes have some effect on behavior; the small annual decline in cigarette sales in Texas may be partially attributed to their cost.

Benefits Received. On the surface, nothing would seem fairer than taxation according to benefits received—let those who benefit from a public service pay for it. Americans have become accustomed to believing that this principle operates in the private sector of the economy and should be applied in the public sector as well.

An example of a **benefits-received tax** in Texas is a 20-cent-per-gallon tax on gasoline and diesel fuel. Three-fourths of the income from taxes on motor fuels is directed into the Texas highway trust fund. The amount of fuel a person uses, and the associated taxes, should represent the benefits that person obtains from highway building and maintenance.

Although not strictly a tax, tuition paid by students in state colleges and universities is based on the benefits-received principle. Most of the cost of public college education in Texas is paid out of state and local tax revenues, but an increasing share of the cost of higher education is paid by student tuitions on the presumption that a student should pay a larger share of the cost of the service from which he or she so greatly benefits. Likewise, revenues from hunting and fishing permits are used for wildlife management.

The benefits-received principle seems reasonable, but few government services are truly special services provided only for special groups. Although the student is a major beneficiary of state-supported higher education, for example, society also benefits from the skills that are added to the bank of human resources. Even the elderly widow who has never owned a car benefits from highways when she buys fresh tomatoes from the supermarket or goes to the hospital in the event of illness. Most government services, such as highways, schools, and law enforcement, take on the character of a public or collective good whose beneficiaries cannot be accurately determined.

Another reason behind government's providing a public service is to make that service available to all. Few people could afford to attend Texas's public colleges and universities, for example, if they had to pay the full cost of higher education.

Ability to Pay. Most taxes are rationalized according to some measure of taxpayers' ability to pay them. The most common **ability-to-pay taxes** are levied on property, sales, and income. Property taxes are based on the premise that the more valuable people's property is, the wealthier they are, and hence, the greater their ability to pay taxes. Sales taxes are based on the premise that the more a person buys, the greater the individual's purchasing power. Income taxes are based on the assumption that the more a person earns, the greater that person's ability to pay.

No base is completely adequate as a measure of a person's ability to pay. During Europe's feudal era, property reflected a person's wealth. With the coming of the commercial revolution, real wealth came to be measured in terms of cash funds rather than land. Nevertheless, the taxes on real estate remain, while more modern forms of ownership, such as stocks, bonds, and other securities, are seldom taxed.

Taxes based on funds (income or expenditure) are also an inadequate measure of true wealth. Income taxes reflect current taxable income and do not account for wealth accumulated in past years. Furthermore, exemptions allow the taxpayer to avoid taxes legally, even on current income. Taxes on consumption and spending (sales taxes) are an even less equitable measure of the ability to pay. Sales taxes measure wealth only as it is spent. Income saved or invested is not spent and so is not taxed. Because it is a general rule of economic behavior that the wealthier a person is, the more the person saves or invests, sales taxes weigh disproportionately on the "have-nots" and "have-littles," who must spend the largest portion of their income on the necessities of life.

Tax Rates. Most people would like to pay as little as possible in taxes, but it turns out that they pay quite a bit (though Texans pay less than most). The average working American works almost one-third of the year (from the first day of January until mid-April) to pay taxes to all levels of government—federal, state, and local.

Averages obscure the real effect of taxes on the individual taxpayer, however. The so-called loopholes in the federal income tax structure have been well publicized, but every tax—federal, state, and local—treats various taxpayers differently. What in the political world is used to justify the unequal burden of taxation?

Progressive Taxes. Progressive taxes are structured like the federal income tax so that rates increase as income increases. Individuals at the very bottom of the financial totem pole have no taxable income and pay nothing, but as incomes increase, the rate increases stepwise from 10 percent to 35 percent. However, the higher rates apply only to *marginal* increments in income. For example, a single individual with $400,000 in taxable income pays 10 percent on the first $8,375, just as lower-income taxpayers do; a rate of 15 percent applies only to taxable income above $8,375 and less than $34,000; and so forth, as shown in Table 27–1.

Liberals and other supporters of progressive taxation argue that persons with higher incomes can better afford to pay higher tax rates and that lower-income persons should be left with a larger share of their incomes to maintain the necessities of life. Lower-income persons also spend a larger share of their incomes on consumption, which is the largest driving force in the economy. Such arguments have not convinced Texans, who adopted a state constitutional amendment that forbids a state income tax unless voters approve. Even then, it can be used only for education and property tax relief.

Regressive Taxes. Texas's taxes are characterized by regressive tax rates, which decline as income increases. For example, the state general sales tax (6.25 percent, among the

TABLE 27–1 Federal Income Tax Rates for Single Individuals, 2010

TAXABLE INCOME	TAX RATE
$0–$8,375	10%
$8,376–$34,000	15%
$34,001–$82,400	25%
$82,401–$171,850	28%
$171,851–$373,650	33%
More than $373,651	35%

Source: Internal Revenue Service.

highest in the nation) is proportional to the value of sales, but because of patterns of consumption, the effective rate actually declines as a person's income increases. Table 27–2 shows that if a family's income increases, so does its general sales tax payment. That fact seems reasonable; we would expect purchases of taxable items to increase as income increases. But note that as income increases, an ever-smaller *percentage* of that income is used for taxable purchases. Presumably, more money is saved, invested, or spent on tax-exempt items. Thus, despite exemptions for certain essential items, the effective rate of the Texas general sales tax declines as family income increases; a working-class individual with an income of $25,000 pays an effective sales tax rate more than twice as high as a person earning $190,000 annually. Similarly, taxpayers pay a smaller percentage of their incomes in property and excise taxes as their incomes increase.

There is a simple explanation for the regressive quality in most consumer taxes—the **declining marginal propensity to consume**. As income increases, a person saves and invests more, thus spending a smaller percentage of that income on consumer items. Compare two smokers: One earns $20,000 per year and the other $200,000 per year. Does the smoker who earns $200,000 per year smoke 10 times as much as the one who earns $20,000? Of course not! Let us assume that each smoker smokes one package of cigarettes per day; each therefore pays $514.65 per year in Texas tobacco taxes. For the low-income individual, tobacco taxes represent almost seven days' earnings, but the other smoker earned the income to pay tobacco taxes in only five hours and 21 minutes.

Consumption of most items follows a similar pattern. The mansion represents a smaller share of income for the millionaire than a shack does for a poor person. Proportionately,

Declining Marginal Propensity to Consume
The tendency, as income increases, for persons to devote a smaller proportion of their income to consumer spending and a larger proportion to savings or investments.

TABLE 27–2 Texas General Sales Tax Paid in Dollars and as a Percentage of Taxable Income, 2009*

TAXABLE INCOME	TEXAS GENERAL SALES TAX	% OF TAXABLE INCOME
$10,000	$259	2.59%
25,000	438	1.75
35,000	534	1.53
45,000	620	1.38
55,000	698	1.27
65,000	771	1.19
75,000	841	1.12
85,000	907	1.07
95,000	970	1.02
110,000	1,055	0.96
130,000	1,173	0.90
150,000	1,279	0.85
170,000	1,386	0.82
190,000	1,485	0.78
1,000,000	1,997	0.20

*For single individuals.
Source: Internal Revenue Service, *Form 1040*, 2009, p. A–13.

the Rolls-Royce is less a burden to its owner than the old Chevrolet to its less affluent owner. Obviously, there are exceptions, but in general, appetites do not increase proportionately with income. Consequently, almost any tax on consumption will not reflect ability to pay. Yet Texas's state and local taxes are based on some form of consumption—property taxes, general sales taxes, gross-receipts taxes, or selective sales taxes.

Even business taxes may be regressive for individuals because of **tax shifting**. Businesses regard their tax burden as part of their operating cost, and they shift much of that cost to customers in the form of higher prices. Thus, business taxes become, in effect, consumer taxes—and, like other consumer taxes, regressive relative to income. Local property taxes are also regressive even when individuals rent their dwellings. When property taxes increase, property owners raise rents.

Taking into account all state and local taxes and tax shifting, Texas has one of the most regressive tax structures among the 50 states. Table 27–3 shows the final incidence of major state and local taxes on Texas families. Those with the lowest fifth of household incomes paid 5.4 percent of their income in general sales taxes—more than three times the portion paid by upper-income households. Lower-income households paid an effective school property tax rate more than twice as high as that of upper-income households. And, for low-income households, the gasoline tax represents more than three times the burden that it does for the upper-income household. Lower-income families even bear a disproportionate share of the state's franchise tax on business.

Conservatives and high-income groups who support regressive taxes argue that taxes on higher-income individuals should be kept low to allow them to save and invest to stimulate the economy; this is known as **supply-side economics**. They argue that applying higher rates to higher incomes is unfair, and that sales and property taxes are easier to collect, more difficult to evade or avoid, and generally less burdensome than progressive income taxes. Some support a national sales tax, also known as the "fair tax," to replace the progressive federal income tax.

Tax Shifting
The practice by which businesses pass taxes to consumers in the form of higher prices.

Supply-Side Economics
The theory that higher-income taxpayers should be taxed less because their savings and investments stimulate the economy.

OTHER REVENUES

Besides state taxes, Texas has several other sources of revenue. The federal government represents an important source of funds, and the state legislature can also borrow funds by issuing bonds, although borrowing is severely restricted. The remainder of the state's revenues comes from miscellaneous sources.

Federal Grants-in-Aid. Federal funds are provided for Texas state and local government programs. For the 2010–2011 period, Texas received about $65.5 billion in federal funds,

TABLE 27–3 Texas Major State and Local Taxes as a Percentage of Household Income, Fiscal Year 2011*

	LOWER INCOME	LOWER MIDDLE	MIDDLE INCOME	UPPER MIDDLE	UPPER INCOME
General Sales Tax	5.4%	3.2%	2.7%	2.4%	1.7%
Franchise (Margins) Tax	0.8	0.5	0.4	0.4	0.3
Gasoline Tax	0.7	0.4	0.4	0.3	0.2
Motor Vehicle Sales Tax	0.5	0.3	0.3	0.3	0.2
School Property Tax	4.8	2.8	2.4	2.4	2.3

*Estimates based on an economic model that takes into account the effect of tax shifting. Household incomes are categorized by quintiles from the lowest one-fifth to the highest one-fifth, each representing 1,818,160 households. Source: Texas Comptroller of Public Accounts, *Exemptions and Tax Incidence*, 2009, February 2009, pp. 47–66.

which represents 36 percent of state revenues (see Figure 27–3). A large majority of Texas's spending for health and human services and more than 45 percent of its spending for transportation originate as federal grants. Although there has been movement toward consolidating federal grant-in-aid programs, they are so numerous that it is only possible to generalize about them.

The evolution of federal grants to state and local governments has a long and controversial history. Although some grants from the national government to the states began as early as 1785, the adoption of the income tax in 1913 drastically altered the financial relationship between the national and state governments by making possible extensive aid to state and local governments.

As discussed in Chapter 3, the Great Depression of the 1930s brought with it a series of financial problems more severe than any that state and local governments had previously experienced. Increased demands for state and local services when revenues were rapidly declining stimulated a long series of New Deal grant-in-aid programs, ranging from welfare to public health and unemployment insurance.

Most of these early grant-in-aid programs were *categorical grants*. Under such aid programs, Congress appropriates funds for a specific purpose and sets up a formula for their distribution. Certain conditions are attached to these grant programs:

1. The receiving government agrees to match the federal funds with its own at a ratio fixed by law (between 10 and 90 percent of the cost of the program).
2. The receiving government administers the program. For example, federal funds are made available for Medicaid, but the state actually pays client benefits.
3. The receiving government must meet minimum standards of federal law. For example, states are forbidden to spend federal funds in any way that promotes racial segregation.

Sometimes additional conditions are attached to categorical grants, such as regional planning and accounting requirements.

FIGURE 27–3 Federal Funds as a Share of All Texas Funds, 2010–2011 (in Billions of Dollars and Percentage of State Revenue)

The pie chart shows that about 36 percent of Texas revenues came from the federal government. Notice that most of these federal funds are for health and human services and stimulus funds for a variety of programs. How can availability of these federal funds impact on policy decisions at the state level?

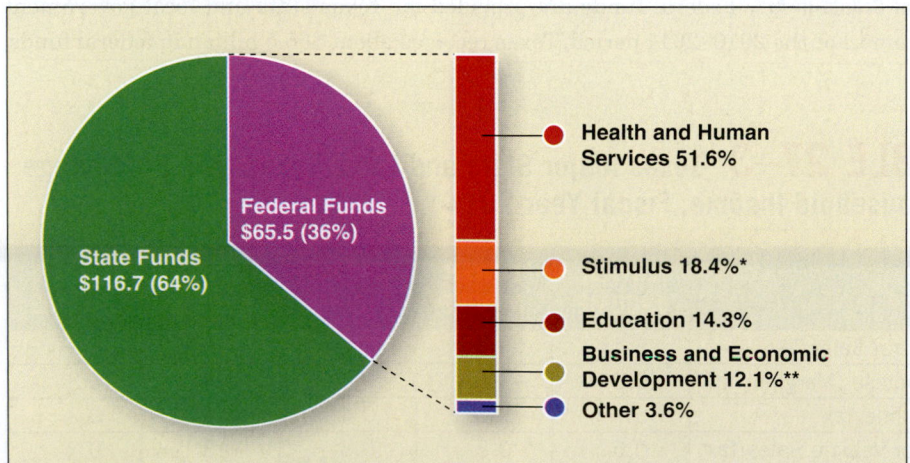

*Stimulus funds are mostly temporary funds made available by the American Recovery and Reinvestment Act of 2009.
**Primarily highways.

Most federal aid, however, now takes the form of newer *block grants* (see Chapter 3) specifying general purposes, such as job training or community development, but allowing the state or local government to determine precisely how the funds should be spent. Conditions may also be established for receipt of block grants, but state and local governments have greater administrative flexibility than with categorical grants. Federal transportation, welfare, and many other grants have been reformed to allow for significant devolution of power to the states through block grants.

The latest expansion of federal grants was a temporary response to the economic collapse that began in 2007. In an attempt to stem the effects of the great recession, Congress passed a series of massive economic stimulus and bailout bills. Among them was the American Recovery and Reinvestment Act of 2009 that pumped $12.1 billion of mostly temporary federal funds into Texas's treasury during the 2010–2011 budget period. More than half of these stimulus grants were spent for education, with much of the remainder going to such state programs as transportation, Medicaid, and unemployment benefits.

Although the infusion of these funds allowed the legislature to balance its budget despite plummeting state tax revenues, these temporary stimulus grants were extremely controversial. Governor Perry took a very high-profile stand against several grants that he believed placed too many restrictions on the state. For example, the state refused about $500 million in unemployment aid because the funds were conditioned on the state expanding eligibility for the program. Such intense resistance to stimulus funds and other increases in federal spending, in Texas and elsewhere, changed the political climate throughout the nation in a way that may dramatically affect future federal aid to state and local governments.

Borrowing. Forty state constitutions or statutes require the legislature to pass a balanced budget. The Texas Constitution is more effective at limiting state borrowing than the constitutions of most other states. At the beginning of each legislative session, the comptroller of public accounts reports to the legislature the total amount of revenues expected from current taxes and other sources, and the legislature can in turn appropriate no more than this amount unless it enacts new tax laws. There are a few exceptions to this general limit: (1) The legislature, by a nearly impossible four-fifths vote, may borrow in emergencies; and (2) the 1876 constitution may be amended to provide for the issuance of bonds for specific programs. Such restrictions have been very effective—Texas has less than one-third the average per capita state debt.

State bonds are classified as (1) **general-obligation bonds** (to be repaid from general revenues), which have been used to finance prison construction, veterans' real estate programs, water development, and higher education; and (2) **revenue bonds**, to be repaid with the revenues from the service they finance, such as higher education bonds financed by tuition revenue.

Other Sources of Revenue. In addition to taxing, grants-in-aid, and borrowing, several miscellaneous sources provide revenue to the Texas government. The state receives a small share of its income from the lottery; various licenses, fines, and fees; dividends from investments; and the sale and leasing of public lands.

General-Obligation Bond
A bond to be repaid from general taxes and other revenues; such bond issues usually must be approved by voters.

Revenue Bond
A bond to be repaid with revenues from the project financed, such as utilities or sports stadiums.

BUDGETING AND SPENDING

Having discussed the various sources of state revenue, we now turn to the other end of the income stream—budgeting and spending. We begin by describing the budgetary process and then discuss spending policies.

THE BUDGETARY PROCESS

The budgetary process includes two basic steps. First, a budget plan must be formulated. Then, the legislature must appropriate the funds necessary to implement the plan.

Budget Planning. Every state has developed some sort of central budgeting agency. Typically, such agencies are set up within the executive branch and are provided with a staff to analyze and evaluate budget requests before submitting a comprehensive budget to the legislature for its consideration. In some states, budget preparation is the joint responsibility of both the legislative and the executive branches.

Texas has established a dual system of budget preparation in which the legislative and executive branches each have separate budget agencies: (1) the Legislative Budget Board (LBB), a legislative agency made up of the presiding officers of the Texas house and senate plus four other members from each of the two houses, and (2) the governor's office.

These two budgeting agencies engage in some joint activities. A full year before the legislature meets, they jointly prepare forms on which the state's operating agencies submit their budgetary requests. After these requests are submitted, joint hearings are held, but the LBB's staff and the governor's staff independently prepare budget proposals. Not surprisingly, these two proposed budgets differ considerably, as each of the two branches, the legislative and the executive, has its own distinct perspectives, goals, and political considerations.

In preparing their budgetary requests, agencies have a strong tendency toward **incremental budgeting**—that is, they tend to base their current budget requests on past appropriations plus some additional amount. In the rush of the short 140-day session, the legislature cannot conscientiously evaluate billions of dollars in budget requests, so it reviews ongoing programs in light of past expenditures, whereas new spending programs are viewed more critically. This process inherently assumes that past appropriations reflect current needs. Reformers frequently advocate **zero-based budgeting**, which would instead evaluate existing programs as if they were new programs for which funding had to be justified.

Appropriations. The legislature legally authorizes the state to spend money to provide its various programs and services through the **appropriations process**. Appropriations bills follow the same steps as other legislation (described in Chapter 24), through standing committee consideration, floor action, conference committee compromise, final voting, and approval by the governor. During most of the legislative process, the recommendations of the LBB carry greater weight than those of the governor, because they usually reflect the wishes of the legislature's powerful presiding officers.

Perhaps the governor's most effective influence in the appropriations process results from the item veto. Like 42 other governors, the Texas chief executive can veto particular items of expenditure without vetoing the whole bill. Although all vetoes can be legally overridden by a two-thirds vote of the legislature, in practice, item vetoes on appropriations bills are final. The legislature finishes its work on the appropriations bill so late in the session that it has usually gone home by the time the governor takes up the bill; obviously, such after-session vetoes are immune to an override attempt.

Despite the importance of the appropriations process, the legislature's control over state expenditures is limited in several ways. **Dedicated funds** prevent the legislature from systematically reviewing the state's expenditures. For example, three-fourths of revenues from motor fuel taxes are dedicated to the State Highway Fund and one-fourth to the Available School Fund. Earnings from state lands are automatically directed to the Permanent University Fund and the Permanent School Fund. Contributions to the Teacher Retirement Fund may be used only for their specified purpose. The Texas

Incremental Budgeting
A budgeting practice in which an agency bases its budget requests on past appropriations plus increases to cover inflation and increased demand for services; this process assumes that past appropriations justify current budgetary requests.

Zero-Based Budgeting
A budgeting practice in which existing programs are evaluated as if they were new programs rather than on the basis of past levels of funding.

Appropriations Process
The process by which a legislative body legally authorizes a government to spend specific sums of money to provide various programs and services.

Dedicated Funds
Revenues dedicated for a specific purpose by the constitution or by statute.

Constitution and state statutes automatically channel 45 percent of state revenues to specified purposes with little or no legislative involvement. Federal grants, court orders, and other restrictions also limit the legislature as it adopts appropriations bills. Only one-fifth of the state's budget is discretionary funding (unaffected by federal, state, statutory, or court requirements).

Biennial legislative sessions make it difficult to spend state funds rationally. It is impossible to predict with precision, say, how many students will enroll in a college for the upcoming semester. Nevertheless, the legislature is expected to predict the state's financial needs two years in advance based on how many students will enroll in all public colleges in the state as well as elementary and secondary schools, how many applicants will be found eligible for unemployment and welfare benefits, how many potholes will develop along state highways, how many criminals will be sentenced to state prison, how many patients will be admitted to state hospitals, and so on. Inevitably, some agencies will be overfunded and others will have too little. Overfunded agencies always find ways to spend whatever money they have, whereas others literally run out of money during the two-year budget period.

THE POLITICS OF SPENDING

A wide variety of factors affects the level of state spending and complicates efforts toward rational budget planning. Nowhere is the dynamic nature of politics as evident as in public finance; nowhere is the conflict between competing economic interests more visible than in the budgetary process. Behind the large figures that represent the state's final budget are vigorous conflict, compromise, and coalition building. Most of society's programs are evaluated not only according to their merit but also in light of the competing demands of other programs and other economic interests. Government programs and problems, including highways, education, urban decay, poverty, crime, and the environment—in short, all the problems and challenges of a modern society—compete for a share of the public treasury.

That if you counted one dollar every second, it would take you about 2,889 years to count the state's annual expenditures?

Powerful political constituencies, interest groups, and their lobbyists join forces with state agencies to defend the programs that benefit them. This alliance between administrative agencies and interest groups brings great pressure to bear on the legislative process. Legislators trade votes (a process called logrolling) to gain funding to benefit their districts or their political supporters.

No single decision better typifies the political character of a state than its budget decision. The whole pattern of spending is, in a sense, a shorthand description of which problems the state has decided to face and which challenges it has chosen to meet. The budget shows how much of which services the state will offer and to whom. Figure 27–4 shows how Texans spent their state revenues in the 2010–2011 budget period. The most costly service in Texas remains education. Public and higher education accounted for 41.4 percent of the state budget. Health and human services (including Medicaid and public assistance), in second place, accounted for 32.8 percent. Transportation, primarily highways, accounted for 10.2 percent. These three services consumed more than four-fifths of the state's budget, with a wide variety of miscellaneous services using up the remainder.

Both individuals and groups benefit from government services, and seeking these benefits is the object of much of the political activity in the state. Political controversy develops because state services affect various groups differently, and these groups evaluate state programs according to their competing self-interests and their conflicting views of the public interest. It is important to outline the state's most significant services and then explore some of the major political issues surrounding them.

FIGURE 27–4 State Appropriations by Function, 2010–2011 (in Billions)

The largest slice of Texas's budget pie goes to education, but the portion spent for health care is rapidly rising. Explain why state spending generates political controversy.

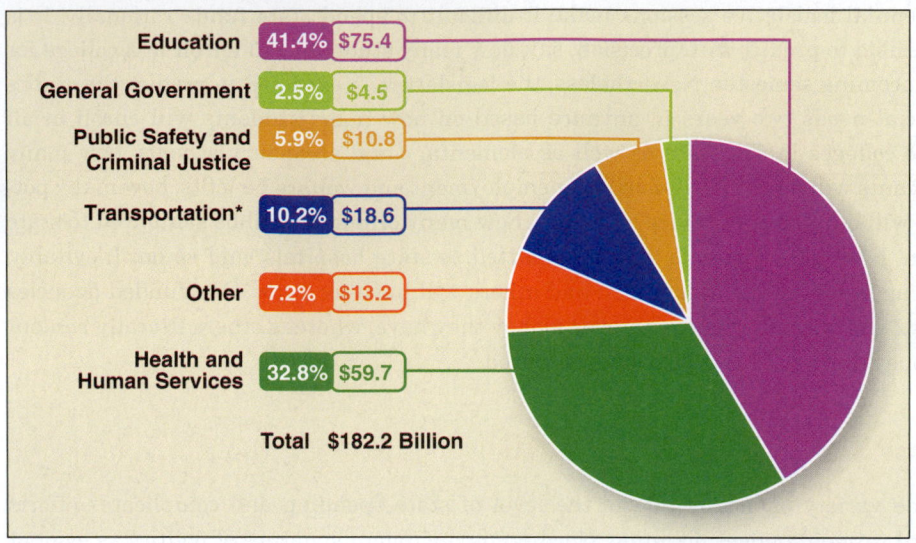

Education	41.4%	$75.4
General Government	2.5%	$4.5
Public Safety and Criminal Justice	5.9%	$10.8
Transportation*	10.2%	$18.6
Other	7.2%	$13.2
Health and Human Services	32.8%	$59.7

Total $182.2 Billion

*Primarily highways.
Source: Legislative Budget Board.

EDUCATION

The educational system in Texas includes elementary and secondary schools (the public schools) and the college and university system (higher education).

ELEMENTARY AND SECONDARY SCHOOLS

Public schools were accepted institutions in the North by the early 19th century, but they did not take root in the South (including Texas) until after the Civil War. Not until the constitution of 1876 provided that alternate sections of public land grants must be set aside to finance schools did the state begin to commit itself to locally administered, optional public schools.

Meaningful state support for public education started with a compulsory attendance law, enacted in 1915, and a constitutional amendment that provided for free textbooks in 1918. In 1949, the Gilmer-Aikin law increased state funding and established the Texas Education Agency (TEA), which carries out the state's educational program.

Recent Trends. Sweeping changes in education resulted when House Bill 72 passed in 1984 to establish statewide **accountability** standards for student test performance and teacher competence. Former President George W. Bush later took the use of high-stakes testing nationwide with his No Child Left Behind program.

Although the standards used to measure public school performance are sometimes controversial, there has been a recent trend toward using them to bring market forces to the public school system. Some teachers and administrators receive merit pay, bonuses for improved student achievement. To introduce the element of competition, the state legislature authorized the State Board of Education to establish schools with special program charters, able to recruit students from across existing school district boundaries. Many state legislators now also favor *privatization* by providing vouchers to help students buy their education from private and religious organizations.

Accountability
Responsibility for a program's results—for example, using measurable standards to hold public schools responsible for their students' performance.

Today, public elementary and secondary education has grown from a fledgling, underfinanced local function into a major state–local partnership. The TEA administers approximately 29 percent of all state expenditures, helping local school districts educate the approximately 90 percent of Texas students who attend public elementary and secondary schools. Public policy decisions affect the knowledge, attitudes, and earning potential of these 4.7 million students and the approximately 300,000 individuals who teach them.

Public School Administration. As in other states, public school administration in Texas has three basic aspects:

1. Substantial local control in a joint state–local partnership.
2. Emphasis on professional administration supervised by laypersons.
3. Independence from the general structure of government.

Next, we consider the relationship of state administration and local administration.

State Administration. The Texas Constitution, the legislature, and the State Board of Education (SBOE) have established the basic decision-making organizations and financial arrangements for public education in the state. The legislature approves the budget for the state's share of the cost of public education and sets certain standards, but it leaves most routine decision making to the TEA and local school districts.

The State Board of Education, which we discussed in Chapter 25, sets curriculum requirements for public schools and establishes general rules and guidelines for the TEA. The SBOE approves organizational plans, recommends a budget to the governor and the Legislative Budget Board, and implements funding formulas established by the legislature. It sets standards for operating public schools and requires management, cost-accounting, and financial reports from local districts.

The commissioner of education is appointed by the governor with the consent of the senate to serve as the state's principal executive officer for education; she or he is assigned several assistant and associate commissioners and has a professional staff. They carry out the regulations and policies established by the legislature and the SBOE concerning public school programs.

DID YOU KNOW?

That Texas students taking the Scholastic Aptitude Test (SAT) in 2008 ranked 46th among the 50 states?

Local Administration. Texas has 1,030 regular school districts (more than any other state), and these districts are the basic structure for local control. Voters in independent school districts elect seven or nine trustees (depending on the district's population) at large or from single-member electoral districts for either three- or four-year terms. These trustees set the district's tax rate and determine school policies within the guidelines established by the TEA. They approve the budget, contract for instructional supplies and construction, and hire and fire personnel. Their most important decision is the hiring of a professional superintendent, who is responsible for the executive or administrative functions of the school district.

Elected state and local school boards traditionally followed the recommendations of professional administrators (the commissioner and the superintendents), and most educational decisions have been made independently of general government. Nevertheless, one should not conclude that independence from general government, localization, or "professionalism" has kept education free of politics. On the contrary, elected boards, especially the State Board of Education, have become quite politically assertive in recent years. Whenever important public decisions are made, political controversy and conflict arise.

The Politics of Public Education. One of the most important decisions concerning public education is what education should be. Should it promote traditional views of society, reinforce the dominant political culture, and teach "acceptable" attitudes? Alternatively, should it teach students to be independent thinkers, capable of evaluating ideas for themselves? Because the Texas state educational system determines the curriculum, selects textbooks, and hires and fires teachers, it must answer these fundamental questions.

Curriculum. The SBOE determines most of the basic curriculum for Texas public schools. Some school districts supplement this basic curriculum with a variety of elective and specialized courses, but in the basic courses—history, civics, biology, and English—students are most likely to be exposed to issues that may fundamentally affect their attitudes. How should a student be exposed to the theory of evolution? What about a course in sex education? In the social sciences, should the political system be pictured in terms of its ideals or as it actually operates, with all of its mistakes and weaknesses? How should the roles of women and minorities be presented? Should students who do not speak standard English be gradually taught English through bilingual education, or should they immediately be immersed in the core curriculum taught in English?

Recent SBOE decisions illustrate how course content can become political. After adopting controversial science and literature curriculum revisions in recent years, Texas's State Board of Education caused an even louder uproar in 2010 when it largely ignored the advice of professional educators and voted along party lines to establish the social studies curriculum standards for the upcoming decade. Critics charged that the SBOE had hijacked the state's educational apparatus to impose a conservative, Christian fundamentalist political agenda on public school students.

Critics focused on standards that require teaching the political beliefs of conservative icons such as Phyllis Schlafly, Newt Gingrich, the Moral Majority, and the National Rifle Association. Meanwhile, students will be taught that Senator Joseph McCarthy's anti-communist crusade may have been justified. Confederate president Jefferson Davis's inaugural address will be taught alongside Abraham Lincoln's speeches, and the role of slavery as a cause of the Civil War will be downplayed.

The requirement that students learn the concept of "responsibility for the common good" (which one board member described as "communistic") has been removed from the curriculum. Students will learn that the United States is a "constitutional republic" rather than a "democratic society" and that the words "separation of church and state" are not in the U.S. Constitution. Students will evaluate how the United Nations undermines U.S. sovereignty and learn about the devaluation of the dollar, including the abandonment of the gold standard. The curriculum standards emphasize the biblical and Judeo-Christian influences on the founding fathers and mandate that students learn the benefits of free enterprise, which is mentioned more than 80 times in the curriculum requirements.

Aside from social and political content, the substance of education in Texas has other important practical consequences as well. Although a large proportion of public school students will never enroll in an institution of higher learning, much educational effort and testing have been directed toward college preparatory courses that provide graduates few, if any, usable job skills. Historically, vocational, agricultural, and home economics programs were viewed as "burial grounds" for pupils who had failed in the traditional academic programs. Today, almost half of public school students are enrolled in "career and technology" programs, and one in five is in "family and consumer sciences." Although program titles have changed, much remains to be done to meet the need for highly skilled technical workers who possess other practical life skills.

DID YOU KNOW?

That the percentage of adults with a high school diploma is lower in Texas than in any other state?

Textbooks. The SBOE selects a list of approved textbooks that the state will buy for public school courses. The selection process generates intense political battles between conservative organizations (such as the Texas Public Policy Foundation and Texas Freedom Works) and liberal groups (such as the Texas Freedom Network). Conservatives have usually dominated the textbook battle, and some publishers have withdrawn their text offerings or changed the content of their texts to satisfy the SBOE.

Legally, the State Board of Education can determine only the accuracy of textbooks, but it has used this power to pressure publishers to submit texts that reflect the political and religious values of its members. One publisher eliminated references to "fossil fuels formed millions of years ago" from a science text because it conflicts with some interpretations of the time line in the Bible. Another publisher eliminated some sections perceived as too kind to Muslims because they had asserted that Osama bin Laden's actions were inconsistent with commonly accepted Islamic teachings. An environmental science text was rejected because it favorably mentioned the Endangered Species Act and warned of the threat of global warming—one group argued that it was unpatriotic to refer to the fact that the United States represents 5 percent of the world's population but produces 25 percent of greenhouse gases. Under pressure from religious conservatives, publishers submitted health textbooks that presented an abstinence-only approach to sex education, excluding essential information about how to prevent unwanted pregnancies and sexually transmitted diseases.

Because Texas controls the second largest textbook market in the nation, the state's textbook decisions have historically determined the content of texts used in public schools in much of the nation. In the future, however, school systems in other states may have more alternatives to Texas-preferred texts. Electronic books, specialty publishing, and custom options are replacing market-dominant, fixed-content texts, and the national textbook market is becoming much more competitive.

Faculties. A 15-member state board for educator certification establishes standards for qualification, conduct, and certification of public school teachers. Actual hiring of teachers is a local matter. Most districts do not follow a publicly announced policy of hiring or dismissing teachers because of their political viewpoints, but in many districts, teachers are carefully screened for their attitudes.

Salary and working conditions are perpetual issues of dissatisfaction among teachers because they affect morale and recruitment. The student-to-teacher ratios in Texas

STATE BOARD OF EDUCATION members are shown at their desks with sample health textbooks presented by publishers hoping for a lucrative position on the state-approved textbook list. Social conservatives and sex education advocates squared off at the final hearing before the board made its selections. (AP Photo/Harry Cabluck)

schools remain similar to those in other states, but increasing public demands for accountability have added reporting and other paperwork to teachers' workloads beyond the standard expectations for lesson planning, grading, and communicating with parents.

Expected income is certainly a factor when people choose their careers, and education simply does not rank favorably among the professions. Texas teachers earn even less than public school teachers in other states. The National Education Association reported that Texas teachers' average salary of $46,179 in 2007–2008 was 11 percent below the national average. The TEA reported that one-third of beginning teachers leave the profession by their fifth year.

Another issue for teachers has been the use of "high-stakes" testing, such as the Texas Assessment of Knowledge and Skills and the National Assessment of Education Progress (the "Nation's Report Card"). Teachers' groups have objected to the use of these test results in retention, promotion, and salary decisions on grounds that they do not accurately measure the full range of teachers' contributions to student knowledge and that their use causes faculty to "teach the test" while ignoring other valuable skills and knowledge that are not included in standardized tests.

Students. Public schools have changed considerably in recent years. The number of students attending Texas public schools has been increasing at a rate of about 2 percent per year, and that increase is expected to continue for the next decade. Students are also more ethnically diverse and are increasingly from low-income backgrounds. Almost two-thirds of them are minorities and 57 percent of them are from low-income families. This changing student population seems to present a challenge to public schools, as a significant achievement gap remains between the performance of Anglo students and that of Latino and African American students.

Scores on the Texas Assessment of Knowledge and Skills (TAKS) test measure student achievement in lower grades, and end-of-course (EOC) exams in core classes are used to evaluate high school student performance. Student accountability programs limit *social promotion* (promotion to the next grade based on age rather than level of learning), and students failing TAKS are offered accelerated instruction in appropriate subjects. Perhaps as a result of these efforts, student performance on standardized tests has been improving somewhat during the past several years, and the performance gaps between ethnic groups has narrowed. Despite these improvements, 24.5 percent more Anglos than African Americans passed TAKS, while 17.7 percent more Anglos than Latinos passed TAKS in 2009.

Public School Finance. In 2007–2008, expenditures for public school operations in Texas were $7,987 per student, ranking Texas 45th among the 50 states (19 percent below the national average). The actual distribution of these funds is governed according to extremely complex rules and mathematical formulas that occupy six chapters totaling over 75,000 words in the Texas Education Code. Although public school accountants and financial officers must understand the nuances of these rules in order to maximize funding for their respective districts, you will need to understand only the system's most basic features in order to engage intelligently in the public debate that surrounds public school finance. The following discussion is organized around the three basic sources of public school funding—federal, state, and local.

Federal grants have increased substantially in recent years. In addition to ongoing federal programs for child nutrition and special-needs, military, and low-income students, the American Recovery and Reinvestment Act of 2009 (known as the stimulus bill) pumped $6 billion into Texas public schools during the 2010–2011 budget period. These temporary federal funds were designed to offset the shortfall in state and local revenues

DID YOU KNOW?

That on average, Texas physicians earn $164,020; lawyers, $124,600; pharmacists, $108,630; and elementary school teachers, $45,860?

DID YOU KNOW?

That Texas per student expenditures were less than in 44 other states?

caused by the recent economic recession. Such funds are not expected to be available in future years, and as a result, the state and local school districts will strain to fill the gap left in the absence of these onetime federal grants.

State funding comes from a variety of sources. The Permanent School Fund invests receipts of rentals, sales, and mineral royalties from Texas's public lands. Only the interest and dividends from this permanent endowment may be spent. Earnings from the Permanent School Fund and one-fourth of the motor fuels tax make up the Available School Fund. Part of this fund is used for textbooks; the remainder is distributed to local school districts based on the number of students in average daily attendance. Basing distribution of state funds on attendance focuses a school district's attention on truancy.

The Foundation School Program (FSP) accounts for the largest portion of state and local funding by far. State funds from general revenues, the margins tax on business (the franchise tax), and a portion of tobacco taxes are distributed to districts according to formulas based on district and student characteristics. The FSP is structured as a state–local partnership to bring some financial equality to local districts, despite vast differences in local tax resources.

Local funding comes primarily from ad valorem property taxes. The market value of property is determined by the county appraisal authority for all local governments within the county, and local district boards then set the property tax rate, stated as an amount per $100 of property value. Local school district trustees may set the property tax rate for maintenance and operations up to $1.17 per $100 valuation.

These property taxes are used to pay about 55 percent of the FSP basic operating expenses, with the state paying for the remainder. The state supplements local funds to ensure that each district has a basic allotment of $4,765 per student and guarantees that each additional cent in local tax above the minimum must yield at least $31.95 per student.

The system of basic allotments and guaranteed yields is designed to provide some financial equity among local school districts. However, local revenues from property taxes vary so much among school districts that the state has been forced to establish certain "recapture" requirements as well. Richer districts such as those with taxable property worth more than $319,000 per student may, under certain circumstances, be required to share their local revenue with poorer districts. They may choose one of several mechanisms to provide aid directly to poorer districts, but most send money to the state for redistribution to other districts.

Some local tax revenues are not subject to these "recapture" requirements. Without aiding poorer districts, wealthier districts may tax up to an additional 50¢ per $100 for construction, capital improvements, and debt service and they may also collect a small amount for educational enrichment.

School-Finance Inequities. The current school-finance system resulted from more than two decades of struggle, litigation, and failed reform efforts. Because the old state funding system could not overcome significant inequalities resulting from heavy dependence on local property taxes, a lawsuit attacking the Texas system of educational finance was filed in federal court. Parents of several students in the Edgewood Independent School District in San Antonio charged that funding inequalities violated the Fourteenth Amendment to the U.S. Constitution, which guarantees that no state shall deny any person the equal protection of the laws. Ultimately, the United States Supreme Court declined to strike down Texas's system of school finance because it failed to find a fundamental U.S. constitutional right to equally funded public education.[1]

---

[1]*San Antonio Independent School District v. Rodriguez*, 411 U.S. 1 (1973).

Later, the battle over inequality shifted to the state level. In 1987, as mentioned in earlier chapters, a state district court decided a different challenge to the funding system, *Edgewood v. Kirby*. The court based its decision on a variety of provisions in the Texas Constitution guaranteeing a suitable and efficient school system. Citing numerous disparities between wealthy and poor districts resulting from heavy reliance on local property taxes, the court found the funding system unconstitutional. In 1989, the Texas Supreme Court unanimously upheld the lower court decision.[2]

After a series of aborted attempts and adverse court rulings, the legislature established the current system. Revenues per student now depend primarily on the school district's tax rate, because the state guarantees that a particular local property tax rate will produce a specific amount of revenue or the state will make up the difference. The requirement that wealthier districts share their revenues with poorer districts outraged some parents and school officials, who described the system as "socialistic" or a "Robin Hood" plan that interfered with local control and their right to educate their children.

Despite the changes, there is still some disparity in revenues per student among school districts. For example, the Dallas Independent School District still has $29,600 more revenues for a class of 20 students than does the Huntsville Independent School District. Yet ironically, the poorer school district's students perform better on standard tests. And despite more equalized revenues, suburban school districts such as Plano and Alamo Heights continue to have far more students passing TAKS than poor, urban, minority school districts such as Dallas and Houston. Table 27–4 shows that student TAKS test scores—and the factors sometimes thought to affect them—vary dramatically from district to district in Texas.

TABLE 27–4 Selected Texas School District Profiles

SCHOOL DISTRICT	ENROLLMENT	PERCENT MINORITY*	PERCENT ECONOMICALLY DISADVANTAGED	STUDENT/ TEACHER RATIO	PERCENT MEETING 2009 TAKS STANDARD†	REVENUE PER STUDENT‡
Houston I.S.D.	199,524	92.2%	81.0%	16.6	69%	$9,969
Dallas I.S.D.	157,174	95.4	86.1	14.4	64	10,248
Plano I.S.D.	53,906	49.3	20.7	13.3	89	10,012
Edgewood I.S.D.	11,608	99.2	90.8	14.5	60	10,626
Huntsville I.S.D.	5,996	52.8	56.5	14.7	75	8,768
Alamo Heights I.S.D.	4,618	38.0	17.3	14.4	85	10,105
West Orange-Cove I.S.D.	2,591	73.4	80.7	13.5	51	9,939
Wink-Loving I.S.D.	322	36.0	36.3	7.4	73	23,161
Statewide	**4,728,204**	**66.0**	**56.7**	**14.4**	**74**	**9,739**

*African American, Hispanic, Native American, Asian, or Pacific Islander.
†The Standard Accountability Indicator among all grades tested.
‡Actual revenues from all sources.
Source: Texas Education Agency, *2008–2009 Academic Excellence Indicator System, District Reports.*

[2]*Edgewood Independent School District v. Kirby*, 777 S.W. 2d 391 (Tex. 1989).

HIGHER EDUCATION

Like public schools, higher education is a major state service, accounting for 12 percent of state expenditures during the 2010–2011 budget period. Texas public institutions of higher education include 35 general academic institutions and universities (with three more scheduled to emerge), nine health-related institutions, and one technical college system with four campuses. Fifty public community colleges operate on 80 campuses.

Figure 27–5 shows that public institutions enroll 90 percent of all students in Texas higher education. The majority of students enroll in public community colleges, where average tuition and fees cost about one-third as much as at public universities.

Administration of Colleges and Universities. The Texas Higher Education Coordinating Board was established to coordinate the complex system of higher education in the state. The governor, with the consent of the senate, appoints its 18 members, who serve for six-year terms. The Coordinating Board appoints the commissioner of higher education to supervise its staff. Together, the board and staff outline the role of each public college and university and determine future needs for programs, curricula, and physical plants.

Because Texas's colleges and universities were not established systematically, the Coordinating Board has difficulty imposing a sensible plan for them to relate to one another. Politically powerful boards of regents compete to impose their views on higher education, as do other groups. Regents and trustees set basic policies for these institutions, within the limits of state law and the rules and guidelines established by the Coordinating Board.

Some boards of regents govern single-campus institutions. Others govern institutions located on several campuses:

- The University of Texas system includes the University of Texas at Austin (with the nation's third largest student population on a single campus) and other campuses located at Arlington, Brownsville, Dallas, El Paso, Permian Basin, San Antonio, and Tyler, as well as the University of Texas—Pan American and several medical and health units.

FIGURE 27–5 Texas Higher Education Enrollments, Fall 2008

Higher education is overwhelmingly a responsibility of the state (left pie chart), and a majority of public college students enroll in community colleges (right pie chart). What challenges do growing enrollments present to Texas's institutions of higher learning? How successful are these institutions at retaining and graduating students who have enrolled in them?

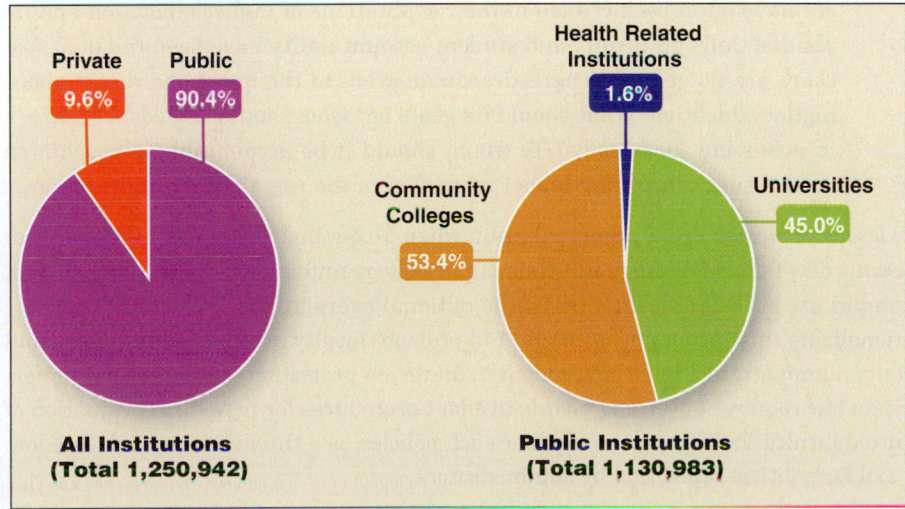

Source: Texas Higher Education Coordinating Board.

- The Texas A&M system has its main campus at College Station, with additional campuses at Corpus Christi, Commerce, Texarkana, Galveston, Kingsville, Prairie View A&M, Tarleton State, West Texas A&M, Texas A&M International, and several smaller campuses.
- The Texas State University system includes Sam Houston State, Texas State University at San Marcos, Sul Ross State, Sul Ross State—Rio Grande Valley, Lamar University, Lamar Institute of Technology, and Lamar State College in Orange and Port Arthur.
- The University of Houston has its main campus in Houston, as well as a downtown campus and campuses at Clear Lake and Victoria.
- The Texas Tech System includes the main campus at Lubbock, several other Western Texas campuses, health science centers, and Angelo State University.

The administrative structure of senior colleges and universities may include systemwide administrators (chancellors), campus presidents, deans, and other officers. The Coordinating Board also generally supervises community colleges, which are authorized and financed largely by the state. Unlike four-year institutions (which are usually designed to attract students from larger regions of the state and nation as well as international students), community colleges are established by voters in one or more school districts primarily to serve area residents. They may be governed either by an independently elected board or by the trustees of a local public school district.

The traditional role of two-year colleges, once referred to as "junior colleges," has been to offer academic courses to first- and second-year students who would later transfer to four-year colleges. Although most of their students are enrolled in transferable academic courses, two-year colleges have responded to the demands resulting from economic diversification by adopting a community college approach—adding adult, continuing, and special education courses as well as technical specialties. The curriculum, low cost, and geographic and financial accessibility of community colleges have resulted in increasing enrollments, especially in academic programs.

The Politics of Higher Education. It is difficult to measure objectively many of the benefits of higher education, such as personal satisfaction and contributions to society. Individual financial benefits, however, are very clear. High school graduates have an average annual income of $31,283; those with an associate's degree earn $39,506; and those with at least a bachelor's degree have an average income of $67,155.[3]

Despite its benefits, legislative bodies and boards of regents and trustees have often been critical in their evaluations of higher education and its results. Calls for faculty and student accountability have been frequent. Yet there are no generally agreed-upon answers to the questions raised about higher education: What should its goals be? How should it measure success in achieving those goals? To whom should it be accountable? We examine some issues concerning higher education in the remainder of this section.

Faculty Issues. Salaries are a perpetual issue when Texas institutions of higher education recruit new faculty. Average full-time public college and university faculty salaries, for example, are still significantly below the national average.

Rationalizing their attempts as an effort to promote faculty accountability, college and university administrators have long sought to dilute job-protection guarantees for professors. State law requires governing boards to adopt procedures for periodic reevaluation of all tenured faculty. Faculties generally fear such policies as a threat to academic freedom and a tool for political repression by administrators.

[3]U.S. Census Bureau, Current Population Survey, *2009 Annual Social and Economic Supplement,* Table PINC-04.

Financial Issues. Financing higher education is a continuing issue. Like elementary and secondary schools, most colleges and universities in Texas must struggle with relatively small budgets. Meanwhile, increasing college enrollments and demands for specialized, high-cost programs are increasing at a time when unemployment compensation, social services, health care, and other services are also placing more demands on depressed state revenues. Revenues in turn are limited by the legislature's reluctance to increase taxes.

Student Accessibility. Proposals to cope with financial pressures include closing institutions with smaller enrollments, reducing duplication, restricting student services, raising tuitions, and delaying construction plans or implementation of new degree programs. Most of these policies have the effect of limiting student access to higher education, but rising costs represent the greatest potential obstacle to a college education for most students.

Since the Texas legislature deregulated tuitions and fees, public college and university boards have dealt with rising costs by raising tuition, mandatory student fees, and residence costs. Between the fall semesters of 2003 and 2009, average tuition and fees for full-time students at Texas public universities rose 72 percent, to $3,323; tuition and fees for the average in-district community college student rose at a similar rate to $743 for 12 hours in the spring semester of 2010.[4] Future financial accessibility of higher education is a growing concern, especially because Pell grants and other forms of financial aid are not keeping pace with rising costs, and students are financing more of the increased cost of higher education by borrowing.

Student Diversity. In addition to affordability, other cultural, structural, and historical factors have limited access to certain populations that have traditionally been underserved by Texas institutions of higher learning. Economically disadvantaged people, those who live in rural areas, and ethnic minorities are notably underrepresented in colleges and universities. Institutions of higher education have struggled with minority student recruitment in an effort to increase **ethnic diversity** and offer more access to underserved populations. Those efforts became especially difficult when the federal Fifth Circuit Court of Appeals ruled that race could not be considered in **affirmative action** admissions policies.[5]

Many states attempted to achieve diversity by considering low family income and other special nonracial obstacles that make it difficult to meet standard admission criteria. The Texas legislature responded by requiring that general academic institutions (except now for the University of Texas at Austin) must automatically admit students from the top 10 percent of their high school graduating class regardless of test scores. More female, African American, Latino, low-income, and rural students have been admitted to state universities under the "10 percent" rule than under traditional admission criteria.

Meanwhile, more recent U.S. Supreme Court decisions have allowed race to be considered directly in college admissions policies as a last resort when other minority recruitment efforts have not produced a diverse student population and so long as specific point advantages are not assigned to minorities.[6] These decisions have, once again, sent some college administrators scrambling to find acceptable affirmative action policies.

Student Retention. Of course, admission to institutions of higher learning is hardly the only measure of success. While students may benefit from even a short experience in

DID YOU KNOW?

That Texas is one of 10 states that charge in-state college tuition to qualified illegal immigrants who graduate from the state's high schools?

Ethnic Diversity
Inclusion of significant numbers of nonwhites such as Latinos, African Americans, Asian Americans, and Native Americans.

Affirmative Action
Positive efforts to recruit ethnic minorities, women, and the economically disadvantaged. Sometimes these efforts are limited to publicity drives among target groups, but such programs sometimes include use of ethnicity or gender as part of the qualification criteria.

---

[4]Texas Higher Education Coordinating Board, *College Costs, Fall 2003–Fall 2009,* http://www.thecb.state.tx.us/Reports/PDF/2010.PDF; Texas Association of Community Colleges, *2003–04 Tuition and Fees* at http://www.tacc.org/pdf/tuition08.pdf and *Spring 2010 Tuition and Fees: Texas Public Community Colleges* at http://www.tacc.org/documents/Sp10tuition_000.pdf.
[5]*Hopwood v. Texas,* 84 F.3d 720 (5th Cir. 1996).
[6]*Grutter v. Bollinger,* 539 U.S. 306 (2003); and *Gratz v. Bollinger,* 539 U.S. 234 (2003).

POLITICS WITH A purpose

Fighting Tuition Hikes

On March 5, 2010, students in 33 states protested rising tuitions at public institutions of higher learning. Their rallies at the University of Texas at Austin and the University of Houston were among the largest in Texas. Many of these students were driven by self-interest because governing boards at Texas's public colleges and universities had raised tuitions more than 70 percent since the state legislature discarded statewide tuition caps in 2003, necessitating ever-rising student debt to pay for these growing costs.

Despite the obviously self-serving purpose of these student protests, the general public may also have a substantial interest in the outcome of the battle over spending at state-supported institutions of higher learning. Broader economic benefits from public investments in higher education seem quite impressive. According to a study funded by the Bill and Melinda Gates Foundation for the Commission for a College Ready Texas, every dollar invested in higher education yields eight dollars in enhanced productivity, greater ongoing capacity, reduced social costs, and stimulus to research and development.* Access to higher education gives workers the skill to be more productive, allows them to pay more in taxes,

*The Perryman Group, *A Tale of Two States—And One Million Jobs,* March 2007, published by the Texas Higher Education Coordinating Board at http://www.thecb.state.tx.us/reports/PDF/1345.PDF?CFID=8408072&CFTO KEN=72550084.

makes them less likely to burden welfare and health care systems, and permits them to contribute their creative talents to economic development.

Nevertheless, student demands for tuition relief faced a difficult political environment. The Texas 2011–2012 budget was strained by a revenue shortfall as a result of economic recession, and many other interest groups presented competing demands on the state's treasury by arguing that their claims served the public interest as well. Legislators have been convinced by benefits received arguments that students should share in the pain of budget restraint by contributing a fair share to the cost of higher education since they are its primary beneficiaries.

While it can be argued that the higher tuitions Texas students are experiencing may limit their access to colleges and universities in the future, student enrollments in the state's institutions of higher learning have recently been growing at a very rapid pace in spite of tuition increases.

college and employers may credit applicants for it, graduation or completion of occupational curriculum programs is society's respected measure of success. Unfortunately, high costs, lack of course availability, inadequate academic preparation, and personal factors all contribute to a problem of student retention. Among full-time degree-seeking students at public universities, 24 percent graduate within four years and 57 percent receive degrees within six years. And community colleges have a much more difficult challenge to retain and graduate students—only 11 percent of them graduate within three years and 20 percent transfer to a senior institution.

Quality. Even graduation rates do not fully measure the success of institutions of higher learning. Successful measures of Texas colleges and universities must take into account their two major functions: (1) teaching; that is, imparting existing knowledge to students, and (2) research; that is, creating new knowledge.

By one measure, Texas has three of the top 100 national public universities in the nation—the University of Texas at Austin ranks 13th; Texas A&M University stands at

22nd; the University of Texas—Dallas comes in at 72nd.[7] Other rankings also show that these are among the most recognized public institutions of higher learning in the state.

Perhaps their rankings partly reflect the resources available to these institutions. General legislative appropriations have been relatively more generous for the University of Texas (UT) at Austin and Texas A&M University. Furthermore, the state constitution has earmarked more than two million acres of public land for the Permanent University Fund (PUF). Two-thirds of the earnings from the PUF are used for construction and other educational enhancements at the University of Texas System campuses, and one-third goes to Texas A&M University campuses. The UT and A&M systems have concentrated many of their resources on their flagship campuses in Austin and College Station rather than on other institutions within their systems.

To help the other universities in Texas, voters amended the state constitution in 2009 to create the National Research University Fund (NRUF) out of the former Permanent Higher Education Fund; it provides funding to enable emerging research universities in Texas to achieve national prominence. Proposed Tier One research universities include the University of Houston, North Texas University, Texas Tech University, and University of Texas campuses at San Antonio, Dallas, Arlington, and El Paso. Of course, the results of these ambitious efforts cannot yet be fully foreseen or evaluated.

HEALTH AND HUMAN SERVICES

The second most costly category of state spending can be broadly classified as health and human services. This category encompasses public assistance, Medicaid for the poor, and a variety of other programs. In the 2010–2011 budget period, these programs cost $59.7 billion (32.8 percent of the state's total budget). About 60 percent of this funding originates as grants-in-aid from the federal government.

The Texas Health and Human Services Commission provides a variety of social services, including Temporary Assistance to Needy Families, Medicaid, and the Children's Health Insurance Program, as shown in Figure 27–6. The commission also coordinates planning, rule making, and budgeting among its four subsidiary social-service agencies: the Department of Aging and Disability Services, the Department of Assistive and Rehabilitative Services, the Department of Family and Protective Services, and the Department of State Health Services. The most important social services include health programs and income support.

HEALTH PROGRAMS

Although opponents of government's assuming responsibility for public health describe it as **"socialized medicine,"** health has been a concern of public authorities since Moses imposed strict hygienic codes on the Jews during their biblical exodus from Egypt. In the United States, the federal government began to provide hospital care to the merchant marine in 1798. Today, health care has evolved into a growing public-private partnership and the second most expensive service that Texas provides.

The state has three levels of involvement in health care: (1) In some instances, the state is the provider of direct health services; for example, it provides health care for certain special populations. (2) In other instances, the state is the payer but not the provider. When it acts as a public health insurer as it does with Medicaid, it pays for the

"Socialized Medicine"
Strictly defined, socialized medicine is a health care system in which the government hires medical practitioners who work at government-owned facilities to directly provide health care as in Great Britain and in U.S. veterans and military hospitals. However, the term is often applied to health care systems in which the government provides health care insurance (such as Medicare), but benefit payments are made to private health care providers.

---

[7] *U.S. News and World Report,* "Best Colleges: Top Public Schools: National Universities," August 19, 2010, at http://colleges.usnews.rankingsandreviews.com/best-colleges/national-top-public. These imperfect rankings are based on reputation, exclusiveness in admissions, and financial resources.

FIGURE 27–6 Texas Health and Human Services Agencies

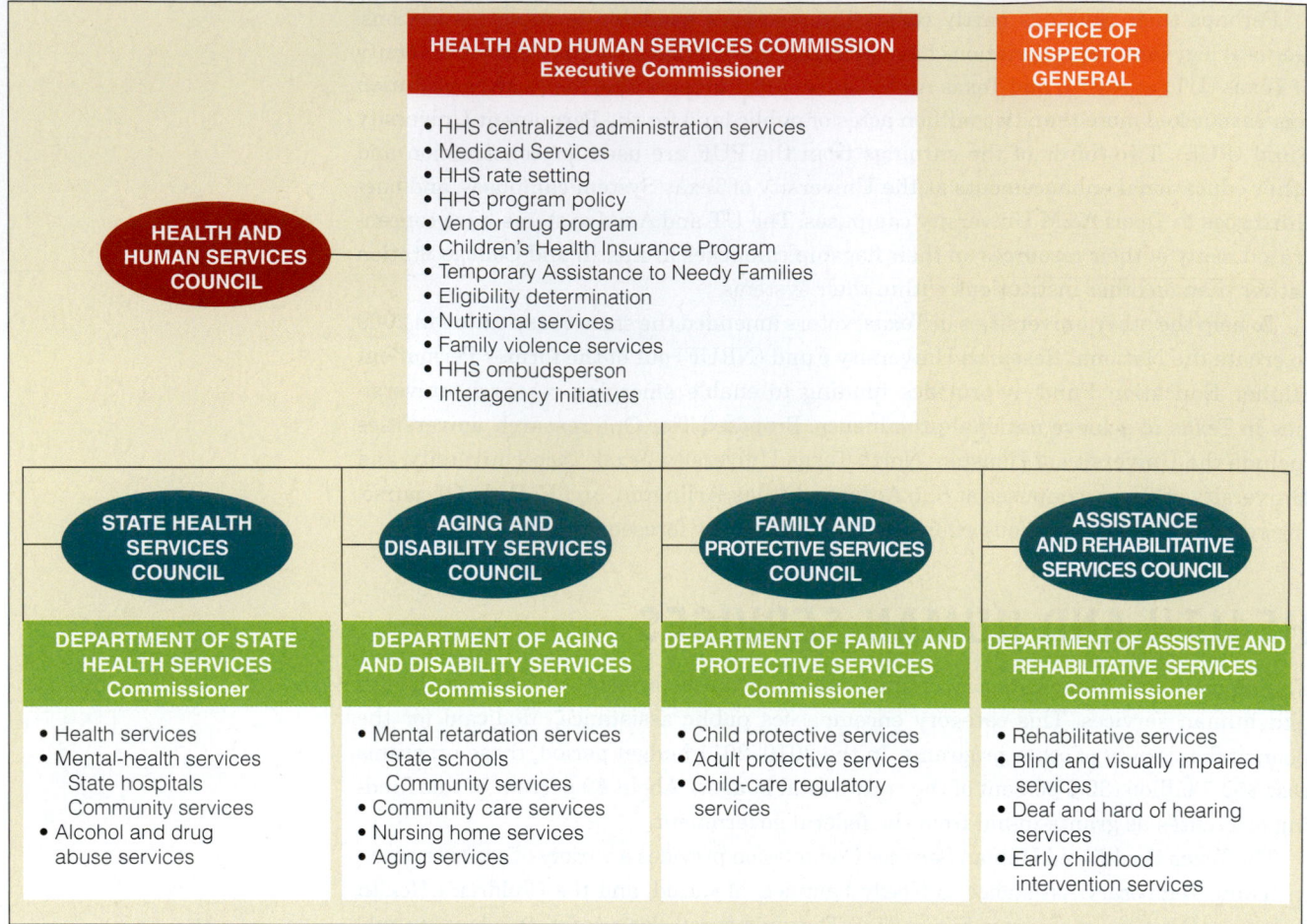

Source: Health and Human Services Commission.

medical services offered by private practitioners. (3) The state also acts as a regulator and buyer of private health insurance.

Direct Health Services. Texas's Department of Health Services (DHS) provides personal health services for special populations. For example, the health department operates a lung and tuberculosis hospital in San Antonio and a general-services hospital in Harlingen. DHS operates general psychiatric hospitals and funds local mental health community centers and chemical dependency programs as well.

County hospitals and clinics are legally responsible for providing medical care for uninsured indigents, and therefore, they have become the health providers of last resort. County hospitals are usually operated by county hospital districts that have the authority to collect property taxes that partially fund their operations. Several government institutions also manage teaching hospitals that provide care to both indigent and nonindigent patients.

Instead of using county-funded hospitals and clinics, many uninsured and indigent patients access medical services through hospital emergency rooms because federal and state laws usually require them to accept patients regardless of their ability to pay. The cost of such treatment is often uncompensated and passed on to paying patients and insurance companies—a practice partially responsible for the recent dramatic increase in health insurance premiums.

State Health Insurance Programs. Texas operates two major health insurance programs for those who qualify. **Medicaid** and the **Children's Health Insurance Program**

Medicaid
A program to provide medical care for qualified low income persons; although funded largely by federal grants-in-aid, it is a state-administered program.

Children's Health Insurance Program (CHIP)
Program to provide health insurance for low income children. It is administered by the state but funded largely by federal grants-in-aid.

(**CHIP**) are fairly comprehensive insurance programs designed to provide a minimal level of care for low-income individuals and families who have enrolled.

Texas spends one-fourth of its state budget on the Medicaid program, but more than 60 percent of Medicaid costs are paid by the federal government. Medicaid reimburses providers for most health services, including eyeglasses, prescription drugs, physicians' fees, laboratory and X-ray services, family planning, ambulance transportation, Medicare Part B premiums, and a wide variety of other medical expenses. Generally, these providers are in managed care (HMO-type) systems.

Medicaid should not be confused with **Medicare**, which is available to all persons age 65 and over regardless of income, and is administered by the U.S. Department of Health and Human Services. In contrast, the Medicaid program is administered by the state and is available only to certain medically indigent individuals: (1) categorically eligible persons eligible for Temporary Assistance for Needy Families (TANF) or Supplemental Security Income (SSI); (2) individuals seeking medical assistance only, low-income persons residing in institutions who qualify for SSI except for certain income requirements; (3) children up to 19 years of age whose family financial status would qualify for TANF but who reside in families with two able-bodied parents; (4) pregnant women who would qualify for TANF but have no other children; (5) children aged six through 18 who reside in families with income below the federal poverty level; (6) children under age six whose families' income is at or below 133 percent of the federal poverty level; (7) pregnant women and infants under one year of age who reside in families with income below 185 percent of the federal poverty level.[8] Of Texas's 3.2 million Medicaid recipients, 90 percent are elderly, disabled, or children.

The Children's Health Insurance Program (CHIP) helps insure children of parents with incomes less than 200 percent of the poverty level and who do not qualify for Medicaid. Even though 500,000 children are insured by CHIP and 2.2 million are enrolled in Medicaid, one in five Texas children remains uninsured.

Private Health Insurance. While about 17 percent of nonelderly Texans have some sort of public insurance coverage such as Medicaid or CHIP, most rely on private insurance companies to pay for their medical expenses. Employer-sponsored plans cover 51 percent of Texans, and 5 percent buy individual policies. The state itself pays private insurance companies for part of the premiums for its employees and teachers. As a result, businesses, government, and individuals have been seriously impacted by health insurance premiums that have skyrocketed more than 80 percent since 2001 and cost about $12,000 for the average family.[9] High premium costs have caused some businesses to drop coverage for their employees, and many individuals have chosen not to buy private coverage, leaving Texas as the state with the largest share of uninsured persons in the nation. In 2008, about 5.9 million Texans, or 27.7 percent of the state's nonelderly population, were uninsured.

Health Care Reform in Texas. As we discussed in Chapter 16, Congress made an effort to cope with the rising cost of private health insurance, the large number of uninsured Americans, and objectionable insurance company practices by passing the controversial Patient Protection and Affordable Care Act of 2010, also known as Health Care Reform (HCR).

Health Care Reform is currently scheduled to impact Texans in stages as its provisions are implemented over time. The act will end some of the most unpopular insurance company practices as its first priority in 2010 and 2011. "Rescissions" will no longer be allowed, as health insurance companies can no longer arbitrarily drop beneficiaries when they get sick or because they have reached lifetime limits. Insurance companies

Medicare
A federal program to provide medical insurance for most persons age sixty-five and over.

---

may not deny insurance to children because of pre-existing conditions, and adults with pre-existing conditions such as diabetes or high blood pressure will be allowed to buy subsidized insurance through a new high-risk pool. Insurance companies must also allow parents to keep their children covered under their family policies until age 26.

Small businesses will be allowed tax credits to help them buy insurance for their employees during the first phase of health reform, but the most significant and controversial elements of the reform package will begin in 2014. Then insurance companies will be subject to a "guaranteed issue" requirement that they must insure all applicants even if they are sick—a requirement that insurance companies will be able to meet only because they will be able to spread risk over a larger pool of customers. Everyone will be required to have health insurance or pay a fine to the federal government—the "individual mandate."

To make health insurance affordable, states (with 90 to 100 percent aid from the federal government) will expand Medicaid eligibility to all persons with incomes below 133 percent of the federal poverty level and maintain their CHIP program. Other uninsured individuals and small businesses will be allowed to buy health insurance through state insurance exchanges, in which insurance companies will compete by offering qualified plans with clear and comparable information on coverage options. States may agree to allow their residents to buy health insurance from an exchange across state lines. Individuals purchasing health insurance on these exchanges will be eligible for subsidies on a sliding scale based on their incomes, up to four times the federal poverty level ($88,200 in 2010). Some low-income individuals will also qualify for subsidies for a portion of out-of-pocket expenses.

Because Texas has the largest percentage of uninsured persons of any state in the nation, HCR will have a more dramatic effect in Texas than in most states. It will expand Medicaid and CHIP eligibility by 2.1 million. Individual mandates, small business subsidies, affordability subsidies for middle-income families, and large business incentives will reduce the number of uninsured by as many as 4.3 million, depending on how many choose to ignore the individual mandate. The remaining uninsured will include illegal immigrants who are ineligible and eligible persons who choose to pay a fine rather than buy health insurance.

The Texas Department of Insurance will be given substantial powers to enforce new federal health insurance regulations and to monitor hikes in insurance premiums. In addition, the state will assume the responsibility for operating an insurance exchange and for qualifying new Medicaid and CHIP clients. And, while the federal government will provide substantial grants to pay for new Medicaid benefits and administrative costs, Health and Human Services Executive Commissioner Tom Suehs estimates the expansion of Medicaid and the Children's Health Insurance Program would cost the state $27 billion between 2014 and 2023.

INCOME SUPPORT PROGRAMS

Temporary Assistance to Needy Families. Among social service programs, Temporary Assistance to Needy Families (TANF) is designed for children whose parents are incapable of providing for their basic needs. More than two-thirds of TANF recipients are children. Unless they are disabled or needed at home to care for very young children, adult TANF and food stamp recipients are referred for employment counseling, assessment, and job placement.

The TANF-Basic program serves those who are deprived of support because of the absence or disability of one or both parents and whose income is at least 87 percent below the poverty level. TANF grants are available for two-parent

DID YOU KNOW?

That one in five Texans lives in poverty?

families in which the principal wage earner is unemployed and the family income does not exceed the criteria established for the basic program.

Federal and state regulations now require recipients to cooperate in identifying an absent parent and, with few exceptions, limit TANF benefits to citizens; adult eligibility is usually limited to two years at a time, with a maximum five-year lifetime benefit. By making welfare less of an entitlement, these welfare reforms were intended to force able-bodied individuals out of dependency and into productive work. Some federal funds now are distributed as block grants to the states to allow them flexibility to develop support services, child care, job training and placement, and rehabilitation programs to help welfare recipients in finding work. These reforms have substantially reduced the number of TANF recipients in Texas.

In 2010–2011, the maximum monthly TANF grant for a family of three was $260, considerably below the national average. Texas's median TANF grant is about half the national median. Adjusting for inflation, TANF benefits have declined considerably over the years. Today, Texas spends only 0.1 percent of its budget for this income assistance program for the poor.

Unemployment Insurance. Whereas TANF is designed as an income supplement for the poor and is administered by the Health and Human Service Commission, unemployment compensation is designed as partial income replacement for those who have lost their jobs. Unlike TANF, which is a welfare program based on need, unemployment compensation is a social insurance program financed by employer-paid premiums and eligibility is based on previous earnings rather than need or family size.

As discussed in Chapter 17, the U.S. Congress established the system of **unemployment insurance** under the Social Security Act of 1935 as a partnership between the states and the federal government. This act imposed a tax on covered employers to establish a nationwide system of unemployment insurance administered by the federal government. However, the act provided that most of this tax would be set aside in all of the states that adopted an acceptable state program. Thus, every state in the union was pressured to adopt state systems of unemployment insurance. Benefits are financed from state taxes on employers, but some administrative costs are paid with federal funds. These programs are actually administered by the states.

In Texas, unemployment insurance is administered by the Texas Workforce Commission (TWC), a three-member board appointed by the governor, with the consent of the senate, for six-year overlapping terms. Outside the authority of the Health and Human Services Commission, the TWC administers benefit payments. Usually, the maximum is 26 weekly benefit payments, but Congress usually extends the period of eligibility and pays for much of cost of the extension during periods of severe recessions when jobs are scarce.

Under Texas's rather restrictive laws, a worker must register for job placement with the TWC and is ineligible to receive benefits (at least for a time) if he or she voluntarily quits or was fired for cause. Since the rate at which employers are taxed is based on claims made by former employees, employers have an interest in contesting employee claims. For these reasons and others, only 35 percent of unemployed Texans received benefits in 2009.

Until recently, handling unemployment insurance claims has not been a major priority among TWC's activities; its major functions have been providing a workforce for employers, gathering employment statistics, enforcing child-labor laws, and providing various special job-training and rehabilitation services. Able-bodied welfare recipients are referred to the TWC for training and child care services. Regional workforce development boards plan one-stop career development centers in 28 areas across the state.

Unemployment Insurance
Benefit program for certain workers losing their employment; a joint federal-state program financed with a tax on employers.

TRANSPORTATION

The third most costly service provided by the state of Texas is transportation. As we mentioned earlier, transportation (primarily highways) accounted for about 10.2 percent of expenditures in 2010–2011.

HIGHWAY PROGRAMS

In the early days of Texas history, road construction was primarily a county responsibility. Most Texas counties still maintain a property tax dedicated to the construction and maintenance of roads, and in rural areas, road building remains a major function of county government. The efforts are too small and too poorly financed, however, to provide the expensive, coordinated, statewide network of roads needed by highly mobile Texans in the modern world.

In contrast to county roads, state highways in Texas are better financed. In 1916, the national government encouraged state governments to assume the major responsibility for highway construction and maintenance. The 1916 Federal Aid Road Act made available federal funds to cover one-half of the construction costs for state highways. To become eligible for those funds, a state was required to establish an agency to develop a coordinated plan for the state highway system and to administer construction and maintenance programs. Texas responded by establishing the Texas Highway Department, now known as the Texas Department of Transportation (TxDOT). The department is supervised by a five-member commission appointed by the governor, with the consent of the senate, for six-year overlapping terms. The commission appoints an executive director, who oversees the department and supervises the work of regional district offices.

Newer federal aid programs and increased funding for existing ones have expanded the responsibilities of the transportation department. The earliest highway-building program was designed to provide only major highways along primary routes. Federal funding later became available for secondary roads, and Texas established the farm-to-market program to assume state maintenance of many county roads as the rural road network was paved, extended, and improved. Finally, beginning in 1956, Congress made funds available for 90 percent of the cost of constructing express, limited-access highways to connect major cities in the United States. Altogether, the 80,000-mile state highway system today carries about three-fourths of the state's motor vehicle traffic (see Table 27–5).

DID YOU KNOW?

That recently, Texas ranked last among the 50 states in per capita spending (30 percent below the national average); Texas per capita expenditures for education ranked 44th among the 50 states; for welfare, its per capita spending ranked 48th; for hospitals, its per capita spending ranked 24th; and per capita expenditures for highways in Texas ranked 28th?

TABLE 27–5 The Texas Highway System

TYPE OF ROADWAY	TOTAL MILES	PERCENTAGE OF TRAFFIC ACCOMMODATED
Interstate highways	10,302	27
Farm-to-market roads	40,969	11
Federal and state highways	28,459	36

Note: Figures do not include more than 225,349 miles of city streets and county roads, which accommodate approximately one-fourth of traffic.
Source: Legislative Budget Board, *Fiscal Size Up, 2010–2011*, p. 425.

THE POLITICS OF TRANSPORTATION

The Good Roads and Transportation Association, a private organization supported by highway contractors and other groups, lobbied for the establishment of the state highway fund and for increases in motor fuel taxes and still attempts to guard the fund against those who would spend any part of it for other purposes. Despite the organization's efforts, per capita state highway funding is slightly below the national average.

Funding for the highway program is a joint federal-state responsibility. In the 2010–2011 period, the federal government, mostly from the federal gasoline tax, provided more than 40 percent of the transportation department's revenues. This large federal contribution has allowed the national government to demand such restrictions as meeting clean-air standards and setting a minimum drinking age of 21 as conditions for receiving federal aid.

State monies account for about 60 percent of TxDOT funding. The state highway fund is mostly supported by motor vehicle registration (license plate) fees and three-fourths of the 20-cent-per-gallon motor fuels tax, which has not been raised since 1991. Although the motor fuels tax is about average for the 50 states, Texas has been maintaining the second most extensive highway network in the nation with limited revenue sources.

As one of the fastest-growing states in the nation, Texas has been forced to look to alternative revenue sources to pay for new highway construction. In a conservative state reluctant to raise motor fuels taxes or general revenue sources such as the state general sales taxes, Governor Perry and other state leaders turned to the idea of privatizing new highways.

Highway Privatization. TxDOT planned to use Comprehensive Development Agreements with private entities to develop a highly ambitious and controversial 50-year program to supplement existing highways. The $200 billion, 4,000-mile Trans-Texas Corridor would have included superhighways (with separate freight and commuter lanes), railways (with high-speed, commuter, and freight lines), and utility corridors (for water, electricity, natural gas, petroleum, fiber-optic telecommunications, and broadband lines). Funded by both state taxes and private investment, the project was to be operated largely by private enterprises such as toll companies.

Pro-business, free market, low-tax conservatives championed the Trans-Texas corridor. They argued that the project was necessary to accommodate cross-border traffic generated by free trade agreements and to relieve congestion resulting from the state's huge population growth in metropolitan areas. Supporters contended that development of the new transport system would stimulate massive economic development with minimum public funding by harnessing private investment capital to keep state taxes low.

Other conservatives, such as property rights advocates, resisted the Trans-Texas Corridor as a state "land grab" of 584,000 privately owned acres. These opponents pointed out that not all of the seized land was to be used for public right-of-way, and land seized for "ancillaries" could legally be leased to investors for any commercial, industrial, or agricultural purpose the government chose. Opponents argued that the state intended to sacrifice property rights to profit influential campaign contributors and foreign investors.

Nativists feared the growing influence of foreign investors in the project, the influx of foreign goods along the vast new network of roads, and the economic integration that resulted from expanding commercial interdependence. Others opposed the project on grounds that the plan bypassed major metropolitan areas and, therefore, would have a minimum impact on urban traffic congestion. Consumer advocates simply opposed the concept of toll roads.

In the face of stiff opposition, TxDOT abandoned the expansive Trans-Texas Corridor plan in favor of smaller, more localized projects, but it has not yet given up on the concept of highway privatization and funding of new highway construction with anticipated toll revenues. The future of highway funding remains a tough political problem for the Texas legislature and the state's political leadership.

Mass Transit
Transport systems that carry multiple passengers such as train and bus systems; whether publicly or privately owned, mass transit systems are available to the general public and usually charge a fare.

Mass Transit. Texans, like most Americans, remain unreceptive to **mass transit** as an alternative to individual motor vehicles. Only 4 to 6 percent of Texas residents regularly commute by urban mass transit, unlike in northeastern areas where mass transportation is a popular, viable alternative to personal vehicles—one-third of all users of urban mass transit live in the New York City metropolitan area.

Automotive transportation is close to the hearts of Texans, and no other mode of transportation seems as convenient because no other is as individualized. Buses and trains cannot take individuals exactly where they want to go exactly when they want to go there. Automobiles have become a way of life, and their manufacture, maintenance, and fueling have become dominant elements of the economy.

Mass transit proponents point to the enormous social and personal costs of automotive transportation. Texas's annual highway death toll is close to 4,000, and thousands more are injured. The motor vehicle is also the single most important contributor to atmospheric pollution, a major factor in climate change, and a significant source of refuse that finds its way into junkyards and landfills. As the least efficient mode of transportation presently available, dependence on the individual motor vehicle is in direct conflict with the need to conserve energy and reduce our "addiction" to foreign oil (a strategic factor in terrorism and foreign wars).

Urban mass transit was widely used before the end of World War II, and supporters of mass transit argue that adequate public funding could once again make railroads and buses rapid and comfortable alternatives to automotive transportation. When gasoline prices rise, more Texans seem to be receptive to using mass transit where it is available.

YOU CAN MAKE A Difference

BECOMING AN INTELLIGENT TAXPAYER AND CONSUMER OF STATE SERVICES

Texas students or their families pay local property taxes either directly, if they are homeowners, or indirectly as hidden taxes if they rent their dwellings. Texas has among the lowest *state* taxes in the nation partly because the state has pushed the cost of many services down to the *local* level. As a result, Texans pay relatively high local property tax rates.

WHY SHOULD YOU CARE?

You (or your family) may be among many local property taxpayers who have seen taxes grow much more rapidly than their incomes. In fact, your property may be taxed disproportionately higher than your neighbors'. Texas is one of a few states that does not require the sales price of many large commercial properties to be made public,

and wealthy property owners hire professionals to fight for reductions in their property valuations. However, you should realize that you can also have a direct impact on the property taxes you (or your family) pay.

WHAT CAN YOU DO?

Your local property taxes are based on the appraised value of your real estate. Local governments in your area use a central countywide appraisal district usually accessible online. It determines the value of your property.

You can protest the appraised value of your property with this appraisal authority. You may find your efforts rewarded—in some jurisdictions, fewer than 10 percent of owners protest their property appraisals, but as many as 75 percent of those who do succeed in lowering their taxes. Be prepared with photos, specific measurements of floor space and land area, and a list of any defects that might diminish the value of the property. How do you know what the appraised value of your property should be? You can research the appraised values of other comparable properties in your neighborhood; these values are a matter of public record and are available in the appraisal district of the county where you live.

You may be eligible for a homestead exemption if you live in a home you own. Such an exemption allows you to pay less in property taxes than you would otherwise. A special exemption is also available for the elderly. It is the taxpayer's responsibility to apply for these exemptions. To locate your county appraisal authority and to find the appraised value of any property, go to www.txcountydata. com; for hints and a slide presentation about how to protest property tax appraisals, go to www.window.state.tx.us.

Much state and federal tuition assistance goes undistributed. Visit your school's financial aid office to determine if you qualify for tuition help. Find help at the Texas Higher Education Coordinating Board Web site at www. collegefortexans.com and the comptroller's Web site at www.everychanceeverytexan.org/.

A parent's failure to make child-support payments may force the other parent to apply for Temporary Assis-tance to Needy Families. If you have this problem, call the attorney general's child-support enforcement office at the number listed in your local telephone directory, or visit the attorney general's Web site at www.oag.state.tx.us/cs/index.shtml.

Find lower electric and telephone rates and stop unwanted telephone solicitations at the Public Utilities Web site at www.puc.state.tx.us.

Those who witness child abuse or neglect should call Protective and Regulatory Services at (800) 252-5400.

See if your family and friends are eligible for state social services by checking links at www.yourtexasbenefits. com/wps/portal. Or, dial 211 for human service needs. Compare health insurance plans and find federal health care reform options at www.texashealthoptions.com.

Before you buy a new vehicle, contact the Texas Department of Motor Vehicles, which maintains "lemon law" records and processes warranty complaints at www. txdmv.gov.

TODAY, many state services can be accessed online at Texas's main Web site at http://www.texas.gov/. (Andresr/Shutterstock.com)

When you buy auto and homeowner's insurance, check with the Texas Department of Insurance, which publishes rates and numbers of customer complaints. Go to www.tdi.state.tx.us/consumer/index.html.

If you need emergency road assistance or wish to report drug trafficking, call the Department of Public Safety at (800) 525-5555.

Apply for a job or unemployment compensation at the Texas Workforce Commission, www.twc.state.tx.us.

KEY TERMS

CHAPTER SUMMARY

1. State tax rates are low in Texas compared with other states and are not rising as a percentage of personal income. Taxes now account for less than half of Texas's revenues, and federal grants-in-aid including temporary stimulus grants account for more than one-third of its funding. Miscellaneous sources and some very limited state borrowing account for the rest.

2. **In the politics of taxation, how are different groups' views of the "public interest" affected by their social and economic positions?** Although taxing decisions may be rationalized as serving some regulatory purpose or reflecting benefits received or ability to pay, groups and individuals often favor taxes that some other social groups pay. Political and economic self-interest motivates much of the discussion of taxes.

3. **What kind of taxes does Texas collect?** Both narrow- and broad-based taxes are used in Texas. The largest single state tax is the general sales tax, which is regressive relative to income because it falls most heavily on middle- and lower-income people. Other state taxes, as well as the ad valorem tax employed by local governments, are also regressive in their effect.

4. The Legislative Budget Board, the state legislature, and the governor become involved in state spending decisions. The process is political. Perhaps no other type of decision evokes more consistent and passionate political efforts from interest groups and administrative agencies.

5. **Which political values do Texas public policy priorities reflect?** Education, health and human services, and transportation are the major services that state government offers, together constituting more than four-fifths of the total cost of Texas's state government. These services have a significant effect on the way Texans live and even on the way they think. It is nearly impossible to evaluate them objectively because they affect various groups so differently, and as a result, policy decisions are made based on fundamental values. Texas spending priorities reflect a conservative political culture that implicitly trusts private enterprise but is skeptical of public services.

6. The educational system of Texas is generally decentralized, and local school districts are mostly independent of the normal course of partisan politics. Statewide educational policies and curricula are conservative, as is much of Texas politics. Compared with other states, per capita expenditures, per student expenditures, and teacher salaries are below average.

7. Health care services are both publicly and privately financed in Texas, as in the rest of the nation, and they are plagued by a similar problem: the rising costs of providing better services to more people. Although a smaller proportion of residents is currently insured in Texas than in any other state, national health care insurance reforms may cover up to four million more of the state's residents in the future.

8. In many ways, the Texas system of public welfare reflects the same values that are present in the state educational and health care systems. It too is poorly financed, and the public-assistance programs that the state has adopted were established only with the financial support of the national government. Few

of these programs are designed to eliminate the root causes of poverty.

9. The highway system has declined as a state spending priority despite the efforts of the Good Roads and Transportation Association, and per capita spending for highways is now less than in most other states. Texans have also been reluctant to substantially increase spending for alternative means of transportation. Privatization of highways has been proposed as an alternative to the inadequate public highway system.

10. Individual and group positions on these and virtually all public policies differ according to who benefits and who pays the cost for which public services. The process of allocating costs and benefits is the very essence of politics.

SELECTED PRINT, MEDIA, AND ONLINE RESOURCES

PRINT RESOURCES

Blau, Joel, and Mimi Abramovitz. *The Dynamics of Social Welfare Policy.* New York: Oxford University Press, 2004. This work examines national social-welfare policy in the context of history, social change, and the economy.

Combs, Susan. *Exemptions and Tax Incidence* (Austin: Office of the Comptroller of Public Accounts, February 2009). This excellent analysis of major Texas taxes demonstrates who bears the burden of each tax and how business taxation ultimately falls on consumers.

Combs, Susan. *Texas in Focus: A Statewide View of Opportunities* (Austin: Office of the Comptroller of Public Accounts, January 2008). This wide-ranging report discusses state problems and programs ranging from education to health to the environment in an authoritative but provocative style.

Heller, Donald E., ed. *The States and Public Higher Education Policy:* Affordability, Access, and Accountability. Balti-more, MD: Johns Hopkins University Press, 2001. In this series of essays, various authors explore some of the most serious issues states face in making decisions about higher education.

Legislative Budget Board. *Fiscal Size-Up, 2010–2011.* Austin, TX: Legislative Budget Board, 2009. This state publication details state taxing and spending programs, as well as recent developments in Texas public policy.

Norton, Peter D. *Fighting Traffic: The Dawn of the Motor Age in the American City.* Cambridge, MA: MIT Press, 2008. This insightful book describes the dramatic changes in society that were necessary to accommodate motor vehicle transportation.

MEDIA RESOURCES

The Battle over School Choice—This PBS *Frontline* video explores the heated debate over whether public school reform or privatization (including voucher plans) is a better choice.

The Merrow Report: In Schools We Trust—Americans rarely agree on what public education should do: Teach basics? Train workers? Inculcate democratic values and tolerance? This PBS video explores varying views on public education.

NOW with Bill Moyers: Medicaid Mess—This PBS feature deals with the tough choices concerning Medicaid and also discusses the cultural values that divide America.

Promoting Prosperity for Texas: Role of State and Local Governments—Produced by Texas's Center for Public Policy Priorities and available at the group's Web site, www.cppp.org, this short feature engages the state's challenges in funding public services.

Tax Me If You Can—Produced by PBS Frontline, this video offers an inside look at how big corporations and wealthy individuals use tax shelters to avoid paying income taxes.

ONLINE RESOURCES

Center for Public Policy Priorities A liberal "think tank" for public policy issues: www.cppp.org

The Education Code provides insight into Texas's complex public school funding system (Chapters 41, 42, and 43): www.statutes.legis.state.tx.us/

Legislative Budget Board provides a wealth of information about tax and budget issues: www.lbb.state.tx.us

Lone Star Foundation presents conservative viewpoints on state services: www.lonestarfoundation.org

Public Citizen presents a liberal, consumer-oriented viewpoint: www.citizen.org/texas

Texans for Public Justice represents progressive viewpoints on state services: www.tpj.org

Texas Education Agency The key site for public education: www.tea.state.tx.us

Texas Public Policy Foundation A conservative "think tank" for public policy issues: www.texaspolicy.com

Texas Taxpayers and Research Association represents the conservative and business perspective on taxation: www.ttara.org

Window on State Government The Comptroller of Public Accounts is the key government site for taxes and the budget: www.window.state.tx.us

28

Leo Bradshaw speaks to the Whitehouse city council during a meeting about the water shortage in Whitehouse, Texas on August 5, 2008. What other local issues are likely to compel members of a community to voice their opinions before the city council? (AP Photo/Tyler Morning Telegraph, Tom Turner)

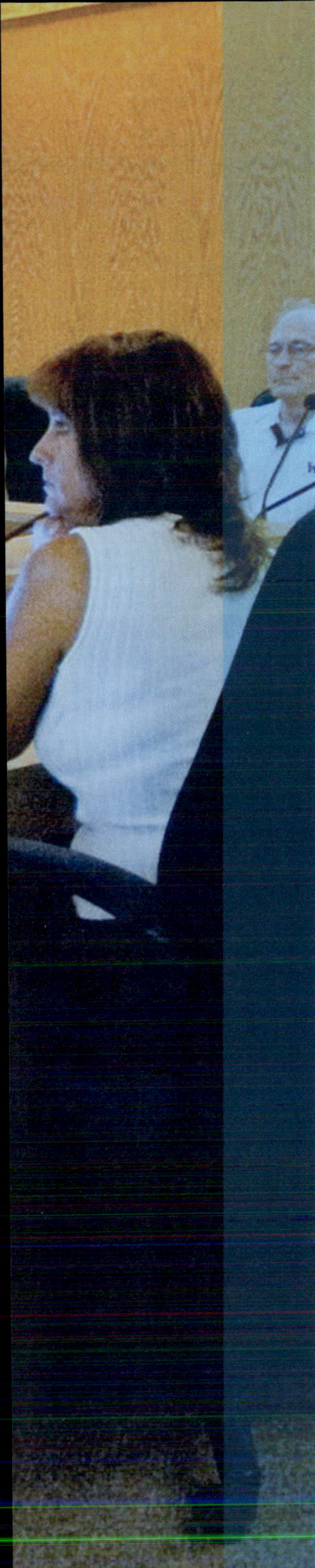

Local Government

QUESTIONS TO CONSIDER

How can voters exert direct influence over municipal governments?

What revenue sources can Texas cities use to meet their budget needs and obligations?

What is the nature of intergovernmental relations at the local level?

CHAPTER CONTENTS

Municipalities

Counties

Special Districts

Councils of Governments

what if...

Texas Cities Appointed Students to City Councils?

BACKGROUND

The Texas governor appoints a student regent to the board of regents of every public university for a one-year term. Student regents enjoy the "powers and duties" that come with board service, except they cannot vote on or second a motion, and their presence will not count toward the quorum needed for the board to meet or cast votes.[*]

Other states have student representation on higher education boards, and in some cases students have voting privileges. City councils throughout the nation appoint high school students to youth commissions in an effort to learn more about the challenges facing young people in their communities. While youth commissioners serve only in an advisory capacity, their perspectives are of great value to mayors and council members whose votes on safety, education, recreation, and health issues can have a direct bearing on a city's youth.

By appointing student regents and creating youth commissions, public officials demonstrate that they value student participation in the political decision-making process. Texas cities could make student input at city hall even more meaningful if they went one step further and added a student seat to their city councils.

Even as a nonvoting member, a student serving on a city council would routinely interact with the mayor, council members, and city staff about council agendas, ordinances, zoning proposals, tax hikes and abatements, and the budget process. City council service would give a student an in-depth look at the inner workings of city government and municipal politics. Mayors and councils would have the benefit of a student's perspective on a wider range of issues than those typically labeled "youth issues."

SERVICE-LEARNING OPPORTUNITIES

Increasingly, students are participating in service-learning activities for high school and college credit. According to the National Service-Learning Clearinghouse, "Service-learning is a teaching and learning strategy that integrates meaningful community service with instruction and reflection to enrich the learning experience, teach civic responsibility,

and strengthen communities."[**] Serving on a city council would give students the chance to fulfill a service-learning requirement in a way that draws a strong connection between classroom knowledge and the nuts and bolts of city politics.

CIVIC ENGAGEMENT

A 2006 survey of local governments reveals that officials recognize a variety of ways the public can make their views known, including attending city council meetings and public hearings, serving on boards and commissions, and completing citizen surveys. But Evelina R. Moulder and Robert J. O'Neill Jr. point out that "There is an important distinction between providing input and participating in the solution."[***] They also note that the survey reveals differences in the amount of resources (such as staff assistance, funding, and budget information) local governments provide to boards and commissions.[****] A student who holds a seat on the city council, even in a nonvoting capacity, would have access to the same resources as the elected members of the council, and that would make the student a more knowledgeable, engaged, and effective participant in the deliberation process.

Appointing a student to the city council would strengthen the student voice in a community in a way that would benefit students, city hall, and society as a whole.

FOR CRITICAL ANALYSIS

1. What qualifications should a student have in order to be appointed to a city council?
2. If the youth commission and the student appointed to serve on the city council disagree on a proposed ordinance, which perspective should the city council weigh more heavily?

---

[*]Texas Education Code, Sections 51.355 and 51.356.

[**]National Service-Learning Clearinghouse, "What Is Service-Learning?," accessed April 4, 2008, at www.servicelearning.org/what_is_service-learning/index.php.
[***]Evelina R. Moulder and Robert J. O'Neill Jr., "Citizen Engagement and Local Government Management," *The Municipal Yearbook 2007* (Washington, DC: the International City/County Management Association), p. 33.
[****]Ibid., p. 34.

SHOULD A CITY place red-light cameras at high-traffic intersections or remove them from these locations? Or annex a neighboring unincorporated area against the wishes of those who live there? Or pass antiloitering laws to curb the presence of the homeless? How should counties provide for mentally ill prisoners or fund the burial of indigents with no known next of kin? These are just a few issues that have been placed on the agendas of local governments throughout the nation, including Texas.

These examples are of a local nature, but a visit to the Web sites of the U.S. Conference of Mayors and the National Association of Counties (NACo) underscores the following point: Issues of national importance are also highly relevant to local governments. In 2008, the U.S. Conference of Mayors emphasized several objectives, including anticrime measures, climate protection, public housing assistance, infrastructure improvements, and youth employment opportunities in "Strong Cities . . . Strong Families . . . for a Strong America: Mayors' 10-Point Plan." That same year, NACo legislative priorities focused on a variety of goals, including food safety, renewable and alternative energy, reauthorization and expansion of the State Children's Health Insurance Program, and improving health care for veterans. It selected the theme of "Protecting Our Children" for National County Week. Both organizations stressed homeland security concerns.

State and local governments adopt measures to address national concerns such as protecting the environment and reducing homelessness. In 2008 the Texas Commission on Environmental Quality's Border Initiative was established to meet environmental needs on the U.S.-Mexico border. Cooperative efforts between cities and counties in both countries include air and water quality monitoring, and scrap tire management. In 2009 the Texas legislature granted $20 million to the eight largest cities in the state to assist these cities in aiding the homeless. The assistance goes to a variety of services including housing, job placement, and shelter facilities. The expenditure is administered by the Texas Department of Housing and Community Affairs.

The sheer number of local governments in Texas can challenge even the most interested members of a community who want to contact local officials occasionally or routinely about pressing concerns, ranging from fixing potholes to the need for better street lighting and more police to the rise in the number of homeless families. (See Table 28–1 below for a comparison of local governments in Texas and in the United States as a whole.) Anyone who lives in a metropolitan area is likely to be governed by several special districts (such as a hospital district, a metropolitan transit authority, and a municipal utility district), in addition to two **general-purpose governments**—the municipal and county governments.

General-Purpose Government
A municipal or county government. In contrast to special districts, general-purpose governments provide a wide range of services.

TABLE 28–1 Local Governments and Public School Systems, United States and Texas, 2007

TOTAL	COUNTY	MUNICIPAL	TOWN OR TOWNSHIP	SPECIAL DISTRICTS	SCHOOL DISTRICTS
United States					
89,476	3,033	19,492	16,519	37,381	13,051
Texas					
4,835	254	1,209	0	2,291	1,081

Source: U.S. Census Bureau, 2007 Census of Governments, www.census.gov/govs/cog/GovOrgTab03ss.html.

While information about local governments is available from a variety of print and electronic media, adequately covering thousands of local governments is no small challenge. Political scientist Doris A. Graber has observed that when it comes to local media, "Reporting, of necessity, becomes highly selective and superficial."[1] Nor can the public depend on local political parties to provide information and generate interest about all local governments. In Texas, political parties do not nominate candidates below the county level. Municipal and special-district elections are nonpartisan—that is, there is no mention of party affiliation on the ballot.

In an effort to shed more light on the inner workings of local government, we examine in the following sections the various institutional features of cities, counties, and special districts. We also look at issues and trends facing local government. Finally, given the growing interest in finding regional solutions to local problems, we discuss the role of councils of governments (COGs) at the local level.

THE USE OF red-light cameras has grown throughout the nation. However, the debate continues about the effectiveness of this device in curtailing traffic accidents. In November 2010, Houston voters approved the removal of red-light cameras. (© Bob Daemmrich/Corbis)

MUNICIPALITIES

How are municipalities relevant to our lives? Cities hire police and firefighters to protect the community. Cities enforce building and safety codes, pass antilitter ordinances, issue garage sale permits, maintain recycling programs, launch antigraffiti programs, impound stray animals for the safety of the community, and enforce curfews. These are just a few examples of how cities routinely affect our day-to-day lives. Some cities have passed ordinances in the interest of public safety and the health of a community. (See Table 28–3 on page 962 for safety and health ordinances passed in Dallas.) In some cases, an ordinance can be subject to amendments, or several ordinances pertaining to one issue are proposed, as was the case with the smoking ban issue in Corpus Christi. (See Figure 28-1.)

Cities also become involved in high-profile, controversial issues. For example, in May 2007, voters in Farmers Branch, a Dallas suburb, approved a ban on the rental of apartments to illegal immigrants (with some exceptions) by more than a two-to-one margin. As of March 2010, two court rulings striking down the ban had not deterred the city council from appealing the rulings. In 2010, a controversial state law was passed in Arizona requiring police officers who stop individuals for lawful reasons to check their immigration status if they suspect they are in the country illegally; the law was amended to ban racial profiling in its enforcement. In reaction to the Arizona law, the Austin City Council passed a resolution banning (with some exceptions) city employee trips to Arizona and official business dealings with the state.

All local governments in Texas are bound by federal and state laws as well as the U.S. and Texas constitutions. The relationship between state and local governments follows from the fact that states, including Texas, have a **unitary system of government**. (We discussed a unitary system of government, as opposed to a federal system, in Chapter 3.) Municipalities—like counties, special districts, and school districts—are

Unitary System of Government
A centralized governmental system in which local or subdivisional governments exercise only those powers given to them by the central government.

---

[1]Doris A. Graber, *Mass Media and American Politics*, 8th ed. (Washington, DC: CQ Press, 2010), p. 267.

TABLE 28–2 Municipal Governments in Texas, 1952–2007

1952	1962	1972	1982	1992	1997	2002	2007
738	866	981	1,121	1,171	1,177	1,196	1,209

Sources: U.S. Census Bureau, *2002 Census of Governments, Volume 1, Number 1, Government Organization,* GC02(1)-1, U.S. Government Printing Office, Washington, DC, 2002, www.census.gov/prod/2003pubs/gc021x1. pdf; U.S. Census Bureau, 2007 Census of Governments, www.census.gov/govs/cog/GovOrgTab03ss.html.

creatures of the state and have only as much power as the Texas Constitution and Texas legislature grant them. Texas has seen a marked increase in the number of municipalities in the state since the 1950s (see Table 28–2).

GENERAL-LAW AND HOME-RULE CITIES

Texas cities are classified as either general-law or home-rule cities. According to the Texas Municipal League, the vast majority of Texas cities—about 75 percent—are general-law cities, and more than 5,000 unincorporated communities have no municipal government.

A **general-law city** is an incorporated community with a population of 5,000 or less and is limited in the subject matter on which it may legislate. A city with a population of more than 5,000 may, by majority vote, become a **home-rule city**. This means it can adopt its own **charter** and structure its local government as it sees fit, as long as these provisions do not conflict with state and national laws and the U.S. and Texas constitutions. Municipal home rule was established in 1912 by a state constitutional amendment. The Texas Constitution allows a home-rule city whose population has dropped to 5,000 or less to retain its home-rule designation.

General-Law City
A city operating under general state laws that apply to all local government units of a similar type. In Texas, cities with a population of 5,000 or less are (in most instances) general-law cities.

Home-Rule City
A city with the state-granted right to frame, adopt, and amend its own charter.

Charter
An organizing document for corporations or municipalities.

FIGURE 28–1 The Many Iterations of an Ordinance

An ordinance may undergo many changes between the time it is first voted on by a governing body and the time it is finally approved.

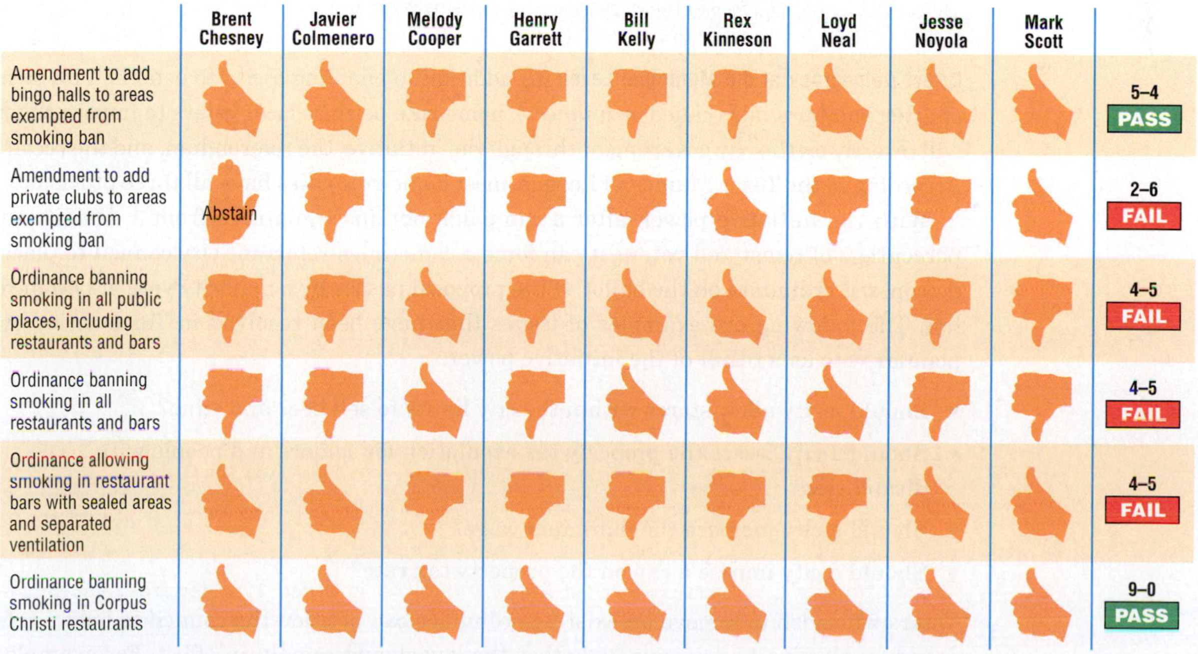

Leanne Libby, "Smoke Ban Passes," *The Corpus Christi Caller-Times,* January 12, 2005, p. A5. © 2004 Caller-Times Publishing Company. Reprinted by permission.

TABLE 28–3 Some Recent Laws Seen as Protecting Dallas Residents from Themselves

YEAR	DALLAS CITY COUNCIL ACTION	STATUS
2000	Require owners to carry pooper-scoopers when walking pets	Few citations written
2003	Ban smoking in most public buildings, including restaurants	Averaging less than one citation per day
2006	Authorize police to impound uninsured vehicles involved in accidents	About 10 cars per day impounded
2006	Ban motorized scooters and "pocket bikes" from streets, sidewalks, and alleys	Few citations written
2006	Authorize 60 red-light cameras to monitor busy intersections	Violations down, as is program revenue; city idled more than one-fourth of its cameras and will rethink strategy
2007	Ban the brandishing of toy guns in a public place	Few citations written
2007	Restrict solicitation, particularly panhandling, further	Thousands of citations written, but less than 1 percent of fines paid
2008	Order additional monitoring of Internet use on public-library computers	Took effect in 2008 as a result of pornography viewing on library computers
2008	Ban motorists from using hand-held cell phones in school zones	Took effect summer 2008

Source: Adapted from *Dallas Morning News* research, from 'can-do' to 'can't do' in "Some Recent Laws Seen as Protecting Dallas Residents from Themselves," accessed March 28, 2008, at www.dallasnews.com/sharedcontent/dws/news/dmn/stories/032908dnmetnannycity.375774a.html.

Direct Democracy at the Municipal Level. In addition to enabling a city to establish its own charter and laws (also called *ordinances*), home rule permits local voters to impose their will directly on the city government through the initiative, the referendum, and the recall. According to the Texas Municipal League, most home-rule cities have all three provisions.

With the initiative power, after a campaign obtains signatures from a designated percentage of registered voters, it can force a sometimes-reluctant city council to place a proposed ordinance on the ballot. If the proposal passes by a majority vote, it becomes law. The following are examples of issues that have been resolved in Texas cities by popular vote as a result of the initiative power:

- Should a city allow stores within the city limits to sell beer and wine?

- Should a city freeze the property tax exemption for seniors and people with disabilities?

- Should a city increase the minimum wage?

- Should a city impose a cap on the property tax rate?

Voters who wish to remove an existing ordinance can petition the council to hold a referendum election to determine whether the law should remain in effect. For example, College Station voters approved by referendum removing red-light cameras. Smoking bans were put to a referendum vote in Lubbock and Baytown. In both cases, voters decided to retain the ban.

Finally, voters can, by petition, force the council to hold a recall election that would permit the people to remove the mayor or a member of the council. Texas Attorney General Greg Abbott ruled that recalled members of a city council must step down once the election results are certified—even if that leaves the council without a quorum.[2]

The Limits of Home Rule. While home-rule cities have wider latitude than general-law cities in their day-to-day operations, they still must contend with state limitations on their authority. For example, state law determines the specific dates on which municipal elections can be held. Voters are free to amend city charters, but the Texas Constitution permits cities to hold charter elections only every two years. In addition, an election establishing a metropolitan transit authority can be held only in cities that meet a population requirement determined by the Texas legislature. Local governments in Texas are subject to "sunshine" laws such as the Public Information Act and the Open Meetings Act. Because Texas is covered under the federal Voting Rights Act, all state and local election law changes must first be approved (the "preclearance" requirement) by the U.S. Justice Department or a federal district court in Washington, D.C.

FORMS OF MUNICIPAL GOVERNMENT

There are three common forms of municipal government: the council-manager system, the mayor-council system, and the commission system.

The Council-Manager System. In a **council-manager system** (see Figure 28–2), an elected city council makes laws and hires a professional manager who is responsible for both executing council policies and managing the day-to-day operations of city government. The manager serves at the pleasure of the council.

Council-Manager System
A municipal system featuring an elected city council and a city manager who is hired by the council. The council makes policy decisions, and the manager is responsible for the day-to-day operations of the city government.

FIGURE 28–2 Common Forms of Municipal Government

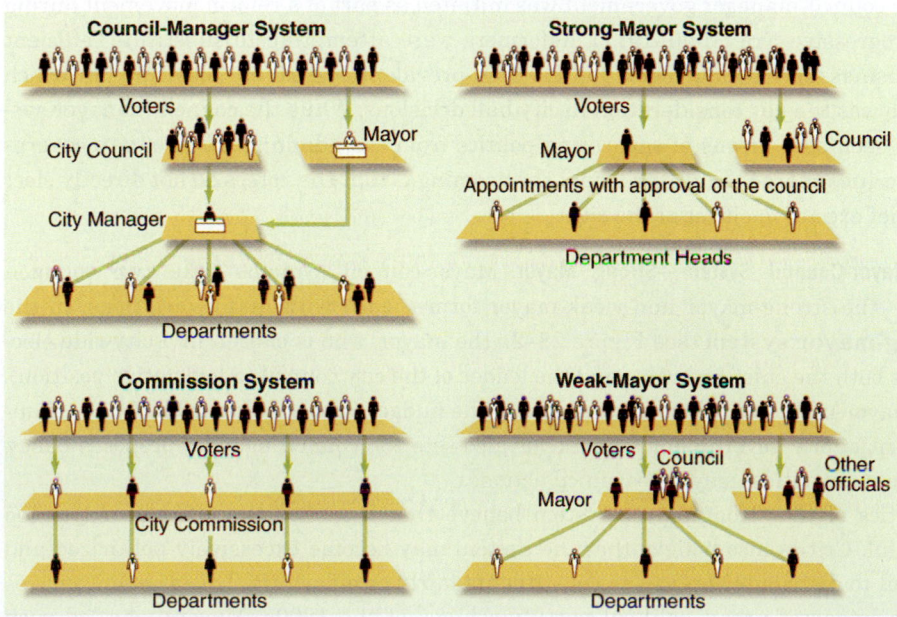

[2]Texas Attorney General Opinion No. GA-0175 (2004).

The powers of the city manager come from the city charter and from the delegation of authority by the council through direct assignment and passage of ordinances. For example, the city manager is responsible for selecting key personnel and for submitting a proposed budget to the council for its approval. The city council will probably seek the manager's opinion on a wide variety of matters, including what tax rate the city should adopt, whether the city should call a bond election, and the feasibility of recommendations made by interest groups. But these issues are ultimately up to the council, and the city manager is expected to implement whatever decisions the council makes.

The Mayor's Role. In a council-manager form of government, a mayor may be either selected by the council from among its members or independently elected by the voters. The mayor presides over council meetings, has limited or no veto power, and has, for the most part, only the same legislative authority as other members of the council. The salaries of the mayor and council members are minimal compared with that of the full-time city manager. However, a 2008 survey of 20 Texas cities conducted by the City of Corpus Christi Legal Department revealed that some council-manager cities provide council members expense or travel allowances, cell phones, laptops, and BlackBerrys— all for official use—and health insurance. In 2008 a district judge ordered the City of Corpus Christi to discontinue allowing members of the city council health insurance benefits because the provision was not in the city charter.

The Powers of the Mayor. The mayor in a council-manager system does have important ceremonial powers, such as signing proclamations and issuing keys to the city to important dignitaries. While the office is institutionally weak, a high-profile mayor can wield considerable influence. Henry Cisneros, who served as Secretary of Housing and Urban Development under President Bill Clinton, first achieved national attention as mayor of San Antonio in the 1980s. Ron Kirk, U.S. Trade Representative in the Obama administration and former Texas secretary of state, made history in 1995 as the first African American elected to the position of Dallas mayor in the city's history. San Antonio and Dallas are the two largest Texas cities that use the council-manager system.

The council-manager government was initiated as part of a reform movement during the Progressive Era (1900–1917). Reformers were attempting to substitute "efficient and businesslike management" for the then-prevalent system of "boss rule," in which politics was the key consideration in city hall decisions. While the council-manager system is seen as a means of separating politics from the administration of city government, critics charge that its principal shortcoming is that the voters do not directly elect the chief executive officer of the city.

The Mayor-Council System—Strong Mayor. Mayor-council systems take two common forms—the strong-mayor and weak-mayor forms—each with many variations. In the **strong-mayor system** (see Figure 28–2), the mayor, who is chosen in a citywide election, is both the chief executive and the leader of the city council (a legislative position). The mayor makes appointments, prepares the budget, and is responsible for the management of city government. The mayor also sets the council agenda, proposes policy, and (in many cities) may veto council actions.

Critics of the strong-mayor system believe that it makes the office of mayor too powerful. Critics also believe that the system may become excessively politicized and will fail to distribute services to constituents fairly or efficiently. This system conjures up the image of urban political party machines of the 1800s. Mayors who led such machines appointed political cronies as department heads, hired campaign workers as city employees, and awarded contracts to supporters.

Strong-Mayor System
A form of municipal government in which substantial authority (such as authority over appointments and the budget) is lodged in the office of the mayor, who is elected in a citywide election.

Although it was criticized by early 20th-century reformers, the strong-mayor form of government did not die out. It was often restructured, however, to include an elected city comptroller (or controller), thus preventing the mayor from having complete control of city finances. (Houston, for example, elects a city controller, who serves as the chief financial officer for the city.) Rules were also adopted to require that contracts be awarded to the lowest and best bidders. Other restrictions in place today that political bosses did not have to contend with include nonpartisan elections; ethics and campaign finance laws; Voting Rights Act coverage in many states, including Texas, that protects minority voting rights; and mayoral and city council term limits in cities throughout the nation.

Houston and Pasadena are the two largest Texas cities with a strong-mayor form of government. El Paso was the second largest city with such a system until 2004. That year, El Paso voters approved the establishment of the council-manager form of government, and a city manager was hired. In 2005, Dallas voters rejected two attempts to replace the city's council-manager system with a strong-mayor form of government.

The Mayor-Council System—Weak Mayor. The **weak-mayor system** (see Figure 28–2) lacks clear lines of authority because the mayor and council share administrative duties. Power, in effect, is decentralized. Under this system, voters may have difficulty determining who should be held accountable when problems and mismanagement occur. This type of government is not common in Texas, although it is used by many small cities.

The Commission System. The **commission system** (see Figure 28–2 on page 963) is another variety of municipal government found across the United States. In this system, voters elect one set of officials, who act as both executives and legislators. The commissioners, sitting together, are the municipal legislature, but each administers a city department individually. A manager or administrative assistant may be employed, but the ultimate administrative authority still remains with the elected commissioners.

Commissioners may possess technical knowledge about city government because they supervise city departments. Because power in the city bureaucracy is fragmented among separately elected commissioners, however, coordination is difficult, and the checks-and-balances system is impaired.

In Texas, home-rule cities are unlikely to use this form of government. The commission system has been largely replaced by the city manager option. The commission system also fell out of favor because of its association with other early 20th-century reform features, including at-large elections, an election system minority groups have challenged in court as diminishing minority voting power.[3] In Texas, a type of commission system is found in general-law cities, but it differs from the plan described previously. According to the Texas Municipal League, "In a general law city, one commissioner, acting alone, has no individual power; only the commission, acting collectively, exercises power."[4]

MUNICIPAL ELECTIONS SYSTEMS

The election systems used by Texas municipalities have sparked a considerable amount of legal and political controversy. The debate has primarily focused on the choice between at-large and single-member district elections.

At-large elections—citywide elections—usually take one of two forms. In the **pure at-large system**, all of the voters elect all of the members of the city council.

Weak-Mayor System
A form of municipal government in which an elected mayor and city council, often along with other elected officers, share administrative responsibilities.

Commission System
A system that allows the members of a city council to serve as heads of city departments.

At-Large Election
A citywide (or, in some states, countywide) election.

Pure At-Large System
An at-large election system in which all voters elect all the members of the city council, and candidates do not run for specific seats.

---

[3]*The Handbook of Texas Online,* http://www.tshaonline.org/handbook/online/; Amy Bridges, *Morning Glories: Municipal Reform in the Southwest* (Princeton, NJ: Princeton University Press), 1997.
[4]*Handbook for Mayors and Councilmembers: General Law Cities* (Austin: Texas Municipal League, 2001), p. 9.

At-Large Place System
An at-large election system in which all voters elect all the members of the city council, and each candidate runs for a specific seat on the council.

Single-Member District
A district in which the voters elect a single member of a legislative body, who runs for election only in that district.

The voters simply choose among all of the candidates to fill the available council seats, and the winning candidates are those who receive the most votes. With the **at-large place system**, each candidate runs for a specific seat on the council (place 1, place 2, and so forth) and is elected by either a plurality or a majority of votes cast citywide for that particular seat. Variations of either system may require that a candidate live in a particular district of the city, but the candidates are still elected by all of the voters in the city. In contrast, with **single-member districts**, each council member is elected from a particular district by the voters who live in that district.

At-Large Systems versus District Systems. Supporters of at-large elections say that they promote the public interest because council members must take a citywide view of problems. They charge that council members elected from districts are focused on the needs of their districts rather than the interests of the community as a whole.

Critics of at-large elections maintain that the system allows a simple majority of voters to elect all council members (who typically come from the upper-income brackets and live in the higher-income areas of town). When a citywide majority elects all council members, the interests of racial, ethnic, and ideological minorities in the community are not represented at city hall. These critics charge that effective neighborhood representation serves the interest of the entire city and is more likely to occur when each district elects its own representative to the council.

Single-Member Districts and Minorities. Although major Texas cities have usually resisted single-member districts, successful legal action in the federal courts by civil rights organizations—such as the Mexican American Legal Defense and Educational Fund, the League of United Latin American Citizens, the American GI Forum, the National Association for the Advancement of Colored People, Texas Rural Legal Aid, and the Southwest Voter Registration Education Project—has forced them to abandon at-large elections. Several cities have instituted a mixed system in which a majority of the council members live in, and are elected from, single-member districts, while the mayor and some additional council members are elected at large. One study found that Mexican American candidates in Texas cities were more likely to win the district positions than the at-large seats in mixed systems.[5] Another investigation drew similar conclusions about African American candidates in the state but found that, for Mexican American candidates, "the pattern was less clear primarily because they were sharply underrepresented in both components."[6]

According to the National Association of Latino Elected and Appointed Officials (NALEO) Educational Fund, in 2007 there were 2,127 locally elected Latino officials in the state. Further, Texas ranks number one among the states in the number of Latinos holding elective offices, and the vast majority (98 percent) are local officials. In 2001, according to the Joint Center for Political and Economic Studies, of the 5,452 African American county and municipal elected officials in the nation, 302 were elected in Texas.

Cumulative Voting (CV)
An at-large election system in which voters can cast one or more votes for a single candidate. For example, a voter who can cast up to five votes in a city council election can cast all five votes for one candidate or spread the votes among several candidates.

Another Alternative: Cumulative Voting. While the single-member district system has been the primary means of increasing minority representation on city councils, some cities have adopted other methods of achieving this goal. One alternative system is **cumulative voting (CV)**. Under this plan, city council members are elected in at-large elections. The number of votes a voter can cast corresponds to the number of seats on the council.

The key characteristic of CV is that the voter can cast more than one vote for a particular candidate. If, for example, there are five seats on the city council, a voter can cast

---

[5]J. L. Polinard, Robert D. Wrinkle, Tomas Longoria, and Norman E. Binder, *Electoral Structure and Urban Policy: The Impact on Mexican-American Communities* (Armonk, NY: M. E. Sharpe, 1994), p. 55.
[6]Robert Brischetto, David R. Richards, Chandler Davidson, and Bernard Grofman, "Texas," in *Quiet Revolution in the South: The Impact of the Voting Rights Act 1965–1990*, eds. Chandler Davidson and Bernard Grofman (Princeton, NJ: Princeton University Press, 1994), p. 252.

all five votes for one candidate or can cast, say, three votes for one candidate and the remaining two votes for another candidate. Theoretically, members of a voting minority in the city could cast all of their votes for a single candidate and increase the chances of that candidate's winning. Two political scientists have concluded, however, that "CV systems . . . guarantee no electoral outcomes. Minority voters must be mobilized and vote cohesively to take advantage of the opportunities CV provides."[7]

According to the organization FairVote, more than 50 local jurisdictions in Texas have adopted CV since the 1990s. Most are school districts. In about 20 percent of the communities where CV is found, both the school board and the city council have adopted the method. Civil rights organizations such as the National Association for the Advancement of Colored People (NAACP) and Mexican American Legal Defense and Educational Fund (MALDEF) have backed cumulative voting in litigation, and the adoption of this election system is credited with leading to the election of minorities in two Texas independent school districts—Atlanta and Amarillo. The Amarillo Independent School District resolved a lawsuit by adopting CV and is the largest jurisdiction in the nation to use this election system.

REVENUE SOURCES AND LIMITATIONS

Sources and amounts of revenue vary greatly among Texas municipalities according to various factors, including the following:

- the size of the city's population.
- the amount and type of taxes the city is allowed and willing to levy.
- the total assessed value of taxable property within the city limits.
- the needs of the residents.

The local political culture determines expectations about appropriate standards of services and tolerable levels of taxation (see Table 28–4). External forces—such as a downturn in the national economy, the closing of a military base, the downsizing of industries, federal and state mandates, and natural disasters—also influence the economic climate of a community. In Texas, state aid represents a considerably lower percentage of municipal revenue than is the norm in many other states. Thus, sales and property taxes are important sources of revenue for Texas cities.

The Sales Tax. A 1 percent municipal **sales tax** was authorized by the legislature in 1968, and since then Texas cities have become heavily dependent on it. Although all taxes are

Sales Tax
A tax collected on the retail price of purchased items.

TABLE 28–4 Property Taxes Levied by Texas Local Governments in 2008 (in Billions of Dollars)

COUNTIES	CITIES	SPECIAL DISTRICTS	SCHOOL DISTRICTS	TOTAL
6.3	6.4	4.9	21.2	**38.9**

Totals may not add due to rounding.
Source: Texas Comptroller of Public Accounts, Property Tax Assistance Division, http://www.window.state.tx.us/taxinfo/proptax/

[7]Robert R. Brischetto and Richard L. Engstrom, "Cumulative Voting and Latino Representation: Exit Surveys in Fifteen Texas Communities," *Social Science Quarterly*, December 1997. For an examination of cumulative voting and representation issues, see Shaun Bowler and Todd Donovan, "Cumulative Voting and Minority Representation: Can It Work?" in *Diversity in Democracy: Minority Representation* in the United States (Charlottesville, VA: University of Virginia Press, pp. 232–250.

DID YOU KNOW?

Grant money from the Governor's Criminal Justice Division was used to launch tattoo-removal programs in four Texas cities—Amarillo, Austin, El Paso, and San Antonio?

Property Tax
A tax on the assessed value of real estate.

affected by economic conditions, sales tax revenues vary more sharply during economic cycles of recession and recovery than do property tax revenues. In addition, the budgetary problems of state and national governments make their assistance to cities unreliable. Cities, therefore, need to build a reserve fund into their budgets to compensate for these somewhat inconsistent sources of revenues.

Property Taxes. Municipalities, school districts, and counties depend heavily on **property taxes**, in which the tax rate is a percentage of the assessed value of real estate. In a community with a low *tax base*, or total assessed value, the local government has a limited capacity to raise taxes from this source. Thus, a poor city must have a high tax rate to provide adequate services. Furthermore, any loss in assessed property values causes a decline in the city's tax base.

Texas has established a countywide appraisal authority for property taxes, and all local governments must accept its property appraisals. However, Texas state law does not require full disclosure when it comes to the price of home sales, which poses challenges when attempting to appraise property with accuracy. According to a 2003 survey by the Texas comptroller's office, chief appraisers concluded that a mandatory disclosure law would increase property values by more than $18 billion. Attempts to pass a mandatory disclosure law in the Texas state legislature in 2007 were unsuccessful.

The property tax rate in general-law cities depends on the size of the city. The maximum property tax rate of a general-law city, however, is $1.50 per $100 of assessed value. Home-rule municipalities can set property tax rates as high as $2.50 per $100 of assessed value.

Limits on Property Taxes. Some Texas cities have taken measures to limit increases in property taxes. For example, the Corpus Christi city charter contains a property tax cap of $0.68 per $100 valuation. (The tax hikes that are tied to voter-approved bonds are not applied toward the cap.) In 2003, Texas voters approved Proposition 13, which allows cities, towns, counties, and junior college districts to freeze property taxes for people who are disabled or elderly. Once the freeze is in place, the governing body cannot repeal it. Texas cities (as well as counties and hospital districts) may also call an election to lower property taxes by raising sales and use taxes.

Voters in non-school-district jurisdictions (cities, counties, and special districts) may petition for a **rollback election** to limit an increase in the property tax rate to no more

Rollback Election
In Texas, an election that permits voters to lower a local property tax increase to 8 percent.

COWBOYS STADIUM in Arlington, Texas, the home of the Dallas Cowboys football team, glows in the night on June 6, 2009, as the George Strait concert lets out. What are the costs and benefits of establishing a sports stadium for a community? What should the public and elected officials take into consideration in order to determine if the benefits outweigh the costs? (© Louis DeLuca/Dallas Morning News/ Corbis)

than 8 percent, plus additional revenue to meet debt-service requirements. For school districts, an election to decide if a tax increase will stand is automatically held if the increase exceeds $0.06 per $100 of assessed valuation; no petition is necessary. According to the Texas comptroller's office, close to 400 local governments have held rollback elections since 1982.

User Fees. When citizens are charged for services received, the charges are called **user fees**. These fees are increasingly popular for two reasons: (1) citizens' opposition to higher taxes and (2) the notion that people should pay for what they actually use. User fees may be collected for city-provided electricity, water, sewage, and garbage collection, as well as for swimming pools, golf courses, and ambulance services. The Texas Municipal League has found that user fees bring in approximately 20 percent of municipal revenue. Permits, business licenses, and inspection fees round out the usual sources of city revenue.

Borrowing. Local governments use **public debt**—normally, bond issues that must be approved by the voters in a referendum—to fund infrastructure projects such as roads, buildings, and public facilities. The amount and use of the debt are determined by the same legal, political, economic, and cultural factors that determine the source and amount of tax revenues. The law in Texas explicitly limits the amount of long-term debt to a percentage of assessed valuation of property within the boundaries of the government. This restriction is intended to keep governments from falling into bankruptcy, as many did during the Great Depression of the 1930s.

TRENDS AND ISSUES

Several trends and issues are important in understanding the current circumstances of Texas municipalities. These include population changes, economic development issues, federal and state mandates, annexation issues, and term limits for local officials.

Population Trends. Table 28–5 on the next page shows the populations of the 15 largest counties and cities in Texas based on 2009 Census Bureau estimates. A community's size as well as its rate of growth can have a significant impact on the public-policy decisions made by local officials. Even a city with overall limited growth may see an internal shift in population, with one area of the city facing dramatic growth in a short span of time, while other areas contend with a loss of population and businesses.

Like other local governments, cities must be aware of demographic changes that produce new demands on city services. For example, a survey of more than 1,000 local governments revealed "challenges in meeting the needs of or planning for older adults," including "accessibility, availability, affordability" when it comes to housing.[8] Cities can also feel the impact of countywide trends on such variables as income. According to the Census Bureau's 2006 American Community Survey, of the 10 counties in the nation with the lowest median incomes, five are in Texas: Lubbock, Nueces, El Paso, Hidalgo, and Cameron.

Economic Development. The **Development Corporation Act** allows many Texas cities to adopt a sales tax for economic development projects, subject to voter approval. The adopting cities have either a 4A or 4B designation, and the classifications determine how the funds can be spent. According to the Texas attorney general's *Economic Development Handbook for Texas Cities (2008)*, 4A status is open only to cities that meet certain population standards, while all cities are eligible for the 4B designation.

DID YOU KNOW?

Eighteen states permit local income taxes but Texas does not?

User Fee
A charge paid by an individual who receives a particular government service, such as water provision or garbage collection.

Public Debt
Sums owed by governments.

Development Corporation Act
A state law that allows select Texas cities to raise the sales tax for economic development, subject to voter approval.

---

[8]Evelina R. Moulder, "The Maturing of America: How Local Governments Are Preparing for a Wave of Retirees," *The Municipal Year Book 2007* (Washington, DC: International City/County Management Association, 2007), p. 9.

TABLE 28–5 2009 Population Estimates and 2000 Census for the 15 Largest Counties and Incorporated Cities in Texas

GEOGRAPHIC AREA	POPULATION		% INCREASE
	2009	2000	
COUNTY			
Harris	4,070,989	3,400,578	19.7%
Dallas	2,451,730	2,218,899	6.8
Tarrant	1,789,900	1,446,219	23.7
Bexar	1,651,448	1,392,931	18.5
Travis	1,026,158	812,280	26.3
Collin	791,631	491,675	61.0
El Paso	751,296	679,622	10.5
Hidalgo	741,152	569,463	30.1
Denton	658,616	432,976	52.1
Fort Bend	556,870	354,452	57.1
Montgomery	447,718	293,768	52.4
Williamson	410,686	249,967	64.2
Cameron	396,371	335,227	18.2
Nueces	323,046	313,645	2.9
Brazoria	309,208	241,767	27.8
CITY			
Houston	2,257,926	1,953,631	15.5%
San Antonio	1,373,668	1,144,646	20.0
Dallas	1,299,543	1,188,580	9.3
Austin	786,386	656,562	19.7
Fort Worth	727,577	534,694	36.0
El Paso	620,456	563,662	10.0
Arlington	380,085	332,969	14.1
Corpus Christi	287,439	277,454	3.5
Plano	273,613	222,030	23.2
Laredo	226,124	176,576	28.0
Lubbock	225,859	199,564	13.1
Garland	222,013	215,768	2.8
Irving	205,541	191,615	7.2
Amarillo	189,392	173,627	9.0
Brownsville	176,859	139,722	26.5

Sources: U.S. Census Bureau, Population Estimates Program. See http://factfinder.census.gov/servlet/
GCTTable?_bm=y&-geo_id=04000US48&-_box_head_nbr=GCT-T1-R&-ds_name=PEP_2009_EST&-_lang=en&
redoLog=false&-mt_name=PEP_2009_EST_GCTT1R_ST2S&-format=ST-2S&-_sse=on and www.census.gov/
popest/cities/SUB-EST2009.html

Sales tax revenue based on 4A status is used for projects related to industry and manufacturing and can be tied to a decrease in the property tax rate. Cities can submit to the voters a joint resolution proposing a 4A sales tax hike and a separate sales tax increase for property tax relief. Voters must either approve or reject the entire joint resolution. The 4B designation is more expansive in scope, allowing cities to use revenue for a wide range of projects, including professional and amateur sports facilities, public park improvements, and affordable housing. Since 1989, more than 500 cities have approved a sales tax hike for economic development under one of the designations, and more than 100 have passed increases under both the 4A and 4B designations. The tax has generated over $370 million for economic development at the local level. The economic development sales tax is particularly popular with small jurisdictions. According to the Texas Economic Development Council, more than half of the cities that have adopted the tax have a population of less than 5,000.

Government Mandates. Texas cities—like most cities in the nation—have seen both a decline in federal and state government dollars and an increase in the number of mandates imposed by these governments. A **mandate** is a law passed by Congress or a state legislature requiring a lower-level government to meet an obligation. Some notable examples of federal mandates are the Americans with Disabilities Act, the National Voter Registration Act (Motor Voter Act), the Help America Vote Act, and the No Child Left Behind Act. Supporters of mandates argue that they permit the federal and state governments to meet important needs in a uniform fashion. Critics charge that mandates—particularly those that are unfunded—impose a heavy financial burden on those governments required to fulfill the obligations.

> **Mandate**
> A requirement or standard imposed on one level of government by a higher level of government.

In the late 1990s, the Texas legislature passed House Bill 66, which established the Unfunded Mandates Interagency Work Group. The state auditor, the state comptroller, the director of the Legislative Budget Board, a senator (selected by the lieutenant governor), and a representative (selected by the speaker) make up the group. Its charge is to record unfunded mandates that are passed by the legislature so that lawmakers have a sense of the impact of these mandates on other governments. Several types of unfunded mandates are exempt from the list, however, including those that are passed in compliance with the Texas Constitution, federal law, or a court order, as well as those that are established as a result of a popular election.

DID YOU KNOW?

According to the Texas Department of State Health Services, more than 250 Texas cities restrict smoking in public places, such as restaurants, bars, and workplaces, but some of the cities have stricter enforcement and punishment than others?

Annexation. Big cities in Texas have not suffered as much as many other U.S. cities from "white flight," urban decay, the evacuation of industry, and declining tax bases. Texas cities have escaped some of the worst of these problems because of the state's liberal annexation laws.

The Municipal Annexation Act establishes a buffer area, known as **extraterritorial jurisdiction (ETJ),** that extends from one-half mile to five miles beyond the city's limits, depending on the city's population. The city may enforce zoning and building codes in the outlying area, and new cities may not be incorporated within the ETJ. The law also gives home-rule cities the power to annex an area equal to 10 percent of their existing area each year without the consent of the inhabitants of the area to be annexed. With this protection and with long-range planning, Texas cities can avoid being boxed in by suburban bedroom cities.

> **Extraterritorial Jurisdiction (ETJ)**
> In Texas, a buffer area that extends beyond a city's limits. Cities can enforce some laws, such as zoning and building codes, in an ETJ.

One strategy involves annexing "fingers" of land outward from the existing city limits and placing the area between the fingers into the ETJ. The unincorporated areas within the ETJ may then be annexed as they become sufficiently populated to warrant it. Central cities that plan ahead are therefore free to extend their boundaries and recapture both the tax base and the population that may have left the city. Increasingly, though, inhabitants of outlying areas are raising objections to the state's municipal annexation laws. These persons resent the fact that their jurisdictions can be annexed without their permission.

The Texas legislature passed a comprehensive annexation bill—the first in more than three decades—in 1999. The measure requires cities to give notice of annexation plans three years in advance, participate in arbitration with areas to be annexed, and deliver services within two and a half years. (Exceptions to the last requirement can be triggered under certain circumstances.) Outlying areas face limits on what they can do if they want to avoid annexation.

A special annexation issue involves **colonias**. A colonia is an unincorporated urban district along the U.S.–Mexican border. They are typically severely impoverished and must contend with a multitude of problems, including substandard housing, unsanitary drinking water, and lack of proper sewage disposal. The Texas attorney general's office has identified more than 1,800 colonias in 29 Texas counties, most of which lie along the U.S.–Mexico border.

These colonias are eligible for financial aid from the state. But what happens to the aid a colonia receives if it is annexed? In 1999, the Texas legislature passed a law that allows a colonia eligible for state aid to continue to receive it for five years after annexation.

Colonia
In Texas, an unincorporated urban district along the U.S.–Mexican border. Colonias are often impoverished and are chiefly inhabited by Mexican Americans.

Term Limit
A restriction on the number of times a person can be elected to a particular office.

Term Limits. While there are no **term limits** for members of Congress, 15 states limit the terms of their state legislatures, according to the National Conference of State Legislatures. In a 2003 survey of cities, responses revealed that only 9 percent have term limits for their chief elected official or the city council, but the measure is more likely to be adopted in larger cities.[9] Proponents of term limits believe that city hall is best governed by new blood and fresh ideas and that limiting the number of terms council members may serve is the best way to achieve that goal. Opponents, though, worry that cities stand to lose experienced, effective council members.

According to the Texas Municipal League, term-limit laws have been approved by the voters in more than 60 cities in the state, with the bulk of the adoptions occurring in the early 1990s. These laws are less than uniform. In Austin, a council member is limited to two consecutive three-year terms, but that limit can be waived with a petition signed by 5 percent of the registered voters represented by the council member. In Dallas, city council members are subject to term limits, but the mayor is not.

Attempts to weaken city term-limit laws through state laws or litigation have been unsuccessful. In 2000, voters in Austin rejected a proposition that would have repealed the city's term-limit law. Four years later, San Antonio voters said no to a ballot measure that would have permitted council members to serve beyond two terms. However, in 2008, a proposal for a limit of four (rather than two) two-year terms passed in San Antonio. Corpus Christi voters decided in November 2010 to tighten term limits. A council member who meets the four two-term limit now must wait six years rather than two before running again for the seat.

DID YOU KNOW?

That Texas has more than 2,000 colonias, which is more than any other state?

COUNTIES

The responsibilities of county governments also have a direct impact on the public. For example, the March 2008 Democratic primary and precinct conventions (caucuses)—commonly referred to as the "Texas two-step"—saw a huge turnout as a result of the intense competition between Barack Obama and Hillary Clinton for the Democratic Party nomination. The county commissioners court decided the precinct voting locations in each county. The county clerk is responsible for early voting, issues marriage licenses, and records birth and death certificates. Property taxes are paid to the county tax office, which

---

[9]Susan A. MacManus and Charles S. Bullock III, "The Form, Structure, and Composition of America's Municipalities in the New Millennium," *The Municipal Year Book 2003* (Washington, DC: International City/County Management Association, 2003), pp. 9, 15.

POLITICS WITH A purpose

Regulating Cell Phone Use

Many Americans believe that using a cell phone while driving an automobile can be dangerous. Many of these same individuals admit to doing so. In a survey conducted by the Insurance Research Council, 84 percent of cell phone users reported that using cell phones while driving could increase the likelihood of accidents, while another 61 percent reported using their cell phones while driving.[a] Some studies have also found delayed reaction time, "especially in the beginning stages of the telephone conversation."[b]

Whether drivers are talking on cell phones or texting, these electronic devices are perceived to be a danger. Given this evidence, state lawmakers are trying to figure out how best to regulate cell phone use in automobiles.

Some states have already taken steps to either ban or limit handheld cell phone use in automobiles. In 2008, California, Connecticut, New Jersey, New York, Utah, and Washington were the only states to ban the use of handheld cell phones while driving. Texas and 19 other states, as well as the District of Columbia, have banned the use of cell phones while operating a school bus. Texas also bans intermediate license holders from using a cell phone for the first six months that they hold this license.[c] In 2009 the Texas state legislature passed a ban on the use of cell phones in school zones. For the law to go into effect, cities or counties must at their own expense first set up signs in school zones indicating the penalty for violating the law.

Some state lawmakers are more concerned with drivers using their cell phones to text-message. In May 2007, Washington became the first state to ban sending and receiving text messages while driving, and New Jersey soon followed. By 2010 thirty states and the District Columbia had banned cell phone texting while driving.[d] If this policy leads to improvements in driving habits, one can expect other states and municipalities to do the same.

Public policy is inspired by a variety of factors. When new technology is introduced into society, lawmakers, like those in the Texas legislature, react to the impact of technology on society and respond to regulate the negative side effects of it. In doing so, lawmakers attempt to limit government intrusion without compromising public safety. Do you think that these attempts have been successful? What do you think about the regulation of cell phone use? What other factors contribute to the enactment of legislation?

[a]Insurance Research Council (IRC), "Cell Phone Owners Prefer to Ignore the Risks," accessed at www.ircweb.org/.
[b]Andrew Parkes and Victor Hooijmeijer, "The influence of the Use of Mobile Phones on Driver Situation Awareness," accessed August 20, 2008, at www-nrd.nhtsa.dot.gov/.

[c]Insurance Institute for Highway Safety: Highway Loss Data Institute, "Cell Phone Laws," accessed August 25, 2008, at www.iihs.org/laws/CellPhoneLaws.aspx.
[d]Ibid, accessed November 8, 2010.

also issues license plates and stickers and processes vehicle transfers. County dispute resolution services help resolve conflicts between landlords and tenants through mediation.

Like the counties in most other states, Texas counties are established and structured by the state constitution and the legislature. The county serves as a general-purpose government and as an administrative arm of the state, carrying out the state's laws and collecting certain state taxes. Although the county is an arm of the state, state supervision is minimal.

County government is far less flexible than municipal government in its organization and functions. Texas counties do not have home rule. At one time, a constitutional provision authorized county home rule. The provision was so poorly written and so difficult to implement that no county in the state was able to use it to reorganize, and it was subsequently repealed.

DID YOU KNOW?

That according to the Texas Hospital Association, approximately 63 Texas counties do not have a hospital?

Because counties cannot pass ordinances unless specifically authorized by the state, new state statutes or constitutional amendments are often necessary to allow a county to deal with contemporary problems. The needs of Harris County, for example, with an estimated population of 4,070,989 in 2009, are significantly different from those of Loving County, which had only an estimated 45 inhabitants in that year. Yet Texas law allows only modest variations in county governments to accommodate these differences. (Many state laws, however, are unique to specific counties because of their population or their location—a law pertaining to a coastal county, for example.)

Counties are also limited in their ability to tax their citizens. Counties can impose property taxes at a maximum rate of $0.80 per $100 of assessed valuation, but they have the power to collect additional taxes beyond this limit—if the voters approve—to cover long-term debt for infrastructure, such as courthouses, criminal justice buildings, farm-to-market roads, flood control, and county road and bridge maintenance.

FUNCTIONS OF COUNTIES

County government is responsible for administering county, state, and national elections, but not those for municipalities, school districts, and other special districts. County government acts for the state in the following areas:

1. Securing rights-of-way for highways.
2. Providing law enforcement.
3. Registering births, deaths, and marriages.
4. Housing state district courts.
5. Registering motor vehicles.
6. Recording land titles and deeds.
7. Collecting some state taxes and fees.

Optional Powers. County government also has optional powers specifically authorized by state law, and these powers are found in various state codes. For example, according to the Local Government Code, a county government may undertake the following activities:

1. Establish and maintain libraries.
2. Operate and maintain parks.
3. Establish recreational and cultural facilities (such as auditoriums and convention centers).
4. Appoint a county historical commission.
5. Regulate sexually oriented businesses.

According to the Health and Safety Code, a county government has the authority to maintain a county hospital.

Intergovernmental Cooperation. A county government may also enter into an agreement with another local government to provide a service or program. For example, the Local Government Code permits county-city partnerships to purchase and maintain parks, museums, and historic sites. The Interlocal Cooperation Act, a part of the code, authorizes various local governments, including counties, cities, and special districts, to contract with each other for the provision of various administrative functions, such as tax assessment and collection and records management. The various governmental units may also jointly provide governmental functions and services, including police and fire protection, maintenance of streets and roads, public health and welfare, and waste disposal.

MAINTAINING LIBRARIES is an optional power of counties. (Marjorie Kamys Cotera/Daemmrich Photography/Image Works)

STRUCTURE AND ORGANIZATION OF COUNTIES

County government consists of several independently elected officials (see Figure 28–3 on the next page). The county governing body, the **commissioners court**, consists of the **county judge** and four **county commissioners**. The commissioners court is not a judicial body but a legislature of limited authority that approves the budget for all operations of the county, sets the tax rate, and passes ordinances.

The commissioners court does not have direct control over the many elected department heads of county government, but it wields considerable influence through its budgetary power. The county **sheriff**, for example, is responsible to county voters for enforcing the law and maintaining order and security in the county jail. The commissioners court, however, must provide the funds to build the jail and must approve its staff; authorize expenditures for each vehicle and its gas and repairs; and authorize deputies, clerks, and their salaries. The sheriff, therefore, is accountable not only to the voters but also to other elected county officials.

County Judges. The county judge is elected for a four-year term from the county at large to preside over the commissioners court. According to the Texas comptroller's office, the powers of the county judge are found in more than 50 provisions of the Local Government Code, as well as many other state codes. The Texas Association of Counties lists many powers held by Texas county judges, including the following:

1. Preparing the budget (a responsibility the county judge shares with the county clerk or auditor in counties with populations under 225,000).
2. Supervising election-related activities (calling elections, posting election notices, and receiving and canvassing election results).
3. Conducting hearings for beer and wine permits.
4. Performing marriage ceremonies.
5. Conducting hearings on state hospital admittance for people with mental illness and other mental disabilities.
6. Serving as the head of civil defense and disaster relief for the county.

Commissioners Court
In Texas, the policy-making body of a county. A commissioners court consists of a county judge (the presiding officer), who is elected in countywide elections, and four county commissioners elected from individual precincts.

County Judge
In Texas, an official elected countywide to preside over the commissioners court and to try certain minor cases.

County Commissioner
One of a group of officials elected to administer a county; in Texas, a member of the commissioners court who is elected from a district or precinct.

Sheriff
The chief law enforcement officer of a county—in most states, an elected official. In Texas, the sheriff's budget must be approved by the commissioners court, which limits the sheriff's authority.

FIGURE 28–3 Texas County Officials Elected by Voters

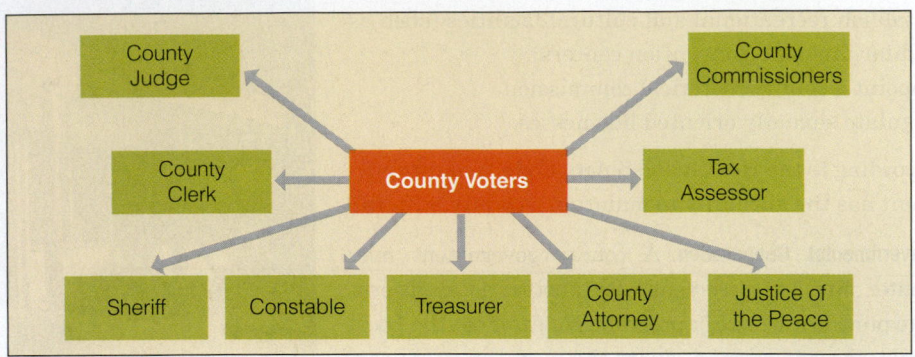

Additionally, a county judge may have judicial authority, but the obligations in this area depend on the county.

The County Commissioners. Four county commissioners make up the remaining membership of the court and are elected for four-year terms. Commissioners are elected in single-member districts (or precincts, as they are called in Texas). In 1968, the United States Supreme Court ruled that commissioner districts must be drawn on the basis of the one-person, one-vote principle.[10] During the next two decades, county governments faced many legal challenges because of malapportioned precincts. For example, between 1974 and 1984, the Mexican American Legal Defense and Educational Fund and the Southwest Voter Registration Education Project filed voting-rights lawsuits in more than 80 counties.[11]

Commissioners are frequently called "road commissioners" because they are responsible for the county roads and bridges within their precincts (unless a county engineer has been hired to do that job). Each commissioner is given a certain amount of revenue and has almost total authority to determine how it will be spent on roads and bridges. Rural residents often consider building and maintenance of rural roads the primary responsibilities of the commissioners.

Law Enforcement Officers. Officers with law enforcement duties include the county sheriff and constables. The sheriff is usually the most powerful county officer, next to the county judge, because he or she has a relatively large budget and a staff of deputies to assist in enforcing state law throughout the county. The sheriff's department usually refrains from patrolling within the corporate limits of cities, the better to use scarce resources and avoid jurisdictional disputes with city police. The department also operates the county jail and delivers and executes court papers (such as court orders).

Constables are elected from the same precincts as justices of the peace and serve as process officers of that court. They are also general law enforcement officers. In metropolitan counties such as Harris and Montgomery, constables have many deputies and are the heads of important law enforcement agencies.

In some counties, the office of constable has remained unfilled for years. Because the office is provided for in the Texas Constitution, however, the only way to abolish it has been by constitutional amendment. In 2002, voters approved an amendment that

Constable
A law enforcement officer. In Texas, constables are elected at the county level and serve as process officers of justice of the peace courts.

---

[10]*Avery v. Midland County*, 390 U.S. 474 (1968).
[11]David Montejano, *Anglos and Mexicans in the Making of Texas, 1836–1986* (Austin: University of Texas Press, 1987), p. 296.

LUPE VALDEZ was reelected sheriff of Dallas County in 2008. With a relatively large budget and staff of deputies to assist them in enforcing state law throughout the county, sheriffs are usually the most powerful county officers, next to county judges. (AP Photo/LM Otero)

allows a commissioners court to abolish a constable office that has been vacant for more than seven years. An abolished office can be restored by the commissioners court or by voter approval.

County Financial Officers. Officials with financial duties include the tax assessor-collector, the treasurer, and the auditor. The **tax assessor-collector** is probably the most important of these. The office has the following responsibilities:

1. Collecting various county taxes and fees.
2. Collecting certain state taxes and fees, particularly motor vehicle registration fees (license plate fees) and the motor vehicle sales tax.
3. Registering voters.

The **county treasurer** is responsible for receiving, depositing, and disbursing funds. Some counties have done away with the treasurer's office. When a county wishes to do this, the commissioners court must petition the legislature for a constitutional amendment to allow its county's voters to eliminate the county treasurer's office. The most likely recipient of the treasurer's duties will be the auditor.

The **county auditor** reviews all county financial records and ensures that expenditures are made in accordance with law. Whereas other key county officials are elected, county auditors are appointed for two-year terms by district judges.

Clerical Officers. Officials with clerical duties include county and district clerks. The **county clerk** serves as the county's chief record keeper and election officer. In some ways, the office parallels that of the Texas secretary of state. The county clerk has the following duties:

1. Serving as clerk for the county commissioners court.
2. Maintaining records for justices of the peace, for county courts, and for district courts in counties with populations of less than 8,000.
3. Recording deeds, mortgages, wills, and contracts.
4. Issuing marriage licenses and maintaining certain records of births and deaths.
5. Serving on the county election board, certifying candidates running for county office, and carrying out other "housekeeping" functions in connection with elections, including preserving the results of state, county, and local elections.

Tax Assessor-Collector
In Texas, a county financial officer whose responsibilities include collecting county taxes or fees and registering voters.

County Treasurer
A county official who is responsible for receiving, depositing, and disbursing county funds.

County Auditor
In Texas, a county financial officer whose duties, depending on the population of the county, may include reviewing county financial records and (in large counties) serving as the chief budget officer.

County Clerk
The chief record keeper and elections officer of a county.

District Clerk
In Texas, the record keeper for the district court in a county with a population that exceeds 8,000.

County Attorney
In Texas, a county legal officer who gives legal advice to the commissioners court, represents the county in court, and prosecutes crimes. If a county has both a county attorney and a district attorney, the latter prosecutes felony crimes.

District Attorney
An official who prosecutes felony cases.

In counties with populations of more than 8,000, the **district clerk** assumes the county clerk's role as record keeper for the district courts. (The county clerk continues to maintain records for the constitutional county court and any county courts-at-law in existence; these courts were discussed in Chapter 26.)

Legal Officers. County attorneys and **district attorneys** perform a variety of functions. Some counties have only one of these officials—either a county or a district attorney. This official prosecutes all criminal cases, gives advisory opinions to county officials that define their authority, and represents the county in civil proceedings.

If a county has both a district attorney and a county attorney, the district attorney specializes in prosecuting cases in district court, while the county attorney handles lesser cases. District attorneys are neither subordinate to nor part of county government in Texas, but their office space and salaries are partly paid by the counties. County attorneys are wholly county officials.

Other Officials. In some counties, commissioners courts or voters have created other executive officers. There may be five or more members of a county board of school trustees, a county superintendent of schools, a county surveyor, a county weigher, and even a county inspector of hides and animals. Counties may also authorize such appointive officers as the county election administrator, county health officer, county medical examiner, county agricultural agent, and home demonstration agent.

ISSUES AND TRENDS

The institutional features of Texas county government date to the 1800s. The demands of modern society are placing an increasingly heavy burden on this level of government. Next, we review some frequent criticisms of county government that follow from outdated structures and discuss the measures counties can take to deal with contemporary problems.

Constitutional Rigidity. The great mass of detailed and restrictive material in the Texas Constitution creates problems of rigidity and inflexibility, and additional controls are scattered throughout the civil statutes. The result is a collection of legal requirements that are applied equally to the four largest counties in the state—Harris, Dallas, Tarrant, and Bexar—and to the scores of counties that have populations of less than 20,000. This standardized approach gives little consideration to the special needs of individual counties. Two political scientists have observed that the nation's "state legislatures have exercised virtually unlimited authority in prescribing the limits of county discretion."[12] This general observation clearly applies to Texas. Under the current system, change has to come from the state legislature.

Long Ballot
An election ballot listing many independently elected offices.

Short Ballot
An election ballot listing only a few independently elected offices.

The Long Ballot. So many county officials are independently elected, and the operations of county government are so decentralized, that voters may find it difficult to monitor the many positions involved in county government. The current system of electing county officials is sometimes said to use a **long ballot**, because the ballot includes a long list of county offices to be filled. Reformers recommend a **short ballot** with fewer elected county officials. More officials would be appointed, and a county-manager system or an

---

[12]David R. Berman and Tanis J. Salant, "The Changing Role of Counties in the Intergovernment System," in *The American County: Frontiers of Knowledge*, ed. Donald C. Menzel (Tuscaloosa: University of Alabama Press, 1996), p. 24.

elected county executive would be established. Defenders of the long ballot counter that the direct election of public officials ensures that government will remain responsive to the needs and demands of the voters.

Unit Road System. One reform that counties are permitted to undertake is to establish a **unit road system**. This system takes the day-to-day responsibility for roads away from individual county commissioners and concentrates it in the hands of a professional engineer, who is responsible to the commissioners court. The voters may petition for an election to establish the unit road system, or commissioners may initiate the change themselves.

Supporters of this system maintain that it brings greater coordination and professionalism to the building of roads in rural areas. The current practice in most counties—dividing funds for roads and bridges among the four commissioners—is defended by those who believe these activities should remain the direct responsibility of elected officials.

Unit Road System
In Texas, a system that concentrates the day-to-day responsibilities of roads in the hands of a professional engineer rather than individual county commissioners. The engineer is ultimately responsible to the commissioners court.

The Civil Service System. Students of government often criticize the use of the spoils system to hire employees. Under this system, political loyalty rather than competence may be the main factor in the recruitment and retention of government workers. A county worker's job security may depend on political allegiance to a particular official and on that official's reelection. When a new official is elected, there may be a substantial turnover of county employees.

Opponents of these practices propose a civil service system that bases employment and promotion on specific qualifications and performance. Because civil service systems also prohibit termination of employment except for proven cause, such systems offer job security, which allegedly attracts qualified personnel. Supporters of this system maintain that it encourages professionalism, increases efficiency, and allows uniform application of equal opportunity requirements.

In contrast, supporters of the spoils system point out that elected officials are responsible for their employees' performance and therefore should have the authority to hire and fire at will. They also argue that an elected official would be foolish to release competent employees simply because they had gained their experience under a predecessor. Finally, they argue that the civil service system provides so much job security that complacency and indifference to the public interest may result.

Eligibility for Civil Service Systems. Texas counties with populations of 200,000 or more may establish a civil service system for county employees, while counties with populations of more than 500,000 may also establish a civil service system for the sheriff's office. According to the Texas Association of Counties, a civil service system exists in half of the 20 counties that meet the eligibility requirement. All seven counties that can establish this system in their sheriff's department have done so.

Consolidation. Students of county government reform point to **city-county consolidation** as a means of reducing both the number of local governments and the duplication of government services, as well as providing greater government efficiency. With consolidation, a county and cities within the county are merged into a single government. According to the National Association of Counties, 41 city-county consolidation proposals have been approved by voters since 1921.

City-County Consolidation
The union of a country and cities within the country to form a single unit of government.

There are several major challenges to the consolidation of governments. Consolidation requires action on the part of the state legislature, followed by local voter approval. Independently elected officials at the local level are likely to resist a move that would merge local responsibilities and reduce the number of political offices. Suzanne M. Leland and Kurt Thurmaier conclude, "The most critical elements that can affect the passage or defeat of the consolidation attempt involve the county sheriff, the status of the new chief executive, taxation, minority representation on the new city-county council, public employees' job security, and the status of minor municipalities."[13]

Additionally, "public choice" theorists maintain that government fragmentation is preferable to a monopoly, that smaller governments are more responsive than larger ones, and that the current system forces governments to be competitive.[14] While many cities and counties enter into agreements to provide services, city-county consolidation bills have failed to win passage in the Texas legislature.

SPECIAL DISTRICTS

Special districts are local governments that provide single or closely related services that are not provided by general-purpose county or municipal governments. (Although the more than 1,000 independent school districts in Texas constitute a type of special-purpose government, other districts are the focus of this chapter. School districts were discussed in Chapter 27.) Special districts do not always receive attention comparable to cities and councils, but they are no less important when it comes to serving the needs of the public. In a suburban area outside the city limits, for example, a special district may be established to provide water and sewer facilities for a housing development. This government unit will have the authority to borrow to build the system and may assess taxes and user fees on property owners and residents.

The number of special districts has grown considerably since the 1950s, as shown in Table 28–6. In fact, special districts are the most numerous of all local governments in Texas (see Table 28–1 on page 959). According to the census bureau, two-thirds of the special districts in Texas provide a single service. The rest are classified as multiple-function districts, and most of those provide sewerage and water supply. Examples of special districts in the state include the following:

- Airport authorities.
- Drainage districts.
- Hospital authorities.
- Municipal utility districts (MUDs).
- Library districts.
- Navigation districts.
- Metropolitan transit authorities (MTAs—see Figure 28–4).

TABLE 28–6 Special Districts in Texas, 1952–2007

1952	1962	1972	1982	1992	2002	2007
491	733	1,215	1,681	2,266	2,245	2,291

Sources: U.S. Census Bureau, *2002 Census of Governments, Volume 1, Number 1, Government Organization*, GC02(1)-1, U.S. Government Printing Office, Washington, DC, 2002, www.census.gov/prod/2003pubs/gc021x1. pdf.; U.S. Census Bureau, 2007 Census of Governments, www.census.gov/govs/cog/GovOrgTab03ss.html.

[13]Suzanne M. Leland and Kurt Thurmaier, "Lessons from 35 Years of City-County Consolidation Attempts," in *The Municipal Year Book, 2006* (Washington, DC: International City/County Management Association, 2006), p. 8.
[14]A thorough discussion of metropolitan fragmentation can be found in Virginia Gray and Peter Eisinger, *American States and Cities*, 2nd ed. (New York: Addison-Wesley Educational Publishers, 1997), Chapter 11.

FIGURE 28–4 Cities and Counties Served by Public Transportation Systems (Metropolitan Transit Authorities, or MTAs)

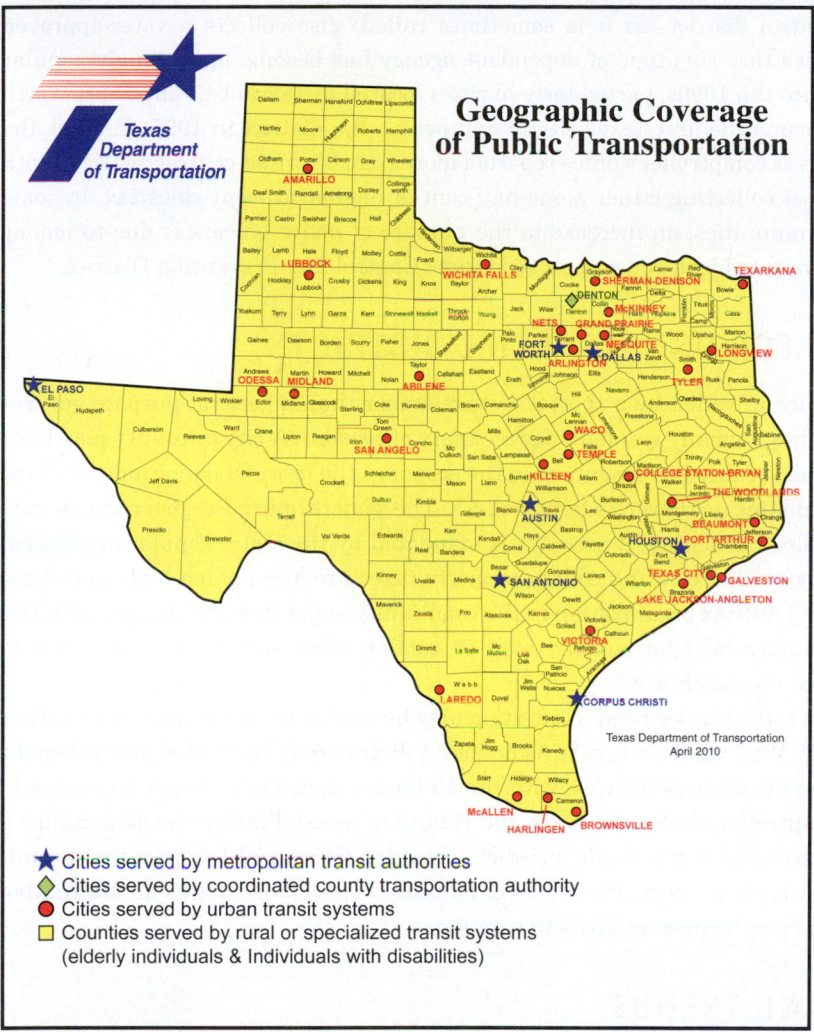

Source: Texas Department of Transportation, 2010.

- River authorities.
- Rural fire-prevention districts.
- Noxious weed-control districts.

Some individuals who serve on the governing boards of special districts are elected, whereas city councils and county commissioners appoint others. In some cases, council members and commissioners serve on these boards themselves.

DEPENDENT AGENCIES

Special districts should not be confused with **dependent agencies**. The U.S. Bureau of the Census recognizes some government entities as dependent agencies rather than special districts because they are closely tied to general-purpose governments and do not have as much independence as special districts in budgeting and administration.

Dependent Agency
A government entity that is closely linked to general-purpose governments. Dependent agencies do not have the independence of special districts.

An example of a dependent agency is a crime-control and prevention district, which is subject to voter approval and remains in existence for only a designated number of years unless the voters approve an extension. A crime-control district (as it is sometimes called) also collects a voter-approved sales tax. This type of dependent agency has become increasingly popular since the 1990s, particularly in cities located in Tarrant County. Fort Worth became the first Texas city to approve such a district in 1995. In 2009, the Texas comptroller's office reported more than 60 crime-control districts, with most collecting either a one-half-cent or one-fourth-cent sales tax. In some communities, an increase in the number of police officers is due to money generated by a voter-approved Crime Control and Prevention District.

REASONS FOR USING SPECIAL DISTRICTS

Having a service provided by a special district rather than a general-purpose government is appealing to many residents for a variety of reasons. A city or county may have limited revenue because of a downturn in the economy, the loss of a major industry, new unfunded mandates, or fewer federal dollars. The general-purpose government may have hit its sales tax ceiling (2 percent) as mandated by the state. Popular or political sentiment may be that city and county property taxes are already too high, and there may be a strong antitax organization in the community eager to make that point. Little or no support may exist for raising taxes or cutting other services to accommodate another service responsibility.

Furthermore, the service need in question may be unique to only a small area within a city or county. Why tax the entire jurisdiction? A district may be created for the benefit of underserved areas, as is the case with the 15 library districts in Texas, according to the Texas comptroller, that serve rural and suburban areas. Finally, the demand for a service may extend beyond a single jurisdiction, calling for a special district that is multicity or multicounty in scope. For a host of reasons, a special district as an alternative revenue source can become an attractive option.

ISSUES AND TRENDS

Special districts can be dissolved. According to the Local Government Code, a municipality can annex a special district. The municipality then takes ownership of the district's property and assets and assumes responsibility for the district's debts, liabilities, and services. The national trend, though, has clearly been toward an increase in the number of special districts, and this trend is also evident in Texas. (See again Table 28–6 on page 980.) Some people believe that the growing number of special districts may be a problem.

"Hidden" Governments. Special districts are sometimes called "hidden" governments. For one thing, the actions of district officials and employees are less visible than if a county or city provided the services. In addition, when elections are held at times or places other than those for general elections, voter turnout is quite low.

Cost. Because special districts are often small, they may purchase in limited quantities at higher prices than larger governments. Additionally, if special districts have little or no authority to tax, they are forced to borrow by issuing revenue bonds, which are paid from fees collected for the service provided, rather than from general-obligation bonds, which are paid from tax revenue.

Because revenue bonds are less secure than general-obligation bonds, residents are forced to pay higher interest rates just to service the bonded indebtedness. Special districts may also have a lower bond rating than larger, general-function governments, which further increases their cost of borrowing.

A study of special districts in more than 300 U.S. metropolitan areas concluded that the special-purpose approach to governing is more costly than the general-purpose approach. Additionally, social-welfare functions (such as hospitals, housing, and welfare) tend to receive more revenue in metropolitan areas with fewer special districts. Housekeeping functions (including fire protection, natural resource management, and police protection) and development functions (including airports, water, and highways) tend to receive more revenue in areas in which special districts are more prevalent.[15]

As stated earlier, local governments sometimes enter into interlocal governments to meet the needs of their respective jurisdictions. Many governments also recognize that problems and fiscal challenges often transcend city, county, and special-district jurisdictions, and that solutions of a regional nature must be sought.

A 2004 survey of city officials conducted by the National League of Cities revealed that "three-fourths of city officials (75 percent) rate their municipality's relations with other cities in their region and metropolitan area as either excellent (28 percent) or good (47 percent),"[16] which is encouraging to those who seek intergovernmental cooperation. However, the survey also shows that the degree of cooperation among municipalities varies depending on the policy. For example, cities are more optimistic about working together on traffic congestion problems and business development issues than on concentrated poverty and the physical conditions of neighborhoods. Furthermore, looking at the three classifications of cities—central, suburban, and rural—the survey concludes: "Different types of cities within a region perceive the benefits of interlocal and regional cooperation in different ways."[17]

COUNCILS OF GOVERNMENTS

Councils of governments (COGs) represent an attempt by the state to encourage coordination of local government activities on a regional basis. The first COG in Texas was formed in 1966, and today there are 24 COGs encompassing all regions of Texas. Figure 28–5 on the next page shows the boundaries, populations, and Web site addresses of the 24 Texas COGs. According to the Texas Association of Regional Councils (TARC), more than 2,000 governments in Texas belong to COGs. Most of the members are municipal and county governments.

DID YOU KNOW?

That Plano was the first Texas city to establish a youth police academy?

A COG is not another government and has no jurisdiction over the various local governments within its borders. Rather, it is a voluntary grouping of governments that have not relinquished any of their self-government rights. COGs provide several significant services to their members, including regional planning, technical services, and help in applying for grants. When requested by member governments, COGs provide research into problem areas and organize and operate training facilities, such as police academies.

One of the major issues on the agenda of Texas COGs is homeland security. The Texas Association of Regional Councils is working with the Texas Engineering Extension Service and the governor's Texas homeland security coordinator to facilitate the implementation of the state's Homeland Security Project. The TARC Web site (**www.txregionalcouncil.org**) lists homeland security training workshops that were held at COGs throughout the state,

---

[15]Kathryn A. Foster, *The Political Economy of Special-Purpose Government* (Washington, DC: Georgetown University Press, 1997), pp. 221–224.
[16]*The State of America's Cities 2004: The Annual Opinion Survey of Municipal Elected Officials* (Washington, DC: National League of Cities, 2004), p. 10.
[17]Ibid.

FIGURE 28–5 Councils of Governments in Texas

This map shows the comptroller's 13 regions and the 24 corresponding regional governments. Regional governing bodies are shown with Web site addresses and the U.S. Census 2000 population. Texas's total population in 2000 was 20,851,820.

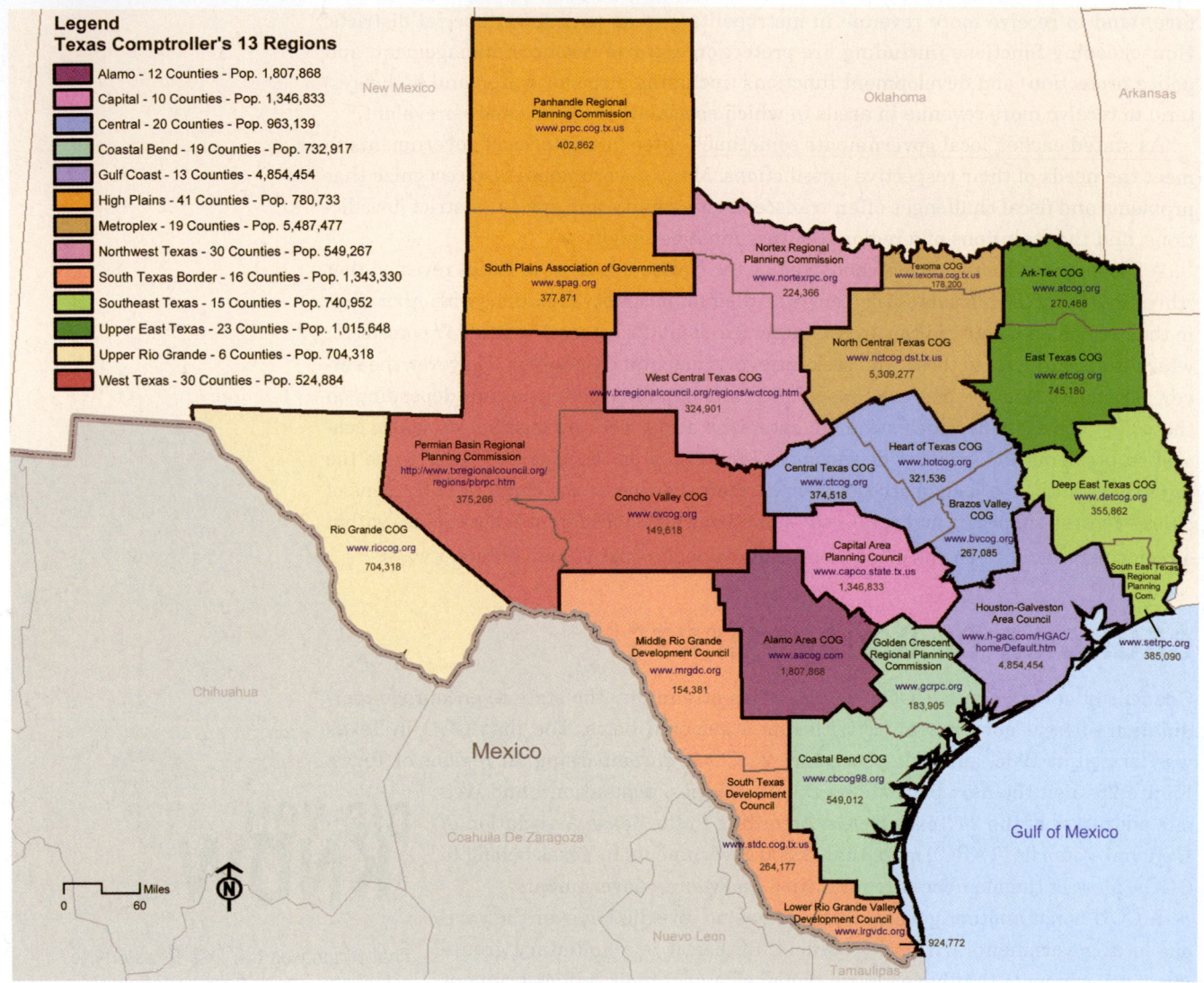

Note: Map data provided "as is" with no warranties of any kind. Colors have no specific representation other than cartographic display.
Sources: ESRI data, Texas comptroller, and U.S. Census Bureau's 2000 Population Statistics Disclaimer.

including workshops entitled "Operational Weapons of Mass Destruction Response for Law Enforcement Train-the-Trainer," "Counterterrorism Training," "Multihazard Program for Schools," and "Radiation Safety Training."

According to the TARC, the South East Texas Regional Planning Commission, Deep East Texas Council of Governments, and the Houston-Galveston Area Council have distributed $40 million of Hurricane Rita relief money to Southeast Texas. In 2008, the Bexar County Commissioners Court commissioned the Alamo Area Council of Governments to establish an inventory of all greenhouse gases in the county.

By bringing local officials together, COGs provide a base for the exchange of ideas and knowledge. Although COGs do not solve the problems facing local governments, they do encourage local officials to recognize the magnitude of these problems and cooperate in managing some of them.

YOU CAN MAKE A Difference

INVOLVEMENT AT THE LOCAL LEVEL

Like the laws handed down by the national and state governments, the policies made by cities, counties, and special districts have a major bearing on our lives. While we can correspond with elected officials and bureaucrats at every level of government in one fashion or another, the best chance of communicating with government officials in an immediate manner—and sometimes even face to face—is at the local level. In addition, we share a common bond with those who fill our local government offices: Like us, they live in our community.

WHY SHOULD YOU CARE?

Local government issues often create strong differences of opinion in the community. Should a city council pass a smoking ban? Should it replace an at-large election system with single-member districts? Should it change from a city-manager to a strong-mayor form of government? Should a municipality and a county government share the expense of a jail, or should they maintain separate jail facilities? Should two neighboring counties join forces to establish and fund a park? Should a metropolitan transit authority change bus routes or suspend service on holidays?

Elected and appointed officials may disagree on what to do about these matters, but unless they decide to take no action at all, they will cast votes or adopt policies that affect everyone in the community. Local government officials should, and often do, seek the views of the public. The public also has many other opportunities to express informed opinions.

WHAT CAN YOU DO?

You can take the following steps to influence local governments:

1. *Observe and learn about local government.* Organize a City Hall Day at your college or university. Hold panel discussions on key issues facing your community. Invite local elected officials (such as the mayor and members of the city council), appointed officials (such as the city manager, the city secretary, and the heads of various city departments), and city hall reporters to serve on the panels. Attend a city council meeting or a county commissioners court meeting. If your local cable system carries these meetings, watch them regularly. Attend a court trial, and watch the county attorney

or district attorney in action. If a constable maintains a ride-along program, ask if you can participate.
2. *Get your message out.* At a meeting of the city council, a special-district board, or the county commissioners court, sign up to speak about an issue that matters to you during the public comments part of the meeting. Write a letter to the editor of a newspaper about a local issue that is important to you. Your letter could spark an exchange of ideas in your community. It might even lead local elected officials to take action.
3. *Participate.* Participate in a local campaign. Candidates often need volunteers to help organize rallies and Get Out the Vote drives, stuff envelopes, work phone banks, and pass out campaign literature.
4. *Advise local lawmakers and officials.* Apply for membership on a city advisory board or commission. Go to your city's official Web site and check out the many boards and commissions that offer you the chance to advise the city council and city officials on matters of critical importance to your community such as health, education, transportation, housing, and ethics.

CITY COUNCILS throughout the nation appoint high school students to youth commissions or councils to advise them on challenges facing young people in their communities. How can youth commissioners effectively share what they learn at City Hall with their peers, the schools and the community as a whole? (Frank Casimiro/ZUMA Press/Newscom)

KEY TERMS

at-large election 965
at-large place system 966
charter 961
city-county consolidation 979
colonia 972
commissioners court 975
commission system 965
constable 976
council-manager system 963
county attorney 978
county auditor 977
county clerk 977
county commissioner 975
county judge 975

county treasurer 977
cumulative voting (CV) 966
dependent agency 981
Development Corporation Act 969
district attorney 978
district clerk 978
extraterritorial jurisdiction (ETJ) 971
general-law city 961
general-purpose government 959
home-rule city 961
long ballot 978
mandate 971
property tax 968

public debt 969
pure at-large system 965
rollback election 968
sales tax 967
sheriff 965
short ballot 978
single-member district 966
strong-mayor system 964
tax assessor-collector 977
term limit 972
unitary system of government 960
unit road system 979
user fee 969
weak-mayor system 965

CHAPTER SUMMARY

1. Municipalities, counties, and special districts provide many services that have a direct impact on our daily lives. It is important, then, to examine these governments in both their historical and contemporary contexts.

2. The municipal reform movement of the early 20th century had a major effect on Texas cities. Key features of the reform era—nonpartisan elections, the council-manager form of government, and at-large elections—are characteristic of many Texas cities. Some cities with Hispanic and African American populations have (often by court order) replaced at-large elections with single-member districts, modified election systems, or cumulative voting to enhance the chances that minority candidates can be elected to the city council.

 3. **How can voters exert direct influence over municipal governments?** While participating in city council elections is a critical means of shaping the direction of city government, several other measures can also be taken by voters to achieve this end. The initiative, the referendum, recall elections, rollback elections, term-limit laws, and economic development sales tax elections offer voters the opportunity to directly influence city government and, in turn, the political and economic climate of a community.

4. Texas county government is largely a product of the 1800s, yet the county is increasingly being called on to resolve problems once considered almost exclusively urban.

5. **What revenue sources can Texas cities use to meet their budget needs and obligations?** Texas municipalities rely on a variety of revenue sources—property and sales taxes, user fees, public debt, and state and federal dollars—to provide services. City officials must decide what measures should be taken when some of these sources meet public opposition or decline because of external factors, such as an economic crisis or demographic changes.

6. **What is the nature of intergovernmental relations at the local level?** With close to 5,000 local governments in Texas, government at this level is largely fragmented. While there can be friction between governments (e.g., in the area of annexation), there can also be cooperation (such as interlocal agreements). Any significant changes in the structural relationship among cities, counties, and special districts, however, will probably be incremental rather than sweeping.

SELECTED PRINT, MEDIA, AND ONLINE RESOURCES

PRINT RESOURCES

Bowler, Shaun, and Todd Andrew Donovan. *Demanding Choices: Opinion, Voting, and Direct Democracy.* Ann Arbor: University of Michigan Press, 1998. The authors give a comprehensive overview of the role the voter plays in referendums.

García, Sonia R., Valerie Martinez-Ebers, Irasema Coronado, Sharon A. Navarro, and Patricia A. Jaramillo. *Políticas: Latina Public Officials in Texas.* Austin: University of Texas Press, 2008. This study includes insightful interviews with some of the first Latinas to serve as mayors or on city councils in the state.

Grey, Lawrence. *How to Win a Local Election: A Complete Step-by-Step Guide,* 3rd ed. New York: M. Evans & Co., 2007. A former Ohio appellate judge offers sound advice on the many aspects of running for local office.

Kaufmann, Karen M. *The Urban Voter: Group Conflict and Mayoral Voting Behavior in American Cities.* Ann Arbor: The University of Michigan Press, 2004. The author explores the role of race when it comes to voting in big-city elections.

Pelissero, John, ed. *Cities, Politics, and Policy: A Comparative Analysis.* Washington, DC: CQ Press, 2003. This book is a collection of articles focusing on major urban issues, including intergovernmental relations, political participation, race and ethnicity, power, decision making, economic development, urban service delivery, finance, and suburban and metropolitan government.

Riordon, William L. *Plunkitt of Tammany Hall: A Series of Very Plain Talks on Very Practical Politics.* Boston, MA: Bedford/St. Martin's, 1994. This book offers the perspective of George Washington Plunkitt, a Tammany Hall ward boss, on why the political machine is preferable to political reform.

Rosales, Rodolfo. *The Illusion of Inclusion: The Untold Political Story of San Antonio.* Austin: University of Texas Press, 2000. The author provides a comprehensive examination of the role of Chicano and Chicana electoral politics in San Antonio municipal elections from the early 1950s to the early 1990s.

Shaw, Catherine. *The Campaign Manager: Running and Winning Local Elections,* 3rd ed. Boulder, CO: Westview Press, 2004. This book offers an in-depth examination of campaigning at the local level.

Strachan, J. Cherie. *High-Tech Grass Roots: The Professionalism of Local Politics.* New York: Rowman & Littlefield Publishers, 2003. This book demonstrates that candidates running for local office in small and medium-sized districts are using resources that in the past were more commonly associated with big-city elections.

Woodworth, James R., W. Robert Gump, and James R. Forrester. *Camelot: A Role Playing Simulation of Political Decision Making,* 5th ed. Belmont, CA: Thomson Wadsworth, 2006. The authors provide a variety of simulation exercises that reveal the inner workings of local political decision making.

MEDIA RESOURCES

City Hall—A 1996 film that depicts a New York mayor (Al Pacino) and the corruption that can surface in big-city politics.

Lone Star—A 1996 murder mystery that depicts the interaction among the residents of a small South Texas border community.

Street Fight—A 2005 documentary on the 2002 Newark, New Jersey, mayoral contest between Cory Booker, a 32-year-old Rhodes Scholar and Yale Law School graduate, and the veteran four-term incumbent, Sharpe James.

ONLINE RESOURCES

Texas Association of Regional Councils Regional planning organizations try to coordinate the activities of local governments in their regions: www.txregionalcouncil.org

Texas Department of Transportation provides information about metropolitan transit authorities (MTAs): www.dot.state.tx.us/

Types of City Government across Major Texas Cities Compare different systems of government. Cities that use the council-manager system include Austin, Dallas, and San Antonio: www.ci.austin.tx.us, www.dallascityhall.com, and www.ci.sat.tx.us. Houston and Pasadena use the mayor-council system: www.houstontx.gov and www.ci.pasadena.tx.us

U.S. Census Bureau's State and County QuickFacts A useful source of information about local government in Texas that provides an abundance of data on all Texas counties and cities: http://quickfacts.census.gov/qfd/index.html

Window on State Government Special districts can provide almost any kind of governmental service. Visit the Texas comptroller's Web site: www.window.state.tx.us/

APPENDIX A

THE DECLARATION
OF INDEPENDENCE

IN CONGRESS, JULY 4, 1776

A Declaration by the Representatives of the United States of America, in General Congress assembled. When in the Course of human Events, it becomes necessary for one People to dissolve the Political Bands which have connected them with another, and to assume among the Powers of the Earth, the separate and equal Station to which the Laws of Nature and of Nature's God entitle them, a decent Respect to the Opinions of Mankind requires that they should declare the causes which impel them to the Separation.

We hold these Truths to be self-evident, that all Men are created equal, that they are endowed by their Creator with certain unalienable Rights, that among these are Life, Liberty, and the Pursuit of Happiness—That to secure these Rights, Governments are instituted among Men, deriving their just Powers from the Consent of the Governed, that whenever any Form of Government becomes destructive of these Ends, it is the Right of the People to alter or to abolish it, and to institute new Government, laying its Foundation on such Principles, and organizing its Powers in such Forms, as to them shall seem most likely to effect their Safety and Happiness. Prudence, indeed, will dictate that Governments long established should not be changed for light and transient Causes; and accordingly all Experience hath shewn, that Mankind are more disposed to suffer, while Evils are sufferable, than to right themselves by abolishing the Forms to which they are accustomed. But when a long Train of Abuses and Usurpations, pursuing invariably the same Object, evinces a Design to reduce them under absolute Despotism, it is their Right, it is their Duty, to throw off such Government, and to provide new Guards for their future Security. Such has been the patient Sufferance of these Colonies; and such is now the Necessity which constrains them to alter their former Systems of Government. The History of the present King of Great-Britain is a History of repeated Injuries and Usurpations, all having in direct Object the Establishment of an absolute Tyranny over these States. To prove this, let Facts be submitted to a candid World.

He has refused his Assent to Laws, the most wholesome and necessary for the public Good.

He has forbidden his Governors to pass Laws of immediate and pressing Importance, unless suspended in their Operation till his Assent should be obtained; and when so suspended, he has utterly neglected to attend to them.

He has refused to pass other Laws for the Accommodation of large Districts of People, unless those People would relinquish the Right of Representation in the Legislature, a Right inestimable to them, and formidable to Tyrants only.

He has called together Legislative Bodies at Places unusual, uncomfortable, and distant from the Depository of their Public Records, for the sole Purpose of fatiguing them into Compliance with his Measures.

He has dissolved Representative Houses repeatedly, for opposing with manly Firmness his Invasions on the Rights of the People.

He has refused for a long Time, after such Dissolutions, to cause others to be elected; whereby the Legislative Powers, incapable of Annihilation, have returned to the People at large for their exercise; the State remaining in the mean time exposed to all the Dangers of Invasion from without, and Convulsions within.

He has endeavoured to prevent the Population of these States; for that Purpose obstructing the Laws for Naturalization of Foreigners; refusing to pass others to encourage their Migrations hither, and raising the Conditions of new Appropriations of Lands.

He has obstructed the Administration of Justice, by refusing his Assent to Laws for establishing Judiciary Powers.

He has made Judges dependent on his Will alone, for the Tenure of their offices, and the Amount and payment of their Salaries.

He has erected a Multitude of new Offices, and sent hither Swarms of Officers to harass our People, and eat out their Substance.

He has kept among us, in Times of Peace, Standing Armies, without the consent of our Legislatures.

He has affected to render the Military independent of, and superior to the Civil Power.

He has combined with others to subject us to a Jurisdiction foreign to our Constitution, and unacknowledged by our Laws; giving his Assent to their Acts of pretended Legislation:

For quartering large Bodies of Armed Troops among us:

For protecting them, by a mock Trial, from Punishment for any Murders which they should commit on the Inhabitants of these States:

For cutting off our Trade with all Parts of the World:

For imposing Taxes on us without our Consent:

For depriving us, in many cases, of the Benefits of Trial by Jury:

For transporting us beyond Seas to be tried for pretended Offences:

For abolishing the free System of English Laws in a neighbouring Province, establishing therein an arbitrary Government, and enlarging its Boundaries, so as to render it at once an Example and fit Instrument for introducing the same absolute Rule into these Colonies:

For taking away our Charters, abolishing our most valuable Laws, and altering fundamentally the Forms of our Governments:

For suspending our own Legislatures, and declaring themselves invested with Power to legislate for us in all Cases whatsoever.

He has abdicated Government here, by declaring us out of his Protection and waging War against us.

He has plundered our Seas, ravaged our Coasts, burnt our towns, and destroyed the Lives of our People.

He is, at this Time, transporting large Armies of foreign Mercenaries to compleat the works of Death, Desolation, and Tyranny, already begun with circumstances of Cruelty and Perfidy, scarcely paralleled in the most barbarous Ages, and totally unworthy the Head of a civilized Nation.

He has constrained our fellow Citizens taken Captive on the high Seas to bear Arms against their Country, to become the Executioners of their Friends and Brethren, or to fall themselves by their Hands.

He has excited domestic Insurrections amongst us, and has endeavoured to bring on the Inhabitants of our Frontiers, the merciless Indian Savages, whose known Rule of Warfare, is an undistinguished Destruction, of all Ages, Sexes and Conditions.

In every state of these Oppressions we have Petitioned for Redress in the most humble Terms: Our repeated Petitions have been answered only by repeated Injury. A Prince, whose Character is thus marked by every act which may define a Tyrant, is unfit to be the Ruler of a free People.

Nor have we been wanting in Attentions to our British Brethren. We have warned them from Time to Time of Attempts by their Legislature to extend an unwarrantable Jurisdiction over us. We have reminded them of the Circumstances of our Emigration and Settlement here. We have appealed to their native Justice and Magnanimity, and we have conjured them by the Ties of our common Kindred to disavow these Usurpations, which, would inevitably interrupt our Connections and Correspondence. They too have been deaf to the Voice of Justice and of Consanguinity. We must, therefore, acquiesce in the Necessity, which denounces our Separation, and hold them, as we hold the rest of Mankind, Enemies in War, in Peace, Friends.

We, therefore, the Representatives of the UNITED STATES OF AMERICA, in General Congress Assembled, appealing to the Supreme Judge of the World for the Rectitude of our Intentions, do, in the Name, and by the Authority of the good People of these Colonies, solemnly Publish and Declare, That these United Colonies are, and of Right ought to be, Free and Independent States; that they are absolved from all Allegiance to the British Crown, and that all political Connection between them and the State of Great-Britain, is and ought to be totally dissolved; and that as Free and Independent States, they have full Power to levy War, conclude Peace, contract Alliances, establish Commerce, and to do all other Acts and Things which Independent States may of right do. And for the support of this declaration, with a firm Reliance on the Protection of divine Providence, we mutually pledge to each other our lives, our Fortunes, and our sacred Honor.

APPENDIX B

THE FEDERALIST PAPERS
Nos. 10 and 51

In 1787, after the newly drafted U.S. Constitution was submitted to the 13 states for ratification, a major political debate ensued between the Federalists (who favored ratification) and the Anti-Federalists (who opposed ratification). Anti-Federalists in New York were particularly critical of the Constitution, and in response to their objections, Federalists Alexander Hamilton, James Madison, and John Jay wrote a series of 85 essays in defense of the Constitution. The essays were published in New York newspapers and reprinted in other newspapers throughout the country.

For students of American government, the essays, collectively known as the Federalist Papers, are particularly important because they provide a glimpse of the founders' political philosophy and intentions in designing the Constitution—and, consequently, in shaping the American philosophy of government.

We have included in this appendix two of these essays: Federalist Papers No. 10 and No. 51. Each essay has been annotated by the authors to indicate its importance in American political thought and to clarify the meaning of particular passages.

FEDERALIST PAPER NO. 10

Federalist Paper No. 10, penned by James Madison, has often been singled out as a key document in American political thought. In this essay, Madison attacks the Anti-Federalists' fear that a republican form of government will inevitably give rise to "factions"—small political parties or groups united by a common interest—that will control the government. Factions will be harmful to the country because they will implement policies beneficial to their own interests but adverse to other people's rights and to the public good. In this essay, Madison attempts to lay to rest this fear by explaining how, in a large republic such as the United States, there will be so many different factions, held together by regional or local interests, that no single one of them will dominate national politics.

Madison opens his essay with a paragraph discussing how important it is to devise a plan of government that can control the "instability, injustice, and confusion" brought about by factions.

Among the numerous advantages promised by a well-constructed Union, none deserves to be more accurately developed than its tendency to break and control the violence of faction. The friend of popular governments never finds himself so much alarmed for their character and fate as when he contemplates their propensity to this dangerous vice. He will not fail, therefore, to set a due value on any plan which, without violating the principles to which he is attached, provides a proper cure for it. The instability, injustice, and confusion introduced into the public councils have, in truth, been the mortal diseases under which popular governments have everywhere perished, as they continue to be the favorite and fruitful topics from which the adversaries to liberty derive their most specious declamations. The valuable improvements made by the American constitutions on the popular models, both ancient and modern, cannot certainly be too much admired; but it would be an unwarrantable partiality to contend that they have as effectually obviated the danger on this side, as was wished and expected. Complaints are everywhere heard from our most considerate and virtuous citizens, equally the friends of public and private faith and of public and personal liberty, that our governments are too unstable, that the public good is disregarded in the conflicts of rival parties, and that measures are too often decided, not according to the rules of justice and the rights of the minor party, but by the superior force of an interested and overbearing majority. However anxiously we may wish that these complaints had no foundation, the evidence of known facts will not permit us to deny that they are in some degree true. It will be found, indeed, on a candid review of our situation, that some of the distresses under which we labor have been erroneously charged on the operation of our governments; but it will be found, at the same time, that other causes will not alone account for many of our heaviest misfortunes; and, particularly, for that prevailing and increasing distrust of public engagements and alarm for private rights which are echoed from one end of the continent to the other. These must be chiefly, if not wholly, effects of the unsteadiness and injustice with which a factious spirit has tainted our public administration.

Madison now defines what he means by the term faction.

By a faction I understand a number of citizens, whether amounting to a majority or minority of the whole, who are united and actuated by some common impulse of passion, or of interest, adverse to the rights of other citizens, or the permanent and aggregate interests of the community.

Madison next contends that there are two methods by which the "mischiefs of faction" can be cured: by removing the causes of faction or by controlling their effects. In the following paragraphs, Madison explains how liberty itself nourishes factions. Therefore, to abolish factions would involve abolishing liberty—a cure "worse than the disease."

There are two methods of curing the mischiefs of faction: the one, by removing its causes; the other, by controlling its effects.

There are again two methods of removing the causes of faction: the one, by destroying the liberty which is essential to its existence; the other, by giving to every citizen the same opinions, the same passions, and the same interests.

It could never be more truly said than of the first remedy that it was worse than the disease. Liberty is to faction what air is to fire, an aliment without which it instantly expires. But it could not be a less folly to abolish liberty, which is essential to political life, because it nourishes faction than it would be to wish the annihilation of air, which is essential to animal life, because it imparts to fire its destructive agency.

The second expedient is as impracticable as the first would be unwise. As long as the reason of man continues fallible, and he is at liberty to exercise it, different opinions will be formed. As long as the connection subsists between his reason and his self-love, his opinions and his passions will have a reciprocal influence on each other; and the former will be objects to which the latter will attach themselves. The diversity in the faculties of men, from which the rights of property originate, is not less an insuperable obstacle to a uniformity of interests. The protection of these faculties is the first object of government. From the protection of different and unequal faculties of acquiring property, the possession of different degrees and kinds of property immediately results; and from the influence of these on the sentiments and views of the respective proprietors ensues a division of the society into different interests and parties.

The latent causes of faction are thus sown in the nature of man; and we see them everywhere brought into different degrees of activity, according to the different circumstances of civil society. A zeal for different opinions concerning religion, concerning government, and many other points, as well of speculation as of practice; an attachment to different leaders ambitiously contending for pre-eminence and power; or to persons of other descriptions whose fortunes have been interesting to the human passions, have, in turn, divided mankind into parties, inflamed them with mutual animosity, and rendered them much more disposed to vex and oppress each other than to co-operate for their common good. So strong is this propensity of mankind to fall into mutual animosities that where no substantial occasion presents itself the most frivolous and fanciful distinctions have been sufficient to kindle their unfriendly passions and excite their most violent conflicts. But the most common and durable source of factions has been the various and unequal distribution of property. Those who hold and those who are without property have ever formed distinct interests in society. Those who are creditors, and those who are debtors, fall under a like discrimination. A landed interest, a manufacturing interest, a mercantile interest, a moneyed interest, with many lesser interests, grow up of necessity in civilized nations, and divide them into different classes, actuated by different sentiments and views. The regulation of these various and interfering interests forms the principal task of modern legislation and involves the spirit of party and faction in the necessary and ordinary operations of government.

No man is allowed to be a judge in his own cause, because his interest would certainly bias his judgment, and, not improbably, corrupt his integrity. With equal, nay with greater reason, a body of men are unfit to be both judges and parties at the same time; yet what are many of the most important acts of legislation but so many judicial determinations, not indeed concerning the rights of single persons, but concerning the rights of large bodies of citizens? And what are the different classes of legislators but advocates and parties to the causes which they determine? Is a law proposed concerning private debts? It is a question to which the creditors are parties on one side and the debtors on the other. Justice ought to hold the balance between them. Yet the parties are, and must be, themselves the judges; and the most numerous party, or in other words, the most powerful faction must be expected to prevail. Shall domestic manufacturers be encouraged, and in what degree, by restrictions on foreign manufacturers? [These] are questions which would be differently decided by the landed and the manufacturing classes, and probably by neither with a sole regard to justice and the public good. The apportionment of taxes on the various descriptions of property is an act which seems to require the most exact impartiality; yet there is, perhaps, no legislative act in which greater opportunity and temptation are given to a predominant party to trample on the rules of justice. Every shilling with which they overburden the inferior number is a shilling saved to their own pockets.

It is in vain to say that enlightened statesmen will be able to adjust these clashing interests and render them all subservient to the public good. Enlightened statesmen will not always be at the helm. Nor, in many cases, can such an adjustment be made at all without taking into view indirect and remote considerations, which will rarely prevail over the immediate interest which one party may find in disregarding the rights of another or the good of the whole.

The inference to which we are brought is that the *causes* of faction cannot be removed and that relief is only to be sought in the means of controlling its *effects*.

Having concluded that "the causes of faction cannot be removed," Madison now looks in some detail at the other method by which factions can be cured—by controlling their effects. This is the heart of his essay. He begins by positing a significant question: How can you have self-government without risking the possibility that a ruling faction, particularly a majority faction, might tyrannize over the rights of others?

If a faction consists of less than a majority, relief is supplied by the republican principle, which enables the majority to defeat its sinister views by regular vote. It may clog the administration, it may convulse the society; but it will be unable to execute and mask its violence under the forms of the Constitution. When a majority is included in a faction, the form of popular government, on the other hand, enables it to sacrifice to its ruling passion or interest both the public good and the rights of other citizens. To secure the public good and private rights against the danger of such a faction, and at the same time to preserve the spirit and the form of popular government, is then the great object to which our inquiries are directed. Let me add that it is the great desideratum by which alone this form of government can be rescued from the opprobrium under which it has so long labored and be recommended to the esteem and adoption of mankind.

Madison now sets forth the idea that one way to control the effects of factions is to ensure that the majority is rendered incapable of acting in concert in order to "carry into effect schemes of oppression." He goes on to state that in a democracy, in which all citizens participate personally in government decision making, there is no way to prevent the majority from communicating with each other and, as a result, acting in concert.

By what means is this object attainable? Evidently by one of two only. Either the existence of the same passion or interest in a majority at the same time must be prevented, or the majority, having such coexistent passion or interest, must be rendered, by their number and local situation, unable to concert and carry into effect schemes of oppression. If the impulse and the opportunity be suffered to coincide, we well know that neither moral nor religious motives can be relied on as an adequate control. They are not found to be such on the injustice and violence of individuals, and lose their efficacy in proportion to the number combined together, that is, in proportion as their efficacy becomes needful.

From this view of the subject it may be concluded that a pure democracy, by which I mean a society consisting of a small number of citizens, who assemble and administer the government in person, can admit of no cure for the mischiefs of faction. A common passion or interest will, in almost every case, be felt by a majority of the whole; a communication and concert results from the form of government itself; and there is nothing to check the inducements to sacrifice the weaker party or an obnoxious individual. Hence it is that such democracies have ever been spectacles of turbulence and contention; have ever been found incompatible with personal security or the rights of property; and have in general been as short in their lives as they have been violent in their deaths. Theoretic politicians, who have patronized this species of government, have erroneously supposed that by reducing mankind to a perfect equality in their political rights, they would at the same time be perfectly equalized and assimilated in their possessions, their opinions, and their passions.

Madison now moves on to discuss the benefits of a republic with respect to controlling the effects of factions. He begins by defining a republic and then pointing out the "two great points of difference" between a republic and a democracy: a republic is governed by a small body of elected representatives, not by the people directly; and a republic can extend over a much larger territory and embrace more citizens than a democracy can.

A republic, by which I mean a government in which the scheme of representation takes place, opens a different prospect and promises the cure for which we are seeking. Let us examine the points in which it varies from pure democracy, and we shall comprehend both the nature of the cure and the efficacy which it must derive from the Union.

The two great points of difference between a democracy and a republic are: first, the delegation of the government, in the latter, to a small number of citizens elected by the rest; secondly, the greater number of citizens and greater sphere of country over which the latter may be extended.

In the following four paragraphs, Madison explains how in a republic, particularly a large republic, the delegation of authority to elected representatives will increase the likelihood that those who govern will be "fit" for their positions and that a proper balance will be achieved between local (factional) interests and national interests. Note how he stresses that the new federal Constitution, by dividing powers between state governments and the national government, provides a "happy combination in this respect."

The effect of the first difference is, on the one hand, to refine and enlarge the public views by passing them through the medium of a chosen body of citizens, whose wisdom may best discern the true interest of their country and whose patriotism and love of justice will be least likely to sacrifice it to temporary or partial considerations. Under such a regulation it may well happen that the public voice, pronounced by the representatives of the people, will be more consonant to the public good than if pronounced by the people themselves, convened for the purpose. On the other hand, the effect may be inverted. Men of factious tempers, of local prejudices, or of sinister designs, may, by intrigue, by corruption, or by other means, first obtain the suffrages, and then betray the interests of the people. The question resulting is, whether small or extensive republics are most favorable to the election of proper guardians of the public weal; and it is clearly decided in favor of the latter by two obvious considerations.

In the first place, it is to be remarked that however small the republic may be the representatives must be raised to a certain number in order to guard against the cabals of a few; and that however large it may be, they must be limited to a certain number in order to guard against the confusion of a multitude. Hence, the number of representatives in the two cases not being in proportion to that of the constituents, and being proportionally greater in the small republic, it follows that if the proportion of fit characters be not less in the large than in the small republic, the former will present a greater option, and consequently a greater probability of a fit choice.

In the next place, as each representative will be chosen by a greater number of citizens in the large than in the small republic, it will be more difficult for unworthy candidates to practice with success the vicious arts by which elections are too often carried; and the suffrages of the people being more free, will be more likely to center on men who possess the most attractive merit and the most diffusive and established characters.

It must be confessed that in this, as in most other cases, there is a mean, on both sides of which inconveniencies will be found to lie. By enlarging too much the number of electors, you render the representative too little acquainted with all their local circumstances and lesser interests; as by reducing it too much, you render him unduly attached to these, and too little fit to comprehend and pursue great and national objects. The federal Constitution forms a happy combination in this respect; the great and aggregate interests being referred to the national, the local and particular to the State legislatures.

Madison now looks more closely at the other difference between a republic and a democracy—namely, that a republic can encompass a larger territory and more citizens than a democracy can. In the remaining paragraphs of his essay, Madison concludes that in a large republic, it will be difficult for factions to act in concert. Although a factious group—religious, political, economic, or otherwise—may control a local or regional government, it will have little chance of gathering a national following. This is because in a large republic, there will be numerous factions whose work will offset the work of any one particular faction ("sect"). As Madison phrases it, these numerous factions will "secure the national councils against any danger from that source."

The other point of difference is the greater number of citizens and extent of territory which may be brought within the compass of republican than of democratic government; and it is this circumstance principally which renders factious combinations less to be dreaded in the former than in the latter. The smaller the society, the fewer probably will be the distinct parties and interests composing it; the fewer the distinct parties and interests, the more frequently will a majority be found of the same party; and the smaller the number of individuals composing a majority, and the smaller the compass within which they are placed, the more easily will they concert and execute their plans of oppression. Extend the sphere and you take in a greater variety of parties and interests; you make it less probable that a majority of the whole will have a common motive to invade the rights of other citizens; or if such a common motive exists, it will be more difficult for all who feel it to discover their own strength and to act in unison with each other. Besides other impediments, it may be remarked that, where there is a consciousness of unjust or dishonorable purposes, communication is always checked by distrust in proportion to the number whose concurrence is necessary.

Hence, it clearly appears that the same advantage which a republic has over a democracy in controlling the effects of faction is enjoyed by a large over a small republic—is enjoyed by the Union over the States composing it. Does this advantage consist in the substitution of representatives whose enlightened views and virtuous sentiments render them superior to local prejudices and to schemes of injustice? It will not be denied that the representation of the Union will be most likely to possess these requisite endowments. Does it consist in the greater security afforded by a greater variety of parties, against the event of any one party being able to outnumber and oppress the rest? In an equal degree does the increased variety of parties comprised within the Union increase this security. Does it, in fine, consist in the greater obstacles opposed to the concert and accomplishment of the secret wishes of an unjust and interested majority? Here again the extent of the Union gives it the most palpable advantage.

The influence of factious leaders may kindle a flame within their particular States but will be unable to spread a general conflagration through the other States. A religious sect may degenerate into a political faction in a part of the Confederacy; but the variety of sects dispersed over the entire face of it must secure the national councils against any danger from that source. A rage for paper money, for an abolition of debts, for an equal division of property, or for any other improper or wicked project, will be less apt to pervade the whole body of the Union than a particular member of it, in the same proportion as such a malady is more likely to taint a particular county or district than an entire State.

In the extent and proper structure of the Union, therefore, we behold a republican remedy for the diseases most incident to republican government. And according to the degree of pleasure and pride we feel in being republicans ought to be our zeal in cherishing the spirit and supporting the character of federalists.

Publius
(James Madison)

FEDERALIST PAPER NO. 51

Federalist Paper No. 51, also authored by James Madison, is another classic in American political theory. Although the Federalists wanted a strong national government, they had not abandoned the traditional American view, particularly notable during the revolutionary era, that those holding powerful government positions could not be trusted to put national interests and the common good above their own personal interests. In this essay, Madison explains why the separation of the national government's powers into three branches— executive, legislative, and judicial—and a federal structure of government offer the best protection against tyranny.

To what expedient, then, shall we finally resort, for maintaining in practice the necessary partition of power among the several departments as laid down in the Constitution? The only answer that can be given is that as all these exterior provisions are found to be inadequate the defect must be supplied, by so contriving the interior structure of the government as that its several constituent parts may, by their mutual relations, be the means of keeping each other in their proper places. Without presuming to undertake a full development of this important idea I will hazard a few general observations which may perhaps place it in a clearer light, and enable us to form a more correct judgment of the principles and structure of the government planned by the convention.

In the next two paragraphs, Madison stresses that for the powers of the different branches (departments) of government to be truly separated, the personnel in one branch should not be dependent on another branch for their appointment or for the "emoluments" (compensation) attached to their offices.

In order to lay a due foundation for that separate and distinct exercise of the different powers of government, which to a certain extent is admitted on all hands to be essential to the preservation of liberty, it is evident that each department should have a will of its own; and consequently should be so constituted that the members of each should have as little agency as possible in the appointment of the members of the others. Were this principle rigorously adhered to, it would require that all the appointments for the supreme executive, legislative, and judiciary magistracies should be drawn from the same fountain of authority, the people, through channels having no communication

whatever with one another. Perhaps such a plan of constructing the several departments would be less difficult in practice than it may in contemplation appear. Some difficulties, however, and some additional expense would attend the execution of it. Some deviations, therefore, from the principle must be admitted. In the constitution of the judiciary department in particular, it might be inexpedient to insist rigorously on the principle: first, because peculiar qualifications being essential in the members, the primary consideration ought to be to select that mode of choice which best secures these qualifications; second, because the permanent tenure by which the appointments are held in that department must soon destroy all sense of dependence on the authority conferring them.

It is equally evident that the members of each department should be as little dependent as possible on those of the others for the emoluments annexed to their offices. Were the executive magistrate, or the judges, not independent of the legislature in this particular, their independence in every other would be merely nominal.

In the following passages, which are among the most widely quoted of Madison's writings, he explains how the separation of the powers of government into three branches helps to counter the effects of personal ambition on government. The separation of powers allows personal motives to be linked to the constitutional rights of a branch of government. In effect, competing personal interests in each branch will help to keep the powers of the three government branches separate and, in so doing, will help to guard the public interest.

But the great security against a gradual concentration of the several powers in the same department consists in giving to those who administer each department the necessary constitutional means and personal motives to resist encroachments of the others. The provision for defense must in this, as in all other cases, be made commensurate to the danger of attack. Ambition must be made to counteract ambition. The interest of the man must be connected with the constitutional rights of the place. It may be a reflection on human nature that such devices should be necessary to control the abuses of government. But what is government itself but the greatest of all reflections on human nature? If men were angels, no government would be necessary. If angels were to govern men, neither external nor internal controls on government would be necessary. In framing a government which is to be administered by men over men, the great difficulty lies in this: you must first enable the government to control the governed; and in the next place oblige it to control itself. A dependence on the people is, no doubt, the primary control on the government; but experience has taught mankind the necessity of auxiliary precautions.

This policy of supplying, by opposite and rival interests, the defect of better motives, might be traced through the whole system of human affairs, private as well as public. We see it particularly displayed in all the subordinate distributions of power, where the constant aim is to divide and arrange the several offices in such a manner as that each may be a check on the other—that the private interest of every individual may be a sentinel over the public rights. These inventions of prudence cannot be less requisite in the distribution of the supreme powers of the State.

Madison now addresses the issue of equality between the branches of government. The legislature will necessarily predominate, but if the executive is given an "absolute negative" (absolute veto power) over legislative actions, this also could lead to an abuse of power. Madison concludes that the division of the legislature into two "branches" (parts, or chambers) will act as a check on the legislature's powers.

But it is not possible to give to each department an equal power of self-defense. In republican government, the legislative authority necessarily predominates. The remedy for this inconveniency is to divide the legislature into different branches; and to render them, by different modes of election and different principles of action, as little connected with each other as the nature of their common functions and their common dependence on the society will admit. It may even be necessary to guard against dangerous encroachments by still further precautions. As the weight of the legislative authority requires that it should be thus divided, the weakness of the executive may require, on the other hand, that it should be fortified. An absolute negative on the legislature appears, at first view, to be the natural defense with which the executive magistrate should be armed. But perhaps it would be neither altogether safe nor alone sufficient. On ordinary occasions it might not be exerted with the requisite firmness, and on extraordinary occasions it might be perfidiously abused. May not this defect of an absolute negative be supplied by some qualified connection between this weaker department and the weaker branch of the stronger department, by which the latter may be led to support the constitutional rights of the former, without being too much detached from the rights of its own department?

If the principles on which these observations are founded be just, as I persuade myself they are, and they be applied as a criterion to the several State constitutions, and to the federal Constitution, it will be found that if the latter does not perfectly correspond with them, the former are infinitely less able to bear such a test.

In the remainder of the essay, Madison discusses how a federal system of government, in which powers are divided between the states and the national government, offers "double security" against tyranny.

There are, moreover, two considerations particularly applicable to the federal system of America, which place that system in a very interesting point of view.

First. In a single republic, all the power surrendered by the people is submitted to the administration of a single government; and the usurpations are guarded against by a division of the government into distinct and separate departments. In the compound republic of America, the power surrendered by the people is first divided between two distinct governments, and then the portion allotted to each subdivided among distinct and separate departments. Hence a double security arises to the rights of the people. The different governments will control each other, at the same time that each will be controlled by itself.

Second. It is of great importance in a republic not only to guard the society against the oppression of its rulers, but to guard one part of the society against the injustice of the other part. Different interests necessarily exist in different classes of citizens. If a majority be united by a common interest, the rights of the minority will be insecure. There are but two methods of providing against this evil: the one by creating a will in the community independent of the majority—that is, of the society itself; the other, by comprehending in the society so many separate descriptions of citizens as will render an unjust combination of a majority of the whole very improbable, if not impracticable. The first method prevails in all governments possessing an hereditary or self-appointed authority. This, at best, is but a precarious security; because a power independent of the society may as well espouse the unjust views of the major as the rightful interests of the minor party, and may possibly be turned against both parties. The second method will be exemplified in the federal republic of the United States. Whilst all authority in it will be derived from and dependent on the society, the society itself will be broken into so many parts, interests and classes of citizens, that the rights of individuals, or of the minority, will be in little danger from interested combinations of the majority.

In a free government the security for civil rights must be the same as that for religious rights. It consists in the one case in the multiplicity of interests, and in the other in the multiplicity of sects. The degree of security in both cases will depend on the number of interests and sects; and this may be presumed to depend on the extent of country and number of people comprehended under the same government. This view of the subject must particularly recommend a proper federal system to all the sincere and considerate friends of republican government, since it shows that in exact proportion as the territory of the Union may be formed into more circumscribed Confederacies, or States, oppressive combinations of a majority will be facilitated; the best security, under the republican forms, for the rights of every class of citizen, will be diminished; and consequently the stability and independence of some member of the government, the only other security, must be proportionally increased. Justice is the end of government. It is the end of civil society. It ever has been and ever will be pursued until it be obtained, or until liberty be lost in the pursuit. In a society under the forms of which the stronger faction can readily unite and oppress the weaker, anarchy may as truly be said to reign as in a state of nature, where the weaker individual is not secured against the violence of the stronger; and as, in the latter state, even the stronger individuals are prompted, by the uncertainty of their condition, to submit to a government which may protect the weak as well as themselves; so, in the former state, will the more powerful factions or parties be gradually induced, by a like motive, to wish for a government which will protect all parties, the weaker as well as the more powerful.

It can be little doubted that if the State of Rhode Island was separated from the Confederacy and left to itself, the insecurity of rights under the popular form of government within such narrow limits would be displayed by such reiterated oppressions of factious majorities that some power altogether independent of the people would soon be called for by the voice of the very factions whose misrule had proved the necessity of it. In the extended republic of the United States, and among the great variety of interests, parties, and sects which it embraces, a coalition of a majority of the whole society could seldom take place on any other principles than those of justice and the general good; whilst there being thus less danger to a minor from the will of a major party, there must be less pretext, also, to provide for the security of the former, by introducing into the government a will not dependent on the latter, or, in other words, a will independent of the society itself. It is no less certain than it is important, notwithstanding the contrary opinions which have been entertained, that the larger the society, provided it lie within a practicable sphere, the more duly capable it will be of self-government. And happily for the republican cause, the practicable sphere may be carried to a very great extent by a judicious modification and mixture of the *federal principle*.

Publius
(James Madison)

GLOSSARY

A

Ability-to-Pay Tax A tax apportioned according to taxpayers' financial capacity.

Access The ability to contact an official either in person or by telephone. Campaign contributions are often given in hopes of gaining access to elected officials.

Accountability Responsibility for a program's results—for example, using measurable standards to hold public schools responsible for their students' performance.

Acquisitive Model A model of bureaucracy that viewstop-level bureaucrats as seeking to expand the size of their budgets and staffs to gain greater power.

Acquitted Found not guilty.

Actual Malice Either knowledge of a defamatory statement's falsity or a reckless disregard for the truth.

Adjutant General The principal staff officer of an army, who passes communications to the commanding general and distributes the general's orders to subordinates. In the example of the Texas National Guard and Texas State Guard, the "commanding general" is the governor. *Adjutant* comes from a Latin word meaning "helper."

Administrative Law Rules and regulations written by administrators to implement laws. The effectiveness of a law is often determined by how the corresponding administrative law is written.

Administrative Agency A federal, state, or local government unit established to perform a specific function. Administrative agencies are created and authorized by legislative bodies to administer and enforce specific laws.

Adversary System A legal system in which parties to a legal action are opponents and are responsible for bringing the facts and law related to their case before the court.

Advice and Consent Terms in the Constitution describing the U.S. Senate's power to review and approve treaties and presidential appointments.

Affirmative Action Positive efforts to recruit ethnic minorities, women, and the economically disadvantaged. Sometimes these efforts are limited to publicity drives among target groups, but such programs sometimes include use of ethnicity or gender as part of the qualification criteria.

Affirm To declare that a court ruling is valid and must stand.

Agenda Setting Determining which public policy questions will be debated or considered.

Anarchy The absence of any form of government or political authority.

Annexation The incorporation of a territory into a larger political unit, such as a country, state, county, or city.

Antitrust Legislation Legislation directed against economic monopolies.

Anti-Federalist An individual who opposed the ratification of the new Constitution in 1787. The Anti-Federalists were opposed to a strong central government.

Appellate Court A court having jurisdiction to review cases and issues that were originally tried in lower courts.

Appellate Jurisdiction The authority vested in an appellate court to review and revise the judicial actions of inferior courts.

Appropriations Process The process by which a legislative body legally authorizes a government to spend specific sums of money to provide various programs and services.

Appointment Power The authority vested in the president to fill a government office or position. Positions filled by presidential appointment include those in the executive branch and the federal judiciary, commissioned officers in the armed forces, and members of the independent regulatory commissions.

Appropriation The passage, by Congress, of a spending bill specifying the amount of authorized funds that actually will be allocated for an agency's use.

Aristocracy Rule by the "best"; in reality, rule by an upper class.

At-Large Election A citywide (or, in some states, countywide) election.

At-Large Place System An at-large election system in which all voters elect all the members of the city council, and each candidate runs for a specific seat on the council.

Attentive Public That portion of the general public that pays attention to policy issues.

Attorney General's Opinion An interpretation of the state's constitution or laws by the state attorney general. Officials may request such opinions, and although the opinions are not legally binding, they are usually followed.

Australian Ballot A secret ballot prepared, distributed, and tabulated by government officials at public expense. Since 1888, all U.S. states have used the Australian ballot rather than an open, public ballot.

Authoritarianism A type of regime in which only the government is fully controlled by the ruler. Social and economic institutions exist that are not under the government's control.

Authorization A formal declaration by a legislative committee that a certain amount of funding may be available to an agency. Some authorizations terminate in a year; others are renewable automatically, without further congressional action.

Automatic, or Built-in, Stabilizers Certain federal programs that cause changes in national income during economic fluctuations without the action of Congress and the president. Examples are the federal income tax system and unemployment compensation.

B

Balance of Trade The difference between the value of a nation's exports of goods and the value of its imports of goods.

Battleground State A state that is likely to be so closely fought that the campaigns devote exceptional effort to winning the popular and electoral vote there.

"Beauty Contest" A presidential primary in which contending candidates compete for popular votes but the results do not control the selection of delegates to the national convention.

Benefits-Received Tax A tax assessed according to the services received by the payers.

Bias An inclination or a preference that interferes with impartial judgment.

Bicameral Legislature A legislature made up of two parts, called chambers. The U.S. Congress, composed of the House of Representatives and the Senate, is a bicameral legislature.

Bicameralism The division of a legislature into two separate assemblies.

Bicultural Encompassing two cultures.

Binational Belonging to two nations.

Black Codes Laws passed by Southern states immediately after the Civil war denying most legal rights to freed slaves.

Blocking Bill In Texas, a bill placed early on the senate calendar that will never actually be considered. A rule—which can be suspended by a two-thirds vote— requires that the senate address bills in chronological order. The blocking bill ensures that a measure must win the vote of two-thirds of the senate even to be considered.

Block Grants Federal programs that provide funds to state and local governments for general functional areas, such as criminal justice or mental health programs.

Blue-Ribbon Commission A commission composed of public personalities or authorities on the subject that is being considered. In Texas, such a commission may have both fact-finding and recommending authority.

Blue Dog Democrats Members of Congress from more moderate states or districts who sometimes "cross over" to vote with Republicans on legislation.

Boards and Commissions In Texas, bodies consisting of three to 18 members that supervise most state agencies.

Boycott A form of pressure or protest—an organized refusal to purchase a particular product or deal with a particular business.

Broad-Based Tax A tax designed to be paid by a large number of taxpayers.

Broad Construction A judicial philosophy that looks to the context and purpose of a law when making an interpretation.

Budgetary Power The power to propose a spending plan to the legislature. The governor of Texas has limited budgetary power because of the competing authority of the Legislative Budget Board.

Budget Deficit Government expenditures that exceed receipts.

Burden of Proof In a court case, a party's duty to convince a judge or jury that the party's version of the facts is true. The standard of proof is higher in a criminal case than in a civil one.

Bureaucracy A large organization that is structured hierarchically to carry out specific functions.

Busing In the context of civil rights, the transportation of public school students from areas where they live to schools in other areas to eliminate school segregation based on residential racial patterns.

C

Cabinet An advisory group selected by the president to aid in making decisions. The Cabinet includes the heads of 15 executive departments and others named by the president.

Cabinet Department One of the 15 departments of the executive branch (State, Treasury, Defense, Justice, Interior, Agriculture, Commerce, Labor, Health and Human Services, Homeland Security, Housing and Urban Development, Education, Energy, Transportation, and Veterans Affairs).

Cabinet System At the state government level, a form of executive organization that allows the governor to appoint and remove top-level administrators, giving the governor more control over the administration.

Calendar In the Texas legislature, the schedule that serves as a conduit for legislation between the committees and the primary legislative body.

Calendars Committee The committee in the Texas house of representatives that assigns bills to the calendars for floor action. (The less important Local and Consent Calendars Committee also performs this function.)

Capture The act by which an industry being regulated by a government agency gains direct or indirect control over agency personnel and decision makers.

Case Law Judicial interpretations of common-law principles and doctrines, as well as interpretations of constitutional law, statutory law, and administrative law.

Casework Personal work for constituents by members of Congress.

Categorical Grants Federal grants to states or local governments that are for specific programs or projects.

Caucus A meeting of party members designed to select candidates and propose policies.

Chad A small fragment of paper produced by the punching of a data card, such as a punch-card ballot.

Change of Venue A change in the site of a trial.

Charter An organizing document for corporations or municipalities.

Charter A document issued by a government that grants to a person, a group of persons, or a corporation the right to carry on one or more specific activities. A state government can grant a charter to a municipality.

Checks and Balances A major principle of the American system of government whereby each branch of the government can check the actions of the others.

Chief Diplomat The role of the president in recognizing foreign governments, making treaties, and effecting executive agreements.

Chief Executive The role of the president as head of the executive branch of the government.

Chief Legislator The role of the president in influencing the making of laws.

Chief of Staff The person who is named to direct the White House Office and advise the president.

Chief of State Nationally, the head of state—the president of the United States, for example. In Texas and other states, the governor—who serves as the symbol of the state and performs ceremonial duties—is the chief of state.

Children's Health Insurance Program (CHIP) Program to provide health insurance for low income children. It is administered by the state but funded largely by federal grants-in-aid.

City-County Consolidation The union of a country and cities within the country to form a single unit of government

Civic Duty A citizen's understood obligation to register, to vote, to be knowledgeable, and to take action to make the community a better place.

Civil Disobedience A nonviolent, public refusal to obey allegedly unjust laws.

Civil Liberties Those personal freedoms that are protected for all individuals. Civil liberties typically involve restraining the government's actions against individuals.

Civil Rights All rights rooted in the Fourteenth Amendment's guarantee of equal protection under the law.

Civil Service A collective term for the body of employees working for the government.

Generally, civil service is understood to apply to all those who gain government employment through a merit system.

Civil Service Commission The initial central personnel agency of the national government, created in 1883.

Class-Action Suit A lawsuit filed by an individual seeking damages for "all persons similarly situated."

Clear and Present Danger Test The test proposed by Justice Oliver Wendell Holmes for determining when government may restrict free speech. Restrictions are permissible, he argued, only when speech creates a *clear and present danger* to the public order.

Clemency Relief from criminal punishment granted by an executive. In Texas, the power of the governor to grant clemency is strictly limited.

Clientele Persons represented by a government agency or a politician.

Cloture An action by which legislative debate is ended so that a floor vote must be taken.

Climate Control The use of public relations techniques to create favorable public opinion toward an interest group, industry, or corporation.

Closed Primary A type of primary in which the voter is limited to choosing candidates of the party of which he or she is a member.

Colonia In Texas, an unincorporated urban district along the U.S.–Mexican border. Colonias are often impoverished and are chiefly inhabited by Mexican Americans.

Commission System A system that allows the members of a city council to serve as heads of city departments.

Commissioners Court In Texas, the policy-making body of a county. A commissioners court consists of a county judge (the presiding officer), who is elected in countywide elections, and four county commissioners elected from individual precincts.

Committee of the Whole An entire legislative body (such as the Texas senate) acting as a committee. The committee's purpose is to allow the body to relax its rules and thereby expedite legislation.

Community Property Any property that a married couple has acquired during their marriage. In certain states, it is divided equally between them in the event of a divorce.

Conflict of Interest A situation that arises when a legislator, bureaucrat, executive official, or judge can make an official decision that results in a personal economic advantage. The result is a potential or real conflict between the personal interests of the officeholder and the general interests of the public.

Constable A law enforcement officer. In Texas, constables are elected at the county level and serve as process officers of justice of the peace courts.

Co-optation The "capturing" of an agency by members of an interest group. In effect, governmental power comes to be exercised by a private interest.

Council-Manager System A municipal system featuring an elected city council and a city manager who is hired by the council. The council makes policy decisions, and the manager is responsible for the day-to-day operations of the city government.

County Attorney In Texas, a county legal officer who gives legal advice to the commissioners court, represents the county in court, and prosecutes crimes. If a county has both a county attorney and a district attorney, the latter prosecutes felony crimes.

County Auditor In Texas, a county financial officer whose duties, depending on the population of the county, may include reviewing county financial records and (in large counties) serving as the chief budget officer.

County Clerk The chief record keeper and elections officer of a county.

County Commissioner One of a group of officials elected to administer a county; in Texas, a member of the commissioners court who is elected from a district or precinct.

County Courts-at-Law In Texas, county courts in addition to the constitutional county court. They are established by the legislature in all but the smallest Texas counties and may have criminal or civil jurisdiction. They form a level of courts superior to justice of the peace and municipal courts but inferior to district courts.

County Judge In Texas, an official elected countywide to preside over the commissioners court and to try certain minor cases.

County Treasurer A county official who is responsible for receiving, depositing, and disbursing county funds.

Coattail Effect The influence of a popular candidate on the electoral success of other candidates on the same party ticket. The effect is increased by the party-column ballot, which encourages straight-ticket voting.

Cold War The ideological, political, and economic confrontation between the United States and the Soviet Union following World War II.

Commander in Chief The role of the president as supreme commander of the military forces of the United States and of the state National Guard units when they are called into federal service.

Commerce Clause The section of the Constitution in which Congress is given the power to regulate trade among the states and with foreign countries.

Commercial Speech Advertising statements, which increasingly have been given First Amendment protection.

Common Law Judge-made law that originated in England from decisions shaped according to prevailing custom. Decisions were applied to similar situations and gradually became common to the nation.

Communications Director A professional specialist who plans the communications strategy and advertising campaign for the candidate.

Communism A revolutionary variant of socialism that favors a partisan (and often totalitarian) dictatorship, government control of all enterprises, and the replacement of free markets by central planning.

Concurrent Powers Powers held jointly by the national and state governments.

Concurring Opinion A separate opinion prepared by a judge who supports the decision of the majority of the court but who wants to make or clarify a particular point or to voice disapproval of the grounds on which the decision was made.

Confederal System A system consisting of a league of independent states, each having essentially sovereign powers. The central government created by such a league has only limited powers over the states.

Confederation A political system in which states or regional governments retain ultimate authority except for those powers they expressly delegate to a central government. A voluntary association of independent states, in which the member states agree to limited restraints on their freedom of action.

Conference Committee A special joint committee appointed to reconcile differences when bills pass the two chambers of Congress in different forms.

Consensus General agreement among the citizenry on an issue.

Consent of the People The idea that governments and laws derive their legitimacy from the consent of the governed.

Conservative Coalition An alliance of Republicans and Southern Democrats that can form in the House or the Senate to oppose liberal legislation and support conservative legislation.

Consolidation The union of two or more governmental units to form a single unit.

Constituent One of the persons represented by a legislator or other elected or appointed official.

Constitutional Initiative An electoral device whereby citizens can propose a constitutional amendment through petitions signed by the required number of registered voters.

Constitutional Power A power vested in the president by Article II of the Constitution.

Consumer Price Index (CPI) A measure of the change in price over time of a specific group of goods and services used by the average household.

Containment A U.S. diplomatic policy adopted by the Truman administration to contain communist power within its existing boundaries.

Continuing Resolution A temporary funding law that Congress passes when an appropriations bill has not been decided by the beginning of the new fiscal year on October 1.

Cooley's Rule The view that cities should be able to govern themselves, presented in an 1871 Michigan decision by Judge Thomas Cooley.

Cooperative Federalism The theory that the states and the national government should cooperate in solving problems.

Corrupt Practices Acts A series of acts passed by Congress in an attempt to limit and regulate the size and sources of contributions and expenditures in political campaigns.

Council of Governments (COG) A voluntary organization of counties and municipalities concerned with area-wide problems.

County The chief governmental unit set up by the state to administer state law and business at the local level. Counties are drawn up by area, rather than by rural or urban criteria.

Credentials Committee A committee used by political parties at their national conventions to determine which delegates may participate. The committee inspects the claim of each prospective delegate to be seated as a legitimate representative of his or her state.

Creole A descendant of European Spanish (or in some regions, French) immigrants to the Americas.

Crossover Voting A circumstance in which members of one political party vote in the other party's primary to influence which nominee is selected by the other party.

Cumulative Voting (CV) An at-large election system in which voters can cast one or more votes for a single candidate. For example, a voter who can cast up to five votes in a city council election can cast all five votes for one candidate or spread the votes among several candidates.

Current Account Balance The current account balance includes the balance of trade in services, unilateral transfers, and other items. This is a wider concept than the balance of trade.

D

***De Facto* Segregation** Racial segregation that occurs because of past social and economic conditions and residential racial patterns.

***De Jure* Segregation** Racial segregation that occurs because of laws or administrative decisions by public agencies.

Deadwood In the context of state government, constitutional provisions made inoperative by changing circumstances or by conflicting federal constitutional or statutory law.

Dealignment A decline in party loyalties that reduces long-term party commitment.

Decentralization In American party politics, distribution of power to state and local party organizations rather than concentration of power in the national organization. In government, distribution of authority to local and regional governments rather than concentration of authority in a central government.

Declining Marginal Propensity to Consume The tendency, as income increases, for persons to devote a smaller proportion of their income to consumer spending and a larger proportion to savings or investments.

Dedicated Funds Revenues dedicated for a specific purpose by the constitution or by statute.

Defamation of Character Wrongfully hurting a person's good reputation. The law imposes a general duty on all persons to refrain from making false, defamatory statements about others.

Defense Policy A subset of national security policies having to do with the U.S. armed forces.

Deferred Adjudication A procedure that allows a judge to postpone final sentencing in a criminal case; charges are dismissed if the defendant completes a satisfactory probationary period.

Democracy A system of government in which political authority is vested in the people. Derived from the Greek words *demos* ("the people") and *kratos* ("authority").

Democratic Party One of the two major American political parties evolving out of the Republican Party of Thomas Jefferson.

Democratic Republic A republic in which representatives elected by the people make and enforce laws and policies.

Dependent Agency A government entity that is closely linked to general-purpose governments. Dependent agencies do not have the independence of special districts.

Détente A French word meaning a relaxation of tensions. The term characterized U.S.-Soviet relations as they developed under President Richard Nixon and Secretary of State Henry Kissinger.

Development Corporation Act A state law that allows select Texas cities to raise the sales tax for economic development, subject to voter approval.

Devolution The transfer of powers from a national or central government to a state or local government.

Dillon's Rule The narrowest possible interpretation of the legal status of local governments, outlined by Judge John E. Dillon, who in 1872 stated that a municipal corporation can exercise only those powers expressly granted by state law.

Direct Primary An intraparty election in which the voters select the candidates who will run on a party's ticket in the subsequent general election. In Texas, nominees must win a majority of the votes, which often means that there are primary runoff elections between the top two candidates.

Directive Authority The power to issue binding orders to state agencies. This power is severely limited for the governor of Texas.

Discretion An official's power to make decisions based on personal judgment rather than on the specific requirements of the law; the freedom to decide or make choices.

District Attorney An official who prosecutes felony cases.

District Clerk In Texas, the record keeper for the district court in a county with a population that exceeds 8,000.

Diplomacy The process by which states carry on political relations with each other; settling conflicts among nations by peaceful means.

Diplomatic Recognition The formal acknowledgment of a foreign government as legitimate.

Direct Democracy A system of government in which political decisions are made by the people directly, rather than by their elected

representatives; probably attained most easily in small political communities.

Direct Primary An intraparty election in which the voters select the candidates who will run on a party's ticket in the subsequent general election.

Direct Technique An interest group activity that involves interaction with government officials to further the group's goals.

Discharge Petition A procedure by which a bill in the House of Representatives may be forced (discharged) out of a committee that has refused to report it for consideration by the House. The petition must be signed by an absolute majority (218) of representatives and is used only on rare occasions.

Dissenting Opinion A separate opinion in which a judge dissents from (disagrees with) the conclusion reached by the majority on the court and expounds his or her own views about the case.

Diversity of Citizenship The condition that exists when the parties to a lawsuit are citizens of different states, or when the parties are citizens of a U.S. state and citizens or the government of a foreign country. Diversity of citizenship can provide a basis for federal jurisdiction.

Divided Government A situation in which one major political party controls the presidency and the other controls the chambers of Congress, or in which one party controls a state governorship and the other controls the state legislature.

Divisive Opinion Public opinion that is polarized between two quite different positions.

Dockets The schedule of court activity.

Domestic Policy Public plans or courses of action that concern internal issues of national importance, such as poverty, crime, and the environment.

Dominant Culture The values, customs, and language established by the group or groups that traditionally have controlled politics and government in a society.

Down-Ticket Describes a candidate for political office relative to others located higher on the ballot.

Dual Federalism A system in which the states and the national government each remains supreme within its own sphere. The doctrine looks on nation and state as coequal sovereign powers. Neither the state government nor the national government should interfere in the other's sphere.

Due Process Established rules and principles for the administration of justice designed to safeguard the rights of the individual. The right to due process of law is provided by the U.S. Constitution and state constitutions.

E

Earmarks Funding appropriations that are specifically designated for a named project in a member's state or district.

Earned-Income Tax Credit (EITC) Program A government program that helps low-income workers by giving back part or all of their Social Security taxes.

Economic Aid Assistance to other nations in the form of grants, loans, or credits to buy the assisting nation's products.

Elastic Clause, or Necessary and Proper Clause The clause in Article I, Section 8, that grants Congress the power to do whatever is necessary to execute its specifically delegated powers.

Election Judge A public official who is responsible for enforcing election rules at a polling place on election day.

Elective Accountability A condition in which officials are directly accountable to the voters for their actions.

Elector A member of the electoral college, which selects the president and vice president. Each state's electors are chosen in each presidential election year according to state laws.

Electoral College A group of persons called *electors* selected by the voters in each state and the District of Columbia; this group officially elects the president and vice president of the United States. The number of electors in each state is equal to the number of each state's representatives in both chambers of Congress.

Electronic Media Communication channels that involve electronic transmissions, such as radio, television, and, to an increasing extent, the Internet.

Elite Theory A perspective holding that society is ruled by a small number of people who exercise power to further their self-interest.

Emergency Power An inherent power exercised by the president during a period of national crisis.

Enabling Act Legislation that confers on appropriate officials the power to implement or enforce the law.

Enabling Legislation A statute enacted by Congress that authorizes the creation of an administrative agency and specifies the name, purpose, composition, functions, and powers of the agency being created.

Energy Policy Laws concerned with how much energy is needed and used.

Enumerated Power A power specifically granted to the national government by the Constitution. The first 17 clauses of Article I, Section 8, specify most of the enumerated powers of Congress.

Environmental Impact Statement (EIS) A report that must show the costs and benefits of major federal actions that could significantly affect the quality of the environment.

Equality As a political value, the idea that all people are of equal worth.

Era of Good Feelings The years from 1817 to 1825, when James Monroe was president and there was, in effect, no political opposition.

Establishment Clause The part of the First Amendment prohibiting the establishment of a church officially supported by the national government. It is applied to questions of state and local government aid to religious organizations and schools, the legality of allowing or requiring school prayers, and the teaching of evolution versus intelligent design.

Ethnic Diversity Inclusion of significant numbers of nonwhites such as Latinos, African Americans, Asian Americans, and Native Americans.

Evangelical Having to do with a broad spectrum of Protestant Christianity that emphasizes salvation and traditional values. Evangelical voters are likely to support culturally conservative politics.

ex officio Having a position by virtue of holding a particular office. For example, the lieutenant governor of Texas serves *ex officio* as the presiding officer of the Texas senate.

Examining Trial A relatively uncommon procedure that may be requested by felony defendants in Texas. In an examining trial, a justice of the peace reviews the facts and decides whether a defendant should have to face trial in criminal court.

Exclusionary Rule A policy forbidding the admission at trial of illegally seized evidence.

Executive Agreement An international agreement made by the president, without senatorial ratification, with the head of a foreign state.

Executive Budget The budget prepared and submitted by the president to Congress.

Executive Office of the President (EOP) An organization established by President Franklin D. Roosevelt to assist the president in carrying out major duties.

Executive Order A rule or regulation issued by the president that has the effect of law. Executive orders can implement and give administrative effect to provisions in the Constitution, to treaties, and to statutes.

Executive Privilege The right of executive officials to withhold information from or to refuse to appear before a legislative committee.

Exports Goods and services produced domestically for sale abroad.

Expressed Power A power of the president that is expressly written into the Constitution or into statutory law.

Extradite To surrender an accused or convicted criminal to the authorities of the state from which he or she has fled; to return a fugitive criminal to the jurisdiction of the accusing state.

Extraterritorial Jurisdiction (ETJ) In Texas, a buffer area that extends beyond a city's limits. Cities can enforce some laws, such as zoning and building codes, in an ETJ.

F

Faction A group or bloc in a legislature or political party acting in pursuit of some special interest or position.

Fall Review The annual process in which the Office of Management and Budget, after receiving formal federal agency requests for funding for the next fiscal year, reviews the requests, makes changes, and submits its recommendations to the president.

Fascism A 20th-century ideology—often totalitarian—that exalts the national collective united behind an absolute ruler. Fascism rejects liberal individualism, values action over rational deliberation, and glorifies war.

FBI Index Crimes A set of crimes reported by the FBI and commonly used as a way of measuring the overall crime rate. The index crimes are murder and non-negligent manslaughter, forcible rape, robbery, aggravated assault, burglary, theft, and motor vehicle theft.

Federal Mandate A requirement in federal legislation that forces states and municipalities to comply with certain rules.

Federal Open Market Committee The most important body within the Federal Reserve System. The Federal Open Market Committee decides how monetary policy should be carried out.

Federal Question A question that has to do with the U.S. Constitution, acts of Congress, or treaties. A federal question provides a basis for federal jurisdiction.

Federal Register A publication of the U.S. government that prints executive orders, rules, and regulations.

Federal Reserve System (the Fed) The agency created by Congress in 1913 to serve as the nation's central banking organization.

Federalism A system of government in which power is divided by a written constitution between a central government and regional or subdivisional governments. Each level must have some domain in which its policies are dominant and some genuine constitutional guarantee of its authority.

Federalist The name given to one who was in favor of the adoption of the U.S. Constitution and the creation of a federal union with a strong central government.

Felony A crime—such as arson, murder, rape, or robbery—that carries the most severe sanctions, usually ranging from one year in prison to death.

Feminism The philosophy of political, economic, and social equality for women and the gender consciousness sufficient to mobilize women for change.

Filibuster The use of the Senate's tradition of unlimited debate as a delaying tactic to block a bill.

Finance Chairperson The campaign professional who directs fundraising, campaign spending, and compliance with campaign finance laws and reporting requirements.

First Budget Resolution A resolution passed by Congress in May that sets overall revenue and spending goals for the following fiscal year.

Fiscal Policy The federal government's use of taxation and spending policies to affect overall business activity.

Fiscal Year (FY) A 12-month period that is used for bookkeeping, or accounting purposes. Usually, the fiscal year does not coincide with the calendar year. For example, the federal government's fiscal year runs from October 1 through September 30.

Floor Leaders Legislators who are responsible for getting party members to vote for or against particular legislation.

Floor The place where a legislative body debates, amends, votes on, enacts, and defeats roposed legislation; the entire house or senate acting as a whole.

Foreclosure The legal process by which a lender takes possession of a mortgaged property when the borrower defaults on the loan.

Formal Powers Legal powers granted to the governor by constitution or statute. Powers of this type, when exercised by the U.S. president, are called *expressed powers*.

Focus Group A small group of individuals who are led in discussion by a professional consultant in order to gather opinions on and responses to candidates and issues.

Food Stamps Benefits issued by the federal government to low-income individuals to be used for the purchase of food; originally provided as coupons, but now typically provided electronically through a card similar to a debit card.

Foreign Policy A nation's external goals and the techniques and strategies used to achieve them.

Foreign Policy Process The steps by which foreign policy goals are decided and acted on.

Fragmentation In state government, a division of power among separately elected executive officials. A plural executive is a fragmented executive.

Freedmen's Bureau The Bureau of Refugees, Freedmen and Abandoned Lands, a federal bureau established in 1865 to aid refugees of the Civil War (including former slaves) and to administer confiscated property. Among other tasks, it sought to provide education to the former slaves. It was disbanded in 1872.

Franking A policy that enables members of Congress to send material through the mail by substituting their facsimile signature (frank) for postage.

Free Exercise Clause The provision of the First Amendment guaranteeing the free exercise of religion.

Free Rider Problem The difficulty interest groups face in recruiting members when the benefits they achieve can be gained without joining the group.

Front-Loading The practice of moving presidential primary elections to the early part of the campaign to maximize the impact of these primaries on the nomination.

Front-Runner The presidential candidate who appears to be ahead at a given time in the primary season.

Full Employment An arbitrary level of unemployment that corresponds to "normal" friction in the labor market. In 1986, a 6.5 percent rate of unemployment was considered full employment. Today, it is assumed to be around 5 percent.

Full Faith and Credit Clause This section of the Constitution requires states to recognize one another's laws and court decisions. It ensures that rights established under deeds, wills, contracts, and other civil matters in one state will be honored by other states.

Functional Consolidation Cooperation by two or more units of local government in providing services to their inhabitants. This is generally done by unifying a set of departments (e.g., the police departments) into a single agency.

G

Gag Order An order issued by a judge restricting the publication of news about a trial or a pretrial hearing to protect the accused's right to a fair trial.

Gender Discrimination Any practice, policy, or procedure that denies equality of treatment to an individual or to a group because of gender.

Gender Gap The difference between the percentage of women who vote for a particular candidate and the percentage of men who vote for the candidate.

General Jurisdiction Exists when a court's authority to hear cases is not significantly restricted. A court of general jurisdiction normally can hear a broad range of cases.

General-Law City A city operating under general state laws that apply to all local government units of a similar type. In Texas, cities with a population of 5,000 or less are (in most instances) general-law cities.

General-Obligation Bond A bond to be repaid from general taxes and other revenues; such bond issues usually must be approved by voters.

General-Purpose Government A municipal or county government. In contrast to special districts, general-purpose governments provide a wide range of services.

General Sales Tax A broad-based tax collected on the retail price of most items.

Generational Effect A long-lasting effect of the events of a particular time on the political opinions of those who came of political age at that time.

Gerrymandering The drawing of legislative district boundary lines to obtain partisan or factional advantage. A district is said to be gerrymandered when its shape is manipulated by the dominant party in the state legislature to maximize electoral strength at the expense of the minority party.

Get Out the Vote (GOTV) This phrase describes the multiple efforts expended by campaigns to get voters out to the polls on election day.

Government Corporation An agency of government that administers a quasi-business enterprise. These corporations are used when activities are primarily commercial.

Government in the Sunshine Act A law that requires all committee-directed federal agencies to conduct their business regularly in public session.

Grand Jury A jury that sits in pretrial proceedings to determine if sufficient evidence exists to try an individual and, therefore, approve an indictment.

Grassroots The lowest organizational level of a political party.

Gross-Receipts Tax A tax on the gross revenues of certain enterprises.

Grandfather Clause A device used by Southern states to disenfranchise African Americans. It restricted voting to those whose grandfathers had voted before 1867.

Great Compromise The compromise between the New Jersey and Virginia plans that created one chamber of the Congress based on population and one chamber representing each state equally; also called the Connecticut Compromise.

Gross Domestic Product (GDP) The dollar value of all final goods and services produced in a one-year period.

Gross Public Debt The net public debt plus interagency borrowings within the government.

H

Hard Money This refers to political contributions and campaign spending that is recorded under the regulations set forth in law and by the Federal Election Commission.

Hatch Act An act passed in 1939 that restricted the political activities of government employees. It also prohibited a political group from spending more than $3 million in any campaign and limited individual contributions to a campaign committee to $5,000.

Hate Crime A criminal offense committed against a person or property that is motivated, in whole or in part, by the offender's bias against a race, color, ethnicity, national origin, sex, gender identity or expression, sexual orientation, disability, age, or religion.

Head of State The role of the president as ceremonial head of the government.

Hidden Tax A tax that is reflected in higher prices of the goods and services sold.

Hillstyle The actions and behaviors of a member of Congress in Washington, D.C., intended to promote policies and the member's own career aspirations.

Home Rule The right of a local government to write a charter establishing any organizational structure or program that does not conflict with state law. The Texas Constitution reserves home rule for municipalities with populations of 5,000 or more.

Home-Rule City A city with the state-granted right to frame, adopt, and amend its own charter.

House and Senate Journals The official public records of the actions of the two chambers of the Texas legislature. The two journals are issued daily during sessions.

Home Rule City A city permitted by the state to let local voters frame, adopt, and amend their own charter.

Homestyle The actions and behaviors of a member of Congress aimed at the constituents and intended to win the support and trust of the voters at home.

I

Ideology A comprehensive set of beliefs about the nature of people and about the role of an institution or government.

Impeachment An action by the House of Representatives to accuse the president, vice president, or other civil officers of the United States of committing "Treason, Bribery, or other high Crimes and Misdemeanors."

Implementation The carrying out of laws by executive officials and the bureaucrats who work for them.

Import Quota A restriction imposed on the value or number of units of a particular good that can be brought into a country. Foreign suppliers are unable to sell more than the amount specified in the import quota.

Imports Goods and services produced outside a country but sold within its borders.

Incarceration Rate The number of persons held in jail or prison for every 100,000 persons in a particular population group.

Income Transfer A transfer of income from some individuals in the economy to other individuals. This is generally done by government action.

Incorporation Theory The view that most of the protections of the Bill of Rights apply to state governments through the Fourteenth Amendment's due process clause.

Incremental Budgeting A budgeting practice in which an agency bases its budget requests on past appropriations plus increases to cover inflation and increased demand for services; this process assumes that past appropriations justify current bud-getary requests.

Incumbent The current holder of an office.

Independent A voter or candidate who does not identify with a political party.

Independent Executive Agency A federal agency that is not part of a Cabinet department but reports directly to the president.

Independent Expenditures Nonregulated contributions from PACs, organizations, and individuals. The funds may be spent on advertising or other campaign activities, so long as those expenditures are not coordinated with those of a candidate.

Independent Regulatory Agency An agency outside the major executive departments charged with making and implementing rules and regulations.

Indictment A formal accusation issued by a grand jury against a party charged with a crime when the jury determines that there is sufficient evidence to bring the accused to trial.

Indirect Appointive Power In Texas, the power of the governor to appoint supervisory boards (but not operational directors) for most state agencies. The supervisory boards and commissions usually appoint the actual heads of most state agencies in Texas.

Indirect Technique A strategy employed by interest groups that uses third parties to influence government officials.

Inflation A sustained rise in the general price level of goods and services.

Informal Powers Powers not directly granted by law. The governor's informal powers may follow from powers granted by law but may also come from the governor's persuasive abilities, which are affected by the governor's personality, popularity, and political support.

Inherent Power A power of the president derived from the statements in the Constitution that "the executive Power shall be vested in a President" and that the president should "take Care that the Laws be faithfully executed"; defined through practice rather than through law.

In-Kind Subsidy A good or service—such as food stamps, housing, or medical care—provided by the government to low-income groups.

Instructed Delegate A legislator who is an agent of the voters who elected him or her and who votes according to the views of constituents regardless of personal beliefs.

Intelligence Community The government agencies that gather information about the capabilities and intentions of foreign governments or that engage in covert actions.

Interest Group An organized group of individuals sharing common objectives who actively attempt to influence policy makers.

Internationality Having family and/or business interests in two or more nations.

Interstate Between two or more states.

Interstate Compact An agreement between two or more states. Agreements on minor matters are made without congressional consent, but any compact that tends to increase the power of the contracting states relative to other states or relative to the national government generally requires the consent of Congress. Such compacts serve as a means by which states can solve regional problems.

Intrastate Within the state.

Iron Texas Star A policy-making coalition that includes interest groups; the lieutenant governor and the speaker of the house; standing committees of the legislature; the governor; and administrators, boards, and commissions.

Iron Curtain The term used to describe the division of Europe between the Soviet bloc and the West; coined by Winston Churchill.

Iron Triangle The three-way alliance among legislators, bureaucrats, and interest groups to make or preserve policies that benefit their respective interests.

Isolationist Foreign Policy A policy of abstaining from an active role in international affairs or alliances, which characterized U.S. foreign policy toward Europe during most of the 1800s.

Issue Advocacy Advertising Advertising paid for by interest groups that support or oppose a candidate or a candidate's position on an issue without mentioning voting or elections.

Issue Network A group of individuals or organizations—which may consist of legislators and legislative staff members, interest group leaders, bureaucrats, the media, scholars, and other experts—that supports a particular policy position on a given issue.

Item Veto The power to veto particular sections or items of an appropriations bill while signing the remainder of the bill into law. The governors of most states have this power.

J

Jim Crow Laws Laws enacted by Southern states that enforced segregation in schools, on transportation, and in public accommodations.

Joint Committee A legislative committee composed of members from both chambers of Congress.

Judicial Activism A doctrine holding that the Supreme Court should take an active role by using its powers to check the activities of governmental bodies when those bodies exceed their authority.

Judicial Implementation The way in which court decisions are translated into action.

Judicial Restraint A doctrine holding that the Supreme Court should defer to the decisions made by the elected representatives of the people in the legislative and executive branches.

Judicial Review The power of the Supreme Court or any court to hold a law or other legal action as unconstitutional.

Jurisdiction The authority of a court to decide certain cases. Not all courts have the authority to decide all cases. Two jurisdictional issues are where a case arises as well as its subject matter.

Justiciable Question A question that may be raised and reviewed in court.

K

Keynesian Economics A school of economic thought that tends to favor active federal government policy making to stabilize economy-wide fluctuations, usually by implementing discretionary fiscal policy.

Kitchen Cabinet The informal advisers to the president.

Ku Klux Klan (KKK) A white supremacist organization. The first Klan was founded during the Reconstruction era following the Civil War.

L

La Raza Unida A party organized in the late 1960s as a means of getting Mexican Americans to unite politically and to identify ethnically as one people.

La Réunion A failed French socialist colony of the 1800s located within the city limits of modern Dallas. Its skilled and educated inhabitants benefited early Dallas.

Labor Movement Generally, the economic and political expression of working-class interests;

politically, the organization of working-class interests.

Late-Train Contribution A contribution given to a candidate in the period that begins after an election and ends 30 days before a regular legislative session.

Latent Interests Public-policy interests that are not recognized or addressed by a group at a particular time.

Lawmaking The process of establishing the legal rules that govern society.

Legislative Audit Committee In Texas, a committee that performs audits of state agencies and departments for the legislature.

Legislative Budget Board The primary budgeting entity for Texas state government.

Legislative Council In Texas, a body that provides research support, information, and bill-drafting assistance to legislators.

Legislature A governmental body primarily responsible for the making of laws.

Libel A written defamation of a person's character, reputation, business, or property rights.

Libertarianism A political ideology based on skepticism or opposition toward almost all government activities.

Life Cycle Effect People change as they grow older because of age-specific experiences and thus people are likely to hold age-specific attitudes.

Limited Jurisdiction Exists when a court's authority to hear cases is restricted to certain types of claims, such as tax claims or bankruptcy petitions.

Line Organization In the federal government, an administrative unit that is directly accountable to the president.

Line-Item Veto The power of an executive to veto individual lines or items within a piece of legislation without vetoing the entire bill.

Literacy Test A test administered as a precondition for voting, often used to prevent African Americans from exercising their right to vote.

Litigate To engage in a legal proceeding or seek relief in a court of law; to carry on a lawsuit.

"Lobby, The" Collectively, the most politically and economically powerful special-interest groups in Texas.

Lobbyist An organization or individual who attempts to influence legislation and the administrative decisions of government.

Long Ballot An election ballot listing many independently elected offices.

Logrolling An arrangement in which two or more members of Congress agree in advance to support each other's bills.

Loophole A legal method by which individuals and businesses are allowed to reduce the tax liabilities owed to the government.

Loose Monetary Policy Monetary policy that makes credit inexpensive and abundant, possibly leading to inflation.

M

Madisonian Model A structure of government proposed by James Madison in which the powers of the government are separated into three branches: executive, legislative, and judicial.

Majoritarianism A political theory holding that in a democracy, the government ought to do what the majority of the people want.

Majority Leader of the House A legislative position held by an important party member in the House of Representatives. The majority leader is selected by the majority party in caucus or conference to foster cohesion among party members and to act as spokesperson for the majority party in the House.

Majority Opinion A court opinion reflecting the views of the majority of the judges.

Managed News Information generated and distributed by the government in such a way as to give government interests priority over candor.

Mandate A requirement or standard imposed on one level of government by a higher level of government.

Maquiladora A factory in the Mexican border region that assembles goods imported duty-free into Mexico for export. In Spanish, it literally means "twin plant."

Mark Up In legislation, to amend, change, or rewrite bills while they are in committee.

Mass Transit Transport systems that carry multiple passengers such as train and bus systems; whether publicly or privately owned, mass transit systems are available to the general public and usually charge a fare.

Material Incentive A reason or motive having to do with economic benefits or opportunities.

Media Channels of mass communication.

Media Access The public's right of access to the media. The Federal Communications Commission and the courts have gradually taken the stance that citizens do have a right to media access.

Medicaid A program to provide medical care for qualified low income persons; although funded largely by federal grants-in-aid, it is a state-administered program.

Medicare A federal program to provide medical insurance for most persons age sixty-five and over.

Merit System The selection, retention, and promotion of government employees on the basis of competitive examinations.

Message Power The ability of a governor (or a U.S. president) to focus the attention of the press, legislators, and citizens on legislative proposals that he or she considers important. The visibility of the office gives the chief executive instant public attention.

Mestizo A person of both Spanish and Native American lineage.

Metroplex The greater Dallas–Fort Worth metropolitan area.

Military-Industrial Complex The mutually beneficial relationship between the armed forces and defense contractors.

Minority Leader of the House The party leader elected by the minority party in the House.

Misdemeanor A lesser crime than a felony, punishable by a fine or imprisonment for up to one year.

Missouri Plan A method of selecting judges that combines appointment and election. Under the plan, the state governor or another official selects judges from nominees chosen by a nonpartisan committee. After a year on the bench, the judges face a popular election to determine whether the public wishes them to remain in office.

Mistrial A trial judged to be invalid because of fundamental error. When a mistrial is declared, the trial may start again, beginning with the selection of a new jury.

Monetary Policy The utilization of changes in the amount of money in circulation to alter credit markets, employment, and the rate of inflation.

Monopolistic Model A model of bureaucracy that compares bureaucracies to monopolistic business firms. Lack of competition in either circumstance leads to inefficient and costly operations.

Monroe Doctrine A policy statement made by President James Monroe in 1823, which set out three principles: (1) European nations should not establish new colonies in the Western Hemisphere; (2) European nations should not intervene in the affairs of independent nations of the Western Hemisphere; and (3) the United States would not interfere in the affairs of European nations.

Moral Idealism A philosophy that sees nations as normally willing to cooperate and to agree on moral standards for conduct.

Municipal Home Rule The power vested in a local unit of government to draft or change its own charter and to manage its own affairs.

N

Narrowcasting Broadcasting that is targeted to one small sector of the population.

National Committee A standing committee of a national political party established to direct and coordinate party activities between national party conventions.

National Convention The meeting held every four years by each major party to select presidential and vice presidential candidates, to write a platform, to choose a national committee, and to conduct party business.

National Health Insurance A plan to provide universal health insurance under which the government provides basic health care coverage to all citizens. In most such plans, the program is funded by taxes on wages or salaries.

National Security Council (NSC) An agency in the Executive Office of the President that advises the president on national security.

National Security Policy Foreign and domestic policy designed to protect the nation's independence and political and economic integrity; policy that is concerned with the safety and defense of the nation.

Natural Rights Rights held to be inherent in natural law, not dependent on governments. John Locke stated that natural law, being superior to human law, specifies certain rights of "life, liberty, and property." These rights, altered to become "life, liberty, and the pursuit of happiness," are asserted in the Declaration of Independence.

Negative Campaigning A strategy in political campaigns of attacking the opposing candidate's issue positions or—especially—his or her character.

Negative Constituents Citizens who openly oppose the government's policies.

Net Public Debt The accumulation of all past federal government deficits; the total amount owed by the federal government to individuals, businesses, and foreigners.

New England Town A governmental unit in the New England states that combines the roles of city and county in one unit.

Nonopinion The lack of an opinion on an issue or policy among the majority.

Normal Trade Relations (NTR) Status A status granted through an international treaty by which each member nation must treat other members at least as well as it treats the country that receives its most favorable treatment. This status was formerly known as most-favored-nation status.

North American Free Trade Agreement (NAFTA) A treaty between Canada, Mexico, and the United States that calls for the gradual removal of tariffs and other trade restrictions. NAFTA came into effect in 1994.

O

Office of Management and Budget (OMB) A division of the Executive Office of the President. The OMB assists the president in preparing the annual budget, clearing and coordinating departmental agency budgets, and supervising the administration of the federal budget.

Office-Block, or Massachusetts, Ballot A form of general-election ballot in which candidates for elective office are grouped together under the title of each office. It emphasizes voting for the office and the individual candidate, rather than for the party.

Ogallala Aquifer A major underground reservoir and a source of water for irrigation and human consumption in northern West Texas and the Texas Panhandle, as well as other states.

Oligarchy Rule by the few in their own interests.

Ombudsperson A person who hears and investigates complaints by private individuals against public officials or agencies.

Open-Meetings Law A law that requires meetings of government decision-making bodies to be open to public scrutiny (with some exceptions).

Open-Records Law A law requiring that records of all government proceedings and decisions are made available to the public.

Open Primary A primary in which any registered voter can vote (but must vote for candidates of only one party).

Opinion Leader One who is able to influence the opinions of others because of position, expertise, or personality.

Opinion Poll A method of systematically questioning a small, selected sample of respondents who are deemed representative of the total population.

Opinion The statement by a judge or a court of the decision reached in a case. The opinion sets forth the applicable law and details the reasoning on which the ruling was based.

Oral Arguments The verbal arguments presented in person by attorneys to an appellate court. Each attorney presents reasons to the court why the court should rule in her or his client's favor.

Order A state of peace and security. Maintaining order by protecting members of society from violence and criminal activity is the oldest purpose of government.

Organic Law The superior law that establishes governing institutions and organizes their formal power relationships.

Original Jurisdiction The authority of a court to consider a case in the first instance; the power to try a case, as opposed to appellate jurisdiction, which involves the power to review cases decided by other courts.

Oversight The process by which Congress follows up on laws it has enacted to ensure that they are being enforced and administered in the way Congress intended.

P

Pairing In political redistricting, placing two incumbent officeholders from the same party in the same district. (Only one of these officeholders can be reelected.)

Pardon A release from the punishment for or legal consequences of a crime; a pardon can be granted by the president before or after a conviction.

Parole Early release from prison under official supervision.

Participation Paradox The fact that people vote even though their individual votes rarely influence the outcome of an election.

Partisan Election An election between candidates who are nominated by their parties and whose party affiliation is designated on the ballot. In Texas, all state and county officials (including judges) are selected in this manner. Only municipal and some special district elections are nonpartisan in Texas.

Partisan Gerrymandering The drawing of district lines for the purpose of providing electoral advantage to members of one political party.

Part-time Legislature A legislative body that meets for short periods of time. Its members are often provided limited resources, including small salaries.

Party Identification Linking oneself to a particular political party.

Party Identifier A person who identifies with a political party.

Party Organization The formal structure and leadership of a political party, including election committees; local, state, and national executives; and paid professional staff.

Party Platform A document drawn up at each national convention outlining the policies, positions, and principles of the party.

Party-Column, or Indiana, Ballot A form of general-election ballot in which all of a party's candidates for elective office are arranged in one column under the party's label and symbol. It emphasizes voting for the party, rather than for the office or individual.

Party-in-Government All of the elected and appointed officials who identify with a political party.

Party-in-the-Electorate Those members of the general public who identify with a political party or who express a preference for one party over another.

Patronage The practice of rewarding faithful party workers and followers with government employment and contracts.

Peer Group A group consisting of members sharing common social characteristics. These groups play an important part in the socialization process, helping to shape attitudes and beliefs.

Pendleton Act (Civil Service Reform Act) An act that established the principle of employment on the basis of merit and created the Civil Service Commission to administer the personnel service.

Permanent Campaign A coordinated and planned strategy carried out by the White House to increase the president's popularity and support.

Permanent School Fund In Texas, a fund that provides support to the public school system. Leases, rents, and royalties from designated public school lands are deposited into the fund.

Personal Recognizance A defendant's personal promise to appear in court.

Picket-Fence Federalism A model of federalism in which specific programs and policies (depicted as vertical pickets in a picket fence) involve all levels of government—national, state, and local (depicted by the horizontal boards in a picket fence).

Pigeonhole The action by which a legislative committee tables a bill and then ignores it.

Plea Bargaining Negotiations that take place between the prosecution and the defense in a criminal case in which the defendant normally is offered a lighter sentence or other benefits in return for a guilty plea.

Plural Executive An executive branch with power divided among several independent officers and a weak chief executive.

Pluralism A theory that views politics as a conflict among interest groups. Political decision making is characterized by bargaining and compromise.

Plurality A number of votes cast for a candidate that is greater than the number of votes for any other candidate but not necessarily a majority.

Points of Order A formal question to the chairperson about the legitimacy of a parliamentary process. A successful point of order can result in the postponement or defeat of legislation.

Pocket Veto A special veto exercised by the chief executive after a legislative body has adjourned. Bills not signed by the chief executive die after a specified period of time. If Congress wishes to reconsider such a bill, it must be reintroduced in the following session of Congress.

Podcasting A method of distributing multimedia files, such as audio or video files, for downloading onto mobile devices or personal computers.

Police Power The authority to legislate for the protection of the health, morals, safety, and welfare of the people. In the United States, most police power is reserved to the states.

Policy Tsar A high-ranking member of the Executive Office of the President appointed to coordinate action in one specific policy area.

Political Action Committee (PAC) A committee set up by and representing a corporation, labor union, or special-interest group. PACs raise and give campaign donations.

Political Consultant A paid professional hired to devise a campaign strategy and manage a campaign.

Political Culture The collection of beliefs and attitudes toward government and the political process held by a community or nation.

Political Party A group of political activists who organize to win elections, operate the government, and determine public policy.

Political Question An issue that a court believes should be decided by the executive or legislative branch.

Political Realism A philosophy that sees each nation as acting principally in its own interest.

Political Socialization The process by which people acquire political beliefs and attitudes.

Political Trust The degree to which individuals express trust in the government and political institutions, usually measured through a specific series of survey questions.

Poll Tax A special tax that must be paid as a qualification for voting. The Twenty-fourth Amendment to the Constitution outlawed the poll tax in national elections, and in 1966, the Supreme Court declared it unconstitutional in all elections.

Pollster The person or firm who conducts public opinion polls for the campaign.

Popular Sovereignty The concept that ultimate political authority is based on the will of the people.

Pork Special projects or appropriations that are intended to benefit a member's district or state; slang term for earmarks.

Pragmatism The philosophy that ideas should be judged by their practical results rather than on an ideological basis. American political parties are usually pragmatic because they are typically more interested in winning elections than in taking clear stands on issues.

Presession Bargaining In Texas and other states, negotiation that lets the governor and legislative leaders reach compromises on particular bills before the beginning of the legislative session. This usually ensures the passage of the bills.

Presiding Officers In Texas, the chief officers of the state senate and house. They are the lieutenant governor, who presides over the senate, and the speaker of the house.

Precedent A court rule bearing on subsequent legal decisions in similar cases. Judges rely on precedents in deciding cases.

President Pro Tempore The temporary presiding officer of the Senate in the absence of the vice president.

Presidential Primary A statewide primary election of delegates to a political party's national convention, held to determine a party's presidential nominee.

Press Secretary The individual who interacts directly with the journalists covering the campaign.

Press Secretary The presidential staff member responsible for handling White House media relations and communications.

Prior Restraint Restraining an action before the activity has actually occurred. When expression is involved, this means censorship.

Privatization The replacement of government services with services provided by private firms.

Privileges and Immunities Special rights and exceptions provided by law. States may not discriminate against one another's citizens.

Probation A sentencing alternative to imprisonment in which the court releases convicted defendants under supervision as long as certain conditions are observed.

Progressive Movement A political movement within both major parties in the early 20th century. Progressives believed that the power of the government should be used to restrain the growing power of large corporations, as well as to provide services for its citizens.

Prohibition Outlawing of the production, sale, and consumption of alcoholic beverages.

Progressive Tax A tax that rises in percentage terms as incomes rise.

Property Tax A tax on the value of real estate. This tax is a particularly important source of revenue for local governments.

Public Debt Sums owed by governments.

Punitive Damages Awards A financial payment that may be awarded to a plaintiff in a civil case to punish the defendant and deter similar conduct in the future.

Pure At-Large System An at-large election system in which all voters elect all the members of the city council, and candidates do not run for specific seats.

Public Agenda Issues that are perceived by the political community as meriting public attention and governmental action.

Public Figure A public official, movie star, or other person known to the public because of his or her position or activities.

Public Interest The best interests of the overall community; the national good, rather than the narrow interests of a particular group.

Public Opinion The aggregate of individual attitudes or beliefs shared by some portion of the adult population.

Purposive Incentive A reason for supporting or participating in the activities of a group that is based on agreement with the goals of the group. For example, someone with a strong interest in human rights might have a purposive incentive to join Amnesty International.

Q

Quasi-Judicial Functions Actions by a branch other than the courts that involve interpreting the law.

Quasi-Legislative Functions Legislative actions by entities other than the legislature; for example, executive branch agencies' adoption of rules and regulations that are binding on citizens.

R

Ranchero Culture A quasi-feudal system whereby a property's owner, or patron, gives workers protection and employment in return for their loyalty and service. The rancher and workers all live on the *ranchero*, or ranch.

Ratification Formal approval.

Rational Ignorance Effect An effect produced when people purposely and rationally decide not to become informed on an issue because they believe that their vote on the issue is not likely to be a deciding one; a lack of incentive to seek the necessary information to cast an intelligent vote.

Realignment A process in which a substantial group of voters switches party allegiance, producing a long-term change in the political landscape.

Reapportionment The allocation of seats in the House of Representatives to each state after each census.

Recession Two or more successive quarters in which the economy shrinks instead of grows.

Redistricting The redrawing of the boundaries of the congressional districts within each state.

Reduction Veto The power of governors in some states (but not Texas) to reduce

amounts in an appropriations bill without striking them out altogether.

Registration The entry of a person's name onto the list of registered voters for elections. To register, a person must meet certain legal requirements of age, citizenship, and residency.

Regressive Tax A tax that falls in percentage terms as incomes rise.

Remand To send a case back to the court that originally heard it.

Reparation Compensation, monetary or nonmonetary (e.g., formal apology), to make amends for a past transgression or harm.

Regular Session A legislative session scheduled by the constitution. Texas regular sessions are biennial (once every two years) rather than annual, as in most states and in Congress.

Regulatory Tax A tax imposed with the intent of exerting social or economic control by reducing taxes on approved behavior or imposing higher taxes on an undesirable activity.

Removal Power The power to dismiss government officials. In Texas, the governor can remove an official that he or she appointed only with the consent of two-thirds of the state senate.

Representation The function of members of Congress as elected officials representing the views of their constituents.

Representative Assembly A legislature composed of individuals who represent the population.

Reprieve A formal postponement of the execution of a sentence imposed by a court of law.

Republic A form of government in which sovereignty rests with the people, as opposed to a king or monarch.

Republican Party One of the two major American political parties. It emerged in the 1850s as an antislavery party and consisted of former Northern Whigs and antislavery Democrats.

Revenue Bond A bond to be repaid with revenues from the project financed, such as utilities or sports stadiums.

Revolving door The interchange of employees among the legislature, government agencies, and related private special-interest groups.

Reverse To annul or make void a court ruling on account of some error or irregularity.

Reverse Discrimination The charge that an affirmative action program discriminates against those who do not have minority status.

Reverse-Income Effect A tendency for wealthier states or regions to favor the Democrats and for less wealthy states or regions to favor the Republicans. The effect appears paradoxical because it reverses traditional patterns of support.

Rollback Election In Texas, an election that permits voters to lower a local property tax increase to 8 percent.

Rule The proposal by the Rules Committee of the House that states the conditions for debate for one piece of legislation.

Rule of Four A United States Supreme Court procedure by which four justices must vote to grant a petition for review if a case is to come before the full court.

Rules Committee A standing committee of the House of Representatives that provides special rules under which specific bills can be debated, amended, and considered by the House.

Rump Convention A meeting of members from a larger convention who secede and organize their own convention elsewhere.

Runoff Primary A second primary election that pits the two top vote-getters from the first primary against each other. Such an election is held in states such as Texas when the winner of the first primary did not receive a majority of the votes.

S

Safe Seat A district that returns the legislator with 55 percent of the vote or more.

Sales Tax A tax collected on the retail price of purchased items.

Sampling Error The difference between a sample's results and the true result if the entire population had been interviewed.

Secession The separation of a territory from a larger political unit. Specifically, the secession of Southern states from the Union in 1860 and 1861.

Second Budget Resolution A resolution passed by Congress in September that sets "binding" limits on taxes and spending for the following fiscal year.

Select Committee A temporary legislative committee established for a limited time period and for a special purpose.

Selective Sales Tax, or Excise Tax A tax levied on specific items only.

Selectperson A member of the governing group of a town.

Senate Majority Leader The chief spokesperson of the majority party in the Senate, who directs the legislative program and party strategy.

Senate Minority Leader The party officer in the Senate who commands the minority party's opposition to the policies of the majority party and directs the legislative program and strategy of his or her party.

Senatorial Courtesy In federal district court judgeship nominations, a tradition allowing a senator to veto a judicial appointment in his or her state.

Seniority System A custom followed in both chambers of Congress specifying that the member of the majority party with the longest term of continuous service will be given preference when a committee chairperson (or a holder of some other significant post) is selected.

Separate-but-Equal Doctrine The 1896 doctrine holding that separate-but-equal facilities do not violate the equal protection clause.

Separation of Powers The principle of dividing governmental powers among different branches of government.

Service Sector The sector of the economy that provides services—such as health care, banking, and education—in contrast to the sector that produces goods.

Sexual Harassment Unwanted physical or verbal conduct or abuse of a sexual nature that interferes with a recipient's job performance, creates a hostile work environment, or carries with it an implicit or explicit threat of adverse employment consequences.

Sheriff The chief law enforcement officer of a county—in most states, an elected official. In Texas, the sheriff's budget must be approved by the commissioners court, which limits the sheriff's authority.

Shivercrat A follower of Governor Allan Shivers of Texas (1949–1957). Shivercrats split their votes between conservative Democrats for state office and Republicans for the U.S. presidency.

Short Ballot An election ballot listing only a few independently elected offices.

Single-Member District A district in which the voters elect a single member of a legislative body, who runs for election only in that district.

Single-Member District System A system that allows only one candidate to be elected from each electoral district. This system discourages the formation of third parties.

Signing Statement A written declaration that a president may make when signing a bill into law. Usually, such statements point out sections of the law that the president deems unconstitutional.

Single-Payer Plan A plan under which one entity has a monopoly on issuing a particular type of insurance. Typically, the entity is the government, and the insurance is basic health coverage.

Slander The public uttering of a false statement that harms the good reputation of another. The statement must be made to, or within the hearing of, persons other than the defamed party.

"Socialized Medicine" Strictly defined, socialized medicine is a health care system in which the government hires medical practitioners who work at government-owned facilities to directly provide health care as in Great Britain and in U.S. veterans and military hospitals. However, the term is often applied to health care systems in which the government provides health care insurance (such as Medicare), but benefit payments are made to private health care providers.

Social Contract A voluntary agreement among individuals to secure their rights and welfare by creating a government and abiding by its rules.

Social Movement A movement that represents the demands of a large segment of the public for political, economic, or social change.

Socialism A political ideology based on strong support for economic and social equality. Socialists traditionally envisioned a society in which major businesses were taken over by the government or by employee cooperatives

Socioeconomic Status The value assigned to a person due to occupation or income. An upper-class person, for example, has high socioeconomic status.

Soft Money Campaign contributions unregulated by federal or state law, usually given to parties and party committees to help fund general party activities.

Solidary Incentive A reason or motive having to do with the desire to associate with others and to share with others a particular interest or hobby.

Sound Bite A brief, memorable comment that can easily be fit into news broadcasts.

Soviet Bloc The Soviet Union and the Eastern European countries that installed communist regimes after World War II and were dominated by the Soviet Union.

Speaker of the House The presiding officer in the House of Representatives. The Speaker is always a member of the majority party and is the most powerful and influential member of the House.

Special Districts A local government that provides services to a jurisdiction that are not provided by general-purpose governments. Examples are municipal utility districts, hospital authorities, and transit authorities.

Special Session Any legislative session that is not specifically scheduled by the constitution or by statute. In some states, the legislature may call itself into special session, but in Texas only the governor may call the legislature into special session.

Spin An interpretation of campaign events or election results that is favorable to the candidate's campaign strategy.

Spin Doctor A political campaign adviser who tries to convince journalists of the truth of a particular interpretation of events.

Spindletop A major oil discovery in 1901 near Beaumont that began the industrialization of Texas.

Splinter Party A new party formed by a dissident faction within a major political party. Often, splinter parties have emerged when a particular personality was at odds with the major party.

Spoils System The awarding of government jobs to political supporters and friends.

Spring Review The annual process in which the Office of Management and Budget requires federal agencies to review their programs, activities, and goals and submit their requests for funding for the next fiscal year.

Statute-like Details Detailed state constitutional provisions characterized by the narrow scope usually found in statutory law.

Statutory Law Law passed by legislatures and eventually compiled in law codes.

Strong-Mayor System A form of municipal government in which substantial authority (such as authority over appointments and the budget) is lodged in the office of the mayor, who is elected in a citywide election.

Standing Committee A permanent committee in the House or Senate that considers bills within a certain subject area.

Stare Decisis To stand on decided cases; the judicial policy of following precedents established by past decisions.

State A group of people occupying a specific area and organized under one government; may be either a nation or a subunit of a nation.

State Central Committee The principal organized structure of each political party within each state. This committee is responsible for carrying out policy decisions of the party's state convention.

State of the Union Message An annual message to Congress in which the president proposes a legislative program. The message is addressed not only to Congress but also to the American people and to the world.

Statutory Power A power created for the president through laws enacted by Congress.

Straight-Ticket Voting Voting exclusively for the candidates of one party.

Strategic Arms Limitation Treaty (SALT I) A treaty between the United States and the Soviet Union to stabilize the nuclear arms competition between the two countries. SALT I talks began in 1969, and agreements were signed on May 26, 1972.

Straw Polls A nonbinding vote, often used to gauge the opinion or will of a group prior to taking a formal, binding vote.

Strict Construction A judicial philosophy that looks to the "letter of the law" when interpreting the Constitution or a particular statute.

Subsidies Grants or special tax exemptions provided by the government to individuals or businesses in the private sector.

Subpoena A legal writ requiring a person's appearance in court to give testimony.

Suffrage The right to vote; the franchise.

Sunset Advisory Commission In Texas, a body that periodically evaluates most government agencies and departments. The commission may recommend the restructuring, abolition, or alteration of the jurisdiction of an agency.

Sunset Legislation Laws requiring that existing programs be reviewed regularly for their effectiveness and be terminated unless specifically extended as a result of these reviews.

Superdelegate A party leader or elected official who is given the right to vote at the party's national convention. Superdelegates are not elected at the state level.

Supplemental Security Income (SSI) A federal program established to provide assistance to elderly persons and persons with disabilities.

Supply-Side Economics The theory that higher-income taxpayers should be taxed less because their savings and investments stimulate the economy.

Supremacy Clause The constitutional provision that makes the Constitution and federal laws superior to all conflicting state and local laws.

Supremacy Doctrine A doctrine that asserts the priority of national law over state laws. This principle is rooted in Article VI of the Constitution, which provides that the Constitution, the laws passed by the national government under its constitutional powers, and all treaties constitute the supreme law of the land.

Suspension of the Rule Setting aside of the rules of a legislative body so that another set of rules can be used.

Swing Voters Voters who frequently swing their support from one party to another.

Symbolic Speech Nonverbal expression of beliefs, which is given substantial protection by the courts.

T

Table In a legislature or similar body, to cease action on a particular measure. A motion to table is not debatable.

Tagging In the Texas senate, a rule that allows a senator to halt a standing committee's consideration of a bill for 48 hours.

Tax Abatement A reduction of or exemption from taxes (usually real estate taxes); typically granted by a local government to businesses in exchange for bringing jobs and investments to a community.

Tax Assessor-Collector In Texas, a county financial officer whose responsibilities include collecting county taxes or fees and registering voters.

Tax Base The object or activity taxed.

Tax Rate The amount of tax per unit of taxable item or activity.

Tax Shifting The practice by which businesses pass taxes to consumers in the form of higher prices.

Tariffs Taxes on imports.

Technical Assistance The practice of sending experts in such areas as agriculture, engineering, or business to aid other nations.

Tenant Farmer A farmer who does not own the land that he or she farms but rents it from a landowner.

Term Limit A restriction on the number of times a person can be elected to a particular office.

Temporary Assistance to Needy Families (TANF) A state-administered program in which grants from the national government are used to provide welfare benefits. The TANF program replaced the Aid to Families with Dependent Children (AFDC) program.

Texas Ethics Commission A constitutionally authorized body that has the power to investigate ethics violations and to penalize violators of Texas ethics laws.

Texas Register A publication that contains all official notices of the Texas state government and some notices of regional bodies. It is found in all university libraries and large municipal libraries in Texas.

Threat to Veto An informal power by which a state governor (or the U.S. president) threatens to veto legislation so as to affect the content of the legislation while it is still in the legislature.

Third Party A political party other than the two major political parties (Republican and Democratic).

Ticket Splitting Voting for candidates of two or more parties for different offices. For example, a voter splits her ticket if she votes for a Republican presidential candidate and a Democratic congressional candidate.

Tidelands A submerged area that extends three leagues (about 10 miles) off the Texas coast. The tidelands controversy developed when offshore oil was discovered and the federal government contended that Texas's jurisdiction extended only three miles into the Gulf of Mexico.

Tight Monetary Policy Monetary policy that makes credit expensive in an effort to slow the economy.

Tipping A phenomenon that occurs when a group that is becoming more numerous over time grows large enough to change the political balance in a district, state, or county.

Tort Reform In civil law, a tort is a wrong or injury (other than a breach of contract). Tort reform is an effort to limit liability in tort cases.

Totalitarian Regime A form of government that controls all aspects of the political and social life of a nation.

Town Manager System A form of town government in which voters elect three selectpersons, who then appoint a professional town manager, who in turn appoints other officials.

Town Meeting The governing authority of a New England town. Qualified voters may participate in the election of officers and the passage of legislation.

Township A rural unit of government based on federal land surveys of the American frontier in the 1780s. Townships have declined significantly in importance.

Tracking Poll A poll taken for the candidate on a nearly daily basis as election day approaches.

Trial Court The court in which most cases begin.

Truman Doctrine The policy adopted by President Harry Truman in 1947 to halt communist expansion in southeastern Europe.

Trustee A legislator who acts according to her or his conscience and the broad interests of the entire society.

Twelfth Amendment An amendment to the Constitution, adopted in 1804, that specifies the separate election of the president and vice president by the electoral college.

Twenty-fifth Amendment A 1967 amendment to the Constitution that establishes procedures for filling presidential and vice presidential vacancies and makes provisions for presidential disability.

Two-Party System A political system in which only two parties have a reasonable chance of winning.

U

Umbrella Organization An organization created by interest groups to promote common goals. Several interest groups may choose this mechanism to coordinate their efforts to influence government when they share the same policy goals. The umbrella organization may be temporary or permanent.

Unanimous Consent Agreement An agreement on the rules of debate for proposed legislation in the Senate that is approved by all the members.

Unanimous Opinion A court opinion or determination on which all judges agree.

Unemployment The inability of those who are in the labor force to find a job; defined as the total number of those in the labor force actively looking for a job but unable to find one.

Unemployment Insurance Benefit program for certain workers losing their employment; a joint federal-state program financed with a tax on employers.

Unfunded Mandate A requirement imposed on a lower level of government by a higher level of government. The requirement is not accompanied by the funds to pay for the resulting expenses.

Unit Road System In Texas, a system that concentrates the day-to-day responsibilities of roads in the hands of a professional engineer rather than individual county commissioners. The engineer is ultimately responsible to the commissioners court.

Unicameral Legislature A legislature with only one legislative chamber, as opposed to a bicameral (two-chamber) legislature, such as the U.S. Congress. Today, Nebraska is the only state in the Union with a unicameral legislature.

Unincorporated Area An area not located within the boundary of a municipality.

Unit Rule A rule by which all of a state's electoral votes are cast for the presidential candidate receiving a plurality of the popular vote in that state.

Unitary System A centralized governmental system in which local or subdivisional governments exercise only those powers given to them by the central government.

Unitary System of Government A centralized governmental system in which local or subdivisional governments exercise only those powers given to them by the central government.

Unorthodox Lawmaking The use of out-of-the-ordinary parliamentary tactics to pass legislation.

U.S. Treasury Bond Debt issued by the federal government.

User-Benefit Theory The principle that the people who benefit from certain types of governmental services should also be the ones to pay the costs for those services.

User Fee A charge paid by an individual who receives a particular government service, such as water provision or garbage collection.

V

Valley (of the Rio Grande), The An area along the Texas side of the Rio Grande River known for its production of citrus fruits.

Veto Message The president's formal explanation of a veto when legislation is returned to Congress.

Victimless Crime A crime in which there does not appear to be a victim—a consensual crime. (Alternatively, the person breaking the law may be considered the primary victim.) Examples often cited include prostitution, gambling, and illegal drug possession.

Vote-Eligible Population (VEP) The total number of persons actually eligible to cast a ballot, excluding noncitizens, felons, and other ineligible persons but including citizens who are temporarily abroad (and who may vote absentee).

Voting-Age Population (VAP) The total number of persons in the United States or a state who are 18 years of age or older, regardless of citizenship, military status, felony conviction, or mental state.

Voter Turnout The percentage of citizens taking part in the election process; the number of eligible voters who actually "turn out" on election day to cast their ballots.

W

Wage and Price Controls Government-imposed controls on the maximum prices that may be charged for specific goods and services, plus controls on permissible wage increases.

War Powers Resolution A law passed in 1973 spelling out the conditions under which the president can commit troops without congressional approval.

Washington Community Individuals regularly involved with politics in Washington, D.C.

Watergate Break-in The 1972 illegal entry into the Democratic National Committee offices by participants in President Richard Nixon's reelection campaign.

Weak-Mayor System A form of municipal government in which an elected mayor and city council, often along with other elected officers, share administrative responsibilities.

Weberian Model A model of bureaucracy developed by the German sociologist Max Weber, who viewed bureaucracies as rational, hierarchical organizations in which decisions are based on logical reasoning.

White Primary The practice of excluding African Americans from Democratic party primary elections in Texas. First enforced by law and later by party rules, this practice was found unconstitutional in *Smith v. Allwright*, 321 U.S. 649 (1944).

Whig Party A major party in the United States during the first half of the 19th century, formally established in 1836. The Whig Party was anti-Jackson and represented a variety of regional interests.

Whip A member of Congress who aids the majority or minority leader of the House or the Senate.

Whistleblower Someone who brings to public attention gross governmental inefficiency or an illegal action.

White House Office The personal office of the president, which tends to presidential political needs and manages the media.

White House Press Corps The reporters assigned full time to cover the presidency.

White Primary A state primary election that restricts voting to whites only; outlawed by the Supreme Court in 1944.

Winter Garden An area of South Texas known for its vegetable production.

Writ of Information In criminal law, a formal accusation filed by a prosecutor against a party charged with a crime. It is an alternative to an indictment and does not involve a grand jury.

Writ of *Certiorari* An order issued by a higher court to a lower court to send up the record of a case for review.

Y

Yellow Journalism A term for sensationalistic, irresponsible journalism. Reputedly, the term is an allusion to the cartoon "The Yellow Kid" in the old *New York World*, a newspaper especially noted for its sensationalism.

Z

Zero-Based Budgeting A budgeting practice in which existing programs are evaluated as if they were new programs rather than on the basis of past levels of funding.

INDEX

U

UFW. *see* United Farm Workers
umbrella organizations, 732
U.N. *see* United Nations
unemployment. *see also* employment
  for African Americans, 174
  for agencies, 106, 174
  American Recovery and Reinvestment Act for, 931
  categorical grant for, 108, 118
  compensation for, 89, 132, 295, 597
  financial crisis for, 555
  as hidden, 592
  insurance for, 592, 949
  measurement of, 592
  politics and, 225, 290
  recession and, 591–592
  as state/local issue, 106
  trends in, 236
  TWC payments for, 949, 953
unemployment compensation, 89, 132, 295, 597
Unfunded Mandates Interagency Work Group, 971
Unfunded Mandates Reform Act (1995), 109
Unidad Hondureña, 254
Union v. Confederacy, 103
United Automobile Workers, 605
United Farm Workers (UFW), 247, 672
United Nations (U.N.), 88, 90, 187
  diplomacy by, 622, 628
  Intergovernmental Panel on Climate Change for, 565
  Security Council for, 635
United States (U.S.)
  bailout funds by, 256, 595, 600, 931
  balance of trade for, 607
  CAFTA-DR for, 606
  demographics for, 23–25
  discrimination in, 167, 666–667
United States Students Association, 248, 255
United States v. Curtiss-Wright Export Corp., 464
United States v. Harriss, 267
United States v. Lopez, 113
United States v. Morrison, 113–114
University of Texas (UT), 662, 666, 727, 728, 729, 941, 944
Unsafe at Any Speed (Nader), 256
Urban League, 246
U.S. Conference of Mayors, 959
U.S. News and World Report (magazine), 379
USA PATRIOT Act, 15, 17, 151, 453, 465, 582
user-benefit theory, in Texas, 789, 926
UT. *see* University of Texas
UT Hearts of Texas, 727

V

Valdez, Lupe, 977
Van Buren, Martin, 460
VAP. *see* voting-age population
Velaquez, Nydia M., 425
Velásquez, Willie, 758
VEP. *see* vote-eligible population
vertical checks and balances by, 98
veterans, benefits for, 590, 945
Veteran's Administration, 667

veto
  by Bush, G.W., 460
  Line Item Veto Act and, 460, 662
  override of, 457–458, 460
  Texas Constitution and, 705, 838, 860–861
  by U.S. presidency, 453, 457–458, 460
vice-presidency, U.S., 472–475
Victims of Crime, Office of, 579
Vietnam War, 134, 186, 193, 213, 218, 266, 283, 285, 318, 358, 452, 596, 627–628, 670
View Point Recovery Centers, 819
Villard, Oswald Garrison, 172
Vinson, Fred, 173
violence
  by armed forces, 5–6
  for busing, 174
  civil rights backlash for, 173, 176
  drug trafficking for, 581–582
  as gender-motivated, 113–114, 187
  private/foreign armies for, 6
  in Texas, 683
Violence against Women Act, 113–114
Virginia Company, of London, 36
Virginia Plan, 46–47. *see also* Constitutional Convention
Virginia Polytechnic Institute and State University, 578–579
Virginia Tech. *see* Virginia Polytechnic Institute and State University
VISTA. *see* Volunteers in Service to America
Vo, Hubert, 825
volunteerism, 212, 343, 344, 364–365, 541–542
Volunteers in Service to America (VISTA), 212
vote-eligible population (VEP), 782
voters/voting
  as absentee, 800, 802
  by African Americans, 11, 45, 54, 103, 104, 111, 167, 170–171, 173, 321, 671
  age for, 4, 193, 212, 317–318, 322, 782
  by armed forces, 326
  by armed services, 326
  ballot for, 9, 179, 320, 325, 326, 328, 363, 789–790, 791, 796, 797–800, 801, 802–803, 804, 978–979
  for Bush, G.W., 179, 284, 323, 325
  buying of, 326
  Civil Rights Acts for, 16, 169, 170, 176, 177–178, 179, 189, 191, 197, 341, 489, 539
  as compulsory, 324, 778
  Constitutional Convention and, 322
  as crossover, 793
  as CV, 966–967
  debates for, 382
  for delegates, 358–359
  in democracy, 314–315, 779
  demographics for, 218–226, 779
  demonstrations for, 43
  as early voting, 802
  education for, 318, 779

Election Assistance Commission for, 329
election judges for, 770, 799–800
for electors, 329
as electronic, 803
felons and, 322–323, 327
Fifteenth Amendment for, 104, 124, 168, 170, 183, 322
fraud in, 326–327
GOTV for, 344, 345, 357, 363, 810
grandfather clause for, 171
Help America Vote Act for, 329
by Hispanics/Latinos, 166, 284, 287, 303, 772, 776
by immigrants, 323, 782
income and, 318
as Independents, 218, 277
inertia in, 757
interest groups and, 727
on Internet, 9, 321
intimidation of, 323, 325
Kids Vote and, 215
League of Women Voters and, 257
literacy test for, 171
by mail, 314, 321, 326, 327
as mandatory, 4
media and, 4, 319, 321, 380–383
by military, 786
by minorities, 966–967
by Native Americans, 54, 167
for naturalized citizens, 325, 447–448
Nineteenth Amendment for, 185–186, 188, 322, 662
as nonvoters, 4, 319, 321
NPV for, 332
for Obama, 212, 217, 340, 361
participation paradox for, 779
Pentagon and, 9
plurality for, 298, 344
Project Vote Smart and, 44
property rights for, 54, 322
race/ethnicity for, 318, 319
registrars for, 321
registration for, 4, 109, 178, 286, 323, 333, 780, 810
requirements for, 4, 12, 333–334
residency for, 781
residency requirement for, 787
restrictions on, 322–323, 325
reverse-income effect and, 290
by slaves, 103, 167
as straight-ticket, 306
strike list for, 781
suffrage and, 11, 168, 178, 179, 183–186, 194, 323, 325, 780, 796, 915
as swing voters, 306
systems for, 324
in Texas, 662, 782–783, 785–788, 792, 795, 800–803, 911–912
Texas ballot for, 796, 797–800, 801
Texas Equal Suffrage Association for, 662
for Texas judges, 911–914
turnout for, 4, 12, 212, 284, 315–321, 324, 325, 380–383, 779, 781–788, 792, 795
Twenty-sixth Amendment for, 193, 318
as uninformed, 4, 12

in U.S. Constitution, 16
VAP/VEP for, 782, 783
Vietnam War and, 193, 318
as voluntary, 4
voter registration drive for, 178, 179, 295, 671
Voting Rights Act (1965) for, 178, 179, 194, 323, 325, 780, 796, 915
white electorate for, 11, 16, 105, 111, 167, 170, 329, 663–664, 735, 786, 788–789
women and, 11, 43, 45, 54, 167–168, 183–186, 266, 322
voting-age population (VAP), 782
Voting Rights Act (1965), 178, 179, 194, 323, 325, 780, 796, 915
vouchers
  for housing, 572
  for school, 129–130, 729–730, 934

W

wage/price controls, 596
wages
  discrimination in, 192–193
  for labor, 25–26
  Lilly Ledbetter Fair Pay Act for, 192, 205
  in third world countries, 604
  of women, 192–193
waivers, for mandates, 109
Wallace, George, 305
Wallace v. Jaffree, 129
Wall Street Journal (newspaper), 394
war. *see also* specific wars
  Congressional declaration of, 62, 453
  consequences of, 212
  presidential powers during, 38, 51, 62, 452–453, 642–643
  rioting during, 171
  through surrogates, 628, 631, 638
  on terrorism, 391, 446, 455, 522, 525–527, 582, 625, 633–634
  War Powers Resolution for, 453, 648
War on Poverty, 111
War Powers Resolution, 453, 648. *see also* Congress, U.S.
Warren, Earl, 153, 173
Warsaw Pact, 627–628
Washington, Denzel, 671
Washington, George, 34, 38, 40, 45, 46, 47, 279, 374, 446, 448, 453, 469, 534, 625, 642, 755
Washington Legal Foundation, 257
Washington Post (newspaper), 134, 378
Washington Times, 645
Washington v. Glucksberg, 150
Watergate scandal, 218, 225, 466, 467. *see also* Nixon, Richard
Wattenberg, Ben, 575
Waxman, Henry, 466
WCTU. *see* Women's Christian Temperance Union
wealth, subculture of, 90